Chambers Seven-Figure Mathematical Tables

consisting of
Logarithms of Numbers 1 to 100 000
Trigonometrical and Other Tables

Part one
College edition

Compiled by
James Pryde F.E.I.S.

chambers
EDINBURGH

Latest Reprint 1977

© **W & R Chambers Ltd**

ISBN 0 550 77803 9

Printed in Great Britain by T & A Constable Ltd, Edinburgh

Contents
Part one

Foreword

CHAMBERS SEVEN-FIGURE MATHEMATICAL
TABLES had their origin in 1844 in a volume entitled
*Mathematical Tables, consisting of Logarithmic and other
Tables required in the various branches of Practical
Mathematics* (xxxi + 316; 8vo). This volume was compiled
by Andrew Bell, at one time mathematics teacher at
Dollar Academy, as an accompaniment to his *Treatise of
Practical Mathematics* (1842) in "Chambers's Educational
Course". Later the original book was enlarged by the
addition of nautical and other tables to form a "necessary
accompaniment" to James Pryde's *Treatise on Navigation*
(1867) in the same series. In 1878 when a new and reset
edition was issued, James Pryde's name appeared on the
title-page, as it has continued to do since that date.
(James Pryde, one of the original Fellows of the Educational Institute of Scotland, was lecturer in mathematics
at the Edinburgh School of Arts, the forerunner of the
present Heriot-Watt University.) In 1930 the book
appeared with a "thoroughly revised and greatly extended
'Explanation of the Tables' by Walter F. Robinson,
F.R.G.S., Lecturer in Surveying, School of Engineering,
Canterbury College, Christchurch, N.Z.". In 1954
appeared the "College Edition" containing only the
logarithm and trigonometrical tables, since it was felt that
the specialised needs of Astronomy and Navigation as far
as the use of tables was concerned were now being met by
specialised books of tables. In response to very numerous
requests, however, the Publishers have restored a number
of tables that continue to have application in certain
calculations mainly connected with surveying in the
revised "Full Edition"; at the same time they have
published separately these additional tables of Part II,
also the Tables of Logarithms on their own.

MATHEMATICAL CONSTANTS

Constant	Number	Log	Constant	Number	Log
π	3·1415 927	0·4971 499	$1/\pi$	0·3183 099	9·5028 501
2π	6·2831 853	0·7981 799	$1/2\pi$	0·1591 549	9·2018 201
$\pi/2$	1·5707 963	0·1961 199	$2/\pi$	0·6366 198	9·8038 801
$\pi/4$	0·7853 982	9·8950 899	$4/\pi$	1·2732 395	0·1049 101
$4\pi/3$	4·1887 902	0·6220 886	$\sqrt[3]{3/4\pi}$	0·6203 505	9·7926 371
π^2	9·8696 044	0·9942 997	$1/\pi^2$	0·1013 212	9·0057 003
$\sqrt{\pi}$	1·7724 539	0·2485 749	$1/\sqrt{\pi}$	0·5641 896	9·7514 251
$\sqrt{2\pi}$	2·5066 283	0·3990 899	$1/\sqrt{2\pi}$	0·3989 423	9·6009 101
$\frac{1}{2}\sqrt{\pi}$	0·8862 269	9·9475 449	$2/\sqrt{\pi}$	1·1283 792	0·0524 551
$\sqrt{\frac{1}{2}\pi}$	1·2533 141	0·0980 599	$\sqrt{2/\pi}$	0·7978 846	9·9019 401
e	2·7182 818	0·4342 945	e^{-1}	0·3678 794	9·5657 055
e^2	7·3890 561	0·8685 890	e^{-2}	0·1353 353	9·1314 110
$\sqrt{e}$	1·6487 213	0·2171 472	$e^{-\frac{1}{2}}$	0·6065 307	9·7828 528
$\sqrt{2}$	1·4142 136	0·1505 150	$\sqrt{\frac{1}{2}}$	0·7071 068	9·8494 850
$\sqrt{3}$	1·7320 508	0·2385 606	$\sqrt[3]{10}$	2·1544 347	0·3333 333
$\sqrt{10}$	3·1622 777	0·5000 000	$\sqrt[3]{100}$	4·6415 888	0·6666 667
$M = \log e$	0·4342 945	9·6377 843	$1/M = \ln 10$	2·3025 851	0·3622 157
ρ	0·4769 363	9·6784 604	$\sqrt{2}\rho$	0·6744 898	9·8289 754
1 radian	57°·2957 795	1·7581 226	$1°$	0^{r}·0174 533	8·2418 774
,,	3437'·7467 708	3·5362 739	$1'$	0^{r}·0002 909	6·4637 261
,,	206264"·8062 471	5·3144 251	$1''$	0^{r}·0000 048	4·6855 749

PRINCIPAL WEIGHTS AND MEASURES: CONVERSION FACTORS

Internationally agreed exact values are given in heavy type. Inverse or reciprocal values are given in brackets; e.g. 1 in = **2·54** cm (0·393 701) indicates that 1 in = 2·54 cm exactly, and 1 cm = 0·393 701 in to six decimals.

1 in = **2·54** cm (0·393 701)
1 ft = **0·304 8** m (3·280 843)
1 yd = **0·914 4** m (1·093 613)
1 mile = **1·609 344** km (0·621 371)

1 in² = **6·451 6** cm² (0·155 000)
1 ft² = 0·092 903 m² (10·763 905)
1 yd² = 0·836 127 m² (1·195 991)
1 sq mile = 2·589 988 km² (0·386 102)
1 acre = 0·404 686 hectares (2·471 052)

1 in³ = 16·387 064 cm³ (0·061 024)
1 ft³ = 0·028 317 m³ (35·314 649)
1 yd³ = 0·764 555 m³ (1·307 950)

1 UK gal = 4·546 092 dm³ (0·219 969)*
= 277·42 in³

1 US gal = 3·785 41 dm³ (0·264 17)*
= 231 in³

1 UK pint = 0·568 261 dm³ (1·759 755)*

1 lb = **0·453 592 37** kg (2·204 623)
1 gr = 0·064 799 g (15·432 359)
1 oz = 28·349 523 g (0·035 274)
1 ton = 1016·047 kg
= 1·016 047 tonne (0·984 206)

1 lbf = **0·453 592 37** kgf (2·204 623)
= 4·448 22 N (0·224 809)
1 kgf = **9·806 65** N (0·101 972)
1 tonf = 9·964 02 kN (0·100 361)
1 pdl = 0·138 255 N (7·233 012)

1 ft lbf = 1·355 82 J (0·737 561)
1 ft pdl = 0·042 14 J (23·730 37)

1 dyn = 10⁻⁵ N
1 erg = 10⁻⁷ J

1 cal$_{\text{IT}}$ = **4·186 8** J (0·238 85)

* The cubic decimetre is known as a litre.

EXPLANATION OF THE TABLES.

COMMON LOGARITHMS

(1) A Table of Logarithms is a collection of auxiliary numbers, so constructed, that by it Multiplication of common numbers can be performed by *addition* of their Logarithms ; Division by their *subtraction ;* Involution, or raising of powers, by their *multiplication ;* and Evolution, or extraction of roots, by their *division.* These auxiliaries or Logarithms are the exponents or powers to which an invariable number called the *base* has to be raised, in order to produce the number of which it is the Logarithm.

The above expressed in algebraic symbols, where A and B represent two numbers, is

(a) Log. $(A \times B)$ $= \log. A + \log. B.$

(b) Log. $\dfrac{A}{B}$ $= \log. A - \log. B.$

(c) Log. A^n $= n \log. A.$

(d) Log. $\sqrt[n]{A} = $ Log. $A^{\frac{1}{n}}$ $= \dfrac{1}{n} \log. A.$

(2) In the following Tables of common logarithms, the base $= 10$, and the power to which 10 has to be raised to produce any number, is therefore the logarithm of that number ; thus,

$$10^1 = 10 \qquad \therefore 1 = \log. 10$$
$$10^2 = 100 \qquad \therefore 2 = \log. 100$$
$$10^3 = 1000 \qquad \therefore 3 = \log. 1000$$
$$10^4 = 10000 \qquad \therefore 4 = \log. 10000$$
$$10^5 = 100000 \qquad \therefore 5 = \log. 100000$$
$$\&c. \qquad\qquad \&c.$$

If, beginning again with 10^1, we divide successively by 10, we obtain the following results :

$$10^1 = 10 \qquad\qquad \therefore 1 = \log. 10$$
$$10^0 = 1 \qquad\qquad \therefore 0 = \log. 1$$
$$10^{-1} = \tfrac{1}{10} = \cdot 1 \qquad \therefore -1 = \log. \cdot 1$$
$$10^{-2} = \tfrac{1}{100} = \cdot 01 \qquad \therefore -2 = \log. \cdot 01$$
$$10^{-3} = \tfrac{1}{1000} = \cdot 001 \qquad \therefore -3 = \log. \cdot 001$$
$$10^{-4} = \tfrac{1}{10000} = \cdot 0001 \qquad \therefore -4 = \log. \cdot 0001$$
$$\&c. \qquad\qquad \&c.$$

When we find from the Table that log. 35 = 1·5440680, this means that $10^{1·5440680} = 10^{\frac{15440680}{10000000}} = 35$; or that, if 10 be raised to a power denoted by the numerator of the fractional exponent, and of the number so found the root indicated by the denominator be extracted, the result will be 35. Other logarithms are to be similarly interpreted.

(3) From the above it appears that the common Log. 1 = 0, that Log. 10 = 1; hence, the logarithms of numbers greater than 1 and less than 10, will be greater than 0 and less than 1; in other words, will be some proper fraction or decimal, without an integer; that the logarithms of all numbers greater than 10 but less than 100, will be greater than 1 and less than 2, or will be 1 + a decimal; while the logarithm of a number consisting of 3 integral figures will be 2 + a decimal, and so on; the integral part of the logarithm being always *one less* than the number of integral figures in the number of which it is the logarithm.

(*a*) **Definition.**—The integral part of a logarithm is called its *characteristic*, and the decimal part is called the *mantissa*.

(4) It also appears that the logarithms of all proper fractions are negative; thus, the logarithm of ¾ or log. ·75 is (1, *b*) log. 3 – log. 4, or ·4771213 – ·6020600 = – ·1249387; but subtracting this from 0, the logarithm of 1, we have $\overline{1}$·8750613, where the *characteristic* only is negative, and the *mantissa* is positive, and consists of the same figures as the *mantissa* of log. 75, which is 1·8750613; from which it appears that the *mantissa* of the logarithm of a number is the same, so long as the digits of the number remain the same, and that the *characteristic* alone changes according to the position of the decimal point; thus,

Log. 43758	= 4·6410575
Log. 4375·8	= 3·6410575
Log. 437·58	= 2·6410575
Log. 43·758	= 1·6410575
Log. 4·3758	= 0·6410575
Log. ·43758	= $\overline{1}$·6410575
Log. ·043758	= $\overline{2}$·6410575
Log. ·0043758	= $\overline{3}$·6410575
&c.	&c.

(*a*) This property of the *characteristic* and *mantissa* is only true of logarithms whose *base* is the same as the root of the scale of arithmetical notation (i.e. 10); it is not true of natural logarithms (to the base *e*, i.e. 2·7182818 . . .); hence, a table of natural logarithms, in order to be universally useful, would require to be infinite in extent. For this reason a table of common logarithms is far more general, and more easily used than logarithms calculated to any other base.

(5) **The Characteristic.**—From what has been said above, and from the fact that only the *mantissa* of the logarithm is put in the Table, the *characteristic*, in each case, must be supplied by the calculator himself. This is done by the following easy Rules.

(a) If the number whose logarithm is sought contain one or more integral figures, *the characteristic is always one less than the number of integral figures in the number*, and is positive.

(b) If the number is wholly a decimal, *its characteristic is the same as the place from the decimal point which its first significant figure occupies*, and is negative: in this case the negative sign is placed over the characteristic, to shew that it alone is negative, the mantissa being always positive.

(6) TO FIND THE LOGARITHM OF A GIVEN NUMBER BY THE TABLES.

(a) If the number consist of not more than *three* figures: the mantissa will be found opposite it on one of the first four pages; and the characteristic must be supplied by (5, a) or (5, b), according as it contains an integer, or is all a decimal.   In this manner is found,

$$\text{Log. } 852 \quad = 2 \cdot 9304396$$
$$\text{and} \quad \text{Log. } \cdot 45 \quad = \bar{1} \cdot 6532125$$

(b) If the number contain *four* digits: the mantissa will be found on pages 2 to 181 under 0 at the top of the page, and opposite the number itself in the column marked No. at the left-hand side of the page; and the proper characteristic must be applied as in the last case.   In this manner is found,

$$\text{Log. } 374 \cdot 5 \quad = 2 \cdot 5734518$$
$$\text{and} \quad \text{Log. } \cdot 03745 \quad = \bar{2} \cdot 5734518$$

(c) If the number contain *five* digits: the mantissa will be found on pages 2 to 181, *opposite* the first four figures on the left-hand side of the page, and *under* the fifth at the top.   In this way it is found that

$$\text{Log. } 87647 \quad = 4 \cdot 9427371$$
$$\text{and} \quad \text{Log. } \cdot 78539 \quad = \bar{1} \cdot 8950854$$

(d) If the number whose logarithm is sought contain six or seven figures: find the mantissa corresponding to the first five figures as directed in (c); then take the difference between this logarithm and the next higher in the table, which is the change in the logarithm corresponding to an increase of 1 or a unit in the fifth figure of the number.   Now, the sixth figure is tenth parts of this unit, and the sixth and seventh are hundredth parts of this unit; in other words, are decimals in reference to it.   Hence, if the difference found above be multiplied by the figures above five, considered as decimals, and the product added to the logarithm found as above, it will be the *true* logarithm sought; thus : Find the logarithm of 387548.

Log. 38754	=	·5883165
Log. 38755	=	·5883277
their difference is		112
and		112 × ·8 = 89·6 or 90 = correction
∴ Log. 387548	=	5·5883255

Find the logarithm of 276·5473.

Here Log. 276·55 $= 2·4417737$
    Log. 276·54 $= 2·4417580$
    their diff. is $=$ 157
    and $157 \times ·73 = 114·61$ or $115 =$ correction.
$\therefore$ Log. 276·5473 $= 2·4417695$

The lines above the figures seen on many of the pages indicate that a change has occurred in the *first three figures* of the mantissa. Thus, on page 2, line 3, the log. of $10024 = 4·0010411$, *not* $4·0000411$.

(7)   PROPORTIONAL PARTS BY INSPECTION.

These corrections can also be more readily made, by means of the columns of proportional parts to be found on the right-hand side of each page; thus, under diff. 112, and opposite 8, is found 90, which being added to the last figures of the log. 38754, gives log. 387548 as above. Also, under the difference 157, and opposite 7, is found 110, and opposite 3 is found 47; but 3 being in the *seventh* place, 47 must be taken as 4·7; which, being nearer to 5 than 4, must be taken as 5; and this added to the 110 gives 115 as the correction to be added to the log. 276·54, to obtain the logarithm of 276·5473; the result being the same as found above.

The differences change so rapidly at the beginning of the Tables, that for want of room, only every *third* difference is given, from page 2 to 9, and every *second* difference, from page 10 to 19: from page 20 to end, *every* difference is given. When the exact difference is not given, use that which differs from it only by *one*, and the result will be sufficiently exact for ordinary purposes; but, when the *greatest accuracy* is required, correct by the *rule (d)* above.

EXERCISES.

1. The logarithm of   729 $=$ 2·8627275
2. The logarithm of   4·385 $=$ 0·6419696
3. The logarithm of   53874 $=$ 4·7313792
4. The logarithm of   53·8745 $=$ 1·7313833
5. The logarithm of   ·003768 $=$ $\bar{3}$·5761109
6. The logarithm of   7853968 $=$ 6·8950891

(8)   TO FIND THE NUMBER CORRESPONDING TO A GIVEN LOGARITHM.

The number of which a given value is the logarithm is frequently called its Antilogarithm, and smaller tables usually give for convenience a separate table of Antilogarithms. For seven figures of decimals such a table would be extensive; it is superfluous, since the user has merely to reverse the process for finding a logarithm, i.e. find from the table which number yields the given logarithm.

When the logarithm is not found in the table, take out the next lower and the five figures of the number belonging to it; then, find the difference between this logarithm and the given one, and under the corresponding tabular difference find the proportional part which is equal to this difference, and opposite it is found the sixth figure of the number: but if the difference is not exactly found among the proportional parts, take the next lower part, and the figure opposite it is the sixth figure of the number; subtract this part from the given difference, annex to the remainder a cipher, consider it as a new proportional part, and find the corresponding figure as before, and it will be the seventh figure of the number.

EXAMPLE.

Find the number (or antilogarithm) whose logarithm is 3·9212074.

Given logarithm	=	3·9212074
Number = 8340·7 to next lower log.	=	3·9212025
		49
Number = ... ·09 to next lower pro. part	=	47
		20
Number = ... ·004 to nearest pro. part	=	21

Hence   8340·794 is the required number or antilogarithm.

COMPUTATION OF NEGATIVE CHARACTERISTICS.

It is usual to make only the characteristic of a logarithm negative, as the calculations can thus be made more conveniently. Calculations with negative characteristics are made according to the rules of algebraic addition and subtraction.

(9) (a) To add two negative characteristics.

Take their sum, and make it negative. Thus $\bar{2}$ added to $\bar{3}$, gives $\bar{5}$.

(b) To add a positive and negative characteristic.

Take their difference, and consider it to be positive or negative according as the positive or negative characteristic is the greater; that is, the difference has the sign of the greater.

Thus 6 and $\bar{2}$ give 4; 5 and $\bar{2}$ give 3; $\bar{5}$ and 2 give $\bar{3}$; $\bar{2}$ and 1 give $\bar{1}$; and so on.

The following examples will easily be performed by attending to these two rules:

EXAMPLES.

1. Add   5·3468541 and $\bar{3}$·2685427
                      5·3468541
                      $\bar{3}$·2685427

                      2·6153968

2. Add   6·3874654 and $\bar{2}$·9245636
                      6·3874654
                      $\bar{2}$·9245636

                      5·3120290

In this example the sum in the first decimal place is 13, and the 1 is carried to 6, which gives 7, then 7 and $\bar{2}$ give 5.

3. Add $\bar{2}$·5632874 and $\bar{3}$·2465281
                      $\bar{2}$·5632874
                      $\bar{3}$·2465281

                      $\bar{6}$·8098155

(10) To subtract a negative characteristic.

Change its sign to plus, and then add it by the preceding rules for addition. Thus, to subtract $\overline{3}$ from 2, the result is found by adding 3 to 2, which gives 5. So $\overline{5}$ subtracted from $\overline{2}$, gives 5 and $\overline{2}$, or 3; also $\overline{3}$ subtracted from $\overline{5}$, gives 3 and $\overline{5}$, or $\overline{2}$.

EXAMPLES.

1. From
$$2 \cdot 6847658 \text{ subtract } \overline{3} \cdot 2468543$$
$$2 \cdot 6847658$$
$$\overline{3} \cdot 2468543$$
$$\overline{}$$
$$5 \cdot 4379115$$

2. From
$$\overline{2} \cdot 3468537 \text{ subtract } \overline{5} \cdot 7654626$$
$$\overline{2} \cdot 3468537$$
$$\overline{5} \cdot 7654626$$
$$\overline{}$$
$$2 \cdot 5813911$$

Here $\overline{5}$ taken from $\overline{2}$, gives 5 and $\overline{2}$, or 3; but in subtracting the first decimal places, there is one to be carried; in other words, 1 is to be subtracted from the upper number $\overline{2}$, which makes it $\overline{3}$, then $\overline{3}$ and 5 give 2.

3. From
$$\overline{5} \cdot 6843252 \text{ subtract } \overline{3} \cdot 7856310$$
$$\overline{5} \cdot 6843252$$
$$\overline{3} \cdot 7856310$$
$$\overline{}$$
$$\overline{3} \cdot 8986942$$

Here $\overline{3}$ taken from 5, gives 3 and $\overline{5}$ or $\overline{2}$, and a 1 of carriage. which is of course to be subtracted, gives $\overline{2}$ and $\overline{1}$ or $\overline{3}$; or the 1 of carriage, with the $\overline{5}$ makes $\overline{6}$, and $\overline{3}$ taken from $\overline{6}$, gives 3 and $\overline{6}$ or $\overline{3}$.

(11) To multiply a logarithm with a negative characteristic.

Multiply the fractional part by the common rules; then multiply the negative characteristic, which will give a negative product, and add the carriage to it by the rule (b) above.

Thus $\overline{2}$, multiplied by 5, gives $\overline{10}$, and if 2 of carriage is to be added, the result is $\overline{8}$.

EXAMPLES.

1. Multiply
$$\overline{2} \cdot 3685464 \text{ by } 2$$
$$\overline{2} \cdot 3685464$$
$$2$$
$$\overline{}$$
$$\overline{4} \cdot 7370928$$

2. Multiply
$$\overline{3} \cdot 7856473 \text{ by } 6$$
$$\overline{3} \cdot 7856473$$
$$6$$
$$\overline{}$$
$$\overline{14} \cdot 7138838$$

Here $\overline{3} \times 6 = \overline{18}$, and $\overline{18}$, with the carriage 4, gives $\overline{14}$.

(12) To divide a logarithm having a negative characteristic.

If the characteristic is divisible by the divisor, write down the quotient with a negative sign, and divide the fractional part by common rules. But if the negative characteristic is not divisible by the divisor, add such a negative number to it as will make it divisible, and prefix an equal positive integer to the fractional part of the logarithm; then divide the increased negative exponent and the other part of the logarithm separately, and the former quotient, taken negatively, will be the characteristic to the fractional part of the quotient.

Thus $\overline{6}$, divided by 3, gives $\overline{2}$. But to divide $\overline{10}$ by 3, add $\overline{2}$ to it, and then $\overline{10}$ is equal to $\overline{12}$ and 2; the former, divided by 3, gives $\overline{4}$, and the latter $\frac{2}{3}$. The quotient, therefore, is $\overline{4}$ and $\frac{2}{3}$.

EXAMPLES.

1. Divide $\qquad\qquad$ $\overline{6}\cdot 3246846$ by 3

$\overline{6}\cdot 3246846 \div 3 = \overline{2}\cdot 1082282$

2. Divide $\qquad\qquad$ $\overline{14}\cdot 3268472$ by 9

$\overline{14}\cdot 3268472 = \overline{18} + 4\cdot 3268472$

and the quotient is $\qquad\qquad = \overline{2}\cdot 4807608$

Here 4 must be added to $\overline{14}$, that the sum $\overline{18}$ may be divisible by 9 ; and as $\overline{4}$ is thus added, therefore 4 must be prefixed to the fractional part, and thus the value of the logarithm is unaltered, for there is added to it $\overline{4}$ and 4, or 0.

(13) To perform Multiplication by Logarithms.

Add the logarithms of the factors, and the sum will be the logarithm of the product.

EXAMPLES.

1. Multiply $\qquad\qquad$ 2·581926 by 345·7291.

L 2·581926 = 0·4119438 $\Big)$

L 345·7291 = 2·5387359 $\Big)$

Product = 892·647, its log. $\qquad$ = $\overline{2}$·9506797 Sum.

2. Multiply $\qquad\qquad$ ·03902, 59·716, and ·00314728.

L ·03902 = $\overline{2}$·5912873 $\Big)$

L 59·716 = 1·7760907 $\Big)$

L ·00314728 = $\overline{3}$·4979353 $\Big)$

Product = ·007333533, its log. $\qquad$ = $\overline{3}$·8653133 Sum.

EXERCISES.

1. Multiply 231·4 and 5·062. $\qquad\qquad\qquad$ Ans. 1171·347.

2. Multiply 35·86, 2·1046, ·8372, and ·00294. $\qquad\qquad$ Ans. ·1857618.

(14) To perform Division by Logarithms.

From the logarithm of the dividend subtract that of the divisor, and the remainder will be the logarithm of the quotient.

EXAMPLES.

1. Divide 371·49 by 52·376.
L 371·49 = 2·5699471 ⎱
L 52·376 = 1·7191323 ⎰

Quotient = 7·092752   0·8508148 Diff.

2. Divide ·07438 by 129·476.
L ·07438 = $\overline{2}$·8714562 ⎱
L 129·476 = 2·1121893 ⎰

Quotient = ·0005744694 $\overline{4}$·7592669 Diff.

EXERCISES.

1. Divide 241·63 by 4·567.   Ans. 52·90782.
2. Divide ·6314 by ·007241.   Ans. 87·19792.

(15) To perform Proportion by Logarithms.

Add together the logarithms of the second and third terms, and from their sum subtract the logarithm of the first, and the remainder will be the logarithm of the fourth term.

(*a*) The *arithmetical complement* of a number is the remainder, after subtracting it from a number consisting of 1, with as many ciphers annexed as the number has of integers. When the index of a logarithm is less than 10, which is generally the case, its arithmetical complement is found by subtracting it from 10.

(*b*) The arithmetical complement of a logarithm is easily found by subtracting its right-hand significant figure from 10, and all those before it from 9.

Instead of subtracting the logarithm of the first term, its arithmetical complement may be added to the logarithms of the second and third, and the sum, after deducting 10 from the index, will be the logarithm of the fourth term.

EXAMPLE.

Find a fourth proportional to 723·4, ·02519, and 3574·862.

As	723·4	2·8593785	ar. com.	7·1406215
To	·02519	$\overline{2}$·4012282		$\overline{2}$·4012282
So is	3574·862	3·5532592		3·5532592
		1·9544874		$\overline{1}$·0951089
To	·1244827	$\overline{1}$·0951089		

In the first method, the logarithms of the second and third terms are added, and that of the first term is then subtracted from the sum ; and in the second method, the arithmetical complement of the logarithm of the first term is added to the logarithms of the second and third, and from 9 the index 10 is subtracted, which gives $\overline{1}$ for a remainder.

(*c*) The *arithmetical complement* of a number is also sometimes understood to be the algebraic remainder after subtracting the number from zero or nothing. Instead of subtracting a number from another, if this arithmetical complement of the former is added to the latter, the sum will be the required difference without deducting 10 or any other number. Thus, in the above example,

$$
\begin{array}{lll}
\text{A. C.* of L } 723\cdot4 & = & \overline{3}\cdot1406215 \\
\text{L } \cdot02519 & = & \overline{2}\cdot4012282 \\
\text{L } 3574\cdot862 & = & 3\cdot5532592 \\
\hline
& & \overline{1}\cdot0951089
\end{array}
$$

which is the same result as before.

(16) To perform Involution by Logarithms.

Multiply the logarithm of the given number by the exponent of the power to which it is to be raised, and the product will be the logarithm of the required power.

EXAMPLE.

Find the cube of $30\cdot7146$.

$$
\begin{array}{l}
\text{L } 30\cdot7146 = 1\cdot4873449 \\
\phantom{\text{L } 30\cdot7146 = } 3 \\
\hline
4\cdot4620347 = \text{L } 28975\cdot75
\end{array}
$$

Hence the cube of $30\cdot7146 = 28975\cdot75$.

EXERCISES.

1. Find the fourth power of $9\cdot163$.	Ans. $7049\cdot38$.
2. Find the 365th power of $1\cdot0045$.	Ans. $5\cdot148888$.

(17) To perform Evolution by Logarithms.

Divide the logarithm of the given number by the exponent of the root which is to be extracted, and the quotient will be the logarithm of the required root.

EXAMPLES.

1. Find the cube root of 12345.

$$
\begin{array}{ll}
& \text{L } 12345 = 4\cdot0914911 \\
\text{Its quotient by 3} & = 1\cdot3638304 = \text{L } 23\cdot11162 \\
\text{Hence} & \sqrt[3]{} \, 12345 = 23\cdot11162
\end{array}
$$

2. Find the fourth root of $\cdot0076542$.

$$
\begin{array}{ll}
& \text{L } \cdot0076542 = \overline{3}\cdot883899\dot{8} \\
\text{Its quotient by 4 (by 12)} & = \overline{1}\cdot4709749 = \text{L } \cdot295784 \\
\text{Hence} & \sqrt[4]{} \, \cdot0076542 = \cdot295784
\end{array}
$$

(18) To find the value of x in the equation $a^x = b$.

By (1, c) we have x Log. $a =$ Log. b.

$$
\therefore x = \log. \, b \div \log. \, a
$$

Let $a = 40$, and $b = 10$

$$
\text{Then } x = \frac{1\cdot0000000}{1\cdot6020600} = \cdot6241964
$$

* A. C. is a contraction for arithmetical complement.

Next,   let $a = \cdot 8$, and $b = 3\cdot 1416$

$$\text{Then } x = \frac{\text{Log. } 3\cdot 1416}{\text{Log. } \cdot 8} = \frac{0\cdot 4971509}{\overline{1}\cdot 9030900}$$

$$= \frac{0\cdot 4971509}{-0\cdot 0969100}$$

$$= -\frac{\cdot 4971509}{\cdot 0969100} = -\frac{4971509}{969100}$$

$$= -5\cdot 130027$$

In this latter case we have to change the divisor $\overline{1}\cdot 9030900$ into $-\cdot 0969100$ before the division can be conveniently performed.

(19) To FIND THE AMOUNT AND PRESENT VALUE OF A SUM OF MONEY AT COMPOUND INTEREST BY LOGARITHMS.

Let $p = $ the principal,
$a = $ " amount,
$t = $ " time or number of payments of interest,
$r = $ " interest of £1 for one period,
$(1 + r) = R = $ " amount of £1 for one period.

Then $a = p\,R^t$ (1)

which, by taking the logarithms of both sides, becomes

Log. $a = $ log. $p + t$ log. R,   (2)

Transposing   Log. $p = $ log. $a - t$ log. R,   (3)

$$\text{Log. } R = \frac{\text{log. } a - \text{log. } p}{t},\quad (4)$$

$$t = \frac{\text{log. } a - \text{log. } p}{\text{log. } R}.\quad (5)$$

Also the interest $= a - p = p\,(R^t - 1)$ (6)

Note.—If in the above formulæ $p = $ the present value of a sum a due t periods hence, they are equally true for the present value ; t, r, and R being the same as above.

When t is large, the logarithm of R, in order to obtain correct results, should be taken with more than seven places of decimals ; for which reason the most common values of R, with their logarithms carried to ten decimals, are inserted in the following table :

LOGARITHMS OF R.

R.	Logarithm.	R.	Logarithm.
1·0025	·00108,43813	1·0325	·01389,00603
1·0050	·00216,60618	1·0350	·01494,03498
1·0075	·00324,50548	1·0375	·01598,81054
1·0100	·00432,13738	1·0400	·01703,33393
1·0125	·00539,50319	1·0425	·01807,60636
1·0150	·00646,60422	1·0450	·01911,62904
1·0175	·00753,44179	1·0475	·02015,40316
1·0200	·00860,01718	1·0500	·02118,92991
1·0225	·00966,33167	1·0525	·02222,21045
1·0250	·01072,38654	1·0550	·02325,24596
1·0275	·01178,18305	1·0575	·02428,03760
1·0300	·01283,72247	1·0600	·02530,58653

EXAMPLE I.

Find the amount and compound interest of £365·50., for 19 years at $4\frac{1}{4}$ per cent.

Since the rate per cent. is 4·25, the rate for £1 $= r = ·0425$, and R $= 1·0425$, $t = 19$, and $p = 365·5$; then by (2),

t log. R $= 19 \times ·0180760636 = 0·3434452084$
$+$ log. $p =$ log. 365·5 $\quad\quad = 2·5628874$
∴ log. $a =$ log. 805·9954 $\quad = 2·9063326$

$$\frac{297}{2908 \div 54 = 54.}$$

Hence the amount $=$ £805·995$+$

Also the interest $= a - p$ by (6) $=$ £805·995 $-$ £365·50 $=$ £440·495.

EXAMPLE II.

Find the present value of £584·775, due 12 years hence, compound interest at $3\frac{1}{2}$ per cent.

Since the rate per cent. is 3·5, the rate for £1 $= r = ·035$, and R $= 1·035$, $t = 12$, and $a =$ £584·775; then by (3),

Log. $a =$ log. 584·775 $\quad\quad = 2·7669888$
$-t$ log. R $= -12 \times ·0149403498 = 0·1792841976$
∴log. $p =$ log. 386·9943 $\quad\quad 2·5877046024$

$$\frac{6997}{113)49024}$$
$$43$$

Hence $p =$ £386·995 $-$

EXAMPLE III.

At what rate per cent. will £365·50 amount to £805·995 in 19 years?

Here $a = 805·995$, $p = 365·5$, and $t = 19$; hence by (4),

$$\text{Log. R} = \frac{\text{log. } a - \text{log. } p}{t}$$

$$= \frac{2·9063324 - 2·5628874}{19}$$

$$= \frac{0·3434450}{19} = ·0180761 \text{ nearly}$$

$$= \text{log. } 1·0425 \quad \therefore R = 1·0425$$

Hence $\quad\quad r = ·0425$, and the rate per cent. is therefore
$\quad\quad\quad\quad = 4·25 = 4\frac{1}{4}$, the rate sought.

EXAMPLE IV.

In what time will £250 amount to £846·59, at 5 per cent. per annum?

Since $a = 846·59$, $p = 250$, R $= 1·05$, by (5),

$$t = \frac{\text{log. } a - \text{log. } p}{\text{log. R}} = \frac{2·9276731 - 2·3979400}{·0211893}$$

$$= \frac{·5297331}{·0211893} = 25 \text{ years, the time sought.}$$

EXAMPLE V.

Find the present value of £3245 due 30 years hence at $4\frac{1}{2}$ per cent., compound interest.

Here $a = 3245$, R $= 1\cdot045$, and $t = 30$; hence by the Note and (3),

$$\text{Log. } p = \text{log. } a - t \text{ log. R,}$$

or log. $p =$ log. $3245 - 30 \times$ log. $1\cdot045$

$$= 3\cdot5112147 - \cdot5734887120$$

$$= 2\cdot937725988 = \text{log. } 866\cdot415$$

$\therefore$ the present value $=$ £866·415.

EXAMPLE VI.

The present value of £596 due 12 years hence, compound interest, is £383·17; what is the rate per cent. per annum?

Here $a = 596$, $p = 383\cdot17$, $t = 12$; hence by the Note and (4),

$$\text{Log. R} = \frac{\text{log. } a - \text{log. } p}{t}$$

$$= \frac{2\cdot7752463 - 2\cdot5833915}{12}$$

$$= \frac{\cdot1918548}{12} = \cdot0159879$$

$$= \text{Log. } 1\cdot0375 = \text{log. R;}$$

$\therefore$ R $= 1\cdot0375$, and the rate per cent. is $3\frac{3}{4}$.

(20) To FIND THE AMOUNT AND PRESENT VALUE OF AN ANNUITY, FOR A GIVEN TIME, AT A GIVEN RATE PER CENT. COMPOUND INTEREST.

Let $p =$ the annual or periodic payment;

A $=$ the amount of the annuity improved at compound interest to the end of the time;

$v =$ the present value of the annuity;

R $=$ the amount of £1 for one period;

and $t =$ the number of years, or periods of payment.

Then
$$\text{A} = p \left(\frac{\text{R}t - 1}{\text{R} - 1} \right), \tag{7}$$

and
$$v = \frac{p(\text{R}t - 1)}{\text{R}t(\text{R} - 1)} = \frac{1}{\text{R}t} \text{A;} \tag{8}$$

$\therefore$ also A $= v\text{R}t.$ (9)

Hence from (7),

$$\text{Log. A} = \text{log. } p + \text{log.}(\text{R}t - 1) - \text{log. } r; \tag{10}$$

from (8),

$$\text{Log. } v = \text{log. } p + \text{log.}(\text{R}t - 1) - \text{log. } r - t \text{ log. R;} \tag{11}$$

and from (9),

$$\text{Log. A} = \text{log. } v + t \text{ log. R.} \tag{12}$$

Transposing (12),

$$\text{Log. R} = \frac{\text{log. A} - \text{log. } v}{t}$$

When the change in a number is small, the change in the logarithm is very nearly proportional to the change in the number.

$$\text{Log. } (n + d) - \text{log. } n = \text{log. } \left(\frac{n + d}{n}\right) = \text{log. } \left(1 + \frac{d}{n}\right).$$

By the theory of logarithms, if μ be

$$\frac{1}{\text{log.}_\epsilon 10} = \frac{1}{2 \cdot 3025809} \text{ or } 0 \cdot 43429448, \text{ Log. }_{10}\left(1 + \frac{d}{n}\right) = \mu\left(\frac{d}{n} - \frac{d^2}{2n^2} + \frac{d^3}{3n^3} - \ldots\ldots\right)$$

If n be greater than 10,000, and if d be not greater than 1, the value of the second term on the right-hand side of the above equation is not greater than $\frac{0 \cdot 434\ldots}{2 \times 10^8} = \cdot 000000002$, while the value of the third term is less than the 10,000th part of this. Therefore if a number be changed from n to $n + d$, the change of logarithm may be expressed as $\frac{0 \cdot 4d}{n}$.

Thus, the logarithm of 5000 is $3 \cdot 6989700$, and the logarithm of 5001 is, very nearly, $3 \cdot 6989700 + \frac{1 \times 0 \cdot 434}{5000} = 3 \cdot 6990567$, being nearly 2 in error in the 7th decimal place.

But there is not much gained by endeavouring to obtain logarithms to more than 7 places by extending the 7-figure logarithms given in the tables, because the 7th figure there given may be too great or too small to the extent of one-half of unity.

In a calculation of the type $a^m - (a + n)^m$, where a and the index m are large, and where n is small, if a fairly accurate result is desired, it is better to write the argument in the form $\left\{a^{\frac{m}{2}} + (a + n)^{\frac{m}{2}}\right\}\left\{a^{\frac{m}{2}} - (a + n)^{\frac{m}{2}}\right\}$, and evaluate it logarithmically.

EXAMPLE.

What is the value of $61^4 - 60^4$?

Twice Log. 61 = $3 \cdot 5706596$, of which the antilog. is 3721
Twice Log. 60 = $3 \cdot 5563026$,   "   "   3600

Sum of antilogs. = 7321, whose logarithm = $3 \cdot 8645704$
Difference "   "   = 121,   "   "   = $2 \cdot 0827854$
Hence $61^4 - 60^4$ = 885841,   "   "   = $5 \cdot 9473558$

The above calculation performed in the ordinary way gives :

$4 \times \text{log. } 61 = 7 \cdot 1413192$, antilog. = 13845837
$4 \times \text{log. } 60 = 7 \cdot 1126052$,   "   = 12960006
                    difference   885831

By ordinary arithmetic the absolutely correct result is 885841.

No.	Log.	No.	Log.	No.	Log.	No.	Log.	No.	Log.
1	0000000	51	7075702	101	0043214	151	1789769	201	3031961
2	3010300	52	7160033	102	0086002	152	1818436	202	3053514
3	4771213	53	7242759	103	0128372	153	1846914	203	3074960
4	6020600	54	7323938	104	0170333	154	1875207	204	3096302
5	6989700	55	7403627	105	0211893	155	1903317	205	3117539
6	7781513	56	7481880	106	0253059	156	1931246	206	3138672
7	8450980	57	7558749	107	0293838	157	1958997	207	3159703
8	9030900	58	7634280	108	0334238	158	1986571	208	3180633
9	9542425	59	7708520	109	0374265	159	2013971	209	3201463
10	0000000	60	7781513	110	0413927	160	2041200	210	3222193
11	0413927	61	7853298	111	0453230	161	2068259	211	3242825
12	0791812	62	7923917	112	0492180	162	2095150	212	3263359
13	1139434	63	7993405	113	0530784	163	2121876	213	3283796
14	1461280	64	8061800	114	0569049	164	2148438	214	3304138
15	1760913	65	8129134	115	0606978	165	2174839	215	3324385
16	2041200	66	8195439	116	0644580	166	2201081	216	3344538
17	2304489	67	8260748	117	0681859	167	2227165	217	3364597
18	2552725	68	8325089	118	0718820	168	2253093	218	3384565
19	2787536	69	8388491	119	0755470	169	2278867	219	3404441
20	3010300	70	8450980	120	0791812	170	2304489	220	3424227
21	3222193	71	8512583	121	0827854	171	2329961	221	3443923
22	3424227	72	8573325	122	0863598	172	2355284	222	3463530
23	3617278	73	8633229	123	0899051	173	2380461	223	3483049
24	3802112	74	8692317	124	0934217	174	2405492	224	3502480
25	3979400	75	8750613	125	0969100	175	2430380	225	3521825
26	4149733	76	8808136	126	1003705	176	2455127	226	3541084
27	4313638	77	8864907	127	1038037	177	2479733	227	3560259
28	4471580	78	8920946	128	1072100	178	2504200	228	3579348
29	4623980	79	8976271	129	1105897	179	2528530	229	3598355
30	4771213	80	9030900	130	1139434	180	2552725	230	3617278
31	4913617	81	9084850	131	1172713	181	2576786	231	3636120
32	5051500	82	9138139	132	1205739	182	2600714	232	3654880
33	5185139	83	9190781	133	1238516	183	2624511	233	3673559
34	5314789	84	9242793	134	1271048	184	2648178	234	3692159
35	5440680	85	9294189	135	1303338	185	2671717	235	3710679
36	5563025	86	9344985	136	1335389	186	2695129	236	3729120
37	5682017	87	9395193	137	1367206	187	2718416	237	3747483
38	5797836	88	9444827	138	1398791	188	2741578	238	3765770
39	5910646	89	9493900	139	1430148	189	2764618	239	3783979
40	6020600	90	9542425	140	1461280	190	2787536	240	3802112
41	6127839	91	9590414	141	1492191	191	2810334	241	3820170
42	6232493	92	9637878	142	1522883	192	2833012	242	3838154
43	6334685	93	9684829	143	1553360	193	2855573	243	3856063
44	6434527	94	9731279	144	1583625	194	2878017	244	3873898
45	6532125	95	9777236	145	1613680	195	2900346	245	3891661
46	6627578	96	9822712	146	1643529	196	2922561	246	3909351
47	6720979	97	9867717	147	1673173	197	2944662	247	3926970
48	6812412	98	9912261	148	1702617	198	2966652	248	3944517
49	6901961	99	9956352	149	1731863	199	2988531	249	3961993
50	6989700	100	0000000	150	1760913	200	3010300	250	3979400

No.	Log.	No.	Log.	No.	Log.	No.	Log.	No.	Log.
251	3996737	301	4785665	351	5453071	401	6031444	451	6541765
252	4014005	302	4800069	352	5465427	402	6042261	452	6551384
253	4031205	303	4814426	353	5477747	403	6053050	453	6560982
254	4048337	304	4828736	354	5490033	404	6063814	454	6570559
255	4065402	305	4842998	355	5502284	405	6074550	455	6580114
256	4082400	306	4857214	356	5514500	406	6085260	456	6589648
257	4099331	307	4871384	357	5526682	407	6095944	457	6599162
258	4116197	308	4885507	358	5538830	408	6106602	458	6608655
259	4132998	309	4899585	359	5550944	409	6117233	459	6618127
260	4149733	310	4913617	360	5563025	410	6127839	460	6627578
261	4166405	311	4927604	361	5575072	411	6138418	461	6637009
262	4183013	312	4941546	362	5587086	412	6148972	462	6646420
263	4199557	313	4955443	363	5599066	413	6159501	463	6655810
264	4216039	314	4969296	364	5611014	414	6170003	464	6665180
265	4232459	315	4983106	365	5622929	415	6180481	465	6674530
266	4248816	316	4996871	366	5634811	416	6190933	466	6683859
267	4265113	317	5010593	367	5646661	417	6201361	467	6693169
268	4281348	318	5024271	368	5658478	418	6211763	468	6702459
269	4297523	319	5037907	369	5670264	419	6222140	469	6711728
270	4313638	320	5051500	370	5682017	420	6232493	470	6720979
271	4329693	321	5065050	371	5693739	421	6242821	471	6730209
272	4345689	322	5078559	372	5705429	422	6253125	472	6739420
273	4361626	323	5092025	373	5717088	423	6263404	473	6748611
274	4377506	324	5105450	374	5728716	424	6273659	474	6757783
275	4393327	325	5118834	375	5740313	425	6283889	475	6766936
276	4409091	326	5132176	376	5751878	426	6294096	476	6776070
277	4424798	327	5145478	377	5763414	427	6304279	477	6785184
278	4440448	328	5158738	378	5774918	428	6314438	478	6794279
279	4456042	329	5171959	379	5786392	429	6324573	479	6803355
280	4471580	330	5185139	380	5797836	430	6334685	480	6812412
281	4487063	331	5198280	381	5809250	431	6344773	481	6821451
282	4502491	332	5211381	382	5820634	432	6354837	482	6830470
283	4517864	333	5224442	383	5831988	433	6364879	483	6839471
284	4533183	334	5237465	384	5843312	434	6374897	484	6848454
285	4548449	335	5250448	385	5854607	435	6384893	485	6857417
286	4563660	336	5263393	386	5865873	436	6394865	486	6866363
287	4578819	337	5276299	387	5877110	437	6404814	487	6875290
288	4593925	338	5289167	388	5888317	438	6414741	488	6884198
289	4608978	339	5301997	389	5899496	439	6424645	489	6893089
290	4623980	340	5314789	390	5910646	440	6434527	490	6901961
291	4638930	341	5327544	391	5921768	441	6444386	491	6910815
292	4653829	342	5340261	392	5932861	442	6454223	492	6919651
293	4668676	343	5352941	393	5943926	443	6464037	493	6928469
294	4683473	344	5365584	394	5954962	444	6473830	494	6937269
295	4698220	345	5378191	395	5965971	445	6483600	495	6946052
296	4712917	346	5390761	396	5976952	446	6493349	496	6954817
297	4727564	347	5403295	397	5987905	447	6503075	497	6963564
298	4742163	348	5415792	398	5998831	448	6512780	498	6972293
299	4756712	349	5428254	399	6009729	449	6522463	499	6981005
300	4771213	350	5440680	400	6020600	450	6532125	500	6989700

No.	Log.	No.	Log.	No.	Log.	No.	Log.	No.	Log.
501	6998377	551	7411516	601	7788745	651	8135810	701	8457180
502	7007037	552	7419391	602	7795965	652	8142476	702	8463371
503	7015680	553	7427251	603	7803173	653	8149132	703	8469553
504	7024305	554	7435098	604	7810369	654	8155777	704	8475727
505	7032914	555	7442930	605	7817554	655	8162413	705	8481891
506	7041505	556	7450748	606	7824726	656	8169038	706	8488047
507	7050080	557	7458552	607	7831887	657	8175654	707	8494194
508	7058637	558	7466342	608	7839036	658	8182259	708	8500333
509	7067178	559	7474118	609	7846173	659	8188854	709	8506462
510	7075702	560	7481880	610	7853298	660	8195439	710	8512583
511	7084209	561	7489629	611	7860412	661	8202015	711	8518696
512	7092700	562	7497363	612	7867514	662	8208580	712	8524800
513	7101174	563	7505084	613	7874605	663	8215135	713	8530895
514	7109631	564	7512791	614	7881684	664	8221681	714	8536982
515	7118072	565	7520484	615	7888751	665	8228216	715	8543060
516	7126497	566	7528164	616	7895807	666	8234742	716	8549130
517	7134905	567	7535831	617	7902852	667	8241258	717	8555192
518	7143298	568	7543483	618	7909885	668	8247765	718	8561244
519	7151674	569	7551123	619	7916906	669	8254261	719	8567289
520	7160033	570	7558749	620	7923917	670	8260748	720	8573325
521	7168377	571	7566361	621	7930916	671	8267225	721	8579353
522	7176705	572	7573960	622	7937904	672	8273693	722	8585372
523	7185017	573	7581546	623	7944880	673	8280151	723	8591383
524	7193313	574	7589119	624	7951846	674	8286599	724	8597386
525	7201593	575	7596678	625	7958800	675	8293038	725	8603380
526	7209857	576	7604225	626	7965743	676	8299467	726	8609366
527	7218106	577	7611758	627	7972675	677	8305887	727	8615344
528	7226339	578	7619278	628	7979596	678	8312297	728	8621314
529	7234557	579	7626786	629	7986506	679	8318698	729	8627275
530	7242759	580	7634280	630	7993405	680	8325089	730	8633229
531	7250945	581	7641761	631	8000294	681	8331471	731	8639174
532	7259116	582	7649230	632	8007171	682	8337844	732	8645111
533	7267272	583	7656686	633	8014037	683	8344207	733	8651040
534	7275413	584	7664128	634	8020893	684	8350561	734	8656961
535	7283538	585	7671559	635	8027737	685	8356906	735	8662873
536	7291648	586	7678976	636	8034571	686	8363241	736	8668778
537	7299743	587	7686381	637	8041394	687	8369567	737	8674675
538	7307823	588	7693773	638	8048207	688	8375884	738	8680564
539	7315888	589	7701153	639	8055009	689	8382192	739	8686444
540	7323938	590	7708520	640	8061800	690	8388491	740	8692317
541	7331973	591	7715875	641	8068580	691	8394780	741	8698182
542	7339993	592	7723217	642	8075350	692	8401061	742	8704039
543	7347998	593	7730547	643	8082110	693	8407332	743	8709888
544	7355989	594	7737864	644	8088859	694	8413595	744	8715729
545	7363965	595	7745170	645	8095597	695	8419848	745	8721563
546	7371926	596	7752463	646	8102325	696	8426092	746	8727388
547	7379873	597	7759743	647	8109043	697	8432328	747	8733206
548	7387806	598	7767012	648	8115750	698	8438554	748	8739016
549	7395723	599	7774268	649	8122447	699	8444772	749	8744818
550	7403627	600	7781513	650	8129134	700	8450980	750	8750613

1c

No.	Log.	No.	Log.	No.	Log.	No.	Log.	No.	Log.
751	8756399	801	9036325	851	9299296	901	9547248	951	9781805
752	8762178	802	9041744	852	9304396	902	9552065	952	9786369
753	8767950	803	9047155	853	9309490	903	9556878	953	9790929
754	8773713	804	9052560	854	9314579	904	9561684	954	9795484
755	8779470	805	9057959	855	9319661	905	9566486	955	9800034
756	8785218	806	9063350	856	9324738	906	9571282	956	9804579
757	8790959	807	9068735	857	9329808	907	9576073	957	9809119
758	8796692	808	9074114	858	9334873	908	9580858	958	9813655
759	8802418	809	9079485	859	9339932	909	9585639	959	9818186
760	8808136	810	9084850	860	9344985	910	9590414	960	9822712
761	8813847	811	9090209	861	9350032	911	9595184	961	9827234
762	8819550	812	9095560	862	9355073	912	9599948	962	9831751
763	8825245	813	9100905	863	9360108	913	9604708	963	9836263
764	8830934	814	9106244	864	9365137	914	9609462	964	9840770
765	8836614	815	9111576	865	9370161	915	9614211	965	9845273
766	8842288	816	9116902	866	9375179	916	9618955	966	9849771
767	8847954	817	9122221	867	9380191	917	9623693	967	9854265
768	8853612	818	9127533	868	9385197	918	9628427	968	9858754
769	8859263	819	9132839	869	9390198	919	9633155	969	9863238
770	8864907	820	9138139	870	9395193	920	9637878	970	9867717
771	8870544	821	9143432	871	9400182	921	9642596	971	9872192
772	8876173	822	9148718	872	9405165	922	9647309	972	9876663
773	8881795	823	9153998	873	9410142	923	9652017	973	9881128
774	8887410	824	9159272	874	9415114	924	9656720	974	9885590
775	8893017	825	9164539	875	9420081	925	9661417	975	9890046
776	8898617	826	9169800	876	9425041	926	9666110	976	9894498
777	8904210	827	9175055	877	9429996	927	9670797	977	9898946
778	8909796	828	9180303	878	9434945	928	9675480	978	9903389
779	8915375	829	9185545	879	9439889	929	9680157	979	9907827
780	8920946	830	9190781	880	9444827	930	9684829	980	9912261
781	8926510	831	9196010	881	9449759	931	9689497	981	9916690
782	8932068	832	9201233	882	9454686	932	9694159	982	9921115
783	8937618	833	9206450	883	9459607	933	9698816	983	9925535
784	8943161	834	9211661	884	9464523	934	9703469	984	9929951
785	8948697	835	9216865	885	9469433	935	9708116	985	9934362
786	8954225	836	9222063	886	9474337	936	9712758	986	9938769
787	8959747	837	9227255	887	9479236	937	9717396	987	9943172
788	8965262	838	9232440	888	9484130	938	9722028	988	9947569
789	8970770	839	9237620	889	9489018	939	9726656	989	9951963
790	8976271	840	9242793	890	9493900	940	9731279	990	9956352
791	8981765	841	9247960	891	9498777	941	9735896	991	9960737
792	8987252	842	9253121	892	9503649	942	9740509	992	9965117
793	8992732	843	9258276	893	9508515	943	9745117	993	9969492
794	8998205	844	9263424	894	9513375	944	9749720	994	9973864
795	9003671	845	9268567	895	9518230	945	9754318	995	9978231
796	9009131	846	9273704	896	9523080	946	9758911	996	9982593
797	9014583	847	9278834	897	9527924	947	9763500	997	9986952
798	9020029	848	9283959	898	9532763	948	9768083	998	9991305
799	9025468	849	9289077	899	9537597	949	9772662	999	9995655
800	9030900	850	9294189	900	9542425	950	9777236		

No.	0	1	2	3	4	5	6	7	8	9	Diff.
1000	000 0000	0434	0869	1303	1737	2171	2605	3039	3473	3907	
01	4341	4775	5208	5642	6076	6510	6943	7377	7810	8244	
02	8677	9111	9544	9977	0̄411	0̄844	1̄277	1̄710	2̄143	2̄576	**433**
03	001 3009	3442	3875	4308	4741	5174	5607	6039	6472	6905	1 43 · 2 87
04	7337	7770	8202	8635	9067	9499	9932	0̄364	0̄796	1̄228	3 130 · 5 217
05	002 1661	2093	2525	2957	3389	3821	4253	4685	5116	5548	4 173
06	5980	6411	6843	7275	7706	8138	8569	9001	9432	9863	6 260 · 7 303
07	003 0295	0726	1157	1588	2019	2451	2882	3313	3744	4174	8 346
08	4605	5036	5467	5898	6328	6759	7190	7620	8051	8481	9 390
09	8912	9342	9772	0̄203	0̄633	1̄063	1̄493	1̄924	2̄354	2̄784	**430**
10	004 3214	3644	4074	4504	4933	5363	5793	6223	6652	7082	1 43 · 2 86
1011	7512	7941	8371	8800	9229	9659	0̄088	0̄517	0̄947	1̄376	3 129 · 4 172
12	005 1805	2234	2663	3092	3521	3950	4379	4808	5237	5666	5 215 · 6 258
13	6094	6523	6952	7380	7809	8238	8666	9094	9523	9951	7 301 · 8 344
14	006 0380	0808	1236	1664	2092	2521	2949	3377	3805	4233	9 387
15	4660	5088	5516	5944	6372	6799	7227	7655	8082	8510	
16	8937	9365	9792	0̄219	0̄647	1̄074	1̄501	1̄928	2̄355	2̄782	**427**
17	007 3210	3637	4064	4490	4917	5344	5771	6198	6624	7051	1 43 · 2 85
18	7478	7904	8331	8757	9184	9610	0̄037	0̄463	0̄889	1̄316	3 128 · 4 171
19	008 1742	2168	2594	3020	3446	3872	4298	4724	5150	5576	5 214 · 6 256
20	6002	6427	6853	7279	7704	8130	8556	8981	9407	9832	7 299 · 8 342
1021	009 0257	0683	1108	1533	1959	2384	2809	3234	3659	4084	9 384
22	4509	4934	5359	5784	6208	6633	7058	7483	7907	8332	
23	8756	9181	9605	0̄030	0̄454	0̄878	1̄303	1̄727	2̄151	2̄575	**424**
24	010 3000	3424	3848	4272	4696	5120	5544	5967	6391	6815	1 42 · 2 85
25	7239	7662	8086	8510	8933	9357	9780	0̄204	0̄627	1̄050	3 127 · 4 170
26	011 1474	1897	2320	2743	3166	3590	4013	4436	4859	5282	5 212 · 6 254
27	5704	6127	6550	6973	7396	7818	8241	8664	9086	9509	7 297 · 8 339
28	9931	0̄354	0̄776	1̄198	1̄621	2̄043	2̄465	2̄887	3̄310	3̄732	9 382
29	012 4154	4576	4998	5420	5842	6264	6685	7107	7529	7951	
30	8372	8794	9215	9637	0̄059	0̄480	0̄901	1̄323	1̄744	2̄165	**421**
1031	013 2587	3008	3429	3850	4271	4692	5113	5534	5955	6376	1 42 · 2 84
32	6797	7218	7639	8059	8480	8901	9321	9742	0̄162	0̄583	3 126 · 4 169
33	014 1003	1424	1844	2264	2685	3105	3525	3945	4365	4785	5 211 · 6 253
34	5205	5625	6045	6465	6885	7305	7725	8144	8564	8984	7 295 · 8 337
35	9403	9823	0̄243	0̄662	1̄082	1̄501	1̄920	2̄340	2̄759	3̄178	9 379
36	015 3598	4017	4436	4855	5274	5693	6112	6531	6950	7369	
37	7788	8206	8625	9044	9462	9881	0̄300	0̄718	1̄137	1̄555	
38	016 1974	2392	2810	3229	3647	4065	4483	4901	5319	5737	**418**
39	6155	6573	6991	7409	7827	8245	8663	9080	9498	9916	1 42 · 2 84
40	017 0333	0751	1168	1586	2003	2421	2838	3256	3673	4090	3 125 · 4 167
1041	4507	4924	5342	5759	6176	6593	7010	7427	7844	8260	5 209 · 6 251
42	8677	9094	9511	9927	0̄344	0̄761	1̄177	1̄594	2̄010	2̄427	7 293 · 8 334
43	018 2843	3259	3676	4092	4508	4925	5341	5757	6173	6589	9 376
44	7005	7421	7837	8253	8669	9084	9500	9916	0̄332	0̄747	
45	019 1163	1578	1994	2410	2825	3240	3656	4071	4486	4902	**415**
46	5317	5732	6147	6562	6977	7392	7807	8222	8637	9052	1 42 · 2 83
47	9467	9882	0̄296	0̄711	1̄126	1̄540	1̄955	2̄369	2̄784	3̄198	3 125 · 4 166
48	020 3613	4027	4442	4856	5270	5684	6099	6513	6927	7341	5 208 · 6 249
49	7755	8169	8583	8997	9411	9824	0̄238	0̄652	1̄066	1̄479	7 291 · 8 332
1050	021 1893	2307	2720	3134	3547	3961	4374	4787	5201	5614	9 374

No.	0	1	2	3	4	5	6	7	8	9	Diff.
1050	021 1893	2307	2720	3134	3547	3961	4374	4787	5201	5614	
51	6027	6440	6854	7267	7680	8093	8506	8919	9332	9745	
52	022 0157	0570	0983	1396	1808	2221	2634	3046	3459	3871	
53	4284	4696	5109	5521	5933	6345	6758	7170	7582	7994	412 1 41 2 82 3 124 4 165 5 206 6 247 7 288 8 330 9 371
54	8406	8818	9230	9642	0054	0466	0878	1289	1701	2113	
55	023 2525	2936	3348	3759	4171	4582	4994	5405	5817	6228	
56	6639	7050	7462	7873	8284	8695	9106	9517	9928	0339	
57	024 0750	1161	1572	1982	2393	2804	3214	3625	4036	4446	
58	4857	5267	5678	6088	6498	6909	7319	7729	8139	8549	
59	8960	9370	9780	0190	0600	1010	1419	1829	2239	2649	409 1 41 2 82 3 123 4 164 5 205 6 245 7 286 8 327 9 368
60	025 3059	3468	3878	4288	4697	5107	5516	5926	6335	6744	
1061	7154	7563	7972	8382	8791	9200	9609	0018	0427	0836	
62	026 1245	1654	2063	2472	2881	3289	3698	4107	4515	4924	
63	5333	5741	6150	6558	6967	7375	7783	8192	8600	9008	
64	9416	9824	0233	0641	1049	1457	1865	2273	2680	3088	
65	027 3496	3904	4312	4719	5127	5535	5942	6350	6757	7165	
66	7572	7979	8387	8794	9201	9609	0016	0423	0830	1237	
67	028 1644	2051	2458	2865	3272	3679	4086	4492	4899	5306	
68	5713	6119	6526	6932	7339	7745	8152	8558	8964	9371	406 1 41 2 81 3 122 4 162 5 203 6 244 7 284 8 325 9 365
69	9777	0183	0590	0996	1402	1808	2214	2620	3026	3432	
70	029 3838	4244	4649	5055	5461	5867	6272	6678	7084	7489	
1071	7895	8300	8706	9111	9516	9922	0327	0732	1138	1543	
72	030 1948	2353	2758	3163	3568	3973	4378	4783	5188	5592	
73	5997	6402	6807	7211	7616	8020	8425	8830	9234	9638	
74	031 0043	0447	0851	1256	1660	2064	2468	2872	3277	3681	
75	4085	4489	4893	5296	5700	6104	6508	6912	7315	7719	
76	8123	8526	8930	9333	9737	0140	0544	0947	1350	1754	403 1 40 2 81 3 121 4 161 5 202 6 242 7 282 8 322 9 363
77	032 2157	2560	2963	3367	3770	4173	4576	4979	5382	5785	
78	6188	6590	6993	7396	7799	8201	8604	9007	9409	9812	
79	033 0214	0617	1019	1422	1824	2226	2629	3031	3433	3835	
80	4238	4640	5042	5444	5846	6248	6650	7052	7453	7855	
1081	8257	8659	9060	9462	9864	0265	0667	1068	1470	1871	
82	034 2273	2674	3075	3477	3878	4279	4680	5081	5482	5884	
83	6285	6686	7087	7487	7888	8289	8690	9091	9491	9892	
84	035 0293	0693	1094	1495	1895	2296	2696	3096	3497	3897	400 1 40 2 80 3 120 4 160 5 200 6 240 7 280 8 320 9 360
85	4297	4698	5098	5498	5898	6298	6698	7098	7498	7898	
86	8298	8698	9098	9498	9898	0297	0697	1097	1496	1896	
87	036 2295	2695	3094	3494	3893	4293	4692	5091	5491	5890	
88	6289	6688	7087	7486	7885	8284	8683	9082	9481	9880	
89	037 0279	0678	1076	1475	1874	2272	2671	3070	3468	3867	
90	4265	4663	5062	5460	5858	6257	6655	7053	7451	7849	
1091	8248	8646	9044	9442	9839	0237	0635	1033	1431	1829	
92	038 2226	2624	3022	3419	3817	4214	4612	5009	5407	5804	397 1 40 2 79 3 119 4 159 5 199 6 238 7 278 8 318 9 357
93	6202	6599	6996	7393	7791	8188	8585	8982	9379	9776	
94	039 0173	0570	0967	1364	1761	2158	2554	2951	3348	3745	
95	4141	4538	4934	5331	5727	6124	6520	6917	7313	7709	
96	8106	8502	8898	9294	9690	0086	0482	0878	1274	1670	
97	040 2066	2462	2858	3254	3650	4045	4441	4837	5232	5628	
98	6023	6419	6814	7210	7605	8001	8396	8791	9187	9582	
99	9977	0372	0767	1162	1557	1952	2347	2742	3137	3532	
1100	041 3927	4322	4716	5111	5506	5900	6295	6690	7084	7479	

No.	0	1	2	3	4	5	6	7	8	9	Diff.
1100	041 3927	4322	4716	5111	5506	5900	6295	6690	7084	7479	394
01	7873	8268	8662	9056	9451	9845	0239	0633	1028	1422	1 39
02	042 1816	2210	2604	2998	3392	3786	4180	4574	4968	5361	2 79
03	5755	6149	6543	6936	7330	7723	8117	8510	8904	9297	3 118
04	9691	0084	0477	0871	1264	1657	2050	2444	2837	3230	4 158
05	043 3623	4016	4409	4802	5195	5587	5980	6373	6766	7159	5 197
06	7551	7944	8337	8729	9122	9514	9907	0299	0692	1084	6 236 / 7 276
07	044 1476	1869	2261	2653	3045	3437	3829	4222	4614	5006	8 315
08	5398	5790	6181	6573	6965	7357	7749	8140	8532	8924	9 355
09	9315	9707	0099	0490	0882	1273	1664	2056	2447	2839	391
10	045 3230	3621	4012	4403	4795	5186	5577	5968	6359	6750	1 39
1111	7141	7531	7922	8313	8704	9095	9485	9876	0267	0657	2 78
12	046 1048	1438	1829	2219	2610	3000	3391	3781	4171	4561	3 117
13	4952	5342	5732	6122	6512	6902	7292	7682	8072	8462	4 156
14	8852	9242	9632	0021	0411	0801	1190	1580	1970	2359	5 196
15	047 2749	3138	3528	3917	4306	4696	5085	5474	5864	6253	6 235 / 7 274
16	6642	7031	7420	7809	8198	8587	8976	9365	9754	0143	8 313
17	048 0532	0921	1309	1698	2087	2475	2864	3253	3641	4030	9 352
18	4418	4806	5195	5583	5972	6360	6748	7136	7525	7913	388
19	8301	8689	9077	9465	9853	0241	0629	1017	1405	1792	1 39
20	049 2180	2568	2956	3343	3731	4119	4506	4894	5281	5669	2 78 / 3 116
1121	6056	6444	6831	7218	7606	7993	8380	8767	9154	9541	4 155
22	9929	0316	0703	1090	1477	1863	2250	2637	3024	3411	5 194
23	050 3798	4184	4571	4958	5344	5731	6117	6504	6890	7277	6 233 / 7 272
24	7663	8049	8436	8822	9208	9595	9981	0367	0753	1139	8 310
25	051 1525	1911	2297	2683	3069	3455	3841	4227	4612	4998	9 349
26	5384	5770	6155	6541	6926	7312	7697	8083	8468	8854	385
27	9239	9624	0010	0395	0780	1166	1551	1936	2321	2706	1 39
28	052 3091	3476	3861	4246	4631	5016	5400	5785	6170	6555	2 77 / 3 116
29	6939	7324	7709	8093	8478	8862	9247	9631	0016	0400	4 154
30	053 0784	1169	1553	1937	2321	2706	3090	3474	3858	4242	5 193 / 6 231
1131	4626	5010	5394	5778	6162	6546	6929	7313	7697	8081	7 270
32	8464	8848	9232	9615	9999	0382	0766	1149	1532	1916	8 308
33	054 2299	2682	3066	3449	3832	4215	4598	4981	5365	5748	9 347
34	6131	6514	6896	7279	7662	8045	8428	8811	9193	9576	
35	9959	0341	0724	1106	1489	1871	2254	2636	3019	3401	382
36	055 3783	4166	4548	4930	5312	5694	6077	6459	6841	7223	1 38
37	7605	7987	8369	8750	9132	9514	9896	0278	0659	1041	2 76 / 3 115
38	056 1423	1804	2186	2567	2949	3330	3712	4093	4475	4856	4 153
39	5237	5619	6000	6381	6762	7143	7524	7905	8287	8668	5 191 / 6 229
40	9049	9429	9810	0191	0572	0953	1334	1714	2095	2476	7 267 / 8 306
1141	057 2856	3237	3618	3998	4379	4759	5140	5520	5900	6281	9 344
42	6661	7041	7422	7802	8182	8562	8942	9322	9702	0082	
43	058 0462	0842	1222	1602	1982	2362	2741	3121	3501	3881	
44	4260	4640	5019	5399	5778	6158	6537	6917	7296	7676	379
45	8055	8434	8813	9193	9572	9951	0330	0709	1088	1467	1 38 / 2 76
46	059 1846	2225	2604	2983	3362	3741	4119	4498	4877	5256	3 114 / 4 152
47	5634	6013	6391	6770	7148	7527	7905	8284	8662	9041	5 190
48	9419	9797	0175	0554	0932	1310	1688	2066	2444	2822	6 227 / 7 265
49	060 3200	3578	3956	4334	4712	5090	5468	5845	6223	6601	8 303
1150	6978	7356	7734	8111	8489	8866	9244	9621	9999	0376	9 341
	061										

4

No.	0	1	2	3	4	5	6	7	8	9	Diff.
1150	060 6978	7356	7734	8111	8489	8866	9244	9621	9999	$\overline{0376}$	
51	061 0753	1131	1508	1885	2262	2639	3017	3394	3771	4148	
52	4525	4902	5279	5656	6032	6409	6786	7163	7540	7916	376
53	8293	8670	9046	9423	9799	$\overline{0176}$	$\overline{0552}$	$\overline{0929}$	$\overline{1305}$	$\overline{1682}$	1 38
54	062 2058	2434	2811	3187	3563	3939	4316	4692	5068	5444	2 75
55	5820	6196	6572	6948	7324	7699	8075	8451	8827	9203	3 113
56	9578	9954	$\overline{0330}$	$\overline{0705}$	$\overline{1081}$	$\overline{1456}$	$\overline{1832}$	$\overline{2207}$	$\overline{2583}$	$\overline{2958}$	4 150
57	063 3334	3709	4084	4460	4835	5210	5585	5960	6335	6711	5 188
58	7086	7461	7836	8211	8585	8960	9335	9710	$\overline{0085}$	$\overline{0460}$	6 226
59	064 0834	1209	1584	1958	2333	2708	3082	3457	3831	4205	7 263
60	4580	4954	5329	5703	6077	6451	6826	7200	7574	7948	8 301
1161	8322	8696	9070	9444	9818	$\overline{0192}$	$\overline{0566}$	$\overline{0940}$	$\overline{1314}$	$\overline{1688}$	9 338
62	065 2061	2435	2809	3182	3556	3930	4303	4677	5050	5424	
63	5797	6171	6544	6917	7291	7664	8037	8410	8784	9157	373
64	9530	9903	$\overline{0276}$	$\overline{0649}$	$\overline{1022}$	$\overline{1395}$	$\overline{1768}$	$\overline{2141}$	$\overline{2514}$	$\overline{2886}$	1 37
65	066 3259	3632	4005	4377	4750	5123	5495	5868	6241	6613	2 75
66	6986	7358	7730	8103	8475	8847	9220	9592	9964	$\overline{0336}$	3 112
67	067 0709	1081	1453	1825	2197	2569	2941	3313	3685	4057	4 149
68	4428	4800	5172	5544	5915	6287	6659	7030	7402	7774	5 187
69	8145	8517	8888	9259	9631	$\overline{0002}$	$\overline{0374}$	$\overline{0745}$	$\overline{1116}$	$\overline{1487}$	6 224
70	068 1859	2230	2601	2972	3343	3714	4085	4456	4827	5198	7 261
1171	5569	5940	6311	6681	7052	7423	7794	8164	8535	8906	8 298
72	9276	9647	$\overline{0017}$	$\overline{0388}$	$\overline{0758}$	$\overline{1129}$	$\overline{1499}$	$\overline{1869}$	$\overline{2240}$	$\overline{2610}$	9 336
73	069 2980	3350	3721	4091	4461	4831	5201	5571	5941	6311	370
74	6681	7051	7421	7791	8160	8530	8900	9270	9639	$\overline{0009}$	1 37
75	070 0379	0748	1118	1487	1857	2226	2596	2965	3335	3704	2 74
76	4073	4442	4812	5181	5550	5919	6288	6658	7027	7396	3 111
77	7765	8134	8503	8871	9240	9609	9978	$\overline{0347}$	$\overline{0715}$	$\overline{1084}$	4 148
78	071 1453	1822	2190	2559	2927	3296	3664	4033	4401	4770	5 185
79	5138	5506	5875	6243	6611	6979	7348	7716	8084	8452	6 222
80	8820	9188	9556	9924	$\overline{0292}$	$\overline{0660}$	$\overline{1028}$	$\overline{1396}$	$\overline{1763}$	$\overline{2131}$	7 259
1181	072 2499	2867	3234	3602	3970	4337	4705	5072	5440	5807	8 296
82	6175	6542	6910	7277	7644	8011	8379	8746	9113	9480	9 333
83	9847	$\overline{0215}$	$\overline{0582}$	$\overline{0949}$	$\overline{1316}$	$\overline{1683}$	$\overline{2050}$	$\overline{2416}$	$\overline{2783}$	$\overline{3150}$	367
84	073 3517	3884	4251	4617	4984	5351	5717	6084	6450	6817	1 37
85	7184	7550	7916	8283	8649	9016	9382	9748	$\overline{0114}$	$\overline{0481}$	2 73
86	074 0847	1213	1579	1945	2311	2677	3043	3409	3775	4141	3 110
87	4507	4873	5239	5605	5970	6336	6702	7068	7433	7799	4 147
88	8164	8530	8895	9261	9626	9992	$\overline{0357}$	$\overline{0723}$	$\overline{1088}$	$\overline{1453}$	5 184
89	075 1819	2184	2549	2914	3279	3644	4010	4375	4740	5105	6 220
90	5470	5835	6199	6564	6929	7294	7659	8024	8388	8753	7 257
1191	9118	9482	9847	$\overline{0211}$	$\overline{0576}$	$\overline{0940}$	$\overline{1305}$	$\overline{1669}$	$\overline{2034}$	$\overline{2398}$	8 294
92	076 2763	3127	3491	3855	4220	4584	4948	5312	5676	6040	9 330
93	6404	6768	7132	7496	7860	8224	8588	8952	9316	9680	364
94	077 0043	0407	0771	1134	1498	1862	2225	2589	2952	3316	1 36
95	3679	4042	4406	4769	5133	5496	5859	6222	6585	6949	2 73
96	7312	7675	8038	8401	8764	9127	9490	9853	$\overline{0216}$	$\overline{0579}$	3 109
97	078 0942	1304	1667	2030	2393	2755	3118	3480	3843	4206	4 146
98	4568	4931	5293	5656	6018	6380	6743	7105	7467	7830	5 182
99	8192	8554	8916	9278	9640	$\overline{0003}$	$\overline{0365}$	$\overline{0727}$	$\overline{1089}$	$\overline{1451}$	6 218
1200	079 1812	2174	2536	2898	3260	3622	3983	4345	4707	5068	7 255

8 291
9 328

No.	0	1	2	3	4	5	6	7	8	9	Diff.
1200	079 1812	2174	2536	2898	3260	3622	3983	4345	4707	5068	
01	5430	5792	6153	6515	6876	7238	7599	7961	8322	8683	361
02	9045	9406	9767	0̅1̅2̅8̅	0̅4̅9̅0̅	0̅8̅5̅1̅	1̅2̅1̅2̅	1̅5̅7̅3̅	1̅9̅3̅4̅	2̅2̅9̅5̅	1 36
03	080 2656	3017	3378	3739	4100	4461	4822	5183	5543	5904	2 72
04	6265	6626	6986	7347	7707	8068	8429	8789	9150	9510	3 108
05	9870	0̅2̅3̅1̅	0̅5̅9̅1̅	0̅9̅5̅2̅	1̅3̅1̅2̅	1̅6̅7̅2̅	2̅0̅3̅2̅	2̅3̅9̅3̅	2̅7̅5̅3̅	3̅1̅1̅3̅	4 144
											5 181
06	081 3473	3833	4193	4553	4913	5273	5633	5993	6353	6713	6 217
07	7073	7432	7792	8152	8512	8871	9231	9591	9950	0̅3̅1̅0̅	7 253
08	082 0669	1029	1388	1748	2107	2467	2826	3185	3545	3904	8 289
09	4263	4622	4981	5341	5700	6059	6418	6777	7136	7495	9 325
10	7854	8213	8571	8930	9289	9648	0̅0̅0̅7̅	0̅3̅6̅5̅	0̅7̅2̅4̅	1̅0̅8̅3̅	
											358
1211	083 1441	1800	2159	2517	2876	3234	3593	3951	4309	4668	1 36
12	5026	5385	5743	6101	6459	6817	7176	7534	7892	8250	2 72
13	8608	8966	9324	9682	0̅0̅4̅0̅	0̅3̅9̅8̅	0̅7̅5̅6̅	1̅1̅1̅4̅	1̅4̅7̅1̅	1̅8̅2̅9̅	3 107
14	084 2187	2545	2902	3260	3618	3975	4333	4690	5048	5405	4 143
15	5763	6120	6478	6835	7192	7550	7907	8264	8621	8979	5 179
											6 215
16	9336	9693	0̅0̅5̅0̅	0̅4̅0̅7̅	0̅7̅6̅4̅	1̅1̅2̅1̅	1̅4̅7̅8̅	1̅8̅3̅5̅	2̅1̅9̅2̅	2̅5̅4̅9̅	7 251
17	085 2906	3263	3619	3976	4333	4690	5046	5403	5760	6116	8 286
18	6473	6829	7186	7542	7899	8255	8612	8968	9324	9681	9 322
19	086 0037	0393	0750	1106	1462	1818	2174	2530	2886	3242	
20	3598	3954	4310	4666	5022	5378	5734	6089	6445	6801	
1221	7157	7512	7868	8224	8579	8935	9290	9646	0̅0̅0̅1̅	0̅3̅5̅7̅	355
22	087 0712	1067	1423	1778	2133	2489	2844	3199	3554	3909	1 36
23	4265	4620	4975	5330	5685	6040	6395	6750	7104	7459	2 71
24	7814	8169	8524	8878	9233	9588	9943	0̅2̅9̅7̅	0̅6̅5̅2̅	1̅0̅0̅6̅	3 107
25	088 1361	1715	2070	2424	2779	3133	3488	3842	4196	4550	4 142
											5 178
26	4905	5259	5613	5967	6321	6676	7030	7384	7738	8092	6 213
27	8446	8800	9153	9507	9861	0̅2̅1̅5̅	0̅5̅6̅9̅	0̅9̅2̅3̅	1̅2̅7̅6̅	1̅6̅3̅0̅	7 249
28	089 1984	2337	2691	3045	3398	3752	4105	4459	4812	5165	8 284
29	5519	5872	6226	6579	6932	7285	7639	7992	8345	8698	9 320
30	9051	9404	9757	0̅1̅1̅0̅	0̅4̅6̅3̅	0̅8̅1̅6̅	1̅1̅6̅9̅	1̅5̅2̅2̅	1̅8̅7̅5̅	2̅2̅2̅8̅	
1231	090 2581	2933	3286	3639	3991	4344	4697	5049	5402	5755	352
32	6107	6460	6812	7164	7517	7869	8222	8574	8926	9279	1 35
33	9631	9983	0̅3̅3̅5̅	0̅6̅8̅7̅	1̅0̅3̅9̅	1̅3̅9̅2̅	1̅7̅4̅4̅	2̅0̅9̅6̅	2̅4̅4̅8̅	2̅8̅0̅0̅	2 70
34	091 3152	3504	3855	4207	4559	4911	5263	5614	5966	6318	3 106
35	6670	7021	7373	7724	8076	8427	8779	9130	9482	9833	4 141
											5 176
36	092 0185	0536	0887	1239	1590	1941	2292	2644	2995	3346	6 211
37	3697	4048	4399	4750	5101	5452	5803	6154	6505	6856	7 246
38	7206	7557	7908	8259	8609	8960	9311	9661	0̅0̅1̅2̅	0̅3̅6̅3̅	8 282
39	093 0713	1064	1414	1764	2115	2465	2816	3166	3516	3867	9 317
40	4217	4567	4917	5267	5618	5968	6318	6668	7018	7368	
1241	7718	8068	8418	8768	9117	9467	9817	0̅1̅6̅7̅	0̅5̅1̅7̅	0̅8̅6̅6̅	
42	094 1216	1566	1915	2265	2614	2964	3313	3663	4012	4362	349
43	4711	5061	5410	5759	6109	6458	6807	7156	7506	7855	1 35
44	8204	8553	8902	9251	9600	9949	0̅2̅9̅8̅	0̅6̅4̅7̅	0̅9̅9̅6̅	1̅3̅4̅5̅	2 70
45	095 1694	2042	2391	2740	3089	3437	3786	4135	4483	4832	3 105
											4 140
46	5180	5529	5877	6226	6574	6923	7271	7620	7968	8316	5 175
47	8665	9013	9361	9709	0̅0̅5̅7̅	0̅4̅0̅6̅	0̅7̅5̅4̅	1̅1̅0̅2̅	1̅4̅5̅0̅	1̅7̅9̅8̅	6 209
48	096 2146	2494	2842	3190	3538	3885	4233	4581	4929	5277	7 244
49	5624	5972	6320	6667	7015	7363	7710	8058	8405	8753	8 279
1250	9100	9448	9795	0̅1̅4̅2̅	0̅4̅9̅0̅	0̅8̅3̅7̅	1̅1̅8̅4̅	1̅5̅3̅1̅	1̅8̅7̅9̅	2̅2̅2̅6̅	9 314
	097										

No.	0	1	2	3	4	5	6	7	8	9	Diff.
1250	096 9100	9448	9795	0142	0490	0837	1184	1531	1879	2226	
51	097 2573	2920	3267	3614	3962	4309	4656	5003	5349	5696	
52	6043	6390	6737	7084	7431	7777	8124	8471	8817	9164	**346**
53	9511	9857	0204	0550	0897	1243	1590	1936	2283	2629	1 35
54	098 2975	3322	3668	4014	4360	4707	5053	5399	5745	6091	2 69
55	6437	6783	7129	7475	7821	8167	8513	8859	9205	9551	3 104 / 4 138
56	9896	0242	0588	0934	1279	1625	1971	2316	2662	3007	5 173
57	099 3353	3698	4044	4389	4735	5080	5425	5771	6116	6461	6 208
58	6806	7152	7497	7842	8187	8532	8877	9222	9567	9912	7 242
59	100 0257	0602	0947	1292	1637	1982	2327	2671	3016	3361	8 277
60	3705	4050	4395	4739	5084	5429	5773	6118	6462	6806	9 311
1261	7151	7495	7840	8184	8528	8873	9217	9561	9905	0249	
62	101 0594	0938	1282	1626	1970	2314	2658	3002	3346	3690	
63	4034	4377	4721	5065	5409	5752	6096	6440	6784	7127	
64	7471	7814	8158	8501	8845	9188	9532	9875	0219	0562	**343**
65	102 0905	1249	1592	1935	2278	2621	2965	3308	3651	3994	1 34
66	4337	4680	5023	5366	5709	6052	6395	6738	7081	7423	2 69 / 3 103
67	7766	8109	8452	8794	9137	9480	9822	0165	0507	0850	4 137
68	103 1193	1535	1877	2220	2562	2905	3247	3589	3932	4274	5 172
69	4616	4958	5301	5643	5985	6327	6669	7011	7353	7695	6 206
70	8037	8379	8721	9063	9405	9747	0089	0430	0772	1114	7 240 / 8 274
1271	104 1456	1797	2139	2480	2822	3164	3505	3847	4188	4530	9 309
72	4871	5213	5554	5895	6237	6578	6919	7260	7602	7943	
73	8284	8625	8966	9307	9648	9989	0331	0671	1012	1353	
74	105 1694	2035	2376	2717	3058	3398	3739	4080	4421	4761	
75	5102	5442	5783	6124	6464	6805	7145	7486	7826	8166	
76	8507	8847	9187	9528	9868	0208	0548	0889	1229	1569	**340**
77	106 1909	2249	2589	2929	3269	3609	3949	4289	4629	4969	1 34
78	5309	5648	5988	6328	6668	7007	7347	7687	8026	8366	2 68
79	8705	9045	9385	9724	0063	0403	0742	1082	1421	1760	3 102 / 4 136
80	107 2100	2439	2778	3117	3457	3796	4135	4474	4813	5152	5 170
1281	5491	5830	6169	6508	6847	7186	7525	7864	8203	8541	6 204
82	8880	9219	9558	9896	0235	0574	0912	1251	1590	1928	7 238 / 8 272
83	108 2267	2605	2944	3282	3620	3959	4297	4635	4974	5312	9 306
84	5650	5988	6327	6665	7003	7341	7679	8017	8355	8693	
85	9031	9369	9707	0045	0383	0721	1059	1396	1734	2072	
86	109 2410	2747	3085	3423	3760	4098	4435	4773	5111	5448	**337**
87	5785	6123	6460	6798	7135	7472	7810	8147	8484	8821	1 34
88	9159	9496	9833	0170	0507	0844	1181	1518	1855	2192	2 67 / 3 101
89	110 2529	2866	3203	3540	3877	4213	4550	4887	5224	5560	4 135 / 5 169
90	5897	6234	6570	6907	7244	7580	7917	8253	8590	8926	6 202
1291	9262	9599	9935	0272	0608	0944	1280	1617	1953	2289	7 236 / 8 270
92	111 2625	2961	3297	3633	3969	4306	4642	4977	5313	5649	9 303
93	5985	6321	6657	6993	7329	7664	8000	8336	8671	9007	**335**
94	9343	9678	0014	0350	0685	1021	1356	1691	2027	2362	1 34
95	112 2698	3033	3368	3704	4039	4374	4709	5045	5380	5715	2 67 / 3 101
96	6050	6385	6720	7055	7390	7725	8060	8395	8730	9065	4 134 / 5 168
97	9400	9735	0069	0404	0739	1074	1408	1743	2078	2412	6 201
98	113 2747	3081	3416	3751	4085	4420	4754	5088	5423	5757	7 235 / 8 268
99	6092	6426	6760	7094	7429	7763	8097	8431	8765	9099	9 302
1300	114 9434	9768	0102	0436	0770	1104	1437	1771	2105	2439	

No.	0	1	2	3	4	5	6	7	8	9
1300	113 9434	9768	0102	0436	0770	1104	1437	1771	2105	2439
01	114 2773	3107	3441	3774	4108	4442	4775	5109	5443	5776
02	6110	6443	6777	7110	7444	7777	8111	8444	8777	9111
03	9444	9777	0111	0444	0777	1110	1444	1777	2110	2443
04	115 2776	3109	3442	3775	4108	4441	4774	5107	5439	5772
05	6105	6438	6771	7103	7436	7769	8101	8434	8767	9099
06	9432	9764	0097	0429	0762	1094	1427	1759	2091	2424
07	116 2756	3088	3420	3753	4085	4417	4749	5081	5413	5745
08	6077	6409	6741	7073	7405	7737	8069	8401	8733	9065
09	9396	9728	0060	0392	0723	1055	1387	1718	2050	2381
10	117 2713	3044	3376	3707	4039	4370	4702	5033	5364	5696
1311	6027	6358	6689	7021	7352	7683	8014	8345	8676	9007
12	9338	9669	0000	0331	0662	0993	1324	1655	1986	2316
13	118 2647	2978	3309	3639	3970	4301	4631	4962	5293	5623
14	5954	6284	6615	6945	7276	7606	7936	8267	8597	8927
15	9258	9588	9918	0248	0578	0909	1239	1569	1899	2229
16	119 2559	2889	3219	3549	3879	4209	4539	4868	5198	5528
17	5858	6187	6517	6847	7177	7506	7836	8165	8495	8825
18	9154	9484	9813	0143	0472	0801	1131	1460	1789	2119
19	120 2448	2777	3106	3436	3765	4094	4423	4752	5081	5410
20	5739	6068	6397	6726	7055	7384	7713	8042	8371	8699
1321	9028	9357	9686	0014	0343	0672	1000	1329	1657	1986
22	121 2315	2643	2972	3300	3628	3957	4285	4614	4942	5270
23	5598	5927	6255	6583	6911	7239	7568	7896	8224	8552
24	8880	9208	9536	9864	0192	0520	0848	1175	1503	1831
25	122 2159	2487	2814	3142	3470	3797	4125	4453	4780	5108
26	5435	5763	6090	6418	6745	7073	7400	7727	8055	8382
27	8709	9036	9364	9691	0018	0345	0672	1000	1327	1654
28	123 1981	2308	2635	2962	3289	3616	3942	4269	4596	4923
29	5250	5577	5903	6230	6557	6883	7210	7537	7863	8190
30	8516	8843	9169	9496	9822	0149	0475	0802	1128	1454
1331	124 1781	2107	2433	2759	3086	3412	3738	4064	4390	4716
32	5042	5368	5694	6020	6346	6672	6998	7324	7650	7976
33	8301	8627	8953	9279	9605	9930	0256	0582	0907	1233
34	125 1558	1884	2209	2535	2860	3186	3511	3837	4162	4487
35	4813	5138	5463	5788	6114	6439	6764	7089	7414	7739
36	8065	8390	8715	9040	9365	9690	0015	0339	0664	0989
37	126 1314	1639	1964	2288	2613	2938	3263	3587	3912	4237
38	4561	4886	5210	5535	5859	6184	6508	6833	7157	7481
39	7806	8130	8454	8779	9103	9427	9751	0076	0400	0724
40	127 1048	1372	1696	2020	2344	2668	2992	3316	3640	3964
1341	4288	4612	4935	5259	5583	5907	6230	6554	6878	7202
42	7525	7849	8172	8496	8819	9143	9466	9790	0113	0437
43	128 0760	1083	1407	1730	2053	2377	2700	3023	3346	3670
44	3993	4316	4639	4962	5285	5608	5931	6254	6577	6900
45	7223	7546	7869	8191	8514	8837	9160	9483	9805	0128
46	129 0451	0773	1096	1418	1741	2064	2386	2709	3031	3354
47	3676	3998	4321	4643	4965	5288	5610	5932	6255	6577
48	6899	7221	7543	7865	8187	8510	8832	9154	9476	9798
49	130 0119	0441	0763	1085	1407	1729	2051	2372	2694	3016
1350	3338	3659	3981	4303	4624	4946	5267	5589	5911	6232

Diff.

332
1	33
2	66
3	100
4	133
5	166
6	199
7	232
8	266
9	299

329
1	33
2	66
3	99
4	132
5	165
6	197
7	230
8	263
9	296

326
1	33
2	65
3	98
4	130
5	163
6	196
7	228
8	261
9	293

323
1	32
2	65
3	97
4	129
5	162
6	194
7	226
8	258
9	291

No.	0	1	2	3	4	5	6	7	8	9	Diff.
1350	130 3338	3659	3981	4303	4624	4946	5267	5589	5911	6232	
51	6553	6875	7196	7518	7839	8161	8482	8803	9124	9446	
52	9767	0088	0409	0730	1052	1373	1694	2015	2336	2657	
53	131 2978	3299	3620	3941	4262	4583	4903	5224	5545	5866	
54	6187	6507	6828	7149	7469	7790	8111	8431	8752	9072	
55	9393	9713	0034	0354	0675	0995	1316	1636	1956	2277	**320**
56	132 2597	2917	3237	3558	3878	4198	4518	4838	5158	5478	1 32
57	5798	6119	6439	6758	7078	7398	7718	8038	8358	8678	2 64
58	8998	9317	9637	9957	0277	0596	0916	1236	1555	1875	3 96
59	133 2195	2514	2834	3153	3473	3792	4112	4431	4750	5070	4 128
60	5389	5708	6028	6347	6666	6985	7305	7624	7943	8262	5 160
											6 192
1361	8581	8900	9219	9538	9857	0176	0495	0814	1133	1452	7 224
62	134 1771	2090	2409	2728	3046	3365	3684	4003	4321	4640	8 256
63	4959	5277	5596	5914	6233	6551	6870	7188	7507	7825	9 288
64	8144	8462	8780	9099	9417	9735	0054	0372	0690	1008	
65	135 1327	1645	1963	2281	2599	2917	3235	3553	3871	4189	
66	4507	4825	5143	5461	5779	6096	6414	6732	7050	7367	
67	7685	8003	8320	8638	8956	9273	9591	9908	0226	0543	**317**
68	136 0861	1178	1496	1813	2131	2448	2765	3083	3400	3717	1 32
69	4034	4352	4669	4986	5303	5620	5937	6255	6572	6889	2 63
70	7206	7523	7840	8157	8473	8790	9107	9424	9741	0058	3 95
											4 127
1371	137 0375	0691	1008	1325	1641	1958	2275	2591	2908	3225	5 159
72	3541	3858	4174	4491	4807	5124	5440	5756	6073	6389	6 190
73	6705	7022	7338	7654	7970	8287	8603	8919	9235	9551	7 222
74	9867	0183	0499	0815	1131	1447	1763	2079	2395	2711	8 254
75	138 3027	3343	3659	3974	4290	4606	4922	5237	5553	5869	9 285
76	6184	6500	6816	7131	7447	7762	8078	8393	8709	9024	
77	9339	9655	9970	0285	0601	0916	1231	1547	1862	2177	
78	139 2492	2807	3122	3438	3753	4068	4383	4698	5013	5328	
79	5643	5958	6272	6587	6902	7217	7532	7847	8161	8476	
80	8791	9106	9420	9735	0050	0364	0679	0993	1308	1622	
											314
1381	140 1937	2251	2566	2880	3195	3509	3823	4138	4452	4766	1 31
82	5080	5395	5709	6023	6337	6651	6966	7280	7594	7908	2 63
83	8222	8536	8850	9164	9478	9792	0106	0419	0733	1047	3 94
84	141 1361	1675	1988	2302	2616	2930	3243	3557	3871	4184	4 126
85	4498	4811	5125	5438	5752	6065	6379	6692	7006	7319	5 157
86	7632	7946	8259	8572	8885	9199	9512	9825	0138	0451	6 188
87	142 0765	1078	1391	1704	2017	2330	2643	2956	3269	3582	7 220
88	3895	4208	4520	4833	5146	5459	5772	6084	6397	6710	8 251
89	7022	7335	7648	7960	8273	8586	8898	9211	9523	9836	9 283
90	143 0148	0460	0773	1085	1398	1710	2022	2335	2647	2959	
1391	3271	3584	3896	4208	4520	4832	5144	5456	5768	6080	
92	6392	6704	7016	7328	7640	7952	8264	8576	8888	9199	
93	9511	9823	0135	0446	0758	1070	1381	1693	2005	2316	**311**
94	144 2628	2939	3251	3562	3874	4185	4497	4808	5119	5431	1 31
95	5742	6053	6365	6676	6987	7298	7610	7921	8232	8543	2 62
											3 93
96	8854	9165	9476	9787	0098	0409	0720	1031	1342	1653	4 124
97	145 1964	2275	2586	2897	3207	3518	3829	4140	4450	4761	5 156
98	5072	5382	5693	6004	6314	6625	6935	7246	7556	7867	6 187
99	8177	8488	8798	9108	9419	9729	0039	0350	0660	0970	7 218
1400	146 1280	1591	1901	2211	2521	2831	3141	3451	3761	4071	8 249
											9 280

9

No.	0	1	2	3	4	5	6	7	8	9	Diff.
1400	146 1280	1591	1901	2211	2521	2831	3141	3451	3761	4071	
01	4381	4691	5001	5311	5621	5931	6241	6551	6861	7170	
02	7480	7790	8100	8409	8719	9029	9338	9648	9958	0267	
03	147 0577	0886	1196	1505	1815	2124	2434	2743	3052	3362	
04	3671	3980	4290	4599	4908	5217	5527	5836	6145	6454	
05	6763	7072	7381	7690	7999	8308	8617	8926	9235	9544	
06	9853	0162	0471	0780	1089	1397	1706	2015	2324	2632	308
07	148 2941	3250	3558	3867	4175	4484	4793	5101	5410	5718	1 31
08	6027	6335	6643	6952	7260	7569	7877	8185	8493	8802	2 62
09	9110	9418	9726	0035	0343	0651	0959	1267	1575	1883	3 92
10	149 2191	2499	2807	3115	3423	3731	4039	4347	4655	4962	4 123
1411	5270	5578	5886	6193	6501	6809	7116	7424	7732	8039	5 154
12	8347	8655	8962	9270	9577	9885	0192	0499	0807	1114	6 185
13	150 1422	1729	2036	2344	2651	2958	3265	3573	3880	4187	7 216
14	4494	4801	5108	5415	5722	6030	6337	6644	6951	7257	8 246
15	7564	7871	8178	8485	8792	9099	9406	9712	0019	0326	9 277
16	151 0633	0939	1246	1553	1859	2166	2472	2779	3085	3392	306
17	3699	4005	4311	4618	4924	5231	5537	5843	6150	6456	1 31
18	6762	7069	7375	7681	7987	8293	8600	8906	9212	9518	2 61
19	9824	0130	0436	0742	1048	1354	1660	1966	2272	2578	3 92
20	152 2883	3189	3495	3801	4107	4412	4718	5024	5329	5635	4 122 / 5 153
1421	5941	6246	6552	6858	7163	7469	7774	8080	8385	8691	6 184
22	8996	9301	9607	9912	0217	0523	0828	1133	1439	1744	7 214
23	153 2049	2354	2659	2964	3270	3575	3880	4185	4490	4795	8 245
24	5100	5405	5710	6015	6320	6625	6929	7234	7539	7844	9 275
25	8149	8453	8758	9063	9368	9672	9977	0281	0586	0891	
26	154 1195	1500	1804	2109	2413	2718	3022	3327	3631	3935	304
27	4240	4544	4848	5153	5457	5761	6065	6370	6674	6978	1 30
28	7282	7586	7890	8194	8498	8802	9106	9410	9714	0018	2 61
29	155 0322	0626	0930	1234	1538	1842	2145	2449	2753	3057	3 91
30	3360	3664	3968	4271	4575	4879	5182	5486	5789	6093	4 122 / 5 152
1431	6396	6700	7003	7307	7610	7914	8217	8520	8824	9127	6 182
32	9430	9733	0037	0340	0643	0946	1249	1553	1856	2159	7 213
33	156 2462	2765	3068	3371	3674	3977	4280	4583	4886	5189	8 243
34	5492	5794	6097	6400	6703	7006	7308	7611	7914	8216	9 274
35	8519	8822	9124	9427	9729	0032	0334	0637	0939	1242	
36	157 1544	1847	2149	2452	2754	3056	3359	3661	3963	4265	302
37	4568	4870	5172	5474	5776	6079	6381	6683	6985	7287	1 30 / 2 60
38	7589	7891	8193	8495	8797	9099	9401	9702	0004	0306	3 91
39	158 0608	0910	1212	1513	1815	2117	2418	2720	3022	3323	4 121 / 5 151
40	3625	3927	4228	4530	4831	5133	5434	5736	6037	6338	6 181
1441	6640	6941	7243	7544	7845	8146	8448	8749	9050	9351	7 211
42	9653	9954	0255	0556	0857	1158	1459	1760	2061	2362	8 242
43	159 2663	2964	3265	3566	3867	4168	4469	4770	5070	5371	9 272
44	5672	5973	6273	6574	6875	7175	7476	7777	8077	8378	300
45	8678	8979	9280	9580	9881	0181	0481	0782	1082	1383	1 30 / 2 60 / 3 90
46	160 1683	1983	2284	2584	2884	3184	3485	3785	4085	4385	4 120 / 5 150
47	4685	4985	5286	5586	5886	6186	6486	6786	7086	7386	6 180
48	7686	7986	8285	8585	8885	9185	9485	9785	0084	0384	7 210
49	161 0684	0984	1283	1583	1883	2182	2482	2781	3081	3380	8 240
1450	3680	3980	4279	4578	4878	5177	5477	5776	6075	6375	9 270

No.	0	1	2	3	4	5	6	7	8	9
1450	161 3680	3980	4279	4578	4878	5177	5477	5776	6075	6375
51	6674	6973	7273	7572	7871	8170	8470	8769	9068	9367
52	9666	9965	0264	0563	0862	1161	1460	1759	2058	2357
53	162 2656	2955	3254	3553	3852	4150	4449	4748	5047	5345
54	5644	5943	6241	6540	6839	7137	7436	7734	8033	8331
55	8630	8928	9227	9525	9824	0122	0420	0719	1017	1315
56	163 1614	1912	2210	2508	2807	3105	3403	3701	3999	4297
57	4596	4894	5192	5490	5788	6086	6384	6682	6979	7277
58	7575	7873	8171	8469	8767	9064	9362	9660	9958	0255
59	164 0553	0851	1148	1446	1743	2041	2339	2636	2934	3231
60	3529	3826	4123	4421	4718	5016	5313	5610	5908	6205
1461	6502	6799	7097	7394	7691	7988	8285	8582	8880	9177
62	9474	9771	0068	0365	0662	0959	1256	1553	1850	2146
63	165 2443	2740	3037	3334	3631	3927	4224	4521	4817	5114
64	5411	5707	6004	6301	6597	6894	7190	7487	7783	8080
65	8376	8673	8969	9265	9562	9858	0155	0451	0747	1043
66	166 1340	1636	1932	2228	2525	2821	3117	3413	3709	4005
67	4301	4597	4893	5189	5485	5781	6077	6373	6669	6965
68	7261	7556	7852	8148	8444	8740	9035	9331	9627	9922
69	167 0218	0514	0809	1105	1400	1696	1991	2287	2582	2878
70	3173	3469	3764	4060	4355	4650	4946	5241	5536	5831
1471	6127	6422	6717	7012	7308	7603	7898	8193	8488	8783
72	9078	9373	9668	9963	0258	0553	0848	1143	1438	1733
73	168 2027	2322	2617	2912	3207	3501	3796	4091	4386	4680
74	4975	5269	5564	5859	6153	6448	6742	7037	7331	7626
75	7920	8215	8509	8803	9098	9392	9686	9981	0275	0569
76	169 0864	1158	1452	1746	2040	2335	2629	2923	3217	3511
77	3805	4099	4393	4687	4981	5275	5569	5863	6157	6450
78	6744	7038	7332	7626	7920	8213	8507	8801	9094	9388
79	9682	9975	0269	0563	0856	1150	1443	1737	2030	2324
80	170 2617	2911	3204	3497	3791	4084	4377	4671	4964	5257
1481	5551	5844	6137	6430	6723	7017	7310	7603	7896	8189
82	8482	8775	9068	9361	9654	9947	0240	0533	0826	1119
83	171 1412	1704	1997	2290	2583	2876	3168	3461	3754	4046
84	4339	4632	4924	5217	5509	5802	6095	6387	6680	6972
85	7265	7557	7849	8142	8434	8727	9019	9311	9604	9896
86	172 0188	0480	0773	1065	1357	1649	1941	2233	2526	2818
87	3110	3402	3694	3986	4278	4570	4862	5154	5446	5737
88	6029	6321	6613	6905	7197	7488	7780	8072	8364	8655
89	8947	9239	9530	9822	0113	0405	0697	0988	1280	1571
90	173 1863	2154	2446	2737	3028	3320	3611	3903	4194	4485
1491	4776	5068	5359	5650	5941	6233	6524	6815	7106	7397
92	7688	7979	8270	8561	8852	9143	9434	9725	0016	0307
93	174 0598	0889	1180	1471	1761	2052	2343	2634	2925	3215
94	3506	3797	4087	4378	4669	4959	5250	5540	5831	6121
95	6412	6702	6993	7283	7574	7864	8155	8445	8735	9026
96	9316	9606	9897	0187	0477	0767	1057	1348	1638	1928
97	175 2218	2508	2798	3088	3378	3668	3958	4248	4538	4828
98	5118	5408	5698	5988	6278	6567	6857	7147	7437	7727
99	8016	8306	8596	8885	9175	9465	9754	0044	0333	0623
1500	176 0913	1202	1492	1781	2071	2360	2649	2939	3228	3518

Diff.

298		296		294		292		290	
1	30	1	30	1	29	1	29	1	29
2	60	2	59	2	59	2	58	2	58
3	89	3	89	3	88	3	88	3	87
4	119	4	118	4	118	4	117	4	116
5	149	5	148	5	147	5	146	5	145
6	179	6	178	6	176	6	175	6	174
7	209	7	207	7	206	7	204	7	203
8	238	8	237	8	235	8	234	8	232
9	268	9	266	9	265	9	263	9	261

11

No.	0	1	2	3	4	5	6	7	8	9	Diff.
1500	176 0913	1202	1492	1781	2071	2360	2649	2939	3228	3518	
01	3807	4096	4386	4675	4964	5253	5543	5832	6121	6410	
02	6699	6988	7278	7567	7856	8145	8434	8723	9012	9301	
03	9590	9879	0168	0457	0745	1034	1323	1612	1901	2190	
04	177 2478	2767	3056	3345	3633	3922	4211	4499	4788	5076	288
05	5365	5654	5942	6231	6519	6808	7096	7385	7673	7961	1 29
06	8250	8538	8826	9115	9403	9691	9980	0268	0556	0844	2 58
07	178 1133	1421	1709	1997	2285	2573	2861	3149	3437	3725	3 86
08	4013	4301	4589	4877	5165	5453	5741	6029	6317	6605	4 115
09	6892	7180	7468	7756	8043	8331	8619	8907	9194	9482	5 144
10	9769	0057	0345	0632	0920	1207	1495	1782	2070	2357	6 173
1511	179 2645	2932	3219	3507	3794	4082	4369	4656	4943	5231	7 202
12	5518	5805	6092	6380	6667	6954	7241	7528	7815	8102	8 230
13	8389	8676	8963	9250	9537	9824	0111	0398	0685	0972	9 259
14	180 1259	1546	1832	2119	2406	2693	2980	3266	3553	3840	286
15	4126	4413	4700	4986	5273	5559	5846	6133	6419	6706	1 29
16	6992	7278	7565	7851	8138	8424	8711	8997	9283	9570	2 57
17	9856	0142	0428	0715	1001	1287	1573	1859	2145	2432	3 86
18	181 2718	3004	3290	3576	3862	4148	4434	4720	5006	5292	4 114
19	5578	5864	6150	6435	6721	7007	7293	7579	7864	8150	5 143
20	8436	8722	9007	9293	9579	9864	0150	0435	0721	1007	6 172
1521	182 1292	1578	1863	2149	2434	2720	3005	3290	3576	3861	7 200
22	4147	4432	4717	5002	5288	5573	5858	6143	6429	6714	8 229
23	6999	7284	7569	7854	8140	8425	8710	8995	9280	9565	9 257
24	9850	0135	0420	0704	0989	1274	1559	1844	2129	2414	
25	183 2698	2983	3268	3553	3837	4122	4407	4691	4976	5261	284
26	5545	5830	6114	6399	6684	6968	7253	7537	7822	8106	1 28
27	8390	8675	8959	9244	9528	9812	0096	0381	0665	0949	2 57
28	184 1234	1518	1802	2086	2370	2654	2939	3223	3507	3791	3 85
29	4075	4359	4643	4927	5211	5495	5779	6063	6347	6630	4 114
30	6914	7198	7482	7766	8050	8333	8617	8901	9185	9468	5 142
1531	9752	0036	0319	0603	0886	1170	1454	1737	2021	2304	6 170
32	185 2588	2871	3155	3438	3721	4005	4288	4572	4855	5138	7 199
33	5422	5705	5988	6271	6555	6838	7121	7404	7687	7970	8 227
34	8254	8537	8820	9103	9386	9669	9952	0235	0518	0801	9 256
35	186 1084	1367	1650	1932	2215	2498	2781	3064	3347	3629	
36	3912	4195	4478	4760	5043	5326	5608	5891	6174	6456	282
37	6739	7021	7304	7586	7869	8151	8434	8716	8999	9281	1 28
38	9563	9846	0128	0410	0693	0975	1257	1540	1822	2104	2 56
39	187 2386	2668	2951	3233	3515	3797	4079	4361	4643	4925	3 85
40	5207	5489	5771	6053	6335	6617	6899	7181	7463	7745	4 113
1541	8026	8308	8590	8872	9154	9435	9717	9999	0280	0562	5 141
42	188 0844	1125	1407	1689	1970	2252	2533	2815	3096	3378	6 169
43	3659	3941	4222	4504	4785	5066	5348	5629	5910	6192	7 197
44	6473	6754	7035	7317	7598	7879	8160	8441	8723	9004	8 226
45	9285	9566	9847	0128	0409	0690	0971	1252	1533	1814	9 254
46	189 2095	2376	2657	2938	3218	3499	3780	4061	4342	4622	
47	4903	5184	5465	5745	6026	6307	6587	6868	7148	7429	
48	7710	7990	8271	8551	8832	9112	9393	9673	9953	0234	
49	190 0514	0795	1075	1355	1636	1916	2196	2476	2757	3037	
1550	3317	3597	3877	4157	4438	4718	4998	5278	5558	5838	

No.	0	1	2	3	4	5	6	7	8	9	Diff.
1550	190 3317	3597	3877	4157	4438	4718	4998	5278	5558	5838	
51	6118	6398	6678	6958	7238	7518	7798	8078	8357	8637	
52	8917	9197	9477	9757	0036	0316	0596	0876	1155	1435	
53	191 1715	1994	2274	2553	2833	3113	3392	3672	3951	4231	279
54	4510	4790	5069	5348	5628	5907	6187	6466	6745	7025	1 28
55	7304	7583	7862	8142	8421	8700	8979	9259	9538	9817	2 56
											3 84
56	192 0096	0375	0654	0933	1212	1491	1770	2049	2328	2607	4 112
57	2886	3165	3444	3723	4002	4281	4559	4838	5117	5396	5 140
58	5675	5953	6232	6511	6789	7068	7347	7625	7904	8183	6 167
59	8461	8740	9018	9297	9575	9854	0132	0411	0689	0968	7 195
60	193 1246	1524	1803	2081	2359	2638	2916	3194	3473	3751	8 223
											9 251
1561	4029	4307	4585	4864	5142	5420	5698	5976	6254	6532	
62	6810	7088	7366	7644	7922	8200	8478	8756	9034	9312	
63	9590	9868	0145	0423	0701	0979	1257	1534	1812	2090	
64	194 2367	2645	2923	3200	3478	3756	4033	4311	4588	4866	277
65	5143	5421	5698	5976	6253	6531	6808	7086	7363	7640	1 28
											2 55
66	7918	8195	8472	8749	9027	9304	9581	9858	0136	0413	3 83
67	195 0690	0967	1244	1521	1798	2075	2353	2630	2907	3184	4 111
68	3461	3738	4014	4291	4568	4845	5122	5399	5676	5953	5 139
69	6229	6506	6783	7060	7336	7613	7890	8167	8443	8720	6 166
70	8997	9273	9550	9826	0103	0379	0656	0932	1209	1485	7 194
											8 222
1571	196 1762	2038	2315	2591	2867	3144	3420	3697	3973	4249	9 249
72	4525	4802	5078	5354	5630	5907	6183	6459	6735	7011	
73	7287	7563	7839	8115	8391	8667	8943	9219	9495	9771	
74	197 0047	0323	0599	0875	1151	1427	1702	1978	2254	2530	
75	2806	3081	3357	3633	3908	4184	4460	4735	5011	5287	275
76	5562	5838	6113	6389	6664	6940	7215	7491	7766	8042	1 28
77	8317	8592	8868	9143	9418	9694	9969	0244	0520	0795	2 55
78	198 1070	1345	1620	1896	2171	2446	2721	2996	3271	3546	3 83
79	3821	4096	4371	4646	4921	5196	5471	5746	6021	6296	4 110
80	6571	6846	7121	7395	7670	7945	8220	8495	8769	9044	5 138
											6 165
1581	9319	9593	9868	0143	0417	0692	0967	1241	1516	1790	7 193
82	199 2065	2339	2614	2888	3163	3437	3712	3986	4260	4535	8 220
83	4809	5083	5358	5632	5906	6181	6455	6729	7003	7278	9 248
84	7552	7826	8100	8374	8648	8922	9197	9471	9745	0019	
85	200 0293	0567	0841	1115	1389	1662	1936	2210	2484	2758	
86	3032	3306	3579	3853	4127	4401	4674	4948	5222	5496	
87	5769	6043	6317	6590	6864	7137	7411	7684	7958	8231	273
88	8505	8778	9052	9325	9599	9872	0146	0419	0692	0966	1 27
89	201 1239	1512	1786	2059	2332	2605	2879	3152	3425	3698	2 55
90	3971	4244	4517	4791	5064	5337	5610	5883	6156	6429	3 82
											4 109
1591	6702	6975	7248	7521	7794	8066	8339	8612	8885	9158	5 137
92	9431	9703	9976	0249	0522	0794	1067	1340	1612	1885	6 164
93	202 2158	2430	2703	2976	3248	3521	3793	4066	4338	4611	7 191
94	4883	5156	5428	5700	5973	6245	6518	6790	7062	7335	8 218
95	7607	7879	8151	8424	8696	8968	9240	9512	9785	0057	9 246
96	203 0329	0601	0873	1145	1417	1689	1961	2233	2505	2777	
97	3049	3321	3593	3865	4137	4409	4681	4952	5224	5496	
98	5768	6040	6311	6583	6855	7126	7398	7670	7941	8213	
99	8485	8756	9028	9299	9571	9842	0114	0385	0657	0928	
1600	204 1200	1471	1743	2014	2285	2557	2828	3099	3371	3642	

No.	0	1	2	3	4	5	6	7	8	9	Diff.
1600	204 1200	1471	1743	2014	2285	2557	2828	3099	3371	3642	
01	3913	4185	4456	4727	4998	5269	5541	5812	6083	6354	
02	6625	6896	7167	7438	7709	7980	8251	8522	8793	9064	
03	9335	9606	9877	0148	0419	0690	0960	1231	1502	1773	
04	205 2044	2314	2585	2856	3127	3397	3668	3939	4209	4480	**270**
05	4750	5021	5292	5562	5833	6103	6374	6644	6915	7185	1 27
06	7455	7726	7996	8267	8537	8807	9078	9348	9618	9889	2 54
07	206 0159	0429	0699	0969	1240	1510	1780	2050	2320	2590	3 81
08	2860	3131	3401	3671	3941	4211	4481	4751	5021	5291	4 108
09	5560	5830	6100	6370	6640	6910	7180	7449	7719	7989	5 135
10	8259	8529	8798	9068	9338	9607	9877	0147	0416	0686	6 162
1611	207 0955	1225	1495	1764	2034	2303	2573	2842	3112	3381	7 189
12	3650	3920	4189	4459	4728	4997	5267	5536	5805	6074	8 216
13	6344	6613	6882	7151	7421	7690	7959	8228	8497	8766	9 243
14	9035	9304	9573	9842	0111	0380	0649	0918	1187	1456	
15	208 1725	1994	2263	2532	2801	3070	3338	3607	3876	4145	
16	4414	4682	4951	5220	5488	5757	6026	6294	6563	6832	
17	7100	7369	7637	7906	8174	8443	8711	8980	9248	9517	**268**
18	9785	0054	0322	0590	0859	1127	1395	1664	1932	2200	1 27
19	209 2468	2737	3005	3273	3541	3810	4078	4346	4614	4882	2 54
20	5150	5418	5686	5954	6222	6490	6758	7026	7294	7562	3 80
1621	7830	8098	8366	8634	8902	9170	9437	9705	9973	0241	4 107
22	210 0508	0776	1044	1312	1579	1847	2115	2382	2650	2918	5 134
23	3185	3453	3720	3988	4255	4523	4790	5058	5325	5593	6 161
24	5860	6128	6395	6662	6930	7197	7464	7732	7999	8266	7 188
25	8534	8801	9068	9335	9603	9870	0137	0404	0671	0938	8 214
26	211 1205	1472	1740	2007	2274	2541	2808	3075	3342	3609	9 241
27	3876	4142	4409	4676	4943	5210	5477	5744	6010	6277	
28	6544	6811	7078	7344	7611	7878	8144	8411	8678	8944	
29	9211	9477	9744	0011	0277	0544	0810	1077	1343	1610	**266**
30	212 1876	2142	2409	2675	2942	3208	3474	3741	4007	4273	1 27
1631	4540	4806	5072	5338	5605	5871	6137	6403	6669	6935	2 53
32	7202	7468	7734	8000	8266	8532	8798	9064	9330	9596	3 80
33	9862	0128	0394	0660	0926	1191	1457	1723	1989	2255	4 106
34	213 2521	2786	3052	3318	3584	3849	4115	4381	4646	4912	5 133
35	5178	5443	5709	5974	6240	6505	6771	7037	7302	7568	6 160
36	7833	8098	8364	8629	8895	9160	9425	9691	9956	0221	7 186
37	214 0487	0752	1017	1283	1548	1813	2078	2343	2609	2874	8 213
38	3139	3404	3669	3934	4199	4464	4730	4995	5260	5525	9 239
39	5790	6055	6319	6584	6849	7114	7379	7644	7909	8174	
40	8438	8703	8968	9233	9498	9762	0027	0292	0556	0821	
1641	215 1086	1350	1615	1880	2144	2409	2673	2938	3203	3467	**264**
42	3732	3996	4260	4525	4789	5054	5318	5583	5847	6111	1 26
43	6376	6640	6904	7169	7433	7697	7961	8226	8490	8754	2 53
44	9018	9282	9546	9811	0075	0339	0603	0867	1131	1395	3 79
45	216 1659	1923	2187	2451	2715	2979	3243	3507	3771	4034	4 106
46	4298	4562	4826	5090	5354	5617	5881	6145	6409	6672	5 132
47	6936	7200	7463	7727	7991	8254	8518	8781	9045	9309	6 158
48	9572	9836	0099	0363	0626	0890	1153	1416	1680	1943	7 185
49	217 2207	2470	2733	2997	3260	3523	3786	4050	4313	4576	8 211
1650	4839	5103	5366	5629	5892	6155	6418	6682	6945	7208	9 238

No.	0	1	2	3	4	5	6	7	8	9
1650	217 4839	5103	5366	5629	5892	6155	6418	6682	6945	7208
51	7471	7734	7997	8260	8523	8786	9049	9312	9575	9838
52	218 0100	0363	0626	0889	1152	1415	1677	1940	2203	2466
53	2729	2991	3254	3517	3779	4042	4305	4567	4830	5092
54	5355	5618	5880	6143	6405	6668	6930	7193	7455	7718
55	7980	8242	8505	8767	9030	9292	9554	9816	0079	0341
56	219 0603	0866	1128	1390	1652	1914	2177	2439	2701	2963
57	3225	3487	3749	4011	4273	4535	4797	5059	5321	5583
58	5845	6107	6369	6631	6893	7155	7417	7678	7940	8202
59	8464	8726	8987	9249	9511	9773	0034	0296	0558	0819
60	220 1081	1342	1604	1866	2127	2389	2650	2912	3173	3435
1661	3696	3958	4219	4481	4742	5003	5265	5526	5788	6049
62	6310	6571	6833	7094	7355	7617	7878	8139	8400	8661
63	8922	9184	9445	9706	9967	0228	0489	0750	1011	1272
64	221 1533	1794	2055	2316	2577	2838	3099	3360	3621	3882
65	4142	4403	4664	4925	5186	5446	5707	5968	6229	6489
66	6750	7011	7271	7532	7793	8053	8314	8574	8835	9095
67	9356	9617	9877	0138	0398	0658	0919	1179	1440	1700
68	222 1960	2221	2481	2741	3002	3262	3522	3783	4043	4303
69	4563	4824	5084	5344	5604	5864	6124	6384	6645	6905
70	7165	7425	7685	7945	8205	8465	8725	8985	9245	9505
1671	9764	0024	0284	0544	0804	1064	1324	1583	1843	2103
72	223 2363	2622	2882	3142	3402	3661	3921	4181	4440	4700
73	4959	5219	5479	5738	5998	6257	6517	6776	7036	7295
74	7555	7814	8073	8333	8592	8852	9111	9370	9630	9889
75	224 0148	0407	0667	0926	1185	1444	1704	1963	2222	2481
76	2740	2999	3258	3517	3777	4036	4295	4554	4813	5072
77	5331	5590	5849	6107	6366	6625	6884	7143	7402	7661
78	7920	8178	8437	8696	8955	9213	9472	9731	9990	0248
79	225 0507	0766	1024	1283	1541	1800	2059	2317	2576	2834
80	3093	3351	3610	3868	4127	4385	4644	4902	5160	5419
1681	5677	5935	6194	6452	6710	6969	7227	7485	7743	8002
82	8260	8518	8776	9034	9293	9551	9809	0067	0325	0583
83	226 0841	1099	1357	1615	1873	2131	2389	2647	2905	3163
84	3421	3679	3937	4194	4452	4710	4968	5226	5484	5741
85	5999	6257	6515	6772	7030	7288	7545	7803	8060	8318
86	8576	8833	9091	9348	9606	9863	0121	0378	0636	0893
87	227 1151	1408	1666	1923	2180	2438	2695	2953	3210	3467
88	3724	3982	4239	4496	4753	5011	5268	5525	5782	6039
89	6296	6554	6811	7068	7325	7582	7839	8096	8353	8610
90	8867	9124	9381	9638	9895	0152	0409	0666	0922	1179
1691	228 1436	1693	1950	2206	2463	2720	2977	3233	3490	3747
92	4004	4260	4517	4774	5030	5287	5543	5800	6057	6313
93	6570	6826	7083	7339	7596	7852	8108	8365	8621	8878
94	9134	9390	9647	9903	0159	0416	0672	0928	1185	1441
95	229 1697	1953	2209	2466	2722	2978	3234	3490	3746	4002
96	4258	4515	4771	5027	5283	5539	5795	6051	6307	6562
97	6818	7074	7330	7586	7842	8098	8354	8609	8865	9121
98	9377	9633	9888	0144	0400	0656	0911	1167	1423	1678
99	230 1934	2189	2445	2701	2956	3212	3467	3723	3978	4234
1700	4489	4745	5000	5256	5511	5766	6022	6277	6532	6788

Diff.

262
1	26
2	52
3	79
4	105
5	131
6	157
7	183
8	210
9	236

260
1	26
2	52
3	78
4	104
5	130
6	156
7	182
8	208
9	234

258
1	26
2	52
3	77
4	103
5	129
6	155
7	181
8	206
9	232

256
1	26
2	51
3	77
4	102
5	128
6	154
7	179
8	205
9	230

No.	0	1	2	3	4	5	6	7	8	9	Diff.
1700	230 4489	4745	5000	5256	5511	5766	6022	6277	6532	6788	
01	7043	7298	7554	7809	8064	8320	8575	8830	9085	9340	
02	9596	9851	0106	0361	0616	0871	1126	1381	1636	1891	
03	231 2146	2401	2656	2911	3166	3421	3676	3931	4186	4441	
04	4696	4951	5206	5460	5715	5970	6225	6480	6734	6989	
05	7244	7499	7753	8008	8263	8517	8772	9026	9281	9536	254
06	9790	0045	0299	0554	0808	1063	1317	1572	1826	2081	1 25
07	232 2335	2590	2844	3098	3353	3607	3861	4116	4370	4624	2 51
08	4879	5133	5387	5641	5896	6150	6404	6658	6912	7166	3 76
09	7421	7675	7929	8183	8437	8691	8945	9199	9453	9707	4 102
10	9961	0215	0469	0723	0977	1231	1485	1739	1992	2246	5 127
											6 152
1711	233 2500	2754	3008	3262	3515	3769	4023	4277	4530	4784	7 178
12	5038	5291	5545	5799	6052	6306	6559	6813	7067	7320	8 203
13	7574	7827	8081	8334	8588	8841	9095	9348	9601	9855	9 229
14	234 0108	0362	0615	0868	1122	1375	1628	1881	2135	2388	
15	2641	2894	3148	3401	3654	3907	4160	4414	4667	4920	
16	5173	5426	5679	5932	6185	6438	6691	6944	7197	7450	
17	7703	7956	8209	8462	8715	8967	9220	9473	9726	9979	
18	235 0232	0484	0737	0990	1243	1495	1748	2001	2253	2506	252
19	2759	3011	3264	3517	3769	4022	4274	4527	4779	5032	1 25
20	5284	5537	5789	6042	6294	6547	6799	7052	7304	7556	2 50
1721	7809	8061	8313	8566	8818	9070	9323	9575	9827	0079	3 76
22	236 0331	0584	0836	1088	1340	1592	1844	2097	2349	2601	4 101
23	2853	3105	3357	3609	3861	4113	4365	4617	4869	5121	5 126
24	5373	5625	5876	6128	6380	6632	6884	7136	7387	7639	6 151
25	7891	8143	8394	8646	8898	9150	9401	9653	9905	0156	7 176
26	237 0408	0660	0911	1163	1414	1666	1917	2169	2420	2672	8 202
27	2923	3175	3426	3678	3929	4181	4432	4683	4935	5186	9 227
28	5437	5689	5940	6191	6443	6694	6945	7196	7448	7699	
29	7950	8201	8452	8703	8955	9206	9457	9708	9959	0210	
30	238 0461	0712	0963	1214	1465	1716	1967	2218	2469	2720	
1731	2971	3222	3472	3723	3974	4225	4476	4727	4977	5228	
32	5479	5730	5980	6231	6482	6732	6983	7234	7484	7735	250
33	7986	8236	8487	8737	8988	9238	9489	9739	9990	0240	1 25
34	239 0491	0741	0992	1242	1493	1743	1993	2244	2494	2744	2 50
35	2995	3245	3495	3746	3996	4246	4496	4747	4997	5247	3 75
36	5497	5747	5998	6248	6498	6748	6998	7248	7498	7748	4 100
37	7998	8248	8498	8748	8998	9248	9498	9748	9998	0248	5 125
38	240 0498	0748	0997	1247	1497	1747	1997	2247	2496	2746	6 150
39	2996	3246	3495	3745	3995	4244	4494	4744	4993	5243	7 175
40	5492	5742	5992	6241	6491	6740	6990	7239	7489	7738	8 200
											9 225
1741	7988	8237	8487	8736	8985	9235	9484	9734	9983	0232	
42	241 0482	0731	0980	1229	1479	1728	1977	2226	2476	2725	
43	2974	3223	3472	3721	3970	4220	4469	4718	4967	5216	
44	5465	5714	5963	6212	6461	6710	6959	7208	7457	7705	
45	7954	8203	8452	8701	8950	9199	9447	9696	9945	0194	
46	242 0442	0691	0940	1189	1437	1686	1935	2183	2432	2680	
47	2929	3178	3426	3675	3923	4172	4420	4669	4917	5166	
48	5414	5663	5911	6160	6408	6656	6905	7153	7401	7650	
49	7898	8146	8395	8643	8891	9139	9388	9636	9884	0132	
1750	243 0380	0629	0877	1125	1373	1621	1869	2117	2365	2613	

No.	0	1	2	3	4	5	6	7	8	9	Diff.
1750	243 0380	0629	0877	1125	1373	1621	1869	2117	2365	2613	
51	2861	3109	3357	3605	3853	4101	4349	4597	4845	5093	
52	5341	5589	5837	6085	6332	6580	6828	7076	7324	7571	
53	7819	8067	8315	8562	8810	9058	9305	9553	9801	0048	
54	244 0296	0543	0791	1039	1286	1534	1781	2029	2276	2524	247
55	2771	3019	3266	3514	3761	4008	4256	4503	4750	4998	1 25
56	5245	5492	5740	5987	6234	6482	6729	6976	7223	7470	2 49
57	7718	7965	8212	8459	8706	8953	9200	9448	9695	9942	3 74
58	245 0189	0436	0683	0930	1177	1424	1671	1918	2165	2411	4 99
59	2658	2905	3152	3399	3646	3893	4140	4386	4633	4880	5 124
60	5127	5373	5620	5867	6114	6360	6607	6854	7100	7347	6 148
1761	7594	7840	8087	8333	8580	8826	9073	9320	9566	9813	7 173
62	246 0059	0306	0552	0798	1045	1291	1538	1784	2030	2277	8 198
63	2523	2769	3016	3262	3508	3755	4001	4247	4493	4740	9 222
64	4986	5232	5478	5724	5970	6217	6463	6709	6955	7201	
65	7447	7693	7939	8185	8431	8677	8923	9169	9415	9661	
66	9907	0153	0399	0645	0891	1136	1382	1628	1874	2120	
67	247 2365	2611	2857	3103	3349	3594	3840	4086	4331	4577	
68	4823	5068	5314	5559	5805	6051	6296	6542	6787	7033	245
69	7278	7524	7769	8015	8260	8506	8751	8997	9242	9487	1 25
70	9733	9978	0223	0469	0714	0959	1205	1450	1695	1940	2 49
1771	248 2186	2431	2676	2921	3166	3412	3657	3902	4147	4392	3 74
72	4637	4882	5127	5372	5617	5862	6107	6352	6597	6842	4 98
73	7087	7332	7577	7822	8067	8312	8557	8802	9047	9291	5 123
74	9536	9781	0026	0271	0515	0760	1005	1249	1494	1739	6 147
75	249 1984	2228	2473	2718	2962	3207	3451	3696	3941	4185	7 172
76	4430	4674	4919	5163	5408	5652	5897	6141	6385	6630	8 196
77	6874	7119	7363	7607	7852	8096	8340	8585	8829	9073	9 221
78	9318	9562	9806	0050	0294	0539	0783	1027	1271	1515	
79	250 1759	2004	2248	2492	2736	2980	3224	3468	3712	3956	
80	4200	4444	4688	4932	5176	5420	5664	5908	6151	6395	
1781	6639	6883	7127	7371	7614	7858	8102	8346	8590	8833	
82	9077	9321	9564	9808	0052	0295	0539	0783	1026	1270	243
83	251 1513	1757	2001	2244	2488	2731	2975	3218	3462	3705	1 24
84	3949	4192	4435	4679	4922	5166	5409	5652	5896	6139	2 49
85	6382	6625	6869	7112	7355	7599	7842	8085	8328	8571	3 73
86	8815	9058	9301	9544	9787	0030	0273	0516	0759	1002	4 97
87	252 1246	1489	1732	1975	2218	2461	2703	2946	3189	3432	5 122
88	3675	3918	4161	4404	4647	4889	5132	5375	5618	5861	6 146
89	6103	6346	6589	6832	7074	7317	7560	7802	8045	8288	7 170
90	8530	8773	9016	9258	9501	9743	9986	0228	0471	0713	8 194
1791	253 0956	1198	1441	1683	1926	2168	2411	2653	2895	3138	9 219
92	3380	3622	3865	4107	4349	4592	4834	5076	5318	5561	
93	5803	6045	6287	6529	6772	7014	7256	7498	7740	7982	
94	8224	8466	8709	8951	9193	9435	9677	9919	0161	0403	
95	254 0645	0886	1128	1370	1612	1854	2096	2338	2580	2822	
96	3063	3305	3547	3789	4030	4272	4514	4756	4997	5239	
97	5481	5722	5964	6206	6447	6689	6931	7172	7414	7655	
98	7897	8138	8380	8621	8863	9104	9346	9587	9829	0070	
99	255 0312	0553	0794	1036	1277	1519	1760	2001	2242	2484	
1800	2725	2966	3208	3449	3690	3931	4172	4414	4655	4896	

No.	0	1	2	3	4	5	6	7	8	9	Diff
1800	255 2725	2966	3208	3449	3690	3931	4172	4414	4655	4896	
01	5137	5378	5619	5860	6102	6343	6584	6825	7066	7307	
02	7548	7789	8030	8271	8512	8753	8994	9235	9475	9716	
03	9957	0198	0439	0680	0921	1161	1402	1643	1884	2125	
04	256 2365	2606	2847	3087	3328	3569	3810	4050	4291	4531	
05	4772	5013	5253	5494	5734	5975	6215	6456	6696	6937	
06	7177	7418	7658	7899	8139	8380	8620	8860	9101	9341	
07	9582	9822	0062	0302	0543	0783	1023	1264	1504	1744	240
08	257 1984	2224	2465	2705	2945	3185	3425	3665	3905	4146	1 24
09	4386	4626	4866	5106	5346	5586	5826	6066	6306	6546	2 48
10	6786	7026	7266	7506	7745	7985	8225	8465	8705	8945	3 72
											4 96
1811	9185	9424	9664	9904	0144	0383	0623	0863	1103	1342	5 120
12	258 1582	1822	2061	2301	2541	2780	3020	3259	3499	3738	6 144
13	3978	4218	4457	4697	4936	5176	5415	5655	5894	6133	7 168
14	6373	6612	6852	7091	7330	7570	7809	8048	8288	8527	8 192
15	8766	9006	9245	9484	9723	9963	0202	0441	0680	0919	9 216
16	259 1158	1398	1637	1876	2115	2354	2593	2832	3071	3310	
17	3549	3788	4027	4266	4505	4744	4983	5222	5461	5700	
18	5939	6178	6417	6655	6894	7133	7372	7611	7849	8088	
19	8327	8566	8804	9043	9282	9521	9759	9998	0237	0475	
20	260 0714	0952	1191	1430	1668	1907	2145	2384	2622	2861	
1821	3099	3338	3576	3815	4053	4292	4530	4769	5007	5245	
22	5484	5722	5960	6199	6437	6675	6914	7152	7390	7628	
23	7867	8105	8343	8581	8820	9058	9296	9534	9772	0010	
24	261 0248	0486	0725	0963	1201	1439	1677	1915	2153	2391	238
25	2629	2867	3105	3343	3580	3818	4056	4294	4532	4770	1 24
26	5008	5246	5483	5721	5959	6197	6435	6672	6910	7148	2 48
27	7385	7623	7861	8099	8336	8574	8811	9049	9287	9524	3 71
28	9762	9999	0237	0475	0712	0950	1187	1425	1662	1900	4 95
29	262 2137	2374	2612	2849	3087	3324	3562	3799	4036	4274	5 119
30	4511	4748	4986	5223	5460	5697	5935	6172	6409	6646	6 143
											7 167
1831	6883	7121	7358	7595	7832	8069	8306	8543	8781	9018	8 190
32	9255	9492	9729	9966	0203	0440	0677	0914	1151	1388	9 214
33	263 1625	1862	2098	2335	2572	2809	3046	3283	3520	3757	
34	3993	4230	4467	4704	4940	5177	5414	5651	5887	6124	
35	6361	6597	6834	7071	7307	7544	7780	8017	8254	8490	
36	8727	8963	9200	9436	9673	9909	0146	0382	0619	0855	
37	264 1092	1328	1564	1801	2037	2273	2510	2746	2982	3219	
38	3455	3691	3928	4164	4400	4636	4873	5109	5345	5581	
39	5817	6053	6290	6526	6762	6998	7234	7470	7706	7942	236
40	8178	8414	8650	8886	9122	9358	9594	9830	0066	0302	1 24
1841	265 0538	0774	1010	1246	1481	1717	1953	2189	2425	2660	2 47
42	2896	3132	3368	3604	3839	4075	4311	4546	4782	5018	3 71
43	5253	5489	5725	5960	6196	6431	6667	6903	7138	7374	4 94
44	7609	7845	8080	8316	8551	8787	9022	9257	9493	9728	5 118
45	9964	0199	0434	0670	0905	1140	1376	1611	1846	2082	6 142
											7 165
46	266 2317	2552	2787	3023	3258	3493	3728	3963	4199	4434	8 189
47	4669	4904	5139	5374	5609	5844	6080	6315	6550	6785	9 212
48	7020	7255	7490	7725	7960	8195	8429	8664	8899	9134	
49	9369	9604	9839	0074	0309	0543	0778	1013	1248	1483	
1850	267 1717	1952	2187	2421	2656	2891	3126	3360	3595	3830	

No.	0	1	2	3	4	5	6	7	8	9	Diff.
1850	267 1717	1952	2187	2421	2656	2891	3126	3360	3595	3830	
51	4064	4299	4533	4768	5003	5237	5472	5706	5941	6175	
52	6410	6644	6879	7113	7348	7582	7817	8051	8285	8520	
53	8754	8989	9223	9457	9692	9926	0160	0394	0629	0863	
54	268 1097	1332	1566	1800	2034	2268	2503	2737	2971	3205	**234**
55	3439	3673	3907	4141	4376	4610	4844	5078	5312	5546	1 23
56	5780	6014	6248	6482	6716	6950	7183	7417	7651	7885	2 47
57	8119	8353	8587	8821	9054	9288	9522	9756	9990	0223	3 70
58	269 0457	0691	0925	1158	1392	1626	1859	2093	2327	2560	4 94
59	2794	3028	3261	3495	3728	3962	4195	4429	4662	4896	5 117
60	5129	5363	5596	5830	6063	6297	6530	6764	6997	7230	6 140
											7 164
1861	7464	7697	7930	8164	8397	8630	8864	9097	9330	9564	8 187
62	9797	0030	0263	0496	0730	0963	1196	1429	1662	1895	9 211
63	270 2129	2362	2595	2828	3061	3294	3527	3760	3993	4226	
64	4459	4692	4925	5158	5391	5624	5857	6090	6323	6555	
65	6788	7021	7254	7487	7720	7953	8185	8418	8651	8884	
66	9116	9349	9582	9815	0047	0280	0513	0745	0978	1211	
67	271 1443	1676	1908	2141	2374	2606	2839	3071	3304	3536	
68	3769	4001	4234	4466	4699	4931	5163	5396	5628	5861	
69	6093	6325	6558	6790	7022	7255	7487	7719	7952	8184	
70	8416	8648	8881	9113	9345	9577	9809	0041	0274	0506	**232**
1871	272 0738	0970	1202	1434	1666	1898	2130	2362	2594	2826	1 23
72	3058	3290	3522	3754	3986	4218	4450	4682	4914	5146	2 46
73	5378	5610	5841	6073	6305	6537	6769	7001	7232	7464	3 70
74	7696	7928	8159	8391	8623	8854	9086	9318	9549	9781	4 93
75	273 0013	0244	0476	0708	0939	1171	1402	1634	1865	2097	5 116
											6 139
76	2328	2560	2791	3023	3254	3486	3717	3949	4180	4411	7 162
77	4643	4874	5105	5337	5568	5799	6031	6262	6493	6725	8 186
78	6956	7187	7418	7650	7881	8112	8343	8574	8806	9037	9 209
79	9268	9499	9730	9961	0192	0423	0654	0885	1116	1347	
80	274 1578	1809	2040	2271	2502	2733	2964	3195	3426	3657	
1881	3888	4119	4350	4581	4811	5042	5273	5504	5735	5965	
82	6196	6427	6658	6888	7119	7350	7581	7811	8042	8273	
83	8503	8734	8964	9195	9426	9656	9887	0117	0348	0578	
84	275 0809	1039	1270	1500	1731	1961	2192	2422	2653	2883	
85	3114	3344	3574	3805	4035	4265	4496	4726	4956	5187	
86	5417	5647	5877	6108	6338	6568	6798	7028	7259	7489	
87	7719	7949	8179	8409	8640	8870	9100	9330	9560	9790	
88	276 0020	0250	0480	0710	0940	1170	1400	1630	1860	2090	
89	2320	2549	2779	3009	3239	3469	3699	3929	4158	4388	
90	4618	4848	5078	5307	5537	5767	5997	6226	6456	6686	**230**
1891	6915	7145	7375	7604	7834	8063	8293	8523	8752	8982	1 23
92	9211	9441	9670	9900	0129	0359	0588	0818	1047	1277	2 46
93	277 1506	1736	1965	2194	2424	2653	2882	3112	3341	3570	3 69
94	3800	4029	4258	4488	4717	4946	5175	5405	5634	5863	4 92
95	6092	6321	6550	6780	7009	7238	7467	7696	7925	8154	5 115
											6 138
96	8383	8612	8841	9070	9299	9528	9757	9986	0215	0444	7 161
97	278 0673	0902	1131	1360	1589	1818	2047	2276	2504	2733	8 184
98	2962	3191	3420	3648	3877	4106	4335	4564	4792	5021	9 207
99	5250	5478	5707	5936	6164	6393	6622	6850	7079	7307	
1900	7536	7765	7993	8222	8450	8679	8907	9136	9364	9593	

No.	0	1	2	3	4	5	6	7	8	9	Diff.
1900	278 7536	7765	7993	8222	8450	8679	8907	9136	9364	9593	
01	9821	0050	0278	0506	0735	0963	1192	1420	1648	1877	
02	279 2105	2333	2562	2790	3018	3247	3475	3703	3931	4160	
03	4388	4616	4844	5072	5301	5529	5757	5985	6213	6441	
04	6669	6898	7126	7354	7582	7810	8038	8266	8494	8722	**228**
05	8950	9178	9406	9634	9862	0090	0317	0545	0773	1001	1 23
06	280 1229	1457	1685	1912	2140	2368	2596	2824	3051	3279	2 46
07	3507	3735	3962	4190	4418	4645	4873	5101	5328	5556	3 68
08	5784	6011	6239	6467	6694	6922	7149	7377	7604	7832	4 91
09	8059	8287	8514	8742	8969	9197	9424	9651	9879	0106	5 114
10	281 0334	0561	0788	1016	1243	1470	1698	1925	2152	2380	6 137
1911	2607	2834	3061	3289	3516	3743	3970	4197	4425	4652	7 160
12	4879	5106	5333	5560	5787	6014	6242	6469	6696	6923	8 182
13	7150	7377	7604	7831	8058	8285	8512	8739	8966	9192	9 205
14	9419	9646	9873	0100	0327	0554	0781	1007	1234	1461	**227**
15	282 1688	1915	2141	2368	2595	2822	3048	3275	3502	3728	1 23
16	3955	4182	4408	4635	4862	5088	5315	5541	5768	5995	2 45
17	6221	6448	6674	6901	7127	7354	7580	7807	8033	8260	3 68
18	8486	8712	8939	9165	9392	9618	9844	0071	0297	0523	4 91
19	283 0750	0976	1202	1429	1655	1881	2107	2334	2560	2786	5 114
20	3012	3238	3465	3691	3917	4143	4369	4595	4821	5048	6 136
1921	5274	5500	5726	5952	6178	6404	6630	6856	7082	7308	7 159
22	7534	7760	7986	8212	8438	8663	8889	9115	9341	9567	8 182
23	9793	0019	0245	0470	0696	0922	1148	1373	1599	1825	9 204
24	284 2051	2276	2502	2728	2953	3179	3405	3630	3856	4082	**226**
25	4307	4533	4759	4984	5210	5435	5661	5886	6112	6337	1 23
26	6563	6788	7014	7239	7465	7690	7916	8141	8366	8592	2 45
27	8817	9043	9268	9493	9719	9944	0169	0394	0620	0845	3 68
28	285 1070	1296	1521	1746	1971	2196	2422	2647	2872	3097	4 90
29	3322	3547	3773	3998	4223	4448	4673	4898	5123	5348	5 113
30	5573	5798	6023	6248	6473	6698	6923	7148	7373	7598	6 136
1931	7823	8048	8273	8497	8722	8947	9172	9397	9622	9846	7 158
32	286 0071	0296	0521	0746	0970	1195	1420	1644	1869	2094	8 181
33	2319	2543	2768	2993	3217	3442	3666	3891	4116	4340	9 203
34	4565	4789	5014	5238	5463	5687	5912	6136	6361	6585	**225**
35	6810	7034	7259	7483	7707	7932	8156	8381	8605	8829	1 23
36	9054	9278	9502	9726	9951	0175	0399	0624	0848	1072	2 45
37	287 1296	1520	1745	1969	2193	2417	2641	2865	3090	3314	3 68
38	3538	3762	3986	4210	4434	4658	4882	5106	5330	5554	4 90
39	5778	6002	6226	6450	6674	6898	7122	7346	7570	7793	5 113
40	8017	8241	8465	8689	8913	9136	9360	9584	9808	0032	6 135
1941	288 0255	0479	0703	0927	1150	1374	1598	1821	2045	2269	7 158
42	2492	2716	2939	3163	3387	3610	3834	4057	4281	4504	8 180
43	4728	4952	5175	5399	5622	5845	6069	6292	6516	6739	9 203
44	6963	7186	7409	7633	7856	8079	8303	8526	8749	8973	**224**
45	9196	9419	9643	9866	0089	0312	0536	0759	0982	1205	1 22
46	289 1428	1652	1875	2098	2321	2544	2767	2990	3213	3436	2 45
47	3660	3883	4106	4329	4552	4775	4998	5221	5444	5667	3 67
48	5890	6112	6335	6558	6781	7004	7227	7450	7673	7896	4 90
49	8118	8341	8564	8787	9010	9232	9455	9678	9901	0123	5 112
1950	290 0346	0569	0792	1014	1237	1460	1682	1905	2127	2350	6 134

Diff. column (for 224): 7 157 · 8 179 · 9 202

No.	0	1	2	3	4	5	6	7	8	9	Diff.
1950	290 0346	0569	0792	1014	1237	1460	1682	1905	2127	2350	
51	2573	2795	3018	3240	3463	3686	3908	4131	4353	4576	
52	4798	5021	5243	5466	5688	5910	6133	6355	6578	6800	
53	7022	7245	7467	7690	7912	8134	8356	8579	8801	9023	
54	9246	9468	9690	9912	0135	0357	0579	0801	1023	1245	222
55	291 1468	1690	1912	2134	2356	2578	2800	3022	3244	3466	1 22
56	3689	3911	4133	4355	4577	4799	5020	5242	5464	5686	2 44 3 67
57	5908	6130	6352	6574	6796	7018	7240	7461	7683	7905	4 89
58	8127	8349	8570	8792	9014	9236	9458	9679	9901	0123	5 111
59	292 0344	0566	0788	1009	1231	1453	1674	1896	2118	2339	6 133
60	2561	2782	3004	3225	3447	3668	3890	4111	4333	4554	7 155
1961	4776	4997	5219	5440	5662	5883	6105	6326	6547	6769	8 178 9 200
62	6990	7211	7433	7654	7875	8097	8318	8539	8760	8982	
63	9203	9424	9645	9867	0088	0309	0530	0751	0973	1194	
64	293 1415	1636	1857	2078	2299	2520	2741	2962	3183	3405	221
65	3626	3847	4068	4289	4510	4730	4951	5172	5393	5614	1 22
66	5835	6056	6277	6498	6719	6940	7160	7381	7602	7823	2 44 3 66
67	8044	8264	8485	8706	8927	9147	9368	9589	9810	0030	4 88
68	294 0251	0472	0692	0913	1134	1354	1575	1795	2016	2237	5 111
69	2457	2678	2898	3119	3339	3560	3780	4001	4221	4442	6 133
70	4662	4883	5103	5324	5544	5764	5985	6205	6426	6646	7 155
1971	6866	7087	7307	7527	7748	7968	8188	8408	8629	8849	8 177 9 199
72	9069	9289	9510	9730	9950	0170	0390	0610	0831	1051	
73	295 1271	1491	1711	1931	2151	2371	2591	2811	3031	3251	
74	3471	3691	3911	4131	4351	4571	4791	5011	5231	5451	220
75	5671	5891	6111	6331	6550	6770	6990	7210	7430	7650	1 22
76	7869	8089	8309	8529	8748	8968	9188	9408	9627	9847	2 44 3 66
77	296 0067	0286	0506	0726	0945	1165	1385	1604	1824	2043	4 88
78	2263	2482	2702	2922	3141	3361	3580	3800	4019	4238	5 110
79	4458	4677	4897	5116	5336	5555	5774	5994	6213	6433	6 132 7 154
80	6652	6871	7091	7310	7529	7748	7968	8187	8406	8626	8 176
1981	8845	9064	9283	9502	9722	9941	0160	0379	0598	0817	9 198
82	297 1037	1256	1475	1694	1913	2132	2351	2570	2789	3008	219
83	3227	3446	3665	3884	4103	4322	4541	4760	4979	5198	1 22
84	5417	5636	5854	6073	6292	6511	6730	6949	7168	7386	2 44
85	7605	7824	8043	8261	8480	8699	8918	9136	9355	9574	3 66
86	9792	0011	0230	0448	0667	0886	1104	1323	1542	1760	4 88 5 110
87	298 1979	2197	2416	2634	2853	3071	3290	3508	3727	3945	6 131
88	4164	4382	4601	4819	5038	5256	5474	5693	5911	6129	7 153
89	6348	6566	6785	7003	7221	7439	7658	7876	8094	8313	8 175
90	8531	8749	8967	9185	9404	9622	9840	0058	0276	0494	9 197
1991	299 0713	0931	1149	1367	1585	1803	2021	2239	2457	2675	
92	2893	3111	3329	3547	3765	3983	4201	4419	4637	4855	218
93	5073	5291	5509	5727	5945	6162	6380	6598	6816	7034	1 22
94	7252	7469	7687	7905	8123	8340	8558	8776	8994	9211	2 44
95	9429	9647	9864	0082	0300	0517	0735	0953	1170	1388	3 65
96	300 1605	1823	2041	2258	2476	2693	2911	3128	3346	3563	4 87 5 109
97	3781	3998	4216	4433	4650	4868	5085	5303	5520	5737	6 131
98	5955	6172	6390	6607	6824	7042	7259	7476	7693	7911	7 153
99	8128	8345	8562	8780	8997	9214	9431	9648	9866	0083	8 174
2000	301 0300	0517	0734	0951	1168	1386	1603	1820	2037	2254	9 196

No.	0	1	2	3	4	5	6	7	8	9	Diff.
2000	301 0300	0517	0734	0951	1168	1386	1603	1820	2037	2254	
01	2471	2688	2905	3122	3339	3556	3773	3990	4207	4424	**217**
02	4641	4858	5075	5291	5508	5725	5942	6159	6376	6593	1 22
03	6809	7026	7243	7460	7677	7893	8110	8327	8544	8760	2 43
04	8977	9194	9411	9627	9844	0061	0277	0494	0711	0927	3 65
05	302 1144	1360	1577	1794	2010	2227	2443	2660	2876	3093	4 87 / 5 109
06	3309	3526	3742	3959	4175	4392	4608	4825	5041	5257	6 130 / 7 152
07	5474	5690	5906	6123	6339	6556	6772	6988	7204	7421	8 174
08	7637	7853	8070	8286	8502	8718	8935	9151	9367	9583	9 195
09	9799	0016	0232	0448	0664	0880	1096	1312	1528	1745	
10	303 1961	2177	2393	2609	2825	3041	3257	3473	3689	3905	**216** / 1 22
2011	4121	4337	4553	4769	4984	5200	5416	5632	5848	6064	2 43
12	6280	6496	6711	6927	7143	7359	7575	7790	8006	8222	3 65
13	8438	8653	8869	9085	9301	9516	9732	9948	0163	0379	4 86
14	304 0595	0810	1026	1242	1457	1673	1888	2104	2319	2535	5 108
15	2751	2966	3182	3397	3613	3828	4043	4259	4474	4690	6 130 / 7 151
16	4905	5121	5336	5552	5767	5982	6198	6413	6628	6844	8 173
17	7059	7274	7490	7705	7920	8135	8351	8566	8781	8996	9 194
18	9212	9427	9642	9857	0072	0288	0503	0718	0933	1148	
19	305 1363	1578	1793	2008	2224	2439	2654	2869	3084	3299	**215**
20	3514	3729	3944	4159	4374	4589	4803	5018	5233	5448	1 22
2021	5663	5878	6093	6308	6523	6737	6952	7167	7382	7597	2 43
22	7812	8026	8241	8456	8671	8885	9100	9315	9529	9744	3 65
23	9959	0174	0388	0603	0817	1032	1247	1461	1676	1891	4 86
24	306 2105	2320	2534	2749	2963	3178	3392	3607	3821	4036	5 108
25	4250	4465	4679	4894	5108	5322	5537	5751	5966	6180	6 129 / 7 151
26	6394	6609	6823	7037	7252	7466	7680	7895	8109	8323	8 172
27	8537	8752	8966	9180	9394	9609	9823	0037	0251	0465	9 194
28	307 0680	0894	1108	1322	1536	1750	1964	2178	2392	2606	**214**
29	2820	3035	3249	3463	3677	3891	4105	4319	4532	4746	1 21
30	4960	5174	5388	5602	5816	6030	6244	6458	6672	6885	2 43
2031	7099	7313	7527	7741	7954	8168	8382	8596	8810	9023	3 64
32	9237	9451	9664	9878	0092	0306	0519	0733	0947	1160	4 86 / 5 107
33	308 1374	1587	1801	2015	2228	2442	2655	2869	3082	3296	6 128
34	3509	3723	3936	4150	4363	4577	4790	5004	5217	5431	7 150
35	5644	5858	6071	6284	6498	6711	6924	7138	7351	7564	8 171 / 9 193
36	7778	7991	8204	8418	8631	8844	9057	9271	9484	9697	
37	9910	0123	0337	0550	0763	0976	1189	1402	1616	1829	
38	309 2042	2255	2468	2681	2894	3107	3320	3533	3746	3959	**213**
39	4172	4385	4598	4811	5024	5237	5450	5663	5876	6089	1 21
40	6302	6515	6727	6940	7153	7366	7579	7792	8004	8217	2 43
2041	8430	8643	8856	9068	9281	9494	9707	9919	0132	0345	3 64 / 4 85
42	310 0557	0770	0983	1195	1408	1621	1833	2046	2258	2471	5 107
43	2684	2896	3109	3321	3534	3746	3959	4171	4384	4596	6 128
44	4809	5021	5234	5446	5659	5871	6084	6296	6508	6721	7 149
45	6933	7145	7358	7570	7783	7995	8207	8419	8632	8844	8 170 / 9 192
46	9056	9269	9481	9693	9905	0117	0330	0542	0754	0966	
47	311 1178	1391	1603	1815	2027	2239	2451	2663	2875	3087	
48	3300	3512	3724	3936	4148	4360	4572	4784	4996	5208	
49	5420	5632	5843	6055	6267	6479	6691	6903	7115	7327	
2050	7539	7750	7962	8174	8386	8598	8810	9021	9233	9445	

No.	0	1	2	3	4	5	6	7	8	9	Diff.
2050	3117539	7750	7962	8174	8386	8598	8810	9021	9233	9445	
51	9657	9868	0080	0292	0504	0715	0927	1139	1350	1562	
52	3121774	1985	2197	2408	2620	2832	3043	3255	3466	3678	
53	3889	4101	4313	4524	4736	4947	5159	5370	5581	5793	
54	6004	6216	6427	6639	6850	7061	7273	7484	7696	7907	
55	8118	8330	8541	8752	8964	9175	9386	9597	9809	0020	**211**

211
1 21
2 42
3 63
4 84
5 106
6 127
7 148
8 169
9 190

No.	0	1	2	3	4	5	6	7	8	9
56	3130231	0442	0654	0865	1076	1287	1498	1709	1921	2132
57	2343	2554	2765	2976	3187	3398	3610	3821	4032	4243
58	4454	4665	4876	5087	5298	5509	5720	5931	6142	6353
59	6563	6774	6985	7196	7407	7618	7829	8040	8251	8461
60	8672	8883	9094	9305	9515	9726	9937	0148	0358	0569
2061	3140780	0991	1201	1412	1623	1833	2044	2255	2465	2676
62	2887	3097	3308	3518	3729	3940	4150	4361	4571	4782
63	4992	5203	5413	5624	5834	6045	6255	6466	6676	6887
64	7097	7307	7518	7728	7939	8149	8359	8570	8780	8990
65	9201	9411	9621	9831	0042	0252	0462	0672	0883	1093

210
1 21
2 42
3 63
4 84
5 105
6 126
7 147
8 168
9 189

No.	0	1	2	3	4	5	6	7	8	9
66	3151303	1513	1724	1934	2144	2354	2564	2774	2985	3195
67	3405	3615	3825	4035	4245	4455	4665	4875	5085	5295
68	5505	5715	5925	6135	6345	6555	6765	6975	7185	7395
69	7605	7815	8025	8235	8444	8654	8864	9074	9284	9494
70	9703	9913	0123	0333	0543	0752	0962	1172	1382	1591
2071	3161801	2011	2220	2430	2640	2849	3059	3269	3478	3688
72	3898	4107	4317	4526	4736	4945	5155	5364	5574	5784
73	5993	6203	6412	6621	6831	7040	7250	7459	7669	7878
74	8088	8297	8506	8716	8925	9134	9344	9553	9762	9972
75	3170181	0390	0600	0809	1018	1227	1437	1646	1855	2064

209
1 21
2 42
3 63
4 84
5 105
6 125
7 146
8 167
9 188

No.	0	1	2	3	4	5	6	7	8	9
76	2273	2483	2692	2901	3110	3319	3528	3738	3947	4156
77	4365	4574	4783	4992	5201	5410	5619	5828	6037	6246
78	6455	6664	6873	7082	7291	7500	7709	7918	8127	8336
79	8545	8754	8963	9172	9380	9589	9798	0007	0216	0425
80	3180633	0842	1051	1260	1468	1677	1886	2095	2303	2512
2081	2721	2929	3138	3347	3556	3764	3973	4181	4390	4599
82	4807	5016	5224	5433	5642	5850	6059	6267	6476	6684
83	6893	7101	7310	7518	7727	7935	8143	8352	8560	8769
84	8977	9186	9394	9602	9811	0019	0227	0436	0644	0852
85	3191061	1269	1477	1685	1894	2102	2310	2518	2727	2935

208
1 21
2 42
3 62
4 83
5 104
6 125
7 146
8 166
9 187

No.	0	1	2	3	4	5	6	7	8	9
86	3143	3351	3559	3768	3976	4184	4392	4600	4808	5016
87	5224	5433	5641	5849	6057	6265	6473	6681	6889	7097
88	7305	7513	7721	7929	8137	8345	8553	8761	8969	9176
89	9384	9592	9800	0008	0216	0424	0632	0839	1047	1255
90	3201463	1671	1878	2086	2294	2502	2709	2917	3125	3333
2091	3540	3748	3956	4163	4371	4579	4786	4994	5202	5409
92	5617	5824	6032	6240	6447	6655	6862	7070	7277	7485
93	7692	7900	8107	8315	8522	8730	8937	9145	9352	9559
94	9767	9974	0182	0389	0596	0804	1011	1218	1426	1633
95	3211840	2048	2255	2462	2669	2877	3084	3291	3498	3706
96	3913	4120	4327	4534	4742	4949	5156	5363	5570	5777
97	5984	6191	6398	6606	6813	7020	7227	7434	7641	7848
98	8055	8262	8469	8676	8883	9090	9297	9504	9711	9917
99	3220124	0331	0538	0745	0952	1159	1366	1572	1779	1986
2100	2193	2400	2607	2813	3020	3227	3434	3640	3847	4054

No.	0	1	2	3	4	5	6	7	8	9	Diff.
2100	322 2193	2400	2607	2813	3020	3227	3434	3640	3847	4054	
01	4261	4467	4674	4881	5087	5294	5501	5707	5914	6121	
02	6327	6534	6740	6947	7153	7360	7567	7773	7980	8186	
03	8393	8599	8806	9012	9219	9425	9632	9838	0045	0251	
04	323 0457	0664	0870	1077	1283	1489	1696	1902	2108	2315	
05	2521	2727	2934	3140	3346	3552	3759	3965	4171	4377	
06	4584	4790	4996	5202	5408	5615	5821	6027	6233	6439	
07	6645	6851	7058	7264	7470	7676	7882	8088	8294	8500	
08	8706	8912	9118	9324	9530	9736	9942	0148	0354	0560	206
09	324 0766	0972	1178	1384	1589	1795	2001	2207	2413	2619	1 21
10	2825	3030	3236	3442	3648	3854	4059	4265	4471	4677	2 41
2111	4882	5088	5294	5499	5705	5911	6117	6322	6528	6734	3 62 / 4 82
12	6939	7145	7350	7556	7762	7967	8173	8378	8584	8789	5 103
13	8995	9201	9406	9612	9817	0023	0228	0433	0639	0844	6 124
14	325 1050	1255	1461	1666	1872	2077	2282	2488	2693	2898	7 144
15	3104	3309	3514	3720	3925	4130	4336	4541	4746	4951	8 165 / 9 185
16	5157	5362	5567	5772	5978	6183	6388	6593	6798	7003	
17	7209	7414	7619	7824	8029	8234	8439	8644	8849	9055	
18	9260	9465	9670	9875	0080	0285	0490	0695	0900	1105	
19	326 1310	1515	1719	1924	2129	2334	2539	2744	2949	3154	205
20	3359	3563	3768	3973	4178	4383	4588	4792	4997	5202	1 21 / 2 41
2121	5407	5611	5816	6021	6226	6430	6635	6840	7044	7249	3 62
22	7454	7658	7863	8068	8272	8477	8682	8886	9091	9295	4 82
23	9500	9705	9909	0114	0318	0523	0727	0932	1136	1341	5 103
24	327 1545	1750	1954	2158	2363	2567	2772	2976	3181	3385	6 123 / 7 144
25	3589	3794	3998	4202	4407	4611	4815	5020	5224	5428	8 164 / 9 185
26	5633	5837	6041	6245	6450	6654	6858	7062	7267	7471	
27	7675	7879	8083	8287	8492	8696	8900	9104	9308	9512	
28	9716	9920	0124	0328	0533	0737	0941	1145	1349	1553	204
29	328 1757	1961	2165	2369	2572	2776	2980	3184	3388	3592	1 20
30	3796	4000	4204	4408	4612	4815	5019	5223	5427	5631	2 41
2131	5834	6038	6242	6446	6650	6853	7057	7261	7465	7668	3 61 / 4 82
32	7872	8076	8279	8483	8687	8890	9094	9298	9501	9705	5 102
33	9909	0112	0316	0519	0723	0926	1130	1334	1537	1741	6 122
34	329 1944	2148	2351	2555	2758	2962	3165	3369	3572	3775	7 143
35	3979	4182	4386	4589	4792	4996	5199	5402	5606	5809	8 163 / 9 184
36	6012	6216	6419	6622	6826	7029	7232	7436	7639	7842	
37	8045	8248	8452	8655	8858	9061	9264	9468	9671	9874	
38	330 0077	0280	0483	0686	0889	1093	1296	1499	1702	1905	
39	2108	2311	2514	2717	2920	3123	3326	3529	3732	3935	203
40	4138	4341	4544	4747	4949	5152	5355	5558	5761	5964	1 20 / 2 41
2141	6167	6370	6572	6775	6978	7181	7384	7586	7789	7992	3 61
42	8195	8397	8600	8803	9006	9208	9411	9614	9816	0019	4 81
43	331 0222	0424	0627	0830	1032	1235	1437	1640	1843	2045	5 102
44	2248	2450	2653	2855	3058	3261	3463	3666	3868	4070	6 122 / 7 142
45	4273	4475	4678	4880	5083	5285	5488	5690	5892	6095	8 162 / 9 183
46	6297	6500	6702	6904	7107	7309	7511	7714	7916	8118	
47	8320	8523	8725	8927	9129	9332	9534	9736	9938	0141	
48	332 0343	0545	0747	0949	1151	1354	1556	1758	1960	2162	
49	2364	2566	2768	2970	3172	3374	3577	3779	3981	4183	
2150	4385	4587	4789	4991	5193	5394	5596	5798	6000	6202	

No.	0	1	2	3	4	5	6	7	8	9	Diff.
2150	332 4385	4587	4789	4991	5193	5394	5596	5798	6000	6202	202
51	6404	6606	6808	7010	7212	7414	7615	7817	8019	8221	1 20
52	8423	8624	8826	9028	9230	9432	9633	9835	0037	0239	2 40
53	333 0440	0642	0844	1045	1247	1449	1650	1852	2054	2255	3 61
54	2457	2659	2860	3062	3263	3465	3667	3868	4070	4271	4 81
55	4473	4674	4876	5077	5279	5480	5682	5883	6085	6286	5 101 / 6 121
56	6488	6689	6890	7092	7293	7495	7696	7897	8099	8300	7 141
57	8501	8703	8904	9105	9307	9508	9709	9911	0112	0313	8 162
58	334 0514	0716	0917	1118	1319	1521	1722	1923	2124	2325	9 182
59	2526	2728	2929	3130	3331	3532	3733	3934	4135	4336	
60	4538	4739	4940	5141	5342	5543	5744	5945	6146	6347	201
2161	6548	6749	6950	7151	7351	7552	7753	7954	8155	8356	1 20
62	8557	8758	8959	9159	9360	9561	9762	9963	0164	0364	2 40
63	335 0565	0766	0967	1168	1368	1569	1770	1970	2171	2372	3 60
64	2573	2773	2974	3175	3375	3576	3777	3977	4178	4378	4 80
65	4579	4780	4980	5181	5381	5582	5782	5983	6183	6384	5 101 / 6 121 / 7 141
66	6585	6785	6986	7186	7386	7587	7787	7988	8188	8389	8 161
67	8589	8790	8990	9190	9391	9591	9791	9992	0192	0392	9 181
68	336 0593	0793	0993	1194	1394	1594	1795	1995	2195	2395	
69	2596	2796	2996	3196	3396	3597	3797	3997	4197	4397	
70	4597	4797	4998	5198	5398	5598	5798	5998	6198	6398	
2171	6598	6798	6998	7198	7398	7598	7798	7998	8198	8398	200
72	8598	8798	8998	9198	9398	9598	9798	9998	0198	0397	1 20
73	337 0597	0797	0997	1197	1397	1596	1796	1996	2196	2396	2 40
74	2595	2795	2995	3195	3394	3594	3794	3994	4193	4393	3 60
75	4593	4792	4992	5192	5391	5591	5791	5990	6190	6389	4 80 / 5 100
76	6589	6788	6988	7188	7387	7587	7786	7986	8185	8385	6 120
77	8584	8784	8983	9183	9382	9582	9781	9981	0180	0379	7 140
78	338 0579	0778	0978	1177	1376	1576	1775	1974	2174	2373	8 160
79	2572	2772	2971	3170	3369	3569	3768	3967	4166	4366	9 180
80	4565	4764	4963	5163	5362	5561	5760	5959	6158	6358	
2181	6557	6756	6955	7154	7353	7552	7751	7950	8149	8348	199
82	8547	8746	8946	9145	9344	9543	9742	9940	0139	0338	1 20
83	339 0537	0736	0935	1134	1333	1532	1731	1930	2129	2327	2 40
84	2526	2725	2924	3123	3322	3520	3719	3918	4117	4316	3 60
85	4514	4713	4912	5111	5309	5508	5707	5906	6104	6303	4 80
86	6502	6700	6899	7098	7296	7495	7693	7892	8091	8289	5 100 / 6 119
87	8488	8686	8885	9084	9282	9481	9679	9878	0076	0275	7 139
88	340 0473	0672	0870	1069	1267	1466	1664	1862	2061	2259	8 159
89	2458	2656	2854	3053	3251	3449	3648	3846	4045	4243	9 179
90	4441	4639	4838	5036	5234	5433	5631	5829	6027	6226	
2191	6424	6622	6820	7018	7217	7415	7613	7811	8009	8207	
92	8405	8604	8802	9000	9198	9396	9594	9792	9990	0188	198
93	341 0386	0584	0782	0980	1178	1376	1574	1772	1970	2168	1 20
94	2366	2564	2762	2960	3158	3356	3554	3752	3950	4147	2 40
95	4345	4543	4741	4939	5137	5334	5532	5730	5928	6126	3 59
96	6323	6521	6719	6917	7114	7312	7510	7708	7905	8103	4 79
97	8301	8498	8696	8894	9091	9289	9486	9684	9882	0079	5 99
98	342 0277	0474	0672	0870	1067	1265	1462	1660	1857	2055	6 119
99	2252	2450	2647	2845	3042	3240	3437	3635	3832	4029	7 139
2200	4227	4424	4622	4819	5016	5214	5411	5608	5806	6003	8 158 / 9 178

25

No.	0	1	2	3	4	5	6	7	8	9	Diff.
2200	342 4227	4424	4622	4819	5016	5214	5411	5608	5806	6003	
01	6200	6398	6595	6792	6990	7187	7384	7581	7779	7976	
02	8173	8370	8568	8765	8962	9159	9356	9554	9751	9948	
03	343 0145	0342	0539	0736	0933	1131	1328	1525	1722	1919	
04	2116	2313	2510	2707	2904	3101	3298	3495	3692	3889	197
05	4086	4283	4480	4677	4874	5071	5268	5464	5661	5858	1 20
											2 39
06	6055	6252	6449	6646	6842	7039	7236	7433	7630	7827	3 59
07	8023	8220	8417	8614	8810	9007	9204	9401	9597	9794	4 79
08	9991	0187	0384	0581	0777	0974	1171	1367	1564	1761	5 99
09	344 1957	2154	2350	2547	2743	2940	3137	3333	3530	3726	6 118
10	3923	4119	4316	4512	4709	4905	5102	5298	5495	5691	7 138
											8 158
2211	5887	6084	6280	6477	6673	6869	7066	7262	7459	7655	9 177
12	7851	8048	8244	8440	8636	8833	9029	9225	9422	9618	
13	9814	0010	0207	0403	0599	0795	0991	1188	1384	1580	
14	345 1776	1972	2168	2365	2561	2757	2953	3149	3345	3541	196
15	3737	3933	4129	4325	4522	4718	4914	5110	5306	5502	1 20
											2 39
16	5698	5894	6090	6285	6481	6677	6873	7069	7265	7461	3 59
17	7657	7853	8049	8245	8440	8636	8832	9028	9224	9420	4 78
18	9615	9811	0007	0203	0399	0594	0790	0986	1182	1377	5 98
19	346 1573	1769	1964	2160	2356	2551	2747	2943	3138	3334	6 118
20	3530	3725	3921	4117	4312	4508	4703	4899	5094	5290	7 137
											8 157
2221	5486	5681	5877	6072	6268	6463	6659	6854	7050	7245	9 176
22	7441	7636	7831	8027	8222	8418	8613	8808	9004	9199	
23	9395	9590	9785	9981	0176	0371	0567	0762	0957	1153	
24	347 1348	1543	1738	1934	2129	2324	2519	2715	2910	3105	
25	3300	3495	3691	3886	4081	4276	4471	4666	4861	5056	
26	5252	5447	5642	5837	6032	6227	6422	6617	6812	7007	195
27	7202	7397	7592	7787	7982	8177	8372	8567	8762	8957	1 20
28	9152	9347	9542	9737	9931	0126	0321	0516	0711	0906	2 39
29	348 1101	1296	1490	1685	1880	2075	2270	2464	2659	2854	3 59
30	3049	3243	3438	3633	3828	4022	4217	4412	4606	4801	4 78
											5 98
2231	4996	5190	5385	5580	5774	5969	6164	6358	6553	6747	6 117
32	6942	7136	7331	7526	7720	7915	8109	8304	8498	8693	7 137
33	8887	9082	9276	9471	9665	9860	0054	0248	0443	0637	8 156
34	349 0832	1026	1220	1415	1609	1804	1998	2192	2387	2581	9 176
35	2775	2970	3164	3358	3552	3747	3941	4135	4330	4524	
36	4718	4912	5106	5301	5495	5689	5883	6077	6272	6466	
37	6660	6854	7048	7242	7436	7630	7825	8019	8213	8407	
38	8601	8795	8989	9183	9377	9571	9765	9959	0153	0347	194
39	350 0541	0735	0929	1123	1317	1511	1705	1898	2092	2286	1 19
40	2480	2674	2868	3062	3256	3449	3643	3837	4031	4225	2 39
2241	4419	4612	4806	5000	5194	5387	5581	5775	5969	6162	3 58
42	6356	6550	6743	6937	7131	7325	7518	7712	7905	8099	4 78
43	8293	8486	8680	8874	9067	9261	9454	9648	9841	0035	5 97
44	351 0229	0422	0616	0809	1003	1196	1390	1583	1777	1970	6 116
45	2163	2357	2550	2744	2937	3131	3324	3517	3711	3904	7 136
											8 155
46	4098	4291	4484	4678	4871	5064	5258	5451	5644	5837	9 175
47	6031	6224	6417	6611	6804	6997	7190	7383	7577	7770	
48	7963	8156	8349	8543	8736	8929	9122	9315	9508	9701	
49	9895	0088	0281	0474	0667	0860	1053	1246	1439	1632	193
2250	352 1825	2018	2211	2404	2597	2790	2983	3176	3369	3562	

No.	0	1	2	3	4	5	6	7	8	9	Diff.
2250	352 1825	2018	2211	2404	2597	2790	2983	3176	3369	3562	193
51	3755	3948	4141	4334	4527	4720	4912	5105	5298	5491	1 19
52	5684	5877	6070	6262	6455	6648	6841	7034	7226	7419	2 39
53	7612	7805	7997	8190	8383	8576	8768	8961	9154	9346	3 58
54	9539	9732	9924	0̄117	0̄310	0̄502	0̄695	0̄888	1̄080	1̄273	4 77
55	353 1465	1658	1851	2043	2236	2428	2621	2813	3006	3198	5 97
											6 116
56	3391	3583	3776	3968	4161	4353	4546	4738	4931	5123	7 135
57	5316	5508	5700	5893	6085	6278	6470	6662	6855	7047	8 154
58	7239	7432	7624	7816	8009	8201	8393	8586	8778	8970	9 174
59	9162	9355	9547	9739	9931	0̄123	0̄316	0̄508	0̄700	0̄892	
60	354 1084	1277	1469	1661	1853	2045	2237	2429	2621	2814	192
											1 19
2261	3006	3198	3390	3582	3774	3966	4158	4350	4542	4734	2 38
62	4926	5118	5310	5502	5694	5886	6078	6270	6462	6654	3 58
63	6846	7037	7229	7421	7613	7805	7997	8189	8381	8572	4 77
64	8764	8956	9148	9340	9531	9723	9915	0̄107	0̄299	0̄490	5 96
65	355 0682	0874	1066	1257	1449	1641	1832	2024	2216	2407	6 115
											7 134
66	2599	2791	2982	3174	3366	3557	3749	3940	4132	4324	8 154
67	4515	4707	4898	5090	5281	5473	5664	5856	6048	6239	9 173
68	6431	6622	6813	7005	7196	7388	7579	7771	7962	8154	
69	8345	8536	8728	8919	9111	9302	9493	9685	9876	0̄067	
70	356 0259	0450	0641	0832	1024	1215	1406	1598	1789	1980	191
											1 19
2271	2171	2363	2554	2745	2936	3127	3319	3510	3701	3892	2 38
72	4083	4274	4466	4657	4848	5039	5230	5421	5612	5803	3 57
73	5994	6185	6376	6568	6759	6950	7141	7332	7523	7714	4 76
74	7905	8096	8287	8478	8668	8859	9050	9241	9432	9623	5 96
75	9814	0005	0̄196	0̄387	0̄578	0̄768	0̄959	1̄150	1̄341	1̄532	6 115
											7 134
76	357 1723	1913	2104	2295	2486	2677	2867	3058	3249	3440	8 153
77	3630	3821	4012	4202	4393	4584	4775	4965	5156	5347	9 172
78	5537	5728	5918	6109	6300	6490	6681	6872	7062	7253	
79	7443	7634	7824	8015	8205	8396	8586	8777	8967	9158	
80	9348	9539	9729	9920	0̄110	0̄301	0̄491	0̄682	0̄872	1̄062	
2281	358 1253	1443	1634	1824	2014	2205	2395	2585	2776	2966	
82	3156	3347	3537	3727	3918	4108	4298	4488	4679	4869	
83	5059	5249	5440	5630	5820	6010	6200	6391	6581	6771	
84	6961	7151	7341	7531	7722	7912	8102	8292	8482	8672	190
85	8862	9052	9242	9432	9622	9812	0̄002	0̄192	0̄382	0̄572	1 19
											2 38
86	359 0762	0952	1142	1332	1522	1712	1902	2092	2282	2472	3 57
87	2662	2852	3041	3231	3421	3611	3801	3991	4181	4370	4 76
88	4560	4750	4940	5130	5319	5509	5699	5889	6078	6268	5 95
89	6458	6648	6837	7027	7217	7406	7596	7786	7976	8165	6 114
90	8355	8544	8734	8924	9113	9303	9493	9682	9872	0̄061	7 133
2291	360 0251	0440	0630	0820	1009	1199	1388	1578	1767	1957	8 152
92	2146	2336	2525	2715	2904	3093	3283	3472	3662	3851	9 171
93	4041	4230	4419	4609	4798	4987	5177	5366	5555	5745	
94	5934	6123	6313	6502	6691	6881	7070	7259	7448	7638	
95	7827	8016	8205	8395	8584	8773	8962	9151	9341	9530	189
96	9719	9908	0̄097	0̄286	0̄475	0̄664	0̄854	1̄043	1̄232	1̄421	
97	361 1610	1799	1988	2177	2366	2555	2744	2933	3122	3311	
98	3500	3689	3878	4067	4256	4445	4634	4823	5012	5201	
99	5390	5579	5768	5956	6145	6334	6523	6712	6901	7090	
2300	7278	7467	7656	7845	8034	8222	8411	8600	8789	8977	

No.	0	1	2	3	4	5	6	7	8	9	Diff.
2300	361 7278	7467	7656	7845	8034	8222	8411	8600	8789	8977	189
01	9166	9355	9544	9732	9921	0110	0298	0487	0676	0865	1 19
02	362 1053	1242	1430	1619	1808	1996	2185	2374	2562	2751	2 38
03	2939	3128	3317	3505	3694	3882	4071	4259	4448	4636	3 57
04	4825	5013	5202	5390	5579	5767	5956	6144	6332	6521	4 76
05	6709	6898	7086	7275	7463	7651	7840	8028	8216	8405	5 95
06	8593	8781	8970	9158	9346	9535	9723	9911	0099	0288	6 113 / 7 132 / 8 151
07	363 0476	0664	0852	1041	1229	1417	1605	1794	1982	2170	9 170
08	2358	2546	2734	2923	3111	3299	3487	3675	3863	4051	
09	4239	4427	4615	4804	4992	5180	5368	5556	5744	5932	188
10	6120	6308	6496	6684	6872	7060	7248	7436	7624	7812	1 19
2311	7999	8187	8375	8563	8751	8939	9127	9315	9503	9690	2 38
12	9878	0066	0254	0442	0630	0817	1005	1193	1381	1569	3 56
13	364 1756	1944	2132	2320	2507	2695	2883	3070	3258	3446	4 75
14	3634	3821	4009	4197	4384	4572	4759	4947	5135	5322	5 94
15	5510	5698	5885	6073	6260	6448	6635	6823	7010	7198	6 113 / 7 132
16	7386	7573	7761	7948	8136	8323	8511	8698	8885	9073	8 150 / 9 169
17	9260	9448	9635	9823	0010	0197	0385	0572	0760	0947	
18	365 1134	1322	1509	1696	1884	2071	2258	2446	2633	2820	
19	3007	3195	3382	3569	3757	3944	4131	4318	4505	4693	
20	4880	5067	5254	5441	5629	5816	6003	6190	6377	6564	
2321	6751	6939	7126	7313	7500	7687	7874	8061	8248	8435	
22	8622	8809	8996	9183	9370	9557	9744	9931	0118	0305	
23	366 0492	0679	0866	1053	1240	1427	1614	1801	1987	2174	
24	2361	2548	2735	2922	3109	3296	3482	3669	3856	4043	
25	4230	4416	4603	4790	4977	5163	5350	5537	5724	5910	
26	6097	6284	6471	6657	6844	7031	7217	7404	7591	7777	187
27	7964	8150	8337	8524	8710	8897	9083	9270	9457	9643	1 19
28	9830	0016	0203	0389	0576	0762	0949	1135	1322	1508	2 37
29	367 1695	1881	2068	2254	2441	2627	2814	3000	3186	3373	3 56 / 4 75
30	3559	3746	3932	4118	4305	4491	4677	4864	5050	5236	5 94
2331	5423	5609	5795	5982	6168	6354	6540	6727	6913	7099	6 112 / 7 131
32	7285	7472	7658	7844	8030	8217	8403	8589	8775	8961	8 150 / 9 168
33	9147	9334	9520	9706	9892	0078	0264	0450	0636	0822	
34	368 1009	1195	1381	1567	1753	1939	2125	2311	2497	2683	
35	2869	3055	3241	3427	3613	3799	3985	4171	4357	4542	
36	4728	4914	5100	5286	5472	5658	5844	6030	6215	6401	
37	6587	6773	6959	7145	7330	7516	7702	7888	8074	8259	
38	8445	8631	8817	9002	9188	9374	9559	9745	9931	0117	186
39	369 0302	0488	0674	0859	1045	1230	1416	1602	1787	1973	1 19
40	2159	2344	2530	2715	2901	3086	3272	3458	3643	3829	2 37 / 3 56
2341	4014	4200	4385	4571	4756	4942	5127	5313	5498	5683	4 74
42	5869	6054	6240	6425	6611	6796	6981	7167	7352	7538	5 93
43	7723	7908	8094	8279	8464	8650	8835	9020	9205	9391	6 112
44	9576	9761	9947	0132	0317	0502	0688	0873	1058	1243	7 130
45	370 1428	1614	1799	1984	2169	2354	2540	2725	2910	3095	8 149 / 9 167
46	3280	3465	3650	3835	4020	4206	4391	4576	4761	4946	
47	5131	5316	5501	5686	5871	6056	6241	6426	6611	6796	
48	6981	7166	7351	7536	7721	7906	8091	8275	8460	8645	
49	8830	9015	9200	9385	9570	9754	9939	0124	0309	0494	
2350	371 0679	0863	1048	1233	1418	1603	1787	1972	2157	2342	

No.	0	1	2	3	4	5	6	7	8	9	Diff.
2350	371 0679	0863	1048	1233	1418	1603	1787	1972	2157	2342	
51	2526	2711	2896	3080	3265	3450	3635	3819	4004	4189	185
52	4373	4558	4742	4927	5112	5296	5481	5666	5850	6035	1 19
53	6219	6404	6588	6773	6957	7142	7327	7511	7696	7880	2 37
54	8065	8249	8434	8618	8802	8987	9171	9356	9540	9725	3 56
55	9909	0094	0278	0462	0647	0831	1015	1200	1384	1569	4 74
56	372 1753	1937	2122	2306	2490	2674	2859	3043	3227	3412	5 93 / 6 111
57	3596	3780	3964	4149	4333	4517	4701	4885	5070	5254	7 130
58	5438	5622	5806	5991	6175	6359	6543	6727	6911	7095	8 148
59	7279	7464	7648	7832	8016	8200	8384	8568	8752	8936	9 167
60	9120	9304	9488	9672	9856	0040	0224	0408	0592	0776	
2361	373 0960	1144	1328	1512	1696	1879	2063	2247	2431	2615	
62	2799	2983	3167	3350	3534	3718	3902	4086	4270	4453	184
63	4637	4821	5005	5189	5372	5556	5740	5924	6107	6291	1 18
64	6475	6658	6842	7026	7210	7393	7577	7761	7944	8128	2 37
65	8311	8495	8679	8862	9046	9230	9413	9597	9780	9964	3 55
66	374 0147	0331	0515	0698	0882	1065	1249	1432	1616	1799	4 74
67	1983	2166	2350	2533	2716	2900	3083	3267	3450	3634	5 92
68	3817	4000	4184	4367	4551	4734	4917	5101	5284	5467	6 110
69	5651	5834	6017	6201	6384	6567	6750	6934	7117	7300	7 129
70	7483	7667	7850	8033	8216	8400	8583	8766	8949	9132	8 147
2371	9316	9499	9682	9865	0048	0231	0414	0598	0781	0964	9 166
72	375 1147	1330	1513	1696	1879	2062	2245	2428	2611	2794	183
73	2977	3160	3343	3526	3709	3892	4075	4258	4441	4624	1 18
74	4807	4990	5173	5356	5539	5722	5905	6088	6270	6453	2 37
75	6636	6819	7002	7185	7368	7550	7733	7916	8099	8282	3 55
76	8464	8647	8830	9013	9195	9378	9561	9744	9926	0109	4 73
77	376 0292	0475	0657	0840	1023	1205	1388	1571	1753	1936	5 92
78	2119	2301	2484	2666	2849	3032	3214	3397	3579	3762	6 110
79	3944	4127	4310	4492	4675	4857	5040	5222	5405	5587	7 128
80	5770	5952	6135	6317	6499	6682	6864	7047	7229	7412	8 146
2381	7594	7776	7959	8141	8323	8506	8688	8871	9053	9235	9 165
82	9418	9600	9782	9965	0147	0329	0511	0694	0876	1058	
83	377 1240	1423	1605	1787	1969	2152	2334	2516	2698	2880	
84	3063	3245	3427	3609	3791	3973	4155	4338	4520	4702	182
85	4884	5066	5248	5430	5612	5794	5976	6158	6340	6522	1 18
86	6704	6886	7068	7250	7432	7614	7796	7978	8160	8342	2 36
87	8524	8706	8888	9070	9252	9434	9616	9798	9979	0161	3 55
88	378 0343	0525	0707	0889	1071	1252	1434	1616	1798	1980	4 73
89	2161	2343	2525	2707	2889	3070	3252	3434	3616	3797	5 91
90	3979	4161	4342	4524	4706	4887	5069	5251	5432	5614	6 109
2391	5796	5977	6159	6341	6522	6704	6885	7067	7249	7430	7 127
92	7612	7793	7975	8156	8338	8519	8701	8882	9064	9245	8 146
93	9427	9608	9790	9971	0153	0334	0516	0697	0879	1060	9 164
94	379 1241	1423	1604	1786	1967	2148	2330	2511	2692	2874	
95	3055	3237	3418	3599	3780	3962	4143	4324	4506	4687	
96	4868	5049	5231	5412	5593	5774	5956	6137	6318	6499	
97	6680	6862	7043	7224	7405	7586	7767	7948	8130	8311	
98	8492	8673	8854	9035	9216	9397	9578	9759	9940	0121	181
99	380 0302	0484	0665	0846	1027	1208	1389	1570	1750	1931	
2400	2112	2293	2474	2655	2836	3017	3198	3379	3560	3741	

No.	0	1	2	3	4	5	6	7	8	9	Diff.
2400	380 2112	2293	2474	2655	2836	3017	3198	3379	3560	3741	181
01	3922	4102	4283	4464	4645	4826	5007	5188	5368	5549	1 18
02	5730	5911	6092	6272	6453	6634	6815	6995	7176	7357	2 36
03	7538	7718	7899	8080	8261	8441	8622	8803	8983	9164	3 54
04	9345	9525	9706	9887	0067	0248	0428	0609	0790	0970	4 72
05	381 1151	1331	1512	1693	1873	2054	2234	2415	2595	2776	5 91
											6 109
06	2956	3137	3317	3498	3678	3859	4039	4220	4400	4580	7 127
07	4761	4941	5122	5302	5483	5663	5843	6024	6204	6384	8 145
08	6565	6745	6926	7106	7286	7467	7647	7827	8007	8188	9 163
09	8368	8548	8729	8909	9089	9269	9450	9630	9810	9990	
10	382 0170	0351	0531	0711	0891	1071	1252	1432	1612	1792	
2411	1972	2152	2332	2512	2693	2873	3053	3233	3413	3593	180
12	3773	3953	4133	4313	4493	4673	4853	5033	5213	5393	1 18
13	5573	5753	5933	6113	6293	6473	6653	6833	7013	7193	2 36
14	7373	7553	7732	7912	8092	8272	8452	8632	8812	8992	3 54
15	9171	9351	9531	9711	9891	0070	0250	0430	0610	0790	4 72
											5 90
16	383 0969	1149	1329	1509	1688	1868	2048	2227	2407	2587	6 108
17	2767	2946	3126	3306	3485	3665	3844	4024	4204	4383	7 126
18	4563	4743	4922	5102	5281	5461	5640	5820	6000	6179	8 144
19	6359	6538	6718	6897	7077	7256	7436	7615	7795	7974	9 162
20	8154	8333	8513	8692	8871	9051	9230	9410	9589	9769	
2421	9948	0127	0307	0486	0665	0845	1024	1203	1383	1562	
22	384 1741	1921	2100	2279	2459	2638	2817	2996	3176	3355	
23	3534	3713	3893	4072	4251	4430	4609	4789	4968	5147	
24	5326	5505	5684	5864	6043	6222	6401	6580	6759	6938	
25	7117	7297	7476	7655	7834	8013	8192	8371	8550	8729	179
26	8908	9087	9266	9445	9624	9803	9982	0161	0340	0519	1 18
27	385 0698	0877	1056	1235	1413	1592	1771	1950	2129	2308	2 36
28	2487	2666	2845	3023	3202	3381	3560	3739	3918	4096	3 54
29	4275	4454	4633	4812	4990	5169	5348	5527	5705	5884	4 72
30	6063	6241	6420	6599	6778	6956	7135	7314	7492	7671	5 90
											6 107
2431	7850	8028	8207	8386	8564	8743	8921	9100	9279	9457	7 125
32	9636	9814	9993	0171	0350	0528	0707	0886	1064	1243	8 143
33	386 1421	1600	1778	1957	2135	2314	2492	2670	2849	3027	9 161
34	3206	3384	3563	3741	3919	4098	4276	4455	4633	4811	
35	4990	5168	5346	5525	5703	5881	6060	6238	6416	6595	
36	6773	6951	7129	7308	7486	7664	7842	8021	8199	8377	
37	8555	8733	8912	9090	9268	9446	9624	9803	9981	0159	
38	387 0337	0515	0693	0871	1049	1228	1406	1584	1762	1940	178
39	2118	2296	2474	2652	2830	3008	3186	3364	3542	3720	1 18
40	3898	4076	4254	4432	4610	4788	4966	5144	5322	5500	2 36
2441	5678	5856	6034	6212	6389	6567	6745	6923	7101	7279	3 53
42	7457	7634	7812	7990	8168	8346	8524	8701	8879	9057	4 71
43	9235	9412	9590	9768	9946	0123	0301	0479	0657	0834	5 89
44	388 1012	1190	1367	1545	1723	1900	2078	2256	2433	2611	6 107
45	2789	2966	3144	3321	3499	3677	3854	4032	4209	4387	7 125
											8 142
46	4565	4742	4920	5097	5275	5452	5630	5807	5985	6162	9 160
47	6340	6517	6695	6872	7050	7227	7404	7582	7759	7937	
48	8114	8292	8469	8646	8824	9001	9178	9356	9533	9711	
49	9888	0065	0243	0420	0597	0774	0952	1129	1306	1484	
2450	389 1661	1838	2015	2193	2370	2547	2724	2902	3079	3256	

No.	0	1	2	3	4	5	6	7	8	9	Diff.
2450	389 1661	1838	2015	2193	2370	2547	2724	2902	3079	3256	
51	3433	3610	3787	3965	4142	4319	4496	4673	4850	5028	
52	5205	5382	5559	5736	5913	6090	6267	6444	6621	6798	**177**
53	6975	7153	7330	7507	7684	7861	8038	8215	8392	8569	1 18
54	8746	8923	9100	9276	9453	9630	9807	9984	0161	0338	2 35
55	390 0515	0692	0869	1046	1223	1399	1576	1753	1930	2107	3 53
56	2284	2460	2637	2814	2991	3168	3344	3521	3698	3875	4 71
57	4052	4228	4405	4582	4759	4935	5112	5289	5465	5642	5 89
58	5819	5995	6172	6349	6525	6702	6879	7055	7232	7409	6 106
59	7585	7762	7939	8115	8292	8468	8645	8821	8998	9175	7 124
60	9351	9528	9704	9881	0057	0234	0410	0587	0763	0940	8 142
2461	391 1116	1293	1469	1646	1822	1998	2175	2351	2528	2704	9 159
62	2880	3057	3233	3410	3586	3762	3939	4115	4291	4468	
63	4644	4820	4997	5173	5349	5526	5702	5878	6055	6231	
64	6407	6583	6760	6936	7112	7288	7464	7641	7817	7993	
65	8169	8345	8522	8698	8874	9050	9226	9402	9578	9755	
66	9931	0107	0283	0459	0635	0811	0987	1163	1339	1515	**176**
67	392 1691	1868	2044	2220	2396	2572	2748	2924	3100	3276	1 18
68	3452	3628	3803	3979	4155	4331	4507	4683	4859	5035	2 35
69	5211	5387	5563	5739	5914	6090	6266	6442	6618	6794	3 53
70	6970	7145	7321	7497	7673	7849	8024	8200	8376	8552	4 70
2471	8727	8903	9079	9255	9430	9606	9782	9958	0133	0309	5 88
72	393 0485	0660	0836	1012	1187	1363	1539	1714	1890	2066	6 106
73	2241	2417	2592	2768	2944	3119	3295	3470	3646	3821	7 123
74	3997	4172	4348	4524	4699	4875	5050	5226	5401	5577	8 141
75	5752	5928	6103	6278	6454	6629	6805	6980	7156	7331	9 158
76	7506	7682	7857	8033	8208	8383	8559	8734	8909	9085	
77	9260	9435	9611	9786	9961	0137	0312	0487	0662	0838	
78	394 1013	1188	1364	1539	1714	1889	2064	2240	2415	2590	
79	2765	2940	3116	3291	3466	3641	3816	3991	4167	4342	
80	4517	4692	4867	5042	5217	5392	5567	5742	5918	6093	
2481	6268	6443	6618	6793	6968	7143	7318	7493	7668	7843	**175**
82	8018	8193	8368	8543	8718	8893	9068	9242	9417	9592	1 18
83	9767	9942	0117	0292	0467	0642	0817	0991	1166	1341	2 35
84	395 1516	1691	1866	2040	2215	2390	2565	2740	2914	3089	3 53
85	3264	3439	3613	3788	3963	4138	4312	4487	4662	4837	4 70
86	5011	5186	5361	5535	5710	5885	6059	6234	6409	6583	5 88
87	6758	6932	7107	7282	7456	7631	7805	7980	8155	8329	6 105
88	8504	8678	8853	9027	9202	9376	9551	9725	9900	0074	7 123
89	396 0249	0423	0598	0772	0947	1121	1296	1470	1645	1819	8 140
90	1993	2168	2342	2517	2691	2865	3040	3214	3389	3563	9 158
2491	3737	3912	4086	4260	4435	4609	4783	4958	5132	5306	
92	5480	5655	5829	6003	6177	6352	6526	6700	6874	7049	
93	7223	7397	7571	7745	7920	8094	8268	8442	8616	8790	**174**
94	8964	9139	9313	9487	9661	9835	0009	0183	0357	0531	1 17
95	397 0705	0880	1054	1228	1402	1576	1750	1924	2098	2272	2 35
											3 52
96	2446	2620	2794	2968	3142	3316	3490	3664	3838	4011	4 70
97	4185	4359	4533	4707	4881	5055	5229	5403	5577	5750	5 87
98	5924	6098	6272	6446	6620	6794	6967	7141	7315	7489	6 104
99	7663	7836	8010	8184	8358	8531	8705	8879	9053	9226	7 122
2500	9400	9574	9748	9921	0095	0269	0442	0616	0790	0963	8 139
	398										9 157

No.	0	1	2	3	4	5	6	7	8	9	Diff.
2500	397 9400	9574	9748	9921	$\overline{0095}$	$\overline{0269}$	$\overline{0442}$	$\overline{0616}$	$\overline{0790}$	$\overline{0963}$	
01	398 1137	1311	1484	1658	1831	2005	2179	2352	2526	2699	
02	2873	3047	3220	3394	3567	3741	3914	4088	4261	4435	
03	4608	4782	4956	5129	5302	5476	5649	5823	5996	6170	
04	6343	6517	6690	6864	7037	7210	7384	7557	7731	7904	
05	8077	8251	8424	8597	8771	8944	9117	9291	9464	9637	
06	9811	9984	$\overline{0157}$	$\overline{0331}$	$\overline{0504}$	$\overline{0677}$	$\overline{0850}$	$\overline{1024}$	$\overline{1197}$	$\overline{1370}$	
07	399 1543	1717	1890	2063	2236	2409	2583	2756	2929	3102	
08	3275	3448	3622	3795	3968	4141	4314	4487	4660	4834	
09	5007	5180	5353	5526	5699	5872	6045	6218	6391	6564	173
10	6737	6910	7083	7256	7429	7602	7775	7948	8121	8294	1 17
2511	8467	8640	8813	8986	9159	9332	9505	9678	9851	$\overline{0023}$	2 35
12	400 0196	0369	0542	0715	0888	1061	1234	1406	1579	1752	3 52
13	1925	2098	2271	2443	2616	2789	2962	3134	3307	3480	4 69
14	3653	3825	3998	4171	4344	4516	4689	4862	5035	5207	5 87
15	5380	5553	5725	5898	6071	6243	6416	6588	6761	6934	6 104
16	7106	7279	7452	7624	7797	7969	8142	8314	8487	8660	7 121
17	8832	9005	9177	9350	9522	9695	9867	$\overline{0040}$	$\overline{0212}$	$\overline{0385}$	8 138
18	401 0557	0730	0902	1075	1247	1420	1592	1764	1937	2109	9 156
19	2282	2454	2626	2799	2971	3144	3316	3488	3661	3833	
20	4005	4178	4350	4522	4695	4867	5039	5212	5384	5556	
2521	5728	5901	6073	6245	6417	6590	6762	6934	7106	7279	
22	7451	7623	7795	7967	8140	8312	8484	8656	8828	9000	
23	9173	9345	9517	9689	9861	$\overline{0033}$	$\overline{0205}$	$\overline{0377}$	$\overline{0549}$	$\overline{0721}$	172
24	402 0894	1066	1238	1410	1582	1754	1926	2098	2270	2442	1 17
25	2614	2786	2958	3130	3302	3474	3646	3818	3990	4162	2 34
26	4333	4505	4677	4849	5021	5193	5365	5537	5709	5881	3 52
27	6052	6224	6396	6568	6740	6912	7083	7255	7427	7599	4 69
28	7771	7942	8114	8286	8458	8630	8801	8973	9145	9317	5 86
29	9488	9660	9832	$\overline{0003}$	$\overline{0175}$	$\overline{0347}$	$\overline{0519}$	$\overline{0690}$	$\overline{0862}$	$\overline{1034}$	6 103
30	403 1205	1377	1549	1720	1892	2063	2235	2407	2578	2750	7 120
2531	2921	3093	3265	3436	3608	3779	3951	4122	4294	4465	8 138
32	4637	4809	4980	5152	5323	5495	5666	5838	6009	6180	9 155
33	6352	6523	6695	6866	7038	7209	7381	7552	7723	7895	
34	8066	8237	8409	8580	8752	8923	9094	9266	9437	9608	
35	9780	9951	$\overline{0122}$	$\overline{0294}$	$\overline{0465}$	$\overline{0636}$	$\overline{0807}$	$\overline{0979}$	$\overline{1150}$	$\overline{1321}$	
36	404 1492	1664	1835	2006	2177	2349	2520	2691	2862	3033	
37	3205	3376	3547	3718	3889	4061	4232	4403	4574	4745	
38	4916	5087	5258	5429	5601	5772	5943	6114	6285	6456	
39	6627	6798	6969	7140	7311	7482	7653	7824	7995	8166	
40	8337	8508	8679	8850	9021	9192	9363	9534	9705	9876	
2541	405 0047	0218	0388	0559	0730	0901	1072	1243	1414	1585	171
42	1755	1926	2097	2268	2439	2610	2780	2951	3122	3293	1 17
43	3464	3634	3805	3976	4147	4317	4488	4659	4830	5000	2 34
44	5171	5342	5512	5683	5854	6025	6195	6366	6537	6707	3 51
45	6878	7049	7219	7390	7560	7731	7902	8072	8243	8413	4 68
46	8584	8755	8925	9096	9266	9437	9607	9778	9948	$\overline{0119}$	5 86
47	406 0289	0460	0630	0801	0971	1142	1312	1483	1653	1824	6 103
48	1994	2165	2335	2506	2676	2846	3017	3187	3358	3528	7 120
49	3698	3869	4039	4209	4380	4550	4721	4891	5061	5231	8 137
2550	5402	5572	5742	5913	6083	6253	6424	6594	6764	6934	9 154

No.	0	1	2	3	4	5	6	7	8	9	Diff.
2550	406 5402	5572	5742	5913	6083	6253	6424	6594	6764	6934	
51	7105	7275	7445	7615	7786	7956	8126	8296	8466	8637	
52	8807	8977	9147	9317	9487	9658	9828	9998	0168	0338	
53	407 0508	0678	0848	1018	1189	1359	1529	1699	1869	2039	
54	2209	2379	2549	2719	2889	3059	3229	3399	3569	3739	
55	3909	4079	4249	4419	4589	4759	4929	5099	5269	5439	
56	5608	5778	5948	6118	6288	6458	6628	6798	6968	7137	**170**
57	7307	7477	7647	7817	7987	8156	8326	8496	8666	8836	1 17
58	9005	9175	9345	9515	9684	9854	0024	0194	0363	0533	2 34
59	408 0703	0873	1042	1212	1382	1551	1721	1891	2060	2230	3 51
60	2400	2569	2739	2909	3078	3248	3417	3587	3757	3926	4 68
2561	4096	4265	4435	4604	4774	4944	5113	5283	5452	5622	5 85
62	5791	5961	6130	6300	6469	6639	6808	6978	7147	7317	6 102
63	7486	7656	7825	7994	8164	8333	8503	8672	8841	9011	7 119
64	9180	9350	9519	9688	9858	0027	0196	0366	0535	0704	8 136
65	409 0874	1043	1212	1382	1551	1720	1889	2059	2228	2397	9 153
66	2567	2736	2905	3074	3243	3413	3582	3751	3920	4089	
67	4259	4428	4597	4766	4935	5105	5274	5443	5612	5781	
68	5950	6119	6288	6458	6627	6796	6965	7134	7303	7472	
69	7641	7810	7979	8148	8317	8486	8655	8824	8993	9162	
70	9331	9500	9669	9838	0007	0176	0345	0514	0683	0852	**169**
2571	410 1021	1190	1359	1527	1696	1865	2034	2203	2372	2541	1 17
72	2710	2878	3047	3216	3385	3554	3723	3891	4060	4229	2 34
73	4398	4567	4735	4904	5073	5242	5410	5579	5748	5917	3 51
74	6085	6254	6423	6592	6760	6929	7098	7266	7435	7604	4 68
75	7772	7941	8110	8278	8447	8616	8784	8953	9121	9290	5 85
76	9459	9627	9796	9964	0133	0301	0470	0639	0807	0976	6 101
77	411 1144	1313	1481	1650	1818	1987	2155	2324	2492	2661	7 118
78	2829	2998	3166	3334	3503	3671	3840	4008	4177	4345	8 135
79	4513	4682	4850	5019	5187	5355	5524	5692	5860	6029	9 152
80	6197	6365	6534	6702	6870	7039	7207	7375	7544	7712	
2581	7880	8048	8217	8385	8553	8721	8890	9058	9226	9394	
82	9562	9731	9899	0067	0235	0403	0571	0740	0908	1076	
83	412 1244	1412	1580	1748	1917	2085	2253	2421	2589	2757	**168**
84	2925	3093	3261	3429	3597	3765	3933	4101	4269	4437	1 17
85	4605	4773	4941	5109	5277	5445	5613	5781	5949	6117	2 34
86	6285	6453	6621	6789	6957	7125	7293	7461	7629	7796	3 50
87	7964	8132	8300	8468	8636	8804	8971	9139	9307	9475	4 67
88	9643	9811	9978	0146	0314	0482	0649	0817	0985	1153	5 84
89	413 1321	1488	1656	1824	1991	2159	2327	2495	2662	2830	6 101
90	2998	3165	3333	3501	3668	3836	4004	4171	4339	4507	7 118
2591	4674	4842	5009	5177	5345	5512	5680	5847	6015	6182	8 134
92	6350	6518	6685	6853	7020	7188	7355	7523	7690	7858	9 151
93	8025	8193	8360	8528	8695	8863	9030	9197	9365	9532	
94	9700	9867	0035	0202	0369	0537	0704	0872	1039	1206	
95	414 1374	1541	1708	1876	2043	2210	2378	2545	2712	2880	
96	3047	3214	3381	3549	3716	3883	4051	4218	4385	4552	
97	4719	4887	5054	5221	5388	5556	5723	5890	6057	6224	
98	6391	6559	6726	6893	7060	7227	7394	7561	7729	7896	
99	8063	8230	8397	8564	8731	8898	9065	9232	9399	9566	**167**
2600	9733	9901	0068	0235	0402	0569	0736	0903	1070	1237	
	415										

No.	0	1	2	3	4	5	6	7	8	9	Diff.
2600	414 9733	9901	0068	0235	0402	0569	0736	0903	1070	1237	
01	415 1404	1570	1737	1904	2071	2238	2405	2572	2739	2906	167
02	3073	3240	3407	3574	3741	3907	4074	4241	4408	4575	1 17
03	4742	4909	5075	5242	5409	5576	5743	5909	6076	6243	2 33
04	6410	6577	6743	6910	7077	7244	7410	7577	7744	7911	3 50
05	8077	8244	8411	8577	8744	8911	9077	9244	9411	9577	4 67
											5 84
06	9744	9911	0077	0244	0411	0577	0744	0911	1077	1244	6 100
07	416 1410	1577	1743	1910	2077	2243	2410	2576	2743	2909	7 117
08	3076	3242	3409	3575	3742	3908	4075	4241	4408	4574	8 134
09	4741	4907	5074	5240	5407	5573	5739	5906	6072	6239	9 150
10	6405	6571	6738	6904	7071	7237	7403	7570	7736	7902	
2611	8069	8235	8401	8568	8734	8900	9067	9233	9399	9565	
12	9732	9898	0064	0231	0397	0563	0729	0895	1062	1228	
13	417 1394	1560	1726	1893	2059	2225	2391	2557	2724	2890	
14	3056	3222	3388	3554	3720	3886	4053	4219	4385	4551	
15	4717	4883	5049	5215	5381	5547	5713	5879	6045	6211	166
16	6377	6543	6709	6875	7041	7207	7373	7539	7705	7871	1 17
17	8037	8203	8369	8535	8701	8867	9033	9199	9365	9531	2 33
18	9696	9862	0028	0194	0360	0526	0692	0857	1023	1189	3 50
19	418 1355	1521	1687	1852	2018	2184	2350	2516	2681	2847	4 66
20	3013	3179	3344	3510	3676	3842	4007	4173	4339	4505	5 83
											6 100
2621	4670	4836	5002	5167	5333	5499	5664	5830	5996	6161	7 116
22	6327	6493	6658	6824	6989	7155	7321	7486	7652	7817	8 133
23	7983	8148	8314	8480	8645	8811	8976	9142	9307	9473	9 149
24	9638	9804	9969	0135	0300	0466	0631	0797	0962	1128	
25	419 1293	1459	1624	1789	1955	2120	2286	2451	2616	2782	
26	2947	3113	3278	3443	3609	3774	3939	4105	4270	4435	
27	4601	4766	4931	5097	5262	5427	5593	5758	5923	6088	
28	6254	6419	6584	6749	6915	7080	7245	7410	7575	7741	
29	7906	8071	8236	8401	8567	8732	8897	9062	9227	9392	
30	9557	9723	9888	0053	0218	0383	0548	0713	0878	1043	
2631	420 1208	1374	1539	1704	1869	2034	2199	2364	2529	2694	165
32	2859	3024	3189	3354	3519	3684	3849	4014	4179	4344	1 17
33	4509	4674	4838	5003	5168	5333	5498	5663	5828	5993	2 33
34	6158	6323	6487	6652	6817	6982	7147	7312	7477	7641	3 50
35	7806	7971	8136	8301	8465	8630	8795	8960	9125	9289	4 66
											5 83
36	9454	9619	9784	9948	0113	0278	0442	0607	0772	0937	6 99
37	421 1101	1266	1431	1595	1760	1925	2089	2254	2419	2583	7 116
38	2748	2913	3077	3242	3406	3571	3736	3900	4065	4229	8 132
39	4394	4558	4723	4888	5052	5217	5381	5546	5710	5875	9 149
40	6039	6204	6368	6533	6697	6862	7026	7191	7355	7520	
2641	7684	7848	8013	8177	8342	8506	8671	8835	8999	9164	
42	9328	9493	9657	9821	9986	0150	0314	0479	0643	0807	
43	422 0972	1136	1300	1465	1629	1793	1957	2122	2286	2450	
44	2615	2779	2943	3107	3271	3436	3600	3764	3928	4093	
45	4257	4421	4585	4749	4913	5078	5242	5406	5570	5734	
46	5898	6063	6227	6391	6555	6719	6883	7047	7211	7375	
47	7539	7703	7868	8032	8196	8360	8524	8688	8852	9016	
48	9180	9344	9508	9672	9836	0000	0164	0328	0492	0656	164
49	423 0820	0984	1147	1311	1475	1639	1803	1967	2131	2295	
2650	2459	2623	2786	2950	3114	3278	3442	3606	3770	3933	

No.	0	1	2	3	4	5	6	7	8	9	Diff.
2650	423 2459	2623	2786	2950	3114	3278	3442	3606	3770	3933	
51	4097	4261	4425	4589	4753	4916	5080	5244	5408	5571	164
52	5735	5899	6063	6226	6390	6554	6718	6881	7045	7209	1 16
53	7372	7536	7700	7864	8027	8191	8355	8518	8682	8846	2 33
54	9009	9173	9336	9500	9664	9827	9991	0154	0318	0482	3 49
55	424 0645	0809	0972	1136	1300	1463	1627	1790	1954	2117	4 66 / 5 82
56	2281	2444	2608	2771	2935	3098	3262	3425	3589	3752	6 98
57	3916	4079	4242	4406	4569	4733	4896	5060	5223	5386	7 115
58	5550	5713	5877	6040	6203	6367	6530	6693	6857	7020	8 131
59	7183	7347	7510	7673	7837	8000	8163	8327	8490	8653	9 148
60	8816	8980	9143	9306	9469	9633	9796	9959	0122	0286	
2661	425 0449	0612	0775	0938	1102	1265	1428	1591	1754	1917	
62	2081	2244	2407	2570	2733	2896	3059	3222	3385	3549	
63	3712	3875	4038	4201	4364	4527	4690	4853	5016	5179	163
64	5342	5505	5668	5831	5994	6157	6320	6483	6646	6809	1 16
65	6972	7135	7298	7461	7624	7787	7950	8113	8276	8439	2 33
66	8601	8764	8927	9090	9253	9416	9579	9742	9904	0067	3 49
67	426 0230	0393	0556	0719	0881	1044	1207	1370	1533	1695	4 65
68	1858	2021	2184	2347	2509	2672	2835	2998	3160	3323	5 82
69	3486	3648	3811	3974	4137	4299	4462	4625	4787	4950	6 98
70	5113	5275	5438	5601	5763	5926	6088	6251	6414	6576	7 114 / 8 130
2671	6739	6901	7064	7227	7389	7552	7714	7877	8039	8202	9 147
72	8365	8527	8690	8852	9015	9177	9340	9502	9665	9827	
73	9990	0152	0315	0477	0639	0802	0964	1127	1289	1452	
74	427 1614	1776	1939	2101	2264	2426	2588	2751	2913	3076	
75	3238	3400	3563	3725	3887	4050	4212	4374	4536	4699	
76	4861	5023	5186	5348	5510	5672	5835	5997	6159	6321	
77	6484	6646	6808	6970	7133	7295	7457	7619	7781	7944	
78	8106	8268	8430	8592	8754	8917	9079	9241	9403	9565	
79	9727	9889	0051	0213	0376	0538	0700	0862	1024	1186	
80	428 1348	1510	1672	1834	1996	2158	2320	2482	2644	2806	
2681	2968	3130	3292	3454	3616	3778	3940	4102	4264	4426	162
82	4588	4750	4912	5073	5235	5397	5559	5721	5883	6045	1 16
83	6207	6369	6530	6692	6854	7016	7178	7340	7501	7663	2 32
84	7825	7987	8149	8311	8472	8634	8796	8958	9119	9281	3 49
85	9443	9605	9766	9928	0090	0252	0413	0575	0737	0898	4 65 / 5 81
86	429 1060	1222	1383	1545	1707	1868	2030	2192	2353	2515	6 97 / 7 113
87	2677	2838	3000	3162	3323	3485	3646	3808	3969	4131	8 130
88	4293	4454	4616	4777	4939	5100	5262	5423	5585	5747	9 146
89	5908	6070	6231	6393	6554	6715	6877	7038	7200	7361	
90	7523	7684	7846	8007	8169	8330	8491	8653	8814	8976	
2691	9137	9298	9460	9621	9782	9944	0105	0267	0428	0589	
92	430 0751	0912	1073	1235	1396	1557	1718	1880	2041	2202	
93	2364	2525	2686	2847	3009	3170	3331	3492	3653	3815	
94	3976	4137	4298	4460	4621	4782	4943	5104	5265	5427	
95	5588	5749	5910	6071	6232	6393	6554	6716	6877	7038	
96	7199	7360	7521	7682	7843	8004	8165	8326	8487	8648	
97	8809	8970	9132	9293	9454	9615	9776	9937	0098	0258	161
98	431 0419	0580	0741	0902	1063	1224	1385	1546	1707	1868	
99	2029	2190	2351	2512	2672	2833	2994	3155	3316	3477	
2700	3638	3798	3959	4120	4281	4442	4603	4763	4924	5085	

No.	0	1	2	3	4	5	6	7	8	9	Diff.
2700	431 3638	3798	3959	4120	4281	4442	4603	4763	4924	5085	
01	5246	5407	5567	5728	5889	6050	6210	6371	6532	6693	161
02	6853	7014	7175	7336	7496	7657	7818	7978	8139	8300	1 16
03	8460	8621	8782	8942	9103	9264	9424	9585	9746	9906	2 32
04	432 0067	0227	0388	0549	0709	0870	1030	1191	1352	1512	3 48
05	1673	1833	1994	2154	2315	2475	2636	2796	2957	3117	4 64 / 5 81
06	3278	3438	3599	3759	3920	4080	4241	4401	4562	4722	6 97
07	4883	5043	5203	5364	5524	5685	5845	6005	6166	6326	7 113
08	6487	6647	6807	6968	7128	7288	7449	7609	7769	7930	8 129
09	8090	8250	8411	8571	8731	8892	9052	9212	9372	9533	9 145
10	9693	9853	0013	0174	0334	0494	0654	0815	0975	1135	
2711	433 1295	1455	1616	1776	1936	2096	2256	2416	2577	2737	
12	2897	3057	3217	3377	3537	3697	3858	4018	4178	4338	
13	4498	4658	4818	4978	5138	5298	5458	5618	5778	5938	
14	6098	6258	6418	6578	6738	6898	7058	7218	7378	7538	
15	7698	7858	8018	8178	8338	8498	8658	8818	8978	9138	
16	9298	9458	9617	9777	9937	0097	0257	0417	0577	0737	
17	434 0896	1056	1216	1376	1536	1696	1855	2015	2175	2335	
18	2495	2654	2814	2974	3134	3293	3453	3613	3773	3932	160
19	4092	4252	4412	4571	4731	4891	5050	5210	5370	5529	1 16
20	5689	5849	6008	6168	6328	6487	6647	6807	6966	7126	2 32 / 3 48
2721	7285	7445	7605	7764	7924	8083	8243	8403	8562	8722	4 64
22	8881	9041	9200	9360	9519	9679	9838	9998	0157	0317	5 80
23	435 0476	0636	0795	0955	1114	1274	1433	1593	1752	1912	6 96
24	2071	2230	2390	2549	2709	2868	3028	3187	3346	3506	7 112
25	3665	3824	3984	4143	4303	4462	4621	4781	4940	5099	8 128 / 9 144
26	5259	5418	5577	5736	5896	6055	6214	6374	6533	6692	
27	6851	7011	7170	7329	7488	7648	7807	7966	8125	8284	
28	8444	8603	8762	8921	9080	9240	9399	9558	9717	9876	
29	436 0035	0194	0354	0513	0672	0831	0990	1149	1308	1467	
30	1626	1786	1945	2104	2263	2422	2581	2740	2899	3058	
2731	3217	3376	3535	3694	3853	4012	4171	4330	4489	4648	
32	4807	4966	5125	5284	5443	5602	5761	5920	6078	6237	159
33	6396	6555	6714	6873	7032	7191	7350	7509	7667	7826	1 16
34	7985	8144	8303	8462	8620	8779	8938	9097	9256	9415	2 32 / 3 48
35	9573	9732	9891	0050	0208	0367	0526	0685	0843	1002	4 64
36	437 1161	1320	1478	1637	1796	1955	2113	2272	2431	2589	5 80
37	2748	2907	3065	3224	3383	3541	3700	3859	4017	4176	6 95
38	4334	4493	4652	4810	4969	5127	5286	5445	5603	5762	7 111
39	5920	6079	6237	6396	6555	6713	6872	7030	7189	7347	8 127
40	7506	7664	7823	7981	8140	8298	8457	8615	8773	8932	9 143
2741	9090	9249	9407	9566	9724	9883	0041	0199	0358	0516	
42	438 0675	0833	0991	1150	1308	1466	1625	1783	1941	2100	
43	2258	2416	2575	2733	2891	3050	3208	3366	3525	3683	
44	3841	3999	4158	4316	4474	4632	4791	4949	5107	5265	
45	5423	5582	5740	5898	6056	6214	6373	6531	6689	6847	
46	7005	7163	7322	7480	7638	7796	7954	8112	8270	8428	
47	8587	8745	8903	9061	9219	9377	9535	9693	9851	0009	
48	439 0167	0325	0483	0641	0799	0957	1115	1273	1431	1589	
49	1747	1905	2063	2221	2379	2537	2695	2853	3011	3169	158
2750	3327	3485	3643	3801	3959	4116	4274	4432	4590	4748	

No.	0	1	2	3	4	5	6	7	8	9	Diff.
2750	439 3327	3485	3643	3801	3959	4116	4274	4432	4590	4748	
51	4906	5064	5222	5379	5537	5695	5853	6011	6169	6326	**158**
52	6484	6642	6800	6958	7115	7273	7431	7589	7747	7904	1 16
53	8062	8220	8378	8535	8693	8851	9009	9166	9324	9482	2 32
54	9639	9797	9955	0112	0270	0428	0585	0743	0901	1058	3 47
55	440 1216	1374	1531	1689	1847	2004	2162	2319	2477	2635	4 63
											5 79
56	2792	2950	3107	3265	3422	3580	3738	3895	4053	4210	6 95
57	4368	4525	4683	4840	4998	5155	5313	5470	5628	5785	7 111
58	5943	6100	6258	6415	6572	6730	6887	7045	7202	7360	8 126
59	7517	7674	7832	7989	8147	8304	8461	8619	8776	8933	9 142
60	9091	9248	9406	9563	9720	9878	0035	0192	0349	0507	
2761	441 0664	0821	0979	1136	1293	1450	1608	1765	1922	2080	
62	2237	2394	2551	2708	2866	3023	3180	3337	3494	3652	
63	3809	3966	4123	4280	4438	4595	4752	4909	5066	5223	
64	5380	5538	5695	5852	6009	6166	6323	6480	6637	6794	
65	6951	7108	7265	7423	7580	7737	7894	8051	8208	8365	**157**
66	8522	8679	8836	8993	9150	9307	9464	9621	9778	9935	1 16
67	442 0092	0249	0405	0562	0719	0876	1033	1190	1347	1504	2 31
68	1661	1818	1975	2132	2288	2445	2602	2759	2916	3073	3 47
69	3230	3386	3543	3700	3857	4014	4171	4327	4484	4641	4 63
70	4798	4954	5111	5268	5425	5582	5738	5895	6052	6209	5 79
											6 94
2771	6365	6522	6679	6835	6992	7149	7306	7462	7619	7776	7 110
72	7932	8089	8246	8402	8559	8716	8872	9029	9185	9342	8 126
73	9499	9655	9812	9969	0125	0282	0438	0595	0751	0908	9 141
74	443 1065	1221	1378	1534	1691	1847	2004	2160	2317	2473	
75	2630	2786	2943	3099	3256	3412	3569	3725	3882	4038	
76	4195	4351	4507	4664	4820	4977	5133	5290	5446	5602	
77	5759	5915	6072	6228	6384	6541	6697	6853	7010	7166	
78	7322	7479	7635	7791	7948	8104	8260	8417	8573	8729	
79	8885	9042	9198	9354	9511	9667	9823	9979	0136	0292	**156**
80	444 0448	0604	0760	0917	1073	1229	1385	1541	1698	1854	1 16
2781	2010	2166	2322	2478	2635	2791	2947	3103	3259	3415	2 31
82	3571	3727	3883	4040	4196	4352	4508	4664	4820	4976	3 47
83	5132	5288	5444	5600	5756	5912	6068	6224	6380	6536	4 62
84	6692	6848	7004	7160	7316	7472	7628	7784	7940	8096	5 78
85	8252	8408	8564	8720	8876	9032	9188	9343	9499	9655	6 94
86	9811	9967	0123	0279	0435	0590	0746	0902	1058	1214	7 109
87	445 1370	1526	1681	1837	1993	2149	2305	2460	2616	2772	8 125
88	2928	3083	3239	3395	3551	3706	3862	4018	4174	4329	9 140
89	4485	4641	4797	4952	5108	5264	5419	5575	5731	5886	
90	6042	6198	6353	6509	6665	6820	6976	7132	7287	7443	
2791	7598	7754	7910	8065	8221	8376	8532	8687	8843	8999	
92	9154	9310	9465	9621	9776	9932	0087	0243	0398	0554	
93	446 0709	0865	1020	1176	1331	1487	1642	1798	1953	2109	
94	2264	2419	2575	2730	2886	3041	3197	3352	3507	3663	
95	3818	3974	4129	4284	4440	4595	4750	4906	5061	5216	
96	5372	5527	5682	5838	5993	6148	6304	6459	6614	6769	**155**
97	6925	7080	7235	7390	7546	7701	7856	8011	8167	8322	
98	8477	8632	8788	8943	9098	9253	9408	9563	9719	9874	
99	447 0029	0184	0339	0494	0650	0805	0960	1115	1270	1425	
2800	1580	1735	1891	2046	2201	2356	2511	2666	2821	2976	

No.	0	1	2	3	4	5	6	7	8	9	Diff.
2800	447 1580	1735	1891	2046	2201	2356	2511	2666	2821	2976	
01	3131	3286	3441	3596	3751	3906	4061	4216	4371	4526	155
02	4681	4836	4991	5146	5301	5456	5611	5766	5921	6076	1 16
03	6231	6386	6541	6696	6851	7006	7161	7315	7470	7625	2 31
04	7780	7935	8090	8245	8400	8554	8709	8864	9019	9174	3 47
05	9329	9483	9638	9793	9948	0103	0258	0412	0567	0722	4 62
											5 78
06	448 0877	1031	1186	1341	1496	1650	1805	1960	2115	2269	6 93
07	2424	2579	2734	2888	3043	3198	3352	3507	3662	3816	7 109
08	3971	4126	4280	4435	4590	4744	4899	5054	5208	5363	8 124
09	5517	5672	5827	5981	6136	6290	6445	6600	6754	6909	9 140
10	7063	7218	7372	7527	7681	7836	7990	8145	8299	8454	
2811	8608	8763	8917	9072	9226	9381	9535	9690	9844	9999	
12	449 0153	0308	0462	0616	0771	0925	1080	1234	1389	1543	
13	1697	1852	2006	2160	2315	2469	2624	2778	2932	3087	
14	3241	3395	3550	3704	3858	4013	4167	4321	4475	4630	
15	4784	4938	5093	5247	5401	5555	5710	5864	6018	6172	154
16	6327	6481	6635	6789	6943	7098	7252	7406	7560	7714	1 15
17	7868	8023	8177	8331	8485	8639	8793	8948	9102	9256	2 31
18	9410	9564	9718	9872	0026	0180	0334	0489	0643	0797	3 46
19	450 0951	1105	1259	1413	1567	1721	1875	2029	2183	2337	4 62
20	2491	2645	2799	2953	3107	3261	3415	3569	3723	3877	5 77
											6 92
2821	4031	4185	4339	4493	4647	4801	4954	5108	5262	5416	7 108
22	5570	5724	5878	6032	6186	6340	6493	6647	6801	6955	8 123
23	7109	7263	7416	7570	7724	7878	8032	8186	8339	8493	9 139
24	8647	8801	8954	9108	9262	9416	9570	9723	9877	0031	
25	451 0185	0338	0492	0646	0799	0953	1107	1261	1414	1568	
26	1722	1875	2029	2183	2336	2490	2644	2797	2951	3104	
27	3258	3412	3565	3719	3873	4026	4180	4333	4487	4640	
28	4794	4948	5101	5255	5408	5562	5715	5869	6022	6176	
29	6329	6483	6636	6790	6943	7097	7250	7404	7557	7711	
30	7864	8018	8171	8325	8478	8632	8785	8938	9092	9245	
2831	9399	9552	9705	9859	0012	0166	0319	0472	0626	0779	
32	452 0932	1086	1239	1393	1546	1699	1853	2006	2159	2312	
33	2466	2619	2772	2926	3079	3232	3385	3539	3692	3845	
34	3998	4152	4305	4458	4611	4765	4918	5071	5224	5377	
35	5531	5684	5837	5990	6143	6297	6450	6603	6756	6909	153
36	7062	7215	7369	7522	7675	7828	7981	8134	8287	8440	1 15
37	8593	8746	8900	9053	9206	9359	9512	9665	9818	9971	2 31
38	453 0124	0277	0430	0583	0736	0889	1042	1195	1348	1501	3 46
39	1654	1807	1960	2113	2266	2419	2572	2725	2878	3030	4 61
40	3183	3336	3489	3642	3795	3948	4101	4254	4407	4559	5 77
											6 92
											7 107
2841	4712	4865	5018	5171	5324	5477	5629	5782	5935	6088	8 122
42	6241	6394	6546	6699	6852	7005	7158	7310	7463	7616	9 138
43	7769	7921	8074	8227	8380	8532	8685	8838	8990	9143	
44	9296	9449	9601	9754	9907	0059	0212	0365	0517	0670	
45	454 0823	0975	1128	1281	1433	1586	1739	1891	2044	2196	
46	2349	2502	2654	2807	2959	3112	3264	3417	3570	3722	
47	3875	4027	4180	4332	4485	4637	4790	4942	5095	5247	
48	5400	5552	5705	5857	6010	6162	6315	6467	6620	6772	
49	6924	7077	7229	7382	7534	7687	7839	7991	8144	8296	
2850	8449	8601	8753	8906	9058	9210	9363	9515	9668	9820	

No.	0	1	2	3	4	5	6	7	8	9	Diff.
2850	454 8449	8601	8753	8906	9058	9210	9363	9515	9668	9820	
51	9972	0125	0277	0429	0581	0734	0886	1038	1191	1343	
52	455 1495	1647	1800	1952	2104	2257	2409	2561	2713	2865	
53	3018	3170	3322	3474	3627	3779	3931	4083	4235	4388	
54	4540	4692	4844	4996	5148	5300	5453	5605	5757	5909	
55	6061	6213	6365	6517	6670	6822	6974	7126	7278	7430	
56	7582	7734	7886	8038	8190	8342	8494	8646	8798	8950	
57	9102	9254	9406	9558	9710	9862	0014	0166	0318	0470	152
58	456 0622	0774	0926	1078	1230	1382	1534	1686	1838	1990	
59	2142	2293	2445	2597	2749	2901	3053	3205	3357	3508	1　15
60	3660	3812	3964	4116	4268	4420	4571	4723	4875	5027	2　30
2861	5179	5330	5482	5634	5786	5938	6089	6241	6393	6545	3　46
62	6696	6848	7000	7152	7303	7455	7607	7758	7910	8062	4　61
63	8213	8365	8517	8669	8820	8972	9124	9275	9427	9578	5　76
64	9730	9882	0033	0185	0337	0488	0640	0791	0943	1095	6　91
65	457 1246	1398	1549	1701	1853	2004	2156	2307	2459	2610	7　106
66	2762	2913	3065	3216	3368	3519	3671	3822	3974	4125	8　122
67	4277	4428	4580	4731	4883	5034	5186	5337	5489	5640	9　137
68	5791	5943	6094	6246	6397	6549	6700	6851	7003	7154	
69	7305	7457	7608	7760	7911	8062	8214	8365	8516	8668	
70	8819	8970	9122	9273	9424	9576	9727	9878	0029	0181	
2871	458 0332	0483	0634	0786	0937	1088	1239	1391	1542	1693	
72	1844	1996	2147	2298	2449	2600	2752	2903	3054	3205	
73	3356	3507	3659	3810	3961	4112	4263	4414	4565	4717	
74	4868	5019	5170	5321	5472	5623	5774	5925	6076	6227	
75	6378	6530	6681	6832	6983	7134	7285	7436	7587	7738	151
76	7889	8040	8191	8342	8493	8644	8795	8946	9097	9248	1　15
77	9399	9550	9701	9851	0002	0153	0304	0455	0606	0757	2　30
78	459 0908	1059	1210	1361	1511	1662	1813	1964	2115	2266	3　45
79	2417	2567	2718	2869	3020	3171	3322	3472	3623	3774	4　60
80	3925	4076	4226	4377	4528	4679	4830	4980	5131	5282	5　76
2881	5433	5583	5734	5885	6036	6186	6337	6488	6638	6789	6　91
82	6940	7090	7241	7392	7542	7693	7844	7994	8145	8296	7　106
83	8446	8597	8748	8898	9049	9200	9350	9501	9651	9802	8　121
84	9953	0103	0254	0404	0555	0705	0856	1007	1157	1308	9　136
85	460 1458	1609	1759	1910	2060	2211	2361	2512	2662	2813	
86	2963	3114	3264	3415	3565	3716	3866	4017	4167	4317	
87	4468	4618	4769	4919	5070	5220	5370	5521	5671	5822	
88	5972	6122	6273	6423	6573	6724	6874	7024	7175	7325	
89	7475	7626	7776	7926	8077	8227	8377	8528	8678	8828	
90	8978	9129	9279	9429	9579	9730	9880	0030	0180	0331	
2891	461 0481	0631	0781	0932	1082	1232	1382	1532	1683	1833	
92	1983	2133	2283	2433	2584	2734	2884	3034	3184	3334	
93	3484	3634	3785	3935	4085	4235	4385	4535	4685	4835	
94	4985	5135	5285	5435	5585	5736	5886	6036	6186	6336	
95	6486	6636	6786	6936	7086	7236	7386	7536	7686	7836	
96	7986	8136	8285	8435	8585	8735	8885	9035	9185	9335	
97	9485	9635	9785	9935	0085	0234	0384	0534	0684	0834	150
98	462 0984	1134	1284	1433	1583	1733	1883	2033	2183	2332	
99	2482	2632	2782	2932	3081	3231	3381	3531	3680	3830	
2900	3980	4130	4279	4429	4579	4729	4878	5028	5178	5328	

No.	0	1	2	3	4	5	6	7	8	9	Diff.
2900	462 3980	4130	4279	4429	4579	4729	4878	5028	5178	5328	
01	5477	5627	5777	5926	6076	6226	6375	6525	6675	6824	**150**
02	6974	7124	7273	7423	7573	7722	7872	8022	8171	8321	1 15
03	8470	8620	8770	8919	9069	9218	9368	9517	9667	9817	2 30
04	9966	0116	0265	0415	0564	0714	0863	1013	1162	1312	3 45
05	463 1461	1611	1760	1910	2059	2209	2358	2508	2657	2807	4 60
											5 75
06	2956	3106	3255	3404	3554	3703	3853	4002	4152	4301	6 90
07	4450	4600	4749	4898	5048	5197	5347	5496	5645	5795	7 105
08	5944	6093	6243	6392	6541	6691	6840	6989	7139	7288	8 120
09	7437	7587	7736	7885	8034	8184	8333	8482	8631	8781	9 135
10	8930	9079	9228	9378	9527	9676	9825	9974	0124	0273	
2911	464 0422	0571	0720	0870	1019	1168	1317	1466	1615	1765	
12	1914	2063	2212	2361	2510	2659	2808	2958	3107	3256	
13	3405	3554	3703	3852	4001	4150	4299	4448	4597	4746	**149**
14	4895	5045	5194	5343	5492	5641	5790	5939	6088	6237	1 15
15	6386	6535	6684	6833	6981	7130	7279	7428	7577	7726	2 30
16	7875	8024	8173	8322	8471	8620	8769	8918	9067	9215	3 45
17	9364	9513	9662	9811	9960	0109	0258	0406	0555	0704	4 60
18	465 0853	1002	1151	1299	1448	1597	1746	1895	2043	2192	5 75
19	2341	2490	2639	2787	2936	3085	3234	3382	3531	3680	6 89
20	3829	3977	4126	4275	4423	4572	4721	4870	5018	5167	7 104
											8 119
2921	5316	5464	5613	5762	5910	6059	6208	6356	6505	6653	9 134
22	6802	6951	7099	7248	7397	7545	7694	7842	7991	8140	
23	8288	8437	8585	8734	8882	9031	9180	9328	9477	9625	
24	9774	9922	0071	0219	0368	0516	0665	0813	0962	1110	
25	466 1259	1407	1556	1704	1853	2001	2149	2298	2446	2595	
26	2743	2892	3040	3188	3337	3485	3634	3782	3930	4079	
27	4227	4376	4524	4672	4821	4969	5117	5266	5414	5562	
28	5711	5859	6007	6156	6304	6452	6601	6749	6897	7045	
29	7194	7342	7490	7639	7787	7935	8083	8232	8380	8528	**148**
30	8676	8824	8973	9121	9269	9417	9565	9714	9862	0010	1 15
2931	467 0158	0306	0455	0603	0751	0899	1047	1195	1343	1492	2 30
32	1640	1788	1936	2084	2232	2380	2528	2676	2824	2973	3 44
33	3121	3269	3417	3565	3713	3861	4009	4157	4305	4453	4 59
34	4601	4749	4897	5045	5193	5341	5489	5637	5785	5933	5 74
35	6081	6229	6377	6525	6673	6821	6969	7117	7265	7413	6 89
36	7561	7708	7856	8004	8152	8300	8448	8596	8744	8892	7 104
37	9039	9187	9335	9483	9631	9779	9927	0074	0222	0370	8 118
38	468 0518	0666	0814	0961	1109	1257	1405	1553	1700	1848	9 133
39	1996	2144	2291	2439	2587	2735	2882	3030	3178	3326	
40	3473	3621	3769	3916	4064	4212	4360	4507	4655	4803	
2941	4950	5098	5246	5393	5541	5689	5836	5984	6131	6279	
42	6427	6574	6722	6870	7017	7165	7312	7460	7607	7755	
43	7903	8050	8198	8345	8493	8640	8788	8935	9083	9231	
44	9378	9526	9673	9821	9968	0116	0263	0411	0558	0706	
45	469 0853	1000	1148	1295	1443	1590	1738	1885	2033	2180	
46	2327	2475	2622	2770	2917	3064	3212	3359	3507	3654	
47	3801	3949	4096	4243	4391	4538	4685	4833	4980	5127	147
48	5275	5422	5569	5717	5864	6011	6159	6306	6453	6600	
49	6748	6895	7042	7190	7337	7484	7631	7778	7926	8073	
2950	8220	8367	8515	8662	8809	8956	9103	9251	9398	9545	

No.	0	1	2	3	4	5	6	7	8	9	Diff.
2950	469 8220	8367	8515	8662	8809	8956	9103	9251	9398	9545	
51	9692	9839	9986	0134	0281	0428	0575	0722	0869	1016	**147**
52	470 1164	1311	1458	1605	1752	1899	2046	2193	2340	2487	1 15
53	2634	2782	2929	3076	3223	3370	3517	3664	3811	3958	2 29
54	4105	4252	4399	4546	4693	4840	4987	5134	5281	5428	3 44
55	5575	5722	5869	6016	6163	6310	6457	6604	6750	6897	4 59 / 5 74
56	7044	7191	7338	7485	7632	7779	7926	8073	8219	8366	6 88
57	8513	8660	8807	8954	9101	9248	9394	9541	9688	9835	7 103
58	9982	0129	0275	0422	0569	0716	0863	1009	1156	1303	8 118
59	471 1450	1596	1743	1890	2037	2183	2330	2477	2624	2770	9 132
60	2917	3064	3211	3357	3504	3651	3797	3944	4091	4237	
2961	4384	4531	4677	4824	4971	5117	5264	5411	5557	5704	
62	5851	5997	6144	6290	6437	6584	6730	6877	7023	7170	
63	7317	7463	7610	7756	7903	8049	8196	8342	8489	8635	
64	8782	8929	9075	9222	9368	9515	9661	9808	9954	0101	
65	472 0247	0393	0540	0686	0833	0979	1126	1272	1419	1565	
66	1711	1858	2004	2151	2297	2444	2590	2736	2883	3029	
67	3175	3322	3468	3615	3761	3907	4054	4200	4346	4493	**146**
68	4639	4785	4932	5078	5224	5371	5517	5663	5809	5956	1 15
69	6102	6248	6395	6541	6687	6833	6980	7126	7272	7418	2 29
70	7564	7711	7857	8003	8149	8296	8442	8588	8734	8880	3 44 / 4 58
2971	9027	9173	9319	9465	9611	9757	9903	0050	0196	0342	5 73
72	473 0488	0634	0780	0926	1073	1219	1365	1511	1657	1803	6 88
73	1949	2095	2241	2387	2533	2679	2825	2972	3118	3264	7 102
74	3410	3556	3702	3848	3994	4140	4286	4432	4578	4724	8 117
75	4870	5016	5162	5308	5454	5600	5746	5891	6037	6183	9 131
76	6329	6475	6621	6767	6913	7059	7205	7351	7497	7642	
77	7788	7934	8080	8226	8372	8518	8664	8809	8955	9101	
78	9247	9393	9539	9684	9830	9976	0122	0268	0413	0559	
79	474 0705	0851	0997	1142	1288	1434	1580	1725	1871	2017	
80	2163	2308	2454	2600	2746	2891	3037	3183	3328	3474	
2981	3620	3765	3911	4057	4202	4348	4494	4639	4785	4931	
82	5076	5222	5368	5513	5659	5805	5950	6096	6241	6387	
83	6533	6678	6824	6969	7115	7260	7406	7552	7697	7843	
84	7988	8134	8279	8425	8570	8716	8861	9007	9152	9298	
85	9443	9589	9734	9880	0025	0171	0316	0462	0607	0753	
86	475 0898	1043	1189	1334	1480	1625	1771	1916	2061	2207	
87	2352	2498	2643	2788	2934	3079	3225	3370	3515	3661	
88	3806	3951	4097	4242	4387	4533	4678	4823	4969	5114	
89	5259	5404	5550	5695	5840	5986	6131	6276	6421	6567	
90	6712	6857	7002	7148	7293	7438	7583	7729	7874	8019	
2991	8164	8309	8455	8600	8745	8890	9035	9180	9326	9471	
92	9616	9761	9906	0051	0196	0342	0487	0632	0777	0922	
93	476 1067	1212	1357	1502	1648	1793	1938	2083	2228	2373	
94	2518	2663	2808	2953	3098	3243	3388	3533	3678	3823	**145**
95	3968	4113	4258	4403	4548	4693	4838	4983	5128	5273	
96	5418	5563	5708	5853	5998	6143	6288	6433	6578	6723	
97	6867	7012	7157	7302	7447	7592	7737	7882	8027	8171	
98	8316	8461	8606	8751	8896	9041	9185	9330	9475	9620	
99	9765	9909	0054	0199	0344	0489	0633	0778	0923	1068	
3000	477 1213	1357	1502	1647	1792	1936	2081	2226	2371	2515	

No.	0	1	2	3	4	5	6	7	8	9	Diff.
3000	477 1213	1357	1502	1647	1792	1936	2081	2226	2371	2515	
01	2660	2805	2949	3094	3239	3383	3528	3673	3818	3962	145
02	4107	4252	4396	4541	4686	4830	4975	5119	5264	5409	1 15
03	5553	5698	5843	5987	6132	6276	6421	6566	6710	6855	2 29
04	6999	7144	7288	7433	7578	7722	7867	8011	8156	8300	3 44
05	8445	8589	8734	8878	9023	9167	9312	9456	9601	9745	4 58
											5 73
06	9890	0034	0179	0323	0468	0612	0757	0901	1045	1190	6 87
07	478 1334	1479	1623	1768	1912	2056	2201	2345	2490	2634	7 102
08	2778	2923	3067	3211	3356	3500	3645	3789	3933	4078	8 116
09	4222	4366	4511	4655	4799	4943	5088	5232	5376	5521	9 131
10	5665	5809	5954	6098	6242	6386	6531	6675	6819	6963	
3011	7108	7252	7396	7540	7684	7829	7973	8117	8261	8405	144
12	8550	8694	8838	8982	9126	9271	9415	9559	9703	9847	1 14
13	9991	0135	0280	0424	0568	0712	0856	1000	1144	1288	2 29
14	479 1432	1577	1721	1865	2009	2153	2297	2441	2585	2729	3 43
15	2873	3017	3161	3305	3449	3593	3737	3881	4025	4169	4 58
											5 72
16	4313	4457	4601	4745	4889	5033	5177	5321	5465	5609	6 86
17	5753	5897	6041	6185	6329	6473	6617	6761	6905	7048	7 101
18	7192	7336	7480	7624	7768	7912	8056	8200	8343	8487	8 115
19	8631	8775	8919	9063	9207	9350	9494	9638	9782	9926	9 130
20	480 0069	0213	0357	0501	0645	0788	0932	1076	1220	1363	
3021	1507	1651	1795	1939	2082	2226	2370	2513	2657	2801	
22	2945	3088	3232	3376	3519	3663	3807	3950	4094	4238	
23	4381	4525	4669	4812	4956	5100	5243	5387	5531	5674	
24	5818	5961	6105	6249	6392	6536	6679	6823	6967	7110	
25	7254	7397	7541	7684	7828	7972	8115	8259	8402	8546	
26	8689	8833	8976	9120	9263	9407	9550	9694	9837	9981	
27	481 0124	0268	0411	0555	0698	0842	0985	1128	1272	1415	
28	1559	1702	1846	1989	2132	2276	2419	2563	2706	2849	
29	2993	3136	3279	3423	3566	3710	3853	3996	4140	4283	
30	4426	4570	4713	4856	5000	5143	5286	5429	5573	5716	
3031	5859	6003	6146	6289	6432	6576	6719	6862	7005	7149	
32	7292	7435	7578	7722	7865	8008	8151	8295	8438	8581	
33	8724	8867	9010	9154	9297	9440	9583	9726	9869	0013	
34	482 0156	0299	0442	0585	0728	0871	1015	1158	1301	1444	
35	1587	1730	1873	2016	2159	2302	2445	2589	2732	2875	
36	3018	3161	3304	3447	3590	3733	3876	4019	4162	4305	
37	4448	4591	4734	4877	5020	5163	5306	5449	5592	5735	143
38	5878	6021	6164	6307	6449	6592	6735	6878	7021	7164	1 14
39	7307	7450	7593	7736	7879	8021	8164	8307	8450	8593	2 29
40	8736	8879	9022	9164	9307	9450	9593	9736	9879	0021	3 43
3041	483 0164	0307	0450	0593	0735	0878	1021	1164	1307	1449	4 57
42	1592	1735	1878	2020	2163	2306	2449	2591	2734	2877	5 72
43	3020	3162	3305	3448	3590	3733	3876	4018	4161	4304	6 86
44	4446	4589	4732	4874	5017	5160	5302	5445	5588	5730	7 100
45	5873	6016	6158	6301	6443	6586	6729	6871	7014	7156	8 114
											9 129
46	7299	7442	7584	7727	7869	8012	8154	8297	8439	8582	
47	8725	8867	9010	9152	9295	9437	9580	9722	9865	0007	
48	484 0150	0292	0435	0577	0720	0862	1004	1147	1289	1432	
49	1574	1717	1859	2002	2144	2286	2429	2571	2714	2856	
3050	2998	3141	3283	3426	3568	3710	3853	3995	4137	4280	

No.	0	1	2	3	4	5	6	7	8	9	Diff.
3050	484 2998	3141	3283	3426	3568	3710	3853	3995	4137	4280	
51	4422	4564	4707	4849	4991	5134	5276	5418	5561	5703	
52	5845	5988	6130	6272	6414	6557	6699	6841	6984	7126	
53	7268	7410	7553	7695	7837	7979	8121	8264	8406	8548	
54	8690	8833	8975	9117	9259	9401	9543	9686	9828	9970	
55	485 0112	0254	0396	0539	0681	0823	0965	1107	1249	1391	
56	1533	1676	1818	1960	2102	2244	2386	2528	2670	2812	
57	2954	3096	3239	3381	3523	3665	3807	3949	4091	4233	142
58	4375	4517	4659	4801	4943	5085	5227	5369	5511	5653	1 14
59	5795	5937	6079	6221	6363	6505	6647	6788	6930	7072	2 28
60	7214	7356	7498	7640	7782	7924	8066	8208	8350	8491	3 43
											4 57
3061	8633	8775	8917	9059	9201	9343	9484	9626	9768	9910	5 71
62	486 0052	0194	0336	0477	0619	0761	0903	1045	1186	1328	6 85
63	1470	1612	1754	1895	2037	2179	2321	2462	2604	2746	7 99
64	2888	3029	3171	3313	3455	3596	3738	3880	4021	4163	8 114
65	4305	4446	4588	4730	4872	5013	5155	5297	5438	5580	9 128
66	5722	5863	6005	6146	6288	6430	6571	6713	6855	6996	
67	7138	7279	7421	7563	7704	7846	7987	8129	8270	8412	
68	8554	8695	8837	8978	9120	9261	9403	9544	9686	9827	
69	9969	0110	0252	0393	0535	0676	0818	0959	1101	1242	
70	487 1384	1525	1667	1808	1950	2091	2232	2374	2515	2657	
3071	2798	2940	3081	3222	3364	3505	3647	3788	3929	4071	
72	4212	4353	4495	4636	4778	4919	5060	5202	5343	5484	
73	5626	5767	5908	6050	6191	6332	6473	6615	6756	6897	
74	7039	7180	7321	7462	7604	7745	7886	8027	8169	8310	
75	8451	8592	8734	8875	9016	9157	9299	9440	9581	9722	
76	9863	0004	0146	0287	0428	0569	0710	0852	0993	1134	
77	488 1275	1416	1557	1698	1839	1981	2122	2263	2404	2545	
78	2686	2827	2968	3109	3251	3392	3533	3674	3815	3956	
79	4097	4238	4379	4520	4661	4802	4943	5084	5225	5366	141
80	5507	5648	5789	5930	6071	6212	6353	6494	6635	6776	1 14
3081	6917	7058	7199	7340	7481	7622	7763	7904	8045	8185	2 28
82	8326	8467	8608	8749	8890	9031	9172	9313	9454	9594	3 42
83	9735	9876	0017	0158	0299	0440	0580	0721	0862	1003	4 56
84	489 1144	1285	1425	1566	1707	1848	1989	2129	2270	2411	5 71
85	2552	2692	2833	2974	3115	3256	3396	3537	3678	3818	6 85
											7 99
86	3959	4100	4241	4381	4522	4663	4804	4944	5085	5226	8 113
87	5366	5507	5648	5788	5929	6070	6210	6351	6492	6632	9 127
88	6773	6914	7054	7195	7335	7476	7617	7757	7898	8038	
89	8179	8320	8460	8601	8741	8882	9023	9163	9304	9444	
90	9585	9725	9866	0006	0147	0287	0428	0569	0709	0850	
3091	490 0990	1131	1271	1412	1552	1693	1833	1973	2114	2254	
92	2395	2535	2676	2816	2957	3097	3238	3378	3518	3659	
93	3799	3940	4080	4220	4361	4501	4642	4782	4922	5063	
94	5203	5343	5484	5624	5765	5905	6045	6186	6326	6466	
95	6607	6747	6887	7027	7168	7308	7448	7589	7729	7869	
96	8010	8150	8290	8430	8571	8711	8851	8991	9132	9272	
97	9412	9552	9693	9833	9973	0113	0253	0394	0534	0674	
98	491 0814	0954	1094	1235	1375	1515	1655	1795	1935	2076	
99	2216	2356	2496	2636	2776	2916	3057	3197	3337	3477	
3100	3617	3757	3897	4037	4177	4317	4457	4597	4738	4878	

No.	0	1	2	3	4	5	6	7	8	9	Diff.
3100	491 3617	3757	3897	4037	4177	4317	4457	4597	4738	4878	
01	5018	5158	5298	5438	5578	5718	5858	5998	6138	6278	**140**
02	6418	6558	6698	6838	6978	7118	7258	7398	7538	7678	1 14
03	7818	7958	8098	8238	8378	8517	8657	8797	8937	9077	2 28
04	9217	9357	9497	9637	9777	9917	0̅0̅5̅7̅	0̅1̅9̅6̅	0̅3̅3̅6̅	0̅4̅7̅6̅	3 42
05	492 0616	0756	0896	1036	1175	1315	1455	1595	1735	1875	4 56
06	2015	2154	2294	2434	2574	2714	2853	2993	3133	3273	5 70
07	3413	3552	3692	3832	3972	4111	4251	4391	4531	4670	6 84
08	4810	4950	5090	5229	5369	5509	5648	5788	5928	6068	7 98
09	6207	6347	6487	6626	6766	6906	7045	7185	7325	7464	8 112
10	7604	7744	7883	8023	8162	8302	8442	8581	8721	8861	9 126
3111	9000	9140	9279	9419	9558	9698	9838	9977	0̅1̅1̅7̅	0̅2̅5̅6̅	
12	493 0396	0535	0675	0815	0954	1094	1233	1373	1512	1652	
13	1791	1931	2070	2210	2349	2489	2628	2768	2907	3047	
14	3186	3326	3465	3604	3744	3883	4023	4162	4302	4441	
15	4581	4720	4859	4999	5138	5278	5417	5556	5696	5835	
16	5974	6114	6253	6393	6532	6671	6811	6950	7089	7229	
17	7368	7507	7647	7786	7925	8065	8204	8343	8483	8622	
18	8761	8900	9040	9179	9318	9457	9597	9736	9875	0̅0̅1̅5̅	
19	494 0154	0293	0432	0571	0711	0850	0989	1128	1268	1407	
20	1546	1685	1824	1964	2103	2242	2381	2520	2659	2799	
3121	2938	3077	3216	3355	3494	3633	3773	3912	4051	4190	
22	4329	4468	4607	4746	4885	5024	5164	5303	5442	5581	
23	5720	5859	5998	6137	6276	6415	6554	6693	6832	6971	
24	7110	7249	7388	7527	7666	7805	7944	8083	8222	8361	**139**
25	8500	8639	8778	8917	9056	9195	9334	9473	9612	9751	1 14
26	9890	0̅0̅2̅9̅	0̅1̅6̅8̅	0̅3̅0̅7̅	0̅4̅4̅5̅	0̅5̅8̅4̅	0̅7̅2̅3̅	0̅8̅6̅2̅	1̅0̅0̅1̅	1̅1̅4̅0̅	2 28
27	495 1279	1418	1557	1695	1834	1973	2112	2251	2390	2529	3 42
28	2667	2806	2945	3084	3223	3362	3500	3639	3778	3917	4 56
29	4056	4194	4333	4472	4611	4750	4888	5027	5166	5305	5 70
30	5443	5582	5721	5860	5998	6137	6276	6415	6553	6692	6 83
3131	6831	6969	7108	7247	7385	7524	7663	7802	7940	8079	7 97
32	8218	8356	8495	8634	8772	8911	9049	9188	9327	9465	8 111
33	9604	9743	9881	0̅0̅2̅0̅	0̅1̅5̅8̅	0̅2̅9̅7̅	0̅4̅3̅6̅	0̅5̅7̅4̅	0̅7̅1̅3̅	0̅8̅5̅1̅	9 125
34	496 0990	1128	1267	1406	1544	1683	1821	1960	2098	2237	
35	2375	2514	2653	2791	2930	3068	3207	3345	3484	3622	
36	3761	3899	4038	4176	4314	4453	4591	4730	4868	5007	
37	5145	5284	5422	5560	5699	5837	5976	6114	6253	6391	
38	6529	6668	6806	6945	7083	7221	7360	7498	7636	7775	
39	7913	8052	8190	8328	8467	8605	8743	8882	9020	9158	
40	9296	9435	9573	9711	9850	9988	0̅1̅2̅6̅	0̅2̅6̅5̅	0̅4̅0̅3̅	0̅5̅4̅1̅	
3141	497 0679	0818	0956	1094	1232	1371	1509	1647	1785	1924	
42	2062	2200	2338	2476	2615	2753	2891	3029	3167	3306	
43	3444	3582	3720	3858	3996	4135	4273	4411	4549	4687	
44	4825	4964	5102	5240	5378	5516	5654	5792	5930	6068	
45	6206	6345	6483	6621	6759	6897	7035	7173	7311	7449	
46	7587	7725	7863	8001	8139	8277	8415	8553	8691	8829	
47	8967	9105	9243	9381	9519	9657	9795	9933	0̅0̅7̅1̅	0̅2̅0̅9̅	**138**
48	498 0347	0485	0623	0761	0899	1037	1175	1313	1451	1589	
49	1727	1865	2002	2140	2278	2416	2554	2692	2830	2968	
3150	3106	3243	3381	3519	3657	3795	3933	4071	4208	4346	

No.	0	1	2	3	4	5	6	7	8	9	Diff.
3150	498 3106	3243	3381	3519	3657	3795	3933	4071	4208	4346	
51	4484	4622	4760	4897	5035	5173	5311	5449	5587	5724	138
52	5862	6000	6138	6275	6413	6551	6689	6826	6964	7102	1 14
53	7240	7377	7515	7653	7791	7928	8066	8204	8341	8479	2 28
54	8617	8755	8892	9030	9168	9305	9443	9581	9718	9856	3 41
55	9994	$\overline{0131}$	$\overline{0269}$	$\overline{0407}$	$\overline{0544}$	$\overline{0682}$	$\overline{0819}$	$\overline{0957}$	$\overline{1095}$	$\overline{1232}$	4 55 / 5 69
56	499 1370	1508	1645	1783	1920	2058	2196	2333	2471	2608	6 83
57	2746	2883	3021	3158	3296	3434	3571	3709	3846	3984	7 97
58	4121	4259	4396	4534	4671	4809	4946	5084	5221	5359	8 110
59	5496	5634	5771	5909	6046	6184	6321	6459	6596	6733	9 124
60	6871	7008	7146	7283	7421	7558	7695	7833	7970	8108	
3161	8245	8382	8520	8657	8794	8932	9069	9207	9344	9481	
62	9619	9756	9893	$\overline{0031}$	$\overline{0168}$	$\overline{0305}$	$\overline{0443}$	$\overline{0580}$	$\overline{0717}$	$\overline{0855}$	
63	500 0992	1129	1267	1404	1541	1678	1816	1953	2090	2227	
64	2365	2502	2639	2777	2914	3051	3188	3325	3463	3600	
65	3737	3874	4012	4149	4286	4423	4560	4698	4835	4972	
66	5109	5246	5383	5521	5658	5795	5932	6069	6206	6344	
67	6481	6618	6755	6892	7029	7166	7303	7440	7578	7715	
68	7852	7989	8126	8263	8400	8537	8674	8811	8948	9085	
69	9222	9359	9496	9634	9771	9908	$\overline{0045}$	$\overline{0182}$	$\overline{0319}$	$\overline{0456}$	137
70	501 0593	0730	0867	1004	1141	1278	1415	1552	1688	1825	1 14 / 2 27
3171	1962	2099	2236	2373	2510	2647	2784	2921	3058	3195	3 41
72	3332	3469	3606	3743	3879	4016	4153	4290	4427	4564	4 55
73	4701	4838	4974	5111	5248	5385	5522	5659	5796	5932	5 69
74	6069	6206	6343	6480	6617	6753	6890	7027	7164	7301	6 82
75	7437	7574	7711	7848	7984	8121	8258	8395	8531	8668	7 96
76	8805	8942	9078	9215	9352	9489	9625	9762	9899	$\overline{0035}$	8 110
77	502 0172	0309	0446	0582	0719	0856	0992	1129	1266	1402	9 123
78	1539	1676	1812	1949	2086	2222	2359	2495	2632	2769	
79	2905	3042	3178	3315	3452	3588	3725	3861	3998	4135	
80	4271	4408	4544	4681	4817	4954	5091	5227	5364	5500	
3181	5637	5773	5910	6046	6183	6319	6456	6592	6729	6865	
82	7002	7138	7275	7411	7548	7684	7821	7957	8093	8230	
83	8366	8503	8639	8776	8912	9049	9185	9321	9458	9594	
84	9731	9867	$\overline{0003}$	$\overline{0140}$	$\overline{0276}$	$\overline{0413}$	$\overline{0549}$	$\overline{0685}$	$\overline{0822}$	$\overline{0958}$	
85	503 1094	1231	1367	1503	1640	1776	1912	2049	2185	2321	
86	2458	2594	2730	2867	3003	3139	3276	3412	3548	3684	
87	3821	3957	4093	4229	4366	4502	4638	4774	4911	5047	
88	5183	5319	5456	5592	5728	5864	6000	6137	6273	6409	
89	6545	6681	6818	6954	7090	7226	7362	7498	7635	7771	
90	7907	8043	8179	8315	8451	8587	8724	8860	8996	9132	
3191	9268	9404	9540	9676	9812	9948	$\overline{0085}$	$\overline{0221}$	$\overline{0357}$	$\overline{0493}$	
92	504 0629	0765	0901	1037	1173	1309	1445	1581	1717	1853	
93	1989	2125	2261	2397	2533	2669	2805	2941	3077	3213	
94	3349	3485	3621	3757	3893	4029	4165	4301	4437	4573	136
95	4709	4845	4980	5116	5252	5388	5524	5660	5796	5932	
96	6068	6204	6339	6475	6611	6747	6883	7019	7155	7291	
97	7426	7562	7698	7834	7970	8106	8241	8377	8513	8649	
98	8785	8920	9056	9192	9328	9464	9599	9735	9871	$\overline{0007}$	
99	505 0142	0278	0414	0550	0685	0821	0957	1093	1228	1364	
3200	1500	1635	1771	1907	2043	2178	2314	2450	2585	2721	

No.	0	1	2	3	4	5	6	7	8	9	Diff.
3200	505 1500	1635	1771	1907	2043	2178	2314	2450	2585	2721	
01	2857	2992	3128	3264	3399	3535	3671	3806	3942	4078	136
02	4213	4349	4485	4620	4756	4891	5027	5163	5298	5434	1 14
03	5569	5705	5841	5976	6112	6247	6383	6518	6654	6790	2 27
04	6925	7061	7196	7332	7467	7603	7738	7874	8009	8145	3 41
05	8280	8416	8551	8687	8822	8958	9093	9229	9364	9500	4 54 / 5 68
06	9635	9771	9906	0042	0177	0312	0448	0583	0719	0854	6 82
07	506 0990	1125	1260	1396	1531	1667	1802	1937	2073	2208	7 95
08	2344	2479	2614	2750	2885	3020	3156	3291	3426	3562	8 109
09	3697	3833	3968	4103	4238	4374	4509	4644	4780	4915	9 122
10	5050	5186	5321	5456	5591	5727	5862	5997	6133	6268	
3211	6403	6538	6674	6809	6944	7079	7214	7350	7485	7620	
12	7755	7891	8026	8161	8296	8431	8567	8702	8837	8972	
13	9107	9242	9378	9513	9648	9783	9918	0053	0188	0324	
14	507 0459	0594	0729	0864	0999	1134	1269	1405	1540	1675	
15	1810	1945	2080	2215	2350	2485	2620	2755	2890	3025	
16	3160	3295	3430	3566	3701	3836	3971	4106	4241	4376	
17	4511	4646	4781	4916	5051	5186	5321	5456	5590	5725	135
18	5860	5995	6130	6265	6400	6535	6670	6805	6940	7075	1 14
19	7210	7345	7480	7614	7749	7884	8019	8154	8289	8424	2 27
20	8559	8694	8828	8963	9098	9233	9368	9503	9638	9772	3 41
3221	9907	0042	0177	0312	0447	0581	0716	0851	0986	1121	4 54 / 5 68
22	508 1255	1390	1525	1660	1794	1929	2064	2199	2334	2468	6 81
23	2603	2738	2873	3007	3142	3277	3411	3546	3681	3816	7 95
24	3950	4085	4220	4354	4489	4624	4758	4893	5028	5163	8 108
25	5297	5432	5567	5701	5836	5970	6105	6240	6374	6509	9 122
26	6644	6778	6913	7047	7182	7317	7451	7586	7720	7855	
27	7990	8124	8259	8393	8528	8663	8797	8932	9066	9201	
28	9335	9470	9604	9739	9873	0008	0142	0277	0411	0546	
29	509 0680	0815	0949	1084	1218	1353	1487	1622	1756	1891	
30	2025	2160	2294	2429	2563	2697	2832	2966	3101	3235	
3231	3370	3504	3638	3773	3907	4042	4176	4310	4445	4579	
32	4714	4848	4982	5117	5251	5385	5520	5654	5788	5923	
33	6057	6191	6326	6460	6594	6729	6863	6997	7132	7266	
34	7400	7534	7669	7803	7937	8072	8206	8340	8474	8609	
35	8743	8877	9011	9146	9280	9414	9548	9682	9817	9951	
36	510 0085	0219	0354	0488	0622	0756	0890	1024	1159	1293	
37	1427	1561	1695	1829	1964	2098	2232	2366	2500	2634	
38	2768	2903	3037	3171	3305	3439	3573	3707	3841	3975	
39	4109	4244	4378	4512	4646	4780	4914	5048	5182	5316	134
40	5450	5584	5718	5852	5986	6120	6254	6388	6522	6656	1 13 / 2 27
3241	6790	6924	7058	7192	7326	7460	7594	7728	7862	7996	3 40
42	8130	8264	8398	8532	8666	8800	8934	9068	9202	9336	4 54
43	9469	9603	9737	9871	0005	0139	0273	0407	0541	0675	5 67
44	511 0808	0942	1076	1210	1344	1478	1612	1745	1879	2013	6 80
45	2147	2281	2415	2548	2682	2816	2950	3084	3218	3351	7 94 / 8 107
46	3485	3619	3753	3887	4020	4154	4288	4422	4555	4689	9 121
47	4823	4957	5090	5224	5358	5492	5625	5759	5893	6026	
48	6160	6294	6428	6561	6695	6829	6962	7096	7230	7363	
49	7497	7631	7764	7898	8032	8165	8299	8433	8566	8700	
3250	8834	8967	9101	9234	9368	9502	9635	9769	9903	0036	

512

No.	0	1	2	3	4	5	6	7	8	9	Diff.
3250	511 8834	8967	9101	9234	9368	9502	9635	9769	9903	0036	
51	512 0170	0303	0437	0570	0704	0838	0971	1105	1238	1372	
52	1505	1639	1772	1906	2040	2173	2307	2440	2574	2707	
53	2841	2974	3108	3241	3375	3508	3642	3775	3909	4042	
54	4175	4309	4442	4576	4709	4843	4976	5110	5243	5377	
55	5510	5643	5777	5910	6044	6177	6310	6444	6577	6711	
56	6844	6977	7111	7244	7377	7511	7644	7778	7911	8044	
57	8178	8311	8444	8578	8711	8844	8978	9111	9244	9377	
58	9511	9644	9777	9911	0044	0177	0311	0444	0577	0710	
59	513 0844	0977	1110	1243	1377	1510	1643	1776	1910	2043	
60	2176	2309	2442	2576	2709	2842	2975	3108	3242	3375	
3261	3508	3641	3774	3908	4041	4174	4307	4440	4573	4706	133
62	4840	4973	5106	5239	5372	5505	5638	5771	5905	6038	1 13
63	6171	6304	6437	6570	6703	6836	6969	7102	7235	7368	2 27
64	7502	7635	7768	7901	8034	8167	8300	8433	8566	8699	3 40
65	8832	8965	9098	9231	9364	9497	9630	9763	9896	0029	4 53
66	514 0162	0295	0428	0561	0694	0827	0960	1093	1225	1358	5 67
67	1491	1624	1757	1890	2023	2156	2289	2422	2555	2688	6 80
68	2820	2953	3086	3219	3352	3485	3618	3751	3883	4016	7 93
69	4149	4282	4415	4548	4681	4813	4946	5079	5212	5345	8 106
70	5478	5610	5743	5876	6009	6142	6274	6407	6540	6673	9 120
3271	6805	6938	7071	7204	7336	7469	7602	7735	7867	8000	
72	8133	8266	8398	8531	8664	8797	8929	9062	9195	9327	
73	9460	9593	9725	9858	9991	0123	0256	0389	0521	0654	
74	515 0787	0919	1052	1185	1317	1450	1583	1715	1848	1980	
75	2113	2246	2378	2511	2643	2776	2909	3041	3174	3306	
76	3439	3571	3704	3837	3969	4102	4234	4367	4499	4632	
77	4764	4897	5029	5162	5294	5427	5560	5692	5825	5957	
78	6089	6222	6354	6487	6619	6752	6884	7017	7149	7282	
79	7414	7547	7679	7811	7944	8076	8209	8341	8474	8606	
80	8738	8871	9003	9136	9268	9400	9533	9665	9798	9930	
3281	516 0062	0195	0327	0459	0592	0724	0856	0989	1121	1253	132
82	1386	1518	1650	1783	1915	2047	2180	2312	2444	2577	1 13
83	2709	2841	2973	3106	3238	3370	3502	3635	3767	3899	2 26
84	4031	4164	4296	4428	4560	4693	4825	4957	5089	5222	3 40
85	5354	5486	5618	5750	5883	6015	6147	6279	6411	6543	4 53
86	6676	6808	6940	7072	7204	7336	7469	7601	7733	7865	5 66
87	7997	8129	8261	8393	8526	8658	8790	8922	9054	9186	6 79
88	9318	9450	9582	9714	9846	9978	0111	0243	0375	0507	7 92
89	517 0639	0771	0903	1035	1167	1299	1431	1563	1695	1827	8 106
90	1959	2091	2223	2355	2487	2619	2751	2883	3015	3147	9 119
3291	3279	3411	3543	3675	3807	3939	4071	4202	4334	4466	
92	4598	4730	4862	4994	5126	5258	5390	5522	5654	5785	
93	5917	6049	6181	6313	6445	6577	6709	6840	6972	7104	
94	7236	7368	7500	7631	7763	7895	8027	8159	8291	8422	
95	8554	8686	8818	8950	9081	9213	9345	9477	9608	9740	
96	9872	0004	0136	0267	0399	0531	0663	0794	0926	1058	
97	518 1189	1321	1453	1585	1716	1848	1980	2111	2243	2375	
98	2507	2638	2770	2902	3033	3165	3297	3428	3560	3692	
99	3823	3955	4086	4218	4350	4481	4613	4745	4876	5008	
3300	5139	5271	5403	5534	5666	5797	5929	6061	6192	6324	

No.	0	1	2	3	4	5	6	7	8	9	Diff.
3300	518 5139	5271	5403	5534	5666	5797	5929	6061	6192	6324	
01	6455	6587	6718	6850	6981	7113	7245	7376	7508	7639	
02	7771	7902	8034	8165	8297	8428	8560	8691	8823	8954	
03	9086	9217	9349	9480	9612	9743	9875	0006	0137	0269	
04	519 0400	0532	0663	0795	0926	1058	1189	1320	1452	1583	
05	1715	1846	1977	2109	2240	2372	2503	2634	2766	2897	
06	3028	3160	3291	3423	3554	3685	3817	3948	4079	4211	
07	4342	4473	4605	4736	4867	4999	5130	5261	5392	5524	
08	5655	5786	5918	6049	6180	6311	6443	6574	6705	6836	
09	6968	7099	7230	7361	7493	7624	7755	7886	8018	8149	
10	8280	8411	8542	8674	8805	8936	9067	9198	9329	9461	
3311	9592	9723	9854	9985	0116	0248	0379	0510	0641	0772	
12	520 0903	1034	1166	1297	1428	1559	1690	1821	1952	2083	
13	2214	2345	2477	2608	2739	2870	3001	3132	3263	3394	
14	3525	3656	3787	3918	4049	4180	4311	4442	4573	4704	
15	4835	4966	5097	5228	5359	5490	5621	5752	5883	6014	
16	6145	6276	6407	6538	6669	6800	6931	7062	7193	7324	
17	7455	7586	7717	7847	7978	8109	8240	8371	8502	8633	
18	8764	8895	9026	9156	9287	9418	9549	9680	9811	9942	
19	521 0073	0203	0334	0465	0596	0727	0858	0988	1119	1250	
20	1381	1512	1642	1773	1904	2035	2166	2296	2427	2558	
3321	2689	2820	2950	3081	3212	3343	3473	3604	3735	3866	
22	3996	4127	4258	4388	4519	4650	4781	4911	5042	5173	
23	5303	5434	5565	5695	5826	5957	6088	6218	6349	6479	
24	6610	6741	6871	7002	7133	7263	7394	7525	7655	7786	
25	7916	8047	8178	8308	8439	8570	8700	8831	8961	9092	
26	9222	9353	9484	9614	9745	9875	0006	0136	0267	0397	
27	522 0528	0659	0789	0920	1050	1181	1311	1442	1572	1703	
28	1833	1964	2094	2225	2355	2486	2616	2747	2877	3007	
29	3138	3268	3399	3529	3660	3790	3921	4051	4181	4312	
30	4442	4573	4703	4834	4964	5094	5225	5355	5486	5616	
3331	5746	5877	6007	6137	6268	6398	6529	6659	6789	6920	
32	7050	7180	7311	7441	7571	7702	7832	7962	8093	8223	
33	8353	8483	8614	8744	8874	9005	9135	9265	9395	9526	
34	9656	9786	9916	0047	0177	0307	0437	0568	0698	0828	
35	523 0958	1089	1219	1349	1479	1609	1740	1870	2000	2130	
36	2260	2391	2521	2651	2781	2911	3041	3172	3302	3432	
37	3562	3692	3822	3952	4083	4213	4343	4473	4603	4733	
38	4863	4993	5124	5254	5384	5514	5644	5774	5904	6034	
39	6164	6294	6424	6554	6684	6814	6945	7075	7205	7335	
40	7465	7595	7725	7855	7985	8115	8245	8375	8505	8635	
3341	8765	8895	9025	9155	9285	9415	9545	9675	9805	9935	
42	524 0064	0194	0324	0454	0584	0714	0844	0974	1104	1234	
43	1364	1494	1624	1753	1883	2013	2143	2273	2403	2533	
44	2663	2793	2922	3052	3182	3312	3442	3572	3702	3831	
45	3961	4091	4221	4351	4481	4610	4740	4870	5000	5130	
46	5259	5389	5519	5649	5779	5908	6038	6168	6298	6427	
47	6557	6687	6817	6946	7076	7206	7336	7465	7595	7725	
48	7854	7984	8114	8244	8373	8503	8633	8762	8892	9022	
49	9151	9281	9411	9540	9670	9800	9929	0059	0189	0318	
3350	525 0448	0578	0707	0837	0967	1096	1226	1355	1485	1615	

Diff. columns:

131
1 13
2 26
3 39
4 52
5 66
6 79
7 92
8 105
9 118

130
1 13
2 26
3 39
4 52
5 65
6 78
7 91
8 104
9 117

No.	0	1	2	3	4	5	6	7	8	9	Diff.
3350	525 0448	0578	0707	0837	0967	1096	1226	1355	1485	1615	
51	1744	1874	2003	2133	2263	2392	2522	2651	2781	2911	
52	3040	3170	3299	3429	3558	3688	3817	3947	4076	4206	
53	4336	4465	4595	4724	4854	4983	5113	5242	5372	5501	
54	5631	5760	5890	6019	6148	6278	6407	6537	6666	6796	
55	6925	7055	7184	7314	7443	7572	7702	7831	7961	8090	
56	8220	8349	8478	8608	8737	8867	8996	9125	9255	9384	
57	9513	9643	9772	9902	0031	0160	0290	0419	0548	0678	
58	526 0807	0936	1066	1195	1324	1454	1583	1712	1841	1971	
59	2100	2229	2359	2488	2617	2746	2876	3005	3134	3264	
60	3393	3522	3651	3781	3910	4039	4168	4297	4427	4556	
3361	4685	4814	4944	5073	5202	5331	5460	5590	5719	5848	
62	5977	6106	6235	6365	6494	6623	6752	6881	7010	7140	129
63	7269	7398	7527	7656	7785	7914	8043	8173	8302	8431	1 13
64	8560	8689	8818	8947	9076	9205	9334	9463	9593	9722	2 26
65	9851	9980	0109	0238	0367	0496	0625	0754	0883	1012	3 39
66	527 1141	1270	1399	1528	1657	1786	1915	2044	2173	2302	4 52 / 5 65
67	2431	2560	2689	2818	2947	3076	3205	3334	3463	·3592	6 77
68	3721	3850	3979	4108	4237	4366	4494	4623	4752	4881	7 90
69	5010	5139	5268	5397	5526	5655	5783	5912	6041	6170	8 103
70	6299	6428	6557	6686	6814	6943	7072	7201	7330	7459	9 116
3371	7588	7716	7845	7974	8103	8232	8360	8489	8618	8747	
72	8876	9004	9133	9262	9391	9520	9648	9777	9906	0035	
73	528 0163	0292	0421	0550	0678	0807	0936	1065	1193	1322	
74	1451	1579	1708	1837	1966	2094	2223	2352	2480	2609	
75	2738	2866	2995	3124	3252	3381	3510	3638	3767	3896	
76	4024	4153	4282	4410	4539	4668	4796	4925	5053	5182	
77	5311	5439	5568	5696	5825	5954	6082	6211	6339	6468	
78	6596	6725	6854	6982	7111	7239	7368	7496	7625	7753	
79	7882	8010	8139	8267	8396	8525	8653	8782	8910	9039	
80	9167	9295	9424	9552	9681	9809	9938	0066	0195	0323	
3381	529 0452	0580	0709	0837	0965	1094	1222	1351	1479	1608	
82	1736	1864	1993	2121	2250	2378	2506	2635	2763	2892	
83	3020	3148	3277	3405	3533	3662	3790	3919	4047	4175	
84	4304	4432	4560	4689	4817	4945	5074	5202	5330	5458	
85	5587	5715	5843	5972	6100	6228	6356	6485	6613	6741	
86	6870	6998	7126	7254	7383	7511	7639	7767	7896	8024	
87	8152	8280	8408	8537	8665	8793	8921	9049	9178	9306	
88	9434	9562	9690	9819	9947	0075	0203	0331	0459	0588	
89	530 0716	0844	0972	1100	1228	1356	1485	1613	1741	1869	
90	1997	2125	2253	2381	2509	2637	2766	2894	3022	3150	
3391	3278	3406	3534	3662	3790	3918	4046	4174	4302	4430	
92	4558	4686	4814	4943	5071	5199	5327	5455	5583	5711	
93	5839	5967	6095	6223	6351	6479	6607	6734	6862	6990	
94	7118	7246	7374	7502	7630	7758	7886	8014	8142	8270	
95	8398	8526	8654	8782	8909	9037	9165	9293	9421	9549	128
96	9677	9805	9933	0060	0188	0316	0444	0572	0700	0828	
97	531 0955	1083	1211	1339	1467	1595	1722	1850	1978	2106	
98	2234	2362	2489	2617	2745	2873	3001	3128	3256	3384	
99	3512	3639	3767	3895	4023	4150	4278	4406	4534	4661	
3400	4789	4917	5045	5172	5300	5428	5556	5683	5811	5939	

No.	0	1	2	3	4	5	6	7	8	9	Diff.
3400	531 4789	4917	5045	5172	5300	5428	5556	5683	5811	5939	
01	6066	6194	6322	6449	6577	6705	6832	6960	7088	7215	128
02	7343	7471	7598	7726	7854	7981	8109	8237	8364	8492	1 13
03	8619	8747	8875	9002	9130	9258	9385	9513	9640	9768	2 26
04	9896	0023	0151	0278	0406	0533	0661	0789	0916	1044	3 38
05	532 1171	1299	1426	1554	1681	1809	1936	2064	2191	2319	4 51 / 5 64
06	2446	2574	2701	2829	2956	3084	3211	3339	3466	3594	6 77
07	3721	3849	3976	4104	4231	4359	4486	4614	4741	4868	7 90
08	4996	5123	5251	5378	5506	5633	5760	5888	6015	6143	8 102
09	6270	6397	6525	6652	6780	6907	7034	7162	7289	7416	9 115
10	7544	7671	7799	7926	8053	8181	8308	8435	8563	8690	
3411	8817	8945	9072	9199	9326	9454	9581	9708	9836	9963	
12	533 0090	0218	0345	0472	0599	0727	0854	0981	1108	1236	
13	1363	1490	1617	1745	1872	1999	2126	2254	2381	2508	
14	2635	2762	2890	3017	3144	3271	3398	3526	3653	3780	
15	3907	4034	4161	4289	4416	4543	4670	4797	4924	5051	
16	5179	5306	5433	5560	5687	5814	5941	6068	6196	6323	
17	6450	6577	6704	6831	6958	7085	7212	7339	7466	7594	
18	7721	7848	7975	8102	8229	8356	8483	8610	8737	8864	
19	8991	9118	9245	9372	9499	9626	9753	9880	0007	0134	
20	534 0261	0388	0515	0642	0769	0896	1023	1150	1277	1404	127
3421	1531	1658	1785	1912	2039	2165	2292	2419	2546	2673	1 13
22	2800	2927	3054	3181	3308	3435	3561	3688	3815	3942	2 25
23	4069	4196	4323	4450	4576	4703	4830	4957	5084	5211	3 38
24	5338	5464	5591	5718	5845	5972	6099	6225	6352	6479	4 51 / 5 64
25	6606	6733	6859	6986	7113	7240	7366	7493	7620	7747	6 76
26	7874	8000	8127	8254	8381	8507	8634	8761	8888	9014	7 89
27	9141	9268	9394	9521	9648	9775	9901	0028	0155	0281	8 102
28	535 0408	0535	0662	0788	0915	1042	1168	1295	1422	1548	9 114
29	1675	1802	1928	2055	2181	2308	2435	2561	2688	2815	
30	2941	3068	3194	3321	3448	3574	3701	3827	3954	4081	
3431	4207	4334	4460	4587	4713	4840	4967	5093	5220	5346	
32	5473	5599	5726	5852	5979	6105	6232	6359	6485	6612	
33	6738	6865	6991	7118	7244	7371	7497	7623	7750	7876	
34	8003	8129	8256	8382	8509	8635	8762	8888	9015	9141	
35	9267	9394	9520	9647	9773	9900	0026	0152	0279	0405	
36	536 0532	0658	0784	0911	1037	1163	1290	1416	1543	1669	
37	1795	1922	2048	2174	2301	2427	2553	2680	2806	2932	
38	3059	3185	3311	3438	3564	3690	3817	3943	4069	4195	
39	4322	4448	4574	4701	4827	4953	5079	5206	5332	5458	
40	5584	5711	5837	5963	6089	6216	6342	6468	6594	6721	
3441	6847	6973	7099	7225	7352	7478	7604	7730	7856	7982	
42	8109	8235	8361	8487	8613	8739	8866	8992	9118	9244	
43	9370	9496	9622	9749	9875	0001	0127	0253	0379	0505	126
44	537 0631	0758	0884	1010	1136	1262	1388	1514	1640	1766	
45	1892	2018	2144	2270	2396	2523	2649	2775	2901	3027	
46	3153	3279	3405	3531	3657	3783	3909	4035	4161	4287	
47	4413	4539	4665	4791	4917	5043	5169	5295	5421	5547	
48	5673	5799	5924	6050	6176	6302	6428	6554	6680	6806	
49	6932	7058	7184	7310	7436	7561	7687	7813	7939	8065	
3450	8191	8317	8443	8569	8694	8820	8946	9072	9198	9324	

No.	0	1	2	3	4	5	6	7	8	9	Diff.
3450	537 8191	8317	8443	8569	8694	8820	8946	9072	9198	9324	
51	9450	9575	9701	9827	9953	0079	0205	0330	0456	0582	126
52	538 0708	0834	0959	1085	1211	1337	1463	1588	1714	1840	1 13
53	1966	2092	2217	2343	2469	2595	2720	2846	2972	3098	2 25
54	3223	3349	3475	3601	3726	3852	3978	4103	4229	4355	3 38
55	4481	4606	4732	4858	4983	5109	5235	5360	5486	5612	4 50
											5 63
56	5737	5863	5989	6114	6240	6366	6491	6617	6743	6868	6 76
57	6994	7119	7245	7371	7496	7622	7747	7873	7999	8124	7 88
58	8250	8375	8501	8627	8752	8878	9003	9129	9255	9380	8 101
59	9506	9631	9757	9882	0008	0133	0259	0384	0510	0635	9 113
60	539 0761	0887	1012	1138	1263	1389	1514	1640	1765	1891	
3461	2016	2141	2267	2392	2518	2643	2769	2894	3020	3145	
62	3271	3396	3522	3647	3772	3898	4023	4149	4274	4400	
63	4525	4650	4776	4901	5027	5152	5277	5403	5528	5653	125
64	5779	5904	6030	6155	6280	6406	6531	6656	6782	6907	1 13
65	7032	7158	7283	7408	7534	7659	7784	7910	8035	8160	2 25
											3 38
66	8286	8411	8536	8661	8787	8912	9037	9163	9288	9413	4 50
67	9538	9664	9789	9914	0039	0165	0290	0415	0540	0666	5 63
68	540 0791	0916	1041	1167	1292	1417	1542	1667	1793	1918	6 75
69	2043	2168	2293	2419	2544	2669	2794	2919	3044	3170	7 88
70	3295	3420	3545	3670	3795	3920	4046	4171	4296	4421	8 100
											9 113
3471	4546	4671	4796	4921	5047	5172	5297	5422	5547	5672	
72	5797	5922	6047	6172	6297	6423	6548	6673	6798	6923	
73	7048	7173	7298	7423	7548	7673	7798	7923	8048	8173	
74	8298	8423	8548	8673	8798	8923	9048	9173	9298	9423	
75	9548	9673	9798	9923	0048	0173	0298	0423	0548	0673	
76	541 0798	0923	1048	1172	1297	1422	1547	1672	1797	1922	
77	2047	2172	2297	2422	2546	2671	2796	2921	3046	3171	
78	3296	3421	3546	3670	3795	3920	4045	4170	4295	4419	
79	4544	4669	4794	4919	5044	5168	5293	5418	5543	5668	
80	5792	5917	6042	6167	6292	6416	6541	6666	6791	6915	
3481	7040	7165	7290	7415	7539	7664	7789	7913	8038	8163	
82	8288	8412	8537	8662	8787	8911	9036	9161	9285	9410	
83	9535	9659	9784	9909	0033	0158	0283	0407	0532	0657	
84	542 0781	0906	1031	1155	1280	1405	1529	1654	1779	1903	
85	2028	2152	2277	2402	2526	2651	2775	2900	3025	3149	
86	3274	3398	3523	3648	3772	3897	4021	4146	4270	4395	
87	4519	4644	4769	4893	5018	5142	5267	5391	5516	5640	
88	5765	5889	6014	6138	6263	6387	6512	6636	6761	6885	
89	7010	7134	7259	7383	7508	7632	7756	7881	8005	8130	
90	8254	8379	8503	8628	8752	8876	9001	9125	9250	9374	
3491	9498	9623	9747	9872	9996	0120	0245	0369	0494	0618	
92	543 0742	0867	0991	1115	1240	1364	1488	1613	1737	1862	
93	1986	2110	2235	2359	2483	2607	2732	2856	2980	3105	
94	3229	3353	3478	3602	3726	3850	3975	4099	4223	4348	
95	4472	4596	4720	4845	4969	5093	5217	5342	5466	5590	
96	5714	5838	5963	6087	6211	6335	6460	6584	6708	6832	
97	6956	7081	7205	7329	7453	7577	7701	7826	7950	8074	
98	8198	8322	8446	8571	8695	8819	8943	9067	9191	9315	
99	9439	9564	9688	9812	9936	0060	0184	0308	0432	0556	124
3500	544 0680	0805	0929	1053	1177	1301	1425	1549	1673	1797	

No.	0	1	2	3	4	5	6	7	8	9	Diff.
3500	544·0680	0805	0929	1053	1177	1301	1425	1549	1673	1797	
01	1921	2045	2169	2293	2417	2541	2665	2789	2913	3037	124
02	3161	3285	3409	3533	3657	3781	3905	4029	4153	4277	1 12
03	4401	4525	4649	4773	4897	5021	5145	5269	5393	5517	2 25
04	5641	5765	5889	6013	6137	6261	6385	6508	6632	6756	3 37
05	6880	7004	7128	7252	7376	7500	7624	7747	7871	7995	4 50
											5 62
06	8119	8243	8367	8491	8615	8738	8862	8986	9110	9234	6 74
07	9358	9481	9605	9729	9853	9977	0̄101	0̄224	0̄348	0̄472	7 87
08	545·0596	0720	0843	0967	1091	1215	1339	1462	1586	1710	8 99
09	1834	1957	2081	2205	2329	2452	2576	2700	2824	2947	9 112
10	3071	3195	3319	3442	3566	3690	3813	3937	4061	4185	
3511	4308	4432	4556	4679	4803	4927	5050	5174	5298	5421	
12	5545	5669	5792	5916	6040	6163	6287	6411	6534	6658	
13	6781	6905	7029	7152	7276	7400	7523	7647	7770	7894	
14	8018	8141	8265	8388	8512	8635	8759	8883	9006	9130	
15	9253	9377	9500	9624	9747	9871	9995	0̄118	0̄242	0̄365	
16	546·0489	0612	0736	0859	0983	1106	1230	1353	1477	1600	
17	1724	1847	1971	2094	2218	2341	2465	2588	2711	2835	
18	2958	3082	3205	3329	3452	3576	3699	3822	3946	4069	
19	4193	4316	4439	4563	4686	4810	4933	5056	5180	5303	
20	5427	5550	5673	5797	5920	6043	6167	6290	6414	6537	
3521	6660	6784	6907	7030	7154	7277	7400	7524	7647	7770	
22	7894	8017	8140	8263	8387	8510	8633	8757	8880	9003	
23	9126	9250	9373	9496	9620	9743	9866	9989	0̄113	0̄236	
24	547·0359	0482	0605	0729	0852	0975	1098	1222	1345	1468	
25	1591	1714	1838	1961	2084	2207	2330	2454	2577	2700	
26	2823	2946	3069	3193	3316	3439	3562	3685	3808	3931	
27	4055	4178	4301	4424	4547	4670	4793	4916	5040	5163	
28	5286	5409	5532	5655	5778	5901	6024	6147	6270	6394	
29	6517	6640	6763	6886	7009	7132	7255	7378	7501	7624	
30	7747	7870	7993	8116	8239	8362	8485	8608	8731	8854	
3531	8977	9100	9223	9346	9469	9592	9715	9838	9961	0̄084	
32	548·0207	0330	0453	0576	0699	0822	0945	1068	1191	1313	
33	1436	1559	1682	1805	1928	2051	2174	2297	2420	2543	
34	2665	2788	2911	3034	3157	3280	3403	3526	3648	3771	123
35	3894	4017	4140	4263	4386	4508	4631	4754	4877	5000	1 12
36	5123	5245	5368	5491	5614	5737	5859	5982	6105	6228	2 25
37	6351	6473	6596	6719	6842	6964	7087	7210	7333	7456	3 37
38	7578	7701	7824	7947	8069	8192	8315	8437	8560	8683	4 49
39	8806	8928	9051	9174	9296	9419	9542	9665	9787	9910	5 62
40	549·0033	0155	0278	0401	0523	0646	0769	0891	1014	1137	6 74
											7 86
3541	1259	1382	1505	1627	1750	1872	1995	2118	2240	2363	8 98
42	2486	2608	2731	2853	2976	3099	3221	3344	3466	3589	9 111
43	3712	3834	3957	4079	4202	4324	4447	4569	4692	4815	
44	4937	5060	5182	5305	5427	5550	5672	5795	5917	6040	
45	6162	6285	6407	6530	6652	6775	6897	7020	7142	7265	
46	7387	7510	7632	7755	7877	8000	8122	8245	8367	8489	
47	8612	8734	8857	8979	9102	9224	9346	9469	9591	9714	
48	9836	9959	0̄081	0̄203	0̄326	0̄448	0̄570	0̄693	0̄815	0̄938	
49	550·1060	1182	1305	1427	1549	1672	1794	1917	2039	2161	
3550	2284	2406	2528	2651	2773	2895	3017	3140	3262	3384	

No.	0	1	2	3	4	5	6	7	8	9	Diff.
3550	550 2284	2406	2528	2651	2773	2895	3017	3140	3262	3384	
51	3507	3629	3751	3874	3996	4118	4240	4363	4485	4607	
52	4730	4852	4974	5096	5219	5341	5463	5585	5708	5830	
53	5952	6074	6197	6319	6441	6563	6685	6808	6930	7052	
54	7174	7296	7419	7541	7663	7785	7907	8030	8152	8274	**122**
55	8396	8518	8640	8763	8885	9007	9129	9251	9373	9495	1 12
56	9618	9740	9862	9984	0106	0228	0350	0472	0594	0717	2 24
57	551 0839	0961	1083	1205	1327	1449	1571	1693	1815	1937	3 37
58	2059	2181	2304	2426	2548	2670	2792	2914	3036	3158	4 49
59	3280	3402	3524	3646	3768	3890	4012	4134	4256	4378	5 61
60	4500	4622	4744	4866	4988	5110	5232	5354	5476	5598	6 73
3561	5720	5842	5964	6086	6208	6329	6451	6573	6695	6817	7 85
62	6939	7061	7183	7305	7427	7549	7671	7793	7914	8036	8 98
63	8158	8280	8402	8524	8646	8768	8890	9011	9133	9255	9 110
64	9377	9499	9621	9743	9864	9986	0108	0230	0352	0474	
65	552 0595	0717	0839	0961	1083	1204	1326	1448	1570	1692	
66	1813	1935	2057	2179	2301	2422	2544	2666	2788	2909	
67	3031	3153	3275	3396	3518	3640	3762	3883	4005	4127	
68	4248	4370	4492	4614	4735	4857	4979	5100	5222	5344	
69	5465	5587	5709	5831	5952	6074	6196	6317	6439	6561	
70	6682	6804	6925	7047	7169	7290	7412	7534	7655	7777	
3571	7899	8020	8142	8263	8385	8507	8628	8750	8871	8993	
72	9115	9236	9358	9479	9601	9722	9844	9965	0087	0209	
73	553 0330	0452	0573	0695	0816	0938	1059	1181	1302	1424	
74	1545	1667	1789	1910	2032	2153	2275	2396	2517	2639	
75	2760	2882	3003	3125	3246	3368	3489	3611	3732	3854	
76	3975	4097	4218	4339	4461	4582	4704	4825	4947	5068	
77	5189	5311	5432	5554	5675	5796	5918	6039	6161	6282	
78	6403	6525	6646	6767	6889	7010	7132	7253	7374	7496	
79	7617	7738	7860	7981	8102	8224	8345	8466	8588	8709	
80	8830	8952	9073	9194	9315	9437	9558	9679	9801	9922	
3581	554 0043	0164	0286	0407	0528	0650	0771	0892	1013	1135	
82	1256	1377	1498	1620	1741	1862	1983	2104	2226	2347	
83	2468	2589	2710	2832	2953	3074	3195	3316	3438	3559	
84	3680	3801	3922	4044	4165	4286	4407	4528	4649	4770	
85	4892	5013	5134	5255	5376	5497	5618	5740	5861	5982	
86	6103	6224	6345	6466	6587	6708	6829	6951	7072	7193	
87	7314	7435	7556	7677	7798	7919	8040	8161	8282	8403	
88	8524	8645	8766	8887	9008	9130	9251	9372	9493	9614	
89	9735	9856	9977	0098	0219	0340	0461	0582	0703	0824	
90	555 0944	1065	1186	1307	1428	1549	1670	1791	1912	2033	**121**
3591	2154	2275	2396	2517	2638	2759	2880	3001	3121	3242	1 12
92	3363	3484	3605	3726	3847	3968	4089	4210	4330	4451	2 24
93	4572	4693	4814	4935	5056	5176	5297	5418	5539	5660	3 36
94	5781	5902	6022	6143	6264	6385	6506	6627	6747	6868	4 48
95	6989	7110	7231	7351	7472	7593	7714	7835	7955	8076	5 61
96	8197	8318	8438	8559	8680	8801	8921	9042	9163	9284	6 73 / 7 85
97	9404	9525	9646	9767	9887	0008	0129	0249	0370	0491	8 97 / 9 109
98	556 0612	0732	0853	0974	1094	1215	1336	1456	1577	1698	
99	1818	1939	2060	2180	2301	2422	2542	2663	2784	2904	
3600	3025	3146	3266	3387	3508	3628	3749	3869	3990	4111	

3600

No.	0	1	2	3	4	5	6	7	8	9	Diff.
3600	556 3025	3146	3266	3387	3508	3628	3749	3869	3990	4111	
01	4231	4352	4472	4593	4714	4834	4955	5075	5196	5317	
02	5437	5558	5678	5799	5919	6040	6160	6281	6402	6522	
03	6643	6763	6884	7004	7125	7245	7366	7486	7607	7727	
04	7848	7968	8089	8209	8330	8450	8571	8691	8812	8932	
05	9053	9173	9294	9414	9535	9655	9775	9896	0016	0137	
06	557 0257	0378	0498	0619	0739	0859	0980	1100	1221	1341	
07	1461	1582	1702	1823	1943	2063	2184	2304	2425	2545	
08	2665	2786	2906	3026	3147	3267	3387	3508	3628	3748	
09	3869	3989	4109	4230	4350	4470	4591	4711	4831	4952	
10	5072	5192	5313	5433	5553	5673	5794	5914	6034	6155	
3611	6275	6395	6515	6636	6756	6876	6996	7117	7237	7357	
12	7477	7598	7718	7838	7958	8079	8199	8319	8439	8559	
13	8680	8800	8920	9040	9160	9281	9401	9521	9641	9761	
14	9881	0002	0122	0242	0362	0482	0602	0723	0843	0963	
15	558 1083	1203	1323	1443	1564	1684	1804	1924	2044	2164	
16	2284	2404	2524	2645	2765	2885	3005	3125	3245	3365	
17	3485	3605	3725	3845	3965	4085	4205	4325	4446	4566	
18	4686	4806	4926	5046	5166	5286	5406	5526	5646	5766	
19	5886	6006	6126	6246	6366	6486	6606	6726	6846	6966	
20	7086	7206	7326	7446	7566	7686	7805	7925	8045	8165	
3621	8285	8405	8525	8645	8765	8885	9005	9125	9245	9365	
22	9484	9604	9724	9844	9964	0084	0204	0324	0444	0563	
23	559 0683	0803	0923	1043	1163	1283	1403	1522	1642	1762	
24	1882	2002	2122	2241	2361	2481	2601	2721	2840	2960	
25	3080	3200	3320	3440	3559	3679	3799	3919	4038	4158	120
26	4278	4398	4518	4637	4757	4877	4997	5116	5236	5356	1 12
27	5476	5595	5715	5835	5954	6074	6194	6314	6433	6553	2 24
28	6673	6792	6912	7032	7152	7271	7391	7511	7630	7750	3 36
29	7870	7989	8109	8229	8348	8468	8588	8707	8827	8947	4 48
30	9066	9186	9306	9425	9545	9664	9784	9904	0023	0143	5 60
3631	560 0262	0382	0502	0621	0741	0860	0980	1100	1219	1339	6 72
32	1458	1578	1698	1817	1937	2056	2176	2295	2415	2534	7 84
33	2654	2774	2893	3013	3132	3252	3371	3491	3610	3730	8 96
34	3849	3969	4088	4208	4327	4447	4566	4686	4805	4925	9 108
35	5044	5164	5283	5403	5522	5641	5761	5880	6000	6119	
36	6239	6358	6478	6597	6716	6836	6955	7075	7194	7314	
37	7433	7552	7672	7791	7911	8030	8149	8269	8388	8508	
38	8627	8746	8866	8985	9104	9224	9343	9463	9582	9701	
39	9821	9940	0059	0179	0298	0417	0537	0656	0775	0895	
40	561 1014	1133	1252	1372	1491	1610	1730	1849	1968	2088	
3641	2207	2326	2445	2565	2684	2803	2922	3042	3161	3280	
42	3399	3519	3638	3757	3876	3996	4115	4234	4353	4472	
43	4592	4711	4830	4949	5069	5188	5307	5426	5545	5665	
44	5784	5903	6022	6141	6260	6380	6499	6618	6737	6856	119
45	6975	7094	7214	7333	7452	7571	7690	7809	7928	8048	
46	8167	8286	8405	8524	8643	8762	8881	9000	9119	9239	
47	9358	9477	9596	9715	9834	9953	0072	0191	0310	0429	
48	562 0548	0667	0786	0905	1024	1144	1263	1382	1501	1620	
49	1739	1858	1977	2096	2215	2334	2453	2572	2691	2810	
3650	2929	3048	3167	3286	3405	3524	3642	3761	3880	3999	

No.	0	1	2	3	4	5	6	7	8	9	Diff.
3650	562 2929	3048	3167	3286	3405	3524	3642	3761	3880	3999	
51	4118	4237	4356	4475	4594	4713	4832	4951	5070	5189	**119**
52	5308	5427	5546	5664	5783	5902	6021	6140	6259	6378	1 12
53	6497	6616	6734	6853	6972	7091	7210	7329	7448	7567	2 24
54	7685	7804	7923	8042	8161	8280	8398	8517	8636	8755	3 36
55	8874	8993	9111	9230	9349	9468	9587	9705	9824	9943	4 48
											5 60
56	563 0062	0181	0299	0418	0537	0656	0775	0893	1012	1131	6 71
57	1250	1368	1487	1606	1725	1843	1962	2081	2200	2318	7 83
58	2437	2556	2674	2793	2912	3031	3149	3268	3387	3505	8 95
59	3624	3743	3861	3980	4099	4218	4336	4455	4574	4692	9 107
60	4811	4930	5048	5167	5285	5404	5523	5641	5760	5879	
3661	5997	6116	6235	6353	6472	6590	6709	6828	6946	7065	
62	7183	7302	7421	7539	7658	7776	7895	8013	8132	8251	
63	8369	8488	8606	8725	8843	8962	9081	9199	9318	9436	
64	9555	9673	9792	9910	0̅0̅2̅9̅	0̅1̅4̅7̅	0̅2̅6̅6̅	0̅3̅8̅4̅	0̅5̅0̅3̅	0̅6̅2̅1̅	
65	564 0740	0858	0977	1095	1214	1332	1451	1569	1688	1806	
66	1925	2043	2162	2280	2398	2517	2635	2754	2872	2991	
67	3109	3228	3346	3464	3583	3701	3820	3938	4056	4175	
68	4293	4412	4530	4648	4767	4885	5004	5122	5240	5359	
69	5477	5595	5714	5832	5951	6069	6187	6306	6424	6542	
70	6661	6779	6897	7016	7134	7252	7371	7489	7607	7726	
3671	7844	7962	8080	8199	8317	8435	8554	8672	8790	8908	
72	9027	9145	9263	9382	9500	9618	9736	9855	9973	0̅0̅9̅1̅	
73	565 0209	0328	0446	0564	0682	0800	0919	1037	1155	1273	
74	1392	1510	1628	1746	1864	1983	2101	2219	2337	2455	
75	2573	2692	2810	2928	3046	3164	3282	3401	3519	3637	
76	3755	3873	3991	4109	4228	4346	4464	4582	4700	4818	
77	4936	5054	5173	5291	5409	5527	5645	5763	5881	5999	
78	6117	6235	6353	6471	6590	6708	6826	6944	7062	7180	
79	7298	7416	7534	7652	7770	7888	8006	8124	8242	8360	
80	8478	8596	8714	8832	8950	9068	9186	9304	9422	9540	
3681	9658	9776	9894	0̅0̅1̅2̅	0̅1̅3̅0̅	0̅2̅4̅8̅	0̅3̅6̅6̅	0̅4̅8̅4̅	0̅6̅0̅2̅	0̅7̅2̅0̅	**118**
82	566 0838	0956	1074	1192	1310	1428	1545	1663	1781	1899	1 12
83	2017	2135	2253	2371	2489	2607	2725	2843	2960	3078	2 24
84	3196	3314	3432	3550	3668	3786	3903	4021	4139	4257	3 35
85	4375	4493	4611	4728	4846	4964	5082	5200	5318	5435	4 47
											5 59
86	5553	5671	5789	5907	6025	6142	6260	6378	6496	6614	6 71
87	6731	6849	6967	7085	7203	7320	7438	7556	7674	7791	7 83
88	7909	8027	8145	8262	8380	8498	8616	8733	8851	8969	8 94
89	9087	9204	9322	9440	9557	9675	9793	9911	0̅0̅2̅8̅	0̅1̅4̅6̅	9 106
90	567 0264	0381	0499	0617	0734	0852	0970	1087	1205	1323	
3691	1440	1558	1676	1793	1911	2029	2146	2264	2382	2499	
92	2617	2735	2852	2970	3087	3205	3323	3440	3558	3675	
93	3793	3911	4028	4146	4263	4381	4499	4616	4734	4851	
94	4969	5086	5204	5322	5439	5557	5674	5792	5909	6027	
95	6144	6262	6379	6497	6615	6732	6850	6967	7085	7202	
96	7320	7437	7555	7672	7790	7907	8025	8142	8260	8377	
97	8495	8612	8729	8847	8964	9082	9199	9317	9434	9552	
98	9669	9787	9904	0̅0̅2̅1̅	0̅1̅3̅9̅	0̅2̅5̅6̅	0̅3̅7̅4̅	0̅4̅9̅1̅	0̅6̅0̅8̅	0̅7̅2̅6̅	
99	568 0843	0961	1078	1196	1313	1430	1548	1665	1782	1900	
3700	2017	2135	2252	2369	2487	2604	2721	2839	2956	3074	

No.	0	1	2	3	4	5	6	7	8	9	Diff.
3700	568 2017	2135	2252	2369	2487	2604	2721	2839	2956	3074	
01	3191	3308	3426	3543	3660	3778	3895	4012	4130	4247	
02	4364	4481	4599	4716	4833	4951	5068	5185	5303	5420	
03	5537	5654	5772	5889	6006	6123	6241	6358	6475	6593	
04	6710	6827	6944	7062	7179	7296	7413	7530	7648	7765	
05	7882	7999	8117	8234	8351	8468	8585	8703	8820	8937	
06	9054	9171	9289	9406	9523	9640	9757	9874	9992	0̅1̅0̅9̅	
07	569 0226	0343	0460	0577	0694	0812	0929	1046	1163	1280	
08	1397	1514	1631	1749	1866	1983	2100	2217	2334	2451	
09	2568	2685	2803	2920	3037	3154	3271	3388	3505	3622	
10	3739	3856	3973	4090	4207	4324	4441	4558	4675	4793	
3711	4910	5027	5144	5261	5378	5495	5612	5729	5846	5963	
12	6080	6197	6314	6431	6548	6665	6782	6899	7016	7133	117
13	7249	7366	7483	7600	7717	7834	7951	8068	8185	8302	1 12
14	8419	8536	8653	8770	8887	9004	9121	9237	9354	9471	2 23
15	9588	9705	9822	9939	0̅0̅5̅6̅	0̅1̅7̅3̅	0̅2̅9̅0̅	0̅4̅0̅6̅	0̅5̅2̅3̅	0̅6̅4̅0̅	3 35
16	570 0757	0874	0991	1108	1225	1341	1458	1575	1692	1809	4 47
17	1926	2042	2159	2276	2393	2510	2627	2743	2860	2977	5 59
18	3094	3211	3327	3444	3561	3678	3795	3911	4028	4145	6 70
19	4262	4379	4495	4612	4729	4846	4962	5079	5196	5313	7 82
20	5429	5546	5663	5780	5896	6013	6130	6247	6363	6480	8 94
											9 105
3721	6597	6713	6830	6947	7064	7180	7297	7414	7530	7647	
22	7764	7880	7997	8114	8230	8347	8464	8580	8697	8814	
23	8930	9047	9164	9280	9397	9514	9630	9747	9863	9980	
24	571 0097	0213	0330	0447	0563	0680	0796	0913	1030	1146	
25	1263	1379	1496	1613	1729	1846	1962	2079	2195	2312	
26	2429	2545	2662	2778	2895	3011	3128	3244	3361	3477	
27	3594	3710	3827	3943	4060	4177	4293	4410	4526	4643	
28	4759	4876	4992	5109	5225	5341	5458	5574	5691	5807	
29	5924	6040	6157	6273	6390	6506	6623	6739	6855	6972	
30	7088	7205	7321	7438	7554	7670	7787	7903	8020	8136	
3731	8252	8369	8485	8602	8718	8834	8951	9067	9184	9300	
32	9416	9533	9649	9765	9882	9998	0̅1̅1̅5̅	0̅2̅3̅1̅	0̅3̅4̅7̅	0̅4̅6̅4̅	
33	572 0580	0696	0813	0929	1045	1162	1278	1394	1511	1627	
34	1743	1859	1976	2092	2208	2325	2441	2557	2674	2790	
35	2906	3022	3139	3255	3371	3487	3604	3720	3836	3952	
36	4069	4185	4301	4417	4534	4650	4766	4882	4999	5115	
37	5231	5347	5463	5580	5696	5812	5928	6044	6161	6277	
38	6393	6509	6625	6742	6858	6974	7090	7206	7322	7438	116
39	7555	7671	7787	7903	8019	8135	8252	8368	8484	8600	1 12
40	8716	8832	8948	9064	9180	9297	9413	9529	9645	9761	2 23
											3 35
3741	9877	9993	0̅1̅0̅9̅	0̅2̅2̅5̅	0̅3̅4̅1̅	0̅4̅5̅7̅	0̅5̅7̅4̅	0̅6̅9̅0̅	0̅8̅0̅6̅	0̅9̅2̅2̅	4 46
42	573 1038	1154	1270	1386	1502	1618	1734	1850	1966	2082	5 58
43	2198	2314	2430	2546	2662	2778	2894	3010	3126	3242	6 70
44	3358	3474	3590	3706	3822	3938	4054	4170	4286	4402	7 81
45	4518	4634	4750	4866	4982	5098	5214	5330	5446	5562	8 93
											9 104
46	5678	5794	5910	6026	6141	6257	6373	6489	6605	6721	
47	6837	6953	7069	7185	7301	7416	7532	7648	7764	7880	
48	7996	8112	8228	8343	8459	8575	8691	8807	8923	9039	
49	9154	9270	9386	9502	9618	9734	9849	9965	0̅0̅8̅1̅	0̅1̅9̅7̅	
3750	574 0313	0428	0544	0660	0776	0892	1007	1123	1239	1355	

No.	0	1	2	3	4	5	6	7	8	9	Diff.
3750	574 0313	0428	0544	0660	0776	0892	1007	1123	1239	1355	
51	1471	1586	1702	1818	1934	2050	2165	2281	2397	2513	
52	2628	2744	2860	2976	3091	3207	3323	3438	3554	3670	
53	3786	3901	4017	4133	4248	4364	4480	4596	4711	4827	
54	4943	5058	5174	5290	5405	5521	5637	5752	5868	5984	
55	6099	6215	6331	6446	6562	6678	6793	6909	7025	7140	
56	7256	7371	7487	7603	7718	7834	7950	8065	8181	8296	
57	8412	8528	8643	8759	8874	8990	9105	9221	9337	9452	
58	9568	9683	9799	9914	0030	0146	0261	0377	0492	0608	
59	575 0723	0839	0954	1070	1185	1301	1416	1532	1647	1763	
60	1878	1994	2109	2225	2340	2456	2571	2687	2802	2918	
3761	3033	3149	3264	3380	3495	3611	3726	3842	3957	4072	
62	4188	4303	4419	4534	4650	4765	4881	4996	5111	5227	
63	5342	5458	5573	5688	5804	5919	6035	6150	6265	6381	
64	6496	6612	6727	6842	6958	7073	7188	7304	7419	7534	
65	7650	7765	7881	7996	8111	8227	8342	8457	8573	8688	
66	8803	8918	9034	9149	9264	9380	9495	9610	9726	9841	
67	9956	0071	0187	0302	0417	0533	0648	0763	0878	0994	
68	576 1109	1224	1339	1455	1570	1685	1800	1916	2031	2146	
69	2261	2377	2492	2607	2722	2837	2953	3068	3183	3298	
70	3414	3529	3644	3759	3874	3989	4105	4220	4335	4450	
3771	4565	4680	4796	4911	5026	5141	5256	5371	5487	5602	115
72	5717	5832	5947	6062	6177	6292	6408	6523	6638	6753	1 12
73	6868	6983	7098	7213	7328	7444	7559	7674	7789	7904	2 23
74	8019	8134	8249	8364	8479	8594	8709	8824	8939	9055	3 35
75	9170	9285	9400	9515	9630	9745	9860	9975	0090	0205	4 46
76	577 0320	0435	0550	0665	0780	0895	1010	1125	1240	1355	5 58
77	1470	1585	1700	1815	1930	2045	2160	2275	2390	2505	6 69
78	2620	2734	2849	2964	3079	3194	3309	3424	3539	3654	7 81
79	3769	3884	3999	4114	4229	4343	4458	4573	4688	4803	8 92
80	4918	5033	5148	5263	5378	5492	5607	5722	5837	5952	9 104
3781	6067	6182	6296	6411	6526	6641	6756	6871	6986	7100	
82	7215	7330	7445	7560	7675	7789	7904	8019	8134	8249	
83	8363	8478	8593	8708	8823	8937	9052	9167	9282	9397	
84	9511	9626	9741	9856	9970	0085	0200	0315	0429	0544	
85	578 0659	0774	0888	1003	1118	1233	1347	1462	1577	1691	
86	1806	1921	2036	2150	2265	2380	2494	2609	2724	2838	
87	2953	3068	3182	3297	3412	3526	3641	3756	3870	3985	
88	4100	4214	4329	4444	4558	4673	4788	4902	5017	5131	
89	5246	5361	5475	5590	5705	5819	5934	6048	6163	6278	
90	6392	6507	6621	6736	6850	6965	7080	7194	7309	7423	
3791	7538	7652	7767	7882	7996	8111	8225	8340	8454	8569	
92	8683	8798	8912	9027	9141	9256	9370	9485	9599	9714	
93	9828	9943	0057	0172	0286	0401	0515	0630	0744	0859	
94	579 0973	1088	1202	1317	1431	1546	1660	1774	1889	2003	
95	2118	2232	2347	2461	2576	2690	2804	2919	3033	3148	
96	3262	3376	3491	3605	3720	3834	3948	4063	4177	4292	
97	4406	4520	4635	4749	4863	4978	5092	5207	5321	5435	
98	5550	5664	5778	5893	6007	6121	6236	6350	6464	6579	
99	6693	6807	6922	7036	7150	7264	7379	7493	7607	7722	
3800	7836	7950	8065	8179	8293	8407	8522	8636	8750	8864	

No.	0	1	2	3	4	5	6	7	8	9	Diff.
3800	579 7836	7950	8065	8179	8293	8407	8522	8636	8750	8864	
01	8979	9093	9207	9321	9436	9550	9664	9778	9893	0007	
02	580 0121	0235	0350	0464	0578	0692	0806	0921	1035	1149	
03	1263	1377	1492	1606	1720	1834	1948	2063	2177	2291	
04	2405	2519	2633	2748	2862	2976	3090	3204	3318	3432	
05	3547	3661	3775	3889	4003	4117	4231	4346	4460	4574	
06	4688	4802	4916	5030	5144	5258	5372	5487	5601	5715	
07	5829	5943	6057	6171	6285	6399	6513	6627	6741	6855	
08	6969	7083	7197	7312	7426	7540	7654	7768	7882	7996	
09	8110	8224	8338	8452	8566	8680	8794	8908	9022	9136	
10	9250	9364	9478	9592	9706	9820	9934	0048	0162	0276	
3811	581 0389	0503	0617	0731	0845	0959	1073	1187	1301	1415	
12	1529	1643	1757	1871	1985	2099	2212	2326	2440	2554	
13	2668	2782	2896	3010	3124	3238	3351	3465	3579	3693	
14	3807	3921	4035	4148	4262	4376	4490	4604	4718	4832	
15	4945	5059	5173	5287	5401	5515	5628	5742	5856	5970	
16	6084	6197	6311	6425	6539	6653	6766	6880	6994	7108	114
17	7222	7335	7449	7563	7677	7790	7904	8018	8132	8245	1 11
18	8359	8473	8587	8700	8814	8928	9042	9155	9269	9383	2 23
19	9497	9610	9724	9838	9951	0065	0179	0293	0406	0520	3 34
20	582 0634	0747	0861	0975	1088	1202	1316	1429	1543	1657	4 46
3821	1770	1884	1998	2111	2225	2339	2452	2566	2680	2793	5 57
22	2907	3020	3134	3248	3361	3475	3589	3702	3816	3929	6 68
23	4043	4157	4270	4384	4497	4611	4725	4838	4952	5065	7 80
24	5179	5292	5406	5520	5633	5747	5860	5974	6087	6201	8 91
25	6314	6428	6541	6655	6769	6882	6996	7109	7223	7336	9 103
26	7450	7563	7677	7790	7904	8017	8131	8244	8358	8471	
27	8585	8698	8812	8925	9039	9152	9265	9379	9492	9606	
28	9719	9833	9946	0060	0173	0287	0400	0513	0627	0740	
29	583 0854	0967	1081	1194	1307	1421	1534	1648	1761	1874	
30	1988	2101	2215	2328	2441	2555	2668	2781	2895	3008	
3831	3122	3235	3348	3462	3575	3688	3802	3915	4028	4142	
32	4255	4368	4482	4595	4708	4822	4935	5048	5162	5275	
33	5388	5501	5615	5728	5841	5955	6068	6181	6295	6408	
34	6521	6634	6748	6861	6974	7087	7201	7314	7427	7540	
35	7654	7767	7880	7993	8107	8220	8333	8446	8560	8673	
36	8786	8899	9012	9126	9239	9352	9465	9578	9692	9805	
37	9918	0031	0144	0258	0371	0484	0597	0710	0823	0937	
38	584 1050	1163	1276	1389	1502	1615	1729	1842	1955	2068	
39	2181	2294	2407	2520	2634	2747	2860	2973	3086	3199	
40	3312	3425	3538	3652	3765	3878	3991	4104	4217	4330	
3841	4443	4556	4669	4782	4895	5008	5121	5234	5348	5461	
42	5574	5687	5800	5913	6026	6139	6252	6365	6478	6591	
43	6704	6817	6930	7043	7156	7269	7382	7495	7608	7721	
44	7834	7947	8060	8173	8286	8399	8512	8625	8738	8850	
45	8963	9076	9189	9302	9415	9528	9641	9754	9867	9980	
46	585 0093	0206	0319	0432	0544	0657	0770	0883	0996	1109	
47	1222	1335	1448	1561	1673	1786	1899	2012	2125	2238	
48	2351	2463	2576	2689	2802	2915	3028	3141	3253	3366	
49	3479	3592	3705	3818	3930	4043	4156	4269	4382	4494	
3850	4607	4720	4833	4946	5058	5171	5284	5397	5510	5622	

No.	0	1	2	3	4	5	6	7	8	9	Diff.
3850	585 4607	4720	4833	4946	5058	5171	5284	5397	5510	5622	
51	5735	5848	5961	6073	6186	6299	6412	6525	6637	6750	
52	6863	6976	7088	7201	7314	7426	7539	7652	7765	7877	113
53	7990	8103	8216	8328	8441	8554	8666	8779	8892	9004	1 11
54	9117	9230	9342	9455	9568	9681	9793	9906	$\overline{0019}$	$\overline{0131}$	2 23
55	586 0244	0356	0469	0582	0694	0807	0920	1032	1145	1258	3 34
56	1370	1483	1596	1708	1821	1933	2046	2159	2271	2384	4 45
57	2496	2609	2722	2834	2947	3059	3172	3285	3397	3510	5 57
58	3622	3735	3847	3960	4072	4185	4298	4410	4523	4635	6 68
59	4748	4860	4973	5085	5198	5310	5423	5535	5648	5761	7 79
60	5873	5986	6098	6211	6323	6436	6548	6661	6773	6886	8 90
3861	6998	7110	7223	7335	7448	7560	7673	7785	7898	8010	9 102
62	8123	8235	8348	8460	8572	8685	8797	8910	9022	9135	
63	9247	9360	9472	9584	9697	9809	9922	$\overline{0034}$	$\overline{0146}$	$\overline{0259}$	
64	587 0371	0484	0596	0708	0821	0933	1045	1158	1270	1383	
65	1495	1607	1720	1832	1944	2057	2169	2281	2394	2506	
66	2618	2731	2843	2955	3068	3180	3292	3405	3517	3629	
67	3742	3854	3966	4079	4191	4303	4416	4528	4640	4752	
68	4865	4977	5089	5201	5314	5426	5538	5651	5763	5875	
69	5987	6100	6212	6324	6436	6549	6661	6773	6885	6997	
70	7110	7222	7334	7446	7559	7671	7783	7895	8007	8120	
3871	8232	8344	8456	8568	8680	8793	8905	9017	9129	9241	
72	9353	9466	9578	9690	9802	9914	$\overline{0026}$	$\overline{0139}$	$\overline{0251}$	$\overline{0363}$	
73	588 0475	0587	0699	0811	0923	1036	1148	1260	1372	1484	
74	1596	1708	1820	1932	2045	2157	2269	2381	2493	2605	
75	2717	2829	2941	3053	3165	3277	3389	3502	3614	3726	112
76	3838	3950	4062	4174	4286	4398	4510	4622	4734	4846	1 11
77	4958	5070	5182	5294	5406	5518	5630	5742	5854	5966	2 22
78	6078	6190	6302	6414	6526	6638	6750	6862	6974	7086	3 34
79	7198	7310	7422	7534	7646	7758	7870	7981	8093	8205	4 45
80	8317	8429	8541	8653	8765	8877	8989	9101	9213	9325	5 56
3881	9436	9548	9660	9772	9884	9996	$\overline{0108}$	$\overline{0220}$	$\overline{0332}$	$\overline{0443}$	6 67
82	589 0555	0667	0779	0891	1003	1115	1227	1338	1450	1562	7 78
83	1674	1786	1898	2009	2121	2233	2345	2457	2569	2680	8 90
84	2792	2904	3016	3128	3239	3351	3463	3575	3687	3798	9 101
85	3910	4022	4134	4246	4357	4469	4581	4693	4804	4916	
86	5028	5140	5251	5363	5475	5587	5698	5810	5922	6034	
87	6145	6257	6369	6481	6592	6704	6816	6927	7039	7151	
88	7263	7374	7486	7598	7709	7821	7933	8044	8156	8268	
89	8379	8491	8603	8714	8826	8938	9049	9161	9273	9384	
90	9496	9608	9719	9831	9943	$\overline{0054}$	$\overline{0166}$	$\overline{0277}$	$\overline{0389}$	$\overline{0501}$	
3891	590 0612	0724	0836	0947	1059	1170	1282	1394	1505	1617	
92	1728	1840	1951	2063	2175	2286	2398	2509	2621	2732	
93	2844	2956	3067	3179	3290	3402	3513	3625	3736	3848	
94	3959	4071	4183	4294	4406	4517	4629	4740	4852	4963	
95	5075	5186	5298	5409	5521	5632	5744	5855	5967	6078	
96	6189	6301	6412	6524	6635	6747	6858	6970	7081	7193	
97	7304	7415	7527	7638	7750	7861	7973	8084	8196	8307	
98	8418	8530	8641	8753	8864	8975	9087	9198	9310	9421	
99	9532	9644	9755	9866	9978	$\overline{0089}$	$\overline{0201}$	$\overline{0312}$	$\overline{0423}$	$\overline{0535}$	
3900	591 0646	0757	0869	0980	1091	1203	1314	1426	1537	1648	

No.	0	1	2	3	4	5	6	7	8	9	Diff.
3900	591 0646	0757	0869	0980	1091	1203	1314	1426	1537	1648	
01	1760	1871	1982	2093	2205	2316	2427	2539	2650	2761	
02	2873	2984	3095	3207	3318	3429	3540	3652	3763	3874	
03	3986	4097	4208	4319	4431	4542	4653	4764	4876	4987	
04	5098	5209	5321	5432	5543	5654	5765	5877	5988	6099	
05	6210	6322	6433	6544	6655	6766	6878	6989	7100	7211	
06	7322	7434	7545	7656	7767	7878	7989	8101	8212	8323	
07	8434	8545	8656	8768	8879	8990	9101	9212	9323	9434	
08	9546	9657	9768	9879	9990	0101	0212	0323	0434	0546	**111**
09	592 0657	0768	0879	0990	1101	1212	1323	1434	1545	1656	1 11
10	1768	1879	1990	2101	2212	2323	2434	2545	2656	2767	2 22
3911	2878	2989	3100	3211	3322	3433	3544	3655	3766	3877	3 33
12	3988	4099	4210	4321	4433	4544	4655	4766	4876	4987	4 44
13	5098	5209	5320	5431	5542	5653	5764	5875	5986	6097	5 56
14	6208	6319	6430	6541	6652	6763	6874	6985	7096	7207	6 67
15	7318	7429	7540	7650	7761	7872	7983	8094	8205	8316	7 78
16	8427	8538	8649	8760	8870	8981	9092	9203	9314	9425	8 89
17	9536	9647	9757	9868	9979	0090	0201	0312	0423	0533	9 100
18	593 0644	0755	0866	0977	1088	1199	1309	1420	1531	1642	
19	1753	1863	1974	2085	2196	2307	2417	2528	2639	2750	
20	2861	2971	3082	3193	3304	3415	3525	3636	3747	3858	
3921	3968	4079	4190	4301	4411	4522	4633	4744	4854	4965	
22	5076	5187	5297	5408	5519	5630	5740	5851	5962	6072	
23	6183	6294	6404	6515	6626	6737	6847	6958	7069	7179	
24	7290	7401	7511	7622	7733	7843	7954	8065	8175	8286	
25	8397	8507	8618	8729	8839	8950	9060	9171	9282	9392	
26	9503	9614	9724	9835	9945	0056	0167	0277	0388	0498	
27	594 0609	0720	0830	0941	1051	1162	1273	1383	1494	1604	
28	1715	1825	1936	2046	2157	2268	2378	2489	2599	2710	
29	2820	2931	3041	3152	3262	3373	3483	3594	3704	3815	
30	3926	4036	4147	4257	4368	4478	4588	4699	4809	4920	
3931	5030	5141	5251	5362	5472	5583	5693	5804	5914	6025	
32	6135	6246	6356	6466	6577	6687	6798	6908	7019	7129	
33	7239	7350	7460	7571	7681	7792	7902	8012	8123	8233	
34	8344	8454	8564	8675	8785	8895	9006	9116	9227	9337	
35	9447	9558	9668	9778	9889	9999	0110	0220	0330	0441	
36	595 0551	0661	0772	0882	0992	1103	1213	1323	1434	1544	
37	1654	1764	1875	1985	2095	2206	2316	2426	2537	2647	
38	2757	2867	2978	3088	3198	3308	3419	3529	3639	3750	
39	3860	3970	4080	4191	4301	4411	4521	4632	4742	4852	
40	4962	5072	5183	5293	5403	5513	5624	5734	5844	5954	
3941	6064	6175	6285	6395	6505	6615	6725	6836	6946	7056	
42	7166	7276	7387	7497	7607	7717	7827	7937	8047	8158	
43	8268	8378	8488	8598	8708	8818	8929	9039	9149	9259	
44	9369	9479	9589	9699	9810	9920	0030	0140	0250	0360	
45	596 0470	0580	0690	0800	0910	1020	1131	1241	1351	1461	
46	1571	1681	1791	1901	2011	2121	2231	2341	2451	2561	
47	2671	2781	2891	3001	3111	3221	3331	3441	3551	3661	
48	3771	3881	3991	4101	4211	4321	4431	4541	4651	4761	
49	4871	4981	5091	5201	5311	5421	5531	5641	5751	5861	
3950	5971	6081	6191	6301	6411	6521	6631	6741	6850	6960	

No.	0	1	2	3	4	5	6	7	8	9	Diff.
3950	596 5971	6081	6191	6301	6411	6521	6631	6741	6850	6960	
51	7070	7180	7290	7400	7510	7620	7730	7840	7950	8059	
52	8169	8279	8389	8499	8609	8719	8829	8939	9048	9158	
53	9268	9378	9488	9598	9708	9817	9927	0037	0147	0257	
54	597 0367	0476	0586	0696	0806	0916	1026	1135	1245	1355	110
55	1465	1575	1684	1794	1904	2014	2124	2233	2343	2453	1 11
56	2563	2673	2782	2892	3002	3112	3221	3331	3441	3551	2 22
57	3661	3770	3880	3990	4099	4209	4319	4429	4538	4648	3 33
58	4758	4868	4977	5087	5197	5306	5416	5526	5636	5745	4 44
59	5855	5965	6074	6184	6294	6403	6513	6623	6733	6842	5 55
60	6952	7062	7171	7281	7391	7500	7610	7719	7829	7939	6 66
3961	8048	8158	8268	8377	8487	8597	8706	8816	8925	9035	7 77
62	9145	9254	9364	9474	9583	9693	9802	9912	0022	0131	8 88
63	598 0241	0350	0460	0569	0679	0789	0898	1008	1117	1227	9 99
64	1336	1446	1556	1665	1775	1884	1994	2103	2213	2322	
65	2432	2541	2651	2761	2870	2980	3089	3199	3308	3418	
66	3527	3637	3746	3856	3965	4075	4184	4294	4403	4513	
67	4622	4731	4841	4950	5060	5169	5279	5388	5498	5607	
68	5717	5826	5936	6045	6154	6264	6373	6483	6592	6702	
69	6811	6920	7030	7139	7249	7358	7467	7577	7686	7796	
70	7905	8014	8124	8233	8343	8452	8561	8671	8780	8890	
3971	8999	9108	9218	9327	9436	9546	9655	9764	9874	9983	
72	599 0092	0202	0311	0420	0530	0639	0748	0858	0967	1076	
73	1186	1295	1404	1514	1623	1732	1841	1951	2060	2169	
74	2279	2388	2497	2606	2716	2825	2934	3044	3153	3262	
75	3371	3481	3590	3699	3808	3918	4027	4136	4245	4355	
76	4464	4573	4682	4791	4901	5010	5119	5228	5338	5447	
77	5556	5665	5774	5884	5993	6102	6211	6320	6429	6539	
78	6648	6757	6866	6975	7084	7194	7303	7412	7521	7630	
79	7739	7849	7958	8067	8176	8285	8394	8503	8612	8722	
80	8831	8940	9049	9158	9267	9376	9485	9594	9704	9813	
3981	9922	0031	0140	0249	0358	0467	0576	0685	0794	0903	
82	600 1013	1122	1231	1340	1449	1558	1667	1776	1885	1994	
83	2103	2212	2321	2430	2539	2648	2757	2866	2975	3084	
84	3193	3302	3411	3520	3629	3738	3847	3956	4065	4174	
85	4283	4392	4501	4610	4719	4828	4937	5046	5155	5264	
86	5373	5482	5591	5700	5809	5918	6027	6136	6244	6353	
87	6462	6571	6680	6789	6898	7007	7116	7225	7334	7443	109
88	7551	7660	7769	7878	7987	8096	8205	8314	8423	8531	1 11
89	8640	8749	8858	8967	9076	9185	9294	9402	9511	9620	2 22
90	9729	9838	9947	0055	0164	0273	0382	0491	0600	0708	3 33
3991	601 0817	0926	1035	1144	1253	1361	1470	1579	1688	1797	4 44
92	1905	2014	2123	2232	2340	2449	2558	2667	2776	2884	5 55
93	2993	3102	3211	3319	3428	3537	3646	3754	3863	3972	6 65
94	4081	4189	4298	4407	4516	4624	4733	4842	4950	5059	7 76
95	5168	5277	5385	5494	5603	5711	5820	5929	6037	6146	8 87
96	6255	6363	6472	6581	6690	6798	6907	7016	7124	7233	9 98
97	7341	7450	7559	7667	7776	7885	7993	8102	8211	8319	
98	8428	8537	8645	8754	8862	8971	9080	9188	9297	9405	
99	9514	9623	9731	9840	9948	0057	0166	0274	0383	0491	
4000	602 0600	0708	0817	0926	1034	1143	1251	1360	1468	1577	

No.	0	1	2	3	4	5	6	7	8	9	Diff.
4000	602 0600	0708	0817	0926	1034	1143	1251	1360	1468	1577	
01	1686	1794	1903	2011	2120	2228	2337	2445	2554	2662	
02	2771	2879	2988	3096	3205	3313	3422	3530	3639	3747	
03	3856	3964	4073	4181	4290	4398	4507	4615	4724	4832	
04	4941	5049	5158	5266	5375	5483	5591	5700	5808	5917	
05	6025	6134	6242	6351	6459	6567	6676	6784	6893	7001	
06	7109	7218	7326	7435	7543	7651	7760	7868	7977	8085	
07	8193	8302	8410	8519	8627	8735	8844	8952	9060	9169	
08	9277	9385	9494	9602	9711	9819	9927	0036	0144	0252	
09	603 0361	0469	0577	0686	0794	0902	1010	1119	1227	1335	**108**
10	1444	1552	1660	1769	1877	1985	2093	2202	2310	2418	1 11
4011	2527	2635	2743	2851	2960	3068	3176	3284	3393	3501	2 22
12	3609	3717	3826	3934	4042	4150	4259	4367	4475	4583	3 32
13	4692	4800	4908	5016	5124	5233	5341	5449	5557	5665	4 43
14	5774	5882	5990	6098	6206	6315	6423	6531	6639	6747	5 54
15	6855	6964	7072	7180	7288	7396	7504	7613	7721	7829	6 65
16	7937	8045	8153	8261	8370	8478	8586	8694	8802	8910	7 76
17	9018	9126	9235	9343	9451	9559	9667	9775	9883	9991	8 86
18	604 0099	0207	0315	0424	0532	0640	0748	0856	0964	1072	9 97
19	1180	1288	1396	1504	1612	1720	1828	1936	2044	2152	
20	2261	2369	2477	2585	2693	2801	2909	3017	3125	3233	
4021	3341	3449	3557	3665	3773	3881	3989	4097	4205	4313	
22	4421	4529	4637	4745	4853	4961	5068	5176	5284	5392	
23	5500	5608	5716	5824	5932	6040	6148	6256	6364	6472	
24	6580	6688	6796	6903	7011	7119	7227	7335	7443	7551	
25	7659	7767	7875	7983	8090	8198	8306	8414	8522	8630	
26	8738	8846	8953	9061	9169	9277	9385	9493	9601	9708	
27	9816	9924	0032	0140	0248	0355	0463	0571	0679	0787	
28	605 0895	1002	1110	1218	1326	1434	1541	1649	1757	1865	
29	1973	2080	2188	2296	2404	2512	2619	2727	2835	2943	
30	3050	3158	3266	3374	3482	3589	3697	3805	3912	4020	
4031	4128	4236	4343	4451	4559	4667	4774	4882	4990	5098	
32	5205	5313	5421	5528	5636	5744	5851	5959	6067	6175	
33	6282	6390	6498	6605	6713	6821	6928	7036	7144	7251	
34	7359	7467	7574	7682	7790	7897	8005	8112	8220	8328	
35	8435	8543	8651	8758	8866	8974	9081	9189	9296	9404	
36	9512	9619	9727	9834	9942	0050	0157	0265	0372	0480	
37	606 0587	0695	0803	0910	1018	1125	1233	1340	1448	1556	
38	1663	1771	1878	1986	2093	2201	2308	2416	2523	2631	
39	2739	2846	2954	3061	3169	3276	3384	3491	3599	3706	
40	3814	3921	4029	4136	4244	4351	4459	4566	4674	4781	
4041	4889	4996	5103	5211	5318	5426	5533	5641	5748	5856	
42	5963	6071	6178	6285	6393	6500	6608	6715	6823	6930	
43	7037	7145	7252	7360	7467	7574	7682	7789	7897	8004	
44	8111	8219	8326	8434	8541	8648	8756	8863	8971	9078	
45	9185	9293	9400	9507	9615	9722	9829	9937	0044	0151	
46	607 0259	0366	0473	0581	0688	0795	0903	1010	1117	1225	**107**
47	1332	1439	1547	1654	1761	1869	1976	2083	2190	2298	
48	2405	2512	2620	2727	2834	2941	3049	3156	3263	3371	
49	3478	3585	3692	3800	3907	4014	4121	4229	4336	4443	
4050	4550	4657	4765	4872	4979	5086	5194	5301	5408	5515	

No.	0	1	2	3	4	5	6	7	8	9	Diff.
4050	607 4550	4657	4765	4872	4979	5086	5194	5301	5408	5515	
51	5622	5730	5837	5944	6051	6158	6266	6373	6480	6587	107
52	6694	6802	6909	7016	7123	7230	7337	7445	7552	7659	1 11
53	7766	7873	7980	8087	8195	8302	8409	8516	8623	8730	2 21
54	8837	8945	9052	9159	9266	9373	9480	9587	9694	9801	3 32
55	9909	0016	0123	0230	0337	0444	0551	0658	0765	0872	4 43
											5 54
56	608 0979	1087	1194	1301	1408	1515	1622	1729	1836	1943	6 64
57	2050	2157	2264	2371	2478	2585	2692	2799	2906	3013	7 75
58	3120	3227	3334	3441	3548	3656	3763	3870	3977	4084	8 86
59	4191	4298	4404	4511	4618	4725	4832	4939	5046	5153	9 96
60	5260	5367	5474	5581	5688	5795	5902	6009	6116	6223	
4061	6330	6437	6544	6651	6758	6865	6972	7078	7185	7292	
62	7399	7506	7613	7720	7827	7934	8041	8148	8254	8361	
63	8468	8575	8682	8789	8896	9003	9110	9216	9323	9430	
64	9537	9644	9751	9858	9964	0071	0178	0285	0392	0499	
65	609 0605	0712	0819	0926	1033	1140	1246	1353	1460	1567	
66	1674	1781	1887	1994	2101	2208	2315	2421	2528	2635	
67	2742	2849	2955	3062	3169	3276	3382	3489	3596	3703	
68	3809	3916	4023	4130	4236	4343	4450	4557	4663	4770	
69	4877	4984	5090	5197	5304	5411	5517	5624	5731	5837	
70	5944	6051	6157	6264	6371	6478	6584	6691	6798	6904	
4071	7011	7118	7224	7331	7438	7544	7651	7758	7864	7971	
72	8078	8184	8291	8398	8504	8611	8718	8824	8931	9037	
73	9144	9251	9357	9464	9571	9677	9784	9890	9997	0104	
74	610 0210	0317	0423	0530	0637	0743	0850	0956	1063	1170	
75	1276	1383	1489	1596	1702	1809	1916	2022	2129	2235	
76	2342	2448	2555	2661	2768	2874	2981	3088	3194	3301	
77	3407	3514	3620	3727	3833	3940	4046	4153	4259	4366	
78	4472	4579	4685	4792	4898	5005	5111	5218	5324	5431	
79	5537	5644	5750	5856	5963	6069	6176	6282	6389	6495	
80	6602	6708	6815	6921	7027	7134	7240	7347	7453	7560	
4081	7666	7772	7879	7985	8092	8198	8304	8411	8517	8624	
82	8730	8836	8943	9049	9156	9262	9368	9475	9581	9687	
83	9794	9900	0007	0113	0219	0326	0432	0538	0645	0751	
84	611 0857	0964	1070	1176	1283	1389	1495	1602	1708	1814	
85	1921	2027	2133	2240	2346	2452	2558	2665	2771	2877	
86	2984	3090	3196	3302	3409	3515	3621	3728	3834	3940	
87	4046	4153	4259	4365	4471	4578	4684	4790	4896	5003	
88	5109	5215	5321	5428	5534	5640	5746	5852	5959	6065	
89	6171	6277	6384	6490	6596	6702	6808	6915	7021	7127	
90	7233	7339	7445	7552	7658	7764	7870	7976	8082	8189	
4091	8295	8401	8507	8613	8719	8826	8932	9038	9144	9250	106
92	9356	9462	9569	9675	9781	9887	9993	0099	0205	0311	1 11
93	612 0417	0524	0630	0736	0842	0948	1054	1160	1266	1372	2 21
94	1478	1584	1691	1797	1903	2009	2115	2221	2327	2433	3 32
95	2539	2645	2751	2857	2963	3069	3175	3281	3387	3493	4 42
96	3599	3706	3812	3918	4024	4130	4236	4342	4448	4554	5 53
97	4660	4766	4872	4978	5084	5190	5296	5402	5508	5614	6 64
98	5720	5826	5931	6037	6143	6249	6355	6461	6567	6673	7 74
99	6779	6885	6991	7097	7203	7309	7415	7521	7627	7733	8 85
4100	7839	7944	8050	8156	8262	8368	8474	8580	8686	8792	9 95

No.	0	1	2	3	4	5	6	7	8	9	Diff.
4100	612 7839	7944	8050	8156	8262	8368	8474	8580	8686	8792	
01	8898	9004	9109	9215	9321	9427	9533	9639	9745	9851	
02	9957	0062	0168	0274	0380	0486	0592	0698	0803	0909	
03	613 1015	1121	1227	1333	1439	1544	1650	1756	1862	1968	
04	2074	2179	2285	2391	2497	2603	2708	2814	2920	3026	
05	3132	3237	3343	3449	3555	3661	3766	3872	3978	4084	
06	4189	4295	4401	4507	4613	4718	4824	4930	5036	5141	
07	5247	5353	5459	5564	5670	5776	5881	5987	6093	6199	
08	6304	6410	6516	6621	6727	6833	6939	7044	7150	7256	
09	7361	7467	7573	7678	7784	7890	7996	8101	8207	8313	
10	8418	8524	8630	8735	8841	8947	9052	9158	9263	9369	
4111	9475	9580	9686	9792	9897	0003	0109	0214	0320	0425	
12	614 0531	0637	0742	0848	0954	1059	1165	1270	1376	1482	
13	1587	1693	1798	1904	2009	2115	2221	2326	2432	2537	
14	2643	2748	2854	2960	3065	3171	3276	3382	3487	3593	
15	3698	3804	3909	4015	4121	4226	4332	4437	4543	4648	
16	4754	4859	4965	5070	5176	5281	5387	5492	5598	5703	
17	5809	5914	6020	6125	6231	6336	6442	6547	6652	6758	
18	6863	6969	7074	7180	7285	7391	7496	7602	7707	7812	
19	7918	8023	8129	8234	8340	8445	8550	8656	8761	8867	
20	8972	9078	9183	9288	9394	9499	9605	9710	9815	9921	
4121	615 0026	0132	0237	0342	0448	0553	0658	0764	0869	0975	
22	1080	1185	1291	1396	1501	1607	1712	1817	1923	2028	
23	2133	2239	2344	2449	2555	2660	2765	2871	2976	3081	
24	3187	3292	3397	3502	3608	3713	3818	3924	4029	4134	
25	4240	4345	4450	4555	4661	4766	4871	4976	5082	5187	
26	5292	5397	5503	5608	5713	5818	5924	6029	6134	6239	
27	6345	6450	6555	6660	6766	6871	6976	7081	7186	7292	
28	7397	7502	7607	7712	7818	7923	8028	8133	8238	8344	
29	8449	8554	8659	8764	8870	8975	9080	9185	9290	9395	
30	9501	9606	9711	9816	9921	0026	0131	0237	0342	0447	
4131	616 0552	0657	0762	0867	0972	1078	1183	1288	1393	1498	
32	1603	1708	1813	1918	2024	2129	2234	2339	2444	2549	
33	2654	2759	2864	2969	3074	3179	3284	3390	3495	3600	
34	3705	3810	3915	4020	4125	4230	4335	4440	4545	4650	
35	4755	4860	4965	5070	5175	5280	5385	5490	5595	5700	
36	5805	5910	6015	6120	6225	6330	6435	6540	6645	6750	
37	6855	6960	7065	7170	7275	7380	7485	7590	7695	7800	
38	7905	8010	8115	8220	8325	8430	8535	8639	8744	8849	
39	8954	9059	9164	9269	9374	9479	9584	9689	9794	9899	
40	617 0003	0108	0213	0318	0423	0528	0633	0738	0843	0947	
4141	1052	1157	1262	1367	1472	1577	1682	1786	1891	1996	
42	2101	2206	2311	2415	2520	2625	2730	2835	2940	3045	
43	3149	3254	3359	3464	3569	3673	3778	3883	3988	4093	
44	4197	4302	4407	4512	4617	4721	4826	4931	5036	5141	
45	5245	5350	5455	5560	5664	5769	5874	5979	6083	6188	
46	6293	6398	6502	6607	6712	6817	6921	7026	7131	7236	
47	7340	7445	7550	7655	7759	7864	7969	8073	8178	8283	
48	8387	8492	8597	8702	8806	8911	9016	9120	9225	9330	
49	9434	9539	9644	9748	9853	9958	0062	0167	0272	0376	
4150	618 0481	0586	0690	0795	0900	1004	1109	1213	1318	1423	

105
1 11
2 21
3 32
4 42
5 53
6 63
7 74
8 84
9 95

No.	0	1	2	3	4	5	6	7	8	9
4150	618 0481	0586	0690	0795	0900	1004	1109	1213	1318	1423
51	1527	1632	1737	1841	1946	2050	2155	2260	2364	2469
52	2573	2678	2783	2887	2992	3096	3201	3306	3410	3515
53	3619	3724	3828	3933	4038	4142	4247	4351	4456	4560
54	4665	4769	4874	4979	5083	5188	5292	5397	5501	5606
55	5710	5815	5919	6024	6128	6233	6337	6442	6546	6651
56	6755	6860	6964	7069	7173	7278	7382	7487	7591	7696
57	7800	7905	8009	8114	8218	8323	8427	8531	8636	8740
58	8845	8949	9054	9158	9263	9367	9471	9576	9680	9785
59	9889	9994	0098	0202	0307	0411	0516	0620	0725	0829
60	619 0933	1038	1142	1246	1351	1455	1560	1664	1768	1873
4161	1977	2082	2186	2290	2395	2499	2603	2708	2812	2916
62	3021	3125	3229	3334	3438	3542	3647	3751	3855	3960
63	4064	4168	4273	4377	4481	4586	4690	4794	4899	5003
64	5107	5212	5316	5420	5524	5629	5733	5837	5942	6046
65	6150	6254	6359	6463	6567	6671	6776	6880	6984	7088
66	7193	7297	7401	7505	7610	7714	7818	7922	8027	8131
67	8235	8339	8443	8548	8652	8756	8860	8964	9069	9173
68	9277	9381	9485	9590	9694	9798	9902	0006	0111	0215
69	620 0319	0423	0527	0631	0736	0840	0944	1048	1152	1256
70	1361	1465	1569	1673	1777	1881	1985	2090	2194	2298
4171	2402	2506	2610	2714	2818	2922	3027	3131	3235	3339
72	3443	3547	3651	3755	3859	3963	4068	4172	4276	4380
73	4484	4588	4692	4796	4900	5004	5108	5212	5316	5420
74	5524	5628	5733	5837	5941	6045	6149	6253	6357	6461
75	6565	6669	6773	6877	6981	7085	7189	7293	7397	7501
76	7605	7709	7813	7917	8021	8125	8229	8333	8437	8541
77	8645	8749	8853	8957	9061	9165	9269	9373	9476	9580
78	9684	9788	9892	9996	0100	0204	0308	0412	0516	0620
79	621 0724	0828	0932	1035	1139	1243	1347	1451	1555	1659
80	1763	1867	1971	2075	2178	2282	2386	2490	2594	2698
4181	2802	2906	3009	3113	3217	3321	3425	3529	3633	3736
82	3840	3944	4048	4152	4256	4359	4463	4567	4671	4775
83	4879	4982	5086	5190	5294	5398	5502	5605	5709	5813
84	5917	6021	6124	6228	6332	6436	6540	6643	6747	6851
85	6955	7058	7162	7266	7370	7473	7577	7681	7785	7888
86	7992	8096	8200	8303	8407	8511	8615	8718	8822	8926
87	9030	9133	9237	9341	9444	9548	9652	9756	9859	9963
88	622 0067	0170	0274	0378	0482	0585	0689	0793	0896	1000
89	1104	1207	1311	1415	1518	1622	1726	1829	1933	2037
90	2140	2244	2348	2451	2555	2658	2762	2866	2969	3073
4191	3177	3280	3384	3487	3591	3695	3798	3902	4006	4109
92	4213	4316	4420	4524	4627	4731	4834	4938	5041	5145
93	5249	5352	5456	5559	5663	5766	5870	5974	6077	6181
94	6284	6388	6491	6595	6698	6802	6906	7009	7113	7216
95	7320	7423	7527	7630	7734	7837	7941	8044	8148	8251
96	8355	8458	8562	8665	8769	8872	8976	9079	9183	9286
97	9390	9493	9597	9700	9804	9907	0011	0114	0217	0321
98	623 0424	0528	0631	0735	0838	0942	1045	1148	1252	1355
99	1459	1562	1666	1769	1872	1976	2079	2183	2286	2389
4200	2493	2596	2700	2803	2906	3010	3113	3217	3320	3423

Diff.

104

1	10
2	21
3	31
4	42
5	52
6	62
7	73
8	83
9	94

No.	0	1	2	3	4	5	6	7	8	9	Diff.
4200	623 2493	2596	2700	2803	2906	3010	3113	3217	3320	3423	
01	3527	3630	3734	3837	3940	4044	4147	4250	4354	4457	
02	4560	4664	4767	4871	4974	5077	5181	5284	5387	5491	
03	5594	5697	5801	5904	6007	6111	6214	6317	6420	6524	
04	6627	6730	6834	6937	7040	7144	7247	7350	7453	7557	
05	7660	7763	7867	7970	8073	8176	8280	8383	8486	8589	
06	8693	8796	8899	9002	9106	9209	9312	9415	9519	9622	
07	9725	9828	9932	0035	0138	0241	0344	0448	0551	0654	
08	624 0757	0861	0964	1067	1170	1273	1377	1480	1583	1686	
09	1789	1892	1996	2099	2202	2305	2408	2511	2615	2718	
10	2821	2924	3027	3130	3234	3337	3440	3543	3646	3749	
4211	3852	3956	4059	4162	4265	4368	4471	4574	4677	4781	
12	4884	4987	5090	5193	5296	5399	5502	5605	5708	5812	
13	5915	6018	6121	6224	6327	6430	6533	6636	6739	6842	
14	6945	7048	7151	7254	7358	7461	7564	7667	7770	7873	
15	7976	8079	8182	8285	8388	8491	8594	8697	8800	8903	
16	9006	9109	9212	9315	9418	9521	9624	9727	9830	9933	
17	625 0036	0139	0242	0345	0448	0551	0654	0757	0860	0963	
18	1066	1169	1272	1375	1478	1581	1683	1786	1889	1992	
19	2095	2198	2301	2404	2507	2610	2713	2816	2919	3022	
20	3125	3227	3330	3433	3536	3639	3742	3845	3948	4051	
4221	4154	4256	4359	4462	4565	4668	4771	4874	4977	5079	
22	5182	5285	5388	5491	5594	5697	5799	5902	6005	6108	
23	6211	6314	6416	6519	6622	6725	6828	6931	7033	7136	
24	7239	7342	7445	7548	7650	7753	7856	7959	8062	8164	
25	8267	8370	8473	8575	8678	8781	8884	8987	9089	9192	
26	9295	9398	9500	9603	9706	9809	9911	0014	0117	0220	
27	626 0322	0425	0528	0631	0733	0836	0939	1042	1144	1247	
28	1350	1453	1555	1658	1761	1863	1966	2069	2171	2274	103
29	2377	2480	2582	2685	2788	2890	2993	3096	3198	3301	1 10
30	3404	3506	3609	3712	3814	3917	4020	4122	4225	4328	2 21
4231	4430	4533	4636	4738	4841	4943	5046	5149	5251	5354	3 31
32	5457	5559	5662	5764	5867	5970	6072	6175	6277	6380	4 41
33	6483	6585	6688	6790	6893	6996	7098	7201	7303	7406	5 52
34	7509	7611	7714	7816	7919	8021	8124	8226	8329	8432	6 62
35	8534	8637	8739	8842	8944	9047	9149	9252	9354	9457	7 72
36	9560	9662	9765	9867	9970	0072	0175	0277	0380	0482	8 82
37	627 0585	0687	0790	0892	0995	1097	1200	1302	1405	1507	9 93
38	1610	1712	1814	1917	2019	2122	2224	2327	2429	2532	
39	2634	2737	2839	2942	3044	3146	3249	3351	3454	3556	
40	3659	3761	3863	3966	4068	4171	4273	4376	4478	4580	
4241	4683	4785	4888	4990	5092	5195	5297	5399	5502	5604	
42	5707	5809	5911	6014	6116	6219	6321	6423	6526	6628	
43	6730	6833	6935	7037	7140	7242	7344	7447	7549	7651	
44	7754	7856	7958	8061	8163	8265	8368	8470	8572	8675	
45	8777	8879	8982	9084	9186	9288	9391	9493	9595	9698	
46	9800	9902	0004	0107	0209	0311	0414	0516	0618	0720	
47	628 0823	0925	1027	1129	1232	1334	1436	1538	1641	1743	
48	1845	1947	2050	2152	2254	2356	2458	2561	2663	2765	
49	2867	2970	3072	3174	3276	3378	3481	3583	3685	3787	
4250	3889	3991	4094	4196	4298	4400	4502	4605	4707	4809	

No.	0	1	2	3	4	5	6	7	8	9	Diff.
4250	628 3889	3991	4094	4196	4298	4400	4502	4605	4707	4809	
51	4911	5013	5115	5218	5320	5422	5524	5626	5728	5830	
52	5933	6035	6137	6239	6341	6443	6545	6647	6750	6852	
53	6954	7056	7158	7260	7362	7464	7566	7669	7771	7873	
54	7975	8077	8179	8281	8383	8485	8587	8689	8792	8894	
55	8996	9098	9200	9302	9404	9506	9608	9710	9812	9914	
56	629 0016	0118	0220	0322	0424	0526	0628	0730	0832	0934	
57	1037	1139	1241	1343	1445	1547	1649	1751	1853	1955	
58	2057	2159	2261	2363	2465	2567	2668	2770	2872	2974	
59	3076	3178	3280	3382	3484	3586	3688	3790	3892	3994	
60	4096	4198	4300	4402	4504	4606	4708	4810	4911	5013	
4261	5115	5217	5319	5421	5523	5625	5727	5829	5931	6033	
62	6134	6236	6338	6440	6542	6644	6746	6848	6950	7051	
63	7153	7255	7357	7459	7561	7663	7765	7866	7968	8070	
64	8172	8274	8376	8478	8579	8681	8783	8885	8987	9089	102
65	9190	9292	9394	9496	9598	9699	9801	9903	0005	0107	1 10
66	630 0209	0310	0412	0514	0616	0717	0819	0921	1023	1125	2 20
67	1226	1328	1430	1532	1634	1735	1837	1939	2041	2142	3 31
68	2244	2346	2448	2549	2651	2753	2855	2956	3058	3160	4 41
69	3262	3363	3465	3567	3668	3770	3872	3974	4075	4177	5 51
70	4279	4380	4482	4584	4686	4787	4889	4991	5092	5194	6 61 / 7 71
4271	5296	5397	5499	5601	5702	5804	5906	6007	6109	6211	8 82
72	6312	6414	6516	6617	6719	6821	6922	7024	7126	7227	9 92
73	7329	7431	7532	7634	7735	7837	7939	8040	8142	8244	
74	8345	8447	8548	8650	8752	8853	8955	9056	9158	9260	
75	9361	9463	9564	9666	9768	9869	9971	0072	0174	0275	
76	631 0377	0479	0580	0682	0783	0885	0986	1088	1189	1291	
77	1393	1494	1596	1697	1799	1900	2002	2103	2205	2306	
78	2408	2509	2611	2712	2814	2915	3017	3118	3220	3321	
79	3423	3524	3626	3727	3829	3930	4032	4133	4235	4336	
80	4438	4539	4641	4742	4844	4945	5046	5148	5249	5351	
4281	5452	5554	5655	5757	5858	5959	6061	6162	6264	6365	
82	6467	6568	6669	6771	6872	6974	7075	7177	7278	7379	
83	7481	7582	7684	7785	7886	7988	8089	8190	8292	8393	
84	8495	8596	8697	8799	8900	9001	9103	9204	9306	9407	
85	9508	9610	9711	9812	9914	0015	0116	0218	0319	0420	
86	632 0522	0623	0724	0826	0927	1028	1130	1231	1332	1434	
87	1535	1636	1737	1839	1940	2041	2143	2244	2345	2446	101
88	2548	2649	2750	2852	2953	3054	3155	3257	3358	3459	1 10
89	3560	3662	3763	3864	3965	4067	4168	4269	4370	4472	2 20 / 3 30
90	4573	4674	4775	4877	4978	5079	5180	5282	5383	5484	4 40
4291	5585	5686	5788	5889	5990	6091	6192	6294	6395	6496	5 51
92	6597	6698	6800	6901	7002	7103	7204	7305	7407	7508	6 61 / 7 71
93	7609	7710	7811	7912	8014	8115	8216	8317	8418	8519	8 81
94	8620	8722	8823	8924	9025	9126	9227	9328	9429	9531	9 91
95	9632	9733	9834	9935	0036	0137	0238	0339	0441	0542	
96	633 0643	0744	0845	0946	1047	1148	1249	1350	1451	1552	
97	1654	1755	1856	1957	2058	2159	2260	2361	2462	2563	
98	2664	2765	2866	2967	3068	3169	3270	3371	3472	3573	
99	3674	3775	3876	3978	4079	4180	4281	4382	4483	4584	
4300	4685	4786	4887	4988	5089	5190	5291	5391	5492	5593	

No.	0	1	2	3	4	5	6	7	8	9	Diff.
4300	633 4685	4786	4887	4988	5089	5190	5291	5391	5492	5593	
01	5694	5795	5896	5997	6098	6199	6300	6401	6502	6603	
02	6704	6805	6906	7007	7108	7209	7310	7411	7512	7613	
03	7713	7814	7915	8016	8117	8218	8319	8420	8521	8622	
04	8723	8824	8924	9025	9126	9227	9328	9429	9530	9631	
05	9732	9832	9933	0034	0135	0236	0337	0438	0539	0639	
06	634 0740	0841	0942	1043	1144	1245	1345	1446	1547	1648	
07	1749	1850	1950	2051	2152	2253	2354	2455	2555	2656	
08	2757	2858	2959	3059	3160	3261	3362	3463	3563	3664	
09	3765	3866	3967	4067	4168	4269	4370	4470	4571	4672	
10	4773	4873	4974	5075	5176	5276	5377	5478	5579	5679	
4311	5780	5881	5982	6082	6183	6284	6385	6485	6586	6687	
12	6788	6888	6989	7090	7190	7291	7392	7492	7593	7694	
13	7795	7895	7996	8097	8197	8298	8399	8499	8600	8701	
14	8801	8902	9003	9103	9204	9305	9405	9506	9607	9707	
15	9808	9909	0009	0110	0211	0311	0412	0512	0613	0714	
16	635 0814	0915	1016	1116	1217	1317	1418	1519	1619	1720	
17	1820	1921	2022	2122	2223	2323	2424	2525	2625	2726	
18	2826	2927	3028	3128	3229	3329	3430	3530	3631	3731	
19	3832	3933	4033	4134	4234	4335	4435	4536	4636	4737	
20	4837	4938	5039	5139	5240	5340	5441	5541	5642	5742	100
4321	5843	5943	6044	6144	6245	6345	6446	6546	6647	6747	1 10
22	6848	6948	7049	7149	7250	7350	7450	7551	7651	7752	2 20
23	7852	7953	8053	8154	8254	8355	8455	8556	8656	8756	3 30
24	8857	8957	9058	9158	9259	9359	9459	9560	9660	9761	4 40
25	9861	9962	0062	0162	0263	0363	0464	0564	0664	0765	5 50
26	636 0865	0966	1066	1166	1267	1367	1467	1568	1668	1769	6 60
27	1869	1969	2070	2170	2270	2371	2471	2571	2672	2772	7 70
28	2873	2973	3073	3174	3274	3374	3475	3575	3675	3776	8 80
29	3876	3976	4076	4177	4277	4377	4478	4578	4678	4779	9 90
30	4879	4979	5080	5180	5280	5380	5481	5581	5681	5782	
4331	5882	5982	6082	6183	6283	6383	6483	6584	6684	6784	
32	6884	6985	7085	7185	7285	7386	7486	7586	7686	7787	
33	7887	7987	8087	8188	8288	8388	8488	8588	8689	8789	
34	8889	8989	9089	9190	9290	9390	9490	9590	9691	9791	
35	9891	9991	0091	0192	0292	0392	0492	0592	0692	0793	
36	637 0893	0993	1093	1193	1293	1394	1494	1594	1694	1794	
37	1894	1994	2094	2195	2295	2395	2495	2595	2695	2795	
38	2895	2996	3096	3196	3296	3396	3496	3596	3696	3796	
39	3897	3997	4097	4197	4297	4397	4497	4597	4697	4797	
40	4897	4997	5097	5197	5298	5398	5498	5598	5698	5798	
4341	5898	5998	6098	6198	6298	6398	6498	6598	6698	6798	
42	6898	6998	7098	7198	7298	7398	7498	7598	7698	7798	
43	7898	7998	8098	8198	8298	8398	8498	8598	8698	8798	
44	8898	8998	9098	9198	9298	9398	9498	9598	9698	9798	
45	9898	9998	0098	0198	0298	0398	0497	0597	0697	0797	
46	638 0897	0997	1097	1197	1297	1397	1497	1597	1697	1796	
47	1896	1996	2096	2196	2296	2396	2496	2596	2696	2795	
48	2895	2995	3095	3195	3295	3395	3495	3594	3694	3794	
49	3894	3994	4094	4194	4294	4393	4493	4593	4693	4793	
4350	4893	4992	5092	5192	5292	5392	5492	5591	5691	5791	

No.	0	1	2	3	4	5	6	7	8	9		
4350	638 4893	4992	5092	5192	5292	5392	5492	5591	5691	5791		
51	5891	5991	6090	6190	6290	6390	6490	6589	6689	6789		
52	6889	6989	7088	7188	7288	7388	7488	7587	7687	7787		
53	7887	7986	8086	8186	8286	8385	8485	8585	8685	8784		
54	8884	8984	9084	9183	9283	9383	9483	9582	9682	9782		
55	9882	9981	0081	0181	0280	0380	0480	0580	0679	0779		
56	639 0879	0978	1078	1178	1277	1377	1477	1577	1676	1776		
57	1876	1975	2075	2175	2274	2374	2474	2573	2673	2773		
58	2872	2972	3072	3171	3271	3371	3470	3570	3669	3769		
59	3869	3968	4068	4168	4267	4367	4466	4566	4666	4765		
60	4865	4965	5064	5164	5263	5363	5463	5562	5662	5761		
4361	5861	5960	6060	6160	6259	6359	6458	6558	6657	6757		
62	6857	6956	7056	7155	7255	7354	7454	7553	7653	7753		
63	7852	7952	8051	8151	8250	8350	8449	8549	8648	8748		
64	8847	8947	9046	9146	9245	9345	9444	9544	9643	9743		
65	9842	9942	0041	0141	0240	0340	0439	0539	0638	0738		
66	640 0837	0937	1036	1136	1235	1335	1434	1534	1633	1732		
67	1832	1931	2031	2130	2230	2329	2429	2528	2627	2727		
68	2826	2926	3025	3125	3224	3323	3423	3522	3622	3721		
69	3820	3920	4019	4119	4218	4317	4417	4516	4616	4715		
70	4814	4914	5013	5113	5212	5311	5411	5510	5609	5709		
4371	5808	5907	6007	6106	6205	6305	6404	6504	6603	6702		
72	6802	6901	7000	7100	7199	7298	7398	7497	7596	7695		
73	7795	7894	7993	8093	8192	8291	8391	8490	8589	8688		
74	8788	8887	8986	9086	9185	9284	9383	9483	9582	9681		
75	9781	9880	9979	0078	0178	0277	0376	0475	0575	0674		
76	641 0773	0872	0972	1071	1170	1269	1369	1468	1567	1666		
77	1765	1865	1964	2063	2162	2262	2361	2460	2559	2658		
78	2758	2857	2956	3055	3154	3254	3353	3452	3551	3650		
79	3749	3849	3948	4047	4146	4245	4344	4444	4543	4642		
80	4741	4840	4939	5039	5138	5237	5336	5435	5534	5633		
4381	5733	5832	5931	6030	6129	6228	6327	6426	6526	6625		
82	6724	6823	6922	7021	7120	7219	7318	7417	7517	7616		
83	7715	7814	7913	8012	8111	8210	8309	8408	8507	8606		
84	8705	8805	8904	9003	9102	9201	9300	9399	9498	9597		
85	9696	9795	9894	9993	0092	0191	0290	0389	0488	0587		
86	642 0686	0785	0884	0983	1082	1181	1280	1379	1478	1577		
87	1676	1775	1874	1973	2072	2171	2270	2369	2468	2567		
88	2666	2765	2864	2963	3062	3161	3260	3359	3458	3557		
89	3656	3755	3854	3953	4052	4151	4249	4348	4447	4546		
90	4645	4744	4843	4942	5041	5140	5239	5338	5437	5535		
4391	5634	5733	5832	5931	6030	6129	6228	6327	6426	6524		
92	6623	6722	6821	6920	7019	7118	7217	7315	7414	7513		
93	7612	7711	7810	7909	8007	8106	8205	8304	8403	8502		
94	8601	8699	8798	8897	8996	9095	9194	9292	9391	9490		
95	9589	9688	9786	9885	9984	0083	0182	0280	0379	0478		
96	643 0577	0676	0774	0873	0972	1071	1170	1268	1367	1466		
97	1565	1663	1762	1861	1960	2058	2157	2256	2355	2454		
98	2552	2651	2750	2848	2947	3046	3145	3243	3342	3441		
99	3540	3638	3737	3836	3935	4033	4132	4231	4329	4428		
4400	4527	4625	4724	4823	4922	5020	5119	5218	5316	5415		

99
1	10
2	20
3	30
4	40
5	50
6	59
7	69
8	79
9	89

No.	0	1	2	3	4	5	6	7	8	9	Diff.
4400	643 4527	4625	4724	4823	4922	5020	5119	5218	5316	5415	
01	5514	5612	5711	5810	5908	6007	6106	6204	6303	6402	
02	6500	6599	6698	6796	6895	6994	7092	7191	7290	7388	
03	7487	7585	7684	7783	7881	7980	8079	8177	8276	8374	
04	8473	8572	8670	8769	8868	8966	9065	9163	9262	9361	
05	9459	9558	9656	9755	9853	9952	0051	0149	0248	0346	
06	644 0445	0543	0642	0741	0839	0938	1036	1135	1233	1332	
07	1431	1529	1628	1726	1825	1923	2022	2120	2219	2317	
08	2416	2514	2613	2711	2810	2908	3007	3105	3204	3302	
09	3401	3499	3598	3696	3795	3893	3992	4090	4189	4287	
10	4386	4484	4583	4681	4780	4878	4977	5075	5174	5272	
4411	5371	5469	5567	5666	5764	5863	5961	6060	6158	6257	
12	6355	6453	6552	6650	6749	6847	6946	7044	7142	7241	
13	7339	7438	7536	7635	7733	7831	7930	8028	8127	8225	
14	8323	8422	8520	8618	8717	8815	8914	9012	9110	9209	
15	9307	9405	9504	9602	9701	9799	9897	9996	0094	0192	
16	645 0291	0389	0487	0586	0684	0782	0881	0979	1077	1176	
17	1274	1372	1471	1569	1667	1766	1864	1962	2061	2159	
18	2257	2355	2454	2552	2650	2749	2847	2945	3043	3142	
19	3240	3338	3437	3535	3633	3731	3830	3928	4026	4124	
20	4223	4321	4419	4517	4616	4714	4812	4910	5009	5107	
4421	5205	5303	5402	5500	5598	5696	5795	5893	5991	6089	
22	6187	6286	6384	6482	6580	6678	6777	6875	6973	7071	
23	7169	7268	7366	7464	7562	7660	7758	7857	7955	8053	
24	8151	8249	8348	8446	8544	8642	8740	8838	8936	9035	
25	9133	9231	9329	9427	9525	9623	9722	9820	9918	0016	
26	646 0114	0212	0310	0408	0507	0605	0703	0801	0899	0997	
27	1095	1193	1291	1390	1488	1586	1684	1782	1880	1978	
28	2076	2174	2272	2370	2468	2566	2665	2763	2861	2959	
29	3057	3155	3253	3351	3449	3547	3645	3743	3841	3939	
30	4037	4135	4233	4331	4429	4527	4625	4723	4821	4919	
4431	5018	5116	5214	5312	5410	5508	5606	5704	5802	5900	
32	5998	6096	6193	6291	6389	6487	6585	6683	6781	6879	
33	6977	7075	7173	7271	7369	7467	7565	7663	7761	7859	
34	7957	8055	8153	8251	8349	8447	8545	8642	8740	8838	
35	8936	9034	9132	9230	9328	9426	9524	9622	9720	9817	
36	9915	0013	0111	0209	0307	0405	0503	0601	0699	0796	
37	647 0894	0992	1090	1188	1286	1384	1482	1579	1677	1775	
38	1873	1971	2069	2167	2264	2362	2460	2558	2656	2754	
39	2851	2949	3047	3145	3243	3341	3438	3536	3634	3732	
40	3830	3928	4025	4123	4221	4319	4417	4514	4612	4710	
4441	4808	4906	5003	5101	5199	5297	5394	5492	5590	5688	
42	5786	5883	5981	6079	6177	6274	6372	6470	6568	6665	
43	6763	6861	6959	7056	7154	7252	7350	7447	7545	7643	
44	7741	7838	7936	8034	8131	8229	8327	8425	8522	8620	
45	8718	8815	8913	9011	9108	9206	9304	9402	9499	9597	
46	9695	9792	9890	9988	0085	0183	0281	0378	0476	0574	
47	648 0671	0769	0867	0964	1062	1160	1257	1355	1453	1550	
48	1648	1745	1843	1941	2038	2136	2234	2331	2429	2526	
49	2624	2722	2819	2917	3015	3112	3210	3307	3405	3503	
4450	3600	3698	3795	3893	3990	4088	4186	4283	4381	4478	

98

1	10
2	20
3	29
4	39
5	49
6	59
7	69
8	78
9	88

4450

No.	0	1	2	3	4	5	6	7	8	9	Diff.
4450	648 3600	3698	3795	3893	3990	4088	4186	4283	4381	4478	
51	4576	4674	4771	4869	4966	5064	5161	5259	5356	5454	
52	5552	5649	5747	5844	5942	6039	6137	6234	6332	6429	
53	6527	6624	6722	6820	6917	7015	7112	7210	7307	7405	
54	7502	7600	7697	7795	7892	7990	8087	8185	8282	8380	
55	8477	8575	8672	8770	8867	8964	9062	9159	9257	9354	
56	9452	9549	9647	9744	9842	9939	0037	0134	0231	0329	
57	649 0426	0524	0621	0719	0816	0914	1011	1108	1206	1303	
58	1401	1498	1595	1693	1790	1888	1985	2083	2180	2277	
59	2375	2472	2570	2667	2764	2862	2959	3056	3154	3251	
60	3349	3446	3543	3641	3738	3835	3933	4030	4128	4225	
4461	4322	4420	4517	4614	4712	4809	4906	5004	5101	5198	
62	5296	5393	5490	5588	5685	5782	5880	5977	6074	6172	
63	6269	6366	6463	6561	6658	6755	6853	6950	7047	7145	
64	7242	7339	7436	7534	7631	7728	7826	7923	8020	8117	
65	8215	8312	8409	8506	8604	8701	8798	8895	8993	9090	
66	9187	9284	9382	9479	9576	9673	9771	9868	9965	0062	
67	650 0160	0257	0354	0451	0548	0646	0743	0840	0937	1034	
68	1132	1229	1326	1423	1520	1618	1715	1812	1909	2006	
69	2104	2201	2298	2395	2492	2589	2687	2784	2881	2978	
70	3075	3172	3270	3367	3464	3561	3658	3755	3852	3950	
4471	4047	4144	4241	4338	4435	4532	4629	4727	4824	4921	
72	5018	5115	5212	5309	5406	5503	5601	5698	5795	5892	
73	5989	6086	6183	6280	6377	6474	6571	6669	6766	6863	
74	6960	7057	7154	7251	7348	7445	7542	7639	7736	7833	
75	7930	8027	8124	8222	8319	8416	8513	8610	8707	8804	
76	8901	8998	9095	9192	9289	9386	9483	9580	9677	9774	
77	9871	9968	0065	0162	0259	0356	0453	0550	0647	0744	
78	651 0841	0938	1035	1132	1229	1326	1423	1520	1617	1714	
79	1811	1908	2005	2102	2198	2295	2392	2489	2586	2683	
80	2780	2877	2974	3071	3168	3265	3362	3459	3556	3653	
4481	3749	3846	3943	4040	4137	4234	4331	4428	4525	4622	
82	4719	4815	4912	5009	5106	5203	5300	5397	5494	5591	
83	5687	5784	5881	5978	6075	6172	6269	6365	6462	6559	
84	6656	6753	6850	6947	7043	7140	7237	7334	7431	7528	
85	7624	7721	7818	7915	8012	8109	8205	8302	8399	8496	
86	8593	8690	8786	8883	8980	9077	9174	9270	9367	9464	
87	9561	9657	9754	9851	9948	0045	0141	0238	0335	0432	
88	652 0528	0625	0722	0819	0916	1012	1109	1206	1303	1399	
89	1496	1593	1690	1786	1883	1980	2076	2173	2270	2367	
90	2463	2560	2657	2754	2850	2947	3044	3140	3237	3334	
4491	3431	3527	3624	3721	3817	3914	4011	4107	4204	4301	
92	4397	4494	4591	4688	4784	4881	4978	5074	5171	5268	
93	5364	5461	5558	5654	5751	5847	5944	6041	6137	6234	
94	6331	6427	6524	6621	6717	6814	6910	7007	7104	7200	
95	7297	7394	7490	7587	7683	7780	7877	7973	8070	8166	
96	8263	8360	8456	8553	8649	8746	8843	8939	9036	9132	
97	9229	9325	9422	9519	9615	9712	9808	9905	0001	0098	
98	653 0195	0291	0388	0484	0581	0677	0774	0870	0967	1063	
99	1160	1256	1353	1450	1546	1643	1739	1836	1932	2029	
4500	2125	2222	2318	2415	2511	2608	2704	2801	2897	2994	

97

1	10
2	19
3	29
4	39
5	49
6	58
7	68
8	78
9	87

No.	0	1	2	3	4	5	6	7	8	9	Diff.
4500	653 2125	2222	2318	2415	2511	2608	2704	2801	2897	2994	
01	3090	3187	3283	3380	3476	3573	3669	3765	3862	3958	
02	4055	4151	4248	4344	4441	4537	4634	4730	4827	4923	
03	5019	5116	5212	5309	5405	5502	5598	5695	5791	5887	
04	5984	6080	6177	6273	6369	6466	6562	6659	6755	6852	
05	6948	7044	7141	7237	7334	7430	7526	7623	7719	7815	
06	7912	8008	8105	8201	8297	8394	8490	8586	8683	8779	
07	8876	8972	9068	9165	9261	9357	9454	9550	9646	9743	
08	9839	9935	0032	0128	0224	0321	0417	0513	0610	0706	
09	654 0802	0899	0995	1091	1188	1284	1380	1477	1573	1669	
10	1765	1862	1958	2054	2151	2247	2343	2439	2536	2632	
4511	2728	2825	2921	3017	3113	3210	3306	3402	3498	3595	
12	3691	3787	3883	3980	4076	4172	4268	4365	4461	4557	
13	4653	4750	4846	4942	5038	5134	5231	5327	5423	5519	
14	5616	5712	5808	5904	6000	6097	6193	6289	6385	6481	
15	6578	6674	6770	6866	6962	7058	7155	7251	7347	7443	
16	7539	7635	7732	7828	7924	8020	8116	8212	8309	8405	
17	8501	8597	8693	8789	8885	8982	9078	9174	9270	9366	
18	9462	9558	9655	9751	9847	9943	0039	0135	0231	0327	
19	655 0423	0520	0616	0712	0808	0904	1000	1096	1192	1288	
20	1384	1480	1577	1673	1769	1865	1961	2057	2153	2249	
4521	2345	2441	2537	2633	2729	2825	2921	3017	3113	3210	
22	3306	3402	3498	3594	3690	3786	3882	3978	4074	4170	
23	4266	4362	4458	4554	4650	4746	4842	4938	5034	5130	
24	5226	5322	5418	5514	5610	5706	5802	5898	5994	6090	
25	6186	6282	6378	6474	6570	6666	6762	6858	6954	7050	
26	7145	7241	7337	7433	7529	7625	7721	7817	7913	8009	
27	8105	8201	8297	8393	8489	8585	8681	8776	8872	8968	
28	9064	9160	9256	9352	9448	9544	9640	9736	9831	9927	
29	656 0023	0119	0215	0311	0407	0503	0599	0694	0790	0886	
30	0982	1078	1174	1270	1365	1461	1557	1653	1749	1845	
4531	1941	2036	2132	2228	2324	2420	2516	2612	2707	2803	
32	2899	2995	3091	3186	3282	3378	3474	3570	3666	3761	
33	3857	3953	4049	4145	4240	4336	4432	4528	4624	4719	
34	4815	4911	5007	5103	5198	5294	5390	5486	5581	5677	
35	5773	5869	5964	6060	6156	6252	6347	6443	6539	6635	
36	6730	6826	6922	7018	7113	7209	7305	7401	7496	7592	
37	7688	7784	7879	7975	8071	8166	8262	8358	8454	8549	
38	8645	8741	8836	8932	9028	9123	9219	9315	9410	9506	
39	9602	9698	9793	9889	9985	0080	0176	0272	0367	0463	
40	657 0559	0654	0750	0845	0941	1037	1132	1228	1324	1419	
4541	1515	1611	1706	1802	1898	1993	2089	2184	2280	2376	
42	2471	2567	2663	2758	2854	2949	3045	3141	3236	3332	
43	3427	3523	3619	3714	3810	3905	4001	4096	4192	4288	
44	4383	4479	4574	4670	4766	4861	4957	5052	5148	5243	
45	5339	5434	5530	5626	5721	5817	5912	6008	6103	6199	
46	6294	6390	6485	6581	6676	6772	6867	6963	7059	7154	
47	7250	7345	7441	7536	7632	7727	7823	7918	8014	8109	
48	8205	8300	8396	8491	8587	8682	8777	8873	8968	9064	
49	9159	9255	9350	9446	9541	9637	9732	9828	9923	0019	
4550	658 0114	0209	0305	0400	0496	0591	0687	0782	0877	0973	

Diff.

96

1	10
2	19
3	29
4	38
5	48
6	58
7	67
8	77
9	86

No.	0	1	2	3	4	5	6	7	8	9	Diff.
4550	658 0114	0209	0305	0400	0496	0591	0687	0782	0877	0973	
51	1068	1164	1259	1355	1450	1545	1641	1736	1832	1927	
52	2023	2118	2213	2309	2404	2500	2595	2690	2786	2881	
53	2977	3072	3167	3263	3358	3453	3549	3644	3740	3835	
54	3930	4026	4121	4216	4312	4407	4502	4598	4693	4788	
55	4884	4979	5074	5170	5265	5361	5456	5551	5647	5742	
56	5837	5932	6028	6123	6218	6314	6409	6504	6600	6695	
57	6790	6886	6981	7076	7171	7267	7362	7457	7553	7648	
58	7743	7838	7934	8029	8124	8220	8315	8410	8505	8601	
59	8696	8791	8886	8982	9077	9172	9267	9363	9458	9553	
60	9648	9744	9839	9934	0029	0125	0220	0315	0410	0506	
4561	659 0601	0696	0791	0886	0982	1077	1172	1267	1362	1458	
62	1553	1648	1743	1838	1934	2029	2124	2219	2314	2410	
63	2505	2600	2695	2790	2885	2981	3076	3171	3266	3361	
64	3456	3552	3647	3742	3837	3932	4027	4122	4218	4313	
65	4408	4503	4598	4693	4788	4883	4979	5074	5169	5264	
66	5359	5454	5549	5644	5740	5835	5930	6025	6120	6215	
67	6310	6405	6500	6595	6690	6786	6881	6976	7071	7166	
68	7261	7356	7451	7546	7641	7736	7831	7926	8021	8117	
69	8212	8307	8402	8497	8592	8687	8782	8877	8972	9067	
70	9162	9257	9352	9447	9542	9637	9732	9827	9922	0017	
4571	660 0112	0207	0302	0397	0492	0587	0682	0777	0872	0967	
72	1062	1157	1252	1347	1442	1537	1632	1727	1822	1917	
73	2012	2107	2202	2297	2392	2487	2582	2677	2772	2867	
74	2962	3057	3151	3246	3341	3436	3531	3626	3721	3816	
75	3911	4006	4101	4196	4291	4386	4481	4575	4670	4765	
76	4860	4955	5050	5145	5240	5335	5430	5524	5619	5714	
77	5809	5904	5999	6094	6189	6284	6378	6473	6568	6663	
78	6758	6853	6948	7042	7137	7232	7327	7422	7517	7612	
79	7706	7801	7896	7991	8086	8181	8275	8370	8465	8560	
80	8655	8750	8844	8939	9034	9129	9224	9318	9413	9508	
4581	9603	9698	9793	9887	9982	0077	0172	0266	0361	0456	
82	661 0551	0646	0740	0835	0930	1025	1120	1214	1309	1404	
83	1499	1593	1688	1783	1878	1972	2067	2162	2257	2351	
84	2446	2541	2636	2730	2825	2920	3015	3109	3204	3299	
85	3393	3488	3583	3678	3772	3867	3962	4056	4151	4246	
86	4341	4435	4530	4625	4719	4814	4909	5003	5098	5193	
87	5287	5382	5477	5571	5666	5761	5855	5950	6045	6139	
88	6234	6329	6423	6518	6613	6707	6802	6897	6991	7086	
89	7181	7275	7370	7464	7559	7654	7748	7843	7938	8032	
90	8127	8221	8316	8411	8505	8600	8695	8789	8884	8978	
4591	9073	9168	9262	9357	9451	9546	9640	9735	9830	9924	
92	662 0019	0113	0208	0303	0397	0492	0586	0681	0775	0870	
93	0964	1059	1154	1248	1343	1437	1532	1626	1721	1815	
94	1910	2004	2099	2194	2288	2383	2477	2572	2666	2761	
95	2855	2950	3044	3139	3233	3328	3422	3517	3611	3706	
96	3800	3895	3989	4084	4178	4273	4367	4462	4556	4651	
97	4745	4840	4934	5028	5123	5217	5312	5406	5501	5595	
98	5690	5784	5879	5973	6067	6162	6256	6351	6445	6540	
99	6634	6729	6823	6917	7012	7106	7201	7295	7389	7484	
4600	7578	7673	7767	7862	7956	8050	8145	8239	8334	8428	

Diff. 95:

	95
1	10
2	19
3	29
4	38
5	48
6	57
7	67
8	76
9	86

No.	0	1	2	3	4	5	6	7	8	9	Diff.
4600	662 7578	7673	7767	7862	7956	8050	8145	8239	8334	8428	
01	8522	8617	8711	8805	8900	8994	9089	9183	9277	9372	
02	9466	9561	9655	9749	9844	9938	0032	0127	0221	0315	
03	663 0410	0504	0598	0693	0787	0881	0976	1070	1164	1259	
04	1353	1447	1542	1636	1730	1825	1919	2013	2108	2202	
05	2296	2391	2485	2579	2674	2768	2862	2956	3051	3145	
06	3239	3334	3428	3522	3616	3711	3805	3899	3994	4088	
07	4182	4276	4371	4465	4559	4653	4748	4842	4936	5030	
08	5125	5219	5313	5407	5502	5596	5690	5784	5879	5973	
09	6067	6161	6256	6350	6444	6538	6632	6727	6821	6915	
10	7009	7103	7198	7292	7386	7480	7574	7669	7763	7857	
4611	7951	8045	8140	8234	8328	8422	8516	8610	8705	8799	
12	8893	8987	9081	9175	9270	9364	9458	9552	9646	9740	
13	9835	9929	0023	0117	0211	0305	0399	0494	0588	0682	
14	664 0776	0870	0964	1058	1152	1247	1341	1435	1529	1623	
15	1717	1811	1905	1999	2093	2188	2282	2376	2470	2564	
16	2658	2752	2846	2940	3034	3128	3222	3317	3411	3505	
17	3599	3693	3787	3881	3975	4069	4163	4257	4351	4445	
18	4539	4633	4727	4821	4915	5009	5104	5198	5292	5386	
19	5480	5574	5668	5762	5856	5950	6044	6138	6232	6326	
20	6420	6514	6608	6702	6796	6890	6984	7078	7172	7266	
4621	7360	7454	7548	7642	7736	7830	7924	8018	8111	8205	
22	8299	8393	8487	8581	8675	8769	8863	8957	9051	9145	
23	9239	9333	9427	9521	9615	9709	9803	9896	9990	0084	
24	665 0178	0272	0366	0460	0554	0648	0742	0836	0930	1023	
25	1117	1211	1305	1399	1493	1587	1681	1775	1869	1962	
26	2056	2150	2244	2338	2432	2526	2620	2713	2807	2901	
27	2995	3089	3183	3277	3370	3464	3558	3652	3746	3840	
28	3934	4027	4121	4215	4309	4403	4497	4590	4684	4778	
29	4872	4966	5059	5153	5247	5341	5435	5529	5622	5716	
30	5810	5904	5998	6091	6185	6279	6373	6466	6560	6654	
4631	6748	6842	6935	7029	7123	7217	7310	7404	7498	7592	
32	7686	7779	7873	7967	8061	8154	8248	8342	8436	8529	
33	8623	8717	8810	8904	8998	9092	9185	9279	9373	9467	
34	9560	9654	9748	9841	9935	0029	0123	0216	0310	0404	
35	666 0497	0591	0685	0778	0872	0966	1060	1153	1247	1341	
36	1434	1528	1622	1715	1809	1903	1996	2090	2184	2277	
37	2371	2465	2558	2652	2746	2839	2933	3027	3120	3214	
38	3307	3401	3495	3588	3682	3776	3869	3963	4056	4150	
39	4244	4337	4431	4525	4618	4712	4805	4899	4993	5086	
40	5180	5273	5367	5461	5554	5648	5741	5835	5929	6022	
4641	6116	6209	6303	6396	6490	6584	6677	6771	6864	6958	
42	7051	7145	7238	7332	7426	7519	7613	7706	7800	7893	
43	7987	8080	8174	8267	8361	8454	8548	8642	8735	8829	
44	8922	9016	9109	9203	9296	9390	9483	9577	9670	9764	
45	9857	9951	0044	0138	0231	0325	0418	0512	0605	0699	
46	667 0792	0886	0979	1072	1166	1259	1353	1446	1540	1633	
47	1727	1820	1914	2007	2101	2194	2287	2381	2474	2568	
48	2661	2755	2848	2941	3035	3128	3222	3315	3409	3502	
49	3595	3689	3782	3876	3969	4063	4156	4249	4343	4436	
4650	4530	4623	4716	4810	4903	4996	5090	5183	5277	5370	

94
1 9
2 19
3 28
4 38
5 47
6 56
7 66
8 75
9 85

No.	0	1	2	3	4	5	6	7	8	9	Diff.
4650	667 4530	4623	4716	4810	4903	4996	5090	5183	5277	5370	
51	5463	5557	5650	5744	5837	5930	6024	6117	6210	6304	
52	6397	6490	6584	6677	6770	6864	6957	7051	7144	7237	
53	7331	7424	7517	7611	7704	7797	7891	7984	8077	8170	
54	8264	8357	8450	8544	8637	8730	8824	8917	9010	9104	
55	9197	9290	9383	9477	9570	9663	9757	9850	9943	0036	
56	668 0130	0223	0316	0410	0503	0596	0689	0783	0876	0969	
57	1062	1156	1249	1342	1435	1529	1622	1715	1808	1902	
58	1995	2088	2181	2275	2368	2461	2554	2647	2741	2834	
59	2927	3020	3114	3207	3300	3393	3486	3580	3673	3766	
60	3859	3952	4046	4139	4232	4325	4418	4511	4605	4698	
4661	4791	4884	4977	5071	5164	5257	5350	5443	5536	5630	
62	5723	5816	5909	6002	6095	6188	6282	6375	6468	6561	
63	6654	6747	6840	6934	7027	7120	7213	7306	7399	7492	
64	7585	7679	7772	7865	7958	8051	8144	8237	8330	8423	
65	8516	8610	8703	8796	8889	8982	9075	9168	9261	9354	
66	9447	9540	9633	9727	9820	9913	0006	0099	0192	0285	
67	669 0378	0471	0564	0657	0750	0843	0936	1029	1122	1215	
68	1308	1402	1495	1588	1681	1774	1867	1960	2053	2146	
69	2239	2332	2425	2518	2611	2704	2797	2890	2983	3076	
70	3169	3262	3355	3448	3541	3634	3727	3820	3913	4006	
4671	4099	4192	4285	4378	4471	4564	4656	4749	4842	4935	
72	5028	5121	5214	5307	5400	5493	5586	5679	5772	5865	
73	5958	6051	6144	6237	6330	6422	6515	6608	6701	6794	
74	6887	6980	7073	7166	7259	7352	7445	7537	7630	7723	
75	7816	7909	8002	8095	8188	8281	8373	8466	8559	8652	
76	8745	8838	8931	9024	9117	9209	9302	9395	9488	9581	
77	9674	9767	9859	9952	0045	0138	0231	0324	0416	0509	
78	670 0602	0695	0788	0881	0974	1066	1159	1252	1345	1438	
79	1530	1623	1716	1809	1902	1995	2087	2180	2273	2366	
80	2459	2551	2644	2737	2830	2922	3015	3108	3201	3294	
4681	3386	3479	3572	3665	3758	3850	3943	4036	4129	4221	
82	4314	4407	4500	4592	4685	4778	4871	4963	5056	5149	
83	5242	5334	5427	5520	5613	5705	5798	5891	5983	6076	
84	6169	6262	6354	6447	6540	6632	6725	6818	6911	7003	
85	7096	7189	7281	7374	7467	7559	7652	7745	7837	7930	
86	8023	8116	8208	8301	8394	8486	8579	8672	8764	8857	
87	8950	9042	9135	9228	9320	9413	9505	9598	9691	9783	
88	9876	9969	0061	0154	0247	0339	0432	0524	0617	0710	
89	671 0802	0895	0988	1080	1173	1265	1358	1451	1543	1636	
90	1728	1821	1914	2006	2099	2191	2284	2377	2469	2562	
4691	2654	2747	2839	2932	3025	3117	3210	3302	3395	3487	
92	3580	3673	3765	3858	3950	4043	4135	4228	4320	4413	
93	4506	4598	4691	4783	4876	4968	5061	5153	5246	5338	
94	5431	5523	5616	5708	5801	5893	5986	6078	6171	6263	
95	6356	6448	6541	6633	6726	6818	6911	7003	7096	7188	
96	7281	7373	7466	7558	7651	7743	7836	7928	8021	8113	
97	8206	8298	8391	8483	8575	8668	8760	8853	8945	9038	
98	9130	9223	9315	9407	9500	9592	9685	9777	9870	9962	
99	672 0054	0147	0239	0332	0424	0517	0609	0701	0794	0886	
4700	0979	1071	1163	1256	1348	1441	1533	1625	1718	1810	

93

1	9
2	19
3	28
4	37
5	47
6	56
7	65
8	74
9	84

No.	0	1	2	3	4	5	6	7	8	9	Diff.
4700	672 0979	1071	1163	1256	1348	1441	1533	1625	1718	1810	
01	1903	1995	2087	2180	2272	2364	2457	2549	2642	2734	
02	2826	2919	3011	3103	3196	3288	3380	3473	3565	3657	
03	3750	3842	3934	4027	4119	4211	4304	4396	4488	4581	
04	4673	4765	4858	4950	5042	5135	5227	5319	5412	5504	
05	5596	5689	5781	5873	5965	6058	6150	6242	6335	6427	
06	6519	6612	6704	6796	6888	6981	7073	7165	7257	7350	
07	7442	7534	7627	7719	7811	7903	7996	8088	8180	8272	
08	8365	8457	8549	8641	8734	8826	8918	9010	9102	9195	
09	9287	9379	9471	9564	9656	9748	9840	9932	0̄025	0̄117	
10	673 0209	0301	0393	0486	0578	0670	0762	0854	0947	1039	
4711	1131	1223	1315	1408	1500	1592	1684	1776	1868	1961	
12	2053	2145	2237	2329	2421	2514	2606	2698	2790	2882	
13	2974	3067	3159	3251	3343	3435	3527	3619	3712	3804	
14	3896	3988	4080	4172	4264	4356	4449	4541	4633	4725	
15	4817	4909	5001	5093	5185	5277	5370	5462	5554	5646	
16	5738	5830	5922	6014	6106	6198	6290	6383	6475	6567	
17	6659	6751	6843	6935	7027	7119	7211	7303	7395	7487	
18	7579	7671	7763	7856	7948	8040	8132	8224	8316	8408	
19	8500	8592	8684	8776	8868	8960	9052	9144	9236	9328	
20	9420	9512	9604	9696	9788	9880	9972	0̄064	0̄156	0̄248	
4721	674 0340	0432	0524	0616	0708	0800	0892	0984	1076	1168	
22	1260	1352	1444	1536	1628	1720	1812	1904	1996	2088	
23	2179	2271	2363	2455	2547	2639	2731	2823	2915	3007	
24	3099	3191	3283	3375	3467	3559	3650	3742	3834	3926	
25	4018	4110	4202	4294	4386	4478	4570	4661	4753	4845	
26	4937	5029	5121	5213	5305	5397	5489	5580	5672	5764	
27	5856	5948	6040	6132	6224	6315	6407	6499	6591	6683	
28	6775	6867	6958	7050	7142	7234	7326	7418	7509	7601	
29	7693	7785	7877	7969	8060	8152	8244	8336	8428	8520	
30	8611	8703	8795	8887	8979	9070	9162	9254	9346	9438	
4731	9529	9621	9713	9805	9897	9988	0̄080	0̄172	0̄264	0̄356	
32	675 0447	0539	0631	0723	0814	0906	0998	1090	1182	1273	
33	1365	1457	1549	1640	1732	1824	1916	2007	2099	2191	
34	2283	2374	2466	2558	2649	2741	2833	2925	3016	3108	
35	3200	3292	3383	3475	3567	3658	3750	3842	3934	4025	
36	4117	4209	4300	4392	4484	4575	4667	4759	4850	4942	
37	5034	5126	5217	5309	5401	5492	5584	5676	5767	5859	
38	5951	6042	6134	6226	6317	6409	6501	6592	6684	6775	
39	6867	6959	7050	7142	7234	7325	7417	7509	7600	7692	
40	7783	7875	7967	8058	8150	8242	8333	8425	8516	8608	
4741	8700	8791	8883	8974	9066	9158	9249	9341	9432	9524	
42	9615	9707	9799	9890	9982	0̄073	0̄165	0̄257	0̄348	0̄440	
43	676 0531	0623	0714	0806	0897	0989	1081	1172	1264	1355	
44	1447	1538	1630	1721	1813	1905	1996	2088	2179	2271	
45	2362	2454	2545	2637	2728	2820	2911	3003	3094	3186	
46	3277	3369	3460	3552	3643	3735	3826	3918	4009	4101	
47	4192	4284	4375	4467	4558	4650	4741	4833	4924	5016	
48	5107	5199	5290	5382	5473	5564	5656	5747	5839	5930	
49	6022	6113	6205	6296	6387	6479	6570	6662	6753	6845	
4750	6936	7028	7119	7210	7302	7393	7485	7576	7667	7759	

92

1	9
2	18
3	28
4	37
5	46
6	55
7	64
8	74
9	83

No.	0	1	2	3	4	5	6	7	8	9	Diff.
4750	676 6936	7028	7119	7210	7302	7393	7485	7576	7667	7759	
51	7850	7942	8033	8125	8216	8307	8399	8490	8582	8673	
52	8764	8856	8947	9038	9130	9221	9313	9404	9495	9587	
53	9678	9770	9861	9952	0044	0135	0226	0318	0409	0500	
54	677 0592	0683	0774	0866	0957	1049	1140	1231	1323	1414	
55	1505	1597	1688	1779	1871	1962	2053	2145	2236	2327	
56	2418	2510	2601	2692	2784	2875	2966	3058	3149	3240	
57	3332	3423	3514	3605	3697	3788	3879	3971	4062	4153	
58	4244	4336	4427	4518	4609	4701	4792	4883	4975	5066	
59	5157	5248	5340	5431	5522	5613	5705	5796	5887	5978	
60	6070	6161	6252	6343	6434	6526	6617	6708	6799	6891	
4761	6982	7073	7164	7255	7347	7438	7529	7620	7712	7803	
62	7894	7985	8076	8168	8259	8350	8441	8532	8623	8715	
63	8806	8897	8988	9079	9171	9262	9353	9444	9535	9626	
64	9718	9809	9900	9991	0082	0173	0264	0356	0447	0538	
65	678 0629	0720	0811	0902	0994	1085	1176	1267	1358	1449	
66	1540	1632	1723	1814	1905	1996	2087	2178	2269	2360	
67	2452	2543	2634	2725	2816	2907	2998	3089	3180	3271	
68	3362	3454	3545	3636	3727	3818	3909	4000	4091	4182	
69	4273	4364	4455	4546	4637	4729	4820	4911	5002	5093	
70	5184	5275	5366	5457	5548	5639	5730	5821	5912	6003	
4771	6094	6185	6276	6367	6458	6549	6640	6731	6822	6913	
72	7004	7095	7186	7277	7368	7459	7550	7641	7732	7823	
73	7914	8005	8096	8187	8278	8369	8460	8551	8642	8733	
74	8824	8915	9006	9097	9188	9279	9370	9461	9552	9643	
75	9734	9825	9916	0007	0098	0188	0279	0370	0461	0552	
76	679 0643	0734	0825	0916	1007	1098	1189	1280	1371	1461	
77	1552	1643	1734	1825	1916	2007	2098	2189	2280	2371	
78	2461	2552	2643	2734	2825	2916	3007	3098	3189	3279	
79	3370	3461	3552	3643	3734	3825	3916	4006	4097	4188	
80	4279	4370	4461	4552	4642	4733	4824	4915	5006	5097	
4781	5187	5278	5369	5460	5551	5642	5732	5823	5914	6005	
82	6096	6187	6277	6368	6459	6550	6641	6731	6822	6913	
83	7004	7095	7185	7276	7367	7458	7549	7639	7730	7821	
84	7912	8002	8093	8184	8275	8366	8456	8547	8638	8729	
85	8819	8910	9001	9092	9182	9273	9364	9455	9545	9636	
86	9727	9818	9908	9999	0090	0181	0271	0362	0453	0544	
87	680 0634	0725	0816	0906	0997	1088	1179	1269	1360	1451	
88	1541	1632	1723	1814	1904	1995	2086	2176	2267	2358	
89	2448	2539	2630	2720	2811	2902	2992	3083	3174	3264	
90	3355	3446	3536	3627	3718	3808	3899	3990	4080	4171	
4791	4262	4352	4443	4534	4624	4715	4806	4896	4987	5077	
92	5168	5259	5349	5440	5531	5621	5712	5802	5893	5984	
93	6074	6165	6256	6346	6437	6527	6618	6709	6799	6890	
94	6980	7071	7161	7252	7343	7433	7524	7614	7705	7796	
95	7886	7977	8067	8158	8248	8339	8430	8520	8611	8701	
96	8792	8882	8973	9063	9154	9244	9335	9426	9516	9607	
97	9697	9788	9878	9969	0059	0150	0240	0331	0421	0512	
98	681 0602	0693	0783	0874	0964	1055	1145	1236	1327	1417	
99	1507	1598	1688	1779	1869	1960	2050	2141	2231	2322	
4800	2412	2503	2593	2684	2774	2865	2955	3046	3136	3227	

Diff.

91

1	9
2	18
3	27
4	36
5	46
6	55
7	64
8	73
9	82

No.	0	1	2	3	4	5	6	7	8	9	Diff.
4800	681 2412	2503	2593	2684	2774	2865	2955	3046	3136	3227	
01	3317	3408	3498	3588	3679	3769	3860	3950	4041	4131	
02	4222	4312	4402	4493	4583	4674	4764	4855	4945	5035	
03	5126	5216	5307	5397	5488	5578	5668	5759	5849	5940	
04	6030	6120	6211	6301	6392	6482	6572	6663	6753	6844	
05	6934	7024	7115	7205	7295	7386	7476	7567	7657	7747	
06	7838	7928	8018	8109	8199	8289	8380	8470	8561	8651	
07	8741	8832	8922	9012	9103	9193	9283	9374	9464	9554	
08	9645	9735	9825	9916	0006	0096	0187	0277	0367	0457	
09	682 0548	0638	0728	0819	0909	0999	1090	1180	1270	1360	
10	1451	1541	1631	1722	1812	1902	1992	2083	2173	2263	
4811	2354	2444	2534	2624	2715	2805	2895	2985	3076	3166	
12	3256	3346	3437	3527	3617	3707	3798	3888	3978	4068	
13	4159	4249	4339	4429	4520	4610	4700	4790	4880	4971	
14	5061	5151	5241	5331	5422	5512	5602	5692	5783	5873	
15	5963	6053	6143	6233	6324	6414	6504	6594	6684	6775	
16	6865	6955	7045	7135	7225	7316	7406	7496	7586	7676	
17	7766	7857	7947	8037	8127	8217	8307	8398	8488	8578	
18	8668	8758	8848	8938	9029	9119	9209	9299	9389	9479	
19	9569	9659	9750	9840	9930	0020	0110	0200	0290	0380	
20	683 0470	0560	0651	0741	0831	0921	1011	1101	1191	1281	
4821	1371	1461	1551	1642	1732	1822	1912	2002	2092	2182	
22	2272	2362	2452	2542	2632	2722	2812	2902	2993	3083	
23	3173	3263	3353	3443	3533	3623	3713	3803	3893	3983	
24	4073	4163	4253	4343	4433	4523	4613	4703	4793	4883	
25	4973	5063	5153	5243	5333	5423	5513	5603	5693	5783	
26	5873	5963	6053	6143	6233	6323	6413	6503	6593	6683	
27	6773	6863	6953	7043	7133	7223	7313	7403	7493	7583	
28	7673	7763	7853	7942	8032	8122	8212	8302	8392	8482	
29	8572	8662	8752	8842	8932	9022	9112	9202	9291	9381	
30	9471	9561	9651	9741	9831	9921	0011	0101	0191	0280	
4831	684 0370	0460	0550	0640	0730	0820	0910	1000	1089	1179	
32	1269	1359	1449	1539	1629	1719	1808	1898	1988	2078	
33	2168	2258	2348	2438	2527	2617	2707	2797	2887	2977	
34	3066	3156	3246	3336	3426	3516	3605	3695	3785	3875	
35	3965	4055	4144	4234	4324	4414	4504	4594	4683	4773	
36	4863	4953	5043	5132	5222	5312	5402	5492	5581	5671	
37	5761	5851	5940	6030	6120	6210	6300	6389	6479	6569	
38	6659	6748	6838	6928	7018	7107	7197	7287	7377	7466	
39	7556	7646	7736	7825	7915	8005	8095	8184	8274	8364	
40	8454	8543	8633	8723	8813	8902	8992	9082	9171	9261	
4841	9351	9441	9530	9620	9710	9799	9889	9979	0068	0158	
42	685 0248	0338	0427	0517	0607	0696	0786	0876	0965	1055	
43	1145	1234	1324	1414	1503	1593	1683	1772	1862	1952	
44	2041	2131	2221	2310	2400	2490	2579	2669	2759	2848	
45	2938	3027	3117	3207	3296	3386	3476	3565	3655	3744	
46	3834	3924	4013	4103	4193	4282	4372	4461	4551	4641	
47	4730	4820	4909	4999	5089	5178	5268	5357	5447	5537	
48	5626	5716	5805	5895	5984	6074	6164	6253	6343	6432	
49	6522	6611	6701	6791	6880	6970	7059	7149	7238	7328	
4850	7417	7507	7596	7686	7776	7865	7955	8044	8134	8223	

90
1 9
2 18
3 27
4 36
5 45
6 54
7 63
8 72
9 81

No.	0	1	2	3	4	5	6	7	8	9	Diff.
4850	685 7417	7507	7596	7686	7776	7865	7955	8044	8134	8223	
51	8313	8402	8492	8581	8671	8760	8850	8939	9029	9118	
52	9208	9297	9387	9476	9566	9655	9745	9834	9924	$\overline{0013}$	
53	686 0103	0192	0282	0371	0461	0550	0640	0729	0819	0908	
54	0998	1087	1177	1266	1356	1445	1535	1624	1713	1803	
55	1892	1982	2071	2161	2250	2340	2429	2518	2608	2697	
56	2787	2876	2966	3055	3145	3234	3323	3413	3502	3592	
57	3681	3770	3860	3949	4039	4128	4217	4307	4396	4486	
58	4575	4665	4754	4843	4933	5022	5111	5201	5290	5380	
59	5469	5558	5648	5737	5826	5916	6005	6095	6184	6273	
60	6363	6452	6541	6631	6720	6809	6899	6988	7078	7167	
4861	7256	7346	7435	7524	7614	7703	7792	7882	7971	8060	
62	8150	8239	8328	8418	8507	8596	8685	8775	8864	8953	
63	9043	9132	9221	9311	9400	9489	9578	9668	9757	9846	
64	9936	$\overline{0025}$	$\overline{0114}$	$\overline{0204}$	$\overline{0293}$	$\overline{0382}$	$\overline{0471}$	$\overline{0561}$	$\overline{0650}$	$\overline{0739}$	
65	687 0828	0918	1007	1096	1186	1275	1364	1453	1543	1632	
66	1721	1810	1900	1989	2078	2167	2257	2346	2435	2524	
67	2613	2703	2792	2881	2970	3060	3149	3238	3327	3416	
68	3506	3595	3684	3773	3863	3952	4041	4130	4219	4309	
69	4398	4487	4576	4665	4755	4844	4933	5022	5111	5200	
70	5290	5379	5468	5557	5646	5735	5825	5914	6003	6092	
4871	6181	6270	6360	6449	6538	6627	6716	6805	6895	6984	
72	7073	7162	7251	7340	7429	7518	7608	7697	7786	7875	
73	7964	8053	8142	8231	8321	8410	8499	8588	8677	8766	
74	8855	8944	9033	9123	9212	9301	9390	9479	9568	9657	
75	9746	9835	9924	$\overline{0013}$	$\overline{0103}$	$\overline{0192}$	$\overline{0281}$	$\overline{0370}$	$\overline{0459}$	$\overline{0548}$	
76	688 0637	0726	0815	0904	0993	1082	1171	1260	1349	1439	
77	1528	1617	1706	1795	1884	1973	2062	2151	2240	2329	
78	2418	2507	2596	2685	2774	2863	2952	3041	3130	3219	
79	3308	3397	3486	3575	3664	3753	3842	3931	4020	4109	
80	4198	4287	4376	4465	4554	4643	4732	4821	4910	4999	
4881	5088	5177	5266	5355	5444	5533	5622	5711	5800	5889	
82	5978	6067	6156	6245	6334	6423	6511	6600	6689	6778	
83	6867	6956	7045	7134	7223	7312	7401	7490	7579	7668	
84	7757	7845	7934	8023	8112	8201	8290	8379	8468	8557	
85	8646	8735	8823	8912	9001	9090	9179	9268	9357	9446	
86	9535	9624	9712	9801	9890	9979	$\overline{0068}$	$\overline{0157}$	$\overline{0246}$	$\overline{0335}$	
87	689 0423	0512	0601	0690	0779	0868	0957	1045	1134	1223	
88	1312	1401	1490	1579	1667	1756	1845	1934	2023	2112	
89	2200	2289	2378	2467	2556	2645	2733	2822	2911	3000	
90	3089	3177	3266	3355	3444	3533	3621	3710	3799	3888	
4891	3977	4065	4154	4243	4332	4421	4509	4598	4687	4776	
92	4864	4953	5042	5131	5220	5308	5397	5486	5575	5663	
93	5752	5841	5930	6018	6107	6196	6285	6373	6462	6551	
94	6640	6728	6817	6906	6995	7083	7172	7261	7350	7438	
95	7527	7616	7704	7793	7882	7971	8059	8148	8237	8325	
96	8414	3503	8591	8680	8769	8858	8946	9035	9124	9212	
97	9301	9390	9478	9567	9656	9744	9833	9922	$\overline{0010}$	$\overline{0099}$	
98	690 0188	0276	0365	0454	0542	0631	0720	0808	0897	0986	
99	1074	1163	1252	1340	1429	1518	1606	1695	1784	1872	
4900	1961	2049	2138	2227	2315	2404	2493	2581	2670	2758	

89

1	9
2	18
3	27
4	36
5	45
6	53
7	62
8	71
9	80

No.	0	1	2	3	4	5	6	7	8	9	Diff.
4900	690 1961	2049	2138	2227	2315	2404	2493	2581	2670	2758	
01	2847	2936	3024	3113	3201	3290	3379	3467	3556	3644	
02	3733	3822	3910	3999	4087	4176	4265	4353	4442	4530	
03	4619	4708	4796	4885	4973	5062	5150	5239	5327	5416	
04	5505	5593	5682	5770	5859	5947	6036	6124	6213	6302	
05	6390	6479	6567	6656	6744	6833	6921	7010	7098	7187	
06	7275	7364	7452	7541	7630	7718	7807	7895	7984	8072	
07	8161	8249	8338	8426	8515	8603	8692	8780	8869	8957	
08	9046	9134	9223	9311	9399	9488	9576	9665	9753	9842	
09	9930	0019	0107	0196	0284	0373	0461	0550	0638	0726	
10	691 0815	0903	0992	1080	1169	1257	1346	1434	1522	1611	
4911	1699	1788	1876	1965	2053	2141	2230	2318	2407	2495	
12	2584	2672	2760	2849	2937	3026	3114	3202	3291	3379	
13	3468	3556	3644	3733	3821	3910	3998	4086	4175	4263	
14	4352	4440	4528	4617	4705	4793	4882	4970	5058	5147	
15	5235	5324	5412	5500	5589	5677	5765	5854	5942	6030	
16	6119	6207	6295	6384	6472	6560	6649	6737	6825	6914	
17	7002	7090	7179	7267	7355	7444	7532	7620	7709	7797	
18	7885	7974	8062	8150	8238	8327	8415	8503	8592	8680	
19	8768	8857	8945	9033	9121	9210	9298	9386	9474	9563	
20	9651	9739	9828	9916	0004	0092	0181	0269	0357	0445	88
4921	692 0534	0622	0710	0798	0887	0975	1063	1151	1240	1328	1 9
22	1416	1504	1593	1681	1769	1857	1945	2034	2122	2210	2 18
23	2298	2387	2475	2563	2651	2739	2828	2916	3004	3092	3 26
24	3180	3269	3357	3445	3533	3621	3710	3798	3886	3974	4 35
25	4062	4151	4239	4327	4415	4503	4591	4680	4768	4856	5 44
26	4944	5032	5120	5209	5297	5385	5473	5561	5649	5737	6 53
27	5826	5914	6002	6090	6178	6266	6354	6443	6531	6619	7 62
28	6707	6795	6883	6971	7059	7148	7236	7324	7412	7500	8 70
29	7588	7676	7764	7853	7941	8029	8117	8205	8293	8381	9 79
30	8469	8557	8645	8733	8822	8910	8998	9086	9174	9262	
4931	9350	9438	9526	9614	9702	9790	9878	9967	0055	0143	
32	693 0231	0319	0407	0495	0583	0671	0759	0847	0935	1023	
33	1111	1199	1287	1375	1463	1551	1639	1727	1815	1903	
34	1991	2079	2167	2256	2344	2432	2520	2608	2696	2784	
35	2872	2960	3048	3136	3224	3312	3400	3488	3576	3664	
36	3752	3839	3927	4015	4103	4191	4279	4367	4455	4543	
37	4631	4719	4807	4895	4983	5071	5159	5247	5335	5423	
38	5511	5599	5687	5775	5863	5951	6039	6126	6214	6302	
39	6390	6478	6566	6654	6742	6830	6918	7006	7094	7182	
40	7269	7357	7445	7533	7621	7709	7797	7885	7973	8061	
4941	8149	8236	8324	8412	8500	8588	8676	8764	8852	8940	
42	9027	9115	9203	9291	9379	9467	9555	9643	9730	9818	
43	9906	9994	0082	0170	0258	0345	0433	0521	0609	0697	
44	694 0785	0872	0960	1048	1136	1224	1312	1399	1487	1575	
45	1663	1751	1839	1926	2014	2102	2190	2278	2366	2453	
46	2541	2629	2717	2805	2892	2980	3068	3156	3244	3331	
47	3419	3507	3595	3682	3770	3858	3946	4034	4121	4209	
48	4297	4385	4472	4560	4648	4736	4824	4911	4999	5087	
49	5175	5262	5350	5438	5526	5613	5701	5789	5877	5964	
4950	6052	6140	6227	6315	6403	6491	6578	6666	6754	6842	

No.	0	1	2	3	4	5	6	7	8	9	Diff.
4950	694 6052	6140	6227	6315	6403	6491	6578	6666	6754	6842	
51	6929	7017	7105	7192	7280	7368	7456	7543	7631	7719	
52	7806	7894	7982	8069	8157	8245	8333	8420	8508	8596	
53	8683	8771	8859	8946	9034	9122	9209	9297	9385	9472	
54	9560	9648	9735	9823	9911	9998	0086	0174	0261	0349	
55	695 0437	0524	0612	0700	0787	0875	0962	1050	1138	1225	
56	1313	1401	1488	1576	1663	1751	1839	1926	2014	2102	
57	2189	2277	2364	2452	2540	2627	2715	2802	2890	2978	
58	3065	3153	3240	3328	3416	3503	3591	3678	3766	3854	
59	3941	4029	4116	4204	4291	4379	4467	4554	4642	4729	
60	4817	4904	4992	5079	5167	5255	5342	5430	5517	5605	
4961	5692	5780	5867	5955	6042	6130	6217	6305	6393	6480	
62	6568	6655	6743	6830	6918	7005	7093	7180	7268	7355	
63	7443	7530	7618	7705	7793	7880	7968	8055	8143	8230	
64	8318	8405	8493	8580	8668	8755	8843	8930	9018	9105	
65	9193	9280	9367	9455	9542	9630	9717	9805	9892	9980	
66	696 0067	0155	0242	0330	0417	0504	0592	0679	0767	0854	
67	0942	1029	1116	1204	1291	1379	1466	1554	1641	1728	
68	1816	1903	1991	2078	2166	2253	2340	2428	2515	2603	
69	2690	2777	2865	2952	3040	3127	3214	3302	3389	3477	
70	3564	3651	3739	3826	3913	4001	4088	4176	4263	4350	
4971	4438	4525	4612	4700	4787	4874	4962	5049	5137	5224	
72	5311	5399	5486	5573	5661	5748	5835	5923	6010	6097	
73	6185	6272	6359	6447	6534	6621	6709	6796	6883	6970	
74	7058	7145	7232	7320	7407	7494	7582	7669	7756	7844	
75	7931	8018	8105	8193	8280	8367	8455	8542	8629	8716	
76	8804	8891	8978	9066	9153	9240	9327	9415	9502	9589	
77	9676	9764	9851	9938	0025	0113	0200	0287	0374	0462	
78	697 0549	0636	0723	0811	0898	0985	1072	1160	1247	1334	
79	1421	1508	1596	1683	1770	1857	1945	2032	2119	2206	
80	2293	2381	2468	2555	2642	2729	2817	2904	2991	3078	
4981	3165	3253	3340	3427	3514	3601	3689	3776	3863	3950	
82	4037	4124	4212	4299	4386	4473	4560	4647	4735	4822	
83	4909	4996	5083	5170	5257	5345	5432	5519	5606	5693	
84	5780	5867	5955	6042	6129	6216	6303	6390	6477	6565	
85	6652	6739	6826	6913	7000	7087	7174	7261	7349	7436	
86	7523	7610	7697	7784	7871	7958	8045	8132	8220	8307	
87	8394	8481	8568	8655	8742	8829	8916	9003	9090	9177	
88	9264	9352	9439	9526	9613	9700	9787	9874	9961	0048	
89	698 0135	0222	0309	0396	0483	0570	0657	0744	0831	0918	
90	1005	1092	1180	1267	1354	1441	1528	1615	1702	1789	
4991	1876	1963	2050	2137	2224	2311	2398	2485	2572	2659	
92	2746	2833	2920	3007	3094	3181	3268	3355	3442	3529	
93	3616	3703	3790	3877	3964	4051	4138	4224	4311	4398	
94	4485	4572	4659	4746	4833	4920	5007	5094	5181	5268	
95	5355	5442	5529	5616	5703	5790	5877	5964	6050	6137	
96	6224	6311	6398	6485	6572	6659	6746	6833	6920	7007	
97	7093	7180	7267	7354	7441	7528	7615	7702	7789	7876	
98	7963	8049	8136	8223	8310	8397	8484	8571	8658	8744	
99	8831	8918	9005	9092	9179	9266	9353	9439	9526	9613	
5000	9700	9787	9874	9961	0047	0134	0221	0308	0395	0482	

699

Diff. 87

1	9
2	17
3	26
4	35
5	44
6	52
7	61
8	70
9	78

No.	0	1	2	3	4	5	6	7	8	9	Diff.
5000	698 9700	9787	9874	9961	0̄047	0̄134	0̄221	0̄308	0̄395	0̄482	
01	699 0569	0655	0742	0829	0916	1003	1090	1176	1263	1350	
02	1437	1524	1611	1697	1784	1871	1958	2045	2131	2218	
03	2305	2392	2479	2565	2652	2739	2826	2913	2999	3086	
04	3173	3260	3347	3433	3520	3607	3694	3780	3867	3954	
05	4041	4128	4214	4301	4388	4475	4561	4648	4735	4822	
06	4908	4995	5082	5169	5255	5342	5429	5516	5602	5689	
07	5776	5863	5949	6036	6123	6210	6296	6383	6470	6556	
08	6643	6730	6817	6903	6990	7077	7163	7250	7337	7424	
09	7510	7597	7684	7770	7857	7944	8031	8117	8204	8291	
10	8377	8464	8551	8637	8724	8811	8897	8984	9071	9157	
5011	9244	9331	9417	9504	9591	9677	9764	9851	9937	0̄024	
12	700 0197	0111	0197	0284	0371	0457	0544	0630	0717	0804	0890	
13	0977	1064	1150	1237	1324	1410	1497	1583	1670	1757	
14	1843	1930	2017	2103	2190	2276	2363	2450	2536	2623	
15	2709	2796	2883	2969	3056	3142	3229	3316	3402	3489	
16	3575	3662	3748	3835	3922	4008	4095	4181	4268	4354	
17	4441	4528	4614	4701	4787	4874	4960	5047	5133	5220	
18	5307	5393	5480	5566	5653	5739	5826	5912	5999	6085	
19	6172	6258	6345	6432	6518	6605	6691	6778	6864	6951	
20	7037	7124	7210	7297	7383	7470	7556	7643	7729	7816	
5021	7902	7989	8075	8162	8248	8335	8421	8508	8594	8681	
22	8767	8854	8940	9027	9113	9199	9286	9372	9459	9545	
23	9632	9718	9805	9891	9978	0̄064	0̄151	0̄237	0̄323	0̄410	
24	701 0496	0583	0669	0756	0842	0929	1015	1101	1188	1274	
25	1361	1447	1534	1620	1706	1793	1879	1966	2052	2138	
26	2225	2311	2398	2484	2570	2657	2743	2830	2916	3002	
27	3089	3175	3262	3348	3434	3521	3607	3694	3780	3866	
28	3953	4039	4125	4212	4298	4385	4471	4557	4644	4730	
29	4816	4903	4989	5075	5162	5248	5334	5421	5507	5594	
30	5680	5766	5853	5939	6025	6112	6198	6284	6371	6457	
5031	6543	6629	6716	6802	6888	6975	7061	7147	7234	7320	
32	7406	7493	7579	7665	7752	7838	7924	8010	8097	8183	
33	8269	8356	8442	8528	8614	8701	8787	8873	8960	9046	
34	9132	9218	9305	9391	9477	9563	9650	9736	9822	9908	
35	9995	0̄081	0̄167	0̄254	0̄340	0̄426	0̄512	0̄598	0̄685	0̄771	
36	702 0857	0943	1030	1116	1202	1288	1375	1461	1547	1633	
37	1720	1806	1892	1978	2064	2151	2237	2323	2409	2495	
38	2582	2668	2754	2840	2926	3013	3099	3185	3271	3357	
39	3444	3530	3616	3702	3788	3874	3961	4047	4133	4219	
40	4305	4392	4478	4564	4650	4736	4822	4909	4995	5081	
5041	5167	5253	5339	5425	5512	5598	5684	5770	5856	5942	
42	6028	6115	6201	6287	6373	6459	6545	6631	6717	6804	
43	6890	6976	7062	7148	7234	7320	7406	7492	7579	7665	
44	7751	7837	7923	8009	8095	8181	8267	8353	8440	8526	
45	8612	8698	8784	8870	8956	9042	9128	9214	9300	9386	
46	9472	9559	9645	9731	9817	9903	9989	0̄075	0̄161	0̄247	
47	703 0333	0419	0505	0591	0677	0763	0849	0935	1021	1107	
48	1193	1279	1366	1452	1538	1624	1710	1796	1882	1968	
49	2054	2140	2226	2312	2398	2484	2570	2656	2742	2828	
5050	2914	3000	3086	3172	3258	3344	3430	3516	3602	3688	

87
1	9
2	17
3	26
4	35
5	44
6	52
7	61
8	70
9	78

No.	0	1	2	3	4	5	6	7	8	9	Diff.
5050	703 2914	3000	3086	3172	3258	3344	3430	3516	3602	3688	
51	3774	3860	3946	4032	4118	4204	4290	4376	4461	4547	
52	4633	4719	4805	4891	4977	5063	5149	5235	5321	5407	
53	5493	5579	5665	5751	5837	5923	6009	6095	6181	6266	
54	6352	6438	6524	6610	6696	6782	6868	6954	7040	7126	
55	7212	7298	7383	7469	7555	7641	7727	7813	7899	7985	
56	8071	8157	8242	8328	8414	8500	8586	8672	8758	8844	
57	8930	9015	9101	9187	9273	9359	9445	9531	9617	9702	
58	9788	9874	9960	0046	0132	0218	0303	0389	0475	0561	
59	704 0647	0733	0818	0904	0990	1076	1162	1248	1334	1419	
60	1505	1591	1677	1763	1848	1934	2020	2106	2192	2278	
5061	2363	2449	2535	2621	2707	2792	2878	2964	3050	3136	
62	3221	3307	3393	3479	3565	3650	3736	3822	3908	3993	
63	4079	4165	4251	4337	4422	4508	4594	4680	4765	4851	
64	4937	5023	5108	5194	5280	5366	5452	5537	5623	5709	
65	5794	5880	5966	6052	6137	6223	6309	6395	6480	6566	
66	6652	6738	6823	6909	6995	7080	7166	7252	7338	7423	
67	7509	7595	7680	7766	7852	7938	8023	8109	8195	8280	
68	8366	8452	8537	8623	8709	8795	8880	8966	9052	9137	
69	9223	9309	9394	9480	9566	9651	9737	9823	9908	9994	
70	705 0080	0165	0251	0337	0422	0508	0594	0679	0765	0850	
5071	0936	1022	1107	1193	1279	1364	1450	1536	1621	1707	
72	1792	1878	1964	2049	2135	2221	2306	2392	2477	2563	
73	2649	2734	2820	2905	2991	3077	3162	3248	3333	3419	
74	3505	3590	3676	3761	3847	3933	4018	4104	4189	4275	
75	4360	4446	4532	4617	4703	4788	4874	4959	5045	5131	
76	5216	5302	5387	5473	5558	5644	5729	5815	5901	5986	
77	6072	6157	6243	6328	6414	6499	6585	6670	6756	6841	
78	6927	7012	7098	7184	7269	7355	7440	7526	7611	7697	
79	7782	7868	7953	8039	8124	8210	8295	8381	8466	8552	
80	8637	8723	8808	8894	8979	9065	9150	9236	9321	9406	
5081	9492	9577	9663	9748	9834	9919	0005	0090	0176	0261	
82	706 0347	0432	0518	0603	0688	0774	0859	0945	1030	1116	
83	1201	1287	1372	1457	1543	1628	1714	1799	1885	1970	
84	2055	2141	2226	2312	2397	2483	2568	2653	2739	2824	
85	2910	2995	3080	3166	3251	3337	3422	3507	3593	3678	
86	3764	3849	3934	4020	4105	4190	4276	4361	4447	4532	
87	4617	4703	4788	4873	4959	5044	5130	5215	5300	5386	
88	5471	5556	5642	5727	5812	5898	5983	6068	6154	6239	
89	6325	6410	6495	6581	6666	6751	6837	6922	7007	7092	
90	7178	7263	7348	7434	7519	7604	7690	7775	7860	7946	
5091	8031	8116	8202	8287	8372	8457	8543	8628	8713	8799	
92	8884	8969	9055	9140	9225	9310	9396	9481	9566	9651	
93	9737	9822	9907	9993	0078	0163	0248	0334	0419	0504	
94	707 0589	0675	0760	0845	0930	1016	1101	1186	1271	1357	
95	1442	1527	1612	1698	1783	1868	1953	2039	2124	2209	
96	2294	2379	2465	2550	2635	2720	2805	2891	2976	3061	
97	3146	3232	3317	3402	3487	3572	3658	3743	3828	3913	
98	3998	4083	4169	4254	4339	4424	4509	4595	4680	4765	
99	4850	4935	5020	5106	5191	5276	5361	5446	5531	5617	
5100	5702	5787	5872	5957	6042	6128	6213	6298	6383	6468	

Diff. 86

1	9
2	17
3	26
4	34
5	43
6	52
7	60
8	69
9	77

No.	0	1	2	3	4	5	6	7	8	9	Diff.
5100	707 5702	5787	5872	5957	6042	6128	6213	6298	6383	6468	
01	6553	6638	6724	6809	6894	6979	7064	7149	7234	7319	
02	7405	7490	7575	7660	7745	7830	7915	8000	8085	8171	
03	8256	8341	8426	8511	8596	8681	8766	8851	8936	9022	
04	9107	9192	9277	9362	9447	9532	9617	9702	9787	9872	
05	9957	0043	0128	0213	0298	0383	0468	0553	0638	0723	
06	708 0808	0893	0978	1063	1148	1233	1318	1403	1488	1574	
07	1659	1744	1829	1914	1999	2084	2169	2254	2339	2424	
08	2509	2594	2679	2764	2849	2934	3019	3104	3189	3274	
09	3359	3444	3529	3614	3699	3784	3869	3954	4039	4124	
10	4209	4294	4379	4464	4549	4634	4719	4804	4889	4974	
5111	5059	5144	5229	5314	5399	5484	5569	5654	5739	5823	
12	5908	5993	6078	6163	6248	6333	6418	6503	6588	6673	
13	6758	6843	6928	7013	7098	7183	7268	7352	7437	7522	
14	7607	7692	7777	7862	7947	8032	8117	8202	8287	8371	
15	8456	8541	8626	8711	8796	8881	8966	9051	9136	9220	
16	9305	9390	9475	9560	9645	9730	9815	9900	9984	0069	
17	709 0154	0239	0324	0409	0494	0579	0663	0748	0833	0918	
18	1003	1088	1173	1257	1342	1427	1512	1597	1682	1766	
19	1851	1936	2021	2106	2191	2275	2360	2445	2530	2615	
20	2700	2784	2869	2954	3039	3124	3209	3293	3378	3463	
5121	3548	3633	3717	3802	3887	3972	4057	4141	4226	4311	
22	4396	4481	4565	4650	4735	4820	4904	4989	5074	5159	
23	5244	5328	5413	5498	5583	5667	5752	5837	5922	6006	
24	6091	6176	6261	6345	6430	6515	6600	6684	6769	6854	
25	6939	7023	7108	7193	7278	7362	7447	7532	7617	7701	
26	7786	7871	7955	8040	8125	8210	8294	8379	8464	8548	
27	8633	8718	8803	8887	8972	9057	9141	9226	9311	9395	
28	9480	9565	9650	9734	9819	9904	9988	0073	0158	0242	
29	710 0327	0412	0496	0581	0666	0750	0835	0920	1004	1089	
30	1174	1258	1343	1428	1512	1597	1682	1766	1851	1936	
5131	2020	2105	2189	2274	2359	2443	2528	2613	2697	2782	
32	2866	2951	3036	3120	3205	3290	3374	3459	3543	3628	
33	3713	3797	3882	3966	4051	4136	4220	4305	4389	4474	
34	4559	4643	4728	4812	4897	4982	5066	5151	5235	5320	
35	5404	5489	5574	5658	5743	5827	5912	5996	6081	6166	
36	6250	6335	6419	6504	6588	6673	6757	6842	6927	7011	
37	7096	7180	7265	7349	7434	7518	7603	7687	7772	7856	
38	7941	8026	8110	8195	8279	8364	8448	8533	8617	8702	
39	8786	8871	8955	9040	9124	9209	9293	9378	9462	9547	
40	9631	9716	9800	9885	9969	0054	0138	0223	0307	0392	
5141	711 0476	0561	0645	0729	0814	0898	0983	1067	1152	1236	
42	1321	1405	1490	1574	1659	1743	1827	1912	1996	2081	
43	2165	2250	2334	2419	2503	2587	2672	2756	2841	2925	
44	3010	3094	3178	3263	3347	3432	3516	3601	3685	3769	
45	3854	3938	4023	4107	4191	4276	4360	4445	4529	4613	
46	4698	4782	4867	4951	5035	5120	5204	5289	5373	5457	
47	5542	5626	5710	5795	5879	5964	6048	6132	6217	6301	
48	6385	6470	6554	6638	6723	6807	6892	6976	7060	7145	
49	7229	7313	7398	7482	7566	7651	7735	7819	7904	7988	
5150	8072	8157	8241	8325	8410	8494	8578	8663	8747	8831	

85

1	9
2	17
3	26
4	34
5	43
6	51
7	60
8	68
9	77

No.	0	1	2	3	4	5	6	7	8	9	Diff.
5150	711 8072	8157	8241	8325	8410	8494	8578	8663	8747	8831	
51	8915	9000	9084	9168	9253	9337	9421	9506	9590	9674	
52	9759	9843	9927	0011	0096	0180	0264	0349	0433	0517	
53	712 0601	0686	0770	0854	0939	1023	1107	1191	1276	1360	
54	1444	1528	1613	1697	1781	1865	1950	2034	2118	2202	
55	2287	2371	2455	2539	2624	2708	2792	2876	2961	3045	
56	3129	3213	3298	3382	3466	3550	3634	3719	3803	3887	
57	3971	4056	4140	4224	4308	4392	4477	4561	4645	4729	
58	4813	4898	4982	5066	5150	5234	5319	5403	5487	5571	
59	5655	5739	5824	5908	5992	6076	6160	6245	6329	6413	
60	6497	6581	6665	6750	6834	6918	7002	7086	7170	7254	
5161	7339	7423	7507	7591	7675	7759	7843	7928	8012	8096	
62	8180	8264	8348	8432	8517	8601	8685	8769	8853	8937	
63	9021	9105	9189	9274	9358	9442	9526	9610	9694	9778	
64	9862	9946	0031	0115	0199	0283	0367	0451	0535	0619	
65	713 0703	0787	0871	0956	1040	1124	1208	1292	1376	1460	
66	1544	1628	1712	1796	1880	1964	2048	2132	2217	2301	
67	2385	2469	2553	2637	2721	2805	2889	2973	3057	3141	
68	3225	3309	3393	3477	3561	3645	3729	3813	3897	3981	
69	4065	4149	4233	4317	4401	4485	4569	4653	4737	4821	
70	4905	4989	5073	5157	5241	5325	5409	5493	5577	5661	
5171	5745	5829	5913	5997	6081	6165	6249	6333	6417	6501	
72	6585	6669	6753	6837	6921	7005	7089	7173	7257	7341	
73	7425	7509	7593	7677	7761	7845	7928	8012	8096	8180	
74	8264	8348	8432	8516	8600	8684	8768	8852	8936	9020	
75	9104	9187	9271	9355	9439	9523	9607	9691	9775	9859	
76	9943	0027	0110	0194	0278	0362	0446	0530	0614	0698	
77	714 0782	0866	0949	1033	1117	1201	1285	1369	1453	1537	
78	1620	1704	1788	1872	1956	2040	2124	2208	2291	2375	
79	2459	2543	2627	2711	2795	2878	2962	3046	3130	3214	
80	3298	3381	3465	3549	3633	3717	3801	3884	3968	4052	
5181	4136	4220	4304	4387	4471	4555	4639	4723	4806	4890	
82	4974	5058	5142	5226	5309	5393	5477	5561	5645	5728	
83	5812	5896	5980	6063	6147	6231	6315	6399	6482	6566	
84	6650	6734	6817	6901	6985	7069	7153	7236	7320	7404	
85	7488	7571	7655	7739	7823	7906	7990	8074	8158	8241	
86	8325	8409	8493	8576	8660	8744	8828	8911	8995	9079	
87	9162	9246	9330	9414	9497	9581	9665	9749	9832	9916	
88	715 0000	0083	0167	0251	0335	0418	0502	0586	0669	0753	
89	0837	0920	1004	1088	1171	1255	1339	1423	1506	1590	
90	1674	1757	1841	1925	2008	2092	2176	2259	2343	2427	
5191	2510	2594	2678	2761	2845	2929	3012	3096	3180	3263	
92	3347	3430	3514	3598	3681	3765	3849	3932	4016	4100	
93	4183	4267	4350	4434	4518	4601	4685	4769	4852	4936	
94	5019	5103	5187	5270	5354	5438	5521	5605	5688	5772	
95	5856	5939	6023	6106	6190	6273	6357	6441	6524	6608	
96	6691	6775	6859	6942	7026	7109	7193	7276	7360	7444	
97	7527	7611	7694	7778	7861	7945	8029	8112	8196	8279	
98	8363	8446	8530	8613	8697	8780	8864	8948	9031	9115	
99	9198	9282	9365	9449	9532	9616	9699	9783	9866	9950	
5200	716 0033	0117	0200	0284	0367	0451	0535	0618	0702	0785	

84

1	8
2	17
3	25
4	34
5	42
6	50
7	59
8	67
9	76

No.	0	1	2	3	4	5	6	7	8	9	Diff.
5200	716 0033	0117	0200	0284	0367	0451	0535	0618	0702	0785	
01	0869	0952	1036	1119	1203	1286	1370	1453	1537	1620	
02	1703	1787	1870	1954	2037	2121	2204	2288	2371	2455	
03	2538	2622	2705	2789	2872	2956	3039	3123	3206	3289	
04	3373	3456	3540	3623	3707	3790	3874	3957	4040	4124	
05	4207	4291	4374	4458	4541	4625	4708	4791	4875	4958	
06	5042	5125	5208	5292	5375	5459	5542	5626	5709	5792	
07	5876	5959	6043	6126	6209	6293	6376	6460	6543	6626	
08	6710	6793	6877	6960	7043	7127	7210	7293	7377	7460	
09	7544	7627	7710	7794	7877	7960	8044	8127	8211	8294	
10	8377	8461	8544	8627	8711	8794	8877	8961	9044	9127	
5211	9211	9294	9377	9461	9544	9627	9711	9794	9877	9961	
12	717 0044	0127	0211	0294	0377	0461	0544	0627	0711	0794	
13	0877	0961	1044	1127	1210	1294	1377	1460	1544	1627	
14	1710	1794	1877	1960	2043	2127	2210	2293	2377	2460	
15	2543	2626	2710	2793	2876	2959	3043	3126	3209	3293	
16	3376	3459	3542	3626	3709	3792	3875	3959	4042	4125	
17	4208	4292	4375	4458	4541	4625	4708	4791	4874	4958	
18	5041	5124	5207	5290	5374	5457	5540	5623	5707	5790	
19	5873	5956	6039	6123	6206	6289	6372	6455	6539	6622	
20	6705	6788	6871	6955	7038	7121	7204	7287	7371	7454	
5221	7537	7620	7703	7786	7870	7953	8036	8119	8202	8286	
22	8369	8452	8535	8618	8701	8784	8868	8951	9034	9117	
23	9200	9283	9367	9450	9533	9616	9699	9782	9865	9949	
24	718 0032	0115	0198	0281	0364	0447	0530	0614	0697	0780	
25	0863	0946	1029	1112	1195	1279	1362	1445	1528	1611	
26	1694	1777	1860	1943	2026	2110	2193	2276	2359	2442	
27	2525	2608	2691	2774	2857	2940	3023	3107	3190	3273	
28	3356	3439	3522	3605	3688	3771	3854	3937	4020	4103	
29	4186	4269	4353	4436	4519	4602	4685	4768	4851	4934	
30	5017	5100	5183	5266	5349	5432	5515	5598	5681	5764	
5231	5847	5930	6013	6096	6179	6262	6345	6428	6511	6594	
32	6677	6760	6843	6926	7009	7092	7175	7258	7341	7424	
33	7507	7590	7673	7756	7839	7922	8005	8088	8171	8254	
34	8337	8420	8503	8586	8669	8752	8835	8918	9001	9084	
35	9167	9250	9333	9416	9499	9582	9665	9748	9830	9913	
36	9996	0079	0162	0245	0328	0411	0494	0577	0660	0743	
37	719 0826	0909	0992	1075	1157	1240	1323	1406	1489	1572	
38	1655	1738	1821	1904	1987	2069	2152	2235	2318	2401	
39	2484	2567	2650	2733	2816	2898	2981	3064	3147	3230	
40	3313	3396	3479	3562	3644	3727	3810	3893	3976	4059	
5241	4142	4224	4307	4390	4473	4556	4639	4722	4804	4887	
42	4970	5053	5136	5219	5302	5384	5467	5550	5633	5716	
43	5799	5881	5964	6047	6130	6213	6296	6378	6461	6544	
44	6627	6710	6792	6875	6958	7041	7124	7207	7289	7372	
45	7455	7538	7621	7703	7786	7869	7952	8034·	8117	8200	
46	8283	8366	8448	8531	8614	8697	8780	8862	8945	9028	
47	9111	9193	9276	9359	9442	9524	9607	9690	9773	9856	
48	9938	0021	0104	0187	0269	0352	0435	0518	0600	0683	
49	720 0766	0848	0931	1014	1097	1179	1262	1345	1428	1510	
5250	1593	1676	1758	1841	1924	2007	2089	2172	2255	2337	

83

1	8
2	17
3	25
4	33
5	42
6	50
7	58
8	66
9	75

No.	0	1	2	3	4	5	6	7	8	9	Diff.
5250	720 1593	1676	1758	1841	1924	2007	2089	2172	2255	2337	
51	2420	2503	2586	2668	2751	2834	2916	2999	3082	3164	
52	3247	3330	3413	3495	3578	3661	3743	3826	3909	3991	
53	4074	4157	4239	4322	4405	4487	4570	4653	4735	4818	
54	4901	4983	5066	5149	5231	5314	5397	5479	5562	5645	
55	5727	5810	5892	5975	6058	6140	6223	6306	6388	6471	
56	6554	6636	6719	6801	6884	6967	7049	7132	7215	7297	
57	7380	7462	7545	7628	7710	7793	7875	7958	8041	8123	
58	8206	8288	8371	8454	8536	8619	8701	8784	8867	8949	
59	9032	9114	9197	9279	9362	9445	9527	9610	9692	9775	
60	9857	9940	0023	0105	0188	0270	0353	0435	0518	0600	
5261	721 0683	0766	0848	0931	1013	1096	1178	1261	1343	1426	
62	1508	1591	1674	1756	1839	1921	2004	2086	2169	2251	
63	2334	2416	2499	2581	2664	2746	2829	2911	2994	3076	
64	3159	3241	3324	3406	3489	3571	3654	3736	3819	3901	
65	3984	4066	4149	4231	4314	4396	4479	4561	4644	4726	
66	4809	4891	4973	5056	5138	5221	5303	5386	5468	5551	
67	5633	5716	5798	5881	5963	6045	6128	6210	6293	6375	
68	6458	6540	6623	6705	6787	6870	6952	7035	7117	7200	
69	7282	7364	7447	7529	7612	7694	7777	7859	7941	8024	
70	8106	8189	8271	8353	8436	8518	8601	8683	8765	8848	
5271	8930	9013	9095	9177	9260	9342	9424	9507	9589	9672	82
72	9754	9836	9919	0001	0084	0166	0248	0331	0413	0495	1 8
73	722 0578	0660	0742	0825	0907	0990	1072	1154	1237	1319	2 16
74	1401	1484	1566	1648	1731	1813	1895	1978	2060	2142	3 25
75	2225	2307	2389	2472	2554	2636	2719	2801	2883	2966	4 33
76	3048	3130	3212	3295	3377	3459	3542	3624	3706	3789	5 41
77	3871	3953	4036	4118	4200	4282	4365	4447	4529	4612	6 49
78	4694	4776	4858	4941	5023	5105	5188	5270	5352	5434	7 57
79	5517	5599	5681	5763	5846	5928	6010	6092	6175	6257	8 66
80	6339	6421	6504	6586	6668	6750	6833	6915	6997	7079	9 74
5281	7162	7244	7326	7408	7491	7573	7655	7737	7820	7902	
82	7984	8066	8148	8231	8313	8395	8477	8559	8642	8724	
83	8806	8888	8971	9053	9135	9217	9299	9382	9464	9546	
84	9628	9710	9792	9875	9957	0039	0121	0203	0286	0368	
85	723 0450	0532	0614	0696	0779	0861	0943	1025	1107	1189	
86	1272	1354	1436	1518	1600	1682	1765	1847	1929	2011	
87	2093	2175	2257	2340	2422	2504	2586	2668	2750	2832	
88	2914	2997	3079	3161	3243	3325	3407	3489	3571	3654	
89	3736	3818	3900	3982	4064	4146	4228	4310	4393	4475	
90	4557	4639	4721	4803	4885	4967	5049	5131	5213	5296	
5291	5378	5460	5542	5624	5706	5788	5870	5952	6034	6116	
92	6198	6280	6362	6445	6527	6609	6691	6773	6855	6937	
93	7019	7101	7183	7265	7347	7429	7511	7593	7675	7757	
94	7839	7921	8003	8085	8167	8250	8332	8414	8496	8578	
95	8660	8742	8824	8906	8988	9070	9152	9234	9316	9398	
96	9480	9562	9644	9726	9808	9890	9972	0054	0136	0218	
97	724 0300	0382	0464	0546	0628	0710	0792	0874	0956	1038	
98	1120	1202	1283	1365	1447	1529	1611	1693	1775	1857	
99	1939	2021	2103	2185	2267	2349	2431	2513	2595	2677	
5300	2759	2841	2923	3005	3086	3168	3250	3332	3414	3496	

No.	0	1	2	3	4	5	6	7	8	9	Diff.
5300	724 2759	2841	2923	3005	3086	3168	3250	3332	3414	3496	
01	3578	3660	3742	3824	3906	3988	4070	4151	4233	4315	
02	4397	4479	4561	4643	4725	4807	4889	4971	5052	5134	
03	5216	5298	5380	5462	5544	5626	5708	5790	5871	5953	
04	6035	6117	6199	6281	6363	6445	6526	6608	6690	6772	
05	6854	6936	7018	7099	7181	7263	7345	7427	7509	7591	
06	7672	7754	7836	7918	8000	8082	8164	8245	8327	8409	
07	8491	8573	8655	8736	8818	8900	8982	9064	9146	9227	
08	9309	9391	9473	9555	9636	9718	9800	9882	9964	0̄045	
09	725 0127	0209	0291	0373	0454	0536	0618	0700	0782	0863	
10	0945	1027	1109	1191	1272	1354	1436	1518	1599	1681	
5311	1763	1845	1927	2008	2090	2172	2254	2335	2417	2499	
12	2581	2662	2744	2826	2908	2989	3071	3153	3235	3316	
13	3398	3480	3562	3643	3725	3807	3889	3970	4052	4134	
14	4216	4297	4379	4461	4542	4624	4706	4788	4869	4951	
15	5033	5114	5196	5278	5360	5441	5523	5605	5686	5768	
16	5850	5931	6013	6095	6176	6258	6340	6422	6503	6585	
17	6667	6748	6830	6912	6993	7075	7157	7238	7320	7402	
18	7483	7565	7647	7728	7810	7892	7973	8055	8137	8218	
19	8300	8382	8463	8545	8626	8708	8790	8871	8953	9035	
20	9116	9198	9280	9361	9443	9524	9606	9688	9769	9851	82
5321	9933	0̄014	0̄096	0̄177	0̄259	0̄341	0̄422	0̄504	0̄585	0̄667	1 8
22	726 0749	0830	0912	0994	1075	1157	1238	1320	1401	1483	2 16
23	1565	1646	1728	1809	1891	1973	2054	2136	2217	2299	3 25
24	2380	2462	2544	2625	2707	2788	2870	2951	3033	3115	4 33
25	3196	3278	3359	3441	3522	3604	3685	3767	3849	3930	5 41
26	4012	4093	4175	4256	4338	4419	4501	4582	4664	4745	6 49
27	4827	4908	4990	5072	5153	5235	5316	5398	5479	5561	7 57
28	5642	5724	5805	5887	5968	6050	6131	6213	6294	6376	8 66
29	6457	6539	6620	6702	6783	6865	6946	7028	7109	7191	9 74
30	7272	7354	7435	7517	7598	7679	7761	7842	7924	8005	
5331	8087	8168	8250	8331	8413	8494	8576	8657	8739	8820	
32	8901	8983	9064	9146	9227	9309	9390	9472	9553	9634	
33	9716	9797	9879	9960	0̄042	0̄123	0̄204	0̄286	0̄367	0̄449	
34	727 0530	0612	0693	0774	0856	0937	1019	1100	1181	1263	
35	1344	1426	1507	1588	1670	1751	1833	1914	1995	2077	
36	2158	2240	2321	2402	2484	2565	2647	2728	2809	2891	
37	2972	3053	3135	3216	3298	3379	3460	3542	3623	3704	
38	3786	3867	3948	4030	4111	4192	4274	4355	4437	4518	
39	4599	4681	4762	4843	4925	5006	5087	5169	5250	5331	
40	5413	5494	5575	5657	5738	5819	5901	5982	6063	6144	
5341	6226	6307	6388	6470	6551	6632	6714	6795	6876	6958	
42	7039	7120	7201	7283	7364	7445	7527	7608	7689	7770	
43	7852	7933	8014	8096	8177	8258	8339	8421	8502	8583	
44	8664	8746	8827	8908	8990	9071	9152	9233	9315	9396	
45	9477	9558	9640	9721	9802	9883	9965	0̄046	0̄127	0̄208	
46	728 0290	0371	0452	0533	0614	0696	0777	0858	0939	1021	
47	1102	1183	1264	1346	1427	1508	1589	1670	1752	1833	
48	1914	1995	2076	2158	2239	2320	2401	2482	2564	2645	
49	2726	2807	2888	2970	3051	3132	3213	3294	3375	3457	
5350	3538	3619	3700	3781	3863	3944	4025	4106	4187	4268	

No.	0	1	2	3	4	5	6	7	8	9	Diff.
5350	728 3538	3619	3700	3781	3863	3944	4025	4106	4187	4268	
51	4350	4431	4512	4593	4674	4755	4836	4918	4999	5080	
52	5161	5242	5323	5404	5486	5567	5648	5729	5810	5891	
53	5972	6054	6135	6216	6297	6378	6459	6540	6621	6703	
54	6784	6865	6946	7027	7108	7189	7270	7351	7433	7514	
55	7595	7676	7757	7838	7919	8000	8081	8162	8244	8325	
56	8406	8487	8568	8649	8730	8811	8892	8973	9054	9135	
57	9216	9298	9379	9460	9541	9622	9703	9784	9865	9946	
58	729 0027	0108	0189	0270	0351	0432	0513	0594	0675	0757	
59	0838	0919	1000	1081	1162	1243	1324	1405	1486	1567	
60	1648	1729	1810	1891	1972	2053	2134	2215	2296	2377	
5361	2458	2539	2620	2701	2782	2863	2944	3025	3106	3187	
62	3268	3349	3430	3511	3592	3673	3754	3835	3916	3997	
63	4078	4159	4240	4321	4402	4483	4564	4645	4726	4807	
64	4888	4969	5050	5131	5212	5292	5373	5454	5535	5616	
65	5697	5778	5859	5940	6021	6102	6183	6264	6345	6426	
66	6507	6588	6669	6749	6830	6911	6992	7073	7154	7235	
67	7316	7397	7478	7559	7640	7721	7801	7882	7963	8044	
68	8125	8206	8287	8368	8449	8530	8610	8691	8772	8853	
69	8934	9015	9096	9177	9258	9338	9419	9500	9581	9662	
70	9743	9824	9905	9985	0066	0147	0228	0309	0390	0471	
5371	730 0552	0632	0713	0794	0875	0956	1037	1118	1198	1279	
72	1360	1441	1522	1603	1683	1764	1845	1926	2007	2088	
73	2168	2249	2330	2411	2492	2573	2653	2734	2815	2896	
74	2977	3057	3138	3219	3300	3381	3461	3542	3623	3704	
75	3785	3865	3946	4027	4108	4189	4269	4350	4431	4512	
76	4593	4673	4754	4835	4916	4997	5077	5158	5239	5320	
77	5400	5481	5562	5643	5723	5804	5885	5966	6046	6127	
78	6208	6289	6369	6450	6531	6612	6692	6773	6854	6935	
79	7015	7096	7177	7258	7338	7419	7500	7581	7661	7742	
80	7823	7903	7984	8065	8146	8226	8307	8388	8468	8549	
5381	8630	8711	8791	8872	8953	9033	9114	9195	9276	9356	
82	9437	9518	9598	9679	9760	9840	9921	0002	0082	0163	
83	731 0244	0324	0405	0486	0567	0647	0728	0809	0889	0970	
84	1051	1131	1212	1292	1373	1454	1534	1615	1696	1776	
85	1857	1938	2018	2099	2180	2260	2341	2422	2502	2583	
86	2663	2744	2825	2905	2986	3067	3147	3228	3309	3389	
87	3470	3550	3631	3712	3792	3873	3953	4034	4115	4195	
88	4276	4356	4437	4518	4598	4679	4759	4840	4921	5001	
89	5082	5162	5243	5324	5404	5485	5565	5646	5727	5807	
90	5888	5968	6049	6129	6210	6291	6371	6452	6532	6613	
5391	6693	6774	6854	6935	7016	7096	7177	7257	7338	7418	
92	7499	7579	7660	7740	7821	7902	7982	8063	8143	8224	
93	8304	8385	8465	8546	8626	8707	8787	8868	8948	9029	
94	9109	9190	9270	9351	9431	9512	9592	9673	9753	9834	
95	9914	9995	0075	0156	0236	0317	0397	0478	0558	0639	
96	732 0719	0800	0880	0961	1041	1122	1202	1283	1363	1444	
97	1524	1605	1685	1766	1846	1927	2007	2087	2168	2248	
98	2329	2409	2490	2570	2651	2731	2812	2892	2972	3053	
99	3133	3214	3294	3375	3455	3535	3616	3696	3777	3857	
5400	3938	4018	4098	4179	4259	4340	4420	4501	4581	4661	

Diff.

81	
1	8
2	16
3	24
4	32
5	41
6	49
7	57
8	65
9	73

No.	0	1	2	3	4	5	6	7	8	9	Diff.
5400	732 3938	4018	4098	4179	4259	4340	4420	4501	4581	4661	
01	4742	4822	4903	4983	5063	5144	5224	5305	5385	5465	
02	5546	5626	5707	5787	5867	5948	6028	6109	6189	6269	
03	6350	6430	6510	6591	6671	6752	6832	6912	6993	7073	
04	7153	7234	7314	7394	7475	7555	7636	7716	7796	7877	
05	7957	8037	8118	8198	8278	8359	8439	8519	8600	8680	
06	8760	8841	8921	9001	9082	9162	9242	9323	9403	9483	
07	9564	9644	9724	9805	9885	9965	0046	0126	0206	0287	
08	733 0367	0447	0527	0608	0688	0768	0849	0929	1009	1090	
09	1170	1250	1330	1411	1491	1571	1652	1732	1812	1892	
10	1973	2053	2133	2213	2294	2374	2454	2535	2615	2695	
5411	2775	2856	2936	3016	3096	3177	3257	3337	3417	3498	
12	3578	3658	3738	3819	3899	3979	4059	4140	4220	4300	
13	4380	4461	4541	4621	4701	4781	4862	4942	5022	5102	
14	5183	5263	5343	5423	5503	5584	5664	5744	5824	5904	
15	5985	6065	6145	6225	6305	6386	6466	6546	6626	6706	
16	6787	6867	6947	7027	7107	7187	7268	7348	7428	7508	
17	7588	7669	7749	7829	7909	7989	8069	8150	8230	8310	
18	8390	8470	8550	8630	8711	8791	8871	8951	9031	9111	
19	9192	9272	9352	9432	9512	9592	9672	9752	9833	9913	
20	9993	0073	0153	0233	0313	0393	0474	0554	0634	0714	80
5421	734 0794	0874	0954	1034	1115	1195	1275	1355	1435	1515	1 8
22	1595	1675	1755	1835	1916	1996	2076	2156	2236	2316	2 16
23	2396	2476	2556	2636	2716	2796	2877	2957	3037	3117	3 24
24	3197	3277	3357	3437	3517	3597	3677	3757	3837	3917	4 32
25	3997	4077	4158	4238	4318	4398	4478	4558	4638	4718	5 40
26	4798	4878	4958	5038	5118	5198	5278	5358	5438	5518	6 48
27	5598	5678	5758	5838	5918	5998	6078	6158	6238	6318	7 56
28	6398	6478	6558	6638	6718	6798	6878	6958	7038	7118	8 64
29	7198	7278	7358	7438	7518	7598	7678	7758	7838	7918	9 72
30	7998	8078	8158	8238	8318	8398	8478	8558	8638	8718	
5431	8798	8878	8958	9038	9118	9198	9278	9358	9438	9518	
32	9598	9678	9758	9837	9917	9997	0077	0157	0237	0317	
33	735 0397	0477	0557	0637	0717	0797	0877	0957	1036	1116	
34	1196	1276	1356	1436	1516	1596	1676	1756	1836	1916	
35	1995	2075	2155	2235	2315	2395	2475	2555	2635	2715	
36	2794	2874	2954	3034	3114	3194	3274	3354	3434	3513	
37	3593	3673	3753	3833	3913	3993	4073	4152	4232	4312	
38	4392	4472	4552	4632	4711	4791	4871	4951	5031	5111	
39	5191	5270	5350	5430	5510	5590	5670	5749	5829	5909	
40	5989	6069	6149	6228	6308	6388	6468	6548	6628	6707	
5441	6787	6867	6947	7027	7107	7186	7266	7346	7426	7506	
42	7585	7665	7745	7825	7905	7984	8064	8144	8224	8304	
43	8383	8463	8543	8623	8702	8782	8862	8942	9022	9101	
44	9181	9261	9341	9420	9500	9580	9660	9740	9819	9899	
45	9979	0059	0138	0218	0298	0378	0457	0537	0617	0697	
46	736 0776	0856	0936	1016	1095	1175	1255	1335	1414	1494	
47	1574	1653	1733	1813	1893	1972	2052	2132	2212	2291	
48	2371	2451	2530	2610	2690	2770	2849	2929	3009	3088	
49	3168	3248	3327	3407	3487	3567	3646	3726	3806	3885	
5450	3965	4045	4124	4204	4284	4363	4443	4523	4602	4682	

No.	0	1	2	3	4	5	6	7	8	9	Diff.
5450	736 3965	4045	4124	4204	4284	4363	4443	4523	4602	4682	
51	4762	4841	4921	5001	5080	5160	5240	5319	5399	5479	
52	5558	5638	5718	5797	5877	5957	6036	6116	6196	6275	
53	6355	6435	6514	6594	6674	6753	6833	6912	6992	7072	
54	7151	7231	7311	7390	7470	7549	7629	7709	7788	7868	
55	7948	8027	8107	8186	8266	8346	8425	8505	8584	8664	
56	8744	8823	8903	8982	9062	9142	9221	9301	9380	9460	
57	9540	9619	9699	9778	9858	9937	0017	0097	0176	0256	
58	737 0335	0415	0494	0574	0654	0733	0813	0892	0972	1051	
59	1131	1210	1290	1370	1449	1529	1608	1688	1767	1847	
60	1926	2006	2086	2165	2245	2324	2404	2483	2563	2642	
5461	2722	2801	2881	2960	3040	3119	3199	3278	3358	3437	
62	3517	3596	3676	3755	3835	3914	3994	4074	4153	4233	
63	4312	4392	4471	4550	4630	4709	4789	4868	4948	5027	
64	5107	5186	5266	5345	5425	5504	5584	5663	5743	5822	
65	5902	5981	6061	6140	6220	6299	6378	6458	6537	6617	
66	6696	6776	6855	6935	7014	7094	7173	7252	7332	7411	
67	7491	7570	7650	7729	7808	7888	7967	8047	8126	8206	
68	8285	8364	8444	8523	8603	8682	8762	8841	8920	9000	
69	9079	9159	9238	9317	9397	9476	9556	9635	9714	9794	
70	9873	9953	0032	0111	0191	0270	0350	0429	0508	0588	
5471	738 0667	0747	0826	0905	0985	1064	1143	1223	1302	1382	
72	1461	1540	1620	1699	1778	1858	1937	2016	2096	2175	
73	2254	2334	2413	2493	2572	2651	2731	2810	2889	2969	
74	3048	3127	3207	3286	3365	3445	3524	3603	3683	3762	
75	3841	3921	4000	4079	4159	4238	4317	4396	4476	4555	
76	4634	4714	4793	4872	4952	5031	5110	5190	5269	5348	
77	5427	5507	5586	5665	5745	5824	5903	5982	6062	6141	
78	6220	6300	6379	6458	6537	6617	6696	6775	6854	6934	
79	7013	7092	7172	7251	7330	7409	7489	7568	7647	7726	
80	7806	7885	7964	8043	8123	8202	8281	8360	8440	8519	
5481	8598	8677	8756	8836	8915	8994	9073	9153	9232	9311	
82	9390	9470	9549	9628	9707	9786	9866	9945	0024	0103	
83	739 0182	0262	0341	0420	0499	0578	0658	0737	0816	0895	
84	0974	1054	1133	1212	1291	1370	1450	1529	1608	1687	
85	1766	1845	1925	2004	2083	2162	2241	2321	2400	2479	
86	2558	2637	2716	2796	2875	2954	3033	3112	3191	3270	
87	3350	3429	3508	3587	3666	3745	3824	3904	3983	4062	
88	4141	4220	4299	4378	4458	4537	4616	4695	4774	4853	
89	4932	5011	5091	5170	5249	5328	5407	5486	5565	5644	
90	5723	5803	5882	5961	6040	6119	6198	6277	6356	6435	
5491	6514	6594	6673	6752	6831	6910	6989	7068	7147	7226	
92	7305	7384	7463	7543	7622	7701	7780	7859	7938	8017	
93	8096	8175	8254	8333	8412	8491	8570	8649	8728	8808	
94	8887	8966	9045	9124	9203	9282	9361	9440	9519	9598	
95	9677	9756	9835	9914	9993	0072	0151	0230	0309	0388	
96	740 0467	0546	0625	0704	0783	0862	0941	1020	1099	1178	
97	1257	1336	1415	1494	1573	1652	1731	1810	1889	1968	
98	2047	2126	2205	2284	2363	2442	2521	2600	2679	2758	
99	2837	2916	2995	3074	3153	3232	3311	3390	3469	3548	
5500	3627	3706	3785	3864	3943	4022	4101	4180	4259	4338	

Diff. 79

1	8
2	16
3	24
4	32
5	40
6	47
7	55
8	63
9	71

No.	0	1	2	3	4	5	6	7	8	9	Diff.
5500	740 3627	3706	3785	3864	3943	4022	4101	4180	4259	4338	
01	4416	4495	4574	4653	4732	4811	4890	4969	5048	5127	
02	5206	5285	5364	5443	5522	5601	5679	5758	5837	5916	
03	5995	6074	6153	6232	6311	6390	6469	6548	6626	6705	
04	6784	6863	6942	7021	7100	7179	7258	7337	7415	7494	
05	7573	7652	7731	7810	7889	7968	8047	8125	8204	8283	
06	8362	8441	8520	8599	8678	8756	8835	8914	8993	9072	
07	9151	9230	9308	9387	9466	9545	9624	9703	9782	9860	
08	9939	$00\overline{18}$	$00\overline{97}$	$01\overline{76}$	$02\overline{55}$	$03\overline{34}$	$04\overline{12}$	$04\overline{91}$	$05\overline{70}$	$06\overline{49}$	
09	741 0728	0807	0885	0964	1043	1122	1201	1280	1358	1437	
10	1516	1595	1674	1752	1831	1910	1989	2068	2146	2225	
5511	2304	2383	2462	2541	2619	2698	2777	2856	2935	3013	
12	3092	3171	3250	3328	3407	3486	3565	3644	3722	3801	
13	3880	3959	4037	4116	4195	4274	4353	4431	4510	4589	
14	4668	4746	4825	4904	4983	5061	5140	5219	5298	5376	
15	5455	5534	5613	5691	5770	5849	5928	6006	6085	6164	
16	6243	6321	6400	6479	6557	6636	6715	6794	6872	6951	
17	7030	7109	7187	7266	7345	7423	7502	7581	7660	7738	
18	7817	7896	7974	8053	8132	8210	8289	8368	8447	8525	
19	8604	8683	8761	8840	8919	8997	9076	9155	9233	9312	
20	9391	9469	9548	9627	9705	9784	9863	9941	$00\overline{20}$	$00\overline{99}$	
5521	742 0177	0256	0335	0413	0492	0571	0649	0728	0807	0885	
22	0964	1043	1121	1200	1279	1357	1436	1515	1593	1672	
23	1750	1829	1908	1986	2065	2144	2222	2301	2379	2458	
24	2537	2615	2694	2773	2851	2930	3008	3087	3166	3244	
25	3323	3401	3480	3559	3637	3716	3794	3873	3952	4030	
26	4109	4187	4266	4345	4423	4502	4580	4659	4737	4816	
27	4895	4973	5052	5130	5209	5288	5366	5445	5523	5602	
28	5680	5759	5837	5916	5995	6073	6152	6230	6309	6387	
29	6466	6544	6623	6702	6780	6859	6937	7016	7094	7173	
30	7251	7330	7408	7487	7565	7644	7722	7801	7880	7958	
5531	8037	8115	8194	8272	8351	8429	8508	8586	8665	8743	
32	8822	8900	8979	9057	9136	9214	9293	9371	9450	9528	
33	9607	9685	9764	9842	9921	9999	$00\overline{78}$	$01\overline{56}$	$02\overline{35}$	$03\overline{13}$	
34	743 0392	0470	0549	0627	0705	0784	0862	0941	1019	1098	
35	1176	1255	1333	1412	1490	1569	1647	1725	1804	1882	
36	1961	2039	2118	2196	2275	2353	2431	2510	2588	2667	
37	2745	2824	2902	2981	3059	3137	3216	3294	3373	3451	
38	3530	3608	3686	3765	3843	3922	4000	4078	4157	4235	
39	4314	4392	4470	4549	4627	4706	4784	4862	4941	5019	
40	5098	5176	5254	5333	5411	5490	5568	5646	5725	5803	
5541	5882	5960	6038	6117	6195	6273	6352	6430	6508	6587	
42	6665	6744	6822	6900	6979	7057	7135	7214	7292	7370	
43	7449	7527	7605	7684	7762	7841	7919	7997	8076	8154	
44	8232	8311	8389	8467	8546	8624	8702	8781	8859	8937	
45	9016	9094	9172	9250	9329	9407	9485	9564	9642	9720	
46	9799	9877	9955	$00\overline{34}$	$01\overline{12}$	$01\overline{90}$	$02\overline{68}$	$03\overline{47}$	$04\overline{25}$	$05\overline{03}$	
47	744 0582	0660	0738	0817	0895	0973	1051	1130	1208	1286	
48	1365	1443	1521	1599	1678	1756	1834	1912	1991	2069	
49	2147	2226	2304	2382	2460	2539	2617	2695	2773	2852	
5550	2930	3008	3086	3165	3243	3321	3399	3478	3556	3634	

79

1	8
2	16
3	24
4	32
5	40
6	47
7	55
8	63
9	71

No.	0	1	2	3	4	5	6	7	8	9	Diff.
5550	744 2930	3008	3086	3165	3243	3321	3399	3478	3556	3634	
51	3712	3791	3869	3947	4025	4103	4182	4260	4338	4416	
52	4495	4573	4651	4729	4807	4886	4964	5042	5120	5199	
53	5277	5355	5433	5511	5590	5668	5746	5824	5902	5981	
54	6059	6137	6215	6293	6372	6450	6528	6606	6684	6762	
55	6841	6919	6997	7075	7153	7232	7310	7388	7466	7544	
56	7622	7701	7779	7857	7935	8013	8091	8170	8248	8326	
57	8404	8482	8560	8638	8717	8795	8873	8951	9029	9107	
58	9185	9264	9342	9420	9498	9576	9654	9732	9810	9889	
59	9967	0045	0123	0201	0279	0357	0435	0514	0592	0670	
60	745 0748	0826	0904	0982	1060	1138	1217	1295	1373	1451	
5561	1529	1607	1685	1763	1841	1919	1998	2076	2154	2232	
62	2310	2388	2466	2544	2622	2700	2778	2856	2934	3013	
63	3091	3169	3247	3325	3403	3481	3559	3637	3715	3793	
64	3871	3949	4027	4105	4183	4261	4340	4418	4496	4574	
65	4652	4730	4808	4886	4964	5042	5120	5198	5276	5354	
66	5432	5510	5588	5666	5744	5822	5900	5978	6056	6134	
67	6212	6290	6368	6446	6524	6602	6680	6758	6836	6914	
68	6992	7070	7148	7226	7304	7382	7460	7538	7616	7694	
69	7772	7850	7928	8006	8084	8162	8240	8318	8396	8474	
70	8552	8630	8708	8786	8864	8942	9020	9098	9176	9254	**78**
5571	9332	9410	9487	9565	9643	9721	9799	9877	9955	0033	1 8
72	746 0111	0189	0267	0345	0423	0501	0579	0657	0735	0813	2 16
73	0890	0968	1046	1124	1202	1280	1358	1436	1514	1592	3 23
74	1670	1748	1825	1903	1981	2059	2137	2215	2293	2371	4 31
75	2449	2527	2605	2682	2760	2838	2916	2994	3072	3150	5 39
76	3228	3306	3383	3461	3539	3617	3695	3773	3851	3929	6 47
77	4006	4084	4162	4240	4318	4396	4474	4552	4629	4707	7 55
78	4785	4863	4941	5019	5097	5174	5252	5330	5408	5486	8 62
79	5564	5641	5719	5797	5875	5953	6031	6108	6186	6264	9 70
80	6342	6420	6498	6575	6653	6731	6809	6887	6965	7042	
5581	7120	7198	7276	7354	7431	7509	7587	7665	7743	7821	
82	7898	7976	8054	8132	8210	8287	8365	8443	8521	8598	
83	8676	8754	8832	8910	8987	9065	9143	9221	9299	9376	
84	9454	9532	9610	9687	9765	9843	9921	9998	0076	0154	
85	747 0232	0310	0387	0465	0543	0621	0698	0776	0854	0932	
86	1009	1087	1165	1243	1320	1398	1476	1554	1631	1709	
87	1787	1864	1942	2020	2098	2175	2253	2331	2409	2486	
88	2564	2642	2719	2797	2875	2953	3030	3108	3186	3263	
89	3341	3419	3497	3574	3652	3730	3807	3885	3963	4040	
90	4118	4196	4273	4351	4429	4507	4584	4662	4740	4817	
5591	4895	4973	5050	5128	5206	5283	5361	5439	5516	5594	
92	5672	5749	5827	5905	5982	6060	6138	6215	6293	6371	
93	6448	6526	6603	6681	6759	6836	6914	6992	7069	7147	
94	7225	7302	7380	7458	7535	7613	7690	7768	7846	7923	
95	8001	8079	8156	8234	8311	8389	8467	8544	8622	8699	
96	8777	8855	8932	9010	9087	9165	9243	9320	9398	9475	
97	9553	9631	9708	9786	9863	9941	0019	0096	0174	0251	
98	748 0329	0407	0484	0562	0639	0717	0794	0872	0950	1027	
99	1105	1182	1260	1337	1415	1492	1570	1648	1725	1803	
5600	1880	1958	2035	2113	2190	2268	2346	2423	2501	2578	

No.	0	1	2	3	4	5	6	7	8	9	Diff.
5600	748 1880	1958	2035	2113	2190	2268	2346	2423	2501	2578	
01	2656	2733	2811	2888	2966	3043	3121	3198	3276	3354	
02	3431	3509	3586	3664	3741	3819	3896	3974	4051	4129	
03	4206	4284	4361	4439	4516	4594	4671	4749	4826	4904	
04	4981	5059	5136	5214	5291	5369	5446	5524	5601	5679	
05	5756	5834	5911	5989	6066	6144	6221	6299	6376	6453	
06	6531	6608	6686	6763	6841	6918	6996	7073	7151	7228	
07	7306	7383	7460	7538	7615	7693	7770	7848	7925	8003	
08	8080	8157	8235	8312	8390	8467	8545	8622	8700	8777	
09	8854	8932	9009	9087	9164	9242	9319	9396	9474	9551	
10	9629	9706	9783	9861	9938	$\overline{0016}$	$\overline{0093}$	$\overline{0170}$	$\overline{0248}$	$\overline{0325}$	
5611	749 0403	0480	0557	0635	0712	0790	0867	0944	1022	1099	
12	1177	1254	1331	1409	1486	1564	1641	1718	1796	1873	
13	1950	2028	2105	2183	2260	2337	2415	2492	2569	2647	
14	2724	2801	2879	2956	3034	3111	3188	3266	3343	3420	
15	3498	3575	3652	3730	3807	3884	3962	4039	4116	4194	
16	4271	4348	4426	4503	4580	4658	4735	4812	4890	4967	
17	5044	5122	5199	5276	5353	5431	5508	5585	5663	5740	
18	5817	5895	5972	6049	6127	6204	6281	6358	6436	6513	
19	6590	6668	6745	6822	6899	6977	7054	7131	7209	7286	
20	7363	7440	7518	7595	7672	7750	7827	7904	7981	8059	
5621	8136	8213	8290	8368	8445	8522	8599	8677	8754	8831	
22	8908	8986	9063	9140	9217	9295	9372	9449	9526	9604	
23	9681	9758	9835	9913	9990	$\overline{0067}$	$\overline{0144}$	$\overline{0221}$	$\overline{0299}$	$\overline{0376}$	
24	750 0453	0530	0608	0685	0762	0839	0916	0994	1071	1148	
25	1225	1302	1380	1457	1534	1611	1688	1766	1843	1920	
26	1997	2074	2152	2229	2306	2383	2460	2538	2615	2692	
27	2769	2846	2924	3001	3078	3155	3232	3309	3387	3464	
28	3541	3618	3695	3772	3850	3927	4004	4081	4158	4235	
29	4312	4390	4467	4544	4621	4698	4775	4853	4930	5007	
30	5084	5161	5238	5315	5392	5470	5547	5624	5701	5778	
5631	5855	5932	6010	6087	6164	6241	6318	6395	6472	6549	
32	6626	6704	6781	6858	6935	7012	7089	7166	7243	7320	
33	7398	7475	7552	7629	7706	7783	7860	7937	8014	8091	
34	8168	8246	8323	8400	8477	8554	8631	8708	8785	8862	
35	8939	9016	9093	9170	9247	9325	9402	9479	9556	9633	
36	9710	9787	9864	9941	$\overline{0018}$	$\overline{0095}$	$\overline{0172}$	$\overline{0249}$	$\overline{0326}$	$\overline{0403}$	
37	751 0480	0557	0634	0711	0789	0866	0943	1020	1097	1174	
38	1251	1328	1405	1482	1559	1636	1713	1790	1867	1944	
39	2021	2098	2175	2252	2329	2406	2483	2560	2637	2714	
40	2791	2868	2945	3022	3099	3176	3253	3330	3407	3484	
5641	3561	3638	3715	3792	3869	3946	4023	4100	4177	4254	
42	4331	4408	4485	4562	4639	4716	4793	4870	4947	5024	
43	5101	5177	5254	5331	5408	5485	5562	5639	5716	5793	
44	5870	5947	6024	6101	6178	6255	6332	6409	6486	6563	
45	6639	6716	6793	6870	6947	7024	7101	7178	7255	7332	
46	7409	7486	7563	7639	7716	7793	7870	7947	8024	8101	
47	8178	8255	8332	8409	8485	8562	8639	8716	8793	8870	
48	8947	9024	9101	9178	9254	9331	9408	9485	9562	9639	
49	9716	9793	9870	9946	$\overline{0023}$	$\overline{0100}$	$\overline{0177}$	$\overline{0254}$	$\overline{0331}$	$\overline{0408}$	
5650	752 0484	0561	0638	0715	0792	0869	0946	1023	1099	1176	

77

1	8
2	15
3	23
4	31
5	39
6	46
7	54
8	62
9	69

No.	0	1	2	3	4	5	6	7	8	9	Diff.
5650	752 0484	0561	0638	0715	0792	0869	0946	1023	1099	1176	
51	1253	1330	1407	1484	1560	1637	1714	1791	1868	1945	
52	2022	2098	2175	2252	2329	2406	2483	2559	2636	2713	
53	2790	2867	2944	3020	3097	3174	3251	3328	3404	3481	
54	3558	3635	3712	3788	3865	3942	4019	4096	4172	4249	
55	4326	4403	4480	4556	4633	4710	4787	4864	4940	5017	
56	5094	5171	5248	5324	5401	5478	5555	5631	5708	5785	
57	5862	5939	6015	6092	6169	6246	6322	6399	6476	6553	
58	6629	6706	6783	6860	6936	7013	7090	7167	7243	7320	
59	7397	7474	7550	7627	7704	7781	7857	7934	8011	8088	
60	8164	8241	8318	8394	8471	8548	8625	8701	8778	8855	
5661	8932	9008	9085	9162	9238	9315	9392	9469	9545	9622	
62	9699	9775	9852	9929	0005	0082	0159	0236	0312	0389	
63	753 0466	0542	0619	0696	0772	0849	0926	1002	1079	1156	
64	1232	1309	1386	1462	1539	1616	1692	1769	1846	1922	
65	1999	2076	2152	2229	2306	2382	2459	2536	2612	2689	
66	2766	2842	2919	2996	3072	3149	3226	3302	3379	3455	
67	3532	3609	3685	3762	3839	3915	3992	4069	4145	4222	
68	4298	4375	4452	4528	4605	4682	4758	4835	4911	4988	
69	5065	5141	5218	5294	5371	5448	5524	5601	5677	5754	
70	5831	5907	5984	6060	6137	6214	6290	6367	6443	6520	
5671	6596	6673	6750	6826	6903	6979	7056	7133	7209	7286	
72	7362	7439	7515	7592	7668	7745	7822	7898	7975	8051	
73	8128	8204	8281	8357	8434	8511	8587	8664	8740	8817	
74	8893	8970	9046	9123	9199	9276	9353	9429	9506	9582	
75	9659	9735	9812	9888	9965	0041	0118	0194	0271	0347	
76	754 0424	0500	0577	0653	0730	0806	0883	0959	1036	1112	
77	1189	1265	1342	1418	1495	1571	1648	1724	1801	1877	
78	1954	2030	2107	2183	2260	2336	2413	2489	2566	2642	
79	2719	2795	2872	2948	3025	3101	3178	3254	3330	3407	
80	3483	3560	3636	3713	3789	3866	3942	4019	4095	4171	
5681	4248	4324	4401	4477	4554	4630	4707	4783	4859	4936	
82	5012	5089	5165	5242	5318	5394	5471	5547	5624	5700	
83	5777	5853	5929	6006	6082	6159	6235	6311	6388	6464	
84	6541	6617	6694	6770	6846	6923	6999	7076	7152	7228	
85	7305	7381	7457	7534	7610	7687	7763	7839	7916	7992	
86	8069	8145	8221	8298	8374	8450	8527	8603	8680	8756	
87	8832	8909	8985	9061	9138	9214	9290	9367	9443	9520	
88	9596	9672	9749	9825	9901	9978	0054	0130	0207	0283	
89	755 0359	0436	0512	0588	0665	0741	0817	0894	0970	1046	
90	1123	1199	1275	1352	1428	1504	1581	1657	1733	1810	
5691	1886	1962	2038	2115	2191	2267	2344	2420	2496	2573	
92	2649	2725	2802	2878	2954	3030	3107	3183	3259	3336	
93	3412	3488	3564	3641	3717	3793	3870	3946	4022	4098	
94	4175	4251	4327	4403	4480	4556	4632	4709	4785	4861	
95	4937	5014	5090	5166	5242	5319	5395	5471	5547	5624	
96	5700	5776	5852	5929	6005	6081	6157	6233	6310	6386	
97	6462	6538	6615	6691	6767	6843	6920	6996	7072	7148	
98	7224	7301	7377	7453	7529	7606	7682	7758	7834	7910	
99	7987	8063	8139	8215	8291	8368	8444	8520	8596	8672	
5700	8749	8825	8901	8977	9053	9130	9206	9282	9358	9434	

77

1	8
2	15
3	23
4	31
5	39
6	46
7	54
8	62
9	69

No.	0	1	2	3	4	5	6	7	8	9	Diff.
5700	755 8749	8825	8901	8977	9053	9130	9206	9282	9358	9434	
01	9510	9587	9663	9739	9815	9891	9967	0044	0120	0196	
02	756 0272	0348	0424	0501	0577	0653	0729	0805	0881	0958	
03	1034	1110	1186	1262	1338	1414	1491	1567	1643	1719	
04	1795	1871	1947	2024	2100	2176	2252	2328	2404	2480	
05	2556	2633	2709	2785	2861	2937	3013	3089	3165	3242	
06	3318	3394	3470	3546	3622	3698	3774	3850	3927	4003	
07	4079	4155	4231	4307	4383	4459	4535	4611	4687	4764	
08	4840	4916	4992	5068	5144	5220	5296	5372	5448	5524	
09	5600	5677	5753	5829	5905	5981	6057	6133	6209	6285	
10	6361	6437	6513	6589	6665	6741	6817	6893	6970	7046	
5711	7122	7198	7274	7350	7426	7502	7578	7654	7730	7806	
12	7882	7958	8034	8110	8186	8262	8338	8414	8490	8566	
13	8642	8718	8794	8870	8946	9022	9098	9174	9250	9326	
14	9402	9478	9554	9630	9706	9782	9858	9934	0010	0086	
15	757 0162	0238	0314	0390	0466	0542	0618	0694	0770	0846	
16	0922	0998	1074	1150	1226	1302	1378	1454	1530	1606	
17	1682	1758	1834	1910	1986	2062	2138	2214	2290	2366	
18	2442	2517	2593	2669	2745	2821	2897	2973	3049	3125	
19	3201	3277	3353	3429	3505	3581	3657	3733	3808	3884	
20	3960	4036	4112	4188	4264	4340	4416	4492	4568	4644	
5721	4719	4795	4871	4947	5023	5099	5175	5251	5327	5403	
22	5479	5554	5630	5706	5782	5858	5934	6010	6086	6162	
23	6237	6313	6389	6465	6541	6617	6693	6769	6845	6920	
24	6996	7072	7148	7224	7300	7376	7451	7527	7603	7679	
25	7755	7831	7907	7982	8058	8134	8210	8286	8362	8438	
26	8513	8589	8665	8741	8817	8893	8968	9044	9120	9196	
27	9272	9348	9423	9499	9575	9651	9727	9803	9878	9954	
28	758 0030	0106	0182	0258	0333	0409	0485	0561	0637	0712	
29	0788	0864	0940	1016	1091	1167	1243	1319	1395	1470	
30	1546	1622	1698	1774	1849	1925	2001	2077	2153	2228	
5731	2304	2380	2456	2531	2607	2683	2759	2835	2910	2986	
32	3062	3138	3213	3289	3365	3441	3516	3592	3668	3744	
33	3819	3895	3971	4047	4122	4198	4274	4350	4425	4501	
34	4577	4653	4728	4804	4880	4956	5031	5107	5183	5258	
35	5334	5410	5486	5561	5637	5713	5789	5864	5940	6016	
36	6091	6167	6243	6319	6394	6470	6546	6621	6697	6773	
37	6848	6924	7000	7076	7151	7227	7303	7378	7454	7530	
38	7605	7681	7757	7832	7908	7984	8060	8135	8211	8287	
39	8362	8438	8514	8589	8665	8741	8816	8892	8968	9043	
40	9119	9195	9270	9346	9422	9497	9573	9649	9724	9800	
5741	9875	9951	0027	0102	0178	0254	0329	0405	0481	0556	
42	759 0632	0708	0783	0859	0934	1010	1086	1161	1237	1313	
43	1388	1464	1539	1615	1691	1766	1842	1917	1993	2069	
44	2144	2220	2296	2371	2447	2522	2598	2674	2749	2825	
45	2900	2976	3052	3127	3203	3278	3354	3429	3505	3581	
46	3656	3732	3807	3883	3959	4034	4110	4185	4261	4336	
47	4412	4488	4563	4639	4714	4790	4865	4941	5016	5092	
48	5168	5243	5319	5394	5470	5545	5621	5696	5772	5848	
49	5923	5999	6074	6150	6225	6301	6376	6452	6527	6603	
5750	6678	6754	6830	6905	6981	7056	7132	7207	7283	7358	

76
1	8
2	15
3	23
4	30
5	38
6	46
7	53
8	61
9	68

No.	0	1	2	3	4	5	6	7	8	9	Diff.
5750	759 6678	6754	6830	6905	6981	7056	7132	7207	7283	7358	
51	7434	7509	7585	7660	7736	7811	7887	7962	8038	8113	
52	8189	8264	8340	8415	8491	8566	8642	8717	8793	8868	
53	8944	9019	9095	9170	9246	9321	9397	9472	9548	9623	
54	9699	9774	9850	9925	0000	0076	0151	0227	0302	0378	
55	760 0453	0529	0604	0680	0755	0831	0906	0981	1057	1132	
56	1208	1283	1359	1434	1510	1585	1661	1736	1811	1887	
57	1962	2038	2113	2189	2264	2339	2415	2490	2566	2641	
58	2717	2792	2867	2943	3018	3094	3169	3245	3320	3395	
59	3471	3546	3622	3697	3772	3848	3923	3999	4074	4149	
60	4225	4300	4376	4451	4526	4602	4677	4753	4828	4903	
5761	4979	5054	5130	5205	5280	5356	5431	5506	5582	5657	
62	5733	5808	5883	5959	6034	6109	6185	6260	6335	6411	
63	6486	6562	6637	6712	6788	6863	6938	7014	7089	7164	
64	7240	7315	7390	7466	7541	7616	7692	7767	7842	7918	
65	7993	8068	8144	8219	8294	8370	8445	8520	8596	8671	
66	8746	8822	8897	8972	9048	9123	9198	9274	9349	9424	
67	9500	9575	9650	9725	9801	9876	9951	0027	0102	0177	
68	761 0253	0328	0403	0478	0554	0629	0704	0780	0855	0930	
69	1005	1081	1156	1231	1307	1382	1457	1532	1608	1683	
70	1758	1833	1909	1984	2059	2134	2210	2285	2360	2435	
5771	2511	2586	2661	2737	2812	2887	2962	3037	3113	3188	
72	3263	3338	3414	3489	3564	3639	3715	3790	3865	3940	
73	4016	4091	4166	4241	4316	4392	4467	4542	4617	4693	
74	4768	4843	4918	4993	5069	5144	5219	5294	5369	5445	
75	5520	5595	5670	5745	5821	5896	5971	6046	6121	6197	
76	6272	6347	6422	6497	6573	6648	6723	6798	6873	6948	
77	7024	7099	7174	7249	7324	7400	7475	7550	7625	7700	
78	7775	7851	7926	8001	8076	8151	8226	8301	8377	8452	
79	8527	8602	8677	8752	8828	8903	8978	9053	9128	9203	
80	9278	9354	9429	9504	9579	9654	9729	9804	9879	9955	
5781	762 0030	0105	0180	0255	0330	0405	0480	0556	0631	0706	
82	0781	0856	0931	1006	1081	1156	1232	1307	1382	1457	
83	1532	1607	1682	1757	1832	1907	1982	2058	2133	2208	
84	2283	2358	2433	2508	2583	2658	2733	2808	2883	2959	
85	3034	3109	3184	3259	3334	3409	3484	3559	3634	3709	
86	3784	3859	3934	4009	4085	4160	4235	4310	4385	4460	
87	4535	4610	4685	4760	4835	4910	4985	5060	5135	5210	
88	5285	5360	5435	5510	5585	5660	5735	5810	5885	5960	
89	6035	6111	6186	6261	6336	6411	6486	6561	6636	6711	
90	6786	6861	6936	7011	7086	7161	7236	7311	7386	7461	
5791	7536	7611	7686	7761	7836	7911	7986	8061	8136	8211	
92	8286	8361	8435	8510	8585	8660	8735	8810	8885	8960	
93	9035	9110	9185	9260	9335	9410	9485	9560	9635	9710	
94	9785	9860	9935	0010	0085	0160	0235	0310	0385	0459	
95	763 0534	0609	0684	0759	0834	0909	0984	1059	1134	1209	
96	1284	1359	1434	1509	1583	1658	1733	1808	1883	1958	
97	2033	2108	2183	2258	2333	2408	2482	2557	2632	2707	
98	2782	2857	2932	3007	3082	3157	3232	3306	3381	3456	
99	3531	3606	3681	3756	3831	3906	3980	4055	4130	4205	
5800	4280	4355	4430	4505	4579	4654	4729	4804	4879	4954	

Diff.

75

1	8
2	15
3	23
4	30
5	38
6	45
7	53
8	60
9	68

No.	0	1	2	3	4	5	6	7	8	9	Diff.
5800	763 4280	4355	4430	4505	4579	4654	4729	4804	4879	4954	
01	5029	5104	5178	5253	5328	5403	5478	5553	5628	5702	
02	5777	5852	5927	6002	6077	6151	6226	6301	6376	6451	
03	6526	6601	6675	6750	6825	6900	6975	7050	7124	7199	
04	7274	7349	7424	7499	7573	7648	7723	7798	7873	7947	
05	8022	8097	8172	8247	8321	8396	8471	8546	8621	8696	
06	8770	8845	8920	8995	9070	9144	9219	9294	9369	9443	
07	9518	9593	9668	9743	9817	9892	9967	0042	0117	0191	
08	764 0266	0341	0416	0490	0565	0640	0715	0789	0864	0939	
09	1014	1089	1163	1238	1313	1388	1462	1537	1612	1687	
10	1761	1836	1911	1986	2060	2135	2210	2285	2359	2434	
5811	2509	2583	2658	2733	2808	2882	2957	3032	3107	3181	
12	3256	3331	3406	3480	3555	3630	3704	3779	3854	3929	
13	4003	4078	4153	4227	4302	4377	4451	4526	4601	4676	
14	4750	4825	4900	4974	5049	5124	5198	5273	5348	5423	
15	5497	5572	5647	5721	5796	5871	5945	6020	6095	6169	
16	6244	6319	6393	6468	6543	6617	6692	6767	6841	6916	
17	6991	7065	7140	7215	7289	7364	7439	7513	7588	7663	
18	7737	7812	7886	7961	8036	8110	8185	8260	8334	8409	
19	8484	8558	8633	8707	8782	8857	8931	9006	9081	9155	
20	9230	9304	9379	9454	9528	9603	9678	9752	9827	9901	
5821	9976	0051	0125	0200	0274	0349	0424	0498	0573	0647	
22	765 0722	0797	0871	0946	1020	1095	1170	1244	1319	1393	
23	1468	1542	1617	1692	1766	1841	1915	1990	2065	2139	
24	2214	2288	2363	2437	2512	2586	2661	2736	2810	2885	
25	2959	3034	3108	3183	3258	3332	3407	3481	3556	3630	
26	3705	3779	3854	3928	4003	4078	4152	4227	4301	4376	
27	4450	4525	4599	4674	4748	4823	4897	4972	5046	5121	
28	5195	5270	5344	5419	5493	5568	5643	5717	5792	5866	
29	5941	6015	6090	6164	6239	6313	6388	6462	6537	6611	
30	6686	6760	6835	6909	6984	7058	7132	7207	7281	7356	
5831	7430	7505	7579	7654	7728	7803	7877	7952	8026	8101	
32	8175	8250	8324	8399	8473	8547	8622	8696	8771	8845	
33	8920	8994	9069	9143	9218	9292	9366	9441	9515	9590	
34	9664	9739	9813	9888	9962	0036	0111	0185	0260	0334	
35	766 0409	0483	0557	0632	0706	0781	0855	0930	1004	1078	
36	1153	1227	1302	1376	1450	1525	1599	1674	1748	1823	
37	1897	1971	2046	2120	2195	2269	2343	2418	2492	2567	
38	2641	2715	2790	2864	2938	3013	3087	3162	3236	3310	
39	3385	3459	3534	3608	3682	3757	3831	3905	3980	4054	
40	4128	4203	4277	4352	4426	4500	4575	4649	4723	4798	
5841	4872	4946	5021	5095	5169	5244	5318	5393	5467	5541	
42	5616	5690	5764	5839	5913	5987	6062	6136	6210	6285	
43	6359	6433	6508	6582	6656	6730	6805	6879	6953	7028	
44	7102	7176	7251	7325	7399	7474	7548	7622	7697	7771	
45	7845	7919	7994	8068	8142	8217	8291	8365	8440	8514	
46	8588	8662	8737	8811	8885	8960	9034	9108	9182	9257	
47	9331	9405	9479	9554	9628	9702	9777	9851	9925	9999	
48	767 0074	0148	0222	0296	0371	0445	0519	0593	0668	0742	
49	0816	0890	0965	1039	1113	1187	1262	1336	1410	1484	
5850	1559	1633	1707	1781	1856	1930	2004	2078	2153	2227	

74

1	7
2	15
3	22
4	30
5	37
6	44
7	52
8	59
9	67

No.	0	1	2	3	4	5	6	7	8	9	Diff.
5850	767 1559	1633	1707	1781	1856	1930	2004	2078	2153	2227	
51	2301	2375	2449	2524	2598	2672	2746	2821	2895	2969	
52	3043	3117	3192	3266	3340	3414	3488	3563	3637	3711	
53	3785	3859	3934	4008	4082	4156	4230	4305	4379	4453	
54	4527	4601	4676	4750	4824	4898	4972	5046	5121	5195	
55	5269	5343	5417	5492	5566	5640	5714	5788	5862	5937	
56	6011	6085	6159	6233	6307	6381	6456	6530	6604	6678	
57	6752	6826	6901	6975	7049	7123	7197	7271	7345	7420	
58	7494	7568	7642	7716	7790	7864	7938	8013	8087	8161	
59	8235	8309	8383	8457	8531	8606	8680	8754	8828	8902	
60	8976	9050	9124	9198	9273	9347	9421	9495	9569	9643	
5861	9717	9791	9865	9940	$\overline{0}$014	$\overline{0}$088	$\overline{0}$162	$\overline{0}$236	$\overline{0}$310	$\overline{0}$384	
62	768 0458	0532	0606	0680	0754	0829	0903	0977	1051	1125	
63	1199	1273	1347	1421	1495	1569	1643	1717	1791	1866	
64	1940	2014	2088	2162	2236	2310	2384	2458	2532	2606	
65	2680	2754	2828	2902	2976	3050	3124	3198	3273	3347	
66	3421	3495	3569	3643	3717	3791	3865	3939	4013	4087	
67	4161	4235	4309	4383	4457	4531	4605	4679	4753	4827	
68	4901	4975	5049	5123	5197	5271	5345	5419	5493	5567	
69	5641	5715	5789	5863	5937	6011	6085	6159	6233	6307	
70	6381	6455	6529	6603	6677	6751	6825	6899	6973	7047	
5871	7121	7195	7269	7343	7417	7491	7565	7639	7713	7787	
72	7860	7934	8008	8082	8156	8230	8304	8378	8452	8526	
73	8600	8674	8748	8822	8896	8970	9044	9118	9192	9265	
74	9339	9413	9487	9561	9635	9709	9783	9857	9931	$\overline{0}$005	
75	769 0079	0153	0227	0300	0374	0448	0522	0596	0670	0744	
76	0818	0892	0966	1040	1114	1187	1261	1335	1409	1483	
77	1557	1631	1705	1779	1852	1926	2000	2074	2148	2222	
78	2296	2370	2444	2517	2591	2665	2739	2813	2887	2961	
79	3035	3108	3182	3256	3330	3404	3478	3552	3626	3699	
80	3773	3847	3921	3995	4069	4143	4216	4290	4364	4438	
5881	4512	4586	4659	4733	4807	4881	4955	5029	5103	5176	
82	5250	5324	5398	5472	5546	5619	5693	5767	5841	5915	
83	5988	6062	6136	6210	6284	6358	6431	6505	6579	6653	
84	6727	6800	6874	6948	7022	7096	7169	7243	7317	7391	
85	7465	7538	7612	7686	7760	7834	7907	7981	8055	8129	
86	8203	8276	8350	8424	8498	8571	8645	8719	8793	8867	
87	8940	9014	9088	9162	9235	9309	9383	9457	9530	9604	
88	9678	9752	9826	9899	9973	$\overline{0}$047	$\overline{0}$121	$\overline{0}$194	$\overline{0}$268	$\overline{0}$342	
89	770 0416	0489	0563	0637	0711	0784	0858	0932	1005	1079	
90	1153	1227	1300	1374	1448	1522	1595	1669	1743	1817	
5891	1890	1964	2038	2111	2185	2259	2333	2406	2480	2554	
92	2627	2701	2775	2849	2922	2996	3070	3143	3217	3291	
93	3364	3438	3512	3585	3659	3733	3807	3880	3954	4028	
94	4101	4175	4249	4322	4396	4470	4543	4617	4691	4764	
95	4838	4912	4985	5059	5133	5206	5280	5354	5427	5501	
96	5575	5648	5722	5796	5869	5943	6017	6090	6164	6238	
97	6311	6385	6459	6532	6606	6679	6753	6827	6900	6974	
98	7048	7121	7195	7269	7342	7416	7489	7563	7637	7710	
99	7784	7858	7931	8005	8078	8152	8226	8299	8373	8447	
5900	8520	8594	8667	8741	8815	8888	8962	9035	9109	9183	

74

1	7
2	15
3	22
4	30
5	37
6	44
7	52
8	59
9	67

No.	0	1	2	3	4	5	6	7	8	9	Diff.
5900	770 8520	8594	8667	8741	8815	8888	8962	9035	9109	9183	
01	9256	9330	9403	9477	9551	9624	9698	9771	9845	9918	
02	9992	0066	0139	0213	0286	0360	0434	0507	0581	0654	
03	771 0728	0801	0875	0949	1022	1096	1169	1243	1316	1390	
04	1463	1537	1611	1684	1758	1831	1905	1978	2052	2125	
05	2199	2273	2346	2420	2493	2567	2640	2714	2787	2861	
06	2934	3008	3081	3155	3229	3302	3376	3449	3523	3596	
07	3670	3743	3817	3890	3964	4037	4111	4184	4258	4331	
08	4405	4478	4552	4625	4699	4772	4846	4919	4993	5066	
09	5140	5213	5287	5360	5434	5507	5581	5654	5728	5801	
10	5875	5948	6022	6095	6169	6242	6316	6389	6463	6536	
5911	6610	6683	6757	6830	6903	6977	7050	7124	7197	7271	
12	7344	7418	7491	7565	7638	7712	7785	7858	7932	8005	
13	8079	8152	8226	8299	8373	8446	8519	8593	8666	8740	
14	8813	8887	8960	9034	9107	9180	9254	9327	9401	9474	
15	9547	9621	9694	9768	9841	9915	9988	0061	0135	0208	
16	772 0282	0355	0428	0502	0575	0649	0722	0795	0869	0942	
17	1016	1089	1162	1236	1309	1383	1456	1529	1603	1676	
18	1750	1823	1896	1970	2043	2117	2190	2263	2337	2410	
19	2483	2557	2630	2704	2777	2850	2924	2997	3070	3144	
20	3217	3290	3364	3437	3510	3584	3657	3731	3804	3877	73
5921	3951	4024	4097	4171	4244	4317	4391	4464	4537	4611	1 7
22	4684	4757	4831	4904	4977	5051	5124	5197	5271	5344	2 15
23	5417	5491	5564	5637	5711	5784	5857	5931	6004	6077	3 22
24	6150	6224	6297	6370	6444	6517	6590	6664	6737	6810	4 29
25	6884	6957	7030	7103	7177	7250	7323	7397	7470	7543	5 37
26	7616	7690	7763	7836	7910	7983	8056	8129	8203	8276	6 44
27	8349	8423	8496	8569	8642	8716	8789	8862	8935	9009	7 51
28	9082	9155	9228	9302	9375	9448	9521	9595	9668	9741	8 58
29	9815	9888	9961	0034	0107	0181	0254	0327	0400	0474	9 66
30	773 0547	0620	0693	0767	0840	0913	0986	1060	1133	1206	
5931	1279	1352	1426	1499	1572	1645	1719	1792	1865	1938	
32	2011	2085	2158	2231	2304	2377	2451	2524	2597	2670	
33	2743	2817	2890	2963	3036	3109	3183	3256	3329	3402	
34	3475	3549	3622	3695	3768	3841	3915	3988	4061	4134	
35	4207	4280	4354	4427	4500	4573	4646	4719	4793	4866	
36	4939	5012	5085	5158	5232	5305	5378	5451	5524	5597	
37	5670	5744	5817	5890	5963	6036	6109	6183	6256	6329	
38	6402	6475	6548	6621	6694	6768	6841	6914	6987	7060	
39	7133	7206	7280	7353	7426	7499	7572	7645	7718	7791	
40	7864	7938	8011	8084	8157	8230	8303	8376	8449	8522	
5941	8596	8669	8742	8815	8888	8961	9034	9107	9180	9253	
42	9326	9400	9473	9546	9619	9692	9765	9838	9911	9984	
43	774 0057	0130	0203	0277	0350	0423	0496	0569	0642	0715	
44	0788	0861	0934	1007	1080	1153	1226	1299	1372	1446	
45	1519	1592	1665	1738	1811	1884	1957	2030	2103	2176	
46	2249	2322	2395	2468	2541	2614	2687	2760	2833	2906	
47	2979	3052	3125	3198	3271	3345	3418	3491	3564	3637	
48	3710	3783	3856	3929	4002	4075	4148	4221	4294	4367	
49	4440	4513	4586	4659	4732	4805	4878	4951	5024	5097	
5950	5170	5243	5316	5389	5462	5535	5608	5681	5754	5827	

No.	0	1	2	3	4	5	6	7	8	9	Diff.
5950	774 5170	5243	5316	5389	5462	5535	5608	5681	5754	5827	
51	5900	5972	6045	6118	6191	6264	6337	6410	6483	6556	
52	6629	6702	6775	6848	6921	6994	7067	7140	7213	7286	
53	7359	7432	7505	7578	7651	7724	7797	7869	7942	8015	
54	8088	8161	8234	8307	8380	8453	8526	8599	8672	8745	
55	8818	8891	8964	9036	9109	9182	9255	9328	9401	9474	
56	9547	9620	9693	9766	9839	9911	9984	0̅0̅5̅7̅	0̅1̅3̅0̅	0̅2̅0̅3̅	
57	775 0276	0349	0422	0495	0568	0641	0713	0786	0859	0932	
58	1005	1078	1151	1224	1297	1369	1442	1515	1588	1661	
59	1734	1807	1880	1952	2025	2098	2171	2244	2317	2390	
60	2463	2535	2608	2681	2754	2827	2900	2973	3046	3118	
5961	3191	3264	3337	3410	3483	3555	3628	3701	3774	3847	
62	3920	3993	4065	4138	4211	4284	4357	4430	4502	4575	
63	4648	4721	4794	4867	4939	5012	5085	5158	5231	5304	
64	5376	5449	5522	5595	5668	5740	5813	5886	5959	6032	
65	6104	6177	6250	6323	6396	6469	6541	6614	6687	6760	
66	6832	6905	6978	7051	7124	7196	7269	7342	7415	7488	
67	7560	7633	7706	7779	7851	7924	7997	8070	8143	8215	
68	8288	8361	8434	8506	8579	8652	8725	8798	8870	8943	
69	9016	9089	9161	9234	9307	9380	9452	9525	9598	9671	
70	9743	9816	9889	9962	0̅0̅3̅4̅	0̅1̅0̅7̅	0̅1̅8̅0̅	0̅2̅5̅3̅	0̅3̅2̅5̅	0̅3̅9̅8̅	
5971	776 0471	0543	0616	0689	0762	0834	0907	0980	1053	1125	
72	1198	1271	1343	1416	1489	1562	1634	1707	1780	1852	
73	1925	1998	2071	2143	2216	2289	2361	2434	2507	2579	
74	2652	2725	2798	2870	2943	3016	3088	3161	3234	3306	
75	3379	3452	3524	3597	3670	3743	3815	3888	3961	4033	
76	4106	4179	4251	4324	4397	4469	4542	4615	4687	4760	
77	4833	4905	4978	5051	5123	5196	5269	5341	5414	5486	
78	5559	5632	5704	5777	5850	5922	5995	6068	6140	6213	
79	6286	6358	6431	6503	6576	6649	6721	6794	6867	6939	
80	7012	7084	7157	7230	7302	7375	7448	7520	7593	7665	
5981	7738	7811	7883	7956	8028	8101	8174	8246	8319	8391	
82	8464	8537	8609	8682	8754	8827	8900	8972	9045	9117	
83	9190	9263	9335	9408	9480	9553	9626	9698	9771	9843	
84	9916	9988	0̅0̅6̅1̅	0̅1̅3̅4̅	0̅2̅0̅6̅	0̅2̅7̅9̅	0̅3̅5̅1̅	0̅4̅2̅4̅	0̅4̅9̅6̅	0̅5̅6̅9̅	
85	777 0642	0714	0787	0859	0932	1004	1077	1149	1222	1295	
86	1367	1440	1512	1585	1657	1730	1802	1875	1947	2020	
87	2093	2165	2238	2310	2383	2455	2528	2600	2673	2745	
88	2818	2890	2963	3035	3108	3181	3253	3326	3398	3471	
89	3543	3616	3688	3761	3833	3906	3978	4051	4123	4196	
90	4268	4341	4413	4486	4558	4631	4703	4776	4848	4921	
5991	4993	5066	5138	5211	5283	5356	5428	5501	5573	5646	
92	5718	5791	5863	5935	6008	6080	6153	6225	6298	6370	
93	6443	6515	6588	6660	6733	6805	6878	6950	7022	7095	
94	7167	7240	7312	7385	7457	7530	7602	7675	7747	7819	
95	7892	7964	8037	8109	8182	8254	8327	8399	8471	8544	
96	8616	8689	8761	8834	8906	8978	9051	9123	9196	9268	
97	9340	9413	9485	9558	9630	9703	9775	9847	9920	9992	
98	778 0065	0137	0209	0282	0354	0427	0499	0571	0644	0716	
99	0789	0861	0933	1006	1078	1151	1223	1295	1368	1440	
6000	1513	1585	1657	1730	1802	1874	1947	2019	2092	2164	

73
1	7
2	15
3	22
4	29
5	37
6	44
7	51
8	58
9	66

No.	0	1	2	3	4	5	6	7	8	9	Diff.
6000	778 1513	1585	1657	1730	1802	1874	1947	2019	2092	2164	
01	2236	2309	2381	2453	2526	2598	2670	2743	2815	2888	
02	2960	3032	3105	3177	3249	3322	3394	3466	3539	3611	
03	3683	3756	3828	3900	3973	4045	4117	4190	4262	4335	
04	4407	4479	4552	4624	4696	4768	4841	4913	4985	5058	
05	5130	5202	5275	5347	5419	5492	5564	5636	5709	5781	
06	5853	5926	5998	6070	6143	6215	6287	6359	6432	6504	
07	6576	6649	6721	6793	6866	6938	7010	7082	7155	7227	
08	7299	7372	7444	7516	7588	7661	7733	7805	7877	7950	
09	8022	8094	8167	8239	8311	8383	8456	8528	8600	8672	
10	8745	8817	8889	8962	9034	9106	9178	9251	9323	9395	
6011	9467	9540	9612	9684	9756	9829	9901	9973	0045	0117	
12	779 0190	0262	0334	0406	0479	0551	0623	0395	0768	0840	
13	0912	0984	1056	1129	1201	1273	1345	1418	1490	1562	
14	1634	1706	1779	1851	1923	1995	2067	2140	2212	2284	
15	2356	2429	2501	2573	2645	2717	2790	2862	2934	3006	
16	3078	3150	3223	3295	3367	3439	3511	3584	3656	3728	
17	3800	3872	3944	4017	4089	4161	4233	4305	4377	4450	
18	4522	4594	4666	4738	4810	4883	4955	5027	5099	5171	
19	5243	5316	5388	5460	5532	5604	5676	5748	5821	5893	
20	5965	6037	6109	6181	6253	6326	6398	6470	6542	6614	
6021	6686	6758	6831	6903	6975	7047	7119	7191	7263	7335	
22	7408	7480	7552	7624	7696	7768	7840	7912	7984	8057	
23	8129	8201	8273	8345	8417	8489	8561	8633	8705	8778	
24	8850	8922	8994	9066	9138	9210	9282	9354	9426	9498	
25	9571	9643	9715	9787	9859	9931	0003	0075	0147	0219	
26	780 0291	0363	0435	0507	0580	0652	0724	0796	0868	0940	
27	1012	1084	1156	1228	1300	1372	1444	1516	1588	1660	
28	1732	1804	1877	1949	2021	2093	2165	2237	2309	2381	
29	2453	2525	2597	2669	2741	2813	2885	2957	3029	3101	
30	3173	3245	3317	3389	3461	3533	3605	3677	3749	3821	
6031	3893	3965	4037	4109	4181	4253	4325	4397	4469	4541	
32	4613	4685	4757	4829	4901	4973	5045	5117	5189	5261	
33	5333	5405	5477	5549	5621	5693	5765	5837	5909	5981	
34	6053	6125	6197	6269	6341	6413	6485	6557	6629	6701	
35	6773	6845	6917	6989	7061	7133	7204	7276	7348	7420	
36	7492	7564	7636	7708	7780	7852	7924	7996	8068	8140	
37	8212	8284	8356	8428	8500	8571	8643	8715	8787	8859	
38	8931	9003	9075	9147	9219	9291	9363	9435	9506	9578	
39	9650	9722	9794	9866	9938	0010	0082	0154	0226	0297	
40	781 0369	0441	0513	0585	0657	0729	0801	0873	0945	1016	
6041	1088	1160	1232	1304	1376	1448	1520	1592	1663	1735	
42	1807	1879	1951	2023	2095	2167	2238	2310	2382	2454	
43	2526	2598	2670	2742	2813	2885	2957	3029	3101	3173	
44	3245	3316	3388	3460	3532	3604	3676	3748	3819	3891	
45	3963	4035	4107	4179	4250	4322	4394	4466	4538	4610	
46	4681	4753	4825	4897	4969	5041	5112	5184	5256	5328	
47	5400	5472	5543	5615	5687	5759	5831	5902	5974	6046	
48	6118	6190	6261	6333	6405	6477	6549	6620	6692	6764	
49	6836	6908	6979	7051	7123	7195	7267	7338	7410	7482	
6050	7554	7626	7697	7769	7841	7913	7984	8056	8128	8200	

72

1	7
2	14
3	22
4	29
5	36
6	43
7	50
8	58
9	65

No.	0	1	2	3	4	5	6	7	8	9	Diff.
6050	781 7554	7626	7697	7769	7841	7913	7984	8056	8128	8200	
51	8272	8343	8415	8487	8559	8630	8702	8774	8846	8917	
52	8989	9061	9133	9204	9276	9348	9420	9491	9563	9635	
53	9707	9778	9850	9922	9994	0065	0137	0209	0281	0352	
54	782 0424	0496	0568	0639	0711	0783	0855	0926	0998	1070	
55	1141	1213	1285	1357	1428	1500	1572	1644	1715	1787	
56	1859	1930	2002	2074	2146	2217	2289	2361	2432	2504	
57	2576	2647	2719	2791	2863	2934	3006	3078	3149	3221	
58	3293	3364	3436	3508	3579	3651	3723	3794	3866	3938	
59	4010	4081	4153	4225	4296	4368	4440	4511	4583	4655	
60	4726	4798	4870	4941	5013	5085	5156	5228	5300	5371	
6061	5443	5514	5586	5658	5729	5801	5873	5944	6016	6088	
62	6159	6231	6303	6374	6446	6518	6589	6661	6732	6804	
63	6876	6947	7019	7091	7162	7234	7305	7377	7449	7520	
64	7592	7664	7735	7807	7878	7950	8022	8093	8165	8236	
65	8308	8380	8451	8523	8594	8666	8738	8809	8881	8952	
66	9024	9096	9167	9239	9310	9382	9454	9525	9597	9668	
67	9740	9812	9883	9955	0026	0098	0169	0241	0313	0384	
68	783 0456	0527	0599	0670	0742	0814	0885	0957	1028	1100	
69	1171	1243	1314	1386	1458	1529	1601	1672	1744	1815	
70	1887	1958	2030	2102	2173	2245	2316	2388	2459	2531	
6071	2602	2674	2745	2817	2888	2960	3032	3103	3175	3246	
72	3318	3389	3461	3532	3604	3675	3747	3818	3890	3961	
73	4033	4104	4176	4247	4319	4390	4462	4533	4605	4676	
74	4748	4819	4891	4962	5034	5105	5177	5248	5320	5391	
75	5463	5534	5606	5677	5749	5820	5892	5963	6035	6106	
76	6178	6249	6321	6392	6464	6535	6606	6678	6749	6821	
77	6892	6964	7035	7107	7178	7250	7321	7393	7464	7536	
78	7607	7678	7750	7821	7893	7964	8036	8107	8179	8250	
79	8321	8393	8464	8536	8607	8679	8750	8821	8893	8964	
80	9036	9107	9179	9250	9322	9393	9464	9536	9607	9679	
6081	9750	9821	9893	9964	0036	0107	0179	0250	0321	0393	
82	784 0464	0536	0607	0678	0750	0821	0893	0964	1035	1107	
83	1178	1250	1321	1392	1464	1535	1607	1678	1749	1821	
84	1892	1963	2035	2106	2178	2249	2320	2392	2463	2534	
85	2606	2677	2749	2820	2891	2963	3034	3105	3177	3248	
86	3319	3391	3462	3534	3605	3676	3748	3819	3890	3962	
87	4033	4104	4176	4247	4318	4390	4461	4532	4604	4675	
88	4746	4818	4889	4960	5032	5103	5174	5246	5317	5388	
89	5460	5531	5602	5674	5745	5816	5888	5959	6030	6102	
90	6173	6244	6316	6387	6458	6529	6601	6672	6743	6815	
6091	6886	6957	7029	7100	7171	7242	7314	7385	7456	7528	
92	7599	7670	7742	7813	7884	7955	8027	8098	8169	8241	
93	8312	8383	8454	8526	8597	8668	8739	8811	8882	8953	
94	9024	9096	9167	9238	9310	9381	9452	9523	9595	9666	
95	9737	9808	9880	9951	0022	0093	0165	0236	0307	0378	
96	785 0450	0521	0592	0663	0735	0806	0877	0948	1019	1091	
97	1162	1233	1304	1376	1447	1518	1589	1661	1732	1803	
98	1874	1945	2017	2088	2159	2230	2301	2373	2444	2515	
99	2586	2658	2729	2800	2871	2942	3014	3085	3156	3227	
6100	3298	3370	3441	3512	3583	3654	3726	3797	3868	3939	

72

1	7
2	14
3	22
4	29
5	36
6	43
7	50
8	58
9	65

No.	0	1	2	3	4	5	6	7	8	9	Diff.
6100	785 3298	3370	3441	3512	3583	3654	3726	3797	3868	3939	
01	4010	4081	4153	4224	4295	4366	4437	4509	4580	4651	
02	4722	4793	4864	4936	5007	5078	5149	5220	5291	5363	
03	5434	5505	5576	5647	5718	5789	5861	5932	6003	6074	
04	6145	6216	6288	6359	6430	6501	6572	6643	6714	6786	
05	6857	6928	6999	7070	7141	7212	7283	7355	7426	7497	
06	7568	7639	7710	7781	7852	7924	7995	8066	8137	8208	
07	8279	8350	8421	8493	8564	8635	8706	8777	8848	8919	
08	8990	9061	9132	9204	9275	9346	9417	9488	9559	9630	
09	9701	9772	9843	9915	9986	0057	0128	0199	0270	0341	
10	786 0412	0483	0554	0625	0696	0767	0839	0910	0981	1052	
6111	1123	1194	1265	1336	1407	1478	1549	1620	1691	1762	
12	1833	1905	1976	2047	2118	2189	2260	2331	2402	2473	
13	2544	2615	2686	2757	2828	2899	2970	3041	3112	3183	
14	3254	3325	3396	3467	3538	3609	3681	3752	3823	3894	
15	3965	4036	4107	4178	4249	4320	4391	4462	4533	4604	
16	4675	4746	4817	4888	4959	5030	5101	5172	5243	5314	
17	5385	5456	5527	5598	5669	5740	5811	5882	5953	6024	
18	6095	6166	6237	6308	6379	6450	6521	6592	6663	6734	
19	6805	6876	6946	7017	7088	7159	7230	7301	7372	7443	
20	7514	7585	7656	7727	7798	7869	7940	8011	8082	8153	
6121	8224	8295	8366	8437	8508	8579	8649	8720	8791	8862	
22	8933	9004	9075	9146	9217	9288	9359	9430	9501	9572	
23	9643	9714	9784	9855	9926	9997	0068	0139	0210	0281	
24	787 0352	0423	0494	0565	0635	0706	0777	0848	0919	0990	
25	1061	1132	1203	1274	1345	1415	1486	1557	1628	1699	
26	1770	1841	1912	1983	2053	2124	2195	2266	2337	2408	
27	2479	2550	2621	2691	2762	2833	2904	2975	3046	3117	
28	3188	3258	3329	3400	3471	3542	3613	3684	3754	3825	
29	3896	3967	4038	4109	4180	4250	4321	4392	4463	4534	
30	4605	4676	4746	4817	4888	4959	5030	5101	5171	5242	
6131	5313	5384	5455	5526	5596	5667	5738	5809	5880	5951	
32	6021	6092	6163	6234	6305	6376	6446	6517	6588	6659	
33	6730	6800	6871	6942	7013	7084	7155	7225	7296	7367	
34	7438	7509	7579	7650	7721	7792	7863	7933	8004	8075	
35	8146	8216	8287	8358	8429	8500	8570	8641	8712	8783	
36	8854	8924	8995	9066	9137	9207	9278	9349	9420	9490	
37	9561	9632	9703	9774	9844	9915	9986	0057	0127	0198	
38	788 0269	0340	0410	0481	0552	0623	0693	0764	0835	0906	
39	0976	1047	1118	1189	1259	1330	1401	1472	1542	1613	
40	1684	1754	1825	1896	1967	2037	2108	2179	2250	2320	
6141	2391	2462	2532	2603	2674	2745	2815	2886	2957	3027	
42	3098	3169	3240	3310	3381	3452	3522	3593	3664	3734	
43	3805	3876	3947	4017	4088	4159	4229	4300	4371	4441	
44	4512	4583	4653	4724	4795	4865	4936	5007	5078	5148	
45	5219	5290	5360	5431	5502	5572	5643	5714	5784	5855	
46	5926	5996	6067	6138	6208	6279	6350	6420	6491	6561	
47	6632	6703	6773	6844	6915	6985	7056	7127	7197	7268	
48	7339	7409	7480	7551	7621	7692	7762	7833	7904	7974	
49	8045	8116	8186	8257	8327	8398	8469	8539	8610	8681	
6150	8751	8822	8892	8963	9034	9104	9175	9245	9316	9387	

71

1	7
2	14
3	21
4	28
5	36
6	43
7	50
8	57
9	64

No.	0	1	2	3	4	5	6	7	8	9	Diff.
6150	788 8751	8822	8892	8963	9034	9104	9175	9245	9316	9387	
51	9457	9528	9598	9669	9740	9810	9881	9951	0022	0093	
52	789 0163	0234	0304	0375	0446	0516	0587	0657	0728	0799	
53	0869	0940	1010	1081	1151	1222	1293	1363	1434	1504	
54	1575	1645	1716	1787	1857	1928	1998	2069	2139	2210	
55	2281	2351	2422	2492	2563	2633	2704	2774	2845	2916	
56	2986	3057	3127	3198	3268	3339	3409	3480	3550	3621	
57	3692	3762	3833	3903	3974	4044	4115	4185	4256	4326	
58	4397	4467	4538	4608	4679	4749	4820	4890	4961	5032	
59	5102	5173	5243	5314	5384	5455	5525	5596	5666	5737	
60	5807	5878	5948	6019	6089	6160	6230	6301	6371	6442	
6161	6512	6583	6653	6724	6794	6865	6935	7005	7076	7146	
62	7217	7287	7358	7428	7499	7569	7640	7710	7781	7851	
63	7922	7992	8063	8133	8204	8274	8344	8415	8485	8556	
64	8626	8697	8767	8838	8908	8979	9049	9119	9190	9260	
65	9331	9401	9472	9542	9613	9683	9753	9824	9894	9965	
66	790 0035	0106	0176	0247	0317	0387	0458	0528	0599	0669	
67	0739	0810	0880	0951	1021	1092	1162	1232	1303	1373	
68	1444	1514	1584	1655	1725	1796	1866	1936	2007	2077	
69	2148	2218	2288	2359	2429	2500	2570	2640	2711	2781	
70	2852	2922	2992	3063	3133	3204	3274	3344	3415	3485	
6171	3555	3626	3696	3767	3837	3907	3978	4048	4118	4189	
72	4259	4330	4400	4470	4541	4611	4681	4752	4822	4892	
73	4963	5033	5103	5174	5244	5315	5385	5455	5526	5596	
74	5666	5737	5807	5877	5948	6018	6088	6159	6229	6299	
75	6370	6440	6510	6581	6651	6721	6792	6862	6932	7003	
76	7073	7143	7214	7284	7354	7424	7495	7565	7635	7706	
77	7776	7846	7917	7987	8057	8128	8198	8268	8338	8409	
78	8479	8549	8620	8690	8760	8831	8901	8971	9041	9112	
79	9182	9252	9323	9393	9463	9533	9604	9674	9744	9814	
80	9885	9955	0025	0096	0166	0236	0306	0377	0447	0517	
6181	791 0587	0658	0728	0798	0868	0939	1009	1079	1150	1220	
82	1290	1360	1431	1501	1571	1641	1711	1782	1852	1922	
83	1992	2063	2133	2203	2273	2344	2414	2484	2554	2625	
84	2695	2765	2835	2905	2976	3046	3116	3186	3257	3327	
85	3397	3467	3537	3608	3678	3748	3818	3889	3959	4029	
86	4099	4169	4240	4310	4380	4450	4520	4591	4661	4731	
87	4801	4871	4942	5012	5082	5152	5222	5292	5363	5433	
88	5503	5573	5643	5714	5784	5854	5924	5994	6064	6135	
89	6205	6275	6345	6415	6486	6556	6626	6696	6766	6836	
90	6906	6977	7047	7117	7187	7257	7327	7398	7468	7538	
6191	7608	7678	7748	7818	7889	7959	8029	8099	8169	8239	
92	8309	8380	8450	8520	8590	8660	8730	8800	8871	8941	
93	9011	9081	9151	9221	9291	9361	9432	9502	9572	9642	
94	9712	9782	9852	9922	9992	0063	0133	0203	0273	0343	
95	792 0413	0483	0553	0623	0694	0764	0834	0904	0974	1044	
96	1114	1184	1254	1324	1394	1465	1535	1605	1675	1745	
97	1815	1885	1955	2025	2095	2165	2235	2306	2376	2446	
98	2516	2586	2656	2726	2796	2866	2936	3006	3076	3146	
99	3216	3286	3356	3427	3497	3567	3637	3707	3777	3847	
6200	3917	3987	4057	4127	4197	4267	4337	4407	4477	4547	

71

1	7
2	14
3	21
4	28
5	36
6	43
7	50
8	57
9	64

No.	0	1	2	3	4	5	6	7	8	9	Diff.
6200	792 3917	3987	4057	4127	4197	4267	4337	4407	4477	4547	
01	4617	4687	4757	4827	4897	4967	5038	5108	5178	5248	
02	5318	5388	5458	5528	5598	5668	5738	5808	5878	5948	
03	6018	6088	6158	6228	6298	6368	6438	6508	6578	6648	
04	6718	6788	6858	6928	6998	7068	7138	7208	7278	7348	
05	7418	7488	7558	7628	7698	7768	7838	7908	7978	8048	
06	8118	8188	8258	8328	8398	8468	8538	8608	8678	8747	
07	8817	8887	8957	9027	9097	9167	9237	9307	9377	9447	
08	9517	9587	9657	9727	9797	9867	9937	0007	0077	0147	
09	793 0217	0287	0356	0426	0496	0566	0636	0706	0776	0846	
10	0916	0986	1056	1126	1196	1266	1336	1406	1475	1545	
6211	1615	1685	1755	1825	1895	1965	2035	2105	2175	2245	
12	2314	2384	2454	2524	2594	2664	2734	2804	2874	2944	
13	3014	3083	3153	3223	3293	3363	3433	3503	3573	3643	
14	3712	3782	3852	3922	3992	4062	4132	4202	4272	4341	
15	4411	4481	4551	4621	4691	4761	4831	4900	4970	5040	
16	5110	5180	5250	5320	5390	5459	5529	5599	5669	5739	
17	5809	5879	5948	6018	6088	6158	6228	6298	6367	6437	
18	6507	6577	6647	6717	6787	6856	6926	6996	7066	7136	
19	7206	7275	7345	7415	7485	7555	7625	7694	7764	7834	
20	7904	7974	8043	8113	8183	8253	8323	8393	8462	8532	
6221	8602	8672	8742	8811	8881	8951	9021	9091	9160	9230	
22	9300	9370	9440	9509	9579	9649	9719	9789	9858	9928	
23	9998	0068	0138	0207	0277	0347	0417	0487	0556	0626	
24	794 0696	0766	0835	0905	0975	1045	1114	1184	1254	1324	
25	1394	1463	1533	1603	1673	1742	1812	1882	1952	2021	
26	2091	2161	2231	2300	2370	2440	2510	2579	2649	2719	
27	2789	2858	2928	2998	3068	3137	3207	3277	3347	3416	
28	3486	3556	3626	3695	3765	3835	3904	3974	4044	4114	
29	4183	4253	4323	4392	4462	4532	4602	4671	4741	4811	
30	4880	4950	5020	5090	5159	5229	5299	5368	5438	5508	
6231	5578	5647	5717	5787	5856	5926	5996	6065	6135	6205	
32	6274	6344	6414	6484	6553	6623	6693	6762	6832	6902	
33	6971	7041	7111	7180	7250	7320	7389	7459	7529	7598	
34	7668	7738	7807	7877	7947	8016	8086	8156	8225	8295	
35	8365	8434	8504	8574	8643	8713	8782	8852	8922	8991	
36	9061	9131	9200	9270	9340	9409	9479	9549	9618	9688	
37	9757	9827	9897	9966	0036	0106	0175	0245	0314	0384	
38	795 0454	0523	0593	0663	0732	0802	0871	0941	1011	1080	
39	1150	1219	1289	1359	1428	1498	1567	1637	1707	1776	
40	1846	1915	1985	2055	2124	2194	2263	2333	2403	2472	
6241	2542	2611	2681	2751	2820	2890	2959	3029	3098	3168	
42	3238	3307	3377	3446	3516	3586	3655	3725	3794	3864	
43	3933	4003	4072	4142	4212	4281	4351	4420	4490	4559	
44	4629	4698	4768	4838	4907	4977	5046	5116	5185	5255	
45	5324	5394	5464	5533	5603	5672	5742	5811	5881	5950	
46	6020	6089	6159	6228	6298	6367	6437	6506	6576	6646	
47	6715	6785	6854	6924	6993	7063	7132	7202	7271	7341	
48	7410	7480	7549	7619	7688	7758	7827	7897	7966	8036	
49	8105	8175	8244	8314	8383	8453	8522	8592	8661	8731	
6250	8800	8870	8939	9009	9078	9148	9217	9287	9356	9426	

70

1	7
2	14
3	21
4	28
5	35
6	42
7	49
8	56
9	63

No.	0	1	2	3	4	5	6	7	8	9	Diff.
6250	795 8800	8870	8939	9009	9078	9148	9217	9287	9356	9426	
51	9495	9564	9634	9703	9773	9842	9912	9981	0051	0120	
52	796 0190	0259	0329	0398	0468	0537	0606	0676	0745	0815	
53	0884	0954	1023	1093	1162	1232	1301	1370	1440	1509	
54	1579	1648	1718	1787	1857	1926	1995	2065	2134	2204	
55	2273	2343	2412	2481	2551	2620	2690	2759	2829	2898	
56	2967	3037	3106	3176	3245	3314	3384	3453	3523	3592	
57	3662	3731	3800	3870	3939	4009	4078	4147	4217	4286	
58	4356	4425	4494	4564	4633	4703	4772	4841	4911	4980	
59	5050	5119	5188	5258	5327	5396	5466	5535	5605	5674	
60	5743	5813	5882	5951	6021	6090	6160	6229	6298	6368	
6261	6437	6506	6576	6645	6714	6784	6853	6923	6992	7061	
62	7131	7200	7269	7339	7408	7477	7547	7616	7685	7755	
63	7824	7893	7963	8032	8101	8171	8240	8309	8379	8448	
64	8517	8587	8656	8725	8795	8864	8933	9003	9072	9141	
65	9211	9280	9349	9419	9488	9557	9627	9696	9765	9835	
66	9904	9973	0043	0112	0181	0250	0320	0389	0458	0528	
67	797 0597	0666	0736	0805	0874	0943	1013	1082	1151	1221	
68	1290	1359	1428	1498	1567	1636	1706	1775	1844	1913	
69	1983	2052	2121	2191	2260	2329	2398	2468	2537	2606	
70	2675	2745	2814	2883	2952	3022	3091	3160	3229	3299	
6271	3368	3437	3507	3576	3645	3714	3784	3853	3922	3991	
72	4060	4130	4199	4268	4337	4407	4476	4545	4614	4684	
73	4753	4822	4891	4961	5030	5099	5168	5237	5307	5376	
74	5445	5514	5584	5653	5722	5791	5860	5930	5999	6068	
75	6137	6207	6276	6345	6414	6483	6553	6622	6691	6760	
76	6829	6899	6968	7037	7106	7175	7245	7314	7383	7452	
77	7521	7590	7660	7729	7798	7867	7936	8006	8075	8144	
78	8213	8282	8351	8421	8490	8559	8628	8697	8766	8836	
79	8905	8974	9043	9112	9181	9251	9320	9389	9458	9527	
80	9596	9666	9735	9804	9873	9942	0011	0080	0150	0219	
6281	798 0288	0357	0426	0495	0565	0634	0703	0772	0841	0910	
82	0979	1048	1118	1187	1256	1325	1394	1463	1532	1601	
83	1671	1740	1809	1878	1947	2016	2085	2154	2224	2293	
84	2362	2431	2500	2569	2638	2707	2776	2846	2915	2984	
85	3053	3122	3191	3260	3329	3398	3467	3536	3606	3675	
86	3744	3813	3882	3951	4020	4089	4158	4227	4296	4366	
87	4435	4504	4573	4642	4711	4780	4849	4918	4987	5056	
88	5125	5194	5263	5333	5402	5471	5540	5609	5678	5747	
89	5816	5885	5954	6023	6092	6161	6230	6299	6368	6437	
90	6506	6575	6645	6714	6783	6852	6921	6990	7059	7128	
6291	7197	7266	7335	7404	7473	7542	7611	7680	7749	7818	
92	7887	7956	8025	8094	8163	8232	8301	8370	8439	8508	
93	8577	8646	8715	8784	8853	8922	8991	9060	9129	9198	
94	9267	9336	9405	9474	9543	9612	9681	9750	9819	9888	
95	9957	0026	0095	0164	0233	0302	0371	0440	0509	0578	
96	799 0647	0716	0785	0854	0923	0992	1061	1130	1199	1268	
97	1337	1406	1475	1544	1613	1682	1751	1820	1889	1958	
98	2027	2096	2164	2233	2302	2371	2440	2509	2578	2647	
99	2716	2785	2854	2923	2992	3061	3130	3199	3268	3337	
6300	3405	3474	3543	3612	3681	3750	3819	3888	3957	4026	

69
1	7
2	14
3	21
4	28
5	35
6	41
7	48
8	55
9	62

No.	0	1	2	3	4	5	6	7	8	9	Diff.
6300	799 3405	3474	3543	3612	3681	3750	3819	3888	3957	4026	
01	4095	4164	4233	4302	4370	4439	4508	4577	4646	4715	
02	4784	4853	4922	4991	5060	5129	5197	5266	5335	5404	
03	5473	5542	5611	5680	5749	5818	5886	5955	6024	6093	
04	6162	6231	6300	6369	6438	6506	6575	6644	6713	6782	
05	6851	6920	6989	7058	7126	7195	7264	7333	7402	7471	
06	7540	7609	7677	7746	7815	7884	7953	8022	8091	8159	
07	8228	8297	8366	8435	8504	8573	8641	8710	8779	8848	
08	8917	8986	9055	9123	9192	9261	9330	9399	9468	9536	
09	9605	9674	9743	9812	9881	9949	0018	0087	0156	0225	
10	800 0294	0362	0431	0500	0569	0638	0707	0775	0844	0913	
6311	0982	1051	1119	1188	1257	1326	1395	1463	1532	1601	
12	1670	1739	1808	1876	1945	2014	2083	2152	2220	2289	
13	2358	2427	2495	2564	2633	2702	2771	2839	2908	2977	
14	3046	3115	3183	3252	3321	3390	3458	3527	3596	3665	
15	3734	3802	3871	3940	4009	4077	4146	4215	4284	4352	
16	4421	4490	4559	4627	4696	4765	4834	4903	4971	5040	
17	5109	5178	5246	5315	5384	5453	5521	5590	5659	5727	
18	5796	5865	5934	6002	6071	6140	6209	6277	6346	6415	
19	6484	6552	6621	6690	6758	6827	6896	6965	7033	7102	
20	7171	7239	7308	7377	7446	7514	7583	7652	7720	7789	
6321	7858	7927	7995	8064	8133	8201	8270	8339	8408	8476	
22	8545	8614	8682	8751	8820	8888	8957	9026	9094	9163	
23	9232	9301	9369	9438	9507	9575	9644	9713	9781	9850	
24	9919	9987	0056	0125	0193	0262	0331	0399	0468	0537	
25	801 0605	0674	0743	0811	0880	0949	1017	1086	1155	1223	
26	1292	1361	1429	1498	1566	1635	1704	1772	1841	1910	
27	1978	2047	2116	2184	2253	2322	2390	2459	2527	2596	
28	2665	2733	2802	2871	2939	3008	3076	3145	3214	3282	
29	3351	3420	3488	3557	3625	3694	3763	3831	3900	3968	
30	4037	4106	4174	4243	4312	4380	4449	4517	4586	4655	
6331	4723	4792	4860	4929	4998	5066	5135	5203	5272	5340	
32	5409	5478	5546	5615	5683	5752	5821	5889	5958	6026	
33	6095	6163	6232	6301	6369	6438	6506	6575	6643	6712	
34	6781	6849	6918	6986	7055	7123	7192	7261	7329	7398	
35	7466	7535	7603	7672	7740	7809	7878	7946	8015	8083	
36	8152	8220	8289	8357	8426	8494	8563	8631	8700	8769	
37	8837	8906	8974	9043	9111	9180	9248	9317	9385	9454	
38	9522	9591	9659	9728	9796	9865	9933	0002	0070	0139	
39	802 0208	0276	0345	0413	0482	0550	0619	0687	0756	0824	
40	0893	0961	1030	1098	1167	1235	1304	1372	1441	1509	
6341	1578	1646	1715	1783	1851	1920	1988	2057	2125	2194	
42	2262	2331	2399	2468	2536	2605	2673	2742	2810	2879	
43	2947	3016	3084	3153	3221	3289	3358	3426	3495	3563	
44	3632	3700	3769	3837	3906	3974	4042	4111	4179	4248	
45	4316	4385	4453	4522	4590	4658	4727	4795	4864	4932	
46	5001	5069	5138	5206	5274	5343	5411	5480	5548	5617	
47	5685	5753	5822	5890	5959	6027	6096	6164	6232	6301	
48	6369	6438	6506	6574	6643	6711	6780	6848	6916	6985	
49	7053	7122	7190	7258	7327	7395	7464	7532	7600	7669	
6350	7737	7806	7874	7942	8011	8079	8148	8216	8284	8353	

69

1	7
2	14
3	21
4	28
5	35
6	41
7	48
8	55
9	62

No.	0	1	2	3	4	5	6	7	8	9	Diff.
6350	802 7737	7806	7874	7942	8011	8079	8148	8216	8284	8353	
51	8421	8490	8558	8626	8695	8763	8831	8900	8968	9037	
52	9105	9173	9242	9310	9378	9447	9515	9583	9652	9720	
53	9789	9857	9925	9994	0062	0130	0199	0267	0335	0404	
54	803 0472	0540	0609	0677	0745	0814	0882	0951	1019	1087	
55	1156	1224	1292	1361	1429	1497	1566	1634	1702	1771	
56	1839	1907	1976	2044	2112	2181	2249	2317	2385	2454	
57	2522	2590	2659	2727	2795	2864	2932	3000	3069	3137	
58	3205	3274	3342	3410	3478	3547	3615	3683	3752	3820	
59	3888	3957	4025	4093	4161	4230	4298	4366	4435	4503	
60	4571	4639	4708	4776	4844	4913	4981	5049	5117	5186	
6361	5254	5322	5391	5459	5527	5595	5664	5732	5800	5868	
62	5937	6005	6073	6141	6210	6278	6346	6414	6483	6551	
63	6619	6687	6756	6824	6892	6960	7029	7097	7165	7233	
64	7302	7370	7438	7506	7575	7643	7711	7779	7848	7916	
65	7984	8052	8121	8189	8257	8325	8393	8462	8530	8598	
66	8666	8735	8803	8871	8939	9007	9076	9144	9212	9280	
67	9348	9417	9485	9553	9621	9690	9758	9826	9894	9962	
68	804 0031	0099	0167	0235	0303	0372	0440	0508	0576	0644	
69	0712	0781	0849	0917	0985	1053	1122	1190	1258	1326	
70	1394	1463	1531	1599	1667	1735	1803	1872	1940	2008	
6371	2076	2144	2212	2281	2349	2417	2485	2553	2621	2690	
72	2758	2826	2894	2962	3030	3098	3167	3235	3303	3371	
73	3439	3507	3575	3644	3712	3780	3848	3916	3984	4052	
74	4121	4189	4257	4325	4393	4461	4529	4598	4666	4734	
75	4802	4870	4938	5006	5074	5143	5211	5279	5347	5415	
76	5483	5551	5619	5687	5756	5824	5892	5960	6028	6096	
77	6164	6232	6300	6368	6437	6505	6573	6641	6709	6777	
78	6845	6913	6981	7049	7118	7186	7254	7322	7390	7458	
79	7526	7594	7662	7730	7798	7866	7934	8003	8071	8139	
80	8207	8275	8343	8411	8479	8547	8615	8683	8751	8819	
6381	8887	8956	9024	9092	9160	9228	9296	9364	9432	9500	
82	9568	9636	9704	9772	9840	9908	9976	0044	0112	0180	
83	805 0248	0316	0385	0453	0521	0589	0657	0725	0793	0861	
84	0929	0997	1065	1133	1201	1269	1337	1405	1473	1541	
85	1609	1677	1745	1813	1881	1949	2017	2085	2153	2221	
86	2289	2357	2425	2493	2561	2629	2697	2765	2833	2901	
87	2969	3037	3105	3173	3241	3309	3377	3445	3513	3581	
88	3649	3717	3785	3853	3921	3989	4057	4125	4193	4261	
89	4329	4397	4465	4533	4601	4669	4737	4805	4873	4941	
90	5009	5077	5145	5212	5280	5348	5416	5484	5552	5620	
6391	5688	5756	5824	5892	5960	6028	6096	6164	6232	6300	
92	6368	6436	6504	6571	6639	6707	6775	6843	6911	6979	
93	7047	7115	7183	7251	7319	7387	7455	7523	7590	7658	
94	7726	7794	7862	7930	7998	8066	8134	8202	8270	8338	
95	8405	8473	8541	8609	8677	8745	8813	8881	8949	9017	
96	9085	9152	9220	9288	9356	9424	9492	9560	9628	9696	
97	9764	9831	9899	9967	0035	0103	0171	0239	0307	0374	
98	806 0442	0510	0578	0646	0714	0782	0850	0917	0985	1053	
99	1121	1189	1257	1325	1393	1460	1528	1596	1664	1732	
6400	1800	1868	1935	2003	2071	2139	2207	2275	2343	2410	

Diff. 68

1	7
2	14
3	20
4	27
5	34
6	41
7	48
8	54
9	61

No.	0	1	2	3	4	5	6	7	8	9	Diff.
6400	806 1800	1868	1935	2003	2071	2139	2207	2275	2343	2410	
01	2478	2546	2614	2682	2750	2817	2885	2953	3021	3089	
02	3157	3225	3292	3360	3428	3496	3564	3632	3699	3767	
03	3835	3903	3971	4038	4106	4174	4242	4310	4378	4445	
04	4513	4581	4649	4717	4784	4852	4920	4988	5056	5124	
05	5191	5259	5327	5395	5463	5530	5598	5666	5734	5802	
06	5869	5937	6005	6073	6141	6208	6276	6344	6412	6479	
07	6547	6615	6683	6751	6818	6886	6954	7022	7089	7157	
08	7225	7293	7361	7428	7496	7564	7632	7699	7767	7835	
09	7903	7970	8038	8106	8174	8242	8309	8377	8445	8513	
10	8580	8648	8716	8784	8851	8919	8987	9055	9122	9190	
6411	9258	9326	9393	9461	9529	9596	9664	9732	9800	9867	
12	9935	0̄003	0̄071	0̄138	0̄206	0̄274	0̄342	0̄409	0̄477	0̄545	
13	807 0612	0680	0748	0816	0883	0951	1019	1086	1154	1222	
14	1290	1357	1425	1493	1560	1628	1696	1764	1831	1899	
15	1967	2034	2102	2170	2237	2305	2373	2440	2508	2576	
16	2644	2711	2779	2847	2914	2982	3050	3117	3185	3253	
17	3320	3388	3456	3523	3591	3659	3726	3794	3862	3929	
18	3997	4065	4132	4200	4268	4335	4403	4471	4538	4606	
19	4674	4741	4809	4877	4944	5012	5080	5147	5215	5283	
20	5350	5418	5486	5553	5621	5689	5756	5824	5891	5959	
6421	6027	6094	6162	6230	6297	6365	6432	6500	6568	6635	
22	6703	6771	6838	6906	6974	7041	7109	7176	7244	7312	
23	7379	7447	7514	7582	7650	7717	7785	7853	7920	7988	
24	8055	8123	8191	8258	8326	8393	8461	8529	8596	8664	
25	8731	8799	8867	8934	9002	9069	9137	9204	9272	9340	
26	9407	9475	9542	9610	9678	9745	9813	9880	9948	0̄015	
27	808 0083.	0151	0218	0286	0353	0421	0488	0556	0624	0691	
28	0759	0826	0894	0961	1029	1096	1164	1232	1299	1367	
29	1434	1502	1569	1637	1704	1772	1840	1907	1975	2042	
30	2110	2177	2245	2312	2380	2447	2515	2582	2650	2718	
6431	2785	2853	2920	2988	3055	3123	3190	3258	3325	3393	
32	3460	3528	3595	3663	3730	3798	3865	3933	4000	4068	
33	4136	4203	4271	4338	4406	4473	4541	4608	4676	4743	
34	4811	4878	4946	5013	5081	5148	5216	5283	5351	5418	
35	5486	5553	5620	5688	5755	5823	5890	5958	6025	6093	
36	6160	6228	6295	6363	6430	6498	6565	6633	6700	6768	
37	6835	6903	6970	7037	7105	7172	7240	7307	7375	7442	
38	7510	7577	7645	7712	7780	7847	7914	7982	8049	8117	
39	8184	8252	8319	8387	8454	8521	8589	8656	8724	8791	
40	8859	8926	8994	9061	9128	9196	9263	9331	9398	9466	
6441	9533	9600	9668	9735	9803	9870	9938	0̄005	0̄072	0̄140	
42	809 0207	0275	0342	0409	0477	0544	0612	0679	0747	0814	
43	0881	0949	1016	1084	1151	1218	1286	1353	1421	1488	
44	1555	1623	1690	1757	1825	1892	1960	2027	2094	2162	
45	2229	2297	2364	2431	2499	2566	2634	2701	2768	2836	
46	2903	2970	3038	3105	3173	3240	3307	3375	3442	3509	
47	3577	3644	3711	3779	3846	3914	3981	4048	4116	4183	
48	4250	4318	4385	4452	4520	4587	4654	4722	4789	4856	
49	4924	4991	5058	5126	5193	5260	5328	5395	5462	5530	
6450	5597	5664	5732	5799	5866	5934	6001	6068	6136	6203	

68

1	7
2	14
3	20
4	27
5	34
6	41
7	48
8	54
9	61

No.	0	1	2	3	4	5	6	7	8	9	Diff.
6450	809 5597	5664	5732	5799	5866	5934	6001	6068	6136	6203	
51	6270	6338	6405	6472	6540	6607	6674	6742	6809	6876	
52	6944	7011	7078	7146	7213	7280	7347	7415	7482	7549	
53	7617	7684	7751	7819	7886	7953	8020	8088	8155	8222	
54	8290	8357	8424	8491	8559	8626	8693	8761	8828	8895	
55	8962	9030	9097	9164	9232	9299	9366	9433	9501	9568	
56	9635	9702	9770	9837	9904	9972	0̄039	0̄106	0̄173	0̄241	
57	810 0308	0375	0442	0510	0577	0644	0711	0779	0846	0913	
58	0980	1048	1115	1182	1249	1317	1384	1451	1518	1586	
59	1653	1720	1787	1855	1922	1989	2056	2123	2191	2258	
60	2325	2392	2460	2527	2594	2661	2729	2796	2863	2930	
6461	2997	3065	3132	3199	3266	3333	3401	3468	3535	3602	
62	3670	3737	3804	3871	3938	4006	4073	4140	4207	4274	
63	4342	4409	4476	4543	4610	4678	4745	4812	4879	4946	
64	5013	5081	5148	5215	5282	5349	5417	5484	5551	5618	
65	5685	5752	5820	5887	5954	6021	6088	6156	6223	6290	
66	6357	6424	6491	6558	6626	6693	6760	6827	6894	6961	
67	7029	7096	7163	7230	7297	7364	7432	7499	7566	7633	
68	7700	7767	7834	7902	7969	8036	8103	8170	8237	8304	
69	8372	8439	8506	8573	8640	8707	8774	8841	8909	8976	
70	9043	9110	9177	9244	9311	9378	9446	9513	9580	9647	
6471	9714	9781	9848	9915	9982	0̄050	0̄117	0̄184	0̄251	0̄318	
72	811 0385	0452	0519	0586	0653	0721	0788	0855	0922	0989	
73	1056	1123	1190	1257	1324	1392	1459	1526	1593	1660	
74	1727	1794	1861	1928	1995	2062	2129	2197	2264	2331	
75	2398	2465	2532	2599	2666	2733	2800	2867	2934	3001	
76	3068	3135	3203	3270	3337	3404	3471	3538	3605	3672	
77	3739	3806	3873	3940	4007	4074	4141	4208	4275	4342	
78	4409	4476	4544	4611	4678	4745	4812	4879	4946	5013	
79	5080	5147	5214	5281	5348	5415	5482	5549	5616	5683	
80	5750	5817	5884	5951	6018	6085	6152	6219	6286	6353	
6481	6420	6487	6554	6621	6688	6755	6822	6889	6956	7023	
82	7090	7157	7224	7291	7358	7425	7492	7559	7626	7693	
83	7760	7827	7894	7961	8028	8095	8162	8229	8296	8363	
84	8430	8497	8564	8631	8698	8765	8832	8899	8966	9033	
85	9100	9167	9234	9301	9368	9435	9502	9569	9636	9702	
86	9769	9836	9903	9970	0̄037	0̄104	0̄171	0̄238	0̄305	0̄372	
87	812 0439	0506	0573	0640	0707	0774	0841	0908	0975	1041	
88	1108	1175	1242	1309	1376	1443	1510	1577	1644	1711	
89	1778	1845	1912	1979	2045	2112	2179	2246	2313	2380	
90	2447	2514	2581	2648	2715	2782	2848	2915	2982	3049	
6491	3116	3183	3250	3317	3384	3451	3518	3584	3651	3718	
92	3785	3852	3919	3986	4053	4120	4186	4253	4320	4387	
93	4454	4521	4588	4655	4722	4788	4855	4922	4989	5056	
94	5123	5190	5257	5323	5390	5457	5524	5591	5658	5725	
95	5792	5858	5925	5992	6059	6126	6193	6260	6326	6393	
96	6460	6527	6594	6661	6728	6794	6861	6928	6995	7062	
97	7129	7196	7262	7329	7396	7463	7530	7597	7663	7730	
98	7797	7864	7931	7998	8064	8131	8198	8265	8332	8399	
99	8465	8532	8599	8666	8733	8799	8866	8933	9000	9067	
6500	9134	9200	9267	9334	9401	9468	9534	9601	9668	9735	

67
1	7
2	13
3	20
4	27
5	34
6	40
7	47
8	54
9	60

No.	0	1	2	3	4	5	6	7	8	9	Diff.
6500	812 9134	9200	9267	9334	9401	9468	9534	9601	9668	9735	
01	9802	9868	9935	0002	0069	0136	0202	0269	0336	0403	
02	813 0470	0536	0603	0670	0737	0804	0870	0937	1004	1071	
03	1138	1204	1271	1338	1405	1471	1538	1605	1672	1739	
04	1805	1872	1939	2006	2072	2139	2206	2273	2339	2406	
05	2473	2540	2607	2673	2740	2807	2874	2940	3007	3074	
06	3141	3207	3274	3341	3408	3474	3541	3608	3675	3741	
07	3808	3875	3942	4008	4075	4142	4209	4275	4342	4409	
08	4475	4542	4609	4676	4742	4809	4876	4943	5009	5076	
09	5143	5209	5276	5343	5410	5476	5543	5610	5676	5743	
10	5810	5877	5943	6010	6077	6143	6210	6277	6344	6410	
6511	6477	6544	6610	6677	6744	6810	6877	6944	7011	7077	
12	7144	7211	7277	7344	7411	7477	7544	7611	7677	7744	
13	7811	7877	7944	8011	8077	8144	8211	8278	8344	8411	
14	8478	8544	8611	8678	8744	8811	8878	8944	9011	9078	
15	9144	9211	9278	9344	9411	9477	9544	9611	9677	9744	
16	9811	9877	9944	0011	0077	0144	0211	0277	0344	0411	
17	814 0477	0544	0610	0677	0744	0810	0877	0944	1010	1077	
18	1144	1210	1277	1343	1410	1477	1543	1610	1677	1743	
19	1810	1876	1943	2010	2076	2143	2210	2276	2343	2409	
20	2476	2543	2609	2676	2742	2809	2876	2942	3009	3075	
6521	3142	3209	3275	3342	3408	3475	3542	3608	3675	3741	
22	3808	3875	3941	4008	4074	4141	4207	4274	4341	4407	
23	4474	4540	4607	4674	4740	4807	4873	4940	5006	5073	
24	5140	5206	5273	5339	5406	5472	5539	5605	5672	5739	
25	5805	5872	5938	6005	6071	6138	6204	6271	6338	6404	
26	6471	6537	6604	6670	6737	6803	6870	6937	7003	7070	
27	7136	7203	7269	7336	7402	7469	7535	7602	7668	7735	
28	7801	7868	7935	8001	8068	8134	8201	8267	8334	8400	
29	8467	8533	8600	8666	8733	8799	8866	8932	8999	9065	
30	9132	9198	9265	9331	9398	9464	9531	9597	9664	9730	
6531	9797	9863	9930	9996	0063	0129	0196	0262	0329	0395	
32	815 0462	0528	0595	0661	0728	0794	0861	0927	0994	1060	
33	1127	1193	1260	1326	1392	1459	1525	1592	1658	1725	
34	1791	1858	1924	1991	2057	2124	2190	2257	2323	2389	
35	2456	2522	2589	2655	2722	2788	2855	2921	2988	3054	
36	3120	3187	3253	3320	3386	3453	3519	3586	3652	3718	
37	3785	3851	3918	3984	4051	4117	4183	4250	4316	4383	
38	4449	4516	4582	4648	4715	4781	4848	4914	4981	5047	
39	5113	5180	5246	5313	5379	5445	5512	5578	5645	5711	
40	5777	5844	5910	5977	6043	6109	6176	6242	6309	6375	
6541	6441	6508	6574	6641	6707	6773	6840	6906	6973	7039	
42	7105	7172	7238	7305	7371	7437	7504	7570	7636	7703	
43	7769	7836	7902	7968	8035	8101	8167	8234	8300	8367	
44	8433	8499	8566	8632	8698	8765	8831	8897	8964	9030	
45	9097	9163	9229	9296	9362	9428	9495	9561	9627	9694	
46	9760	9826	9893	9959	0025	0092	0158	0224	0291	0357	
47	816 0423	0490	0556	0622	0689	0755	0821	0888	0954	1020	
48	1087	1153	1219	1286	1352	1418	1485	1551	1617	1684	
49	1750	1816	1883	1949	2015	2081	2148	2214	2280	2347	
6550	2413	2479	2546	2612	2678	2745	2811	2877	2943	3010	

67

1	7
2	13
3	20
4	27
5	34
6	40
7	47
8	54
9	60

No.	0	1	2	3	4	5	6	7	8	9	Diff.
6550	816 2413	2479	2546	2612	2678	2745	2811	2877	2943	3010	
51	3076	3142	3209	3275	3341	3407	3474	3540	3606	3673	
52	3739	3805	3871	3938	4004	4070	4137	4203	4269	4335	
53	4402	4468	4534	4600	4667	4733	4799	4866	4932	4998	
54	5064	5131	5197	5263	5329	5396	5462	5528	5594	5661	
55	5727	5793	5859	5926	5992	6058	6124	6191	6257	6323	
56	6389	6456	6522	6588	6654	6721	6787	6853	6919	6986	
57	7052	7118	7184	7251	7317	7383	7449	7515	7582	7648	
58	7714	7780	7847	7913	7979	8045	8111	8178	8244	8310	
59	8376	8443	8509	8575	8641	8707	8774	8840	8906	8972	
60	9038	9105	9171	9237	9303	9369	9436	9502	9568	9634	
6561	9700	9767	9833	9899	9965	0031	0098	0164	0230	0296	
62	817 0362	0428	0495	0561	0627	0693	0759	0826	0892	0958	
63	1024	1090	1156	1223	1289	1355	1421	1487	1553	1620	
64	1686	1752	1818	1884	1950	2017	2083	2149	2215	2281	
65	2347	2413	2480	2546	2612	2678	2744	2810	2876	2943	
66	3009	3075	3141	3207	3273	3339	3406	3472	3538	3604	
67	3670	3736	3802	3869	3935	4001	4067	4133	4199	4265	
68	4331	4398	4464	4530	4596	4662	4728	4794	4860	4927	
69	4993	5059	5125	5191	5257	5323	5389	5455	5521	5588	
70	5654	5720	5786	5852	5918	5984	6050	6116	6182	6249	
6571	6315	6381	6447	6513	6579	6645	6711	6777	6843	6909	
72	6976	7042	7108	7174	7240	7306	7372	7438	7504	7570	
73	7636	7702	7768	7835	7901	7967	8033	8099	8165	8231	
74	8297	8363	8429	8495	8561	8627	8693	8759	8825	8892	
75	8958	9024	9090	9156	9222	9288	9354	9420	9486	9552	
76	9618	9684	9750	9816	9882	9948	0014	0080	0146	0212	
77	818 0278	0344	0410	0477	0543	0609	0675	0741	0807	0873	
78	0939	1005	1071	1137	1203	1269	1335	1401	1467	1533	
79	1599	1665	1731	1797	1863	1929	1995	2061	2127	2193	
80	2259	2325	2391	2457	2523	2589	2655	2721	2787	2853	
6581	2919	2985	3051	3117	3183	3249	3315	3381	3447	3513	
82	3579	3645	3711	3777	3843	3909	3975	4041	4107	4173	
83	4239	4305	4370	4436	4502	4568	4634	4700	4766	4832	
84	4898	4964	5030	5096	5162	5228	5294	5360	5426	5492	
85	5558	5624	5690	5756	5822	5888	5953	6019	6085	6151	
86	6217	6283	6349	6415	6481	6547	6613	6679	6745	6811	
87	6877	6943	7008	7074	7140	7206	7272	7338	7404	7470	
88	7536	7602	7668	7734	7800	7866	7931	7997	8063	8129	
89	8195	8261	8327	8393	8459	8525	8591	8656	8722	8788	
90	8854	8920	8986	9052	9118	9184	9250	9315	9381	9447	
6591	9513	9579	9645	9711	9777	9843	9908	9974	0040	0106	
92	819 0172	0238	0304	0370	0436	0501	0567	0633	0699	0765	
93	0831	0897	0962	1028	1094	1160	1226	1292	1358	1424	
94	1489	1555	1621	1687	1753	1819	1885	1950	2016	2082	
95	2148	2214	2280	2346	2411	2477	2543	2609	2675	2741	
96	2806	2872	2938	3004	3070	3136	3202	3267	3333	3399	
97	3465	3531	3597	3662	3728	3794	3860	3926	3991	4057	
98	4123	4189	4255	4321	4386	4452	4518	4584	4650	4715	
99	4781	4847	4913	4979	5045	5110	5176	5242	5308	5374	
6600	5439	5505	5571	5637	5703	5768	5834	5900	5966	6032	

66

1	7
2	13
3	20
4	26
5	33
6	40
7	46
8	53
9	59

No.	0	1	2	3	4	5	6	7	8	9	Diff.
6600	819 5439	5505	5571	5637	5703	5768	5834	5900	5966	6032	
01	6097	6163	6229	6295	6360	6426	6492	6558	6624	6689	
02	6755	6821	6887	6953	7018	7084	7150	7216	7281	7347	
03	7413	7479	7545	7610	7676	7742	7808	7873	7939	8005	
04	8071	8136	8202	8268	8334	8399	8465	8531	8597	8662	
05	8728	8794	8860	8925	8991	9057	9123	9188	9254	9320	
06	9386	9451	9517	9583	9649	9714	9780	9846	9912	9977	
07	820 0043	0109	0175	0240	0306	0372	0437	0503	0569	0635	
08	0700	0766	0832	0898	0963	1029	1095	1160	1226	1292	
09	1358	1423	1489	1555	1620	1686	1752	1817	1883	1949	
10	2015	2080	2146	2212	2277	2343	2409	2474	2540	2606	
6611	2672	2737	2803	2869	2934	3000	3066	3131	3197	3263	
12	3328	3394	3460	3525	3591	3657	3723	3788	3854	3920	
13	3985	4051	4117	4182	4248	4314	4379	4445	4511	4576	
14	4642	4708	4773	4839	4905	4970	5036	5102	5167	5233	
15	5298	5364	5430	5495	5561	5627	5692	5758	5824	5889	
16	5955	6021	6086	6152	6218	6283	6349	6414	6480	6546	
17	6611	6677	6743	6808	6874	6939	7005	7071	7136	7202	
18	7268	7333	7399	7464	7530	7596	7661	7727	7793	7858	
19	7924	7989	8055	8121	8186	8252	8317	8383	8449	8514	
20	8580	8645	8711	8777	8842	8908	8973	9039	9105	9170	
6621	9236	9301	9367	9433	9498	9564	9629	9695	9761	9826	
22	9892	9957	0023	0089	0154	0220	0285	0351	0416	0482	
23	821 0548	0613	0679	0744	0810	0875	0941	1007	1072	1138	
24	1203	1269	1334	1400	1465	1531	1597	1662	1728	1793	
25	1859	1924	1990	2055	2121	2187	2252	2318	2383	2449	
26	2514	2580	2645	2711	2776	2842	2908	2973	3039	3104	
27	3170	3235	3301	3366	3432	3497	3563	3628	3694	3759	
28	3825	3891	3956	4022	4087	4153	4218	4284	4349	4415	
29	4480	4546	4611	4677	4742	4808	4873	4939	5004	5070	
30	5135	5201	5266	5332	5397	5463	5528	5594	5659	5725	
6631	5790	5856	5921	5987	6052	6118	6183	6249	6314	6380	
32	6445	6511	6576	6642	6707	6773	6838	6904	6969	7034	
33	7100	7165	7231	7296	7362	7427	7493	7558	7624	7689	
34	7755	7820	7886	7951	8017	8082	8147	8213	8278	8344	
35	8409	8475	8540	8606	8671	8737	8802	8867	8933	8998	
36	9064	9129	9195	9260	9326	9391	9456	9522	9587	9653	
37	9718	9784	9849	9914	9980	0045	0111	0176	0242	0307	
38	822 0372	0438	0503	0569	0634	0700	0765	0830	0896	0961	
39	1027	1092	1158	1223	1288	1354	1419	1485	1550	1615	
40	1681	1746	1812	1877	1942	2008	2073	2139	2204	2269	
6641	2335	2400	2466	2531	2596	2662	2727	2793	2858	2923	
42	2989	3054	3119	3185	3250	3316	3381	3446	3512	3577	
43	3643	3708	3773	3839	3904	3969	4035	4100	4166	4231	
44	4296	4362	4427	4492	4558	4623	4688	4754	4819	4884	
45	4950	5015	5081	5146	5211	5277	5342	5407	5473	5538	
46	5603	5669	5734	5799	5865	5930	5995	6061	6126	6191	
47	6257	6322	6387	6453	6518	6583	6649	6714	6779	6845	
48	6910	6975	7041	7106	7171	7237	7302	7367	7433	7498	
49	7563	7629	7694	7759	7825	7890	7955	8021	8086	8151	
6650	8216	8282	8347	8412	8478	8543	8608	8674	8739	8804	

66

1	7
2	13
3	20
4	26
5	33
6	40
7	46
8	53
9	59

No.	0	1	2	3	4	5	6	7	8	9	Diff.
6650	822 8216	8282	8347	8412	8478	8543	8608	8674	8739	8804	
51	8869	8935	9000	9065	9131	9196	9261	9327	9392	9457	
52	9522	9588	9653	9718	9784	9849	9914	9979	0045	0110	
53	823 0175	0241	0306	0371	0436	0502	0567	0632	0697	0763	
54	0828	0893	0958	1024	1089	1154	1220	1285	1350	1415	
55	1481	1546	1611	1676	1742	1807	1872	1937	2003	2068	
56	2133	2198	2264	2329	2394	2459	2525	2590	2655	2720	
57	2786	2851	2916	2981	3047	3112	3177	3242	3307	3373	
58	3438	3503	3568	3634	3699	3764	3829	3894	3960	4025	
59	4090	4155	4221	4286	4351	4416	4481	4547	4612	4677	
60	4742	4808	4873	4938	5003	5068	5134	5199	5264	5329	
6661	5394	5460	5525	5590	5655	5720	5786	5851	5916	5981	
62	6046	6111	6177	6242	6307	6372	6437	6503	6568	6633	
63	6698	6763	6828	6894	6959	7024	7089	7154	7220	7285	
64	7350	7415	7480	7545	7611	7676	7741	7806	7871	7936	
65	8002	8067	8132	8197	8262	8327	8392	8458	8523	8588	
66	8653	8718	8783	8849	8914	8979	9044	9109	9174	9239	
67	9305	9370	9435	9500	9565	9630	9695	9761	9826	9891	
68	9956	0021	0086	0151	0216	0282	0347	0412	0477	0542	
69	824 0607	0672	0737	0803	0868	0933	0998	1063	1128	1193	
70	1258	1323	1389	1454	1519	1584	1649	1714	1779	1844	
6671	1909	1975	2040	2105	2170	2235	2300	2365	2430	2495	
72	2560	2625	2691	2756	2821	2886	2951	3016	3081	3146	
73	3211	3276	3341	3406	3472	3537	3602	3667	3732	3797	
74	3862	3927	3992	4057	4122	4187	4252	4318	4383	4448	
75	4513	4578	4643	4708	4773	4838	4903	4968	5033	5098	
76	5163	5228	5293	5358	5423	5489	5554	5619	5684	5749	
77	5814	5879	5944	6009	6074	6139	6204	6269	6334	6399	
78	6464	6529	6594	6659	6724	6789	6854	6919	6984	7049	
79	7114	7179	7244	7310	7375	7440	7505	7570	7635	7700	
80	7765	7830	7895	7960	8025	8090	8155	8220	8285	8350	
6681	8415	8480	8545	8610	8675	8740	8805	8870	8935	9000	
82	9065	9130	9195	9260	9325	9390	9455	9520	9585	9650	
83	9715	9780	9845	9910	9975	0040	0105	0169	0234	0299	
84	825 0364	0429	0494	0559	0624	0689	0754	0819	0884	0949	
85	1014	1079	1144	1209	1274	1339	1404	1469	1534	1599	
86	1664	1729	1794	1859	1924	1988	2053	2118	2183	2248	
87	2313	2378	2443	2508	2573	2638	2703	2768	2833	2898	
88	2963	3028	3093	3157	3222	3287	3352	3417	3482	3547	
89	3612	3677	3742	3807	3872	3937	4002	4066	4131	4196	
90	4261	4326	4391	4456	4521	4586	4651	4716	4780	4845	
6691	4910	4975	5040	5105	5170	5235	5300	5365	5430	5494	
92	5559	5624	5689	5754	5819	5884	5949	6014	6078	6143	
93	6208	6273	6338	6403	6468	6533	6598	6662	6727	6792	
94	6857	6922	6987	7052	7117	7181	7246	7311	7376	7441	
95	7506	7571	7636	7700	7765	7830	7895	7960	8025	8090	
96	8154	8219	8284	8349	8414	8479	8544	8608	8673	8738	
97	8803	8868	8933	8998	9062	9127	9192	9257	9322	9387	
98	9451	9516	9581	9646	9711	9776	9840	9905	9970	0035	
99	826 0100	0165	0229	0294	0359	0424	0489	0554	0618	0683	
6700	0748	0813	0878	0942	1007	1072	1137	1202	1267	1331	

65
1	7
2	13
3	20
4	26
5	33
6	39
7	46
8	52
9	59

No.	0	1	2	3	4	5	6	7	8	9	Diff.
6700	826 0748	0813	0878	0942	1007	1072	1137	1202	1267	1331	
01	1396	1461	1526	1591	1655	1720	1785	1850	1915	1979	
02	2044	2109	2174	2239	2303	2368	2433	2498	2563	2627	
03	2692	2757	2822	2887	2951	3016	3081	3146	3210	3275	
04	3340	3405	3470	3534	3599	3664	3729	3794	3858	3923	
05	3988	4053	4117	4182	4247	4312	4376	4441	4506	4571	
06	4635	4700	4765	4830	4895	4959	5024	5089	5154	5218	
07	5283	5348	5413	5477	5542	5607	5672	5736	5801	5866	
08	5931	5995	6060	6125	6190	6254	6319	6384	6448	6513	
09	6578	6643	6707	6772	6837	6902	6966	7031	7096	7160	
10	7225	7290	7355	7419	7484	7549	7614	7678	7743	7808	
6711	7872	7937	8002	8067	8131	8196	8261	8325	8390	8455	
12	8519	8584	8649	8714	8778	8843	8908	8972	9037	9102	
13	9166	9231	9296	9361	9425	9490	9555	9619	9684	9749	
14	9813	9878	9943	0007	0072	0137	0201	0266	0331	0395	
15	827 0460	0525	0590	0654	0719	0784	0848	0913	0978	1042	
16	1107	1172	1236	1301	1366	1430	1495	1560	1624	1689	
17	1753	1818	1883	1947	2012	2077	2141	2206	2271	2335	
18	2400	2465	2529	2594	2659	2723	2788	2852	2917	2982	
19	3046	3111	3176	3240	3305	3370	3434	3499	3563	3628	
20	3693	3757	3822	3887	3951	4016	4080	4145	4210	4274	
6721	4339	4404	4468	4533	4597	4662	4727	4791	4856	4920	
22	4985	5050	5114	5179	5244	5308	5373	5437	5502	5567	
23	5631	5696	5760	5825	5889	5954	6019	6083	6148	6212	
24	6277	6342	6406	6471	6535	6600	6665	6729	6794	6858	
25	6923	6987	7052	7117	7181	7246	7310	7375	7439	7504	
26	7569	7633	7698	7762	7827	7891	7956	8021	8085	8150	
27	8214	8279	8343	8408	8473	8537	8602	8666	8731	8795	
28	8860	8924	8989	9053	9118	9183	9247	9312	9376	9441	
29	9505	9570	9634	9699	9763	9828	9893	9957	0022	0086	
30	828 0151	0215	0280	0344	0409	0473	0538	0602	0667	0731	
6731	0796	0860	0925	0989	1054	1119	1183	1248	1312	1377	
32	1441	1506	1570	1635	1699	1764	1828	1893	1957	2022	
33	2086	2151	2215	2280	2344	2409	2473	2538	2602	2667	
34	2731	2796	2860	2925	2989	3054	3118	3183	3247	3312	
35	3376	3440	3505	3569	3634	3698	3763	3827	3892	3956	
36	4021	4085	4150	4214	4279	4343	4408	4472	4537	4601	
37	4665	4730	4794	4859	4923	4988	5052	5117	5181	5246	
38	5310	5375	5439	5503	5568	5632	5697	5761	5826	5890	
39	5955	6019	6083	6148	6212	6277	6341	6406	6470	6535	
40	6599	6663	6728	6792	6857	6921	6986	7050	7114	7179	
6741	7243	7308	7372	7437	7501	7565	7630	7694	7759	7823	
42	7887	7952	8016	8081	8145	8210	8274	8338	8403	8467	
43	8532	8596	8660	8725	8789	8854	8918	8982	9047	9111	
44	9176	9240	9304	9369	9433	9498	9562	9626	9691	9755	
45	9820	9884	9948	0013	0077	0141	0206	0270	0335	0399	
46	829 0463	0528	0592	0656	0721	0785	0850	0914	0978	1043	
47	1107	1171	1236	1300	1365	1429	1493	1558	1622	1686	
48	1751	1815	1879	1944	2008	2073	2137	2201	2266	2330	
49	2394	2459	2523	2587	2652	2716	2780	2845	2909	2973	
6750	3038	3102	3166	3231	3295	3359	3424	3488	3552	3617	

65

1	7
2	13
3	20
4	26
5	33
6	39
7	46
8	52
9	59

No.	0	1	2	3	4	5	6	7	8	9	Diff.
6750	829 3038	3102	3166	3231	3295	3359	3424	3488	3552	3617	
51	3681	3745	3810	3874	3938	4003	4067	4131	4196	4260	
52	4324	4389	4453	4517	4582	4646	4710	4775	4839	4903	
53	4967	5032	5096	5160	5225	5289	5353	5418	5482	5546	
54	5611	5675	5739	5803	5868	5932	5996	6061	6125	6189	
55	6254	6318	6382	6446	6511	6575	6639	6704	6768	6832	
56	6896	6961	7025	7089	7154	7218	7282	7346	7411	7475	
57	7539	7603	7668	7732	7796	7861	7925	7989	8053	8118	
58	8182	8246	8310	8375	8439	8503	8567	8632	8696	8760	
59	8824	8889	8953	9017	9081	9146	9210	9274	9338	9403	
60	9467	9531	9595	9660	9724	9788	9852	9917	9981	0045	
6761	830 0109	0174	0238	0302	0366	0431	0495	0559	0623	0687	
62	0752	0816	0880	0944	1009	1073	1137	1201	1265	1330	
63	1394	1458	1522	1587	1651	1715	1779	1843	1908	1972	
64	2036	2100	2164	2229	2293	2357	2421	2485	2550	2614	
65	2678	2742	2806	2871	2935	2999	3063	3127	3192	3256	
66	3320	3384	3448	3512	3577	3641	3705	3769	3833	3898	
67	3962	4026	4090	4154	4218	4283	4347	4411	4475	4539	
68	4604	4668	4732	4796	4860	4924	4988	5053	5117	5181	
69	5245	5309	5373	5438	5502	5566	5630	5694	5758	5823	
70	5887	5951	6015	6079	6143	6207	6272	6336	6400	6464	64
6771	6528	6592	6656	6721	6785	6849	6913	6977	7041	7105	1 6
72	7169	7234	7298	7362	7426	7490	7554	7618	7683	7747	2 13
73	7811	7875	7939	8003	8067	8131	8195	8260	8324	8388	3 19
74	8452	8516	8580	8644	8708	8772	8837	8901	8965	9029	4 26
75	9093	9157	9221	9285	9349	9413	9478	9542	9606	9670	5 32
76	9734	9798	9862	9926	9990	0054	0119	0183	0247	0311	6 38 7 45
77	831 0375	0439	0503	0567	0631	0695	0759	0823	0887	0952	8 51
78	1016	1080	1144	1208	1272	1336	1400	1464	1528	1592	9 58
79	1656	1720	1784	1849	1913	1977	2041	2105	2169	2233	
80	2297	2361	2425	2489	2553	2617	2681	2745	2809	2873	
6781	2937	3001	3066	3130	3194	3258	3322	3386	3450	3514	
82	3578	3642	3706	3770	3834	3898	3962	4026	4090	4154	
83	4218	4282	4346	4410	4474	4538	4602	4666	4730	4794	
84	4858	4922	4986	5050	5114	5178	5242	5306	5371	5435	
85	5499	5563	5627	5691	5755	5819	5883	5947	6011	6075	
86	6139	6203	6267	6331	6395	6459	6523	6587	6651	6715	
87	6778	6842	6906	6970	7034	7098	7162	7226	7290	7354	
88	7418	7482	7546	7610	7674	7738	7802	7866	7930	7994	
89	8058	8122	8186	8250	8314	8378	8442	8506	8570	8634	
90	8698	8762	8826	8890	8954	9018	9081	9145	9209	9273	
6791	9337	9401	9465	9529	9593	9657	9721	9785	9849	9913	
92	9977	0041	0105	0169	0233	0296	0360	0424	0488	0552	
93	832 0616	0680	0744	0808	0872	0936	1000	1064	1128	1192	
94	1255	1319	1383	1447	1511	1575	1639	1703	1767	1831	
95	1895	1959	2022	2086	2150	2214	2278	2342	2406	2470	
96	2534	2598	2662	2725	2789	2853	2917	2981	3045	3109	
97	3173	3237	3300	3364	3428	3492	3556	3620	3684	3748	
98	3812	3875	3939	4003	4067	4131	4195	4259	4323	4387	
99	4450	4514	4578	4642	4706	4770	4834	4898	4961	5025	
6800	5089	5153	5217	5281	5345	5408	5472	5536	5600	5664	

No.	0	1	2	3	4	5	6	7	8	9	Diff.
6800	332 5089	5153	5217	5281	5345	5408	5472	5536	5600	5664	
01	5728	5792	5855	5919	5983	6047	6111	6175	6239	6302	
02	6366	6430	6494	6558	6622	6686	6749	6813	6877	6941	
03	7005	7069	7132	7196	7260	7324	7388	7452	7515	7579	
04	7643	7707	7771	7835	7898	7962	8026	8090	8154	8217	
05	8281	8345	8409	8473	8537	8600	8664	8728	8792	8856	
06	8919	8983	9047	9111	9175	9238	9302	9366	9430	9494	
07	9558	9621	9685	9749	9813	9877	9940	0004	0068	0132	
08	333 0195	0259	0323	0387	0451	0514	0578	0642	0706	0770	
09	0833	0897	0961	1025	1088	1152	1216	1280	1344	1407	
10	1471	1535	1599	1662	1726	1790	1854	1918	1981	2045	
6811	2109	2173	2236	2300	2364	2428	2491	2555	2619	2683	
12	2746	2810	2874	2938	3001	3065	3129	3193	3256	3320	
13	3384	3448	3511	3575	3639	3703	3766	3830	3894	3958	
14	4021	4085	4149	4212	4276	4340	4404	4467	4531	4595	
15	4659	4722	4786	4850	4913	4977	5041	5105	5168	5232	
16	5296	5360	5423	5487	5551	5614	5678	5742	5806	5869	
17	5933	5997	6060	6124	6188	6251	6315	6379	6443	6506	
18	6570	6634	6697	6761	6825	6888	6952	7016	7080	7143	
19	7207	7271	7334	7398	7462	7525	7589	7653	7716	7780	
20	7844	7907	7971	8035	8098	8162	8226	8289	8353	8417	
6821	8480	8544	8608	8672	8735	8799	8862	8926	8990	9053	64
22	9117	9181	9244	9308	9372	9435	9499	9563	9626	9690	1 6
23	9754	9817	9881	9945	0008	0072	0136	0199	0263	0327	2 13
24	334 0390	0454	0517	0581	0645	0708	0772	0836	0899	0963	3 19
25	1027	1090	1154	1217	1281	1345	1408	1472	1536	1599	4 26
26	1663	1726	1790	1854	1917	1981	2045	2108	2172	2235	5 32
27	2299	2363	2426	2490	2553	2617	2681	2744	2808	2872	6 38
28	2935	2999	3062	3126	3190	3253	3317	3380	3444	3508	7 45
29	3571	3635	3698	3762	3826	3889	3953	4016	4080	4143	8 51
30	4207	4271	4334	4398	4461	4525	4589	4652	4716	4779	9 58
6831	4843	4906	4970	5034	5097	5161	5224	5288	5351	5415	
32	5479	5542	5606	5669	5733	5796	5860	5924	5987	6051	
33	6114	6178	6241	6305	6368	6432	6496	6559	6623	6686	
34	6750	6813	6877	6940	7004	7067	7131	7195	7258	7322	
35	7385	7449	7512	7576	7639	7703	7766	7830	7893	7957	
36	8021	8084	8148	8211	8275	8338	8402	8465	8529	8592	
37	8656	8719	8783	8846	8910	8973	9037	9100	9164	9227	
38	9291	9354	9418	9481	9545	9609	9672	9736	9799	9863	
39	9926	9990	0053	0117	0180	0244	0307	0371	0434	0498	
40	335 0561	0625	0688	0751	0815	0878	0942	1005	1069	1132	
6841	1196	1259	1323	1386	1450	1513	1577	1640	1704	1767	
42	1831	1894	1958	2021	2085	2148	2212	2275	2338	2402	
43	2465	2529	2592	2656	2719	2783	2846	2910	2973	3037	
44	3100	3163	3227	3290	3354	3417	3481	3544	3608	3671	
45	3735	3798	3861	3925	3988	4052	4115	4179	4242	4306	
46	4369	4432	4496	4559	4623	4686	4750	4813	4876	4940	
47	5003	5067	5130	5194	5257	5320	5384	5447	5511	5574	
48	5638	5701	5764	5828	5891	5955	6018	6081	6145	6208	
49	6272	6335	6398	6462	6525	6589	6652	6716	6779	6842	
6850	6906	6969	7033	7096	7159	7223	7286	7349	7413	7476	

No.	0	1	2	3	4	5	6	7	8	9	Diff.
6850	835 6906	6969	7033	7096	7159	7223	7286	7349	7413	7476	
51	7540	7603	7666	7730	7793	7857	7920	7983	8047	8110	
52	8174	8237	8300	8364	8427	8490	8554	8617	8681	8744	
53	8807	8871	8934	8997	9061	9124	9188	9251	9314	9378	
54	9441	9504	9568	9631	9694	9758	9821	9885	9948	$\overline{0011}$	
55	836 0075	0138	0201	0265	0328	0391	0455	0518	0581	0645	
56	0708	0771	0835	0898	0961	1025	1088	1151	1215	1278	
57	1341	1405	1468	1531	1595	1658	1721	1785	1848	1911	
58	1975	2038	2101	2165	2228	2291	2355	2418	2481	2545	
59	2608	2671	2735	2798	2861	2925	2988	3051	3115	3178	
60	3241	3304	3368	3431	3494	3558	3621	3684	3748	3811	
6861	3874	3937	4001	4064	4127	4191	4254	4317	4381	4444	
62	4507	4570	4634	4697	4760	4824	4887	4950	5013	5077	
63	5140	5203	5267	5330	5393	5456	5520	5583	5646	5709	
64	5773	5836	5899	5963	6026	6089	6152	6216	6279	6342	
65	6405	6469	6532	6595	6658	6722	6785	6848	6911	6975	
66	7038	7101	7164	7228	7291	7354	7417	7481	7544	7607	
67	7670	7734	7797	7860	7923	7987	8050	8113	8176	8240	
68	8303	8366	8429	8493	8556	8619	8682	8745	8809	8872	
69	8935	8998	9062	9125	9188	9251	9314	9378	9441	9504	
70	9567	9631	9694	9757	9820	9883	9947	$\overline{0010}$	$\overline{0073}$	$\overline{0136}$	
6871	837 0199	0263	0326	0389	0452	0516	0579	0642	0705	0768	63
72	0832	0895	0958	1021	1084	1147	1211	1274	1337	1400	1 6
73	1463	1527	1590	1653	1716	1779	1843	1906	1969	2032	2 13
74	2095	2158	2222	2285	2348	2411	2474	2538	2601	2664	3 19
75	2727	2790	2853	2917	2980	3043	3106	3169	3232	3296	4 25
76	3359	3422	3485	3548	3611	3674	3738	3801	3864	3927	5 32
77	3990	4053	4117	4180	4243	4306	4369	4432	4495	4559	6 38
78	4622	4685	4748	4811	4874	4937	5001	5064	5127	5190	7 44
79	5253	5316	5379	5442	5506	5569	5632	5695	5758	5821	8 50
80	5884	5948	6011	6074	6137	6200	6263	6326	6389	6452	9 57
6881	6516	6579	6642	6705	6768	6831	6894	6957	7020	7084	
82	7147	7210	7273	7336	7399	7462	7525	7588	7652	7715	
83	7778	7841	7904	7967	8030	8093	8156	8219	8282	8346	
84	8409	8472	8535	8598	8661	8724	8787	8850	8913	8976	
85	9039	9103	9166	9229	9292	9355	9418	9481	9544	9607	
86	9670	9733	9796	9859	9922	9986	$\overline{0049}$	$\overline{0112}$	$\overline{0175}$	$\overline{0238}$	
87	838 0301	0364	0427	0490	0553	0616	0679	0742	0805	0868	
88	0931	0994	1057	1121	1184	1247	1310	1373	1436	1499	
89	1562	1625	1688	1751	1814	1877	1940	2003	2066	2129	
90	2192	2255	2318	2381	2444	2507	2570	2633	2696	2759	
6891	2822	2886	2949	3012	3075	3138	3201	3264	3327	3390	
92	3453	3516	3579	3642	3705	3768	3831	3894	3957	4020	
93	4083	4146	4209	4272	4335	4398	4461	4524	4587	4650	
94	4713	4776	4839	4902	4965	5028	5091	5154	5217	5280	
95	5343	5406	5469	5532	5595	5658	5721	5784	5847	5910	
96	5973	6036	6098	6161	6224	6287	6350	6413	6476	6539	
97	6602	6665	6728	6791	6854	6917	6980	7043	7106	7169	
98	7232	7295	7358	7421	7484	7547	7610	7673	7736	7798	
99	7861	7924	7987	8050	8113	8176	8239	8302	8365	8428	
6900	8491	8554	8617	8680	8743	8806	8869	8931	8994	9057	

No.	0	1	2	3	4	5	6	7	8	9	Diff.
6900	838 8491	8554	8617	8680	8743	8806	8869	8931	8994	9057	
01	9120	9183	9246	9309	9372	9435	9498	9561	9624	9687	
02	9750	9812	9875	9938	0001	0064	0127	0190	0253	0316	
03	839 0379	0442	0505	0567	0630	0693	0756	0819	0882	0945	
04	1008	1071	1134	1197	1259	1322	1385	1448	1511	1574	
05	1637	1700	1763	1826	1888	1951	2014	2077	2140	2203	
06	2266	2329	2392	2454	2517	2580	2643	2706	2769	2832	
07	2895	2957	3020	3083	3146	3209	3272	3335	3398	3460	
08	3523	3586	3649	3712	3775	3838	3900	3963	4026	4089	
09	4152	4215	4278	4341	4403	4466	4529	4592	4655	4718	
10	4780	4843	4906	4969	5032	5095	5158	5220	5283	5346	
6911	5409	5472	5535	5597	5660	5723	5786	5849	5912	5974	
12	6037	6100	6163	6226	6289	6351	6414	6477	6540	6603	
13	6666	6728	6791	6854	6917	6980	7042	7105	7168	7231	
14	7294	7357	7419	7482	7545	7608	7671	7733	7796	7859	
15	7922	7985	8047	8110	8173	8236	8299	8361	8424	8487	
16	8550	8613	8675	8738	8801	8864	8927	8989	9052	9115	
17	9178	9241	9303	9366	9429	9492	9554	9617	9680	9743	
18	9806	9868	9931	9994	0057	0119	0182	0245	0308	0371	
19	840 0433	0496	0559	0622	0684	0747	0810	0873	0935	0998	
20	1061	1124	1186	1249	1312	1375	1437	1500	1563	1626	
6921	1688	1751	1814	1877	1939	2002	2065	2128	2190	2253	
22	2316	2379	2441	2504	2567	2630	2692	2755	2818	2881	
23	2943	3006	3069	3132	3194	3257	3320	3382	3445	3508	
24	3571	3633	3696	3759	3821	3884	3947	4010	4072	4135	
25	4198	4260	4323	4386	4449	4511	4574	4637	4699	4762	
26	4825	4888	4950	5013	5076	5138	5201	5264	5326	5389	
27	5452	5515	5577	5640	5703	5765	5828	5891	5953	6016	
28	6079	6141	6204	6267	6330	6392	6455	6518	6580	6643	
29	6706	6768	6831	6894	6956	7019	7082	7144	7207	7270	
30	7332	7395	7458	7520	7583	7646	7708	7771	7834	7896	
6931	7959	8022	8084	8147	8210	8272	8335	8398	8460	8523	
32	8586	8648	8711	8773	8836	8899	8961	9024	9087	9149	
33	9212	9275	9337	9400	9463	9525	9588	9650	9713	9776	
34	9838	9901	9964	0026	0089	0152	0214	0277	0339	0402	
35	841 0465	0527	0590	0653	0715	0778	0840	0903	0966	1028	
36	1091	1153	1216	1279	1341	1404	1467	1529	1592	1654	
37	1717	1780	1842	1905	1967	2030	2093	2155	2218	2280	
38	2343	2406	2468	2531	2593	2656	2719	2781	2844	2906	
39	2969	3031	3094	3157	3219	3282	3344	3407	3470	3532	
40	3595	3657	3720	3782	3845	3908	3970	4033	4095	4158	
6941	4220	4283	4346	4408	4471	4533	4596	4658	4721	4784	
42	4846	4909	4971	5034	5096	5159	5221	5284	5347	5409	
43	5472	5534	5597	5659	5722	5784	5847	5909	5972	6035	
44	6097	6160	6222	6285	6347	6410	6472	6535	6597	6660	
45	6723	6785	6848	6910	6973	7035	7098	7160	7223	7285	
46	7348	7410	7473	7535	7598	7660	7723	7785	7848	7910	
47	7973	8036	8098	8161	8223	8286	8348	8411	8473	8536	
48	8598	8661	8723	8786	8848	8911	8973	9036	9098	9161	
49	9223	9286	9348	9411	9473	9536	9598	9661	9723	9786	
6950	9848	9911	9973	0036	0098	0160	0223	0285	0348	0410	
	842										

63
1	6
2	13
3	19
4	25
5	32
6	38
7	44
8	50
9	57

No.	0	1	2	3	4	5	6	7	8	9	Diff.
6950	841 9848	9911	9973	0̄036	0̄098	0̄160	0̄223	0̄285	0348	0̄410	
51	842 0473	0535	0598	0660	0723	0785	0848	0910	0973	1035	
52	1098	1160	1223	1285	1348	1410	1472	1535	1597	1660	
53	1722	1785	1847	1910	1972	2035	2097	2160	2222	2284	
54	2347	2409	2472	2534	2597	2659	2722	2784	2846	2909	
55	2971	3034	3096	3159	3221	3284	3346	3408	3471	3533	
56	3596	3658	3721	3783	3845	3908	3970	4033	4095	4158	
57	4220	4282	4345	4407	4470	4532	4595	4657	4719	4782	
58	4844	4907	4969	5031	5094	5156	5219	5281	5344	5406	
59	5468	5531	5593	5656	5718	5780	5843	5905	5968	6030	
60	6092	6155	6217	6280	6342	6404	6467	6529	6592	6654	
6961	6716	6779	6841	6904	6966	7028	7091	7153	7215	7278	
62	7340	7403	7465	7527	7590	7652	7714	7777	7839	7902	
63	7964	8026	8089	8151	8213	8276	8338	8401	8463	8525	
64	8588	8650	8712	8775	8837	8899	8962	9024	9086	9149	
65	9211	9274	9336	9398	9461	9523	9585	9648	9710	9772	
66	9835	9897	9959	0̄022	0̄084	0̄146	0̄209	0̄271	0̄333	0̄396	
67	843 0458	0520	0583	0645	0707	0770	0832	0894	0957	1019	
68	1081	1144	1206	1268	1331	1393	1455	1518	1580	1642	
69	1705	1767	1829	1892	1954	2016	2079	2141	2203	2265	
70	2328	2390	2452	2515	2577	2639	2702	2764	2826	2889	
6971	2951	3013	3075	3138	3200	3262	3325	3387	3449	3511	
72	3574	3636	3698	3761	3823	3885	3948	4010	4072	4134	
73	4197	4259	4321	4383	4446	4508	4570	4633	4695	4757	
74	4819	4882	4944	5006	5069	5131	5193	5255	5318	5380	
75	5442	5504	5567	5629	5691	5753	5816	5878	5940	6002	
76	6065	6127	6189	6251	6314	6376	6438	6500	6563	6625	
77	6687	6749	6812	6874	6936	6998	7061	7123	7185	7247	
78	7310	7372	7434	7496	7559	7621	7683	7745	7808	7870	
79	7932	7994	8056	8119	8181	8243	8305	8368	8430	8492	
80	8554	8616	8679	8741	8803	8865	8928	8990	9052	9114	
6981	9176	9239	9301	9363	9425	9487	9550	9612	9674	9736	
82	9798	9861	9923	9985	0̄047	0̄109	0̄172	0̄234	0̄296	0̄358	
83	844 0420	0483	0545	0607	0669	0731	0794	0856	0918	0980	
84	1042	1104	1167	1229	1291	1353	1415	1478	1540	1602	
85	1664	1726	1788	1851	1913	1975	2037	2099	2161	2224	
86	2286	2348	2410	2472	2534	2597	2659	2721	2783	2845	
87	2907	2970	3032	3094	3156	3218	3280	3343	3405	3467	
88	3529	3591	3653	3715	3778	3840	3902	3964	4026	4088	
89	4150	4213	4275	4337	4399	4461	4523	4585	4647	4710	
90	4772	4834	4896	4958	5020	5082	5145	5207	5269	5331	
6991	5393	5455	5517	5579	5642	5704	5766	5828	5890	5952	
92	6014	6076	6138	6201	6263	6325	6387	6449	6511	6573	
93	6635	6697	6759	6822	6884	6946	7008	7070	7132	7194	
94	7256	7318	7380	7443	7505	7567	7629	7691	7753	7815	
95	7877	7939	8001	8063	8126	8188	8250	8312	8374	8436	
96	8498	8560	8622	8684	8746	8808	8870	8933	8995	9057	
97	9119	9181	9243	9305	9367	9429	9491	9553	9615	9677	
98	9739	9801	9863	9926	9988	0̄050	0̄112	0̄174	0̄236	0̄298	
99	845 0360	0422	0484	0546	0608	0670	0732	0794	0856	0918	
7000	0980	1042	1104	1167	1229	1291	1353	1415	1477	1539	

62

1	6
2	12
3	19
4	25
5	31
6	37
7	43
8	50
9	56

No.	0	1	2	3	4	5	6	7	8	9	Diff.
7000	845 0980	1042	1104	1167	1229	1291	1353	1415	1477	1539	
01	1601	1663	1725	1787	1849	1911	1973	2035	2097	2159	
02	2221	2283	2345	2407	2469	2531	2593	2655	2717	2779	
03	2841	2903	2965	3027	3089	3151	3213	3275	3337	3399	
04	3461	3523	3585	3647	3709	3771	3833	3895	3957	4019	
05	4081	4143	4205	4267	4329	4391	4453	4515	4577	4639	
06	4701	4763	4825	4887	4949	5011	5073	5135	5197	5259	
07	5321	5383	5445	5507	5569	5631	5693	5755	5817	5879	
08	5941	6003	6065	6127	6189	6251	6313	6375	6437	6499	
09	6561	6623	6685	6746	6808	6870	6932	6994	7056	7118	
10	7180	7242	7304	7366	7428	7490	7552	7614	7676	7738	
7011	7800	7862	7924	7986	8047	8109	8171	8233	8295	8357	
12	8419	8481	8543	8605	8667	8729	8791	8853	8915	8976	
13	9038	9100	9162	9224	9286	9348	9410	9472	9534	9596	
14	9658	9720	9781	9843	9905	9967	0029	0091	0153	0215	
15	846 0277	0339	0401	0462	0524	0586	0648	0710	0772	0834	
16	0896	0958	1020	1082	1143	1205	1267	1329	1391	1453	
17	1515	1577	1639	1700	1762	1824	1886	1948	2010	2072	
18	2134	2196	2257	2319	2381	2443	2505	2567	2629	2691	
19	2752	2814	2876	2938	3000	3062	3124	3186	3247	3309	
20	3371	3433	3495	3557	3619	3680	3742	3804	3866	3928	
7021	3990	4052	4113	4175	4237	4299	4361	4423	4485	4546	
22	4608	4670	4732	4794	4856	4917	4979	5041	5103	5165	
23	5227	5289	5350	5412	5474	5536	5598	5660	5721	5783	
24	5845	5907	5969	6031	6092	6154	6216	6278	6340	6401	
25	6463	6525	6587	6649	6711	6772	6834	6896	6958	7020	
26	7081	7143	7205	7267	7329	7391	7452	7514	7576	7638	
27	7700	7761	7823	7885	7947	8009	8070	8132	8194	8256	
28	8318	8379	8441	8503	8565	8626	8688	8750	8812	8874	
29	8935	8997	9059	9121	9183	9244	9306	9368	9430	9491	
30	9553	9615	9677	9739	9800	9862	9924	9986	0047	0109	
7031	847 0171	0233	0295	0356	0418	0480	0542	0603	0665	0727	
32	0789	0850	0912	0974	1036	1097	1159	1221	1283	1344	
33	1406	1468	1530	1591	1653	1715	1777	1838	1900	1962	
34	2024	2085	2147	2209	2271	2332	2394	2456	2518	2579	
35	2641	2703	2764	2826	2888	2950	3011	3073	3135	3197	
36	3258	3320	3382	3443	3505	3567	3629	3690	3752	3814	
37	3876	3937	3999	4061	4122	4184	4246	4307	4369	4431	
38	4493	4554	4616	4678	4739	4801	4863	4925	4986	5048	
39	5110	5171	5233	5295	5356	5418	5480	5542	5603	5665	
40	5727	5788	5850	5912	5973	6035	6097	6158	6220	6282	
7041	6343	6405	6467	6528	6590	6652	6714	6775	6837	6899	
42	6960	7022	7084	7145	7207	7269	7330	7392	7454	7515	
43	7577	7639	7700	7762	7824	7885	7947	8009	8070	8132	
44	8193	8255	8317	8378	8440	8502	8563	8625	8687	8748	
45	8810	8872	8933	8995	9057	9118	9180	9241	9303	9365	
46	9426	9488	9550	9611	9673	9735	9796	9858	9919	9981	
47	848 0043	0104	0166	0228	0289	0351	0412	0474	0536	0597	
48	0659	0721	0782	0844	0905	0967	1029	1090	1152	1213	
49	1275	1337	1398	1460	1522	1583	1645	1706	1768	1830	
7050	1891	1953	2014	2076	2138	2199	2261	2322	2384	2446	

62

1	6
2	12
3	19
4	25
5	31
6	37
7	43
8	50
9	56

No.	0	1	2	3	4	5	6	7	8	9	Diff.
7050	848 1891	1953	2014	2076	2138	2199	2261	2322	2384	2446	
51	2507	2569	2630	2692	2754	2815	2877	2938	3000	3061	
52	3123	3185	3246	3308	3369	3431	3493	3554	3616	3677	
53	3739	3800	3862	3924	3985	4047	4108	4170	4231	4293	
54	4355	4416	4478	4539	4601	4662	4724	4786	4847	4909	
55	4970	5032	5093	5155	5216	5278	5340	5401	5463	5524	
56	5586	5647	5709	5770	5832	5893	5955	6017	6078	6140	
57	6201	6263	6324	6386	6447	6509	6570	6632	6693	6755	
58	6817	6878	6940	7001	7063	7124	7186	7247	7309	7370	
59	7432	7493	7555	7616	7678	7739	7801	7862	7924	7985	
60	8047	8109	8170	8232	8293	8355	8416	8478	8539	8601	
7061	8662	8724	8785	8847	8908	8970	9031	9093	9154	9216	
62	9277	9339	9400	9462	9523	9585	9646	9708	9769	9831	
63	9892	9954	0015	0077	0138	0199	0261	0322	0384	0445	
64	849 0507	0568	0630	0691	0753	0814	0876	0937	0999	1060	
65	1122	1183	1245	1306	1368	1429	1490	1552	1613	1675	
66	1736	1798	1859	1921	1982	2044	2105	2167	2228	2289	
67	2351	2412	2474	2535	2597	2658	2720	2781	2843	2904	
68	2965	3027	3088	3150	3211	3273	3334	3396	3457	3518	
69	3580	3641	3703	3764	3826	3887	3948	4010	4071	4133	
70	4194	4256	4317	4378	4440	4501	4563	4624	4686	4747	
7071	4808	4870	4931	4993	5054	5115	5177	5238	5300	5361	
72	5423	5484	5545	5607	5668	5730	5791	5852	5914	5975	
73	6037	6098	6159	6221	6282	6344	6405	6466	6528	6589	
74	6651	6712	6773	6835	6896	6958	7019	7080	7142	7203	
75	7264	7326	7387	7449	7510	7571	7633	7694	7755	7817	
76	7878	7940	8001	8062	8124	8185	8246	8308	8369	8431	
77	8492	8553	8615	8676	8737	8799	8860	8922	8983	9044	
78	9106	9167	9228	9290	9351	9412	9474	9535	9596	9658	
79	9719	9780	9842	9903	9965	0026	0087	0149	0210	0271	
80	850 0333	0394	0455	0517	0578	0639	0701	0762	0823	0885	
7081	0946	1007	1069	1130	1191	1253	1314	1375	1437	1498	
82	1559	1621	1682	1743	1805	1866	1927	1988	2050	2111	
83	2172	2234	2295	2356	2418	2479	2540	2602	2663	2724	
84	2786	2847	2908	2969	3031	3092	3153	3215	3276	3337	
85	3399	3460	3521	3582	3644	3705	3766	3828	3889	3950	
86	4011	4073	4134	4195	4257	4318	4379	4440	4502	4563	
87	4624	4686	4747	4808	4869	4931	4992	5053	5115	5176	
88	5237	5298	5360	5421	5482	5543	5605	5666	5727	5788	
89	5850	5911	5972	6034	6095	6156	6217	6279	6340	6401	
90	6462	6524	6585	6646	6707	6769	6830	6891	6952	7014	
7091	7075	7136	7197	7259	7320	7381	7442	7504	7565	7626	
92	7687	7749	7810	7871	7932	7993	8055	8116	8177	8238	
93	8300	8361	8422	8483	8545	8606	8667	8728	8789	8851	
94	8912	8973	9034	9095	9157	9218	9279	9340	9402	9463	
95	9524	9585	9646	9708	9769	9830	9891	9952	0014	0075	
96	851 0136	0197	0258	0320	0381	0442	0503	0564	0626	0687	
97	0748	0809	0870	0932	0993	1054	1115	1176	1238	1299	
98	1360	1421	1482	1544	1605	1666	1727	1788	1849	1911	
99	1972	2033	2094	2155	2216	2278	2339	2400	2461	2522	
7100	2583	2645	2706	2767	2828	2889	2950	3012	3073	3134	

61

1	6
2	12
3	18
4	24
5	31
6	37
7	43
8	49
9	55

No.	0	1	2	3	4	5	6	7	8	9	Diff.
7100	851 2583	2645	2706	2767	2828	2889	2950	3012	3073	3134	
01	3195	3256	3317	3379	3440	3501	3562	3623	3684	3746	
02	3807	3868	3929	3990	4051	4112	4174	4235	4296	4357	
03	4418	4479	4540	4602	4663	4724	4785	4846	4907	4968	
04	5030	5091	5152	5213	5274	5335	5396	5457	5519	5580	
05	5641	5702	5763	5824	5885	5946	6008	6069	6130	6191	
06	6252	6313	6374	6435	6496	6558	6619	6680	6741	6802	
07	6863	6924	6985	7046	7108	7169	7230	7291	7352	7413	
08	7474	7535	7596	7657	7719	7780	7841	7902	7963	8024	
09	8085	8146	8207	8268	8329	8391	8452	8513	8574	8635	
10	8696	8757	8818	8879	8940	9001	9062	9124	9185	9246	
7111	9307	9368	9429	9490	9551	9612	9673	9734	9795	9856	
12	9917	9979	0040	0101	0162	0223	0284	0345	0406	0467	
13	852 0528	0589	0650	0711	0772	0833	0894	0955	1017	1078	
14	1139	1200	1261	1322	1383	1444	1505	1566	1627	1688	
15	1749	1810	1871	1932	1993	2054	2115	2176	2237	2298	
16	2359	2420	2481	2542	2604	2665	2726	2787	2848	2909	
17	2970	3031	3092	3153	3214	3275	3336	3397	3458	3519	
18	3580	3641	3702	3763	3824	3885	3946	4007	4068	4129	
19	4190	4251	4312	4373	4434	4495	4556	4617	4678	4739	
20	4800	4861	4922	4983	5044	5105	5166	5227	5288	5349	
7121	5410	5471	5532	5593	5654	5715	5776	5837	5898	5959	
22	6020	6081	6142	6203	6264	6325	6386	6447	6508	6568	
23	6629	6690	6751	6812	6873	6934	6995	7056	7117	7178	
24	7239	7300	7361	7422	7483	7544	7605	7666	7727	7788	
25	7849	7910	7971	8032	8092	8153	8214	8275	8336	8397	
26	8458	8519	8580	8641	8702	8763	8824	8885	8946	9007	
27	9068	9129	9189	9250	9311	9372	9433	9494	9555	9616	
28	9677	9738	9799	9860	9921	9982	0042	0103	0164	0225	
29	853 0286	0347	0408	0469	0530	0591	0652	0713	0773	0834	
30	0895	0956	1017	1078	1139	1200	1261	1322	1383	1443	
7131	1504	1565	1626	1687	1748	1809	1870	1931	1992	2052	
32	2113	2174	2235	2296	2357	2418	2479	2540	2600	2661	
33	2722	2783	2844	2905	2966	3027	3088	3148	3209	3270	
34	3331	3392	3453	3514	3575	3635	3696	3757	3818	3879	
35	3940	4001	4062	4122	4183	4244	4305	4366	4427	4488	
36	4548	4609	4670	4731	4792	4853	4914	4974	5035	5096	
37	5157	5218	5279	5340	5400	5461	5522	5583	5644	5705	
38	5765	5826	5887	5948	6009	6070	6130	6191	6252	6313	
39	6374	6435	6495	6556	6617	6678	6739	6800	6860	6921	
40	6982	7043	7104	7165	7225	7286	7347	7408	7469	7530	
7141	7590	7651	7712	7773	7834	7894	7955	8016	8077	8138	
42	8198	8259	8320	8381	8442	8502	8563	8624	8685	8746	
43	8807	8867	8928	8989	9050	9110	9171	9232	9293	9354	
44	9414	9475	9536	9597	9658	9718	9779	9840	9901	9962	
45	854 0022	0083	0144	0205	0265	0326	0387	0448	0509	0569	
46	0630	0691	0752	0812	0873	0934	0995	1056	1116	1177	
47	1238	1299	1359	1420	1481	1542	1602	1663	1724	1785	
48	1845	1906	1967	2028	2088	2149	2210	2271	2331	2392	
49	2453	2514	2574	2635	2696	2757	2817	2878	2939	3000	
7150	3060	3121	3182	3243	3303	3364	3425	3486	3546	3607	

61

1	6
2	12
3	18
4	24
5	31
6	37
7	43
8	49
9	55

No.	0	1	2	3	4	5	6	7	8	9	Diff.
7150	854 3060	3121	3182	3243	3303	3364	3425	3486	3546	3607	
51	3668	3729	3789	3850	3911	3971	4032	4093	4154	4214	
52	4275	4336	4397	4457	4518	4579	4639	4700	4761	4822	
53	4882	4943	5004	5064	5125	5186	5247	5307	5368	5429	
54	5489	5550	5611	5671	5732	5793	5854	5914	5975	6036	
55	6096	6157	6218	6278	6339	6400	6461	6521	6582	6643	
56	6703	6764	6825	6885	6946	7007	7067	7128	7189	7249	
57	7310	7371	7432	7492	7553	7614	7674	7735	7796	7856	
58	7917	7978	8038	8099	8160	8220	8281	8342	8402	8463	
59	8524	8584	8645	8706	8766	8827	8888	8948	9009	9070	
60	9130	9191	9252	9312	9373	9433	9494	9555	9615	9676	
7161	9737	9797	9858	9919	9979	0040	0101	0161	0222	0283	
62	855 0343	0404	0464	0525	0586	0646	0707	0768	0828	0889	
63	0950	1010	1071	1131	1192	1253	1313	1374	1435	1495	
64	1556	1616	1677	1738	1798	1859	1919	1980	2041	2101	
65	2162	2223	2283	2344	2404	2465	2526	2586	2647	2707	
66	2768	2829	2889	2950	3010	3071	3132	3192	3253	3313	
67	3374	3435	3495	3556	3616	3677	3738	3798	3859	3919	
68	3980	4041	4101	4162	4222	4283	4343	4404	4465	4525	
69	4586	4646	4707	4768	4828	4889	4949	5010	5070	5131	
70	5192	5252	5313	5373	5434	5494	5555	5616	5676	5737	
7171	5797	5858	5918	5979	6039	6100	6161	6221	6282	6342	
72	6403	6463	6524	6584	6645	6706	6766	6827	6887	6948	
73	7008	7069	7129	7190	7250	7311	7372	7432	7493	7553	
74	7614	7674	7735	7795	7856	7916	7977	8037	8098	8159	
75	8219	8280	8340	8401	8461	8522	8582	8643	8703	8764	
76	8824	8885	8945	9006	9066	9127	9187	9248	9308	9369	
77	9429	9490	9550	9611	9672	9732	9793	9853	9914	9974	
78	856 0035	0095	0156	0216	0277	0337	0398	0458	0519	0579	
79	0640	0700	0761	0821	0882	0942	1002	1063	1123	1184	
80	1244	1305	1365	1426	1486	1547	1607	1668	1728	1789	
7181	1849	1910	1970	2031	2091	2152	2212	2273	2333	2394	
82	2454	2514	2575	2635	2696	2756	2817	2877	2938	2998	
83	3059	3119	3180	3240	3301	3361	3421	3482	3542	3603	
84	3663	3724	3784	3845	3905	3965	4026	4086	4147	4207	
85	4268	4328	4389	4449	4509	4570	4630	4691	4751	4812	
86	4872	4933	4993	5053	5114	5174	5235	5295	5356	5416	
87	5476	5537	5597	5658	5718	5779	5839	5899	5960	6020	
88	6081	6141	6202	6262	6322	6383	6443	6504	6564	6624	
89	6685	6745	6806	6866	6926	6987	7047	7108	7168	7229	
90	7289	7349	7410	7470	7531	7591	7651	7712	7772	7832	
7191	7893	7953	8014	8074	8134	8195	8255	8316	8376	8436	
92	8497	8557	8618	8678	8738	8799	8859	8919	8980	9040	
93	9101	9161	9221	9282	9342	9402	9463	9523	9584	9644	
94	9704	9765	9825	9885	9946	0006	0067	0127	0187	0248	
95	857 0308	0368	0429	0489	0549	0610	0670	0730	0791	0851	
96	0912	0972	1032	1093	1153	1213	1274	1334	1394	1455	
97	1515	1575	1636	1696	1756	1817	1877	1937	1998	2058	
98	2118	2179	2239	2299	2360	2420	2480	2541	2601	2661	
99	2722	2782	2842	2903	2963	3023	3084	3144	3204	3265	
7200	3325	3385	3446	3506	3566	3627	3687	3747	3807	3868	

Diff. 61

1	6
2	12
3	18
4	24
5	31
6	37
7	43
8	49
9	55

No.	0	1	2	3	4	5	6	7	8	9	Diff.
7200	857 3325	3385	3446	3506	3566	3627	3687	3747	3807	3868	
01	3928	3988	4049	4109	4169	4230	4290	4350	4411	4471	
02	4531	4591	4652	4712	4772	4833	4893	4953	5014	5074	
03	5134	5194	5255	5315	5375	5436	5496	5556	5616	5677	
04	5737	5797	5858	5918	5978	6038	6099	6159	6219	6280	
05	6340	6400	6460	6521	6581	6641	6701	6762	6822	6882	
06	6943	7003	7063	7123	7184	7244	7304	7364	7425	7485	
07	7545	7605	7666	7726	7786	7847	7907	7967	8027	8088	
08	8148	8208	8268	8329	8389	8449	8509	8570	8630	8690	
09	8750	8810	8871	8931	8991	9051	9112	9172	9232	9292	
10	9353	9413	9473	9533	9594	9654	9714	9774	9835	9895	
7211	9955	0015	0075	0136	0196	0256	0316	0377	0437	0497	
12	858 0557	0617	0678	0738	0798	0858	0918	0979	1039	1099	
13	1159	1220	1280	1340	1400	1460	1521	1581	1641	1701	
14	1761	1822	1882	1942	2002	2062	2123	2183	2243	2303	
15	2363	2424	2484	2544	2604	2664	2724	2785	2845	2905	
16	2965	3025	3086	3146	3206	3266	3326	3387	3447	3507	
17	3567	3627	3687	3748	3808	3868	3928	3988	4048	4109	
18	4169	4229	4289	4349	4409	4470	4530	4590	4650	4710	
19	4770	4831	4891	4951	5011	5071	5131	5192	5252	5312	
20	5372	5432	5492	5552	5613	5673	5733	5793	5853	5913	
7221	5973	6034	6094	6154	6214	6274	6334	6394	6455	6515	
22	6575	6635	6695	6755	6815	6876	6936	6996	7056	7116	
23	7176	7236	7296	7357	7417	7477	7537	7597	7657	7717	
24	7777	7837	7898	7958	8018	8078	8138	8198	8258	8318	
25	8379	8439	8499	8559	8619	8679	8739	8799	8859	8919	
26	8980	9040	9100	9160	9220	9280	9340	9400	9460	9520	
27	9581	9641	9701	9761	9821	9881	9941	0001	0061	0121	
28	859 0181	0242	0302	0362	0422	0482	0542	0602	0662	0722	
29	0782	0842	0902	0962	1023	1083	1143	1203	1263	1323	
30	1383	1443	1503	1563	1623	1683	1743	1803	1863	1924	
7231	1984	2044	2104	2164	2224	2284	2344	2404	2464	2524	
32	2584	2644	2704	2764	2824	2884	2944	3005	3065	3125	
33	3185	3245	3305	3365	3425	3485	3545	3605	3665	3725	
34	3785	3845	3905	3965	4025	4085	4145	4205	4265	4325	
35	4385	4445	4505	4565	4625	4685	4746	4806	4866	4926	
36	4986	5046	5106	5166	5226	5286	5346	5406	5466	5526	
37	5586	5646	5706	5766	5826	5886	5946	6006	6066	6126	
38	6186	6246	6306	6366	6426	6486	6546	6606	6666	6726	
39	6786	6846	6906	6966	7026	7086	7146	7206	7266	7326	
40	7386	7446	7506	7566	7626	7686	7746	7806	7866	7925	
7241	7985	8045	8105	8165	8225	8285	8345	8405	8465	8525	
42	8585	8645	8705	8765	8825	8885	8945	9005	9065	9125	
43	9185	9245	9305	9365	9425	9485	9545	9605	9665	9724	
44	9784	9844	9904	9964	0024	0084	0144	0204	0264	0324	
45	860 0384	0444	0504	0564	0624	0684	0744	0803	0863	0923	
46	0983	1043	1103	1163	1223	1283	1343	1403	1463	1523	
47	1583	1643	1702	1762	1822	1882	1942	2002	2062	2122	
48	2182	2242	2302	2362	2422	2481	2541	2601	2661	2721	
49	2781	2841	2901	2961	3021	3081	3140	3200	3260	3320	
7250	3380	3440	3500	3560	3620	3680	3739	3799	3859	3919	

Diff.

60

1	6
2	12
3	18
4	24
5	30
6	36
7	42
8	48
9	54

No.	0	1	2	3	4	5	6	7	8	9	Diff.
7250	860 3380	3440	3500	3560	3620	3680	3739	3799	3859	3919	
51	3979	4039	4099	4159	4219	4279	4338	4398	4458	4518	
52	4578	4638	4698	4758	4817	4877	4937	4997	5057	5117	
53	5177	5237	5297	5356	5416	5476	5536	5596	5656	5716	
54	5776	5835	5895	5955	6015	6075	6135	6195	6254	6314	
55	6374	6434	6494	6554	6614	6673	6733	6793	6853	6913	
56	6973	7033	7092	7152	7212	7272	7332	7392	7452	7511	
57	7571	7631	7691	7751	7811	7870	7930	7990	8050	8110	
58	8170	8229	8289	8349	8409	8469	8529	8588	8648	8708	
59	8768	8828	8888	8947	9007	9067	9127	9187	9247	9306	
60	9366	9426	9486	9546	9605	9665	9725	9785	9845	9905	
7261	9964	$\overline{0024}$	$\overline{0084}$	$\overline{0144}$	$\overline{0204}$	$\overline{0263}$	$\overline{0323}$	$\overline{0383}$	$\overline{0443}$	$\overline{0503}$	
62	861 0562	0622	0682	0742	0802	0861	0921	0981	1041	1101	
63	1160	1220	1280	1340	1400	1459	1519	1579	1639	1699	
64	1758	1818	1878	1938	1997	2057	2117	2177	2237	2296	
65	2356	2416	2476	2536	2595	2655	2715	2775	2834	2894	
66	2954	3014	3073	3133	3193	3253	3313	3372	3432	3492	
67	3552	3611	3671	3731	3791	3850	3910	3970	4030	4089	
68	4149	4209	4269	4328	4388	4448	4508	4567	4627	4687	
69	4747	4806	4866	4926	4986	5045	5105	5165	5225	5284	
70	5344	5404	5464	5523	5583	5643	5703	5762	5822	5882	
7271	5941	6001	6061	6121	6180	6240	6300	6360	6419	6479	60
72	6539	6598	6658	6718	6778	6837	6897	6957	7016	7076	1 6
73	7136	7196	7255	7315	7375	7434	7494	7554	7614	7673	2 12
74	7733	7793	7852	7912	7972	8031	8091	8151	8211	8270	3 18
75	8330	8390	8449	8509	8569	8628	8688	8748	8808	8867	4 24
76	8927	8987	9046	9106	9166	9225	9285	9345	9404	9464	5 30
77	9524	9583	9643	9703	9762	9822	9882	9941	$\overline{0001}$	$\overline{0061}$	6 36 / 7 42
78	862 0121	0180	0240	0300	0359	0419	0479	0538	0598	0658	8 48
79	0717	0777	0837	0896	0956	1016	1075	1135	1194	1254	9 54
80	1314	1373	1433	1493	1552	1612	1672	1731	1791	1851	
7281	1910	1970	2030	2089	2149	2209	2268	2328	2387	2447	
82	2507	2566	2626	2686	2745	2805	2865	2924	2984	3043	
83	3103	3163	3222	3282	3342	3401	3461	3520	3580	3640	
84	3699	3759	3819	3878	3938	3997	4057	4117	4176	4236	
85	4296	4355	4415	4474	4534	4594	4653	4713	4772	4832	
86	4892	4951	5011	5070	5130	5190	5249	5309	5368	5428	
87	5488	5547	5607	5666	5726	5786	5845	5905	5964	6024	
88	6084	6143	6203	6262	6322	6382	6441	6501	6560	6620	
89	6680	6739	6799	6858	6918	6977	7037	7097	7156	7216	
90	7275	7335	7394	7454	7514	7573	7633	7692	7752	7811	
7291	7871	7931	7990	8050	8109	8169	8228	8288	8347	8407	
92	8467	8526	8586	8645	8705	8764	8824	8883	8943	9003	
93	9062	9122	9181	9241	9300	9360	9419	9479	9539	9598	
94	9658	9717	9777	9836	9896	9955	$\overline{0015}$	$\overline{0074}$	$\overline{0134}$	$\overline{0193}$	
95	863 0253	0312	0372	0432	0491	0551	0610	0670	0729	0789	
96	0848	0908	0967	1027	1086	1146	1205	1265	1324	1384	
97	1443	1503	1562	1622	1682	1741	1801	1860	1920	1979	
98	2039	2098	2158	2217	2277	2336	2396	2455	2515	2574	
99	2634	2693	2753	2812	2872	2931	2991	3050	3110	3169	
7300	3229	3288	3348	3407	3467	3526	3586	3645	3705	3764	

No.	0	1	2	3	4	5	6	7	8	9	Diff.
7300	863 3229	3288	3348	3407	3467	3526	3586	3645	3705	3764	
01	3823	3883	3942	4002	4061	4121	4180	4240	4299	4359	
02	4418	4478	4537	4597	4656	4716	4775	4835	4894	4954	
03	5013	5072	5132	5191	5251	5310	5370	5429	5489	5548	
04	5608	5667	5727	5786	5845	5905	5964	6024	6083	6143	
05	6202	6262	6321	6381	6440	6499	6559	6618	6678	6737	
06	6797	6856	6916	6975	7034	7094	7153	7213	7272	7332	
07	7391	7451	7510	7569	7629	7688	7748	7807	7867	7926	
08	7985	8045	8104	8164	8223	8283	8342	8401	8461	8520	
09	8580	8639	8698	8758	8817	8877	8936	8996	9055	9114	
10	9174	9233	9293	9352	9411	9471	9530	9590	9649	9708	
7311	9768	9827	9887	9946	0005	0065	0124	0184	0243	0302	
12	864 0362	0421	0481	0540	0599	0659	0718	0778	0837	0896	
13	0956	1015	1075	1134	1193	1253	1312	1371	1431	1490	
14	1550	1609	1668	1728	1787	1846	1906	1965	2025	2084	
15	2143	2203	2262	2321	2381	2440	2500	2559	2618	2678	
16	2737	2796	2856	2915	2974	3034	3093	3152	3212	3271	
17	3331	3390	3449	3509	3568	3627	3687	3746	3805	3865	
18	3924	3983	4043	4102	4161	4221	4280	4339	4399	4458	
19	4517	4577	4636	4695	4755	4814	4873	4933	4992	5051	
20	5111	5170	5229	5289	5348	5407	5467	5526	5585	5645	
7321	5704	5763	5823	5882	5941	6001	6060	6119	6179	6238	
22	6297	6357	6416	6475	6534	6594	6653	6712	6772	6831	
23	6890	6950	7009	7068	7128	7187	7246	7305	7365	7424	
24	7483	7543	7602	7661	7721	7780	7839	7898	7958	8017	
25	8076	8136	8195	8254	8313	8373	8432	8491	8551	8610	
26	8669	8728	8788	8847	8906	8966	9025	9084	9143	9203	
27	9262	9321	9380	9440	9499	9558	9618	9677	9736	9795	
28	9855	9914	9973	0032	0092	0151	0210	0269	0329	0388	
29	865 0447	0506	0566	0625	0684	0743	0803	0862	0921	0980	
30	1040	1099	1158	1217	1277	1336	1395	1454	1514	1573	
7331	1632	1691	1751	1810	1869	1928	1988	2047	2106	2165	
32	2225	2284	2343	2402	2461	2521	2580	2639	2698	2758	
33	2817	2876	2935	2995	3054	3113	3172	3231	3291	3350	
34	3409	3468	3527	3587	3646	3705	3764	3824	3883	3942	
35	4001	4060	4120	4179	4238	4297	4356	4416	4475	4534	
36	4593	4652	4712	4771	4830	4889	4948	5008	5067	5126	
37	5185	5244	5304	5363	5422	5481	5540	5600	5659	5718	
38	5777	5836	5895	5955	6014	6073	6132	6191	6251	6310	
39	6369	6428	6487	6546	6606	6665	6724	6783	6842	6901	
40	6961	7020	7079	7138	7197	7256	7316	7375	7434	7493	
7341	7552	7611	7671	7730	7789	7848	7907	7966	8025	8085	
42	8144	8203	8262	8321	8380	8440	8499	8558	8617	8676	
43	8735	8794	8854	8913	8972	9031	9090	9149	9208	9268	
44	9327	9386	9445	9504	9563	9622	9681	9741	9800	9859	
45	9918	9977	0036	0095	0155	0214	0273	0332	0391	0450	
46	866 0509	0568	0627	0687	0746	0805	0864	0923	0982	1041	
47	1100	1160	1219	1278	1337	1396	1455	1514	1573	1632	
48	1691	1751	1810	1869	1928	1987	2046	2105	2164	2223	
49	2282	2342	2401	2460	2519	2578	2637	2696	2755	2814	
7350	2873	2932	2992	3051	3110	3169	3228	3287	3346	3405	

59

1	6
2	12
3	18
4	24
5	30
6	35
7	41
8	47
9	53

No.	0	1	2	3	4	5	6	7	8	9	Diff.
7350	866 2873	2932	2992	3051	3110	3169	3228	3287	3346	3405	
51	3464	3523	3582	3641	3701	3760	3819	3878	3937	3996	
52	4055	4114	4173	4232	4291	4350	4409	4468	4528	4587	
53	4646	4705	4764	4823	4882	4941	5000	5059	5118	5177	
54	5236	5295	5354	5413	5472	5532	5591	5650	5709	5768	
55	5827	5886	5945	6004	6063	6122	6181	6240	6299	6358	
56	6417	6476	6535	6594	6653	6712	6771	6830	6889	6949	
57	7008	7067	7126	7185	7244	7303	7362	7421	7480	7539	
58	7598	7657	7716	7775	7834	7893	7952	8011	8070	8129	
59	8188	8247	8306	8365	8424	8483	8542	8601	8660	8719	
60	8778	8837	8896	8955	9014	9073	9132	9191	9250	9309	
7361	9368	9427	9486	9545	9604	9663	9722	9781	9840	9899	
62	9958	0017	0076	0135	0194	0253	0312	0371	0430	0489	
63	867 0548	0607	0666	0725	0784	0843	0902	0961	1020	1079	
64	1138	1197	1256	1315	1374	1433	1492	1551	1610	1669	
65	1728	1786	1845	1904	1963	2022	2081	2140	2199	2258	
66	2317	2376	2435	2494	2553	2612	2671	2730	2789	2848	
67	2907	2966	3025	3084	3142	3201	3260	3319	3378	3437	
68	3496	3555	3614	3673	3732	3791	3850	3909	3968	4027	
69	4086	4145	4203	4262	4321	4380	4439	4498	4557	4616	
70	4675	4734	4793	4852	4911	4970	5028	5087	5146	5205	
7371	5264	5323	5382	5441	5500	5559	5618	5677	5735	5794	
72	5853	5912	5971	6030	6089	6148	6207	6266	6325	6383	
73	6442	6501	6560	6619	6678	6737	6796	6855	6914	6972	
74	7031	7090	7149	7208	7267	7326	7385	7444	7502	7561	
75	7620	7679	7738	7797	7856	7915	7974	8032	8091	8150	
76	8209	8268	8327	8386	8445	8503	8562	8621	8680	8739	
77	8798	8857	8916	8974	9033	9092	9151	9210	9269	9328	
78	9387	9445	9504	9563	9622	9681	9740	9799	9857	9916	
79	9975	0034	0093	0152	0211	0269	0328	0387	0446	0505	
80	868 0564	0622	0681	0740	0799	0858	0917	0976	1034	1093	
7381	1152	1211	1270	1329	1387	1446	1505	1564	1623	1682	
82	1740	1799	1858	1917	1976	2035	2093	2152	2211	2270	
83	2329	2388	2446	2505	2564	2623	2682	2740	2799	2858	
84	2917	2976	3035	3093	3152	3211	3270	3329	3387	3446	
85	3505	3564	3623	3681	3740	3799	3858	3917	3975	4034	
86	4093	4152	4211	4269	4328	4387	4446	4505	4563	4622	
87	4681	4740	4799	4857	4916	4975	5034	5093	5151	5210	
88	5269	5328	5386	5445	5504	5563	5622	5680	5739	5798	
89	5857	5915	5974	6033	6092	6151	6209	6268	6327	6386	
90	6444	6503	6562	6621	6679	6738	6797	6856	6915	6973	
7391	7032	7091	7150	7208	7267	7326	7385	7443	7502	7561	
92	7620	7678	7737	7796	7855	7913	7972	8031	8090	8148	
93	8207	8266	8325	8383	8442	8501	8560	8618	8677	8736	
94	8794	8853	8912	8971	9029	9088	9147	9206	9264	9323	
95	9382	9441	9499	9558	9617	9675	9734	9793	9852	9910	
96	9969	0028	0086	0145	0204	0263	0321	0380	0439	0497	
97	869 0556	0615	0674	0732	0791	0850	0908	0967	1026	1085	
98	1143	1202	1261	1319	1378	1437	1495	1554	1613	1672	
99	1730	1789	1848	1906	1965	2024	2082	2141	2200	2259	
7400	2317	2376	2435	2493	2552	2611	2669	2728	2787	2845	

Diff. 59

1	6
2	12
3	18
4	24
5	30
6	35
7	41
8	47
9	53

No.	0	1	2	3	4	5	6	7	8	9	Diff.
7400	869 2317	2376	2435	2493	2552	2611	2669	2728	2787	2845	
01	2904	2963	3021	3080	3139	3197	3256	3315	3373	3432	
02	3491	3549	3608	3667	3725	3784	3843	3901	3960	4019	
03	4077	4136	4195	4253	4312	4371	4429	4488	4547	4605	
04	4664	4723	4781	4840	4899	4957	5016	5075	5133	5192	
05	5251	5309	5368	5427	5485	5544	5603	5661	5720	5778	
06	5837	5896	5954	6013	6072	6130	6189	6248	6306	6365	
07	6423	6482	6541	6599	6658	6717	6775	6834	6892	6951	
08	7010	7068	7127	7186	7244	7303	7361	7420	7479	7537	
09	7596	7655	7713	7772	7830	7889	7948	8006	8065	8123	
10	8182	8241	8299	8358	8417	8475	8534	8592	8651	8710	
7411	8768	8827	8885	8944	9003	9061	9120	9178	9237	9296	
12	9354	9413	9471	9530	9588	9647	9706	9764	9823	9881	
13	9940	9999	0057	0116	0174	0233	0292	0350	0409	0467	
14	870 0526	0584	0643	0702	0760	0819	0877	0936	0994	1053	
15	1112	1170	1229	1287	1346	1404	1463	1522	1580	1639	
16	1697	1756	1814	1873	1931	1990	2049	2107	2166	2224	
17	2283	2341	2400	2458	2517	2576	2634	2693	2751	2810	
18	2868	2927	2985	3044	3102	3161	3220	3278	3337	3395	
19	3454	3512	3571	3629	3688	3746	3805	3863	3922	3981	
20	4039	4098	4156	4215	4273	4332	4390	4449	4507	4566	59
7421	4624	4683	4741	4800	4858	4917	4975	5034	5092	5151	1 6
22	5210	5268	5327	5385	5444	5502	5561	5619	5678	5736	2 12
23	5795	5853	5912	5970	6029	6087	6146	6204	6263	6321	3 18
24	6380	6438	6497	6555	6614	6672	6731	6789	6848	6906	4 24
25	6965	7023	7082	7140	7199	7257	7316	7374	7432	7491	5 30
26	7549	7608	7666	7725	7783	7842	7900	7959	8017	8076	6 35
27	8134	8193	8251	8310	8368	8427	8485	8544	8602	8660	7 41
28	8719	8777	8836	8894	8953	9011	9070	9128	9187	9245	8 47
29	9304	9362	9421	9479	9537	9596	9654	9713	9771	9830	9 53
30	9888	9947	0005	0063	0122	0180	0239	0297	0356	0414	
7431	871 0473	0531	0589	0648	0706	0765	0823	0882	0940	0999	
32	1057	1115	1174	1232	1291	1349	1408	1466	1524	1583	
33	1641	1700	1758	1817	1875	1933	1992	2050	2109	2167	
34	2226	2284	2342	2401	2459	2518	2576	2634	2693	2751	
35	2810	2868	2927	2985	3043	3102	3160	3219	3277	3335	
36	3394	3452	3511	3569	3627	3686	3744	3803	3861	3919	
37	3978	4036	4095	4153	4211	4270	4328	4387	4445	4503	
38	4562	4620	4679	4737	4795	4854	4912	4970	5029	5087	
39	5146	5204	5262	5321	5379	5437	5496	5554	5613	5671	
40	5729	5788	5846	5904	5963	6021	6080	6138	6196	6255	
7441	6313	6371	6430	6488	6546	6605	6663	6722	6780	6838	
42	6897	6955	7013	7072	7130	7188	7247	7305	7363	7422	
43	7480	7539	7597	7655	7714	7772	7830	7889	7947	8005	
44	8064	8122	8180	8239	8297	8355	8414	8472	8530	8589	
45	8647	8705	8764	8822	8880	8939	8997	9055	9114	9172	
46	9230	9289	9347	9405	9464	9522	9580	9639	9697	9755	
47	9814	9872	9930	9988	0047	0105	0163	0222	0280	0338	
48	872 0397	0455	0513	0572	0630	0688	0747	0805	0863	0921	
49	0980	1038	1096	1155	1213	1271	1330	1388	1446	1504	
7450	1563	1621	1679	1738	1796	1854	1912	1971	2029	2087	

No.	0	1	2	3	4	5	6	7	8	9	Diff.
7450	872 1563	1621	1679	1738	1796	1854	1912	1971	2029	2087	
51	2146	2204	2262	2320	2379	2437	2495	2554	2612	2670	
52	2728	2787	2845	2903	2962	3020	3078	3136	3195	3253	
53	3311	3369	3428	3486	3544	3603	3661	3719	3777	3836	
54	3894	3952	4010	4069	4127	4185	4243	4302	4360	4418	
55	4476	4535	4593	4651	4709	4768	4826	4884	4942	5001	
56	5059	5117	5175	5234	5292	5350	5408	5467	5525	5583	
57	5641	5700	5758	5816	5874	5933	5991	6049	6107	6166	
58	6224	6282	6340	6398	6457	6515	6573	6631	6690	6748	
59	6806	6864	6923	6981	7039	7097	7155	7214	7272	7330	
60	7388	7446	7505	7563	7621	7679	7738	7796	7854	7912	
7461	7970	8029	8087	8145	8203	8261	8320	8378	8436	8494	
62	8552	8611	8669	8727	8785	8843	8902	8960	9018	9076	
63	9134	9193	9251	9309	9367	9425	9484	9542	9600	9658	
64	9716	9774	9833	9891	9949	0007	0065	0124	0182	0240	
65	873 0298	0356	0414	0473	0531	0589	0647	0705	0764	0822	
66	0880	0938	0996	1054	1113	1171	1229	1287	1345	1403	
67	1462	1520	1578	1636	1694	1752	1810	1869	1927	1985	
68	2043	2101	2159	2218	2276	2334	2392	2450	2508	2566	
69	2625	2683	2741	2799	2857	2915	2973	3032	3090	3148	
70	3206	3264	3322	3380	3439	3497	3555	3613	3671	3729	
7471	3787	3845	3904	3962	4020	4078	4136	4194	4252	4311	
72	4369	4427	4485	4543	4601	4659	4717	4775	4834	4892	
73	4950	5008	5066	5124	5182	5240	5298	5357	5415	5473	
74	5531	5589	5647	5705	5763	5821	5880	5938	5996	6054	
75	6112	6170	6228	6286	6344	6402	6461	6519	6577	6635	
76	6693	6751	6809	6867	6925	6983	7041	7100	7158	7216	
77	7274	7332	7390	7448	7506	7564	7622	7680	7738	7797	
78	7855	7913	7971	8029	8087	8145	8203	8261	8319	8377	
79	8435	8493	8551	8610	8668	8726	8784	8842	8900	8958	
80	9016	9074	9132	9190	9248	9306	9364	9422	9480	9538	
7481	9597	9655	9713	9771	9829	9887	9945	0003	0061	0119	
82	874 0177	0235	0293	0351	0409	0467	0525	0583	0641	0699	
83	0757	0815	0874	0932	0990	1048	1106	1164	1222	1280	
84	1338	1396	1454	1512	1570	1628	1686	1744	1802	1860	
85	1918	1976	2034	2092	2150	2208	2266	2324	2382	2440	
86	2498	2556	2614	2672	2730	2788	2846	2904	2962	3020	
87	3078	3136	3194	3252	3310	3368	3426	3484	3542	3600	
88	3658	3716	3774	3832	3890	3948	4006	4064	4122	4180	
89	4238	4296	4354	4412	4470	4528	4586	4644	4702	4760	
90	4818	4876	4934	4992	5050	5108	5166	5224	5282	5340	
7491	5398	5456	5514	5572	5630	5688	5746	5804	5862	5920	
92	5978	6036	6094	6152	6210	6268	6325	6383	6441	6499	
93	6557	6615	6673	6731	6789	6847	6905	6963	7021	7079	
94	7137	7195	7253	7311	7369	7427	7485	7543	7600	7658	
95	7716	7774	7832	7890	7948	8006	8064	8122	8180	8238	
96	8296	8354	8412	8470	8528	8585	8643	8701	8759	8817	
97	8875	8933	8991	9049	9107	9165	9223	9281	9339	9396	
98	9454	9512	9570	9628	9686	9744	9802	9860	9918	9976	
99	875 0034	0091	0149	0207	0265	0323	0381	0439	0497	0555	
7500	0613	0671	0728	0786	0844	0902	0960	1018	1076	1134	

58
1	6
2	12
3	17
4	23
5	29
6	35
7	41
8	46
9	52

No.	0	1	2	3	4	5	6	7	8	9	Diff.
7500	875 0613	0671	0728	0786	0844	0902	0960	1018	1076	1134	
01	1192	1250	1307	1365	1423	1481	1539	1597	1655	1713	
02	1771	1828	1886	1944	2002	2060	2118	2176	2234	2292	
03	2349	2407	2465	2523	2581	2639	2697	2755	2813	2870	
04	2928	2986	3044	3102	3160	3218	3275	3333	3391	3449	
05	3507	3565	3623	3681	3738	3796	3854	3912	3970	4028	
06	4086	4143	4201	4259	4317	4375	4433	4491	4548	4606	
07	4664	4722	4780	4838	4896	4953	5011	5069	5127	5185	
08	5243	5300	5358	5416	5474	5532	5590	5648	5705	5763	
09	5821	5879	5937	5995	6052	6110	6168	6226	6284	6342	
10	6399	6457	6515	6573	6631	6689	6746	6804	6862	6920	
7511	6978	7035	7093	7151	7209	7267	7325	7382	7440	7498	
12	7556	7614	7671	7729	7787	7845	7903	7960	8018	8076	
13	8134	8192	8249	8307	8365	8423	8481	8539	8596	8654	
14	8712	8770	8828	8885	8943	9001	9059	9116	9174	9232	
15	9290	9348	9405	9463	9521	9579	9637	9694	9752	9810	
16	9868	9925	9983	0041	0099	0157	0214	0272	0330	0388	
17	876 0446	0503	0561	0619	0677	0734	0792	0850	0908	0965	
18	1023	1081	1139	1197	1254	1312	1370	1428	1485	1543	
19	1601	1659	1716	1774	1832	1890	1947	2005	2063	2121	
20	2178	2236	2294	2352	2409	2467	2525	2583	2640	2698	
7521	2756	2814	2871	2929	2987	3045	3102	3160	3218	3276	
22	3333	3391	3449	3506	3564	3622	3680	3737	3795	3853	
23	3911	3968	4026	4084	4142	4199	4257	4315	4372	4430	
24	4488	4546	4603	4661	4719	4776	4834	4892	4950	5007	
25	5065	5123	5180	5238	5296	5354	5411	5469	5527	5584	
26	5642	5700	5758	5815	5873	5931	5988	6046	6104	6161	
27	6219	6277	6335	6392	6450	6508	6565	6623	6681	6738	
28	6796	6854	6911	6969	7027	7085	7142	7200	7258	7315	
29	7373	7431	7488	7546	7604	7661	7719	7777	7834	7892	
30	7950	8007	8065	8123	8180	8238	8296	8353	8411	8469	
7531	8526	8584	8642	8699	8757	8815	8872	8930	8988	9045	
32	9103	9161	9218	9276	9334	9391	9449	9507	9564	9622	
33	9680	9737	9795	9853	9910	9968	0026	0083	0141	0199	
34	877 0256	0314	0371	0429	0487	0544	0602	0660	0717	0775	
35	0833	0890	0948	1005	1063	1121	1178	1236	1294	1351	
36	1409	1467	1524	1582	1639	1697	1755	1812	1870	1928	
37	1985	2043	2100	2158	2216	2273	2331	2388	2446	2504	
38	2561	2619	2677	2734	2792	2849	2907	2965	3022	3080	
39	3137	3195	3253	3310	3368	3425	3483	3541	3598	3656	
40	3713	3771	3829	3886	3944	4001	4059	4117	4174	4232	
7541	4289	4347	4405	4462	4520	4577	4635	4693	4750	4808	
42	4865	4923	4980	5038	5096	5153	5211	5268	5326	5384	
43	5441	5499	5556	5614	5671	5729	5787	5844	5902	5959	
44	6017	6074	6132	6189	6247	6305	6362	6420	6477	6535	
45	6592	6650	6708	6765	6823	6880	6938	6995	7053	7110	
46	7168	7226	7283	7341	7398	7456	7513	7571	7628	7686	
47	7743	7801	7859	7916	7974	8031	8089	8146	8204	8261	
48	8319	8376	8434	8492	8549	8607	8664	8722	8779	8837	
49	8894	8952	9009	9067	9124	9182	9239	9297	9354	9412	
7550	9470	9527	9585	9642	9700	9757	9815	9872	9930	9987	

58

1	6
2	12
3	17
4	23
5	29
6	35
7	41
8	46
9	52

No.	0	1	2	3	4	5	6	7	8	9	Diff.
7550	877 9470	9527	9585	9642	9700	9757	9815	9872	9930	9987	
51	878 0045	0102	0160	0217	0275	0332	0390	0447	0505	0562	
52	0620	0677	0735	0792	0850	0907	0965	1022	1080	1137	
53	1195	1252	1310	1367	1425	1482	1540	1597	1655	1712	
54	1770	1827	1885	1942	2000	2057	2115	2172	2230	2287	
55	2345	2402	2460	2517	2575	2632	2690	2747	2805	2862	
56	2919	2977	3034	3092	3149	3207	3264	3322	3379	3437	
57	3494	3552	3609	3667	3724	3782	3839	3896	3954	4011	
58	4069	4126	4184	4241	4299	4356	4414	4471	4529	4586	
59	4643	4701	4758	4816	4873	4931	4988	5046	5103	5161	
60	5218	5275	5333	5390	5448	5505	5563	5620	5678	5735	
7561	5792	5850	5907	5965	6022	6080	6137	6194	6252	6309	
62	6367	6424	6482	6539	6596	6654	6711	6769	6826	6884	
63	6941	6998	7056	7113	7171	7228	7286	7343	7400	7458	
64	7515	7573	7630	7687	7745	7802	7860	7917	7975	8032	
65	8089	8147	8204	8262	8319	8376	8434	8491	8549	8606	
66	8663	8721	8778	8836	8893	8950	9008	9065	9123	9180	
67	9237	9295	9352	9410	9467	9524	9582	9639	9696	9754	
68	9811	9869	9926	9983	0041	0098	0156	0213	0270	0328	
69	879 0385	0442	0500	0557	0615	0672	0729	0787	0844	0901	
70	0959	1016	1074	1131	1188	1246	1303	1360	1418	1475	
7571	1532	1590	1647	1705	1762	1819	1877	1934	1991	2049	
72	2106	2163	2221	2278	2335	2393	2450	2508	2565	2622	
73	2680	2737	2794	2852	2909	2966	3024	3081	3138	3196	
74	3253	3310	3368	3425	3482	3540	3597	3654	3712	3769	
75	3826	3884	3941	3998	4056	4113	4170	4228	4285	4342	
76	4400	4457	4514	4572	4629	4686	4744	4801	4858	4916	
77	4973	5030	5088	5145	5202	5259	5317	5374	5431	5489	
78	5546	5603	5661	5718	5775	5833	5890	5947	6004	6062	
79	6119	6176	6234	6291	6348	6406	6463	6520	6577	6635	
80	6692	6749	6807	6864	6921	6979	7036	7093	7150	7208	
7581	7265	7322	7380	7437	7494	7551	7609	7666	7723	7781	
82	7838	7895	7952	8010	8067	8124	8181	8239	8296	8353	
83	8411	8468	8525	8582	8640	8697	8754	8811	8869	8926	
84	8983	9041	9098	9155	9212	9270	9327	9384	9441	9499	
85	9556	9613	9670	9728	9785	9842	9899	9957	0014	0071	
86	880 0128	0186	0243	0300	0357	0415	0472	0529	0586	0644	
87	0701	0758	0815	0873	0930	0987	1044	1102	1159	1216	
88	1273	1330	1388	1445	1502	1559	1617	1674	1731	1788	
89	1846	1903	1960	2017	2074	2132	2189	2246	2303	2361	
90	2418	2475	2532	2589	2647	2704	2761	2818	2875	2933	
7591	2990	3047	3104	3162	3219	3276	3333	3390	3448	3505	
92	3562	3619	3676	3734	3791	3848	3905	3962	4020	4077	
93	4134	4191	4248	4306	4363	4420	4477	4534	4592	4649	
94	4706	4763	4820	4877	4935	4992	5049	5106	5163	5221	
95	5278	5335	5392	5449	5507	5564	5621	5678	5735	5792	
96	5850	5907	5964	6021	6078	6135	6193	6250	6307	6364	
97	6421	6478	6536	6593	6650	6707	6764	6821	6879	6936	
98	6993	7050	7107	7164	7222	7279	7336	7393	7450	7507	
99	7564	7622	7679	7736	7793	7850	7907	7964	8022	8079	
7600	8136	8193	8250	8307	8364	8422	8479	8536	8593	8650	

Diff. column:

57

1	6
2	11
3	17
4	23
5	29
6	34
7	40
8	46
9	51

No.	0	1	2	3	4	5	6	7	8	9	Diff.
7600	880 8136	8193	8250	8307	8364	8422	8479	8536	8593	8650	
01	8707	8764	8822	8879	8936	8993	9050	9107	9164	9222	
02	9279	9336	9393	9450	9507	9564	9621	9679	9736	9793	
03	9850	9907	9964	0021	0078	0136	0193	0250	0307	0364	
04	881 0421	0478	0535	0592	0650	0707	0764	0821	0878	0935	
05	0992	1049	1106	1163	1221	1278	1335	1392	1449	1506	
06	1563	1620	1677	1735	1792	1849	1906	1963	2020	2077	
07	2134	2191	2248	2305	2363	2420	2477	2534	2591	2648	
08	2705	2762	2819	2876	2933	2990	3048	3105	3162	3219	
09	3276	3333	3390	3447	3504	3561	3618	3675	3732	3789	
10	3847	3904	3961	4018	4075	4132	4189	4246	4303	4360	
7611	4417	4474	4531	4588	4645	4703	4760	4817	4874	4931	
12	4988	5045	5102	5159	5216	5273	5330	5387	5444	5501	
13	5558	5615	5672	5729	5786	5844	5901	5958	6015	6072	
14	6129	6186	6243	6300	6357	6414	6471	6528	6585	6642	
15	6699	6756	6813	6870	6927	6984	7041	7098	7155	7212	
16	7269	7326	7383	7440	7497	7554	7611	7669	7726	7783	
17	7840	7897	7954	8011	8068	8125	8182	8239	8296	8353	
18	8410	8467	8524	8581	8638	8695	8752	8809	8866	8923	
19	8980	9037	9094	9151	9208	9265	9322	9379	9436	9493	
20	9550	9607	9664	9721	9778	9835	9892	9949	0006	0063	
7621	882 0120	0177	0234	0291	0348	0405	0462	0519	0575	0632	
22	0689	0746	0803	0860	0917	0974	1031	1088	1145	1202	
23	1259	1316	1373	1430	1487	1544	1601	1658	1715	1772	
24	1829	1886	1943	2000	2057	2114	2171	2228	2285	2342	
25	2398	2455	2512	2569	2626	2683	2740	2797	2854	2911	
26	2968	3025	3082	3139	3196	3253	3310	3367	3424	3481	
27	3537	3594	3651	3708	3765	3822	3879	3936	3993	4050	
28	4107	4164	4221	4278	4335	4392	4448	4505	4562	4619	
29	4676	4733	4790	4847	4904	4961	5018	5075	5132	5188	
30	5245	5302	5359	5416	5473	5530	5587	5644	5701	5758	
7631	5815	5871	5928	5985	6042	6099	6156	6213	6270	6327	
32	6384	6441	6497	6554	6611	6668	6725	6782	6839	6896	
33	6953	7010	7066	7123	7180	7237	7294	7351	7408	7465	
34	7522	7578	7635	7692	7749	7806	7863	7920	7977	8034	
35	8090	8147	8204	8261	8318	8375	8432	8489	8545	8602	
36	8659	8716	8773	8830	8887	8944	9000	9057	9114	9171	
37	9228	9285	9342	9399	9455	9512	9569	9626	9683	9740	
38	9797	9853	9910	9967	0024	0081	0138	0195	0251	0308	
39	883 0365	0422	0479	0536	0593	0649	0706	0763	0820	0877	
40	0934	0990	1047	1104	1161	1218	1275	1331	1388	1445	
7641	1502	1559	1616	1673	1729	1786	1843	1900	1957	2014	
42	2070	2127	2184	2241	2298	2354	2411	2468	2525	2582	
43	2639	2695	2752	2809	2866	2923	2980	3036	3093	3150	
44	3207	3264	3320	3377	3434	3491	3548	3604	3661	3718	
45	3775	3832	3889	3945	4002	4059	4116	4173	4229	4286	
46	4343	4400	4457	4513	4570	4627	4684	4741	4797	4854	
47	4911	4968	5024	5081	5138	5195	5252	5308	5365	5422	
48	5479	5536	5592	5649	5706	5763	5819	5876	5933	5990	
49	6047	6103	6160	6217	6274	6330	6387	6444	6501	6558	
7650	6614	6671	6728	6785	6841	6898	6955	7012	7068	7125	

Diff. 57
1 6
2 11
3 17
4 23
5 29
6 34
7 40
8 46
9 51

No.	0	1	2	3	4	5	6	7	8	9	Diff.
7650	883 6614	6671	6728	6785	6841	6898	6955	7012	7068	7125	
51	7182	7239	7296	7352	7409	7466	7523	7579	7636	7693	
52	7750	7806	7863	7920	7977	8033	8090	8147	8204	8260	
53	8317	8374	8431	8487	8544	8601	8658	8714	8771	8828	
54	8885	8941	8998	9055	9112	9168	9225	9282	9338	9395	
55	9452	9509	9565	9622	9679	9736	9792	9849	9906	9963	
56	884 0019	0076	0133	0189	0246	0303	0360	0416	0473	0530	
57	0586	0643	0700	0757	0813	0870	0927	0983	1040	1097	
58	1154	1210	1267	1324	1380	1437	1494	1551	1607	1664	
59	1721	1777	1834	1891	1948	2004	2061	2118	2174	2231	
60	2288	2344	2401	2458	2514	2571	2628	2685	2741	2798	
7661	2855	2911	2968	3025	3081	3138	3195	3251	3308	3365	
62	3421	3478	3535	3592	3648	3705	3762	3818	3875	3932	
63	3988	4045	4102	4158	4215	4272	4328	4385	4442	4498	
64	4555	4612	4668	4725	4782	4838	4895	4952	5008	5065	
65	5122	5178	5235	5292	5348	5405	5462	5518	5575	5631	
66	5688	5745	5801	5858	5915	5971	6028	6085	6141	6198	
67	6255	6311	6368	6425	6481	6538	6594	6651	6708	6764	
68	6821	6878	6934	6991	7048	7104	7161	7217	7274	7331	
69	7387	7444	7501	7557	7614	7671	7727	7784	7840	7897	
70	7954	8010	8067	8124	8180	8237	8293	8350	8407	8463	
7671	8520	8576	8633	8690	8746	8803	8860	8916	8973	9029	
72	9086	9143	9199	9256	9312	9369	9426	9482	9539	9595	
73	9652	9709	9765	9822	9878	9935	9992	0048	0105	0161	
74	885 0218	0275	0331	0388	0444	0501	0557	0614	0671	0727	
75	0784	0840	0897	0954	1010	1067	1123	1180	1237	1293	
76	1350	1406	1463	1519	1576	1633	1689	1746	1802	1859	
77	1915	1972	2029	2085	2142	2198	2255	2311	2368	2425	
78	2481	2538	2594	2651	2707	2764	2820	2877	2934	2990	
79	3047	3103	3160	3216	3273	3329	3386	3443	3499	3556	
80	3612	3669	3725	3782	3838	3895	3951	4008	4065	4121	
7681	4178	4234	4291	4347	4404	4460	4517	4573	4630	4686	
82	4743	4800	4856	4913	4969	5026	5082	5139	5195	5252	
83	5308	5365	5421	5478	5534	5591	5647	5704	5761	5817	
84	5874	5930	5987	6043	6100	6156	6213	6269	6326	6382	
85	6439	6495	6552	6608	6665	6721	6778	6834	6891	6947	
86	7004	7060	7117	7173	7230	7286	7343	7399	7456	7512	
87	7569	7625	7682	7738	7795	7851	7908	7964	8021	8077	
88	8134	8190	8247	8303	8360	8416	8473	8529	8586	8642	
89	8699	8755	8812	8868	8925	8981	9037	9094	9150	9207	
90	9263	9320	9376	9433	9489	9546	9602	9659	9715	9772	
7691	9828	9885	9941	9998	0054	0110	0167	0223	0280	0336	
92	886 0393	0449	0506	0562	0619	0675	0732	0788	0844	0901	
93	0957	1014	1070	1127	1183	1240	1296	1352	1409	1465	
94	1522	1578	1635	1691	1748	1804	1860	1917	1973	2030	
95	2086	2143	2199	2256	2312	2368	2425	2481	2538	2594	
96	2651	2707	2763	2820	2876	2933	2989	3046	3102	3158	
97	3215	3271	3328	3384	3441	3497	3553	3610	3666	3723	
98	3779	3835	3892	3948	4005	4061	4118	4174	4230	4287	
99	4343	4400	4456	4512	4569	4625	4682	4738	4794	4851	
7700	4907	4964	5020	5076	5133	5189	5246	5302	5358	5415	

57

1	6
2	11
3	17
4	23
5	29
6	34
7	40
8	46
9	51

No.	0	1	2	3	4	5	6	7	8	9	Diff.
7700	886 4907	4964	5020	5076	5133	5189	5246	5302	5358	5415	
01	5471	5528	5584	5640	5697	5753	5810	5866	5922	5979	
02	6035	6092	6148	6204	6261	6317	6373	6430	6486	6543	
03	6599	6655	6712	6768	6824	6881	6937	6994	7050	7106	
04	7163	7219	7275	7332	7388	7445	7501	7557	7614	7670	
05	7726	7783	7839	7896	7952	8008	8065	8121	8177	8234	
06	8290	8346	8403	8459	8515	8572	8628	8685	8741	8797	
07	8854	8910	8966	9023	9079	9135	9192	9248	9304	9361	
08	9417	9473	9530	9586	9642	9699	9755	9811	9868	9924	
09	9980	0̅0̅3̅7̅	0̅0̅9̅3̅	0̅1̅4̅9̅	0̅2̅0̅6̅	0̅2̅6̅2̅	0̅3̅1̅8̅	0̅3̅7̅5̅	0̅4̅3̅1̅	0̅4̅8̅7̅	
10	887 0544	0600	0656	0713	0769	0825	0882	0938	0994	1051	
7711	1107	1163	1220	1276	1332	1389	1445	1501	1558	1614	
12	1670	1727	1783	1839	1895	1952	2008	2064	2121	2177	
13	2233	2290	2346	2402	2459	2515	2571	2627	2684	2740	
14	2796	2853	2909	2965	3022	3078	3134	3190	3247	3303	
15	3359	3416	3472	3528	3584	3641	3697	3753	3810	3866	
16	3922	3978	4035	4091	4147	4204	4260	4316	4372	4429	
17	4485	4541	4598	4654	4710	4766	4823	4879	4935	4991	
18	5048	5104	5160	5217	5273	5329	5385	5442	5498	5554	
19	5610	5667	5723	5779	5835	5892	5948	6004	6060	6117	
20	6173	6229	6286	6342	6398	6454	6511	6567	6623	6679	
7721	6736	6792	6848	6904	6961	7017	7073	7129	7185	7242	56
22	7298	7354	7410	7467	7523	7579	7635	7692	7748	7804	1 6
23	7860	7917	7973	8029	8085	8142	8198	8254	8310	8366	2 11
24	8423	8479	8535	8591	8648	8704	8760	8816	8872	8929	3 17
25	8985	9041	9097	9154	9210	9266	9322	9378	9435	9491	4 22
26	9547	9603	9659	9716	9772	9828	9884	9941	9997	0̅0̅5̅3̅	5 28
27	888 0109	0165	0222	0278	0334	0390	0446	0503	0559	0615	6 34
28	0671	0727	0784	0840	0896	0952	1008	1064	1121	1177	7 39
29	1233	1289	1345	1402	1458	1514	1570	1626	1683	1739	8 45
30	1795	1851	1907	1963	2020	2076	2132	2188	2244	2301	9 50
7731	2357	2413	2469	2525	2581	2638	2694	2750	2806	2862	
32	2918	2975	3031	3087	3143	3199	3255	3312	3368	3424	
33	3480	3536	3592	3649	3705	3761	3817	3873	3929	3986	
34	4042	4098	4154	4210	4266	4322	4379	4435	4491	4547	
35	4603	4659	4715	4772	4828	4884	4940	4996	5052	5108	
36	5165	5221	5277	5333	5389	5445	5501	5558	5614	5670	
37	5726	5782	5838	5894	5950	6007	6063	6119	6175	6231	
38	6287	6343	6400	6456	6512	6568	6624	6680	6736	6792	
39	6848	6905	6961	7017	7073	7129	7185	7241	7297	7353	
40	7410	7466	7522	7578	7634	7690	7746	7802	7858	7915	
7741	7971	8027	8083	8139	8195	8251	8307	8363	8419	8476	
42	8532	8588	8644	8700	8756	8812	8868	8924	8980	9037	
43	9093	9149	9205	9261	9317	9373	9429	9485	9541	9597	
44	9653	9710	9766	9822	9878	9934	9990	0̅0̅4̅6̅	0̅1̅0̅2̅	0̅1̅5̅8̅	
45	889 0214	0270	0326	0382	0439	0495	0551	0607	0663	0719	
46	0775	0831	0887	0943	0999	1055	1111	1167	1223	1279	
47	1336	1392	1448	1504	1560	1616	1672	1728	1784	1840	
48	1896	1952	2008	2064	2120	2176	2232	2288	2345	2401	
49	2457	2513	2569	2625	2681	2737	2793	2849	2905	2961	
7750	3017	3073	3129	3185	3241	3297	3353	3409	3465	3521	

No.	0	1	2	3	4	5	6	7	8	9	Diff.
7750	889 3017	3073	3129	3185	3241	3297	3353	3409	3465	3521	
51	3577	3633	3689	3745	3801	3858	3914	3970	4026	4082	
52	4138	4194	4250	4306	4362	4418	4474	4530	4586	4642	
53	4698	4754	4810	4866	4922	4978	5034	5090	5146	5202	
54	5258	5314	5370	5426	5482	5538	5594	5650	5706	5762	
55	5818	5874	5930	5986	6042	6098	6154	6210	6266	6322	
56	6378	6434	6490	6546	6602	6658	6714	6770	6826	6882	
57	6938	6994	7050	7106	7162	7218	7274	7330	7386	7442	
58	7498	7554	7610	7666	7722	7778	7834	7890	7946	8002	
59	8058	8113	8169	8225	8281	8337	8393	8449	8505	8561	
60	8617	8673	8729	8785	8841	8897	8953	9009	9065	9121	
7761	9177	9233	9289	9345	9401	9457	9513	9569	9624	9680	
62	9736	9792	9848	9904	9960	0016	0072	0128	0184	0240	
63	890 0296	0352	0408	0464	0520	0576	0632	0687	0743	0799	
64	0855	0911	0967	1023	1079	1135	1191	1247	1303	1359	
65	1415	1471	1526	1582	1638	1694	1750	1806	1862	1918	
66	1974	2030	2086	2142	2198	2253	2309	2365	2421	2477	
67	2533	2589	2645	2701	2757	2813	2869	2924	2980	3036	
68	3092	3148	3204	3260	3316	3372	3428	3484	3539	3595	
69	3651	3707	3763	3819	3875	3931	3987	4043	4098	4154	
70	4210	4266	4322	4378	4434	4490	4546	4601	4657	4713	56
7771	4769	4825	4881	4937	4993	5049	5104	5160	5216	5272	1 6
72	5328	5384	5440	5496	5551	5607	5663	5719	5775	5831	2 11
73	5887	5943	5998	6054	6110	6166	6222	6278	6334	6389	3 17
74	6445	6501	6557	6613	6669	6725	6781	6836	6892	6948	4 22
75	7004	7060	7116	7172	7227	7283	7339	7395	7451	7507	5 28
76	7563	7618	7674	7730	7786	7842	7898	7953	8009	8065	6 34
77	8121	8177	8233	8289	8344	8400	8456	8512	8568	8624	7 39
78	8679	8735	8791	8847	8903	8959	9014	9070	9126	9182	8 45
79	9238	9294	9349	9405	9461	9517	9573	9629	9684	9740	9 50
80	9796	9852	9908	9963	0019	0075	0131	0187	0243	0298	
7781	891 0354	0410	0466	0522	0577	0633	0689	0745	0801	0856	
82	0912	0968	1024	1080	1135	1191	1247	1303	1359	1415	
83	1470	1526	1582	1638	1694	1749	1805	1861	1917	1972	
84	2028	2084	2140	2196	2251	2307	2363	2419	2475	2530	
85	2586	2642	2698	2754	2809	2865	2921	2977	3032	3088	
86	3144	3200	3256	3311	3367	3423	3479	3534	3590	3646	
87	3702	3758	3813	3869	3925	3981	4036	4092	4148	4204	
88	4259	4315	4371	4427	4482	4538	4594	4650	4706	4761	
89	4817	4873	4929	4984	5040	5096	5152	5207	5263	5319	
90	5375	5430	5486	5542	5598	5653	5709	5765	5821	5876	
7791	5932	5988	6044	6099	6155	6211	6266	6322	6378	6434	
92	6489	6545	6601	6657	6712	6768	6824	6880	6935	6991	
93	7047	7102	7158	7214	7270	7325	7381	7437	7493	7548	
94	7604	7660	7715	7771	7827	7883	7938	7994	8050	8105	
95	8161	8217	8273	8328	8384	8440	8495	8551	8607	8663	
96	8718	8774	8830	8885	8941	8997	9053	9108	9164	9220	
97	9275	9331	9387	9442	9498	9554	9610	9665	9721	9777	
98	9832	9888	9944	9999	0055	0111	0166	0222	0278	0334	
99	892 0389	0445	0501	0556	0612	0668	0723	0779	0835	0890	
7800	0946	1002	1057	1113	1169	1224	1280	1336	1391	1447	

No.	0	1	2	3	4	5	6	7	8	9	Diff.
7800	892 0946	1002	1057	1113	1169	1224	1280	1336	1391	1447	
01	1503	1558	1614	1670	1725	1781	1837	1892	1948	2004	
02	2059	2115	2171	2226	2282	2338	2393	2449	2505	2560	
03	2616	2672	2727	2783	2839	2894	2950	3006	3061	3117	
04	3173	3228	3284	3340	3395	3451	3506	3562	3618	3673	
05	3729	3785	3840	3896	3952	4007	4063	4119	4174	4230	
06	4285	4341	4397	4452	4508	4564	4619	4675	4731	4786	
07	4842	4897	4953	5009	5064	5120	5176	5231	5287	5342	
08	5398	5454	5509	5565	5621	5676	5732	5787	5843	5899	
09	5954	6010	6065	6121	6177	6232	6288	6344	6399	6455	
10	6510	6566	6622	6677	6733	6788	6844	6900	6955	7011	
7811	7066	7122	7178	7233	7289	7344	7400	7456	7511	7567	
12	7622	7678	7734	7789	7845	7900	7956	8011	8067	8123	
13	8178	8234	8289	8345	8401	8456	8512	8567	8623	8678	
14	8734	8790	8845	8901	8956	9012	9068	9123	9179	9234	
15	9290	9345	9401	9457	9512	9568	9623	9679	9734	9790	
16	9846	9901	9957	0012	0068	0123	0179	0234	0290	0346	
17	893 0401	0457	0512	0568	0623	0679	0734	0790	0846	0901	
18	0957	1012	1068	1123	1179	1234	1290	1345	1401	1457	
19	1512	1568	1623	1679	1734	1790	1845	1901	1956	2012	
20	2068	2123	2179	2234	2290	2345	2401	2456	2512	2567	56
7821	2623	2678	2734	2789	2845	2900	2956	3012	3067	3123	1 6
22	3178	3234	3289	3345	3400	3456	3511	3567	3622	3678	2 11
23	3733	3789	3844	3900	3955	4011	4066	4122	4177	4233	3 17
24	4288	4344	4399	4455	4510	4566	4621	4677	4732	4788	4 22
25	4843	4899	4954	5010	5065	5121	5176	5232	5287	5343	5 28
26	5398	5454	5509	5565	5620	5676	5731	5787	5842	5898	6 34
27	5953	6009	6064	6120	6175	6231	6286	6342	6397	6453	7 39
28	6508	6564	6619	6675	6730	6786	6841	6897	6952	7007	8 45
29	7063	7118	7174	7229	7285	7340	7396	7451	7507	7562	9 50
30	7618	7673	7729	7784	7839	7895	7950	8006	8061	8117	
7831	8172	8228	8283	8339	8394	8450	8505	8560	8616	8671	
32	8727	8782	8838	8893	8949	9004	9059	9115	9170	9226	
33	9281	9337	9392	9448	9503	9558	9614	9669	9725	9780	
34	9836	9891	9947	0002	0057	0113	0168	0224	0279	0335	
35	894 0390	0445	0501	0556	0612	0667	0723	0778	0833	0889	
36	0944	1000	1055	1111	1166	1221	1277	1332	1388	1443	
37	1498	1554	1609	1665	1720	1776	1831	1886	1942	1997	
38	2053	2108	2163	2219	2274	2330	2385	2440	2496	2551	
39	2607	2662	2717	2773	2828	2884	2939	2994	3050	3105	
40	3161	3216	3271	3327	3382	3438	3493	3548	3604	3659	
7841	3715	3770	3825	3881	3936	3991	4047	4102	4158	4213	
42	4268	4324	4379	4435	4490	4545	4601	4656	4711	4767	
43	4822	4878	4933	4988	5044	5099	5154	5210	5265	5320	
44	5376	5431	5487	5542	5597	5653	5708	5763	5819	5874	
45	5929	5985	6040	6096	6151	6206	6262	6317	6372	6428	
46	6483	6538	6594	6649	6704	6760	6815	6870	6926	6981	
47	7037	7092	7147	7203	7258	7313	7369	7424	7479	7535	
48	7590	7645	7701	7756	7811	7867	7922	7977	8033	8088	
49	8143	8199	8254	8309	8365	8420	8475	8531	8586	8641	
7850	8697	8752	8807	8863	8918	8973	9028	9084	9139	9194	

No.	0	1	2	3	4	5	6	7	8	9	Diff.
7850	894 8697	8752	8807	8863	8918	8973	9028	9084	9139	9194	
51	9250	9305	9360	9416	9471	9526	9582	9637	9692	9748	
52	9803	9858	9914	9969	0024	0079	0135	0190	0245	0301	
53	895 0356	0411	0467	0522	0577	0632	0688	0743	0798	0854	
54	0909	0964	1020	1075	1130	1185	1241	1296	1351	1407	
55	1462	1517	1572	1628	1683	1738	1794	1849	1904	1959	
56	2015	2070	2125	2181	2236	2291	2346	2402	2457	2512	
57	2568	2623	2678	2733	2789	2844	2899	2954	3010	3065	
58	3120	3176	3231	3286	3341	3397	3452	3507	3562	3618	
59	3673	3728	3783	3839	3894	3949	4004	4060	4115	4170	
60	4225	4281	4336	4391	4446	4502	4557	4612	4667	4723	
7861	4778	4833	4888	4944	4999	5054	5109	5165	5220	5275	
62	5330	5386	5441	5496	5551	5607	5662	5717	5772	5828	
63	5883	5938	5993	6048	6104	6159	6214	6269	6325	6380	
64	6435	6490	6545	6601	6656	6711	6766	6822	6877	6932	
65	6987	7042	7098	7153	7208	7263	7319	7374	7429	7484	
66	7539	7595	7650	7705	7760	7815	7871	7926	7981	8036	
67	8092	8147	8202	8257	8312	8368	8423	8478	8533	8588	
68	8644	8699	8754	8809	8864	8919	8975	9030	9085	9140	
69	9195	9251	9306	9361	9416	9471	9527	9582	9637	9692	
70	9747	9803	9858	9913	9968	0023	0078	0134	0189	0244	
7871	896 0299	0354	0409	0465	0520	0575	0630	0685	0741	0796	
72	0851	0906	0961	1016	1072	1127	1182	1237	1292	1347	
73	1403	1458	1513	1568	1623	1678	1733	1789	1844	1899	
74	1954	2009	2064	2120	2175	2230	2285	2340	2395	2450	
75	2506	2561	2616	2671	2726	2781	2837	2892	2947	3002	
76	3057	3112	3167	3222	3278	3333	3388	3443	3498	3553	
77	3608	3664	3719	3774	3829	3884	3939	3994	4050	4105	
78	4160	4215	4270	4325	4380	4435	4491	4546	4601	4656	
79	4711	4766	4821	4876	4931	4987	5042	5097	5152	5207	
80	5262	5317	5372	5428	5483	5538	5593	5648	5703	5758	
7881	5813	5868	5923	5979	6034	6089	6144	6199	6254	6309	
82	6364	6419	6475	6530	6585	6640	6695	6750	6805	6860	
83	6915	6970	7025	7081	7136	7191	7246	7301	7356	7411	
84	7466	7521	7576	7631	7686	7742	7797	7852	7907	7962	
85	8017	8072	8127	8182	8237	8292	8347	8403	8458	8513	
86	8568	8623	8678	8733	8788	8843	8898	8953	9008	9063	
87	9118	9173	9229	9284	9339	9394	9449	9504	9559	9614	
88	9669	9724	9779	9834	9889	9944	9999	0054	0109	0165	
89	897 0220	0275	0330	0385	0440	0495	0550	0605	0660	0715	
90	0770	0825	0880	0935	0990	1045	1100	1155	1210	1265	
7891	1320	1375	1431	1486	1541	1596	1651	1706	1761	1816	
92	1871	1926	1981	2036	2091	2146	2201	2256	2311	2366	
93	2421	2476	2531	2586	2641	2696	2751	2806	2861	2916	
94	2971	3026	3081	3136	3191	3246	3301	3356	3411	3466	
95	3521	3576	3631	3686	3741	3796	3851	3906	3961	4016	
96	4071	4126	4181	4236	4291	4346	4401	4456	4511	4566	
97	4621	4676	4731	4786	4841	4896	4951	5006	5061	5116	
98	5171	5226	5281	5336	5391	5446	5501	5556	5611	5666	
99	5721	5776	5831	5886	5941	5996	6051	6106	6161	6216	
7900	6271	6326	6381	6436	6491	6546	6601	6656	6711	6766	

55
1	6
2	11
3	17
4	22
5	28
6	33
7	39
8	44
9	50

No.	0	1	2	3	4	5	6	7	8	9	Diff.
7900	897 6271	6326	6381	6436	6491	6546	6601	6656	6711	6766	
01	6821	6876	6931	6986	7040	7095	7150	7205	7260	7315	
02	7370	7425	7480	7535	7590	7645	7700	7755	7810	7865	
03	7920	7975	8030	8085	8140	8195	8250	8304	8359	8414	
04	8469	8524	8579	8634	8689	8744	8799	8854	8909	8964	
05	9019	9074	9129	9184	9238	9293	9348	9403	9458	9513	
06	9568	9623	9678	9733	9788	9843	9898	9953	$\overline{0}008$	$\overline{0}062$	
07	898 0117	0172	0227	0282	0337	0392	0447	0502	0557	0612	
08	0667	0722	0776	0831	0886	0941	0996	1051	1106	1161	
09	1216	1271	1326	1380	1435	1490	1545	1600	1655	1710	
10	1765	1820	1875	1930	1984	2039	2094	2149	2204	2259	
7911	2314	2369	2424	2479	2533	2588	2643	2698	2753	2808	
12	2863	2918	2973	3027	3082	3137	3192	3247	3302	3357	
13	3412	3467	3521	3576	3631	3686	3741	3796	3851	3906	
14	3960	4015	4070	4125	4180	4235	4290	4345	4399	4454	
15	4509	4564	4619	4674	4729	4784	4838	4893	4948	5003	
16	5058	5113	5168	5222	5277	5332	5387	5442	5497	5552	
17	5606	5661	5716	5771	5826	5881	5936	5990	6045	6100	
18	6155	6210	6265	6320	6374	6429	6484	6539	6594	6649	
19	6703	6758	6813	6868	6923	6978	7032	7087	7142	7197	
20	7252	7307	7361	7416	7471	7526	7581	7636	7690	7745	
7921	7800	7855	7910	7965	8019	8074	8129	8184	8239	8294	
22	8348	8403	8458	8513	8568	8622	8677	8732	8787	8842	
23	8897	8951	9006	9061	9116	9171	9225	9280	9335	9390	
24	9445	9499	9554	9609	9664	9719	9774	9828	9883	9938	
25	9993	$\overline{0}048$	$\overline{0}102$	$\overline{0}157$	$\overline{0}212$	$\overline{0}267$	$\overline{0}321$	$\overline{0}376$	$\overline{0}431$	$\overline{0}486$	
26	899 0541	0595	0650	0705	0760	0815	0869	0924	0979	1034	
27	1089	1143	1198	1253	1308	1363	1417	1472	1527	1582	
28	1636	1691	1746	1801	1856	1910	1965	2020	2075	2129	
29	2184	2239	2294	2348	2403	2458	2513	2568	2622	2677	
30	2732	2787	2841	2896	2951	3006	3060	3115	3170	3225	
7931	3279	3334	3389	3444	3499	3553	3608	3663	3718	3772	
32	3827	3882	3937	3991	4046	4101	4156	4210	4265	4320	
33	4375	4429	4484	4539	4594	4648	4703	4758	4812	4867	
34	4922	4977	5031	5086	5141	5196	5250	5305	5360	5415	
35	5469	5524	5579	5634	5688	5743	5798	5852	5907	5962	
36	6017	6071	6126	6181	6235	6290	6345	6400	6454	6509	
37	6564	6619	6673	6728	6783	6837	6892	6947	7002	7056	
38	7111	7166	7220	7275	7330	7384	7439	7494	7549	7603	
39	7658	7713	7767	7822	7877	7932	7986	8041	8096	8150	
40	8205	8260	8314	8369	8424	8479	8533	8588	8643	8697	
7941	8752	8807	8861	8916	8971	9025	9080	9135	9189	9244	
42	9299	9354	9408	9463	9518	9572	9627	9682	9736	9791	
43	9846	9900	9955	$\overline{0}010$	$\overline{0}064$	$\overline{0}119$	$\overline{0}174$	$\overline{0}228$	$\overline{0}283$	$\overline{0}338$	
44	900 0392	0447	0502	0556	0611	0666	0720	0775	0830	0884	
45	0939	0994	1048	1103	1158	1212	1267	1322	1376	1431	
46	1486	1540	1595	1650	1704	1759	1814	1868	1923	1977	
47	2032	2087	2141	2196	2251	2305	2360	2415	2469	2524	
48	2579	2633	2688	2743	2797	2852	2906	2961	3016	3070	
49	3125	3180	3234	3289	3344	3398	3453	3507	3562	3617	
7950	3671	3726	3781	3835	3890	3944	3999	4054	4108	4163	

Diff.

55

1	6
2	11
3	17
4	22
5	28
6	33
7	39
8	44
9	50

No.	0	1	2	3	4	5	6	7	8	9	Diff.
7950	900 3671	3726	3781	3835	3890	3944	3999	4054	4108	4163	
51	4218	4272	4327	4381	4436	4491	4545	4600	4654	4709	
52	4764	4818	4873	4928	4982	5037	5091	5146	5201	5255	
53	5310	5364	5419	5474	5528	5583	5637	5692	5747	5801	
54	5856	5910	5965	6020	6074	6129	6183	6238	6293	6347	
55	6402	6456	6511	6566	6620	6675	6729	6784	6839	6893	
56	6948	7002	7057	7112	7166	7221	7275	7330	7384	7439	
57	7494	7548	7603	7657	7712	7766	7821	7876	7930	7985	
58	8039	8094	8148	8203	8258	8312	8367	8421	8476	8530	
59	8585	8640	8694	8749	8803	8858	8912	8967	9022	9076	
60	9131	9185	9240	9294	9349	9403	9458	9513	9567	9622	
7961	9676	9731	9785	9840	9894	9949	0004	0058	0113	0167	
62	901 0222	0276	0331	0385	0440	0494	0549	0604	0658	0713	
63	0767	0822	0876	0931	0985	1040	1094	1149	1203	1258	
64	1313	1367	1422	1476	1531	1585	1640	1694	1749	1803	
65	1858	1912	1967	2021	2076	2130	2185	2239	2294	2349	
66	2403	2458	2512	2567	2621	2676	2730	2785	2839	2894	
67	2948	3003	3057	3112	3166	3221	3275	3330	3384	3439	
68	3493	3548	3602	3657	3711	3766	3820	3875	3929	3984	
69	4038	4093	4147	4202	4256	4311	4365	4420	4474	4529	
70	4583	4638	4692	4747	4801	4856	4910	4965	5019	5074	
7971	5128	5183	5237	5292	5346	5401	5455	5509	5564	5618	
72	5673	5727	5782	5836	5891	5945	6000	6054	6109	6163	
73	6218	6272	6327	6381	6436	6490	6544	6599	6653	6708	
74	6762	6817	6871	6926	6980	7035	7089	7144	7198	7252	
75	7307	7361	7416	7470	7525	7579	7634	7688	7743	7797	
76	7851	7906	7960	8015	8069	8124	8178	8233	8287	8341	
77	8396	8450	8505	8559	8614	8668	8723	8777	8831	8886	
78	8940	8995	9049	9104	9158	9212	9267	9321	9376	9430	
79	9485	9539	9594	9648	9702	9757	9811	9866	9920	9974	
80	902 0029	0083	0138	0192	0247	0301	0355	0410	0464	0519	
7981	0573	0628	0682	0736	0791	0845	0900	0954	1008	1063	
82	1117	1172	1226	1280	1335	1389	1444	1498	1552	1607	
83	1661	1716	1770	1824	1879	1933	1988	2042	2096	2151	
84	2205	2260	2314	2368	2423	2477	2532	2586	2640	2695	
85	2749	2804	2858	2912	2967	3021	3076	3130	3184	3239	
86	3293	3347	3402	3456	3511	3565	3619	3674	3728	3782	
87	3837	3891	3946	4000	4054	4109	4163	4217	4272	4326	
88	4381	4435	4489	4544	4598	4652	4707	4761	4815	4870	
89	4924	4979	5033	5087	5142	5196	5250	5305	5359	5413	
90	5468	5522	5577	5631	5685	5740	5794	5848	5903	5957	
7991	6011	6066	6120	6174	6229	6283	6337	6392	6446	6500	
92	6555	6609	6663	6718	6772	6826	6881	6935	6989	7044	
93	7098	7152	7207	7261	7315	7370	7424	7478	7533	7587	
94	7641	7696	7750	7804	7859	7913	7967	8022	8076	8130	
95	8185	8239	8293	8348	8402	8456	8511	8565	8619	8674	
96	8728	8782	8836	8891	8945	8999	9054	9108	9162	9217	
97	9271	9325	9380	9434	9488	9542	9597	9651	9705	9760	
98	9814	9868	9923	9977	0031	0085	0140	0194	0248	0303	
99	903 0357	0411	0466	0520	0574	0628	0683	0737	0791	0846	
8000	0900	0954	1008	1063	1117	1171	1226	1280	1334	1388	

55

1	6
2	11
3	17
4	22
5	28
6	33
7	39
8	44
9	50

No.	0	1	2	3	4	5	6	7	8	9	Diff.
8000	903 0900	0954	1008	1063	1117	1171	1226	1280	1334	1388	
01	1443	1497	1551	1606	1660	1714	1768	1823	1877	1931	
02	1985	2040	2094	2148	2203	2257	2311	2365	2420	2474	
03	2528	2582	2637	2691	2745	2799	2854	2908	2962	3017	
04	3071	3125	3179	3234	3288	3342	3396	3451	3505	3559	
05	3613	3668	3722	3776	3830	3885	3939	3993	4047	4102	
06	4156	4210	4264	4319	4373	4427	4481	4536	4590	4644	
07	4698	4753	4807	4861	4915	4969	5024	5078	5132	5186	
08	5241	5295	5349	5403	5458	5512	5566	5620	5674	5729	
09	5783	5837	5891	5946	6000	6054	6108	6163	6217	6271	
10	6325	6379	6434	6488	6542	6596	6650	6705	6759	6813	
8011	6867	6922	6976	7030	7084	7138	7193	7247	7301	7355	
12	7409	7464	7518	7572	7626	7680	7735	7789	7843	7897	
13	7951	8006	8060	8114	8168	8222	8277	8331	8385	8439	
14	8493	8548	8602	8656	8710	8764	8819	8873	8927	8981	
15	9035	9089	9144	9198	9252	9306	9360	9415	9469	9523	
16	9577	9631	9685	9740	9794	9848	9902	9956	$\overline{0010}$	$\overline{0065}$	
17	904 0119	0173	0227	0281	0336	0390	0444	0498	0552	0606	
18	0661	0715	0769	0823	0877	0931	0985	1040	1094	1148	
19	1202	1256	1310	1365	1419	1473	1527	1581	1635	1690	
20	1744	1798	1852	1906	1960	2014	2069	2123	2177	2231	
8021	2285	2339	2393	2448	2502	2556	2610	2664	2718	2772	
22	2827	2881	2935	2989	3043	3097	3151	3206	3260	3314	
23	3368	3422	3476	3530	3584	3639	3693	3747	3801	3855	
24	3909	3963	4017	4072	4126	4180	4234	4288	4342	4396	
25	4450	4505	4559	4613	4667	4721	4775	4829	4883	4937	
26	4992	5046	5100	5154	5208	5262	5316	5370	5424	5479	
27	5533	5587	5641	5695	5749	5803	5857	5911	5965	6020	
28	6074	6128	6182	6236	6290	6344	6398	6452	6506	6560	
29	6615	6669	6723	6777	6831	6885	6939	6993	7047	7101	
30	7155	7210	7264	7318	7372	7426	7480	7534	7588	7642	
8031	7696	7750	7804	7858	7913	7967	8021	8075	8129	8183	
32	8237	8291	8345	8399	8453	8507	8561	8615	8670	8724	
33	8778	8832	8886	8940	8994	9048	9102	9156	9210	9264	
34	9318	9372	9426	9480	9534	9589	9643	9697	9751	9805	
35	9859	9913	9967	$\overline{0021}$	$\overline{0075}$	$\overline{0129}$	$\overline{0183}$	$\overline{0237}$	$\overline{0291}$	$\overline{0345}$	
36	905 0399	0453	0507	0561	0615	0669	0724	0778	0832	0886	
37	0940	0994	1048	1102	1156	1210	1264	1318	1372	1426	
38	1480	1534	1588	1642	1696	1750	1804	1858	1912	1966	
39	2020	2074	2128	2182	2236	2290	2344	2398	2452	2506	
40	2560	2615	2669	2723	2777	2831	2885	2939	2993	3047	
8041	3101	3155	3209	3263	3317	3371	3425	3479	3533	3587	
42	3641	3695	3749	3803	3857	3911	3965	4019	4073	4127	
43	4181	4235	4289	4343	4397	4451	4505	4559	4613	4667	
44	4721	4775	4829	4883	4937	4991	5045	5099	5153	5207	
45	5260	5314	5368	5422	5476	5530	5584	5638	5692	5746	
46	5800	5854	5908	5962	6016	6070	6124	6178	6232	6286	
47	6340	6394	6448	6502	6556	6610	6664	6718	6772	6826	
48	6880	6934	6988	7042	7096	7149	7203	7257	7311	7365	
49	7419	7473	7527	7581	7635	7689	7743	7797	7851	7905	
8050	7959	8013	8067	8121	8175	8229	8282	8336	8390	8444	

54
1 5
2 11
3 16
4 22
5 27
6 32
7 38
8 43
9 49

No.	0	1	2	3	4	5	6	7	8	9	Diff.
8050	905 7959	8013	8067	8121	8175	8229	8282	8336	8390	8444	
51	8498	8552	8606	8660	8714	8768	8822	8876	8930	8984	
52	9038	9092	9146	9199	9253	9307	9361	9415	9469	9523	
53	9577	9631	9685	9739	9793	9847	9901	9954	0008	0062	
54	906 0116	0170	0224	0278	0332	0386	0440	0494	0548	0602	
55	0655	0709	0763	0817	0871	0925	0979	1033	1087	1141	
56	1195	1248	1302	1356	1410	1464	1518	1572	1626	1680	
57	1734	1788	1841	1895	1949	2003	2057	2111	2165	2219	
58	2273	2327	2380	2434	2488	2542	2596	2650	2704	2758	
59	2812	2865	2919	2973	3027	3081	3135	3189	3243	3297	
60	3350	3404	3458	3512	3566	3620	3674	3728	3781	3835	
8061	3889	3943	3997	4051	4105	4159	4212	4266	4320	4374	
62	4428	4482	4536	4590	4643	4697	4751	4805	4859	4913	
63	4967	5020	5074	5128	5182	5236	5290	5344	5397	5451	
64	5505	5559	5613	5667	5721	5774	5828	5882	5936	5990	
65	6044	6098	6151	6205	6259	6313	6367	6421	6474	6528	
66	6582	6636	6690	6744	6798	6851	6905	6959	7013	7067	
67	7121	7174	7228	7282	7336	7390	7444	7497	7551	7605	
68	7659	7713	7767	7820	7874	7928	7982	8036	8090	8143	
69	8197	8251	8305	8359	8412	8466	8520	8574	8628	8682	
70	8735	8789	8843	8897	8951	9004	9058	9112	9166	9220	
8071	9273	9327	9381	9435	9489	9543	9596	9650	9704	9758	
72	9812	9865	9919	9973	0027	0081	0134	0188	0242	0296	
73	907 0350	0403	0457	0511	0565	0618	0672	0726	0780	0834	
74	0887	0941	0995	1049	1103	1156	1210	1264	1318	1372	
75	1425	1479	1533	1587	1640	1694	1748	1802	1856	1909	
76	1963	2017	2071	2124	2178	2232	2286	2340	2393	2447	
77	2501	2555	2608	2662	2716	2770	2823	2877	2931	2985	
78	3038	3092	3146	3200	3254	3307	3361	3415	3469	3522	
79	3576	3630	3684	3737	3791	3845	3899	3952	4006	4060	
80	4114	4167	4221	4275	4329	4382	4436	4490	4544	4597	
8081	4651	4705	4759	4812	4866	4920	4974	5027	5081	5135	
82	5188	5242	5296	5350	5403	5457	5511	5565	5618	5672	
83	5726	5780	5833	5887	5941	5994	6048	6102	6156	6209	
84	6263	6317	6370	6424	6478	6532	6585	6639	6693	6747	
85	6800	6854	6908	6961	7015	7069	7123	7176	7230	7284	
86	7337	7391	7445	7498	7552	7606	7660	7713	7767	7821	
87	7874	7928	7982	8036	8089	8143	8197	8250	8304	8358	
88	8411	8465	8519	8573	8626	8680	8734	8787	8841	8895	
89	8948	9002	9056	9109	9163	9217	9270	9324	9378	9432	
90	9485	9539	9593	9646	9700	9754	9807	9861	9915	9968	
8091	908 0022	0076	0129	0183	0237	0290	0344	0398	0451	0505	
92	0559	0612	0666	0720	0773	0827	0881	0934	0988	1042	
93	1095	1149	1203	1256	1310	1364	1417	1471	1525	1578	
94	1632	1686	1739	1793	1847	1900	1954	2008	2061	2115	
95	2169	2222	2276	2329	2383	2437	2490	2544	2598	2651	
96	2705	2759	2812	2866	2920	2973	3027	3080	3134	3188	
97	3241	3295	3349	3402	3456	3510	3563	3617	3670	3724	
98	3778	3831	3885	3939	3992	4046	4099	4153	4207	4260	
99	4314	4368	4421	4475	4528	4582	4636	4689	4743	4797	
8100	4850	4904	4957	5011	5065	5118	5172	5225	5279	5333	

54
1	5
2	11
3	16
4	22
5	27
6	32
7	38
8	43
9	49

No.	0	1	2	3	4	5	6	7	8	9	Diff.
8100	908 4850	4904	4957	5011	5065	5118	5172	5225	5279	5333	
01	5386	5440	5494	5547	5601	5654	5708	5762	5815	5869	
02	5922	5976	6030	6083	6137	6190	6244	6298	6351	6405	
03	6458	6512	6566	6619	6673	6726	6780	6834	6887	6941	
04	6994	7048	7102	7155	7209	7262	7316	7369	7423	7477	
05	7530	7584	7637	7691	7745	7798	7852	7905	7959	8012	
06	8066	8120	8173	8227	8280	8334	8387	8441	8495	8548	
07	8602	8655	8709	8762	8816	8870	8923	8977	9030	9084	
08	9137	9191	9245	9298	9352	9405	9459	9512	9566	9619	
09	9673	9727	9780	9834	9887	9941	9994	0048	0101	0155	
10	909 0209	0262	0316	0369	0423	0476	0530	0583	0637	0690	
8111	0744	0798	0851	0905	0958	1012	1065	1119	1172	1226	
12	1279	1333	1386	1440	1494	1547	1601	1654	1708	1761	
13	1815	1868	1922	1975	2029	2082	2136	2189	2243	2297	
14	2350	2404	2457	2511	2564	2618	2671	2725	2778	2832	
15	2885	2939	2992	3046	3099	3153	3206	3260	3313	3367	
16	3420	3474	3527	3581	3634	3688	3741	3795	3848	3902	
17	3955	4009	4062	4116	4169	4223	4276	4330	4383	4437	
18	4490	4544	4597	4651	4704	4758	4811	4865	4918	4972	
19	5025	5079	5132	5186	5239	5293	5346	5400	5453	5507	
20	5560	5614	5667	5721	5774	5828	5881	5935	5988	6042	
8121	6095	6149	6202	6256	6309	6362	6416	6469	6523	6576	
22	6630	6683	6737	6790	6844	6897	6951	7004	7058	7111	
23	7165	7218	7271	7325	7378	7432	7485	7539	7592	7646	
24	7699	7753	7806	7860	7913	7966	8020	8073	8127	8180	
25	8234	8287	8341	8394	8447	8501	8554	8608	8661	8715	
26	8768	8822	8875	8929	8982	9035	9089	9142	9196	9249	
27	9303	9356	9409	9463	9516	9570	9623	9677	9730	9784	
28	9837	9890	9944	9997	0051	0104	0158	0211	0264	0318	
29	910 0371	0425	0478	0532	0585	0638	0692	0745	0799	0852	
30	0905	0959	1012	1066	1119	1173	1226	1279	1333	1386	
8131	1440	1493	1546	1600	1653	1707	1760	1813	1867	1920	
32	1974	2027	2081	2134	2187	2241	2294	2348	2401	2454	
33	2508	2561	2615	2668	2721	2775	2828	2882	2935	2988	
34	3042	3095	3148	3202	3255	3309	3362	3415	3469	3522	
35	3576	3629	3682	3736	3789	3842	3896	3949	4003	4056	
36	4109	4163	4216	4270	4323	4376	4430	4483	4536	4590	
37	4643	4697	4750	4803	4857	4910	4963	5017	5070	5123	
38	5177	5230	5284	5337	5390	5444	5497	5550	5604	5657	
39	5710	5764	5817	5871	5924	5977	6031	6084	6137	6191	
40	6244	6297	6351	6404	6457	6511	6564	6618	6671	6724	
8141	6778	6831	6884	6938	6991	7044	7098	7151	7204	7258	
42	7311	7364	7418	7471	7524	7578	7631	7684	7738	7791	
43	7844	7898	7951	8004	8058	8111	8164	8218	8271	8324	
44	8378	8431	8484	8538	8591	8644	8698	8751	8804	8858	
45	8911	8964	9018	9071	9124	9177	9231	9284	9337	9391	
46	9444	9497	9551	9604	9657	9711	9764	9817	9871	9924	
47	9977	0030	0084	0137	0190	0244	0297	0350	0404	0457	
48	911 0510	0564	0617	0670	0723	0777	0830	0883	0937	0990	
49	1043	1096	1150	1203	1256	1310	1363	1416	1470	1523	
8150	1576	1629	1683	1736	1789	1843	1896	1949	2002	2056	

54

1	5
2	11
3	16
4	22
5	27
6	32
7	38
8	43
9	49

No.	0	1	2	3	4	5	6	7	8	9	Diff.
8150	911 1576	1629	1683	1736	1789	1843	1896	1949	2002	2056	
51	2109	2162	2215	2269	2322	2375	2429	2482	2535	2588	
52	2642	2695	2748	2802	2855	2908	2961	3015	3068	3121	
53	3174	3228	3281	3334	3387	3441	3494	3547	3601	3654	
54	3707	3760	3814	3867	3920	3973	4027	4080	4133	4186	
55	4240	4293	4346	4399	4453	4506	4559	4612	4666	4719	
56	4772	4825	4879	4932	4985	5038	5092	5145	5198	5251	
57	5305	5358	5411	5464	5518	5571	5624	5677	5731	5784	
58	5837	5890	5943	5997	6050	6103	6156	6210	6263	6316	
59	6369	6423	6476	6529	6582	6635	6689	6742	6795	6848	
60	6902	6955	7008	7061	7114	7168	7221	7274	7327	7381	
8161	7434	7487	7540	7593	7647	7700	7753	7806	7859	7913	
62	7966	8019	8072	8126	8179	8232	8285	8338	8392	8445	
63	8498	8551	8604	8658	8711	8764	8817	8870	8924	8977	
64	9030	9083	9136	9190	9243	9296	9349	9402	9456	9509	
65	9562	9615	9668	9721	9775	9828	9881	9934	9987	$\overline{0041}$	
66	912 0094	0147	0200	0253	0306	0360	0413	0466	0519	0572	
67	0626	0679	0732	0785	0838	0891	0945	0998	1051	1104	
68	1157	1210	1264	1317	1370	1423	1476	1529	1583	1636	
69	1689	1742	1795	1848	1902	1955	2008	2061	2114	2167	
70	2221	2274	2327	2380	2433	2486	2539	2593	2646	2699	
8171	2752	2805	2858	2912	2965	3018	3071	3124	3177	3230	
72	3284	3337	3390	3443	3496	3549	3602	3656	3709	3762	
73	3815	3868	3921	3974	4028	4081	4134	4187	4240	4293	
74	4346	4399	4453	4506	4559	4612	4665	4718	4771	4824	
75	4878	4931	4984	5037	5090	5143	5196	5249	5303	5356	
76	5409	5462	5515	5568	5621	5674	5728	5781	5834	5887	
77	5940	5993	6046	6099	6152	6206	6259	6312	6365	6418	
78	6471	6524	6577	6630	6683	6737	6790	6843	6896	6949	
79	7002	7055	7108	7161	7214	7268	7321	7374	7427	7480	
80	7533	7586	7639	7692	7745	7798	7852	7905	7958	8011	
8181	8064	8117	8170	8223	8276	8329	8382	8436	8489	8542	
82	8595	8648	8701	8754	8807	8860	8913	8966	9019	9072	
83	9126	9179	9232	9285	9338	9391	9444	9497	9550	9603	
84	9656	9709	9762	9815	9868	9922	9975	$\overline{0028}$	$\overline{0081}$	$\overline{0134}$	
85	913 0187	0240	0293	0346	0399	0452	0505	0558	0611	0664	
86	0717	0770	0824	0877	0930	0983	1036	1089	1142	1195	
87	1248	1301	1354	1407	1460	1513	1566	1619	1672	1725	
88	1778	1831	1884	1937	1990	2044	2097	2150	2203	2256	
89	2309	2362	2415	2468	2521	2574	2627	2680	2733	2786	
90	2839	2892	2945	2998	3051	3104	3157	3210	3263	3316	
8191	3369	3422	3475	3528	3581	3634	3687	3740	3793	3846	
92	3899	3952	4005	4058	4111	4165	4218	4271	4324	4377	
93	4430	4483	4536	4589	4642	4695	4748	4801	4854	4907	
94	4960	5013	5066	5119	5172	5225	5278	5331	5384	5437	
95	5490	5543	5596	5649	5702	5755	5808	5861	5914	5967	
96	6019	6072	6125	6178	6231	6284	6337	6390	6443	6496	
97	6549	6602	6655	6708	6761	6814	6867	6920	6973	7026	
98	7079	7132	7185	7238	7291	7344	7397	7450	7503	7556	
99	7609	7662	7715	7768	7821	7874	7927	7980	8033	8086	
8200	8139	8191	8244	8297	8350	8403	8456	8509	8562	8615	

53
1	5
2	11
3	16
4	21
5	27
6	32
7	37
8	42
9	48

No.	0	1	2	3	4	5	6	7	8	9	Diff.
8200	913 8139	8191	8244	8297	8350	8403	8456	8509	8562	8615	
01	8668	8721	8774	8827	8880	8933	8986	9039	9092	9145	
02	9198	9251	9304	9356	9409	9462	9515	9568	9621	9674	
03	9727	9780	9833	9886	9939	9992	0045	0098	0151	0204.	
04	914 0257	0309	0362	0415	0468	0521	0574	0627	0680	0733.	
05	0786	0839	0892	0945	0998	1050	1103	1156	1209	1262	
06	1315	1368	1421	1474	1527	1580	1633	1686	1738	1791	
07	1844	1897	1950	2003	2056	2109	2162	2215	2268	2321	
08	2373	2426	2479	2532	2585	2638	2691	2744	2797	2850	
09	2903	2955	3008	3061	3114	3167	3220	3273	3326	3379	
10	3432	3484	3537	3590	3643	3696	3749	3802	3855	3908	
8211	3961	4013	4066	4119	4172	4225	4278	4331	4384	4437	
12	4489	4542	4595	4648	4701	4754	4807	4860	4912	4965	
13	5018	5071	5124	5177	5230	5283	5335	5388	5441	5494	
14	5547	5600	5653	5706	5758	5811	5864	5917	5970	6023	
15	6076	6129	6181	6234	6287	6340	6393	6446	6499	6551	
16	6604	6657	6710	6763	6816	6869	6921	6974	7027	7080	
17	7133	7186	7239	7291	7344	7397	7450	7503	7556	7609	
18	7661	7714	7767	7820	7873	7926	7978	8031	8084	8137	
19	8190	8243	8295	8348	8401	8454	8507	8560	8613	8665	
20	8718	8771	8824	8877	8930	8982	9035	9088	9141	9194	53
8221	9246	9299	9352	9405	9458	9511	9563	9616	9669	9722	1 5
22	9775	9828	9880	9933	9986	0039	0092	0144	0197	0250	2 11
23	915 0303	0356	0409	0461	0514	0567	0620	0673	0725	0778	3 16
24	0831	0884	0937	0989	1042	1095	1148	1201	1253	1306	4 21
25	1359	1412	1465	1517	1570	1623	1676	1729	1781	1834	5 27
26	1887	1940	1993	2045	2098	2151	2204	2257	2309	2362	6 32
27	2415	2468	2521	2573	2626	2679	2732	2784	2837	2890	7 37
28	2943	2996	3048	3101	3154	3207	3260	3312	3365	3418	8 42
29	3471	3523	3576	3629	3682	3734	3787	3840	3893	3946	9 48
30	3998	4051	4104	4157	4209	4262	4315	4368	4420	4473	
8231	4526	4579	4632	4684	4737	4790	4843	4895	4948	5001	
32	5054	5106	5159	5212	5265	5317	5370	5423	5476	5528	
33	5581	5634	5687	5739	5792	5845	5898	5950	6003	6056	
34	6109	6161	6214	6267	6320	6372	6425	6478	6531	6583	
35	6636	6689	6742	6794	6847	6900	6952	7005	7058	7111	
36	7163	7216	7269	7322	7374	7427	7480	7532	7585	7638	
37	7691	7743	7796	7849	7902	7954	8007	8060	8112	8165	
38	8218	8271	8323	8376	8429	8481	8534	8587	8640	8692	
39	8745	8798	8850	8903	8956	9009	9061	9114	9167	9219	
40	9272	9325	9378	9430	9483	9536	9588	9641	9694	9746	
8241	9799	9852	9905	9957	0010	0063	0115	0168	0221	0273	
42	916 0326	0379	0431	0484	0537	0590	0642	0695	0748	0800	
43	0853	0906	0958	1011	1064	1116	1169	1222	1274	1327	
44	1380	1433	1485	1538	1591	1643	1696	1749	1801	1854	
45	1907	1959	2012	2065	2117	2170	2223	2275	2328	2381	
46	2433	2486	2539	2591	2644	2697	2749	2802	2855	2907	
47	2960	3013	3065	3118	3171	3223	3276	3329	3381	3434	
48	3487	3539	3592	3644	3697	3750	3802	3855	3908	3960	
49	4013	4066	4118	4171	4224	4276	4329	4382	4434	4487	
8250	4539	4592	4645	4697	4750	4803	4855	4908	4961	5013	

No.	0	1	2	3	4	5	6	7	8	9	Diff.
8250	916 4539	4592	4645	4697	4750	4803	4855	4908	4961	5013	
51	5066	5119	5171	5224	5276	5329	5382	5434	5487	5540	
52	5592	5645	5697	5750	5803	5855	5908	5961	6013	6066	
53	6118	6171	6224	6276	6329	6382	6434	6487	6539	6592	
54	6645	6697	6750	6802	6855	6908	6960	7013	7066	7118	
55	7171	7223	7276	7329	7381	7434	7486	7539	7592	7644	
56	7697	7749	7802	7855	7907	7960	8012	8065	8118	8170	
57	8223	8275	8328	8381	8433	8486	8538	8591	8644	8696	
58	8749	8801	8854	8907	8959	9012	9064	9117	9169	9222	
59	9275	9327	9380	9432	9485	9538	9590	9643	9695	9748	
60	9800	9853	9906	9958	0011	0063	0116	0169	0221	0274	
8261	917 0326	0379	0431	0484	0537	0589	0642	0694	0747	0799	
62	0852	0904	0957	1010	1062	1115	1167	1220	1272	1325	
63	1378	1430	1483	1535	1588	1640	1693	1745	1798	1851	
64	1903	1956	2008	2061	2113	2166	2218	2271	2323	2376	
65	2429	2481	2534	2586	2639	2691	2744	2796	2849	2901	
66	2954	3007	3059	3112	3164	3217	3269	3322	3374	3427	
67	3479	3532	3584	3637	3690	3742	3795	3847	3900	3952	
68	4005	4057	4110	4162	4215	4267	4320	4372	4425	4477	
69	4530	4582	4635	4687	4740	4793	4845	4898	4950	5003	
70	5055	5108	5160	5213	5265	5318	5370	5423	5475	5528	52
8271	5580	5633	5685	5738	5790	5843	5895	5948	6000	6053	1 5
72	6105	6158	6210	6263	6315	6368	6420	6473	6525	6578	2 10
73	6630	6683	6735	6788	6840	6893	6945	6998	7050	7103	3 16
74	7155	7208	7260	7313	7365	7418	7470	7523	7575	7628	4 21
75	7680	7733	7785	7837	7890	7942	7995	8047	8100	8152	5 26
76	8205	8257	8310	8362	8415	8467	8520	8572	8625	8677	6 31
77	8730	8782	8834	8887	8939	8992	9044	9097	9149	9202	7 36
78	9254	9307	9359	9412	9464	9517	9569	9621	9674	9726	8 42
79	9779	9831	9884	9936	9989	0041	0094	0146	0198	0251	9 47
80	918 0303	0356	0408	0461	0513	0566	0618	0671	0723	0775	
8281	0828	0880	0933	0985	1038	1090	1143	1195	1247	1300	
82	1352	1405	1457	1510	1562	1614	1667	1719	1772	1824	
83	1877	1929	1981	2034	2086	2139	2191	2244	2296	2348	
84	2401	2453	2506	2558	2611	2663	2715	2768	2820	2873	
85	2925	2978	3030	3082	3135	3187	3240	3292	3344	3397	
86	3449	3502	3554	3607	3659	3711	3764	3816	3869	3921	
87	3973	4026	4078	4131	4183	4235	4288	4340	4393	4445	
88	4497	4550	4602	4655	4707	4759	4812	4864	4917	4969	
89	5021	5074	5126	5179	5231	5283	5336	5388	5441	5493	
90	5545	5598	5650	5702	5755	5807	5860	5912	5964	6017	
8291	6069	6122	6174	6226	6279	6331	6383	6436	6488	6541	
92	6593	6645	6698	6750	6802	6855	6907	6960	7012	7064	
93	7117	7169	7221	7274	7326	7378	7431	7483	7536	7588	
94	7640	7693	7745	7797	7850	7902	7954	8007	8059	8112	
95	8164	8216	8269	8321	8373	8426	8478	8530	8583	8635	
96	8687	8740	8792	8844	8897	8949	9002	9054	9106	9159	
97	9211	9263	9316	9368	9420	9473	9525	9577	9630	9682	
98	9734	9787	9839	9891	9944	9996	0048	0101	0153	0205	
99	919 0258	0310	0362	0415	0467	0519	0572	0624	0676	0729	
8300	0781	0833	0886	0938	0990	1043	1095	1147	1200	1252	

No.	0	1	2	3	4	5	6	7	8	9	Diff.
8300	919 0781	0833	0886	0938	0990	1043	1095	1147	1200	1252	
01	1304	1356	1409	1461	1513	1566	1618	1670	1723	1775	
02	1827	1880	1932	1984	2037	2089	2141	2193	2246	2298	
03	2350	2403	2455	2507	2560	2612	2664	2717	2769	2821	
04	2873	2926	2978	3030	3083	3135	3187	3239	3292	3344	
05	3396	3449	3501	3553	3606	3658	3710	3762	3815	3867	
06	3919	3972	4024	4076	4128	4181	4233	4285	4338	4390	
07	4442	4494	4547	4599	4651	4703	4756	4808	4860	4913	
08	4965	5017	5069	5122	5174	5226	5279	5331	5383	5435	
09	5488	5540	5592	5644	5697	5749	5801	5853	5906	5958	
10	6010	6062	6115	6167	6219	6272	6324	6376	6428	6481	
8311	6533	6585	6637	6690	6742	6794	6846	6899	6951	7003	
12	7055	7108	7160	7212	7264	7317	7369	7421	7473	7526	
13	7578	7630	7682	7735	7787	7839	7891	7943	7996	8048	
14	8100	8152	8205	8257	8309	8361	8414	8466	8518	8570	
15	8623	8675	8727	8779	8831	8884	8936	8988	9040	9093	
16	9145	9197	9249	9301	9354	9406	9458	9510	9563	9615	
17	9667	9719	9771	9824	9876	9928	9980	0033	0085	0137	
18	920 0189	0241	0294	0346	0398	0450	0502	0555	0607	0659	
19	0711	0763	0816	0868	0920	0972	1024	1077	1129	1181	
20	1233	1285	1338	1390	1442	1494	1546	1599	1651	1703	52
8321	1755	1807	1860	1912	1964	2016	2068	2121	2173	2225	1 5
22	2277	2329	2381	2434	2486	2538	2590	2642	2695	2747	2 10
23	2799	2851	2903	2955	3008	3060	3112	3164	3216	3269	3 16
24	3321	3373	3425	3477	3529	3582	3634	3686	3738	3790	4 21
25	3842	3895	3947	3999	4051	4103	4155	4208	4260	4312	5 26
26	4364	4416	4468	4521	4573	4625	4677	4729	4781	4833	6 31
27	4886	4938	4990	5042	5094	5146	5199	5251	5303	5355	7 36
28	5407	5459	5511	5564	5616	5668	5720	5772	5824	5876	8 42
29	5929	5981	6033	6085	6137	6189	6241	6294	6346	6398	9 47
30	6450	6502	6554	6606	6659	6711	6763	6815	6867	6919	
8331	6971	7023	7076	7128	7180	7232	7284	7336	7388	7440	
32	7493	7545	7597	7649	7701	7753	7805	7857	7910	7962	
33	8014	8066	8118	8170	8222	8274	8327	8379	8431	8483	
34	8535	8587	8639	8691	8743	8796	8848	8900	8952	9004	
35	9056	9108	9160	9212	9264	9317	9369	9421	9473	9525	
36	9577	9629	9681	9733	9785	9838	9890	9942	9994	0046	
37	921 0098	0150	0202	0254	0306	0358	0411	0463	0515	0567	
38	0619	0671	0723	0775	0827	0879	0931	0983	1036	1088	
39	1140	1192	1244	1296	1348	1400	1452	1504	1556	1608	
40	1661	1713	1765	1817	1869	1921	1973	2025	2077	2129	
8341	2181	2233	2285	2337	2389	2442	2494	2546	2598	2650	
42	2702	2754	2806	2858	2910	2962	3014	3066	3118	3170	
43	3222	3274	3327	3379	3431	3483	3535	3587	3639	3691	
44	3743	3795	3847	3899	3951	4003	4055	4107	4159	4211	
45	4263	4315	4367	4420	4472	4524	4576	4628	4680	4732	
46	4784	4836	4888	4940	4992	5044	5096	5148	5200	5252	
47	5304	5356	5408	5460	5512	5564	5616	5668	5720	5772	
48	5824	5876	5928	5980	6032	6085	6137	6189	6241	6293	
49	6345	6397	6449	6501	6553	6605	6657	6709	6761	6813	
8350	6865	6917	6969	7021	7073	7125	7177	7229	7281	7333	

No.	0	1	2	3	4	5	6	7	8	9	Diff.
8350	921 6865	6917	6969	7021	7073	7125	7177	7229	7281	7333	
51	7385	7437	7489	7541	7593	7645	7697	7749	7801	7853	
52	7905	7957	8009	8061	8113	8165	8217	8269	8321	8373	
53	8425	8477	8529	8581	8633	8685	8737	8789	8841	8893	
54	8945	8997	9049	9101	9153	9205	9257	9309	9361	9413	
55	9465	9517	9569	9620	9672	9724	9776	9828	9880	9932	
56	9984	$\overline{0036}$	$\overline{0088}$	$\overline{0140}$	$\overline{0192}$	$\overline{0244}$	$\overline{0296}$	$\overline{0348}$	$\overline{0400}$	$\overline{0452}$	
57	922 0504	0556	0608	0660	0712	0764	0816	0868	0920	0972	
58	1024	1076	1128	1180	1232	1283	1335	1387	1439	1491	
59	1543	1595	1647	1699	1751	1803	1855	1907	1959	2011	
60	2063	2115	2167	2219	2271	2323	2374	2426	2478	2530	
8361	2582	2634	2686	2738	2790	2842	2894	2946	2998	3050	
62	3102	3154	3206	3257	3309	3361	3413	3465	3517	3569	
63	3621	3673	3725	3777	3829	3881	3933	3984	4036	4088	
64	4140	4192	4244	4296	4348	4400	4452	4504	4556	4608	
65	4659	4711	4763	4815	4867	4919	4971	5023	5075	5127	
66	5179	5231	5282	5334	5386	5438	5490	5542	5594	5646	
67	5698	5750	5801	5853	5905	5957	6009	6061	6113	6165	
68	6217	6269	6321	6372	6424	6476	6528	6580	6632	6684	
69	6736	6788	6839	6891	6943	6995	7047	7099	7151	7203	
70	7255	7306	7358	7410	7462	7514	7566	7618	7670	7722	
8371	7773	7825	7877	7929	7981	8033	8085	8137	8188	8240	52
72	8292	8344	8396	8448	8500	8552	8603	8655	8707	8759	1 5
73	8811	8863	8915	8967	9018	9070	9122	9174	9226	9278	2 10
74	9330	9381	9433	9485	9537	9589	9641	9693	9744	9796	3 16
75	9848	9900	9952	$\overline{0004}$	$\overline{0056}$	$\overline{0107}$	$\overline{0159}$	$\overline{0211}$	$\overline{0263}$	$\overline{0315}$	4 21
76	923 0367	0419	0470	0522	0574	0626	0678	0730	0781	0833	5 26
77	0885	0937	0989	1041	1093	1144	1196	1248	1300	1352	6 31
78	1404	1455	1507	1559	1611	1663	1715	1766	1818	1870	7 36
79	1922	1974	2026	2077	2129	2181	2233	2285	2337	2388	8 42
80	2440	2492	2544	2596	2647	2699	2751	2803	2855	2907	9 47
8381	2958	3010	3062	3114	3166	3217	3269	3321	3373	3425	
82	3477	3528	3580	3632	3684	3736	3787	3839	3891	3943	
83	3995	4046	4098	4150	4202	4254	4305	4357	4409	4461	
84	4513	4564	4616	4668	4720	4772	4823	4875	4927	4979	
85	5031	5082	5134	5186	5238	5290	5341	5393	5445	5497	
86	5549	5600	5652	5704	5756	5808	5859	5911	5963	6015	
87	6066	6118	6170	6222	6274	6325	6377	6429	6481	6532	
88	6584	6636	6688	6740	6791	6843	6895	6947	6998	7050	
89	7102	7154	7205	7257	7309	7361	7413	7464	7516	7568	
90	7620	7671	7723	7775	7827	7878	7930	7982	8034	8085	
8391	8137	8189	8241	8292	8344	8396	8448	8499	8551	8603	
92	8655	8707	8758	8810	8862	8913	8965	9017	9069	9120	
93	9172	9224	9276	9327	9379	9431	9483	9534	9586	9638	
94	9690	9741	9793	9845	9897	9948	$\overline{0000}$	$\overline{0052}$	$\overline{0104}$	$\overline{0155}$	
95	924 0207	0259	0310	0362	0414	0466	0517	0569	0621	0673	
96	0724	0776	0828	0879	0931	0983	1035	1086	1138	1190	
97	1242	1293	1345	1397	1448	1500	1552	1604	1655	1707	
98	1759	1810	1862	1914	1966	2017	2069	2121	2172	2224	
99	2276	2328	2379	2431	2483	2534	2586	2638	2689	2741	
8400	2793	2845	2896	2948	3000	3051	3103	3155	3206	3258	

No.	0	1	2	3	4	5	6	7	8	9	Diff.
8400	924 2793	2845	2896	2948	3000	3051	3103	3155	3206	3258	
01	3310	3362	3413	3465	3517	3568	3620	3672	3723	3775	
02	3827	3878	3930	3982	4034	4085	4137	4189	4240	4292	
03	4344	4395	4447	4499	4550	4602	4654	4705	4757	4809	
04	4860	4912	4964	5015	5067	5119	5170	5222	5274	5326	
05	5377	5429	5481	5532	5584	5636	5687	5739	5791	5842	
06	5894	5946	5997	6049	6101	6152	6204	6255	6307	6359	
07	6410	6462	6514	6565	6617	6669	6720	6772	6824	6875	
08	6927	6979	7030	7082	7134	7185	7237	7289	7340	7392	
09	7444	7495	7547	7598	7650	7702	7753	7805	7857	7908	
10	7960	8012	8063	8115	8167	8218	8270	8321	8373	8425	
8411	8476	8528	8580	8631	8683	8734	8786	8838	8889	8941	
12	8993	9044	9096	9148	9199	9251	9302	9354	9406	9457	
13	9509	9561	9612	9664	9715	9767	9819	9870	9922	9973	
14	925 0025	0077	0128	0180	0232	0283	0335	0386	0438	0490	
15	0541	0593	0644	0696	0748	0799	0851	0902	0954	1006	
16	1057	1109	1160	1212	1264	1315	1367	1418	1470	1522	
17	1573	1625	1676	1728	1780	1831	1883	1934	1986	2038	
18	2089	2141	2192	2244	2296	2347	2399	2450	2502	2554	
19	2605	2657	2708	2760	2811	2863	2915	2966	3018	3069	
20	3121	3172	3224	3276	3327	3379	3430	3482	3534	3585	
8421	3637	3688	3740	3791	3843	3895	3946	3998	4049	4101	
22	4152	4204	4256	4307	4359	4410	4462	4513	4565	4616	
23	4668	4720	4771	4823	4874	4926	4977	5029	5080	5132	
24	5184	5235	5287	5338	5390	5441	5493	5544	5596	5648	
25	5699	5751	5802	5854	5905	5957	6008	6060	6111	6163	
26	6215	6266	6318	6369	6421	6472	6524	6575	6627	6678	
27	6730	6781	6833	6885	6936	6988	7039	7091	7142	7194	
28	7245	7297	7348	7400	7451	7503	7554	7606	7657	7709	
29	7761	7812	7864	7915	7967	8018	8070	8121	8173	8224	
30	8276	8327	8379	8430	8482	8533	8585	8636	8688	8739	
8431	8791	8842	8894	8945	8997	9048	9100	9151	9203	9254	
32	9306	9357	9409	9460	9512	9563	9615	9667	9718	9770	
33	9821	9873	9924	9975	0027	0078	0130	0181	0233	0284	
34	926 0336	0387	0439	0490	0542	0593	0645	0696	0748	0799	
35	0851	0902	0954	1005	1057	1108	1160	1211	1263	1314	
36	1366	1417	1469	1520	1572	1623	1675	1726	1778	1829	
37	1880	1932	1983	2035	2086	2138	2189	2241	2292	2344	
38	2395	2447	2498	2550	2601	2653	2704	2755	2807	2858	
39	2910	2961	3013	3064	3116	3167	3219	3270	3322	3373	
40	3424	3476	3527	3579	3630	3682	3733	3785	3836	3888	
8441	3939	3990	4042	4093	4145	4196	4248	4299	4351	4402	
42	4453	4505	4556	4608	4659	4711	4762	4814	4865	4916	
43	4968	5019	5071	5122	5174	5225	5277	5328	5379	5431	
44	5482	5534	5585	5637	5688	5739	5791	5842	5894	5945	
45	5997	6048	6099	6151	6202	6254	6305	6357	6408	6459	
46	6511	6562	6614	6665	6716	6768	6819	6871	6922	6974	
47	7025	7076	7128	7179	7231	7282	7333	7385	7436	7488	
48	7539	7590	7642	7693	7745	7796	7847	7899	7950	8002	
49	8053	8105	8156	8207	8259	8310	8362	8413	8464	8516	
8450	8567	8618	8670	8721	8773	8824	8875	8927	8978	9030	

52

1	5
2	10
3	16
4	21
5	26
6	31
7	36
8	42
9	47

No.	0	1	2	3	4	5	6	7	8	9	Diff.
8450	926 8567	8618	8670	8721	8773	8824	8875	8927	8978	9030	
51	9081	9132	9184	9235	9287	9338	9389	9441	9492	9543	
52	9595	9646	9698	9749	9800	9852	9903	9955	0006	0057	
53	927 0109	0160	0211	0263	0314	0366	0417	0468	0520	0571	
54	0622	0674	0725	0777	0828	0879	0931	0982	1033	1085	
55	1136	1187	1239	1290	1342	1393	1444	1496	1547	1598	
56	1650	1701	1752	1804	1855	1907	1958	2009	2061	2112	
57	2163	2215	2266	2317	2369	2420	2471	2523	2574	2625	
58	2677	2728	2780	2831	2882	2934	2985	3036	3088	3139	
59	3190	3242	3293	3344	3396	3447	3498	3550	3601	3652	
60	3704	3755	3806	3858	3909	3960	4012	4063	4114	4166	
8461	4217	4268	4320	4371	4422	4474	4525	4576	4628	4679	
62	4730	4782	4833	4884	4935	4987	5038	5089	5141	5192	
63	5243	5295	5346	5397	5449	5500	5551	5603	5654	5705	
64	5757	5808	5859	5910	5962	6013	6064	6116	6167	6218	
65	6270	6321	6372	6424	6475	6526	6577	6629	6680	6731	
66	6783	6834	6885	6937	6988	7039	7090	7142	7193	7244	
67	7296	7347	7398	7449	7501	7552	7603	7655	7706	7757	
68	7808	7860	7911	7962	8014	8065	8116	8167	8219	8270	
69	8321	8373	8424	8475	8526	8578	8629	8680	8732	8783	
70	8834	8885	8937	8988	9039	9090	9142	9193	9244	9296	
8471	9347	9398	9449	9501	9552	9603	9654	9706	9757	9808	
72	9859	9911	9962	0013	0065	0116	0167	0218	0270	0321	
73	928 0372	0423	0475	0526	0577	0628	0680	0731	0782	0833	
74	0885	0936	0987	1038	1090	1141	1192	1243	1295	1346	
75	1397	1448	1500	1551	1602	1653	1705	1756	1807	1858	
76	1909	1961	2012	2063	2114	2166	2217	2268	2319	2371	
77	2422	2473	2524	2576	2627	2678	2729	2780	2832	2883	
78	2934	2985	3037	3088	3139	3190	3241	3293	3344	3395	
79	3446	3498	3549	3600	3651	3702	3754	3805	3856	3907	
80	3959	4010	4061	4112	4163	4215	4266	4317	4368	4419	
8481	4471	4522	4573	4624	4675	4727	4778	4829	4880	4931	
82	4983	5034	5085	5136	5187	5239	5290	5341	5392	5443	
83	5495	5546	5597	5648	5699	5751	5802	5853	5904	5955	
84	6007	6058	6109	6160	6211	6263	6314	6365	6416	6467	
85	6518	6570	6621	6672	6723	6774	6826	6877	6928	6979	
86	7030	7081	7133	7184	7235	7286	7337	7389	7440	7491	
87	7542	7593	7644	7696	7747	7798	7849	7900	7951	8003	
88	8054	8105	8156	8207	8258	8310	8361	8412	8463	8514	
89	8565	8616	8668	8719	8770	8821	8872	8923	8975	9026	
90	9077	9128	9179	9230	9282	9333	9384	9435	9486	9537	
8491	9588	9640	9691	9742	9793	9844	9895	9946	9998	0049	
92	929 0100	0151	0202	0253	0304	0356	0407	0458	0509	0560	
93	0611	0662	0714	0765	0816	0867	0918	0969	1020	1071	
94	1123	1174	1225	1276	1327	1378	1429	1480	1532	1583	
95	1634	1685	1736	1787	1838	1889	1941	1992	2043	2094	
96	2145	2196	2247	2298	2350	2401	2452	2503	2554	2605	
97	2656	2707	2758	2810	2861	2912	2963	3014	3065	3116	
98	3167	3218	3269	3321	3372	3423	3474	3525	3576	3627	
99	3678	3729	3780	3832	3883	3934	3985	4036	4087	4138	
8500	4189	4240	4291	4343	4394	4445	4496	4547	4598	4649	

51

1	5
2	10
3	15
4	20
5	26
6	31
7	36
8	41
9	46

No.	0	1	2	3	4	5	6	7	8	9	Diff.
8500	929 4189	4240	4291	4343	4394	4445	4496	4547	4598	4649	
01	4700	4751	4802	4853	4905	4956	5007	5058	5109	5160	
02	5211	5262	5313	5364	5415	5466	5517	5569	5620	5671	
03	5722	5773	5824	5875	5926	5977	6028	6079	6130	6181	
04	6233	6284	6335	6386	6437	6488	6539	6590	6641	6692	
05	6743	6794	6845	6896	6947	6998	7050	7101	7152	7203	
06	7254	7305	7356	7407	7458	7509	7560	7611	7662	7713	
07	7764	7815	7866	7917	7969	8020	8071	8122	8173	8224	
08	8275	8326	8377	8428	8479	8530	8581	8632	8683	8734	
09	8785	8836	8887	8938	8989	9040	9091	9142	9194	9245	
10	9296	9347	9398	9449	9500	9551	9602	9653	9704	9755	
8511	9806	9857	9908	9959	0010	0061	0112	0163	0214	0265	
12	930 0316	0367	0418	0469	0520	0571	0622	0673	0724	0775	
13	0826	0877	0928	0979	1030	1081	1132	1183	1234	1285	
14	1336	1387	1438	1489	1540	1591	1643	1694	1745	1796	
15	1847	1898	1949	2000	2051	2102	2153	2204	2255	2306	
16	2357	2408	2459	2510	2561	2612	2663	2713	2764	2815	
17	2866	2917	2968	3019	3070	3121	3172	3223	3274	3325	
18	3376	3427	3478	3529	3580	3631	3682	3733	3784	3835	
19	3886	3937	3988	4039	4090	4141	4192	4243	4294	4345	
20	4396	4447	4498	4549	4600	4651	4702	4753	4804	4855	
8521	4906	4957	5008	5059	5110	5160	5211	5262	5313	5364	51
22	5415	5466	5517	5568	5619	5670	5721	5772	5823	5874	1　5
23	5925	5976	6027	6078	6129	6180	6231	6282	6333	6383	2　10
24	6434	6485	6536	6587	6638	6689	6740	6791	6842	6893	3　15
25	6944	6995	7046	7097	7148	7199	7250	7300	7351	7402	4　20
26	7453	7504	7555	7606	7657	7708	7759	7810	7861	7912	5　26
27	7963	8014	8064	8115	8166	8217	8268	8319	8370	8421	6　31
28	8472	8523	8574	8625	8676	8727	8777	8828	8879	8930	7　36
29	8981	9032	9083	9134	9185	9236	9287	9338	9388	9439	8　41
30	9490	9541	9592	9643	9694	9745	9796	9847	9898	9949	9　46
8531	9999	0050	0101	0152	0203	0254	0305	0356	0407	0458	
32	931 0508	0559	0610	0661	0712	0763	0814	0865	0916	0967	
33	1017	1068	1119	1170	1221	1272	1323	1374	1425	1475	
34	1526	1577	1628	1679	1730	1781	1832	1883	1933	1984	
35	2035	2086	2137	2188	2239	2290	2341	2391	2442	2493	
36	2544	2595	2646	2697	2748	2798	2849	2900	2951	3002	
37	3053	3104	3155	3205	3256	3307	3358	3409	3460	3511	
38	3562	3612	3663	3714	3765	3816	3867	3918	3968	4019	
39	4070	4121	4172	4223	4274	4324	4375	4426	4477	4528	
40	4579	4630	4680	4731	4782	4833	4884	4935	4986	5036	
8541	5087	5138	5189	5240	5291	5341	5392	5443	5494	5545	
42	5596	5647	5697	5748	5799	5850	5901	5952	6002	6053	
43	6104	6155	6206	6257	6307	6358	6409	6460	6511	6562	
44	6612	6663	6714	6765	6816	6867	6917	6968	7019	7070	
45	7121	7171	7222	7273	7324	7375	7426	7476	7527	7578	
46	7629	7680	7731	7781	7832	7883	7934	7985	8035	8086	
47	8137	8188	8239	8289	8340	8391	8442	8493	8544	8594	
48	8645	8696	8747	8798	8848	8899	8950	9001	9052	9102	
49	9153	9204	9255	9306	9356	9407	9458	9509	9560	9610	
8550	9661	9712	9763	9814	9864	9915	9966	0017	0067	0118	

932

No.	0	1	2	3	4	5	6	7	8	9	Diff.
8550	931 9661	9712	9763	9814	9864	9915	9966	0017	0067	0118	
51	932 0169	0220	0271	0321	0372	0423	0474	0525	0575	0626	
52	0677	0728	0778	0829	0880	0931	0982	1032	1083	1134	
53	1185	1235	1286	1337	1388	1439	1489	1540	1591	1642	
54	1692	1743	1794	1845	1896	1946	1997	2048	2099	2149	
55	2200	2251	2302	2352	2403	2454	2505	2555	2606	2657	
56	2708	2759	2809	2860	2911	2962	3012	3063	3114	3165	
57	3215	3266	3317	3368	3418	3469	3520	3571	3621	3672	
58	3723	3774	3824	3875	3926	3977	4027	4078	4129	4180	
59	4230	4281	4332	4382	4433	4484	4535	4585	4636	4687	
60	4738	4788	4839	4890	4941	4991	5042	5093	5144	5194	
8561	5245	5296	5346	5397	5448	5499	5549	5600	5651	5702	
62	5752	5803	5854	5904	5955	6006	6057	6107	6158	6209	
63	6259	6310	6361	6412	6462	6513	6564	6614	6665	6716	
64	6767	6817	6868	6919	6969	7020	7071	7122	7172	7223	
65	7274	7324	7375	7426	7476	7527	7578	7629	7679	7730	
66	7781	7831	7882	7933	7983	8034	8085	8136	8186	8237	
67	8288	8338	8389	8440	8490	8541	8592	8643	8693	8744	
68	8795	8845	8896	8947	8997	9048	9099	9149	9200	9251	
69	9301	9352	9403	9453	9504	9555	9606	9656	9707	9758	
70	9808	9859	9910	9960	0011	0062	0112	0163	0214	0264	
8571	933 0315	0366	0416	0467	0518	0568	0619	0670	0720	0771	51
72	0822	0872	0923	0974	1024	1075	1126	1176	1227	1278	1 5
73	1328	1379	1430	1480	1531	1582	1632	1683	1733	1784	2 10
74	1835	1885	1936	1987	2037	2088	2139	2189	2240	2291	3 15
75	2341	2392	2443	2493	2544	2595	2645	2696	2746	2797	4 20
76	2848	2898	2949	3000	305)	3101	3152	3202	3253	3303	5 26
77	3354	3405	3455	3506	3557	3607	3658	3709	3759	3810	6 31
78	3860	3911	3962	4012	4063	4114	4164	4215	4265	4316	7 36
79	4367	4417	4468	4519	4569	4620	4670	4721	4772	4822	8 41
80	4873	4923	4974	5025	5075	5126	5177	5227	5278	5328	9 46
8581	5379	5430	5480	5531	5581	5632	5683	5733	5784	5834	
82	5885	5936	5986	6037	6088	6138	6189	6239	6290	6341	
83	6391	6442	6492	6543	6594	6644	6695	6745	6796	6846	
84	6897	6948	6998	7049	7099	7150	7201	7251	7302	7352	
85	7403	7454	7504	7555	7605	7656	7707	7757	7808	7858	
86	7909	7959	8010	8061	8111	8162	8212	8263	8313	8364	
87	8415	8465	8516	8566	8617	8668	8718	8769	8819	8870	
88	8920	8971	9021	9072	9123	9173	9224	9274	9325	9375	
89	9426	9477	9527	9578	9628	9679	9729	9780	9831	9881	
90	9932	9982	0033	0083	0134	0184	0235	0286	0336	0387	
8591	934 0437	0488	0538	0589	0639	0690	0740	0791	0842	0892	
92	0943	0993	1044	1094	1145	1195	1246	1296	1347	1398	
93	1448	1499	1549	1600	1650	1701	1751	1802	1852	1903	
94	1953	2004	2055	2105	2156	2206	2257	2307	2358	2408	
95	2459	2509	2560	2610	2661	2711	2762	2812	2863	2914	
96	2964	3015	3065	3116	3166	3217	3267	3318	3368	3419	
97	3469	3520	3570	3621	3671	3722	3772	3823	3873	3924	
98	3974	4025	4075	4126	4176	4227	4277	4328	4378	4429	
99	4479	4530	4580	4631	4682	4732	4783	4833	4884	4934	
8600	4985	5035	5086	5136	5187	5237	5287	5338	5388	5439	

No.	0	1	2	3	4	5	6	7	8	9	Diff.
8600	934 4985	5035	5086	5136	5187	5237	5287	5338	5388	5439	
01	5489	5540	5590	5641	5691	5742	5792	5843	5893	5944	
02	5994	6045	6095	6146	6196	6247	6297	6348	6398	6449	
03	6499	6550	6600	6651	6701	6752	6802	6853	6903	6954	
04	7004	7054	7105	7155	7206	7256	7307	7357	7408	7458	
05	7509	7559	7610	7660	7711	7761	7812	7862	7912	7963	
06	8013	8064	8114	8165	8215	8266	8316	8367	8417	8468	
07	8518	8568	8619	8669	8720	8770	8821	8871	8922	8972	
08	9023	9073	9123	9174	9224	9275	9325	9376	9426	9477	
09	9527	9578	9628	9678	9729	9779	9830	9880	9931	9981	
10	935 0032	0082	0132	0183	0233	0284	0334	0385	0435	0485	
8611	0536	0586	0637	0687	0738	0788	0838	0889	0939	0990	
12	1040	1091	1141	1191	1242	1292	1343	1393	1444	1494	
13	1544	1595	1645	1696	1746	1797	1847	1897	1948	1998	
14	2049	2099	2150	2200	2250	2301	2351	2402	2452	2502	
15	2553	2603	2654	2704	2754	2805	2855	2906	2956	3006	
16	3057	3107	3158	3208	3259	3309	3359	3410	3460	3511	
17	3561	3611	3662	3712	3763	3813	3863	3914	3964	4015	
18	4065	4115	4166	4216	4266	4317	4367	4418	4468	4518	
19	4569	4619	4670	4720	4770	4821	4871	4922	4972	5022	
20	5073	5123	5173	5224	5274	5325	5375	5425	5476	5526	
8621	5576	5627	5677	5728	5778	5828	5879	5929	5979	6030	
22	6080	6131	6181	6231	6282	6332	6382	6433	6483	6533	
23	6584	6634	6685	6735	6785	6836	6886	6936	6987	7037	
24	7087	7138	7188	7239	7289	7339	7390	7440	7490	7541	
25	7591	7641	7692	7742	7792	7843	7893	7943	7994	8044	
26	8095	8145	8195	8246	8296	8346	8397	8447	8497	8548	
27	8598	8648	8699	8749	8799	8850	8900	8950	9001	9051	
28	9101	9152	9202	9252	9303	9353	9403	9454	9504	9554	
29	9605	9655	9705	9756	9806	9856	9907	9957	0007	0058	
30	936 0108	0158	0209	0259	0309	0360	0410	0460	0511	0561	
8631	0611	0661	0712	0762	0812	0863	0913	0963	1014	1064	
32	1114	1165	1215	1265	1316	1366	1416	1466	1517	1567	
33	1617	1668	1718	1768	1819	1869	1919	1970	2020	2070	
34	2120	2171	2221	2271	2322	2372	2422	2473	2523	2573	
35	2623	2674	2724	2774	2825	2875	2925	2975	3026	3076	
36	3126	3177	3227	3277	3327	3378	3428	3478	3529	3579	
37	3629	3679	3730	3780	3830	3881	3931	3981	4031	4082	
38	4132	4182	4233	4283	4333	4383	4434	4484	4534	4584	
39	4635	4685	4735	4786	4836	4886	4936	4987	5037	5087	
40	5137	5188	5238	5288	5338	5389	5439	5489	5540	5590	
8641	5640	5690	5741	5791	5841	5891	5942	5992	6042	6092	
42	6143	6193	6243	6293	6344	6394	6444	6494	6545	6595	
43	6645	6695	6746	6796	6846	6896	6947	6997	7047	7097	
44	7148	7198	7248	7298	7349	7399	7449	7499	7550	7600	
45	7650	7700	7750	7801	7851	7901	7951	8002	8052	8102	
46	8152	8203	8253	8303	8353	8403	8454	8504	8554	8604	
47	8655	8705	8755	8805	8855	8906	8956	9006	9056	9107	
48	9157	9207	9257	9307	9358	9408	9458	9508	9559	9609	
49	9659	9709	9759	9810	9860	9910	9960	0010	0061	0111	
8650	937 0161	0211	0261	0312	0362	0412	0462	0513	0563	0613	

50

1	5
2	10
3	15
4	20
5	25
6	30
7	35
8	40
9	45

No.	0	1	2	3	4	5	6	7	8	9	Diff.
8650	937 0161	0211	0261	0312	0362	0412	0462	0513	0563	0613	
51	0663	0713	0764	0814	0864	0914	0964	1015	1065	1115	
52	1165	1215	1265	1316	1366	1416	1466	1516	1567	1617	
53	1667	1717	1767	1818	1868	1918	1968	2018	2069	2119	
54	2169	2219	2269	2319	2370	2420	2470	2520	2570	2621	
55	2671	2721	2771	2821	2871	2922	2972	3022	3072	3122	
56	3172	3223	3273	3323	3373	3423	3474	3524	3574	3624	
57	3674	3724	3775	3825	3875	3925	3975	4025	4075	4126	
58	4176	4226	4276	4326	4376	4427	4477	4527	4577	4627	
59	4677	4728	4778	4828	4878	4928	4978	5028	5079	5129	
60	5179	5229	5279	5329	5380	5430	5480	5530	5580	5630	
8661	5680	5731	5781	5831	5881	5931	5981	6031	6082	6132	
62	6182	6232	6282	6332	6382	6432	6483	6533	6583	6633	
63	6683	6733	6783	6834	6884	6934	6984	7034	7084	7134	
64	7184	7235	7285	7335	7385	7435	7485	7535	7585	7636	
65	7686	7736	7786	7836	7886	7936	7986	8037	8087	8137	
66	8187	8237	8287	8337	8387	8437	8488	8538	8588	8638	
67	8688	8738	8788	8838	8888	8939	8989	9039	9089	9139	
68	9189	9239	9289	9339	9389	9440	9490	9540	9590	9640	
69	9690	9740	9790	9840	9890	9941	9991	0̅0̅4̅1̅	0̅0̅9̅1̅	0̅1̅4̅1̅	
70	938 0191	0241	0291	0341	0391	0441	0492	0542	0592	0642	
8671	0692	0742	0792	0842	0892	0942	0992	1042	1093	1143	
72	1193	1243	1293	1343	1393	1443	1493	1543	1593	1643	
73	1693	1744	1794	1844	1894	1944	1994	2044	2094	2144	
74	2194	2244	2294	2344	2394	2445	2495	2545	2595	2645	
75	2695	2745	2795	2845	2895	2945	2995	3045	3095	3145	
76	3195	3245	3296	3346	3396	3446	3496	3546	3596	3646	
77	3696	3746	3796	3846	3896	3946	3996	4046	4096	4146	
78	4196	4246	4297	4347	4397	4447	4497	4547	4597	4647	
79	4697	4747	4797	4847	4897	4947	4997	5047	5097	5147	
80	5197	5247	5297	5347	5397	5447	5497	5547	5598	5648	
8681	5698	5748	5798	5848	5898	5948	5998	6048	6098	6148	
82	6198	6248	6298	6348	6398	6448	6498	6548	6598	6648	
83	6698	6748	6798	6848	6898	6948	6998	7048	7098	7148	
84	7198	7248	7298	7348	7398	7448	7498	7548	7598	7648	
85	7698	7748	7798	7848	7898	7948	7998	8048	8098	8148	
86	8198	8248	8298	8348	8398	8448	8498	8548	8598	8648	
87	8698	8748	8798	8848	8898	8948	8998	9048	9098	9148	
88	9198	9248	9298	9348	9398	9448	9498	9548	9598	9648	
89	9698	9748	9798	9848	9898	9948	9998	0̅0̅4̅8̅	0̅0̅9̅8̅	0̅1̅4̅8̅	
90	939 0198	0248	0298	0348	0398	0448	0498	0548	0598	0648	
8691	0697	0747	0797	0847	0897	0947	0997	1047	1097	1147	
92	1197	1247	1297	1347	1397	1447	1497	1547	1597	1647	
93	1697	1747	1797	1847	1897	1947	1997	2046	2096	2146	
94	2196	2246	2296	2346	2396	2446	2496	2546	2596	2646	
95	2696	2746	2796	2846	2896	2946	2996	3045	3095	3145	
96	3195	3245	3295	3345	3395	3445	3495	3545	3595	3645	
97	3695	3745	3795	3845	3894	3944	3994	4044	4094	4144	
98	4194	4244	4294	4344	4394	4444	4494	4544	4593	4643	
99	4693	4743	4793	4843	4893	4943	4993	5043	5093	5143	
8700	5193	5242	5292	5342	5392	5442	5492	5542	5592	5642	

50

1	5
2	10
3	15
4	20
5	25
6	30
7	35
8	40
9	45

No.	0	1	2	3	4	5	6	7	8	9	Diff.
8700	939 5193	5242	5292	5342	5392	5442	5492	5542	5592	5642	
01	5692	5742	5792	5841	5891	5941	5991	6041	6091	6141	
02	6191	6241	6291	6341	6390	6440	6490	6540	6590	6640	
03	6690	6740	6790	6840	6889	6939	6989	7039	7089	7139	
04	7189	7239	7289	7339	7388	7438	7488	7538	7588	7638	
05	7688	7738	7788	7837	7887	7937	7987	8037	8087	8137	
06	8187	8237	8286	8336	8386	8436	8486	8536	8586	8636	
07	8685	8735	8785	8835	8885	8935	8985	9035	9084	9134	
08	9184	9234	9284	9334	9384	9434	9483	9533	9583	9633	
09	9683	9733	9783	9833	9882	9932	9982	0032	0082	0132	
10	940 0182	0231	0281	0331	0381	0431	0481	0531	0580	0630	
8711	0680	0730	0780	0830	0880	0929	0979	1029	1079	1129	
12	1179	1229	1278	1328	1378	1428	1478	1528	1577	1627	
13	1677	1727	1777	1827	1877	1926	1976	2026	2076	2126	
14	2176	2225	2275	2325	2375	2425	2475	2524	2574	2624	
15	2674	2724	2774	2823	2873	2923	2973	3023	3073	3122	
16	3172	3222	3272	3322	3372	3421	3471	3521	3571	3621	
17	3670	3720	3770	3820	3870	3920	3969	4019	4069	4119	
18	4169	4218	4268	4318	4368	4418	4468	4517	4567	4617	
19	4667	4717	4766	4816	4866	4916	4966	5015	5065	5115	
20	5165	5215	5264	5314	5364	5414	5464	5513	5563	5613	
8721	5663	5713	5762	5812	5862	5912	5962	6011	6061	6111	
22	6161	6211	6260	6310	6360	6410	6460	6509	6559	6609	
23	6659	6709	6758	6808	6858	6908	6957	7007	7057	7107	
24	7157	7206	7256	7306	7356	7405	7455	7505	7555	7605	
25	7654	7704	7754	7804	7853	7903	7953	8003	8053	8102	
26	8152	8202	8252	8301	8351	8401	8451	8500	8550	8600	
27	8650	8700	8749	8799	8849	8899	8948	8998	9048	9098	
28	9147	9197	9247	9297	9346	9396	9446	9496	9545	9595	
29	9645	9695	9744	9794	9844	9894	9943	9993	0043	0093	
30	941 0142	0192	0242	0292	0341	0391	0441	0491	0540	0590	
8731	0640	0690	0739	0789	0839	0889	0938	0988	1038	1088	
32	1137	1187	1237	1286	1336	1386	1436	1485	1535	1585	
33	1635	1684	1734	1784	1834	1883	1933	1983	2032	2082	
34	2132	2182	2231	2281	2331	2380	2430	2480	2530	2579	
35	2629	2679	2729	2778	2828	2878	2927	2977	3027	3077	
36	3126	3176	3226	3275	3325	3375	3425	3474	3524	3574	
37	3623	3673	3723	3772	3822	3872	3922	3971	4021	4071	
38	4120	4170	4220	4270	4319	4369	4419	4468	4518	4568	
39	4617	4667	4717	4766	4816	4866	4916	4965	5015	5065	
40	5114	5164	5214	5263	5313	5363	5412	5462	5512	5562	
8741	5611	5661	5711	5760	5810	5860	5909	5959	6009	6058	
42	6108	6158	6207	6257	6307	6356	6406	6456	6505	6555	
43	6605	6654	6704	6754	6803	6853	6903	6952	7002	7052	
44	7101	7151	7201	7250	7300	7350	7399	7449	7499	7548	
45	7598	7648	7697	7747	7797	7846	7896	7946	7995	8045	
46	8095	8144	8194	8244	8293	8343	8393	8442	8492	8542	
47	8591	8641	8691	8740	8790	8840	8889	8939	8988	9038	
48	9088	9137	9187	9237	9286	9336	9386	9435	9485	9535	
49	9584	9634	9683	9733	9783	9832	9882	9932	9981	0031	
8750	942 0081	0130	0180	0229	0279	0329	0378	0428	0478	0527	

50
1	5
2	10
3	15
4	20
5	25
6	30
7	35
8	40
9	45

No.	0	1	2	3	4	5	6	7	8	9	Diff.
8750	942 0081	0130	0180	0229	0279	0329	0378	0428	0478	0527	
51	0577	0626	0676	0726	0775	0825	0875	0924	0974	1023	
52	1073	1123	1172	1222	1272	1321	1371	1420	1470	1520	
53	1569	1619	1669	1718	1768	1817	1867	1917	1966	2016	
54	2065	2115	2165	2214	2264	2313	2363	2413	2462	2512	
55	2562	2611	2661	2710	2760	2810	2859	2909	2958	3008	
56	3058	3107	3157	3206	3256	3306	3355	3405	3454	3504	
57	3553	3603	3653	3702	3752	3801	3851	3901	3950	4000	
58	4049	4099	4149	4198	4248	4297	4347	4397	4446	4496	
59	4545	4595	4644	4694	4744	4793	4843	4892	4942	4991	
60	5041	5091	5140	5190	5239	5289	5339	5388	5438	5487	
8761	5537	5586	5636	5686	5735	5785	5834	5884	5933	5983	
62	6032	6082	6132	6181	6231	6280	6330	6379	6429	6479	
63	6528	6578	6627	6677	6726	6776	6825	6875	6925	6974	
64	7024	7073	7123	7172	7222	7271	7321	7371	7420	7470	
65	7519	7569	7618	7668	7717	7767	7816	7866	7916	7965	
66	8015	8064	8114	8163	8213	8262	8312	8361	8411	8461	
67	8510	8560	8609	8659	8708	8758	8807	8857	8906	8956	
68	9005	9055	9104	9154	9204	9253	9303	9352	9402	9451	
69	9501	9550	9600	9649	9699	9748	9798	9847	9897	9946	
70	9996	0045	0095	0144	0194	0244	0293	0343	0392	0442	**49**
8771	943 0491	0541	0590	0640	0689	0739	0788	0838	0887	0937	1 5
72	0986	1036	1085	1135	1184	1234	1283	1333	1382	1432	2 10
73	1481	1531	1580	1630	1679	1729	1778	1828	1877	1927	3 15
74	1976	2026	2075	2125	2174	2224	2273	2323	2372	2422	4 20
75	2471	2521	2570	2620	2669	2719	2768	2818	2867	2917	5 25
76	2966	3016	3065	3115	3164	3214	3263	3313	3362	3412	6 29 / 7 34
77	3461	3510	3560	3609	3659	3708	3758	3807	3857	3906	8 39
78	3956	4005	4055	4104	4154	4203	4253	4302	4352	4401	9 44
79	4450	4500	4549	4599	4648	4698	4747	4797	4846	4896	
80	4945	4995	5044	5094	5143	5192	5242	5291	5341	5390	
8781	5440	5489	5539	5588	5638	5687	5737	5786	5835	5885	
82	5934	5984	6033	6083	6132	6182	6231	6280	6330	6379	
83	6429	6478	6528	6577	6627	6676	6726	6775	6824	6874	
84	6923	6973	7022	7072	7121	7170	7220	7269	7319	7368	
85	7418	7467	7517	7566	7615	7665	7714	7764	7813	7863	
86	7912	7961	8011	8060	8110	8159	8209	8258	8307	8357	
87	8406	8456	8505	8555	8604	8653	8703	8752	8802	8851	
88	8900	8950	8999	9049	9098	9148	9197	9246	9296	9345	
89	9395	9444	9493	9543	9592	9642	9691	9741	9790	9839	
90	9889	9938	9988	0037	0086	0136	0185	0235	0284	0333	
8791	944 0383	0432	0482	0531	0580	0630	0679	0729	0778	0827	
92	0877	0926	0976	1025	1074	1124	1173	1223	1272	1321	
93	1371	1420	1470	1519	1568	1618	1667	1716	1766	1815	
94	1865	1914	1963	2013	2062	2112	2161	2210	2260	2309	
95	2358	2408	2457	2507	2556	2605	2655	2704	2753	2803	
96	2852	2902	2951	3000	3050	3099	3148	3198	3247	3297	
97	3346	3395	3445	3494	3543	3593	3642	3691	3741	3790	
98	3840	3889	3938	3988	4037	4086	4136	4185	4234	4284	
99	4333	4383	4432	4481	4531	4580	4629	4679	4728	4777	
8800	4827	4876	4925	4975	5024	5073	5123	5172	5222	5271	

No.	0	1	2	3	4	5	6	7	8	9	Diff.
8800	944 4827	4876	4925	4975	5024	5073	5123	5172	5222	5271	
01	5320	5370	5419	5468	5518	5567	5616	5666	5715	5764	
02	5814	5863	5912	5962	6011	6060	6110	6159	6208	6258	
03	6307	6356	6406	6455	6504	6554	6603	6652	6702	6751	
04	6800	6850	6899	6948	6998	7047	7096	7146	7195	7244	
05	7294	7343	7392	7442	7491	7540	7590	7639	7688	7737	
06	7787	7836	7885	7935	7984	8033	8083	8132	8181	8231	
07	8280	8329	8379	8428	8477	8527	8576	8625	8674	8724	
08	8773	8822	8872	8921	8970	9020	9069	9118	9167	9217	
09	9266	9315	9365	9414	9463	9513	9562	9611	9660	9710	
10	9759	9808	9858	9907	9956	0006	0055	0104	0153	0203	
8811	945 0252	0301	0351	0400	0449	0498	0548	0597	0646	0696	
12	0745	0794	0843	0893	0942	0991	1041	1090	1139	1188	
13	1238	1287	1336	1386	1435	1484	1533	1583	1632	1681	
14	1730	1780	1829	1878	1928	1977	2026	2075	2125	2174	
15	2223	2272	2322	2371	2420	2469	2519	2568	2617	2667	
16	2716	2765	2814	2864	2913	2962	3011	3061	3110	3159	
17	3208	3258	3307	3356	3405	3455	3504	3553	3602	3652	
18	3701	3750	3799	3849	3898	3947	3996	4046	4095	4144	
19	4193	4243	4292	4341	4390	4440	4489	4538	4587	4637	
20	4686	4735	4784	4834	4883	4932	4981	5031	5080	5129	
8821	5178	5227	5277	5326	5375	5424	5474	5523	5572	5621	
22	5671	5720	5769	5818	5867	5917	5966	6015	6064	6114	
23	6163	6212	6261	6310	6360	6409	6458	6507	6557	6606	
24	6655	6704	6753	6803	6852	6901	6950	7000	7049	7098	
25	7147	7196	7246	7295	7344	7393	7442	7492	7541	7590	
26	7639	7688	7738	7787	7836	7885	7934	7984	8033	8082	
27	8131	8180	8230	8279	8328	8377	8426	8476	8525	8574	
28	8623	8672	8722	8771	8820	8869	8918	8968	9017	9066	
29	9115	9164	9214	9263	9312	9361	9410	9459	9509	9558	
30	9607	9656	9705	9755	9804	9853	9902	9951	0000	0050	
8831	946 0099	0148	0197	0246	0296	0345	0394	0443	0492	0541	
32	0591	0640	0689	0738	0787	0836	0886	0935	0984	1033	
33	1082	1131	1181	1230	1279	1328	1377	1426	1476	1525	
34	1574	1623	1672	1721	1771	1820	1869	1918	1967	2016	
35	2066	2115	2164	2213	2262	2311	2360	2410	2459	2508	
36	2557	2606	2655	2705	2754	2803	2852	2901	2950	2999	
37	3049	3098	3147	3196	3245	3294	3343	3393	3442	3491	
38	3540	3589	3638	3687	3737	3786	3835	3884	3933	3982	
39	4031	4080	4130	4179	4228	4277	4326	4375	4424	4474	
40	4523	4572	4621	4670	4719	4768	4817	4867	4916	4965	
8841	5014	5063	5112	5161	5210	5260	5309	5358	5407	5456	
42	5505	5554	5603	5652	5702	5751	5800	5849	5898	5947	
43	5996	6045	6094	6144	6193	6242	6291	6340	6389	6438	
44	6487	6536	6586	6635	6684	6733	6782	6831	6880	6929	
45	6978	7027	7077	7126	7175	7224	7273	7322	7371	7420	
46	7469	7518	7568	7617	7666	7715	7764	7813	7862	7911	
47	7960	8009	8058	8108	8157	8206	8255	8304	8353	8402	
48	8451	8500	8549	8598	8647	8697	8746	8795	8844	8893	
49	8942	8991	9040	9089	9138	9187	9236	9285	9335	9384	
8850	9433	9482	9531	9580	9629	9678	9727	9776	9825	9874	

49

1	5
2	10
3	15
4	20
5	25
6	29
7	34
8	39
9	44

No.	0	1	2	3	4	5	6	7	8	9	Diff.
8850	946 9433	9482	9531	9580	9629	9678	9727	9776	9825	9874	
51	9923	9972	0022	0071	0120	0169	0218	0267	0316	0365	
52	947 0414	0463	0512	0561	0610	0659	0708	0757	0807	0856	
53	0905	0954	1003	1052	1101	1150	1199	1248	1297	1346	
54	1395	1444	1493	1542	1591	1640	1689	1739	1788	1837	
55	1886	1935	1984	2033	2082	2131	2180	2229	2278	2327	
56	2376	2425	2474	2523	2572	2621	2670	2719	2768	2817	
57	2866	2915	2965	3014	3063	3112	3161	3210	3259	3308	
58	3357	3406	3455	3504	3553	3602	3651	3700	3749	3798	
59	3847	3896	3945	3994	4043	4092	4141	4190	4239	4288	
60	4337	4386	4435	4484	4533	4582	4631	4680	4729	4778	
8861	4827	4876	4925	4974	5023	5072	5121	5170	5219	5268	
62	5317	5366	5415	5464	5513	5562	5611	5660	5709	5758	
63	5807	5856	5905	5954	6003	6052	6101	6150	6199	6248	
64	6297	6346	6395	6444	6493	6542	6591	6640	6689	6738	
65	6787	6836	6885	6934	6983	7032	7081	7130	7179	7228	
66	7277	7326	7375	7424	7473	7522	7571	7620	7669	7718	
67	7767	7816	7865	7914	7963	8012	8061	8110	8159	8208	
68	8257	8306	8355	8404	8453	8502	8551	8600	8649	8698	
69	8747	8796	8844	8893	8942	8991	9040	9089	9138	9187	
70	9236	9285	9334	9383	9432	9481	9530	9579	9628	9677	
8871	9726	9775	9824	9873	9922	9971	0020	0068	0117	0166	
72	948 0215	0264	0313	0362	0411	0460	0509	0558	0607	0656	
73	0705	0754	0803	0852	0901	0950	0998	1047	1096	1145	
74	1194	1243	1292	1341	1390	1439	1488	1537	1586	1635	
75	1684	1733	1781	1830	1879	1928	1977	2026	2075	2124	
76	2173	2222	2271	2320	2369	2418	2467	2515	2564	2613	
77	2662	2711	2760	2809	2858	2907	2956	3005	3054	3102	
78	3151	3200	3249	3298	3347	3396	3445	3494	3543	3592	
79	3641	3689	3738	3787	3836	3885	3934	3983	4032	4081	
80	4130	4179	4227	4276	4325	4374	4423	4472	4521	4570	
8881	4619	4668	4717	4765	4814	4863	4912	4961	5010	5059	
82	5108	5157	5205	5254	5303	5352	5401	5450	5499	5548	
83	5597	5646	5694	5743	5792	5841	5890	5939	5988	6037	
84	6085	6134	6183	6232	6281	6330	6379	6428	6477	6525	
85	6574	6623	6672	6721	6770	6819	6868	6916	6965	7014	
86	7063	7112	7161	7210	7259	7307	7356	7405	7454	7503	
87	7552	7601	7650	7698	7747	7796	7845	7894	7943	7992	
88	8040	8089	8138	8187	8236	8285	8334	8382	8431	8480	
89	8529	8578	8627	8676	8724	8773	8822	8871	8920	8969	
90	9018	9066	9115	9164	9213	9262	9311	9360	9408	9457	
8891	9506	9555	9604	9653	9701	9750	9799	9848	9897	9946	
92	9995	0043	0092	0141	0190	0239	0288	0336	0385	0434	
93	949 0483	0532	0581	0629	0678	0727	0776	0825	0874	0922	
94	0971	1020	1069	1118	1167	1215	1264	1313	1362	1411	
95	1460	1508	1557	1606	1655	1704	1752	1801	1850	1899	
96	1948	1997	2045	2094	2143	2192	2241	2289	2338	2387	
97	2436	2485	2534	2582	2631	2680	2729	2778	2826	2875	
98	2924	2973	3022	3070	3119	3168	3217	3266	3314	3363	
99	3412	3461	3510	3558	3607	3656	3705	3754	3802	3851	
8900	3900	3949	3998	4046	4095	4144	4193	4242	4290	4339	

Diff.

49

1	5
2	10
3	15
4	20
5	25
6	29
7	34
8	39
9	44

No.	0	1	2	3	4	5	6	7	8	9	Diff.
8900	949 3900	3949	3998	4046	4095	4144	4193	4242	4290	4339	
01	4388	4437	4486	4534	4583	4632	4681	4730	4778	4827	
02	4876	4925	4973	5022	5071	5120	5169	5217	5266	5315	
03	5364	5413	5461	5510	5559	5608	5656	5705	5754	5803	
04	5852	5900	5949	5998	6047	6095	6144	6193	6242	6290	
05	6339	6388	6437	6486	6534	6583	6632	6681	6729	6778	
06	6827	6876	6924	6973	7022	7071	7119	7168	7217	7266	
07	7315	7363	7412	7461	7510	7558	7607	7656	7705	7753	
08	7802	7851	7900	7948	7997	8046	8095	8143	8192	8241	
09	8290	8338	8387	8436	8485	8533	8582	8631	8680	8728	
10	8777	8826	8875	8923	8972	9021	9069	9118	9167	9216	
8911	9264	9313	9362	9411	9459	9508	9557	9606	9654	9703	
12	9752	9801	9849	9898	9947	9995	0044	0093	0142	0190	
13	950 0239	0288	0337	0385	0434	0483	0531	0580	0629	0678	
14	0726	0775	0824	0872	0921	0970	1019	1067	1116	1165	
15	1213	1262	1311	1360	1408	1457	1506	1554	1603	1652	
16	1701	1749	1798	1847	1895	1944	1993	2042	2090	2139	
17	2188	2236	2285	2334	2382	2431	2480	2529	2577	2626	
18	2675	2723	2772	2821	2869	2918	2967	3016	3064	3113	
19	3162	3210	3259	3308	3356	3405	3454	3502	3551	3600	
20	3649	3697	3746	3795	3843	3892	3941	3989	4038	4087	
8921	4135	4184	4233	4281	4330	4379	4427	4476	4525	4574	
22	4622	4671	4720	4768	4817	4866	4914	4963	5012	5060	
23	5109	5158	5206	5255	5304	5352	5401	5450	5498	5547	
24	5596	5644	5693	5742	5790	5839	5888	5936	5985	6034	
25	6082	6131	6180	6228	6277	6326	6374	6423	6472	6520	
26	6569	6617	6666	6715	6763	6812	6861	6909	6958	7007	
27	7055	7104	7153	7201	7250	7299	7347	7396	7445	7493	
28	7542	7590	7639	7688	7736	7785	7834	7882	7931	7980	
29	8028	8077	8126	8174	8223	8271	8320	8369	8417	8466	
30	8515	8563	8612	8660	8709	8758	8806	8855	8904	8952	
8931	9001	9050	9098	9147	9195	9244	9293	9341	9390	9439	
32	9487	9536	9584	9633	9682	9730	9779	9827	9876	9925	
33	9973	0022	0071	0119	0168	0216	0265	0314	0362	0411	
34	951 0459	0508	0557	0605	0654	0703	0751	0800	0848	0897	
35	0946	0994	1043	1091	1140	1189	1237	1286	1334	1383	
36	1432	1480	1529	1577	1626	1675	1723	1772	1820	1869	
37	1918	1966	2015	2063	2112	2161	2209	2258	2306	2355	
38	2404	2452	2501	2549	2598	2646	2695	2744	2792	2841	
39	2889	2938	2987	3035	3084	3132	3181	3229	3278	3327	
40	3375	3424	3472	3521	3569	3618	3667	3715	3764	3812	
8941	3861	3910	3958	4007	4055	4104	4152	4201	4250	4298	
42	4347	4395	4444	4492	4541	4589	4638	4687	4735	4784	
43	4832	4881	4929	4978	5027	5075	5124	5172	5221	5269	
44	5318	5366	5415	5464	5512	5561	5609	5658	5706	5755	
45	5803	5852	5901	5949	5998	6046	6095	6143	6192	6240	
46	6289	6337	6386	6435	6483	6532	6580	6629	6677	6726	
47	6774	6823	6871	6920	6969	7017	7066	7114	7163	7211	
48	7260	7308	7357	7405	7454	7502	7551	7599	7648	7697	
49	7745	7794	7842	7891	7939	7988	8036	8085	8133	8182	
8950	8230	8279	8327	8376	8424	8473	8521	8570	8619	8667	

49
1	5
2	10
3	15
4	20
5	25
6	29
7	34
8	39
9	44

No.	0	1	2	3	4	5	6	7	8	9	Diff.
8950	951 8230	8279	8327	8376	8424	8473	8521	8570	8619	8667	
51	8716	8764	8813	8861	8910	8958	9007	9055	9104	9152	
52	9201	9249	9298	9346	9395	9443	9492	9540	9589	9637	
53	9686	9734	9783	9831	9880	9928	9977	0025	0074	0122	
54	952 0171	0219	0268	0316	0365	0413	0462	0510	0559	0607	
55	0656	0704	0753	0801	0850	0898	0947	0995	1044	1092	
56	1141	1189	1238	1286	1335	1383	1432	1480	1529	1577	
57	1626	1674	1723	1771	1820	1868	1917	1965	2014	2062	
58	2111	2159	2208	2256	2305	2353	2401	2450	2498	2547	
59	2595	2644	2692	2741	2789	2838	2886	2935	2983	3032	
60	3080	3129	3177	3226	3274	3322	3371	3419	3468	3516	
8961	3565	3613	3662	3710	3759	3807	3856	3904	3952	4001	
62	4049	4098	4146	4195	4243	4292	4340	4389	4437	4486	
63	4534	4582	4631	4679	4728	4776	4825	4873	4922	4970	
64	5018	5067	5115	5164	5212	5261	5309	5358	5406	5454	
65	5503	5551	5600	5648	5697	5745	5794	5842	5890	5939	
66	5987	6036	6084	6133	6181	6230	6278	6326	6375	6423	
67	6472	6520	6569	6617	6665	6714	6762	6811	6859	6908	
68	6956	7004	7053	7101	7150	7198	7247	7295	7343	7392	
69	7440	7489	7537	7586	7634	7682	7731	7779	7828	7876	
70	7924	7973	8021	8070	8118	8167	8215	8263	8312	8360	
8971	8409	8457	8505	8554	8602	8651	8699	8747	8796	8844	48
72	8893	8941	8989	9038	9086	9135	9183	9231	9280	9328	1 5
73	9377	9425	9473	9522	9570	9619	9667	9715	9764	9812	2 10
74	9861	9909	9957	0006	0054	0103	0151	0199	0248	0296	3 14
75	953 0345	0393	0441	0490	0538	0587	0635	0683	0732	0780	4 19
76	0828	0877	0925	0974	1022	1070	1119	1167	1215	1264	5 24
77	1312	1361	1409	1457	1506	1554	1603	1651	1699	1748	6 29
78	1796	1844	1893	1941	1989	2038	2086	2135	2183	2231	7 34
79	2280	2328	2376	2425	2473	2522	2570	2618	2667	2715	8 38
80	2763	2812	2860	2908	2957	3005	3054	3102	3150	3199	9 43
8981	3247	3295	3344	3392	3440	3489	3537	3585	3634	3682	
82	3731	3779	3827	3876	3924	3972	4021	4069	4117	4166	
83	4214	4262	4311	4359	4407	4456	4504	4552	4601	4649	
84	4697	4746	4794	4842	4891	4939	4987	5036	5084	5132	
85	5181	5229	5277	5326	5374	5422	5471	5519	5567	5616	
86	5664	5712	5761	5809	5857	5906	5954	6002	6051	6099	
87	6147	6196	6244	6292	6341	6389	6437	6486	6534	6582	
88	6631	6679	6727	6776	6824	6872	6921	6969	7017	7065	
89	7114	7162	7210	7259	7307	7355	7404	7452	7500	7549	
90	7597	7645	7694	7742	7790	7838	7887	7935	7983	8032	
8991	8080	8128	8177	8225	8273	8321	8370	8418	8466	8515	
92	8563	8611	8660	8708	8756	8804	8853	8901	8949	8998	
93	9046	9094	9143	9191	9239	9287	9336	9384	9432	9481	
94	9529	9577	9625	9674	9722	9770	9819	9867	9915	9963	
95	954 0012	0060	0108	0157	0205	0253	0301	0350	0398	0446	
96	0494	0543	0591	0639	0688	0736	0784	0832	0881	0929	
97	0977	1025	1074	1122	1170	1219	1267	1315	1363	1412	
98	1460	1508	1556	1605	1653	1701	1749	1798	1846	1894	
99	1943	1991	2039	2087	2136	2184	2232	2280	2329	2377	
9000	2425	2473	2522	2570	2618	2666	2715	2763	2811	2859	

No.	0	1	2	3	4	5	6	7	8	9	Diff.
9000	954 2425	2473	2522	2570	2618	2666	2715	2763	2811	2859	
01	2908	2956	3004	3052	3101	3149	3197	3245	3294	3342	
02	3390	3438	3487	3535	3583	3631	3680	3728	3776	3824	
03	3873	3921	3969	4017	4065	4114	4162	4210	4258	4307	
04	4355	4403	4451	4500	4548	4596	4644	4692	4741	4789	
05	4837	4885	4934	4982	5030	5078	5127	5175	5223	5271	
06	5319	5368	5416	5464	5512	5561	5609	5657	5705	5753	
07	5802	5850	5898	5946	5994	6043	6091	6139	6187	6236	
08	6284	6332	6380	6428	6477	6525	6573	6621	6669	6718	
09	6766	6814	6862	6910	6959	7007	7055	7103	7152	7200	
10	7248	7296	7344	7393	7441	7489	7537	7585	7634	7682	
9011	7730	7778	7826	7874	7923	7971	8019	8067	8115	8164	
12	8212	8260	8308	8356	8405	8453	8501	8549	8597	8646	
13	8694	8742	8790	8838	8886	8935	8983	9031	9079	9127	
14	9176	9224	9272	9320	9368	9416	9465	9513	9561	9609	
15	9657	9705	9754	9802	9850	9898	9946	9995	0043	0091	
16	955 0139	0187	0235	0284	0332	0380	0428	0476	0524	0573	
17	0621	0669	0717	0765	0813	0862	0910	0958	1006	1054	
18	1102	1150	1199	1247	1295	1343	1391	1439	1488	1536	
19	1584	1632	1680	1728	1776	1825	1873	1921	1969	2017	
20	2065	2114	2162	2210	2258	2306	2354	2402	2451	2499	
9021	2547	2595	2643	2691	2739	2788	2836	2884	2932	2980	
22	3028	3076	3125	3173	3221	3269	3317	3365	3413	3461	
23	3510	3558	3606	3654	3702	3750	3798	3846	3895	3943	
24	3991	4039	4087	4135	4183	4231	4280	4328	4376	4424	
25	4472	4520	4568	4616	4665	4713	4761	4809	4857	4905	
26	4953	5001	5050	5098	5146	5194	5242	5290	5338	5386	
27	5434	5483	5531	5579	5627	5675	5723	5771	5819	5867	
28	5916	5964	6012	6060	6108	6156	6204	6252	6300	6348	
29	6397	6445	6493	6541	6589	6637	6685	6733	6781	6829	
30	6878	6926	6974	7022	7070	7118	7166	7214	7262	7310	
9031	7358	7407	7455	7503	7551	7599	7647	7695	7743	7791	
32	7839	7887	7935	7984	8032	8080	8128	8176	8224	8272	
33	8320	8368	8416	8464	8512	8560	8609	8657	8705	8753	
34	8801	8849	8897	8945	8993	9041	9089	9137	9185	9234	
35	9282	9330	9378	9426	9474	9522	9570	9618	9666	9714	
36	9762	9810	9858	9906	9954	0003	0051	0099	0147	0195	
37	956 0243	0291	0339	0387	0435	0483	0531	0579	0627	0675	
38	0723	0771	0819	0868	0916	0964	1012	1060	1108	1156	
39	1204	1252	1300	1348	1396	1444	1492	1540	1588	1636	
40	1684	1732	1780	1828	1876	1925	1973	2021	2069	2117	
9041	2165	2213	2261	2309	2357	2405	2453	2501	2549	2597	
42	2645	2693	2741	2789	2837	2885	2933	2981	3029	3077	
43	3125	3173	3221	3269	3317	3365	3413	3461	3509	3558	
44	3606	3654	3702	3750	3798	3846	3894	3942	3990	4038	
45	4086	4134	4182	4230	4278	4326	4374	4422	4470	4518	
46	4566	4614	4662	4710	4758	4806	4854	4902	4950	4998	
47	5046	5094	5142	5190	5238	5286	5334	5382	5430	5478	
48	5526	5574	5622	5670	5718	5766	5814	5862	5910	5958	
49	6006	6054	6102	6150	6198	6246	6294	6342	6390	6438	
9050	6486	6534	6582	6630	6678	6726	6774	6822	6870	6918	

48
1 5
2 10
3 14
4 19
5 24
6 29
7 34
8 38
9 43

No.	0	1	2	3	4	5	6	7	8	9	Diff.
9050	956 6486	6534	6582	6630	6678	6726	6774	6822	6870	6918	
51	6966	7014	7062	7110	7158	7206	7254	7302	7349	7397	
52	7445	7493	7541	7589	7637	7685	7733	7781	7829	7877	
53	7925	7973	8021	8069	8117	8165	8213	8261	8309	8357	
54	8405	8453	8501	8549	8597	8645	8693	8741	8789	8837	
55	8885	8933	8980	9028	9076	9124	9172	9220	9268	9316	
56	9364	9412	9460	9508	9556	9604	9652	9700	9748	9796	
57	9844	9892	9940	9988	0035	0083	0131	0179	0227	0275	
58	957 0323	0371	0419	0467	0515	0563	0611	0659	0707	0755	
59	0803	0851	0898	0946	0994	1042	1090	1138	1186	1234	
60	1282	1330	1378	1426	1474	1522	1570	1618	1665	1713	
9061	1761	1809	1857	1905	1953	2001	2049	2097	2145	2193	
62	2241	2289	2336	2384	2432	2480	2528	2576	2624	2672	
63	2720	2768	2816	2864	2911	2959	3007	3055	3103	3151	
64	3199	3247	3295	3343	3391	3439	3486	3534	3582	3630	
65	3678	3726	3774	3822	3870	3918	3966	4013	4061	4109	
66	4157	4205	4253	4301	4349	4397	4445	4492	4540	4588	
67	4636	4684	4732	4780	4828	4876	4924	4971	5019	5067	
68	5115	5163	5211	5259	5307	5355	5402	5450	5498	5546	
69	5594	5642	5690	5738	5786	5833	5881	5929	5977	6025	
70	6073	6121	6169	6217	6264	6312	6360	6408	6456	6504	
9071	6552	6600	6647	6695	6743	6791	6839	6887	6935	6983	
72	7030	7078	7126	7174	7222	7270	7318	7366	7413	7461	
73	7509	7557	7605	7653	7701	7748	7796	7844	7892	7940	
74	7988	8036	8083	8131	8179	8227	8275	8323	8371	8418	
75	8466	8514	8562	8610	8658	8706	8753	8801	8849	8897	
76	8945	8993	9041	9088	9136	9184	9232	9280	9328	9376	
77	9423	9471	9519	9567	9615	9663	9710	9758	9806	9854	
78	9902	9950	9997	0045	0093	0141	0189	0237	0284	0332	
79	958 0380	0428	0476	0524	0571	0619	0667	0715	0763	0811	
80	0858	0906	0954	1002	1050	1098	1145	1193	1241	1289	
9081	1337	1385	1432	1480	1528	1576	1624	1672	1719	1767	
82	1815	1863	1911	1958	2006	2054	2102	2150	2198	2245	
83	2293	2341	2389	2437	2484	2532	2580	2628	2676	2723	
84	2771	2819	2867	2915	2962	3010	3058	3106	3154	3202	
85	3249	3297	3345	3393	3441	3488	3536	3584	3632	3680	
86	3727	3775	3823	3871	3919	3966	4014	4062	4110	4157	
87	4205	4253	4301	4349	4396	4444	4492	4540	4588	4635	
88	4683	4731	4779	4827	4874	4922	4970	5018	5065	5113	
89	5161	5209	5257	5304	5352	5400	5448	5495	5543	5591	
90	5639	5687	5734	5782	5830	5878	5925	5973	6021	6069	
9091	6117	6164	6212	6260	6308	6355	6403	6451	6499	6547	
92	6594	6642	6690	6738	6785	6833	6881	6929	6976	7024	
93	7072	7120	7167	7215	7263	7311	7358	7406	7454	7502	
94	7549	7597	7645	7693	7741	7788	7836	7884	7932	7979	
95	8027	8075	8123	8170	8218	8266	8314	8361	8409	8457	
96	8505	8552	8600	8648	8695	8743	8791	8839	8886	8934	
97	8982	9030	9077	9125	9173	9221	9268	9316	9364	9412	
98	9459	9507	9555	9603	9650	9698	9746	9793	9841	9889	
99	9937	9984	0032	0080	0128	0175	0223	0271	0318	0366	
9100	959 0414	0462	0509	0557	0605	0653	0700	0748	0796	0843	

48

1	5
2	10
3	14
4	19
5	24
6	29
7	34
8	38
9	43

No.	0	1	2	3	4	5	6	7	8	9	Diff.
9100	959 0414	0462	0509	0557	0605	0653	0700	0748	0796	0843	
01	0891	0939	0987	1034	1082	1130	1177	1225	1273	1321	
02	1368	1416	1464	1511	1559	1607	1655	1702	1750	1798	
03	1845	1893	1941	1989	2036	2084	2132	2179	2227	2275	
04	2322	2370	2418	2466	2513	2561	2609	2656	2704	2752	
05	2800	2847	2895	2943	2990	3038	3086	3133	3181	3229	
06	3276	3324	3372	3420	3467	3515	3563	3610	3658	3706	
07	3753	3801	3849	3896	3944	3992	4039	4087	4135	4183	
08	4230	4278	4326	4373	4421	4469	4516	4564	4612	4659	
09	4707	4755	4802	4850	4898	4945	4993	5041	5088	5136	
10	5184	5231	5279	5327	5374	5422	5470	5517	5565	5613	
9111	5660	5708	5756	5803	5851	5899	5946	5994	6042	6089	
12	6137	6185	6232	6280	6328	6375	6423	6471	6518	6566	
13	6614	6661	6709	6757	6804	6852	6900	6947	6995	7043	
14	7090	7138	7186	7233	7281	7328	7376	7424	7471	7519	
15	7567	7614	7662	7710	7757	7805	7853	7900	7948	7996	
16	8043	8091	8138	8186	8234	8281	8329	8377	8424	8472	
17	8520	8567	8615	8662	8710	8758	8805	8853	8901	8948	
18	8996	9044	9091	9139	9186	9234	9282	9329	9377	9425	
19	9472	9520	9567	9615	9663	9710	9758	9806	9853	9901	
20	9948	9996	0044	0091	0139	0186	0234	0282	0329	0377	
9121	960 0425	0472	0520	0567	0615	0663	0710	0758	0805	0853	
22	0901	0948	0996	1044	1091	1139	1186	1234	1282	1329	
23	1377	1424	1472	1520	1567	1615	1662	1710	1758	1805	
24	1853	1900	1948	1996	2043	2091	2138	2186	2234	2281	
25	2329	2376	2424	2472	2519	2567	2614	2662	2709	2757	
26	2805	2852	2900	2947	2995	3043	3090	3138	3185	3233	
27	3281	3328	3376	3423	3471	3518	3566	3614	3661	3709	
28	3756	3804	3851	3899	3947	3994	4042	4089	4137	4184	
29	4232	4280	4327	4375	4422	4470	4517	4565	4613	4660	
30	4708	4755	4803	4850	4898	4946	4993	5041	5088	5136	
9131	5183	5231	5279	5326	5374	5421	5469	5516	5564	5611	
32	5659	5707	5754	5802	5849	5897	5944	5992	6039	6087	
33	6135	6182	6230	6277	6325	6372	6420	6467	6515	6563	
34	6610	6658	6705	6753	6800	6848	6895	6943	6990	7038	
35	7086	7133	7181	7228	7276	7323	7371	7418	7466	7513	
36	7561	7608	7656	7704	7751	7799	7846	7894	7941	7989	
37	8036	8084	8131	8179	8226	8274	8321	8369	8416	8464	
38	8512	8559	8607	8654	8702	8749	8797	8844	8892	8939	
39	8987	9034	9082	9129	9177	9224	9272	9319	9367	9414	
40	9462	9509	9557	9605	9652	9700	9747	9795	9842	9890	
9141	9937	9985	0032	0080	0127	0175	0222	0270	0317	0365	
42	961 0412	0460	0507	0555	0602	0650	0697	0745	0792	0840	
43	0887	0935	0982	1030	1077	1125	1172	1220	1267	1315	
44	1362	1410	1457	1505	1552	1600	1647	1695	1742	1790	
45	1837	1885	1932	1980	2027	2075	2122	2170	2217	2264	
46	2312	2359	2407	2454	2502	2549	2597	2644	2692	2739	
47	2787	2834	2882	2929	2977	3024	3072	3119	3167	3214	
48	3262	3309	3357	3404	3451	3499	3546	3594	3641	3689	
49	3736	3784	3831	3879	3926	3974	4021	4069	4116	4163	
9150	4211	4258	4306	4353	4401	4448	4496	4543	4591	4638	

48
1 5
2 10
3 14
4 19
5 24
6 29
7 34
8 38
9 43

No.	0	1	2	3	4	5	6	7	8	9	Diff.
9150	961 4211	4258	4306	4353	4401	4448	4496	4543	4591	4638	
51	4686	4733	4780	4828	4875	4923	4970	5018	5065	5113	
52	5160	5208	5255	5302	5350	5397	5445	5492	5540	5587	
53	5635	5682	5730	5777	5824	5872	5919	5967	6014	6062	
54	6109	6157	6204	6251	6299	6346	6394	6441	6489	6536	
55	6583	6631	6678	6726	6773	6821	6868	6916	6963	7010	
56	7058	7105	7153	7200	7248	7295	7342	7390	7437	7485	
57	7532	7580	7627	7674	7722	7769	7817	7864	7912	7959	
58	8006	8054	8101	8149	8196	8243	8291	8338	8386	8433	
59	8481	8528	8575	8623	8670	8718	8765	8812	8860	8907	
60	8955	9002	9050	9097	9144	9192	9239	9287	9334	9381	
9161	9429	9476	9524	9571	9618	9666	9713	9761	9808	9855	
62	9903	9950	9998	0045	0092	0140	0187	0235	0282	0329	
63	962 0377	0424	0472	0519	0566	0614	0661	0709	0756	0803	
64	0851	0898	0946	0993	1040	1088	1135	1183	1230	1277	
65	1325	1372	1419	1467	1514	1562	1609	1656	1704	1751	
66	1799	1846	1893	1941	1988	2035	2083	2130	2178	2225	
67	2272	2320	2367	2414	2462	2509	2557	2604	2651	2699	
68	2746	2793	2841	2888	2936	2983	3030	3078	3125	3172	
69	3220	3267	3314	3362	3409	3457	3504	3551	3599	3646	
70	3693	3741	3788	3835	3883	3930	3978	4025	4072	4120	
9171	4167	4214	4262	4309	4356	4404	4451	4498	4546	4593	
72	4640	4688	4735	4783	4830	4877	4925	4972	5019	5067	
73	5114	5161	5209	5256	5303	5351	5398	5445	5493	5540	
74	5587	5635	5682	5729	5777	5824	5871	5919	5966	6013	
75	6061	6108	6155	6203	6250	6297	6345	6392	6439	6487	
76	6534	6581	6629	6676	6723	6771	6818	6865	6913	6960	
77	7007	7055	7102	7149	7197	7244	7291	7339	7386	7433	
78	7481	7528	7575	7622	7670	7717	7764	7812	7859	7906	
79	7954	8001	8048	8096	8143	8190	8238	8285	8332	8380	
80	8427	8474	8521	8569	8616	8663	8711	8758	8805	8853	
9181	8900	8947	8994	9042	9089	9136	9184	9231	9278	9326	
82	9373	9420	9467	9515	9562	9609	9657	9704	9751	9799	
83	9846	9893	9940	9988	0035	0082	0130	0177	0224	0271	
84	963 0319	0366	0413	0461	0508	0555	0602	0650	0697	0744	
85	0792	0839	0886	0933	0981	1028	1075	1123	1170	1217	
86	1264	1312	1359	1406	1454	1501	1548	1595	1643	1690	
87	1737	1784	1832	1879	1926	1974	2021	2068	2115	2163	
88	2210	2257	2304	2352	2399	2446	2493	2541	2588	2635	
89	2683	2730	2777	2824	2872	2919	2966	3013	3061	3108	
90	3155	3202	3250	3297	3344	3391	3439	3486	3533	3580	
9191	3628	3675	3722	3769	3817	3864	3911	3958	4006	4053	
92	4100	4147	4195	4242	4289	4336	4384	4431	4478	4525	
93	4573	4620	4667	4714	4762	4809	4856	4903	4951	4998	
94	5045	5092	5139	5187	5234	5281	5328	5376	5423	5470	
95	5517	5565	5612	5659	5706	5753	5801	5848	5895	5942	
96	5990	6037	6084	6131	6179	6226	6273	6320	6367	6415	
97	6462	6509	6556	6604	6651	6698	6745	6792	6840	6887	
98	6934	6981	7028	7076	7123	7170	7217	7265	7312	7359	
99	7406	7453	7501	7548	7595	7642	7689	7737	7784	7831	
9200	7878	7925	7973	8020	8067	8114	8161	8209	8256	8303	

47

1	5
2	9
3	14
4	19
5	24
6	28
7	33
8	38
9	42

No.	0	1	2	3	4	5	6	7	8	9	Diff.
9200	963 7878	7925	7973	8020	8067	8114	8161	8209	8256	8303	
01	8350	8398	8445	8492	8539	8586	8634	8681	8728	8775	
02	8822	8869	8917	8964	9011	9058	9105	9153	9200	9247	
03	9294	9341	9389	9436	9483	9530	9577	9625	9672	9719	
04	9766	9813	9860	9908	9955	0002	0049	0096	0144	0191	
05	964 0238	0285	0332	0379	0427	0474	0521	0568	0615	0663	
06	0710	0757	0804	0851	0898	0946	0993	1040	1087	1134	
07	1181	1229	1276	1323	1370	1417	1464	1512	1559	1606	
08	1653	1700	1747	1795	1842	1889	1936	1983	2030	2078	
09	2125	2172	2219	2266	2313	2361	2408	2455	2502	2549	
10	2596	2643	2691	2738	2785	2832	2879	2926	2974	3021	
9211	3068	3115	3162	3209	3256	3304	3351	3398	3445	3492	
12	3539	3586	3634	3681	3728	3775	3822	3869	3916	3964	
13	4011	4058	4105	4152	4199	4246	4294	4341	4388	4435	
14	4482	4529	4576	4623	4671	4718	4765	4812	4859	4906	
15	4953	5001	5048	5095	5142	5189	5236	5283	5330	5378	
16	5425	5472	5519	5566	5613	5660	5707	5755	5802	5849	
17	5896	5943	5990	6037	6084	6131	6179	6226	6273	6320	
18	6367	6414	6461	6508	6555	6603	6650	6697	6744	6791	
19	6838	6885	6932	6979	7027	7074	7121	7168	7215	7262	
20	7309	7356	7403	7451	7498	7545	7592	7639	7686	7733	47
9221	7780	7827	7874	7922	7969	8016	8063	8110	8157	8204	1　5
22	8251	8298	8345	8392	8440	8487	8534	8581	8628	8675	2　9
23	8722	8769	8816	8863	8910	8958	9005	9052	9099	9146	3　14
24	9193	9240	9287	9334	9381	9428	9475	9523	9570	9617	4　19
25	9664	9711	9758	9805	9852	9899	9946	9993	0040	0087	5　24
26	965 0135	0182	0229	0276	0323	0370	0417	0464	0511	0558	6　28
27	0605	0652	0699	0746	0793	0841	0888	0935	0982	1029	7　33
28	1076	1123	1170	1217	1264	1311	1358	1405	1452	1499	8　38
29	1546	1594	1641	1688	1735	1782	1829	1876	1923	1970	9　42
30	2017	2064	2111	2158	2205	2252	2299	2346	2393	2440	
9231	2488	2535	2582	2629	2676	2723	2770	2817	2864	2911	
32	2958	3005	3052	3099	3146	3193	3240	3287	3334	3381	
33	3428	3475	3522	3569	3617	3664	3711	3758	3805	3852	
34	3899	3946	3993	4040	4087	4134	4181	4228	4275	4322	
35	4369	4416	4463	4510	4557	4604	4651	4698	4745	4792	
36	4839	4886	4933	4980	5027	5074	5121	5168	5215	5262	
37	5309	5356	5403	5450	5497	5545	5592	5639	5686	5733	
38	5780	5827	5874	5921	5968	6015	6062	6109	6156	6203	
39	6250	6297	6344	6391	6438	6485	6532	6579	6626	6673	
40	6720	6767	6814	6861	6908	6955	7002	7049	7096	7143	
9241	7190	7237	7284	7331	7378	7425	7472	7519	7566	7613	
42	7660	7707	7754	7801	7848	7895	7942	7989	8036	8083	
43	8130	8177	8224	8270	8317	8364	8411	8458	8505	8552	
44	8599	8646	8693	8740	8787	8834	8881	8928	8975	9022	
45	9069	9116	9163	9210	9257	9304	9351	9398	9445	9492	
46	9539	9586	9633	9680	9727	9774	9821	9868	9915	9962	
47	966 0009	0056	0103	0149	0196	0243	0290	0337	0384	0431	
48	0478	0525	0572	0619	0666	0713	0760	0807	0854	0901	
49	0948	0995	1042	1089	1136	1183	1230	1276	1323	1370	
9250	1417	1464	1511	1558	1605	1652	1699	1746	1793	1840	

No.	0	1	2	3	4	5	6	7	8	9	Diff.
9250	966 1417	1464	1511	1558	1605	1652	1699	1746	1793	1840	
51	1887	1934	1981	2028	2075	2122	2168	2215	2262	2309	
52	2356	2403	2450	2497	2544	2591	2638	2685	2732	2779	
53	2826	2873	2919	2966	3013	3060	3107	3154	3201	3248	
54	3295	3342	3389	3436	3483	3530	3577	3623	3670	3717	
55	3764	3811	3858	3905	3952	3999	4046	4093	4140	4187	
56	4233	4280	4327	4374	4421	4468	4515	4562	4609	4656	
57	4703	4750	4796	4843	4890	4937	4984	5031	5078	5125	
58	5172	5219	5266	5312	5359	5406	5453	5500	5547	5594	
59	5641	5688	5735	5782	5828	5875	5922	5969	6016	6063	
60	6110	6157	6204	6251	6297	6344	6391	6438	6485	6532	
9261	6579	6626	6673	6720	6766	6813	6860	6907	6954	7001	
62	7048	7095	7142	7188	7235	7282	7329	7376	7423	7470	
63	7517	7564	7610	7657	7704	7751	7798	7845	7892	7939	
64	7985	8032	8079	8126	8173	8220	8267	8314	8360	8407	
65	8454	8501	8548	8595	8642	8689	8735	8782	8829	8876	
66	8923	8970	9017	9064	9110	9157	9204	9251	9298	9345	
67	9392	9438	9485	9532	9579	9626	9673	9720	9767	9813	
68	9860	9907	9954	0001	0048	0095	0141	0188	0235	0282	
69	967 0329	0376	0423	0469	0516	0563	0610	0657	0704	0750	
70	0797	0844	0891	0938	0985	1032	1078	1125	1172	1219	47
9271	1266	1313	1359	1406	1453	1500	1547	1594	1641	1687	1　5
72	1734	1781	1828	1875	1922	1968	2015	2062	2109	2156	2　9
73	2203	2249	2296	2343	2390	2437	2484	2530	2577	2624	3　14
74	2671	2718	2765	2811	2858	2905	2952	2999	3046	3092	4　19
75	3139	3186	3233	3280	3326	3373	3420	3467	3514	3561	5　24
76	3607	3654	3701	3748	3795	3841	3888	3935	3982	4029	6　28
77	4076	4122	4169	4216	4263	4310	4356	4403	4450	4497	7　33
78	4544	4590	4637	4684	4731	4778	4825	4871	4918	4965	8　38
79	5012	5059	5105	5152	5199	5246	5293	5339	5386	5433	9　42
80	5480	5527	5573	5620	5667	5714	5761	5807	5854	5901	
9281	5948	5995	6041	6088	6135	6182	6228	6275	6322	6369	
82	6416	6462	6509	6556	6603	6650	6696	6743	6790	6837	
83	6884	6930	6977	7024	7071	7117	7164	7211	7258	7305	
84	7351	7398	7445	7492	7538	7585	7632	7679	7726	7772	
85	7819	7866	7913	7959	8006	8053	8100	8146	8193	8240	
86	8287	8334	8380	8427	8474	8521	8567	8614	8661	8708	
87	8754	8801	8848	8895	8942	8988	9035	9082	9129	9175	
88	9222	9269	9316	9362	9409	9456	9503	9549	9596	9643	
89	9690	9736	9783	9830	9877	9923	9970	0017	0064	0110	
90	968 0157	0204	0251	0297	0344	0391	0438	0484	0531	0578	
9291	0625	0671	0718	0765	0812	0858	0905	0952	0999	1045	
92	1092	1139	1185	1232	1279	1326	1372	1419	1466	1513	
93	1559	1606	1653	1700	1746	1793	1840	1886	1933	1980	
94	2027	2073	2120	2167	2214	2260	2307	2354	2400	2447	
95	2494	2541	2587	2634	2681	2728	2774	2821	2868	2914	
96	2961	3008	3055	3101	3148	3195	3241	3288	3335	3382	
97	3428	3475	3522	3568	3615	3662	3709	3755	3802	3849	
98	3895	3942	3989	4036	4082	4129	4176	4222	4269	4316	
99	4362	4409	4456	4503	4549	4596	4643	4689	4736	4783	
9300	4829	4876	4923	4970	5016	5063	5110	5156	5203	5250	

No.	0	1	2	3	4	5	6	7	8	9	Diff.
9300	968 4829	4876	4923	4970	5016	5063	5110	5156	5203	5250	
01	5296	5343	5390	5437	5483	5530	5577	5623	5670	5717	
02	5763	5810	5857	5903	5950	5997	6043	6090	6137	6184	
03	6230	6277	6324	6370	6417	6464	6510	6557	6604	6650	
04	6697	6744	6790	6837	6884	6930	6977	7024	7070	7117	
05	7164	7210	7257	7304	7350	7397	7444	7490	7537	7584	
06	7630	7677	7724	7770	7817	7864	7910	7957	8004	8050	
07	8097	8144	8190	8237	8284	8330	8377	8424	8470	8517	
08	8564	8610	8657	8704	8750	8797	8844	8890	8937	8984	
09	9030	9077	9124	9170	9217	9264	9310	9357	9404	9450	
10	9497	9543	9590	9637	9683	9730	9777	9823	9870	9917	
9311	9963	$\overline{0010}$	$\overline{0057}$	$\overline{0103}$	$\overline{0150}$	$\overline{0196}$	$\overline{0243}$	$\overline{0290}$	$\overline{0336}$	$\overline{0383}$	
12	969 0430	0476	0523	0570	0616	0663	0709	0756	0803	0849	
13	0896	0943	0989	1036	1083	1129	1176	1222	1269	1316	
14	1362	1409	1456	1502	1549	1595	1642	1689	1735	1782	
15	1829	1875	1922	1968	2015	2062	2108	2155	2202	2248	
16	2295	2341	2388	2435	2481	2528	2574	2621	2668	2714	
17	2761	2808	2854	2901	2947	2994	3041	3087	3134	3180	
18	3227	3274	3320	3367	3413	3460	3507	3553	3600	3647	
19	3693	3740	3786	3833	3880	3926	3973	4019	4066	4113	
20	4159	4206	4252	4299	4346	4392	4439	4485	4532	4578	
9321	4625	4672	4718	4765	4811	4858	4905	4951	4998	5044	
22	5091	5138	5184	5231	5277	5324	5371	5417	5464	5510	
23	5557	5603	5650	5697	5743	5790	5836	5883	5929	5976	
24	6023	6069	6116	6162	6209	6256	6302	6349	6395	6442	
25	6488	6535	6582	6628	6675	6721	6768	6814	6861	6908	
26	6954	7001	7047	7094	7140	7187	7234	7280	7327	7373	
27	7420	7466	7513	7559	7606	7653	7699	7746	7792	7839	
28	7885	7932	7978	8025	8072	8118	8165	8211	8258	8304	
29	8351	8397	8444	8491	8537	8584	8630	8677	8723	8770	
30	8816	8863	8910	8956	9003	9049	9096	9142	9189	9235	
9331	9282	9328	9375	9422	9468	9515	9561	9608	9654	9701	
32	9747	9794	9840	9887	9933	9980	$\overline{0027}$	$\overline{0073}$	$\overline{0120}$	$\overline{0166}$	
33	970 0213	0259	0306	0352	0399	0445	0492	0538	0585	0631	
34	0678	0724	0771	0818	0864	0911	0957	1004	1050	1097	
35	1143	1190	1236	1283	1329	1376	1422	1469	1515	1562	
36	1608	1655	1701	1748	1794	1841	1888	1934	1981	2027	
37	2074	2120	2167	2213	2260	2306	2353	2399	2446	2492	
38	2539	2585	2632	2678	2725	2771	2818	2864	2911	2957	
39	3004	3050	3097	3143	3190	3236	3283	3329	3376	3422	
40	3469	3515	3562	3608	3655	3701	3748	3794	3841	3887	
9341	3934	3980	4027	4073	4120	4166	4213	4259	4306	4352	
42	4399	4445	4492	4538	4585	4631	4678	4724	4771	4817	
43	4863	4910	4956	5003	5049	5096	5142	5189	5235	5282	
44	5328	5375	5421	5468	5514	5561	5607	5654	5700	5747	
45	5793	5840	5886	5932	5979	6025	6072	6118	6165	6211	
46	6258	6304	6351	6397	6444	6490	6537	6583	6629	6676	
47	6722	6769	6815	6862	6908	6955	7001	7048	7094	7141	
48	7187	7233	7280	7326	7373	7419	7466	7512	7559	7605	
49	7652	7698	7745	7791	7837	7884	7930	7977	8023	8070	
9350	8116	8163	8209	8255	8302	8348	8395	8441	8488	8534	

Diff.

47

1	5
2	9
3	14
4	19
5	24
6	28
7	33
8	38
9	42

No.	0	1	2	3	4	5	6	7	8	9	Diff.
9350	970 8116	8163	8209	8255	8302	8348	8395	8441	8488	8534	
51	8581	8627	8673	8720	8766	8813	8859	8906	8952	8999	
52	9045	9091	9138	9184	9231	9277	9324	9370	9416	9463	
53	9509	9556	9602	9649	9695	9742	9788	9834	9881	9927	
54	9974	0020	0067	0113	0159	0206	0252	0299	0345	0391	
55	971 0438	0484	0531	0577	0624	0670	0716	0763	0809	0856	
56	0902	0949	0995	1041	1088	1134	1181	1227	1273	1320	
57	1366	1413	1459	1506	1552	1598	1645	1691	1738	1784	
58	1830	1877	1923	1970	2016	2062	2109	2155	2202	2248	
59	2294	2341	2387	2434	2480	2526	2573	2619	2666	2712	
60	2758	2805	2851	2898	2944	2990	3037	3083	3130	3176	
9361	3222	3269	3315	3362	3408	3454	3501	3547	3594	3640	
62	3686	3733	3779	3826	3872	3918	3965	4011	4057	4104	
63	4150	4197	4243	4289	4336	4382	4429	4475	4521	4568	
64	4614	4660	4707	4753	4800	4846	4892	4939	4985	5031	
65	5078	5124	5171	5217	5263	5310	5356	5402	5449	5495	
66	5542	5588	5634	5681	5727	5773	5820	5866	5912	5959	
67	6005	6052	6098	6144	6191	6237	6283	6330	6376	6422	
68	6469	6515	6562	6608	6654	6701	6747	6793	6840	6886	
69	6932	6979	7025	7071	7118	7164	7211	7257	7303	7350	
70	7396	7442	7489	7535	7581	7628	7674	7720	7767	7813	46
9371	7859	7906	7952	7998	8045	8091	8137	8184	8230	8276	1 5
72	8323	8369	8415	8462	8508	8554	8601	8647	8694	8740	2 9
73	8786	8833	8879	8925	8972	9018	9064	9111	9157	9203	3 14
74	9249	9296	9342	9388	9435	9481	9527	9574	9620	9666	4 18
75	9713	9759	9805	9852	9898	9944	9991	0037	0083	0130	5 23
											6 28
76	972 0176	0222	0269	0315	0361	0408	0454	0500	0547	0593	7 32
77	0639	0685	0732	0778	0824	0871	0917	0963	1010	1056	8 37
78	1102	1149	1195	1241	1288	1334	1380	1426	1473	1519	9 41
79	1565	1612	1658	1704	1751	1797	1843	1889	1936	1982	
80	2028	2075	2121	2167	2214	2260	2306	2352	2399	2445	
9381	2491	2538	2584	2630	2677	2723	2769	2815	2862	2908	
82	2954	3001	3047	3093	3139	3186	3232	3278	3325	3371	
83	3417	3463	3510	3556	3602	3649	3695	3741	3787	3834	
84	3880	3926	3973	4019	4065	4111	4158	4204	4250	4296	
85	4343	4389	4435	4482	4528	4574	4620	4667	4713	4759	
86	4805	4852	4898	4944	4991	5037	5083	5129	5176	5222	
87	5268	5314	5361	5407	5453	5500	5546	5592	5638	5685	
88	5731	5777	5823	5870	5916	5962	6008	6055	6101	6147	
89	6193	6240	6286	6332	6378	6425	6471	6517	6563	6610	
90	6656	6702	6748	6795	6841	6887	6933	6980	7026	7072	
9391	7118	7165	7211	7257	7303	7350	7396	7442	7488	7535	
92	7581	7627	7673	7720	7766	7812	7858	7905	7951	7997	
93	8043	8089	8136	8182	8228	8274	8321	8367	8413	8459	
94	8506	8552	8598	8644	8690	8737	8783	8829	8875	8922	
95	8968	9014	9060	9107	9153	9199	9245	9291	9338	9384	
96	9430	9476	9523	9569	9615	9661	9707	9754	9800	9846	
97	9892	9938	9985	0031	0077	0123	0170	0216	0262	0308	
98	973 0354	0401	0447	0493	0539	0585	0632	0678	0724	0770	
99	0816	0863	0909	0955	1001	1048	1094	1140	1186	1232	
9400	1279	1325	1371	1417	1463	1510	1556	1602	1648	1694	

No.	0	1	2	3	4	5	6	7	8	9	Diff.
9400	973 1279	1325	1371	1417	1463	1510	1556	1602	1648	1694	
01	1741	1787	1833	1879	1925	1972	2018	2064	2110	2156	
02	2202	2249	2295	2341	2387	2433	2480	2526	2572	2618	
03	2664	2711	2757	2803	2849	2895	2941	2988	3034	3080	
04	3126	3172	3219	3265	3311	3357	3403	3449	3496	3542	
05	3588	3634	3680	3727	3773	3819	3865	3911	3957	4004	
06	4050	4096	4142	4188	4234	4281	4327	4373	4419	4465	
07	4511	4558	4604	4650	4696	4742	4788	4835	4881	4927	
08	4973	5019	5065	5112	5158	5204	5250	5296	5342	5389	
09	5435	5481	5527	5573	5619	5665	5712	5758	5804	5850	
10	5896	5942	5989	6035	6081	6127	6173	6219	6265	6312	
9411	6358	6404	6450	6496	6542	6588	6635	6681	6727	6773	
12	6819	6865	6911	6958	7004	7050	7096	7142	7188	7234	
13	7281	7327	7373	7419	7465	7511	7557	7604	7650	7696	
14	7742	7788	7834	7880	7926	7973	8019	8065	8111	8157	
15	8203	8249	8295	8342	8388	8434	8480	8526	8572	8618	
16	8664	8711	8757	8803	8849	8895	8941	8987	9033	9080	
17	9126	9172	9218	9264	9310	9356	9402	9449	9495	·9541	
18	9587	9633	9679	9725	9771	9817	9864	9910	9956	$\overline{0}$002	
19	974 0048	0094	0140	0186	0232	0279	0325	0371	0417	0463	
20	0509	0555	0601	0647	0693	0740	0786	0832	0878	0924	
9421	0970	1016	1062	1108	1154	1201	1247	1293	1339	1385	
22	1431	1477	1523	1569	1615	1661	1708	1754	1800	1846	
23	1892	1938	1984	2030	2076	2122	2168	2215	2261	2307	
24	2353	2399	2445	2491	2537	2583	2629	2675	2721	2768	
25	2814	2860	2906	2952	2998	3044	3090	3136	3182	3228	
26	3274	3320	3367	3413	3459	3505	3551	3597	3643	3689	
27	3735	3781	3827	3873	3919	3965	4011	4058	4104	4150	
28	4196	4242	4288	4334	4380	4426	4472	4518	4564	4610	
29	4656	4702	4748	4795	4841	4887	4933	4979	5025	5071	
30	5117	5163	5209	5255	5301	5347	5393	5439	5485	5531	
9431	5577	5623	5670	5716	5762	5808	5854	5900	5946	5992	
32	6038	6084	6130	6176	6222	6268	6314	6360	6406	6452	
33	6498	6544	6590	6636	6683	6729	6775	6821	6867	6913	
34	6959	7005	7051	7097	7143	7189	7235	7281	7327	7373	
35	7419	7465	7511	7557	7603	7649	7695	7741	7787	7833	
36	7879	7925	7971	8017	8063	8109	8155	8201	8248	8294	
37	8340	8386	8432	8478	8524	8570	8616	8662	8708	8754	
38	8800	8846	8892	8938	8984	9030	9076	9122	9168	9214	
39	9260	9306	9352	9398	9444	9490	9536	9582	9628	9674	
40	9720	9766	9812	9858	9904	9950	9996	$\overline{0}$042	$\overline{0}$088	$\overline{0}$134	
9441	975 0180	0226	0272	0318	0364	0410	0456	0502	0548	0594	
42	0640	0686	0732	0778	0824	0870	0916	0962	1008	1054	
43	1100	1146	1192	1238	1284	1330	1376	1422	1468	1514	
44	1560	1606	1652	1698	1744	1790	1836	1882	1928	1974	
45	2020	2066	2112	2158	2204	2250	2296	2341	2387	2433	
46	2479	2525	2571	2617	2663	2709	2755	2801	2847	2893	
47	2939	2985	3031	3077	3123	3169	3215	3261	3307	3353	
48	3399	3445	3491	3537	3583	3629	3675	3721	3767	3813	
49	3858	3904	3950	3996	4042	4088	4134	4180	4226	4272	
9450	4318	4364	4410	4456	4502	4548	4594	4640	4686	4732	

46
1	5
2	9
3	14
4	18
5	23
6	28
7	32
8	37
9	41

No.	0	1	2	3	4	5	6	7	8	9	Diff.
9450	975 4318	4364	4410	4456	4502	4548	4594	4640	4686	4732	
51	4778	4824	4870	4915	4961	5007	5053	5099	5145	5191	
52	5237	5283	5329	5375	5421	5467	5513	5559	5605	5651	
53	5697	5743	5788	5834	5880	5926	5972	6018	6064	6110	
54	6156	6202	6248	6294	6340	6386	6432	6478	6523	6569	
55	6615	6661	6707	6753	6799	6845	6891	6937	6983	7029	
56	7075	7121	7166	7212	7258	7304	7350	7396	7442	7488	
57	7534	7580	7626	7672	7718	7763	7809	7855	7901	7947	
58	7993	8039	8085	8131	8177	8223	8269	8315	8360	8406	
59	8452	8498	8544	8590	8636	8682	8728	8774	8820	8865	
60	8911	8957	9003	9049	9095	9141	9187	9233	9279	9325	
9461	9370	9416	9462	9508	9554	9600	9646	9692	9738	9784	
62	9829	9875	9921	9967	0013	0059	0105	0151	0197	0243	
63	976 0288	0334	0380	0426	0472	0518	0564	0610	0656	0701	
64	0747	0793	0839	0885	0931	0977	1023	1069	1114	1160	
65	1206	1252	1298	1344	1390	1436	1481	1527	1573	1619	
66	1665	1711	1757	1803	1849	1894	1940	1986	2032	2078	
67	2124	2170	2216	2261	2307	2353	2399	2445	2491	2537	
68	2582	2628	2674	2720	2766	2812	2858	2904	2949	2995	
69	3041	3087	3133	3179	3225	3270	3316	3362	3408	3454	
70	3500	3546	3592	3637	3683	3729	3775	3821	3867	3913	
9471	3958	4004	4050	4096	4142	4188	4233	4279	4325	4371	
72	4417	4463	4509	4554	4600	4646	4692	4738	4784	4830	
73	4875	4921	4967	5013	5059	5105	5150	5196	5242	5288	
74	5334	5380	5425	5471	5517	5563	5609	5655	5701	5746	
75	5792	5838	5884	5930	5976	6021	6067	6113	6159	6205	
76	6251	6296	6342	6388	6434	6480	6525	6571	6617	6663	
77	6709	6755	6800	6846	6892	6938	6984	7030	7075	7121	
78	7167	7213	7259	7305	7350	7396	7442	7488	7534	7579	
79	7625	7671	7717	7763	7808	7854	7900	7946	7992	8038	
80	8083	8129	8175	8221	8267	8312	8358	8404	8450	8496	
9481	8541	8587	8633	8679	8725	8770	8816	8862	8908	8954	
82	9000	9045	9091	9137	9183	9229	9274	9320	9366	9412	
83	9458	9503	9549	9595	9641	9686	9732	9778	9824	9870	
84	9915	9961	0007	0053	0099	0144	0190	0236	0282	0328	
85	977 0373	0419	0465	0511	0556	0602	0648	0694	0740	0785	
86	0831	0877	0923	0969	1014	1060	1106	1152	1197	1243	
87	1289	1335	1381	1426	1472	1518	1564	1609	1655	1701	
88	1747	1793	1838	1884	1930	1976	2021	2067	2113	2159	
89	2204	2250	2296	2342	2388	2433	2479	2525	2571	2616	
90	2662	2708	2754	2799	2845	2891	2937	2982	3028	3074	
9491	3120	3165	3211	3257	3303	3349	3394	3440	3486	3532	
92	3577	3623	3669	3715	3760	3806	3852	3898	3943	3989	
93	4035	4081	4126	4172	4218	4264	4309	4355	4401	4447	
94	4492	4538	4584	4630	4675	4721	4767	4812	4858	4904	
95	4950	4995	5041	5087	5133	5178	5224	5270	5316	5361	
96	5407	5453	5499	5544	5590	5636	5681	5727	5773	5819	
97	5864	5910	5956	6002	6047	6093	6139	6184	6230	6276	
98	6322	6367	6413	6459	6505	6550	6596	6642	6687	6733	
99	6779	6825	6870	6916	6962	7007	7053	7099	7145	7190	
9500	7236	7282	7327	7373	7419	7465	7510	7556	7602	7647	

Diff. 46

1	5
2	9
3	14
4	18
5	23
6	28
7	32
8	37
9	41

No.	0	1	2	3	4	5	6	7	8	9	Diff.
9500	977 7236	7282	7327	7373	7419	7465	7510	7556	7602	7647	
01	7693	7739	7785	7830	7876	7922	7967	8013	8059	8105	
02	8150	8196	8242	8287	8333	8379	8424	8470	8516	8562	
03	8607	8653	8699	8744	8790	8836	8881	8927	8973	9019	
04	9064	9110	9156	9201	9247	9293	9338	9384	9430	9476	
05	9521	9567	9613	9658	9704	9750	9795	9841	9887	9932	
06	9978	0024	0069	0115	0161	0207	0252	0298	0344	0389	
07	978 0435	0481	0526	0572	0618	0663	0709	0755	0800	0846	
08	0892	0937	0983	1029	1074	1120	1166	1211	1257	1303	
09	1348	1394	1440	1485	1531	1577	1622	1668	1714	1760	
10	1805	1851	1897	1942	1988	2033	2079	2125	2170	2216	
9511	2262	2307	2353	2399	2444	2490	2536	2581	2627	2673	
12	2718	2764	2810	2855	2901	2947	2992	3038	3084	3129	
13	3175	3221	3266	3312	3358	3403	3449	3495	3540	3586	
14	3631	3677	3723	3768	3814	3860	3905	3951	3997	4042	
15	4088	4134	4179	4225	4270	4316	4362	4407	4453	4499	
16	4544	4590	4636	4681	4727	4773	4818	4864	4909	4955	
17	5001	5046	5092	5138	5183	5229	5274	5320	5366	5411	
18	5457	5503	5548	5594	5640	5685	5731	5776	5822	5868	
19	5913	5959	6005	6050	6096	6141	6187	6233	6278	6324	
20	6369	6415	6461	6506	6552	6598	6643	6689	6734	6780	
9521	6826	6871	6917	6962	7008	7054	7099	7145	7191	7236	
22	7282	7327	7373	7419	7464	7510	7555	7601	7647	7692	
23	7738	7783	7829	7875	7920	7966	8011	8057	8103	8148	
24	8194	8239	8285	8331	8376	8422	8467	8513	8559	8604	
25	8650	8695	8741	8787	8832	8878	8923	8969	9015	9060	
26	9106	9151	9197	9243	9288	9334	9379	9425	9470	9516	
27	9562	9607	9653	9698	9744	9790	9835	9881	9926	9972	
28	979 0017	0063	0109	0154	0200	0245	0291	0337	0382	0428	
29	0473	0519	0564	0610	0656	0701	0747	0792	0838	0883	
30	0929	0975	1020	1066	1111	1157	1202	1248	1294	1339	
9531	1385	1430	1476	1521	1567	1613	1658	1704	1749	1795	
32	1840	1886	1931	1977	2023	2068	2114	2159	2205	2250	
33	2296	2341	2387	2433	2478	2524	2569	2615	2660	2706	
34	2751	2797	2843	2888	2934	2979	3025	3070	3116	3161	
35	3207	3253	3298	3344	3389	3435	3480	3526	3571	3617	
36	3662	3708	3754	3799	3845	3890	3936	3981	4027	4072	
37	4118	4163	4209	4254	4300	4346	4391	4437	4482	4528	
38	4573	4619	4664	4710	4755	4801	4846	4892	4937	4983	
39	5028	5074	5120	5165	5211	5256	5302	5347	5393	5438	
40	5484	5529	5575	5620	5666	5711	5757	5802	5848	5893	
9541	5939	5984	6030	6076	6121	6167	6212	6258	6303	6349	
42	6394	6440	6485	6531	6576	6622	6667	6713	6758	6804	
43	6849	6895	6940	6986	7031	7077	7122	7168	7213	7259	
44	7304	7350	7395	7441	7486	7532	7577	7623	7668	7714	
45	7759	7805	7850	7896	7941	7987	8032	8078	8123	8169	
46	8214	8260	8305	8351	8396	8442	8487	8533	8578	8624	
47	8669	8715	8760	8806	8851	8897	8942	8988	9033	9079	
48	9124	9170	9215	9261	9306	9352	9397	9442	9488	9533	
49	9579	9624	9670	9715	9761	9806	9852	9897	9943	9988	
9550	980 0034	0079	0125	0170	0216	0261	0307	0352	0398	0443	

46

1	5
2	9
3	14
4	18
5	23
6	28
7	32
8	37
9	41

No.	0	1	2	3	4	5	6	7	8	9	Diff.
9550	980 0034	0079	0125	0170	0216	0261	0307	0352	0398	0443	
51	0488	0534	0579	0625	0670	0716	0761	0807	0852	0898	
52	0943	0989	1034	1080	1125	1170	1216	1261	1307	1352	
53	1398	1443	1489	1534	1580	1625	1671	1716	1761	1807	
54	1852	1898	1943	1989	2034	2080	2125	2171	2216	2261	
55	2307	2352	2398	2443	2489	2534	2580	2625	2671	2716	
56	2761	2807	2852	2898	2943	2989	3034	3080	3125	3170	
57	3216	3261	3307	3352	3398	3443	3489	3534	3579	3625	
58	3670	3716	3761	3807	3852	3897	3943	3988	4034	4079	
59	4125	4170	4215	4261	4306	4352	4397	4443	4488	4533	
60	4579	4624	4670	4715	4761	4806	4851	4897	4942	4988	
9561	5033	5079	5124	5169	5215	5260	5306	5351	5397	5442	
62	5487	5533	5578	5624	5669	5714	5760	5805	5851	5896	
63	5942	5987	6032	6078	6123	6169	6214	6259	6305	6350	
64	6396	6441	6486	6532	6577	6623	6668	6714	6759	6804	
65	6850	6895	6941	6986	7031	7077	7122	7168	7213	7258	
66	7304	7349	7395	7440	7485	7531	7576	7622	7667	7712	
67	7758	7803	7849	7894	7939	7985	8030	8075	8121	8166	
68	8212	8257	8302	8348	8393	8439	8484	8529	8575	8620	
69	8666	8711	8756	8802	8847	8892	8938	8983	9029	9074	
70	9119	9165	9210	9256	9301	9346	9392	9437	9482	9528	
9571	9573	9619	9664	9709	9755	9800	9845	9891	9936	9982	
72	981 0027	0072	0118	0163	0208	0254	0299	0344	0390	0435	
73	0481	0526	0571	0617	0662	0707	0753	0798	0844	0889	
74	0934	0980	1025	1070	1116	1161	1206	1252	1297	1342	
75	1388	1433	1479	1524	1569	1615	1660	1705	1751	1796	
76	1841	1887	1932	1977	2023	2068	2113	2159	2204	2250	
77	2295	2340	2386	2431	2476	2522	2567	2612	2658	2703	
78	2748	2794	2839	2884	2930	2975	3020	3066	3111	3156	
79	3202	3247	3292	3338	3383	3428	3474	3519	3564	3610	
80	3655	3700	3746	3791	3836	3882	3927	3972	4018	4063	
9581	4108	4154	4199	4244	4290	4335	4380	4426	4471	4516	
82	4562	4607	4652	4698	4743	4788	4834	4879	4924	4970	
83	5015	5060	5106	5151	5196	5241	5287	5332	5377	5423	
84	5468	5513	5559	5604	5649	5695	5740	5785	5831	5876	
85	5921	5966	6012	6057	6102	6148	6193	6238	6284	6329	
86	6374	6420	6465	6510	6555	6601	6646	6691	6737	6782	
87	6827	6873	6918	6963	7008	7054	7099	7144	7190	7235	
88	7280	7326	7371	7416	7461	7507	7552	7597	7643	7688	
89	7733	7778	7824	7869	7914	7960	8005	8050	8095	8141	
90	8186	8231	8277	8322	8367	8412	8458	8503	8548	8594	
9591	8639	8684	8729	8775	8820	8865	8911	8956	9001	9046	
92	9092	9137	9182	9228	9273	9318	9363	9409	9454	9499	
93	9544	9590	9635	9680	9726	9771	9816	9861	9907	9952	
94	9997	0042	0088	0133	0178	0223	0269	0314	0359	0405	
95	982 0450	0495	0540	0586	0631	0676	0721	0767	0812	0857	
96	0902	0948	0993	1038	1083	1129	1174	1219	1264	1310	
97	1355	1400	1445	1491	1536	1581	1626	1672	1717	1762	
98	1807	1853	1898	1943	1988	2034	2079	2124	2169	2215	
99	2260	2305	2350	2396	2441	2486	2531	2577	2622	2667	
9600	2712	2758	2803	2848	2893	2939	2984	3029	3074	3119	

45

1	5
2	9
3	14
4	18
5	23
6	27
7	32
8	36
9	41

No.	0	1	2	3	4	5	6	7	8	9	Diff.
9600	982 2712	2758	2803	2848	2893	2939	2984	3029	3074	3119	
01	3165	3210	3255	3300	3346	3391	3436	3481	3527	3572	
02	3617	3662	3707	3753	3798	3843	3888	3934	3979	4024	
03	4069	4115	4160	4205	4250	4295	4341	4386	4431	4476	
04	4522	4567	4612	4657	4702	4748	4793	4838	4883	4928	
05	4974	5019	5064	5109	5155	5200	5245	5290	5335	5381	
06	5426	5471	5516	5561	5607	5652	5697	5742	5787	5833	
07	5878	5923	5968	6014	6059	6104	6149	6194	6240	6285	
08	6330	6375	6420	6466	6511	6556	6601	6646	6692	6737	
09	6782	6827	6872	6918	6963	7008	7053	7098	7143	7189	
10	7234	7279	7324	7369	7415	7460	7505	7550	7595	7641	
9611	7686	7731	7776	7821	7867	7912	7957	8002	8047	8092	
12	8138	8183	8228	8273	8318	8364	8409	8454	8499	8544	
13	8589	8635	8680	8725	8770	8815	8860	8906	8951	8996	
14	9041	9086	9132	9177	9222	9267	9312	9357	9403	9448	
15	9493	9538	9583	9628	9674	9719	9764	9809	9854	9899	
16	9945	9990	$\overline{0035}$	$\overline{0080}$	$\overline{0125}$	$\overline{0170}$	$\overline{0216}$	$\overline{0261}$	$\overline{0306}$	$\overline{0351}$	
17	983 0396	0441	0486	0532	0577	0622	0667	0712	0757	0803	
18	0848	0893	0938	0983	1028	1073	1119	1164	1209	1254	
19	1299	1344	1390	1435	1480	1525	1570	1615	1660	1706	
20	1751	1796	1841	1886	1931	1976	2022	2067	2112	2157	
9621	2202	2247	2292	2338	2383	2428	2473	2518	2563	2608	
22	2654	2699	2744	2789	2834	2879	2924	2969	3015	3060	
23	3105	3150	3195	3240	3285	3331	3376	3421	3466	3511	
24	3556	3601	3646	3692	3737	3782	3827	3872	3917	3962	
25	4007	4053	4098	4143	4188	4233	4278	4323	4368	4413	
26	4459	4504	4549	4594	4639	4684	4729	4774	4819	4865	
27	4910	4955	5000	5045	5090	5135	5180	5225	5271	5316	
28	5361	5406	5451	5496	5541	5586	5631	5677	5722	5767	
29	5812	5857	5902	5947	5992	6037	6082	6128	6173	6218	
30	6263	6308	6353	6398	6443	6488	6533	6579	6624	6669	
9631	6714	6759	6804	6849	6894	6939	6984	7029	7075	7120	
32	7165	7210	7255	7300	7345	7390	7435	7480	7525	7571	
33	7616	7661	7706	7751	7796	7841	7886	7931	7976	8021	
34	8066	8111	8157	8202	8247	8292	8337	8382	8427	8472	
35	8517	8562	8607	8652	8697	8743	8788	8833	8878	8923	
36	8968	9013	9058	9103	9148	9193	9238	9283	9328	9374	
37	9419	9464	9509	9554	9599	9644	9689	9734	9779	9824	
38	9869	9914	9959	$\overline{0004}$	$\overline{0049}$	0095	0140	0185	0230	0275	
39	984 0320	0365	0410	0455	0500	0545	0590	0635	0680	0725	
40	0770	0815	0860	0905	0951	0996	1041	1086	1131	1176	
9641	1221	1266	1311	1356	1401	1446	1491	1536	1581	1626	
42	1671	1716	1761	1806	1851	1896	1942	1987	2032	2077	
43	2122	2167	2212	2257	2302	2347	2392	2437	2482	2527	
44	2572	2617	2662	2707	2752	2797	2842	2887	2932	2977	
45	3022	3067	3112	3157	3202	3247	3292	3338	3383	3428	
46	3473	3518	3563	3608	3653	3698	3743	3788	3833	3878	
47	3923	3968	4013	4058	4103	4148	4193	4238	4283	4328	
48	4373	4418	4463	4508	4553	4598	4643	4688	4733	4778	
49	4823	4868	4913	4958	5003	5048	5093	5138	5183	5228	
9650	5273	5318	5363	5408	5453	5498	5543	5588	5633	5678	

45

1	5
2	9
3	14
4	18
5	23
6	27
7	32
8	36
9	41

No.	0	1	2	3	4	5	6	7	8	9	Diff.
9650	984 5273	5318	5363	5408	5453	5498	5543	5588	5633	5678	
51	5723	5768	5813	5858	5903	5948	5993	6038	6083	6128	
52	6173	6218	6263	6308	6353	6398	6443	6488	6533	6578	
53	6623	6668	6713	6758	6803	6848	6893	6938	6983	7028	
54	7073	7118	7163	7208	7253	7298	7343	7388	7433	7478	
55	7523	7568	7613	7658	7703	7748	7793	7838	7883	7928	
56	7973	8018	8063	8107	8152	8197	8242	8287	8332	8377	
57	8422	8467	8512	8557	8602	8647	8692	8737	8782	8827	
58	8872	8917	8962	9007	9052	9097	9142	9187	9232	9277	
59	9322	9367	9412	9457	9502	9546	9591	9636	9681	9726	
60	9771	9816	9861	9906	9951	9996	0̅0̅4̅1̅	0̅0̅8̅6̅	0̅1̅3̅1̅	0̅1̅7̅6̅	
9661	985 0221	0266	0311	0356	0401	0446	0491	0535	0580	0625	
62	0670	0715	0760	0805	0850	0895	0940	0985	1030	1075	
63	1120	1165	1210	1255	1300	1345	1389	1434	1479	1524	
64	1569	1614	1659	1704	1749	1794	1839	1884	1929	1974	
65	2019	2064	2108	2153	2198	2243	2288	2333	2378	2423	
66	2468	2513	2558	2603	2648	2693	2737	2782	2827	2872	
67	2917	2962	3007	3052	3097	3142	3187	3232	3277	3321	
68	3366	3411	3456	3501	3546	3591	3636	3681	3726	3771	
69	3816	3861	3905	3950	3995	4040	4085	4130	4175	4220	
70	4265	4310	4355	4399	4444	4489	4534	4579	4624	4669	
9671	4714	4759	4804	4849	4893	4938	4983	5028	5073	5118	
72	5163	5208	5253	5298	5342	5387	5432	5477	5522	5567	
73	5612	5657	5702	5747	5791	5836	5881	5926	5971	6016	
74	6061	6106	6151	6196	6240	6285	6330	6375	6420	6465	
75	6510	6555	6600	6644	6689	6734	6779	6824	6869	6914	
76	6959	7003	7048	7093	7138	7183	7228	7273	7318	7363	
77	7407	7452	7497	7542	7587	7632	7677	7722	7766	7811	
78	7856	7901	7946	7991	8036	8081	8125	8170	8215	8260	
79	8305	8350	8395	8440	8484	8529	8574	8619	8664	8709	
80	8754	8798	8843	8888	8933	8978	9023	9068	9112	9157	
9681	9202	9247	9292	9337	9382	9426	9471	9516	9561	9606	
82	9651	9696	9740	9785	9830	9875	9920	9965	0̅0̅1̅0̅	0̅0̅5̅4̅	
83	986 0099	0144	0189	0234	0279	0324	0368	0413	0458	0503	
84	0548	0593	0637	0682	0727	0772	0817	0862	0907	0951	
85	0996	1041	1086	1131	1176	1220	1265	1310	1355	1400	
86	1445	1489	1534	1579	1624	1669	1714	1758	1803	1848	
87	1893	1938	1983	2027	2072	2117	2162	2207	2252	2296	
88	2341	2386	2431	2476	2521	2565	2610	2655	2700	2745	
89	2790	2834	2879	2924	2969	3014	3058	3103	3148	3193	
90	3238	3283	3327	3372	3417	3462	3507	3551	3596	3641	
9691	3686	3731	3776	3820	3865	3910	3955	4000	4044	4089	
92	4134	4179	4224	4268	4313	4358	4403	4448	4493	4537	
93	4582	4627	4672	4717	4761	4806	4851	4896	4941	4985	
94	5030	5075	5120	5165	5209	5254	5299	5344	5389	5433	
95	5478	5523	5568	5613	5657	5702	5747	5792	5836	5881	
96	5926	5971	6016	6060	6105	6150	6195	6240	6284	6329	
97	6374	6419	6464	6508	6553	6598	6643	6687	6732	6777	
98	6822	6867	6911	6956	7001	7046	7090	7135	7180	7225	
99	7270	7314	7359	7404	7449	7493	7538	7583	7628	7673	
9700	7717	7762	7807	7852	7896	7941	7986	8031	8076	8120	

45

1	5
2	9
3	14
4	18
5	23
6	27
7	32
8	36
9	41

No.	0	1	2	3	4	5	6	7	8	9	Diff.
9700	986 7717	7762	7807	7852	7896	7941	7986	8031	8076	8120	
01	8165	8210	8255	8299	8344	8389	8434	8478	8523	8568	
02	8613	8657	8702	8747	8792	8837	8881	8926	8971	9016	
03	9060	9105	9150	9195	9239	9284	9329	9374	9418	9463	
04	9508	9553	9597	9642	9687	9732	9776	9821	9866	9911	
05	9955	0000	0045	0090	0134	0179	0224	0269	0313	0358	
06	987 0403	0448	0492	0537	0582	0627	0671	0716	0761	0806	
07	0850	0895	0940	0985	1029	1074	1119	1163	1208	1253	
08	1298	1342	1387	1432	1477	1521	1566	1611	1656	1700	
09	1745	1790	1834	1879	1924	1969	2013	2058	2103	2148	
10	2192	2237	2282	2326	2371	2416	2461	2505	2550	2595	
9711	2640	2684	2729	2774	2818	2863	2908	2953	2997	3042	
12	3087	3131	3176	3221	3266	3310	3355	3400	3444	3489	
13	3534	3579	3623	3668	3713	3757	3802	3847	3892	3936	
14	3981	4026	4070	4115	4160	4205	4249	4294	4339	4383	
15	4428	4473	4517	4562	4607	4652	4696	4741	4786	4830	
16	4875	4920	4964	5009	5054	5099	5143	5188	5233	5277	
17	5322	5367	5411	5456	5501	5545	5590	5635	5680	5724	
18	5769	5814	5858	5903	5948	5992	6037	6082	6126	6171	
19	6216	6261	6305	6350	6395	6439	6484	6529	6573	6618	
20	6663	6707	6752	6797	6841	6886	6931	6975	7020	7065	
9721	7109	7154	7199	7243	7288	7333	7377	7422	7467	7511	
22	7556	7601	7646	7690	7735	7780	7824	7869	7914	7958	
23	8003	8048	8092	8137	8182	8226	8271	8316	8360	8405	
24	8450	8494	8539	8583	8628	8673	8717	8762	8807	8851	
25	8896	8941	8985	9030	9075	9119	9164	9209	9253	9298	
26	9343	9387	9432	9477	9521	9566	9611	9655	9700	9745	
27	9789	9834	9878	9923	9968	0012	0057	0102	0146	0191	
28	988 0236	0280	0325	0370	0414	0459	0503	0548	0593	0637	
29	0682	0727	0771	0816	0861	0905	0950	0994	1039	1084	
30	1128	1173	1218	1262	1307	1352	1396	1441	1485	1530	
9731	1575	1619	1664	1709	1753	1798	1842	1887	1932	1976	
32	2021	2066	2110	2155	2200	2244	2289	2333	2378	2423	
33	2467	2512	2556	2601	2646	2690	2735	2780	2824	2869	
34	2913	2958	3003	3047	3092	3136	3181	3226	3270	3315	
35	3360	3404	3449	3493	3538	3583	3627	3672	3716	3761	
36	3806	3850	3895	3939	3984	4029	4073	4118	4162	4207	
37	4252	4296	4341	4386	4430	4475	4519	4564	4609	4653	
38	4698	4742	4787	4831	4876	4921	4965	5010	5054	5099	
39	5144	5188	5233	5277	5322	5367	5411	5456	5500	5545	
40	5590	5634	5679	5723	5768	5813	5857	5902	5946	5991	
9741	6035	6080	6125	6169	6214	6258	6303	6348	6392	6437	
42	6481	6526	6570	6615	6660	6704	6749	6793	6838	6882	
43	6927	6972	7016	7061	7105	7150	7194	7239	7284	7328	
44	7373	7417	7462	7506	7551	7596	7640	7685	7729	7774	
45	7818	7863	7908	7952	7997	8041	8086	8130	8175	8220	
46	8264	8309	8353	8398	8442	8487	8531	8576	8621	8665	
47	8710	8754	8799	8843	8888	8932	8977	9022	9066	9111	
48	9155	9200	9244	9289	9333	9378	9423	9467	9512	9556	
49	9601	9645	9690	9734	9779	9823	9868	9913	9957	0002	
9750	989 0046	0091	0135	0180	0224	0269	0313	0358	0402	0447	

45
1	5
2	9
3	14
4	18
5	23
6	27
7	32
8	36
9	41

No.	0	1	2	3	4	5	6	7	8	9	Diff.
9750	989 0046	0091	0135	0180	0224	0269	0313	0358	0402	0447	
51	0492	0536	0581	0625	0670	0714	0759	0803	0848	0892	
52	0937	0981	1026	1071	1115	1160	1204	1249	1293	1338	
53	1382	1427	1471	1516	1560	1605	1649	1694	1738	1783	
54	1828	1872	1917	1961	2006	2050	2095	2139	2184	2228	
55	2273	2317	2362	2406	2451	2495	2540	2584	2629	2673	
56	2718	2762	2807	2851	2896	2940	2985	3030	3074	3119	
57	3163	3208	3252	3297	3341	3386	3430	3475	3519	3564	
58	3608	3653	3697	3742	3786	3831	3875	3920	3964	4009	
59	4053	4098	4142	4187	4231	4276	4320	4365	4409	4454	
60	4498	4543	4587	4632	4676	4721	4765	4810	4854	4899	
9761	4943	4988	5032	5077	5121	5166	5210	5255	5299	5344	
62	5388	5433	5477	5521	5566	5610	5655	5699	5744	5788	
63	5833	5877	5922	5966	6011	6055	6100	6144	6189	6233	
64	6278	6322	6367	6411	6456	6500	6545	6589	6634	6678	
65	6722	6767	6811	6856	6900	6945	6989	7034	7078	7123	
66	7167	7212	7256	7301	7345	7390	7434	7478	7523	7567	
67	7612	7656	7701	7745	7790	7834	7879	7923	7968	8012	
68	8057	8101	8145	8190	8234	8279	8323	8368	8412	8457	
69	8501	8546	8590	8634	8679	8723	8768	8812	8857	8901	
70	8946	8990	9035	9079	9123	9168	9212	9257	9301	9346	
9771	9390	9435	9479	9523	9568	9612	9657	9701	9746	9790	44
72	9835	9879	9923	9968	$\overline{0012}$	$\overline{0057}$	$\overline{0101}$	$\overline{0146}$	$\overline{0190}$	$\overline{0235}$	1 4
73	990 0279	0323	0368	0412	0457	0501	0546	0590	0634	0679	2 9
74	0723	0768	0812	0857	0901	0946	0990	1034	1079	1123	3 13
75	1168	1212	1257	1301	1345	1390	1434	1479	1523	1568	4 18
76	1612	1656	1701	1745	1790	1834	1878	1923	1967	2012	5 22
77	2056	2101	2145	2189	2234	2278	2323	2367	2411	2456	6 26
78	2500	2545	2589	2634	2678	2722	2767	2811	2856	2900	7 31
79	2944	2989	3033	3078	3122	3167	3211	3255	3300	3344	8 35
80	3389	3433	3477	3522	3566	3611	3655	3699	3744	3788	9 40
9781	3833	3877	3921	3966	4010	4055	4099	4143	4188	4232	
82	4277	4321	4365	4410	4454	4499	4543	4587	4632	4676	
83	4721	4765	4809	4854	4898	4942	4987	5031	5076	5120	
84	5164	5209	5253	5298	5342	5386	5431	5475	5520	5564	
85	5608	5653	5697	5741	5786	5830	5875	5919	5963	6008	
86	6052	6096	6141	6185	6230	6274	6318	6363	6407	6452	
87	6496	6540	6585	6629	6673	6718	6762	6806	6851	6895	
88	6940	6984	7028	7073	7117	7161	7206	7250	7295	7339	
89	7383	7428	7472	7516	7561	7605	7649	7694	7738	7783	
90	7827	7871	7916	7960	8004	8049	8093	8137	8182	8226	
9791	8271	8315	8359	8404	8448	8492	8537	8581	8625	8670	
92	8714	8758	8803	8847	8891	8936	8980	9025	9069	9113	
93	9158	9202	9246	9291	9335	9379	9424	9468	9512	9557	
94	9601	9645	9690	9734	9778	9823	9867	9911	9956	$\overline{0000}$	
95	991 0044	0089	0133	0177	0222	0266	0310	0355	0399	0443	
96	0488	0532	0576	0621	0665	0709	0754	0798	0842	0887	
97	0931	0975	1020	1064	1108	1153	1197	1241	1286	1330	
98	1374	1419	1463	1507	1552	1596	1640	1685	1729	1773	
99	1818	1862	1906	1951	1995	2039	2083	2128	2172	2216	
9800	2261	2305	2349	2394	2438	2482	2527	2571	2615	2660	

9800

No.	0	1	2	3	4	5	6	7	8	9	Diff.
9800	991 2261	2305	2349	2394	2438	2482	2527	2571	2615	2660	
01	2704	2748	2793	2837	2881	2925	2970	3014	3058	3103	
02	3147	3191	3236	3280	3324	3369	3413	3457	3501	3546	
03	3590	3634	3679	3723	3767	3812	3856	3900	3944	3989	
04	4033	4077	4122	4166	4210	4255	4299	4343	4387	4432	
05	4476	4520	4565	4609	4653	4697	4742	4786	4830	4875	
06	4919	4963	5007	5052	5096	5140	5185	5229	5273	5317	
07	5362	5406	5450	5495	5539	5583	5627	5672	5716	5760	
08	5805	5849	5893	5937	5982	6026	6070	6115	6159	6203	
09	6247	6292	6336	6380	6424	6469	6513	6557	6602	6646	
10	6690	6734	6779	6823	6867	6911	6956	7000	7044	7088	
9811	7133	7177	7221	7266	7310	7354	7398	7443	7487	7531	
12	7575	7620	7664	7708	7752	7797	7841	7885	7929	7974	
13	8018	8062	8107	8151	8195	8239	8284	8328	8372	8416	
14	8461	8505	8549	8593	8638	8682	8726	8770	8815	8859	
15	8903	8947	8992	9036	9080	9124	9169	9213	9257	9301	
16	9345	9390	9434	9478	9522	9567	9611	9655	9699	9744	
17	9788	9832	9876	9921	9965	$\overline{0009}$	$\overline{0053}$	$\overline{0098}$	$\overline{0142}$	$\overline{0186}$	
18	992 0230	0275	0319	0363	0407	0451	0496	0540	0584	0628	
19	0673	0717	0761	0805	0850	0894	0938	0982	1026	1071	
20	1115	1159	1203	1248	1292	1336	1380	1424	1469	1513	
9821	1557	1601	1646	1690	1734	1778	1822	1867	1911	1955	44
22	1999	2044	2088	2132	2176	2220	2265	2309	2353	2397	1 4
23	2441	2486	2530	2574	2618	2662	2707	2751	2795	2839	2 9
24	2884	2928	2972	3016	3060	3105	3149	3193	3237	3281	3 13
25	3326	3370	3414	3458	3502	3547	3591	3635	3679	3723	4 18
26	3768	3812	3856	3900	3944	3989	4033	4077	4121	4165	5 22
27	4210	4254	4298	4342	4386	4431	4475	4519	4563	4607	6 26
28	4651	4696	4740	4784	4828	4872	4917	4961	5005	5049	7 31
29	5093	5138	5182	5226	5270	5314	5358	5403	5447	5491	8 35
30	5535	5579	5624	5668	5712	5756	5800	5844	5889	5933	9 40
9831	5977	6021	6065	6109	6154	6198	6242	6286	6330	6375	
32	6419	6463	6507	6551	6595	6640	6684	6728	6772	6816	
33	6860	6905	6949	6993	7037	7081	7125	7170	7214	7258	
34	7302	7346	7390	7435	7479	7523	7567	7611	7655	7699	
35	7744	7788	7832	7876	7920	7964	8009	8053	8097	8141	
36	8185	8229	8274	8318	8362	8406	8450	8494	8538	8583	
37	8627	8671	8715	8759	8803	8847	8892	8936	8980	9024	
38	9068	9112	9156	9201	9245	9289	9333	9377	9421	9465	
39	9510	9554	9598	9642	9686	9730	9774	9819	9863	9907	
40	9951	9995	$\overline{0039}$	$\overline{0083}$	$\overline{0128}$	$\overline{0172}$	$\overline{0216}$	$\overline{0260}$	$\overline{0304}$	$\overline{0348}$	
9841	993 0392	0436	0481	0525	0569	0613	0657	0701	0745	0789	
42	0834	0878	0922	0966	1010	1054	1098	1142	1187	1231	
43	1275	1319	1363	1407	1451	1495	1540	1584	1628	1672	
44	1716	1760	1804	1848	1893	1937	1981	2025	2069	2113	
45	2157	2201	2245	2290	2334	2378	2422	2466	2510	2554	
46	2598	2642	2687	2731	2775	2819	2863	2907	2951	2995	
47	3039	3083	3128	3172	3216	3260	3304	3348	3392	3436	
48	3480	3524	3569	3613	3657	3701	3745	3789	3833	3877	
49	3921	3965	4010	4054	4098	4142	4186	4230	4274	4318	
9850	4362	4406	4450	4495	4539	4583	4627	4671	4715	4759	

No.	0	1	2	3	4	5	6	7	8	9	Diff.
9850	993 4362	4406	4450	4495	4539	4583	4627	4671	4715	4759	
51	4803	4847	4891	4935	4980	5024	5068	5112	5156	5200	
52	5244	5288	5332	5376	5420	5464	5509	5553	5597	5641	
53	5685	5729	5773	5817	5861	5905	5949	5993	6037	6082	
54	6126	6170	6214	6258	6302	6346	6390	6434	6478	6522	
55	6566	6610	6654	6698	6743	6787	6831	6875	6919	6963	
56	7007	7051	7095	7139	7183	7227	7271	7315	7359	7404	
57	7448	7492	7536	7580	7624	7668	7712	7756	7800	7844	
58	7888	7932	7976	8020	8064	8108	8152	8197	8241	8285	
59	8329	8373	8417	8461	8505	8549	8593	8637	8681	8725	
60	8769	8813	8857	8901	8945	8989	9033	9077	9122	9166	
9861	9210	9254	9298	9342	9386	9430	9474	9518	9562	9606	
62	9650	9694	9738	9782	9826	9870	9914	9958	0̄002	0̄046	
63	994 0090	0134	0178	0222	0266	0310	0355	0399	0443	0487	
64	0531	0575	0619	0663	0707	0751	0795	0839	0883	0927	
65	0971	1015	1059	1103	1147	1191	1235	1279	1323	1367	
66	1411	1455	1499	1543	1587	1631	1675	1719	1763	1807	
67	1851	1895	1939	1983	2027	2071	2115	2159	2203	2247	
68	2291	2335	2379	2423	2467	2511	2555	2599	2643	2687	
69	2731	2775	2820	2864	2908	2952	2996	3040	3084	3128	
70	3172	3216	3260	3304	3348	3392	3436	3480	3524	3568	
9871	3612	3656	3700	3744	3788	3831	3875	3919	3963	4007	44
72	4051	4095	4139	4183	4227	4271	4315	4359	4403	4447	1 4
73	4491	4535	4579	4623	4667	4711	4755	4799	4843	4887	2 9
74	4931	4975	5019	5063	5107	5151	5195	5239	5283	5327	3 13
75	5371	5415	5459	5503	5547	5591	5635	5679	5723	5767	4 18
76	5811	5855	5899	5943	5987	6031	6075	6119	6163	6207	5 22
77	6251	6295	6338	6382	6426	6470	6514	6558	6602	6646	6 26
78	6690	6734	6778	6822	6866	6910	6954	6998	7042	7086	7 31
79	7130	7174	7218	7262	7306	7350	7394	7438	7482	7525	8 35
80	7569	7613	7657	7701	7745	7789	7833	7877	7921	7965	9 40
9881	8009	8053	8097	8141	8185	8229	8273	8317	8361	8405	
82	8448	8492	8536	8580	8624	8668	8712	8756	8800	8844	
83	8888	8932	8976	9020	9064	9108	9152	9196	9239	9283	
84	9327	9371	9415	9459	9503	9547	9591	9635	9679	9723	
85	9767	9811	9855	9899	9942	9986	0̄030	0̄074	0̄118	0̄162	
86	995 0206	0250	0294	0338	0382	0426	0470	0514	0557	0601	
87	0645	0689	0733	0777	0821	0865	0909	0953	0997	1041	
88	1085	1128	1172	1216	1260	1304	1348	1392	1436	1480	
89	1524	1568	1612	1656	1699	1743	1787	1831	1875	1919	
90	1963	2007	2051	2095	2139	2182	2226	2270	2314	2358	
9891	2402	2446	2490	2534	2578	2622	2665	2709	2753	2797	
92	2841	2885	2929	2973	3017	3061	3104	3148	3192	3236	
93	3280	3324	3368	3412	3456	3500	3543	3587	3631	3675	
94	3719	3763	3807	3851	3895	3939	3982	4026	4070	4114	
95	4158	4202	4246	4290	4334	4377	4421	4465	4509	4553	
96	4597	4641	4685	4729	4772	4816	4860	4904	4948	4992	
97	5036	5080	5123	5167	5211	5255	5299	5343	5387	5431	
98	5474	5518	5562	5606	5650	5694	5738	5782	5825	5869	
99	5913	5957	6001	6045	6089	6133	6176	6220	6264	6308	
9900	6352	6396	6440	6484	6527	6571	6615	6659	6703	6747	

No.	0	1	2	3	4	5	6	7	8	9	Diff.
9900	995 6352	6396	6440	6484	6527	6571	6615	6659	6703	6747	
01	6791	6834	6878	6922	6966	7010	7054	7098	7142	7185	
02	7229	7273	7317	7361	7405	7449	7492	7536	7580	7624	
03	7668	7712	7755	7799	7843	7887	7931	7975	8019	8062	
04	8106	8150	8194	8238	8282	8326	8369	8413	8457	8501	
05	8545	8589	8632	8676	8720	8764	8808	8852	8896	8939	
06	8983	9027	9071	9115	9159	9202	9246	9290	9334	9378	
07	9422	9465	9509	9553	9597	9641	9685	9728	9772	9816	
08	9860	9904	9948	9991	0035	0079	0123	0167	0211	0254	
09	996 0298	0342	0386	0430	0474	0517	0561	0605	0649	0693	
10	0737	0780	0824	0868	0912	0956	0999	1043	1087	1131	
9911	1175	1219	1262	1306	1350	1394	1438	1481	1525	1569	
12	1613	1657	1701	1744	1788	1832	1876	1920	1963	2007	
13	2051	2095	2139	2182	2226	2270	2314	2358	2402	2445	
14	2489	2533	2577	2621	2664	2708	2752	2796	2840	2883	
15	2927	2971	3015	3059	3102	3146	3190	3234	3278	3321	
16	3365	3409	3453	3497	3540	3584	3628	3672	3716	3759	
17	3803	3847	3891	3935	3978	4022	4066	4110	4153	4197	
18	4241	4285	4329	4372	4416	4460	4504	4548	4591	4635	
19	4679	4723	4766	4810	4854	4898	4942	4985	5029	5073	
20	5117	5161	5204	5248	5292	5336	5379	5423	5467	5511	44
9921	5554	5598	5642	5686	5730	5773	5817	5861	5905	5948	1 4
22	5992	6036	6080	6124	6167	6211	6255	6299	6342	6386	2 9
23	6430	6474	6517	6561	6605	6649	6693	6736	6780	6824	3 13
24	6868	6911	6955	6999	7043	7086	7130	7174	7218	7261	4 18
25	7305	7349	7393	7436	7480	7524	7568	7611	7655	7699	5 22
26	7743	7786	7830	7874	7918	7961	8005	8049	8093	8136	6 26 7 31
27	8180	8224	8268	8311	8355	8399	8443	8486	8530	8574	8 35
28	8618	8661	8705	8749	8793	8836	8880	8924	8968	9011	9 40
29	9055	9099	9143	9186	9230	9274	9318	9361	9405	9449	
30	9492	9536	9580	9624	9667	9711	9755	9799	9842	9886	
9931	9930	9974	0017	0061	0105	0148	0192	0236	0280	0323	
32	997 0367	0411	0455	0498	0542	0586	0629	0673	0717	0761	
33	0804	0848	0892	0936	0979	1023	1067	1110	1154	1198	
34	1242	1285	1329	1373	1416	1460	1504	1548	1591	1635	
35	1679	1722	1766	1810	1854	1897	1941	1985	2028	2072	
36	2116	2160	2203	2247	2291	2334	2378	2422	2465	2509	
37	2553	2597	2640	2684	2728	2771	2815	2859	2903	2946	
38	2990	3034	3077	3121	3165	3208	3252	3296	3340	3383	
39	3427	3471	3514	3558	3602	3645	3689	3733	3776	3820	
40	3864	3908	3951	3995	4039	4082	4126	4170	4213	4257	
9941	4301	4344	4388	4432	4475	4519	4563	4607	4650	4694	
42	4738	4781	4825	4869	4912	4956	5000	5043	5087	5131	
43	5174	5218	5262	5305	5349	5393	5436	5480	5524	5567	
44	5611	5655	5699	5742	5786	5830	5873	5917	5961	6004	
45	6048	6092	6135	6179	6223	6266	6310	6354	6397	6441	
46	6485	6528	6572	6616	6659	6703	6747	6790	6834	6878	
47	6921	6965	7009	7052	7096	7139	7183	7227	7270	7314	
48	7358	7401	7445	7489	7532	7576	7620	7663	7707	7751	
49	7794	7838	7882	7925	7969	8013	8056	8100	8144	8187	
9950	8231	8274	8318	8362	8405	8449	8493	8536	8580	8624	

No.	0	1	2	3	4	5	6	7	8	9	Diff.
9950	997 8231	8274	8318	8362	8405	8449	8493	8536	8580	8624	
51	8667	8711	8755	8798	8842	8885	8929	8973	9016	9060	
52	9104	9147	9191	9235	9278	9322	9365	9409	9453	9496	
53	9540	9584	9627	9671	9715	9758	9802	9845	9889	9933	
54	9976	0020	0064	0107	0151	0195	0238	0282	0325	0369	
55	998 0413	0456	0500	0544	0587	0631	0674	0718	0762	0805	
56	0849	0893	0936	0980	1023	1067	1111	1154	1198	1241	
57	1285	1329	1372	1416	1460	1503	1547	1590	1634	1678	
58	1721	1765	1808	1852	1896	1939	1983	2026	2070	2114	
59	2157	2201	2245	2288	2332	2375	2419	2463	2506	2550	
60	2593	2637	2681	2724	2768	2811	2855	2899	2942	2986	
9961	3029	3073	3117	3160	3204	3247	3291	3335	3378	3422	
62	3465	3509	3553	3596	3640	3683	3727	3771	3814	3858	
63	3901	3945	3988	4032	4076	4119	4163	4206	4250	4294	
64	4337	4381	4424	4468	4512	4555	4599	4642	4686	4729	
65	4773	4817	4860	4904	4947	4991	5035	5078	5122	5165	
66	5209	5252	5296	5340	5383	5427	5470	5514	5557	5601	
67	5645	5688	5732	5775	5819	5862	5906	5950	5993	6037	
68	6080	6124	6167	6211	6255	6298	6342	6385	6429	6472	
69	6516	6560	6603	6647	6690	6734	6777	6821	6864	6908	
70	6952	6995	7039	7082	7126	7169	7213	7256	7300	7344	
9971	7387	7431	7474	7518	7561	7605	7648	7692	7736	7779	43
72	7823	7866	7910	7953	7997	8040	8084	8128	8171	8215	1 4
73	8258	8302	8345	8389	8432	8476	8519	8563	8607	8650	2 9
74	8694	8737	8781	8824	8868	8911	8955	8998	9042	9086	3 13
75	9129	9173	9216	9260	9303	9347	9390	9434	9477	9521	4 17
76	9564	9608	9651	9695	9739	9782	9826	9869	9913	9956	5 22
77	999 0000	0043	0087	0130	0174	0217	0261	0304	0348	0391	6 26
78	0435	0479	0522	0566	0609	0653	0696	0740	0783	0827	7 30
79	0870	0914	0957	1001	1044	1088	1131	1175	1218	1262	8 34
80	1305	1349	1392	1436	1479	1523	1567	1610	1654	1697	9 39
9981	1741	1784	1828	1871	1915	1958	2002	2045	2089	2132	
82	2176	2219	2263	2306	2350	2393	2437	2480	2524	2567	
83	2611	2654	2698	2741	2785	2828	2872	2915	2959	3002	
84	3046	3089	3133	3176	3220	3263	3307	3350	3394	3437	
85	3481	3524	3568	3611	3655	3698	3742	3785	3829	3872	
86	3916	3959	4003	4046	4090	4133	4177	4220	4264	4307	
87	4350	4394	4437	4481	4524	4568	4611	4655	4698	4742	
88	4785	4829	4872	4916	4959	5003	5046	5090	5133	5177	
89	5220	5264	5307	5351	5394	5438	5481	5524	5568	5611	
90	5655	5698	5742	5785	5829	5872	5916	5959	6003	6046	
9991	6090	6133	6177	6220	6263	6307	6350	6394	6437	6481	
92	6524	6568	6611	6655	6698	6742	6785	6828	6872	6915	
93	6959	7002	7046	7089	7133	7176	7220	7263	7307	7350	
94	7393	7437	7480	7524	7567	7611	7654	7698	7741	7785	
95	7828	7871	7915	7958	8002	8045	8089	8132	8176	8219	
96	8262	8306	8349	8393	8436	8480	8523	8567	8610	8653	
97	8697	8740	8784	8827	8871	8914	8958	9001	9044	9088	
98	9131	9175	9218	9262	9305	9349	9392	9435	9479	9522	
99	9566	9609	9653	9696	9739	9783	9826	9870	9913	9957	
10000	0000 0000	0434	0869	1303	1737	2171	2606	3040	3474	3908	

REDUCTION OF COMMON TO NATURAL LOGARITHMS.

Com. Log.	Natural Log.	Com. Log.	Natural Log	Com. Log.	Natural Log.	Com. Log.	Natural Log.
1	2·80258509	26	59·86721242	51	117·43183974	76	174·99646707
2	4·60517019	27	62·16979751	52	119·73442484	77	177·29905216
3	6·90775528	28	64·47238260	53	122·03700993	78	179·60163725
4	9·21034037	29	66·77496770	54	124·33959502	79	181·90422235
5	11·51292546	30	69·07755279	55	126·64218011	80	184·20680744
6	13·81551056	31	71·38013788	56	128·94476521	81	186·50939253
7	16·11809565	32	73·68272298	57	131·24735030	82	188·81197763
8	18·42068074	33	75·98530807	58	133·54993539	83	191·11456272
9	20·72326584	34	78·28789316	59	135·85252049	84	193·41714781
10	23·02585093	35	80·59047825	60	138·15510558	85	195·71973290
11	25·32843602	36	82·89306335	61	140·45769067	86	198·02231800
12	27·63102112	37	85·19564844	62	142·76027576	87	200·32490309
13	29·93360621	38	87·49822353	63	145·06286086	88	202·62748818
14	32·23619130	39	89·80081863	64	147·36544595	89	204·93007328
15	34·53877639	40	92·10340372	65	149·66803104	90	207·23265837
16	36·84136149	41	94·40598881	66	151·97061614	91	209·53524346
17	39·14394658	42	96·70857391	67	154·27320123	92	211·83782856
18	41·44653167	43	99·01115900	68	156·57578632	93	214·14041365
19	43·74911677	44	101·31374409	69	158·87837142	94	216·44299874
20	46·05170186	45	103·61632918	70	161·18095651	95	218·74558383
21	48·35428695	46	105·91891428	71	163·48354160	96	221·04816893
22	50·65687205	47	108·22149937	72	165·78612670	97	223·35075402
23	52·95945714	48	110·52408446	73	168·08871179	98	225·65333911
24	55·26204223	49	112·82666956	74	170·39129688	99	227·95592421
25	57·56462732	50	115·12925465	75	172·69388197	100	230·25850930

REDUCTION OF NATURAL TO COMMON LOGARITHMS.

Nat. Log.	Common Log.	Nat. Log.	Common Log.	Nat. Log.	Common Log.	Nat Log.	Common Log.
1	0·43429448	26	11·29165653	51	22·14901858	76	33·00638062
2	0·86858896	27	11·72595101	52	22·58331306	77	33·44067511
3	1·30288345	28	12·16024549	53	23·01760754	78	33·87496959
4	1·73717793	29	12·59453998	54	23·45190202	79	34·30926407
5	2·17147241	30	13·02883446	55	23·88619650	80	34·74355855
6	2·60576689	31	13·46312894	56	24·32049099	81	35·17785303
7	3·04006137	32	13·89742342	57	24·75478547	82	35·61214752
8	3·47435586	33	14·33171790	58	25·18907995	83	36·04644200
9	3·90865034	34	14·76601238	59	25·62337443	84	36·48073648
10	4·34294482	35	15·20030687	60	26·05766891	85	36·91503096
11	4·77723930	36	15·63460135	61	26·49196340	86	37·34932544
12	5·21153378	37	16·06889583	62	26·92625788	87	37·78361993
13	5·64582826	38	16·50319031	63	27·36055236	88	38·21791441
14	6·08012275	39	16·93748479	64	27·79484684	89	38·65220889
15	6·51441723	40	17·37177928	65	28·22914132	90	39·08650337
16	6·94871171	41	17·80607376	66	28·66343581	91	39·52079785
17	7·38300619	42	18·24036824	67	29·09773029	92	39·95509234
18	7·81730067	43	18·67466272	68	29·53202477	93	40·38938682
19	8·25159516	44	19·10895720	69	29·96631925	94	40·82368130
20	8·68588964	45	19·54325169	70	30·40061373	95	41·25797578
21	9·12018412	46	19·97754617	71	30·83490822	96	41·69227026
22	9·55447860	47	20·41184065	72	31·26920270	97	42·12656474
23	9·98877308	48	20·84613513	73	31·70349718	98	42·56085923
24	10·42306757	49	21·28042961	74	32·13779166	99	42·99515371
25	10·85736205	50	21·71472410	75	32·57208614	100	43·42944819

REDUCTION OF COMMON TO NATURAL LOGARITHMS
AND *VICE VERSA*

For occasional use these reductions may be effected by means of the conversion tables on page 182. The procedure for using these will be evident from the two examples given below. It is obviously most important that the values in the successive lines are placed in their correct decimal position.

1. Find the natural logarithm corresponding to the common logarithm 0·9542425.

Com. Log.				Nat. Log.
·95	...	...	...	2·18745584
42	...	...	...	967086
42	...	...	...	9671
5	...	...	...	115
·9542425				2·19722456

2. Find the common logarithm corresponding to the natural logarithm 2·19722456.

Nat. Log.				Com. Log.
2·	...	...	...	·86858896
19	...	...	...	8251595
72	...	...	...	312692
24	...	...	...	1042
56	...	...	...	24
2·19722456				·95424249

If the common logarithm to be converted is that of a number less than 1, say 0·09, it will almost certainly be in the form $\bar{2}$·9542425, where the characteristic is negative ($\bar{2}$) and the mantissa positive (·9542425). In such a case the converted value (positive) of the mantissa (2·19722456) must be *subtracted* from the tabular value (expressed as negative) of the characteristic (i.e. $-4\cdot60517019$), the whole resulting natural logarithm being negative ($-2\cdot40794563$).

To convert a wholly negative natural logarithm to the corresponding common logarithm, it is probably easier to convert the whole of the former. The resulting common logarithm is then wholly negative, but may be rendered in the conventional form by subtracting the mantissa from 1, and increasing the characteristic by 1 and marking it negative (e.g. $\bar{2}$).

Frequent users of natural logarithms will find it much more to their advantage to use the table of natural logarithms given in *Chambers Six-Figure Mathematical Tables*.

No.	Square	Cube	Reciprocal	Multiples of π	No.	Square	Cube	Reciprocal	Multiples of π
x	x^2	x^3	x^{-1}		x	x^2	x^3	x^{-1}	
1	1	1	1·0000 000	3·142	50	25 00	125 000	0·0200 000	157·080
2	4	8	0·5000 000	6·283	51	26 01	132 651	·0196 078	160·221
3	9	27	·3333 333	9·425	52	27 04	140 608	·0192 308	163·363
4	16	64	·2500 000	12·566	53	28 09	148 877	·0188 679	166·504
					54	29 16	157 464	·0185 185	169·646
5	25	125	0·2000 000	15·708	55	30 25	166 375	0·0181 818	172·788
6	36	216	·1666 667	18·850	56	31 36	175 616	·0178 571	175·929
7	49	343	·1428 571	21·991	57	32 49	185 193	·0175 439	179·071
8	64	512	·1250 000	25·133	58	33 64	195 112	·0172 414	182·212
9	81	729	·1111 111	28·274	59	34 81	205 379	·0169 492	185·354
10	1 00	1 000	0·1000 000	31·416	60	36 00	216 000	0·0166 667	188·496
11	1 21	1 331	·0909 091	34·558	61	37 21	226 981	·0163 934	191·637
12	1 44	1 728	·0833 333	37·699	62	38 44	238 328	·0161 290	194·779
13	1 69	2 197	·0769 231	40·841	63	39 69	250 047	·0158 730	197·920
14	1 96	2 744	·0714 286	43·982	64	40 96	262 144	·0156 250	201·062
15	2 25	3 375	0·0666 667	47·124	65	42 25	274 625	0·0153 846	204·204
16	2 56	4 096	·0625 000	50·265	66	43 56	287 496	·0151 515	207·345
17	2 89	4 913	·0588 235	53·407	67	44 89	300 763	·0149 254	210·487
18	3 24	5 832	·0555 556	56·549	68	46 24	314 432	·0147 059	213·628
19	3 61	6 859	·0526 316	59·690	69	47 61	328 509	·0144 928	216·770
20	4 00	8 000	0·0500 000	62·832	70	49 00	343 000	0·0142 857	219·911
21	4 41	9 261	·0476 190	65·973	71	50 41	357 911	·0140 845	223·053
22	4 84	10 648	·0454 545	69·115	72	51 84	373 248	·0138 889	226·195
23	5 29	12 167	·0434 783	72·257	73	53 29	389 017	·0136 986	229·336
24	5 76	13 824	·0416 667	75·398	74	54 76	405 224	·0135 135	232·478
25	6 25	15 625	0·0400 000	78·540	75	56 25	421 875	0·0133 333	235·619
26	6 76	17 576	·0384 615	81·681	76	57 76	438 976	·0131 579	238·761
27	7 29	19 683	·0370 370	84·823	77	59 29	456 533	·0129 870	241·903
28	7 84	21 952	·0357 143	87·965	78	60 84	474 552	·0128 205	245·044
29	8 41	24 389	·0344 828	91·106	79	62 41	493 039	·0126 582	248·186
30	9 00	27 000	0·0333 333	94·248	80	64 00	512 000	0·0125 000	251·327
31	9 61	29 791	·0322 581	97·389	81	65 61	531 441	·0123 457	254·469
32	10 24	32 768	·0312 500	100·531	82	67 24	551 368	·0121 951	257·611
33	10 89	35 937	·0303 030	103·673	83	68 89	571 787	·0120 482	260·752
34	11 56	39 304	·0294 118	106·814	84	70 56	592 704	·0119 048	263·894
35	12 25	42 875	0·0285 714	109·956	85	72 25	614 125	0·0117 647	267·035
36	12 96	46 656	·0277 778	113·097	86	73 96	636 056	·0116 279	270·177
37	13 69	50 653	·0270 270	116·239	87	75 69	658 503	·0114 943	273·319
38	14 44	54 872	·0263 158	119·381	88	77 44	681 472	·0113 636	276·460
39	15 21	59 319	·0256 410	122·522	89	79 21	704 969	·0112 360	279·602
40	16 00	64 000	0·0250 000	125·664	90	81 00	729 000	0·0111 111	282·743
41	16 81	68 921	·0243 902	128·805	91	82 81	753 571	·0109 890	285·885
42	17 64	74 088	·0238 095	131·947	92	84 64	778 688	·0108 696	289·027
43	18 49	79 507	·0232 558	135·088	93	86 49	804 357	·0107 527	292·168
44	19 36	85 184	·0227 273	138·230	94	88 36	830 584	·0106 383	295·310
45	20 25	91 125	0·0222 222	141·372	95	90 25	857 375	0·0105 263	298·451
46	21 16	97 336	·0217 391	144·513	96	92 16	884 736	·0104 167	301·593
47	22 09	103 823	·0212 766	147·655	97	94 09	912 673	·0103 093	304·734
48	23 04	110 592	·0208 333	150·796	98	96 04	941 192	·0102 041	307·876
49	24 01	117 649	·0204 082	153·938	99	98 01	970 299	·0101 010	311·018
50	25 00	125 000	0·0200 000	157·080	100	100 00	1000 000	0·0100 000	314·159

LOGARITHMIC SINES, TANGENTS, AND SECANTS.
(PAGES 183-227.)

The logarithmic sines, tangents, &c. are the logarithms of the numbers that express the lengths of these lines for any given arc, supposing the radius of the circle to be 10,000,000,000.

(22) To FIND THE LOGARITHMIC SINE OF AN ARC.

(a) When the arc contains degrees and minutes only.

If the number of degrees is under 45, find them at the top of the table, and in the column marked sine at the top, and opposite to the number of minutes in the left-hand column, is the required logarithm.

If the number of degrees exceeds 45, and is less than 90, they will be found at the foot of the page; and in the column marked sine at the foot, and opposite to the number of minutes in the right-hand column, will be found the required logarithm.

The same rule applies to tangents, cotangents, and all the other trigonometrical quantities.

EXAMPLES.

The log. sine of			36° 24′	is	9·7733614
"	"	secant	36° 50′	"	10·0967023
"	"	cotangent	53° 36′	"	9·8676228
"	"	tangent	53° 40′	"	10·1334356

(b) When the arc contains degrees, minutes, and seconds.

Find the logarithm for the number of degrees and minutes as before, and multiply the tabular difference in the difference column next this logarithm by the number of seconds; divide the product by 60, and add the quotient as a proportional part to the preceding logarithm.

If the given quantity is a cosine, cotangent, or cosecant, the proportional part for the seconds must be subtracted from the logarithm for the degrees and minutes.

EXAMPLES.

1. Find the logarithmic tangent of 36° 40′ 50″.

Log. tan. 36° 40′	=	9·8718486
Proportional part = 2637 × $\frac{50}{60}$	=	2197
Log. tan. 36° 40′ 50″	=	9·8720683

2. To find the logarithmic cosecant of 53° 20′ 24″.

Log. cosec. 53° 20′	=	10·0957589
Prop. part = 940 × $\frac{24}{60}$	=	− 376
Log. cosec. 53° 20′ 24″	=	10·0957213

The rule depends on this principle: The tabular difference for any logarithm is the difference between it and the next higher, and therefore is the difference corresponding to $60''$; hence if D denote the tabular difference, and d the proportional part to be added for the number of seconds n, then

$$60 : n = \mathrm{D} : d, \text{ and } d = \frac{n\mathrm{D}}{60}$$

This supposes the differences to be constant, which is nearly the case for several consecutive logarithms.

(23) To FIND THE NUMBER OF DEGREES, MINUTES, AND SECONDS CORRES-PONDING TO ANY LOGARITHMIC SINE, TANGENT, OR SECANT.

(a) When the logarithm is found in the tables.

The number of degrees will be found at the top or foot of the page, according as the name of the logarithm is at the top or foot of the column, and the minutes are found in the proper column, as in (22).

EXAMPLES.

1. The log. tan. 9·8673583 corresponds to 36° 23′.
2. The log. cos. 9·7776128 corresponds to 53° 11′.

(b) When the given logarithm is not found in the table exactly.

Find the next lower logarithm in the proper column, and take the degrees and minutes corresponding to it when it is a sine, tangent, or secant; find the difference between this logarithm and the given one; multiply this difference by 60, and divide by the tabular difference, and the quotient will be the number of seconds required.

(c) When the given logarithm is that of a cosine, cotangent, or cosecant, it is to be taken from the next higher logarithm in the table, and the seconds found from the remainder as above.

EXAMPLES.

1. Find the degrees, minutes, and seconds corresponding to the logarithmic sine 9·9047423.

Next lower	9·9047106 = log. sine 53° 25′
Given log.	9·9047423
Difference =	317, and tab. diff. = 937.

Hence $n = \dfrac{317 \times 60}{937} = 20''\cdot3$

and $\qquad 9\cdot9047423 = \text{log. sine } 53° 25' 20''\cdot3.$

2. Find the number of degrees, minutes, and seconds corresponding to the logarithmic cosecant 10·2280452.

Next higher	10·2281850 = log. cosec. 36° 15′
Given log.	10·2280452
Difference	1398, and tab. diff. = 1722

Hence $n = \dfrac{1398 \times 60}{1722} = 48''\cdot7$

and $\qquad$ $10 \cdot 2280452 = $ log. cosec. $36° 15' 48'' \cdot 7$

The rule depends on the proportion in article 22, or

$$D : d = 60 : n, \text{ and } n = \frac{60d}{D}.$$

RULES FOR SMALL ARCS.

(24) It should be noted that both the logarithmic and the natural sines and cosecants of angles near 90° vary slowly and nearly regularly, and that, while the logarithmic cosines and secants of such angles vary rapidly and irregularly, their natural cosines and secants vary rapidly but nearly regularly. It therefore follows that both the logarithmic and natural tangents and cotangents of angles near 90° vary rapidly and irregularly.

On the other hand, in the case of small angles, the natural and logarithmic cosines vary slowly and regularly, the logarithmic sines vary rapidly and irregularly, while the natural sines vary rapidly and regularly.

Hence in trigonometrical equations where exactitude of solution is desired, a sine formula should not be used if the answer or root is an angle of near 90°; while if the answer is a small angle, a cosine formula should not be used.

It is evident from the above that when dealing with small angles, say, under 3°, containing fractional portions of a minute, ordinary interpolation by proportional parts will not give exact results, and one or other of the following rules must be used:

(25) To FIND THE LOGARITHMIC SINE OF A SMALL ARC.

To the logarithm of the arc reduced to seconds add $4 \cdot 6855749$, and from the sum subtract one-third of its logarithmic secant, the index of the latter logarithm being previously diminished by 10; the remainder is the required logarithmic sine.

EXAMPLE.

Find the logarithmic sine of $1° 44' 36'' \cdot 8$.

$$a = 1° \ 44' \ 36'' \cdot 8 = 6276'' \cdot 8, \text{ and its log.} \ = \ 3 \cdot 7977383$$
$$\text{Constant number} \ = \ 4 \cdot 6855749$$

$$\overline{\qquad\qquad\qquad 8 \cdot 4833132}$$

$$- \tfrac{1}{3} \ (\text{Log. sec. } a - 10) = \tfrac{1}{3} \times \cdot 0002011 \ = \ 0 \cdot 0000670$$

Hence log. sine of $1° 44' 36'' \cdot 8$ $\qquad = \ 8 \cdot 4832462$

This may also be determined by the use of natural sines, thus:

$$\text{Sine } 1°44' \ = \ 0 \cdot 0302478$$
$$\text{Proportional part} = 2907 \times \frac{36 \cdot 8}{60} \ = \ 1783$$

$$\overline{\qquad\qquad\qquad 0 \cdot 0304261}$$

Hence log. sine $1° 44' 36'' \cdot 8$ $\qquad = \ \text{log. } 0 \cdot 0304261$
$$= \ \overline{2} \cdot 4832463$$

(26) To find the logarithmic tangent of a small arc.

To the logarithm of the arc reduced to seconds add 4·6855749, and two-thirds of the logarithmic secant, the index of the latter logarithm being previously diminished by 10; the sum is the required logarithmic tangent.

EXAMPLE.

Find the logarithmic tangent of 1° 44′ 36″·8.

$$a = 1° \ 44′ \ 36″·8 = 6276″·8, \text{ and its log.} = 3·7977383$$
$$\text{Constant number} = 4·6855749$$
$$\rule{3cm}{0.4pt}$$
$$8·4833132$$
$$+ \tfrac{2}{3} (\text{Log. sec. } a - 10) = \tfrac{2}{3} \times ·0002011 = 0·0001341$$
$$\rule{3cm}{0.4pt}$$

Hence log. tangent of 1° 44′ 36″·8 = 8·4834473

(27) To find a small arc of which the logarithmic sine is given.

To the given logarithmic sine add 5̄·3144251, and one-third of the corresponding logarithmic secant, the index of the latter logarithm being previously diminished by 10; the sum is the logarithm of the number of seconds in the arc.

EXAMPLE.

Find the arc corresponding to the logarithmic sine 8·4832462.

The arc is found in the ordinary way to be 1° 44′ 36″, and the logarithmic secant of this arc is 10·0002011; hence

Given log. sine	=	8·4832462
Constant number	=	5̄·3144251
$\tfrac{1}{3}$ (Log. sec. − 10)	=	0·0000670
L 6276″·8	=	3·7977383

Hence $a = 6276″·8 = 1° \ 44′ \ 36″·8$.

(28) To find a small arc, of which the logarithmic tangent is given.

To the given logarithmic tangent add 5̄·3144251, and from this sum subtract two-thirds of the corresponding logarithmic secant, previously diminishing its index by 10; the remainder is the logarithm of the number of seconds in the arc.

EXAMPLE.

The logarithmic tangent of a small arc is 8·4834473; required the arc.

It is found in the usual way that the arc is nearly 1° 44′ 36″, and its log. secant = 10·0002011.

Given log. tangent	=	8·4834473
Constant number	=	5̄·3144251
		3·7978724
$-\tfrac{2}{3}$ (Log. sec. − 10)	=	0·0001341
L 6276·8	=	3·7977383

Hence $a = 6276″·8 = 1° \ 44′ \ 36″·8$.

CIRCULAR MEASURE OF ANGLES, OR RADIANS
ARCS TO RADIUS = 1. (Pages 228–239.)

(33) To find the circular measure of an arc, the angular measure of which is given; and conversely.

(a) Find the degrees in the arc at the top of the page, and the minutes at the left-hand side; then, under the degrees and opposite the minutes, is the length sought; but if the angle contain seconds, to this result add the number opposite the seconds on the right-hand side of the page, and the sum will be the length sought.

(b) Conversely: When the length or circular measure is given, find the given length in the table; then the degrees at the top and the minutes at the left-hand side give the angular measure sought when the length is found in the table exactly; but if the length is not found exactly in the table, take the degrees and minutes corresponding to the next less arc, and subtract this next less arc from the given one, and opposite the remainder on the right-hand side of the page will be found the seconds in the arc.

This table provides a rapid and exact means of converting angles from circular measure to degrees, minutes, and seconds, and conversely.

It is obvious that the parts for seconds of arc, tabulated at the right-hand side of the pages, are uniformly applicable to any angle, irrespective of its magnitude.

The table is specially useful in railway surveying, because the length of any circular curve can be found almost by inspection, if the radius and the central angle θ be given.

EXAMPLE.

The angle of deviation formed by two straights of a railway is 10° 50′ 20″. The straights are to be connected by a curve of radius 4000 feet. What is the length of the curve ?

Circular measure of 10° 50′	=	0·1890773
Difference for 20″	=	0·0000970
		0·1891743
Radius	=	4000
Length of curve	=	756·7 feet

NATURAL SINES, COSINES, VERSED SINES, AND CHORDS.
(Pages 240–284.)

(34) The natural sines, cosines, versed sines, chords, &c., contained in this table, are the lengths of these functions of arcs of a circle whose radius = 1. They are all decimal fractions, though the point is not prefixed except where they are equal to or greater than 1, in which case the point is inserted. Or, they are the lengths of the same functions, in integers, to radius = 10,000,000.

The natural sines and cosines of arcs, also the arcs for any given natural sines or cosines, are found from the table by the same method as that used for logarithmic sines and cosines.

The natural sines and cosines of arcs are easily found from the logarithmic sines and cosines, by merely subtracting 10 from the indices of the latter, and then the number corresponding to this logarithm is the natural sine or cosine required. In the same manner the natural tangents, secants, &c. can be found.

Let s = the natural sine of an arc,
and S = the sine of the same arc, whose logarithm is
              the logarithmic sine :
then S = 10,000,000,000 s
and LS = 10 + L s
or L s = LS − 10.

EXAMPLE.

Given the logarithmic sine of 36° 44′, namely, 9·7767676, to find the natural sine of the same arc.

$$
\begin{array}{lll}
\text{L sine 36° 44′} & = & 9\cdot7767676 \\
\text{Subtract} & & 10\cdot \\
\hline
\text{L nat. sine} & & \bar{1}\cdot7767676 \\
\text{Hence natural sine} & = & \cdot5980915
\end{array}
$$

If the chord of an arc greater than 90° be required, take *twice* the natural sine of *half* that arc, and it will be the chord required. Or, let c =the chord of its supplement; then the square root of $(2+c)$ $(2-c)$ =the required chord, i.e. the chord sought = $\sqrt{4-c^2}$.

Note.—This table can be used for finding the length of a degree of longitude corresponding to any given latitude; thus, multiply the natural cosine of the given latitude by 60, and the product will be the length of a degree of longitude in geographical or nautical miles; or multiply the same by 69·121, and the product will be the length in English miles, the earth being considered as a sphere of radius 3960 miles.

The table of chords is convenient for finding the lengths of the chords required in setting out railway and other curves.

EXAMPLE.

What is the chordal distance between two points 250 ft. apart along a curve of 700 ft. radius?

θ, the central angle, is $\dfrac{250}{700}$, or 0·3571, which, by table, p. 230, is 20° 27′ 30″, the chord of which, by table, is 0·3551. 0·3551 × 700 =248·57 ft. the chordal length required.

The table of chords is also useful in setting out angles, either on paper, or in the field by chain only. The versines are useful in reducing chainages taken on the slope, with a 'long' or 'compound' chain, to their horizontal equivalents.

EXAMPLE.

Find the horizontal equivalent of 463·7 ft. measured on a slope of 3° 46′.

$$\text{Horizontal correction} = 463\text{·}7\ (1 - \cos.\ 3°\ 46')$$
$$= 463\text{·}7 \times \text{versine}\ 3°\ 46'$$
$$= 463\text{·}7 \times 0\text{·}002$$
$$= 0\text{·}9$$

Therefore horizontal distance = 462·8 ft.

NATURAL TANGENTS AND COTANGENTS, SECANTS AND COSECANTS.   (PAGES 285-310.)

(35) This cable is used in the same manner as the table of natural sines and cosines, namely, the degrees are found at the top of the page, and the minutes of the angle at the left-hand side of the page, when the quantity sought is a *tangent* or *secant;* but the degrees must be found at the bottom of the page, and the minutes at the right-hand side of the page, when the quantity sought is a *cotangent* or *cosecant;* the quantity sought will then be found at the angle of intersection of these columns, or it is the only quantity which is common to both columns.

If the given angle contain seconds, find the difference between the quantity corresponding to the minutes in the given angle, and that corresponding to the next higher minute, which will give the change for 1′ = 60″, which call D, and let d be the correction corresponding to the seconds in the given angle, which call s; then

$$60'' : s'' :: D : d$$
$$\therefore d = \frac{s\,D}{60} = \text{the correction sought.}$$

This correction must be applied by *addition* if the quantity sought be a tangent or secant, but by *subtraction* if it be a cotangent or cosecant.

If the angle be sought which corresponds to a given tangent or secant, cotangent or cosecant, find the next less, if it be not found exactly in the table, when the given quantity is a tangent or secant, but the next greater when it is a cotangent or cosecant, and take the difference between it and the given quantity, which call d; also take the difference between this tabular quantity and that corresponding to the next higher minute, which call D; then

$$D : d :: 60'' : s \text{ (the seconds sought)},$$
$$\therefore s = \frac{60\,d}{D}$$

EXAMPLE I.

Find the natural tangent of 42° 17′ 43″.

Natural tangent of 42° 17′	=	·9093984 +
" " 42° 18′	=	·9099300
Difference for 60″ = D	=	5316
$d = \dfrac{43\,\mathrm{D}}{60} = \dfrac{43 \times 5316}{60}$	=	3810 +
∴ natural tangent 42° 17′ 43″	=	·9097794

EXAMPLE II.

Find the natural cotangent of 42° 17′ 43″.

Natural cotangent of 42° 17′	=	1·0996281 +
" " 42° 18′	=	1·0989857
Difference for 60″ = D	=	6424
$d = \dfrac{43\,\mathrm{D}}{60} = \dfrac{43 \times 6424}{60}$	=	4604 −
∴ natural cotangent 42° 17′ 43″	=	1·0991677

EXAMPLE III.

Find the angle whose natural tangent is ·7342856.

Given natural tangent	=	·7342856
Natural tangent 36° 17′	=	·7341253
∴ d	=	1603
Also natural tangent 36° 18′	=	·7345730
∴ D	=	4477

But $s = \dfrac{60\,d}{\mathrm{D}} = \dfrac{60 \times 1603}{4477} = \dfrac{96180}{4477} = 21″·5.$

Hence ·7342856 = natural tangent of 36° 17′ 21″·5.

EXAMPLE IV.

Find the angle whose natural cotangent is 2·1583764.

Given natural cotangent	=	2·1583764
Natural cotangent of 24° 51′	=	2·1592476
∴ d	=	8712
Also natural cotangent of 24° 52′	=	2·1576015
∴ D	=	16461

But $s = \dfrac{60 \times d}{\mathrm{D}} = \dfrac{60 \times 8712}{16461} = \dfrac{522720}{16461} = 31″·8.$

Hence 2·1583764 = natural cotangent of 24° 51′ 31″·8.

(36) The calculations for the secants and cosecants, where the angle involves seconds, is the same as those given above for tangents and cotangents.

′	Sine	Diff.	Cosec.	Tang.	Diff.	Cotang.	Secant	D.	Cosine	′
0	In. Neg.	Infin.	Infinite	In. Neg.	Infin.	Infinite	10·0000000	0	10·0000000	60
1	6·4637261		13·5362739	6·4637261		13·5362739	10·0000000	0	10·0000000	59
2	6·7647561	3010300	13·2352439	6·7647562	3010301	13·2352438	10·0000001	1	9·9999999	58
3	6·9408473	1760912	13·0591527	6·9408475	1760913	13·0591525	10·0000002	1	9·9999998	57
4	7·0657860	1249387	12·9342140	7·0657863	1249388	12·9342137	10·0000003	1	9·9999997	56
5	7·1626960	969100	12·8373040	7·1626964	969101	12·8373036	10·0000005	2	9·9999995	55
		791811			791814			1		
6	7·2418771		12·7581229	7·2418778		12·7581222	10·0000007	2	9·9999993	54
7	7·3088239	669468	12·6911761	7·3088248	669470	12·6911752	10·0000009	3	9·9999991	53
8	7·3668157	579918	12·6331843	7·3668169	579921	12·6331831	10·0000012	3	9·9999988	52
9	7·4179681	511524	12·5820319	7·4179696	511527	12·5820304	10·0000015	3	9·9999985	51
10	7·4637255	457574	12·5362745	7·4637273	457577	12·5362727	10·0000018	3	9·9999982	50
		413926			413930			3		
11	7·5051181		12·4948819	7·5051203		12·4948797	10·0000022	4	9·9999978	49
12	7·5429065	377884	12·4570935	7·5429091	377888	12·4570909	10·0000026	4	9·9999974	48
13	7·5776684	347619	12·4223316	7·5776715	347624	12·4223285	10·0000031	5	9·9999969	47
14	7·6098530	321846	12·3901470	7·6098566	321851	12·3901434	10·0000036	5	9·9999964	46
15	7·6398160	299630	12·3601840	7·6398201	299635	12·3601799	10·0000041	5	9·9999959	45
		280285			280291			6		
16	7·6678445		12·3321555	7·6678492		12·3321508	10·0000047	6	9·9999953	44
17	7·6941733	263288	12·3058267	7·6941786	263294	12·3058214	10·0000053	6	9·9999947	43
18	7·7189966	248233	12·2810034	7·7190026	248240	12·2809974	10·0000060	7	9·9999940	42
19	7·7424775	234809	12·2575225	7·7424841	234815	12·2575159	10·0000066	6	9·9999934	41
20	7·7647537	222762	12·2352463	7·7647610	222769	12·2352390	10·0000073	7	9·9999927	40
		211890			211898			8		
21	7·7859427		12·2140573	7·7859508		12·2140492	10·0000081	8	9·9999919	39
22	7·8061458	202031	12·1938542	7·8061547	202039	12·1938453	10·0000089	8	9·9999911	38
23	7·8254507	193049	12·1745493	7·8254604	193057	12·1745396	10·0000097	9	9·9999903	37
24	7·8439338	184831	12·1560662	7·8439444	184840	12·1560556	10·0000106	9	9·9999894	36
25	7·8616623	177285	12·1383377	7·8616738	177294	12·1383262	10·0000115	9	9·9999885	35
		170330			170339			9		
26	7·8786953		12·1213047	7·8787077		12·1212923	10·0000124	10	9·9999876	34
27	7·8950854	163901	12·1049146	7·8950988	163911	12·1049012	10·0000134	10	9·9999866	33
28	7·9108793	157939	12·0891207	7·9108938	157950	12·0891062	10·0000144	11	9·9999856	32
29	7·9261190	152397	12·0738810	7·9261344	152406	12·0738656	10·0000155	10	9·9999845	31
30	7·9408419	147229	12·0591581	7·9408584	147240	12·0591416	10·0000165	12	9·9999835	30
		142400			142412			11		
31	7·9550819		12·0449181	7·9550996		12·0449004	10·0000177	11	9·9999823	29
32	7·9688698	137879	12·0311302	7·9688886	137890	12·0311114	10·0000188	12	9·9999812	28
33	7·9822334	133636	12·0177668	7·9822534	133648	12·0177466	10·0000200	12	9·9999800	27
34	7·9951980	129646	12·0048020	7·9952192	129658	12·0047808	10·0000212	13	9·9999788	26
35	8·0077867	125887	11·9922133	8·0078092	125900	11·9921908	10·0000225	13	9·9999775	25
		122340			122353			13		
36	8·0200207		11·9799793	8·0200445		11·9799505	10·0000238	14	9·9999762	24
37	8·0319195	118988	11·9680805	8·0319446	119001	11·9680554	10·0000252	13	9·9999748	23
38	8·0435009	115814	11·9564991	8·0435274	115828	11·9564726	10·0000265	14	9·9999735	22
39	8·0547814	112805	11·9452186	8·0548094	112820	11·9451906	10·0000279	15	9·9999721	21
40	8·0657763	109949	11·9342237	8·0658057	109963	11·9341943	10·0000294	15	9·9999706	20
		107234			107249			15		
41	8·0764997		11·9235003	8·0765306		11·9234694	10·0000309	15	9·9999691	19
42	8·0869646	104649	11·9130354	8·0869970	104664	11·9130030	10·0000324	16	9·9999676	18
43	8·0971832	102186	11·9028168	8·0972172	102202	11·9027828	10·0000340	16	9·9999660	17
44	8·1071669	99837	11·8928331	8·1072025	99853	11·8927975	10·0000356	16	9·9999644	16
45	8·1169262	97593	11·8830738	8·1169634	97609	11·8830366	10·0000372	16	9·9999628	15
		95448			95465			17		
46	8·1264710		11·8735290	8·1265099		11·8734901	10·0000389	17	9·9999611	14
47	8·1358104	93394	11·8641896	8·1358510	93411	11·8641490	10·0000406	17	9·9999594	13
48	8·1449532	91428	11·8550468	8·1449956	91446	11·8550044	10·0000423	17	9·9999577	12
49	8·1539075	89543	11·8460925	8·1539516	89560	11·8460484	10·0000441	18	9·9999559	11
50	8·1626808	87733	11·8373192	8·1627267	87751	11·8372733	10·0000459	18	9·9999541	10
		85996			86015			19		
51	8·1712804		11·8287196	8·1713282		11·8286718	10·0000478	19	9·9999522	9
52	8·1797129	84325	11·8202871	8·1797626	84344	11·8202374	10·0000497	19	9·9999503	8
53	8·1879848	82719	11·8120152	8·1880364	82738	11·8119636	10·0000516	20	9·9999484	7
54	8·1961020	81172	11·8038980	8·1961556	81192	11·8038444	10·0000536	20	9·9999464	6
55	8·2040703	79683	11·7959297	8·2041259	79703	11·7958741	10·0000556	20	9·9999444	5
		78246			78267			20		
56	8·2118949		11·7881051	8·2119526		11·7880474	10·0000576	21	9·9999424	4
57	8·2195811	76862	11·7804189	8·2196408	76882	11·7803592	10·0000597	21	9·9999403	3
58	8·2271335	75524	11·7728665	8·2271953	75545	11·7728047	10·0000618	22	9·9999382	2
59	8·2345568	74233	11·7654432	8·2346208	74255	11·7653792	10·0000640	22	9·9999360	1
60	8·2418553	72985	11·7581447	8·2419215	73007	11·7580785	10·0000662	22	9·9999338	0

′	Cosine	Diff.	Secant	Cotang.	Diff.	Tang.	Cosec.	D.	Sine	′

89 Deg.

'	Sine	Diff.	Cosec.	Tang.	Diff.	Cotang.	Secant	D.	Cosine	'
0	8·2418553	71779	11·7581447	8·2419215	71800	11·7580785	10·0000662	22	9·9999338	60
1	8·2490332	70611	11·7509668	8·2491015	70634	11·7508985	10·0009684	22	9·9999316	59
2	8·2560943	69481	11·7439057	8·2561649	69504	11·7438351	10·0000706	23	9·9999294	58
3	8·2630424	68386	11·7369576	8·2631153	68410	11·7368847	10·0000729	23	9·9999271	57
4	8·2698810	67326	11·7301190	8·2699563	67349	11·7300437	10·0000753	24	9·9999247	56
5	8·2766136	66293	11·7233864	8·2766912	66322	11·7233088	10·0000776	24	9·9999224	55
6	8·2832434	65300	11·7167566	8·2833234	65325	11·7166766	10·0000800	25	9·9999200	54
7	8·2897734	64333	11·7102266	8·2898559	64358	11·7101441	10·0000825	25	9·9999175	53
8	8·2962067	63393	11·7037933	8·2962917	63418	11·7037083	10·0000850	25	9·9999150	52
9	8·3025460	62481	11·6974540	8·3026335	62507	11·6973665	10·0000875	25	9·9999125	51
10	8·3087941	61595	11·6912059	8·3088842	61620	11·6911158	10·0000900	26	9·9999100	50
11	8·3149536	60733	11·6850464	8·3150462	60759	11·6849538	10·0000926	27	9·9999074	49
12	8·3210269	59894	11·6789731	8·3211221	59922	11·6788779	10·0000953	26	9·9999047	48
13	8·3270163	59080	11·6729837	8·3271143	59106	11·6728857	10·0000979	27	9·9999021	47
14	8·3329243	58286	11·6670757	8·3330249	58314	11·6669751	10·0001006	28	9·9998994	46
15	8·3387529	57514	11·6612471	8·3388563	57542	11·6611437	10·0001034	27	9·9998966	45
16	8·3445043	56762	11·6554957	8·3446105	56790	11·6553895	10·0001061	28	9·9998939	44
17	8·3501805	56030	11·6498195	8·3502895	56058	11·6497105	10·0001089	28	9·9998911	43
18	8·3557835	55315	11·6442165	8·3558953	55344	11·6441047	10·0001118	29	9·9998882	42
19	8·3613150	54619	11·6386850	8·3614297	54648	11·6385703	10·0001147	29	9·9998853	41
20	8·3667769	53941	11·6332231	8·3668945	53970	11·6331055	10·0001176	30	9·9998824	40
21	8·3721710	53278	11·6278290	8·3722915	53308	11·6277085	10·0001206	30	9·9998794	39
22	8·3774988	52632	11·6225012	8·3776223	52663	11·6223777	10·0001236	30	9·9998764	38
23	8·3827620	52002	11·6172380	8·3828886	52032	11·6171114	10·0001266	31	9·9998734	37
24	8·3879622	51386	11·6120378	8·3880918	51418	11·6119082	10·0001297	31	9·9998703	36
25	8·3931008	50785	11·6068992	8·3932336	50816	11·6067664	10·0001328	31	9·9998672	35
26	8·3981793	50197	11·6018207	8·3983152	50229	11·6016848	10·0001359	32	9·9998641	34
27	8·4031990	49624	11·5968010	8·4033381	49656	11·5966619	10·0001391	32	9·9998609	33
28	8·4081614	49062	11·5918386	8·4083037	49095	11·5916963	10·0001423	33	9·9998577	32
29	8·4130676	48514	11·5869324	8·4132132	48547	11·5867868	10·0001456	33	9·9998544	31
30	8·4179190	47978	11·5820810	8·4180679	48011	11·5819321	10·0001489	33	9·9998511	30
31	8·4227168	47453	11·5772832	8·4228690	47486	11·5771310	10·0001522	33	9·9998478	29
32	8·4274621	46940	11·5725379	8·4276176	46973	11·5723824	10·0001555	34	9·9998445	28
33	8·4321561	46438	11·5678439	8·4323150	46472	11·5676850	10·0001589	35	9·9998411	27
34	8·4367999	45945	11·5632001	8·4369622	45981	11·5630378	10·0001624	35	9·9998376	26
35	8·4413944	45465	11·5586056	8·4415603	45500	11·5584397	10·0001659	35	9·9998341	25
36	8·4459409	44993	11·5540591	8·4461103	45028	11·5538897	10·0001694	35	9·9998306	24
37	8·4504402	44532	11·5495598	8·4506131	44568	11·5493869	10·0001727	36	9·9998271	23
38	8·4548934	44079	11·5451066	8·4550699	44115	11·5449301	10·0001765	36	9·9998235	22
39	8·4593013	43636	11·5406987	8·4594814	43672	11·5405186	10·0001801	37	9·9998199	21
40	8·4636649	43201	11·5363351	8·4638486	43239	11·5361514	10·0001838	37	9·9998162	20
41	8·4679850	42776	11·5320150	8·4681725	42813	11·5318275	10·0001875	37	9·9998125	19
42	8·4722626	42358	11·5277374	8·4724538	42395	11·5275462	10·0001912	38	9·9998088	18
43	8·4764984	41948	11·5235016	8·4766933	41987	11·5233067	10·0001950	38	9·9998050	17
44	8·4806932	41547	11·5193068	8·4808920	41585	11·5191080	10·0001988	38	9·9998012	16
45	8·4848479	41153	11·5151521	8·4850505	41191	11·5149495	10·0002026	39	9·9997974	15
46	8·4889632	40766	11·5110368	8·4891696	40806	11·5108304	10·0002065	39	9·9997935	14
47	8·4930398	40386	11·5069602	8·4932502	40426	11·5067498	10·0002104	40	9·9997896	13
48	8·4970784	40014	11·5029216	8·4972928	40054	11·5027072	10·0002144	39	9·9997856	12
49	8·5010798	39649	11·4989202	8·5012982	39689	11·4987018	10·0002183	41	9·9997817	11
50	8·5050447	39289	11·4949553	8·5052671	39330	11·4947329	10·0002224	40	9·9997776	10
51	8·5089736	38937	11·4910264	8·5092001	38977	11·4907999	10·0002264	41	9·9997736	9
52	8·5128673	38591	11·4871327	8·5130978	38632	11·4869022	10·0002305	42	9·9997695	8
53	8·5167264	38250	11·4832736	8·5169610	38292	11·4830390	10·0002347	41	9·9997653	7
54	8·5205514	37916	11·4794486	8·5207902	37958	11·4792098	10·0002388	42	9·9997612	6
55	8·5243430	37587	11·4756570	8·5245860	37630	11·4754140	10·0002430	43	9·9997570	5
56	8·5281017	37264	11·4718983	8·5283490	37307	11·4716510	10·0002473	43	9·9997527	4
57	8·5318281	36947	11·4681719	8·5320797	36990	11·4679203	10·0002516	43	9·9997484	3
58	8·5355228	36635	11·4644772	8·5357787	36679	11·4642213	10·0002559	43	9·9997441	2
59	8·5391863	36329	11·4608137	8·5394466	36372	11·4605534	10·0002602	44	9·9997398	1
60	8·5428192		11·4571808	8·5430838		11·4569162	10·0002646		9·9997354	0

'	Cosine	Diff.	Secant	Cotang.	Diff.	Tang.	Cosec.	D.	Sine	'

2 Deg.

′	Sine	Diff.	Cosec.	Tang.	Diff.	Cotang.	Secant	D.	Cosine	′
0	8·5428192	36026	11·4571808	8·5430838	36071	11·4569162	10·0002646	45	9·9997354	60
1	8·5464218	35730	11·4535782	8·5466909	35774	11·4533091	10·0002691	44	9·9997309	59
2	8·5499948	35438	11·4500052	8·5502683	35483	11·4497317	10·0002735	45	9·9997265	58
3	8·5535386	35150	11·4464614	8·5538166	35196	11·4461834	10·0002780	46	9·9997220	57
4	8·5570536	34868	11·4429464	8·5573362	34914	11·4426638	10·0002826	46	9·9997174	56
5	8·5605404	34590	11·4394596	8·5608276	34636	11·4391724	10·0002872	46	9·9997128	55
6	8·5639994	34316	11·4360006	8·5642912	34363	11·4357088	10·0002918	46	9·9997082	54
7	8·5674310	34047	11·4325690	8·5677275	34093	11·4322725	10·0002964	47	9·9997036	53
8	8·5708357	33782	11·4291643	8·5711368	33829	11·4288632	10·0003011	47	9·9996989	52
9	8·5742139	33521	11·4257861	8·5745197	33569	11·4254803	10·0003058	48	9·9996942	51
10	8·5775660	33263	11·4224340	8·5778766	33311	11·4221234	10·0003106	48	9·9996894	50
11	8·5808923	33010	11·4191077	8·5812077	33059	11·4187923	10·0003154	48	9·9996846	49
12	8·5841933	32761	11·4158067	8·5845136	32809	11·4154864	10·0003202	48	9·9996798	48
13	8·5874694	32514	11·4125306	8·5877945	32564	11·4122055	10·0003251	49	9·9996749	47
14	8·5907209	32274	11·4092791	8·5910509	32323	11·4089491	10·0003300	49	9·9996700	46
15	8·5939483	32034	11·4060517	8·5942832	32085	11·4057168	10·0003350	49	9·9996650	45
16	8·5971517	31800	11·4028483	8·5974917	31850	11·4025083	10·0003399	51	9·9996601	44
17	8·6003317	31569	11·3996683	8·6006767	31619	11·3993233	10·0003450	51	9·9996550	43
18	8·6034886	31340	11·3965114	8·6038386	31391	11·3961614	10·0003500	51	9·9996500	42
19	8·6066226	31115	11·3933774	8·6069777	31166	11·3930223	10·0003551	51	9·9996449	41
20	8·6097341	30894	11·3902659	8·6100943	30946	11·3899057	10·0003602	52	9·9996398	40
21	8·6128235	30675	11·3871765	8·6131889	30727	11·3868111	10·0003654	52	9·9996346	39
22	8·6158910	30459	11·3841090	8·6162616	30511	11·3837384	10·0003706	52	9·9996294	38
23	8·6189369	30247	11·3810603	8·6193127	30300	11·3806873	10·0003758	53	9·9996242	37
24	8·6219616	30037	11·3780384	8·6223427	30091	11·3776573	10·0003811	53	9·9996189	36
25	8·6249653	29831	11·3750347	8·6253518	29884	11·3746482	10·0003864	54	9·9996136	35
26	8·6279484	29627	11·3720516	8·6283402	29681	11·3716598	10·0003918	54	9·9996082	34
27	8·6309111	29426	11·3690889	8·6313083	29480	11·3686917	10·0003972	54	9·9996028	33
28	8·6338537	29227	11·3661463	8·6342563	29282	11·3657437	10·0004026	55	9·9995974	32
29	8·6367764	29032	11·3632236	8·6371845	29086	11·3628155	10·0004081	55	9·9995919	31
30	8·6396796	28838	11·3603204	8·6400931	28894	11·3599069	10·0004135	56	9·9995865	30
31	8·6425634	28648	11·3574366	8·6429825	28703	11·3570175	10·0004191	56	9·9995809	29
32	8·6454282	28460	11·3545718	8·6458528	28516	11·3541472	10·0004247	56	9·9995753	28
33	8·6482742	28274	11·3517258	8·6487044	28331	11·3512956	10·0004303	56	9·9995697	27
34	8·6511016	28091	11·3488984	8·6515375	28147	11·3484625	10·0004359	57	9·9995641	26
35	8·6539107	27910	11·3460893	8·6543522	27968	11·3456478	10·0004416	57	9·9995584	25
36	8·6567017	27731	11·3432983	8·6571490	27789	11·3428510	10·0004473	58	9·9995527	24
37	8·6594748	27555	11·3405252	8·6599279	27612	11·3400721	10·0004531	58	9·9995469	23
38	8·6622303	27381	11·3377697	8·6626891	27440	11·3373109	10·0004589	58	9·9995411	22
39	8·6649684	27209	11·3350316	8·6654331	27267	11·3345669	10·0004647	58	9·9995353	21
40	8·6676893	27039	11·3323107	8·6681598	27099	11·3318402	10·0004705	59	9·9995295	20
41	8·6703932	26872	11·3296068	8·6708697	26931	11·3291303	10·0004764	60	9·9995236	19
42	8·6730804	26706	11·3269196	8·6735628	26765	11·3264372	10·0004824	60	9·9995176	18
43	8·6757510	26542	11·3242490	8·6762393	26603	11·3237607	10·0004884	60	9·9995116	17
44	8·6784052	26381	11·3215948	8·6788996	26441	11·3211004	10·0004944	60	9·9995056	16
45	8·6810433	26221	11·3189567	8·6815437	26282	11·3184563	10·0005004	61	9·9994996	15
46	8·6836654	26064	11·3163346	8·6841719	26125	11·3158281	10·0005065	61	9·9994935	14
47	8·6862718	25907	11·3137282	8·6867844	25969	11·3132156	10·0005126	62	9·9994874	13
48	8·6888625	25754	11·3111375	8·6893813	25816	11·3106187	10·0005188	62	9·9994812	12
49	8·6914379	25601	11·3085621	8·6919629	25663	11·3080371	10·0005250	62	9·9994750	11
50	8·6939980	25451	11·3060020	8·6945292	25514	11·3054708	10·0005312	63	9·9994688	10
51	8·6965431	25303	11·3034569	8·6970806	25366	11·3029194	10·0005375	63	9·9994625	9
52	8·6990734	25155	11·3009266	8·6996172	25218	11·3003828	10·0005438	64	9·9994562	8
53	8·7015889	25010	11·2984111	8·7021390	25075	11·2978610	10·0005502	63	9·9994498	7
54	8·7040899	24867	11·2959101	8·7046465	24930	11·2953535	10·0005565	65	9·9994435	6
55	8·7065766	24724	11·2934234	8·7071395	24790	11·2928605	10·0005630	64	9·9994370	5
56	8·7090490	24585	11·2909510	8·7096185	24649	11·2903815	10·0005694	65	9·9994306	4
57	8·7115075	24445	11·2884925	8·7120834	24511	11·2879166	10·0005759	65	9·9994241	3
58	8·7139520	24309	11·2860480	8·7145345	24374	11·2854655	10·0005824	66	9·9994176	2
59	8·7163829	24173	11·2836171	8·7169719	24239	11·2830281	10·0005890	66	9·9994110	1
60	8·7188002		11·2811998	8·7193958		11·2806042	10·0005956		9·9994044	0

′	Cosine	Diff.	Secant	Cotang.	Diff.	Tang.	Cosec.	D	Sine	′

87 Deg.

′	Sine	Diff.	Cosec.	Tang.	Diff.	Cotang.	Secant	D.	Cosine	′
0	8·7188002	24038	11·2811998	8·7193958	24105	11·2806042	10·0005956	66	9·9994044	60
1	8·7212040	23906	11·2787960	8·7218063	23972	11·2781937	10·0006022	67	9·9993978	59
2	8·7235946	23775	11·2764054	8·7242035	23842	11·2757965	10·0006089	67	9·9993911	58
3	8·7259721	23645	11·2740279	8·7265877	23712	11·2734123	10·0006156	68	9·9993844	57
4	8·7283366	23516	11·2716634	8·7289589	23585	11·2710411	10·0006224	68	9·9993776	56
5	8·7306882	23390	11·2693118	8·7313174	23457	11·2686826	10·0006292	68	9·9993708	55
6	8·7330272	23263	11·2669728	8·7336631	23333	11·2663369	10·0006360	68	9·9993640	54
7	8·7353535	23140	11·2646465	8·7359964	23208	11·2640036	10·0006428	69	9·9993572	53
8	8·7376675	23016	11·2623325	8·7383172	23086	11·2616828	10·0006497	69	9·9993503	52
9	8·7399691	22895	11·2600309	8·7406258	22964	11·2593742	10·0006567	70	9·9993433	51
10	8·7422586	22774	11·2577414	8·7429222	22845	11·2570778	10·0006636	69	9·9993364	50
11	8·7445360	22655	11·2554640	8·7452067	22725	11·2547933	10·0006707	70	9·9993293	49
12	8·7468015	22538	11·2531985	8·7474792	22608	11·2525208	10·0006777	71	9·9993223	48
13	8·7490553	22420	11·2509447	8·7497400	22492	11·2502600	10·0006848	71	9·9993152	47
14	8·7512973	22305	11·2487027	8·7519892	22377	11·2480108	10·0006919	72	9·9993081	46
15	8·7535278	22191	11·2464722	8·7542269	22262	11·2457731	10·0006991	71	9·9993009	45
16	8·7557469	22077	11·2442531	8·7564531	22150	11·2435469	10·0007062	73	9·9992938	44
17	8·7579546	21966	11·2420454	8·7586681	22038	11·2413319	10·0007135	72	9·9992865	43
18	8·7601512	21854	11·2398488	8·7608719	21928	11·2391281	10·0007207	73	9·9992793	42
19	8·7623366	21745	11·2376634	8·7630647	21818	11·2369353	10·0007280	73	9·9992720	41
20	8·7645111	21636	11·2354889	8·7652465	21710	11·2347535	10·0007354	74	9·9992646	40
21	8·7666747	21528	11·2333253	8·7674175	21602	11·2325825	10·0007428	74	9·9992572	39
22	8·7688275	21422	11·2311725	8·7695777	21497	11·2304223	10·0007502	74	9·9992498	38
23	8·7709697	21317	11·2290303	8·7717274	21391	11·2282726	10·0007576	74	9·9992424	37
24	8·7731014	21212	11·2268986	8·7738665	21287	11·2261335	10·0007651	75	9·9992349	36
25	8·7752226	21108	11·2247774	8·7759952	21184	11·2240048	10·0007726	75	9·9992274	35
26	8·7773334	21006	11·2226666	8·7781136	21082	11·2218864	10·0007802	76	9·9992198	34
27	8·7794340	20904	11·2205660	8·7802218	20981	11·2197782	10·0007878	76	9·9992122	33
28	8·7815244	20804	11·2184756	8·7823199	20880	11·2176801	10·0007954	77	9·9992046	32
29	8·7836048	20705	11·2163952	8·7844079	20782	11·2155921	10·0008031	77	9·9991969	31
30	8·7856753	20606	11·2143247	8·7864861	20683	11·2135139	10·0008108	77	9·9991892	30
31	8·7877359	20508	11·2122641	8·7885544	20586	11·2114456	10·0008185	78	9·9991815	29
32	8·7897867	20411	11·2102133	8·7906130	20490	11·2093870	10·0008263	78	9·9991737	28
33	8·7918278	20316	11·2081722	8·7926620	20394	11·2073380	10·0008341	79	9·9991659	27
34	8·7938594	20220	11·2061406	8·7947014	20299	11·2052986	10·0008420	79	9·9991580	26
35	8·7958814	20127	11·2041186	8·7967313	20206	11·2032687	10·0008499	79	9·9991501	25
36	8·7978941	20033	11·2021059	8·7987519	20113	11·2012481	10·0008578	80	9·9991422	24
37	8·7998974	19941	11·2001026	8·8007632	20021	11·1992368	10·0008658	80	9·9991342	23
38	8·8018915	19849	11·1981085	8·8027653	19930	11·1972347	10·0008738	80	9·9991262	22
39	8·8038764	19759	11·1961236	8·8047583	19839	11·1952417	10·0008818	81	9·9991182	21
40	8·8058523	19669	11·1941477	8·8067422	19750	11·1932578	10·0008899	81	9·9991101	20
41	8·8078192	19580	11·1921808	8·8087172	19662	11·1912828	10·0008980	82	9·9991020	19
42	8·8097772	19492	11·1902228	8·8106834	19573	11·1893166	10·0009062	82	9·9990938	18
43	8·8117264	19404	11·1882736	8·8126407	19487	11·1873593	10·0009144	82	9·9990856	17
44	8·8136668	19317	11·1863332	8·8145894	19400	11·1854106	10·0009226	83	9·9990774	16
45	8·8155985	19232	11·1844015	8·8165294	19314	11·1834706	10·0009309	83	9·9990691	15
46	8·8175217	19146	11·1824783	8·8184608	19230	11·1815392	10·0009392	83	9·9990608	14
47	8·8194363	19062	11·1805637	8·8203838	19146	11·1796162	10·0009475	84	9·9990525	13
48	8·8213425	18979	11·1786575	8·8222984	19062	11·1777016	10·0009559	84	9·9990441	12
49	8·8232404	18895	11·1767596	8·8242046	18980	11·1757954	10·0009643	84	9·9990357	11
50	8·8251299	18813	11·1748701	8·8261026	18898	11·1738974	10·0009727	85	9·9990273	10
51	8·8270112	18732	11·1729888	8·8279924	18817	11·1720076	10·0009812	85	9·9990188	9
52	8·8288844	18651	11·1711156	8·8298741	18737	11·1701259	10·0009897	86	9·9990103	8
53	8·8307495	18571	11·1692505	8·8317478	18656	11·1682522	10·0009983	86	9·9990017	7
54	8·8326066	18491	11·1673934	8·8336134	18578	11·1663866	10·0010069	86	9·9989931	6
55	8·8344557	18412	11·1655443	8·8354712	18499	11·1645288	10·0010155	87	9·9989845	5
56	8·8362969	18335	11·1637031	8·8373211	18422	11·1626789	10·0010242	87	9·9989758	4
57	8·8381304	18257	11·1618696	8·8391633	18344	11·1608367	10·0010329	87	9·9989671	3
58	8·8399561	18180	11·1600439	8·8409977	18268	11·1590023	10·0010416	88	9·9989584	2
59	8·8417741	18104	11·1582259	8·8428245	18192	11·1571755	10·0010504	88	9·9989496	1
60	8·8435845		11·1564155	8·8446437		11·1553563	10·0010592		9·9989408	0

′	Cosine	Diff.	Secant	Cotang.	Diff.	Tang.	Cosec.	D.	Sine	′

′	Sine	Diff.	Cosec.	Tang.	Diff.	Cotang.	Secant	D.	Cosine	′
0	8·8435845	18029	11·1564155	8·8446437	18117	11·1553563	10·0010592	89	9·9989408	60
1	8·8453874	17953	11·1546126	8·8464554	18043	11·1535446	10·0010681	89	9·9989319	59
2	8·8471827	17880	11·1528173	8·8482597	17969	11·1517403	10·0010770	89	9·9989230	58
3	8·8489707	17805	11·1510293	8·8500566	17895	11·1499434	10·0010859	89	9·9989141	57
4	8·8507512	17733	11·1492488	8·8518461	17822	11·1481539	10·0010948	90	9·9989052	56
5	8·8525245	17660	11·1474755	8·8536283	17751	11·1463717	10·0011038	91	9·9988962	55
6	8·8542905	17588	11·1457095	8·8554034	17679	11·1445966	10·0011129	91	9·9988871	54
7	8·8560493	17517	11·1439507	8·8571713	17608	11·1428287	10·0011220	91	9·9988780	53
8	8·8578010	17447	11·1421990	8·8589321	17538	11·1410679	10·0011311	91	9·9988689	52
9	8·8595457	17376	11·1404543	8·8606859	17468	11·1393141	10·0011402	92	9·9988598	51
10	8·8612833	17306	11·1387167	8·8624327	17398	11·1375673	10·0011494	92	9·9988506	50
11	8·8630139	17237	11·1369861	8·8641725	17330	11·1358275	10·0011586	93	9·9988414	49
12	8·8647376	17169	11·1352624	8·8659055	17262	11·1340945	10·0011679	93	9·9988321	48
13	8·8664545	17101	11·1335455	8·8676317	17194	11·1323683	10·0011772	93	9·9988228	47
14	8·8681646	17034	11·1318354	8·8693511	17127	11·1306489	10·0011865	94	9·9988135	46
15	8·8698680	16966	11·1301320	8·8710638	17061	11·1289362	10·0011959	94	9·9988041	45
16	8·8715646	16900	11·1284354	8·8727699	16995	11·1272301	10·0012053	94	9·9987947	44
17	8·8732546	16835	11·1267454	8·8744694	16929	11·1255306	10·0012147	95	9·9987853	43
18	8·8749381	16769	11·1250619	8·8761623	16864	11·1238377	10·0012242	95	9·9987758	42
19	8·8766150	16704	11·1233850	8·8778487	16799	11·1221513	10·0012337	96	9·9987663	41
20	8·8782854	16639	11·1217146	8·8795286	16736	11·1204714	10·0012433	96	9·9987567	40
21	8·8799493	16576	11·1200507	8·8812022	16672	11·1187978	10·0012529	96	9·9987471	39
22	8·8816069	16512	11·1183931	8·8828604	16609	11·1171396	10·0012625	97	9·9987375	38
23	8·8832581	16450	11·1167419	8·8845303	16547	11·1154697	10·0012722	97	9·9987278	37
24	8·8849031	16387	11·1150969	8·8861850	16484	11·1138150	10·0012819	97	9·9987181	36
25	8·8865418	16325	11·1134582	8·8878334	16423	11·1121666	10·0012916	98	9·9987084	35
26	8·8881743	16264	11·1118257	8·8894757	16362	11·1105243	10·0013014	98	9·9986986	34
27	8·8898007	16202	11·1101993	8·8911119	16301	11·1088881	10·0013112	98	9·9986888	33
28	8·8914209	16142	11·1085791	8·8927420	16240	11·1072580	10·0013210	99	9·9986790	32
29	8·8930351	16082	11·1069649	8·8943660	16182	11·1056340	10·0013309	99	9·9986691	31
30	8·8946433	16022	11·1053567	8·8959842	16121	11·1040158	10·0013409	100	9·9986591	30
31	8·8962455	15963	11·1037545	8·8975963	16063	11·1024037	10·0013508	100	9·9086492	29
32	8·8978418	15904	11·1021582	8·8992026	16004	11·1007974	10·0013608	100	9·9986392	28
33	8·8994322	15846	11·1005678	8·9008030	15947	11·0991970	10·0013708	101	9·9986292	27
34	8·9010168	15787	11·0989832	8·9023977	15889	11·0976023	10·0013809	101	9·9986191	26
35	8·9025955	15730	11·0974045	8·9039866	15831	11·0960134	10·0013910	102	9·9986090	25
36	8·9041685	15673	11·0958315	8·9055697	15775	11·0944303	10·0014012	102	9·9985988	24
37	8·9057358	15617	11·0942642	8·9071472	15718	11·0928528	10·0014114	102	9·9985886	23
38	8·9072975	15560	11·0927025	8·9087190	15663	11·0912810	10·0014216	102	9·9985784	22
39	8·9088535	15504	11·0911465	8·9102853	15607	11·0897147	10·0014318	103	9·9985682	21
40	8·9104039	15448	11·0895961	8·9118460	15552	11·0881540	10·0014421	103	9·9985579	20
41	8·9119487	15394	11·0880513	8·9134012	15497	11·0865988	10·0014525	103	9·9985475	19
42	8·9134881	15338	11·0865119	8·9149509	15443	11·0850491	10·0014628	104	9·9985372	18
43	8·9150219	15285	11·0849781	8·9164952	15388	11·0835048	10·0014732	105	9·9985268	17
44	8·9165504	15230	11·0834496	8·9180340	15335	11·0819660	10·0014837	105	9·9985163	16
45	8·9180734	15177	11·0819266	8·9195675	15282	11·0804325	10·0014942	105	9·9985058	15
46	8·9195911	15123	11·0804089	8·9210957	15229	11·0789043	10·0015047	105	9·9984953	14
47	8·9211034	15071	11·0788966	8·9226186	15177	11·0773814	10·0015152	106	9·9984848	13
48	8·9226105	15018	11·0773895	8·9241363	15124	11·0758637	10·0015258	106	9·9984742	12
49	8·9241123	14966	11·0758877	8·9256487	15073	11·0743513	10·0015364	107	9·9984636	11
50	8·9256089	14914	11·0743911	8·9271560	15021	11·0728440	10·0015471	107	9·9984529	10
51	8·9271003	14863	11·0728997	8·9286581	14971	11·0713419	10·0015578	107	9·9984422	9
52	8·9285866	14812	11·0714134	8·9301552	14919	11·0698448	10·0015685	108	9·9984315	8
53	8·9300678	14761	11·0699322	8·9316471	14869	11·0683529	10·0015793	108	9·9984207	7
54	8·9315439	14711	11·0684561	8·9331340	14820	11·0668660	10·0015901	109	9·9984099	6
55	8·9330150	14661	11·0669850	8·9346160	14769	11·0653840	10·0016010	109	9·9983990	5
56	8·9344811	14611	11·0655189	8·9360929	14721	11·0639071	10·0016119	109	9·9983881	4
57	8·9359422	14561	11·0640578	8·9375650	14671	11·0624350	10·0016228	109	9·9983772	3
58	8·9373983	14513	11·0626017	8·9390321	14623	11·0609679	10·0016337	110	9·9983663	2
59	8·9388496	14464	11·0611504	8·9404944	14574	11·0595056	10·0016447	111	9·9983553	1
60	8·9402960		11·0597040	8·9419518		11·0580482	10·0016558		9·9983442	0

| ′ | Cosine | Diff. | Secant | Cotang. | Diff. | Tang. | Cosec. | D. | Sine | ′ |

′	Sine	Diff.	Cosec.	Tang.	Diff.	Cotang.	Secant	D.	Cosine	′
0	8·9402960	14416	11·0597040	8·9419518	14526	11·0580482	10·0016558	110	9·9983442	60
1	8·9417376	14367	11·0582624	8·9434044	14479	11·0565956	10·0016668	112	9·9983332	59
2	8·9431743	14320	11·0568257	8·9448523	14431	11·0551477	10·0016780	111	9·9983220	58
3	8·9446063	14272	11·0553937	8·9462954	14384	11·0537046	10·0016891	112	9·9983109	57
4	8·9460335	14226	11·0539665	8·9477338	14338	11·0522662	10·0017003	112	9·9982997	56
5	8·9474561	14178	11·0525439	8·9491676	14291	11·0508324	10·0017115	113	9·9982885	55
6	8·9488739	14132	11·0511261	8·9505967	14244	11·0494033	10·0017228	112	9·9982772	54
7	8·9502871	14086	11·0497129	8·9520211	14199	11·0479789	10·0017340	114	9·9982660	53
8	8·9516957	14039	11·0483043	8·9534410	14154	11·0465590	10·0017454	113	9·9982546	52
9	8·9530996	13995	11·0469004	8·9548564	14108	11·0451436	10·0017567	115	9·9982433	51
10	8·9544991	13949	11·0455009	8·9562672	14063	11·0437328	10·0017682	114	9·9982318	50
11	8·9558940	13903	11·0441060	8·9576735	14019	11·0423265	10·0017796	115	9·9982204	49
12	8·9572843	13860	11·0427157	8·9590754	13974	11·0409246	10·0017911	115	9·9982089	48
13	8·9586703	13814	11·0413297	8·9604728	13931	11·0395272	10·0018026	115	9·9981974	47
14	8·9600517	13771	11·0399483	8·9618659	13886	11·0381341	10·0018141	116	9·9981859	46
15	8·9614288	13726	11·0385712	8·9632545	13843	11·0367455	10·0018257	117	9·9981743	45
16	8·9628014	13683	11·0371986	8·9646388	13800	11·0353612	10·0018374	116	9·9981626	44
17	8·9641697	13640	11·0358303	8·9660188	13756	11·0339812	10·0018490	117	9·9981510	43
18	8·9655337	13597	11·0344663	8·9673944	13714	11·0326056	10·0018607	118	9·9981393	42
19	8·9668934	13553	11·0331066	8·9687658	13672	11·0312342	10·0018725	117	9·9981275	41
20	8·9682487	13512	11·0317513	8·9701330	13629	11·0298670	10·0018842	118	9·9981158	40
21	8·9695999	13469	11·0304001	8·9714959	13588	11·0285041	10·0018960	119	9·9981040	39
22	8·9709468	13427	11·0290532	8·9728547	13545	11·0271453	10·0019079	119	9·9980921	38
23	8·9722895	13385	11·0277105	8·9742092	13505	11·0257908	10·0019198	119	9·9980802	37
24	8·9736280	13344	11·0263720	8·9755597	13463	11·0244403	10·0019317	120	9·9980683	36
25	8·9749624	13302	11·0250376	8·9769060	13423	11·0230940	10·0019437	120	9·9980563	35
26	8·9762926	13262	11·0237074	8·9782483	13382	11·0217517	10·0019557	120	9·9980443	34
27	8·9776188	13220	11·0223812	8·9795865	13341	11·0204135	10·0019677	121	9·9980323	33
28	8·9789408	13181	11·0210592	8·9809206	13301	11·0190794	10·0019798	121	9·9980202	32
29	8·9802589	13140	11·0197411	8·9822507	13262	11·0177493	10·0019919	121	9·9980081	31
30	8·9815729	13100	11·0184271	8·9835769	13222	11·0164231	10·0020040	122	9·9979960	30
31	8·9828829	13060	11·0171171	8·9848991	13182	11·0151009	10·0020162	122	9·9979838	29
32	8·9841889	13021	11·0158111	8·9862173	13144	11·0137827	10·0020284	122	9·9979716	28
33	8·9854910	12981	11·0145090	8·9875317	13104	11·0124683	10·0020407	123	9·9979593	27
34	8·9867891	12943	11·0132109	8·9888421	13066	11·0111579	10·0020530	123	9·9979470	26
35	8·9880834	12903	11·0119166	8·9901487	13027	11·0098513	10·0020653	123	9·9979347	25
36	8·9893737	12865	11·0106263	8·9914514	12989	11·0085486	10·0020777	124	9·9979223	24
37	8·9906602	12827	11·0093398	8·9927503	12951	11·0072497	10·0020901	124	9·9979099	23
38	8·9919429	12788	11·0080571	8·9940454	12913	11·0059546	10·0021025	125	9·9978975	22
39	8·9932217	12751	11·0067783	8·9953367	12876	11·0046633	10·0021150	125	9·9978850	21
40	8·9944968	12713	11·0055032	8·9966243	12838	11·0033757	10·0021275	126	9·9978725	20
41	8·9957681	12675	11·0042319	8·9979081	12802	11·0020919	10·0021401	126	9·9978599	19
42	8·9970356	12638	11·0029644	8·9991883	12764	11·0008117	10·0021527	126	9·9978473	18
43	8·9982994	12601	11·0017006	9·0004647	12728	10·9995353	10·0021653	127	9·9978347	17
44	8·9995595	12565	11·0004405	9·0017375	12691	10·9982625	10·0021780	127	9·9978220	16
45	9·0008160	12527	10·9991840	9·0030066	12655	10·9969934	10·0021907	127	9·9978093	15
46	9·0020687	12492	10·9979313	9·0042721	12619	10·9957279	10·0022034	128	9·9977966	14
47	9·0033179	12455	10·9966821	9·0055340	12584	10·9944660	10·0022162	128	9·9977838	13
48	9·0045634	12419	10·9954366	9·0067924	12547	10·9932076	10·0022290	128	9·9977710	12
49	9·0058053	12383	10·9941947	9·0080471	12513	10·9919529	10·0022418	129	9·9977582	11
50	9·0070436	12348	10·9929564	9·0092984	12477	10·9907016	10·0022547	130	9·9977453	10
51	9·0082784	12312	10·9917216	9·0105461	12442	10·9894539	10·0022677	129	9·9977323	9
52	9·0095096	12278	10·9904904	9·0117903	12407	10·9882097	10·0022806	130	9·9977194	8
53	9·0107374	12242	10·9892626	9·0130310	12372	10·9869690	10·0022936	131	9·9977064	7
54	9·0119616	12207	10·9880384	9·0142682	12339	10·9857318	10·0023067	130	9·9976933	6
55	9·0131823	12173	10·9868177	9·0155021	12304	10·9844979	10·0023197	131	9·9976803	5
56	9·0143996	12139	10·9856004	9·0167325	12269	10·9832675	10·0023328	132	9·9976672	4
57	9·0156135	12104	10·9843865	9·0179594	12237	10·9820406	10·0023460	132	9·9976540	3
58	9·0168239	12070	10·9831761	9·0191831	12202	10·9808169	10·0023592	132	9·9976408	2
59	9·0180309	12037	10·9819691	9·0204033	12169	10·9795967	10·0023724	133	9·9976276	1
60	9·0192346		10·9807654	9·0216202		10·9783798	10·0023857		9·9976143	0

| ′ | Cosine | Diff. | Secant | Cotang. | Diff. | Tang. | Cosec. | D. | Sine | ′ |

	Sine	Diff.	Cosec.	Tang.	Diff.	Cotang.	Secant	D.	Cosine	'
0	9·0192346	12002	10·9807654	9·0216202	12136	10·9783798	10·0023857	132	8·3976143	60
1	9·0204348	11970	10·9795652	9·0228338	12103	10·9771662	10·0023989	134	9·9976011	59
2	9·0216318	11936	10·9783682	9·0240441	12069	10·9759559	10·0024123	134	9·9975877	58
3	9·0228254	11903	10·9771746	9·0252510	12038	10·9747490	10·0024257	134	9·9975743	57
4	9·0240157	11870	10·9759843	9·0264548	12004	10·9735452	10·0024395	134	9·9975609	56
5	9·0252027	11838	10·9747973	9·0276552	11972	10·9723448	10·0024525	135	9·9975475	55
6	9·0263865	11804	10·9736135	9·0288524	11940	10·9711476	10·0024660	135	9·9975340	54
7	9·0275669	11773	10·9724331	9·0300464	11909	10·9699536	10·0024795	136	9·9975205	53
8	9·0287442	11740	10·9712558	9·0312373	11876	10·9687627	10·0024931	136	9·9975069	52
9	9·0299182	11708	10·9700818	9·0324249	11844	10·9675751	10·0025067	136	9·9974933	51
10	9·0310890	11677	10·9689110	9·0336093	11813	10·9663907	10·0025203	137	9·9974797	50
11	9·0322567	11645	10·9677433	9·0347906	11782	10·9652094	10·0025340	137	9·9974660	49
12	9·0334212	11613	10·9665788	9·0359688	11751	10·9640312	10·0025477	137	9·9974523	48
13	9·0345825	11582	10·9654175	9·0371439	11720	10·9628561	10·0025614	138	9·9974386	47
14	9·0357407	11551	10·9642593	9·0383159	11689	10·9616841	10·0025752	138	9·9974248	46
15	9·0368958	11519	10·9631042	9·0394848	11658	10·9605152	10·0025890	139	9·9974110	45
16	9·0380477	11489	10·9619523	9·0406506	11628	10·9593494	10·0026029	138	9·9973971	44
17	9·0391966	11458	10·9608034	9·0418134	11597	10·9581866	10·0026167	140	9·9973833	43
18	9·0403424	11428	10·9596576	9·0429731	11568	10·9570269	10·0026307	139	9·9973693	42
19	9·0414852	11397	10·9585148	9·0441299	11537	10·9558701	10·0026446	140	9·9973554	41
20	9·0426249	11368	10·9573751	9·0452836	11507	10·9547164	10·0026586	141	9·9973414	40
21	9·0437617	11337	10·9562383	9·0464343	11478	10·9535657	10·0026727	141	9·9973273	39
22	9·0448954	11307	10·9551046	9·0475821	11449	10·9524179	10·0026868	141	9·9973132	38
23	9·0460261	11277	10·9539739	9·0487270	11419	10·9512730	10·0027009	141	9·9972991	37
24	9·0471538	11248	10·9528462	9·0498689	11389	10·9501311	10·0027150	142	9·9972850	36
25	9·0482786	11219	10·9517214	9·0510078	11361	10·9489922	10·0027292	142	9·9972708	35
26	9·0494005	11189	10·9505995	9·0521439	11332	10·9478561	10·0027434	143	9·9972566	34
27	9·0505194	11160	10·9494806	9·0532771	11303	10·9467229	10·0027577	143	9·9972423	33
28	9·0516354	11131	10·9483646	9·0544074	11275	10·9455926	10·0027720	143	9·9972280	32
29	9·0527485	11103	10·9472515	9·0555349	11246	10·9444651	10·0027863	144	9·9972137	31
30	9·0538588	11073	10·9461412	9·0566595	11218	10·9433405	10·0028007	144	9·9971993	30
31	9·0549661	11045	10·9450339	9·0577813	11189	10·9422187	10·0028151	145	9·9971849	29
32	9·0560706	11017	10·9439299	9·0589002	11162	10·9410998	10·0028296	145	9·9971704	28
33	9·0571723	10988	10·9428277	9·0600164	11133	10·9399836	10·0028441	145	9·9971559	27
34	9·0582711	10961	10·9417289	9·0611297	11106	10·9388703	10·0028586	146	9·9971414	26
35	9·0593672	10932	10·9406328	9·0622403	11079	10·9377597	10·0028732	146	9·9971268	25
36	9·0604604	10905	10·9395396	9·0633482	11051	10·9366518	10·0028878	146	9·9971122	24
37	9·0615509	10877	10·9384491	9·0644533	11023	10·9355467	10·0029024	147	9·9970976	23
38	9·0626386	10849	10·9373614	9·0655556	10997	10·9344444	10·0029171	147	9·9970829	22
39	9·0637235	10822	10·9362765	9·0666553	10969	10·9333447	10·0029318	147	9·9970682	21
40	9·0648057	10795	10·9351943	9·0677522	10943	10·9322478	10·0029465	148	9·9970535	20
41	9·0658852	10767	10·9341148	9·0688465	10916	10·9311535	10·0029613	148	9·9970387	19
42	9·0669619	10741	10·9330381	9·0699381	10889	10·9300619	10·0029761	149	9·9970239	18
43	9·0680360	10714	10·9319640	9·0710270	10863	10·9289730	10·0029910	149	9·9970090	17
44	9·0691074	10687	10·9308926	9·0721133	10836	10·9278867	10·0030059	149	9·9969941	16
45	9·0701761	10660	10·9298239	9·0731969	10810	10·9268031	10·0030208	150	9·9969792	15
46	9·0712421	10634	10·9287579	9·0742779	10784	10·9257221	10·0030358	150	9·9969642	14
47	9·0723055	10608	10·9276945	9·0753563	10758	10·9246437	10·0030508	150	9·9969492	13
48	9·0733663	10581	10·9266337	9·0764321	10732	10·9235679	10·0030658	151	9·9969342	12
49	9·0744244	10555	10·9255756	9·0775053	10707	10·9224947	10·0030809	151	9·9969191	11
50	9·0754799	10530	10·9245201	9·0785760	10681	10·9214240	10·0030960	152	9·9969040	10
51	9·0765329	10503	10·9234671	9·0796441	10655	10·9203559	10·0031112	152	9·9968888	9
52	9·0775832	10478	10·9224168	9·0807096	10630	10·9192904	10·0031264	152	9·9968736	8
53	9·0786310	10452	10·9213690	9·0817726	10605	10·9182274	10·0031416	153	9·9968584	7
54	9·0796762	10427	10·9203228	9·0828331	10580	10·9171669	10·0031569	153	9·9968431	6
55	9·0807189	10401	10·9192811	9·0838911	10555	10·9161089	10·0031722	153	9·9968278	5
56	9·0817590	10376	10·9182410	9·0849466	10530	10·9150534	10·0031875	154	9·9968125	4
57	9·0827966	10351	10·9172034	9·0859996	10505	10·9140004	10·0032029	154	9·9967971	3
58	9·0838317	10326	10·9161683	9·0870501	10480	10·9129499	10·0032183	154	9·9967817	2
59	9·0848643	10302	10·9151357	9·0880981	10457	10·9119019	10·0032338	155	9·9967662	1
60	9·0858945		10·9141055	9·0891438		10·9108562	10·0032493	155	9·9967507	0
'	Cosine	Diff.	Secant	Cotang.	Diff.	Tang.	Cosec.	D.	Sine	'

LOGARITHMIC SINES,

′	Sine	Diff.	Cosec.	Tang.	Diff.	Cotang.	Secant	D.	Cosine	′
0	9·0858945	10276	10·9141055	9·0891438	10431	10·9108562	10·0032493	155	9·9967507	60
1	9·0869221	10252	10·9130779	9·0901869	10408	10·9098131	10·0032648	156	9·9967352	59
2	9·0879473	10227	10·9120527	9·0912277	10383	10·9087723	10·0032804	156	9·9967196	58
3	9·0889700	10203	10·9110300	9·0922660	10360	10·9077340	10·0032960	156	9·9967040	57
4	9·0899903	10179	10·9100097	9·0933020	10335	10·9066980	10·0033116	157	9·9966884	56
5	9·0910082	10155	10·9089918	9·0943355	10312	10·9056645	10·0033273	157	9·9966727	55
6	9·0920237	10130	10·9079763	9·0953667	10288	10·9046333	10·0033430	158	9·9966570	54
7	9·0930367	10107	10·9069633	9·0963955	10264	10·9036045	10·0033588	158	9·9966412	53
8	9·0940474	10082	10·9059526	9·0974219	10241	10·9025781	10·0033746	158	9·9966254	52
9	9·0950556	10059	10·9049444	9·0984460	10218	10·9015540	10·0033904	159	9·9966096	51
10	9·0960615	10036	10·9039385	9·0994678	10194	10·9005322	10·0034063	159	9·9965937	50
11	9·0970651	10011	10·9029349	9·1004872	10172	10·8995128	10·0034222	159	9·9965778	49
12	9·0980662	9989	10·9019338	9·1015044	10148	10·8984956	10·0034381	160	9·9965619	48
13	9·0990651	9965	10·9009349	9·1025192	10125	10·8974808	10·0034541	160	9·9965459	47
14	9·1000616	9942	10·8999384	9·1035317	10103	10·8964683	10·0034701	161	9·9965299	46
15	9·1010558	9919	10·8989442	9·1045420	10080	10·8954580	10·0034862	161	9·9965138	45
16	9·1020477	9896	10·8979523	9·1055500	10057	10·8944500	10·0035023	161	9·9964977	44
17	9·1030373	9873	10·8969627	9·1065557	10034	10·8934443	10·0035184	161	9·9964816	43
18	9·1040246	9850	10·8959754	9·1075591	10013	10·8924409	10·0035345	162	9·9964655	42
19	9·1050096	9828	10·8949904	9·1085604	9990	10·8914396	10·0035507	162	9·9964493	41
20	9·1059924	9805	10·8940076	9·1095594	9968	10·8904406	10·0035670	163	9·9964330	40
21	9·1069729	9783	10·8930271	9·1105562	9946	10·8894438	10·0035833	163	9·9964167	39
22	9·1079512	9760	10·8920488	9·1115508	9923	10·8884492	10·0035996	163	9·9964004	38
23	9·1089272	9738	10·8910728	9·1125431	9902	10·8874569	10·0036159	163	9·9963841	37
24	9·1099010	9716	10·8900990	9·1135333	9880	10·8864667	10·0036323	164	9·9963677	36
25	9·1108726	9694	10·8891274	9·1145213	9859	10·8854787	10·0036487	165	9·9963513	35
26	9·1118420	9672	10·8881580	9·1155072	9837	10·8844928	10·0036652	165	9·9963348	34
27	9·1128092	9650	10·8871908	9·1164909	9815	10·8835091	10·0036817	165	9·9963183	33
28	9·1137742	9628	10·8862258	9·1174724	9794	10·8825276	10·0036982	166	9·9963018	32
29	9·1147370	9607	10·8852630	9·1184518	9773	10·8815482	10·0037148	166	9·9962852	31
30	9·1156977	9585	10·8843023	9·1194291	9752	10·8805709	10·0037314	167	9·9962686	30
31	9·1166562	9563	10·8833438	9·1204043	9730	10·8795957	10·0037481	167	9·9962519	29
32	9·1176125	9542	10·8823875	9·1213773	9709	10·8786227	10·0037648	167	9·9962352	28
33	9·1185667	9521	10·8814333	9·1223482	9689	10·8776518	10·0037815	168	9·9962185	27
34	9·1195188	9500	10·8804812	9·1233171	9668	10·8766829	10·0037983	168	9·9962017	26
35	9·1204688	9479	10·8795312	9·1242839	9647	10·8757161	10·0038151	168	9·9961849	25
36	9·1214167	9457	10·8785833	9·1252486	9626	10·8747514	10·0038319	169	9·9961681	24
37	9·1223624	9437	10·8776376	9·1262112	9606	10·8737888	10·0038488	169	9·9961512	23
38	9·1233061	9416	10·8766939	9·1271718	9585	10·8728282	10·0038657	169	9·9961343	22
39	9·1242477	9395	10·8757523	9·1281303	9565	10·8718697	10·0038826	170	9·9961174	21
40	9·1251872	9374	10·8748128	9·1290868	9545	10·8709132	10·0038996	170	9·9961004	20
41	9·1261246	9354	10·8738754	9·1300413	9524	10·8699587	10·0039166	171	9·9960834	19
42	9·1270600	9334	10·8729400	9·1309937	9505	10·8690063	10·0039337	171	9·9960663	18
43	9·1279934	9313	10·8720066	9·1319442	9484	10·8680558	10·0039508	171	9·9960492	17
44	9·1289247	9292	10·8710753	9·1328926	9465	10·8671074	10·0039679	172	9·9960321	16
45	9·1298539	9273	10·8701461	9·1338391	9444	10·8661609	10·0039851	172	9·9960149	15
46	9·1307812	9252	10·8692188	9·1347835	9425	10·8652165	10·0040023	173	9·9959977	14
47	9·1317064	9233	10·8682936	9·1357260	9405	10·8642740	10·0040196	173	9·9959804	13
48	9·1326297	9212	10·8673703	9·1366665	9386	10·8633335	10·0040369	173	9·9959631	12
49	9·1335509	9193	10·8664491	9·1376051	9366	10·8623949	10·0040542	173	9·9959458	11
50	9·1344702	9173	10·8655298	9·1385417	9347	10·8614583	10·0040716	174	9·9959284	10
51	9·1353875	9153	10·8646125	9·1394764	9328	10·8605236	10·0040889	175	9·9959111	9
52	9·1363028	9133	10·8636972	9·1404092	9308	10·8595908	10·0041064	175	9·9958936	8
53	9·1372161	9114	10·8627839	9·1413400	9289	10·8586600	10·0041239	175	9·9958761	7
54	9·1381275	9095	10·8618725	9·1422689	9270	10·8577311	10·0041414	175	9·9958586	6
55	9·1390370	9075	10·8609630	9·1431959	9251	10·8568041	10·0041589	176	9·9958411	5
56	9·1399445	9056	10·8600555	9·1441210	9232	10·8558790	10·0041765	176	9·9958235	4
57	9·1408501	9036	10·8591499	9·1450442	9213	10·8549558	10·0041941	176	9·9958059	3
58	9·1417537	9018	10·8582463	9·1459655	9194	10·8540345	10·0042118	177	9·9957882	2
59	9·1426555	8998	10·8573445	9·1468849	9176	10·8531151	10·0042295	177	9·9957705	1
60	9·1435553		10·8564447	9·1478025		10·8521975	10·0042472	177	9·9957528	0

| ′ | Cosine | Diff. | Secant | Cotang. | Diff. | Tang. | Cosec. | D. | Sine | ′ |

′	Sine	Diff.	Cosec.	Tang.	Diff.	Cotang.	Secant	D.	Cosine	′
0	9·1435553	8979	10·8564447	9·1478025	9157	10·8521975	10·0042472	178	9·9957528	60
1	9·1444532	8961	10·8555468	9·1487182	9139	10·8512818	10·0042650	178	9·9957350	59
2	9·1453493	8942	10·8546507	9·1496321	9120	10·8503679	10·0042828	178	9·9957172	58
3	9·1462435	8923	10·8537565	9·1505441	9102	10·8494559	10·0043007	179	9·9956993	57
4	9·1471358	8904	10·8528642	9·1514543	9084	10·8485457	10·0043185	178	9·9956815	56
5	9·1480262	8886	10·8519738	9·1523627	9065	10·8476373	10·0043365	180	9·9956635	55
								179		
6	9·1489148	8867	10·8510852	9·1532692	9047	10·8467308	10·0043544	180	9·9956456	54
7	9·1498015	8849	10·8501985	9·1541739	9030	10·8458261	10·0043724	180	9·9956276	53
8	9·1506864	8830	10·8493136	9·1550769	9011	10·8449231	10·0043905	181	9·9956095	52
9	9·1515694	8813	10·8484306	9·1559780	8993	10·8440220	10·0044085	180	9·9955915	51
10	9·1524507	8794	10·8475493	9·1568773	8975	10·8431227	10·0044266	181	9·9955734	50
								182		
11	9·1533301	8775	10·8466699	9·1577748	8958	10·8422252	10·0044448	182	9·9955552	49
12	9·1542076	8758	10·8457924	9·1586706	8940	10·8413294	10·0044630	182	9·9955370	48
13	9·1550834	8740	10·8449166	9·1595646	8923	10·8404354	10·0044812	183	9·9955188	47
14	9·1559574	8722	10·8440426	9·1604569	8904	10·8395431	10·0044995	183	9·9955005	46
15	9·1568296	8704	10·8431704	9·1613473	8888	10·8386527	10·0045178	183	9·9954822	45
								183		
16	9·1577000	8686	10·8423000	9·1622361	8870	10·8377639	10·0045361	184	9·9954639	44
17	9·1585686	8668	10·8414314	9·1631231	8852	10·8368769	10·0045545	184	9·9954455	43
18	9·1594354	8651	10·8405646	9·1640083	8836	10·8359917	10·0045729	184	9·9954271	42
19	9·1603005	8634	10·8396995	9·1648919	8818	10·8351081	10·0045913	185	9·9954087	41
20	9·1611639	8615	10·8388361	9·1657737	8801	10·8342263	10·0046098	185	9·9953902	40
								185		
21	9·1620254	8599	10·8379746	9·1666538	8784	10·8333462	10·0046283	186	9·9953717	39
22	9·1628853	8581	10·8371147	9·1675322	8767	10·8324678	10·0046469	186	9·9953531	38
23	9·1637434	8564	10·8362566	9·1684089	8750	10·8315911	10·0046655	186	9·9953345	37
24	9·1645998	8546	10·8354002	9·1692839	8733	10·8307161	10·0046841	187	9·9953159	36
25	9·1654544	8530	10·8345456	9·1701572	8717	10·8298428	10·0047028	187	9·9952972	35
								187		
26	9·1663074	8512	10·8336926	9·1710289	8700	10·8289711	10·0047215	188	9·9952785	34
27	9·1671586	8495	10·8328414	9·1718989	8683	10·8281011	10·0047403	188	9·9952597	33
28	9·1680081	8478	10·8319919	9·1727672	8666	10·8272328	10·0047591	188	9·9952409	32
29	9·1688559	8462	10·8311441	9·1736338	8650	10·8263662	10·0047779	188	9·9952221	31
30	9·1697021	8444	10·8302979	9·1744988	8634	10·8255012	10·0047967	189	9·9952033	30
								189		
31	9·1705465	8428	10·8294535	9·1753622	8617	10·8246378	10·0048156	190	9·9951844	29
32	9·1713893	8412	10·8286107	9·1762239	8601	10·8237761	10·0048346	190	9·9951654	28
33	9·1722305	8394	10·8277695	9·1770840	8585	10·8229160	10·0048536	190	9·9951464	27
34	9·1730699	8378	10·8269301	9·1779425	8568	10·8220575	10·0048726	190	9·9951274	26
35	9·1739077	8362	10·8260923	9·1787993	8553	10·8212007	10·0048916	189	9·9951084	25
								191		
36	9·1747439	8345	10·8252561	9·1796546	8536	10·8203454	10·0049107	191	9·9950893	24
37	9·1755784	8328	10·8244216	9·1805082	8520	10·8194918	10·0049298	192	9·9950702	23
38	9·1764112	8313	10·8235888	9·1813602	8504	10·8186398	10·0049490	192	9·9950510	22
39	9·1772425	8296	10·8227575	9·1822106	8489	10·8177894	10·0049682	192	9·9950318	21
40	9·1780721	8280	10·8219279	9·1830595	8473	10·8169405	10·0049874	193	9·9950126	20
								193		
41	9·1789001	8264	10·8210999	9·1839068	8457	10·8160932	10·0050067	193	9·9949933	19
42	9·1797265	8247	10·8202735	9·1847525	8441	10·8152475	10·0050260	194	9·9949740	18
43	9·1805512	8232	10·8194488	9·1855966	8426	10·8144034	10·0050454	194	9·9949546	17
44	9·1813744	8216	10·8186256	9·1864392	8410	10·8135608	10·0050648	194	9·9949352	16
45	9·1821960	8200	10·8178040	9·1872802	8394	10·8127198	10·0050842	194	9·9949158	15
								194		
46	9·1830160	8184	10·8169840	9·1881196	8379	10·8118804	10·0051036	195	9·9948964	14
47	9·1838344	8168	10·8161656	9·1889575	8364	10·8110425	10·0051231	195	9·9948769	13
48	9·1846512	8153	10·8153488	9·1897939	8348	10·8102061	10·0051427	196	9·9948573	12
49	9·1854665	8137	10·8145335	9·1906287	8334	10·8093713	10·0051623	196	9·9948377	11
50	9·1862802	8121	10·8137198	9·1914621	8318	10·8085379	10·0051819	196	9·9948181	10
								196		
51	9·1870923	8106	10·8129077	9·1922939	8302	10·8077061	10·0052015	197	9·9947985	9
52	9·1879029	8091	10·8120971	9·1931241	8288	10·8068759	10·0052212	197	9·9947788	8
53	9·1887120	8075	10·8112880	9·1939529	8273	10·8060471	10·0052409	198	9·9947591	7
54	9·1895195	8059	10·8104805	9·1947802	8257	10·8052198	10·0052607	198	9·9947393	6
55	9·1903254	8045	10·8096746	9·1956059	8243	10·8043941	10·0052805	198	9·9947195	5
								198		
56	9·1911299	8029	10·8088701	9·1964302	8228	10·8035698	10·0053003	199	9·9946997	4
57	9·1919328	8014	10·8080672	9·1972530	8213	10·8027470	10·0053202	199	9·9946798	3
58	9·1927342	7999	10·8072658	9·1980743	8198	10·8019257	10·0053401	199	9·9946599	2
59	9·1935341	7983	10·8064659	9·1988941	8184	10·8011059	10·0053601	200	9·9946399	1
60	9·1943324		10·8056676	9·1997125		10·8002875	10·0053801	200	9·9946199	0
′	Cosine	Diff.	Secant	Cotang.	Diff.	Tang.	Cosec.	D.	Sine	′

′	Sine	Diff.	Cosec.	Tang.	Diff.	Cotang.	Secant	D.	Cosine	′
0	9·1943324	7969	10·8056676	9·1997125	8169	10·8002875	10·0053801	200	9·9946199	60
1	9·1951293	7954	10·8048707	9·2005294	8155	10·7994706	10·0054001	201	9·9945999	59
2	9·1959247	7939	10·8040753	9·2013449	8139	10·7986551	10·0054202	201	9·9945798	58
3	9·1967186	7924	10·8032814	9·2021588	8126	10·7978412	10·0054403	201	9·9945597	57
4	9·1975110	7909	10·8024890	9·2029714	8111	10·7970286	10·0054604	202	9·9945396	56
5	9·1983019	7894	10·8016981	9·2037825	8097	10·7962175	10·0054806	202	9·9945194	55
6	9·1990913	7880	10·8009087	9·2045922	8082	10·7954078	10·0055008	202	9·9944992	54
7	9·1998793	7865	10·8001207	9·2054004	8068	10·7945996	10·0055211	202	9·9944789	53
8	9·2006658	7851	10·7993342	9·2062072	8054	10·7937928	10·0055413	204	9·9944587	52
9	9·2014509	7836	10·7985491	9·2070126	8039	10·7929874	10·0055617	203	9·9944383	51
10	9·2022345	7822	10·7977655	9·2078165	8026	10·7921835	10·0055820	205	9·9944180	50
11	9·2030167	7807	10·7969833	9·2086191	8012	10·7913809	10·0056025	204	9·9943975	49
12	9·2037974	7792	10·7962026	9·2094203	7997	10·7905797	10·0056229	205	9·9943771	48
13	9·2045766	7779	10·7954234	9·2102200	7984	10·7897800	10·0056434	205	9·9943566	47
14	9·2053545	7764	10·7946455	9·2110184	7969	10·7889816	10·0056639	205	9·9943361	46
15	9·2061309	7750	10·7938691	9·2118153	7956	10·7881847	10·0056844	206	9·9943156	45
16	9·2069059	7736	10·7930941	9·2126109	7942	10·7873891	10·0057050	207	9·9942950	44
17	9·2076795	7721	10·7923205	9·2134051	7929	10·7865949	10·0057257	206	9·9942743	43
18	9·2084516	7708	10·7915484	9·2141980	7914	10·7858020	10·0057463	207	9·9942537	42
19	9·2092224	7693	10·7907776	9·2149894	7901	10·7850106	10·0057670	208	9·9942330	41
20	9·2099917	7680	10·7900083	9·2157795	7888	10·7842205	10·0057878	208	9·9942122	40
21	9·2107597	7666	10·7892403	9·2165683	7873	10·7834317	10·0058086	208	9·9941914	39
22	9·2115263	7651	10·7884737	9·2173556	7861	10·7826444	10·0058294	208	9·9941706	38
23	9·2122914	7638	10·7877086	9·2181417	7847	10·7818583	10·0058502	209	9·9941498	37
24	9·2130552	7624	10·7869448	9·2189264	7833	10·7810736	10·0058711	210	9·9941289	36
25	9·2138176	7611	10·7861824	9·2197097	7820	10·7802903	10·0058921	209	9·9941079	35
26	9·2145787	7597	10·7854213	9·2204917	7807	10·7795083	10·0059130	211	9·9940870	34
27	9·2153384	7583	10·7846616	9·2212724	7794	10·7787276	10·0059341	210	9·9940659	33
28	9·2160967	7569	10·7839033	9·2220518	7780	10·7779482	10·0059551	211	9·9940449	32
29	9·2168536	7556	10·7831464	9·2228298	7767	10·7771702	10·0059762	211	9·9940238	31
30	9·2176092	7543	10·7823908	9·2236065	7754	10·7763935	10·0059973	212	9·9940027	30
31	9·2183635	7529	10·7816365	9·2243819	7742	10·7756181	10·0060185	212	9·9939815	29
32	9·2191164	7516	10·7808836	9·2251561	7728	10·7748439	10·0060397	212	9·9939603	28
33	9·2198680	7502	10·7801320	9·2259289	7715	10·7740711	10·0060609	213	9·9939391	27
34	9·2206182	7489	10·7793818	9·2267004	7702	10·7732996	10·0060822	213	9·9939178	26
35	9·2213671	7476	10·7786329	9·2274706	7689	10·7725294	10·0061035	213	9·9938965	25
36	9·2221147	7462	10·7778853	9·2282395	7676	10·7717605	10·0061248	214	9·9938752	24
37	9·2228609	7450	10·7771391	9·2290071	7664	10·7709929	10·0061462	214	9·9938538	23
38	9·2236059	7436	10·7763941	9·2297735	7651	10·7702265	10·0061676	215	9·9938324	22
39	9·2243495	7423	10·7756505	9·2305386	7638	10·7694614	10·0061891	215	9·9938109	21
40	9·2250918	7410	10·7749082	9·2313024	7626	10·7686976	10·0062106	215	9·9937894	20
41	9·2258328	7397	10·7741672	9·2320650	7612	10·7679350	10·0062321	216	9·9937679	19
42	9·2265725	7385	10·7734273	9·2328262	7601	10·7671738	10·0062537	216	9·9937463	18
43	9·2273110	7371	10·7726890	9·2335863	7588	10·7664137	10·0062753	217	9·9937247	17
44	9·2280481	7358	10·7719519	9·2343451	7575	10·7656549	10·0062970	217	9·9937030	16
45	9·2287839	7346	10·7712161	9·2351026	7563	10·7648974	10·0063187	217	9·9936813	15
46	9·2295185	7333	10·7704815	9·2358589	7550	10·7641411	10·0063404	218	9·9936596	14
47	9·2302518	7320	10·7697482	9·2366139	7539	10·7633861	10·0063622	218	9·9936378	13
48	9·2309838	7307	10·7690162	9·2373678	7525	10·7626322	10·0063840	218	9·9936160	12
49	9·2317145	7295	10·7682855	9·2381203	7514	10·7618797	10·0064058	219	9·9935942	11
50	9·2324440	7282	10·7675560	9·2388717	7501	10·7611283	10·0064277	219	9·9935723	10
51	9·2331722	7270	10·7668278	9·2396218	7490	10·7603782	10·0064496	219	9·9935504	9
52	9·2338992	7257	10·7661008	9·2403708	7477	10·7596292	10·0064715	220	9·9935285	8
53	9·2346249	7245	10·7653751	9·2411185	7465	10·7588815	10·0064935	221	9·9935065	7
54	9·2353494	7232	10·7646506	9·2418650	7453	10·7581350	10·0065156	220	9·9934844	6
55	9·2360726	7220	10·7639274	9·2426103	7440	10·7573897	10·0065376	221	9·9934624	5
56	9·2367946	7207	10·7632054	9·2433543	7429	10·7566457	10·0065597	222	9·9934403	4
57	9·2375153	7196	10·7624847	9·2440972	7417	10·7559028	10·0065819	222	9·9934181	3
58	9·2382349	7183	10·7617651	9·2448389	7405	10·7551611	10·0066041	222	9·9933959	2
59	9·2389532	7170	10·7610468	9·2455794	7394	10·7544206	10·0066263	222	9·9933737	1
60	9·2396702		10·7603298	9·2463188		10·7536812	10·0066485		9·9933515	0
′	Cosine	Diff.	Secant	Cotang.	Diff.	Tang.	Cosec.	D.	Sine	′

10 Deg.

′	Sine	Diff.	Cosec.	Tang.	Diff.	Cotang.	Secant	D.	Cosine	′
0	9·2396702		10·7603298	9·2463188		10·7536812	10·0066485		9·9933515	60
1	9·2403861	7159	10·7596139	9·2470569	7381	10·7529431	10·0066708	223	9·9933292	59
2	9·2411007	7146	10·7588993	9·2477939	7370	10·7522061	10·0066932	224	9·9933068	58
3	9·2418141	7134	10·7581859	9·2485297	7358	10·7514703	10·0067155	223	9·9932845	57
4	9·2425264	7123	10·7574736	9·2492643	7346	10·7507357	10·0067379	224	9·9932621	56
5	9·2432374	7110	10·7567626	9·2499978	7335	10·7500022	10·0067604	225	9·9932396	55
6	9·2439472	7098	10·7560528	9·2507301	7323	10·7492699	10·0067829	225	9·9932171	54
7	9·2446558	7086	10·7553442	9·2514612	7311	10·7485388	10·0068054	225	9·9931946	53
8	9·2453632	7074	10·7546368	9·2521912	7300	10·7478088	10·0068280	226	9·9931720	52
9	9·2460695	7063	10·7539305	9·2529200	7288	10·7470800	10·0068506	226	9·9931494	51
10	9·2467746	7051	10·7532254	9·2536477	7277	10·7463523	10·0068732	226	9·9931268	50
11	9·2474784	7038	10·7525216	9·2543743	7266	10·7456257	10·0068959	227	9·9931041	49
12	9·2481811	7027	10·7518189	9·2550997	7254	10·7449003	10·0069186	227	9·9930814	48
13	9·2488827	7016	10·7511173	9·2558240	7243	10·7441760	10·0069413	227	9·9930587	47
14	9·2495830	7003	10·7504170	9·2565472	7232	10·7434528	10·0069641	228	9·9930359	46
15	9·2502822	6992	10·7497178	9·2572692	7220	10·7427308	10·0069869	228	9·9930131	45
16	9·2509803	6981	10·7490197	9·2579901	7209	10·7420099	10·0070098	229	9·9929902	44
17	9·2516772	6969	10·7483228	9·2587099	7198	10·7412901	10·0070327	229	9·9929673	43
18	9·2523729	6957	10·7476271	9·2594285	7186	10·7405715	10·0070556	229	9·9929444	42
19	9·2530675	6946	10·7469325	9·2601461	7176	10·7398539	10·0070786	230	9·9929214	41
20	9·2537609	6934	10·7462391	9·2608625	7164	10·7391375	10·0071016	230	9·9928984	40
21	9·2544532	6923	10·7455468	9·2615779	7154	10·7384221	10·0071247	231	9·9928753	39
22	9·2551444	6912	10·7448556	9·2622921	7142	10·7377079	10·0071478	231	9·9928522	38
23	9·2558344	6900	10·7441656	9·2630053	7132	10·7369947	10·0071709	231	9·9928291	37
24	9·2565233	6889	10·7434767	9·2637173	7120	10·7362827	10·0071941	232	9·9928059	36
25	9·2572110	6877	10·7427890	9·2644283	7110	10·7355717	10·0072173	232	9·9927827	35
26	9·2578977	6867	10·7421023	9·2651382	7099	10·7348618	10·0072405	232	9·9927595	34
27	9·2585832	6855	10·7414168	9·2658470	7088	10·7341530	10·0072638	233	9·9927362	33
28	9·2592676	6844	10·7407324	9·2665547	7077	10·7334453	10·0072871	233	9·9927129	32
29	9·2599509	6833	10·7400491	9·2672613	7066	10·7327387	10·0073105	234	9·9926895	31
30	9·2606330	6821	10·7393670	9·2679669	7056	10·7320331	10·0073339	234	9·9926661	30
31	9·2613141	6811	10·7386859	9·2686714	7045	10·7313286	10·0073573	234	9·9926427	29
32	9·2619941	6800	10·7380059	9·2693749	7035	10·7306251	10·0073808	235	9·9926192	28
33	9·2626729	6788	10·7373271	9·2700772	7023	10·7299228	10·0074043	235	9·9925957	27
34	9·2633507	6778	10·7366493	9·2707786	7014	10·7292214	10·0074278	235	9·9925722	26
35	9·2640274	6767	10·7359726	9·2714788	7002	10·7285212	10·0074514	236	9·9925486	25
36	9·2647030	6756	10·7352970	9·2721780	6992	10·7278220	10·0074750	236	9·9925250	24
37	9·2653775	6745	10·7346225	9·2728762	6982	10·7271238	10·0074987	237	9·9925013	23
38	9·2660509	6734	10·7339491	9·2735733	6971	10·7264267	10·0075224	237	9·9924776	22
39	9·2667232	6723	10·7332768	9·2742694	6961	10·7257306	10·0075461	237	9·9924539	21
40	9·2673945	6713	10·7326055	9·2749644	6950	10·7250356	10·0075699	238	9·9924301	20
41	9·2680647	6702	10·7319353	9·2756584	6940	10·7243416	10·0075937	238	9·9924063	19
42	9·2687338	6691	10·7312662	9·2763514	6930	10·7236486	10·0076176	239	9·9923824	18
43	9·2694019	6681	10·7305981	9·2770434	6920	10·7229566	10·0076415	239	9·9923585	17
44	9·2700689	6670	10·7299311	9·2777343	6909	10·7222657	10·0076654	239	9·9923346	16
45	9·2707348	6659	10·7292652	9·2784242	6899	10·7215758	10·0076894	240	9·9923106	15
46	9·2713997	6649	10·7286003	9·2791131	6889	10·7208869	10·0077134	240	9·9922866	14
47	9·2720635	6638	10·7279365	9·2798009	6878	10·7201991	10·0077374	240	9·9922626	13
48	9·2727263	6628	10·7272737	9·2804878	6869	10·7195122	10·0077615	241	9·9922385	12
49	9·2733880	6617	10·7266120	9·2811736	6858	10·7188264	10·0077856	241	9·9922144	11
50	9·2740487	6607	10·7259513	9·2818585	6849	10·7181415	10·0078098	242	9·9921902	10
51	9·2747083	6596	10·7252917	9·2825423	6838	10·7174577	10·0078340	242	9·9921660	9
52	9·2753669	6586	10·7246331	9·2832251	6828	10·7167749	10·0078582	242	9·9921418	8
53	9·2760245	6576	10·7239755	9·2839070	6819	10·7160930	10·0078825	243	9·9921175	7
54	9·2766811	6566	10·7233189	9·2845878	6808	10·7154122	10·0079068	243	9·9920932	6
55	9·2773366	6555	10·7226634	9·2852677	6799	10·7147323	10·0079311	243	9·9920689	5
56	9·2779911	6545	10·7220089	9·2859466	6789	10·7140534	10·0079555	244	9·9920445	4
57	9·2786445	6534	10·7213555	9·2866245	6779	10·7133755	10·0079799	244	9·9920201	3
58	9·2792970	6525	10·7207030	9·2873014	6769	10·7126986	10·0080044	245	9·9919956	2
59	9·2799484	6514	10·7200516	9·2879773	6759	10·7120227	10·0080289	245	9·9919711	1
60	9·2805988	6504	10·7194012	9·2886523	6750	10·7113477	10·0080534	245	9·9919466	0

| ′ | Cosine | Diff. | Secant | Cotang. | Diff. | Tang. | Cosec. | D. | Sine | ′ |

79 Deg.

′	Sine	Diff.	Cosec.	Tang.	Diff.	Cotang.	Secant	D.	Cosine	′
0	9·2805988	6495	10·7194012	9·2886523	6740	10·7113477	10·0080534	246	9·9919466	60
1	9·2812483	6484	10·7187517	9·2893263	6730	10·7106737	10·0080780	246	9·9919220	59
2	9·2818967	6474	10·7181033	9·2899993	6720	10·7100007	10·0081026	247	9·9918974	58
3	9·2825441	6464	10·7174559	9·2906713	6711	10·7093287	10·0081273	247	9·9918727	57
4	9·2831905	6454	10·7168095	9·2913424	6702	10·7086576	10·0081520	247	9·9918480	56
5	9·2838359	6444	10·7161641	9·2920126	6691	10·7079874	10·0081767	247	9·9918233	55
6	9·2844803	6434	10·7155197	9·2926817	6683	10·7073183	10·0082014	249	9·9917986	54
7	9·2851237	6424	10·7148763	9·2933500	6672	10·7066500	10·0082263	248	9·9917737	53
8	9·2857661	6415	10·7142339	9·2940172	6664	10·7059828	10·0082511	249	9·9917489	52
9	9·2864076	6404	10·7135924	9·2946836	6653	10·7053164	10·0082760	249	9·9917240	51
10	9·2870480	6395	10·7129520	9·2953489	6645	10·7046511	10·0083009	250	9·9916991	50
11	9·2876875	6385	10·7123125	9·2960134	6635	10·7039866	10·0083259	249	9·9916741	49
12	9·2883260	6376	10·7116740	9·2966769	6626	10·7033231	10·0083508	251	9·9916492	48
13	9·2889636	6365	10·7110364	9·2973395	6616	10·7026605	10·0083759	251	9·9916241	47
14	9·2896001	6356	10·7103999	9·2980011	6607	10·7019989	10·0084010	251	9·9915990	46
15	9·2902357	6347	10·7097643	9·2986618	6598	10·7013382	10·0084261	251	9·9915739	45
16	9·2908704	6336	10·7091296	9·2993216	6588	10·7006784	10·0084512	252	9·9915488	44
17	9·2915040	6327	10·7084960	9·2999804	6579	10·7000196	10·0084764	252	9·9915236	43
18	9·2921367	6318	10·7078633	9·3006383	6571	10·6993617	10·0085016	253	9·9914984	42
19	9·2927685	6308	10·7072315	9·3012954	6560	10·6987046	10·0085269	253	9·9914731	41
20	9·2933993	6298	10·7066007	9·3019514	6552	10·6980486	10·0085522	253	9·9914478	40
21	9·2940291	6289	10·7059709	9·3026066	6543	10·6973934	10·0085775	254	9·9914225	39
22	9·2946580	6279	10·7053420	9·3032609	6534	10·6967391	10·0086029	254	9·9913971	38
23	9·2952859	6270	10·7047141	9·3039143	6524	10·6960857	10·0086283	255	9·9913717	37
24	9·2959129	6261	10·7040871	9·3045667	6516	10·6954333	10·0086538	255	9·9913462	36
25	9·2965390	6251	10·7034610	9·3052183	6506	10·6947817	10·0086793	255	9·9913207	35
26	9·2971641	6242	10·7028359	9·3058689	6498	10·6941311	10·0087048	256	9·9912952	34
27	9·2977883	6233	10·7022117	9·3065187	6488	10·6934813	10·0087304	256	9·9912696	33
28	9·2984116	6223	10·7015884	9·3071675	6480	10·6928325	10·0087560	256	9·9912440	32
29	9·2990339	6214	10·7009661	9·3078155	6471	10·6921845	10·0087816	257	9·9912184	31
30	9·2996553	6205	10·7003447	9·3084626	6462	10·6915374	10·0088073	257	9·9911927	30
31	9·3002758	6195	10·6997242	9·3091088	6453	10·6908912	10·0088330	258	9·9911670	29
32	9·3008953	6187	10·6991047	9·3097541	6444	10·6902459	10·0088588	258	9·9911412	28
33	9·3015140	6177	10·6984860	9·3103985	6436	10·6896015	10·0088846	258	9·9911154	27
34	9·3021317	6168	10·6978683	9·3110421	6427	10·6889579	10·0089104	259	9·9910896	26
35	9·3027485	6159	10·6972515	9·3116848	6418	10·6883152	10·0089363	259	9·9910637	25
36	9·3033644	6150	10·6966356	9·3123266	6409	10·6876734	10·0089622	259	9·9910378	24
37	9·3039794	6140	10·6960206	9·3129675	6401	10·6870325	10·0089881	260	9·9910119	23
38	9·3045934	6132	10·6954066	9·3136076	6392	10·6863924	10·0090141	261	9·9909859	22
39	9·3052066	6123	10·6947934	9·3142468	6383	10·6857532	10·0090402	260	9·9909598	21
40	9·3058189	6114	10·6941811	9·3148851	6375	10·6851149	10·0090662	261	9·9909338	20
41	9·3064303	6104	10·6935697	9·3155226	6366	10·6844774	10·0090923	262	9·9909077	19
42	9·3070407	6096	10·6929593	9·3161592	6358	10·6838408	10·0091185	262	9·9908815	18
43	9·3076503	6087	10·6923497	9·3167950	6349	10·6832050	10·0091447	262	9·9908553	17
44	9·3082590	6078	10·6917410	9·3174299	6341	10·6825701	10·0091709	262	9·9908291	16
45	9·3088668	6069	10·6911332	9·3180640	6332	10·6819360	10·0091971	263	9·9908029	15
46	9·3094737	6061	10·6905263	9·3186972	6323	10·6813028	10·0092234	264	9·9907766	14
47	9·3100798	6051	10·6899202	9·3193295	6316	10·6806705	10·0092498	263	9·9907502	13
48	9·3106849	6043	10·6893151	9·3199611	6307	10·6800389	10·0092761	265	9·9907239	12
49	9·3112892	6034	10·6887108	9·3205918	6298	10·6794082	10·0093026	264	9·9906974	11
50	9·3118926	6025	10·6881074	9·3212216	6290	10·6787784	10·0093290	265	9·9906710	10
51	9·3124951	6017	10·6875049	9·3218506	6282	10·6781494	10·0093555	265	9·9906445	9
52	9·3130968	6008	10·6869032	9·3224788	6273	10·6775212	10·0093820	266	9·9906180	8
53	9·3136976	5999	10·6863024	9·3231061	6266	10·6768939	10·0094086	266	9·9905914	7
54	9·3142975	5990	10·6857025	9·3237327	6257	10·6762673	10·0094352	266	9·9905648	6
55	9·3148965	5982	10·6851035	9·3243584	6248	10·6756416	10·0094618	267	9·9905382	5
56	9·3154947	5974	10·6845053	9·3249832	6241	10·6750168	10·0094885	267	9·9905115	4
57	9·3160921	5964	10·6839079	9·3256073	6232	10·6743927	10·0095152	268	9·9904848	3
58	9·3166885	5956	10·6833115	9·3262305	6224	10·6737695	10·0095420	268	9·9904580	2
59	9·3172841	5948	10·6827159	9·3268529	6216	10·6731471	10·0095688	268	9·9904312	1
60	9·3178789		10·6821211	9·3274745		10·6725255	10·0095956		9·9904044	0

′	Cosine	Diff.	Secant	Cotang.	Diff.	Tang.	Cosec.	D.	Sine	′

78 Deg.

′	Sine	Diff.	Cosec.	Tang.	Diff.	Cotang.	Secant	D.	Cosine	′
0	9·3178789	5939	10·6821211	9·3274745	6208	10·6725255	10·0095956	269	9·9904044	60
1	9·3184728	5931	10·6815272	9·3280953	6200	10·6719047	10·0096225	269	9·9903775	59
2	9·3190659	5922	10·6809341	9·3287153	6192	10·6712847	10·0096494	269	9·9903506	58
3	9·3196581	5914	10·6803419	9·3293345	6183	10·6706655	10·0096763	270	9·9903237	57
4	9·3202495	5905	10·6797505	9·3299528	6176	10·6700472	10·0097033	270	9·9902967	56
5	9·3208400	5897	10·6791600	9·3305704	6168	10·6694296	10·0097303	271	9·9902697	55
6	9·3214297	5889	10·6785703	9·3311872	6159	10·6688128	10·0097574	271	9·9902426	54
7	9·3220186	5880	10·6779814	9·3318031	6152	10·6681969	10·0097845	272	9·9902155	53
8	9·3226066	5872	10·6773934	9·3324183	6144	10·6675817	10·0098117	271	9·9901883	52
9	9·3231938	5864	10·6768062	9·3330327	6136	10·6669673	10·0098388	273	9·9901612	51
10	9·3237802	5855	10·6762198	9·3336463	6128	10·6663537	10·0098661	272	9·9901339	50
11	9·3243657	5848	10·6756343	9·3342591	6120	10·6657409	10·0098933	273	9·9901067	49
12	9·3249505	5839	10·6750495	9·3348711	6112	10·6651289	10·0099206	273	9·9900794	48
13	9·3255344	5830	10·6744656	9·3354823	6104	10·6645177	10·0099479	274	9·9900521	47
14	9·3261174	5823	10·6738826	9·3360927	6097	10·6639073	10·0099753	274	9·9900247	46
15	9·3266997	5814	10·6733003	9·3367024	6089	10·6632976	10·0100027	275	9·9899973	45
16	9·3272811	5806	10·6727189	9·3373113	6081	10·6626887	10·0100302	275	9·9899698	44
17	9·3278617	5799	10·6721383	9·3379194	6073	10·6620806	10·0100577	275	9·9899423	43
18	9·3284416	5790	10·6715584	9·3385267	6066	10·6614733	10·0100852	275	9·9899148	42
19	9·3290206	5782	10·6709794	9·3391333	6058	10·6608667	10·0101127	276	9·9898873	41
20	9·3295988	5773	10·6704012	9·3397391	6050	10·6602609	10·0101403	277	9·9898597	40
21	9·3301761	5766	10·6698239	9·3403441	6043	10·6596559	10·0101680	277	9·9898320	39
22	9·3307527	5758	10·6692473	9·3409484	6035	10·6590516	10·0101957	277	9·9898043	38
23	9·3313285	5750	10·6686715	9·3415519	6027	10·6584481	10·0102234	277	9·9897766	37
24	9·3319035	5742	10·6680965	9·3421546	6020	10·6578454	10·0102511	278	9·9897489	36
25	9·3324777	5734	10·6675223	9·3427566	6012	10·6572434	10·0102789	279	9·9897211	35
26	9·3330511	5726	10·6669489	9·3433578	6005	10·6566422	10·0103068	278	9·9896932	34
27	9·3336237	5718	10·6663763	9·3439583	5997	10·6560417	10·0103346	280	9·9896654	33
28	9·3341955	5710	10·6658045	9·3445580	5990	10·6554420	10·0103626	279	9·9896374	32
29	9·3347665	5703	10·6652335	9·3451570	5982	10·6548430	10·0103905	280	9·9896095	31
30	9·3353368	5694	10·6646632	9·3457552	5975	10·6542448	10·0104185	280	9·9895815	30
31	9·3359062	5687	10·6640938	9·3463527	5967	10·6536473	10·0104465	281	9·9895535	29
32	9·3364749	5679	10·6635251	9·3469494	5960	10·6530506	10·0104746	281	9·9895254	28
33	9·3370428	5671	10·6629572	9·3475454	5953	10·6524546	10·0105027	281	9·9894973	27
34	9·3376099	5663	10·6623901	9·3481407	5945	10·6518593	10·0105308	282	9·9894692	26
35	9·3381762	5656	10·6618238	9·3487352	5938	10·6512648	10·0105590	282	9·9894410	25
36	9·3387418	5647	10·6612582	9·3493290	5930	10·6506710	10·0105872	283	9·9894128	24
37	9·3393065	5641	10·6606935	9·3499220	5923	10·6500780	10·0106155	283	9·9893845	23
38	9·3398706	5632	10·6601294	9·3505143	5916	10·6494857	10·0106438	283	9·9893562	22
39	9·3404338	5625	10·6595662	9·3511059	5909	10·6488941	10·0106721	284	9·9893279	21
40	9·3409963	5617	10·6590037	9·3516968	5901	10·6483032	10·0107005	284	9·9892995	20
41	9·3415580	5610	10·6584420	9·3522869	5894	10·6477131	10·0107289	284	9·9892711	19
42	9·3421190	5602	10·6578810	9·3528763	5887	10·6471237	10·0107573	285	9·9892427	18
43	9·3426792	5594	10·6573208	9·3534650	5880	10·6465350	10·0107858	286	9·9892142	17
44	9·3432386	5587	10·6567614	9·3540530	5872	10·6459470	10·0108144	285	9·9891856	16
45	9·3437973	5579	10·6562027	9·3546402	5865	10·6453598	10·0108429	286	9·9891571	15
46	9·3443552	5572	10·6556448	9·3552267	5859	10·6447733	10·0108715	287	9·9891285	14
47	9·3449124	5564	10·6550876	9·3558126	5851	10·6441874	10·0109002	287	9·9890998	13
48	9·3454688	5557	10·6545312	9·3563977	5844	10·6436023	10·0109289	287	9·9890711	12
49	9·3460245	5549	10·6539755	9·3569821	5837	10·6430179	10·0109576	287	9·9890424	11
50	9·3465794	5542	10·6534206	9·3575658	5829	10·6424342	10·0109863	288	9·9890137	10
51	9·3471336	5534	10·6528664	9·3581487	5823	10·6418513	10·0110151	289	9·9889849	9
52	9·3476870	5527	10·6523130	9·3587310	5816	10·6412690	10·0110440	289	9·9889560	8
53	9·3482397	5520	10·6517603	9·3593126	5809	10·6406874	10·0110729	289	9·9889271	7
54	9·3487917	5512	10·6512083	9·3598935	5801	10·6401065	10·0111018	289	9·9888982	6
55	9·3493429	5505	10·6506571	9·3604736	5795	10·6395264	10·0111307	290	9·9888693	5
56	9·3498934	5498	10·6501066	9·3610531	5788	10·6389469	10·0111597	290	9·9888403	4
57	9·3504432	5490	10·6495568	9·3616319	5781	10·6383681	10·0111887	291	9·9888113	3
58	9·3509922	5483	10·6490078	9·3622100	5774	10·6377900	10·0112178	291	9·9887822	2
59	9·3515405	5475	10·6484595	9·3627874	5767	10·6372126	10·0112469	292	9·9887531	1
60	9·3520880		10·6479120	9·3633641		10·6366359	10·0112761		9·9887239	0

′	Cosine	Diff.	Secant	Cotang.	Diff.	Tang.	Cosec.	D.	Sine	′

′	Sine	Diff.	Cosec.	Tang.	Diff.	Cotang.	Secant	D.	Cosine	′
0	9·3520880	5469	10·6479120	9·3633641	5760	10·6366359	10·0112761	292	9·9887239	60
1	9·3526349	5461	10·6473651	9·3639401	5754	10·6360599	10·0113053	292	9·9886947	59
2	9·3531810	5454	10·6468190	9·3645155	5746	10·6354845	10·0113345	292	9·9886655	58
3	9·3537264	5446	10·6462736	9·3650901	5740	10·6349099	10·0113637	293	9·9886363	57
4	9·3542710	5440	10·6457290	9·3656641	5733	10·6343353	10·0113930	294	9·9886070	56
5	9·3548150	5432	10·6451850	9·3662374	5726	10·6337626	10·0114224	294	9·9885776	55
6	9·3553582	5425	10·6446418	9·3668100	5719	10·6331900	10·0114518	294	9·9885482	54
7	9·3559007	5419	10·6440993	9·3673819	5713	10·6326181	10·0114812	294	9·9885188	53
8	9·3564426	5410	10·6435574	9·3679532	5706	10·6320468	10·0115106	295	9·9884894	52
9	9·3569836	5404	10·6430164	9·3685238	5699	10·6314762	10·0115401	296	9·9884599	51
10	9·3575240	5397	10·6424760	9·3690937	5692	10·6309063	10·0115697	296	9·9884303	50
11	9·3580637	5390	10·6419363	9·3696629	5686	10·6303371	10·0115992	296	9·9884008	49
12	9·3586027	5382	10·6413973	9·3702315	5679	10·6297685	10·0116288	297	9·9883712	48
13	9·3591409	5376	10·6408591	9·3707994	5673	10·6292006	10·0116585	297	9·9883415	47
14	9·3596785	5369	10·6403215	9·3713667	5666	10·6286333	10·0116882	297	9·9883118	46
15	9·3602154	5361	10·6397846	9·3719333	5659	10·6280667	10·0117179	298	9·9882821	45
16	9·3607515	5355	10·6392485	9·3724992	5653	10·6275008	10·0117477	298	9·9882523	44
17	9·3612870	5347	10·6387130	9·3730645	5646	10·6269355	10·0117775	298	9·9882225	43
18	9·3618217	5341	10·6381783	9·3736291	5639	10·6263709	10·0118073	299	9·9881927	42
19	9·3623558	5334	10·6376442	9·3741930	5633	10·6258070	10·0118372	299	9·9881628	41
20	9·3628892	5327	10·6371108	9·3747563	5627	10·6252437	10·0118671	300	9·9881329	40
21	9·3634219	5320	10·6365781	9·3753190	5620	10·6246810	10·0118971	300	9·9881029	39
22	9·3639539	5313	10·6360461	9·3758810	5613	10·6241190	10·0119271	300	9·9880729	38
23	9·3644852	5306	10·6355148	9·3764423	5607	10·6235577	10·0119571	301	9·9880429	37
24	9·3650158	5300	10·6349842	9·3770030	5601	10·6229970	10·0119872	301	9·9880128	36
25	9·3655458	5292	10·6344542	9·3775631	5594	10·6224369	10·0120173	302	9·9879827	35
26	9·3660750	5286	10·6339250	9·3781225	5588	10·6218775	10·0120475	302	9·9879525	34
27	9·3666036	5279	10·6333964	9·3786813	5581	10·6213187	10·0120777	302	9·9879223	33
28	9·3671315	5272	10·6328685	9·3792394	5575	10·6207606	10·0121079	303	9·9878921	32
29	9·3676587	5266	10·6323413	9·3797969	5568	10·6202031	10·0121382	303	9·9878618	31
30	9·3681853	5258	10·6318147	9·3803537	5563	10·6196463	10·0121685	303	9·9878315	30
31	9·3687111	5252	10·6312889	9·3809100	5555	10·6190900	10·0121988	304	9·9878012	29
32	9·3692363	5245	10·6307637	9·3814655	5550	10·6185345	10·0122292	304	9·9877708	28
33	9·3697608	5239	10·6302392	9·3820205	5543	10·6179795	10·0122596	304	9·9877404	27
34	9·3702847	5232	10·6297153	9·3825748	5537	10·6174252	10·0122901	305	9·9877099	26
35	9·3708079	5225	10·6291921	9·3831285	5531	10·6168715	10·0123206	305	9·9876794	25
36	9·3713304	5219	10·6286606	9·3836816	5524	10·6163184	10·0123512	306	9·9876488	24
37	9·3718523	5212	10·6281477	9·3842340	5518	10·6157660	10·0123817	307	9·9876183	23
38	9·3723735	5205	10·6276265	9·3847858	5512	10·6152142	10·0124124	306	9·9875876	22
39	9·3728940	5199	10·6271060	9·3853370	5506	10·6146630	10·0124430	307	9·9875570	21
40	9·3734139	5192	10·6265861	9·3858876	5500	10·6141124	10·0124737	307	9·9875263	20
41	9·3739331	5186	10·6260669	9·3864376	5493	10·6135624	10·0125045	307	9·9874955	19
42	9·3744517	5179	10·6255448	9·3869869	5487	10·6130131	10·0125352	309	9·9874648	18
43	9·3749696	5172	10·6250304	9·3875356	5481	10·6124644	10·0125661	308	9·9874339	17
44	9·3754868	5166	10·6245132	9·3880837	5475	10·6119163	10·0125969	309	9·9874031	16
45	9·3760034	5160	10·6239966	9·3886312	5469	10·6113688	10·0126278	309	9·9873722	15
46	9·3765194	5153	10·6234806	9·3891781	5463	10·6108219	10·0126587	310	9·9873413	14
47	9·3770347	5146	10·6229653	9·3897244	5456	10·6102756	10·0126897	310	9·9873103	13
48	9·3775493	5140	10·6224507	9·3902700	5451	10·6097300	10·0127207	311	9·9872793	12
49	9·3780633	5134	10·6219367	9·3908151	5444	10·6091849	10·0127518	311	9·9872482	11
50	9·3785767	5127	10·6214233	9·3913595	5439	10·6086405	10·0127829	311	9·9872171	10
51	9·3790894	5121	10·6209106	9·3919034	5432	10·6080966	10·0128140	311	9·9871860	9
52	9·3796015	5114	10·6203985	9·3924466	5427	10·6075534	10·0128451	313	9·9871549	8
53	9·3801129	5108	10·6198871	9·3929893	5420	10·6070107	10·0128764	312	9·9871236	7
54	9·3806237	5102	10·6193763	9·3935313	5414	10·6064687	10·0129076	313	9·9870924	6
55	9·3811339	5095	10·6188661	9·3940727	5409	10·6059273	10·0129389	313	9·9870611	5
56	9·3816434	5089	10·6183566	9·3946136	5402	10·6053864	10·0129702	314	9·9870298	4
57	9·3821523	5082	10·6178477	9·3951538	5397	10·6048462	10·0130016	314	9·9869984	3
58	9·3826605	5077	10·6173395	9·3956935	5391	10·6043065	10·0130330	314	9·9869670	2
59	9·3831682	5070	10·6168318	9·3962326	5385	10·6037674	10·0130644	315	9·9869356	1
60	9·3836752		10·6163248	9·3967711		10·6032289	10·0130959		9·9869041	0

′	Cosine	Diff.	Secant	Cotang.	Diff.	Tang.	Cosec.	D.	Sine	′

′	Sine	Diff.	Cosec.	Tang.	Diff.	Cotang.	Secant	D.	Cosine	′
0	9·3836752	5063	10·6163248	9·3967711	5378	10·6032289	10·0130959	315	9·9869041	60
1	9·3841815	5058	10·6158185	9·3973089	5374	10·6026911	10·0131274	316	9·9868726	59
2	9·3846873	5051	10·6153127	9·3978463	5367	10·6021537	10·0131590	316	9·9868410	58
3	9·3851924	5045	10·6148076	9·3983830	5361	10·6016170	10·0131906	316	9·9868094	57
4	9·3856969	5039	10·6143031	9·3989191	5356	10·6010809	10·0132222	317	9·9867778	56
5	9·3862008	5032	10·6137992	9·3994547	5349	10·6005453	10·0132539	317	9·9867461	55
6	9·3867040	5027	10·6132960	9·3999896	5344	10·6000104	10·0132856	317	9·9867144	54
7	9·3872067	5020	10·6127933	9·4005240	5338	10·5994760	10·0133173	318	9·9866827	53
8	9·3877087	5014	10·6122913	9·4010578	5332	10·5989422	10·0133491	318	9·9866509	52
9	9·3882101	5008	10·6117899	9·4015910	5327	10·5984090	10·0133809	318	9·9866191	51
10	9·3887109	5002	10·6112891	9·4021237	5321	10·5978763	10·0134128	319	9·9865872	50
11	9·3892111	4995	10·6107889	9·4026558	5315	10·5973442	10·0134447	320	9·9865553	49
12	9·3897106	4990	10·6102894	9·4031873	5309	10·5968127	10·0134767	320	9·9865233	48
13	9·3902096	4983	10·6097904	9·4037182	5304	10·5962818	10·0135087	320	9·9864913	47
14	9·3907079	4978	10·6092921	9·4042486	5298	10·5957514	10·0135407	320	9·9864593	46
15	9·3912057	4971	10·6087943	9·4047784	5292	10·5952216	10·0135727	321	9·9864273	45
16	9·3917028	4965	10·6082972	9·4053076	5287	10·5946924	10·0136048	322	9·9863952	44
17	9·3921993	4959	10·6078007	9·4058363	5281	10·5941637	10·0136370	322	9·9863630	43
18	9·3926952	4953	10·6073048	9·4063644	5275	10·5936356	10·0136692	322	9·9863308	42
19	9·3931905	4947	10·6068095	9·4068919	5270	10·5931081	10·0137014	323	9·9862986	41
20	9·3936852	4942	10·6063148	9·4074189	5264	10·5925811	10·0137337	323	9·9862663	40
21	9·3941794	4935	10·6058206	9·4079453	5259	10·5920547	10·0137660	323	9·9862340	39
22	9·3946729	4929	10·6053271	9·4084712	5253	10·5915288	10·0137983	324	9·9862017	38
23	9·3951658	4923	10·6048342	9·4089965	5247	10·5910035	10·0138307	324	9·9861693	37
24	9·3956581	4918	10·6043419	9·4095212	5242	10·5904788	10·0138631	324	9·9861369	36
25	9·3961499	4911	10·6038501	9·4100454	5236	10·5899546	**10·**0138955	325	9·9861045	35
26	9·3966410	4905	10·6033590	9·4105690	5231	10·5894310	10·0139280	326	9·9860720	34
27	9·3971315	4900	10·6028685	9·4110921	5225	10·5889079	10·0139606	326	9·9860394	33
28	9·3976215	4894	10·6023785	9·4116146	5220	10·5883864	10·0139931	326	9·9860069	32
29	9·3981109	4887	10·6018891	9·4121366	5215	10·5878634	10·0140258	327	9·9859742	31
30	9·3985996	4882	10·6014004	9·4126581	5208	10·5873419	10·0140584	327	9·9859416	30
31	9·3990878	4876	10·6009122	9·4131789	5204	10·5868211	10·0140911	327	9·9859089	29
32	9·3995754	4871	10·6004246	9·4136993	5198	10·5863007	10·0141238	328	9·9858762	28
33	9·4000625	4864	10·5999375	9·4142191	5192	10·5857809	10·0141566	328	9·9858434	27
34	9·4005489	4859	10·5994511	9·4147383	5187	10·5852617	10·0141894	329	9·9858106	26
35	9·4010348	4853	10·5989652	9·4152570	5182	10·5847430	10·0142223	328	9·9857777	25
36	9·4015201	4847	10·5984799	9·4157752	5176	10·5842248	10·0142551	330	9·9857449	24
37	9·4020048	4841	10·5979952	9·4162928	5171	10·5837072	10·0142881	329	9·9857119	23
38	9·4024889	4835	10·5975111	9·4168099	5166	10·5831901	10·0143210	330	9·9856790	22
39	9·4029724	4830	10·5970276	9·4173265	5160	10·5826735	10·0143540	331	9·9856460	21
40	9·4034554	4824	10·5965446	9·4178425	5155	10·5821575	10·0143871	331	9·9856129	20
41	9·4039378	4818	10·5960622	9·4183580	5149	10·5816420	10·0144202	331	9·9855798	19
42	9·4044196	4813	10·5955804	9·4188729	5145	10·5811271	10·0144533	332	9·9855467	18
43	9·4049009	4807	10·5950991	9·4193874	5139	10·5806126	10·0144865	332	9·9855135	17
44	9·4053816	4801	10·5946184	9·4199013	5133	10·5800987	10·0145197	332	9·9854803	16
45	9·4058617	4796	10·5941383	9·4204146	5129	10·5795854	10·0145529	333	9·9854471	15
46	9·4063413	4790	10·5936587	9·4209275	5123	10·5790725	10·0145862	333	9·9854138	14
47	9·4068203	4784	10·5931797	9·4214398	5117	10·5785602	10·0146195	334	9·9853805	13
48	9·4072987	4779	10·5927013	9·4219515	5113	10·5780485	10·0146529	333	9·9853471	12
49	9·4077766	4773	10·5922234	9·4224628	5107	10·5775372	10·0146862	335	9·9853138	11
50	9·4082539	4767	10·5917461	9·4229735	5103	10·5770265	10·0147197	335	9·9852803	10
51	9·4087306	4762	10·5912694	9·4234838	5097	10·5765162	10·0147532	335	9·9852468	9
52	9·4092068	4756	10·5907932	9·4239935	5091	10·5760065	10·0147867	335	9·9852133	8
53	9·4096824	4751	10·5903176	9·4245026	5087	10·5754974	10·0148202	336	9·9851798	7
54	9·4101575	4745	10·5898425	9·4250113	5081	10·5749887	10·0148538	337	9·9851462	6
55	9·4106320	4739	10·5893680	9·4255194	5077	10·5744806	10·0148875	336	9·9851125	5
56	9·4111059	4734	10·5888941	9·4260271	5071	10·5739729	10·0149211	337	9·9850789	4
57	9·4115793	4729	10·5884207	9·4265342	5066	10·5734658	10·0149548	338	9·9850452	3
58	9·4120522	4723	10·5879478	9·4270408	5061	10·5729592	10·0149886	338	9·9850114	2
59	9·4125245	4717	10·5874755	9·4275469	5056	10·5724531	10·0150224	338	9·9849776	1
60	9·4129962		10·5870038	9·4280525		10·5719475	10·0150562		9·9849438	0

′	Cosine	Diff.	Secant	Cotang.	Diff.	Tang.	Cosec.	D.	Sine	′

15 Deg.

′	Sine	Diff.	Cosec.	Tang.	Diff.	Cotang.	Secant	D.	Cosine	′
0	9·4129962	4712	10·5870038	9·4280525	5050	10·5719475	10·0150562	339	9·9849438	60
1	9·4134674	4707	10·5865326	9·4285575	5046	10·5714425	10·0150901	339	9·9849099	59
2	9·4139381	4701	10·5860619	9·4290621	5040	10·5709379	10·0151240	340	9·9848760	58
3	9·4144082	4696	10·5855918	9·4295661	5036	10·5704339	10·0151580	339	9·9848420	57
4	9·4148778	4690	10·5851222	9·4300697	5030	10·5699303	10·0151919	341	9·9848081	56
5	9·4153468	4684	10·5846532	9·4305727	5026	10·5694273	10·0152260	340	9·9847740	55
6	9·4158152	4680	10·5841848	9·4310753	5020	10·5689247	10·0152600	341	9·9847400	54
7	9·4162832	4674	10·5837168	9·4315773	5016	10·5684227	10·0152941	342	9·9847059	53
8	9·4167506	4668	10·5832494	9·4320789	5010	10·5679211	10·0153283	342	9·9846717	52
9	9·4172174	4663	10·5827826	9·4325799	5005	10·5674201	10·0153625	342	9·9846375	51
10	9·4176837	4658	10·5823163	9·4330804	5001	10·5669196	10·0153967	343	9·9846033	50
11	9·4181495	4653	10·5818505	9·4335805	4995	10·5664195	10·0154310	343	9·9845690	49
12	9·4186148	4647	10·5813852	9·4340800	4991	10·5659200	10·0154653	343	9·9845347	48
13	9·4190795	4641	10·5809205	9·4345791	4985	10·5654209	10·0154996	344	9·9845004	47
14	9·4195436	4637	10·5804564	9·4350776	4981	10·5649224	10·0155340	344	9·9844660	46
15	9·4200073	4631	10·5799927	9·4355757	4976	10·5644243	10·0155684	345	9·9844316	45
16	9·4204704	4626	10·5795296	9·4360733	4971	10·5639267	10·0156029	345	9·9843971	44
17	9·4209330	4620	10·5790670	9·4365704	4966	10·5634296	10·0156374	345	9·9843626	43
18	9·4213950	4616	10·5786050	9·4370670	4961	10·5629330	10·0156719	346	9·9843281	42
19	9·4218566	4610	10·5781434	9·4375631	4956	10·5624369	10·0157065	346	9·9842935	41
20	9·4223176	4604	10·5776824	9·4380587	4951	10·5619413	10·0157411	347	9·9842589	40
21	9·4227780	4600	10·5772220	9·4385538	4947	10·5614462	10·0157758	347	9·9842242	39
22	9·4232380	4594	10·5767620	9·4390485	4941	10·5609515	10·0158105	347	9·9841895	38
23	9·4236974	4589	10·5763026	9·4395426	4937	10·5604574	10·0158452	348	9·9841548	37
24	9·4241563	4584	10·5758437	9·4400363	4932	10·5599637	10·0158800	348	9·9841200	36
25	9·4246147	4579	10·5753853	9·4405295	4927	10·5594705	10·0159148	349	9·9840852	35
26	9·4250726	4573	10·5749274	9·4410222	4923	10·5589778	10·0159497	349	9·9840503	34
27	9·4255299	4568	10·5744701	9·4415145	4917	10·5584855	10·0159846	349	9·9840154	33
28	9·4259867	4563	10·5740133	9·4420062	4913	10·5579938	10·0160195	350	9·9839805	32
29	9·4264430	4558	10·5735570	9·4424975	4908	10·5575025	10·0160545	350	9·9839455	31
30	9·4268988	4553	10·5731012	9·4429883	4903	10·5570117	10·0160895	350	9·9839105	30
31	9·4273541	4548	10·5726459	9·4434786	4899	10·5565214	10·0161245	351	9·9838755	29
32	9·4278089	4542	10·5721911	9·4439685	4894	10·5560315	10·0161596	352	9·9838404	28
33	9·4282631	4538	10·5717369	9·4444579	4889	10·5555421	10·0161948	351	9·9838052	27
34	9·4287169	4532	10·5712831	9·4449468	4884	10·5550532	10·0162299	353	9·9837701	26
35	9·4291701	4527	10·5708299	9·4454352	4880	10·5545648	10·0162652	352	9·9837348	25
36	9·4296228	4522	10·5703772	9·4459232	4875	10·5540768	10·0163004	353	9·9836996	24
37	9·4300750	4517	10·5699250	9·4464107	4871	10·5535893	10·0163357	353	9·9836643	23
38	9·4305267	4512	10·5694733	9·4468978	4865	10·5531022	10·0163710	354	9·9836290	22
39	9·4309779	4507	10·5690221	9·4473843	4861	10·5526157	10·0164064	354	9·9835936	21
40	9·4314286	4502	10·5685714	9·4478704	4857	10·5521296	10·0164418	355	9·9835582	20
41	9·4318788	4497	10·5681212	9·4483561	4852	10·5516439	10·0164773	355	9·9835227	19
42	9·4323285	4492	10·5676715	9·4488413	4847	10·5511587	10·0165128	355	9·9834872	18
43	9·4327777	4487	10·5672223	9·4493260	4842	10·5506740	10·0165483	356	9·9834517	17
44	9·4332264	4482	10·5667736	9·4498102	4838	10·5501898	10·0165839	356	9·9834161	16
45	9·4336746	4477	10·5663254	9·4502940	4834	10·5497060	10·0166195	356	9·9833805	15
46	9·4341223	4471	10·5658777	9·4507774	4828	10·5492226	10·0166551	357	9·9833449	14
47	9·4345694	4467	10·5654306	9·4512602	4825	10·5487398	10·0166908	357	9·9833092	13
48	9·4350161	4462	10·5649839	9·4517427	4819	10·5482573	10·0167265	358	9·9832735	12
49	9·4354623	4457	10·5645377	9·4522246	4815	10·5477754	10·0167623	358	9·9832377	11
50	9·4359080	4452	10·5640920	9·4527061	4811	10·5472939	10·0167981	358	9·9832019	10
51	9·4363532	4448	10·5636468	9·4531872	4806	10·5468128	10·0168339	359	9·9831661	9
52	9·4367980	4442	10·5632020	9·4536678	4801	10·5463322	10·0168698	360	9·9831302	8
53	9·4372422	4437	10·5627578	9·4541479	4797	10·5458521	10·0169058	359	9·9830942	7
54	9·4376859	4433	10·5623141	9·4546276	4793	10·5453724	10·0169417	360	9·9830583	6
55	9·4381292	4427	10·5618708	9·4551069	4788	10·5448931	10·0169777	361	9·9830223	5
56	9·4385719	4423	10·5614281	9·4555857	4784	10·5444143	10·0170138	361	9·9829862	4
57	9·4390142	4418	10·5609858	9·4560641	4779	10·5439359	10·0170499	361	9·9829501	3
58	9·4394560	4413	10·5605440	9·4565420	4774	10·5434580	10·0170860	362	9·9829140	2
59	9·4398973	4408	10·5601027	9·4570194	4770	10·5429806	10·0171222	362	9·9828778	1
60	9·4403381		10·5596619	9·4574964		10·5425036	10·0171584		9·9828416	0
′	Cosine	Diff.	Secant	Cotang.	Diff.	Tang.	Cosec.	D.	Sine	′

198

16 Deg.

′	Sine	Diff.	Cosec.	Tang.	Diff.	Cotang.	Secant	D.	Cosine	′
0	9·4403381	4403	10·5596619	9·4574964	4766	10·5425036	10·0171584	362	9·9828416	60
1	9·4407784	4398	10·5592216	9·4579730	4761	10·5420270	10·0171946	363	9·9828054	59
2	9·4412182	4394	10·5587818	9·4584491	4757	10·5415509	10·0172309	363	9·9827691	58
3	9·4416576	4389	10·5583424	9·4589248	4753	10·5410752	10·0172672	364	9·9827328	57
4	9·4420965	4384	10·5579035	9·4594001	4748	10·5405999	10·0173036	364	9·9826964	56
5	9·4425349	4379	10·5574651	9·4598749	4743	10·5401251	10·0173400	364	9·9826600	55
6	9·4429728	4375	10·5570272	9·4603492	4740	10·5396508	10·0173764	365	9·9826236	54
7	9·4434103	4369	10·5565897	9·4608232	4735	10·5391768	10·0174129	365	9·9825871	53
8	9·4438472	4365	10·5561528	9·4612967	4730	10·5387033	10·0174494	366	9·9825506	52
9	9·4442837	4360	10·5557163	9·4617697	4726	10·5382303	10·0174860	366	9·9825140	51
10	9·4447197	4356	10·5552803	9·4622423	4722	10·5377577	10·0175226	366	9·9824774	50
11	9·4451553	4351	10·5548447	9·4627145	4718	10·5372855	10·0175592	367	9·9824408	49
12	9·4455904	4346	10·5544096	9·4631863	4713	10·5368137	10·0175959	367	9·9824041	48
13	9·4460250	4341	10·5539750	9·4636576	4709	10·5363424	10·0176326	368	9·9823674	47
14	9·4464591	4336	10·5535409	9·4641285	4705	10·5358715	10·0176694	368	9·9823306	46
15	9·4468927	4332	10·5531073	9·4645990	4700	10·5354010	10·0177062	369	9·9822938	45
16	9·4473259	4327	10·5526741	9·4650690	4696	10·5349310	10·0177431	369	9·9822569	44
17	9·4477586	4323	10·5522414	9·4655386	4692	10·5344614	10·0177799	370	9·9822201	43
18	9·4481909	4318	10·5518091	9·4660078	4687	10·5339922	10·0178169	369	9·9821831	42
19	9·4486227	4313	10·5513773	9·4664765	4683	10·5335235	10·0178538	370	9·9821462	41
20	9·4490540	4309	10·5509460	9·4669448	4679	10·5330552	10·0178908	371	9·9821092	40
21	9·4494849	4304	10·5505151	9·4674127	4675	10·5325873	10·0179279	370	9·9820721	39
22	9·4499153	4299	10·5500847	9·4678802	4671	10·5321198	10·0179649	372	9·9820351	38
23	9·4503452	4295	10·5496548	9·4683473	4666	10·5316527	10·0180021	371	9·9819979	37
24	9·4507747	4290	10·5492253	9·4688139	4662	10·5311861	10·0180392	372	9·9819608	36
25	9·4512037	4285	10·5487963	9·4692801	4658	10·5307199	10·0180764	373	9·9819236	35
26	9·4516322	4281	10·5483678	9·4697459	4653	10·5302541	10·0181137	373	9·9818863	34
27	9·4520603	4276	10·5479397	9·4702112	4650	10·5297888	10·0181510	373	9·9818490	33
28	9·4524879	4272	10·5475121	9·4706762	4645	10·5293238	10·0181883	373	9·9818117	32
29	9·4529151	4267	10·5470849	9·4711407	4641	10·5288593	10·0182256	374	9·9817744	31
30	9·4533418	4263	10·5466582	9·4716048	4637	10·5283952	10·0182630	375	9·9817370	30
31	9·4537681	4258	10·5462319	9·4720685	4633	10·5279315	10·0183005	375	9·9816995	29
32	9·4541939	4253	10·5458061	9·4725318	4629	10·5274682	10·0183380	375	9·9816620	28
33	9·4546192	4249	10·5453808	9·4729947	4625	10·5270053	10·0183755	375	9·9816245	27
34	9·4550441	4245	10·5449559	9·4734572	4620	10·5265428	10·0184130	376	9·9815870	26
35	9·4554686	4240	10·5445314	9·4739192	4616	10·5260808	10·0184506	377	9·9815494	25
36	9·4558926	4235	10·5441074	9·4743808	4613	10·5256192	10·0184883	377	9·9815117	24
37	9·4563161	4231	10·5436839	9·4748421	4608	10·5251579	10·0185260	377	9·9814740	23
38	9·4567392	4226	10·5432608	9·4753029	4604	10·5246971	10·0185637	377	9·9814363	22
39	9·4571618	4222	10·5428382	9·4757633	4600	10·5242367	10·0186014	378	9·9813986	21
40	9·4575840	4218	10·5424160	9·4762233	4596	10·5237767	10·0186392	379	9·9813608	20
41	9·4580058	4213	10·5419942	9·4766829	4592	10·5233171	10·0186771	379	9·9813229	19
42	9·4584271	4209	10·5415729	9·4771421	4588	10·5228579	10·0187150	379	9·9812850	18
43	9·4588480	4204	10·5411520	9·4776009	4583	10·5223991	10·0187529	380	9·9812471	17
44	9·4592684	4200	10·5407316	9·4780592	4580	10·5219408	10·0187909	380	9·9812091	16
45	9·4596884	4195	10·5403116	9·4785172	4576	10·5214828	10·0188289	380	9·9811711	15
46	9·4601079	4191	10·5398921	9·4789748	4571	10·5210252	10·0188669	381	9·9811331	14
47	9·4605270	4186	10·5394730	9·4794319	4568	10·5205681	10·0189050	381	9·9810950	13
48	9·4609456	4182	10·5390544	9·4798887	4564	10·5201113	10·0189431	382	9·9810569	12
49	9·4613638	4178	10·5386362	9·4803451	4560	10·5196549	10·0189813	382	9·9810187	11
50	9·4617816	4173	10·5382184	9·4808011	4555	10·5191989	10·0190195	382	9·9809805	10
51	9·4621989	4169	10·5378011	9·4812566	4552	10·5187434	10·0190577	383	9·9809423	9
52	9·4626158	4165	10·5373842	9·4817118	4548	10·5182882	10·0190960	383	9·9809040	8
53	9·4630323	4160	10·5369677	9·4821666	4544	10·5178334	10·0191343	383	9·9808657	7
54	9·4634483	4156	10·5365517	9·4826210	4540	10·5173790	10·0191727	384	9·9808273	6
55	9·4638639	4151	10·5361361	9·4830750	4536	10·5169250	10·0192111	384	9·9807889	5
56	9·4642790	4148	10·5357210	9·4835286	4532	10·5164714	10·0192495	385	9·9807505	4
57	9·4646938	4143	10·5353062	9·4839818	4528	10·5160182	10·0192880	385	9·9807120	3
58	9·4651081	4138	10·5348919	9·4844346	4524	10·5155654	10·0193265	386	9·9806735	2
59	9·4655219	4134	10·5344781	9·4848870	4520	10·5151130	10·0193651	386	9·9806349	1
60	9·4659353		10·5340647	9·4853390		10·5146610	10·0194037	386	9·9805963	0

′	Cosine	Diff.	Secant	Cotang.	Diff.	Tang.	Cosec.	D.	Sine	′

′	Sine	Diff.	Cosec.	Tang.	Diff.	Cotang.	Secant	D.	Cosine	′
0	9·4659353	4130	10·5340647	9·4853390	4517	10·5146610	10·0194037	386	9·9805963	60
1	9·4663483	4126	10·5336517	9·4857907	4512	10·5142093	10·0194423	387	9·9805577	59
2	9·4667609	4121	10·5332391	9·4862419	4509	10·5137581	10·0194810	387	9·9805190	58
3	9·4671730	4118	10·5328270	9·4866928	4505	10·5133072	10·0195197	388	9·9804803	57
4	9·4675848	4112	10·5324152	9·4871433	4500	10·5128567	10·0195585	388	9·9804415	56
5	9·4679960	4109	10·5320040	9·4875933	4497	10·5124067	10·0195973	388	9·9804027	55
6	9·4684069	4104	10·5315931	9·4880430	4494	10·5119570	10·0196361	389	9·9803639	54
7	9·4688173	4100	10·5311827	9·4884924	4489	10·5115076	10·0196750	389	9·9803250	53
8	9·4692273	4096	10·5307727	9·4889413	4485	10·5110587	10·0197140	390	9·9802860	52
9	9·4696369	4092	10·5303631	9·4893898	4482	10·5106102	10·0197529	389	9·9802471	51
10	9·4700461	4087	10·5299539	9·4898380	4478	10·5101620	10·0197919	390	9·9802081	50
11	9·4704548	4083	10·5295452	9·4902858	4474	10·5097142	10·0198310	391	9·9801690	49
12	9·4708631	4079	10·5291369	9·4907332	4470	10·5092668	10·0198701	391	9·9801299	48
13	9·4712710	4075	10·5287290	9·4911802	4467	10·5088198	10·0199092	392	9·9800908	47
14	9·4716785	4071	10·5283215	9·4916269	4462	10·5083731	10·0199484	392	9·9800516	46
15	9·4720856	4066	10·5279144	9·4920731	4459	10·5079269	10·0199876	392	9·9800124	45
16	9·4724922	4063	10·5275078	9·4925190	4456	10·5074810	10·0200268	393	9·9799732	44
17	9·4728985	4058	10·5271015	9·4929646	4451	10·5070354	10·0200661	393	9·9799339	43
18	9·4733043	4054	10·5266957	9·4934097	4448	10·5065903	10·0201054	394	9·9798946	42
19	9·4737097	4049	10·5262903	9·4938545	4443	10·5061455	10·0201448	394	9·9798552	41
20	9·4741146	4046	10·5258854	9·4942988	4441	10·5057012	10·0201842	394	9·9798158	40
21	9·4745192	4042	10·5254808	9·4947429	4436	10·5052571	10·0202236	395	9·9797764	39
22	9·4749234	4037	10·5250766	9·4951865	4433	10·5048135	10·0202631	395	9·9797369	38
23	9·4753271	4033	10·5246729	9·4956298	4429	10·5043702	10·0203027	396	9·9796973	37
24	9·4757304	4030	10·5242696	9·4960727	4425	10·5039273	10·0203422	396	9·9796578	36
25	9·4761334	4025	10·5238666	9·4965152	4422	10·5034848	10·0203818	397	9·9796182	35
26	9·4765359	4021	10·5234641	9·4969574	4417	10·5030426	10·0204215	397	9·9795785	34
27	9·4769380	4016	10·5230620	9·4973991	4415	10·5026009	10·0204612	397	9·9795388	33
28	9·4773396	4013	10·5226604	9·4978406	4410	10·5021594	10·0205009	398	9·9794991	32
29	9·4777409	4009	10·5222591	9·4982816	4407	10·5017184	10·0205407	398	9·9794593	31
30	9·4781418	4005	10·5218582	9·4987223	4403	10·5012777	10·0205805	399	9·9794195	30
31	9·4785423	4000	10·5214577	9·4991626	4400	10·5008374	10·0206204	398	9·9793796	29
32	9·4789423	3997	10·5210577	9·4996026	4396	10·5003974	10·0206602	400	9·9793398	28
33	9·4793420	3992	10·5206580	9·5000422	4392	10·4999578	10·0207002	399	9·9792998	27
34	9·4797412	3989	10·5202588	9·5004814	4389	10·4995186	10·0207401	401	9·9792599	26
35	9·4801401	3984	10·5198599	9·5009203	4385	10·4990797	10·0207802	400	9·9792198	25
36	9·4805385	3981	10·5194615	9·5013588	4381	10·4986412	10·0208202	401	9·9791798	24
37	9·4809366	3976	10·5190634	9·5017969	4378	10·4982031	10·0208603	401	9·9791397	23
38	9·4813342	3973	10·5186658	9·5022347	4374	10·4977653	10·0209004	402	9·9790996	22
39	9·4817315	3968	10·5182685	9·5026721	4371	10·4973279	10·0209406	402	9·9790594	21
40	9·4821283	3965	10·5178717	9·5031092	4367	10·4968908	10·0209808	403	9·9790192	20
41	9·4825248	3960	10·5174752	9·5035459	4363	10·4964541	10·0210211	403	9·9789789	19
42	9·4829208	3957	10·5170792	9·5039822	4360	10·4960178	10·0210614	403	9·9789386	18
43	9·4833165	3952	10·5166835	9·5044182	4356	10·4955818	10·0211017	404	9·9788983	17
44	9·4837117	3949	10·5162883	9·5048538	4353	10·4951462	10·0211421	404	9·9788579	16
45	9·4841066	3944	10·5158934	9·5052891	4349	10·4947109	10·0211825	405	9·9788175	15
46	9·4845010	3941	10·5154990	9·5057240	4346	10·4942760	10·0212230	405	9·9787770	14
47	9·4848951	3937	10·5151049	9·5061586	4342	10·4938414	10·0212635	405	9·9787365	13
48	9·4852888	3932	10·5147112	9·5065928	4339	10·4934072	10·0213040	406	9·9786960	12
49	9·4856820	3929	10·5143180	9·5070267	4335	10·4929733	10·0213446	406	9·9786554	11
50	9·4860749	3925	10·5139251	9·5074602	4331	10·4925398	10·0213852	407	9·9786148	10
51	9·4864674	3921	10·5135326	9·5078933	4328	10·4921067	10·0214259	407	9·9785741	9
52	9·4868595	3917	10·5131405	9·5083261	4325	10·4916739	10·0214666	407	9·9785334	8
53	9·4872512	3914	10·5127488	9·5087586	4321	10·4912414	10·0215073	408	9·9784927	7
54	9·4876426	3909	10·5123574	9·5091907	4317	10·4908093	10·0215481	408	9·9784519	6
55	9·4880335	3905	10·5119665	9·5096224	4315	10·4903776	10·0215889	409	9·9784111	5
56	9·4884240	3902	10·5115760	9·5100539	4310	10·4899461	10·0216298	409	9·9783702	4
57	9·4888142	3898	10·5111858	9·5104849	4307	10·4895151	10·0216707	410	9·9783293	3
58	9·4892040	3894	10·5107960	9·5109156	4304	10·4890844	10·0217117	409	9·9782883	2
59	9·4895934	3890	10·5104066	9·5113460	4300	10·4886540	10·0217526	411	9·9782474	1
60	9·4899824		10·5100176	9·5117760		10·4882240	10·0217937		9·9782063	0

| ′ | Cosine | Diff. | Secant | Cotang. | Diff. | Tang. | Cosec. | D. | Sine | ′ |

TANGENTS, AND SECANTS.

′	Sine	Diff.	Cosec.	Tang.	Diff.	Cotang.	Secant	D.	Cosine	′
0	9·4899824	3886	10·5100176	9·5117760	4297	10·4882240	10·0217937	410	9·9782063	60
1	9·4903710	3882	10·5096290	9·5122057	4294	10·4877943	10·0218347	412	9·9781653	59
2	9·4907592	3879	10·5092408	9·5126351	4290	10·4873649	10·0218759	411	9·9781241	58
3	9·4911471	3874	10·5088529	9·5130641	4286	10·4869359	10·0219170	412	9·9780830	57
4	9·4915345	3871	10·5084655	9·5134927	4283	10·4865073	10·0219582	412	9·9780418	56
5	9·4919216	3867	10·5080784	9·5139210	4280	10·4860790	10·0219994	413	9·9780006	55
6	9·4923083	3863	10·5076917	9·5143490	4276	10·4856510	10·0220407	413	9·9779593	54
7	9·4926946	3860	10·5073054	9·5147766	4273	10·4852234	10·0220820	414	9·9779180	53
8	9·4930806	3855	10·5069194	9·5152039	4270	10·4847961	10·0221234	413	9·9778766	52
9	9·4934661	3852	10·5065339	9·5156309	4266	10·4843691	10·0221647	415	9·9778353	51
10	9·4938513	3848	10·5061487	9·5160575	4263	10·4839425	10·0222062	415	9·9777938	50
11	9·4942361	3844	10·5057639	9·5164838	4259	10·4835162	10·0222477	415	9·9777523	49
12	9·4946205	3841	10·5053795	9·5169097	4256	10·4830903	10·0222892	415	9·9777108	48
13	9·4950046	3837	10·5049954	9·5173353	4253	10·4826647	10·0223307	416	9·9776693	47
14	9·4953883	3833	10·5046117	9·5177606	4249	10·4822394	10·0223723	417	9·9776277	46
15	9·4957716	3829	10·5042284	9·5181855	4246	10·4818145	10·0224140	416	9·9775860	45
16	9·4961545	3825	10·5038455	9·5186101	4243	10·4813899	10·0224556	418	9·9775444	44
17	9·4965370	3822	10·5034630	9·5190344	4239	10·4809656	10·0224974	417	9·9775026	43
18	9·4969192	3818	10·5030808	9·5194583	4236	10·4805417	10·0225391	418	9·9774609	42
19	9·4973010	3814	10·5026990	9·5198819	4233	10·4801181	10·0225809	419	9·9774191	41
20	9·4976824	3811	10·5023176	9·5203052	4230	10·4796948	10·0226228	418	9·9773772	40
21	9·4980635	3807	10·5019365	9·5207282	4226	10·4792718	10·0226646	420	9·9773354	39
22	9·4984442	3803	10·5015558	9·5211508	4222	10·4788492	10·0227066	419	9·9772934	38
23	9·4988245	3800	10·5011755	9·5215730	4220	10·4784270	10·0227485	420	9·9772515	37
24	9·4992045	3795	10·5007955	9·5219950	4216	10·4780050	10·0227905	421	9·9772095	36
25	9·4995840	3793	10·5004160	9·5224166	4213	10·4775834	10·0228326	421	9·9771674	35
26	9·4999633	3788	10·5000367	9·5228379	4210	10·4771621	10·0228747	421	9·9771253	34
27	9·5003421	3785	10·4996579	9·5232589	4206	10·4767411	10·0229168	422	9·9770832	33
28	9·5007206	3781	10·4992794	9·5236795	4204	10·4763205	10·0229590	422	9·9770410	32
29	9·5010987	3777	10·4989013	9·5240999	4200	10·4759001	1C·0230012	422	9·9769988	31
30	9·5014764	3774	10·4985236	9·5245199	4196	10·4754801	1C·0230434	423	9·9769566	30
31	9·5018538	3770	10·4981462	9·5249395	4194	10·4750605	10·0230857	423	9·9769143	29
32	9·5022308	3767	10·4977692	9·5253589	4190	10·4746411	10·0231280	424	9·9768720	28
33	9·5026075	3763	10·4973925	9·5257779	4187	10·4742221	10·0231704	424	9·9768296	27
34	9·5029838	3759	10·4970162	9·5261966	4184	10·4738034	10·0232128	425	9·9767872	26
35	9·5033597	3756	10·4966403	9·5266150	4181	10·4733850	10·0232553	425	9·9767447	25
36	9·5037353	3752	10·4962647	9·5270331	4177	10·4729669	10·0232978	425	9·9767022	24
37	9·5041105	3748	10·4958895	9·5274508	4174	10·4725492	10·0233403	426	9·9766597	23
38	9·5044853	3745	10·4955147	9·5278682	4171	10·4721318	10·0233829	426	9·9766171	22
39	9·5048598	3741	10·4951402	9·5282853	4168	10·4717147	10·0234255	427	9·9765745	21
40	9·5052339	3738	10·4947661	9·5287021	4165	10·4712979	10·0234682	427	9·9765318	20
41	9·5056077	3734	10·4943923	9·5291186	4161	10·4708814	10·0235109	427	9·9764891	19
42	9·5059811	3731	10·4940189	9·5295347	4158	10·4704653	10·0235536	428	9·9764464	18
43	9·5063542	3727	10·4936458	9·5299505	4156	10·4700495	10·0235964	428	9·9764036	17
44	9·5067269	3723	10·4932731	9·5303661	4152	10·4696339	10·0236392	429	9·9763608	16
45	9·5070992	3720	10·4929008	9·5307813	4148	10·4692187	10·0236821	429	9·9763179	15
46	9·5074712	3716	10·4925288	9·5311961	4146	10·4688039	10·0237250	429	9·9762750	14
47	9·5078428	3713	10·4921572	9·5316107	4143	10·4683893	10·0237679	430	9·9762321	13
48	9·5082141	3709	10·4917859	9·5320250	4139	10·4679750	10·0238109	430	9·9761891	12
49	9·5085850	3706	10·4914150	9·5324389	4137	10·4675611	10·0238539	431	9·9761461	11
50	9·5089556	3702	10·4910444	9·5328526	4133	10·4671474	10·0238970	431	9·9761030	10
51	9·5093258	3698	10·4906742	9·5332659	4130	10·4667341	10·0239401	432	9·9760599	9
52	9·5096956	3695	10·4903044	9·5336789	4127	10·4663211	10·0239833	431	9·9760167	8
53	9·5100651	3692	10·4899349	9·5340916	4124	10·4659084	10·0240264	433	9·9759736	7
54	9·5104343	3688	10·4895657	9·5345040	4121	10·4654960	10·0240697	433	9·9759303	6
55	9·5108031	3685	10·4891969	9·5349161	4117	10·4650839	10·0241130	433	9·9758870	5
56	9·5111716	3681	10·4888284	9·5353278	4115	10·4646722	10·0241563	433	9·9758437	4
57	9·5115397	3677	10·4884603	9·5357393	4112	10·4642607	10·0241996	434	9·9758004	3
58	9·5119074	3675	10·4880926	9·5361505	4108	10·4638495	10·0242430	435	9·9757570	2
59	9·5122749	3670	10·4877251	9·5365613	4106	10·4634387	10·0242865	434	9·9757135	1
60	9·5126419		10·4873581	9·5369719		10·4630281	10·0243299		9·9756701	0

′	Cosine	Diff.	Secant	Cotang.	Diff.	Tang.	Cosec.	D.	Sine	′

201

′	Sine	Diff.	Cosec.	Tang.	Diff.	Cotang.	Secant	D.	Cosine	′
0	9·5126419	3667	10·4873581	9·5369719	4102	10·4630281	10·0243299	436	9·9756701	60
1	9·5130086	3664	10·4869914	9·5373821	4099	10·4626179	10·0243735	435	9·9756265	59
2	9·5133750	3660	10·4866250	9·5377920	4097	10·4622080	10·0244170	436	9·9755830	58
3	9·5137410	3657	10·4862590	9·5382017	4093	10·4617983	10·0244606	437	9·9755394	57
4	9·5141067	3654	10·4858933	9·5386110	4090	10·4613890	10·0245043	436	9·9754957	56
5	9·5144721	3650	10·4855279	9·5390200	4087	10·4609800	10·0245479	438	9·9754521	55
6	9·5148371	3646	10·4851629	9·5394287	4084	10·4605713	10·0245917	437	9·9754083	54
7	9·5152017	3643	10·4847983	9·5398371	4082	10·4601629	10·0246354	438	9·9753646	53
8	9·5155660	3640	10·4844340	9·5402453	4078	10·4597547	10·0246792	439	9·9753208	52
9	9·5159300	3636	10·4840700	9·5406531	4075	10·4593469	10·0247231	439	9·9752769	51
10	9·5162936	3633	10·4837064	9·5410606	4072	10·4589394	10·0247670	439	9·9752330	50
11	9·5166569	3629	10·4833431	9·5414678	4069	10·4585322	10·0248109	440	9·9751891	49
12	9·5170198	3626	10·4829802	9·5418747	4066	10·4581253	10·0248549	440	9·9751451	48
13	9·5173824	3623	10·4826176	9·5422813	4064	10·4577187	10·0248989	441	9·9751011	47
14	9·5177447	3619	10·4822553	9·5426877	4060	10·4573123	10·0249430	441	9·9750570	46
15	9·5181066	3616	10·4818934	9·5430937	4057	10·4569063	10·0249871	441	9·9750129	45
16	9·5184682	3613	10·4815318	9·5434994	4054	10·4565006	10·0250312	442	9·9749688	44
17	9·5188295	3609	10·4811705	9·5439048	4052	10·4560952	10·0250754	442	9·9749246	43
18	9·5191904	3606	10·4808096	9·5443100	4048	10·4556900	10·0251196	443	9·9748804	42
19	9·5195510	3602	10·4804490	9·5447148	4045	10·4552852	10·0251639	443	9·9748361	41
20	9·5199112	3599	10·4800888	9·5451193	4043	10·4548807	10·0252082	443	9·9747918	40
21	9·5202711	3596	10·4797289	9·5455236	4040	10·4544764	10·0252525	444	9·9747475	39
22	9·5206307	3592	10·4793693	9·5459276	4036	10·4540724	10·0252969	444	9·9747031	38
23	9·5209899	3589	10·4790101	9·5463312	4034	10·4536688	10·0253413	444	9·9746587	37
24	9·5213488	3586	10·4786512	9·5467346	4031	10·4532654	10·0253858	445	9·9746142	36
25	9·5217074	3582	10·4782926	9·5471377	4028	10·4528623	10·0254303	445	9·9745697	35
26	9·5220656	3579	10·4779344	9·5475405	4025	10·4524595	10·0254748	445	9·9745252	34
27	9·5224235	3576	10·4775765	9·5479430	4022	10·4520570	10·0255194	446	9·9744806	33
28	9·5227811	3572	10·4772189	9·5483452	4019	10·4516548	10·0255641	446	9·9744359	32
29	9·5231383	3570	10·4768617	9·5487471	4016	10·4512529	10·0256087	447	9·9743913	31
30	9·5234953	3565	10·4765047	9·5491487	4013	10·4508513	10·0256534	448	9·9743466	30
31	9·5238518	3563	10·4761482	9·5495500	4011	10·4504500	10·0256982	448	9·9743018	29
32	9·5242081	3559	10·4757919	9·5499511	4008	10·4500489	10·0257430	448	9·9742570	28
33	9·5245640	3556	10·4754360	9·5503519	4004	10·4496481	10·0257878	449	9·9742122	27
34	9·5249196	3553	10·4750804	9·5507523	4002	10·4492477	10·0258327	449	9·9741673	26
35	9·5252749	3549	10·4747251	9·5511525	3999	10·4488475	10·0258776	450	9·9741224	25
36	9·5256298	3546	10·4743702	9·5515524	3997	10·4484476	10·0259226	450	9·9740774	24
37	9·5259844	3543	10·4740156	9·5519521	3993	10·4480479	10·0259676	451	9·9740324	23
38	9·5263387	3540	10·4736613	9·5523514	3990	10·4476486	10·0260127	451	9·9739873	22
39	9·5266927	3536	10·4733073	9·5527504	3988	10·4472496	10·0260578	451	9·9739422	21
40	9·5270463	3534	10·4729537	9·5531492	3985	10·4468508	10·0261029	452	9·9738971	20
41	9·5273997	3529	10·4726003	9·5535477	3982	10·4464523	10·0261481	452	9·9738519	19
42	9·5277526	3527	10·4722474	9·5539459	3979	10·4460541	10·0261933	452	9·9738067	18
43	9·5281053	3524	10·4718947	9·5543438	3977	10·4456562	10·0262385	453	9·9737615	17
44	9·5284577	3520	10·4715423	9·5547415	3973	10·4452585	10·0262838	453	9·9737162	16
45	9·5288097	3517	10·4711903	9·5551388	3971	10·4448612	10·0263291	453	9·9736709	15
46	9·5291614	3514	10·4708386	9·5555359	3968	10·4444641	10·0263745	454	9·9736255	14
47	9·5295128	3510	10·4704872	9·5559327	3965	10·4440673	10·0264199	455	9·9735801	13
48	9·5298648	3508	10·4701362	9·5563292	3963	10·4436708	10·0264654	455	9·9735346	12
49	9·5302146	3504	10·4697854	9·5567255	3959	10·4432745	10·0265109	456	9·9734891	11
50	9·5305650	3501	10·4694350	9·5571214	3957	10·4428786	10·0265565	455	9·9734435	10
51	9·5309151	3498	10·4690849	9·5575171	3954	10·4424829	10·0266020	456	9·9733980	9
52	9·5312649	3494	10·4687351	9·5579125	3952	10·4420875	10·0266477	456	9·9733523	8
53	9·5316143	3492	10·4683857	9·5583077	3948	10·4416923	10·0266933	457	9·9733067	7
54	9·5319635	3488	10·4680365	9·5587025	3946	10·4412975	10·0267390	457	9·9732610	6
55	9·5323123	3485	10·4676877	9·5590971	3943	10·4409029	10·0267848	458	9·9732152	5
56	9·5326608	3482	10·4673392	9·5594914	3940	10·4405086	10·0268306	458	9·9731694	4
57	9·5330090	3479	10·4669910	9·5598854	3938	10·4401146	10·0268764	459	9·9731236	3
58	9·5333569	3475	10·4666431	9·5602792	3935	10·4397208	10·0269223	459	9·9730777	2
59	9·5337044	3473	10·4662956	9·5606727	3932	10·4393273	10·0269682	460	9·9730318	1
60	9·5340517		10·4659483	9·5610659		10·4389341	10·0270142		9·9729858	0
′	Cosine	Diff.	Secant	Cotang.	Diff.	Tang.	Cosec.	D.	Sine	′

′	Sine	Diff.	Cosec.	Tang.	Diff.	Cotang.	Secant	D.	Cosine	′
0	9·5340517	3469	10·4659483	9·5610659	3929	10·4389341	10·0270142	460	9·9729858	60
1	9·5343986	3466	10·4656014	9·5614588	3927	10·4385412	10·0270602	460	9·9729398	59
2	9·5347452	3463	10·4652548	9·5618515	3924	10·4381485	10·0271062	461	9·9728938	58
3	9·5350915	3460	10·4649085	9·5622439	3921	10·4377561	10·0271523	461	9·9728477	57
4	9·5354375	3457	10·4645625	9·5626360	3918	10·4373640	10·0271984	462	9·9728016	56
5	9·5357832	3454	10·4642168	9·5630278	3916	10·4369722	10·0272446	462	9·9727554	55
6	9·5361286	3451	10·4638714	9·5634194	3913	10·4365806	10·0272908	463	9·9727092	54
7	9·5364737	3447	10·4635263	9·5638107	3911	10·4361893	10·0273371	463	9·9726629	53
8	9·5368184	3445	10·4631816	9·5642018	3907	10·4357982	10·0273834	463	9·9726166	52
9	9·5371629	3441	10·4628371	9·5645925	3906	10·4354075	10·0274297	464	9·9725703	51
10	9·5375070	3438	10·4624930	9·5649831	3902	10·4350169	10·0274761	464	9·9725239	50
11	9·5378508	3435	10·4621492	9·5653733	3900	10·4346267	10·0275225	465	9·9724775	49
12	9·5381943	3432	10·4618057	9·5657683	3897	10·4342367	10·0275690	465	9·9724310	48
13	9·5385375	3429	10·4614625	9·5661530	3894	10·4338470	10·0276155	465	9·9723845	47
14	9·5388804	3426	10·4611196	9·5665424	3892	10·4334576	10·0276620	466	9·9723380	46
15	9·5392230	3423	10·4607770	9·5669316	3889	10·4330684	10·0277086	466	9·9722914	45
16	9·5395653	3420	10·4604347	9·5673205	3886	10·4326795	10·0277552	467	9·9722448	44
17	9·5399073	3416	10·4600927	9·5677091	3884	10·4322909	10·0278019	467	9·9721981	43
18	9·5402489	3414	10·4597511	9·5680975	3881	10·4319025	10·0278486	467	9·9721514	42
19	9·5405903	3411	10·4594097	9·5684856	3879	10·4315144	10·0278953	468	9·9721047	41
20	9·5409314	3407	10·4590686	9·5688735	3876	10·4311265	10·0279421	469	9·9720579	40
21	9·5412721	3405	10·4587279	9·5692611	3873	10·4307389	10·0279890	468	9·9720110	39
22	9·5416126	3401	10·4583874	9·5696484	3871	10·4303516	10·0280358	470	9·9719642	38
23	9·5419527	3399	10·4580473	9·5700355	3868	10·4299645	10·0280828	469	9·9719172	37
24	9·5422926	3395	10·4577074	9·5704223	3865	10·4295777	10·0281297	470	9·9718703	36
25	9·5426321	3392	10·4573679	9·5708088	3863	10·4291912	10·0281767	471	9·9718233	35
26	9·5429713	3390	10·4570287	9·5711951	3860	10·4288049	10·0282238	471	9·9717762	34
27	9·5433103	3386	10·4566897	9·5715811	3858	10·4284189	10·0282709	471	9·9717291	33
28	9·5436489	3384	10·4563511	9·5719669	3855	10·4280331	10·0283180	472	9·9716820	32
29	9·5439873	3380	10·4560127	9·5723524	3853	10·4276476	10·0283652	472	9·9716348	31
30	9·5443253	3377	10·4·56747	9·5727377	3850	10·4272623	10·0284124	472	9·9715876	30
31	9·5446630	3375	10·4553370	9·5731227	3847	10·4268773	10·0284596	473	9·9715404	29
32	9·5450005	3371	10·4649995	9·5735074	3845	10·4264926	10·0285069	473	9·9714931	28
33	9·5453376	3369	10·4546624	9·5738919	3842	10·4261081	10·0285543	474	9·9714457	27
34	9·5456745	3365	10·4543255	9·5742761	3840	10·4257239	10·0286016	473	9·9713984	26
35	9·5460110	3362	10·4539890	9·5746601	3837	10·4253399	10·02·6491	475	9·9713509	25
36	9·5463472	3360	10·4536528	9·5750438	3834	10·4249562	10·0286965	474	9·9713035	24
37	9·5466832	3357	10·4533168	9·5754272	3832	10·4245728	10·0287440	475	9·9712560	23
38	9·5470189	3353	10·4529811	9·5758104	3830	10·4241896	10·0287916	476	9·9712084	22
39	9·5473542	3351	10·4526458	9·5761934	3827	10·4238066	10·0288392	476	9·9711608	21
40	9·5476893	3347	10·4523107	9·5765761	3824	10·4234239	10·0288868	476	9·9711132	20
41	9·5480240	3345	10·4519760	9·5769585	3822	10·4230415	10·0289345	477	9·9710655	19
42	9·5483585	3342	10·4516415	9·5773407	3819	10·4226593	10·0289822	477	9·9710178	18
43	9·5486927	3339	10·4513073	9·5777226	3817	10·4222774	10·0290299	478	9·9709701	17
44	9·5490266	3336	10·4509734	9·5781043	3815	10·4218957	10·0290777	479	9·9709223	16
45	9·5493602	3333	10·4506398	9·5784858	3811	10·4215142	10·0291256	479	9·9708744	15
46	9·5496935	3330	10·4503065	9·5788669	3810	10·4211331	10·0291735	479	9·9708265	14
47	9·5500265	3327	10·4499735	9·5792479	3807	10·4207521	10·0292214	480	9·9707786	13
48	9·5503592	3324	10·4496408	9·5796286	3804	10·4203714	10·0292694	480	9·9707306	12
49	9·5506916	3321	10·4493084	9·5800090	3802	10·4199910	10·0293174	480	9·9706826	11
50	9·5510237	3319	10·4489763	9·5803892	3799	10·4196108	10·0293654	481	9·9706346	10
51	9·5513556	3315	10·4486444	9·5807691	3797	10·4192309	10·0294135	482	9·9705865	9
52	9·5516871	3313	10·4483129	9·5811488	3794	10·4188512	10·0294617	481	9·9705383	8
53	9·5520184	3310	10·4479816	9·5815282	3792	10·4184718	10·0295098	483	9·9704902	7
54	9·5523494	3307	10·4476506	9·5819074	3790	10·4180926	10·0295581	482	9·9704419	6
55	9·5526801	3304	10·4473199	9·5822864	3787	10·4177136	10·0296063	483	9·9703937	5
56	9·5530105	3301	10·4469895	9·5826651	3784	10·4173349	10·0296546	484	9·9703454	4
57	9·5533406	3298	10·4466594	9·5830435	3782	10·4169565	10·0297030	484	9·9702970	3
58	9·5536704	3295	10·4463296	9·5834217	3780	10·4165783	10·0297514	484	9·9702486	2
59	9·5539999	3293	10·4460001	9·5837997	3777	10·4162003	10·0297998	485	9·9702002	1
60	9·5543292		10·4456708	9·5841774		10·4158226	10·0298483		9·9701517	0

′	Cosine	Diff.	Secant	Cotang.	Diff.	Tang.	Cosec.	D.	Sine	′

′	Sine	Diff.	Cosec.	Tang.	Diff.	Cotang.	Secant	D.	Cosine	′
0	9·5543292	3289	10·4456708	9·5841774	3775	10·4158226	10·0298483	485	9·9701517	60
1	9·5546581	3287	10·4453419	9·5845549	3772	10·4154451	10·0298968	485	9·9701032	59
2	9·5549868	3284	10·4450132	9·5849321	3770	10·4150679	10·0299453	486	9·9700547	58
3	9·5553152	3281	10·4446848	9·5853091	3768	10·4146909	10·0299939	487	9·9700061	57
4	9·5556433	3278	10·4443567	9·5856859	3765	10·4143141	10·0300426	487	9·9699574	56
5	9·5559711	3276	10·4440289	9·5860624	3762	10·4139376	10·0300913	487	9·9699087	55
6	9·5562987	3272	10·4437013	9·5864386	3761	10·4135614	10·0301400	488	9·9698600	54
7	9·5566259	3270	10·4433741	9·5868147	3757	10·4131853	10·0301888	488	9·9698112	53
8	9·5569529	3267	10·4430471	9·5871904	3756	10·4128096	10·0302376	488	9·9697624	52
9	9·5572796	3264	10·4427204	9·5875660	3753	10·4124340	10·0302864	489	9·9697136	51
10	9·5576060	3261	10·4423940	9·5879413	3750	10·4120587	10·0303353	488	9·9696647	50
11	9·5579321	3258	10·4420679	9·5883163	3749	10·4116837	10·0303842	490	9·9696158	49
12	9·5582579	3256	10·4417421	9·5886912	3745	10·4113088	10·0304332	491	9·9695668	48
13	9·5585835	3253	10·4414165	9·5890657	3744	10·4109343	10·0304823	490	9·9695177	47
14	9·5589088	3250	10·4410912	9·5894401	3741	10·4105599	10·0305313	491	9·9694687	46
15	9·5592338	3247	10·4407662	9·5898142	3739	10·4101858	10·0305804	492	9·9694196	45
16	9·5595585	3244	10·4404415	9·5901881	3736	10·4098119	10·0306296	492	9·9693704	44
17	9·5598829	3242	10·4401171	9·5905617	3734	10·4094383	10·0306788	492	9·9693212	43
18	9·5602071	3239	10·4397929	9·5909351	3731	10·4090649	10·0307280	493	9·9692720	42
19	9·5605310	3236	10·4394690	9·5913082	3730	10·4086918	10·0307773	493	9·9692227	41
20	9·5608546	3233	10·4391454	9·5916812	3727	10·4083188	10·0308266	493	9·9691734	40
21	9·5611779	3231	10·4388221	9·5920539	3724	10·4079461	10·0308759	495	9·9691241	39
22	9·5615010	3227	10·4384990	9·5924263	3722	10·4075737	10·0309254	494	9·9690746	38
23	9·5618237	3225	10·4381763	9·5927985	3720	10·4072015	10·0309748	495	9·9690252	37
24	9·5621462	3223	10·4378538	9·5931705	3718	10·4068295	10·0310243	495	9·9689757	36
25	9·5624685	3219	10·4375315	9·5935423	3715	10·4064577	10·0310738	496	9·9689262	35
26	9·5627904	3217	10·4372096	9·5939138	3713	10·4060862	10·0311234	496	9·9688766	34
27	9·5631121	3214	10·4368879	9·5942851	3710	10·4057149	10·0311730	497	9·9688270	33
28	9·5634335	3211	10·4365665	9·5946561	3708	10·4053439	10·0312227	497	9·9687773	32
29	9·5637546	3208	10·4362454	9·5950269	3706	10·4049731	10·0312724	497	9·9687276	31
30	9·5640754	3206	10·4359246	9·5953975	3704	10·4046025	10·0313221	498	9·9686779	30
31	9·5643960	3203	10·4356040	9·5957679	3701	10·4042321	10·0313719	498	9·9686281	29
32	9·5647163	3200	10·4352837	9·5961380	3699	10·4038620	10·0314217	499	9·9685783	28
33	9·5650363	3198	10·4349637	9·5965079	3697	10·4034921	10·0314716	499	9·9685284	27
34	9·5653561	3195	10·4346439	9·5968776	3694	10·4031224	10·0315215	499	9·9684785	26
35	9·5656756	3192	10·4343244	9·5972470	3692	10·4027530	10·0315714	500	9·9684286	25
36	9·5659948	3189	10·4340052	9·5976162	3690	10·4023838	10·0316214	501	9·9683786	24
37	9·5663137	3187	10·4336863	9·5979852	3688	10·4020148	10·0316715	501	9·9683285	23
38	9·5666324	3184	10·4333676	9·5983540	3685	10·4016460	10·0317216	501	9·9682784	22
39	9·5669508	3181	10·4330492	9·5987225	3683	10·4012775	10·0317717	502	9·9682283	21
40	9·5672689	3179	10·4327311	9·5990908	3680	10·4009092	10·0318219	502	9·9681781	20
41	9·5675868	3176	10·4324132	9·5994588	3679	10·4005412	10·0318721	502	9·9681279	19
42	9·5679044	3173	10·4320956	9·5998267	3676	10·4001733	10·0319223	503	9·9680777	18
43	9·5682217	3170	10·4317783	9·6001943	3674	10·3998057	10·0319726	503	9·9680274	17
44	9·5685387	3168	10·4314613	9·6005617	3672	10·3994383	10·0320229	504	9·9679771	16
45	9·5688555	3166	10·4311445	9·6009289	3669	10·3990711	10·0320733	504	9·9679267	15
46	9·5691721	3162	10·4308279	9·6012958	3667	10·3987042	10·0321237	505	9·9678763	14
47	9·5694883	3160	10·4305117	9·6016625	3665	10·3983375	10·0321742	505	9·9678258	13
48	9·5698043	3157	10·4301957	9·6020290	3663	10·3979710	10·0322247	506	9·9677753	12
49	9·5701200	3155	10·4298800	9·6023953	3660	10·3976047	10·0322753	506	9·9677247	11
50	9·5704355	3151	10·4295645	9·6027613	3658	10·3972387	10·0323259	506	9·9676741	10
51	9·5707506	3150	10·4292494	9·6031271	3656	10·3968729	10·0323765	507	9·9676235	9
52	9·5710656	3146	10·4289344	9·6034927	3654	10·3965073	10·0324272	507	9·9675728	8
53	9·5713802	3144	10·4286198	9·6038581	3652	10·3961419	10·0324779	508	9·9675221	7
54	9·5716946	3141	10·4283054	9·6042233	3649	10·3957767	10·0325287	508	9·9674713	6
55	9·5720087	3139	10·4279913	9·6045882	3647	10·3954118	10·0325795	508	9·9674205	5
56	9·5723226	3136	10·4276774	9·6049529	3645	10·3950471	10·0326303	509	9·9673697	4
57	9·5726362	3133	10·4273638	9·6053174	3643	10·3946826	10·0326812	509	9·9673188	3
58	9·5729495	3131	10·4270505	9·6056817	3640	10·3943183	19·0327321	510	9·9672679	2
59	9·5732626	3128	10·4267374	9·6060457	3639	10·3939543	10·0327831	510	9·9672169	1
60	9·5735754		10·4264246	9·6064096		10·3935904	10·0328341		9·9671659	0

′	Cosine	Diff.	Secant	Cotang.	Diff.	Tang.	Cosec.	D.	Sine	′

′	Sine	Diff.	Cosec.	Tang.	Diff.	Cotang.	Secant	D.	Cosine	′
0	9·5735754	3126	10·4264246	9·6064096	3636	10·3935904	10·0328341	511	9·9671659	60
1	9·5738880	3123	10·4261120	9·6067732	3634	10·3932268	10·0328852	511	9·9671148	59
2	9·5742003	3120	10·4257997	9·6071366	3631	10·3928634	10·0329363	512	9·9670637	58
3	9·5745123	3117	10·4254877	9·6074997	3630	10·3925003	10·0329875	511	9·9670125	57
4	9·5748240	3116	10·4251760	9·6078627	3627	10·3921373	10·0330386	513	9·9669614	56
5	9·5751356	3112	10·4248644	9·6082254	3626	10·3917746	10·0330899	513	9·9669101	55
6	9·5754468	3110	10·4245532	9·6085880	3623	10·3914120	10·0331412	513	9·9668588	54
7	9·5757578	3107	10·4242422	9·6089503	3621	10·3910497	10·0331925	513	9·9668075	53
8	9·5760685	3105	10·4239315	9·6093124	3618	10·3906876	10·0332438	514	9·9667562	52
9	9·5763790	3102	10·4236210	9·6096742	3617	10·3903258	10·0332952	515	9·9667048	51
10	9·5766892	3099	10·4233108	9·6100359	3614	10·3899641	10·0333467	515	9·9666533	50
11	9·5769991	3007	10·4230009	9·6103973	3613	10·3896027	10·0333982	515	9·9666018	49
12	9·5773088	3005	10·4226912	9·6107586	3610	10·3892414	10·0334497	516	9·9665503	48
13	9·5776183	3092	10·4223817	9·6111196	3608	10·3888804	10·0335013	516	9·9664987	47
14	9·5779275	3089	10·4220725	9·6114804	3605	10·3885196	10·0335529	517	9·9664471	46
15	9·5782364	3086	10·4217636	9·6118409	3604	10·3881591	10·0336046	517	9·9663954	45
16	9·5785450	3085	10·4214550	9·6122013	3602	10·3877987	10·0336563	517	9·9663437	44
17	9·5788535	3081	10·4211465	9·6125615	3599	10·3874385	10·0337080	518	9·9662920	43
18	9·5791616	3079	10·4208384	9·6129214	3598	10·3870786	10·0337598	518	9·9662402	42
19	9·5794695	3077	10·4205305	9·6132812	3595	10·3867188	10·0338116	519	9·9661884	41
20	9·5797772	3073	10·4202228	9·6136407	3593	10·3863593	10·0338635	519	9·9661365	40
21	9·5800845	3072	10·4199155	9·6140000	3591	10·3860000	10·0339154	520	9·9660846	39
22	9·5803917	3069	10·4196083	9·6143591	3589	10·3856409	10·0339674	520	9·9660326	38
23	9·5806986	3066	10·4193014	9·6147180	3586	10·3852820	10·0340194	520	9·9659806	37
24	9·5810052	3064	10·4189948	9·6150766	3585	10·3849234	10·0340715	521	9·9659285	36
25	9·5813116	3061	10·4186884	9·6154351	3583	10·3845649	10·0341236	521	9·9658764	35
26	9·5816177	3059	10·4183823	9·6157934	3580	10·3842066	10·0341757	522	9·9658243	34
27	9·5819236	3056	10·4180764	9·6161514	3579	10·3838486	10·0342279	522	9·9657721	33
28	9·5822292	3053	10·4177708	9·6165093	3576	10·3834907	10·0342801	522	9·9657199	32
29	9·5825345	3052	10·4174655	9·6168669	3574	10·3831331	10·0343323	523	9·9656677	31
30	9·5828397	3048	10·4171603	9·6172243	3572	10·3827757	10·0343847	523	9·9656153	30
31	9·5831445	3046	10·4168555	9·6175815	3570	10·3824185	10·0344370	524	9·9655630	29
32	9·5834491	3044	10·4165509	9·6179385	3568	10·3820615	10·0344894	524	9·9655106	28
33	9·5837535	3041	10·4162465	9·6182953	3566	10·3817047	10·0345418	524	9·9654582	27
34	9·5840576	3039	10·4159424	9·6186519	3564	10·3813481	10·0345943	525	9·9654057	26
35	9·5843615	3036	10·4156385	9·6190083	3562	10·3809917	10·0346468	525	9·9653532	25
36	9·5846651	3034	10·4153349	9·6193645	3560	10·3806355	10·0346994	526	9·9653006	24
37	9·5849685	3031	10·4150315	9·6197205	3557	10·3802795	10·0347520	526	9·9652480	23
38	9·5852716	3029	10·4147284	9·6200762	3556	10·3799238	10·0348047	527	9·9651953	22
39	9·5855745	3026	10·4144255	9·6204318	3554	10·3795682	10·0348574	527	9·9651426	21
40	9·5858771	3024	10·4141229	9·6207872	3551	10·3792128	10·0349101	527	9·9650899	20
41	9·5861795	3021	10·4138205	9·6211423	3550	10·3788577	10·0349629	528	9·9650371	19
42	9·5864816	3019	10·4135184	9·6214973	3547	10·3785027	10·0350157	528	9·9649843	18
43	9·5867835	3016	10·4132165	9·6218520	3545	10·3781480	10·0350686	529	9·9649314	17
44	9·5870851	3014	10·4129149	9·6222066	3543	10·3777934	10·0351215	529	9·9648785	16
45	9·5873865	3011	10·4126135	9·6225609	3541	10·3774391	10·0351744	530	9·9648256	15
46	9·5876876	3009	10·4123124	9·6229150	3540	10·3770850	10·0352274	531	9·9647726	14
47	9·5879885	3007	10·4120115	9·6232690	3537	10·3767310	10·0352805	530	9·9647195	13
48	9·5882892	3004	10·4117108	9·6236227	3536	10·3763773	10·0353335	532	9·9646665	12
49	9·5885896	3001	10·4114104	9·6239763	3533	10·3760237	10·0353867	531	9·9646133	11
50	9·5888897	2996	10·4111103	9·6243296	3533	10·3756704	10·0354398	532	9·9645602	10
51	9·5891897	2996	10·4108103	9·6246827	3529	10·3753173	10·0354931	532	9·9645069	9
52	9·5894893	2995	10·4105107	9·6250356	3528	10·3749644	10·0355463	533	9·9644537	8
53	9·5897888	2992	10·4102112	9·6253884	3525	10·3746116	10·0355996	533	9·9644004	7
54	9·5900880	2989	10·4099120	9·6257409	3523	10·3742591	10·0356530	534	9·9643470	6
55	9·5903869	2987	10·4096131	9·6260932	3522	10·3739068	10·0357063	533	9·9642937	5
56	9·5906856	2985	10·4093144	9·6264454	3519	10·3735546	10·0357598	535	9·9642402	4
57	9·5909841	2982	10·4090159	9·6267973	3518	10·3732027	10·0358132	534	9·9641868	3
58	9·5912823	2980	10·4087177	9·6271491	3515	10·3728509	10·0358668	536	9·9641332	2
59	9·5915803	2977	10·4084197	9·6275006	3513	10·3724994	10·0359203	535	9·9640797	1
60	9·5918780		10·4081220	9·6278519		10·3721481	10·0359739	536	9·9640261	0

′	Cosine	Diff.	Secant	Cotang.	Diff.	Tang.	Cosec.	D.	Sine	′

67 Deg.

23 Deg.

′	Sine	Diff.	Cosec.	Tang.	Diff.	Cotang.	Secant	D.	Cosine	′
0	9·5918780	2975	10·4081220	9·6278519	3512	10·3721481	10·0359739	537	9·9640261	60
1	9·5921755	2973	10·4078245	9·6282031	3509	10·3717969	10·0360276	537	9·9639724	59
2	9·5924728	2970	10·4075272	9·6285540	3508	10·3714460	10·0360813	537	9·9639187	58
3	9·5927698	2968	10·4072302	9·6289048	3505	10·3710952	10·0361350	538	9·9638650	57
4	9·5930666	2965	10·4069334	9·6292553	3504	10·3707447	10·0361888	538	9·9638112	56
5	9·5933631	2963	10·4066369	9·6296057	3501	10·3703943	10·0362426	538	9·9637574	55
6	9·5936594	2961	10·4063406	9·6299558	3500	10·3700442	10·0362964	540	9·9637036	54
7	9·5939555	2958	10·4060445	9·6303058	3498	10·3696942	10·0363504	539	9·9636496	53
8	9·5942513	2956	10·4057487	9·6306556	3496	10·3693444	10·0364043	540	9·9635957	52
9	9·5945469	2953	10·4054531	9·6310052	3493	10·3389948	10·0364583	540	9·9635417	51
10	9·5948422	2951	10·4051578	9·6313545	3492	10·3686455	10·0365123	541	9·9634877	50
11	9·5951373	2949	10·4048627	9·6317037	3490	10·3682963	10·0365664	541	9·9634336	49
12	9·5954322	2946	10·4045678	9·6320527	3488	10·3679473	10·0366205	542	9·9633795	48
13	9·5957268	2944	10·4042732	9·6324015	3486	10·3675985	10·0366747	542	9·9633253	47
14	9·5960212	2942	10·4039788	9·6327501	3484	10·3672499	10·0367289	543	9·9632711	46
15	9·5963154	2939	10·4036846	9·6330985	3483	10·3669015	10·0367832	543	9·9632168	45
16	9·5966093	2937	10·4033907	9·6334468	3480	10·3665532	10·0368375	543	9·9631625	44
17	9·5969030	2935	10·4030970	9·6337948	3478	10·3662052	10·0368918	544	9·9631082	43
18	9·5971965	2932	10·4028035	9·6341426	3477	10·3658574	10·0369462	544	9·9630538	42
19	9·5974897	2930	10·4025103	9·6344903	3475	10·3655097	10·0370006	545	9·9629994	41
20	9·5977827	2927	10·4022173	9·6348378	3472	10·3651622	10·0370551	545	9·9629449	40
21	9·5980754	2925	10·4019246	9·6351850	3471	10·3648150	10·0371096	546	9·9628904	39
22	9·5983679	2923	10·4016321	9·6355321	3469	10·3644679	10·0371642	546	9·9628358	38
23	9·5986602	2921	10·4013398	9·6358790	3467	10·3641210	10·0372188	546	9·9627812	37
24	9·5989523	2918	10·4010477	9·6362257	3465	10·3637743	10·0372734	546	9·9627266	36
25	9·5992441	2916	10·4007559	9·6365722	3463	10·3634278	10·0373281	547	9·9626719	35
26	9·5995357	2913	10·4004643	9·6369185	3461	10·3630815	10·0373828	548	9·9626172	34
27	9·5998270	2911	10·4001730	9·6372646	3460	10·3627354	10·0374376	548	9·9625624	33
28	9·6001181	2909	10·3998819	9·6376106	3457	10·3623894	10·0374924	548	9·9625076	32
29	9·6004090	2907	10·3995910	9·6379563	3456	10·3620437	10·0375473	549	9·9624527	31
30	9·6006997	2904	10·3993003	9·6383019	3454	10·3616981	10·0376022	549	9·9623978	30
31	9·6009901	2902	10·3990099	9·6386473	3452	10·3613527	10·0376572	550	9·9623428	29
32	9·6012803	2900	10·3987197	9·6389925	3450	10·3610075	10·0377122	550	9·9622878	28
33	9·6015703	2897	10·3984297	9·6393375	3448	10·3606625	10·0377672	550	9·9622328	27
34	9·6013600	2895	10·3981400	9·6396823	3446	10·3603177	10·0378223	551	9·9621777	26
35	9·6021495	2893	10·3978505	9·6400269	3445	10·3599731	10·0378774	551	9·9621226	25
36	9·6024388	2890	10·3975612	9·6403714	3442	10·3596286	10·0379326	552	9·9620674	24
37	9·6027278	2888	10·3972722	9·6407156	3441	10·3592844	10·0379878	552	9·9620122	23
38	9·6030166	2886	10·3969834	9·6410597	3439	10·3589403	10·0380431	553	9·9619569	22
39	9·6033052	2884	10·3966948	9·6414036	3437	10·3585964	10·0380984	553	9·9619016	21
40	9·6035936	2881	10·3964064	9·6417473	3435	10·3582527	10·0381537	553	9·9618463	20
41	9·6038817	2879	10·3961183	9·6420908	3434	10·3579092	10·0382091	554	9·9617909	19
42	9·6041696	2877	10·3958304	9·6424342	3431	10·3575658	10·0382645	554	9·9617355	18
43	9·6044573	2875	10·3955427	9·6427773	3430	10·3572227	10·0383200	555	9·9616800	17
44	9·6047448	2872	10·3952552	9·6431203	3428	10·3568797	10·0383755	555	9·9616245	16
45	9·6050320	2870	10·3949680	9·6434631	3426	10·3565369	10·0384311	556	9·9615689	15
46	9·6053190	2867	10·3946810	9·6438057	3424	10·3561943	10·0384867	557	9·9615133	14
47	9·6056057	2866	10·3943943	9·6441481	3422	10·3558519	10·0385424	556	9·9614576	13
48	9·6058923	2863	10·3941077	9·6444903	3421	10·3555097	10·0385980	557	9·9614020	12
49	9·6061786	2861	10·3938214	9·6448324	3419	10·3551676	10·0386538	558	9·9613462	11
50	9·6064647	2859	10·3935353	9·6451743	3417	10·3548257	10·0387096	558	9·9612904	10
51	9·6067506	2856	10·3932494	9·6455160	3415	10·3544840	10·0387654	559	9·9612346	9
52	9·6070362	2854	10·3929638	9·6458575	3413	10·3541425	10·0388213	559	9·9611787	8
53	9·6073216	2852	10·3926784	9·6461988	3412	10·3538012	10·0388772	560	9·9611228	7
54	9·6076068	2850	10·3923932	9·6465400	3410	10·3534600	10·0389332	560	9·9610668	6
55	9·6078918	2847	10·3921082	9·6468810	3407	10·3531190	10·0389892	560	9·9610108	5
56	9·6081765	2846	10·3918235	9·6472217	3407	10·3527783	10·0390452	561	9·9609548	4
57	9·6084611	2843	10·3915389	9·6475624	3404	10·3524376	10·0391013	561	9·9608987	3
58	9·6087454	2840	10·3912546	9·6479028	3403	10·3520972	10·0391574	562	9·9608426	2
59	9·6090294	2839	10·3909706	9·6482431	3400	10·3517569	10·0392136	562	9·9607864	1
60	9·6093133		10·3906867	9·6485831		10·3514169	10·0392698		9·9607302	0

′	Cosine	Diff.	Secant	Cotang.	Diff.	Tang.	Cosec.	D.	Sine	′

24 Deg.

′	Sine	Diff.	Cosec.	Tang.	Diff.	Cotang.	Secant	D.	Cosine	′
0	9·6093133	2836	10·3906867	9·6485831	3399	10·3514169	10·0392698	563	9·9607302	60
1	9·6095969	2834	10·3904031	9·6489230	3398	10·3510770	10·0393261	563	9·9606739	59
2	9·6098803	2832	10·3901197	9·6492628	3395	10·3507372	10·0393824	564	9·9606176	58
3	9·6101635	2830	10·3898365	9·6496023	3394	10·3503977	10·0394388	564	9·9605612	57
4	9·6104465	2828	10·3895535	9·6499417	3392	10·3500583	10·0394952	564	9·9605048	56
5	9·6107293	2825	10·3892707	9·6502809	3390	10·3497191	10·0395516	565	9·9604484	55
6	9·6110118	2823	10·3889882	9·6506199	3388	10·3493801	10·0396081	565	9·9603919	54
7	9·6112941	2821	10·3887059	9·6509587	3387	10·3490413	10·0396646	566	9·9603354	53
8	9·6115762	2818	10·3884238	9·6512974	3385	10·3487026	10·0397212	566	9·9602788	52
9	9·6118580	2817	10·3881420	9·6516359	3383	10·3483641	10·0397778	567	9·9602222	51
10	9·6121397	2814	10·3878603	9·6519742	3381	10·3480258	10·0398345	567	9·9601655	50
11	9·6124211	2812	10·3875789	9·6523123	3380	10·3476877	10·0398912	568	9·9601088	49
12	9·6127023	2810	10·3872977	9·6526503	3378	10·3473497	10·0399480	568	9·9600520	48
13	9·6129833	2808	10·3870167	9·6529881	3376	10·3470119	10·0400048	568	9·9599952	47
14	9·6132641	2805	10·3867359	9·6533257	3374	10·3466743	10·0400616	569	9·9599384	46
15	9·6135446	2804	10·3864554	9·6536631	3373	10·3463369	10·0401185	569	9·9598815	45
16	9·6138250	2801	10·3861750	9·6540004	3371	10·3459996	10·0401754	570	9·9598246	44
17	9·6141051	2799	10·3858949	9·6543375	3369	10·3456625	10·0402324	570	9·9597676	43
18	9·6143850	2797	10·3856150	9·6546744	3368	10·3453256	10·0402894	571	9·9597106	42
19	9·6146647	2794	10·3853353	9·6550112	3365	10·3449888	10·0403465	571	9·9596535	41
20	9·6149441	2793	10·3850559	9·6553477	3364	10·3446523	10·0404036	571	9·9595964	40
21	9·6152234	2790	10·3847766	9·6556841	3363	10·3443159	10·0404607	572	9·9595393	39
22	9·6155024	2788	10·3844976	9·6560204	3360	10·3439796	10·0405179	573	9·9594821	38
23	9·6157812	2787	10·3842188	9·6563564	3359	10·3436436	10·0405752	573	9·9594248	37
24	9·6160599	2783	10·3839401	9·6566923	3357	10·3433077	10·0406325	573	9·9593675	36
25	9·6163382	2782	10·3836618	9·6570280	3356	10·3429720	10·0406898	574	9·9593102	35
26	9·6166164	2780	10·3833836	9·6573636	3353	10·3426364	10·0407472	574	9·9592528	34
27	9·6168944	2777	10·3831056	9·6576989	3352	10·3423011	10·0408046	574	9·9591954	33
28	9·6171721	2775	10·3828279	9·6580341	3351	10·3419659	10·0408620	575	9·9591380	32
29	9·6174496	2774	10·3825504	9·6583692	3349	10·3416308	10·0409195	576	9·9590805	31
30	9·6177270	2771	10·3822730	9·6587041	3346	10·3412959	10·0409771	576	9·9590229	30
31	9·6180041	2768	10·3819959	9·6590387	3346	10·3409613	10·0410347	576	9·9589653	29
32	9·6182809	2767	10·3817191	9·6593783	3343	10·3406267	10·0410923	577	9·9589077	28
33	9·6185576	2765	10·3814424	9·6597076	3342	10·3402924	10·0411500	577	9·9588500	27
34	9·6188341	2762	10·3811659	9·6600418	3340	10·3399582	10·0412077	578	9·9587923	26
35	9·6191103	2761	10·3808897	9·6603758	3339	10·3396242	10·0412655	578	9·9587345	25
36	9·6193864	2758	10·3806136	9·6607097	3337	10·3392903	10·0413233	579	9·9586767	24
37	9·6196622	2756	10·3803378	9·6610434	3335	10·3389566	10·0413812	579	9·9586188	23
38	9·6199378	2754	10·3800622	9·6613769	3334	10·3386231	10·0414391	579	9·9585609	22
39	9·6202132	2752	10·3797868	9·6617103	3331	10·3382897	10·0414970	580	9·9585030	21
40	9·6204884	2750	10·3795116	9·6620434	3331	10·3379566	10·0415550	581	9·9584450	20
41	9·6207634	2748	10·3792366	9·6623765	3328	10·3376235	10·0416131	581	9·9583869	19
42	9·6210382	2745	10·3789618	9·6627093	3327	10·3372907	10·0416712	581	9·9583288	18
43	9·6213127	2744	10·3786873	9·6630420	3325	10·3369580	10·0417293	582	9·9582707	17
44	9·6215871	2741	10·3784129	9·6633745	3324	10·3366255	10·0417875	582	9·9582125	16
45	9·6218612	2739	10·3781388	9·6637069	3322	10·3362931	10·0418457	582	9·9581543	15
46	9·6221351	2737	10·3778649	9·6640391	3320	10·3359609	10·0419039	583	9·9580961	14
47	9·6224088	2736	10·3775912	9·6643711	3319	10·3356289	10·0419622	584	9·9580378	13
48	9·6226824	2733	10·3773176	9·6647030	3316	10·3352970	10·0420206	584	9·9579794	12
49	9·6229557	2730	10·3770443	9·6650346	3316	10·3349654	10·0420790	584	9·9579210	11
50	9·6232287	2729	10·3767713	9·6653662	3313	10·3346338	10·0421374	585	9·9578626	10
51	9·6235016	2727	10·3764984	9·6656975	3313	10·3343025	10·0421959	585	9·9578041	9
52	9·6237743	2725	10·3762257	9·6660288	3310	10·3339712	10·0422544	586	9·9577456	8
53	9·6240468	2722	10·3759532	9·6663598	3309	10·3336402	10·0423130	586	9·9576870	7
54	9·6243190	2721	10·3756810	9·6666907	3307	10·3333093	10·0423716	587	9·9576284	6
55	9·6245911	2718	10·3754089	9·6670214	3305	10·3329786	10·0424303	587	9·9575697	5
56	9·6248629	2717	10·3751371	9·6673519	3304	10·3326481	10·0424890	588	9·9575110	4
57	9·6251346	2714	10·3748654	9·6676823	3303	10·3323177	10·0425478	588	9·9574522	3
58	9·6254060	2712	10·3745940	9·6680126	3300	10·3319874	10·0426066	588	9·9573934	2
59	9·6256772	2711	10·3743228	9·6683426	3299	10·3316574	10·0426654	589	9·9573346	1
60	9·6259483		10·3740517	9·6686725		10·3313275	10·0427243		9·9572757	0

′	Cosine	Diff.	Secant	Cotang.	Diff.	Tang.	Cosec.	D.	Sine	′

65 Deg.

25 Deg.

′	Sine	Diff.	Cosec.	Tang.	Diff.	Cotang.	Secant	D.	Cosine	′
0	9·6259483	2708	10·3740517	9·6686725	3298	10·3313275	10·0427243	589	9·9572757	60
1	9·6262191	2706	10·3737809	9·6690023	3296	10·3309977	10·0427832	590	9·9572168	59
2	9·6264897	2704	10·3735103	9·6693319	3294	10·3306681	10·0428422	590	9·9571578	58
3	9·6267601	2702	10·3732399	9·6696613	3293	10·3303387	10·0429012	591	9·9570988	57
4	9·6270303	2700	10·3729697	9·6699906	3291	10·3300094	10·0429603	591	9·9570397	56
5	9·6273003	2698	10·3726997	9·6703197	3289	10·3296803	10·0430194	591	9·9569806	55
6	9·6275701	2696	10·3724299	9·6706486	3288	10·3293514	10·0430785	592	9·9569215	54
7	9·6278397	2693	10·3721603	9·6709774	3286	10·3290226	10·0431377	593	9·9568623	53
8	9·6281090	2692	10·3718910	9·6713060	3285	10·3286940	10·0431970	593	9·9568030	52
9	9·6283782	2690	10·3716218	9·6716345	3283	10·3283655	10·0432563	593	9·9567437	51
10	9·6286472	2688	10·3713528	9·6719628	3282	10·3280372	10·0433156	594	9·9566844	50
11	9·6289160	2685	10·3710840	9·6722910	3280	10·3277090	10·0433750	594	9·9566250	49
12	9·6291845	2684	10·3708155	9·6726190	3278	10·3273810	10·0434344	595	9·9565656	48
13	9·6294529	2682	10·3705471	9·6729468	3277	10·3270532	10·0434939	595	9·9565061	47
14	9·6297211	2679	10·3702789	9·6732745	3275	10·3267255	10·0435534	596	9·9564466	46
15	9·6299890	2678	10·3700110	9·6736020	3274	10·3263980	10·0436130	596	9·9563870	45
16	9·6302568	2675	10·3697432	9·6739294	3272	10·3260706	10·0436726	596	9·9563274	44
17	9·6305243	2674	10·3694757	9·6742566	3270	10·3257434	10·0437322	597	9·9562678	43
18	9·6307917	2672	10·3692083	9·6745836	3269	10·3254164	10·0437919	597	9·9562081	42
19	9·6310589	2669	10·3689411	9·6749105	3267	10·3250895	10·0438517	598	9·9561483	41
20	9·6313258	2668	10·3686742	9·6752372	3266	10·3247628	10·0439114	599	9·9560886	40
21	9·6315926	2665	10·3684074	9·6755638	3265	10·3244362	10·0439713	598	9·9560287	39
22	9·6318591	2664	10·3681409	9·6758903	3262	10·3241097	10·0440311	600	9·9559689	38
23	9·6321255	2661	10·3678745	9·6762165	3261	10·3237885	10·0440911	599	9·9559089	37
24	9·6323916	2660	10·3676084	9·6765426	3260	10·3234574	10·0441510	600	9·9558490	36
25	9·6326576	2657	10·3673424	9·6768686	3258	10·3231314	10·0442110	601	9·9557890	35
26	9·6329233	2656	10·3670767	9·6771944	3257	10·3228056	10·0442711	596	9·9557289	34
27	9·6331889	2653	10·3668111	9·6775201	3255	10·3224799	10·0443312	601	9·9556688	33
28	9·6334542	2652	10·3665458	9·6778456	3253	10·3221544	10·0443913	601	9·9556087	32
29	9·6337194	2650	10·3662806	9·6781709	3252	10·3218291	10·0444515	602	9·9555485	31
30	9·6339844	2647	10·3660156	9·6784961	3250	10·3215039	10·0445118	603	9·9555482	30
31	9·6342491	2646	10·3657509	9·6788211	3249	10·3211789	10·0445720	604	9·9554280	29
32	9·6345137	2643	10·3654863	9·6791460	3248	10·3208540	10·0446324	603	9·9553676	28
33	9·6347780	2642	10·3652220	9·6794708	3245	10·3205292	10·0446927	604	9·9553073	27
34	9·6350422	2640	10·3649578	9·6797953	3245	10·3202047	10·0447531	605	9·9552469	26
35	9·6353062	2637	10·3646938	9·6801198	3242	10·3198802	10·0448136	605	9·9551864	25
36	9·6355699	2636	10·3644301	9·6804440	3242	10·3195560	10·0448741	606	9·9551259	24
37	9·6358335	2634	10·3641665	9·6807682	3239	10·3192318	10·0449347	606	9·9550653	23
38	9·6360969	2632	10·3639031	9·6810921	3239	10·3189079	10·0449953	606	9·9550047	22
39	9·6363601	2630	10·3636399	9·6814160	3236	10·3185840	10·0450559	607	9·9549441	21
40	9·6366231	2628	10·3633769	9·6817396	3236	10·3182604	10·0451166	607	9·9548834	20
41	9·6368859	2625	10·3631141	9·6820632	3233	10·3179368	10·0451773	608	9·9548227	19
42	9·6371484	2624	10·3628516	9·6823865	3233	10·3176135	10·0452381	608	9·9547619	18
43	9·6374108	2623	10·3625892	9·6827098	3230	10·3172902	10·0452989	609	9·9547011	17
44	9·6376731	2620	10·3623269	9·6830323	3229	10·3169672	10·0453598	609	9·9546402	16
45	9·6379351	2618	10·3620649	9·6833557	3228	10·3166443	10·0454207	609	9·9545793	15
46	9·6381969	2616	10·3618031	9·6836785	3226	10·3163215	10·0454816	610	9·9545184	14
47	9·6384585	2614	10·3615415	9·6840011	3225	10·3159989	10·0455426	611	9·9544574	13
48	9·6387199	2613	10·3612801	9·6843236	3223	10·3156764	10·0456037	611	9·9543963	12
49	9·6389812	2610	10·3610188	9·6846459	3222	10·3153541	10·0456648	611	9·9543352	11
50	9·6392422	2608	10·3607578	9·6849681	3220	10·3150319	10·0457259	612	9·9542741	10
51	9·6395030	2607	10·3604970	9·6852901	3219	10·3147099	10·0457871	612	9·9542129	9
52	9·6397637	2604	10·3602363	9·6856120	3218	10·3143880	10·0458483	613	9·9541517	8
53	9·6400241	2603	10·3599759	9·6859338	3215	10·3140662	10·0459096	613	9·9540904	7
54	9·6402844	2601	10·3597156	9·6862553	3215	10·3137447	10·0459709	614	9·9540291	6
55	9·6405445	2599	10·3594555	9·6865768	3213	10·3134232	10·0460323	614	9·9539677	5
56	9·6408044	2596	10·3591956	9·6868981	3211	10·3131019	10·0460937	615	9·9539063	4
57	9·6410640	2595	10·3589360	9·6872192	3210	10·3127808	10·0461552	615	9·9538448	3
58	9·6413235	2593	10·3586765	9·6875402	3209	10·3124598	10·0462167	615	9·9537833	2
59	9·6415828	2592	10·3584172	9·6878611	3207	10·3121389	10·0462782	616	9·9537218	1
60	9·6418420		10·3581580	9·6881818		10·3118182	10·0463398		9·9536602	0

| ′ | Cosine | Diff. | Secant | Cotang. | Diff. | Tang. | Cosec. | D. | Sine | ′ |

64 Deg.

′	Sine	Diff.	Cosec.	Tang.	Diff.	Cotang.	Secant	D.	Cosine	′
0	9·6418420	2589	10·3581580	9·6881818	3205	10·3118182	10·0463398	617	9·9536602	60
1	9·6421009	2587	10·3578991	9·6885023	3204	10·3114977	10·0464015	616	9·9535985	59
2	9·6423596	2586	10·3576404	9·6888227	3203	10·3111773	10·0464631	618	9·9535369	58
3	9·6426182	2583	10·3573818	9·6891430	3201	10·3108570	10·0465249	617	9·9534751	57
4	9·6428765	2582	10·3571235	9·6894631	32..0	10·3105369	10·0465866	619	9·9534134	56
5	9·6431347	2579	10·3568653	9·6897831	3199	10·3102169	10·0466485	618	9·9533515	55
6	9·6433926	2578	10·3566074	9·6901030	3196	10·3098970	10·0467103	619	9·9532897	54
7	9·6436504	2576	10·3563496	9·6904226	3196	10·3095774	10·0467722	620	9·9532278	53
8	9·6439080	2574	10·3560920	9·6907422	3194	10·3092578	10·0468342	620	9·9531658	52
9	9·6441654	2572	10·3558346	9·6910616	3193	10·3089384	10·0468962	620	9·9531038	51
10	9·6444226	2570	10·3555774	9·6913809	3191	10·3086191	10·0469582	621	9·9530418	50
11	9·6446796	2569	10·3553204	9·6917000	3189	10·3083000	10·0470203	622	9·9529797	49
12	9·6449365	2566	10·3550635	9·6920189	3189	10·3079811	10·0470825	622	9·9529175	48
13	9·6451931	2565	10·3548069	9·6923378	3187	10·3076622	10·0471447	622	9·9528553	47
14	9·6454496	2562	10·3545504	9·6926565	3185	10·3073435	10·0472069	623	9·9527931	46
15	9·6457058	2561	10·3542942	9·6929750	3184	10·3070250	10·0472692	623	9·9527308	45
16	9·6459619	2559	10·3540381	9·6932934	3183	10·3067066	10·0473315	624	9·9526685	44
17	9·6462178	2557	10·3537822	9·6936117	3181	10·3063883	10·0473939	624	9·9526061	43
18	9·6464735	2555	10·3535265	9·6939298	3180	10·3060702	10·0474563	624	9·9525437	42
19	9·6467290	2554	10·3532710	9·6942478	3178	10·3057522	10·0475187	625	9·9524813	41
20	9·6469844	2551	10·3530156	9·6945656	3177	10·3054344	10·0475812	626	9·9524188	40
21	9·6472395	2550	10·3527605	9·6948833	3176	10·3051167	10·0476438	626	9·9523562	39
22	9·6474945	2547	10·3525055	9·6952009	3174	10·3047991	10·0477064	626	9·9522936	38
23	9·6477492	2546	10·3522508	9·6955183	3172	10·3044817	10·0477690	627	9·9522310	37
24	9·6480038	2544	10·3519962	9·6958355	3172	10·3041645	10·0478317	628	9·9521683	36
25	9·6482582	2542	10·3517418	9·6961527	3170	10·3038473	10·0478945	627	9·9521055	35
26	9·6485124	2541	10·3514876	9·6964697	3168	10·3035303	10·0479572	629	9·9520428	34
27	9·6487665	2538	10·3512335	9·6967865	3167	10·3032135	10·0480201	628	9·9519799	33
28	9·6490203	2537	10·3509797	9·6971032	3166	10·3028968	10·0480829	630	9·9519171	32
29	9·6492740	2534	10·3507260	9·6974198	3165	10·3025802	10·0481459	629	9·9518541	31
30	9·6495274	2533	10·3504726	9·6977363	3163	10·3022637	10·0482088	630	9·9517912	30
31	9·6497807	2531	10·3502193	9·6980526	3161	10·3019474	10·0482718	631	9·9517282	29
32	9·6500338	2530	10·3499662	9·6983687	3160	10·3016313	10·0483349	631	9·9516651	28
33	9·6502868	2527	10·3497132	9·6986847	3159	10·3013153	10·0483980	631	9·9516020	27
34	9·6505395	2525	10·3494605	9·6990006	3158	10·3009994	10·0484611	632	9·9515389	26
35	9·6507920	2524	10·3492080	9·6993164	3156	10·3006836	10·0485243	633	9·9514757	25
36	9·6510444	2522	10·3489556	9·6996320	3154	10·3003680	10·0485876	632	9·9514124	24
37	9·6512966	2520	10·3487034	9·6999474	3154	10·3000526	10·0486508	634	9·9513492	23
38	9·6515486	2518	10·3484514	9·7002628	3152	10·2997372	10·0487142	634	9·9512858	22
39	9·6518004	2517	10·3481996	9·7005780	3150	10·2994220	10·0487776	634	9·9512224	21
40	9·6520521	2514	10·3479479	9·7008930	3150	10·2991070	10·0488410	634	9·9511590	20
41	9·6523035	2513	10·3476965	9·7012080	3147	10·2987920	10·0489044	636	9·9510956	19
42	9·6525548	2511	10·3474452	9·7015227	3147	10·2984773	10·0489680	635	9·9510320	18
43	9·6528059	2509	10·3471941	9·7018374	3145	10·2981626	10·0490315	636	9·9509685	17
44	9·6530568	2507	10·3469432	9·7021519	3144	10·2978481	10·0490951	637	9·9509049	16
45	9·6533075	2506	10·3466925	9·7024663	3142	10·2975337	10·0491588	637	9·9508412	15
46	9·6535581	2503	10·3464419	9·7027805	3141	10·2972195	10·0492225	637	9·9507775	14
47	9·6538084	2502	10·3461916	9·7030946	3140	10·2969054	10·0492862	638	9·9507138	13
48	9·6540586	2500	10·3459414	9·7034086	3139	10·2965914	10·0493500	639	9·9506500	12
49	9·6543086	2498	10·3456914	9·7037225	3137	10·2962775	10·0494139	638	9·9505861	11
50	9·6545584	2497	10·3454416	9·7040362	3135	10·2959638	10·0494777	640	9·9505223	10
51	9·6548081	2494	10·3451919	9·7043497	3135	10·2956503	10·0495417	639	9·9504583	9
52	9·6550575	2493	10·3449425	9·7046632	3133	10·2953368	10·0496056	641	9·9503944	8
53	9·6553068	2491	10·3446932	9·7049765	3132	10·2950235	10·0496697	640	9·9503303	7
54	9·6555559	2489	10·3444441	9·7052897	3130	10·2947103	10·0497337	641	9·9502663	6
55	9·6558048	2488	10·3441952	9·7056027	3129	10·2943973	10·0497978	642	9·9502022	5
56	9·6560536	2485	10·3439464	9·7059156	3128	10·2940844	10·0498620	642	9·9501380	4
57	9·6563021	2484	10·3436979	9·7062284	3126	10·2937716	10·0499262	643	9·9500738	3
58	9·6565505	2482	10·3434495	9·7065410	3125	10·2934590	10·0499905	643	9·9500095	2
59	9·6567987	2481	10·3432013	9·7068535	3124	10·2931465	10·0500548	643	9·9499452	1
60	9·6570468		10·3429532	9·7071659		10·2928341	10·0501191		9·9498809	0
′	Cosine	Diff.	Secant	Cotang.	Diff.	Tang.	Cosec.	D.	Sine	′

′	Sine	Diff.	Cosec.	Tang.	Diff.	Cotang.	Secant	D.	Cosine	′
0	9·6570468	2478	10·3429532	9·7071659	3122	10·2928341	10·0501191	644	9·9498809	60
1	9·6572946	2477	10·3427054	9·7074781	3121	10·2925219	10·0501835	644	9·9498165	59
2	9·6575423	2475	10·3424577	9·7077902	3120	10·2922098	10·0502479	645	9·9497521	58
3	9·6577898	2473	10·3422102	9·7081022	3119	10·2918978	10·0503124	646	9·9496876	57
4	9·6580371	2471	10·3419629	9·7084141	3117	10·2915859	10·0503770	645	9·9496230	56
5	9·6582842	2470	10·3417158	9·7087258	3116	10·2912742	10·0504415	647	9·9495585	55
6	9·6585312	2468	10·3414688	9·7090374	3114	10·2909626	10·0505062	646	9·9494938	54
7	9·6587780	2466	10·3412220	9·7093488	3113	10·2906512	10·0505708	647	9·9494292	53
8	9·6590246	2464	10·3409754	9·7096601	3112	10·2903399	10·0506355	648	9·9493645	52
9	9·6592710	2463	10·3407290	9·7099713	3111	10·2900287	10·0507003	648	9·9492997	51
10	9·6595173	2460	10·3404827	9·7102824	3109	10·2897176	10·0507651	649	9·9492349	50
11	9·6597633	2460	10·3402367	9·7105933	3108	10·2894067	10·0508300	649	9·9491700	49
12	9·6600093	2457	10·3399907	9·7109041	3107	10·2890959	10·0508949	649	9·9491051	48
13	9·6602550	2455	10·3397450	9·7112148	3106	10·2887852	10·0509598	650	9·9490402	47
14	9·6605005	2454	10·3394995	9·7115254	3104	10·2884746	10·0510248	651	9·9489752	46
15	9·6607459	2452	10·3392541	9·7118358	3103	10·2881642	10·0510899	651	9·9489101	45
16	9·6609911	2450	10·3390089	9·7121461	3101	10·2878539	10·0511550	651	9·9488450	44
17	9·6612361	2449	10·3387639	9·7124562	3100	10·2875438	10·0512201	652	9·9487799	43
18	9·6614810	2447	10·3385190	9·7127662	3099	10·2872338	10·0512853	652	9·9487147	42
19	9·6617257	2445	10·3382743	9·7130761	3098	10·2869239	10·0513505	653	9·9486495	41
20	9·6619702	2443	10·3380298	9·7133859	3097	10·2866141	10·0514158	653	9·9485842	40
21	9·6622145	2441	10·3377855	9·7136956	3095	10·2863044	10·0514811	654	9·9485189	39
22	9·6624586	2440	10·3375414	9·7140051	3094	10·2859949	10·0515465	654	9·9484535	38
23	9·6627026	2438	10·3372974	9·7143145	3092	10·2856855	10·0516119	654	9·9483881	37
24	9·6629464	2436	10·3370536	9·7146237	3092	10·2853763	10·0516773	655	9·9483227	36
25	9·6631900	2435	10·3368100	9·7149329	3090	10·2850671	10·0517428	656	9·9482572	35
26	9·6634335	2433	10·3365665	9·7152419	3089	10·2847581	10·0518084	656	9·9481916	34
27	9·6636768	2431	10·3363232	9·7155508	3087	10·2844492	10·0518740	656	9·9481260	33
28	9·6639199	2429	10·3360801	9·7158595	3087	10·2841405	10·0519396	657	9·9480604	32
29	9·6641628	2428	10·3358372	9·7161682	3085	10·2838318	10·0520053	658	9·9479947	31
30	9·6644056	2426	10·3355944	9·7164767	3084	10·2835233	10·0520711	658	9·9479289	30
31	9·6646482	2424	10·3353518	9·7167851	3082	10·2832149	10·0521369	658	9·9478631	29
32	9·6648906	2423	10·3351094	9·7170933	3081	10·2829067	10·0522027	659	9·9477973	28
33	9·6651329	2420	10·3348671	9·7174014	3080	10·2825986	10·0522686	659	9·9477314	27
34	9·6653749	2419	10·3346251	9·7177094	3079	10·2822906	10·0523345	660	9·9476655	26
35	9·6656168	2418	10·3343832	9·7180173	3078	10·2819827	10·0524005	660	9·9475995	25
36	9·6658586	2415	10·3341414	9·7183251	3076	10·2816749	10·0524665	661	9·9475335	24
37	9·6661001	2414	10·3338999	9·7186327	3075	10·2813673	10·0525326	661	9·9474674	23
38	9·6663415	2413	10·3336585	9·7189402	3074	10·2810598	10·0525987	661	9·9474013	22
39	9·6665828	2410	10·3334172	9·7192476	3073	10·2807524	10·0526648	663	9·9473352	21
40	9·6668238	2409	10·3331762	9·7195549	3071	10·2804451	10·0527311	662	9·9472689	20
41	9·6670647	2407	10·3329353	9·7198620	3070	10·2801380	10·0527973	663	9·9472027	19
42	9·6673054	2405	10·3326946	9·7201690	3069	10·2798310	10·0528636	664	9·9471364	18
43	9·6675459	2404	10·3324541	9·7204759	3068	10·2795241	10·0529300	664	9·9470700	17
44	9·6677863	2402	10·3322137	9·7207827	3066	10·2792173	10·0529964	664	9·9470036	16
45	9·6680265	2400	10·3319735	9·7210893	3065	10·2789107	10·0530628	665	9·9469372	15
46	9·6682665	2399	10·3317335	9·7213958	3064	10·2786042	10·0531293	665	9·9468707	14
47	9·6685064	2397	10·3314936	9·7217022	3063	10·2782978	10·0531958	666	9·9468042	13
48	9·6687461	2395	10·3312539	9·7220085	3062	10·2779915	10·0532624	666	9·9467376	12
49	9·6689856	2394	10·3310144	9·7223147	3060	10·2776853	10·0533290	667	9·9466710	11
50	9·6692250	2392	10·3307750	9·7226207	3059	10·2773793	10·0533957	667	9·9466043	10
51	9·6694642	2390	10·3305358	9·7229266	3058	10·2770734	10·0534624	668	9·9465376	9
52	9·6697032	2388	10·3302968	9·7232324	3057	10·2767676	10·0535292	668	9·9464708	8
53	9·6699420	2387	10·3300580	9·7235381	3055	10·2764619	10·0535960	669	9·9464040	7
54	9·6701807	2385	10·3298193	9·7238436	3054	10·2761564	10·0536629	669	9·9463371	6
55	9·6704192	2384	10·3295808	9·7241490	3053	10·2758510	10·0537298	670	9·9462702	5
56	9·6706576	2382	10·3293424	9·7244543	3052	10·2755457	10·0537968	670	9·9462032	4
57	9·6708958	2380	10·3291042	9·7247595	3051	10·2752405	10·0538638	670	9·9461362	3
58	9·6711338	2378	10·3288662	9·7250645	3049	10·2749354	10·0539308	671	9·9460692	2
59	9·6713716	2377	10·3286284	9·7253695	3049	10·2746305	10·0539979	672	9·9460021	1
60	9·6716093		10·3283907	9·7256744		10·2743256	10·0540651		9·9459349	0

′	Cosine	Diff.	Secant	Cotang.	Diff.	Tang.	Cosec.	D.	Sine	′

28 Deg.

′	Sine	Diff.	Cosec.	Tang.	Diff.	Cotang.	Secant	D.	Cosine	′
0	9·6716093	2375	10·3283907	9·7256744	3047	10·2743256	10·0540651	672	9·9459349	60
1	9·6718468	2373	10·3281532	9·7259791	3046	10·2740209	10·0541323	672	9·9458677	59
2	9·6720841	2372	10·3279159	9·7262837	3044	10·2737163	10·0541995	672	9·9458005	58
3	9·6723213	2370	10·3276787	9·7265881	3044	10·2734119	10·0542668	673	9·9457332	57
4	9·6725583	2369	10·3274417	9·7268925	3042	10·2731075	10·0543341	673	9·9456659	56
5	9·6727952	2367	10·3272048	9·7271967	3041	10·2728033	10·0544015	674	9·9455985	55
6	9·6730319	2365	10·3269681	9·7275008	3040	10·2724992	10·0544690	675	9·9455310	54
7	9·6732684	2363	10·3267316	9·7278048	3039	10·2721952	10·0545364	674	9·9454636	53
8	9·6735047	2362	10·3264953	9·7281087	3037	10·2718913	10·0546040	676	9·9453960	52
9	9·6737409	2360	10·3262591	9·7284124	3037	10·2715876	10·0546715	675	9·9453285	51
10	9·6739769	2359	10·3260231	9·7287161	3035	10·2712839	10·0547391	676	9·9452609	50
11	9·6742128	2357	10·3257872	9·7290196	3034	10·2709804	10·0548068	677	9·9451932	49
12	9·6744485	2355	10·3255515	9·7293230	3033	10·2706770	10·0548745	677	9·9451255	48
13	9·6746840	2354	10·3253160	9·7296263	3032	10·2703737	10·0549423	678	9·9450577	47
14	9·6749194	2352	10·3250806	9·7299295	3030	10·2700705	10·0550101	678	9·9449899	46
15	9·6751546	2350	10·3248454	9·7302325	3029	10·2697675	10·0550780	679	9·9449220	45
16	9·6753896	2349	10·3246104	9·7305354	3029	10·2694646	10·0551459	679	9·9448541	44
17	9·6756245	2347	10·3243755	9·7308383	3027	10·2691617	10·0552138	680	9·9447862	43
18	9·6758592	2345	10·3241408	9·7311410	3026	10·2688590	10·0552818	681	9·9447182	42
19	9·6760937	2344	10·3239063	9·7314436	3024	10·2685564	10·0553499	680	9·9446501	41
20	9·6763281	2342	10·3236719	9·7317460	3024	10·2682540	10·0554179	682	9·9445821	40
21	9·6765623	2340	10·3234377	9·7320484	3022	10·2679516	10·0554861	682	9·9445139	39
22	9·6767963	2339	10·3232037	9·7323506	3021	10·2676494	10·0555543	682	9·9444457	38
23	9·6770302	2338	10·3229698	9·7326527	3020	10·2673473	10·0556225	683	9·9443775	37
24	9·6772640	2335	10·3227360	9·7329547	3019	10·2670453	10·0556908	683	9·9443092	36
25	9·6774975	2334	10·3225025	9·7332566	3018	10·2667434	10·0557591	684	9·9442409	35
26	9·6777309	2333	10·3222691	9·7335584	3017	10·2664416	10·0558275	684	9·9441725	34
27	9·6779642	2330	10·3220358	9·7338601	3015	10·2661399	10·0558959	685	9·9441041	33
28	9·6781972	2329	10·3218028	9·7341616	3015	10·2658384	10·0559644	685	9·9440356	32
29	9·6784301	2328	10·3215699	9·7344631	3013	10·2655369	10·0560329	686	9·9439671	31
30	9·6786629	2326	10·3213371	9·7347644	3012	10·2652356	10·0561015	686	9·9438985	30
31	9·6788955	2324	10·3211045	9·7350656	3011	10·2649344	10·0561701	687	9·9438299	29
32	9·6791279	2323	10·3208721	9·7353667	3010	10·2646333	10·0562388	687	9·9437612	28
33	9·6793602	2321	10·3206398	9·7356677	3008	10·2643323	10·0563075	687	9·9436925	27
34	9·6795923	2320	10·3204077	9·7359685	3008	10·2640315	10·0563762	689	9·9436238	26
35	9·6798243	2317	10·3201757	9·7362693	3006	10·2637307	10·0564451	688	9·9435549	25
36	9·6800560	2317	10·3199440	9·7365699	3006	10·2634301	10·0565139	689	9·9434861	24
37	9·6802877	2314	10·3197123	9·7368705	3004	10·2631295	10·0565828	690	9·9434172	23
38	9·6805191	2313	10·3194809	9·7371709	3003	10·2628291	10·0566518	690	9·9433482	22
39	9·6807504	2312	10·3192496	9·7374712	3002	10·2625288	10·0567208	690	9·9432792	21
40	9·6809816	2310	10·3190184	9·7377714	3001	10·2622286	10·0567898	691	9·9432102	20
41	9·6812126	2308	10·3187874	9·7380715	2999	10·2619285	10·0568589	691	9·9431411	19
42	9·6814434	2307	10·3185566	9·7383714	2999	10·2616286	10·0569280	692	9·9430720	18
43	9·6816741	2305	10·3183259	9·7386713	2997	10·2613287	10·0569972	693	9·9430028	17
44	9·6819046	2303	10·3180954	9·7389710	2997	10·2610290	10·0570665	692	9·9429335	16
45	9·6821349	2302	10·3178651	9·7392707	2995	10·2607293	10·0571357	694	9·9428643	15
46	9·6823651	2301	10·3176349	9·7395702	2994	10·2604298	10·0572051	694	9·9427949	14
47	9·6825952	2298	10·3174048	9·7398696	2993	10·2601304	10·0572745	694	9·9427255	13
48	9·6828250	2298	10·3171750	9·7401689	2992	10·2598311	10·0573439	695	9·9426561	12
49	9·6830548	2295	10·3169452	9·7404681	2991	10·2595319	10·0574134	695	9·9425866	11
50	9·6832843	2294	10·3167157	9·7407672	2990	10·2592328	10·0574829	695	9·9425171	10
51	9·6835137	2293	10·3164863	9·7410662	2988	10·2589338	10·0575524	697	9·9424476	9
52	9·6837430	2290	10·3162570	9·7413650	2988	10·2586350	10·0576221	696	9·9423779	8
53	9·6839720	2290	10·3160280	9·7416638	2986	10·2583362	10·0576917	697	9·9423083	7
54	9·6842010	2287	10·3157990	9·7419624	2985	10·2580376	10·0577614	698	9·9422386	6
55	9·6844297	2286	10·3155703	9·7422609	2985	10·2577391	10·0578312	698	9·9421688	5
56	9·6846583	2285	10·3153417	9·7425594	2983	10·2574406	10·0579010	699	9·9420990	4
57	9·6848868	2283	10·3151132	9·7428577	2982	10·2571423	10·0579709	699	9·9420291	3
58	9·6851151	2281	10·3148849	9·7431559	2981	10·2568441	10·0580408	699	9·9419592	2
59	9·6853432	2280	10·3146568	9·7434540	2980	10·2565460	10·0581107	700	9·9418893	1
60	9·6855712		10·3144288	9·7437520		10·2562480	10·0581807		9·9418193	0

| ′ | Cosine | Diff. | Secant | Cotang. | Diff | Tang. | Cosec. | D. | Sine | ′ |

211

29 Deg.

′	Sine	Diff.	Cosec.	Tang.	Diff.	Cotang.	Secant	D.	Cosine	′
0	9·6855712	2279	10·3144288	9·7437520	2979	10·2562480	10·0581807	701	9·9418193	60
1	9·6857901	2276	10·3142009	9·7440499	2977	10·2559501	10·0582508	701	9·9417492	59
2	9·6860267	2275	10·3139733	9·7443476	2977	10·2556524	10·0583209	701	9·9416791	58
3	9·6862542	2274	10·3137458	9·7446453	2975	10·2553547	10·0583910	702	9·9416090	57
4	9·6864816	2272	10·3135184	9·7449428	2975	10·2550572	10·0584612	703	9·9415388	56
5	9·6867088	2271	10·3132912	9·7452403	2973	10·2547597	10·0585315	703	9·9414685	55
6	9·6869359	2269	10·3130641	9·7455376	2973	10·2544624	10·0586018	703	9·9413982	54
7	9·6871628	2267	10·3128372	9·7458349	2971	10·2541651	10·0586721	704	9·9413279	53
8	9·6873895	2266	10·3126105	9·7461320	2970	10·2538680	10·0587425	704	9·9412575	52
9	9·6876161	2264	10·3123839	9·7464290	2969	10·2535710	10·0588129	705	9·9411871	51
10	9·6878425	2263	10·3121575	9·7467259	2968	10·2532741	10·0588834	705	9·9411166	50
11	9·6880688	2261	10·3119312	9·7470227	2967	10·2529773	10·0589539	706	9·9410461	49
12	9·6882949	2260	10·3117051	9·7473194	2966	10·2526806	10·0590245	707	9·9409755	48
13	9·6885209	2258	10·3114791	9·7476160	2965	10·2523840	10·0590952	706	9·9409048	47
14	9·6887467	2256	10·3112533	9·7479125	2964	10·2520875	10·0591658	708	9·9408342	46
15	9·6889723	2255	10·3110277	9·7482089	2963	10·2517911	10·0592366	707	9·9407634	45
16	9·6891978	2254	10·3108022	9·7485052	2961	10·2514948	10·0593073	708	9·9406927	44
17	9·6894232	2252	10·3105768	9·7488013	2961	10·2511987	10·0593781	709	9·9406219	43
18	9·6896484	2250	10·3103516	9·7490974	2960	10·2509026	10·0594490	709	9·9405510	42
19	9·6898734	2249	10·3101266	9·7493934	2958	10·2506066	10·0595199	710	9·9404801	41
20	9·6900983	2248	10·3099017	9·7496892	2958	10·2503108	10·0595909	710	9·9404091	40
21	9·6903231	2245	10·3096769	9·7499850	2956	10·2500150	10·0596619	711	9·9403381	39
22	9·6905476	2245	10·3094524	9·7502806	2956	10·2497194	10·0597330	711	9·9402670	38
23	9·6907721	2243	10·3092279	9·7505762	2954	10·2494238	10·0598041	711	9·9401959	37
24	9·6909964	2241	10·3090036	9·7508716	2953	10·2491284	10·0598752	713	9·9401248	36
25	9·6912205	2240	10·3087795	9·7511669	2953	10·2488331	10·0599465	712	9·9400535	35
26	9·6914445	2238	10·3085555	9·7514622	2951	10·2485378	10·0600177	713	9·9399823	34
27	9·6916683	2236	10·3083317	9·7517573	2950	10·2482427	10·0600890	713	9·9399110	33
28	9·6918919	2236	10·3081081	9·7520523	2949	10·2479477	10·0601604	714	9·9398396	32
29	9·6921155	2233	10·3078845	9·7523472	2948	10·2476528	10·0602318	714	9·9397682	31
30	9·6923388	2232	10·3076612	9·7526420	2948	10·2473580	10·0603032	715	9·9396968	30
31	9·6925620	2231	10·3074380	9·7529368	2946	10·2470632	10·0603747	716	9·9396253	29
32	9·6927851	2229	10·3072149	9·7532314	2945	10·2467686	10·0604463	716	9·9395537	28
33	9·6930080	2228	10·3069920	9·7535259	2944	10·2464741	10·0605179	716	9·9394821	27
34	9·6932308	2226	10·3067692	9·7538203	2943	10·2461797	10·0605895	717	9·9394105	26
35	9·6934534	2224	10·3065466	9·7541146	2942	10·2458854	10·0606612	717	9·9393388	25
36	9·6936758	2223	10·3063242	9·7544088	2941	10·2455912	10·0607329	718	9·9392671	24
37	9·6938981	2222	10·3061019	9·7547029	2940	10·2452971	10·0608047	719	9·9391953	23
38	9·6941203	2220	10·3058797	9·7549969	2039	10·2450031	10·0608766	719	9·9391234	22
39	9·6943423	2219	10·3056577	9·7552908	2938	10·2447092	10·0609485	719	9·9390515	21
40	9·6945642	2217	10·3054358	9·7555846	2937	10·2444154	10·0610204	720	9·9389796	20
41	9·6947859	2215	10·3052141	9·7558783	2935	10·2441217	10·0610024	720	9·9389076	19
42	9·6950074	2214	10·3049926	9·7561718	2935	10·2438282	10·0611644	721	9·9388356	18
43	9·6952288	2213	10·3047712	9·7564653	2934	10·2435347	10·0612365	721	9·9387635	17
44	9·6954501	2211	10·3045499	9·7567587	2933	10·2432413	10·0613086	722	9·9386914	16
45	9·6956712	2210	10·3043288	9·7570520	2932	10·2429480	10·0613808	722	9·9386192	15
46	9·6958922	2208	10·3041078	9·7573452	2931	10·2426548	10·0614530	723	9·9385470	14
47	9·6961130	2206	10·3038870	9·7576383	2930	10·2423617	10·0615253	723	9·9384747	13
48	9·6963336	2205	10·3036664	9·7579313	2929	10·2420687	10·0615976	724	9·9384024	12
49	9·6965541	2204	10·3034459	9·7582242	2928	10·2417758	10·0616700	724	9·9383300	11
50	9·6967745	2202	10·3032255	9·7585170	2926	10·2414830	10·0617424	725	9·9382576	10
51	9·6969947	2201	10·3030053	9·7588096	2926	10·2411904	10·0618149	725	9·9381851	9
52	9·6972148	2199	10·3027852	9·7591022	2925	10·2408978	10·0618874	726	9·9381126	8
53	9·6974347	2198	10·3025653	9·7593947	2924	10·2406053	10·0619600	726	9·9380400	7
54	9·6976545	2196	10·3023455	9·7596871	2923	10·2403129	10·0620326	727	9·9379674	6
55	9·6978741	2195	10·3021259	9·7599794	2922	10·2400206	10·0621053	727	9·9378947	5
56	9·6980936	2193	10·3019064	9·7602716	2921	10·2397284	10·0621780	728	9·9378220	4
57	9·6983129	2192	10·3016871	9·7605637	2920	10·2394363	10·0622508	728	9·9377492	3
58	9·6985321	2190	10·3014679	9·7608557	2919	10·2391443	10·0623236	729	9·9376764	2
59	9·6987511	2189	10·3012489	9·7611476	2918	10·2388524	10·0623965	729	9·9376035	1
60	9·6989700		10·3010300	9·7614394		10·2385606	10·0624694		9·9375306	0
′	Cosine	Diff.	Secant	Cotang.	Diff.	Tang.	Cosec.	D.	Sine	′

212

30 Deg.

′	Sine	Diff.	Cosec.	Tang.	Diff.	Cotang.	Secant	D.	Cosine	′
0	9·6989700	2187	10·3010300	9·7614394	2917	10·2385606	10·0624694	729	9·9375306	60
1	9·6991887	2186	10·3008113	9·7617311	2916	10·2382689	10·0625423	730	9·9374577	59
2	9·6994073	2185	10·3005927	9·7620227	2915	10·2379773	10·0626153	731	9·9373847	58
3	9·6996258	2183	10·3003742	9·7623142	2914	10·2376858	10·0626884	731	9·9373116	57
4	9·6998441	2181	10·3001559	9·7626056	2913	10·2373944	10·0627615	732	9·9372385	56
5	9·7000622	2180	10·2999378	9·7628969	2912	10·2371031	10·0628347	732	9·9371653	55
6	9·7002802	2179	10·2997198	9·7631881	2911	10·2368119	10·0629079	732	9·9370921	54
7	9·7004981	2177	10·2995019	9·7634792	2910	10·2365208	10·0629811	733	9·9370189	53
8	9·7007158	2176	10·2992842	9·7637702	2910	10·2362298	10·0630544	734	9·9369456	52
9	9·7009334	2174	10·2990666	9·7640612	2908	10·2359388	10·0631278	734	9·9368722	51
10	9·7011508	2173	10·2988492	9·7643520	2907	10·2356480	10·0632012	734	9·9367988	50
11	9·7013681	2171	10·2986319	9·7646427	2907	10·2353573	10·0632746	735	9·9367254	49
12	9·7015852	2170	10·2984148	9·7649334	2905	10·2350666	10·0633481	736	9·9366519	48
13	9·7018022	2168	10·2981978	9·7652239	2904	10·2347761	10·0634217	736	9·9365783	47
14	9·7020190	2167	10·2979810	9·7655143	2904	10·2344857	10·0634953	736	9·9365047	46
15	9·7022357	2166	10·2977643	9·7658047	2902	10·2341953	10·0635689	737	9·9364311	45
16	9·7024523	2164	10·2975477	9·7660949	2902	10·2339051	10·0636426	738	9·9363574	44
17	9·7026687	2162	10·2973313	9·7663851	2900	10·2336149	10·0637164	738	9·9362836	43
18	9·7028849	2162	10·2971151	9·7666751	2900	10·2333249	10·0637902	738	9·9362098	42
19	9·7031011	2159	10·2968989	9·7669651	2899	10·2330349	10·0638640	739	9·9361360	41
20	9·7033170	2159	10·2966830	9·7672550	2898	10·2327450	10·0639379	740	9·9360621	40
21	9·7035329	2157	10·2964671	9·7675448	2896	10·2324552	10·0640119	740	9·9359881	39
22	9·7037486	2155	10·2962514	9·7678344	2896	10·2321656	10·0640859	740	9·9359141	38
23	9·7039641	2154	10·2960359	9·7681240	2895	10·2318760	10·0641599	741	9·9358401	37
24	9·7041795	2152	10·2958205	9·7684135	2894	10·2315865	10·0642340	742	9·9357630	36
25	9·7043947	2152	10·2956053	9·7687029	2893	10·2312971	10·0643082	741	9·9356918	35
26	9·7046099	2149	10·2953901	9·7689922	2892	10·2310078	10·0643823	743	9·9356177	34
27	9·7048248	2149	10·2951752	9·7692814	2891	10·2307186	10·0644566	743	9·9355434	33
28	9·7050397	2146	10·2949603	9·7695705	2891	10·2304295	10·0645309	743	9·9354691	32
29	9·7052543	2146	10·2947457	9·7698596	2889	10·2301404	10·0646052	744	9·9353944	31
30	9·7054689	2144	10·2945311	9·7701485	2888	10·2298515	10·0646796	745	9·9353204	30
31	9·7056833	2142	10·2943167	9·7704373	2888	10·2295627	10·0647541	744	9·9352459	29
32	9·7058975	2141	10·2941025	9·7707261	2886	10·2292739	10·0648285	746	9·9351715	28
33	9·7061116	2140	10·2938884	9·7710147	2886	10·2289853	10·0649031	746	9·9350969	27
34	9·7063256	2138	10·2936744	9·7713033	2884	10·2286967	10·0649777	746	9·9350223	26
35	9·7065394	2137	10·2934606	9·7715917	2884	10·2284083	10·0650523	747	9·9349477	25
36	9·7067531	2136	10·2932469	9·7718801	2883	10·2281199	10·0651270	747	9·9348730	24
37	9·7069667	2134	10·2930333	9·7721684	2882	10·2278316	10·0652017	748	9·9347983	23
38	9·7071801	2132	10·2928199	9·7724566	2881	10·2275434	10·0652765	749	9·9347235	22
39	9·7073933	2131	10·2926067	9·7727447	2880	10·2272553	10·0653514	748	9·9346486	21
40	9·7076064	2130	10·2923936	9·7730327	2879	10·2269673	10·0654262	750	9·9345738	20
41	9·7078194	2129	10·2921806	9·7733206	2878	10·2266794	10·0655012	750	9·9344988	19
42	9·7080323	2127	10·2919677	9·7736084	2877	10·2263916	10·0655762	750	9·9344238	18
43	9·7082450	2125	10·2917550	9·7738961	2877	10·2261039	10·0656512	751	9·9343488	17
44	9·7084575	2124	10·2915425	9·7741838	2875	10·2258162	10·0657263	751	9·9342737	16
45	9·7086699	2123	10·2913301	9·7744713	2875	10·2255287	10·0658014	752	9·9341986	15
46	9·7088822	2121	10·2911178	9·7747588	2874	10·2252412	10·0658766	752	9·9341234	14
47	9·7090943	2120	10·2909057	9·7750462	2872	10·2249538	10·0659518	753	9·9340482	13
48	9·7093063	2119	10·2906937	9·7753334	2872	10·2246666	10·0660271	753	9·9339729	12
49	9·7095182	2117	10·2904818	9·7756206	2871	10·2243794	10·0661024	754	9·9338976	11
50	9·7097299	2116	10·2902701	9·7759077	2870	10·2240923	10·0661778	754	9·9338222	10
51	9·7099415	2114	10·2900585	9·7761947	2869	10·2238053	10·0662533	754	9·9337467	9
52	9·7101529	2113	10·2898471	9·7764816	2869	10·2235184	10·0663287	756	9·9336713	8
53	9·7103642	2111	10·2896358	9·7767685	2867	10·2232315	10·0664043	756	9·9335957	7
54	9·7105753	2110	10·2894247	9·7770552	2866	10·2229448	10·0664799	756	9·9335201	6
55	9·7107863	2109	10·2892137	9·7773418	2866	10·2226582	10·0665555	757	9·9334445	5
56	9·7109972	2108	10·2890028	9·7776284	2865	10·2223716	10·0666312	757	9·9333688	4
57	9·7112080	2106	10·2887920	9·7779149	2863	10·2220851	10·0667069	758	9·9332931	3
58	9·7114186	2104	10·2885814	9·7782012	2863	10·2217988	10·0667827	758	9·9332173	2
59	9·7116290	2103	10·2883710	9·7784875	2862	10·2215125	10·0668585	759	9·9331415	1
60	9·7118393		10·2881607	9·7787737		10·2212263	10·0669344		9·9330656	0
′	Cosine	Diff.	Secant	Cotang.	Diff.	Tang.	Cosec.	D.	Sine	′

59 Deg.

31 Deg.

′	Sine	Diff.	Cosec.	Tang.	Diff.	Cotang.	Secant	D.	Cosine	′
0	9·7118393	2102	10·2881607	9·7787737	2862	10·2212263	10·0669344	759	9·9330656	60
1	9·7120495	2101	10·2879505	9·7790599	2860	10·2209401	10·0670103	760	9·9329897	59
2	9·7122596	2099	10·2877404	9·7793459	2859	10·2206541	10·0670863	761	9·9329137	58
3	9·7124695	2097	10·2875305	9·7796318	2859	10·2203682	10·0671624	760	9·9328376	57
4	9·7126792	2097	10·2873208	9·7799177	2857	10·2200823	10·0672384	762	9·9327616	56
5	9·7128889	2094	10·2871111	9·7802034	2857	10·2197966	10·0673146	762	9·9326854	55
6	9·7130983	2094	10·2869017	9·7804891	2856	10·2195109	10·0673908	762	9·9326092	54
7	9·7133077	2092	10·2866923	9·7807747	2855	10·2192253	10·0674670	763	9·9325330	53
8	9·7135169	2091	10·2864831	9·7810602	2854	10·2189398	10·0675433	763	9·9324567	52
9	9·7137260	2089	10·2862740	9·7813456	2853	10·2186544	10·0676196	764	9·9323804	51
10	9·7139349	2088	10·2860651	9·7816309	2853	10·2183691	10·0676960	764	9·9323040	50
11	9·7141437	2087	10·2858563	9·7819162	2851	10·2180838	10·0677724	765	9·9322276	49
12	9·7143524	2085	10·2856476	9·7822013	2851	10·2177987	10·0678489	765	9·9321511	48
13	9·7145609	2084	10·2854391	9·7824864	2849	10·2175136	10·0679254	766	9·9320746	47
14	9·7147693	2083	10·2852307	9·7827713	2849	10·2172287	10·0680020	767	9·9319980	46
15	9·7149776	2081	10·2850224	9·7830562	2848	10·2169438	10·0680787	766	9·9319213	45
16	9·7151857	2080	10·2848143	9·7833410	2848	10·2166590	10·0681553	768	9·9318447	44
17	9·7153937	2078	10·2846063	9·7836258	2846	10·2163742	10·0682321	768	9·9317679	43
18	9·7156015	2077	10·2843985	9·7839104	2845	10·2160896	10·0683089	768	9·9316911	42
19	9·7158092	2076	10·2841908	9·7841949	2845	10·2158051	10·0683857	769	9·9316143	41
20	9·7160168	2075	10·2839832	9·7844794	2844	10·2155206	10·0684626	769	9·9315374	40
21	9·7162243	2073	10·2837757	9·7847638	2843	10·2152362	10·0685395	770	9·9314605	39
22	9·7164316	2071	10·2835684	9·7850481	2842	10·2149519	10·0686165	770	9·9313835	38
23	9·7166387	2071	10·2833613	9·7853323	2841	10·2146677	10·0686935	771	9·9313065	37
24	9·7168458	2068	10·2831542	9·7856164	2840	10·2143836	10·0687706	772	9·9312294	36
25	9·7170526	2068	10·2829474	9·7859004	2840	10·2140996	10·0688478	772	9·9311522	35
26	9·7172594	2066	10·2827406	9·7861844	2838	10·2138156	10·0689250	772	9·9310750	34
27	9·7174660	2065	10·2825340	9·7864682	2838	10·2135318	10·0690022	773	9·9309978	33
28	9·7176725	2064	10·2823275	9·7867520	2837	10·2132480	10·0690795	773	9·9309205	32
29	9·7178789	2062	10·2821211	9·7870357	2836	10·2129643	10·0691568	774	9·9308432	31
30	9·7180851	2061	10·2819149	9·7873193	2835	10·2126807	10·0692342	775	9·9307658	30
31	9·7182912	2059	10·2817088	9·7876028	2835	10·2123972	10·0693117	774	9·9306883	29
32	9·7184971	2059	10·2815029	9·7878863	2833	10·2121137	10·0693891	776	9·9306109	28
33	9·7187030	2056	10·2812970	9·7881696	2833	10·2118304	10·0694667	776	9·9305333	27
34	9·7189086	2056	10·2810914	9·7884529	2832	10·2115471	10·0695443	776	9·9304557	26
35	9·7191142	2054	10·2808858	9·7887361	2831	10·2112639	10·0696219	777	9·9303781	25
36	9·7193196	2053	10·2806804	9·7890192	2831	10·2109808	10·0696996	778	9·9303004	24
37	9·7195249	2051	10·2804751	9·7893023	2829	10·2106977	10·0697774	778	9·9302226	23
38	9·7197300	2050	10·2802700	9·7895852	2829	10·2104148	10·0698552	778	9·9301448	22
39	9·7199350	2049	10·2800650	9·7898681	2827	10·2101319	10·0699330	779	9·9300670	21
40	9·7201399	2048	10·2798601	9·7901508	2827	10·2098492	10·0700109	779	9·9299891	20
41	9·7203447	2046	10·2796553	9·7904335	2826	10·2095665	10·0700888	780	9·9299112	19
42	9·7205493	2045	10·2794507	9·7907161	2826	10·2092839	10·0701668	781	9·9298332	18
43	9·7207538	2043	10·2792462	9·7909987	2824	10·2090013	10·0702449	781	9·9297551	17
44	9·7209581	2042	10·2790419	9·7912811	2824	10·2087189	10·0703230	781	9·9296770	16
45	9·7211623	2041	10·2788377	9·7915635	2823	10·2084365	10·0704011	782	9·9295989	15
46	9·7213664	2040	10·2786336	9·7918458	2822	10·2081542	10·0704793	783	9·9295207	14
47	9·7215704	2038	10·2784296	9·7921280	2821	10·2078720	10·0705576	783	9·9294424	13
48	9·7217742	2037	10·2782258	9·7924101	2820	10·2075899	10·0706359	784	9·9293641	12
49	9·7219779	2035	10·2780221	9·7926921	2820	10·2073079	10·0707143	784	9·9292857	11
50	9·7221814	2034	10·2778186	9·7929741	2819	10·2070259	10·0707927	784	9·9292073	10
51	9·7223848	2033	10·2776152	9·7932560	2818	10·2067440	10·0708711	785	9·9291289	9
52	9·7225881	2032	10·2774119	9·7935378	2817	10·2064622	10·0709496	786	9·9290504	8
53	9·7227913	2030	10·2772087	9·7938195	2816	10·2061805	10·0710282	786	9·9289718	7
54	9·7229943	2029	10·2770057	9·7941011	2816	10·2058989	10·0711068	787	9·9288932	6
55	9·7231972	2028	10·2768028	9·7943827	2814	10·2056173	10·0711855	787	9·9288145	5
56	9·7234000	2026	10·2766000	9·7946641	2814	10·2053359	10·0712642	787	9·9287358	4
57	9·7236026	2025	10·2763974	9·7949455	2813	10·2050545	10·0713429	788	9·9286571	3
58	9·7238051	2024	10·2761949	9·7952268	2813	10·2047732	10·0714217	789	9·9285783	2
59	9·7240075	2022	10·2759925	9·7955081	2811	10·2044919	10·0715006	789	9·9284994	1
60	9·7242097		10·2757903	9·7957892		10·2042108	10·0715795		9·9284205	0

′	Cosine	Diff.	Secant	Cotang.	Diff.	Tang.	Cosec.	D.	Sine	′

′	Sine	Diff.	Cosec.	Tang.	Diff.	Cotang.	Secant	D.	Cosine	′
0	9·7242097	2021	10·2757903	9·7957892	2811	10·2042108	10·0715795	790	9·9284205	60
1	9·7244118	2020	10·2755882	9·7960703	2810	10·2039297	10·0716585	790	9·9283415	59
2	9·7246138	2018	10·2753862	9·7963513	2809	10·2036487	10·0717375	791	9·9282625	58
3	9·7248156	2018	10·2751844	9·7966322	2808	10·2033678	10·0718166	791	9·9281834	57
4	9·7250174	2015	10·2749826	9·7969130	2808	10·2030870	10·0718957	792	9·9281043	56
5	9·7252189	2015	10·2747811	9·7971938	2807	10·2028062	10·0719749	792	9·9280251	55
6	9·7254204	2013	10·2745796	9·7974745	2806	10·2025255	10·0720541	793	9·9279459	54
7	9·7256217	2012	10·2743783	9·7977551	2805	10·2022449	10·0721334	793	9·9278666	53
8	9·7258229	2011	10·2741771	9·7980356	2805	10·2019644	10·0722127	794	9·9277873	52
9	9·7260240	2009	10·2739760	9·7983160	2804	10·2016840	10·0722921	794	9·9277079	51
10	9·7262249	2008	10·2737751	9·7985964	2804	10·2014036	10·0723715	795	9·9276285	50
11	9·7264257	2007	10·2735743	9·7988767	2803	10·2011233	10·0724510	795	9·9275490	49
12	9·7266264	2005	10·2733736	9·7991569	2802	10·2008431	10·0725305	796	9·9274695	48
13	9·7268269	2004	10·2731731	9·7994370	2801	10·2005630	10·0726101	796	9·9273899	47
14	9·7270273	2003	10·2729727	9·7997170	2800	10·2002830	10·0726897	797	9·9273103	46
15	9·7272276	2002	10·2727724	9·7999970	2800	10·2000030	10·0727694	797	9·9272306	45
16	9·7274278	2000	10·2725722	9·8002769	2799	10·1997231	10·0728491	798	9·9271509	44
17	9·7276278	1999	10·2723722	9·8005567	2798	10·1994433	10·0729289	798	9·9270711	43
18	9·7278277	1998	10·2721723	9·8008365	2798	10·1991635	10·0730087	799	9·9269913	42
19	9·7280275	1996	10·2719725	9·8011161	2796	10·1988839	10·0730886	800	9·9269114	41
20	9·7282271	1996	10·2717729	9·8013957	2796	10·1986043	10·0731686	800	9·9268314	40
21	9·7284267	1993	10·2715733	9·8016752	2795	10·1983248	10·0732486	800	9·9267514	39
22	9·7286260	1993	10·2713740	9·8019546	2794	10·1980454	10·0733286	801	9·9266714	38
23	9·7288253	1991	10·2711747	9·8022340	2794	10·1977660	10·0734087	801	9·9265913	37
24	9·7290244	1990	10·2709756	9·8025133	2793	10·1974867	10·0734888	802	9·9265112	36
25	9·7292234	1989	10·2707766	9·8027925	2792	10·1972075	10·0735690	803	9·9264310	35
26	9·7294223	1988	10·2705777	9·8030716	2791	10·1969284	10·0736493	803	9·9263507	34
27	9·7296211	1986	10·2703789	9·8033506	2790	10·1966494	10·0737296	803	9·9262704	33
28	9·7298197	1985	10·2701803	9·8036296	2790	10·1963704	10·0738099	805	9·9261901	32
29	9·7300182	1983	10·2699818	9·8039085	2789	10·1960915	10·0738904	805	9·9261096	31
30	9·7302165	1983	10·2697835	9·8041873	2788	10·1958127	10·0739708	804	9·9260292	30
31	9·7304148	1981	10·2695852	9·8044661	2788	10·1955339	10·0740513	806	9·9259487	29
32	9·7306129	1980	10·2693871	9·8047447	2786	10·1952553	10·0741319	806	9·9258681	28
33	9·7308109	1978	10·2691891	9·8050233	2786	10·1949767	10·0742125	806	9·9257875	27
34	9·7310087	1977	10·2689913	9·8053019	2786	10·1946981	10·0742931	808	9·9257069	26
35	9·7312064	1976	10·2687936	9·8055803	2784	10·1944197	10·0743739	807	9·9256261	25
36	9·7314040	1975	10·2685960	9·8058587	2784	10·1941413	10·0744546	808	9·9255454	24
37	9·7316015	1974	10·2683985	9·8061370	2783	10·1938630	10·0745354	809	9·9254646	23
38	9·7317989	1972	10·2682011	9·8064152	2782	10·1935848	10·0746163	809	9·9253837	22
39	9·7319961	1971	10·2680039	9·8066933	2781	10·1933067	10·0746972	810	9·9253028	21
40	9·7321932	1970	10·2678068	9·8069714	2781	10·1930286	10·0747782	810	9·9252218	20
41	9·7323902	1968	10·2676098	9·8072494	2780	10·1927506	10·0748592	811	9·9251408	19
42	9·7325870	1967	10·2674130	9·8075273	2779	10·1924727	10·0749403	811	9·9250597	18
43	9·7327837	1966	10·2672163	9·8078052	2779	10·1921948	10·0750214	812	9·9249786	17
44	9·7329803	1965	10·2670197	9·8080829	2777	10·1919171	10·0751026	813	9·9248974	16
45	9·7331768	1963	10·2668232	9·8083606	2777	10·1916394	10·0751839	812	9·9248161	15
46	9·7333731	1962	10·2666269	9·8086383	2777	10·1913617	10·0752651	814	9·9247349	14
47	9·7335693	1961	10·2664307	9·8089158	2775	10·1910842	10·0753465	814	9·9246535	13
48	9·7337654	1960	10·2662346	9·8091933	2775	10·1908067	10·0754279	814	9·9245721	12
49	9·7339614	1958	10·2660386	9·8094707	2774	10·1905293	10·0755093	815	9·9244907	11
50	9·7341572	1957	10·2658428	9·8097480	2773	10·1902520	10·0755908	815	9·9244092	10
51	9·7343529	1956	10·2656471	9·8100253	2773	10·1899747	10·0756723	816	9·9243277	9
52	9·7345485	1955	10·2654515	9·8103025	2772	10·1896975	10·0757539	817	9·9242461	8
53	9·7347440	1953	10·2652560	9·8105796	2771	10·1894204	10·0758356	817	9·9241644	7
54	9·7349393	1952	10·2650607	9·8108566	2770	10·1891434	10·0759173	817	9·9240827	6
55	9·7351345	1951	10·2648655	9·8111336	2770	10·1888664	10·0759990	819	9·9240010	5
56	9·7353296	1950	10·2646704	9·8114105	2769	10·1885895	10·0760809	818	9·9239191	4
57	9·7355246	1949	10·2644754	9·8116873	2768	10·1883127	10·0761627	819	9·9238373	3
58	9·7357195	1947	10·2642805	9·8119641	2768	10·1880359	10·0762446	820	9·9237554	2
59	9·7359142	1946	10·2640858	9·8122408	2767	10·1877592	10·0763266	820	9·9236734	1
60	9·7361088		10·2638912	9·8125174	2766	10·1874826	10·0764086		9·9235914	0

| ′ | Cosine | Diff. | Secant | Cotang. | Diff. | Tang. | Cosec. | D. | Sine | ′ |

33 Deg.

′	Sine	Diff.	Cosec.	Tang.	Diff.	Cotang.	Secant	D.	Cosine	′
0	9·7361088	1944	10·2638912	9·8125174	2765	10·1874826	10·0764086	821	9·9235914	60
1	9·7363032	1944	10·2636968	9·8127939	2765	10·1872061	10·0764907	821	9·9235093	59
2	9·7364976	1942	10·2635024	9·8130704	2764	10·1869296	10·0765728	822	9·9234272	58
3	9·7366918	1941	10·2633082	9·8133468	2763	10·1866532	10·0766550	822	9·9233450	57
4	9·7368859	1940	10·2631141	9·8136231	2762	10·1863769	10·0767372	823	9·9232628	56
5	9·7370799	1938	10·2629201	9·8138993	2762	10·1861007	10·0768195	823	9·9231805	55
6	9·7372737	1938	10·2627263	9·8141755	2761	10·1858245	10·0769018	824	9·9230982	54
7	9·7374675	1936	10·2625325	9·8144516	2761	10·1855484	10·0769842	824	9·9230158	53
8	9·7376611	1935	10·2623389	9·8147277	2759	10·1852723	10·0770666	825	9·9229334	52
9	9·7378546	1933	10·2621454	9·8150036	2759	10·1849964	10·0771491	825	9·9228509	51
10	9·7380479	1933	10·2619521	9·8152795	2759	10·1847205	10·0772316	826	9·9227684	50
11	9·7382412	1931	10·2617588	9·8155554	2757	10·1844446	10·0773142	826	9·9226858	49
12	9·7384343	1930	10·2615657	9·8158311	2757	10·1841689	10·0773968	827	9·9226032	48
13	9·7386273	1928	10·2613727	9·8161068	2756	10·1838932	10·0774795	828	9·9225205	47
14	9·7388201	1928	10·2611799	9·8163824	2756	10·1836176	10·0775623	828	9·9224377	46
15	9·7390129	1926	10·2609871	9·8166580	2755	10·1833420	10·0776451	828	9·9223549	45
16	9·7392055	1925	10·2607945	9·8169335	2754	10·1830665	10·0777279	830	9·9222721	44
17	9·7393980	1924	10·2606020	9·8172089	2753	10·1827911	10·0778109	829	9·9221891	43
18	9·7395904	1923	10·2604096	9·8174842	2753	10·1825158	10·0778938	830	9·9221062	42
19	9·7397827	1921	10·2602173	9·8177595	2752	10·1822405	10·0779768	831	9·9220232	41
20	9·7399748	1920	10·2600252	9·8180347	2751	10·1819653	10·0780599	831	9·9219401	40
21	9·7401668	1919	10·2598332	9·8183098	2751	10·1816902	10·0781430	832	9·9218570	39
22	9·7403587	1918	10·2596413	9·8185849	2750	10·1814151	10·0782262	832	9·9217738	38
23	9·7405505	1916	10·2594495	9·8188599	2749	10·1811401	10·0783094	833	9·9216906	37
24	9·7407421	1916	10·2592579	9·8191348	2748	10·1808652	10·0783927	833	9·9216073	36
25	9·7409337	1914	10·2590663	9·8194096	2748	10·1805904	10·0784760	834	9·9215240	35
26	9·7411251	1913	10·2588749	9·8196844	2748	10·1803156	10·0785594	834	9·9214406	34
27	9·7413164	1911	10·2586836	9·8199592	2746	10·1800408	10·0786428	835	9·9213572	33
28	9·7415075	1911	10·2584925	9·8202338	2746	10·1797662	10·0787263	835	9·9212737	32
29	9·7416986	1909	10·2583014	9·8205084	2745	10·1794916	10·0788098	836	9·9211902	31
30	9·7418895	1908	10·2581105	9·8207829	2745	10·1792171	10·0788934	837	9·9211066	30
31	9·7420803	1907	10·2579197	9·8210574	2743	10·1789426	10·0789771	836	9·9210229	29
32	9·7422710	1906	10·2577290	9·8213317	2743	10·1786683	10·0790607	838	9·9209393	28
33	9·7424616	1904	10·2575384	9·8216060	2743	10·1783940	10·0791445	838	9·9208555	27
34	9·7426520	1903	10·2573480	9·8218803	2742	10·1781197	10·0792283	839	9·9207717	26
35	9·7428423	1902	10·2571577	9·8221545	2741	10·1778455	10·0793122	839	9·9206878	25
36	9·7430325	1901	10·2569675	9·8224286	2740	10·1775714	10·0793961	839	9·9206039	24
37	9·7432226	1900	10·2567774	9·8227026	2740	10·1772974	10·0794800	840	9·9205200	23
38	9·7434126	1898	10·2565874	9·8229766	2739	10·1770234	10·0795640	841	9·9204360	22
39	9·7436024	1897	10·2563976	9·8232505	2739	10·1767495	10·0796481	841	9·9203519	21
40	9·7437921	1896	10·2562079	9·8235244	2737	10·1764756	10·0797322	842	9·9202678	20
41	9·7439817	1895	10·2560183	9·8237981	2738	10·1762019	10·0798164	842	9·9201836	19
42	9·7441712	1894	10·2558288	9·8240719	2736	10·1759281	10·0799006	843	9·9200994	18
43	9·7443606	1892	10·2556394	9·8243455	2736	10·1756545	10·0799849	843	9·9200151	17
44	9·7445498	1892	10·2554502	9·8246191	2735	10·1753809	10·0800692	844	9·9199308	16
45	9·7447390	1890	10·2552610	9·8248926	2734	10·1751074	10·0801536	845	9·9198464	15
46	9·7449280	1889	10·2550720	9·8251660	2734	10·1748340	10·0802381	844	9·9197619	14
47	9·7451169	1887	10·2548831	9·8254394	2733	10·1745606	10·0803225	846	9·9196775	13
48	9·7453056	1887	10·2546944	9·8257127	2733	10·1742873	10·0804071	846	9·9195929	12
49	9·7454943	1885	10·2545057	9·8259860	2732	10·1740140	10·0804917	846	9·9195083	11
50	9·7456828	1884	10·2543172	9·8262592	2731	10·1737408	10·0805763	847	9·9194237	10
51	9·7458712	1883	10·2541288	9·8265323	2730	10·1734677	10·0806610	848	9·9193390	9
52	9·7460595	1882	10·2539405	9·8268053	2730	10·1731947	10·0807458	848	9·9192542	8
53	9·7462477	1881	10·2537523	9·8270783	2730	10·1729217	10·0808306	849	9·9191694	7
54	9·7464358	1879	10·2535642	9·8273513	2728	10·1726487	10·0809155	849	9·9190845	6
55	9·7466237	1878	10·2533763	9·8276241	2728	10·1723759	10·0810004	850	9·9189996	5
56	9·7468115	1877	10·2531885	9·8278969	2727	10·1721031	10·0810854	850	9·9189146	4
57	9·7469992	1876	10·2530008	9·8281696	2727	10·1718304	10·0811704	851	9·9188296	3
58	9·7471868	1875	10·2528132	9·8284423	2726	10·1715577	10·0812555	851	9·9187445	2
59	9·7473743	1874	10·2526257	9·8287149	2725	10·1712851	10·0813406	852	9·9186594	1
60	9·7475617		10·2524383	9·8289874		10·1710126	10·0814258		9·9185742	0

′	Cosine	Diff.	Secant	Cotang.	Diff.	Tang.	Cosec.	D.	Sine	′

′	Sine	Diff.	Cosec.	Tang.	Diff.	Cotang.	Secant	D.	Cosine	′
0	9·7475617	1872	10·2524383	9·8289874	2725	10·1710126	10·0814258	852	9·9185742	60
1	9·7477489	1871	10·2522511	9·8292599	2724	10·1707401	10·0815110	853	9·9184890	59
2	9·7479360	1870	10·2520640	9·8295323	2724	10·1704677	10·0815963	854	9·9184037	58
3	9·7481230	1869	10·2518770	9·8298047	2722	10·1701953	10·0816817	854	9·9183183	57
4	9·7483099	1863	10·2516901	9·8300769	2723	10·1699231	10·0817671	854	9·9182329	56
5	9·7484967	1866	10·2515033	9·8303492	2721	10·1696508	10·0818525	855	9·9181475	55
6	9·7486833	1865	10·2513167	9·8306213	2721	10·1693787	10·0819380	856	9·9180620	54
7	9·7488698	1864	10·2511302	9·8308934	2720	10·1691066	10·0820236	856	9·9179764	53
8	9·7490562	1863	10·2509438	9·8311654	2720	10·1688346	10·0821092	857	9·9178908	52
9	9·7492425	1862	10·2507575	9·8314374	2719	10·1685626	10·0821949	857	9·9178051	51
10	9·7494287	1861	10·2505713	9·8317093	2718	10·1682907	10·0822806	858	9·9177194	50
11	9·7496148	1859	10·2503852	9·8319811	2718	10·1680189	10·0823664	858	9·9176336	49
12	9·7498007	1859	10·2501993	9·8322529	2717	10·1677471	10·0824522	859	9·9175478	48
13	9·7499866	1857	10·2500134	9·8325246	2717	10·1674754	10·0825381	859	9·9174619	47
14	9·7501723	1856	10·2498277	9·8327963	2716	10·1672037	10·0826240	860	9·9173760	46
15	9·7503579	1855	10·2496421	9·8330679	2715	10·1669321	10·0827100	860	9·9172040	45
16	9·7505434	1853	10·2494566	9·8333394	2715	10·1666606	10·0827960	861	9·9172040	44
17	9·7507287	1853	10·2492713	9·8336109	2714	10·1663891	10·0828821	862	9·9171179	43
18	9·7509140	1851	10·2490860	9·8338823	2713	10·1661177	10·0829683	862	9·9170317	42
19	9·7510991	1851	10·2489009	9·8341536	2713	10·1658464	10·0830545	862	9·9169455	41
20	9·7512842	1849	10·2487158	9·8344249	2712	10·1655751	10·0831407	863	9·9168593	40
21	9·7514691	1847	10·2485309	9·8346961	2712	10·1653039	10·0832270	864	9·9167730	39
22	9·7516538	1847	10·2483462	9·8349673	2711	10·1650327	10·0833134	864	9·9166866	38
23	9·7518385	1846	10·2481615	9·8352384	2710	10·1647616	10·0833998	865	9·9166002	37
24	9·7520231	1844	10·2479769	9·8355094	2710	10·1644906	10·0834863	865	9·9165137	36
25	9·7522075	1844	10·2477925	9·8357804	2709	10·1642196	10·0835728	866	9·9164272	35
26	9·7523919	1842	10·2476081	9·8360513	2708	10·1639487	10·0836594	867	9·9163406	34
27	9·7525761	1841	10·2474239	9·8363221	2708	10·1636779	10·0837461	866	9·9162539	33
28	9·7527602	1840	10·2472398	9·8365929	2707	10·1634071	10·0838327	868	9·9161673	32
29	9·7529442	1838	10·2470558	9·8368636	2707	10·1631364	10·0839195	868	9·9160805	31
30	9·7531280	1838	10·2468720	9·8371343	2706	10·1628657	10·0840063	868	9·9159937	30
31	9·7533118	1836	10·2466882	9·8374049	2706	10·1625951	10·0840931	869	9·9159069	29
32	9·7534954	1836	10·2465046	9·8376755	2705	10·1623245	10·0841800	870	9·9158200	28
33	9·7536790	1834	10·2463210	9·8379460	2704	10·1620540	10·0842670	870	9·9157330	27
34	9·7538624	1833	10·2461376	9·8382164	2703	10·1617836	10·0843540	871	9·9156460	26
35	9·7540457	1831	10·2459543	9·8384867	2704	10·1615133	10·0844411	871	9·9155580	25
36	9·7542288	1831	10·2457712	9·8387571	2702	10·1612429	10·0845282	872	9·9154718	24
37	9·7544119	1830	10·2455881	9·8390273	2702	10·1609727	10·0846154	872	9·9153846	23
38	9·7545949	1828	10·2454051	9·8392975	2701	10·1607025	10·0847026	873	9·9152974	22
39	9·7547777	1827	10·2452223	9·8395676	2701	10·1604324	10·0847899	873	9·9152101	21
40	9·7549604	1827	10·2450396	9·8398377	2700	10·1601623	10·0848772	874	9·9151228	20
41	9·7551431	1825	10·2448569	9·8401077	2699	10·1598923	10·0849646	875	9·9150354	19
42	9·7553256	1824	10·2446744	9·8403776	2699	10·1596224	10·0850521	875	9·9149479	18
43	9·7555080	1822	10·2444920	9·8406475	2699	10·1593525	10·0851396	875	9·9148604	17
44	9·7556902	1822	10·2443098	9·8409174	2697	10·1590826	10·0852271	877	9·9147729	16
45	9·7558724	1820	10·2441276	9·8411871	2698	10·1588129	10·0853148	876	9·9146852	15
46	9·7560544	1820	10·2439456	9·8414569	2696	10·1585431	10·0854024	877	9·9145976	14
47	9·7562364	1818	10·2437636	9·8417265	2696	10·1582735	10·0854901	878	9·9145099	13
48	9·7564182	1817	10·2435818	9·8419961	2696	10·1580039	10·0855779	879	9·9144221	12
49	9·7565999	1816	10·2434001	9·8422657	2694	10·1577343	10·0856658	878	9·9143342	11
50	9·7567815	1815	10·2432185	9·8425351	2695	10·1574649	10·0857536	880	9·9142464	10
51	9·7569630	1814	10·2430370	9·8428046	2693	10·1571954	10·0858416	880	9·9141584	9
52	9·7571444	1812	10·2428556	9·8430739	2693	10·1569261	10·0859296	880	9·9140704	8
53	9·7573256	1812	10·2426744	9·8433432	2693	10·1566568	10·0860176	881	9·9139824	7
54	9·7575068	1810	10·2424932	9·8436125	2692	10·1563875	10·0861057	882	9·9138943	6
55	9·7576878	1809	10·2423122	9·8438817	2691	10·1561183	10·0861939	882	9·9138061	5
56	9·7578687	1808	10·2421313	9·8441508	2691	10·1558492	10·0862821	883	9·9137179	4
57	9·7580495	1807	10·2419505	9·8444199	2690	10·1555801	10·0863704	883	9·9136296	3
58	9·7582302	1806	10·2417698	9·8446889	2690	10·1553111	10·0864587	883	9·9135413	2
59	9·7584108	1805	10·2415892	9·8449579	2689	10·1550421	10·0865470	885	9·9134530	1
60	9·7585913		10·2414087	9·8452268		10·1547732	10·0866355		9·9133645	0

| ′ | Cosine | Diff. | Secant | Cotang. | Diff. | Tang. | Cosec. | D. | Sine | ′ |

35 Deg.

′	Sine	Diff.	Cosec.	Tang.	Diff.	Cotang.	Secant	D.	Cosine	′
0	9·7585913		10·2414087	9·8452268		10·1547732	10·0866355		9·9133645	60
1	9·7587717	1804	10·2412283	9·8454956	2688	10·1545044	10·0867240	885	9·9132760	59
2	9·7589519	1802	10·2410481	9·8457644	2688	10·1542356	10·0868125	885	9·9131875	58
3	9·7591321	1802	10·2408679	9·8460332	2688	10·1539668	10·0869011	886	9·9130989	57
4	9·7593121	1800	10·2406879	9·8463018	2686	10·1536982	10·0869898	887	9·9130102	56
5	9·7594920	1799	10·2405080	9·8465705	2687	10·1534295	10·0870785	887	9·9129215	55
		1798			2685			887		
6	9·7596718	1797	10·2403282	9·8468390	2685	10·1531610	10·0871672	888	9·9128328	54
7	9·7598515	1796	10·2401485	9·8471075	2685	10·1528925	10·0872560	889	9·9127440	53
8	9·7600311	1795	10·2399689	9·8473760	2684	10·1526240	10·0873449	889	9·9126551	52
9	9·7602106	1793	10·2397894	9·8476444	2683	10·1523556	10·0874338	890	9·9125662	51
10	9·7603899	1793	10·2396101	9·8479127	2683	10·1520873	10·0875228	890	9·9124772	50
11	9·7605692	1791	10·2394308	9·8481810	2682	10·1518190	10·0876118	891	9·9123882	49
12	9·7607483	1791	10·2392517	9·8484492	2682	10·1515508	10·0877009	892	9·9122991	48
13	9·7609274	1789	10·2390726	9·8487174	2681	10·1512826	10·0877901	892	9·9122099	47
14	9·7611063	1788	10·2388937	9·8489855	2681	10·1510145	10·0878793	892	9·9121207	46
15	9·7612851	1787	10·2387149	9·8492536	2680	10·1507464	10·0879685	893	9·9120315	45
16	9·7614638	1786	10·2385362	9·8495216	2680	10·1504784	10·0880578	894	9·9119422	44
17	9·7616424	1784	10·2383576	9·8497896	2679	10·1502104	10·0881472	894	9·9118528	43
18	9·7618208	1784	10·2381792	9·8500575	2678	10·1499425	10·0882366	895	9·9117634	42
19	9·7619992	1783	10·2380008	9·8503253	2678	10·1496747	10·0883261	895	9·9116739	41
20	9·7621775	1781	10·2378225	9·8505931	2677	10·1494069	10·0884156	896	9·9115844	40
21	9·7623556	1781	10·2376444	9·8508608	2677	10·1491392	10·0885052	897	9·9114948	39
22	9·7625337	1779	10·2374663	9·8511285	2676	10·1488715	10·0885949	896	9·9114051	38
23	9·7627116	1778	10·2372884	9·8513961	2676	10·1486039	10·0886845	898	9·9113155	37
24	9·7628894	1777	10·2371106	9·8516637	2675	10·1483363	10·0887743	898	9·9112257	36
25	9·7630671	1776	10·2369329	9·8519312	2675	10·1480688	10·0888641	899	9·9111359	35
26	9·7632447	1775	10·2367553	9·8521987	2674	10·1478013	10·0889540	899	9·9110460	34
27	9·7634222	1774	10·2365778	9·8524661	2674	10·1475339	10·0890439	900	9·9109561	33
28	9·7635996	1773	10·2364004	9·8527335	2673	10·1472665	10·0891339	900	9·9108661	32
29	9·7637769	1771	10·2362231	9·8530008	2672	10·1469992	10·0892239	901	9·9107761	31
30	9·7639540	1771	10·2360460	9·8532680	2672	10·1467320	10·0893140	901	9·9106860	30
31	9·7641311	1769	10·2358689	9·8535352	2671	10·1464648	10·0894041	902	9·9105959	29
32	9·7643080	1769	10·2356920	9·8538023	2671	10·1461977	10·0894943	902	9·9105057	28
33	9·7644849	1767	10·2355151	9·8540694	2671	10·1459306	10·0895845	904	9·9104155	27
34	9·7646616	1766	10·2353384	9·8543365	2669	10·1456635	10·0896749	903	9·9103251	26
35	9·7648382	1765	10·2351618	9·8546034	2670	10·1453966	10·0897652	904	9·9102348	25
36	9·7650147	1764	10·2349853	9·8548704	2668	10·1451296	10·0898556	905	9·9101444	24
37	9·7651911	1763	10·2348089	9·8551372	2669	10·1448628	10·0899461	905	9·9100539	23
38	9·7653674	1762	10·2346326	9·8554041	2667	10·1445959	10·0900366	906	9·9099634	22
39	9·7655436	1761	10·2344564	9·8556708	2668	10·1443292	10·0901272	907	9·9098728	21
40	9·7657197	1760	10·2342803	9·8559376	2666	10·1440624	10·0902179	906	9·9097821	20
41	9·7658957	1758	10·2341043	9·8562042	2666	10·1437958	10·0903085	908	9·9096915	19
42	9·7660715	1758	10·2339285	9·8564708	2666	10·1435292	10·0903993	908	9·9096007	18
43	9·7662473	1756	10·2337527	9·8567374	2665	10·1432626	10·0904901	909	9·9095099	17
44	9·7664229	1756	10·2335771	9·8570039	2665	10·1429961	10·0905810	909	9·9094190	16
45	9·7665985	1754	10·2334015	9·8572704	2664	10·1427296	10·0906719	910	9·9093281	15
46	9·7667739	1753	10·2332261	9·8575368	2663	10·1424632	10·0907629	910	9·9092371	14
47	9·7669492	1752	10·2330508	9·8578031	2663	10·1421969	10·0908539	911	9·9091461	13
48	9·7671244	1752	10·2328756	9·8580694	2663	10·1419306	10·0909450	911	9·909·550	12
49	9·7672996	1750	10·2327004	9·8583357	2662	10·1416643	10·0910361	912	9·9089639	11
50	9·7674746	1748	10·2325254	9·8586019	2661	10·1413981	10·0911273	913	9·9088727	10
51	9·7676494	1748	10·2323506	9·8588680	2661	10·1411320	10·0912186	913	9·9087814	9
52	9·7678242	1747	10·2321758	9·8591341	2661	10·1408659	10·0913099	913	9·9086901	8
53	9·7679989	1746	10·2320011	9·8594002	2659	10·1405998	10·0914012	915	9·9085988	7
54	9·7681735	1745	10·2318265	9·8596661	2660	10·1403339	10·0914927	914	9·9085073	6
55	9·7683480	1743	10·2316520	9·8599321	2659	10·1400679	10·0915841	916	9·9084159	5
56	9·7685223	1743	10·2314777	9·8601980	2658	10·1398020	10·0916757	916	9·9083243	4
57	9·7686966	1741	10·2313034	9·8604638	2658	10·1395362	10·0917673	916	9·9082327	3
58	9·7688707	1741	10·2311293	9·8607296	2658	10·1392704	10·0918589	917	9·9081411	2
59	9·7690448	1739	10·2309552	9·8609954	2656	10·1390046	10·0919506	918	9·9080494	1
60	9·7692187		10·2307813	9·8612610		10·1387390	10·0920424		9·9079576	0

| ′ | Cosine | Diff. | Secant | Cotang. | Diff. | Tang. | Cosec. | D. | Sine | ′ |

36 Deg.

′	Sine	Diff.	Cosec.	Tang.	Diff.	Cotang.	Secant	D.	Cosine	′
0	9·7692187	1738	10·2307813	9·8612610	2657	10·1387390	10·0920424	918	9·9079576	60
1	9·7693925	1737	10·2306075	9·8615267	2656	10·1384733	10·0921342	918	9·9078658	59
2	9·7695662	1736	10·2304338	9·8617923	2655	10·1382077	10·0922260	920	9·9077740	58
3	9·7697398	1736	10·2302602	9·8620578	2655	10·1379422	10·0923180	919	9·9076820	57
4	9·7699134	1734	10·2300866	9·8623233	2654	10·1376767	10·0924099	921	9·9075901	56
5	9·7700868	1733	10·2299132	9·8625887	2654	10·1374113	10·0925020	921	9·9074980	55
6	9·7702601	1731	10·2297399	9·8628541	2654	10·1371459	10·0925941	921	9·9074059	54
7	9·7704332	1731	10·2295668	9·8631195	2653	10·1368805	10·0926862	922	9·9073138	53
8	9·7706063	1730	10·2293937	9·8633848	2652	10·1366152	10·0927784	923	9·9072216	52
9	9·7707793	1729	10·2292207	9·8636500	2652	10·1363500	10·0928707	923	9·9071293	51
10	9·7709522	1727	10·2290478	9·8639152	2651	10·1360848	10·0929630	924	9·9070370	50
11	9·7711249	1727	10·2288751	9·8641803	2651	10·1358197	10·0930554	924	9·9069446	49
12	9·7712976	1726	10·2287024	9·8644454	2651	10·1355546	10·0931478	925	9·9068522	48
13	9·7714702	1724	10·2285298	9·8647105	2650	10·1352895	10·0932403	926	9·9067597	47
14	9·7716426	1724	10·2283574	9·8649755	2649	10·1350245	10·0933329	926	9·9066671	46
15	9·7718150	1722	10·2281850	9·8652404	2649	10·1347596	10·0934255	926	9·9065745	45
16	9·7719872	1721	10·2280128	9·8655053	2649	10·1344947	10·0935181	927	9·9064819	44
17	9·7721593	1721	10·2278407	9·8657702	2648	10·1342298	10·0936108	928	9·9063892	43
18	9·7723314	1719	10·2276686	9·8660350	2647	10·1339650	10·0937036	928	9·9062964	42
19	9·7725033	1718	10·2274967	9·8662997	2647	10·1337003	10·0937964	929	9·9062036	41
20	9·7726751	1717	10·2273249	9·8665644	2647	10·1334356	10·0938893	930	9·9061107	40
21	9·7728468	1717	10·2271532	9·8668291	2646	10·1331709	10·0939823	930	9·9060177	39
22	9·7730185	1715	10·2269815	9·8670937	2646	10·1329063	10·0940753	930	9·9059247	38
23	9·7731900	1714	10·2268100	9·8673583	2645	10·1326417	10·0941683	931	9·9058317	37
24	9·7733614	1713	10·2266386	9·8676228	2645	10·1323772	10·0942614	932	9·9057386	36
25	9·7735327	1712	10·2264673	9·8678873	2644	10·1321127	10·0943546	932	9·9056454	35
26	9·7737039	1710	10·2262961	9·8681517	2643	10·1318483	10·0944478	933	9·9055522	34
27	9·7738749	1710	10·2261251	9·8684160	2644	10·1315840	10·0945411	933	9·9054589	33
28	9·7740459	1709	10·2259541	9·8686804	2642	10·1313196	10·0946344	934	9·9053656	32
29	9·7742168	1708	10·2257832	9·8689446	2643	10·1310554	10·0947278	935	9·9052722	31
30	9·7743876	1707	10·2256124	9·8692089	2642	10·1307911	10·0948213	935	9·9051787	30
31	9·7745583	1705	10·2254417	9·8694731	2641	10·1305269	10·0949148	936	9·9050852	29
32	9·7747288	1705	10·2252712	9·8697372	2641	10·1302628	10·0950084	936	9·9049916	28
33	9·7748993	1704	10·2251007	9·8700013	2640	10·1299987	10·0951020	937	9·9048980	27
34	9·7750697	1702	10·2249303	9·8702653	2640	10·1297347	10·0951957	937	9·9048043	26
35	9·7752399	1702	10·2247601	9·8705293	2640	10·1294707	10·0952894	938	9·9047106	25
36	9·7754101	1700	10·2245899	9·8707933	2639	10·1292067	10·0953832	938	9·9046168	24
37	9·7755801	1700	10·2244199	9·8710572	2638	10·1289428	10·0954770	939	9·9045230	23
38	9·7757501	1698	10·2242499	9·8713210	2638	10·1286790	10·0955709	940	9·9044291	22
39	9·7759199	1698	10·2240801	9·8715848	2638	10·1284152	10·0956649	940	9·9043351	21
40	9·7760897	1696	10·2239103	9·8718486	2637	10·1281514	10·0957589	941	9·9042411	20
41	9·7762593	1696	10·2237407	9·8721123	2637	10·1278877	10·0958530	941	9·9041470	19
42	9·7764289	1694	10·2235711	9·8723760	2636	10·1276240	10·0959471	942	9·9040529	18
43	9·7765983	1693	10·2234017	9·8726396	2636	10·1273604	10·0960413	943	9·9039587	17
44	9·7767676	1693	10·2232324	9·8729032	2636	10·1270968	10·0961356	943	9·9038644	16
45	9·7769369	1691	10·2230631	9·8731668	2634	10·1268332	10·0962299	944	9·9037701	15
46	9·7771060	1690	10·2228940	9·8734302	2635	10·1265698	10·0963243	944	9·9036757	14
47	9·7772750	1689	10·2227250	9·8736937	2634	10·1263063	10·0964187	945	9·9035813	13
48	9·7774439	1689	10·2225561	9·8739571	2633	10·1260429	10·0965132	945	9·9034868	12
49	9·7776128	1687	10·2223872	9·8742204	2634	10·1257796	10·0966077	946	9·9033923	11
50	9·7777815	1686	10·2222185	9·8744838	2632	10·1255162	10·0967023	946	9·9032977	10
51	9·7779501	1685	10·2220499	9·8747470	2632	10·1252530	10·0967969	947	9·9032031	9
52	9·7781186	1684	10·2218814	9·8750102	2632	10·1249898	10·0968916	948	9·9031084	8
53	9·7782870	1683	10·2217130	9·8752734	2631	10·1247266	10·0969864	948	9·9030136	7
54	9·7784553	1682	10·2215447	9·8755365	2631	10·1244635	10·0970812	949	9·9029188	6
55	9·7786235	1681	10·2213765	9·8757996	2631	10·1242004	10·0971761	950	9·9028239	5
56	9·7787916	1680	10·2212084	9·8760627	2630	10·1239373	10·0972711	950	9·9027289	4
57	9·7789596	1679	10·2210404	9·8763257	2629	10·1236743	10·0973661	950	9·9026339	3
58	9·7791275	1678	10·2208725	9·8765886	2629	10·1234114	10·0974611	951	9·9025389	2
59	9·7792953	1677	10·2207047	9·8768515	2629	10·1231485	10·0975562	952	9·9024438	1
60	9·7794630		10·2205370	9·8771144		10·1228856	10·0976514		9·9023486	0

′	Cosine	Diff.	Secant	Cotang.	Diff.	Tang.	Cosec.	D.	Sine	′

37 Deg.

′	Sine	Diff.	Cosec.	Tang.	Diff.	Cotang.	Secant	D.	Cosine	′
0	9·7794630		10·2205370	9·8771144		10·1228856	10·0976514		9·9023486	60
1	9·7796306	1676	10·2203694	9·8773772	2628	10·1226228	10·0977466	952	9·9022534	59
2	9·7797981	1675	10·2202019	9·8776400	2628	10·1223600	10·0978419	953	9·9021581	58
3	9·7799655	1674	10·2200345	9·8779027	2627	10·1220973	10·0979372	953	9·9020628	57
4	9·7801328	1673	10·2198672	9·8781654	2627	10·1218346	10·0980326	954	9·9019674	56
5	9·7803000	1672	10·2197000	9·8784281	2627	10·1215719	10·0981281	955	9·9018719	55
		1671			2626			955		
6	9·7804671	1670	10·2195329	9·8786907	2626	10·1213093	10·0982236	956	9·9017764	54
7	9·7806341	1669	10·2193659	9·8789533	2625	10·1210467	10·0983192	956	9·9016808	53
8	9·7808010	1667	10·2191990	9·8792158	2624	10·1207842	10·0984148	957	9·9015852	52
9	9·7809677	1667	10·2190323	9·8794782	2625	10·1205218	10·0985105	957	9·9014895	51
10	9·7811344	1666	10·2188656	9·8797407	2624	10·1202593	10·0986062	958	9·9013938	50
11	9·7813010	1665	10·2186990	9·8800031	2623	10·1199969	10·0987020	959	9·9012980	49
12	9·7814675	1664	10·2185325	9·8802654	2623	10·1197346	10·0987979	959	9·9012021	48
13	9·7816339	1663	10·2183661	9·8805277	2623	10·1194723	10·0988938	960	9·9011062	47
14	9·7818002	1662	10·2181998	9·8807900	2622	10·1192100	10·0989898	960	9·9010102	46
15	9·7819664	1660	10·2180336	9·8810522	2622	10·1189478	10·0990858	961	9·9009142	45
16	9·7821324	1660	10·2178676	9·8813144	2621	10·1186856	10·0991819	962	9·9008181	44
17	9·7822984	1659	10·2177016	9·8815765	2621	10·1184235	10·0992781	962	9·9007219	43
18	9·7824643	1658	10·2175357	9·8818386	2621	10·1181614	10·0993743	963	9·9006257	42
19	9·7826301	1657	10·2173699	9·8821007	2620	10·1178993	10·0994706	963	9·9005294	41
20	9·7827958	1656	10·2172042	9·8823627	2619	10·1176373	10·0995669	964	9·9004331	40
21	9·7829614	1654	10·2170386	9·8826246	2620	10·1173754	10·0996633	964	9·9003367	39
22	9·7831268	1654	10·2168732	9·8828866	2618	10·1171134	10·0997597	965	9·9002403	38
23	9·7832922	1653	10·2167078	9·8831484	2619	10·1168516	10·0998562	966	9·9001438	37
24	9·7834575	1652	10·2165425	9·8834103	2618	10·1165897	10·0999528	966	9·9000472	36
25	9·7836227	1651	10·2163773	9·8836721	2617	10·1163279	10·1000494	967	9·8999506	35
26	9·7837878	1650	10·2162122	9·8839338	2618	10·1160662	10·1001461	967	9·8998539	34
27	9·7839528	1649	10·2160472	9·8841956	2616	10·1158044	10·1002428	968	9·8997572	33
28	9·7841177	1647	10·2158823	9·8844572	2616	10·1155428	10·1003396	968	9·8996604	32
29	9·7842824	1647	10·2157176	9·8847189	2616	10·1152811	10·1004364	969	9·8995636	31
30	9·7844471	1646	10·2155529	9·8849805	2615	10·1150195	10·1005333	970	9·8994667	30
31	9·7846117	1645	10·2153883	9·8852420	2615	10·1147580	10·1006303	970	9·8993697	29
32	9·7847762	1644	10·2152238	9·8855035	2615	10·1144965	10·1007273	971	9·8992727	28
33	9·7849406	1643	10·2150594	9·8857650	2614	10·1142350	10·1008244	972	9·8991756	27
34	9·7851049	1642	10·2148951	9·8860264	2614	10·1139736	10·1009216	972	9·8990784	26
35	9·7852691	1641	10·2147309	9·8862878	2614	10·1137122	10·1010188	972	9·8989812	25
36	9·7854332	1640	10·2145668	9·8865492	2613	10·1134508	10·1011160	973	9·8988840	24
37	9·7855972	1639	10·2144028	9·8868105	2613	10·1131895	10·1012133	974	9·8987867	23
38	9·7857611	1638	10·2142389	9·8870718	2612	10·1129282	10·1013107	974	9·8986893	22
39	9·7859249	1637	10·2140751	9·8873330	2612	10·1126670	10·1014081	975	9·8985919	21
40	9·7860886	1636	10·2139114	9·8875942	2612	10·1124058	10·1015056	976	9·8984944	20
41	9·7862522	1635	10·2137478	9·8878554	2611	10·1121446	10·1016032	976	9·8983968	19
42	9·7864157	1634	10·2135843	9·8881165	2610	10·1118835	10·1017008	977	9·8982992	18
43	9·7865791	1633	10·2134209	9·8883777	2611	10·1116225	10·1017985	977	9·8982015	17
44	9·7867424	1632	10·2132576	9·8886386	2610	10·1113614	10·1018962	978	9·8981038	16
45	9·7869056	1631	10·2130944	9·8888996	2609	10·1111004	10·1019940	978	9·8980060	15
46	9·7870687	1630	10·2129313	9·8891605	2609	10·1108395	10·1020918	979	9·8979082	14
47	9·7872317	1629	10·2127683	9·8894214	2609	10·1105786	10·1021897	980	9·8978103	13
48	9·7873946	1628	10·2126054	9·8896823	2609	10·1103177	10·1022877	980	9·8977123	12
49	9·7875574	1628	10·2124426	9·8899432	2608	10·1100568	10·1023857	981	9·8976143	11
50	9·7877202	1626	10·2122798	9·8902040	2607	10·1097960	10·1024838	981	9·8975162	10
51	9·7878828	1625	10·2121172	9·8904647	2607	10·1095353	10·1025819	982	9·8974181	9
52	9·7880453	1624	10·2119547	9·8907254	2607	10·1092746	10·1026801	983	9·8973199	8
53	9·7882077	1624	10·2117923	9·8909861	2607	10·1090139	10·1027784	983	9·8972216	7
54	9·7883701	1622	10·2116299	9·8912468	2606	10·1087532	10·1028767	984	9·8971233	6
55	9·7885323	1621	10·2114677	9·8915074	2605	10·1084926	10·1029751	984	9·8970249	5
56	9·7886944	1621	10·2113056	9·8917679	2606	10·1082321	10·1030735	985	9·8969265	4
57	9·7888565	1619	10·2111435	9·8920285	2605	10·1079715	10·1031720	986	9·8968320	3
58	9·7890184	1618	10·2109816	9·8922890	2604	10·1077110	10·1032706	986	9·8967294	2
59	9·7891802	1618	10·2108198	9·8925494	2604	10·1074506	10·1033692	987	9·8966308	1
60	9·7893420		10·2106580	9·8928098		10·1071902	10·1034679		9·8965321	0
′	Cosine	Diff.	Secant	Cotang.	Diff.	Tang.	Cosec.	D.	Sine	′

52 Deg.

′	Sine	Diff.	Cosec.	Tang.	Diff.	Cotang.	Secant	Diff.	Cosine	′
0	9·7893420	1616	10·2106580	9·8928098	2604	10·1071902	10·1034679	987	9·8965321	60
1	9·7895036	1616	10·2104964	9·8930702	2604	10·1069298	10·1035666	988	9·8964334	59
2	9·7896652	1614	10·2103348	9·8933306	2603	10·1066694	10·1036654	988	9·8963346	58
3	9·7898266	1614	10·2101734	9·8935909	2602	10·1064091	10·1037642	989	9·8962358	57
4	9·7899880	1613	10·2100120	9·8938511	2603	10·1061489	10·1038631	990	9·8961369	56
5	9·7901493	1611	10·2098507	9·8941114	2601	10·1058886	10·1039621	990	9·8960379	55
6	9·7903104	1611	10·2096896	9·8943715	2602	10·1056285	10·1040611	991	9·8959389	54
7	9·7904715	1610	10·2095285	9·8946317	2601	10·1053683	10·1041602	992	9·8958398	53
8	9·7906325	1608	10·2093675	9·8948918	2601	10·1051082	10·1042594	992	9·8957406	52
9	9·7907933	1608	10·2092067	9·8951519	2600	10·1048481	10·1043586	992	9·8956414	51
10	9·7909541	1607	10·2090459	9·8954119	2600	10·1045881	10·1044578	993	9·8955422	50
11	9·7911148	1606	10·2088852	9·8956719	2600	10·1043281	10·1045571	994	9·8954429	49
12	9·7912754	1605	10·2087246	9·8959319	2599	10·1040681	10·1046565	994	9·8953435	48
13	9·7914359	1604	10·2085641	9·8961918	2599	10·1038082	10·1047560	995	9·8952440	47
14	9·7915963	1603	10·2084037	9·8964517	2599	10·1035483	10·1048555	995	9·8951445	46
15	9·7917566	1602	10·2082434	9·8967116	2598	10·1032884	10·1049550	997	9·8950450	45
16	9·7919168	1601	10·2080832	9·8969714	2598	10·1030286	10·1050547	996	9·8949453	44
17	9·7920769	1600	10·2079231	9·8972312	2598	10·1027688	10·1051543	998	9·8948457	43
18	9·7922369	1599	10·2077631	9·8974910	2597	10·1025090	10·1052541	998	9·8947459	42
19	9·7923968	1598	10·2076032	9·8977507	2597	10·1022493	10·1053539	998	9·8946461	41
20	9·7925566	1597	10·2074434	9·8980104	2596	10·1019896	10·1054537	1000	9·8945463	40
21	9·7927163	1597	10·2072837	9·8982700	2596	10·1017300	10·1055537	999	9·8944463	39
22	9·7928760	1595	10·2071240	9·8985296	2596	10·1014704	10·1056536	1001	9·8943464	38
23	9·7930355	1594	10·2069645	9·8987892	2595	10·1012108	10·1057537	1001	9·8942463	37
24	9·7931949	1594	10·2068051	9·8990487	2595	10·1009513	10·1058538	1001	9·8941462	36
25	9·7933543	1592	10·2066457	9·8993082	2595	10·1006918	10·1059539	1003	9·8940461	35
26	9·7935135	1592	10·2064865	9·8995677	2594	10·1004323	10·1060542	1002	9·8939458	34
27	9·7936727	1590	10·2063273	9·8998271	2594	10·1001729	10·1061544	1004	9·8938456	33
28	9·7938317	1590	10·2061683	9·9000865	2594	10·0999135	10·1062548	1004	9·8937452	32
29	9·7939907	1589	10·2060093	9·9003459	2593	10·0996541	10·1063552	1004	9·8936448	31
30	9·7941496	1587	10·2058504	9·9006052	2593	10·0993948	10·1064556	1005	9·8935444	30
31	9·7943083	1587	10·2056917	9·9008645	2592	10·0991355	10·1065561	1006	9·8934439	29
32	9·7944670	1586	10·2055330	9·9011237	2593	10·0988763	10·1066567	1007	9·8933433	28
33	9·7946256	1585	10·2053744	9·9013830	2592	10·0986170	10·1067574	1007	9·8932426	27
34	9·7947841	1584	10·2052159	9·9016422	2591	10·0983578	10·1068581	1007	9·8931419	26
35	9·7949425	1583	10·2050575	9·9019013	2591	10·0980987	10·1069588	1008	9·8930412	25
36	9·7951008	1582	10·2048992	9·9021604	2591	10·0978396	10·1070596	1009	9·8929404	24
37	9·7952590	1581	10·2047410	9·9024195	2591	10·0975805	10·1071605	1010	9·8928395	23
38	9·7954171	1580	10·2045829	9·9026786	2590	10·0973214	10·1072615	1010	9·8927385	22
39	9·7955751	1579	10·2044249	9·9029376	2590	10·0970624	10·1073625	1010	9·8926375	21
40	9·7957330	1579	10·2042670	9·9031966	2589	10·0968034	10·1074635	1011	9·8925365	20
41	9·7958909	1577	10·2041091	9·9034555	2589	10·0965445	10·1075646	1012	9·8924354	19
42	9·7960486	1576	10·2039514	9·9037144	2589	10·0962856	10·1076658	1013	9·8923342	18
43	9·7962062	1576	10·2037938	9·9039733	2589	10·0960267	10·1077671	1013	9·8922329	17
44	9·7963638	1574	10·2036362	9·9042321	2589	10·0957679	10·1078684	1013	9·8921316	16
45	9·7965212	1574	10·2034788	9·9044910	2587	10·0955090	10·1079697	1014	9·8920303	15
46	9·7966786	1573	10·2033214	9·9047497	2588	10·0952503	10·1080711	1015	9·8919289	14
47	9·7968359	1571	10·2031641	9·9050085	2587	10·0949915	10·1081726	1016	9·8918274	13
48	9·7969930	1571	10·2030070	9·9052672	2587	10·0947328	10·1082742	1016	9·8917258	12
49	9·7971501	1570	10·2028499	9·9055259	2586	10·0944741	10·1083758	1016	9·8916242	11
50	9·7973071	1569	10·2026929	9·9057845	2586	10·0942155	10·1084774	1018	9·8915226	10
51	9·7974640	1568	10·2025360	9·9060431	2586	10·0939569	10·1085792	1017	9·8914208	9
52	9·7976208	1567	10·2023792	9·9063017	2586	10·0936983	10·1086809	1019	9·8913191	8
53	9·7977775	1566	10·2022225	9·9065603	2585	10·0934397	10·1087828	1019	9·8912172	7
54	9·7979341	1565	10·2020659	9·9068188	2585	10·0931812	10·1088847	1020	9·8911153	6
55	9·7980906	1564	10·2019094	9·9070773	2584	10·0929227	10·1089867	1020	9·8910133	5
56	9·7982470	1564	10·2017530	9·9073357	2584	10·0926643	10·1090887	1021	9·8909113	4
57	9·7984034	1562	10·2015966	9·9075941	2584	10·0924059	10·1091908	1021	9·8908092	3
58	9·7985596	1562	10·2014404	9·9078525	2584	10·0921475	10·1092929	1022	9·8907071	2
59	9·7987158	1560	10·2012842	9·9081109	2583	10·0918891	10·1093951	1023	9·8906049	1
60	9·7988718		10·2011282	9·9083692		10·0916308	10·1094974		9·8905026	0

| ′ | Cosine | Diff. | Secant | Cotang. | Diff. | Tang. | Cosec. | Diff. | Sine | ′ |

′	Sine	Diff.	Cosec.	Tang.	Diff.	Cotang.	Secant	Diff.	Cosine	′
0	9·7988718	1560	10·2011282	9·9083692	2583	10·0916308	10·1094974	1023	9·8905026	60
1	9·7990278	1558	10·2009722	9·9086275	2583	10·0913725	10·1095997	1024	9·8904003	59
2	9·7991836	1558	10·2008164	9·9088858	2582	10·0911142	10·1097021	1025	9·8902979	58
3	9·7993394	1557	10·2006606	9·9091440	2582	10·0908560	10·1098046	1025	9·8901954	57
4	9·7994951	1556	10·2005049	9·9094022	2581	10·0905978	10·1099071	1026	9·8900929	56
5	9·7996507	1555	10·2003493	9·9096603	2582	10·0903397	10·1100097	1026	9·8899903	55
6	9·7998062	1554	10·2001938	9·9099185	2581	10·0900815	10·1101123	1027	9·8898877	54
7	9·7999616	1553	10·2000384	9·9101766	2581	10·0898234	10·1102150	1028	9·8897850	53
8	9·8001169	1552	10·1998831	9·9104347	2580	10·0895653	10·1103178	1028	9·8896822	52
9	9·8002721	1551	10·1997279	9·9106927	2580	10·0893073	10·1104206	1029	9·8895794	51
10	9·8004272	1551	10·1995728	9·9109507	2580	10·0890493	10·1105235	1029	9·8894765	50
11	9·8005823	1549	10·1994177	9·9112087	2579	10·0887913	10·1106264	1030	9·8893736	49
12	9·8007372	1549	10·1992628	9·9114666	2579	10·0885334	10·1107294	1031	9·8892706	48
13	9·8008921	1547	10·1991079	9·9117245	2579	10·0882755	10·1108325	1031	9·8891675	47
14	9·8010468	1547	10·1989532	9·9119824	2579	10·0880176	10·1109356	1032	9·8890644	46
15	9·8012015	1546	10·1987985	9·9122403	2578	10·0877597	10·1110388	1032	9·8889612	45
16	9·8013561	1545	10·1986439	9·9124981	2578	10·0875019	10·1111420	1033	9·8888580	44
17	9·8015106	1543	10·1984894	9·9127559	2578	10·0872441	10·1112453	1034	9·8887547	43
18	9·8016649	1543	10·1983351	9·9130137	2577	10·0869863	10·1113487	1034	9·8886513	42
19	9·8018192	1543	10·1981808	9·9132714	2577	10·0867286	10·1114521	1035	9·8885479	41
20	9·8019735	1541	10·1980265	9·9135291	2577	10·0864709	10·1115556	1036	9·8884444	40
21	9·8021276	1540	10·1978724	9·9137868	2576	10·0862132	10·1116592	1036	9·8883408	39
22	9·8022816	1539	10·1977184	9·9140444	2576	10·0859556	10·1117628	1037	9·8882372	38
23	9·8024355	1539	10·1975645	9·9143020	2576	10·0856980	10·1118665	1037	9·8881335	37
24	9·8025894	1537	10·1974106	9·9145596	2575	10·0854404	10·1119702	1038	9·8880298	36
25	9·8027431	1537	10·1972569	9·9148171	2576	10·0851829	10·1120740	1039	9·8879260	35
26	9·8028968	1536	10·1971032	9·9150747	2575	10·0849253	10·1121779	1039	9·8878221	34
27	9·8030504	1534	10·1969496	9·9153322	2575	10·0846678	10·1122818	1040	9·8877182	33
28	9·8032038	1534	10·1967962	9·9155896	2574	10·0844104	10·1123858	1040	9·8876142	32
29	9·8033572	1533	10·1966428	9·9158471	2574	10·0841529	10·1124898	1041	9·8875102	31
30	9·8035105	1532	10·1964895	9·9161045	2573	10·0838955	10·1125939	1042	9·8874061	30
31	9·8036637	1531	10·1963363	9·9163618	2574	10·0836382	10·1126981	1042	9·8873019	29
32	9·8038168	1531	10·1961832	9·9166192	2573	10·0833808	10·1128023	1043	9·8871977	28
33	9·8039699	1529	10·1960301	9·9168765	2573	10·0831235	10·1129066	1044	9·8870934	27
34	9·8041228	1529	10·1958772	9·9171338	2573	10·0828662	10·1130110	1044	9·8869890	26
35	9·8042757	1527	10·1957243	9·9173911	2572	10·0826089	10·1131154	1045	9·8868846	25
36	9·8044284	1527	10·1955716	9·9176483	2572	10·0823517	10·1132199	1045	9·8867801	24
37	9·8045811	1525	10·1954189	9·9179055	2572	10·0820945	10·1133244	1046	9·8866756	23
38	9·8047336	1525	10·1952664	9·9181627	2571	10·0818373	10·1134290	1047	9·8865710	22
39	9·8048861	1524	10·1951139	9·9184198	2571	10·0815802	10·1135337	1047	9·8864663	21
40	9·8050385	1523	10·1949615	9·9186769	2571	10·0813231	10·1136384	1048	9·8863616	20
41	9·8051908	1522	10·1948092	9·9189340	2571	10·0810660	10·1137432	1049	9·8862568	19
42	9·8053430	1521	10·1946570	9·9191911	2570	10·0808089	10·1138481	1049	9·8861519	18
43	9·8054951	1521	10·1945049	9·9194481	2570	10·0805519	10·1139530	1050	9·8860470	17
44	9·8056472	1519	10·1943528	9·9197051	2570	10·0802949	10·1140580	1050	9·8859420	16
45	9·8057991	1519	10·1942009	9·9199621	2570	10·0800379	10·1141630	1051	9·8858370	15
46	9·8059510	1517	10·1940490	9·9202191	2569	10·0797809	10·1142681	1052	9·8857319	14
47	9·8061027	1517	10·1938973	9·9204760	2569	10·0795240	10·1143733	1052	9·8856267	13
48	9·8062544	1516	10·1937456	9·9207329	2569	10·0792671	10·1144785	1053	9·8855215	12
49	9·8064060	1515	10·1935940	9·9209898	2568	10·0790102	10·1145838	1053	9·8854162	11
50	9·8065575	1514	10·1934425	9·9212466	2568	10·0787534	10·1146891	1054	9·8853109	10
51	9·8067089	1513	10·1932911	9·9215034	2568	10·0784966	10·1147945	1055	9·8852055	9
52	9·8068602	1512	10·1931398	9·9217602	2568	10·0782398	10·1149000	1055	9·8851000	8
53	9·8070114	1512	10·1929886	9·9220170	2567	10·0779830	10·1150055	1056	9·8849945	7
54	9·8071626	1510	10·1928374	9·9222737	2567	10·0777263	10·1151111	1057	9·8848889	6
55	9·8073136	1510	10·1926864	9·9225304	2567	10·0774696	10·1152168	1057	9·8847832	5
56	9·8074646	1508	10·1925354	9·9227871	2566	10·0772129	10·1153225	1058	9·8846775	4
57	9·8076154	1508	10·1923846	9·9230437	2567	10·0769563	10·1154283	1058	9·8845717	3
58	9·8077662	1507	10·1922338	9·9233004	2566	10·0766996	10·1155341	1060	9·8844659	2
59	9·8079169	1506	10·1920831	9·9235570	2565	10·0764430	10·1156401	1059	9·8843599	1
60	9·8080675		10·1919325	9·9238135		10·0761865	10·1157460		9·8842540	0
′	Cosine	Diff.	Secant	Cotang.	Diff.	Tang.	Cosec.	Diff.	Sine	′

′	Sine	Diff.	Cosec.	Tang.	Diff.	Cotang.	Secant	Diff.	Cosine	′
0	9·8080675	1505	10·1919325	9·9238135	2566	10·0761865	10·1157460	1061	9·8842540	60
1	9·8082180	1504	10·1917820	9·9240701	2565	10·0759299	10·1158521	1061	9·8841479	59
2	9·8083684	1504	10·1916316	9·9243266	2565	10·0756734	10·1159582	1061	9·8840418	58
3	9·8085188	1502	10·1914812	9·9245831	2565	10·0754169	10·1160643	1063	9·8839357	57
4	9·8086690	1502	10·1913310	9·9248396	2564	10·0751604	10·1161706	1062	9·8838294	56
5	9·8088192	1500	10·1911808	9·9250960	2564	10·0749040	10·1162768	1064	9·8837232	55
6	9·8089692	1500	10·1910308	9·9253524	2564	10·0746476	10·1163832	1064	9·8836168	54
7	9·8091192	1499	10·1908808	9·9256088	2564	10·0743912	10·1164896	1065	9·8835104	53
8	9·8092691	1498	10·1907309	9·9258652	2563	10·0741348	10·1165961	1065	9·8834039	52
9	9·8094189	1497	10·1905811	9·9261215	2563	10·0738785	10·1167026	1066	9·8832974	51
10	9·8095686	1496	10·1904314	9·9263778	2563	10·0736222	10·1168092	1067	9·8831908	50
11	9·8097182	1496	10·1902818	9·9266341	2563	10·0733659	10·1169159	1067	9·8830841	49
12	9·8098678	1494	10·1901322	9·9268904	2562	10·0731096	10·1170226	1068	9·8829774	48
13	9·8100172	1494	10·1899828	9·9271466	2562	10·0728534	10·1171294	1068	9·8828706	47
14	9·8101666	1493	10·1898334	9·9274028	2562	10·0725972	10·1172362	1068	9·8827638	46
15	9·8103159	1491	10·1896841	9·9276590	2562	10·0723410	10·1173432	1069	9·8826568	45
16	9·8104650	1491	10·1895350	9·9279152	2561	10·0720848	10·1174501	1071	9·8825499	44
17	9·8106141	1490	10·1893859	9·9281713	2561	10·0718287	10·1175572	1071	9·8824428	43
18	9·8107631	1490	10·1892369	9·9284274	2561	10·0715726	10·1176643	1072	9·8823357	42
19	9·8109121	1488	10·1890879	9·9286835	2561	10·0713165	10·1177715	1072	9·8822285	41
20	9·8110609	1487	10·1889391	9·9289396	2560	10·0710604	10·1178787	1073	9·8821213	40
21	9·8112096	1487	10·1887904	9·9291956	2560	10·0708044	10·1179860	1073	9·8820140	39
22	9·8113583	1486	10·1886417	9·9294516	2560	10·0705484	10·1180933	1073	9·8819067	38
23	9·8115069	1485	10·1884931	9·9297076	2560	10·0702924	10·1182008	1074	9·8817992	37
24	9·8116554	1484	10·1883446	9·9299636	2560	10·0700364	10·1183082	1076	9·8816918	36
25	9·8118038	1483	10·1881962	9·9302195	2560	10·0697805	10·1184158	1076	9·8815842	35
26	9·8119521	1482	10·1880479	9·9304755	2559	10·0695245	10·1185234	1077	9·8814766	34
27	9·8121003	1481	10·1878997	9·9307314	2558	10·0692686	10·1186311	1077	9·8813689	33
28	9·8122484	1481	10·1877516	9·9309872	2559	10·0690128	10·1187388	1078	9·8812612	32
29	9·8123965	1479	10·1876035	9·9312431	2558	10·0687569	10·1188466	1079	9·8811534	31
30	9·8125444	1479	10·1874556	9·9314989	2558	10·0685011	10·1189545	1079	9·8810455	30
31	9·8126923	1478	10·1873077	9·9317547	2558	10·0682453	10·1190624	1080	9·8809376	29
32	9·8128401	1477	10·1871599	9·9320105	2557	10·0679895	10·1191704	1080	9·8808296	28
33	9·8129878	1476	10·1870122	9·9322662	2558	10·0677338	10·1192785	1081	9·8807215	27
34	9·8131354	1475	10·1868646	9·9325220	2557	10·0674780	10·1193866	1081	9·8806134	26
35	9·8132829	1474	10·1867171	9·9327777	2557	10·0672223	10·1194948	1082	9·8805052	25
36	9·8134303	1474	10·1865697	9·9330334	2556	10·0669666	10·1196030	1082	9·8803970	24
37	9·8135777	1473	10·1864223	9·9332890	2556	10·0667110	10·1197113	1083	9·8802887	23
38	9·8137250	1471	10·1862750	9·9335446	2556	10·0664554	10·1198197	1084	9·8801803	22
39	9·8138721	1471	10·1861279	9·9338003	2556	10·0661997	10·1199281	1084	9·8800719	21
40	9·8140192	1470	10·1859808	9·9340559	2555	10·0659441	10·1200366	1085	9·8799634	20
41	9·8141662	1469	10·1858338	9·9343114	2556	10·0656886	10·1201452	1086	9·8798548	19
42	9·8143131	1469	10·1856869	9·9345670	2555	10·0654330	10·1202538	1086	9·8797462	18
43	9·8144600	1467	10·1855400	9·9348225	2555	10·0651775	10·1203625	1087	9·8796375	17
44	9·8146067	1467	10·1853933	9·9350780	2555	10·0649220	10·1204713	1088	9·8795287	16
45	9·8147534	1465	10·1852466	9·9353335	2554	10·0646665	10·1205801	1088	9·8794199	15
46	9·8148999	1465	10·1851001	9·9355889	2555	10·0644111	10·1206890	1089	9·8793110	14
47	9·8150464	1464	10·1849536	9·9358444	2554	10·0641556	10·1207979	1089	9·8792021	13
48	9·8151928	1463	10·1848072	9·9360998	2554	10·0639002	10·1209070	1091	9·8790930	12
49	9·8153391	1463	10·1846609	9·9363552	2553	10·0636448	10·1210160	1090	9·8789840	11
50	9·8154854	1461	10·1845146	9·9366105	2554	10·0633895	10·1211252	1092	9·8788748	10
51	9·8156315	1461	10·1843685	9·9368659	2553	10·0631341	10·1212344	1092	9·8787656	9
52	9·8157776	1459	10·1842224	9·9371212	2553	10·0628788	10·1213437	1093	9·8786563	8
53	9·8159235	1459	10·1840765	9·9373765	2553	10·0626235	10·1214530	1093	9·8785470	7
54	9·8160694	1458	10·1839306	9·9376318	2553	10·0623682	10·1215624	1094	9·8784376	6
55	9·8162152	1457	10·1837848	9·9378871	2552	10·0621129	10·1216719	1095	9·8783281	5
56	9·8163609	1457	10·1836391	9·9381423	2552	10·0618577	10·1217814	1095	9·8782186	4
57	9·8165066	1455	10·1834934	9·9383975	2552	10·0616025	10·1218910	1096	9·8781090	3
58	9·8166521	1454	10·1833479	9·9386527	2552	10·0613473	10·1220006	1096	9·8779994	2
59	9·8167975	1454	10·1832025	9·9389079	2552	10·0610921	10·1221104	1098	9·8778896	1
60	9·8169429		10·1830571	9·9391631		10·0608369	10·1222201	1097	9·8777799	0
′	Cosine	Diff.	Secant	Cotang.	Diff.	Tang.	Cosec.	Diff.	Sine	′

223

′	Sine	Diff.	Cosec.	Tang.	Diff.	Cotang.	Secant	Diff.	Cosine	′
0	9·8169429	1453	10·1830571	9·9391631	2551	10·0608369	10·1222201	1099	9·8777799	60
1	9·8170882	1452	10·1829118	9·9394182	2551	10·0605818	10·1223300	1099	9·8776700	59
2	9·8172334	1451	10·1827666	9·9396733	2551	10·0603267	10·1224399	1100	9·8775601	58
3	9·8173785	1450	10·1826215	9·9399284	2551	10·0600716	10·1225499	1100	9·8774501	57
4	9·8175235	1450	10·1824765	9·9401835	2550	10·0598165	10·1226599	1101	9·8773401	56
5	9·8176685	1448	10·1823315	9·9404385	2551	10·0595615	10·1227700	1102	9·8772300	55
6	9·8178133	1448	10·1821867	9·9406936	2550	10·0593064	10·1228802	1102	9·8771198	54
7	9·8179581	1447	10·1820419	9·9409486	2550	10·0590514	10·1229904	1103	9·8770096	53
8	9·8181028	1446	10·1818972	9·9412036	2550	10·0587964	10·1231007	1104	9·8768993	52
9	9·8182474	1445	10·1817526	9·9414585	2549	10·0585415	10·1232111	1104	9·8767889	51
10	9·8183919	1445	10·1816081	9·9417135	2550	10·0582865	10·1233215	1105	9·8766785	50
11	9·8185364	1443	10·1814636	9·9419684	2549	10·0580316	10·1234320	1106	9·8765680	49
12	9·8186807	1443	10·1813193	9·9422233	2549	10·0577767	10·1235426	1106	9·8764574	48
13	9·8188250	1442	10·1811750	9·9424782	2549	10·0575218	10·1236532	1107	9·8763468	47
14	9·8189692	1441	10·1810308	9·9427331	2548	10·0572669	10·1237639	1108	9·8762361	46
15	9·8191133	1440	10·1808867	9·9429879	2549	10·0570121	10·1238747	1108	9·8761253	45
16	9·8192573	1439	10·1807427	9·9432428	2548	10·0567572	10·1239855	1109	9·8760145	44
17	9·8194012	1438	10·1805988	9·9434976	2548	10·0565024	10·1240964	1109	9·8759036	43
18	9·8195450	1438	10·1804550	9·9437524	2548	10·0562476	10·1242073	1110	9·8757927	42
19	9·8196888	1437	10·1803112	9·9440072	2547	10·0559928	10·1243184	1110	9·8756816	41
20	9·8198325	1436	10·1801675	9·9442619	2547	10·0557381	10·1244294	1112	9·8755706	40
21	9·8199761	1435	10·1800239	9·9445166	2548	10·0554834	10·1245406	1112	9·8754594	39
22	9·8201196	1434	10·1798804	9·9447714	2547	10·0552286	10·1246518	1113	9·8753482	38
23	9·8202630	1433	10·1797370	9·9450261	2546	10·0549739	10·1247631	1113	9·8752369	37
24	9·8204063	1433	10·1795937	9·9452807	2547	10·0547193	10·1248744	1114	9·8751256	36
25	9·8205496	1431	10·1794504	9·9455354	2546	10·0544646	10·1249858	1115	9·8750142	35
26	9·8206927	1431	10·1793073	9·9457900	2547	10·0542100	10·1250973	1115	9·8749027	34
27	9·8208358	1430	10·1791642	9·9460447	2546	10·0539553	10·1252088	1117	9·8747912	33
28	9·8209788	1429	10·1790212	9·9462993	2546	10·0537007	10·1253205	1116	9·8746705	32
29	9·8211217	1429	10·1788783	9·9465539	2545	10·0534461	10·1254321	1118	9·8745679	31
30	9·8212646	1427	10·1787354	9·9468084	2546	10·0531916	10·1255439	1118	9·8744561	30
31	9·8214073	1427	10·1785027	9·9470630	2545	10·0529370	10·1256557	1118	9·8743443	29
32	9·8215500	1426	10·1784500	9·9473175	2545	10·0526825	10·1257675	1120	9·8742325	28
33	9·8216926	1425	10·1783074	9·9475720	2545	10·0524280	10·1258795	1120	9·8741205	27
34	9·8218351	1424	10·1781649	9·9478265	2545	10·0521735	10·1259915	1120	9·8740085	26
35	9·8219775	1423	10·1780225	9·9480810	2545	10·0519190	10·1261035	1121	9·8738965	25
36	9·8221198	1423	10·1778802	9·9483355	2544	10·0516645	10·1262156	1122	9·8737844	24
37	9·8222621	1421	10·1777379	9·9485899	2544	10·0514101	10·1263278	1123	9·8736722	23
38	9·8224042	1421	10·1775958	9·9488443	2544	10·0511557	10·1264401	1123	9·8735599	22
39	9·8225463	1420	10·1774537	9·9490987	2544	10·0509013	10·1265524	1124	9·8734476	21
40	9·8226883	1419	10·1773117	9·9493531	2544	10·0506469	10·1266648	1125	9·8733352	20
41	9·8228302	1419	10·1771698	9·9496075	2544	10·0503925	10·1267773	1125	9·8732227	19
42	9·8229721	1417	10·1770279	9·9498619	2543	10·0501381	10·1268898	1126	9·8731102	18
43	9·8231138	1417	10·1768862	9·9501162	2543	10·0498838	10·1270024	1127	9·8729976	17
44	9·8232555	1416	10·1767445	9·9503705	2543	10·0496295	10·1271151	1127	9·8728849	16
45	9·8233971	1415	10·1766029	9·9506248	2543	10·0493752	10·1272278	1128	9·8727722	15
46	9·8235386	1414	10·1764614	9·9508791	2543	10·0491209	10·1273406	1128	9·8726594	14
47	9·8236800	1413	10·1763200	9·9511334	2542	10·0488666	10·1274534	1129	9·8725466	13
48	9·8238213	1413	10·1761787	9·9513876	2543	10·0486124	10·1275663	1130	9·8724337	12
49	9·8239626	1411	10·1760374	9·9516419	2542	10·0483581	10·1276793	1131	9·8723207	11
50	9·8241037	1411	10·1758963	9·9518961	2542	10·0481039	10·1277924	1131	9·8722076	10
51	9·8242448	1410	10·1757552	9·9521503	2542	10·0478497	10·1279055	1132	9·8720945	9
52	9·8243858	1409	10·1756142	9·9524045	2542	10·0475955	10·1280187	1132	9·8719813	8
53	9·8245267	1409	10·1754733	9·9526587	2541	10·0473413	10·1281319	1133	9·8718681	7
54	9·8246676	1407	10·1753324	9·9529128	2542	10·0470872	10·1282452	1134	9·8717548	6
55	9·8248083	1407	10·1751917	9·9531670	2541	10·0468330	10·1283586	1135	9·8716414	5
56	9·8249490	1406	10·1750510	9·9534221	2541	10·0465789	10·1284721	1135	9·8715279	4
57	9·8250896	1405	10·1749104	9·9536752	2541	10·0463248	10·1285856	1136	9·8714144	3
58	9·8252301	1404	10·1747699	9·9539293	2541	10·0460707	10·1286992	1136	9·8713008	2
59	9·8253705	1404	10·1746295	9·9541834	2540	10·0458166	10·1288128	1137	9·8711872	1
60	9·8255109		10·1744891	9·9544374		10·0455626	10·1289265		9·8710735	0
′	Cosine	Diff.	Secant	Cotang.	Diff.	Tang.	Cosec.	Diff.	Sine	′

′	Sine	Diff.	Cosec.	Tang.	Diff.	Cotang.	Secant	Diff.	Cosine	′
0	9·8255109	1403	10·1744891	9·9544374	2541	10·0455626	10·1289265	1138	9·8710735	60
1	9·8256512	1401	10·1743488	9·9546915	2540	10·0453085	10·1290403	1139	9·8709597	59
2	9·8257913	1401	10·1742087	9·9549455	2540	10·0450545	10·1291542	1139	9·8708458	58
3	9·8259314	1401	10·1740686	9·9551995	2540	10·0448005	10·1292681	1140	9·8707319	57
4	9·8260715	1399	10·1739285	9·9554535	2540	10·0445465	10·1293821	1140	9·8706179	56
5	9·8262114	1398	10·1737886	9·9557075	2540	10·0442925	10·1294961	1141	9·8705039	55
6	9·8263512	1398	10·1736488	9·9559615	2539	10·0440385	10·1296102	1142	9·8703898	54
7	9·8264910	1397	10·1735090	9·9562154	2540	10·0437846	10·1297244	1143	9·8702756	53
8	9·8266307	1396	10·1733693	9·9564694	2539	10·0435306	10·1298387	1143	9·8701613	52
9	9·8267703	1395	10·1732297	9·9567233	2539	10·0432767	10·1299530	1144	9·8700470	51
10	9·8269098	1395	10·1730902	9·9569772	2539	10·0430228	10·1300674	1144	9·8699326	50
11	9·8270493	1394	10·1729507	9·9572311	2539	10·0427689	10·1301818	1145	9·8698182	49
12	9·8271887	1392	10·1728113	9·9574850	2539	10·0425150	10·1302963	1146	9·8697037	48
13	9·8273279	1392	10·1726727	9·9577389	2538	10·0422611	10·1304109	1147	9·8695891	47
14	9·8274671	1392	10·1725329	9·9579927	2538	10·0420073	10·1305256	1147	9·8694744	46
15	9·8276063	1390	10·1723937	9·9582465	2539	10·0417535	10·1306403	1148	9·8693597	45
16	9·8277453	1390	10·1722547	9·9585004	2538	10·0414996	10·1307551	1148	9·8692449	44
17	9·8278843	1388	10·1721157	9·9587542	2538	10·0412458	10·1308699	1149	9·8691301	43
18	9·8280231	1388	10·1719769	9·9590080	2538	10·0409920	10·1309848	1150	9·8690152	42
19	9·8281619	1387	10·1718381	9·9592618	2538	10·0407382	10·1310998	1151	9·8689002	41
20	9·8283006	1387	10·1716994	9·9595155	2538	10·0404845	10·1312149	1151	9·8687851	40
21	9·8284393	1385	10·1715607	9·9597693	2537	10·0402307	10·1313300	1152	9·8686700	39
22	9·8285778	1385	10·1714222	9·9600230	2537	10·0399770	10·1314452	1152	9·8685548	38
23	9·8287163	1384	10·1712837	9·9602767	2538	10·0397233	10·1315604	1154	9·8684296	37
24	9·8288547	1383	10·1711453	9·9605305	2537	10·0394695	10·1316758	1154	9·8683242	36
25	9·8289930	1382	10·1710070	9·9607842	2536	10·0392158	10·1317912	1154	9·8682088	35
26	9·8291312	1382	10·1708608	9·9610378	2537	10·0389622	10·1319066	1155	9·8680934	34
27	9·8292694	1381	10·1707306	9·9612915	2537	10·0387085	10·1320221	1156	9·8679779	33
28	9·8294075	1379	10·1705925	9·9615452	2536	10·0384548	10·1321377	1157	9·8678623	32
29	9·8295454	1379	10·1704546	9·9617988	2537	10·0382012	10·1322534	1157	9·8677446	31
30	9·8296833	1379	10·1703167	9·9620525	2536	10·0379475	10·1323691	1158	9·8676309	30
31	9·8298212	1377	10·1701788	9·9623061	2536	10·0376939	10·1324849	1159	9·8675151	29
32	9·8299589	1377	10·1700411	9·9625597	2536	10·0374403	10·1326008	1159	9·8673992	28
33	9·8300966	1376	10·1699034	9·9628133	2536	10·0371867	10·1327167	1160	9·8672833	27
34	9·8302342	1375	10·1697658	9·9630669	2535	10·0369331	10·1328327	1161	9·8671673	26
35	9·8303717	1374	10·1696283	9·9633204	2536	10·0366796	10·1329488	1161	9·8670512	25
36	9·8305091	1373	10·1694909	9·9635740	2535	10·0364260	10·1330649	1162	9·8669351	24
37	9·8306464	1373	10·1693536	9·9638275	2536	10·0361725	10·1331811	1163	9·8668189	23
38	9·8307837	1372	10·1692163	9·9640811	2535	10·0359189	10·1332974	1163	9·8667026	22
39	9·8309209	1371	10·1690791	9·9643346	2535	10·0356654	10·1334137	1164	9·8665863	21
40	9·8310580	1370	10·1689420	9·9645881	2535	10·0354119	10·1335301	1165	9·8664699	20
41	9·8311950	1370	10·1688050	9·9648416	2535	10·0351584	10·1336466	1165	9·8663534	19
42	9·8313320	1368	10·1686680	9·9650951	2535	10·0349049	10·1337631	1166	9·8662369	18
43	9·8314688	1368	10·1685312	9·9653486	2534	10·0346514	10·1338797	1167	9·8661203	17
44	9·8316056	1367	10·1683944	9·9656020	2535	10·0343980	10·1339964	1168	9·8660036	16
45	9·8317423	1366	10·1682577	9·9658555	2534	10·0341445	10·1341132	1168	9·8658868	15
46	9·8318789	1366	10·1681211	9·9661089	2534	10·0338911	10·1342300	1169	9·8657700	14
47	9·8320155	1364	10·1679845	9·9663623	2534	10·0336377	10·1343469	1169	9·8656531	13
48	9·8321519	1364	10·1678481	9·9666157	2535	10·0333843	10·1344638	1170	9·8655362	12
49	9·8322883	1363	10·1677117	9·9668692	2533	10·0331308	10·1345808	1171	9·8654192	11
50	9·8324246	1363	10·1675754	9·9671225	2534	10·0328775	10·1346979	1172	9·8653021	10
51	9·8325609	1361	10·1674391	9·9673759	2534	10·0326241	10·1348151	1172	9·8651849	9
52	9·8326970	1361	10·1673030	9·9676293	2534	10·0323707	10·1349323	1173	9·8650677	8
53	9·8328331	1360	10·1671669	9·9678827	2533	10·0321173	10·1350496	1173	9·8649504	7
54	9·8329691	1359	10·1670309	9·9681360	2533	10·0318640	10·1351669	1175	9·8648331	6
55	9·8331050	1358	10·1668950	9·9683893	2534	10·0316107	10·1352844	1175	9·8647156	5
56	9·8332408	1358	10·1667592	9·9686427	2533	10·0313573	10·1354019	1175	9·8645981	4
57	9·8333766	1356	10·1666234	9·9688960	2533	10·0311040	10·1355194	1177	9·8644806	3
58	9·8335122	1356	10·1664878	9·9691493	2533	10·0308507	10·1356371	1177	9·8643629	2
59	9·8336478	1355	10·1663522	9·9694026	2533	10·0305974	10·1357548	1177	9·8642452	1
60	9·8337833		10·1662167	9·9696559		10·0303441	10·1358725		9·8641275	0

′	Cosine	Diff.	Secant	Cotang.	Diff.	Tang.	Cosec.	Diff.	Sine	′

225

43 Deg.

′	Sine	Diff.	Cosec.	Tang.	Diff.	Cotang.	Secant	Diff.	Cosine	′
0	9·8337833	1355	10·1662167	9·9696559	2532	10·0303441	10·1358725	1179	9·8641275	60
1	9·8339188	1353	10·1660812	9·9699091	2533	10·0300909	10·1359904	1179	9·8640096	59
2	9·8340541	1353	10·1659459	9·9701624	2533	10·0298376	10·1361083	1180	9·8638917	58
3	9·8341894	1352	10·1658106	9·9704157	2532	10·0295843	10·1362263	1180	9·8637737	57
4	9·8343246	1351	10·1656754	9·9706689	2532	10·0293311	10·1363443	1181	9·8636557	56
5	9·8344597	1351	10·1655403	9·9709221	2533	10·0290779	10·1364624	1182	9·8635376	55
6	9·8345948	1349	10·1654052	9·9711754	2532	10·0288246	10·1365806	1183	9·8634194	54
7	9·8347297	1349	10·1652703	9·9714286	2632	10·0285714	10·1366989	1183	9·8633011	53
8	9·8348646	1348	10·1651354	9·9716818	2532	10·0283182	10·1368172	1184	9·8631828	52
9	9·8349994	1347	10·1650006	9·9719350	2532	10·0280650	10·1369356	1184	9·8630644	51
10	9·8351341	1347	10·1648659	9·9721882	2531	10·0278118	10·1370540	1186	9·8629460	50
11	9·8352688	1345	10·1647312	9·9724413	2532	10·0275587	10·1371726	1186	9·8628274	49
12	9·8354033	1345	10·1645967	9·9726945	2532	10·0273055	10·1372912	1186	9·8627088	48
13	9·8355378	1344	10·1644622	9·9729477	2531	10·0270523	10·1374098	1188	9·8625902	47
14	9·8356722	1344	10·1643278	9·9732008	2531	10·0267992	10·1375286	1188	9·8624714	46
15	9·8358066	1342	10·1641934	9·9734539	2532	10·0265461	10·1376474	1188	9·8623526	45
16	9·8359408	1342	10·1640592	9·9737071	2531	10·0262929	10·1377662	1190	9·8622338	44
17	9·8360750	1341	10·1639250	9·9739602	2531	10·0260398	10·1378852	1190	9·8621148	43
18	9·8362091	1340	10·1637909	9·9742133	2531	10·0257867	10·1380042	1191	9·8619958	42
19	9·8363431	1340	10·1636569	9·9744664	2531	10·0255336	10·1381233	1191	9·8618767	41
20	9·8364771	1338	10·1635229	9·9747195	2531	10·0252805	10·1382424	1193	9·8617576	40
21	9·8366109	1338	10·1633891	9·9749726	2531	10·0250274	10·1383617	1193	9·8616383	39
22	9·8367447	1337	10·1632553	9·9752257	2530	10·0247743	10·1384810	1193	9·8615190	38
23	9·8368784	1337	10·1631216	9·9754787	2531	10·0245213	10·1386003	1194	9·8613997	37
24	9·8370121	1335	10·1629879	9·9757318	2531	10·0242682	10·1387197	1195	9·8612803	36
25	9·8371456	1335	10·1628544	9·9759849	2530	10·0240151	10·1388392	1196	9·8611608	35
26	9·8372791	1334	10·1627209	9·9762379	2530	10·0237621	10·1389588	1197	9·8610412	34
27	9·8374125	1333	10·1625875	9·9764909	2531	10·0235091	10·1390785	1197	9·8609215	33
28	9·8375458	1332	10·1624542	9·9767440	2530	10·0232560	10·1391982	1197	9·8608018	32
29	9·8376790	1332	10·1623210	9·9769970	2530	10·0230030	10·1393179	1199	9·8606821	31
30	9·8378122	1331	10·1621878	9·9772500	2530	10·0227500	10·1394378	1199	9·8605622	30
31	9·8379453	1330	10·1620547	9·9775030	2530	10·0224970	10·1395577	1200	9·8604423	29
32	9·8380783	1329	10·1619217	9·9777560	2530	10·0222440	10·1396777	1201	9·8603223	28
33	9·8382112	1329	10·1617888	9·9780090	2530	10·0219910	10·1397978	1201	9·8602022	27
34	9·8383441	1328	10·1616559	9·9782620	2529	10·0217380	10·1399179	1202	9·8600821	26
35	9·8384769	1327	10·1615231	9·9785149	2530	10·0214851	10·1400381	1203	9·8599619	25
36	9·8386096	1326	10·1613904	9·9787679	2530	10·0212321	10·1401584	1203	9·8598416	24
37	9·8387422	1325	10·1612578	9·9790209	2529	10·0209791	10·1402787	1204	9·8597213	23
38	9·8388747	1325	10·1611253	9·9792738	2529	10·0207262	10·1403991	1205	9·8596009	22
39	9·8390072	1324	10·1609928	9·9795268	2529	10·0204732	10·1405196	1205	9·8594804.	21
40	9·8391396	1323	10·1608604	9·9797797	2529	10·0202203	10·1406401	1206	9·8593599	20
41	9·8392719	1322	10·1607281	9·9800326	2530	10·0199674	10·1407607	1207	9·8592393	19
42	9·8394041	1322	10·1605959	9·9802856	2529	10·0197144	10·1408814	1208	9·8591186	18
43	9·8395363	1321	10·1604637	9·9805385	2529	10·0194615	10·1410022	1208	9·8589978	17
44	9·8396684	1320	10·1603316	9·9807914	2529	10·0192086	10·1411230	1209	9·8588770	16
45	9·8398004	1319	10·1601996	9·9810443	2529	10·0189557	10·1412439	1210	9·8587561	15
46	9·8399323	1319	10·1600677	9·9812972	2529	10·0187028	10·1413649	1210	9·8586351	14
47	9·8400642	1317	10·1599358	9·9815501	2529	10·0184499	10·1414859	1212	9·8585141	13
48	9·8401959	1317	10·1598041	9·9818030	2529	10·0181970	10·1416071	1211	9·8583929	12
49	9·8403276	1317	10·1596724	9·9820559	2529	10·0179441	10·1417282	1213	9·8582718	11
50	9·8404593	1315	10·1595407	9·9823087	2529	10·0176913	10·1418495	1213	9·8581505	10
51	9·8405908	1315	10·1594092	9·9825616	2529	10·0174384	10·1419708	1214	9·8580292	9
52	9·8407223	1314	10·1592777	9·9828145	2528	10·0171855	10·1420922	1215	9·8579078	8
53	9·8408537	1313	10·1591463	9·9830673	2529	10·0169327	10·1422137	1215	9·8577863	7
54	9·8409850	1312	10·1590150	9·9833202	2528	10·0166798	10·1423352	1216	9·8576648	6
55	9·8411162	1312	10·1588838	9·9835730	2529	10·0164270	10·1424568	1217	9·8575432	5
56	9·8412474	1311	10·1587526	9·9838259	2528	10·0161741	10·1425785	1217	9·8574215	4
57	9·8413785	1310	10·1586215	9·9840787	2528	10·0159213	10·1427002	1219	9·8572998	3
58	9·8415095	1309	10·1584905	9·9843315	2529	10·0156685	10·1428221	1218	9·8571779	2
59	9·8416404	1309	10·1583596	9·9845844	2528	10·0154156	10·1429439	1220	9·8570561	1
60	9·8417713		10·1582287	9·9848372		10·0151628	10·1430659		9·8569341	0

′	Cosine	Diff.	Secant	Cotang.	Diff.	Tang.	Cosec.	Diff.	Sine	′

46 Deg.

′	Sine	Diff.	Cosec.	Tang.	Diff.	Cotang.	Secant	Diff.	Cosine	′
0	9·8417713	1308	10·1582287	9·9848372	2528	10·0151628	10·1430659	1220	9·8569341	60
1	9·8419021	1307	10·1580979	9·9850900	2528	10·0149100	10·1431879	1221	9·8568121	59
2	9·8420328	1306	10·1579672	9·9853428	2528	10·0146572	10·1433100	1222	9·8566900	58
3	9·8421634	1305	10·1578366	9·9855956	2528	10·0144044	10·1434322	1223	9·8565678	57
4	9·8422939	1305	10·1577061	9·9858484	2528	10·0141516	10·1435545	1223	9·8564455	56
5	9·8424244	1304	10·1575756	9·9861012	2528	10·0138988	10·1436768	1224	9·8563232	55
6	9·8425548	1303	10·1574452	9·9863540	2528	10·0136460	10·1437992	1224	9·8562008	54
7	9·8426851	1303	10·1573149	9·9866068	2528	10·0133932	10·1439216	1226	9·8560784	53
8	9·8428154	1302	10·1571846	9·9868596	2527	10·0131404	10·1440442	1226	9·8559558	52
9	9·8429456	1301	10·1570544	9·9871123	2528	10·0128877	10·1441668	1226	9·8558332	51
10	9·8430757	1300	10·1569243	9·9873651	2528	10·0126349	10·1442894	1228	9·8557106	50
11	9·8432057	1299	10·1567943	9·9876179	2527	10·0123821	10·1444122	1228	9·8555878	49
12	9·8433356	1299	10·1566644	9·9878706	2528	10·0121294	10·1445350	1229	9·8554650	48
13	9·8434655	1298	10·1565345	9·9881234	2527	10·0118766	10·1446579	1229	9·8553421	47
14	9·8435953	1297	10·1564047	9·9883761	2528	10·0116239	10·1447808	1231	9·8552192	46
15	9·8437250	1297	10·1562750	9·9886289	2527	10·0113711	10·1449039	1231	9·8550961	45
16	9·8438547	1295	10·1561453	9·9888816	2528	10·0111184	10·1450270	1231	9·8549730	44
17	9·8439842	1295	10·1560158	9·9891344	2527	10·0108656	10·1451501	1233	9·8548499	43
18	9·8441137	1295	10·1558863	9·9893871	2528	10·0106129	10·1452734	1233	9·8547266	42
19	9·8442432	1293	10·1557568	9·9896399	2527	10·0103601	10·1453967	1234	9·8546033	41
20	9·8443725	1293	10·1556275	9·9898926	2527	10·0101074	10·1455201	1235	9·8544799	40
21	9·8445018	1292	10·1554982	9·9901453	2528	10·0098547	10·1456436	1235	9·8543564	39
22	9·8446310	1291	10·1553690	9·9903981	2527	10·0096019	10·1457671	1236	9·8542329	38
23	9·8447601	1290	10·1552399	9·9906508	2527	10·0093492	10·1458907	1237	9·8541093	37
24	9·8448891	1290	10·1551109	9·9909035	2527	10·0090965	10·1460144	1237	9·8539856	36
25	9·8450181	1289	10·1549819	9·9911562	2527	10·0088438	10·1461381	1238	9·8538619	35
26	9·8451470	1288	10·1548530	9·9914089	2527	10·0085911	10·1462619	1239	9·8537381	34
27	9·8452758	1287	10·1547242	9·9916616	2527	10·0083384	10·1463858	1240	9·8536142	33
28	9·8454045	1287	10·1545955	9·9919143	2527	10·0080857	10·1465098	1240	9·8534902	32
29	9·8455332	1286	10·1544668	9·9921670	2527	10·0078330	10·1466338	1241	9·8533662	31
30	9·8456618	1285	10·1543382	9·9924197	2527	10·0075803	10·1467579	1242	9·8532421	30
31	9·8457903	1285	10·1542097	9·9926724	2527	10·0073276	10·1468821	1243	9·8531179	29
32	9·8459188	1283	10·1540812	9·9929251	2527	10·0070749	10·1470064	1243	9·8529936	28
33	9·8460471	1283	10·1539529	9·9931778	2527	10·0068222	10·1471307	1244	9·8528693	27
34	9·8461754	1282	10·1538246	9·9934305	2527	10·0065695	10·1472551	1245	9·8527449	26
35	9·8463036	1282	10·1536964	9·9936832	2527	10·0063168	10·1473796	1245	9·8526204	25
36	9·8464318	1281	10·1535682	9·9939359	2527	10·0060641	10·1475041	1246	9·8524959	24
37	9·8465599	1280	10·1534401	9·9941886	2527	10·0058114	10·1476287	1247	9·8523713	23
38	9·8466879	1279	10·1533121	9·9944413	2527	10·0055587	10·1477534	1248	9·8522466	22
39	9·8468158	1278	10·1531842	9·9946940	2526	10·0053060	10·1478782	1248	9·8521218	21
40	9·8469436	1278	10·1530564	9·9949466	2527	10·0050534	10·1480030	1249	9·8519970	20
41	9·8470714	1277	10·1529286	9·9951993	2527	10·0048007	10·1481279	1250	9·8518721	19
42	9·8471991	1276	10·1528009	9·9954520	2527	10·0045480	10·1482529	1251	9·8517471	18
43	9·8473267	1276	10·1526733	9·9957047	2526	10·0042953	10·1483780	1251	9·8516220	17
44	9·8474543	1274	10·1525457	9·9959573	2527	10·0040427	10·1485031	1252	9·8514969	16
45	9·8475817	1274	10·1524183	9·9962100	2527	10·0037900	10·1486283	1252	9·8513717	15
46	9·8477091	1274	10·1522909	9·9964627	2527	10·0035373	10·1487535	1254	9·8512465	14
47	9·8478365	1272	10·1521635	9·9967154	2526	10·0032846	10·1488789	1254	9·8511211	13
48	9·8479637	1272	10·1520363	9·9969680	2527	10·0030320	10·1490043	1255	9·8509957	12
49	9·8480909	1271	10·1519091	9·9972207	2527	10·0027793	10·1491298	1256	9·8508702	11
50	9·8482180	1270	10·1517820	9·9974734	2526	10·0025266	10·1492554	1256	9·8507446	10
51	9·8483450	1270	10·1516550	9·9977260	2527	10·0022740	10·1493810	1257	9·8506190	9
52	9·8484720	1269	10·1515280	9·9979787	2527	10·0020213	10·1495067	1258	9·8504933	8
53	9·8485989	1268	10·1514011	9·9982314	2526	10·0017686	10·1496325	1258	9·8503675	7
54	9·8487257	1267	10·1512743	9·9984840	2527	10·0015160	10·1497583	1260	9·8502417	6
55	9·8488524	1267	10·1511476	9·9987367	2526	10·0012633	10·1498843	1260	9·8501157	5
56	9·8489791	1266	10·1510209	9·9989893	2527	10·0010107	10·1500103	1260	9·8499897	4
57	9·8491057	1265	10·1508943	9·9992420	2527	10·0007580	10·1501363	1262	9·8498637	3
58	9·8492322	1264	10·1507678	9·9994947	2526	10·0005053	10·1502625	1262	9·8497375	2
59	9·8493586	1264	10·1506414	9·9997473	2527	10·0002527	10·1503887	1263	9·8496113	1
60	9·8494850		10·1505150	10·0000000		10·0000000	10·1505150		9·8494850	0

′	Cosine	Diff.	Secant	Cotang.	Diff.	Tang.	Cosec.	Diff.	Sine	′

′	0°	1°	2°	3°	4°	5°	6°	7°	″	
0	·0000000	·0174533	·0349066	·0523599	·0698132	·0872665	·1047198	·1221730	0	·0000000
1	·0002909	·0177442	·0351975	·0526508	·0701041	·0875574	·1050106	·1224639	1	·0000048
2	·0005818	·0180351	·0354884	·0529417	·0703949	·0878482	·1053015	·1227548	2	·0000097
3	·0008727	·0183260	·0357792	·0532325	·0706858	·0881391	·1055924	·1230457	3	·0000145
4	·0011636	·0186168	·0360701	·0535234	·0709767	·0884300	·1058833	·1233366	4	·0000194
5	·0014544	·0189077	·0363610	·0538143	·0712676	·0887209	·1061742	·1236275	5	·0000242
6	·0017453	·0191986	·0366519	·0541052	·0715585	·0890118	·1064651	·1239184	6	·0000291
7	·0020362	·0194895	·0369428	·0543961	·0718494	·0893027	·1067560	·1242093	7	·0000339
8	·0023271	·0197804	·0372337	·0546870	·0721403	·0895936	·1070469	·1245002	8	·0000388
9	·0026180	·0200713	·0375246	·0549779	·0724312	·0898845	·1073377	·1247910	9	·0000436
10	·0029089	·0203622	·0378155	·0552688	·0727221	·0901753	·1076286	·1250819	10	·0000485
11	·0031998	·0206531	·0381064	·0555596	·0730129	·0904662	·1079195	·1253728	11	·0000533
12	·0034907	·0209440	·0383972	·0558505	·0733038	·0907571	·1082104	·1256637	12	·0000582
13	·0037815	·0212348	·0386881	·0561414	·0735947	·0910480	·1085013	·1259546	13	·0000630
14	·0040724	·0215257	·0389790	·0564323	·0738856	·0913389	·1087922	·1262455	14	·0000679
15	·0043633	·0218166	·0392699	·0567232	·0741765	·0916298	·1090831	·1265364	15	·0000727
16	·0046542	·0221075	·0395608	·0570141	·0744674	·0919207	·1093740	·1268273	16	·0000776
17	·0049451	·0223984	·0398517	·0573050	·0747583	·0922116	·1096649	·1271181	17	·0000824
18	·0052360	·0226893	·0401426	·0575959	·0750492	·0925025	·1099557	·1274090	18	·0000873
19	·0055269	·0229802	·0404335	·0578868	·0753400	·0927933	·1102466	·1276999	19	·0000921
20	·0058178	·0232711	·0407243	·0581776	·0756309	·0930842	·1105375	·1279908	20	·0000970
21	·0061087	·0235619	·0410152	·0584685	·0759218	·0933751	·1108284	·1282817	21	·0001018
22	·0063995	·0238528	·0413061	·0587594	·0762127	·0936660	·1111193	·1285726	22	·0001067
23	·0066904	·0241437	·0415970	·0590503	·0765036	·0939569	·1114102	·1288635	23	·0001115
24	·0069813	·0244346	·0418879	·0593412	·0767945	·0942478	·1117011	·1291544	24	·0001164
25	·0072722	·0247255	·0421788	·0596321	·0770854	·0945387	·1119920	·1294453	25	·0001212
26	·0075631	·0250164	·0424697	·0599230	·0773763	·0948296	·1122828	·1297361	26	·0001261
27	·0078540	·0253073	·0427606	·0602139	·0776672	·0951204	·1125737	·1300270	27	·0001309
28	·0081449	·0255982	·0430515	·0605047	·0779580	·0954113	·1128646	·1303179	28	·0001357
29	·0084358	·0258891	·0433423	·0607956	·0782489	·0957022	·1131555	·1306088	29	·0001406
30	·0087266	·0261799	·0436332	·0610865	·0785398	·0959931	·1134464	·1308997	30	·0001454
31	·0090175	·0264708	·0439241	·0613774	·0788307	·0962840	·1137373	·1311906	31	·0001503
32	·0093084	·0267617	·0442150	·0616683	·0791216	·0965749	·1140282	·1314815	32	·0001551
33	·0095993	·0270526	·0445059	·0619592	·0794125	·0968658	·1143191	·1317724	33	·0001600
34	·0098902	·0273435	·0447968	·0622501	·0797034	·0971567	·1146100	·1320632	34	·0001648
35	·0101811	·0276344	·0450877	·0625410	·0799943	·0974475	·1149008	·1323541	35	·0001697
36	·0104720	·0279253	·0453786	·0628319	·0802851	·0977384	·1151917	·1326450	36	·0001745
37	·0107629	·0282162	·0456694	·0631227	·0805760	·0980293	·1154826	·1329359	37	·0001794
38	·0110538	·0285070	·0459603	·0634136	·0808669	·0983202	·1157735	·1332268	38	·0001842
39	·0113446	·0287979	·0462512	·0637045	·0811578	·0986111	·1160644	·1335177	39	·0001891
40	·0116355	·0290888	·0465421	·0639954	·0814487	·0989020	·1163553	·1338086	40	·0001939
41	·0119264	·0293797	·0468330	·0642863	·0817396	·0991929	·1166462	·1340995	41	·0001988
42	·0122173	·0296706	·0471239	·0645772	·0820305	·0994838	·1169371	·1343904	42	·0002036
43	·0125082	·0299615	·0474148	·0648681	·0823214	·0997747	·1172279	·1346812	43	·0002085
44	·0127991	·0302524	·0477057	·0651590	·0826123	·1000655	·1175188	·1349721	44	·0002133
45	·0130900	·0305433	·0479966	·0654498	·0829031	·1003564	·1178097	·1352630	45	·0002182
46	·0133809	·0308342	·0482874	·0657407	·0831940	·1006473	·1181006	·1355539	46	·0002230
47	·0136717	·0311250	·0485783	·0660316	·0834849	·1009382	·1183915	·1358448	47	·0002279
48	·0139626	·0314159	·0488692	·0663225	·0837758	·1012291	·1186824	·1361357	48	·0002327
49	·0142535	·0317068	·0491601	·0666134	·0840667	·1015200	·1189733	·1364266	49	·0002376
50	·0145444	·0319977	·0494510	·0669043	·0843576	·1018109	·1192642	·1367175	50	·0002424
51	·0148353	·0322886	·0497419	·0671952	·0846485	·1021018	·1195551	·1370083	51	·0002473
52	·0151262	·0325795	·0500328	·0674861	·0849394	·1023926	·1198459	·1372992	52	·0002521
53	·0154171	·0328704	·0503237	·0677770	·0852302	·1026835	·1201368	·1375901	53	·0002570
54	·0157080	·0331613	·0506145	·0680678	·0855211	·1029744	·1204277	·1378810	54	·0002618
55	·0159989	·0334521	·0509054	·0683587	·0858120	·1032653	·1207186	·1381719	55	·0002666
56	·0162897	·0337430	·0511963	·0686496	·0861029	·1035562	·1210095	·1384628	56	·0002715
57	·0165806	·0340339	·0514872	·0689405	·0863938	·1038471	·1213004	·1387537	57	·0002763
58	·0168715	·0343248	·0517781	·0692314	·0866847	·1041380	·1215913	·1390446	58	·0002812
59	·0171624	·0346157	·0520690	·0695223	·0869756	·1044289	·1218822	·1393355	59	·0002860
60	·0174533	·0349066	·0523599	·0698132	·0872665	·1047198	·1221730	·1396263	60	·0002909

'	8°	9°	10°	11°	12°	13°	14°	15°	"	
0	·1396263	·1570796	·1745329	·1919862	·2094395	·2268928	·2443461	·2617994	0	·0000000
1	·1399172	·1573705	·1748238	·1922771	·2097304	·2271837	·2446370	·2620903	1	·0000048
2	·1402081	·1576614	·1751147	·1925680	·2100213	·2274746	·2449279	·2623812	2	·0000097
3	·1404990	·1579523	·1754056	·1928589	·2103122	·2277655	·2452188	·2626721	3	·0000145
4	·1407899	·1582432	·1756965	·1931498	·2106031	·2280564	·2455096	·2629629	4	·0000194
5	·1410808	·1585341	·1759874	·1934407	·2108940	·2283472	·2458005	·2632538	5	·0000242
6	·1413717	·1588250	·1762783	·1937315	·2111848	·2286381	·2460914	·2635447	6	·0000291
7	·1416626	·1591159	·1765691	·1940224	·2114757	·2289290	·2463823	·2638356	7	·0000339
8	·1419534	·1594067	·1768600	·1943133	·2117666	·2292199	·2466732	·2641265	8	·0000388
9	·1422443	·1596976	·1771509	·1946042	·2120575	·2295108	·2469641	·2644174	9	·0000436
10	·1425352	·1599885	·1774418	·1948951	·2123484	·2298017	·2472550	·2647083	10	·0000485
11	·1428261	·1602794	·1777327	·1951860	·2126393	·2300926	·2475459	·2649992	11	·0000533
12	·1431170	·1605703	·1780236	·1954769	·2129302	·2303835	·2478368	·2652901	12	·0000582
13	·1434079	·1608612	·1783145	·1957678	·2132211	·2306743	·2481276	·2655809	13	·0000630
14	·1436988	·1611521	·1786054	·1960587	·2135119	·2309652	·2484185	·2658718	14	·0000679
15	·1439897	·1614430	·1788962	·1963495	·2138028	·2312561	·2487094	·2661627	15	·0000727
16	·1442806	·1617338	·1791871	·1966404	·2140937	·2315470	·2490003	·2664536	16	·0000776
17	·1445714	·1620247	·1794780	·1969313	·2143846	·2318379	·2492912	·2667445	17	·0000824
18	·1448623	·1623156	·1797689	·1972222	·2146755	·2321288	·2495821	·2670354	18	·0000873
19	·1451532	·1626065	·1800598	·1975131	·2149664	·2324197	·2498730	·2673263	19	·0000921
20	·1454441	·1628974	·1803507	·1978040	·2152573	·2327106	·2501639	·2676172	20	·0000970
21	·1457350	·1631883	·1806416	·1980949	·2155482	·2330015	·2504547	·2679080	21	·0001018
22	·1460259	·1634792	·1809325	·1983858	·2158391	·2332923	·2507456	·2681989	22	·0001067
23	·1463168	·1637701	·1812234	·1986766	·2161299	·2335832	·2510365	·2684898	23	·0001115
24	·1466077	·1640609	·1815142	·1989675	·2164208	·2338741	·2513274	·2687807	24	·0001164
25	·1468985	·1643518	·1818051	·1992584	·2167117	·2341650	·2516183	·2690716	25	·0001212
26	·1471894	·1646427	·1820960	·1995493	·2170026	·2344559	·2519092	·2693625	26	·0001261
27	·1474803	·1649336	·1823869	·1998402	·2172935	·2347468	·2522001	·2696534	27	·0001309
28	·1477712	·1652245	·1826778	·2001311	·2175844	·2350377	·2524910	·2699443	28	·0001357
29	·1480621	·1655154	·1829687	·2004220	·2178753	·2353286	·2527819	·2702351	29	·0001406
30	·1483530	·1658063	·1832596	·2007129	·2181662	·2356194	·2530727	·2705260	30	·0001454
31	·1486439	·1660972	·1835505	·2010038	·2184570	·2359103	·2533636	·2708169	31	·0001503
32	·1489348	·1663881	·1838413	·2012946	·2187479	·2362012	·2536545	·2711078	32	·0001551
33	·1492257	·1666789	·1841322	·2015855	·2190388	·2364921	·2539454	·2713987	33	·0001600
34	·1495165	·1669698	·1844231	·2018764	·2193297	·2367830	·2542363	·2716896	34	·0001648
35	·1498074	·1672607	·1847140	·2021673	·2196206	·2370739	·2545272	·2719805	35	·0001697
36	·1500983	·1675516	·1850049	·2024582	·2199115	·2373648	·2548181	·2722714	36	·0001745
37	·1503892	·1678425	·1852958	·2027491	·2202024	·2376557	·2551090	·2725623	37	·0001794
38	·1506801	·1681334	·1855867	·2030400	·2204933	·2379466	·2553998	·2728531	38	·0001842
39	·1509710	·1684243	·1858776	·2033309	·2207842	·2382374	·2556907	·2731440	39	·0001891
40	·1512619	·1687152	·1861685	·2036217	·2210750	·2385283	·2559816	·2734349	40	·0001939
41	·1515528	·1690060	·1864593	·2039126	·2213659	·2388192	·2562725	·2737258	41	·0001988
42	·1518436	·1692969	·1867502	·2042035	·2216568	·2391101	·2565634	·2740167	42	·0002036
43	·1521345	·1695878	·1870411	·2044944	·2219477	·2394010	·2568543	·2743076	43	·0002085
44	·1524254	·1698787	·1873320	·2047853	·2222386	·2396919	·2571452	·2745985	44	·0002133
45	·1527163	·1701696	·1876229	·2050762	·2225295	·2399828	·2574361	·2748894	45	·0002182
46	·1530072	·1704605	·1879138	·2053671	·2228204	·2402737	·2577270	·2751802	46	·0002230
47	·1532981	·1707514	·1882047	·2056580	·2231113	·2405645	·2580178	·2754711	47	·0002279
48	·1535890	·1710423	·1884956	·2059489	·2234021	·2408554	·2583087	·2757620	48	·0002327
49	·1538799	·1713332	·1887864	·2062397	·2236930	·2411463	·2585996	·2760529	49	·0002376
50	·1541708	·1716240	·1890773	·2065306	·2239839	·2414372	·2588905	·2763438	50	·0002424
51	·1544616	·1719149	·1893682	·2068215	·2242748	·2417281	·2591814	·2766347	51	·0002473
52	·1547525	·1722058	·1896591	·2071124	·2245657	·2420190	·2594723	·2769256	52	·0002521
53	·1550434	·1724967	·1899500	·2074033	·2248566	·2423099	·2597632	·2772165	53	·0002570
54	·1553343	·1727876	·1902409	·2076942	·2251475	·2426008	·2600541	·2775073	54	·0002618
55	·1556252	·1730785	·1905318	·2079851	·2254384	·2428917	·2603449	·2777982	55	·0002666
56	·1559161	·1733694	·1908227	·2082760	·2257292	·2431825	·2606358	·2780891	56	·0002715
57	·1562070	·1736603	·1911136	·2085668	·2260201	·2434734	·2609267	·2783800	57	·0002763
58	·1564979	·1739511	·1914044	·2088577	·2263110	·2437643	·2612176	·2786709	58	·0002812
59	·1567887	·1742420	·1916953	·2091486	·2266019	·2440552	·2615085	·2789618	59	·0002860
60	·1570796	·1745329	·1919862	·2094395	·2268928	·2443461	·2617994	·2792527	60	·0002909

′	16°	17°	18°	19°	20°	21°	22°	23°	″	
0	·2792527	·2967060	·3141593	·3316126	·3490659	·3665191	·3839724	·4014257	0	·0000000
1	·2795436	·2969969	·3144502	·3319034	·3493567	·3668100	·3842633	·4017166	1	·0000048
2	·2798345	·2972877	·3147410	·3321943	·3496476	·3671009	·3845542	·4020075	2	·0000097
3	·2801253	·2975786	·3150319	·3324852	·3499385	·3673918	·3848451	·4022984	3	·0000145
4	·2804162	·2978695	·3153228	·3327761	·3502294	·3676827	·3851360	·4025893	4	·0000194
5	·2807071	·2981604	·3156137	·3330670	·3505203	·3679736	·3854269	·4028802	5	·0000242
6	·2809980	·2984513	·3159046	·3333579	·3508112	·3682645	·3857178	·4031711	6	·0000291
7	·2812889	·2987422	·3161955	·3336488	·3511021	·3685554	·3860087	·4034619	7	·0000339
8	·2815798	·2990331	·3164864	·3339397	·3513930	·3688462	·3862995	·4037528	8	·0000388
9	·2818707	·2993240	·3167773	·3342306	·3516838	·3691371	·3865904	·4040437	9	·0000436
10	·2821616	·2996149	·3170681	·3345214	·3519747	·3694280	·3868813	·4043346	10	·0000485
11	·2824525	·2999057	·3173590	·3348123	·3522656	·3697189	·3871722	·4046255	11	·0000533
12	·2827433	·3001966	·3176499	·3351032	·3525565	·3700098	·3874631	·4049164	12	·0000582
13	·2830342	·3004875	·3179408	·3353941	·3528474	·3703007	·3877540	·4052073	13	·0000630
14	·2833251	·3007784	·3182317	·3356850	·3531383	·3705916	·3880449	·4054982	14	·0000679
15	·2836160	·3010693	·3185226	·3359759	·3534292	·3708825	·3883358	·4057891	15	·0000727
16	·2839069	·3013602	·3188135	·3362668	·3537201	·3711734	·3886266	·4060799	16	·0000776
17	·2841978	·3016511	·3191044	·3365577	·3540109	·3714642	·3889175	·4063708	17	·0000824
18	·2844887	·3019420	·3193953	·3368485	·3543018	·3717551	·3892084	·4066617	18	·0000873
19	·2847796	·3022328	·3196861	·3371394	·3545927	·3720460	·3894993	·4069526	19	·0000921
20	·2850704	·3025237	·3199770	·3374303	·3548836	·3723369	·3897902	·4072435	20	·0000970
21	·2853613	·3028146	·3202679	·3377212	·3551745	·3726278	·3900811	·4075344	21	·0001018
22	·2856522	·3031055	·3205588	·3380121	·3554654	·3729187	·3903720	·4078253	22	·0001067
23	·2859431	·3033964	·3208497	·3383030	·3557563	·3732096	·3906629	·4081162	23	·0001115
24	·2862340	·3036873	·3211406	·3385939	·3560472	·3735005	·3909538	·4084070	24	·0001164
25	·2865249	·3039782	·3214315	·3388848	·3563381	·3737913	·3912446	·4086979	25	·0001212
26	·2868158	·3042691	·3217224	·3391757	·3566289	·3740822	·3915355	·4089888	26	·0001261
27	·2871067	·3045600	·3220132	·3394665	·3569198	·3743731	·3918264	·4092797	27	·0001309
28	·2873976	·3048508	·3223041	·3397574	·3572107	·3746640	·3921173	·4095706	28	·0001357
29	·2876884	·3051417	·3225950	·3400483	·3575016	·3749549	·3924082	·4098615	29	·0001406
30	·2879793	·3054326	·3228859	·3403392	·3577925	·3752458	·3926991	·4101524	30	·0001454
31	·2882702	·3057235	·3231767	·3406301	·3580834	·3755367	·3929900	·4104433	31	·0001503
32	·2885611	·3060144	·3234677	·3409210	·3583743	·3758276	·3932809	·4107342	32	·0001551
33	·2888520	·3063053	·3237586	·3412119	·3586652	·3761185	·3935717	·4110250	33	·0001600
34	·2891429	·3065962	·3240495	·3415028	·3589560	·3764093	·3938626	·4113159	34	·0001648
35	·2894338	·3068871	·3243404	·3417936	·3592469	·3767002	·3941535	·4116068	35	·0001697
36	·2897247	·3071779	·3246312	·3420845	·3595378	·3769911	·3944444	·4118977	36	·0001745
37	·2900155	·3074688	·3249221	·3423754	·3598287	·3772820	·3947353	·4121886	37	·0001794
38	·2903064	·3077597	·3252130	·3426663	·3601196	·3775729	·3950262	·4124795	38	·0001842
39	·2905973	·3080506	·3255039	·3429572	·3604105	·3778638	·3953171	·4127704	39	·0001891
40	·2908882	·3083415	·3257948	·3432481	·3607014	·3781547	·3956080	·4130613	40	·0001939
41	·2911791	·3086324	·3260857	·3435390	·3609923	·3784456	·3958989	·4133521	41	·0001988
42	·2914700	·3089233	·3263766	·3438299	·3612832	·3787364	·3961897	·4136430	42	·0002036
43	·2917609	·3092142	·3266675	·3441207	·3615740	·3790273	·3964806	·4139339	43	·0002085
44	·2920518	·3095051	·3269583	·3444116	·3618649	·3793182	·3967715	·4142248	44	·0002133
45	·2923426	·3097959	·3272492	·3447025	·3621558	·3796091	·3970624	·4145157	45	·0002182
46	·2926335	·3100868	·3275401	·3449934	·3624467	·3799000	·3973533	·4148066	46	·0002230
47	·2929244	·3103777	·3278310	·3452843	·3627376	·3801909	·3976442	·4150975	47	·0002279
48	·2932153	·3106686	·3281219	·3455752	·3630285	·3804818	·3979351	·4153884	48	·0002327
49	·2935062	·3109595	·3284128	·3458661	·3633194	·3807727	·3982260	·4156793	49	·0002376
50	·2937971	·3112504	·3287037	·3461570	·3636103	·3810636	·3985163	·4159701	50	·0002424
51	·2940880	·3115413	·3289946	·3464479	·3639011	·3813544	·3988077	·4162610	51	·0002473
52	·2943789	·3118322	·3292855	·3467387	·3641920	·3816453	·3990986	·4165519	52	·0002521
53	·2946698	·3121230	·3295763	·3470296	·3644829	·3819362	·3993895	·4168428	53	·0002570
54	·2949606	·3124139	·3298672	·3473205	·3647738	·3822271	·3996804	·4171337	54	·0002618
55	·2952515	·3127048	·3301581	·3476114	·3650647	·3825180	·3999713	·4174246	55	·0002666
56	·2955424	·3129957	·3304490	·3479023	·3653556	·3828089	·4002622	·4177155	56	·0002715
57	·2958333	·3132866	·3307399	·3481932	·3656465	·3830998	·4005531	·4180064	57	·0002763
58	·2961242	·3135775	·3310308	·3484841	·3659374	·3833907	·4008440	·4182972	58	·0002812
59	·2964151	·3138684	·3313217	·3487750	·3662283	·3836815	·4011348	·4185881	59	·0002860
60	·2967060	·3141593	·3316126	·3490659	·3665191	·3839724	·4014257	·4188790	60	·0002909

′	24°	25°	26°	27°	28°	29°	30°	31°	″	
0	·4188790	·4363323	·4537856	·4712389	·4886922	·5061455	·5235988	·5410521	0	·0000000
1	·4191699	·4366232	·4540765	·4715298	·4889831	·5064364	·5238897	·5413429	1	·0000048
2	·4194608	·4369141	·4543674	·4718207	·4892740	·5067273	·5241806	·5416338	2	·0000097
3	·4197517	·4372050	·4546583	·4721116	·4895649	·5070181	·5244714	·5419247	3	·0000145
4	·4200426	·4374959	·4549492	·4724025	·4898557	·5073090	·5247623	·5422156	4	·0000194
5	·4203335	·4377868	·4552400	·4726933	·4901466	·5075999	·5250532	·5425065	5	·0000242
6	·4206243	·4380776	·4555309	·4729842	·4904375	·5078908	·5253441	·5427974	6	·0000291
7	·4209152	·4383685	·4558218	·4732751	·4907284	·5081817	·5256350	·5430883	7	·0000339
8	·4212061	·4386594	·4561127	·4735660	·4910193	·5084726	·5259259	·5433792	8	·0000388
9	·4214970	·4389503	·4564036	·4738569	·4913102	·5087635	·5262168	·5436701	9	·0000436
10	·4217879	·4392412	·4566945	·4741478	·4916011	·5090544	·5265077	·5439610	10	·0000485
11	·4220788	·4395321	·4569854	·4744387	·4918920	·5093453	·5267985	·5442518	11	·0000533
12	·4223697	·4398230	·4572763	·4747296	·4921828	·5096361	·5270894	·5445427	12	·0000582
13	·4226606	·4401139	·4575672	·4750204	·4924737	·5099270	·5273803	·5448336	13	·0000630
14	·4229515	·4404047	·4578580	·4753113	·4927646	·5102179	·5276712	·5451245	14	·0000679
15	·4232423	·4406956	·4581489	·4756022	·4930555	·5105088	·5279621	·5454154	15	·0000727
16	·4235332	·4409865	·4584398	·4758931	·4933464	·5107997	·5282530	·5457063	16	·0000776
17	·4238241	·4412774	·4587307	·4761840	·4936373	·5110906	·5285439	·5459972	17	·0000824
18	·4241150	·4415683	·4590216	·4764749	·4939282	·5113815	·5288348	·5462880	18	·0000873
19	·4244059	·4418592	·4593125	·4767658	·4942191	·5116724	·5291257	·5465789	19	·0000921
20	·4246968	·4421501	·4596034	·4770567	·4945100	·5119632	·5294165	·5468698	20	·0000970
21	·4249877	·4424409	·4598943	·4773476	·4948008	·5122541	·5297074	·5471607	21	·0001018
22	·4252786	·4427318	·4601851	·4776384	·4950917	·5125450	·5299983	·5474516	22	·0001067
23	·4255694	·4430227	·4604760	·4779293	·4953826	·5128359	·5302892	·5477425	23	·0001115
24	·4258603	·4433136	·4607669	·4782202	·4956735	·5131268	·5305801	·5480334	24	·0001164
25	·4261512	·4436045	·4610578	·4785111	·4959644	·5134177	·5308710	·5483243	25	·0001212
26	·4264421	·4438954	·4613487	·4788020	·4962553	·5137086	·5311619	·5486152	26	·0001261
27	·4267330	·4441863	·4616396	·4790929	·4965462	·5139995	·5314527	·5489060	27	·0001309
28	·4270239	·4444772	·4619305	·4793838	·4968371	·5142904	·5317436	·5491969	28	·0001357
29	·4273148	·4447681	·4622214	·4796747	·4971279	·5145812	·5320345	·5494878	29	·0001406
30	·4276057	·4450590	·4625123	·4799655	·4974188	·5148721	·5323254	·5497787	30	·0001454
31	·4278966	·4453498	·4628031	·4802564	·4977097	·5151630	·5326163	·5500696	31	·0001503
32	·4281874	·4456407	·4630940	·4805473	·4980006	·5154539	·5329072	·5503605	32	·0001551
33	·4284783	·4459316	·4633849	·4808382	·4982915	·5157448	·5331981	·5506514	33	·0001600
34	·4287692	·4462225	·4636758	·4811291	·4985824	·5160357	·5334890	·5509423	34	·0001648
35	·4290601	·4465134	·4639667	·4814200	·4988733	·5163266	·5337798	·5512332	35	·0001697
36	·4293510	·4468043	·4642576	·4817109	·4991642	·5166175	·5340707	·5515240	36	·0001745
37	·4296419	·4470952	·4645485	·4820018	·4994551	·5169083	·5343616	·5518149	37	·0001794
38	·4299328	·4473861	·4648394	·4822926	·4997459	·5171992	·5346525	·5521058	38	·0001842
39	·4302237	·4476770	·4651302	·4825835	·5000368	·5174901	·5349434	·5523967	39	·0001891
40	·4305145	·4479678	·4654211	·4828744	·5003277	·5177810	·5352343	·5526876	40	·0001939
41	·4308054	·4482587	·4657120	·4831653	·5006186	·5180719	·5355252	·5529785	41	·0001988
42	·4310963	·4485496	·4660029	·4834562	·5009095	·5183628	·5358161	·5532694	42	·0002036
43	·4313872	·4488405	·4662938	·4837471	·5012004	·5186537	·5361070	·5535603	43	·0002085
44	·4316781	·4491314	·4665847	·4840380	·5014913	·5189446	·5363979	·5538511	44	·0002133
45	·4319690	·4494223	·4668756	·4843289	·5017822	·5192355	·5366887	·5541420	45	·0002182
46	·4322599	·4497132	·4671665	·4846198	·5020730	·5195263	·5369796	·5544329	46	·0002230
47	·4325508	·4500041	·4674574	·4849106	·5023639	·5198172	·5372705	·5547238	47	·0002279
48	·4328417	·4502949	·4677482	·4852015	·5026548	·5201081	·5375614	·5550147	48	·0002327
49	·4331325	·4505858	·4680391	·4854924	·5029457	·5203990	·5378523	·5553056	49	·0002376
50	·4334234	·4508767	·4683300	·4857833	·5032366	·5206899	·5381432	·5555965	50	·0002424
51	·4337143	·4511676	·4686209	·4860742	·5035275	·5209808	·5384341	·5558874	51	·0002473
52	·4340052	·4514585	·4689118	·4863651	·5038184	·5212717	·5387250	·5561783	52	·0002521
53	·4342961	·4517494	·4692027	·4866560	·5041093	·5215626	·5390159	·5564691	53	·0002570
54	·4345870	·4520403	·4694936	·4869469	·5044002	·5218534	·5393067	·5567600	54	·0002618
55	·4348779	·4523312	·4697845	·4872377	·5046910	·5221443	·5395976	·5570509	55	·0002666
56	·4351688	·4526221	·4700753	·4875286	·5049819	·5224352	·5398885	·5573418	56	·0002715
57	·4354596	·4529129	·4703662	·4878195	·5052728	·5227261	·5401794	·5576327	57	·0002763
58	·4357505	·4532038	·4706571	·4881104	·5055637	·5230170	·5404703	·5579236	58	·0002812
59	·4360414	·4534947	·4709480	·4884013	·5058546	·5233079	·5407612	·5582145	59	·0002860
60	·4363323	·4537856	·4712389	·4886922	·5061455	·5235988	·5410521	·5585054	60	·0002909

′	32°	33°	34°	35°	36°	37°	38°	39°	″	
0	·5585054	·5759587	·5934119	·6108652	·6283185	·6457718	·6632251	·6806784	0	·0000000
1	·5587962	·5762495	·5937028	·6111561	·6286094	·6460627	·6635160	·6809693	1	·0000048
2	·5590871	·5765404	·5939937	·6114470	·6289003	·6463536	·6638069	·6812602	2	·0000097
3	·5593780	·5768313	·5942846	·6117379	·6291912	·6466445	·6640978	·6815511	3	·0000145
4	·5596689	·5771222	·5945755	·6120288	·6294821	·6469354	·6643887	·6818420	4	·0000194
5	·5599598	·5774131	·5948664	·6123197	·6297730	·6472263	·6646796	·6821328	5	·0000242
6	·5602507	·5777040	·5951573	·6126106	·6300639	·6475172	·6649704	·6824237	6	·0000291
7	·5605416	·5779949	·5954482	·6129015	·6303547	·6478080	·6652613	·6827146	7	·0000339
8	·5608325	·5782858	·5957391	·6131923	·6306456	·6480989	·6655522	·6830055	8	·0000388
9	·5611233	·5785766	·5960299	·6134832	·6309365	·6483898	·6658431	·6832964	9	·0000436
10	·5614142	·5788675	·5963208	·6137741	·6312274	·6486807	·6661340	·6835873	10	·0000485
11	·5617051	·5791584	·5966117	·6140650	·6315183	·6489716	·6664249	·6838782	11	·0000533
12	·5619960	·5794493	·5969026	·6143559	·6318092	·6492625	·6667158	·6841691	12	·0000582
13	·5622869	·5797402	·5971935	·6146468	·6321001	·6495534	·6670067	·6844600	13	·0000630
14	·5625778	·5800311	·5974844	·6149377	·6323910	·6498443	·6672976	·6847508	14	·0000679
15	·5628687	·5803220	·5977753	·6152286	·6326819	·6501351	·6675884	·6850417	15	·0000727
16	·5631596	·5806129	·5980662	·6155194	·6329727	·6504260	·6678793	·6853326	16	·0000776
17	·5634505	·5809038	·5983570	·6158103	·6332636	·6507169	·6681702	·6856235	17	·0000824
18	·5637413	·5811946	·5986479	·6161012	·6335545	·6510078	·6684611	·6859144	18	·0000873
19	·5640322	·5814855	·5989388	·6163921	·6338454	·6512987	·6687520	·6862053	19	·0000921
20	·5643231	·5817764	·5992297	·6166830	·6341363	·6515896	·6690429	·6864962	20	·0000970
21	·5646140	·5820673	·5995206	·6169739	·6344272	·6518805	·6693338	·6867871	21	·0001018
22	·5649049	·5823582	·5998115	·6172648	·6347181	·6521714	·6696247	·6870779	22	·0001067
23	·5651958	·5826491	·6001024	·6175557	·6350090	·6524623	·6699155	·6873688	23	·0001115
24	·5654867	·5829400	·6003933	·6178466	·6352998	·6527531	·6702064	·6876597	24	·0001164
25	·5657776	·5832309	·6006842	·6181374	·6355907	·6530440	·6704973	·6879506	25	·0001212
26	·5660685	·5835217	·6009750	·6184283	·6358816	·6533349	·6707882	·6882415	26	·0001261
27	·5663593	·5838126	·6012659	·6187192	·6361725	·6536258	·6710791	·6885324	27	·0001309
28	·5666502	·5841035	·6015568	·6190101	·6364634	·6539167	·6713700	·6888233	28	·0001357
29	·5669411	·5843944	·6018477	·6193010	·6367543	·6542076	·6716609	·6891142	29	·0001406
30	·5672320	·5846853	·6021386	·6195919	·6370452	·6544985	·6719518	·6894051	30	·0001454
31	·5675229	·5849762	·6024295	·6198828	·6373361	·6547894	·6722427	·6896959	31	·0001503
32	·5678138	·5852671	·6027204	·6201737	·6376270	·6550803	·6725335	·6899868	32	·0001551
33	·5681047	·5855580	·6030113	·6204645	·6379178	·6553711	·6728244	·6902777	33	·0001600
34	·5683955	·5858489	·6033022	·6207554	·6382087	·6556620	·6731153	·6905686	34	·0001648
35	·5686864	·5861397	·6035930	·6210463	·6384996	·6559529	·6734062	·6908595	35	·0001697
36	·5689773	·5864306	·6038839	·6213372	·6387905	·6562438	·6736971	·6911504	36	·0001745
37	·5692682	·5867215	·6041748	·6216281	·6390814	·6565347	·6739880	·6914413	37	·0001794
38	·5695591	·5870124	·6044657	·6219190	·6393723	·6568256	·6742789	·6917322	38	·0001842
39	·5698500	·5873033	·6047566	·6222099	·6396632	·6571165	·6745698	·6920230	39	·0001891
40	·5701409	·5875942	·6050475	·6225008	·6399541	·6574074	·6748606	·6923139	40	·0001939
41	·5704318	·5878851	·6053384	·6227917	·6402449	·6576982	·6751515	·6926048	41	·0001988
42	·5707227	·5881760	·6056293	·6230825	·6405358	·6579891	·6754424	·6928957	42	·0002036
43	·5710135	·5884668	·6059201	·6233734	·6408267	·6582800	·6757333	·6931866	43	·0002085
44	·5713044	·5887577	·6062110	·6236643	·6411176	·6585709	·6760242	·6934775	44	·0002133
45	·5715953	·5890486	·6065019	·6239552	·6414085	·6588618	·6763151	·6937684	45	·0002182
46	·5718862	·5893395	·6067928	·6242461	·6416994	·6591527	·6766060	·6940593	46	·0002230
47	·5721771	·5896304	·6070837	·6245370	·6419903	·6594436	·6768969	·6943502	47	·0002279
48	·5724680	·5899213	·6073746	·6248279	·6422812	·6597345	·6771877	·6946410	48	·0002327
49	·5727589	·5902122	·6076655	·6251188	·6425721	·6600253	·6774786	·6949319	49	·0002376
50	·5730498	·5905031	·6079564	·6254096	·6428629	·6603162	·6777695	·6952228	50	·0002424
51	·5733407	·5907940	·6082472	·6257005	·6431538	·6606071	·6780604	·6955137	51	·0002473
52	·5736315	·5910848	·6085381	·6259914	·6434447	·6608980	·6783513	·6958046	52	·0002521
53	·5739224	·5913757	·6088290	·6262823	·6437356	·6611889	·6786422	·6960955	53	·0002570
54	·5742133	·5916666	·6091199	·6265732	·6440265	·6614798	·6789331	·6963864	54	·0002618
55	·5745042	·5919575	·6094108	·6268641	·6443174	·6617707	·6792240	·6966773	55	·0002666
56	·5747951	·5922484	·6097017	·6271550	·6446083	·6620616	·6795149	·6969681	56	·0002715
57	·5750860	·5925393	·6099926	·6274459	·6448992	·6623525	·6798057	·6972590	57	·0002763
58	·5753769	·5928302	·6102835	·6277368	·6451900	·6626433	·6800966	·6975499	58	·0002812
59	·5756678	·5931211	·6105743	·6280276	·6454809	·6629342	·6803875	·6978408	59	·0002860
60	·5759587	·5934119	·6108652	·6283185	·6457718	·6632251	·6806784	·6981317	60	·0002909

CIRCULAR MEASURE OF ANGLES,

′	40°	41°	42°	43°	44°	45°	46°	47°	″	
0	·6981317	·7155850	·7330383	·7504916	·7679449	·7853982	·8028515	·8203047	0	·0000000
1	·6984226	·7158759	·7333292	·7507825	·7682358	·7856891	·8031423	·8205956	1	·0000048
2	·6987135	·7161668	·7336201	·7510734	·7685266	·7859799	·8034332	·8208865	2	·0000097
3	·6990044	·7164577	·7339110	·7513642	·7688175	·7862708	·8037241	·8211774	3	·0000145
4	·6992953	·7167485	·7342018	·7516551	·7691084	·7865617	·8040150	·8214683	4	·0000194
5	·6995861	·7170394	·7344927	·7519460	·7693993	·7868526	·8043059	·8217592	5	·0000242
6	·6998770	·7173303	·7347836	·7522369	·7696902	·7871435	·8045968	·8220501	6	·0000291
7	·7001679	·7176212	·7350745	·7525278	·7699811	·7874344	·8048877	·8223410	7	·0000339
8	·7004588	·7179121	·7353654	·7528187	·7702720	·7877253	·8051785	·8226319	8	·0000388
9	·7007497	·7182030	·7356563	·7531096	·7705629	·7880162	·8054694	·8229227	9	·0000436
10	·7010406	·7184939	·7359472	·7534005	·7708538	·7883070	·8057603	·8232136	10	·0000485
11	·7013315	·7187848	·7362381	·7536913	·7711446	·7885979	·8060512	·8235045	11	·0000533
12	·7016224	·7190757	·7365289	·7539822	·7714355	·7888888	·8063421	·8237954	12	·0000582
13	·7019132	·7193665	·7368198	·7542731	·7717264	·7891797	·8066330	·8240863	13	·0000630
14	·7022041	·7196574	·7371107	·7545640	·7720173	·7894706	·8069239	·8243772	14	·0000679
15	·7024950	·7199483	·7374016	·7548549	·7723082	·7897615	·8072148	·8246681	15	·0000727
16	·7027859	·7202392	·7376925	·7551458	·7725991	·7900524	·8075057	·8249590	16	·0000776
17	·7030768	·7205301	·7379834	·7554367	·7728900	·7903433	·8077966	·8252498	17	·0000824
18	·7033677	·7208210	·7382743	·7557276	·7731809	·7906342	·8080874	·8255407	18	·0000873
19	·7036586	·7211119	·7385652	·7560185	·7734717	·7909250	·8083783	·8258316	19	·0000921
20	·7039495	·7214028	·7388561	·7563093	·7737626	·7912159	·8086692	·8261225	20	·0000970
21	·7042404	·7216936	·7391469	·7566002	·7740535	·7915068	·8089601	·8264134	21	·0001018
22	·7045312	·7219845	·7394378	·7568911	·7743444	·7917977	·8092510	·8267043	22	·0001067
23	·7048221	·7222754	·7397287	·7571820	·7746353	·7920886	·8095419	·8269952	23	·0001115
24	·7051130	·7225663	·7400196	·7574729	·7749262	·7923795	·8098328	·8272861	24	·0001164
25	·7054039	·7228572	·7403105	·7577638	·7752171	·7926704	·8101237	·8275770	25	·0001212
26	·7056948	·7231481	·7406014	·7580547	·7755080	·7929613	·8104145	·8278678	26	·0001261
27	·7059857	·7234390	·7408923	·7583456	·7757989	·7932521	·8107054	·8281587	27	·0001309
28	·7062766	·7237299	·7411832	·7586364	·7760897	·7935430	·8109963	·8284496	28	·0001357
29	·7065675	·7240208	·7414740	·7589273	·7763806	·7938339	·8112872	·8287405	29	·0001406
30	·7068583	·7243116	·7417649	·7592182	·7766715	·7941248	·8115781	·8290314	30	·0001454
31	·7071492	·7246025	·7420558	·7595091	·7769624	·7944157	·8118690	·8293223	31	·0001503
32	·7074401	·7248934	·7423467	·7598000	·7772533	·7947066	·8121599	·8296132	32	·0001551
33	·7077310	·7251843	·7426376	·7600909	·7775442	·7949975	·8124508	·8299041	33	·0001600
34	·7080219	·7254752	·7429285	·7603818	·7778351	·7952884	·8127417	·8301949	34	·0001648
35	·7083128	·7257661	·7432194	·7606727	·7781260	·7955793	·8130325	·8304858	35	·0001697
36	·7086037	·7260570	·7435103	·7609635	·7784168	·7958701	·8133234	·8307767	36	·0001745
37	·7088946	·7263479	·7438011	·7612544	·7787077	·7961610	·8136143	·8310676	37	·0001794
38	·7091855	·7266387	·7440920	·7615453	·7789986	·7964519	·8139052	·8313585	38	·0001842
39	·7094763	·7269296	·7443829	·7618362	·7792895	·7967428	·8141961	·8316494	39	·0001891
40	·7097672	·7272205	·7446738	·7621271	·7795804	·7970337	·8144870	·8319403	40	·0001939
41	·7100581	·7275114	·7449647	·7624180	·7798713	·7973246	·8147779	·8322312	41	·0001988
42	·7103490	·7278023	·7452556	·7627089	·7801622	·7976155	·8150688	·8325220	42	·0002036
43	·7106399	·7280932	·7455465	·7629998	·7804531	·7979064	·8153596	·8328129	43	·0002085
44	·7109308	·7283841	·7458374	·7632907	·7807439	·7981972	·8156505	·8331038	44	·0002133
45	·7112217	·7286750	·7461283	·7635815	·7810348	·7984881	·8159414	·8333947	45	·0002182
46	·7115126	·7289659	·7464192	·7638724	·7813257	·7987790	·8162323	·8336856	46	·0002230
47	·7118034	·7292567	·7467100	·7641633	·7816166	·7990699	·8165232	·8339765	47	·0002279
48	·7120943	·7295476	·7470009	·7644542	·7819075	·7993608	·8168141	·8342674	48	·0002327
49	·7123852	·7298385	·7472918	·7647451	·7821984	·7996517	·8171050	·8345583	49	·0002376
50	·7126761	·7301294	·7475827	·7650360	·7824893	·7999426	·8173959	·8348492	50	·0002424
51	·7129670	·7304203	·7478736	·7653269	·7827802	·8002335	·8176868	·8351400	51	·0002473
52	·7132579	·7307112	·7481645	·7656178	·7830711	·8005244	·8179776	·8354309	52	·0002521
53	·7135488	·7310021	·7484554	·7659086	·7833619	·8008152	·8182685	·8357218	53	·0002570
54	·7138397	·7312930	·7487462	·7661995	·7836528	·8011061	·8185594	·8360127	54	·0002618
55	·7141306	·7315838	·7490371	·7664904	·7839437	·8013970	·8188503	·8363036	55	·0002666
56	·7144214	·7318747	·7493280	·7667813	·7842346	·8016879	·8191412	·8365945	56	·0002715
57	·7147123	·7321656	·7496189	·7670722	·7845255	·8019788	·8194321	·8368854	57	·0002763
58	·7150032	·7324565	·7499098	·7673631	·7848164	·8022697	·8197230	·8371763	58	·0002812
59	·7152941	·7327474	·7502007	·7676540	·7851073	·8025606	·8200139	·8374672	59	·0002860
60	·7155850	·7330383	·7504916	·7679449	·7853982	·8028515	·8203047	·8377580	60	·0002909

′	48°	49°	50°	51°	52°	53°	54°	55°	″	
0	·8377580	·8552113	·8726646	·8901179	·9075712	·9250245	·9424778	·9599311	0	·0000000
1	·8380489	·8555022	·8729555	·8904088	·9078621	·9253154	·9427687	·9602220	1	·0000048
2	·8383398	·8557931	·8732464	·8906997	·9081530	·9256063	·9430596	·9605129	2	·0000097
3	·8386307	·8560840	·8735373	·8909906	·9084439	·9258972	·9433505	·9608038	3	·0000145
4	·8389216	·8563749	·8738282	·8912815	·9087348	·9261881	·9436414	·9610946	4	·0000194
5	·8392125	·8566658	·8741191	·8915724	·9090257	·9264789	·9439323	·9613855	5	·0000242
6	·8395034	·8569567	·8744100	·8918632	·9093165	·9267698	·9442231	·9616764	6	·0000291
7	·8397943	·8572476	·8747008	·8921541	·9096074	·9270607	·9445140	·9619673	7	·0000339
8	·8400851	·8575384	·8749917	·8924450	·9098983	·9273516	·9448049	·9622582	8	·0000388
9	·8403760	·8578293	·8752826	·8927359	·9101892	·9276425	·9450958	·9625491	9	·0000436
10	·8406669	·8581202	·8755735	·8930268	·9104801	·9279334	·9453867	·9628400	10	·0000485
11	·8409578	·8584111	·8758644	·8933177	·9107710	·9282243	·9456776	·9631309	11	·0000533
12	·8412487	·8587020	·8761553	·8936086	·9110619	·9285152	·9459685	·9634217	12	·0000582
13	·8415396	·8589929	·8764462	·8938995	·9113528	·9288061	·9462593	·9637126	13	·0000630
14	·8418305	·8592838	·8767371	·8941904	·9116436	·9290969	·9465502	·9640035	14	·0000679
15	·8421214	·8595747	·8770279	·8944812	·9119345	·9293878	·9468411	·9642944	15	·0000727
16	·8424123	·8598655	·8773188	·8947721	·9122254	·9296787	·9471320	·9645853	16	·0000776
17	·8427031	·8601564	·8776097	·8950630	·9125163	·9299696	·9474229	·9648762	17	·0000824
18	·8429940	·8604473	·8779006	·8953539	·9128072	·9302605	·9477138	·9651671	18	·0000873
19	·8432849	·8607382	·8781915	·8956448	·9130981	·9305514	·9480047	·9654580	19	·0000921
20	·8435758	·8610291	·8784824	·8959357	·9133890	·9308423	·9482956	·9657489	20	·0000970
21	·8438667	·8613200	·8787733	·8962266	·9136799	·9311332	·9485864	·9660397	21	·0001018
22	·8441576	·8616109	·8790642	·8965175	·9139708	·9314240	·9488773	·9663306	22	·0001067
23	·8444485	·8619018	·8793551	·8968083	·9142616	·9317149	·9491682	·9666215	23	·0001115
24	·8447394	·8621927	·8796459	·8970992	·9145525	·9320058	·9494591	·9669124	24	·0001164
25	·8450302	·8624835	·8799368	·8973901	·9148434	·9322967	·9497500	·9672033	25	·0001212
26	·8453211	·8627744	·8802277	·8976810	·9151343	·9325876	·9500409	·9674942	26	·0001261
27	·8456120	·8630653	·8805186	·8979719	·9154252	·9328785	·9503318	·9677851	27	·0001309
28	·8459029	·8633562	·8808095	·8982628	·9157161	·9331694	·9506227	·9680760	28	·0001357
29	·8461938	·8636471	·8811004	·8985537	·9160070	·9334603	·9509136	·9683668	29	·0001406
30	·8464847	·8639380	·8813913	·8988446	·9162979	·9337511	·9512044	·9686577	30	·0001454
31	·8467756	·8642289	·8816822	·8991355	·9165887	·9340420	·9514953	·9689486	31	·0001503
32	·8470665	·8645198	·8819730	·8994263	·9168796	·9343329	·9517862	·9692395	32	·0001551
33	·8473574	·8648106	·8822639	·8997172	·9171705	·9346238	·9520771	·9695304	33	·0001600
34	·8476482	·8651015	·8825548	·9000081	·9174614	·9349147	·9523680	·9698213	34	·0001648
35	·8479391	·8653924	·8828457	·9002990	·9177523	·9352056	·9526589	·9701122	35	·0001697
36	·8482300	·8656833	·8831366	·9005899	·9180432	·9354965	·9529498	·9704031	36	·0001745
37	·8485209	·8659742	·8834275	·9008808	·9183341	·9357874	·9532407	·9706940	37	·0001794
38	·8488118	·8662651	·8837184	·9011717	·9186250	·9360783	·9535315	·9709848	38	·0001842
39	·8491027	·8665560	·8840093	·9014626	·9189159	·9363691	·9538224	·9712757	39	·0001891
40	·8493936	·8668469	·8843002	·9017534	·9192067	·9366600	·9541133	·9715666	40	·0001939
41	·8496845	·8671378	·8845910	·9020443	·9194976	·9369509	·9544042	·9718575	41	·0001988
42	·8499753	·8674286	·8848819	·9023352	·9197885	·9372418	·9546951	·9721484	42	·0002036
43	·8502662	·8677195	·8851728	·9026261	·9200794	·9375327	·9549860	·9724393	43	·0002085
44	·8505571	·8680104	·8854637	·9029170	·9203703	·9378236	·9552769	·9727302	44	·0002133
45	·8508480	·8683013	·8857546	·9032079	·9206612	·9381145	·9555678	·9730211	45	·0002182
46	·8511389	·8685922	·8860455	·9034988	·9209521	·9384054	·9558587	·9733119	46	·0002230
47	·8514298	·8688831	·8863364	·9037897	·9212430	·9386962	·9561495	·9736028	47	·0002279
48	·8517207	·8691740	·8866273	·9040806	·9215338	·9389871	·9564404	·9738937	48	·0002327
49	·8520116	·8694649	·8869181	·9043714	·9218247	·9392780	·9567313	·9741846	49	·0002376
50	·8523025	·8697557	·8872090	·9046623	·9221156	·9395689	·9570222	·9744755	50	·0002424
51	·8525933	·8700466	·8874999	·9049532	·9224065	·9398598	·9573131	·9747664	51	·0002473
52	·8528842	·8703375	·8877908	·9052441	·9226974	·9401507	·9576040	·9750573	52	·0002521
53	·8531751	·8706284	·8880817	·9055350	·9229883	·9404416	·9578949	·9753482	53	·0002570
54	·8534660	·8709193	·8883726	·9058259	·9232792	·9407325	·9581858	·9756391	54	·0002618
55	·8537569	·8712102	·8886635	·9061168	·9235701	·9410234	·9584766	·9759299	55	·0002666
56	·8540478	·8715011	·8889544	·9064077	·9238610	·9413142	·9587675	·9762208	56	·0002715
57	·8543387	·8717920	·8892453	·9066985	·9241518	·9416051	·9590584	·9765117	57	·0002763
58	·8546296	·8720828	·8895361	·9069894	·9244427	·9418960	·9593493	·9768026	58	·0002812
59	·8549204	·8723737	·8898270	·9072803	·9247336	·9421869	·9596402	·9770935	59	·0002860
60	·8552113	·8726646	·8901179	·9075712	·9250245	·9424778	·9599311	·9773844	60	·0002909

′	56°	57°	58°	59°	60°	61°	62°	″	
0	·9773844	·9948377	1·0122910	1·0297443	1·0471976	1·0646508	1·0821041	0	·0000000
1	·9776753	·9951286	1·0125819	1·0300351	1·0474884	1·0649417	1·0823950	1	·0000048
2	·9779662	·9954194	1·0128727	1·0303260	1·0477793	1·0652326	1·0826859	2	·0000097
3	·9782570	·9957103	1·0131636	1·0306169	1·0480702	1·0655235	1·0829768	3	·0000145
4	·9785479	·9960012	1·0134545	1·0309078	1·0483611	1·0658144	1·0832677	4	·0000194
5	·9788388	·9962921	1·0137454	1·0311987	1·0486520	1·0661053	1·0835586	5	·0000242
6	·9791297	·9965830	1·0140363	1·0314896	1·0489429	1·0663962	1·0838495	6	·0000291
7	·9794206	·9968739	1·0143272	1·0317805	1·0492338	1·0666871	1·0841404	7	·0000339
8	·9797115	·9971648	1·0146181	1·0320714	1·0495247	1·0669779	1·0844312	8	·0000388
9	·9800024	·9974557	1·0149090	1·0323623	1·0498155	1·0672688	1·0847221	9	·0000436
10	·9802933	·9977466	1·0151998	1·0326531	1·0501064	1·0675597	1·0850130	10	·0000485
11	·9805842	·9980374	1·0154907	1·0329440	1·0503973	1·0678506	1·0853039	11	·0000533
12	·9808750	·9983283	1·0157816	1·0332349	1·0506882	1·0681415	1·0855948	12	·0000582
13	·9811659	·9986192	1·0160725	1·0335258	1·0509791	1·0684324	1·0858857	13	·0000630
14	·9814568	·9989101	1·0163634	1·0338167	1·0512700	1·0687233	1·0861766	14	·0000679
15	·9817477	·9992010	1·0166543	1·0341076	1·0515609	1·0690142	1·0864675	15	·0000727
16	·9820386	·9994919	1·0169452	1·0343985	1·0518518	1·0693051	1·0867583	16	·0000776
17	·9823295	·9997828	1·0172361	1·0346894	1·0521427	1·0695959	1·0870492	17	·0000824
18	·9826204	1·0000737	1·0175270	1·0349802	1·0524335	1·0698868	1·0873401	18	·0000873
19	·9829113	1·0003645	1·0178178	1·0352711	1·0527244	1·0701777	1·0876310	19	·0000921
20	·9832021	1·0006554	1·0181087	1·0355620	1·0530153	1·0704686	1·0879219	20	·0000970
21	·9834930	1·0009463	1·0183996	1·0358529	1·0533062	1·0707595	1·0882128	21	·0001018
22	·9837839	1·0012372	1·0186905	1·0361438	1·0535971	1·0710504	1·0885037	22	·0001067
23	·9840748	1·0015281	1·0189814	1·0364347	1·0538880	1·0713413	1·0887946	23	·0001115
24	·9843657	1·0018190	1·0192723	1·0367256	1·0541789	1·0716322	1·0890854	24	·0001164
25	·9846566	1·0021099	1·0195632	1·0370165	1·0544698	1·0719230	1·0893763	25	·0001212
26	·9849475	1·0024008	1·0198541	1·0373074	1·0547606	1·0722139	1·0896672	26	·0001261
27	·9852384	1·0026917	1·0201449	1·0375982	1·0550515	1·0725048	1·0899581	27	·0001309
28	·9855293	1·0029825	1·0204358	1·0378891	1·0553424	1·0727957	1·0902490	28	·0001357
29	·9858201	1·0032734	1·0207267	1·0381800	1·0556333	1·0730866	1·0905399	29	·0001406
30	·9861110	1·0035643	1·0210176	1·0384709	1·0559242	1·0733775	1·0908308	30	·0001454
31	·9864019	1·0038552	1·0213085	1·0387618	1·0562151	1·0736684	1·0911217	31	·0001503
32	·9866928	1·0041461	1·0215994	1·0390527	1·0565060	1·0739593	1·0914126	32	·0001551
33	·9869837	1·0044370	1·0218903	1·0393436	1·0567969	1·0742502	1·0917034	33	·0001600
34	·9872746	1·0047279	1·0221812	1·0396344	1·0570877	1·0745410	1·0919943	34	·0001648
35	·9875655	1·0050188	1·0224721	1·0399253	1·0573786	1·0748319	1·0922852	35	·0001697
36	·9878564	1·0053096	1·0227629	1·0402162	1·0576695	1·0751228	1·0925761	36	·0001745
37	·9881472	1·0056005	1·0230538	1·0405071	1·0579604	1·0754137	1·0928670	37	·0001794
38	·9884381	1·0058914	1·0233447	1·0407980	1·0582513	1·0757046	1·0931579	38	·0001842
39	·9887290	1·0061823	1·0236356	1·0410889	1·0585422	1·0759955	1·0934488	39	·0001891
40	·9890199	1·0064732	1·0239265	1·0413798	1·0588331	1·0762864	1·0937397	40	·0001939
41	·9893108	1·0067641	1·0242174	1·0416707	1·0591240	1·0765773	1·0940306	41	·0001988
42	·9896017	1·0070550	1·0245083	1·0419616	1·0594149	1·0768681	1·0943214	42	·0002036
43	·9898926	1·0073459	1·0247992	1·0422525	1·0597057	1·0771590	1·0946123	43	·0002085
44	·9901835	1·0076368	1·0250900	1·0425433	1·0599966	1·0774499	1·0949032	44	·0002133
45	·9904744	1·0079276	1·0253809	1·0428342	1·0602875	1·0777408	1·0951941	45	·0002182
46	·9907652	1·0082185	1·0256718	1·0431251	1·0605784	1·0780317	1·0954850	46	·0002230
47	·9910561	1·0085094	1·0259627	1·0434160	1·0608693	1·0783226	1·0957759	47	·0002279
48	·9913470	1·0088003	1·0262536	1·0437069	1·0611602	1·0786135	1·0960668	48	·0002327
49	·9916379	1·0090912	1·0265445	1·0439978	1·0614511	1·0789044	1·0963577	49	·0002376
50	·9919288	1·0093821	1·0268354	1·0442887	1·0617420	1·0791953	1·0966485	50	·0002424
51	·9922197	1·0096730	1·0271263	1·0445796	1·0620328	1·0794861	1·0969394	51	·0002473
52	·9925106	1·0099639	1·0274172	1·0448704	1·0623237	1·0797770	1·0972303	52	·0002521
53	·9928015	1·0102547	1·0277080	1·0451613	1·0626146	1·0800679	1·0975212	53	·0002570
54	·9930923	1·0105456	1·0279989	1·0454522	1·0629055	1·0803588	1·0978121	54	·0002618
55	·9933832	1·0108365	1·0282898	1·0457431	1·0631964	1·0806497	1·0981030	55	·0002666
56	·9936741	1·0111274	1·0285807	1·0460340	1·0634873	1·0809406	1·0983939	56	·0002715
57	·9939650	1·0114183	1·0288716	1·0463249	1·0637782	1·0812315	1·0986848	57	·0002763
58	·9942559	1·0117092	1·0291625	1·0466158	1·0640691	1·0815224	1·0989757	58	·0002812
59	·9945468	1·0120001	1·0294534	1·0469067	1·0643600	1·0818132	1·0992665	59	·0002860
60	·9948377	1·0122910	1·0297443	1·0471976	1·0646508	1·0821041	1·0995574	60	·0002909

′	63°	64°	65°	66°	67°	68°	69°	″	
0	1·0995574	1·1170107	1·1344640	1·1519173	1·1693706	1·1868239	1·2042772	0	·0000000
1	1·0998483	1·1173016	1·1347549	1·1522082	1·1696615	1·1871148	1·2045681	1	·0000048
2	1·1001392	1·1175925	1·1350458	1·1524991	1·1699524	1·1874057	1·2048590	2	·0000097
3	1·1004301	1·1178834	1·1353367	1·1527900	1·1702433	1·1876966	1·2051498	3	·0000145
4	1·1007210	1·1181743	1·1356276	1·1530809	1·1705342	1·1879874	1·2054407	4	·0000194
5	1·1010119	1·1184652	1·1359185	1·1533717	1·1708250	1·1882783	1·2057316	5	·0000242
6	1·1013028	1·1187561	1·1362093	1·1536626	1·1711159	1·1885692	1·2060225	6	·0000291
7	1·1015936	1·1190469	1·1365002	1·1539535	1·1714068	1·1888601	1·2063134	7	·0000339
8	1·1018845	1·1193378	1·1367911	1·1542444	1·1716977	1·1891510	1·2066043	8	·0000388
9	1·1021754	1·1196287	1·1370820	1·1545353	1·1719886	1·1894419	1·2068952	9	·0000436
10	1·1024663	1·1199196	1·1373729	1·1548262	1·1722795	1·1897328	1·2071861	10	·0000485
11	1·1027572	1·1202105	1·1376638	1·1551171	1·1725704	1·1900237	1·2074770	11	·0000533
12	1·1030481	1·1205014	1·1379547	1·1554080	1·1728613	1·1903145	1·2077678	12	·0000582
13	1·1033390	1·1207923	1·1382456	1·1556989	1·1731521	1·1906054	1·2080587	13	·0000630
14	1·1036299	1·1210832	1·1385364	1·1559897	1·1734430	1·1908963	1·2083496	14	·0000679
15	1·1039208	1·1213740	1·1388273	1·1562806	1·1737339	1·1911872	1·2086405	15	·0000727
16	1·1042116	1·1216649	1·1391182	1·1565715	1·1740248	1·1914781	1·2089314	16	·0000776
17	1·1045025	1·1219558	1·1394091	1·1568624	1·1743157	1·1917690	1·2092223	17	·0000824
18	1·1047934	1·1222467	1·1397000	1·1571533	1·1746066	1·1920599	1·2095132	18	·0000873
19	1·1050843	1·1225376	1·1399909	1·1574442	1·1748975	1·1923508	1·2098041	19	·0000921
20	1·1053752	1·1228285	1·1402818	1·1577351	1·1751884	1·1926417	1·2100949	20	·0000970
21	1·1056661	1·1231194	1·1405727	1·1580260	1·1754793	1·1929325	1·2103858	21	·0001018
22	1·1059570	1·1234103	1·1408636	1·1583168	1·1757701	1·1932234	1·2106767	22	·0001067
23	1·1062479	1·1237012	1·1411544	1·1586077	1·1760610	1·1935143	1·2109676	23	·0001115
24	1·1065387	1·1239921	1·1414453	1·1588986	1·1763519	1·1938052	1·2112585	24	·0001164
25	1·1068296	1·1242829	1·1417362	1·1591895	1·1766428	1·1940961	1·2115494	25	·0001212
26	1·1071205	1·1245738	1·1420271	1·1594804	1·1769337	1·1943870	1·2118403	26	·0001261
27	1·1074114	1·1248647	1·1423180	1·1597713	1·1772246	1·1946779	1·2121312	27	·0001309
28	1·1077023	1·1251556	1·1426089	1·1600622	1·1775155	1·1949688	1·2124221	28	·0001357
29	1·1079932	1·1254465	1·1428998	1·1603531	1·1778064	1·1952596	1·2127129	29	·0001406
30	1·1082841	1·1257374	1·1431907	1·1606440	1·1780972	1·1955505	1·2130038	30	·0001454
31	1·1085750	1·1260283	1·1434815	1·1609348	1·1783881	1·1958414	1·2132947	31	·0001503
32	1·1088659	1·1263191	1·1437724	1·1612257	1·1786790	1·1961323	1·2135856	32	·0001551
33	1·1091567	1·1266100	1·1440633	1·1615166	1·1789699	1·1964232	1·2138765	33	·0001600
34	1·1094476	1·1269009	1·1443542	1·1618075	1·1792608	1·1967141	1·2141674	34	·0001648
35	1·1097385	1·1271918	1·1446451	1·1620984	1·1795517	1·1970050	·2144583	35	·0001697
36	1·1100294	1·1274827	1·1449360	1·1623893	1·1798426	1·1972959	1·2147492	36	·0001745
37	1·1103203	1·1277736	1·1452269	1·1626802	1·1801335	1·1975868	1·2150400	37	·0001794
38	1·1106112	1·1280645	1·1455178	1·1629711	1·1804244	1·1978776	1·2153309	38	·0001842
39	1·1109021	1·1283554	1·1458087	1·1632619	1·1807152	1·1981685	1·2156218	39	·0001891
40	1·1111930	1·1286462	1·1460995	1·1635528	1·1810061	1·1984594	1·2159127	40	·0001939
41	1·1114838	1·1289371	1·1463904	1·1638437	1·1812970	1·1987503	1·2162036	41	·0001988
42	1·1117747	1·1292280	1·1466813	1·1641346	1·1815879	1·1990412	1·2164945	42	·0002036
43	1·1120656	1·1295189	1·1469722	1·1644255	1·1818788	1·1993321	1·2167854	43	·0002085
44	1·1123565	1·1298098	1·1472631	1·1647164	1·1821697	1·1996230	1·2170763	44	·0002133
45	1·1126474	1·1301007	1·1475540	1·1650073	1·1824606	1·1999139	1·2173672	45	·0002182
46	1·1129383	1·1303916	1·1478449	1·1652982	1·1827515	1·2002047	1·2176580	46	·0002230
47	1·1132292	1·1306825	1·1481358	1·1655891	1·1830423	1·2004956	1·2179489	47	·0002279
48	1·1135201	1·1309734	1·1484267	1·1658799	1·1833332	1·2007865	1·2182398	48	·0002327
49	1·1138110	1·1312642	1·1487175	1·1661708	1·1836241	1·2010774	1·2185307	49	·0002376
50	1·1141018	1·1315551	1·1490084	1·1664617	1·1839150	1·2013683	1·2188216	50	·0002424
51	1·1143927	1·1318460	1·1492993	1·1667526	1·1842059	1·2016592	1·2191125	51	·0002473
52	1·1146836	1·1321369	1·1495902	1·1670435	1·1844968	1·2019501	1·2194034	52	·0002521
53	1·1149745	1·1324278	1·1498811	1·1673344	1·1847877	1·2022410	1·2196943	53	·0002570
54	1·1152654	1·1327187	1·1501720	1·1676253	1·1850786	1·2025319	1·2199851	54	·0002618
55	1·1155563	1·1330096	1·1504629	1·1679162	1·1853695	1·2028227	1·2202760	55	·0002666
56	1·1158472	1·1333005	1·1507538	1·1682070	1·1856603	1·2031136	1·2205669	56	·0002715
57	1·1161381	1·1335913	1·1510446	1·1684979	1·1859512	1·2034045	1·2208578	57	·0002763
58	1·1164289	1·1338822	1·1513355	1·1687888	1·1862421	1·2036954	1·2211487	58	·0002812
59	1·1167198	1·1341731	1·1516264	1·1690797	1·1865330	1·2039863	1·2214396	59	·0002860
60	1·1170107	1·1344640	1·1519173	1·1693706	1·1868239	1·2042772	1·2217305	60	·0002909

′	70°	71°	72°	73°	74°	75°	76°	″	
0	1·2217305	1·2391838	1·2566371	1·2740904	1·2915436	1·3089969	1·3264502	0	·0000000
1	1·2220214	1·2394747	1·2569279	1·2743812	1·2918345	1·3092878	1·3267411	1	·0000048
2	1·2223122	1·2397655	1·2572188	1·2746721	1·2921254	1·3095787	1·3270320	2	·0000097
3	1·2226031	1·2400564	1·2575097	1·2749630	1·2924163	1·3098696	1·3273229	3	·0000145
4	1·2228940	1·2403473	1·2578006	1·2752539	1·2927072	1·3101605	1·3276138	4	·0000194
5	1·2231849	1·2406382	1·2580915	1·2755448	1·2929981	1·3104514	1·3279047	5	·0000242
6	1·2234758	1·2409291	1·2583824	1·2758357	1·2932890	1·3107423	1·3281956	6	·0000291
7	1·2237667	1·2412200	1·2586733	1·2761266	1·2935799	1·3110332	1·3284864	7	·0000339
8	1·2240576	1·2415109	1·2589642	1·2764175	1·2938708	1·3113240	1·3287773	8	·0000388
9	1·2243485	1·2418018	1·2592551	1·2767083	1·2941616	1·3116149	1·3290682	9	·0000436
10	1·2246394	1·2420927	1·2595459	1·2769992	1·2944525	1·3119058	1·3293591	10	·0000485
11	1·2249302	1·2423835	1·2598368	1·2772901	1·2947434	1·3121967	1·3296500	11	·0000533
12	1·2252211	1·2426744	1·2601277	1·2775810	1·2950343	1·3124876	1·3299409	12	·0000582
13	1·2255120	1·2429653	1·2604186	1·2778719	1·2953252	1·3127785	1·3302318	13	·0000630
14	1·2258029	1·2432562	1·2607095	1·2781628	1·2956161	1·3130694	1·3305227	14	·0000679
15	1·2260938	1·2435471	1·2610004	1·2784537	1·2959070	1·3133603	1·3308136	15	·0000727
16	1·2263847	1·2438380	1·2612913	1·2787446	1·2961979	1·3136512	1·3311044	16	·0000776
17	1·2266756	1·2441289	1·2615822	1·2790355	1·2964887	1·3139420	1·3313953	17	·0000824
18	1·2269665	1·2444198	1·2618730	1·2793263	1·2967796	1·3142329	1·3316862	18	·0000873
19	1·2272574	1·2447106	1·2621639	1·2796172	1·2970705	1·3145238	1·3319771	·19	·0000921
20	1·2275482	1·2450015	1·2624548	1·2799081	1·2973614	1·3148147	1·3322680	20	·0000970
21	1·2278391	1·2452924	1·2627457	1·2801990	1·2976523	1·3151056	1·3325589	21	·0001018
22	1·2281300	1·2455833	1·2630366	1·2804899	1·2979432	1·3153965	1·3328498	22	·0001067
23	1·2284209	1·2458742	1·2633275	1·2807808	1·2982341	1·3156874	1·3331407	23	·0001115
24	1·2287118	1·2461651	1·2636184	1·2810717	1·2985250	1·3159783	1·3334315	24	·0001164
25	1·2290027	1·2464560	1·2639093	1·2813626	1·2988159	1·3162691	1·3337224	25	·0001212
26	1·2292936	1·2467469	1·2642002	1·2816534	1·2991067	1·3165600	1·3340133	26	·0001261
27	1·2295845	1·2470378	1·2644910	1·2819443	1·2993976	1·3168509	1·3343042	27	·0001309
28	1·2298753	1·2473286	1·2647819	1·2822352	1·2996885	1·3171418	1·3345951	28	·0001357
29	1·2301662	1·2476195	1·2650728	1·2825261	1·2999794	1·3174327	1·3348860	29	·0001406
30	1·2304571	1·2479104	1·2653637	1·2828170	1·3002703	1·3177236	1·3351769	30	·0001454
31	1·2307480	1·2482013	1·2656546	1·2831079	1·3005612	1·3180145	1·3354678	31	·0001503
32	1·2310389	1·2484922	1·2659455	1·2833988	1·3008521	1·3183054	1·3357587	32	·0001551
33	1·2313298	1·2487831	1·2662364	1·2836897	1·3011430	1·3185962	1·3360495	33	·0001600
34	1·2316207	1·2490740	1·2665272	1·2839806	1·3014338	1·3188871	1·3363404	34	·0001648
35	1·2319116	1·2493649	1·2668181	1·2842714	1·3017247	1·3191780	1·3366313	35	·0001697
36	1·2322025	1·2496557	1·2671090	1·2845623	1·3020156	1·3194689	1·3369222	36	·0001745
37	1·2324933	1·2499466	1·2673999	1·2848532	1·3023065	1·3197598	1·3372131	37	·0001794
38	1·2327842	1·2502375	1·2676908	1·2851441	1·3025974	1·3200507	1·3375040	38	·0001842
39	1·2330751	1·2505284	1·2679817	1·2854350	1·3028883	1·3203416	1·3377949	39	·0001891
40	1·2333660	1·2508193	1·2682726	1·2857259	1·3031792	1·3206325	1·3380858	40	·0001939
41	1·2336569	1·2511102	1·2685635	1·2860168	1·3034701	1·3209234	1·3383766	41	·0001988
42	1·2339478	1·2514011	1·2688544	1·2863077	1·3037610	1·3212142	1·3386675	42	·0002036
43	1·2342387	1·2516920	1·2691453	1·2865985	1·3040518	1·3215051	1·3389584	43	·0002085
44	1·2345296	1·2519829	1·2694361	1·2868894	1·3043427	1·3217960	1·3392493	44	·0002133
45	1·2348204	1·2522737	1·2697270	1·2871803	1·3046336	1·3220869	1·3395402	45	·0002182
46	1·2351113	1·2525646	1·2700179	1·2874712	1·3049245	1·3223778	1·3398311	46	·0002230
47	1·2354022	1·2528555	1·2703088	1·2877621	1·3052154	1·3226687	1·3401220	47	·0002279
48	1·2356931	1·2531464	1·2705997	1·2880530	1·3055063	1·3229596	1·3404129	48	·0002327
49	1·2359840	1·2534373	1·2708906	1·2883439	1·3057972	1·3232505	1·3407038	49	·0002376
50	1·2362749	1·2537282	1·2711815	1·2886348	1·3060881	1·3235413	1·3409946	50	·0002424
51	1·2365658	1·2540191	1·2714724	1·2889257	1·3063789	1·3238322	1·3412855	51	·0002473
52	1·2368567	1·2543100	1·2717632	1·2892165	1·3066698	1·3241231	1·3415764	52	·0002521
53	1·2371476	1·2546008	1·2720541	1·2895074	1·3069607	1·3244140	1·3418673	53	·0002570
54	1·2374384	1·2548917	1·2723450	1·2897983	1·3072516	1·3247049	1·3421582	54	·0002618
55	1·2377293	1·2551826	1·2726359	1·2900892	1·3075425	1·3249958	1·3424491	55	·0002666
56	1·2380202	1·2554735	1·2729268	1·2903801	1·3078334	1·3252867	1·3427400	56	·0002715
57	1·2383111	1·2557644	1·2732177	1·2906710	1·3081243	1·3255776	1·3430309	57	·0002763
58	1·2386020	1·2560553	1·2735086	1·2909619	1·3084152	1·3258685	1·3433217	58	·0002812
59	1·2388929	1·2563462	1·2737995	1·2912528	1·3087061	1·3261593	1·3436126	59	·0002860
60	1·2391838	1·2566371	1·2740904	1·2915436	1·3089969	1·3264502	1·3439035	60	·0002909

′	77°	78°	79°	80°	81°	82°	83°	″	
0	1·3439035	1·3613568	1·3788101	1·3962634	1·4137167	1·4311700	1·4486233	0	·0000000
1	1·3441944	1·3616477	1·3791010	1·3965543	1·4140076	1·4314609	1·4489142	1	·0000048
2	1·3444853	1·3619386	1·3793919	1·3968452	1·4142985	1·4317518	1·4492051	2	·0000097
3	1·3447762	1·3622295	1·3796828	1·3971361	1·4145894	1·4320427	1·4494959	3	·0000145
4	1·3450671	1·3625204	1·3799737	1·3974270	1·4148802	1·4323335	1·4497868	4	·0000194
5	1·3453580	1·3628113	1·3802645	1·3977178	1·4151711	1·4326244	1·4500777	5	·0000242
6	1·3456489	1·3631021	1·3805554	1·3980087	1·4154620	1·4329153	1·4503686	6	·0000291
7	1·3459397	1·3633930	1·3808463	1·3982996	1·4157529	1·4332062	1·4506595	7	·0000339
8	1·3462306	1·3636839	1·3811372	1·3985905	1·4160438	1·4334971	1·4509504	8	·0000388
9	1·3465215	1·3639748	1·3814281	1·3988814	1·4163347	1·4337880	1·4512413	9	·0000436
10	1·3468124	1·3642657	1·3817190	1·3991723	1·4166256	1·4340789	1·4515322	10	·0000485
11	1·3471033	1·3645566	1·3820099	1·3994632	1·4169165	1·4343698	1·4518230	11	·0000533
12	1·3473942	1·3648475	1·3823008	1·3997541	1·4172074	1·4346606	1·4521139	12	·0000582
13	1·3476851	1·3651384	1·3825917	1·4000449	1·4174982	1·4349515	1·4524048	13	·0000630
14	1·3479760	1·3654293	1·3828825	1·4003358	1·4177891	1·4352424	1·4526957	14	·0000679
15	1·3482668	1·3657201	1·3831734	1·4006267	1·4180800	1·4355333	1·4529866	15	·0000727
16	1·3485577	1·3660110	1·3834643	1·4009176	1·4183709	1·4358242	1·4532775	16	·0000776
17	1·3488486	1·3663019	1·3837552	1·4012085	1·4186618	1·4361151	1·4535684	17	·0000824
18	1·3491395	1·3665928	1·3840461	1·4014994	1·4189527	1·4364060	1·4538593	18	·0000873
19	1·3494304	1·3668837	1·3843370	1·4017903	1·4192436	1·4366969	1·4541502	19	·0000921
20	1·3497213	1·3671746	1·3846279	1·4020812	1·4195344	1·4369878	1·4544410	20	·0000970
21	1·3500122	1·3674655	1·3849188	1·4023721	1·4198253	1·4372786	1·4547319	21	·0001018
22	1·3503031	1·3677564	1·3852096	1·4026629	1·4201162	1·4375695	1·4550228	22	·0001067
23	1·3505940	1·3680472	1·3855005	1·4029583	1·4204071	1·4378604	1·4553137	23	·0001115
24	1·3508848	1·3683381	1·3857914	1·4032447	1·4206980	1·4381513	1·4556046	24	·0001164
25	1·3511757	1·3686290	1·3860823	1·4035356	1·4209889	1·4384422	1·4558955	25	·0001212
26	1·3514666	1·3689199	1·3863732	1·4038265	1·4212798	1·4387331	1·4561864	26	·0001261
27	1·3517575	1·3692108	1·3866641	1·4041174	1·4215707	1·4390240	1·4564773	27	·0001309
28	1·3520484	1·3695017	1·3869550	1·4044083	1·4218616	1·4393149	1·4567681	28	·0001357
29	1·3523393	1·3697926	1·3872459	1·4046992	1·4221525	1·4396057	1·4570590	29	·0001406
30	1·3526302	1·3700835	1·3875368	1·4049900	1·4224433	1·4398966	1·4573499	30	·0001454
31	1·3529211	1·3703744	1·3878276	1·4052809	1·4227342	1·4401875	1·4576408	31	·0001503
32	1·3532119	1·3706652	1·3881185	1·4055718	1·4230251	1·4404784	1·4579317	32	·0001551
33	1·3535028	1·3709561	1·3884094	1·4058627	1·4233160	1·4407693	1·4582226	33	·0001600
34	1·3537937	1·3712470	1·3887003	1·4061536	1·4236069	1·4410601	1·4585135	34	·0001648
35	1·3540846	1·3715379	1·3889912	1·4064445	1·4238978	1·4413511	1·4588044	35	·0001697
36	1·3543755	1·3718288	1·3892821	1·4067354	1·4241887	1·4416420	1·4590953	36	·0001745
37	1·3546664	1·3721197	1·3895730	1·4070263	1·4244796	1·4419329	1·4593861	37	·0001794
38	1·3549573	1·3724106	1·3898639	1·4073172	1·4247704	1·4422237	1·4596770	38	·0001842
39	1·3552482	1·3727015	1·3901547	1·4076080	1·4250613	1·4425146	1·4599679	39	·0001891
40	1·3555391	1·3729923	1·3904456	1·4078989	1·4253522	1·4428055	1·4602588	40	·0001939
41	1·3558299	1·3732832	1·3907365	1·4081898	1·4256431	1·4430964	1·4605497	41	·0001988
42	1·3561208	1·3735741	1·3910274	1·4084807	1·4259340	1·4433873	1·4608406	42	·0002036
43	1·3564117	1·3738650	1·3913183	1·4087716	1·4262249	1·4436782	1·4611315	43	·0002085
44	1·3567026	1·3741559	1·3916092	1·4090625	1·4265158	1·4439691	1·4614224	44	·0002133
45	1·3569935	1·3744468	1·3919001	1·4093534	1·4268067	1·4442600	1·4617132	45	·0002182
46	1·3572844	1·3747377	1·3921910	1·4096443	1·4270976	1·4445508	1·4620041	46	·0002230
47	1·3575753	1·3750286	1·3924819	1·4099351	1·4273884	1·4448417	1·4622950	47	·0002279
48	1·3578662	1·3753195	1·3927727	1·4102260	1·4276793	1·4451326	1·4625859	48	·0002327
49	1·3581570	1·3756103	1·3930636	1·4105169	1·4279702	1·4454235	1·4628768	49	·0002376
50	1·3584479	1·3759012	1·3933545	1·4108078	1·4282611	1·4457144	1·4631677	50	·0002424
51	1·3587388	1·3761921	1·3936454	1·4110987	1·4285520	1·4460053	1·4634586	51	·0002473
52	1·3590297	1·3764830	1·3939363	1·4113896	1·4288429	1·4462962	1·4637495	52	·0002521
53	1·3593206	1·3767739	1·3942272	1·4116805	1·4291338	1·4465871	1·4640404	53	·0002570
54	1·3596115	1·3770648	1·3945181	1·4119714	1·4294247	1·4468779	1·4643312	54	·0002618
55	1·3599024	1·3773557	1·3948090	1·4122623	1·4297155	1·4471688	1·4646221	55	·0002666
56	1·3601933	1·3776466	1·3950998	1·4125531	1·4300064	1·4474597	1·4649130	56	·0002715
57	1·3604842	1·3779374	1·3953907	1·4128440	1·4302973	1·4477506	1·4652039	57	·0002763
58	1·3607750	1·3782283	1·3956816	1·4131349	1·4305882	1·4480415	1·4654948	58	·0002812
59	1·3610659	1·3785192	1·3959725	1·4134258	1·4308791	1·4483324	1·4657857	59	·0002860
60	1·3613568	1·3788101	1·3962634	1·4137167	1·4311700	1·4486233	1·4660766	60	·0002909

CIRCULAR MEASURE OF ANGLES, OR, LENGTH OF ARCS TO RADIUS = 1.

′	84°	85°	86°	87°	88°	89°	90°	″	
0	1·4660766	1·4835299	1·5009832	1·5184364	1·5358897	1·5533430	1·5707963	0	·0000000
1	1·4663675	1·4838208	1·5012740	1·5187273	1·5361806	1·5536339	1·5710872	1	·0000048
2	1·4666583	1·4841116	1·5015649	1·5190182	1·5364715	1·5539248	1·5713781	2	·0000097
3	1·4669492	1·4844025	1·5018558	1·5193091	1·5367624	1·5542157	1·5716690	3	·0000145
4	1·4672401	1·4846934	1·5021467	1·5196000	1·5370533	1·5545066	1·5719599	4	·0000194
5	1·4675310	1·4849843	1·5024376	1·5198909	1·5373442	1·5547975	1·5722508	5	·0000242
6	1·4678219	1·4852752	1·5027285	1·5201818	1·5376351	1·5550884	1·5725417	6	·0000291
7	1·4681128	1·4855661	1·5030194	1·5204727	1·5379260	1·5553793	1·5728325	7	·0000339
8	1·4684037	1·4858570	1·5033103	1·5207656	1·5382168	1·5556701	1·5731234	8	·0000388
9	1·4686946	1·4861479	1·5036012	1·5210544	1·5385077	1·5559610	1·5734143	9	·0000436
10	1·4689855	1·4864387	1·5038920	1·5213453	1·5387986	1·5562519	1·5737052	10	·0000485
11	1·4692763	1·4867296	1·5041829	1·5216362	1·5390895	1·5565428	1·5739961	11	·0000533
12	1·4695672	1·4870205	1·5044738	1·5219271	1·5393804	1·5568337	1·5742870	12	·0000582
13	1·4698581	1·4873114	1·5047647	1·5222180	1·5396713	1·5571246	1·5745779	13	·0000630
14	1·4701490	1·4876023	1·5050556	1·5225089	1·5399622	1·5574155	1·5748688	14	·0000679
15	1·4704399	1·4878932	1·5053465	1·5227998	1·5402531	1·5577064	1·5751596	15	·0000727
16	1·4707308	1·4881841	1·5056374	1·5230906	1·5405440	1·5579972	1·5754505	16	·0000776
17	1·4710217	1·4884750	1·5059283	1·5233815	1·5408348	1·5582881	1·5757414	17	·0000824
18	1·4713126	1·4887659	1·5062191	1·5236724	1·5411257	1·5585790	1·5760323	18	·0000873
19	1·4716034	1·4890567	1·5065100	1·5239633	1·5414166	1·5588699	1·5763232	19	·0000921
20	1·4718943	1·4893476	1·5068009	1·5242542	1·5417075	1·5591608	1·5766141	20	·0000970
21	1·4721852	1·4896385	1·5070918	1·5245451	1·5419984	1·5594517	1·5769050	21	·0001018
22	1·4724761	1·4899294	1·5073827	1·5248360	1·5422893	1·5597426	1·5771959	22	·0001067
23	1·4727670	1·4902203	1·5076736	1·5251269	1·5425802	1·5600335	1·5774868	23	·0001115
24	1·4730579	1·4905112	1·5079645	1·5254178	1·5428711	1·5603244	1·5777776	24	·0001164
25	1·4733488	1·4908021	1·5082554	1·5257087	1·5431619	1·5606152	1·5780685	25	·0001212
26	1·4736397	1·4910930	1·5085463	1·5259995	1·5434528	1·5609061	1·5783594	26	·0001261
27	1·4739306	1·4913838	1·5088371	1·5262904	1·5437437	1·5611970	1·5786503	27	·0001309
28	1·4742214	1·4916747	1·5091280	1·5265813	1·5440346	1·5614879	1·5789412	28	·0001357
29	1·4745123	1·4919656	1·5094189	1·5268722	1·5443255	1·5617788	1·5792321	29	·0001406
30	1·4748032	1·4922565	1·5097098	1·5271631	1·5446164	1·5620697	1·5795230	30	·0001454
31	1·4750941	1·4925474	1·5100007	1·5274540	1·5449073	1·5623606	1·5798139	31	·0001503
32	1·4753850	1·4928383	1·5102916	1·5277449	1·5451982	1·5626515	1·5801047	32	·0001551
33	1·4756759	1·4931292	1·5105825	1·5280358	1·5454891	1·5629423	1·5803956	33	·0001600
34	1·4759668	1·4934201	1·5108734	1·5283266	1·5457799	1·5632332	1·5806865	34	·0001648
35	1·4762577	1·4937110	1·5111642	1·5286175	1·5460708	1·5635241	1·5809774	35	·0001697
36	1·4765485	1·4940018	1·5114551	1·5289084	1·5463617	1·5638150	1·5812683	36	·0001745
37	1·4768394	1·4942927	1·5117460	1·5291993	1·5466526	1·5641059	1·5815592	37	·0001794
38	1·4771303	1·4945836	1·5120369	1·5294902	1·5469435	1·5643968	1·5818501	38	·0001842
39	1·4774212	1·4948745	1·5123278	1·5297811	1·5472344	1·5646877	1·5821410	39	·0001891
40	1·4777121	1·4951654	1·5126187	1·5300720	1·5475253	1·5649786	1·5824319	40	·0001939
41	1·4780030	1·4954563	1·5129096	1·5303629	1·5478162	1·5652695	1·5827227	41	·0001988
42	1·4782939	1·4957472	1·5132005	1·5306538	1·5481070	1·5655603	1·5830136	42	·0002036
43	1·4785848	1·4960381	1·5134913	1·5309446	1·5483979	1·5658512	1·5833045	43	·0002085
44	1·4788757	1·4963289	1·5137822	1·5312355	1·5486888	1·5661421	1·5835954	44	·0002133
45	1·4791665	1·4966198	1·5140731	1·5315264	1·5489797	1·5664330	1·5838863	45	·0002182
46	1·4794574	1·4969107	1·5143640	1·5318173	1·5492706	1·5667239	1·5841772	46	·0002230
47	1·4797483	1·4972016	1·5146549	1·5321082	1·5495615	1·5670148	1·5844681	47	·0002279
48	1·4800392	1·4974925	1·5149458	1·5323991	1·5498524	1·5673057	1·5847590	48	·0002327
49	1·4803301	1·4977834	1·5152367	1·5326900	1·5501433	1·5675966	1·5850498	49	·0002376
50	1·4806210	1·4980743	1·5155276	1·5329809	1·5504342	1·5678874	1·5853407	50	·0002424
51	1·4809119	1·4983652	1·5158185	1·5332717	1·5507250	1·5681783	1·5856316	51	·0002473
52	1·4812028	1·4986561	1·5161093	1·5335626	1·5510159	1·5684692	1·5859225	52	·0002521
53	1·4814936	1·4989469	1·5164002	1·5338535	1·5513068	1·5687601	1·5862134	53	·0002570
54	1·4817845	1·4992378	1·5166911	1·5341444	1·5515977	1·5690510	1·5865043	54	·0002618
55	1·4820754	1·4995287	1·5169820	1·5344353	1·5518886	1·5693419	1·5867952	55	·0002666
56	1·4823663	1·4998196	1·5172729	1·5347262	1·5521795	1·5696328	1·5870861	56	·0002715
57	1·4826572	1·5001105	1·5175638	1·5350171	1·5524704	1·5699237	1·5873770	57	·0002763
58	1·4829481	1·5004014	1·5178547	1·5353080	1·5527613	1·5702145	1·5876678	58	·0002812
59	1·4832390	1·5006923	1·5181456	1·5355989	1·5530521	1·5705054	1·5879587	59	·0002860
60	1·4835299	1·5009832	1·5184364	1·5358897	1·5533430	1·5707963	1·5882496	60	·0002909

′	Sine	Diff.	Covers.	Chord	Co-chord	Vers.	Diff.	Cosine	′
0	0000000		1·0000000	0000000	1·4142136	0000000	0	1·0000000	60
1	0002909	2909	9997091	0002909	1·4140079	0000000	0	1·0000000	59
2	0005818	2909	9994182	0005818	1·4138022	0000002	2	9999998	58
3	0008727	2909	9991273	0008727	1·4135964	0000004	2	9999996	57
4	0011636	2909	9988364	0011636	1·4133906	0000007	3	9999993	56
5	0014544	2908	9985456	0014544	1·4131847	0000011	4	9999989	·55
		2909					4		
6	0017453	2909	9982547	0017453	1·4129788	0000015	6	9999985	54
7	0020362	2909	9979638	0020362	1·4127729	0000021	6	9999979	53
8	0023271	2909	9976729	0023271	1·4125670	0000027	7	9999973	52
9	0026180	2909	9973820	0026180	1·4123611	0000034	8	9999966	51
10	0029089	2909	9970911	0029089	1·4121552	0000042	9	9999958	50
11	0031998	2909	9968002	0031998	1·4119492	0000051	10	9999949	49
12	0034907	2908	9965093	0034907	1·4117432	0000061	11	9999939	48
13	0037815	2909	9962185	0037815	1·4115371	0000072	11	9999928	47
14	0040724	2909	9959276	0040724	1·4113310	0000083	12	9999917	46
15	0043633	2909	9956367	0043633	1·4111249	0000095	13	9999905	45
16	0046542	2909	9953458	0046542	1·4109188	0000108	14	9999892	44
17	0049451	2909	9950549	0049451	1·4107126	0000122	15	9999878	43
18	0052360	2908	9947640	0052360	1·4105064	0000137	16	9999863	42
19	0055268	2909	9944732	0055269	1·4103001	0000153	16	9999847	41
20	0058177	2909	9941823	0058178	1·4100938	0000169	18	9999831	40
21	0061086		9938914	0061087	1·4098875	0000187	18	9999813	39
22	0063995	2909	9936005	0063995	1·4096812	0000205	19	9999795	38
23	0066904	2909	9933096	0066904	1·4094748	0000224	20	9999776	37
24	0069813	2909	9930187	0069813	1·4092684	0000244	20	9999756	36
25	0072721	2908	9927279	0072722	1·4090620	0000264	22	9999736	35
		2909					22		
26	0075630	2909	9924370	0075630	1·4088556	0000286	22	9999714	34
27	0078539	2909	9921461	0078539	1·4086491	0000308	24	9999692	33
28	0081448	2909	9918552	0081448	1·4084426	0000332	24	9999668	32
29	0084357	2908	9915643	0084357	1·4082360	0000356	25	9999644	31
30	0087265	2909	9912735	0087266	1·4080294	0000381	26	9999619	30
31	0090174	2909	9909826	0090175	1·4078228	0000407	26	9999593	29
32	0093083	2909	9906917	0093084	1·4076162	0000433	28	9999567	28
33	0095992	2908	9904008	0095993	1·4074095	0000461	28	9999539	27
34	0098900	2909	9901100	0098902	1·4072028	0000489	29	9999511	26
35	0101809	2909	9898191	0101811	1·4069961	0000518	30	9999482	25
36	0104718	2909	9895282	0104720	1·4067894	0000548	31	9999452	24
37	0107627	2908	9892373	0107628	1·4065826	0000579	32	9999421	23
38	0110535	2909	9889465	0110536	1·4063758	0000611	32	9999389	22
39	0113444	2909	9886556	0113445	1·4061690	0000643	34	9999357	21
40	0116353	2908	9883647	0116354	1·4059622	0000677	34	9999323	20
41	0119261	2909	9880739	0119263	1·4057552	0000711	35	9999289	19
42	0122170	2909	9877830	0122172	1·4055482	0000746	36	9999254	18
43	0125079	2908	9874921	0125081	1·4053413	0000782	37	9999218	17
44	0127987	2909	9872013	0127990	1·4051344	0000819	38	9999181	16
45	0130896	2909	9869104	0130899	1·4049273	0000857	38	9999143	15
46	0133805	2908	9866195	0133808	1·4047202	0000895	40	9999105	14
47	0136713	2909	9863287	0136717	1·4045132	0000935	40	9999065	13
48	0139622	2908	9860378	0139626	1·4043062	0000975	41	9999025	12
49	0142530	2909	9857470	0142534	1·4040990	0001016	42	9998984	11
50	0145439	2909	9854561	0145442	1·4038918	0001058	42	9998942	10
51	0148348	2908	9851652	0148351	1·4036846	0001100	44	9998900	9
52	0151256	2909	9848744	0151260	1·4034774	0001144	44	9998856	8
53	0154165	2908	9845835	0154169	1·4032701	0001188	46	9998812	7
54	0157073	2909	9842927	0157078	1·4030628	0001234	46	9998766	6
55	0159982	2908	9840018	0159987	1·4028555	0001280	47	9998720	5
56	0162890	2909	9837110	0162896	1·4026482	0001327	48	9998673	4
57	0165799	2908	9834201	0165805	1·4024408	0001375	48	9998625	3
58	0168707	2909	9831293	0168714	1·4022334	0001423	50	9998577	2
59	0171616	2908	9828384	0171622	1·4020260	0001473	50	9998527	1
60	0174524		9825476	0174530	1·4018186	0001523		9998477	0
′	Cosine	Diff.	Vers.	Co-chord	Chord	Covers.	Diff.	Sine	′

′	Sine	Diff.	Covers.	Chord	Co-chord	Vers.	Diff.	Cosine	′
0	0174524	2908	9825476	0174530	1·4018186	0001523	51	9998477	60
1	0177432	2909	9822568	0177439	1·4016111	0001574	52	9998426	59
2	0180341	2908	9819659	0180348	1·4014036	0001626	53	9998374	58
3	0183249	2908	9816751	0183257	1·4011960	0001679	54	9998321	57
4	0186158	2908	9813842	0186166	1·4009884	0001733	54	9998267	56
5	0189066	2908	9810934	0189075	1·4007808	0001787	56	9998213	55
6	0191974	2909	9808026	0191984	1·4005732	0001843	56	9998157	54
7	0194883	2908	9805117	0194892	1·4003655	0001899	57	9998101	53
8	0197791	2908	9802209	0197800	1·4001578	0001956	57	9998044	52
9	0200699	2909	9799301	0200709	1·3999500	0002014	59	9997986	51
10	0203608	2908	9796392	0203618	1·3997422	0002073	60	9997927	50
11	0206516	2908	9793484	0206527	1·3995344	0002133	60	9997867	49
12	0209424	2908	9790576	0209436	1·3993266	0002193	62	9997807	48
13	0212332	2909	9787668	0212345	1·3991188	0002255	62	9997745	47
14	0215241	2908	9784759	0215254	1·3989110	0002317	63	9997683	46
15	0218149	2908	9781851	0218162	1·3987031	0002380	64	9997620	45
16	0221057	2908	9778943	0221070	1·3984952	0002444	64	9997556	44
17	0223965	2908	9776035	0223979	1·3982872	0002508	66	9997492	43
18	0226873	2908	9773127	0226888	1·3980792	0002574	66	9997426	42
19	0229781	2908	9770219	0229797	1·3978711	0002640	68	9997360	41
20	0232690	2908	9767310	0232706	1·3976630	0002708	68	9997292	40
21	0235598	2908	9764402	0235614	1·3974549	0002776	68	9997224	39
22	0238506	2908	9761494	0238522	1·3972468	0002844	70	9997156	38
23	0241414	2908	9758586	0241431	1·3970387	0002914	71	9997086	37
24	0244322	2908	9755678	0244340	1·3968306	0002985	72	9997015	36
25	0247230	2908	9752770	0247249	1·3966224	0003057	72	9996943	35
26	0250138	2908	9749862	0250158	1·3964142	0003129	73	9996871	34
27	0253046	2908	9746954	0253066	1·3962059	0003202	74	9996798	33
28	0255954	2908	9744046	0255974	1·3959976	0003276	74	9996724	32
29	0258862	2907	9741138	0258883	1·3957893	0003351	76	9996649	31
30	0261769	2908	9738231	0261792	1·3955810	0003427	76	9996573	30
31	0264677	2908	9735323	0264701	1·3953726	0003503	78	9996497	29
32	0267585	2908	9732415	0267610	1·3951642	0003581	78	9996419	28
33	0270493	2908	9729507	0270518	1·3949557	0003659	79	9996341	27
34	0273401	2908	9726599	0273426	1·3947472	0003738	80	9996262	26
35	0276309	2907	9723691	0276335	1·3945387	0003818	81	9996182	25
36	0279216	2908	9720784	0279244	1·3943302	0003899	81	9996101	24
37	0282124	2908	9717876	0282152	1·3941216	0003980	83	9996020	23
38	0285032	2908	9714968	0285060	1·3939130	0004063	83	9995937	22
39	0287940	2908	9712060	0287969	1·3937044	0004146	84	9995854	21
40	0290847	2908	9709153	0290878	1·3934958	0004230	86	9995770	20
41	0293755	2907	9706245	0293787	1·3932871	0004316	85	9995684	19
42	0296662	2908	9703338	0296696	1·3930784	0004401	87	9995599	18
43	0299570	2908	9700430	0299604	1·3928697	0004488	88	9995512	17
44	0302478	2907	9697522	0302512	1·3926610	0004576	88	9995424	16
45	0305385	2908	9694615	0305421	1·3924522	0004664	89	9995336	15
46	0308293	2907	9691707	0308330	1·3922434	0004753	90	9995247	14
47	0311200	2908	9688800	0311238	1·3920345	0004843	91	9995157	13
48	0314108	2907	9685892	0314146	1·3918256	0004934	92	9995066	12
49	0317015	2907	9682985	0317055	1·3916167	0005026	93	9994974	11
50	0319922	2908	9680078	0319964	1·3914078	0005119	93	9994881	10
51	0322830	2907	9677170	0322872	1·3911988	0005212	95	9994788	9
52	0325737	2907	9674263	0325780	1·3909898	0005307	95	9994693	8
53	0328644	2908	9671356	0328689	1·3907807	0005402	96	9994598	7
54	0331552	2907	9668448	0331598	1·3905716	0005498	97	9994502	6
55	0334459	2907	9665541	0334506	1·3903625	0005595	97	9994405	5
56	0337366	2908	9662634	0337414	1·3901534	0005692	99	9994308	4
57	0340274	2907	9659726	0340323	1·3899443	0005791	99	9994209	3
58	0343181	2907	9656819	0343232	1·3897352	0005890	101	9994110	2
59	0346088	2907	9653912	0346140	1·3895260	0005991	101	9994009	1
60	0348995		9651005	0349048	1·3893168	0006092		9993908	0
′	Cosine	Diff.	Vers.	Co-chord	Chord	Covers.	Diff.	Sine	′

,	Sine	Diff.	Covers.	Chord	Co-chord	Vers.	Diff.	Cosine	,
0	0348995	2907	9651005	0349048	1·3893168	0000092	102	9993908	60
1	0351902	2907	9648098	0351956	1·3891075	0006194	102	9993806	59
2	0354809	2907	9645191	0354864	1·3888982	0006296	104	9993704	58
3	0357716	2907	9642284	0357773	1·3886889	0006400	105	9993600	57
4	0360623	2907	9639377	0360682	1·3884796	0006505	105	9993495	56
5	0363530	2907	9636470	0363590	1·3882702	0006610	106	9993390	55
6	0366437	2907	9633563	0366498	1·3880608	0006716	107	9993284	54
7	0369344	2907	9630656	0369407	1·3878513	0006823	108	9993177	53
8	0372251	2907	9627749	0372316	1·3876418	0006931	109	9993069	52
9	0375158	2907	9624842	0375224	1·3874323	0007040	109	9992960	51
10	0378065	2906	9621935	0378132	1·3872228	0007149	111	9992851	50
11	0380971	2907	9619029	0381040	1·3870132	0007260	111	9992740	49
12	0383878	2907	9616122	0383948	1·3868036	0007371	112	9992629	48
13	0386785	2907	9613215	0386857	1·3865940	0007483	113	9992517	47
14	0389692	2906	9610308	0389766	1·3863844	0007596	114	9992404	46
15	0392598	2907	9607402	0392674	1·3861747	0007710	114	9992290	45
16	0395505	2906	9604495	0395582	1·3859650	0007824	116	9992176	44
17	0398411	2907	9601589	0398490	1·3857553	0007940	116	9992060	43
18	0401318	2906	9598682	0401398	1·3855456	0008056	117	9991944	42
19	0404224	2907	9595776	0404307	1·3853358	0008173	118	9991827	41
20	0407131	2906	9592869	0407216	1·3851260	0008291	119	9991709	40
21	0410037	2907	9589963	0410124	1·3849161	0008410	120	9991590	39
22	0412944	2906	9587056	0413032	1·3847062	0008530	120	9991470	38
23	0415850	2907	9584150	0415940	1·3844963	0008650	122	9991350	37
24	0418757	2906	9581243	0418848	1·3842864	0008772	122	9991228	36
25	0421663	2906	9578337	0421756	1·3840764	0008894	123	9991106	35
26	0424569	2906	9575431	0424664	1·3838664	0009017	124	9990983	34
27	0427475	2907	9572525	0427573	1·3836564	0009141	125	9990859	33
28	0430382	2906	9569618	0430482	1·3834464	0009266	125	9990734	32
29	0433288	2906	9566712	0433390	1·3832363	0009391	127	9990609	31
30	0436194	2906	9563806	0436298	1·3830262	0009518	127	9990482	30
31	0439100	2906	9560900	0439206	1·3928160	0009645	128	9990355	29
32	0442006	2906	9557994	0442114	1·3826058	0009773	129	9990227	28
33	0444912	2906	9555088	0445022	1·3823956	0009902	130	9990098	27
34	0447818	2906	9552182	0447930	1·3821854	0010032	131	9989968	26
35	0450724	2906	9549276	0450838	1·3819751	0010163	131	9989837	25
36	0453630	2906	9546370	0453746	1·3817648	0010294	133	9989706	24
37	0456536	2906	9543464	0456654	1·3815545	0010427	133	9989573	23
38	0459442	2905	9540558	0459562	1·3813442	0010560	134	9989440	22
39	0462347	2906	9537653	0462471	1·3811338	0010694	135	9989306	21
40	0465253	2906	9534747	0465380	1·3809234	0010829	136	9989171	20
41	0468159	2906	9531841	0468288	1·3807129	0010965	136	9989035	19
42	0471065	2905	9528935	0471196	1·3805024	0011101	138	9988899	18
43	0473970	2906	9526030	0474104	1·3802919	0011239	138	9988761	17
44	0476876	2905	9523124	0477012	1·3800814	0011377	139	9988623	16
45	0479781	2906	9520219	0479920	1·3798709	0011516	140	9988484	15
46	0482687	2905	9517313	0482828	1·3796604	0011656	141	9988344	14
47	0485592	2906	9514408	0485736	1·3794497	0011797	142	9988203	13
48	0488498	2905	9511502	0488644	1·3792390	0011939	142	9988061	12
49	0491403	2905	9508597	0491552	1·3790284	0012081	144	9987919	11
50	0494308	2906	9505692	0494460	1·3788178	0012225	144	9987775	10
51	0497214	2905	9502786	0497368	1·3786070	0012369	145	9987631	9
52	0500119	2905	9499881	0500276	1·3783962	0012514	146	9987486	8
53	0503024	2905	9496976	0503184	1·3781854	0012660	146	9987340	7
54	0505929	2906	9494071	0506092	1·3779746	0012806	148	9987194	6
55	0508835	2905	9491165	0509000	1·3777638	0012954	148	9987046	5
56	0511740	2905	9488260	0511908	1·3775530	0013102	150	9986898	4
57	0514645	2905	9485355	0514816	1·3773420	0013252	150	9986748	3
58	0517550	2905	9482450	0517724	1·3771310	0013402	151	9986598	2
59	0520455	2905	9479545	0520631	1·3769201	0013553	152	9986447	1
60	0523360		9476640	0523528	1·3767092	0013705		9986295	0
,	Cosine	Diff.	Vers.	Co-chord	Chord	Covers.	Diff.	Sine	,

′	Sine	Diff.	Covers.	Chord	Co-chord	Vers.	Diff.	Cosine	′
0	0523360	2904	9476640	0523538	1·3767092	0013705	152	9986295	60
1	0526264	2905	9473736	0526446	1·3764981	0013857	154	9986143	59
2	0529169	2905	9470831	0529354	1·3762870	0014011	154	9985989	58
3	0532074	2905	9467926	0532262	1·3760760	0014165	155	9985835	57
4	0534979	2904	9465021	0535170	1·3758650	0014320	156	9985680	56
5	0537883	2905	9462117	0538078	1·3756538	0014476	157	9985524	55
6	0540788	2905	9459212	0540986	1·3754426	0014633	158	9985367	54
7	0543693	2904	9456307	0543894	1·3752314	0014791	159	9985209	53
8	0546597	2905	9453403	0546802	1·3750202	0014950	159	9985050	52
9	0549502	2904	9450498	0549710	1·3748089	0015109	160	9984891	51
10	0552406	2905	9447594	0552618	1·3745976	0015269	161	9984731	50
11	0555311	2904	9444689	0555525	1·3743863	0015430	162	9984570	49
12	0558215	2904	9441785	0558432	1·3741750	0015592	163	9984408	48
13	0561119	2905	9438881	0561340	1·3739636	0015755	164	9984245	47
14	0564024	2904	9435976	0564248	1·3737522	0015919	164	9984081	46
15	0566928	2904	9433072	0567156	1·3735408	0016083	166	9983917	45
16	0569832	2904	9430168	0570064	1·3733294	0016249	166	9983751	44
17	0572736	2904	9427264	0572972	1·3731179	0016415	167	9983585	43
18	0575640	2904	9424360	0575880	1·3729064	0016582	168	9983418	42
19	0578544	2904	9421456	0578787	1·3726948	0016750	168	9983250	41
20	0581448	2904	9418552	0581694	1·3724832	0016918	170	9983082	40
21	0584352	2904	9415648	0584602	1·3722716	0017088	170	9982912	39
22	0587256	2904	9412744	0587510	1·3720600	0017258	172	9982742	38
23	0590160	2904	9409840	0590417	1·3718484	0017430	172	9982570	37
24	0593064	2903	9406936	0593324	1·3716368	0017602	173	9982398	36
25	0595967	2904	9404033	0596232	1·3714250	0017775	173	9982225	35
26	0598871	2904	9401129	0599140	1·3712132	0017948	175	9982052	34
27	0601775	2903	9398225	0602048	1·3710014	0018123	176	9981877	33
28	0604678	2904	9395322	0604956	1·3707896	0018299	176	9981701	32
29	0607582	2903	9392418	0607863	1·3705778	0018475	177	9981525	31
30	0610485	2904	9389515	0610770	1·3703660	0018652	178	9981348	30
31	0613389	2903	9386611	0613678	1·3701541	0018830	179	9981170	29
32	0616292	2904	9383708	0616586	1·3699422	0019009	180	9980991	28
33	0619196	2903	9380804	0619493	1·3697302	0019189	180	9980811	27
34	0622099	2903	9377901	0622400	1·3695182	0019369	181	9980631	26
35	0625002	2903	9374998	0625308	1·3693062	0019550	183	9980450	25
36	0627905	2903	9372095	0628216	1·3690942	0019733	183	9980267	24
37	0630808	2903	9369192	0631123	1·3688821	0019916	184	9980084	23
38	0633711	2903	9366289	0634030	1·3686700	0020100	184	9979900	22
39	0636614	2903	9363386	0636937	1·3684579	0020284	186	9979716	21
40	0639517	2903	9360483	0639844	1·3682458	0020470	187	9979530	20
41	0642420	2903	9357580	0642752	1·3680336	0020657	187	9979343	19
42	0645323	2903	9354677	0645660	1·3678214	0020844	188	9979156	18
43	0648226	2903	9351774	0648567	1·3676091	0021032	189	9978968	17
44	0651129	2902	9348871	0651474	1·3673968	0021221	190	9978779	16
45	0654031	2903	9345969	0654381	1·3671845	0021411	190	9978589	15
46	0656934	2902	9343066	0657288	1·3669722	0021601	192	9978399	14
47	0659836	2903	9340164	0660196	1·3667599	0021793	192	9978207	13
48	0662739	2902	9337261	0663104	1·3665476	0021985	194	9978015	12
49	0665641	2903	9334359	0666011	1·3663351	0022179	194	9977821	11
50	0668544	2902	9331456	0668918	1·3661226	0022373	194	9977627	10
51	0671446	2903	9328554	0671825	1·3659102	0022567	196	9977433	9
52	0674349	2902	9325651	0674732	1·3656978	0022763	197	9977237	8
53	0677251	2902	9322749	0677640	1·3654852	0022960	197	9977040	7
54	0680153	2902	9319847	0680548	1·3652726	0023157	198	9976843	6
55	0683055	2902	9316945	0683455	1·3650600	0023355	200	9976645	5
56	0685957	2902	9314043	0686362	1·3648474	0023555	200	9976445	4
57	0688859	2902	9311141	0689269	1·3646348	0023755	200	9976245	3
58	0691761	2902	9308239	0692176	1·3644222	0023955	202	9976045	2
59	0694663	2902	9305337	0695083	1·3642095	0024157	202	9975843	1
60	0697565	2902	9302435	0697990	1·3639968	0024359		9975641	0

′	Cosine	Diff.	Vers.	Co-chord	Chord	Covers.	Diff.	Sine	′

′	Sine	Diff.	Covers.	Chord	Co-chord	Vers.	Diff.	Cosine	′
0	0697565	2902	9302435	0697990	1·3639968	0024359	204	9975641	60
1	0700467	2901	9299533	0700897	1·3637840	0024563	204	9975437	59
2	0703368	2902	9296632	0703804	1·3635712	0024767	205	9975233	58
3	0706270	2901	9293730	0706711	1·3633584	0024972	206	9975028	57
4	0709171	2902	9290829	0709618	1·3631456	0025178	207	9974822	56
5	0712073	2901	9287927	0712525	1·3629327	0025385	207	9974615	55
6	0714974	2902	9285026	0715432	1·3627198	0025592	209	9974408	54
7	0717876	2901	9282124	0718339	1·3625068	0025801	209	9974199	53
8	0720777	2901	9279223	0721246	1·3622938	0026010	210	9973990	52
9	0723678	2902	9276322	0724153	1·3620808	0026220	211	9973780	51
10	0726580	2901	9273420	0727060	1·3618678	0026431	212	9973569	50
11	0729481	2901	9270519	0729967	1·3616548	0026643	212	9973357	49
12	0732382	2901	9267618	0732874	1·3614418	0026855	214	9973145	48
13	0735283	2901	9264717	0735781	1·3612287	0027069	214	9972931	47
14	0738184	2901	9261816	0738688	1·3610156	0027283	215	9972717	46
15	0741085	2901	9258915	0741595	1·3608024	0027498	216	9972502	45
16	0743986	2901	9256014	0744502	1·3605892	0027714	217	9972286	44
17	0746887	2900	9253113	0747409	1·3603759	0027931	218	9972069	43
18	0749787	2901	9250213	0750316	1·3601626	0028149	218	9971851	42
19	0752688	2901	9247312	0753223	1·3599494	0028367	220	9971633	41
20	0755589	2900	9244411	0756130	1·3597362	0028587	220	9971413	40
21	0758489	2901	9241511	0759036	1·3595228	0028807	221	9971193	39
22	0761390	2900	9238610	0761942	1·3593094	0029028	222	9970972	38
23	0764290	2900	9235710	0764849	1·3590960	0029250	222	9970750	37
24	0767190	2901	9232810	0767756	1·3588826	0029472	224	9970528	36
25	0770091	2900	9229909	0770663	1·3586691	0029696	224	9970304	35
26	0772991	2900	9227009	0773570	1·3584556	0029920	226	9970080	34
27	0775891	2900	9224109	0776477	1·3582421	0030146	226	9969854	33
28	0778791	2900	9221209	0779384	1·3580286	0030372	227	9969628	32
29	0781691	2900	9218309	0782290	1·3578150	0030599	228	9969401	31
30	0784591	2900	9215409	0785196	1·3576014	0030827	228	9969173	30
31	0787491	2900	9212509	0788103	1·3573878	0031055	230	9968945	29
32	0790391	2899	9209609	0791010	1·3571742	0031285	230	9968715	28
33	0793290	2900	9206710	0793916	1·3569605	0031515	231	9968485	27
34	0796190	2900	9203810	0796822	1·3567468	0031746	232	9968254	26
35	0799090	2899	9200910	0799729	1·3565331	0031978	233	9968022	25
36	0801989	2900	9198011	0802636	1·3563194	0032211	234	9967789	24
37	0804889	2899	9195111	0805542	1·3561056	0032445	234	9967555	23
38	0807788	2899	9192212	0808448	1·3558918	0032679	236	9967321	22
39	0810687	2900	9189313	0811355	1·3556779	0032915	236	9967085	21
40	0813587	2899	9186413	0814262	1·3554640	0033151	237	9966849	20
41	0816486	2899	9183514	0817168	1·3552501	0033388	238	9966612	19
42	0819385	2899	9180615	0820074	1·3550362	0033626	239	9966374	18
43	0822284	2899	9177716	0822981	1·3548222	0033865	240	9966135	17
44	0825183	2899	9174817	0825888	1·3546082	0034105	240	9965895	16
45	0828082	2899	9171918	0828794	1·3543942	0034345	241	9965655	15
46	0830981	2899	9169019	0831700	1·3541802	0034586	242	9965414	14
47	0833880	2898	9166120	0834607	1·3539661	0034828	243	9965172	13
48	0836778	2899	9163222	0837514	1·3537520	0035071	244	9964929	12
49	0839677	2899	9160323	0840420	1·3535378	0035315	245	9964685	11
50	0842576	2898	9157424	0843326	1·3533236	0035560	245	9964440	10
51	0845474	2899	9154526	0846232	1·3531094	0035805	247	9964195	9
52	0848373	2898	9151627	0849138	1·3528952	0036052	247	9963948	8
53	0851271	2898	9148729	0852044	1·3526809	0036299	248	9963701	7
54	0854169	2898	9145831	0854950	1·3524666	0036547	249	9963453	6
55	0857067	2899	9142933	0857857	1·3522523	0036796	250	9963204	5
56	0859966	2898	9140034	0860764	1·3520380	0037046	250	9962954	4
57	0862864	2898	9137136	0863670	1·3518236	0037296	252	9962704	3
58	0865762	2898	9134238	0866576	1·3516092	0037548	252	9962452	2
59	0868660	2897	9131340	0869482	1·3513948	0037800	253	9962200	1
60	0871557		9128443	0872388	1·3511804	0038053		9961947	0

′	Cosine	Diff.	Vers.	Co-chord	Chord	Covers.	Diff.	Sine	′

′	Sine	Diff.	Covers.	Chord	Co-chord	Vers.	Diff.	Cosine	′
0	0871557	2898	9128443	0872388	1·3511804	0038053	254	9961947	60
1	0874455	2898	9125545	0875294	1·3509659	0038307	255	9961693	59
2	0877353	2898	9122647	0878200	1·3507514	0038562	255	9961438	58
3	0880251	2897	9119749	0881106	1·3505369	0038817	257	9961183	57
4	0883148	2898	9116852	0884012	1·3503224	0039074	257	9960926	56
5	0886046	2897	9113954	0886918	1·3501078	0039331	258	9960669	55
6	0888943	2897	9111057	0889824	1·3498932	0039589	259	9960411	54
7	0891840	2898	9108160	0892730	1·3496785	0039848	260	9960152	53
8	0894738	2897	9105262	0895636	1·3494638	0040108	261	9959892	52
9	0897635	2897	9102365	0898542	1·3492491	0040369	261	9959631	51
10	0900532	2897	9099468	0901448	1·3490344	0040630	263	9959370	50
11	0903429	2897	9096571	0904354	1·3488196	0040893	263	9959107	49
12	0906326	2897	9093674	0907260	1·3486048	0041156	264	9958844	48
13	0909223	2896	9090777	0910166	1·3483900	0041420	265	9958580	47
14	0912119	2897	9087881	0913072	1·3481752	0041685	266	9958315	46
15	0915016	2897	9084984	0915978	1·3479603	0041951	266	9958049	45
16	0917913	2896	9082087	0918884	1·3477454	0042217	268	9957783	44
17	0920809	2897	9079191	0921789	1·3475304	0042485	268	9957515	43
18	0923706	2896	9076294	0924694	1·3473154	0042753	269	9957247	42
19	0926602	2897	9073398	0927600	1·3471004	0043022	270	9956978	41
20	0929499	2896	9070501	0930506	1·3468854	0043292	271	9956708	40
21	0932395	2896	9067605	0933412	1·3466703	0043563	272	9956437	39
22	0935291	2896	9064709	0936318	1·3464552	0043835	272	9956165	38
23	0938187	2896	9061813	0939224	1·3462401	0044107	273	9955893	37
24	0941083	2896	9058917	0942130	1·3460250	0044380	275	9955620	36
25	0943979	2896	9056021	0945035	1·3458098	0044655	275	9955345	35
26	0946875	2896	9053125	0947940	1·3455946	0044930	275	9955070	34
27	0949771	2895	9050229	0950846	1·3453794	0045205	277	9954795	33
28	0952666	2896	9047334	0953752	1·3451642	0045482	278	9954518	32
29	0955562	2896	9044438	0956657	1·3449489	0045760	278	9954240	31
30	0958458	2895	9041542	0959562	1·3447336	0046038	279	9953962	30
31	0961353	2895	9038647	0962468	1·3445183	0046317	280	9953683	29
32	0964248	2896	9035752	0965374	1·3443030	0046597	281	9953403	28
33	0967144	2895	9032856	0968279	1·3440876	0046878	282	9953122	27
34	0970039	2895	9029961	0971184	1·3438722	0047160	283	9952840	26
35	0972934	2895	9027066	0974090	1·3436567	0047443	283	9952557	25
36	0975829	2895	9024171	0976996	1·3434412	0047726	284	9952274	24
37	0978724	2895	9021276	0979901	1·3432257	0048010	285	9951990	23
38	0981619	2895	9018381	0982806	1·3430102	0048295	286	9951705	22
39	0984514	2894	9015486	0985711	1·3427946	0048581	287	9951419	21
40	0987408	2894	9012592	0988616	1·3425790	0048868	288	9951132	20
41	0990303	2894	9009697	0991522	1·3423634	0049156	288	9950844	19
42	0993197	2895	9006803	0994428	1·3421478	0049444	290	9950556	18
43	0996092	2894	9003908	0997333	1·3419321	0049734	290	9950266	17
44	0998986	2895	9001014	1000238	1·3417164	0050024	291	9949976	16
45	1001881	2894	8998119	1003143	1·3415006	0050315	292	9949685	15
46	1004775	2894	8995225	1006048	1·3412848	0050607	292	9949393	14
47	1007669	2894	8992331	1008953	1·3410690	0050899	294	9949101	13
48	1010563	2894	8989437	1011858	1·3408532	0051193	294	9948807	12
49	1013457	2894	8986543	1014764	1·3406374	0051487	296	9948513	11
50	1016351	2894	8983649	1017670	1·3404216	0051783	296	9948217	10
51	1019245	2893	8980755	1020575	1·3402056	0052079	296	9947921	9
52	1022138	2894	8977862	1023480	1·3399896	0052375	298	9947625	8
53	1025032	2893	8974968	1026385	1·3397737	0052673	299	9947327	7
54	1027925	2894	8972075	1029290	1·3395578	0052972	299	9947028	6
55	1030819	2893	8969181	1032195	1·3393417	0053271	301	9946729	5
56	1033712	2893	8966288	1035100	1·3391256	0053572	301	9946428	4
57	1036605	2894	8963395	1038005	1·3389096	0053873	302	9946127	3
58	1039499	2893	8960501	1040910	1·3386936	0054175	302	9945825	2
59	1042392	2893	8957608	1043815	1·3384774	0054477	304	9945523	1
60	1045285	2893	8954715	1046720	1·3382612	0054781		9945219	0
′	Cosine	Diff.	Vers.	Co-chord	Chord	Covers.	Diff.	Sine	′

'	Sine	Diff.	Covers.	Chord	Co-chord	Vers.	Diff.	Cosine	'
0	1045285		8954715	1046720	1·3382612	0054781		9945219	60
1	1048178	2893	8951822	1049624	1·3380450	0055086	305	9944914	59
2	1051070	2892	8948930	1052528	1·3378288	0055391	305	9944609	58
3	1053963	2893	8946037	1055433	1·3376125	0055697	306	9944303	57
4	1056856	2893	8943144	1058338	1·3373962	0056004	307	9943996	56
5	1059748	2892	8940252	1061243	1·3371799	0056312	308	9943688	55
		2893					309		
6	1062641	2892	8937359	1064148	1·3369636	0056621	309	9943379	54
7	1065533	2892	8934467	1067053	1·3367473	0056930	310	9943070	53
8	1068425	2893	8931575	1069958	1·3365310	0057240	312	9942760	52
9	1071318	2892	8928682	1072862	1·3363145	0057552	312	9942448	51
10	1074210	2892	8925790	1075766	1·3360980	0057864	313	9942136	50
11	1077102	2892	8922898	1078671	1·3358816	0058177	313	9941823	49
12	1079994	2891	8920006	1081576	1·3356652	0058490	315	9941510	48
13	1082885	2892	8917115	1084481	1·3354486	0058805	315	9941195	47
14	1085777	2892	8914223	1087386	1·3352320	0059120	317	9940880	46
15	1088668	2891	8911331	1090290	1·3350154	0059437	317	9940563	45
16	1091560	2892	8908440	1093194	1·3347988	0059754	318	9940246	44
17	1094452	2891	8905548	1096099	1·3345822	0060072	318	9939928	43
18	1097343	2891	8902657	1099004	1·3343656	0060390	320	9939610	42
19	1100234	2892	8899766	1101908	1·3341489	0060710	321	9939290	41
20	1103126	2891	8896874	1104812	1·3339322	0061031	321	9938969	40
21	1106017	2891	8893983	1107717	1·3337154	0061352	322	9938648	39
22	1108908	2891	8891092	1110622	1·3334986	0061674	323	9938326	38
23	1111799	2890	8888201	1113526	1·3332818	0061997	324	9938003	37
24	1114689	2891	8885311	1116430	1·3330650	0062321	324	9937679	36
25	1117580	2891	8882420	1119334	1·3328481	0062645	326	9937355	35
26	1120471	2890	8879529	1122238	1·3326312	0062971	326	9937029	34
27	1123361	2891	8876639	1125143	1·3324143	0063297	328	9936703	33
28	1126252	2890	8873748	1128048	1·3321974	0063625	328	9936375	32
29	1129142	2890	8870858	1130952	1·3319804	0063953	328	9936047	31
30	1132032	2890	8867968	1133856	1·3317634	0064281	330	9935719	30
31	1134922	2890	8865078	1136760	1·3315463	0064611	331	9935389	29
32	1137812	2890	8862188	1139664	1·3313292	0064942	331	9935058	28
33	1140702	2890	8859298	1142568	1·3311121	0065273	332	9934727	27
34	1143592	2890	8856408	1145472	1·3308950	0065605	333	9934395	26
35	1146482	2890	8853518	1148376	1·3306779	0065938	334	9934062	25
36	1149372	2889	8850628	1151280	1·3304608	0066272	335	9933728	24
37	1152261	2890	8847739	1154184	1·3302435	0066607	336	9933393	23
38	1155151	2889	8844849	1157088	1·3300262	0066943	336	9933057	22
39	1158040	2889	8841960	1159992	1·3298090	0067279	337	9932721	21
40	1160929	2889	8839071	1162896	1·3295918	0067616	339	9932384	20
41	1163818	2889	8836182	1165800	1·3293744	0067955	339	9932045	19
42	1166707	2889	8833293	1168704	1·3291570	0068294	339	9931706	18
43	1169596	2889	8830404	1171608	1·3289397	0068633	341	9931367	17
44	1172485	2889	8827515	1174512	1·3287224	0068974	341	9931026	16
45	1175374	2889	8824626	1177416	1·3285049	0069315	343	9930685	15
46	1178263	2888	8821737	1180320	1·3282874	0069658	343	9930342	14
47	1181151	2889	8818849	1183224	1·3280699	0070001	344	9929999	13
48	1184040	2888	8815960	1186128	1·3278524	0070345	345	9929655	12
49	1186928	2888	8813072	1189031	1·3276349	0070690	345	9929310	11
50	1189816	2888	8810184	1191934	1·3274174	0071035	347	9928965	10
51	1192704	2889	8807296	1194838	1·3271997	0071382	347	9928618	9
52	1195593	2888	8804407	1197742	1·3269820	0071729	349	9928271	8
53	1198481	2887	8801519	1200646	1·3267644	0072078	349	9927922	7
54	1201368	2888	8798632	1203550	1·3265468	0072427	349	9927573	6
55	1204256	2888	8795744	1206453	1·3263291	0072776	351	9927224	5
56	1207144	2887	8792856	1209356	1·3261114	0073127	352	9926873	4
57	1210031	2888	8789969	1212260	1·3258936	0073479	352	9926521	3
58	1212919	2887	8787081	1215164	1·3256758	0073831	353	9926169	2
59	1215806	2887	8784194	1218067	1·3254579	0074184	354	9925816	1
60	1218693	2887	8781307	1220970	1·3252400	0074538		9925462	0
'	Cosine	Diff.	Vers.	Co-chord	Chord	Covers.	Diff.	Sine	'

7 Deg.

′	Sine	Diff.	Covers.	Chord	Co-chord	Vers.	Diff.	Cosine	′
0	1218693	2888	8781307	1220970	1·3252400	0074538	355	9925462	60
1	1221581	2887	8778419	1223874	1·3250222	0074893	356	9925107	59
2	1224468	2887	8775532	1226778	1·3248044	0075249	357	9924751	58
3	1227355	2886	8772645	1229681	1·3245864	0075606	357	9924394	57
4	1230241	2887	8769759	1232584	1·3243684	0075963	358	9924037	56
5	1233128	2887	8766872	1235488	1·3241504	0076321	360	9923679	55
6	1236015	2886	8763985	1238392	1·3239324	0076681	360	9923319	54
7	1238901	2887	8761099	1241295	1·3237144	0077041	360	9922959	53
8	1241788	2886	8758212	1244198	1·3234964	0077401	362	9922599	52
9	1244674	2886	8755326	1247101	1·3232782	0077763	363	9922237	51
10	1247560	2886	8752440	1250004	1·3230600	0078126	363	9921874	50
11	1250446	2886	8749554	1252907	1·3228419	0078489	364	9921511	49
12	1253332	2886	8746668	1255810	1·3226238	0078853	365	9921147	48
13	1256218	2886	8743782	1258713	1·3224055	0079218	366	9920782	47
14	1259104	2886	8740896	1261616	1·3221872	0079584	367	9920416	46
15	1261990	2885	8738010	1264519	1·3219690	0079951	367	9920049	45
16	1264875	2886	8735125	1267422	1·3217508	0080318	368	9919682	44
17	1267761	2885	8732239	1270325	1·3215324	0080686	370	9919314	43
18	1270646	2885	8729354	1273228	1·3213140	0081056	370	9918944	42
19	1273531	2885	8726469	1276131	1·3210956	0081426	370	9918574	41
20	1276416	2886	8723584	1279034	1·3208772	0081796	372	9918204	40
21	1279302	2884	8720698	1281937	1·3206588	0082168	373	9917832	39
22	1282186	2885	8717814	1284840	1·3204404	0082541	373	9917459	38
23	1285071	2885	8714929	1287743	1·3202219	0082914	374	9917086	37
24	1287956	2885	8712044	1290646	1·3200034	0083288	375	9916712	36
25	1290841	2884	8709159	1293549	1·3197848	0083663	376	9916337	35
26	1293725	2884	8706275	1296452	1·3195662	0084039	377	9915961	34
27	1296609	2885	8703391	1299355	1·3193476	0084416	378	9915584	33
28	1299494	2884	8700506	1302258	1·3191290	0084794	378	9915206	32
29	1302378	2884	8697622	1305160	1·3189103	0085172	379	9914828	31
30	1305262	2884	8694738	1308062	1·3186916	0085551	380	9914449	30
31	1308146	2884	8691854	1310965	1·3184729	0085931	381	9914069	29
32	1311030	2883	8688970	1313868	1·3182542	0086312	382	9913688	28
33	1313913	2884	8686087	1316770	1·3180354	0086694	383	9913306	27
34	1316797	2884	8683203	1319672	1·3178166	0087077	383	9912923	26
35	1319681	2883	8680319	1322575	1·3175978	0087460	385	9912540	25
36	1322564	2883	8677436	1325478	1·3173790	0087845	385	9912155	24
37	1325447	2883	8674553	1328380	1·3171601	0088230	386	9911770	23
38	1328330	2883	8671670	1331282	1·3169412	0088616	387	9911384	22
39	1331213	2883	8668787	1334185	1·3167222	0089003	387	9910997	21
40	1334096	2883	8665904	1337088	1·3165032	0089390	389	9910610	20
41	1336979	2883	8663021	1339990	1·3162842	0089779	389	9910221	19
42	1339862	2882	8660138	1342892	1·3160652	0090168	390	9909832	18
43	1342744	2883	8657256	1345795	1·3158461	0090558	391	9909442	17
44	1345627	2882	8654373	1348698	1·3156270	0090949	392	9909051	16
45	1348509	2883	8651491	1351600	1·3154079	0091341	393	9908659	15
46	1351392	2882	8648608	1354502	1·3151888	0091734	393	9908266	14
47	1354274	2882	8645726	1357404	1·3149696	0092127	395	9907873	13
48	1357156	2882	8642844	1360306	1·3147504	0092522	395	9907478	12
49	1360038	2881	8639962	1363208	1·3145312	0092917	396	9907083	11
50	1362919	2882	8637081	1366110	1·3143120	0093313	397	9906687	10
51	1365801	2882	8634199	1369012	1·3140927	0093710	397	9906290	9
52	1368683	2881	8631317	1371914	1·3138734	0094107	399	9905893	8
53	1371564	2881	8628436	1374816	1·3136541	0094506	399	9905494	7
54	1374445	2882	8625555	1377718	1·3134348	0094905	401	9905095	6
55	1377327	2881	8622673	1380620	1·3132154	0095306	401	9904694	5
56	1380208	2881	8619792	1383522	1·3129960	0095707	402	9904293	4
57	1383089	2881	8616911	1386424	1·3127765	0096109	402	9903891	3
58	1385970	2880	8614030	1389326	1·3125570	0096511	404	9903489	2
59	1388850	2881	8611150	1392228	1·3123375	0096915	404	9903085	1
60	1391731		8608269	1395130	1·3121180	0097319		9902681	0
′	Cosine	Diff.	Vers.	Co-chord	Chord	Covers.	Diff.	Sine	′

NATURAL SINES, COSINES, &c. Deg. 82.

′	Sine	Diff.	Covers.	Chord	Co-chord	Vers.	Diff.	Cosine	′
0	1391731	2881	8608269	1395130	1·3121180	0097319	406	9902681	60
1	1394612	2880	8605388	1398032	1·3118985	0097725	406	9902275	59
2	1397492	2880	8602508	1400934	1·3116790	0098131	407	9901869	58
3	1400372	2880	8599628	1403835	1·3114593	0098538	407	9901462	57
4	1403252	2880	8596748	1406736	1·3112396	0098945	409	9901055	56
5	1406132	2880	8593868	1409638	1·3110200	0099354	409	9900646	55
6	1409012	2880	8590988	1412540	1·3108004	0099763	411	9900237	54
7	1411892	2880	8588108	1415441	1·3105806	0100174	411	9899826	53
8	1414772	2879	8585228	1418342	1·3103608	0100585	412	9899415	52
9	1417651	2880	8582349	1421244	1·3101411	0100997	413	9899003	51
10	1420531	2879	8579469	1424146	1·3099214	0101410	413	9898590	50
11	1423410	2879	8576590	1427047	1·3097015	0101823	415	9898177	49
12	1426289	2879	8573711	1429948	1·3094816	0102238	415	9897762	48
13	1429168	2879	8570832	1432850	1·3092617	0102653	416	9897347	47
14	1432047	2879	8567953	1435752	1·3090418	0103069	417	9896931	46
15	1434926	2879	8565074	1438653	1·3088219	0103486	418	9896514	45
16	1437805	2879	8562195	1441554	1·3086020	0103904	419	9896096	44
17	1440684	2878	8559316	1444455	1·3083820	0104323	419	9895677	43
18	1443562	2878	8556438	1447356	1·3081620	0104742	420	9895258	42
19	1446440	2879	8553560	1450258	1·3079419	0105162	422	9894838	41
20	1449319	2878	8550681	1453160	1·3077218	0105584	422	9894416	40
21	1452197	2878	8547803	1456061	1·3075017	0106006	422	9893994	39
22	1455075	2878	8544925	1458962	1·3072816	0106428	424	9893572	38
23	1457953	2878	8542047	1461863	1·3070614	0106852	425	9893148	37
24	1460830	2877	8539170	1464764	1·3068412	0107277	425	9892723	36
25	1463708	2878	8536292	1467665	1·3066210	0107702	426	9892298	35
26	1466585	2877	8533415	1470566	1·3064008	0108128	427	9891872	34
27	1469463	2878	8530537	1473467	1·3061805	0108555	428	9891445	33
28	1472340	2877	8527660	1476368	1·3059602	0108983	429	9891017	32
29	1475217	2877	8524783	1479269	1·3057399	0109412	429	9890588	31
30	1478094	2877	8521906	1482170	1·3055196	0109841	431	9890159	30
31	1480971	2877	8519029	1485071	1·3052992	0110272	431	9889728	29
32	1483848	2876	8516152	1487972	1·3050788	0110703	432	9889297	28
33	1486724	2877	8513276	1490873	1·3048583	0111135	433	9888865	27
34	1489601	2876	8510399	1493774	1·3046378	0111568	434	9888432	26
35	1492477	2876	8507523	1496674	1·3044173	0112002	434	9887998	25
36	1495353	2877	8504647	1499574	1·3041968	0112436	436	9887564	24
37	1498230	2876	8501770	1502475	1·3039762	0112872	436	9887128	23
38	1501106	2875	8498894	1505376	1·3037556	0113308	437	9886692	22
39	1503981	2876	8496019	1508277	1·3035350	0113745	438	9886255	21
40	1506857	2876	8493143	1511178	1·3033144	0114183	439	9885817	20
41	1509733	2875	8490267	1514078	1·3030938	0114622	439	9885378	19
42	1512608	2876	8487392	1516978	1·3028732	0115061	441	9884939	18
43	1515484	2875	8484516	1519879	1·3026524	0115502	441	9884498	17
44	1518359	2875	8481641	1522780	1·3024316	0115943	442	9884057	16
45	1521234	2875	8478766	1525680	1·3022109	0116385	443	9883615	15
46	1524109	2875	8475891	1528580	1·3019902	0116828	444	9883172	14
47	1526984	2874	8473016	1531480	1·3017693	0117272	444	9882728	13
48	1529858	2875	8470142	1534380	1·3015484	0117716	446	9882284	12
49	1532733	2874	8467267	1537281	1·3013275	0118162	446	9881838	11
50	1535607	2875	8464393	1540182	1·3011066	0118608	447	9881392	10
51	1538482	2874	8461518	1543082	1·3008857	0119055	448	9880945	9
52	1541356	2874	8458644	1545982	1·3006648	0119503	449	9880497	8
53	1544230	2874	8455770	1548882	1·3004438	0119952	449	9880048	7
54	1547104	2874	8452896	1551782	1·3002228	0120401	451	9879599	6
55	1549978	2873	8450022	1554682	1·3000017	0120852	451	9879148	5
56	1552851	2874	8447149	1557582	1·2997806	0121303	452	9878697	4
57	1555725	2873	8444275	1560482	1·2995595	0121755	453	9878245	3
58	1558598	2874	8441402	1563382	1·2993384	0122208	454	9877792	2
59	1561472	2873	8438528	1566282	1·2991172	0122662	455	9877338	1
60	1564345		8435655	1569182	1·2988960	0123117		9876883	0
′	Cosine	Diff.	Vers.	Co-chord	Chord	Covers.	Diff.	Sine	′

 Deg. 81.

′	Sine	Diff.	Covers.	Chord	Co-chord	Vers.	Diff.	Cosine	′
0	1564345	2873	8435655	1569182	1·2988960	0123117	455	9876883	60
1	1567218	2873	8432782	1572082	1·2986748	0123572	456	9876428	59
2	1570091	2872	8429909	1574982	1·2984536	0124028	458	9875972	58
3	1572963	2873	8427037	1577882	1·2982324	0124486	457	9875514	57
4	1575836	2872	8424164	1580782	1·2980112	0124943	459	9875057	56
5	1578708	2873	8421292	1583681	1·2977898	0125402	460	9874598	55
6	1581581	2872	8418419	1586580	1·2975684	0125862	460	9874138	54
7	1584453	2872	8415547	1589480	1·2973470	0126322	462	9873678	53
8	1587325	2872	8412675	1592380	1·2971256	0126784	462	9873216	52
9	1590197	2872	8409803	1595280	1·2969042	0127246	462	9872754	51
10	1593069	2871	8406931	1598180	1·2966828	0127709	463	9872291	50
11	1595940	2872	8404060	1601079	1·2964613	0128173	464	9871827	49
12	1598812	2871	8401188	1603978	1·2962398	0128637	464	9871363	48
13	1601683	2872	8398317	1606878	1·2960183	0129103	466	9870897	47
14	1604555	2871	8395445	1609778	1·2957968	0129569	466	9870431	46
15	1607426	2871	8392574	1612677	1·2955751	0130036	467	9869964	45
16	1610297	2870	8389703	1615576	1·2953534	0130504	468	9869496	44
17	1613167	2871	8386833	1618475	1·2951318	0130973	469	9869027	43
18	1616038	2871	8383962	1621374	1·2949102	0131443	470	9868557	42
19	1618909	2870	8381091	1624274	1·2946885	0131913	470	9868087	41
20	1621779	2871	8378221	1627174	1·2944668	0132385	472	9867615	40
21	1624650	2870	8375350	1630073	1·2942450	0132857	472	9867143	39
22	1627520	2870	8372480	1632972	1·2940232	0133330	473	9866670	38
23	1630390	2870	8369610	1635871	1·2938014	0133804	474	9866196	37
24	1633260	2869	8366740	1638770	1·2935796	0134278	474	9865722	36
25	1636129	2870	8363871	1641669	1·2933577	0134754	476	9865246	35
26	1638999	2869	8361001	1644568	1·2931358	0135230	476	9864770	34
27	1641868	2870	8358132	1647467	1·2929139	0135707	477	9864293	33
28	1644738	2869	8355262	1650366	1·2926920	0136185	478	9863815	32
29	1647607	2869	8352393	1653265	1·2924700	0136664	479	9863336	31
30	1650476	2869	8349524	1656164	1·2922480	0137144	480	9862856	30
31	1653345	2869	8346655	1659063	1·2920259	0137625	481	9862375	29
32	1656214	2868	8343786	1661962	1·2918038	0138106	481	9861894	28
33	1659082	2869	8340918	1664861	1·2915817	0138588	482	9861412	27
34	1661951	2868	8338049	1667760	1·2913596	0139071	483	9860929	26
35	1664819	2868	8335181	1670658	1·2911375	0139555	484	9860445	25
36	1667687	2869	8332313	1673556	1·2909154	0140040	485	9859960	24
37	1670556	2867	8329444	1676455	1·2906932	0140525	485	9859475	23
38	1673423	2868	8326577	1679354	1·2904710	0141012	487	9858988	22
39	1676291	2868	8323709	1682253	1·2902487	0141499	487	9858501	21
40	1679159	2867	8320841	1685152	1·2900264	0141987	488	9858013	20
41	1682026	2868	8317974	1688050	1·2898041	0142476	489	9857524	19
42	1684894	2867	8315106	1690948	1·2895818	0142965	489	9857035	18
43	1687761	2867	8312239	1693847	1·2893594	0143456	491	9856544	17
44	1690628	2867	8309372	1696746	1·2891370	0143947	491	9856053	16
45	1693495	2867	8306505	1699644	1·2889146	0144439	492	9855561	15
46	1696362	2866	8303638	1702542	1·2886922	0144932	493	9855068	14
47	1699228	2867	8300772	1705440	1·2884697	0145426	494	9854574	13
48	1702095	2866	8297905	1708338	1·2882472	0145921	495	9854079	12
49	1704961	2867	8295039	1711236	1·2880247	0146417	496	9853583	11
50	1707828	2866	8292172	1714134	1·2878022	0146913	496	9853087	10
51	1710694	2866	8289306	1717033	1·2875796	0147410	497	9852590	9
52	1713560	2865	8286440	1719932	1·2873570	0147908	498	9852092	8
53	1716425	2866	8283575	1722830	1·2871344	0148407	499	9851593	7
54	1719291	2865	8280709	1725728	1·2869118	0148907	500	9851093	6
55	1722156	2866	8277844	1728626	1·2866891	0149407	500	9850593	5
56	1725022	2865	8274978	1731524	1·2864664	0149909	502	9850091	4
57	1727887	2865	8272113	1734422	1·2862436	0150411	502	9849589	3
58	1730752	2865	8269248	1737320	1·2860208	0150914	503	9849086	2
59	1733617	2865	8266383	1740217	1·2857980	0151418	504	9848582	1
60	1736482		8263518	1743114	1·2855752	0151922	504	9848078	0

| ′ | Cosine | Diff. | Vers. | Co-chord | Chord | Covers. | Diff. | Sine | ′ |

'	Sine	Diff.	Covers.	Chord	Co-chord	Vers.	Diff.	Cosine	'
0	1736482	2864	8263518	1743114	1·2855752	0151922	506	9848078	60
1	1739346	2865	8260654	1746012	1·2853523	0152428	506	9847572	59
2	1742211	2864	8257789	1748910	1·2851294	0152934	508	9847066	58
3	1745075	2864	8254925	1751808	1·2849065	0153442	508	9846558	57
4	1747939	2864	8252061	1754706	1·2846836	0153950	508	9846050	56
5	1750803	2864	8249197	1757604	1·2844607	0154458	510	9845542	55
6	1753667	2864	8246333	1760502	1·2842378	0154968	511	9845032	54
7	1756531	2864	8243469	1763399	1·2840147	0155479	511	9844521	53
8	1759395	2863	8240605	1766296	1·2837916	0155990	512	9844010	52
9	1762258	2863	8237742	1769194	1·2835686	0156502	513	9843498	51
10	1765121	2863	8234879	1772092	1·2833456	0157015	514	9842985	50
11	1767984	2863	8232016	1774989	1·2831224	0157529	515	9842471	49
12	1770847	2863	8229153	1777886	1·2828992	0158044	515	9841956	48
13	1773710	2863	8226290	1780783	1·2826760	0158559	517	9841441	47
14	1776573	2862	8223427	1783680	1·2824528	0159076	517	9840924	46
15	1779435	2863	8220565	1786578	1·2822296	0159593	518	9840407	45
16	1782298	2862	8217702	1789476	1·2820064	0160111	519	9839889	44
17	1785160	2862	8214840	1792373	1·2817831	0160630	520	9839370	43
18	1788022	2862	8211978	1795270	1·2815598	0161150	520	9838850	42
19	1790884	2862	8209116	1798167	1·2813365	0161670	522	9838330	41
20	1793746	2861	8206254	1801064	1·2811132	0162192	522	9837808	40
21	1796607	2862	8203393	1803961	1·2808898	0162714	523	9837286	39
22	1799469	2861	8200531	1806858	1·2806664	0163237	524	9836763	38
23	1802330	2861	8197670	1809755	1·2804429	0163761	524	9836239	37
24	1805191	2861	8194809	1812652	1·2802194	0164285	526	9835715	36
25	1808052	2861	8191948	1815549	1·2799959	0164811	526	9835189	35
26	1810913	2861	8189087	1818446	1·2797724	0165337	527	9834663	34
27	1813774	2861	8186226	1821342	1·2795488	0165864	528	9834136	33
28	1816635	2860	8183365	1824238	1·2793252	0166392	529	9833608	32
29	1819495	2860	8180505	1827135	1·2791016	0166921	530	9833079	31
30	1822355	2860	8177645	1830032	1·2788780	0167451	530	9832549	30
31	1825215	2860	8174785	1832929	1·2786543	0167981	532	9832019	29
32	1828075	2860	8171925	1835826	1·2784306	0168513	532	9831487	28
33	1830935	2860	8169065	1838722	1·2782069	0169045	533	9830955	27
34	1833795	2859	8166205	1841618	1·2779832	0169578	534	9830422	26
35	1836654	2860	8163346	1844515	1·2777594	0170112	535	9829888	25
36	1839514	2859	8160486	1847412	1·2775356	0170647	535	9829353	24
37	1842373	2859	8157627	1850308	1·2773118	0171182	536	9828818	23
38	1845232	2859	8154768	1853204	1·2770880	0171718	538	9828282	22
39	1848091	2858	8151909	1856101	1·2768641	0172256	538	9827744	21
40	1850949	2859	8149051	1858998	1·2766402	0172794	538	9827206	20
41	1853808	2858	8146192	1861894	1·2764162	0173332	540	9826668	19
42	1856666	2858	8143334	1864790	1·2761922	0173872	541	9826128	18
43	1859524	2858	8140476	1867686	1·2759682	0174413	541	9825587	17
44	1862382	2858	8137618	1870582	1·2757442	0174954	542	9825046	16
45	1865240	2858	8134760	1873478	1·2755202	0175496	543	9824504	15
46	1868098	2858	8131902	1876374	1·2752962	0176039	544	9823961	14
47	1870956	2857	8129044	1879270	1·2750721	0176583	544	9823417	13
48	1873813	2857	8126187	1882166	1·2748480	0177127	546	9822873	12
49	1876670	2858	8123330	1885062	1·2746238	0177673	546	9822327	11
50	1879528	2857	8120472	1887958	1·2743996	0178219	547	9821781	10
51	1882385	2856	8117615	1890854	1·2741754	0178766	548	9821234	9
52	1885241	2857	8114759	1893750	1·2739512	0179314	549	9820686	8
53	1888098	2856	8111902	1896646	1·2737269	0179863	550	9820137	7
54	1890954	2857	8109046	1899542	1·2735026	0180413	550	9819587	6
55	1893811	2856	8106189	1902437	1·2732783	0180963	552	9819037	5
56	1896667	2856	8103333	1905332	1·2730540	0181515	552	9818485	4
57	1899523	2856	8100477	1908228	1·2728296	0182067	553	9817933	3
58	1902379	2855	8097621	1911124	1·2726052	0182620	554	9817380	2
59	1905234	2856	8094766	1914020	1·2723808	0183174	554	9816826	1
60	1908090		8091910	1916916	1·2721564	0183728		9816272	0

'	Cosine	Diff.	Vers.	Co-chord	Chord	Covers.	Diff.	Sine	'

′	Sine	Diff.	Covers.	Chord	Co-chord	Vers.	Diff.	Cosine	′
0	1908090		8091910	1916916	1·2721564	0183728		9816272	60
1	1910945	2855	8089055	1919811	1·2719319	0184284	556	9815716	59
2	1913801	2856	8086199	1922706	1·2717074	0184840	556	9815160	58
3	1916656	2855	8083344	1925601	1·2714829	0185397	557	9814603	57
4	1919510	2854	8080490	1928496	1·2712584	0185955	558	9814045	56
5	1922365	2855	8077635	1931392	1·2710338	0186514	559	9813486	55
		2855					559		
6	1925220		8074780	1934288	1·2708092	0187073		9812927	54
7	1928074	2854	8071926	1937183	1·2705846	0187634	561	9812366	53
8	1930928	2854	8069072	1940078	1·2703600	0188195	561	9811805	52
9	1933782	2854	8066218	1942973	1·2701353	0188757	562	9811243	51
10	1936636	2854	8063364	1945868	1·2699106	0189320	563	9810680	50
		2854					564		
11	1939490		8060510	1948763	1·2696858	0189884		9810116	49
12	1942344	2854	8057656	1951658	1·2694610	0190448	564	9809552	48
13	1945197	2853	8054803	1954553	1·2692362	0191014	566	9808986	47
14	1948050	2853	8051950	1957448	1·2690114	0191580	566	9808420	46
15	1950903	2853	8049097	1960343	1·2687865	0192147	567	9807853	45
		2853					568		
16	1953756		8046244	1963238	1·2685616	0192715		9807285	44
17	1956609	2853	8043391	1966133	1·2683367	0193284	569	9806716	43
18	1959461	2852	8040539	1969028	1·2681118	0193853	569	9806147	42
19	1962314	2853	8037686	1971922	1·2678869	0194424	571	9805576	41
20	1965166	2852	8034834	1974816	1·2676620	0194995	571	9805005	40
		2852					572		
21	1968018		8031982	1977711	1·2674369	0195567		9804433	39
22	1970870	2852	8029130	1980606	1·2672118	0196140	573	9803860	38
23	1973722	2852	8026278	1983500	1·2669868	0196714	574	9803286	37
24	1976573	2851	8023427	1986394	1·2667618	0197288	574	9802712	36
25	1979425	2852	8020575	1989289	1·2665366	0197864	576	9802136	35
		2851					576		
26	1982276		8017724	1992184	1·2663114	0198440		9801560	34
27	1985127	2851	8014873	1995078	1·2660863	0199017	577	9800983	33
28	1987978	2851	8012022	1997972	1·2658612	0199595	578	9800405	32
29	1990829	2851	8009171	2000867	1·2656359	0200173	578	9799827	31
30	1993679	2850	8006321	2003762	1·2654106	0200753	580	9799247	30
		2851					580		
31	1996530		8003470	2006656	1·2651853	0201333		9798667	29
32	1999380	2850	8000620	2009550	1·2649600	0201914	581	9798086	28
33	2002230	2850	7997770	2012444	1·2647347	0202496	582	9797504	27
34	2005080	2850	7994920	2015338	1·2645094	0203079	583	9796921	26
35	2007930	2850	7992070	2018232	1·2642840	0203663	584	9796337	25
		2849					585		
36	2010779		7989221	2021126	1·2640586	0204248		9795752	24
37	2013629	2850	7986371	2024020	1·2638332	0204833	585	9795167	23
38	2016478	2849	7983522	2026914	1·2636078	0205419	586	9794581	22
39	2019327	2849	7980673	2029808	1·2633823	0206006	587	9793994	21
40	2022176	2849	7977824	2032702	1·2631568	0206594	588	9793406	20
		2848					588		
41	2025024		7974976	2035596	1·2629312	0207182		9792818	19
42	2027873	2849	7972127	2038490	1·2627056	0207772	590	9792228	18
43	2030721	2848	7969279	2041383	1·2624800	0208362	590	9791638	17
44	2033569	2848	7966431	2044276	1·2622544	0208953	591	9791047	16
45	2036418	2849	7963582	2047170	1·2620287	0209545	592	9790455	15
		2847					593		
46	2039265		7960735	2050064	1·2618030	0210138		9789862	14
47	2042113	2848	7957887	2052957	1·2615773	0210732	594	9789268	13
48	2044961	2848	7955039	2055850	1·2613516	0211326	594	9788674	12
49	2047808	2847	7952192	2058744	1·2611258	0211921	595	9788079	11
50	2050655	2847	7949345	2061638	1·2609000	0212517	596	9787483	10
		2847					597		
51	2053502		7946498	2064531	1·2606742	0213114		9786886	9
52	2056349	2847	7943651	2067424	1·2604484	0213712	598	9786288	8
53	2059195	2846	7940805	2070317	1·2602225	0214311	599	9785689	7
54	2062042	2847	7937958	2073210	1·2599966	0214910	599	9785090	6
55	2064888	2846	7935112	2076104	1·2597707	0215510	600	9784490	5
		2846					601		
56	2067734		7932266	2078998	1·2595448	0216111		9783889	4
57	2070580	2846	7929420	2081891	1·2593188	0216713	602	9783287	3
58	2073426	2846	7926574	2084784	1·2590928	0217316	603	9782684	2
59	2076272	2846	7923728	2087677	1·2588668	0217920	604	9782080	1
60	2079117	2845	7920883	2090570	1·2586408	0218524	604	9781476	0

′	Cosine	Diff.	Vers.	Co-chord	Chord	Covers.	Diff.	Sine	′

′	Sine	Diff.	Covers.	Chord	Co-chord	Vers.	Diff.	Cosine	′
0	2079117	2845	7920883	2090570	1·2586408	0218524	605	9781476	60
1	2081962	2845	7918038	2093463	1·2584147	0219129	606	9780871	59
2	2084807	2845	7915193	2096356	1·2581886	0219735	607	9780265	58
3	2087652	2845	7912348	2099248	1·2579625	0220342	608	9779658	57
4	2090497	2844	7909503	2102140	1·2577364	0220950	608	9779050	56
5	2093341	2845	7906659	2105033	1·2575102	0221558	610	9778442	55
6	2096186	2844	7903814	2107926	1·2572840	0222168	610	9777832	54
7	2099030	2844	7900970	2110819	1·2570577	0222778	611	9777222	53
8	2101874	2844	7898126	2113712	1·2568314	0223389	612	9776611	52
9	2104718	2843	7895282	2116604	1·2566051	0224001	612	9775999	51
10	2107561	2844	7892439	2119496	1·2563788	0224613	614	9775387	50
11	2110405	2843	7889595	2122389	1·2561525	0225227	614	9774773	49
12	2113248	2843	7886752	2125282	1·2559262	0225841	615	9774159	48
13	2116091	2843	7883909	2128174	1·2556997	0226456	616	9773544	47
14	2118934	2843	7881066	2131066	1·2554732	0227072	617	9772928	46
15	2121777	2842	7878223	2133958	1·2552468	0227689	618	9772311	45
16	2124619	2843	7875381	2136850	1·2550204	0228307	618	9771693	44
17	2127462	2842	7872538	2139743	1·2547939	0228925	619	9771075	43
18	2130304	2842	7869696	2142636	1·2545674	0229544	620	9770456	42
19	2133146	2842	7866854	2145528	1·2543408	0230164	621	9769836	41
20	2135988	2841	7864012	2148420	1·2541142	0230785	622	9769215	40
21	2138829	2842	7861171	2151312	1·2538876	0231407	623	9768593	39
22	2141671	2841	7858329	2154204	1·2536610	0232030	623	9767970	38
23	2144512	2841	7855488	2157096	1·2534343	0232653	624	9767347	37
24	2147353	2841	7852647	2159988	1·2532076	0233277	625	9766723	36
25	2150194	2841	7849806	2162879	1·2529809	0233902	626	9766098	35
26	2153035	2841	7846965	2165770	1·2527542	0234528	627	9765472	34
27	2155876	2840	7844124	2168662	1·2525274	0235155	627	9764845	33
28	2158716	2840	7841284	2171554	1·2523006	0235782	629	9764218	32
29	2161556	2840	7838444	2174446	1·2520738	0236411	629	9763589	31
30	2164396	2840	7835604	2177338	1·2518470	0237040	630	9762960	30
31	2167236	2840	7832764	2180229	1·2516201	0237670	631	9762330	29
32	2170076	2839	7829924	2183120	1·2513932	0238301	631	9761699	28
33	2172915	2839	7827085	2186012	1·2511662	0238932	633	9761068	27
34	2175754	2839	7824246	2188904	1·2509392	0239565	633	9760435	26
35	2178593	2839	7821407	2191795	1·2507123	0240198	634	9759802	25
36	2181432	2839	7818568	2194686	1·2504854	0240832	635	9759168	24
37	2184271	2839	7815729	2197577	1·2502583	0241467	636	9758533	23
38	2187110	2838	7812890	2200468	1·2500312	0242103	637	9757897	22
39	2189948	2838	7810052	2203360	1·2498041	0242740	637	9757260	21
40	2192786	2838	7807214	2206252	1·2495770	0243377	638	9756623	20
41	2195624	2838	7804376	2209143	1·2493499	0244015	640	9755985	19
42	2198462	2838	7801538	2212034	1·2491228	0244655	639	9755345	18
43	2201300	2837	7798700	2214925	1·2488956	0245294	641	9754706	17
44	2204137	2837	7795863	2217816	1·2486684	0245935	642	9754065	16
45	2206974	2837	7793026	2220707	1·2484411	0246577	642	9753423	15
46	2209811	2837	7790189	2223598	1·2482138	0247219	643	9752781	14
47	2212648	2837	7787352	2226488	1·2479865	0247862	644	9752138	13
48	2215485	2836	7784515	2229378	1·2477592	0248506	645	9751494	12
49	2218321	2837	7781679	2232269	1·2475318	0249151	646	9750849	11
50	2221158	2836	7778842	2235160	1·2473044	0249797	647	9750203	10
51	2223994	2836	7776006	2238051	1·2470770	0250444	647	9749556	9
52	2226830	2836	7773170	2240942	1·2468496	0251091	648	9748909	8
53	2229666	2835	7770334	2243832	1·2466222	0251739	649	9748261	7
54	2232501	2836	7767499	2246722	1·2463948	0252388	650	9747612	6
55	2235337	2835	7764663	2249613	1·2461672	0253038	651	9746962	5
56	2238172	2835	7761828	2252504	1·2459396	0253689	651	9746311	4
57	2241007	2835	7758993	2255394	1·2457121	0254340	652	9745660	3
58	2243842	2834	7756158	2258284	1·2454846	0254992	653	9745008	2
59	2246676	2835	7753324	2261174	1·2452569	0255645	654	9744355	1
60	2249511		7750489	2264064	1·2450292	0256299		9743701	0
′	Cosine	Diff.	Vers.	Co-chord	Chord	Covers.	Diff.	Sine	′

′	Sine	Diff.	Covers.	Chord	Co-chord	Vers.	Diff.	Cosine	′
0	2249511	2834	7750489	2264064	1·2450292	0256299	655	9743701	60
1	2252345	2834	7747655	2266954	1·2448016	0256954	656	9743046	59
2	2255179	2834	7744821	2269844	1·2445740	0257610	656	9742390	58
3	2258013	2833	7741987	2272734	1·2443462	0258266	657	9741734	57
4	2260846	2834	7739154	2275624	1·2441184	0258923	658	9741077	56
5	2263680	2833	7736320	2278514	1·2438906	0259581	659	9740419	55
6	2266513	2833	7733487	2281404	1·2436628	0260240	660	9739760	54
7	2269346	2833	7730654	2284294	1·2434350	0260900	661	9739100	53
8	2272179	2833	7727821	2287184	1·2432072	0261561	661	9738439	52
9	2275012	2832	7724988	2290074	1·2429793	0262222	662	9737778	51
10	2277844	2833	7722156	2292964	1·2427514	0262884	663	9737116	50
11	2280677	2832	7719323	2295854	1·2425235	0263547	664	9736453	49
12	2283509	2832	7716491	2298744	1·2422956	0264211	665	9735789	48
13	2286341	2831	7713659	2301633	1·2420676	0264876	665	9735124	47
14	2289172	2832	7710828	2304522	1·2418396	0265541	666	9734459	46
15	2292004	2831	7707996	2307412	1·2416115	0266207	668	9733793	45
16	2294835	2831	7705165	2310302	1·2413834	0266875	667	9733125	44
17	2297666	2831	7702334	2313191	1·2411553	0267542	669	9732458	43
18	2300497	2831	7699503	2316080	1·2409272	0268211	670	9731789	42
19	2303328	2831	7696672	2318969	1·2406991	0268881	670	9731119	41
20	2306159	2830	7693841	2321858	1·2404710	0269551	672	9730449	40
21	2308989	2830	7691011	2324747	1·2402428	0270223	672	9729777	39
22	2311819	2830	7688181	2327636	1·2400146	0270895	673	9729105	38
23	2314649	2830	7685351	2330525	1·2397863	0271568	673	9728432	37
24	2317479	2830	7682521	2333414	1·2395580	0272241	675	9727759	36
25	2320309	2829	7679691	2336303	1·2393297	0272916	675	9727084	35
26	2323138	2829	7676862	2339192	1·2391014	0273591	676	9726409	34
27	2325967	2829	7674033	2342081	1·2388731	0274267	677	9725733	33
28	2328796	2829	7671204	2344970	1·2386448	0274944	678	9725056	32
29	2331625	2829	7668375	2347859	1·2384163	0275622	679	9724378	31
30	2334454	2828	7665546	2350748	1·2381878	0276301	679	9723699	30
31	2337282	2828	7662718	2353637	1·2379594	0276980	681	9723020	29
32	2340110	2828	7659890	2356526	1·2377310	0277661	681	9722339	28
33	2342938	2828	7657062	2359414	1·2375025	0278342	682	9721658	27
34	2345766	2828	7654234	2362302	1·2372740	0279024	682	9720976	26
35	2348594	2827	7651406	2365191	1·2370454	0279706	684	9720294	25
36	2351421	2827	7648579	2368080	1·2368168	0280390	684	9719610	24
37	2354248	2827	7645752	2370968	1·2365882	0281074	686	9718926	23
38	2357075	2827	7642925	2373856	1·2363596	0281760	686	9718240	22
39	2359902	2827	7640098	2376744	1·2361309	0282446	687	9717554	21
40	2362729	2826	7637271	2379632	1·2359022	0283133	687	9716867	20
41	2365555	2826	7634445	2382520	1·2356735	0283820	689	9716180	19
42	2368381	2826	7631619	2385408	1·2354448	0284509	689	9715491	18
43	2371207	2826	7628793	2388297	1·2352160	0285198	690	9714802	17
44	2374033	2826	7625967	2391186	1·2349872	0285888	691	9714112	16
45	2376859	2825	7623141	2394074	1·2347584	0286579	692	9713421	15
46	2379684	2826	7620316	2396962	1·2345296	0287271	693	9712729	14
47	2382510	2825	7617490	2399849	1·2343007	0287964	693	9712036	13
48	2385335	2824	7614665	2402736	1·2340718	0288657	694	9711343	12
49	2388159	2825	7611841	2405624	1·2338428	0289351	696	9710649	11
50	2390984	2824	7609016	2408512	1·2336138	0290047	695	9709953	10
51	2393808	2825	7606192	2411400	1·2333849	0290742	697	9709258	9
52	2396633	2824	7603367	2414288	1·2331560	0291439	698	9708561	8
53	2399457	2823	7600543	2417175	1·2329269	0292137	698	9707863	7
54	2402280	2824	7597720	2420062	1·2326978	0292835	699	9707165	6
55	2405104	2823	7594896	2422950	1·2324687	0293534	700	9706466	5
56	2407927	2824	7592073	2425838	1·2322396	0294234	701	9705766	4
57	2410751	2823	7589249	2428725	1·2320105	0294935	702	9705065	3
58	2413574	2822	7586426	2431612	1·2317814	0295637	702	9704363	2
59	2416396	2823	7583604	2434499	1·2315522	0296339	704	9703661	1
60	2419219		7580781	2437386	1·2313230	0297043		9702957	0
′	Cosine	Diff.	Vers.	Co-chord	Chord	Covers.	Diff.	Sine	′

′	Sine	Diff.	Covers.	Chord	Co-chord	Vers.	Diff.	Cosine	′
0	2419219		7580781	2437386	1·2313230	0297043		9702957	60
1	2422041	2822	7577959	2440274	1·2310937	0297747	704	9702253	59
2	2424863	2822	7575137	2443162	1·2308644	0298452	705	9701548	58
3	2427685	2822	7572315	2446049	1·2306351	0299158	706	9700842	57
4	2430507	2822	7569493	2448936	1·2304058	0299864	706	9700136	56
5	2433329	2822	7566671	2451823	1·2301765	0300572	708	9699428	55
6	2436150	2821	7563850	2454710	1·2299472	0301280	708	9698720	54
7	2438971	2821	7561029	2457596	1·2297178	0301989	709	9698011	53
8	2441792	2821	7558208	2460482	1·2294884	0302699	710	9697301	52
9	2444613	2821	7555387	2463369	1·2292589	0303409	710	9696591	51
10	2447433	2820	7552567	2466256	1·2290294	0304121	712	9695879	50
11	2450254	2821	7549746	2469143	1·2287999	0304833	712	9695167	49
12	2453074	2820	7546926	2472030	1·2285704	0305547	714	9694453	48
13	2455894	2820	7544106	2474916	1·2283408	0306260	713	9693740	47
14	2458713	2819	7541287	2477802	1·2281112	0306975	715	9693025	46
15	2461533	2820	7538467	2480689	1·2278816	0307691	716	9692309	45
16	2464352	2819	7535648	2483576	1·2276520	0308407	716	9691593	44
17	2467171	2819	7532829	2486462	1·2274224	0309125	718	9690875	43
18	2469990	2819	7530010	2489348	1·2271928	0309843	718	9690157	42
19	2472809	2819	7527191	2492234	1·2269630	0310562	719	9689438	41
20	2475627	2818	7524373	2495120	1·2267332	0311281	719	9688719	40
21	2478445	2818	7521555	2498006	1·2265035	0312002	721	9687998	39
22	2481263	2818	7518737	2500892	1·2262738	0312723	721	9687277	38
23	2484081	2818	7515919	2503778	1·2260440	0313445	722	9686555	37
24	2486899	2818	7513101	2506664	1·2258142	0314168	723	9685832	36
25	2489716	2817	7510284	2509550	1·2255843	0314892	724	9685108	35
26	2492533	2817	7507467	2512436	1·2253544	0315617	725	9684383	34
27	2495350	2817	7504650	2515322	1·2251245	0316342	725	9683658	33
28	2498167	2817	7501833	2518208	1·2248946	0317069	727	9682931	32
29	2500984	2817	7499016	2521094	1·2246646	0317796	727	9682204	31
30	2503800	2816	7496200	2523980	1·2244346	0318524	728	9681476	30
31	2506616	2816	7493384	2526865	1·2242046	0319252	728	9680748	29
32	2509432	2816	7490568	2529750	1·2239746	0319982	730	9680018	28
33	2512248	2816	7487752	2532636	1·2237445	0320712	730	9679288	27
34	2515063	2815	7484937	2535522	1·2235144	0321443	731	9678557	26
35	2517879	2816	7482121	2538407	1·2232842	0322175	732	9677825	25
36	2520694	2815	7479306	2541292	1·2230540	0322908	733	9677092	24
37	2523508	2814	7476492	2544177	1·2228239	0323642	734	9676358	23
38	2526323	2815	7473677	2547062	1·2225938	0324376	734	9675624	22
39	2529137	2814	7470863	2549947	1·2223635	0325112	736	9674888	21
40	2531952	2815	7468048	2552832	1·2221332	0325848	736	9674152	20
41	2534766	2814	7465234	2555718	1·2219029	0326585	737	9673415	19
42	2537579	2813	7462421	2558604	1·2216726	0327322	737	9672678	18
43	2540393	2814	7459607	2561488	1·2214423	0328061	739	9671939	17
44	2543206	2813	7456794	2564372	1·2212120	0328800	739	9671200	16
45	2546019	2813	7453981	2567257	1·2209816	0329541	741	9670459	15
46	2548832	2813	7451168	2570142	1·2207512	0330282	741	9669718	14
47	2551645	2813	7448355	2573027	1·2205208	0331023	741	9668977	13
48	2554458	2813	7445542	2575912	1·2202904	0331766	743	9668234	12
49	2557270	2812	7442730	2578797	1·2200599	0332510	744	9667490	11
50	2560082	2812	7439918	2581682	1·2198294	0333254	744	9666746	10
51	2562894	2812	7437106	2584566	1·2195988	0333999	745	9666001	9
52	2565705	2811	7434295	2587450	1·2193682	0334745	746	9665255	8
53	2568517	2812	7431483	2590334	1·2191376	0335492	747	9664508	7
54	2571328	2811	7428672	2593218	1·2189070	0336239	747	9663761	6
55	2574139	2811	7425861	2596103	1·2186764	0336988	749	9663012	5
56	2576950	2811	7423050	2598988	1·2184458	0337737	749	9662263	4
57	2579760	2810	7420240	2601872	1·2182151	0338487	750	9661513	3
58	2582570	2810	7417430	2604756	1·2179844	0339238	751	9660762	2
59	2585381	2811	7414619	2607640	1·2177536	0339989	751	9660011	1
60	2588190	2809	7411810	2610524	1·2175228	0340742	753	9659258	0
′	Cosine	Diff.	Vers.	Co-chord	Chord	Covers.	Diff.	Sine	′

′	Sine	Diff.	Covers.	Chord	Co-chord	Vers.	Diff.	Cosine	′
0	2588190	2810	7411810	2610524	1·2175223	0340742	753	9659258	60
1	2591000	2810	7409000	2613408	1·2172920	0341495	754	9658505	59
2	2593810	2809	7406190	2616292	1·2170612	0342249	755	9657751	58
3	2596619	2809	7403381	2619176	1·2168304	0343004	756	9656996	57
4	2599428	2809	7400572	2622060	1·2165996	0343760	756	9656240	56
5	2602237	2808	7397763	2624943	1·2163687	0344516	758	9655484	55
6	2605045	2808	7394955	2627826	1·2161378	0345274	758	9654726	54
7	2607853	2809	7392147	2630710	1·2159068	0346032	759	9653968	53
8	2610662	2807	7389338	2633594	1·2156758	0346791	760	9653209	52
9	2613469	2808	7386531	2636478	1·2154448	0347551	760	9652449	51
10	2616277	2808	7383723	2639362	1·2152138	0348311	762	9651689	50
11	2619085	2807	7380915	2642245	1·2149827	0349073	762	9650927	49
12	2621892	2807	7378108	2645128	1·2147516	0349835	763	9650165	48
13	2624699	2807	7375301	2648011	1·2145205	0350598	764	9649402	47
14	2627506	2806	7372494	2650894	1·2142894	0351362	765	9648638	46
15	2630312	2806	7369688	2653777	1·2140583	0352127	765	9647873	45
16	2633118	2807	7366882	2656660	1·2138272	0352892	767	9647108	44
17	2635925	2805	7364075	2659543	1·2135960	0353659	767	9646341	43
18	2638730	2806	7361270	2662426	1·2133648	0354426	768	9645574	42
19	2641536	2806	7358464	2665309	1·2131335	0355194	769	9644806	41
20	2644342	2805	7355658	2668192	1·2129022	0355963	769	9644037	40
21	2647147	2805	7352853	2671075	1·2126709	0356732	771	9643268	39
22	2649952	2805	7350048	2673958	1·2124396	0357503	771	9642497	38
23	2652757	2804	7347243	2676841	1·2122082	0358274	772	9641726	37
24	2655561	2805	7344439	2679724	1·2119768	0359046	773	9640954	36
25	2658366	2804	7341634	2682606	1·2117454	0359819	774	9640181	35
26	2661170	2803	7338830	2685488	1·2115140	0360593	774	9639407	34
27	2663973	2804	7336027	2688371	1·2112825	0361367	775	9638633	33
28	2666777	2804	7333223	2691254	1·2110510	0362142	777	9637858	32
29	2669581	2803	7330419	2694136	1·2108195	0362919	776	9637081	31
30	2672384	2803	7327616	2697018	1·2105880	0363695	778	9636305	30
31	2675187	2802	7324813	2699901	1·2103564	0364473	779	9635527	29
32	2677989	2803	7322011	2702784	1·2101248	0365252	779	9634748	28
33	2680792	2802	7319208	2705666	1·2098932	0366031	780	9633969	27
34	2683594	2802	7316406	2708548	1·2096616	0366811	781	9633189	26
35	2686396	2802	7313604	2711430	1·2094299	0367592	782	9632408	25
36	2689198	2802	7310802	2714312	1·2091982	0368374	783	9631626	24
37	2692000	2801	7308000	2717194	1·2089665	0369157	783	9630843	23
38	2694801	2801	7305199	2720076	1·2087348	0369940	785	9630060	22
39	2697602	2801	7302398	2722957	1·2085030	0370725	785	9629275	21
40	2700403	2801	7299597	2725838	1·2082712	0371510	786	9628490	20
41	2703204	2800	7296796	2728720	1·2080394	0372296	787	9627704	19
42	2706004	2801	7293996	2731602	1·2078076	0373083	787	9626917	18
43	2708805	2800	7291195	2734484	1·2075757	0373870	788	9626130	17
44	2711605	2799	7288395	2737366	1·2073438	0374658	790	9625342	16
45	2714404	2800	7285596	2740247	1·2071119	0375448	790	9624552	15
46	2717204	2799	7282796	2743128	1·2068800	0376238	790	9623762	14
47	2720003	2799	7279997	2746009	1·2066480	0377028	792	9622972	13
48	2722802	2799	7277198	2748890	1·2064160	0377820	793	9622180	12
49	2725601	2799	7274399	2751772	1·2061840	0378613	793	9621387	11
50	2728400	2798	7271600	2754654	1·2059520	0379406	794	9620594	10
51	2731198	2799	7268802	2757535	1·2057199	0380200	795	9619800	9
52	2733997	2797	7266003	2760416	1·2054878	0380995	795	9619005	8
53	2736794	2798	7263206	2763297	1·2052556	0381790	797	9618210	7
54	2739592	2798	7260408	2766178	1·2050234	0382587	797	9617413	6
55	2742390	2797	7257610	2769059	1·2047912	0383384	798	9616616	5
56	2745187	2797	7254813	2771940	1·2045590	0384182	799	9615818	4
57	2747984	2797	7252016	2774820	1·2043268	0384981	800	9615019	3
58	2750781	2796	7249219	2777700	1·2040946	0385781	801	9614219	2
59	2753577	2797	7246423	2780581	1·2038623	0386582	801	9613418	1
60	2756374		7243626	2783462	1·2036300	0387383		9612617	0
′	Cosine	Diff.	Vers.	Co-chord	Chord	Covers.	Diff.	Sine	′

′	Sine	Diff.	Covers.	Chord	Co-chord	Vers.	Diff.	Cosine	′
0	2756374	2796	7243626	2783462	1·2036300	0387383	802	9612617	60
1	2759170	2795	7240830	2786343	1·2033977	0388185	803	9611815	59
2	2761965	2796	7238035	2789224	1·2031654	0388988	804	9611012	58
3	2764761	2795	7235239	2792104	1·2029330	0389792	805	9610208	57
4	2767556	2796	7232444	2794984	1·2027006	0390597	805	9609403	56
5	2770352	2795	7229648	2797864	1·2024682	0391402	806	9608598	55
6	2773147	2794	7226853	2800744	1·2022358	0392208	808	9607792	54
7	2775941	2795	7224059	2803624	1·2020033	0393016	807	9606984	53
8	2778736	2794	7221264	2806504	1·2017708	0393823	809	9606177	52
9	2781530	2794	7218470	2809384	1·2015382	0394632	810	9605368	51
10	2784324	2794	7215676	2812264	1·2013056	0395442	810	9604558	50
11	2787118	2793	7212882	2815144	1·2010730	0396252	811	9603748	49
12	2789911	2793	7210089	2818024	1·2008404	0397063	812	9602937	48
13	2792704	2793	7207296	2820904	1·2006078	0397875	813	9602125	47
14	2795497	2793	7204503	2823784	1·2003752	0398688	813	9601312	46
15	2798290	2793	7201710	2826664	1·2001425	0399501	815	9600499	45
16	2801083	2792	7198917	2829544	1·1999098	0400316	815	9599684	44
17	2803875	2792	7196125	2832423	1·1996770	0401131	816	9598869	43
18	2806667	2792	7193333	2835302	1·1994442	0401947	817	9598053	42
19	2809459	2792	7190541	2838182	1·1992114	0402764	818	9597236	41
20	2812251	2791	7187749	2841062	1·1989786	0403582	818	9596418	40
21	2815042	2791	7184958	2843941	1·1987458	0404400	819	9595600	39
22	2817833	2791	7182167	2846820	1·1985130	0405219	820	9594781	38
23	2820624	2791	7179376	2849699	1·1982801	0406039	821	9593961	37
24	2823415	2790	7176585	2852578	1·1980472	0406860	822	9593140	36
25	2826205	2790	7173795	2855457	1·1978142	0407682	822	9592318	35
26	2828995	2790	7171005	2858336	1·1975812	0408504	824	9591496	34
27	2831785	2790	7168215	2861215	1·1973483	0409328	824	9590672	33
28	2834575	2789	7165425	2864094	1·1971154	0410152	825	9589848	32
29	2837364	2789	7162636	2866973	1·1968823	0410977	826	9589023	31
30	2840153	2789	7159847	2869852	1·1966492	0411803	826	9588197	30
31	2842942	2789	7157058	2872731	1·1964161	0412629	828	9587371	29
32	2845731	2789	7154269	2875610	1·1961830	0413457	828	9586543	28
33	2848520	2788	7151480	2878489	1·1959498	0414285	829	9585715	27
34	2851308	2788	7148692	2881368	1·1957166	0415114	830	9584886	26
35	2854096	2788	7145904	2884246	1·1954834	0415944	830	9584056	25
36	2856884	2787	7143116	2887124	1·1952502	0416774	832	9583226	24
37	2859671	2787	7140329	2890002	1·1950170	0417606	832	9582394	23
38	2862458	2788	7137542	2892880	1·1947838	0418438	833	9581562	22
39	2865246	2786	7134754	2895759	1·1945505	0419271	834	9580729	21
40	2868032	2787	7131968	2898638	1·1943172	0420105	835	9579895	20
41	2870819	2786	7129181	2901516	1·1940838	0420940	835	9579060	19
42	2873605	2786	7126395	2904394	1·1938504	0421775	836	9578225	18
43	2876391	2786	7123609	2907272	1·1936170	0422611	837	9577389	17
44	2879177	2786	7120823	2910150	1·1933836	0423448	838	9576552	16
45	2881963	2785	7118037	2913028	1·1931502	0424286	839	9575714	15
46	2884748	2785	7115252	2915906	1·1929168	0425125	840	9574875	14
47	2887533	2785	7112467	2918783	1·1926833	0425965	840	9574035	13
48	2890318	2785	7109682	2921660	1·1924498	0426805	841	9573195	12
49	2893103	2784	7106897	2924538	1·1922162	0427646	842	9572354	11
50	2895887	2784	7104113	2927416	1·1919826	0428488	843	9571512	10
51	2898671	2784	7101329	2930293	1·1917490	0429331	844	9570669	9
52	2901455	2784	7098545	2933170	1·1915154	0430175	844	9569825	8
53	2904239	2783	7095761	2936048	1·1912818	0431019	845	9568981	7
54	2907022	2783	7092978	2938926	1·1910482	0431864	846	9568136	6
55	2909805	2783	7090195	2941803	1·1908145	0432710	847	9567290	5
56	2912588	2783	7087412	2944680	1·1905808	0433557	848	9566443	4
57	2915371	2782	7084629	2947557	1·1903470	0434405	848	9565595	3
58	2918153	2782	7081847	2950434	1·1901132	0435253	849	9564747	2
59	2920935	2782	7079065	2953311	1·1898794	0436102	850	9563898	1
60	2923717	2782	7076283	2956188	1·1896456	0436952		9563048	0
′	Cosine	Diff.	Vers.	Co-chord	Chord	Covers.	Diff.	Sine	′

17 Deg.

′	Sine	Diff.	Covers.	Chord	Co-chord	Vers.	Diff.	Cosine	′
0	2923717	2782	7076283	2956188	1·1896456	0436952	851	9563048	60
1	2926499	2781	7073501	2959065	1·1894117	0437803	852	9562197	59
2	2929280	2781	7070720	2961942	1·1891778	0438655	853	9561345	58
3	2932061	2781	7067939	2964819	1·1889439	0439508	853	9560492	57
4	2934842	2781	7065158	2967696	1·1887100	0440361	854	9559639	56
5	2937623	2780	7062377	2970572	1·1884761	0441215	855	9558785	55
6	2940403	2780	7059597	2973448	1·1882422	0442070	856	9557930	54
7	2943183	2780	7056817	2976325	1·1880082	0442926	856	9557074	53
8	2945963	2780	7054037	2979202	1·1877742	0443782	857	9556218	52
9	2948743	2779	7051257	2082078	1·1875401	0444639	859	9555361	51
10	2951522	2780	7048478	2984954	1·1873060	0445498	859	9554502	50
11	2954302	2779	7045698	2987830	1·1870719	0446357	859	9553643	49
12	2957081	2778	7042919	2990706	1·1868378	0447216	861	9552784	48
13	2959859	2779	7040141	2993583	1·1866036	0448077	861	9551923	47
14	2962638	2778	7037362	2996460	1·1863694	0448938	863	9551062	46
15	2965416	2778	7034584	2999336	1·1861352	0449801	863	9550199	45
16	2968194	2777	7031806	3002212	1·1859010	0450664	863	9549336	44
17	2970971	2778	7029029	3005087	1·1856668	0451527	865	9548473	43
18	2973749	2777	7026251	3007962	1·1854326	0452392	865	9547608	42
19	2976526	2777	7023474	3010838	1·1851982	0453257	867	9546743	41
20	2979303	2776	7020697	3013714	1·1849638	0454124	867	9545876	40
21	2982079	2777	7017921	3016590	1·1847295	0454991	868	9545009	39
22	2984856	2776	7015144	3019466	1·1844952	0455859	868	9544141	38
23	2987632	2776	7012368	3022341	1·1842608	0456727	870	9543273	37
24	2990408	2776	7009592	3025216	1·1840264	0457597	870	9542403	36
25	2993184	2775	7006816	3028092	1·1837919	0458467	871	9541533	35
26	2995959	2775	7004041	3030968	1·1835574	0459338	872	9540662	34
27	2998734	2775	7001266	3033843	1·1833229	0460210	873	9539790	33
28	3001509	2775	6998491	3036718	1·1830884	0461083	873	9538917	32
29	3004284	2774	6995716	3039593	1·1828538	0461956	873	9538044	31
30	3007058	2774	6992942	3042468	1·1826192	0462830	876	9537170	30
31	3009832	2774	6990168	3045343	1·1823846	0463706	876	9536294	29
32	3012606	2774	6987394	3048218	1·1821500	0464582	876	9535418	28
33	3015380	2773	6984620	3051093	1·1819154	0465458	878	9534542	27
34	3018153	2773	6981847	3053968	1·1816808	0466336	878	9533664	26
35	3020926	2773	6979074	3056842	1·1814461	0467214	879	9532786	25
36	3023699	2772	6976301	3059716	1·1812114	0468093	880	9531907	24
37	3026471	2773	6973529	3062591	1·1809766	0468973	881	9531027	23
38	3029244	2772	6970756	3065466	1·1807418	0469854	882	9530146	22
39	3032016	2772	6967984	3068340	1·1805070	0470736	882	9529264	21
40	3034788	2771	6965212	3071214	1·1802722	0471618	883	9528382	20
41	3037559	2772	6962441	3074089	1·1800373	0472501	884	9527499	19
42	3040331	2771	6959669	3076964	1·1798024	0473385	885	9526615	18
43	3043102	2770	6956898	3079838	1·1795675	0474270	886	9525730	17
44	3045872	2771	6954128	3082712	1·1793326	0475156	886	9524844	16
45	3048643	2770	6951357	3085586	1·1790977	0476042	887	9523958	15
46	3051413	2770	6948587	3088460	1·1788628	0476929	888	9523071	14
47	3054183	2770	6945817	3091334	1·1786278	0477817	889	9522183	13
48	3056953	2770	6943047	3094208	1·1783928	0478706	890	9521294	12
49	3059723	2769	6940277	3097082	1·1781577	0479596	890	9520404	11
50	3062492	2769	6937508	3099956	1·1779226	0480486	891	9519514	10
51	3065261	2769	6934739	3102829	1·1776875	0481377	892	9518623	9
52	3068030	2768	6931970	3105702	1·1774524	0482269	893	9517731	8
53	3070798	2768	6929202	3108576	1·1772172	0483162	894	9516838	7
54	3073566	2768	6926434	3111450	1·1769820	0484056	894	9515944	6
55	3076334	2768	6923666	3114323	1·1767468	0484950	896	9515050	5
56	3079102	2767	6920898	3117196	1·1765116	0485846	896	9514154	4
57	3081869	2767	6918131	3120070	1·1762764	0486742	897	9513258	3
58	3084636	2767	6915364	3122944	1·1760412	0487639	897	9512361	2
59	3087403	2767	6912597	3125817	1·1758059	0488536	899	9511464	1
60	3090170		6909830	3128690	1·1755706	0489435		9510565	0

′	Cosine	Diff.	Vers.	Co-chord	Chord	Covers.	Diff.	Sine	′

Deg. 72.

′	Sine	Diff.	Covers.	Chord	Co-chord	Vers.	Diff.	Cosine	′
0	3090170		6909830	3128690	1·1755706	0489435		9510565	60
1	3092936	2766	6907064	3131563	1·1753352	0490334	899	9509666	59
2	3095702	2766	6904298	3134436	1·1750998	0491234	900	9508766	58
3	3098468	2766	6901532	3137309	1·1748644	0492135	901	9507865	57
4	3101234	2766	6898766	3140182	1·1746290	0493037	902	9506963	56
5	3103999	2765	6896001	3143054	1·1743935	0493939	902	9506061	55
		2765					904		
6	3106764	2765	6893236	3145926	1·1741580	0494843		9505157	54
7	3109529	2765	6890471	3148799	1·1739225	0495747	904	9504253	53
8	3112294	2764	6887706	3151672	1·1736870	0496652	905	9503348	52
9	3115058	2764	6884942	3154544	1·1734515	0497557	905	9502443	51
10	3117822	2764	6882178	3157416	1·1732160	0498464	907	9501536	50
		2764					907		
11	3120586	2763	6879414	3160289	1·1729804	0499371		9500629	49
12	3123349	2763	6876651	3163162	1·1727448	0500279	908	9499721	48
13	3126112	2763	6873888	3166034	1·1725091	0501188	909	9498812	47
14	3128875	2763	6871125	3168906	1·1722734	0502098	910	9497902	46
15	3131638	2762	6868362	3171778	1·1720377	0503009	911	9496991	45
							911		
16	3134400	2763	6865600	3174650	1·1718020	0503920		9496080	44
17	3137163	2702	6862837	3177522	1·1715662	0504832	912	9495168	43
18	3139925	2761	6860075	3180394	1·1713304	0505745	913	9494255	42
19	3142686	2762	6857314	3183266	1·1710946	0506659	914	9493341	41
20	3145448	2761	6854552	3186138	1·1708588	0507574	915	9492426	40
							915		
21	3148209	2760	6851791	3189009	1·1706230	0508489		9491511	39
22	3150969	2761	6849031	3191880	1·1703872	0509405	916	9490595	38
23	3153730	2760	6846270	3194752	1·1701513	0510322	917	9489678	37
24	3156490	2760	6843510	3197624	1·1699154	0511240	918	9488760	36
25	3159250	2760	6840750	3200495	1·1696794	0512158	918	9487842	35
							920		
26	3162010	2760	6837990	3203366	1·1694434	0513078		9486922	34
27	3164770	2759	6835230	3206238	1·1692074	0513998	920	9486002	33
28	3167529	2759	6832471	3209110	1·1689714	0514919	921	9485081	32
29	3170288	2759	6829712	3211981	1·1687354	0515841	922	9484159	31
30	3173047	2758	6826953	3214852	1·1684994	0516763	922	9483237	30
							924		
31	3175805	2758	6824195	3217723	1·1682633	0517687		9482313	29
32	3178563	2758	6821437	3220594	1·1680272	0518611	924	9481389	28
33	3181321	2758	6818679	3223464	1·1677910	0519536	925	9480464	27
34	3184079	2757	6815921	3226334	1·1675548	0520462	926	9479538	26
35	3186836	2757	6813164	3229205	1·1673186	0521388	926	9478612	25
							928		
36	3189593	2757	6810407	3232076	1·1670824	0522316		9477684	24
37	3192350	2756	6807650	3234947	1·1668462	0523244	928	9476756	23
38	3195106	2757	6804894	3237818	1·1666100	0524173	929	9475827	22
39	3197863	2756	6802137	3240688	1·1663737	0525103	930	9474897	21
40	3200619	2755	6799381	3243558	1·1661374	0526034	931	9473966	20
							931		
41	3203374	2756	6796626	3246429	1·1659010	0526965		9473035	19
42	3206130	2755	6793870	3249300	1·1656646	0527897	932	9472103	18
43	3208885	2755	6791115	3252170	1·1654282	0528830	933	9471170	17
44	3211640	2755	6788360	3255040	1·1651918	0529764	934	9470236	16
45	3214395	2754	6785605	3257910	1·1649554	0530699	935	9469301	15
							935		
46	3217149	2754	6782851	3260780	1·1647190	0531634		9468366	14
47	3219903	2754	6780097	3263650	1·1644825	0532570	936	9467430	13
48	3222657	2754	6777343	3266520	1·1642460	0533507	937	9466493	12
49	3225411	2753	6774589	3269389	1·1640094	0534445	938	9465555	11
50	3228164	2753	6771836	3272258	1·1637729	0535384	939	9464616	10
							939		
51	3230917	2753	6769083	3275128	1·1635362	0536323		9463677	9
52	3233670	2752	6766330	3277998	1·1632996	0537264	941	9462736	8
53	3236422	2752	6763578	3280867	1·1630630	0538205	941	9461795	7
54	3239174	2752	6760826	3283736	1·1628264	0539146	941	9460854	6
55	3241926	2752	6758074	3286606	1·1625897	0540089	943	9459911	5
							943		
56	3244678	2751	6755322	3289476	1·1623530	0541032		9458968	4
57	3247429	2751	6752571	3292345	1·1621162	0541977	945	9458023	3
58	3250180	2751	6749820	3295214	1·1618794	0542922	945	9457078	2
59	3252931	2751	6747069	3298083	1·1616427	0543868	946	9456132	1
60	3255682	2751	6744318	3300952	1·1614060	0544814	946	9455186	0

| ′ | Cosine | Diff. | Vers. | Co-chord | Chord | Covers. | Diff. | Sine | ′ |

′	Sine	Diff.	Covers.	Chord	Co-chord	Vers.	Diff.	Cosine	′
0	3255682		6744318	3300952	1·1614060	0544814		9455186	60
1	3258432	2750	6741568	3303821	1·1611691	0545762	948	9454238	59
2	3261182	2750	6738818	3306690	1·1609322	0546710	948	9453290	58
3	3263932	2750	6736068	3309559	1·1606953	0547659	949	9452341	57
4	3266681	2749	6733319	3312428	1·1604584	0548609	950	9451391	56
5	3269430	2749	6730570	3315296	1·1602215	0549559	950	9450441	55
6	3272179	2749	6727821	3318164	1·1599846	0550511	952	9449489	54
7	3274928	2749	6725072	3321033	1·1597476	0551463	952	9448537	53
8	3277676	2748	6722324	3323902	1·1595106	0552416	953	9447584	52
9	3280424	2748	6719576	3326770	1·1592736	0553370	954	9446630	51
10	3283172	2748	6716828	3329638	1·1590366	0554325	955	9445675	50
11	3285919	2747	6714021	3332506	1·1587995	0555280	955	9444720	49
12	3288666	2747	6711334	3335374	1·1585624	0556236	956	9443764	48
13	3291413	2747	6708587	3338243	1·1583252	0557193	957	9442807	47
14	3294160	2747	6705840	3341112	1·1580880	0558151	958	9441849	46
15	3296906	2746	6703094	3343979	1·1578509	0559110	959	9440890	45
16	3299653	2747	6700347	3346846	1·1576138	0560069	959	9439931	44
17	3302398	2745	6697602	3349714	1·1573765	0561029	960	9438971	43
18	3305144	2746	6694856	3352582	1·1571392	0561990	961	9438010	42
19	3307889	2745	6692111	3355450	1·1569019	0562952	962	9437048	41
20	3310634	2745	6689366	3358318	1·1566646	0563915	963	9436085	40
21	3313379	2745	6686621	3361185	1·1564273	0564878	963	9435122	39
22	3316123	2744	6683877	3364052	1·1561900	0565843	965	9434157	38
23	3318867	2744	6681133	3366920	1·1559526	0566808	965	9433192	37
24	3321611	2744	6678389	3369788	1·1557152	0567773	965	9432227	36
25	3324355	2744	6675645	3372655	1·1554778	0568740	967	9431260	35
26	3327098	2743	6672902	3375522	1·1552404	0569707	967	9430293	34
27	3329841	2743	6670159	3378389	1·1550029	0570676	969	9429324	33
28	3332584	2743	6667416	3381256	1·1547654	0571645	969	9428355	32
29	3335326	2742	6664674	3384123	1·1545279	0572614	969	9427386	31
30	3338069	2743	6661931	3386990	1·1542904	0573585	971	9426415	30
31	3340810	2741	6659190	3389857	1·1540528	0574556	971	9425444	29
32	3343552	2742	6656448	3392724	1·1538152	0575529	973	9424471	28
33	3346293	2741	6653707	3395590	1·1535776	0576502	973	9423498	27
34	3349034	2741	6650966	3398456	1·1533400	0577475	973	9422525	26
35	3351775	2741	6648225	3401323	1·1531023	0578450	975	9421550	25
36	3354516	2741	6645484	3404190	1·1528646	0579425	975	9420575	24
37	3357256	2740	6642744	3407056	1·1526269	0580402	977	9419598	23
38	3359996	2740	6640004	3409922	1·1523892	0581379	977	9418621	22
39	3362735	2739	6637265	3412789	1·1521514	0582356	977	9417644	21
40	3365475	2740	6634525	3415656	1·1519136	0583335	979	9416665	20
41	3368214	2739	6631786	3418522	1·1516758	0584314	979	9415686	19
42	3370953	2739	6629047	3421388	1·1514380	0585295	981	9414705	18
43	3373691	2738	6626309	3424254	1·1512001	0586276	981	9413724	17
44	3376429	2738	6623571	3427120	1·1509622	0587257	981	9412743	16
45	3379167	2738	6620833	3429985	1·1507243	0588240	983	9411760	15
46	3381905	2738	6618095	3432850	1·1504864	0589223	983	9410777	14
47	3384642	2737	6615358	3435716	1·1502485	0590207	984	9409793	13
48	3387379	2737	6612621	3438582	1·1500106	0591192	985	9408808	12
49	3390116	2737	6609884	3441447	1·1497725	0592178	986	9407822	11
50	3392852	2736	6607148	3444312	1·1495344	0593165	987	9406835	10
51	3395589	2737	6604411	3447178	1·1492964	0594152	987	9405848	9
52	3398325	2736	6601675	3450044	1·1490584	0595140	988	9404860	8
53	3401060	2735	6598940	3452909	1·1488203	0596129	989	9403871	7
54	3403796	2736	6596204	3455774	1·1485822	0597119	990	9402881	6
55	3406531	2735	6593469	3458639	1·1483440	0598109	990	9401891	5
56	3409265	2734	6590735	3461504	1·1481058	0599101	992	9400899	4
57	3412000	2735	6588000	3464369	1·1478676	0600093	992	9399907	3
58	3414734	2734	6585266	3467234	1·1476294	0601086	993	9398914	2
59	3417468	2734	6582532	3470099	1·1473911	0602079	993	9397921	1
60	3420201	2733	6579799	3472964	1·1471528	0603074	995	9396926	0

′	Cosine	Diff.	Vers.	Co-chord	Chord	Covers.	Diff.	Sine	′

′	Sine	Diff.	Covers.	Chord	Co-chord	Vers.	Diff.	Cosine	′
0	3420201		6579799	3472964	1·1471528	0603074		9396926	60
1	3422935	2734	6577065	3475828	1·1469145	0604069	995	9395931	59
2	3425668	2733	6574332	3478692	1·1466762	0605065	996	9394935	58
3	3428400	2732	6571600	3481557	1·1464379	0606062	997	9393938	57
4	3431133	2733	6568867	3484422	1·1461996	0607060	998	9392940	56
5	3433865	2732	6566135	3487286	1·1459612	0608058	998	9391942	55
6	3436597	2732	6563403	3490150	1·1457228	0609057	999	9390943	54
7	3439329	2732	6560671	3493014	1·1454843	0610058	1001	9389942	53
8	3442060	2731	6557940	3495878	1·1452458	0611058	1000	9388942	52
9	3444791	2731	6555209	3498742	1·1450073	0612060	1002	9387940	51
10	3447521	2730	6552479	3501606	1·1447688	0613062	1002	9386938	50
11	3450252	2731	6549748	3504470	1·1445303	0614066	1004	9385934	49
12	3452982	2730	6547018	3507334	1·1442918	0615070	1004	9384930	48
13	3455712	2730	6544288	3510198	1·1440532	0616075	1005	9383925	47
14	3458441	2729	6541559	3513062	1·1438146	0617080	1005	9382920	46
15	3461171	2730	6538829	3515926	1·1435759	0618087	1007	9381913	45
16	3463900	2729	6536100	3518790	1·1433372	0619094	1007	9380906	44
17	3466628	2728	6533372	3521653	1·1430985	0620102	1008	9379898	43
18	3469357	2729	6530643	3524516	1·1428598	0621111	1009	9378889	42
19	3472085	2728	6527915	3527379	1·1426211	0622120	1009	9377880	41
20	3474812	2727	6525188	3530242	1·1423824	0623131	1011	9376869	40
21	3477540	2728	6522460	3533105	1·1421436	0624142	1011	9375858	39
22	3480267	2727	6519733	3535968	1·1419048	0625154	1012	9374846	38
23	3482994	2727	6517006	3538831	1·1416660	0626167	1013	9373833	37
24	3485720	2726	6514280	3541694	1·1414272	0627180	1013	9372820	36
25	3488447	2727	6511553	3544557	1·1411883	0628194	1014	9371806	35
26	3491173	2726	6508827	3547420	1·1409494	0629210	1016	9370790	34
27	3493898	2725	6506102	3550283	1·1407104	0630226	1016	9369774	33
28	3496624	2726	6503376	3553146	1·1404714	0631242	1016	9368758	32
29	3499349	2725	6500651	3556008	1·1402325	0632260	1018	9367740	31
30	3502074	2725	6497926	3558870	1·1399936	0633278	1018	9366722	30
31	3504798	2724	6495202	3561733	1·1397545	0634297	1019	9365703	29
32	3507523	2725	6492477	3564596	1·1395154	0635317	1020	9364683	28
33	3510247	2724	6489753	3567458	1·1392764	0636338	1021	9363662	27
34	3512970	2724	6487030	3570320	1·1390374	0637359	1021	9362641	26
35	3515693	2723	6484307	3573182	1·1387982	0638382	1023	9361618	25
36	3518416	2723	6481584	3576044	1·1385590	0639405	1023	9360595	24
37	3521139	2723	6478861	3578906	1·1383198	0640429	1024	9359571	23
38	3523862	2723	6476138	3581768	1·1380806	0641453	1024	9358547	22
39	3526584	2722	6473416	3584630	1·1378414	0642479	1026	9357521	21
40	3529306	2722	6470694	3587492	1·1376022	0643505	1026	9356495	20
41	3532027	2721	6467973	3590353	1·1373630	0644532	1027	9355468	19
42	3534748	2721	6465252	3593214	1·1371238	0645560	1028	9354440	18
43	3537469	2721	6462531	3596076	1·1368844	0646588	1028	9353412	17
44	3540190	2721	6459810	3598938	1·1366450	0647618	1030	9352382	16
45	3542910	2720	6457090	3601799	1·1364057	0648648	1030	9351352	15
46	3545630	2720	6454370	3604660	1·1361664	0649679	1031	9350321	14
47	3548350	2720	6451650	3607521	1·1359269	0650711	1032	9349289	13
48	3551070	2720	6448930	3610382	1·1356874	0651743	1032	9348257	12
49	3553789	2719	6446211	3613243	1·1354480	0652777	1034	9347223	11
50	3556508	2719	6443492	3616104	1·1352086	0653811	1034	9346189	10
51	3559226	2718	6440774	3618965	1·1349691	0654846	1035	9345154	9
52	3561944	2718	6438056	3621826	1·1347296	0655881	1035	9344119	8
53	3564662	2718	6435338	3624687	1·1344900	0656918	1037	9343082	7
54	3567380	2718	6432620	3627548	1·1342504	0657955	1037	9342045	6
55	3570097	2717	6429903	3630409	1·1340108	0658993	1038	9341007	5
56	3572814	2717	6427186	3633270	1·1337712	0660032	1039	9339968	4
57	3575531	2717	6424469	3636130	1·1335315	0661072	1040	9338928	3
58	3578248	2717	6421752	3638990	1·1332918	0662112	1040	9337888	2
59	3580964	2716	6419036	3641850	1·1330521	0663154	1042	9336846	1
60	3583679	2715	6416321	3644710	1·1328124	0664196	1042	9335804	0
′	Cosine	Diff.	Vers.	Co-chord	Chord	Covers.	Diff.	Sine	′

′	Sine	Diff.	Covers.	Chord	Co-chord	Vers.	Diff.	Cosine	′
0	3583679	2716	6416321	3644710	1·1328124	0664196	1043	9335804	60
1	3586395	2715	6413605	3647570	1·1325727	0665239	1043	9334761	59
2	3589110	2715	6410890	3650430	1·1323330	0666282	1045	9333718	58
3	3591825	2715	6408175	3653290	1·1320932	0667327	1045	9332673	57
4	3594540	2714	6405460	3656150	1·1318534	0668372	1046	9331628	56
5	3597254	2714	6402746	3659010	1·1316135	0669418	1047	9330582	55
6	3599968	2714	6400032	3661870	1·1313736	0670465	1047	9329535	54
7	3602682	2713	6397318	3664730	1·1311337	0671512	1049	9328488	53
8	3605395	2713	6394605	3667590	1·1308938	0672561	1049	9327439	52
9	3608108	2713	6391892	3670449	1·1306539	0673610	1050	9326390	51
10	3610821	2713	6389179	3673308	1·1304140	0674660	1050	9325340	50
11	3613534	2712	6386466	3676168	1·1301740	0675710	1052	9324290	49
12	3616246	2712	6383754	3679028	1·1299340	0676762	1052	9323238	48
13	3618958	2711	6381042	3681887	1·1296940	0677814	1053	9322186	47
14	3621669	2711	6378331	3684746	1·1294540	0678867	1054	9321133	46
15	3624380	2711	6375620	3687605	1·1292139	0679921	1055	9320079	45
16	3627091	2711	6372909	3690464	1·1289738	0680976	1055	9319024	44
17	3629802	2710	6370198	3693323	1·1287336	0682031	1057	9317969	43
18	3632512	2710	6367488	3696182	1·1284934	0683088	1057	9316912	42
19	3635222	2710	6364778	3699040	1·1282533	0684145	1058	9315855	41
20	3637932	2709	6362068	3701898	1·1280132	0685203	1058	9314797	40
21	3640641	2710	6359359	3704757	1·1277729	0686261	1060	9313739	39
22	3643351	2708	6356649	3707616	1·1275326	0687321	1060	9312679	38
23	3646059	2709	6353941	3710474	1·1272923	0688381	1061	9311619	37
24	3648768	2708	6351232	3713332	1·1270520	0689442	1062	9310558	36
25	3651476	2708	6348524	3716190	1·1268117	0690504	1062	9309496	35
26	3654184	2707	6345816	3719048	1·1265714	0691566	1064	9308434	34
27	3656891	2708	6343109	3721906	1·1263310	0692630	1064	9307370	33
28	3659599	2707	6340401	3724764	1·1260906	0693694	1065	9306306	32
29	3662306	2706	6337694	3727622	1·1258502	0694759	1065	9305241	31
30	3665012	2707	6334988	3730480	1·1256098	0695824	1067	9304176	30
31	3667719	2706	6332281	3733338	1·1253694	0696891	1067	9303109	29
32	3670425	2705	6329575	3736196	1·1251290	0697958	1068	9302042	28
33	3673130	2706	6326870	3739054	1·1248884	0699026	1069	9300974	27
34	3675836	2705	6324164	3741912	1·1246478	0700095	1070	9299905	26
35	3678541	2705	6321459	3744769	1·1244073	0701165	1070	9298835	25
36	3681246	2704	6318754	3747626	1·1241668	0702235	1071	9297765	24
37	3683950	2704	6316050	3750483	1·1239262	0703306	1072	9296694	23
38	3686654	2704	6313346	3753340	1·1236856	0704378	1073	9295622	22
39	3689358	2703	6310642	3756198	1·1234449	0705451	1074	9294549	21
40	3692061	2704	6307939	3759056	1·1232042	0706525	1074	9293475	20
41	3694765	2703	6305235	3761913	1·1229635	0707599	1075	9292401	19
42	3697468	2702	6302532	3764770	1·1227228	0708674	1076	9291326	18
43	3700170	2702	6299830	3767626	1·1224820	0709750	1077	9290250	17
44	3702872	2702	6297128	3770482	1·1222412	0710827	1077	9289173	16
45	3705574	2702	6294426	3773339	1·1220004	0711904	1079	9288096	15
46	3708276	2701	6291724	3776196	1·1217596	0712983	1079	9287017	14
47	3710977	2701	6289023	3779052	1·1215188	0714062	1080	9285938	13
48	3713678	2701	6286322	3781908	1·1212780	0715142	1080	9284858	12
49	3716379	2700	6283621	3784765	1·1210371	0716222	1082	9283778	11
50	3719079	2701	6280921	3787622	1·1207962	0717304	1082	9282696	10
51	3721780	2699	6278220	3790478	1·1205553	0718386	1083	9281614	9
52	3724479	2700	6275521	3793334	1·1203144	0719469	1084	9280531	8
53	3727179	2699	6272821	3796190	1·1200734	0720553	1084	9279447	7
54	3729878	2699	6270122	3799046	1·1198324	0721637	1086	9278363	6
55	3732577	2698	6267423	3801902	1·1195913	0722723	1086	9277277	5
56	3735275	2698	6264725	3804758	1·1193502	0723809	1087	9276191	4
57	3737973	2698	6262027	3807613	1·1191091	0724896	1088	9275104	3
58	3740671	2698	6259329	3810468	1·1188680	0725984	1088	9274016	2
59	3743369	2697	6256631	3813324	1·1186269	0727072	1089	9272928	1
60	3746066		6253934	3816180	1·1183858	0728161		9271839	0

′	Cosine	Diff.	Vers.	Co-chord	Chord	Covers.	Diff.	Sine	′

′	Sine	Diff.	Covers.	Chord	Co-chord	Vers.	Diff.	Cosine	′
0	3746066	2697	6253934	3816180	1·1183858	0728161	1091	9271839	60
1	3748763	2696	6251237	3819035	1·1181446	0729252	1090	9270748	59
2	3751459	2697	6248541	3821890	1·1179034	0730342	1092	9269658	58
3	3754156	2696	6245844	3824746	1·1176622	0731434	1092	9268566	57
4	3756852	2695	6243148	3827602	1·1174210	0732526	1094	9267474	56
5	3759547	2696	6240453	3830457	1·1171797	0733620	1094	9266380	55
6	3762243	2695	6237757	3833312	1·1169384	0734714	1094	9265286	54
7	3764938	2694	6235062	3836166	1·1166971	0735808	1096	9264192	53
8	3767632	2695	6232368	3839020	1·1164558	0736904	1096	9263096	52
9	3770327	2694	6229673	3841875	1·1162144	0738000	1098	9262000	51
10	3773021	2693	6226979	3844730	1·1159730	0739098	1097	9260902	50
11	3775714	2694	6224286	3847585	1·1157316	0740195	1099	9259805	49
12	3778408	2693	6221592	3850440	1·1154902	0741294	1100	9258706	48
13	3781101	2693	6218899	3853294	1·1152487	0742394	1100	9257606	47
14	3783794	2692	6216206	3856148	1·1150072	0743494	1101	9256506	46
15	3786486	2692	6213514	3859002	1·1147657	0744595	1102	9255405	45
16	3789178	2692	6210822	3861856	1·1145242	0745697	1102	9254303	44
17	3791870	2692	6208130	3864710	1·1142827	0746799	1104	9253201	43
18	3794562	2691	6205438	3867564	1·1140412	0747903	1104	9252097	42
19	3797253	2691	6202747	3870418	1·1137996	0749007	1105	9250993	41
20	3799944	2690	6200056	3873272	1·1135580	0750112	1106	9249888	40
21	3802634	2690	6197366	3876126	1·1133163	0751218	1106	9248782	39
22	3805324	2690	6194676	3878980	1·1130746	0752324	1108	9247676	38
23	3808014	2690	6191986	3881834	1·1128329	0753432	1108	9246568	37
24	3810704	2689	6189296	3884688	1·1125912	0754540	1109	9245460	36
25	3813393	2689	6186607	3887541	1·1123495	0755649	1109	9244351	35
26	3816082	2688	6183918	3890394	1·1121078	0756758	1111	9243242	34
27	3818770	2689	6181230	3893247	1·1118660	0757869	1111	9242131	33
28	3821459	2688	6178541	3896100	1·1116242	0758980	1112	9241020	32
29	3824147	2687	6175853	3898953	1·1113823	0760092	1113	9239908	31
30	3826834	2688	6173166	3901806	1·1111404	0761205	1113	9238795	30
31	3829522	2687	6170478	3904659	1·1108985	0762318	1115	9237682	29
32	3832209	2686	6167791	3907512	1·1106566	0763433	1115	9236567	28
33	3834895	2687	6165105	3910365	1·1104147	0764548	1116	9235452	27
34	3837582	2686	6162418	3913218	1·1101728	0765664	1116	9234336	26
35	3840268	2685	6159732	3916070	1·1099308	0766780	1118	9233220	25
36	3842953	2686	6157047	3918922	1·1096888	0767898	1118	9232102	24
37	3845639	2685	6154361	3921775	1·1094468	0769016	1119	9230984	23
38	3848324	2684	6151676	3924628	1·1092048	0770135	1120	9229865	22
39	3851008	2685	6148992	3927480	1·1089627	0771255	1121	9228745	21
40	3853693	2684	6146307	3930332	1·1087206	0772376	1121	9227624	20
41	3856377	2683	6143623	3933184	1·1084785	0773497	1122	9226503	19
42	3859060	2684	6140940	3936036	1·1082364	0774619	1123	9225381	18
43	3861744	2683	6138256	3938888	1·1079942	0775742	1124	9224258	17
44	3864427	2683	6135573	3941740	1·1077520	0776866	1124	9223134	16
45	3867110	2682	6132890	3944592	1·1075098	0777990	1126	9222010	15
46	3869792	2682	6130208	3947444	1·1072676	0779116	1126	9220884	14
47	3872474	2682	6127526	3950295	1·1070253	0780242	1126	9219758	13
48	3875156	2681	6124844	3953146	1·1067830	0781368	1128	9218632	12
49	3877837	2681	6122163	3955998	1·1065407	0782496	1129	9217504	11
50	3880518	2681	6119482	3958850	1·1062984	0783625	1129	9216375	10
51	3883199	2681	6116801	3961701	1·1060561	0784754	1130	9215246	9
52	3885880	2680	6114120	3964552	1·1058138	0785884	1130	9214116	8
53	3888560	2680	6111440	3967403	1·1055714	0787014	1132	9212986	7
54	3891240	2679	6108760	3970254	1·1053290	0788146	1132	9211854	6
55	3893919	2679	6106081	3973105	1·1050865	0789278	1133	9210722	5
56	3896598	2679	6103402	3975956	1·1048440	0790411	1134	9209589	4
57	3899277	2678	6100723	3978807	1·1046015	0791545	1135	9208455	3
58	3901955	2678	6098045	3981658	1·1043590	0792680	1135	9207320	2
59	3904633	2678	6095367	3984508	1·1041165	0793815	1136	9206185	1
60	3907311		6092689	3987358	1·1038740	0794951		9205049	0
′	Cosine	Diff.	Vers.	Co-chord	Chord	Covers.	Diff.	Sine	′

′	Sine	Diff.	Covers.	Chord	Co-chord	Vers.	Diff.	Cosine	′
0	3907311	2678	6092689	3987358	1·1038740	0794951	1137	9205049	60
1	3909989	2677	6090011	3990209	1·1036314	0796088	1138	9203912	59
2	3912666	2677	6087334	3993060	1·1033888	0797226	1139	9202774	58
3	3915343	2676	6084657	3995910	1·1031462	0798365	1139	9201635	57
4	3918019	2676	6081981	3998760	1·1029036	0799504	1140	9200496	56
5	3920695	2676	6079305	4001610	1·1026609	0800644	1141	9199356	55
6	3923371	2676	6076629	4004460	1·1024182	0801785	1142	9198215	54
7	3926047	2675	6073953	4007310	1·1021754	0802927	1142	9197073	53
8	3928722	2675	6071278	4010160	1·1019326	0804069	1143	9195931	52
9	3931397	2674	6068603	4013010	1·1016899	0805212	1144	9194788	51
10	3934071	2674	6065929	4015860	1·1014472	0806356	1145	9193644	50
11	3936745	2674	6063255	4018709	1·1012043	0807501	1146	9192499	49
12	3939419	2674	6060581	4021558	1·1009614	0808647	1146	9191353	48
13	3942093	2673	6057907	4024408	1·1007186	0809793	1147	9190207	47
14	3944766	2673	6055234	4027258	1·1004758	0810940	1148	9189060	46
15	3947439	2672	6052561	4030107	1·1002329	0812088	1149	9187912	45
16	3950111	2672	6049889	4032956	1·0999900	0813237	1149	9186763	44
17	3952783	2672	6047217	4035805	1·0997470	0814386	1150	9185614	43
18	3955455	2672	6044545	4038654	1·0995040	0815536	1151	9184464	42
19	3958127	2671	6041873	4041503	1·0992610	0816687	1152	9183313	41
20	3960798	2670	6039202	4044352	1·0990180	0817839	1152	9182161	40
21	3963468	2671	6036532	4047200	1·0987749	0818991	1154	9181009	39
22	3966139	2670	6033861	4050048	1·0985318	0820145	1154	9179855	38
23	3968809	2670	6031191	4052897	1·0982887	0821299	1155	9178701	37
24	3971479	2669	6028521	4055746	1·0980456	0822454	1155	9177546	36
25	3974148	2670	6025852	4058594	1·0978025	0823609	1157	9176391	35
26	3976818	2668	6023182	4061442	1·0975594	0824766	1157	9175234	34
27	3979486	2669	6020514	4064290	1·0973162	0825923	1158	9174077	33
28	3982155	2668	6017845	4067138	1·0970730	0827081	1159	9172919	32
29	3984823	2668	6015177	4069987	1·0968297	0828240	1159	9171760	31
30	3987491	2667	6012509	4072836	1·0965864	0829399	1161	9170601	30
31	3990158	2667	6009842	4075683	1·0963431	0830560	1161	9169440	29
32	3992825	2667	6007175	4078530	1·0960998	0831721	1161	9168279	28
33	3995492	2666	6004508	4081378	1·0958565	0832882	1163	9167118	27
34	3998158	2667	6001842	4084226	1·0956132	0834045	1164	9165955	26
35	4000825	2665	5999175	4087074	1·0953698	0835209	1164	9164791	25
36	4003490	2666	5996510	4089922	1·0951264	0836373	1165	9163627	24
37	4006156	2665	5993844	4092769	1·0948830	0837538	1165	9162462	23
38	4008821	2665	5991179	4095616	1·0946396	0838703	1167	9161297	22
39	4011486	2664	5988514	4098463	1·0943961	0839870	1167	9160130	21
40	4014150	2664	5985850	4101310	1·0941526	0841037	1168	9158963	20
41	4016814	2664	5983186	4104157	1·0939091	0842205	1169	9157795	19
42	4019478	2663	5980522	4107004	1·0936656	0843374	1170	9156626	18
43	4022141	2663	5977859	4109851	1·0934220	0844544	1170	9155456	17
44	4024804	2663	5975196	4112698	1·0931784	0845714	1171	9154286	16
45	4027467	2662	5972533	4115544	1·0929348	0846885	1172	9153115	15
46	4030129	2662	5969871	4118390	1·0926912	0848057	1173	9151943	14
47	4032791	2662	5967209	4121237	1·0924476	0849230	1173	9150770	13
48	4035453	2661	5964547	4124084	1·0922040	0850403	1175	9149597	12
49	4038114	2661	5961886	4126930	1·0919603	0851578	1175	9148422	11
50	4040775	2661	5959225	4129776	1·0917166	0852753	1175	9147247	10
51	4043436	2660	5956564	4132622	1·0914728	0853928	1177	9146072	9
52	4046096	2660	5953904	4135468	1·0912290	0855105	1177	9144895	8
53	4048756	2660	5951244	4138314	1·0909852	0856282	1178	9143718	7
54	4051416	2659	5948584	4141160	1·0907414	0857460	1179	9142540	6
55	4054075	2659	5945925	4144006	1·0904976	0858639	1180	9141361	5
56	4056734	2659	5943266	4146852	1·0902538	0859819	1180	9140181	4
57	4059393	2658	5940607	4149698	1·0900099	0860999	1182	9139001	3
58	4062051	2658	5937949	4152544	1·0897660	0862181	1182	9137819	2
59	4064709	2657	5935291	4155389	1·0895220	0863363	1182	9136637	1
60	4067366		5932634	4158234	1·0892780	0864545		9135455	0
′	Cosine	Diff.	Vers.	Co-chord	Chord	Covers.	Diff.	Sine	′

′	Sine	Diff.	Covers.	Chord	Co-chord	Vers.	Diff.	Cosine	′
0	4067366	2658	5932634	4158234	1·0892780	0864545	1184	9135455	60
1	4070024	2657	5929976	4161079	1·0890341	0865729	1184	9134271	59
2	4072681	2656	5927319	4163924	1·0887902	0866913	1185	9133087	58
3	4075337	2656	5924663	4166769	1·0885461	0868098	1186	9131902	57
4	4077993	2656	5922007	4169614	1·0883020	0869284	1187	9130716	56
5	4080649	2656	5919351	4172459	1·0880579	0870471	1187	9129529	55
6	4083305	2655	5916695	4175304	1·0878138	0871658	1188	9128342	54
7	4085960	2655	5914040	4178149	1·0875697	0872846	1189	9127154	53
8	4088615	2654	5911385	4180994	1·0873256	0874035	1190	9125965	52
9	4091269	2654	5908731	4183838	1·0870815	0875225	1191	9124775	51
10	4093923	2654	5906077	4186682	1·0868374	0876416	1191	9123584	50
11	4096577	2653	5903423	4189527	1·0865931	0877607	1192	9122393	49
12	4099230	2653	5900770	4192372	1·0863488	0878799	1193	9121201	48
13	4101883	2653	5898117	4195216	1·0861046	0879992	1193	9120008	47
14	4104536	2653	5895464	4198060	1·0858604	0881185	1195	9118815	46
15	4107189	2652	5892811	4200904	1·0856161	0882380	1195	9117620	45
16	4109841	2651	5890159	4203748	1·0853718	0883575	1196	9116425	44
17	4112492	2652	5887508	4206592	1·0851274	0884771	1196	9115229	43
18	4115144	2651	5884856	4209436	1·0848830	0885967	1198	9114033	42
19	4117795	2650	5882205	4212279	1·0846386	0887165	1198	9112835	41
20	4120445	2651	5879555	4215122	1·0843942	0888363	1199	9111637	40
21	4123096	2649	5876904	4217966	1·0841498	0889562	1200	9110438	39
22	4125745	2650	5874255	4220810	1·0839054	0890762	1200	9109238	38
23	4128395	2649	5871605	4223653	1·0836609	0891962	1201	9108038	37
24	4131044	2649	5868956	4226496	1·0834164	0893163	1202	9106837	36
25	4133693	2649	5866307	4229339	1·0831719	0894365	1203	9105635	35
26	4136342	2648	5863658	4232182	1·0829274	0895568	1204	9104432	34
27	4138990	2648	5861010	4235025	1·0826828	0896772	1204	9103228	33
28	4141638	2647	5858362	4237868	1·0824382	0897976	1205	9102024	32
29	4144285	2647	5855715	4240711	1·0821936	0899181	1206	9100819	31
30	4146932	2647	5853068	4243554	1·0819490	0900387	1207	9099613	30
31	4149579	2647	5850421	4246396	1·0817043	0901594	1207	9098406	29
32	4152226	2646	5847774	4249238	1·0814596	0902801	1209	9097199	28
33	4154872	2645	5845128	4252081	1·0812149	0904010	1209	9095990	27
34	4157517	2646	5842483	4254924	1·0809702	0905219	1209	9094781	26
35	4160163	2645	5839837	4257766	1·0807254	0906428	1211	9093572	25
36	4162808	2645	5837192	4260608	1·0804806	0907639	1211	9092361	24
37	4165453	2644	5834547	4263450	1·0802358	0908850	1212	9091150	23
38	4168097	2644	5831903	4266292	1·0799910	0910062	1213	9089938	22
39	4170741	2644	5829259	4269134	1·0797462	0911275	1214	9088725	21
40	4173385	2643	5826615	4271976	1·0795014	0912489	1214	9087511	20
41	4176028	2643	5823972	4274817	1·0792565	0913703	1215	9086297	19
42	4178671	2642	5821329	4277658	1·0790116	0914918	1216	9085082	18
43	4181313	2643	5818687	4280500	1·0787666	0916134	1217	9083866	17
44	4183956	2641	5816044	4283342	1·0785216	0917351	1217	9082649	16
45	4186597	2642	5813403	4286183	1·0782766	0918568	1218	9081432	15
46	4189239	2641	5810761	4289024	1·0780316	0919786	1219	9080214	14
47	4191880	2641	5808120	4291865	1·0777866	0921005	1220	9078995	13
48	4194521	2640	5805479	4294706	1·0775416	0922225	1221	9077775	12
49	4197161	2640	5802839	4297547	1·0772965	0923446	1221	9076554	11
50	4199801	2640	5800199	4300388	1·0770514	0924667	1222	9075333	10
51	4202441	2639	5797559	4303229	1·0768063	0925889	1223	9074111	9
52	4205080	2639	5794920	4306070	1·0765612	0927112	1223	9072888	8
53	4207719	2639	5792281	4308911	1·0763160	0928335	1225	9071665	7
54	4210358	2638	5789642	4311752	1·0760708	0929560	1225	9070440	6
55	4212996	2638	5787004	4314592	1·0758256	0930785	1226	9069215	5
56	4215634	2638	5784366	4317432	1·0755804	0932011	1227	9067989	4
57	4218272	2637	5781728	4320272	1·0753351	0933238	1227	9066762	3
58	4220909	2637	5779091	4323112	1·0750898	0934465	1228	9065535	2
59	4223546	2637	5776454	4325952	1·0748445	0935693	1229	9064307	1
60	4226183		5773817	4328792	1·0745992	0936922		9063078	0
′	Cosine	Diff.	Vers.	Co-chord	Chord	Covers.	Diff.	Sine	′

′	Sine	Diff.	Covers.	Chord	Co-chord	Vers.	Diff.	Cosine	′
0	4226183	2636	5773817	4328792	1·0745992	0936922	1230	9063078	60
1	4228819	2636	5771181	4331632	1·0743539	0938152	1230	9061848	59
2	4231455	2635	5768545	4334472	1·0741086	0939382	1232	9060618	58
3	4234090	2635	5765910	4337312	1·0738632	0940614	1232	9059386	57
4	4236725	2635	5763275	4340152	1·0736178	0941846	1232	9058154	56
5	4239360	2634	5760640	4342991	1·0733723	0943078	1224	9056922	55
6	4241994	2634	5758006	4345830	1·0731268	0944312	1234	9055688	54
7	4244628	2634	5755372	4348669	1·0728813	0945546	1235	9054454	53
8	4247262	2633	5752738	4351508	1·0726358	0946781	1236	9053219	52
9	4249895	2633	5750105	4354347	1·0723903	0948017	1237	9051983	51
10	4252528	2633	5747472	4357186	1·0721448	0949254	1237	9050746	50
11	4255161	2632	5744839	4360025	1·0718992	0950491	1238	9049509	49
12	4257793	2632	5742207	4362864	1·0716536	0951729	1239	9048271	48
13	4260425	2631	5739575	4365703	1·0714080	0952968	1240	9047032	47
14	4263056	2631	5736944	4368542	1·0711624	0954208	1241	9045792	46
15	4265687	2631	5734313	4371381	1·0709167	0955449	1241	9044551	45
16	4268318	2631	5731682	4374220	1·0706710	0956690	1242	9043310	44
17	4270949	2630	5729051	4377058	1·0704253	0957932	1243	9042068	43
18	4273579	2629	5726421	4379896	1·0701796	0959175	1243	9040825	42
19	4276208	2630	5723792	4382734	1·0699338	0960418	1244	9039582	41
20	4278838	2629	5721162	4385572	1·0696880	0961662	1245	9038338	40
21	4281467	2628	5718533	4388410	1·0694422	0962907	1246	9037093	39
22	4284095	2628	5715905	4391248	1·0691964	0964153	1247	9035847	38
23	4286723	2628	5713277	4394086	1·0689505	0965400	1247	9034600	37
24	4289351	2628	5710649	4396924	1·0687046	0966647	1248	9033353	36
25	4291979	2627	5708021	4399762	1·0684588	0967895	1249	9032105	35
26	4294606	2627	5705394	4402600	1·0682130	0969144	1250	9030856	34
27	4297233	2626	5702767	4405437	1·0679670	0970394	1250	9029606	33
28	4299859	2626	5700141	4408274	1·0677210	0971644	1251	9028356	32
29	4302485	2626	5697515	4411111	1·0674750	0972895	1252	9027105	31
30	4305111	2625	5694889	4413948	1·0672290	0974147	1253	9025853	30
31	4307736	2625	5692264	4416785	1·0669830	0975400	1253	9024600	29
32	4310361	2625	5689639	4419622	1·0667370	0976653	1255	9023347	28
33	4312986	2624	5687014	4422459	1·0664909	0977908	1254	9022092	27
34	4315610	2624	5684390	4425296	1·0662448	0979162	1256	9020838	26
35	4318234	2623	5681766	4428133	1·0659987	0980418	1257	9019582	25
36	4320857	2624	5679143	4430970	1·0657526	0981675	1257	9018325	24
37	4323481	2622	5676519	4433806	1·0655064	0982932	1258	9017068	23
38	4326103	2623	5673897	4436642	1·0652602	0984190	1259	9015810	22
39	4328726	2622	5671274	4439479	1·0650140	0985449	1259	9014551	21
40	4331348	2622	5668652	4442316	1·0647678	0986708	1261	9013292	20
41	4333970	2621	5666030	4445152	1·0645215	0987969	1261	9012031	19
42	4336591	2621	5663409	4447988	1·0642752	0989230	1262	9010770	18
43	4339212	2620	5660788	4450824	1·0640289	0990492	1262	9009508	17
44	4341832	2621	5658168	4453660	1·0637826	0991754	1264	9008246	16
45	4344453	2619	5655547	4456496	1·0635363	0993018	1264	9006982	15
46	4347072	2620	5652928	4459332	1·0632900	0994282	1265	9005718	14
47	4349692	2619	5650308	4462167	1·0630436	0995547	1265	9004453	13
48	4352311	2619	5647689	4465002	1·0627972	0996812	1267	9003188	12
49	4354930	2618	5645070	4467838	1·0625507	0998079	1267	9001921	11
50	4357548	2618	5642452	4470674	1·0623042	0999346	1268	9000654	10
51	4360166	2618	5639834	4473509	1·0620578	1000614	1269	8999386	9
52	4362784	2617	5637216	4476344	1·0618114	1001883	1269	8998117	8
53	4365401	2617	5634599	4479179	1·0615648	1003152	1270	8996848	7
54	4368018	2616	5631982	4482014	1·0613182	1004422	1271	8995578	6
55	4370634	2617	5629366	4484849	1·0610716	1005693	1272	8994307	5
56	4373251	2615	5626749	4487684	1·0608250	1006965	1272	8993035	4
57	4375866	2616	5624134	4490518	1·0605784	1008237	1274	8991763	3
58	4378482	2615	5621518	4493352	1·0603318	1009511	1274	8990489	2
59	4381097	2614	5618903	4496187	1·0600852	1010785	1275	8989215	1
60	4383711		5616289	4499022	1·0598386	1012060		8987940	0
′	Cosine	Diff.	Vers.	Co-chord	Chord	Covers.	Diff.	Sine	′

′	Sine	Diff.	Covers.	Chord	Co-chord	Vers.	Diff.	Cosine	′
0	4383711	2615	5616289	4499022	1·0598386	1012060	1275	8987940	60
1	4386326	2614	5613674	4501856	1·0595919	1013335	1276	8986665	59
2	4388940	2613	5611060	4504690	1·0593452	1014611	1277	8985389	58
3	4391553	2613	5608447	4507524	1·0590984	1015888	1278	8984112	57
4	4394166	2613	5605834	4510358	1·0588516	1017166	1279	8982834	56
5	4396779	2613	5603221	4513192	1·0586048	1018445	1279	8981555	55
6	4399392	2612	5600608	4516026	1·0583580	1019724	1280	8980276	54
7	4402004	2611	5597996	4518859	1·0581112	1021004	1281	8978996	53
8	4404615	2612	5595385	4521692	1·0578644	1022285	1282	8977715	52
9	4407227	2611	5592773	4524526	1·0576175	1023567	1282	8976433	51
10	4409838	2610	5590162	4527360	1·0573706	1024849	1283	8975151	50
11	4412448	2611	5587552	4530193	1·0571236	1026132	1284	8973868	49
12	4415059	2609	5584941	4533026	1·0568766	1027416	1285	8972584	48
13	4417668	2610	5582332	4535859	1·0566297	1028701	1285	8971299	47
14	4420278	2609	5579722	4538692	1·0563828	1029986	1287	8970014	46
15	4422887	2609	5577113	4541525	1·0561357	1031273	1287	8968727	45
16	4425496	2608	5574504	4544358	1·0558886	1032560	1287	8967440	44
17	4428104	2608	5571896	4547191	1·0556416	1033847	1289	8966153	43
18	4430712	2607	5569288	4550024	1·0553946	1035136	1289	8964864	42
19	4433319	2608	5566681	4552856	1·0551475	1036425	1290	8963575	41
20	4435927	2607	5564073	4555688	1·0549004	1037715	1291	8962285	40
21	4438534	2606	5561466	4558521	1·0546532	1039006	1291	8960994	39
22	4441140	2606	5558860	4561354	1·0544060	1040297	1292	8959703	38
23	4443746	2606	5556254	4564186	1·0541588	1041589	1293	8958411	37
24	4446352	2605	5553648	4567018	1·0539116	1042882	1294	8957118	36
25	4448957	2605	5551043	4569850	1·0536643	1044176	1295	8955824	35
26	4451562	2605	5548438	4572682	1·0534170	1045471	1295	8954529	34
27	4454167	2604	5545833	4575513	1·0531698	1046766	1296	8953234	33
28	4456771	2604	5543229	4578344	1·0529226	1048062	1296	8951938	32
29	4459375	2603	5540625	4581176	1·0526752	1049359	1297	8950641	31
30	4461978	2603	5538022	4584008	1·0524278	1050656	1299	8949344	30
31	4464581	2603	5535419	4586839	1·0521804	1051955	1299	8948045	29
32	4467184	2602	5532816	4589670	1·0519330	1053254	1300	8946746	28
33	4469786	2602	5530214	4592501	1·0516856	1054554	1300	8945446	27
34	4472388	2602	5527612	4595332	1·0514382	1055854	1302	8944146	26
35	4474990	2601	5525010	4598163	1·0511908	1057156	1302	8942844	25
36	4477591	2601	5522409	4600994	1·0509434	1058458	1302	8941542	24
37	4480192	2600	5519808	4603825	1·0506958	1059760	1304	8940240	23
38	4482792	2600	5517203	4606656	1·0504482	1061064	1304	8938936	22
39	4485392	2600	5514608	4609487	1·0502007	1062368	1306	8937632	21
40	4487992	2599	5512008	4612318	1·0499532	1063674	1305	8936326	20
41	4490591	2599	5509409	4615148	1·0497056	1064979	1307	8935021	19
42	4493190	2599	5506810	4617978	1·0494580	1066286	1308	8933714	18
43	4495789	2598	5504211	4620808	1·0492103	1067594	1308	8932406	17
44	4498387	2597	5501613	4623638	1·0489626	1068902	1309	8931098	16
45	4500984	2598	5499016	4626468	1·0487149	1070211	1309	8929789	15
46	4503582	2597	5496418	4629298	1·0484672	1071520	1311	8928480	14
47	4506179	2596	5493821	4632128	1·0482195	1072831	1311	8927169	13
48	4508775	2597	5491225	4634958	1·0479718	1074142	1312	8925858	12
49	4511372	2595	5488623	4637788	1·0477240	1075454	1312	8924546	11
50	4513967	2596	5486033	4640618	1·0474762	1076766	1314	8923234	10
51	4516563	2595	5483437	4643447	1·0472284	1078080	1314	8921920	9
52	4519158	2595	5480842	4646276	1·0469806	1079394	1315	8920606	8
53	4521753	2594	5478247	4649105	1·0467327	1080709	1316	8919291	7
54	4524347	2594	5475653	4651934	1·0464848	1082025	1316	8917975	6
55	4526941	2594	5473059	4654763	1·0462369	1083341	1317	8916659	5
56	4529535	2593	5470465	4657592	1·0459890	1084658	1318	8915342	4
57	4532128	2593	5467872	4660421	1·0457411	1085976	1319	8914024	3
58	4534721	2592	5465279	4663250	1·0454932	1087295	1320	8912705	2
59	4537313	2592	5462687	4666079	1·0452452	1088615	1320	8911385	1
60	4539905		5460095	4668908	1·0449972	1089935		8910065	0
′	Cosine	Diff.	Vers.	Co-chord	Chord	Covers.	Diff.	Sine	′

′	Sine	Diff.	Covers.	Chord	Co-chord	Vers.	Diff.	Cosine	′
0	4539905	2592	5460095	4668908	1·0449972	1089935	1321	8910065	60
1	4542497	2591	5457503	4671736	1·0447491	1091256	1321	8908744	59
2	4545088	2591	5454912	4674564	1·0445010	1092577	1323	8907423	58
3	4547679	2590	5452321	4677392	1·0442529	1093900	1323	8906100	57
4	4550269	2590	5449731	4680220	1·0440048	1095223	1324	8904777	56
5	4552859	2590	5447141	4683048	1·0437567	1096547	1325	8903453	55
6	4555449	2589	5444551	4685876	1·0435086	1097872	1325	8902128	54
7	4558038	2589	5441962	4688704	1·0432604	1099197	1327	8900803	53
8	4560627	2589	5439373	4691532	1·0430122	1100524	1327	8899476	52
9	4563216	2588	5436784	4694360	1·0427640	1101851	1327	8898149	51
10	4565804	2588	5434196	4697188	1·0425158	1103178	1329	8896822	50
11	4568392	2587	5431608	4700015	1·0422675	1104507	1329	8895493	49
12	4570979	2587	5429021	4702842	1·0420192	1105836	1330	8894164	48
13	4573566	2587	5426434	4705669	1·0417709	1107166	1331	8892834	47
14	4576153	2586	5423847	4708496	1·0415226	1108497	1332	8891503	46
15	4578739	2586	5421261	4711323	1·0412743	1109829	1332	8890171	45
16	4581325	2585	5418675	4714150	1·0410260	1111161	1333	8888839	44
17	4583910	2586	5416090	4716977	1·0407776	1112494	1334	8887506	43
18	4586496	2584	5413504	4719804	1·0405292	1113828	1334	8886172	42
19	4589080	2585	5410920	4722631	1·0402807	1115162	1335	8884838	41
20	4591665	2583	5408335	4725458	1·0400322	1116497	1337	8883503	40
21	4594248	2584	5405752	4728284	1·0397837	1117834	1336	8882166	39
22	4596832	2583	5403168	4731110	1·0395352	1119170	1338	8880830	38
23	4599415	2583	5400585	4733936	1·0392867	1120508	1338	8879492	37
24	4601998	2582	5398002	4736762	1·0390382	1121846	1339	8878154	36
25	4604580	2582	5395420	4739588	1·0387896	1123185	1340	8876815	35
26	4607162	2582	5392838	4742414	1·0385410	1124525	1341	8875475	34
27	4609744	2581	5390256	4745240	1·0382924	1125866	1341	8874134	33
28	4612325	2581	5387675	4748066	1·0380438	1127207	1342	8872793	32
29	4614906	2580	5385094	4750892	1·0377952	1128549	1343	8871451	31
30	4617486	2580	5382514	4753718	1·0375466	1129892	1343	8870108	30
31	4620066	2580	5379934	4756543	1·0372979	1131235	1345	8868765	29
32	4622646	2579	5377354	4759368	1·0370492	1132580	1345	8867420	28
33	4625225	2579	5374775	4762194	1·0368004	1133925	1345	8866075	27
34	4627804	2578	5372196	4765020	1·0365516	1135270	1347	8864730	26
35	4630382	2578	5369618	4767845	1·0363028	1136617	1347	8863383	25
36	4632960	2578	5367040	4770670	1·0360540	1137964	1348	8862036	24
37	4635538	2577	5364462	4773494	1·0358052	1139312	1349	8860688	23
38	4638115	2577	5361885	4776318	1·0355564	1140661	1350	8859339	22
39	4640692	2577	5359308	4779143	1·0353075	1142011	1350	8857989	21
40	4643269	2576	5356731	4781968	1·0350586	1143361	1351	8856639	20
41	4645845	2575	5354155	4784792	1·0348097	1144712	1352	8855288	19
42	4648420	2576	5351580	4787616	1·0345608	1146064	1352	8853936	18
43	4650996	2575	5349004	4790441	1·0343118	1147416	1354	8852584	17
44	4653571	2574	5346429	4793266	1 0340628	1148770	1354	8851230	16
45	4656145	2574	5343855	4796090	1·0338138	1150124	1354	8849876	15
46	4658719	2574	5341281	4798914	1·0335648	1151478	1356	8848522	14
47	4661293	2573	5338707	4801737	1·0333157	1152834	1356	8847166	13
48	4663866	2573	5336134	4804560	1·0330666	1154190	1357	8845810	12
49	4666439	2573	5333561	4807384	1·0328175	1155547	1358	8844453	11
50	4669012	2572	5330988	4810208	1·0325684	1156905	1359	8843095	10
51	4671584	2572	5328416	4813031	1·0323193	1158264	1359	8841736	9
52	4674156	2571	5325844	4815854	1·0320702	1159623	1360	8840377	8
53	4676727	2571	5323273	4818678	1·0318210	1160983	1361	8839017	7
54	4679298	2571	5320702	4821502	1·0315718	1162344	1361	8837656	6
55	4681869	2570	5318131	4824325	1·0313226	1163705	1362	8836295	5
56	4684439	2570	5315561	4827148	1·0310734	1165067	1364	8834933	4
57	4687009	2569	5312991	4829970	1·0308241	1166431	1363	8833569	3
58	4689578	2569	5310422	4832792	1·0305748	1167794	1365	8832206	2
59	4692147	2569	5307853	4835615	1·0303255	1169159	1365	8830841	1
60	4694716		5305284	4838438	1·0300762	1170524		8829476	0
′	Cosine	Diff.	Vers.	Co-chord	Chord	Covers.	Diff.	Sine	′

′	Sine	Diff.	Covers.	Chord	Co-chord	Vers.	Diff.	Cosine	′
0	4694716	2568	5305284	4838438	1·0300762	1170524	1366	8829476	60
1	4697284	2568	5302716	4841260	1·0298268	1171890	1367	8828110	59
2	4699852	2567	5300148	4844082	1·0295774	1173257	1367	8826743	58
3	4702419	2567	5297581	4846904	1·0293280	1174624	1369	8825376	57
4	4704986	2567	5295014	4849726	1·0290786	1175993	1369	8824007	56
5	4707553	2566	5292447	4852548	1·0288292	1177362	1369	8822638	55
6	4710119	2566	5289881	4855370	1·0285798	1178731	1371	8821269	54
7	4712685	2565	5287315	4858192	1·0283303	1180102	1371	8819898	53
8	4715250	2565	5284750	4861014	1·0280808	1181473	1372	8818527	52
9	4717815	2565	5282185	4863836	1·0278312	1182845	1373	8817155	51
10	4720380	2564	5279620	4866658	1·0275816	1184218	1373	8815782	50
11	4722944	2564	5277056	4869479	1·0273321	1185591	1374	8814409	49
12	4725508	2563	5274492	4872300	1·0270826	1186965	1375	8813035	48
13	4728071	2563	5271929	4875121	1·0268329	1188340	1376	8811660	47
14	4730634	2563	5269366	4877942	1·0265832	1189716	1377	8810284	46
15	4733197	2562	5266803	4880763	1·0263336	1191093	1377	8808907	45
16	4735759	2562	5264241	4883584	1·0260840	1192470	1378	8807530	44
17	4738321	2561	5261679	4886405	1·0258343	1193848	1378	8806152	43
18	4740882	2561	5259118	4889226	1·0255846	1195226	1380	8804774	42
19	4743443	2561	5256557	4892046	1·0253348	1196606	1380	8803394	41
20	4746004	2560	5253996	4894866	1·0250850	1197986	1381	8802014	40
21	4748564	2560	5251436	4897687	1·0248352	1199367	1382	8800633	39
22	4751124	2559	5248876	4900508	1·0245854	1200749	1382	8799251	38
23	4753683	2559	5246317	4903328	1·0243356	1202131	1383	8797869	37
24	4756242	2559	5243758	4906148	1·0240858	1203514	1384	8796486	36
25	4758801	2558	5241199	4908968	1·0238359	1204898	1385	8795102	35
26	4761359	2558	5238641	4911788	1·0235860	1206283	1385	8793717	34
27	4763917	2557	5236083	4914607	1·0233361	1207668	1386	8792332	33
28	4766474	2557	5233526	4917426	1·0230862	1209054	1387	8790946	32
29	4769031	2557	5230969	4920246	1·0228362	1210441	1388	8789559	31
30	4771588	2556	5228412	4923066	1·0225862	1211829	1388	8788171	30
31	4774144	2556	5225856	4925885	1·0223362	1213217	1389	8786783	29
32	4776700	2555	5223300	4928704	1·0220862	1214606	1390	8785394	28
33	4779255	2555	5220745	4931523	1·0218361	1215996	1391	8784004	27
34	4781810	2554	5218190	4934342	1·0215860	1217387	1391	8782613	26
35	4784364	2555	5215636	4937161	1·0213359	1218778	1392	8781222	25
36	4786919	2553	5213081	4939980	1·0210858	1220170	1393	8779830	24
37	4789472	2554	5210528	4942799	1·0208357	1221563	1394	8778437	23
38	4792026	2553	5207974	4945618	1·0205856	1222957	1394	8777043	22
39	4794579	2552	5205421	4948436	1·0203354	1224351	1395	8775649	21
40	4797131	2552	5202869	4951254	1·0200852	1225746	1396	8774254	20
41	4799683	2552	5200317	4954072	1·0198350	1227142	1396	8772858	19
42	4802235	2551	5197765	4956890	1·0195848	1228538	1398	8771462	18
43	4804786	2551	5195214	4959708	1·0193345	1229936	1398	8770064	17
44	4807337	2551	5192663	4962526	1·0190842	1231334	1398	8768666	16
45	4809888	2550	5190112	4965344	1·0188339	1232732	1400	8767268	15
46	4812438	2549	5187562	4968162	1·0185836	1234132	1400	8765868	14
47	4814987	2550	5185013	4970980	1·0183332	1235532	1401	8764468	13
48	4817537	2549	5182463	4973798	1·0180828	1236933	1402	8763067	12
49	4820086	2548	5179914	4976615	1·0178324	1238335	1402	8761665	11
50	4822634	2548	5177366	4979432	1·0175820	1239737	1404	8760263	10
51	4825182	2548	5174818	4982249	1·0173316	1241141	1404	8758859	9
52	4827730	2547	5172270	4985066	1·0170812	1242545	1404	8757455	8
53	4830277	2547	5169723	4987883	1·0168307	1243949	1406	8756051	7
54	4832824	2546	5167176	4990700	1·0165802	1245355	1406	8754645	6
55	4835370	2546	5164630	4993517	1·0163297	1246761	1407	8753239	5
56	4837916	2546	5162084	4996334	1·0160792	1248168	1407	8751832	4
57	4840462	2545	5159538	4999151	1·0158286	1249575	1409	8750425	3
58	4843007	2545	5156993	5001968	1·0155780	1250984	1409	8749016	2
59	4845552	2544	5154448	5004784	1·0153274	1252393	1410	8747607	1
60	4848096		5151904	5007600	1·0150768	1253803		8746197	0
′	Cosine	Diff.	Vers.	Co-chord	Chord	Covers.	Diff.	Sine	′

′	Sine	Diff.	Covers.	Chord	Co-chord	Vers.	Diff.	Cosine	′
0	4848096	2544	5151904	5007600	1·0150768	1253803	1411	8746197	60
1	4850640	2544	5149360	5010416	1·0148261	1255214	1411	8744786	59
2	4853184	2543	5146816	5013232	1·0145754	1256625	1412	8743375	58
3	4855727	2543	5144273	5016048	1·0143247	1258037	1413	8741963	57
4	4858270	2542	5141730	5018864	1·0140740	1259450	1413	8740550	56
5	4860812	2542	5139188	5021680	1·0138233	1260863	1415	8739137	55
6	4863354	2541	5136646	5024496	1·0135726	1262278	1415	8737722	54
7	4865895	2541	5134105	5027311	1·0133218	1263693	1416	8736307	53
8	4868436	2541	5131564	5030126	1·0130710	1265109	1416	8734891	52
9	4870977	2540	5129023	5032942	1·0128201	1266525	1417	8733475	51
10	4873517	2540	5126483	5035758	1·0125692	1267942	1418	8732058	50
11	4876057	2540	5123943	5038573	1·0123184	1269360	1419	8730640	49
12	4878597	2539	5121403	5041388	1·0120676	1270779	1420	8729221	48
13	4881136	2538	5118864	5044202	1·0118166	1272199	1420	8727801	47
14	4883674	2538	5116326	5047016	1·0115656	1273619	1421	8726381	46
15	4886212	2538	5113788	5049831	1·0113147	1275040	1422	8724960	45
16	4888750	2538	5111250	5052646	1·0110638	1276462	1422	8723538	44
17	4891288	2537	5108712	5055460	1·0108128	1277884	1423	8722116	43
18	4893825	2536	5106175	5058274	1·0105618	1279307	1424	8720693	42
19	4896361	2536	5103639	5061089	1·0103107	1280731	1425	8719269	41
20	4898897	2536	5101103	5063904	1·0100596	1282156	1425	8717844	40
21	4901433	2535	5098567	5066718	1·0098086	1283581	1426	8716419	39
22	4903968	2535	5096032	5069532	1·0095576	1285007	1427	8714993	38
23	4906503	2535	5093497	5072345	1·0093064	1286434	1428	8713566	37
24	4909038	2534	5090962	5075158	1·0090552	1287862	1428	8712138	36
25	4911572	2533	5088428	5077972	1·0088041	1289290	1429	8710710	35
26	4914105	2533	5085895	5080786	1·0085530	1290719	1430	8709281	34
27	4916638	2533	5083362	5083599	1·0083017	1292149	1431	8707851	33
28	4919171	2533	5080829	5086412	1·0080504	1293580	1431	8706420	32
29	4921704	2532	5078296	5089225	1·0077992	1295011	1432	8704989	31
30	4924236	2531	5075764	5092038	1·0075480	1296443	1433	8703557	30
31	4926767	2531	5073233	5094851	1·0072967	1297876	1433	8702124	29
32	4929298	2531	5070702	5097664	1·0070454	1299309	1435	8700691	28
33	4931829	2530	5068171	5100477	1·0067940	1300744	1435	8699256	27
34	4934359	2530	5065641	5103290	1·0065426	1302179	1435	8697821	26
35	4936889	2530	5063111	5106103	1·0062912	1303614	1437	8696386	25
36	4939419	2529	5060581	5108916	1·0060398	1305051	1437	8694949	24
37	4941948	2528	5058052	5111728	1·0057884	1306488	1438	8693512	23
38	4944476	2529	5055524	5114540	1·0055370	1307926	1438	8692074	22
39	4947005	2527	5052995	5117352	1·0052855	1309364	1440	8690636	21
40	4949532	2528	5050468	5120164	1·0050340	1310804	1440	8689196	20
41	4952060	2527	5047940	5122976	1·0047825	1312244	1441	8687756	19
42	4954587	2526	5045413	5125788	1·0045310	1313685	1441	8686315	18
43	4957113	2526	5042887	5128599	1·0042795	1315126	1443	8684874	17
44	4959639	2526	5040361	5131410	1·0040280	1316569	1443	8683431	16
45	4962165	2525	5037835	5134222	1·0037764	1318012	1444	8681988	15
46	4964690	2525	5035310	5137034	1·0035248	1319456	1444	8680544	14
47	4967215	2525	5032785	5139845	1·0032732	1320900	1445	8679100	13
48	4969740	2524	5030260	5142656	1·0030214	1322345	1446	8677655	12
49	4972264	2523	5027736	5145467	1·0027698	1323791	1447	8676209	11
50	4974787	2523	5025213	5148278	1·0025182	1325238	1448	8674762	10
51	4977310	2523	5022690	5151089	1·0022664	1326686	1448	8673314	9
52	4979833	2522	5020167	5153900	1·0020146	1328134	1449	8671866	8
53	4982355	2522	5017645	5156710	1·0017629	1329583	1450	8670417	7
54	4984877	2522	5015123	5159520	1·0015112	1331033	1450	8668967	6
55	4987399	2521	5012601	5162330	1·0012593	1332483	1451	8667517	5
56	4989920	2521	5010080	5165140	1·0010074	1333934	1452	8666066	4
57	4992441	2520	5007559	5167951	1·0007556	1335386	1453	8664614	3
58	4994961	2520	5005039	5170762	1·0005038	1336839	1453	8663161	2
59	4997481	2519	5002519	5173571	1·0002519	1338292	1454	8661708	1
60	5000000		5000000	5176380	1·0000000	1339746		8660254	0
′	Cosine	Diff.	Vers.	Co-chord	Chord	Covers.	Diff.	Sine	′

′	Sine	Diff.	Covers.	Chord	Co-chord	Vers.	Diff.	Cosine	′
0	5000000	2519	5000000	5176380	1·0000000	1339746	1455	8660254	60
1	5002519	2518	4997481	5179190	9997481	1341201	1455	8658799	59
2	5005037	2519	4994963	5182000	9994962	1342656	1457	8657344	58
3	5007556	2517	4992444	5184810	9992442	1344113	1457	8655887	57
4	5010073	2518	4989927	5187620	9989922	1345570	1457	8654430	56
5	5012591	2516	4987409	5190429	9987402	1347027	1459	8652973	55
6	5015107	2517	4984893	5193238	9984882	1348486	1459	8651514	54
7	5017624	2516	4982376	5196047	9982361	1349945	1460	8650055	3
8	5020140	2515	4979860	5198856	9979840	1351405	1461	8648595	52
9	5022655	2515	4977345	5201665	9977319	1352866	1461	8647134	51
10	5025170	2515	4974830	5204474	9974798	1354327	1462	8645673	50
11	5027685	2514	4972315	5207282	9972276	1355789	1463	8644211	49
12	5030199	2514	4969801	5210090	9969754	1357252	1464	8642748	48
13	5032713	2514	4967287	5212898	9967232	1358716	1464	8641284	47
14	5035227	2513	4964773	5215706	9964710	1360180	1465	8639820	46
15	5037740	2512	4962260	5218515	9962188	1361645	1466	8638355	45
16	5040252	2513	4959748	5221324	9959666	1363111	1466	8636889	44
17	5042765	2511	4957235	5224131	9957143	1364577	1467	8635423	43
18	5045276	2512	4954724	5226938	9954620	1366044	1468	8633956	42
19	5047788	2510	4952212	5229746	9952097	1367512	1469	8632488	41
20	5050298	2511	4949702	5232554	9949574	1368981	1470	8631019	40
21	5052809	2510	4947191	5235362	9947051	1370451	1470	8629549	39
22	5055319	2509	4944681	5238170	9944528	1371921	1471	8628079	38
23	5057828	2510	4942172	5240977	9942004	1373392	1471	8626608	37
24	5060338	2508	4939662	5243784	9939480	1374863	1473	8625137	36
25	5062846	2509	4937154	5246591	9936955	1376336	1473	8623664	35
26	5065355	2508	4934645	5249398	9934430	1377809	1474	8622191	34
27	5067863	2507	4932137	5252205	9931905	1379283	1474	8620717	33
28	5070370	2507	4929630	5255012	9929380	1380757	1475	8619243	32
29	5072877	2507	4927123	5257818	9926855	1382232	1476	8617768	31
30	5075384	2506	4924616	5260624	9924330	1383708	1477	8616292	30
31	5077890	2506	4922110	5263430	9921804	1385185	1478	8614815	29
32	5080396	2505	4919604	5266236	9919278	1386663	1478	8613337	28
33	5082901	2505	4917099	5269043	9916752	1388141	1479	8611859	27
34	5085406	2504	4914594	5271850	9914226	1389620	1479	8610380	26
35	5087910	2504	4912090	5274655	9911700	1391099	1481	8608901	25
36	5090414	2504	4909586	5277460	9909174	1392580	1481	8607420	24
37	5092918	2503	4907082	5280266	9906647	1394061	1482	8605939	23
38	5095421	2503	4904579	5283072	9904120	1395543	1482	8604457	22
39	5097924	2502	4902076	5285878	9901592	1397025	1484	8602975	21
40	5100426	2502	4899574	5288684	9899064	1398509	1484	8601491	20
41	5102928	2501	4897072	5291489	9896537	1399993	1484	8600007	19
42	5105429	2501	4894571	5294294	9894010	1401477	1486	8598523	18
43	5107930	2501	4892070	5297099	9891481	1402963	1486	8597037	17
44	5110431	2500	4889569	5299904	9888952	1404449	1487	8595551	16
45	5112931	2500	4887069	5302709	9886424	1405936	1488	8594064	15
46	5115431	2499	4884569	5305514	9883896	1407424	1488	8592576	14
47	5117930	2499	4882070	5308318	9881367	1408912	1489	8591088	13
48	5120429	2498	4879571	5311122	9878838	1410401	1490	8589599	12
49	5122927	2498	4877073	5313927	9876308	1411891	1490	8588109	11
50	5125425	2498	4874575	5316732	9873778	1413381	1492	8586619	10
51	5127923	2497	4872077	5319536	9871248	1414873	1492	8585127	9
52	5130420	2496	4869580	5322340	9868718	1416365	1492	8583635	8
53	5132916	2497	4867084	5325143	9866188	1417857	1494	8582143	7
54	5135413	2495	4864587	5327946	9863658	1419351	1494	8580649	6
55	5137908	2496	4862092	5330750	9861127	1420845	1495	8579155	5
56	5140404	2495	4859596	5333554	9858596	1422340	1496	8577660	4
57	5142899	2494	4857101	5336358	9856065	1423836	1496	8576164	3
58	5145393	2494	4854607	5339162	9853534	1425332	1497	8574668	2
59	5147887	2494	4852113	5341965	9851003	1426829	1498	8573171	1
60	5150381		4849619	5344768	9848472	1428327		8571673	0

| ′ | Cosine | Diff. | Vers. | Co-chord | Chord | Covers. | Diff. | Sine | ′ |

′	Sine	Diff.	Covers.	Chord	Co-chord	Vers.	Diff.	Cosine	′
0	5150381	2493	4849619	5344768	9848472	1428327	1499	8571673	60
1	5152874	2493	4847126	5347571	9845940	1429826	1499	8570174	59
2	5155367	2492	4844633	5350374	9843408	1431325	1500	8568675	58
3	5157859	2492	4842141	5353176	9840875	1432825	1501	8567175	57
4	5160351	2491	4839649	5355978	9838342	1434326	1501	8565674	56
5	5162842	2491	4837158	5358781	9835809	1435827	1502	8564173	55
6	5165333	2491	4834667	5361584	9833276	1437329	1503	8562671	54
7	5167824	2490	4832176	5364386	9830743	1438832	1504	8561168	53
8	5170314	2490	4829686	5367188	9828210	1440336	1504	8559664	52
9	5172804	2489	4827196	5369990	9825677	1441840	1505	8558160	51
10	5175293	2489	4824707	5372792	9823144	1443345	1506	8556655	50
11	5177782	2488	4822218	5375594	9820610	1444851	1506	8555149	49
12	5180270	2488	4819730	5378396	9818076	1446357	1508	8553643	48
13	5182758	2488	4817242	5381198	9815541	1447865	1508	8552135	47
14	5185246	2487	4814754	5384000	9813006	1449373	1508	8550627	46
15	5187733	2486	4812267	5386801	9810471	1450881	1510	8549119	45
16	5190219	2486	4809781	5389602	9807936	1452391	1510	8547609	44
17	5192705	2486	4807295	5392403	9805401	1453901	1511	8546099	43
18	5195191	2485	4804809	5395204	9802866	1455412	1511	8544588	42
19	5197676	2485	4802324	5398005	9800330	1456923	1513	8543077	41
20	5200161	2485	4799839	5400806	9797794	1458436	1513	8541564	40
21	5202646	2484	4797354	5403607	9795258	1459949	1513	8540051	39
22	5205130	2483	4794870	5406408	9792722	1461462	1515	8538538	38
23	5207613	2483	4792387	5409208	9790186	1462977	1515	8537023	37
24	5210096	2483	4789904	5412008	9787650	1464492	1516	8535508	36
25	5212579	2482	4787421	5414809	9785113	1466008	1517	8533992	35
26	5215061	2482	4784939	5417610	9782576	1467525	1517	8532475	34
27	5217543	2481	4782457	5420410	9780038	1469042	1518	8530958	33
28	5220024	2481	4779976	5423210	9777500	1470560	1519	8529440	32
29	5222505	2481	4777495	5426009	9774962	1472079	1519	8527921	31
30	5224986	2480	4775014	5428808	9772424	1473598	1521	8526402	30
31	5227466	2479	4772534	5431608	9769886	1475119	1521	8524881	29
32	5229945	2479	4770055	5434408	9767348	1476640	1521	8523360	28
33	5232424	2479	4767576	5437207	9764810	1478161	1523	8521839	27
34	5234903	2478	4765097	5440006	9762272	1479684	1523	8520316	26
35	5237381	2478	4762619	5442805	9759733	1481207	1524	8518793	25
36	5239859	2477	4760141	5445604	9757194	1482731	1524	8517269	24
37	5242336	2477	4757664	5448403	9754654	1484255	1526	8515745	23
38	5244813	2477	4755187	5451202	9752114	1485781	1526	8514219	22
39	5247290	2476	4752710	5454001	9749574	1487307	1526	8512693	21
40	5249766	2475	4750234	5456800	9747034	1488833	1528	8511167	20
41	5252241	2476	4747759	5459598	9744494	1490361	1528	8509639	19
42	5254717	2474	4745283	5462396	9741954	1491889	1529	8508111	18
43	5257191	2474	4742809	5465195	9739413	1493418	1529	8506582	17
44	5259665	2474	4740335	5467994	9736872	1494947	1531	8505053	16
45	5262139	2474	4737861	5470791	9734331	1496478	1531	8503522	15
46	5264613	2472	4735387	5473588	9731790	1498009	1532	8501991	14
47	5267085	2473	4732915	5476386	9729249	1499541	1532	8500459	13
48	5269558	2472	4730442	5479184	9726708	1501073	1533	8498927	12
49	5272030	2472	4727970	5481982	9724166	1502606	1534	8497394	11
50	5274502	2471	4725498	5484780	9721624	1504140	1535	8495860	10
51	5276973	2470	4723027	5487577	9719082	1505675	1535	8494325	9
52	5279443	2471	4720557	5490374	9716540	1507210	1536	8492790	8
53	5281914	2469	4718086	5493171	9713997	1508746	1537	8491254	7
54	5284383	2470	4715617	5495968	9711454	1510283	1538	8489717	6
55	5286853	2469	4713147	5498765	9708911	1511821	1538	8488179	5
56	5289322	2468	4710678	5501562	9706368	1513359	1539	8486641	4
57	5291790	2468	4708210	5504358	9703824	1514898	1540	8485102	3
58	5294258	2468	4705742	5507154	9701280	1516438	1540	8483562	2
59	5296726	2467	4703274	5509951	9698736	1517978	1541	8482022	1
60	5299193		4700807	5512748	9696192	1519519		8480481	0

′	Cosine	Diff.	Vers.	Co-chord	Chord	Covers.	Diff.	Sine	′

′	Sine	Diff.	Covers.	Chord	Co-chord	Vers.	Diff.	Cosine	′
0	5299193		4700807	5512748	9696192	1519519		8480481	60
1	5301659	2466	4698341	5515544	9693648	1521061	1542	8478939	59
2	5304125	2466	4695875	5518340	9691104	1522603	1542	8477397	58
3	5306591	2466	4693409	5521135	9688559	1524147	1544	8475853	57
4	5309057	2466	4690943	5523930	9686014	1525691	1544	8474309	56
5	5311521	2464	4688479	5526726	9683469	1527235	1544	8472765	55
		2465					1546		
6	5313986	2464	4686014	5529522	9680924	1528781	1546	8471219	54
7	5316450	2463	4683550	5532317	9678378	1530327	1547	8469673	53
8	5318913	2463	4681087	5535112	9675832	1531874	1547	8468126	52
9	5321376	2463	4678624	5537908	9673286	1533421	1549	8466579	51
10	5323839	2462	4676161	5540704	9670740	1534970	1549	8465030	50
11	5326301	2462	4673699	5543499	9668194	1536519	1549	8463481	49
12	5328763	2461	4671237	5546294	9665648	1538068	1551	8461932	48
13	5331224	2461	4668776	5549088	9663101	1539619	1551	8460381	47
14	5333685	2460	4666315	5551882	9660554	1541170	1552	8458830	46
15	5336145	2460	4663855	5554677	9658007	1542722	1552	8457278	45
16	5338605	2460	4661395	5557472	9655460	1544274	1554	8455726	44
17	5341065	2458	4658935	5560266	9652912	1545828	1554	8454172	43
18	5343523	2459	4656477	5563060	9650364	1547382	1554	8452618	42
19	5345982	2458	4654018	5565854	9647816	1548936	1556	8451064	41
20	5348440	2458	4651560	5568648	9645268	1550492	1556	8449508	40
21	5350898	2457	4649102	5571442	9642720	1552048	1557	8447952	39
22	5353355	2457	4646645	5574236	9640172	1553605	1557	8446395	38
23	5355812	2456	4644188	5577029	9637623	1555162	1559	8444838	37
24	5358268	2456	4641732	5579822	9635074	1556721	1559	8443279	36
25	5360724	2455	4639276	5582615	9632524	1558280	1559	8441720	35
26	5363179	2455	4636821	5585408	9629974	1559839	1561	8440161	34
27	5365634	2455	4634366	5588201	9627425	1561400	1561	8438600	33
28	5368089	2454	4631911	5590994	9624876	1562961	1562	8437039	32
29	5370543	2453	4629457	5593787	9622326	1564523	1563	8435477	31
30	5372996	2453	4627004	5596580	9619776	1566086	1563	8433914	30
31	5375449	2453	4624551	5599373	9617225	1567649	1564	8432351	29
32	5377902	2452	4622098	5602166	9614674	1569213	1565	8430787	28
33	5380354	2452	4619646	5604958	9612123	1570778	1565	8429222	27
34	5382806	2451	4617194	5607750	9609572	1572343	1566	8427657	26
35	5385257	2451	4614743	5610542	9607021	1573909	1567	8426091	25
36	5387708	2450	4612292	5613334	9604470	1575476	1568	8424524	24
37	5390158	2450	4609842	5616126	9601918	1577044	1568	8422956	23
38	5392608	2450	4607392	5618918	9599366	1578612	1569	8421388	22
39	5395058	2449	4604942	5621710	9596814	1580181	1570	8419819	21
40	5397507	2448	4602493	5624502	9594262	1581751	1570	8418249	20
41	5399955	2448	4600045	5627293	9591710	1583321	1571	8416679	19
42	5402403	2448	4597597	5630084	9589158	1584892	1572	8415108	18
43	5404851	2447	4595149	5632875	9586605	1586464	1573	8413536	17
44	5407298	2447	4592702	5635666	9584052	1588037	1573	8411963	16
45	5409745	2446	4590255	5638457	9581498	1589610	1574	8410390	15
46	5412191	2446	4587809	5641248	9578944	1591184	1575	8408816	14
47	5414637	2445	4585363	5644039	9576391	1592759	1575	8407241	13
48	5417082	2445	4582918	5646830	9573888	1594334	1576	8405666	12
49	5419527	2444	4580473	5649620	9571283	1595910	1577	8404090	11
50	5421971	2444	4578029	5652410	9568728	1597487	1577	8402513	10
51	5424415	2444	4575585	5655200	9566174	1599064	1579	8400936	9
52	5426859	2443	4573141	5657990	9563620	1600643	1579	8399357	8
53	5429302	2442	4570698	5660780	9561065	1602222	1579	8397778	7
54	5431744	2443	4568256	5663570	9558510	1603801	1581	8396199	6
55	5434187	2441	4565813	5666360	9555955	1605382	1581	8394618	5
56	5436628	2441	4563372	5669150	9553400	1606963	1582	8393037	4
57	5439069	2441	4560931	5671939	9550844	1608545	1582	8391455	3
58	5441510	2441	4558490	5674728	9548288	1610127	1583	8389873	2
59	5443951	2439	4556049	5677517	9545732	1611710	1584	8388290	1
60	5446390		4553610	5680306	9543176	1613294		8386706	0

′	Cosine	Diff.	Vers.	Co-chord	Chord	Covers.	Diff.	Sine	′

′	Sine	Diff.	Covers.	Chord	Co-chord	Vers.	Diff.	Cosine	′
0	5446390	2440	4553610	5680306	9543176	1613294	1585	8386706	60
1	5448830	2439	4551170	5683095	9540619	1614879	1585	8385121	59
2	5451269	2438	4548731	5685884	9538062	1616464	1586	8383536	58
3	5453707	2438	4546293	5688673	9535505	1618050	1587	8381950	57
4	5456145	2438	4543855	5691462	9532948	1619637	1588	8380363	56
5	5458583	2437	4541417	5694251	9530391	1621225	1588	8378775	55
6	5461020	2436	4538980	5697040	9527834	1622813	1589	8377187	54
7	5463456	2436	4536544	5699828	9525276	1624402	1589	8375598	53
8	5465892	2436	4534108	5702616	9522718	1625991	1591	8374009	52
9	5468328	2435	4531672	5705404	9520160	1627582	1591	8372418	51
10	5470763	2435	4529237	5708192	9517602	1629173	1591	8370827	50
11	5473198	2434	4526802	5710980	9515043	1630764	1593	8369236	49
12	5475632	2434	4524368	5713768	9512484	1632357	1593	8367643	48
13	5478066	2433	4521934	5716555	9509925	1633950	1594	8366050	47
14	5480499	2433	4519501	5719342	9507366	1635544	1594	8364456	46
15	5482932	2433	4517068	5722129	9504807	1637138	1596	8362862	45
16	5485365	2432	4514635	5724916	9502248	1638734	1596	8361266	44
17	5487797	2431	4512203	5727704	9499688	1640330	1596	8359670	43
18	5490228	2431	4509772	5730492	9497128	1641926	1598	8358074	42
19	5492659	2431	4507341	5733278	9494568	1643524	1598	8356476	41
20	5495090	2430	4504910	5736064	9492008	1645122	1599	8354878	40
21	5497520	2430	4502480	5738851	9489447	1646721	1599	8353279	39
22	5499950	2429	4500050	5741638	9486886	1648320	1600	8351680	38
23	5502379	2428	4497621	5744424	9484325	1649920	1601	8350080	37
24	5504807	2429	4495193	5747210	9481764	1651521	1602	8348479	36
25	5507236	2427	4492764	5749996	9479203	1653123	1602	8346877	35
26	5509663	2428	4490337	5752782	9476642	1654725	1603	8345275	34
27	5512091	2427	4487909	5755568	9474080	1656328	1604	8343672	33
28	5514518	2426	4485482	5758354	9471518	1657932	1605	8342068	32
29	5516944	2426	4483056	5761140	9468956	1659537	1605	8340463	31
30	5519370	2425	4480630	5763926	9466394	1661142	1606	8338858	30
31	5521795	2425	4478205	5766711	9463831	1662748	1606	8337252	29
32	5524220	2425	4475780	5769496	9461268	1664354	1608	8335646	28
33	5526645	2424	4473355	5772281	9458705	1665962	1608	8334038	27
34	5529069	2423	4470931	5775066	9456142	1667570	1608	8332430	26
35	5531492	2423	4468508	5777851	9453579	1669178	1610	8330822	25
36	5533915	2423	4466085	5780636	9451016	1670788	1610	8329212	24
37	5536338	2422	4463662	5783421	9448452	1672398	1611	8327602	23
38	5538760	2422	4461240	5786206	9445888	1674009	1611	8325991	22
39	5541182	2421	4458818	5788990	9443324	1675620	1612	8324380	21
40	5543603	2421	4456397	5791774	9440760	1677232	1613	8322768	20
41	5546024	2420	4453976	5794558	9438195	1678845	1614	8321155	19
42	5548444	2420	4451556	5797342	9435630	1680459	1614	8319541	18
43	5550864	2419	4449136	5800126	9433065	1682073	1615	8317927	17
44	5553283	2419	4446717	5802910	9430500	1683688	1616	8316312	16
45	5555702	2419	4444298	5805694	9427935	1685304	1616	8314696	15
46	5558121	2418	4441879	5808478	9425370	1686920	1617	8313080	14
47	5560539	2417	4439461	5811261	9422804	1688537	1618	8311463	13
48	5562956	2417	4437044	5814044	9420238	1690155	1619	8309845	12
49	5565373	2417	4434627	5816827	9417672	1691774	1619	8308226	11
50	5567790	2416	4432210	5819610	9415106	1693393	1620	8306607	10
51	5570206	2415	4429794	5822393	9412539	1695013	1621	8304987	9
52	5572621	2415	4427379	5825176	9409972	1696634	1621	8303366	8
53	5575036	2415	4424964	5827959	9407405	1698255	1622	8301745	7
54	5577451	2414	4422549	5830742	9404838	1699877	1623	8300123	6
55	5579865	2414	4420135	5833524	9402271	1701500	1623	8298500	5
56	5582279	2413	4417721	5836306	9399704	1703123	1625	8296877	4
57	5584692	2413	4415308	5839088	9397136	1704748	1624	8295252	3
58	5587105	2412	4412895	5841870	9394568	1706372	1626	8293628	2
59	5589517	2412	4410483	5844652	9392000	1707998	1626	8292002	1
60	5591929		4408071	5847434	9388432	1709624		8290376	0
′	Cosine	Diff.	Vers.	Co-chord	Chord	Covers.	Diff.	Sine	′

′	Sine	Diff.	Covers.	Chord	Co-chord	Vers.	Diff.	Cosine	′
0	5591929	2411	4408071	5847434	9389432	1709624	1627	8290376	60
1	5594340	2411	4405660	5850216	9386863	1711251	1628	8288749	59
2	5596751	2411	4403249	5852998	9384294	1712879	1628	8287121	58
3	5599162	2410	4400838	5855779	9381725	1714507	1629	8285493	57
4	5601572	2409	4398428	5858560	9379156	1716136	1630	8283864	56
5	5603981	2409	4396019	5861341	9376587	1717766	1631	8282234	55
6	5606390	2408	4393610	5864122	9374018	1719397	1631	8280603	54
7	5608798	2408	4391202	5866903	9371448	1721028	1632	8278972	53
8	5611206	2408	4388794	5869684	9368878	1722660	1632	8277340	52
9	5613614	2407	4386386	5872465	9366308	1724292	1634	8275708	51
10	5616021	2407	4383979	5875246	9363738	1725926	1634	8274074	50
11	5618428	2406	4381572	5878026	9361167	1727560	1634	8272440	49
12	5620834	2405	4379166	5880806	9358596	1729194	1636	8270806	48
13	5623239	2406	4376761	5883586	9356025	1730830	1636	8269170	47
14	5625645	2404	4374355	5886366	9353454	1732466	1637	8267534	46
15	5628049	2404	4371951	5889146	9350883	1734103	1637	8265897	45
16	5630453	2404	4369547	5891926	9348312	1735740	1638	8264260	44
17	5632857	2403	4367143	5894706	9345740	1737378	1639	8262622	43
18	5635260	2403	4364740	5897486	9343168	1739017	1640	8260983	42
19	5637663	2403	4362337	5900265	9340596	1740657	1640	8259343	41
20	5640066	2401	4359934	5903044	9338024	1742297	1641	8257703	40
21	5642467	2402	4357533	5905824	9335451	1743938	1642	8256062	39
22	5644869	2401	4355131	5908604	9332878	1745580	1642	8254420	38
23	5647270	2400	4352730	5911383	9330305	1747222	1643	8252778	37
24	5649670	2400	4350330	5914162	9327732	1748865	1644	8251135	36
25	5652070	2399	4347930	5916940	9325159	1750509	1644	8249491	35
26	5654469	2399	4345531	5919718	9322586	1752153	1645	8247847	34
27	5656868	2399	4343132	5922497	9320012	1753798	1646	8246202	33
28	5659267	2398	4340733	5925276	9317438	1755444	1647	8244556	32
29	5661665	2397	4338335	5928054	9314864	1757091	1647	8242909	31
30	5664062	2397	4335938	5930832	9312290	1758738	1648	8241262	30
31	5666459	2397	4333541	5933610	9309716	1760386	1649	8239614	29
32	5668856	2396	4331144	5936388	9307142	1762035	1649	8237965	28
33	5671252	2396	4328748	5939165	9304567	1763684	1650	8236316	27
34	5673648	2395	4326352	5941942	9301992	1765334	1651	8234666	26
35	5676043	2394	4323957	5944720	9299416	1766985	1651	8233015	25
36	5678437	2395	4321563	5947498	9296840	1768636	1652	8231364	24
37	5680832	2393	4319168	5950275	9294265	1770288	1653	8229712	23
38	5683225	2394	4316775	5953052	9291690	1771941	1654	8228059	22
39	5685619	2392	4314381	5955829	9289114	1773595	1654	8226405	21
40	5688011	2392	4311989	5958606	9286538	1775249	1655	8224751	20
41	5690403	2392	4309597	5961382	9283961	1776904	1656	8223096	19
42	5692795	2392	4307205	5964158	9281384	1778560	1656	8221440	18
43	5695187	2390	4304813	5966935	9278807	1780216	1657	8219784	17
44	5697577	2391	4302423	5969712	9276230	1781873	1658	8218127	16
45	5699968	2389	4300032	5972488	9273653	1783531	1658	8216469	15
46	5702357	2390	4297643	5975264	9271076	1785189	1659	8214811	14
47	5704747	2389	4295253	5978040	9268498	1786848	1660	8213152	13
48	5707136	2388	4292864	5980816	9265920	1788508	1660	8211492	12
49	5709524	2388	4290476	5983592	9263342	1790168	1662	8209832	11
50	5711912	2387	4288088	5986368	9260764	1791830	1661	8208170	10
51	5714299	2387	4285701	5989143	9258186	1793491	1663	8206509	9
52	5716686	2387	4283314	5991918	9255608	1795154	1663	8204846	8
53	5719073	2386	4280927	5994693	9253029	1796817	1664	8203183	7
54	5721459	2385	4278541	5997468	9250450	1798481	1665	8201519	6
55	5723844	2385	4276156	6000243	9247871	1800146	1665	8199854	5
56	5726229	2385	4273771	6003018	9245292	1801811	1666	8198189	4
57	5728614	2384	4271386	6005793	9242712	1803477	1667	8196523	3
58	5730998	2383	4269002	6008568	9240132	1805144	1667	8194856	2
59	5733381	2383	4266619	6011342	9237552	1806811	1669	8193189	1
60	5735764		4264236	6014116	9234972	1808480		8191520	0
′	Cosine	Diff.	Vers.	Co-chord	Chord	Covers.	Diff.	Sine	′

′	Sine	Diff.	Covers.	Chord	Co-chord	Vers.	Diff.	Cosine	′
0	5735764	2383	4264236	6014116	9234972	1808480	1668	8191520	60
1	5738147	2382	4261853	6016890	9232392	1810148	1670	8189852	59
2	5740529	2382	4259471	6019664	9229812	1811818	1670	8188182	58
3	5742911	2381	4257089	6022438	9227231	1813488	1671	8186512	57
4	5745292	2380	4254708	6025212	9224650	1815159	1672	8184841	56
5	5747672	2381	4252328	6027986	9222069	1816831	1672	8183169	55
6	5750053	2379	4249947	6030760	9219488	1818503	1673	8181497	54
7	5752432	2379	4247568	6033533	9216906	1820176	1673	8179824	53
8	5754811	2379	4245189	6036306	9214324	1821849	1675	8178151	52
9	5757190	2378	4242810	6039079	9211742	1823524	1675	8176476	51
10	5759568	2378	4240432	6041852	9209160	1825199	1676	8174801	50
11	5761946	2377	4238054	6044625	9206578	1826875	1676	8173125	49
12	5764323	2377	4235677	6047398	9203996	1828551	1677	8171449	48
13	5766700	2376	4233300	6050170	9201413	1830228	1678	8169772	47
14	5769076	2376	4230924	6052942	9198830	1831906	1678	8168094	46
15	5771452	2375	4228548	6055715	9196247	1833584	1680	8166416	45
16	5773827	2375	4226173	6058488	9193664	1835264	1680	8164736	44
17	5776202	2374	4223798	6061260	9191080	1836944	1680	8163056	43
18	5778576	2374	4221424	6064032	9188496	1838624	1681	8161376	42
19	5780950	2373	4219050	6066804	9185913	1840305	1682	8159695	41
20	5783323	2373	4216677	6069576	9183330	1841987	1683	8158013	40
21	5785696	2373	4214304	6072347	9180745	1843670	1683	8156330	39
22	5788069	2371	4211931	6075118	9178160	1845353	1684	8154647	38
23	5790440	2372	4209560	6077890	9175576	1847037	1685	8152963	37
24	5792812	2371	4207188	6080662	9172992	1848722	1685	8151278	36
25	5795183	2370	4204817	6083433	9170406	1850407	1687	8149593	35
26	5797553	2370	4202447	6086204	9167820	1852094	1686	8147906	34
27	5799923	2369	4200077	6088974	9165235	1853780	1688	8146220	33
28	5802292	2369	4197708	6091744	9162650	1855468	1688	8144532	32
29	5804661	2369	4195339	6094515	9160064	1857156	1689	8142844	31
30	5807030	2367	4192970	6097286	9157478	1858845	1689	8141155	30
31	5809397	2368	4190603	6100056	9154892	1860534	1691	8139466	29
32	5811765	2367	4188235	6102826	9152306	1862225	1691	8137775	28
33	5814132	2366	4185868	6105596	9149719	1863916	1691	8136084	27
34	5816498	2366	4183502	6108366	9147132	1865607	1692	8134393	26
35	5818864	2366	4181136	6111136	9144545	1867299	1693	8132701	25
36	5821230	2365	4178770	6113906	9141958	1868992	1694	8131008	24
37	5823595	2364	4176405	6116676	9139371	1870686	1694	8129314	23
38	5825959	2364	4174041	6119446	9136784	1872380	1695	8127620	22
39	5828323	2364	4171677	6122215	9134196	1874075	1696	8125925	21
40	5830687	2363	4169313	6124984	9131608	1875771	1697	8124229	20
41	5833050	2362	4166950	6127753	9129020	1877468	1697	8122532	19
42	5835412	2362	4164588	6130522	9126432	1879165	1698	8120835	18
43	5837774	2362	4162226	6133291	9123843	1880863	1698	8119137	17
44	5840136	2361	4159864	6136060	9121254	1882561	1699	8117439	16
45	5842497	2360	4157503	6138828	9118665	1884260	1700	8115740	15
46	5844857	2360	4155143	6141596	9116076	1885960	1701	8114040	14
47	5847217	2360	4152783	6144364	9113487	1887661	1701	8112339	13
48	5849577	2359	4150423	6147132	9110898	1889362	1702	8110638	12
49	5851936	2358	4148064	6149900	9108308	1891064	1702	8108936	11
50	5854294	2358	4145706	6152668	9105718	1892766	1704	8107234	10
51	5856652	2358	4143348	6155436	9103128	1894470	1704	8105530	9
52	5859010	2357	4140990	6158204	9100538	1896174	1704	8103826	8
53	5861367	2357	4138633	6160971	9097948	1897878	1706	8102122	7
54	5863724	2356	4136276	6163738	9095358	1899584	1706	8100416	6
55	5866080	2355	4133920	6166505	9092767	1901290	1706	8098710	5
56	5868435	2355	4131565	6169272	9090176	1902996	1708	8097004	4
57	5870790	2355	4129210	6172039	9087585	1904704	1708	8095296	3
58	5873145	2354	4126855	6174806	9084994	1906412	1709	8093588	2
59	5875499	2354	4124501	6177573	9082402	1908121	1709	8091879	1
60	5877853		4122147	6180340	9079810	1909830		8090170	0

′	Cosine	Diff.	Vers.	Co-chord	Chord	Covers.	Diff.	Sine	′

′	Sine	Diff.	Covers.	Chord	Co-chord	Vers.	Diff.	Cosine	′
0	5877853		4122147	6180340	9079810	1909830		8090170	60
1	5880206	2353	4119794	6183106	9077218	1911540	1710	8088460	59
2	5882558	2352	4117442	6185872	9074626	1913251	1711	8086749	58
3	5884910	2352	4115090	6188638	9072034	1914963	1712	8085037	57
4	5887262	2352	4112738	6191404	9069442	1916675	1712	8083325	56
5	5889613	2351	4110387	6194170	9066849	1918388	1713	8081612	55
6	5891964	2351	4108036	6196936	9064256	1920101	1713	8079899	54
7	5894314	2350	4105686	6199702	9061663	1921815	1714	8078185	53
8	5896663	2349	4103337	6202468	9059070	1923530	1715	8076470	52
9	5899012	2349	4100988	6205233	9056476	1925246	1716	8074754	51
10	5901361	2349	4098639	6207998	9053882	1926962	1716	8073038	50
11	5903709	2348	4096291	6210763	9051288	1928679	1717	8071321	49
12	5906057	2348	4093943	6213528	9048694	1930397	1718	8069603	48
13	5908404	2347	4091596	6216293	9046100	1932115	1718	8067885	47
14	5910750	2346	4089250	6219058	9043506	1933834	1719	8066166	46
15	5913096	2346	4086904	6221823	9040911	1935554	1720	8064446	45
16	5915442	2346	4084558	6224588	9038316	1937274	1720	8062726	44
17	5917787	2345	4082213	6227352	9035721	1938995	1721	8061005	43
18	5920132	2345	4079868	6230116	9033126	1940717	1722	8059283	42
19	5922476	2344	4077524	6232880	9030530	1942440	1723	8057560	41
20	5924819	2343	4075181	6235644	9027934	1944163	1723	8055837	40
21	5927163	2344	4072837	6238408	9025339	1945887	1724	8054113	39
22	5929505	2342	4070495	6241172	9022744	1947611	1724	8052389	38
23	5931847	2342	4068153	6243935	9020147	1949336	1725	8050664	37
24	5934189	2342	4065811	6246698	9017550	1951062	1726	8048938	36
25	5936530	2341	4063470	6249461	9014954	1952789	1727	8047211	35
26	5938871	2341	4061129	6252224	9012358	1954516	1727	8045484	34
27	5941211	2340	4058789	6254987	9009761	1956244	1728	8043756	33
28	5943550	2339	4056450	6257750	9007164	1957972	1728	8042028	32
29	5945889	2339	4054111	6260513	9004566	1959701	1729	8040299	31
30	5948228	2339	4051772	6263276	9001968	1961431	1730	8038569	30
31	5950566	2338	4049434	6266038	8999371	1963162	1731	8036838	29
32	5952904	2338	4047096	6268800	8996774	1964893	1731	8035107	28
33	5955241	2337	4044759	6271563	8994176	1966625	1732	8033375	27
34	5957577	2336	4042423	6274326	8991578	1968358	1733	8031642	26
35	5959913	2336	4040087	6277088	8988979	1970091	1733	8029909	25
36	5962249	2336	4037751	6279850	8986380	1971825	1734	8028175	24
37	5964584	2335	4035416	6282611	8983781	1973560	1735	8026440	23
38	5966918	2334	4033082	6285372	8981182	1975295	1735	8024705	22
39	5969252	2334	4030748	6288134	8978583	1977031	1736	8022969	21
40	5971586	2334	4028414	6290896	8975984	1978768	1737	8021232	20
41	5973919	2333	4026081	6293657	8973384	1980505	1737	8019495	19
42	5976251	2332	4023749	6296418	8970784	1982244	1739	8017756	18
43	5978583	2332	4021417	6299178	8968184	1983982	1738	8016018	17
44	5980915	2332	4019085	6301938	8965584	1985722	1740	8014278	16
45	5983246	2331	4016754	6304699	8962984	1987462	1740	8012538	15
46	5985577	2331	4014423	6307460	8960384	1989203	1741	8010797	14
47	5987906	2329	4012094	6310220	8957783	1990944	1741	8009056	13
48	5990236	2330	4009764	6312980	8955182	1992686	1742	8007314	12
49	5992565	2329	4007435	6315740	8952581	1994429	1743	8005571	11
50	5994893	2328	4005107	6318500	8949980	1996173	1744	8003827	10
51	5997221	2328	4002779	6321260	8047378	1997917	1744	8002083	9
52	5999549	2328	4000451	6324020	8944776	1999662	1745	8000338	8
53	6001876	2327	3998124	6326780	8942174	2001407	1745	7998503	7
54	6004202	2326	3995798	6329540	8939572	2003153	1746	7996847	6
55	6006528	2326	3993472	6332299	8936970	2004900	1747	7995100	5
56	6008854	2326	3991146	6335058	8934368	2006648	1748	7993352	4
57	6011179	2325	3988821	6337817	8931765	2008396	1748	7991604	3
58	6013503	2324	3986497	6340576	8929162	2010145	1749	7989855	2
59	6015827	2324	3984173	6343335	8926559	2011895	1750	7988105	1
60	6018150	2323	3981850	6346094	8923956	2013645	1750	7986355	0
′	Cosine	Diff.	Vers.	Co-chord	Chord	Covers.	Diff.	Sine	′

′	Sine	Diff.	Covers.	Chord	Co-chord	Vers.	Diff.	Cosine	′
0	6018150	2323	3981850	6346094	8923956	2013645	1751	7986355	60
1	6020473	2322	3979527	6348852	8921353	2015396	1751	7984604	59
2	6022795	2322	3977205	6351610	8918750	2017147	1753	7982853	58
3	6025117	2322	3974883	6354368	8916146	2018900	1753	7981100	57
4	6027439	2321	3972561	6357126	8913542	2020653	1753	7979347	56
5	6029760	2320	3970240	6359884	8910938	2022406	1755	7977594	55
6	6032080	2320	3967920	6362642	8908334	2024161	1755	7975839	54
7	6034400	2319	3965600	6365400	8905729	2025916	1755	7974084	53
8	6036719	2319	3963281	6368158	8903124	2027671	1757	7972329	52
9	6039038	2318	3960962	6370915	8900519	2029428	1757	7970572	51
10	6041356	2318	3958644	6373672	8897914	2031185	1757	7968815	50
11	6043674	2317	3956326	6376429	8895309	2032942	1759	7967058	49
12	6045991	2317	3954009	6379186	8892704	2034701	1759	7965299	48
13	6048308	2316	3951692	6381943	8890098	2036460	1760	7963540	47
14	6050624	2316	3949376	6384700	8887492	2038220	1760	7961780	46
15	6052940	2315	3947060	6387456	8884886	2039980	1761	7960020	45
16	6055255	2315	3944745	6390212	8882280	2041741	1762	7958259	44
17	6057570	2314	3942430	6392969	8879674	2043503	1762	7956497	43
18	6059884	2314	3940116	6395726	8877068	2045265	1763	7954735	42
19	6062198	2313	3937802	6398482	8874461	2047028	1764	7952972	41
20	6064511	2313	3935489	6401238	8871854	2048792	1764	7951208	40
21	6066824	2312	3933176	6403993	8869246	2050556	1766	7949444	39
22	6069136	2311	3930864	6406748	8866638	2052322	1765	7947678	38
23	6071447	2311	3928553	6409504	8864031	2054087	1767	7945913	37
24	6073758	2311	3926242	6412260	8861424	2055854	1767	7944146	36
25	6076069	2310	3923931	6415015	8858816	2057621	1768	7942379	35
26	6078379	2310	3921621	6417770	8856208	2059389	1768	7940611	34
27	6080689	2309	3919311	6420525	8853600	2061157	1769	7938843	33
28	6082998	2308	3917002	6423280	8850992	2062926	1770	7937074	32
29	6085306	2308	3914694	6426035	8848383	2064696	1771	7935304	31
30	6087614	2308	3912386	6428790	8845774	2066467	1771	7933533	30
31	6089922	2307	3910078	6431544	8843165	2068238	1772	7931762	29
32	6092229	2306	3907771	6434298	8840556	2070010	1772	7929990	28
33	6094535	2306	3905465	6437052	8837946	2071782	1773	7928218	27
34	6096841	2306	3903159	6439806	8835336	2073555	1774	7926445	26
35	6099147	2305	3900853	6442560	8832727	2075329	1775	7924671	25
36	6101452	2304	3898548	6445314	8830118	2077104	1775	7922896	24
37	6103756	2304	3896244	6448068	8827507	2078879	1776	7921121	23
38	6106060	2303	3893940	6450822	8824896	2080655	1776	7919345	22
39	6108363	2303	3891637	6453575	8822296	2082431	1777	7917560	21
40	6110666	2303	3889334	6456328	8819676	2084208	1778	7915792	20
41	6112969	2301	3887031	6459081	8817065	2085986	1779	7914014	19
42	6115270	2302	3884730	6461834	8814454	2087765	1779	7912235	18
43	6117572	2301	3882428	6464587	8811842	2089544	1780	7910456	17
44	6119873	2300	3880127	6467340	8809230	2091324	1780	7908676	16
45	6122173	2300	3877827	6470092	8806619	2093104	1781	7906896	15
46	6124473	2299	3875527	6472844	8804008	2094885	1782	7905115	14
47	6126772	2299	3873228	6475596	8801396	2096667	1783	7903333	13
48	6129071	2298	3870929	6478348	8798784	2098450	1783	7901550	12
49	6131369	2297	3868631	6481100	8796171	2100233	1784	7899767	11
50	6133666	2298	3866334	6483852	8793558	2102017	1785	7897983	10
51	6135964	2296	3864036	6486604	8790945	2103802	1785	7896198	9
52	6138260	2296	3861740	6489356	8788332	2105587	1786	7894413	8
53	6140556	2296	3859444	6492107	8785719	2107373	1786	7892627	7
54	6142852	2295	3857148	6494858	8783106	2109159	1787	7890841	6
55	6145147	2295	3854853	6497609	8780493	2110946	1788	7889054	5
56	6147442	2294	3852558	6500360	8777880	2112734	1789	7887266	4
57	6149736	2293	3850264	6503111	8775266	2114523	1789	7885477	3
58	6152029	2293	3847971	6505862	8772652	2116312	1790	7883688	2
59	6154322	2293	3845678	6508613	8770037	2118102	1790	7881898	1
60	6156615		3843385	6511364	8767422	2119892		7880108	0

′	Cosine	Diff.	Vers.	Co-chord	Chord	Covers.	Diff.	Sine	′

′	Sine	Diff.	Covers.	Chord	Co-chord	Vers.	Diff.	Cosine	′
0	6156615		3843385	6511364	8767422	2119892		7880108	60
1	6158907	2292	3841093	6514114	8764808	2121684	1792	7878316	59
2	6161198	2291	3838802	6516864	8762194	2123476	1792	7876524	58
3	6163489	2291	3836511	6519614	8759579	2125268	1792	7874732	57
4	6165780	2291	3834220	6522364	8756964	2127061	1793	7872939	56
5	6168069	2289	3831931	6525114	8754348	2128855	1794	7871145	55
		2290					1795		
6	6170359	2289	3829641	6527864	8751732	2130650	1795	7869350	54
7	6172648	2288	3827352	6530613	8749117	2132445	1796	7867555	53
8	6174936	2288	3825064	6533362	8746502	2134241	1796	7865759	52
9	6177224	2287	3822776	6536111	8743885	2136037	1798	7863963	51
10	6179511	2287	3820489	6538860	8741268	2137835	1798	7862165	50
11	6181798	2286	3818202	6541609	8738652	2139633	1798	7860367	49
12	6184084	2286	3815916	6544358	8736036	2141431	1799	7858569	48
13	6186370	2285	3813630	6547107	8733419	2143230	1800	7856770	47
14	6188655	2284	3811345	6549856	8730802	2145030	1801	7854970	46
15	6190939	2285	3809061	6552604	8728185	2146831	1801	7853169	45
16	6193224	2283	3806776	6555352	8725568	2148632	1802	7851368	44
17	6195507	2283	3804493	6558100	8722950	2150434	1802	7849566	43
18	6197790	2283	3802210	6560848	8720332	2152236	1803	7847764	42
19	6200073	2282	3799927	6563596	8717714	2154039	1804	7845961	41
20	6202355	2281	3797645	6566344	8715096	2155843	1805	7844157	40
21	6204636	2281	3795364	6569091	8712478	2157648	1805	7842352	39
22	6206917	2281	3793083	6571838	8709860	2159453	1806	7840547	38
23	6209198	2280	3790802	6574585	8707241	2161259	1806	7838741	37
24	6211478	2279	3788522	6577332	8704622	2163065	1808	7836935	36
25	6213757	2279	3786243	6580079	8702003	2164873	1807	7835127	35
26	6216036	2278	3783964	6582826	8699384	2166680	1809	7833320	34
27	6218314	2278	3781686	6585573	8696764	2168489	1809	7831511	33
28	6220592	2278	3779408	6588320	8694144	2170298	1810	7829702	32
29	6222870	2276	3777130	6591066	8691525	2172108	1810	7827892	31
30	6225146	2277	3774854	6593812	8688906	2173918	1812	7826082	30
31	6227423	2275	3772577	6596559	8686285	2175730	1811	7824270	29
32	6229698	2276	3770302	6599306	8683664	2177541	1813	7822459	28
33	6231974	2274	3768026	6602051	8681044	2179354	1813	7820646	27
34	6234248	2274	3765752	6604796	8678424	2181167	1813	7818833	26
35	6236522	2274	3763478	6607542	8675803	2182981	1814	7817019	25
36	6238796	2273	3761204	6610288	8673182	2184795	1814	7815205	24
37	6241069	2273	3758931	6613033	8670561	2186610	1815	7813390	23
38	6243342	2272	3756658	6615778	8667940	2188426	1816	7811574	22
39	6245614	2271	3754386	6618523	8665318	2190243	1817	7809757	21
40	6247885	2271	3752115	6621268	8662696	2192060	1817	7807940	20
41	6250156	2271	3749844	6624013	8660074	2193877	1817	7806123	19
42	6252427	2269	3747573	6626758	8657452	2195696	1819	7804304	18
43	6254696	2270	3745304	6629502	8654829	2197515	1819	7802485	17
44	6256966	2269	3743034	6632246	8652206	2199335	1820	7800665	16
45	6259235	2268	3740765	6634990	8649584	2201155	1820	7798845	15
46	6261503	2268	3738497	6637734	8646962	2202976	1821	7797024	14
47	6263771	2267	3736229	6640478	8644338	2204798	1822	7795202	13
48	6266038	2267	3733962	6643222	8641714	2206620	1822	7793380	12
49	6268305	2266	3731695	6645966	8639091	2208443	1823	7791557	11
50	6270571	2266	3729429	6648710	8636468	2210267	1824	7789733	10
51	6272837	2265	3727163	6651453	8633844	2212091	1824	7787909	9
52	6275102	2264	3724898	6654196	8631220	2213916	1825	7786084	8
53	6277366	2265	3722634	6656939	8628596	2215742	1826	7784258	7
54	6279631	2263	3720369	6659682	8625972	2217569	1827	7782431	6
55	6281894	2263	3718106	6662425	8623347	2219396	1827	7780604	5
56	6284157	2263	3715843	6665168	8620722	2221223	1827	7778777	4
57	6286420	2262	3713580	6667910	8618097	2223051	1828	7776949	3
58	6288682	2261	3711318	6670652	8615472	2224880	1829	7775120	2
59	6290943	2261	3709057	6673395	8612847	2226710	1830	7773290	1
60	6293204		3706796	6676138	8610222	2228540	1830	7771460	0
′	Cosine	Diff.	Vers.	Co-chord	Chord	Covers.	Diff.	Sine	′

′	Sine	Diff.	Covers.	Chord	Co-chord	Vers.	Diff.	Cosine	′
0	6293204	2260	3706796	6676138	8610222	2228540	1831	7771460	60
1	6295464	2260	3704536	6678879	8607596	2230371	1832	7769629	59
2	6297724	2259	3702276	6681620	8604970	2232203	1832	7767797	58
3	6299983	2259	3700017	6684362	8602344	2234035	1833	7765965	57
4	6302242	2258	3697758	6687104	8599718	2235868	1834	7764132	56
5	6304500	2258	3695500	6689845	8597092	2237702	1834	7762298	55
6	6306758	2257	3693242	6692586	8594466	2239536	1835	7760464	54
7	6309015	2257	3690985	6695327	8591839	2241371	1835	7758629	53
8	6311272	2256	3688728	6698068	8589212	2243206	1837	7756794	52
9	6313528	2256	3686472	6700809	8586585	2245043	1836	7754957	51
10	6315784	2255	3684216	6703550	8583958	2246879	1838	7753121	50
11	6318039	2254	3681961	6706291	8581330	2248717	1838	7751283	49
12	6320293	2254	3679707	6709032	8578702	2250555	1839	7749445	48
13	6322547	2253	3677453	6711772	8576074	2252394	1839	7747606	47
14	6324800	2253	3675200	6714512	8573446	2254233	1841	7745767	46
15	6327053	2253	3672947	6717252	8570818	2256074	1840	7743926	45
16	6329306	2251	3670694	6719992	8568190	2257914	1842	7742086	44
17	6331557	2252	3668443	6722731	8565562	2259756	1842	7740244	43
18	6333809	2250	3666191	6725470	8562934	2261598	1843	7738402	42
19	6336059	2251	3663941	6728210	8560305	2263441	1843	7736559	41
20	6338310	2249	3661690	6730950	8557676	2265284	1844	7734716	40
21	6340559	2249	3659441	6733689	8555046	2267128	1845	7732872	39
22	6342808	2249	3657192	6736428	8552416	2268973	1845	7731027	38
23	6345057	2248	3654943	6739167	8549787	2270818	1846	7729182	37
24	6347305	2248	3652695	6741906	8547158	2272664	1847	7727336	36
25	6349553	2247	3650447	6744644	8544528	2274511	1847	7725489	35
26	6351800	2246	3648200	6747382	8541898	2276358	1848	7723642	34
27	6354046	2246	3645954	6750120	8539267	2278206	1849	7721794	33
28	6356292	2245	3643708	6752858	8536636	2280055	1849	7719945	32
29	6358537	2245	3641463	6755596	8534005	2281904	1850	7718096	31
30	6360782	2244	3639218	6758334	8531374	2283754	1851	7716246	30
31	6363026	2244	3636974	6761072	8528743	2285605	1851	7714395	29
32	6365270	2243	3634730	6763810	8526112	2287456	1852	7712544	28
33	6367513	2243	3632487	6766547	8523481	2289308	1852	7710692	27
34	6369756	2242	3630244	6769284	8520850	2291160	1854	7708840	26
35	6371998	2242	3628002	6772021	8518218	2293014	1854	7706986	25
36	6374240	2241	3625760	6774758	8515586	2294868	1854	7705132	24
37	6376481	2240	3623519	6777495	8512954	2296722	1855	7703278	23
38	6378721	2240	3621279	6780232	8510322	2298577	1856	7701423	22
39	6380961	2240	3619039	6782968	8507689	2300433	1857	7699567	21
40	6383201	2239	3616799	6785704	8505056	2302290	1857	7697710	20
41	6385440	2238	3614560	6788441	8502423	2304147	1857	7695853	19
42	6387678	2238	3612322	6791178	8499790	2306004	1859	7693996	18
43	6389916	2237	3610084	6793914	8497157	2307863	1859	7692137	17
44	6392153	2237	3607847	6796650	8494524	2309722	1860	7690278	16
45	6394390	2236	3605610	6799385	8491890	2311582	1860	7688418	15
46	6396626	2236	3603374	6802120	8489256	2313442	1861	7686558	14
47	6398862	2235	3601138	6804856	8486622	2315303	1862	7684697	13
48	6401097	2235	3598903	6807592	8483988	2317165	1862	7682835	12
49	6403332	2234	3596668	6810327	8481354	2319027	1863	7680973	11
50	6405566	2233	3594434	6813062	8478720	2320890	1864	7679110	10
51	6407799	2233	3592201	6815796	8476085	2322754	1864	7677246	9
52	6410032	2232	3589968	6818530	8473450	2324618	1865	7675382	8
53	6412264	2232	3587736	6821265	8470815	2326483	1865	7673517	7
54	6414496	2232	3585504	6824000	8468180	2328348	1867	7671652	6
55	6416728	2230	3583272	6826734	8465545	2330215	1867	7669785	5
56	6418958	2231	3581042	6829468	8462910	2332082	1867	7667918	4
57	6421189	2229	3578811	6832202	8460274	2333949	1868	7666051	3
58	6423418	2229	3576582	6834936	8457638	2335817	1869	7664183	2
59	6425647	2229	3574353	6837669	8455002	2337686	1870	7662314	1
60	6427876		3572124	6840402	8452366	2339556		7660444	0

′	Cosine	Diff.	Vers.	Co-chord	Chord	Covers.	Diff.	Sine	′

′	Sine	Diff.	Covers.	Chord	Co-chord	Vers.	Diff.	Cosine	′
0	6427876	2228	3572124	6840402	8452366	2339556	1870	7660444	60
1	6430104	2228	3569896	6843136	8449729	2341426	1870	7658574	59
2	6432332	2227	3567668	6845870	8447092	2343296	1872	7656704	58
3	6434559	2226	3565441	6848603	8444455	2345168	1872	7654832	57
4	6436785	2226	3563215	6851336	8441818	2347040	1873	7652960	56
5	6439011	2225	3560989	6854068	8439181	2348913	1873	7651087	55
6	6441236	2225	3558764	6856800	8436544	2350786	1874	7649214	54
7	6443461	2224	3556539	6859533	8433906	2352660	1875	7647340	53
8	6445685	2224	3554315	6862266	8431268	2354535	1875	7645465	52
9	6447909	2223	3552091	6864998	8428630	2356410	1876	7643590	51
10	6450132	2223	3549868	6867730	8425992	2358286	1876	7641714	50
11	6452355	2222	3547645	6870462	8423354	2360162	1878	7639838	49
12	6454577	2221	3545423	6873194	8420716	2362040	1878	7637960	48
13	6456798	2221	3543202	6875925	8418077	2363918	1878	7636082	47
14	6459019	2221	3540981	6878658	8415438	2365796	1879	7634204	46
15	6461240	2220	3538760	6881389	8412799	2367675	1880	7632325	45
16	6463460	2219	3536540	6884120	8410160	2369555	1881	7630445	44
17	6465679	2219	2534321	6886851	8407521	2371436	1881	7628564	43
18	6467898	2218	3532102	6889582	8404882	2373317	1881	7626683	42
19	6470116	2218	3529884	6892312	8402242	2375198	1883	7624802	41
20	6472334	2217	3527666	6895042	8399602	2377081	1883	7622919	40
21	6474551	2216	3525449	6897773	8396962	2378964	1884	7621036	39
22	6476767	2217	3523233	6900504	8394322	2380848	1884	7619152	38
23	6478984	2215	3521016	6903234	8391682	2382732	1885	7617268	37
24	6481199	2215	3518801	6905964	8389042	2384617	1886	7615383	36
25	6483414	2214	3516586	6908694	8386401	2386503	1886	7613497	35
26	6485628	2214	3514372	6911424	8383760	2388389	1887	7611611	34
27	6487842	2214	3512158	6914153	8381119	2390276	1887	7609724	33
28	6490056	2212	3509944	6916882	8378478	2392163	1888	7607837	32
29	6492268	2212	3507732	6919612	8375836	2394051	1889	7605949	31
30	6494480	2212	3505520	6922342	8373194	2395940	1890	7604060	30
31	6496692	2211	3503308	6925071	8370553	2397830	1890	7602170	29
32	6498903	2211	3501097	6927800	8367912	2399720	1891	7600280	28
33	6501114	2210	3498886	6930528	8365269	2401611	1891	7598389	27
34	6503324	2209	3496676	6933256	8362626	2403502	1892	7596498	26
35	6505533	2209	3494467	6935985	8359984	2405394	1893	7594606	25
36	6507742	2209	3492258	6938714	8357342	2407287	1893	7592713	24
37	6509951	2207	3490049	6941442	8354699	2409180	1894	7590820	23
38	6512158	2208	3487842	6944170	8352056	2411074	1895	7588926	22
39	6514366	2206	3485634	6946897	8349413	2412969	1895	7587031	21
40	6516572	2206	3483428	6949624	8346770	2414864	1896	7585136	20
41	6518778	2206	3481222	6952352	8344126	2416760	1897	7583240	19
42	6520984	2205	3479016	6955080	8341482	2418657	1897	7581343	18
43	6523189	2205	3476811	6957807	8338838	2420554	1898	7579446	17
44	6525394	2204	3474606	6960534	8336194	2422452	1898	7577548	16
45	6527598	2203	3472402	6963261	8333550	2424350	1899	7575650	15
46	6529801	2203	3470199	6965988	8330906	2426249	1900	7573751	14
47	6532004	2202	3467996	6968714	8328261	2428149	1900	7571851	13
48	6534206	2202	3465794	6971440	8325616	2430049	1901	7569951	12
49	6536408	2201	3463592	6974167	8322971	2431950	1902	7568050	11
50	6538609	2201	3461391	6976894	8320326	2433852	1902	7566148	10
51	6540810	2200	3459190	6979620	8317680	2435754	1903	7564246	9
52	6543010	2199	3456990	6982346	8315034	2437657	1904	7562343	8
53	6545209	2199	3454791	6985071	8312389	2439561	1904	7560439	7
54	6547408	2199	3452592	6987796	8309744	2441465	1905	7558535	6
55	6549607	2197	3450393	6990522	8307098	2443370	1906	7556630	5
56	6551804	2198	3448196	6993248	8304452	2445276	1906	7554724	4
57	6554002	2196	3445998	6995973	8301805	2447182	1907	7552818	3
58	6556198	2197	3443802	6998698	8299158	2449089	1907	7550911	2
59	6558395	2195	3441605	7001423	8296511	2450996	1908	7549004	1
60	6560590		3439410	7004148	8293864	2452904		7547096	0
′	Cosine	Diff.	Vers.	Co-chord	Chord	Covers.	Diff.	Sine	′

′	Sine	Diff.	Covers.	Chord	Co-chord	Vers.	Diff.	Cosine	′
0	6560590	2195	3439410	7004148	8293864	2452904	1909	7547096	60
1	6562785	2195	3437215	7006872	8291217	2454813	1909	7545187	59
2	6564980	2194	3435020	7009596	8288570	2456722	1910	7543278	58
3	6567174	2193	3432826	7012321	8285923	2458632	1911	7541368	57
4	6569367	2193	3430633	7015046	8283276	2460543	1911	7539457	56
5	6571560	2192	3428440	7017769	8280628	2462454	1912	7537546	55
6	6573752	2192	3426248	7020492	8277980	2464366	1913	7535634	54
7	6575944	2191	3424056	7023216	8275332	2466279	1913	7533721	53
8	6578135	2191	3421865	7025940	8272684	2468192	1914	7531808	52
9	6580326	2190	3419674	7028663	8270035	2470106	1914	7529894	51
10	6582516	2190	3417484	7031386	8267386	2472020	1915	7527980	50
11	6584706	2189	3415294	7034109	8264737	2473935	1916	7526065	49
12	6586895	2188	3413105	7036832	8262088	2475851	1916	7524149	48
13	6589083	2188	3410917	7039555	8259439	2477767	1917	7522233	47
14	6591271	2187	3408729	7042278	8256790	2479684	1918	7520316	46
15	6593458	2187	3406542	7045001	8254140	2481602	1918	7518398	45
16	6595645	2186	3404355	7047724	8251490	2483520	1919	7516480	44
17	6597831	2186	3402169	7050446	8248841	2485439	1920	7514561	43
18	6600017	2185	3399983	7053168	8246192	2487359	1920	7512641	42
19	6602202	2184	3397798	7055890	8243541	2489279	1921	7510721	41
20	6604386	2184	3395614	7058612	8240890	2491200	1921	7508800	40
21	6606570	2184	3393430	7061333	8238240	2493121	1922	7506879	39
22	6608754	2182	3391246	7064054	8235590	2495043	1923	7504957	38
23	6610936	2183	3389064	7066775	8232939	2496966	1923	7503034	37
24	6613119	2181	3386881	7069496	8230288	2498889	1924	7501111	36
25	6615300	2182	3384700	7072217	8227636	2500813	1925	7499187	35
26	6617482	2180	3382518	7074938	8224984	2502738	1925	7497262	34
27	6619662	2180	3380338	7077659	8222333	2504663	1926	7495337	33
28	6621842	2180	3378158	7080380	8219682	2506589	1927	7493411	32
29	6624022	2178	3375978	7083100	8217030	2508516	1927	7491484	31
30	6626200	2179	3373800	7085820	8214378	2510443	1928	7489557	30
31	6628379	2178	3371621	7088540	8211725	2512371	1928	7487629	29
32	6630557	2177	3369443	7091260	8209072	2514299	1929	7485701	28
33	6632734	2176	3367266	7093980	8206419	2516228	1930	7483772	27
34	6634910	2177	3365090	7096700	8203766	2518158	1930	7481842	26
35	6637087	2175	3362913	7099420	8201113	2520088	1931	7479912	25
36	6639262	2175	3360738	7102140	8198460	2522019	1932	7477981	24
37	6641437	2175	3358563	7104859	8195807	2523951	1932	7476049	23
38	6643612	2173	3356388	7107578	8193154	2525883	1933	7474117	22
39	6645785	2174	3354215	7110297	8190500	2527816	1933	7472184	21
40	6647959	2172	3352041	7113016	8187846	2529749	1934	7470251	20
41	6650131	2173	3349869	7115734	8185192	2531683	1935	7468317	19
42	6652304	2171	3347696	7118452	8182538	2533618	1936	7466382	18
43	6654475	2171	3345525	7121170	8179884	2535554	1936	7464446	17
44	6656646	2171	3343354	7123888	8177230	2537490	1936	7462510	16
45	6658817	2170	3341183	7126606	8174575	2539426	1938	7460574	15
46	6660987	2169	3339013	7129324	8171920	2541364	1937	7458636	14
47	6663156	2169	3336844	7132042	8169265	2543301	1939	7456699	13
48	6665325	2168	3334675	7134760	8166610	2545240	1939	7454760	12
49	6667493	2168	3332507	7137477	8163954	2547179	1940	7452821	11
50	6669661	2167	3330339	7140194	8161298	2549119	1940	7450881	10
51	6671828	2166	3328172	7142911	8158642	2551059	1942	7448941	9
52	6673994	2166	3326006	7145628	8155986	2553001	1941	7446999	8
53	6676160	2166	3323840	7148345	8153330	2554942	1943	7445058	7
54	6678326	2164	3321674	7151062	8150674	2556885	1942	7443115	6
55	6680490	2165	3319510	7153779	8148018	2558827	1944	7441173	5
56	6682655	2163	3317345	7156496	8145362	2560771	1944	7439229	4
57	6684818	2163	3315182	7159212	8142705	2562715	1945	7437285	3
58	6686981	2163	3313019	7161928	8140048	2564660	1946	7435340	2
59	6689144	2162	3310856	7164643	8137390	2566606	1946	7433394	1
60	6691306		3308694	7167358	8134732	2568552		7431448	0

′	Cosine	Diff.	Vers.	Co-chord	Chord	Covers.	Diff.	Sine	′

′	Sine	Diff.	Covers.	Chord	Co-chord	Vers.	Diff.	Cosine	′
0	6691306	2162	3308694	7167358	8134732	2568552	1946	7431448	60
1	6693468	2160	3306532	7170074	8132075	2570498	1948	7429502	59
2	6695628	2161	3304372	7172790	8129418	2572446	1948	7427554	58
3	6697789	2159	3302211	7175505	8126760	2574394	1948	7425606	57
4	6699948	2160	3300052	7178220	8124102	2576342	1950	7423658	56
5	6702108	2158	3297892	7180935	8121444	2578292	1950	7421708	55
6	6704266	2158	3295734	7183650	8118786	2580242	1950	7419758	54
7	6706424	2158	3293576	7186365	8116127	2582192	1951	7417808	53
8	6708582	2157	3291418	7189080	8113468	2584143	1952	7415857	52
9	6710739	2156	3289261	7191794	8110809	2586095	1952	7413905	51
10	6712895	2156	3287105	7194508	8108150	2588047	1953	7411953	50
11	6715051	2155	3284949	7197222	8105491	2590000	1954	7410000	49
12	6717206	2155	3282794	7199936	8102832	2591954	1954	7408046	48
13	6719361	2154	3280639	7202650	8100172	2593908	1955	7406092	47
14	6721515	2153	3278485	7205364	8097512	2595863	1956	7404137	46
15	6723668	2153	3276332	7208077	8094852	2597819	1956	7402181	45
16	6725821	2152	3274179	7210790	8092192	2599775	1957	7400225	44
17	6727973	2152	3272027	7213503	8089532	2601732	1957	7398268	43
18	6730125	2151	3269875	7216216	8086872	2603689	1958	7396311	42
19	6732276	2151	3267724	7218929	8084211	2605647	1959	7394353	41
20	6734427	2150	3265573	7221642	8081550	2607606	1959	7392394	40
21	6736577	2150	3263423	7224355	8078889	2609565	1960	7390435	39
22	6738727	2149	3261273	7227068	8076228	2611525	1960	7388475	38
23	6740876	2148	3259124	7229780	8073567	2613485	1962	7386515	37
24	6743024	2148	3256976	7232492	8070906	2615447	1961	7384553	36
25	6745172	2147	3254828	7235204	8068244	2617408	1963	7382592	35
26	6747319	2147	3252681	7237916	8065582	2619371	1963	7380629	34
27	6749466	2146	3250534	7240627	8062920	2621334	1963	7378666	33
28	6751612	2145	3248388	7243338	8060258	2623297	1965	7376703	32
29	6753757	2145	3246243	7246049	8057596	2625262	1965	7374738	31
30	6755902	2144	3244098	7248760	8054934	2627227	1965	7372773	30
31	6758046	2144	3241954	7251471	8052271	2629192	1966	7370808	29
32	6760190	2143	3239810	7254182	8049608	2631158	1967	7368842	28
33	6762333	2143	3237667	7256893	8046945	2633125	1967	7366875	27
34	6764476	2142	3235524	7259604	8044282	2635092	1968	7364908	26
35	6766618	2142	3233382	7262314	8041619	2637060	1969	7362940	25
36	6768760	2141	3231240	7265024	8038956	2639029	1969	7360971	24
37	6770901	2140	3229099	7267734	8036292	2640998	1970	7359002	23
38	6773041	2140	3226959	7270444	8033628	2642968	1971	7357032	22
39	6775181	2139	3224819	7273154	8030964	2644939	1971	7355061	21
40	6777320	2139	3222680	7275864	8028300	2646910	1972	7353090	20
41	6779459	2138	3220541	7278573	8025636	2648882	1972	7351118	19
42	6781597	2137	3218403	7281282	8022972	2650854	1973	7349146	18
43	6783734	2137	3216266	7283992	8020307	2652827	1974	7347173	17
44	6785871	2136	3214129	7286702	8017642	2654801	1974	7345199	16
45	6788007	2136	3211993	7289410	8014977	2656775	1975	7343225	15
46	6790143	2135	3209857	7292118	8012312	2658750	1975	7341250	14
47	6792278	2135	3207722	7294827	8009646	2660725	1976	7339275	13
48	6794413	2134	3205587	7297536	8006980	2662701	1977	7337299	12
49	6796547	2134	3203453	7300244	8004315	2664678	1977	7335322	11
50	6798681	2132	3201319	7302952	8001650	2666655	1978	7333345	10
51	6800813	2133	3199187	7305660	7998983	2668633	1979	7331367	9
52	6802946	2132	3197054	7308368	7996316	2670612	1979	7329388	8
53	6805078	2131	3194922	7311075	7993650	2672591	1980	7327409	7
54	6807209	2130	3192791	7313782	7990984	2674571	1980	7325429	6
55	6809339	2130	3190661	7316490	7988317	2676551	1982	7323449	5
56	6811469	2130	3188531	7319198	7985650	2678533	1981	7321467	4
57	6813599	2129	3186401	7321905	7982983	2680514	1983	7319486	3
58	6815728	2128	3184272	7324612	7980316	2682497	1982	7317503	2
59	6817856	2128	3182144	7327318	7977649	2684479	1984	7315521	1
60	6819984		3180016	7330024	7974982	2686463		7313537	0
′	Cosine	Diff.	Vers.	Co-chord	Chord	Covers.	Diff.	Sine	′

′	Sine	Diff.	Covers.	Chord	Co-chord	Vers.	Diff.	Cosine	′
0	6819984	2127	3180016	7330024	7974982	2686463	1984	7313537	60
1	6822111	2126	3177889	7332731	7972314	2688447	1985	7311553	59
2	6824237	2126	3175763	7335438	7969646	2690432	1985	7309568	58
3	6826363	2126	3173637	7338144	7966978	2692417	1986	7307583	57
4	6828489	2124	3171511	7340850	7964310	2694403	1987	7305597	56
5	6830613	2125	3169387	7343555	7961641	2696390	1987	7303610	55
6	6832738	2123	3167262	7346260	7958972	2698377	1988	7301623	54
7	6834861	2123	3165139	7348966	7956304	2700365	1989	7299635	53
8	6836984	2123	3163016	7351672	7953636	2702354	1989	7297646	52
9	6839107	2122	3160893	7354377	7950966	2704343	1989	7295657	51
10	6841229	2121	3158771	7357082	7948296	2706332	1991	7293668	50
11	6843350	2121	3156650	7359787	7945627	2708323	1991	7291677	49
12	6845471	2120	3154529	7362492	7942958	2710314	1991	7289686	48
13	6847591	2120	3152409	7365196	7940288	2712305	1992	7287695	47
14	6849711	2119	3150289	7367900	7937618	2714297	1993	7285703	46
15	6851830	2118	3148170	7370604	7934948	2716290	1994	7283710	45
16	6853948	2118	3146052	7373308	7932278	2718284	1994	7281716	44
17	6856066	2118	3143934	7376012	7929607	2720278	1994	7279722	43
18	6858184	2116	3141816	7378716	7926936	2722272	1996	7277728	42
19	6860300	2116	3139700	7381419	7924266	2724268	1996	7275732	41
20	6862416	2116	3137584	7384122	7921596	2726264	1996	7273736	40
21	6864532	2115	3135468	7386826	7918925	2728260	1997	7271740	39
22	6866647	2114	3133353	7389530	7916254	2730257	1998	7269743	38
23	6868761	2114	3131239	7392233	7913582	2732255	1998	7267745	37
24	6870875	2113	3129125	7394936	7910910	2734253	1999	7265747	36
25	6872988	2113	3127012	7397638	7908238	2736252	2000	7263748	35
26	6875101	2112	3124899	7400340	7905566	2738252	2000	7261748	34
27	6877213	2112	3122787	7403042	7902894	2740252	2001	7259748	33
28	6879325	2110	3120675	7405744	7900222	2742253	2001	7257747	32
29	6881435	2111	3118565	7408446	7897550	2744254	2002	7255746	31
30	6883546	2109	3116454	7411148	7894878	2746256	2003	7253744	30
31	6885655	2110	3114345	7413850	7892205	2748259	2003	7251741	29
32	6887765	2108	3112235	7416552	7889532	2750262	2004	7249738	28
33	6889873	2108	3110127	7419253	7886859	2752266	2005	7247734	27
34	6891981	2108	3108019	7421954	7884186	2754271	2005	7245729	26
35	6894089	2106	3105911	7424655	7881512	2756276	2005	7243724	25
36	6896195	2107	3103805	7427356	7878838	2758281	2007	7241719	24
37	6898302	2105	3101698	7430057	7876164	2760288	2007	7239712	23
38	6900407	2105	3099593	7432758	7873490	2762295	2007	7237705	22
39	6902512	2105	3097488	7435458	7870816	2764302	2008	7235698	21
40	6904617	2104	3095383	7438158	7868142	2766310	2009	7233690	20
41	6906721	2103	3093279	7440859	7865468	2768319	2010	7231681	19
42	6908824	2103	3091176	7443560	7862794	2770329	2010	7229671	18
43	6910927	2102	3089073	7446259	7860119	2772339	2010	7227661	17
44	6913029	2102	3086971	7448958	7857444	2774349	2011	7225651	16
45	6915131	2101	3084869	7451658	7854769	2776360	2012	7223640	15
46	6917232	2100	3082768	7454358	7852094	2778372	2013	7221628	14
47	6919332	2100	3080668	7457057	7849418	2780385	2013	7219615	13
48	6921432	2099	3078568	7459756	7846742	2782398	2013	7217602	12
49	6923531	2099	3076469	7462455	7844066	2784411	2015	7215589	11
50	6925630	2098	3074370	7465154	7841390	2786426	2015	7213574	10
51	6927728	2097	3072272	7467852	7838714	2788441	2015	7211559	9
52	6929825	2097	3070175	7470550	7836038	2790456	2016	7209544	8
53	6931922	2096	3068078	7473248	7833362	2792472	2017	7207528	7
54	6934018	2096	3065982	7475946	7830686	2794489	2017	7205511	6
55	6936114	2095	3063886	7478644	7828009	2796506	2018	7203494	5
56	6938209	2095	3061791	7481342	7825332	2798524	2019	7201476	4
57	6940304	2094	3059696	7484040	7822655	2800543	2019	7199457	3
58	6942398	2093	3057602	7486738	7819978	2802562	2020	7197438	2
59	6944491	2093	3055509	7489435	7817300	2804582	2020	7195418	1
60	6946584		3053416	7492132	7814622	2806602		7193398	0

′	Cosine	Diff.	Vers.	Co-chord	Chord	Covers.	Diff.	Sine	′

′	Sine	Diff.	Covers.	Chord	Co-chord	Vers.	Diff.	Cosine	′
0	6946584	2092	3053416	7492132	7814622	2806602	2021	7193398	60
1	6948676	2091	3051324	7494829	7811944	2808623	2022	7191377	59
2	6950767	2091	3049233	7497526	7809266	2810645	2022	7189355	58
3	6952858	2091	3047142	7500222	7806588	2812667	2023	7187333	57
4	6954949	2090	3045051	7502918	7803910	2814690	2023	7185310	56
5	6957039	2089	3042961	7505615	7801232	2816713	2024	7183287	55
6	6959128	2089	3040872	7508312	7798554	2818737	2025	7181263	54
7	6961217	2088	3038783	7511008	7795875	2820762	2025	7179238	53
8	6963305	2087	3036695	7513704	7793196	2822787	2026	7177213	52
9	6965392	2087	3034608	7516399	7790517	2824813	2026	7175187	51
10	6967479	2086	3032521	7519094	7787838	2826839	2027	7173161	50
11	6969565	2086	3030435	7521790	7785159	2828866	2028	7171134	49
12	6971651	2085	3028349	7524486	7782480	2830894	2028	7169106	48
13	6973736	2085	3026264	7527181	7779800	2832922	2029	7167078	47
14	6975821	2084	3024179	7529876	7777120	2834951	2030	7165049	46
15	6977905	2083	3022095	7532570	7774440	2836981	2030	7163019	45
16	6979988	2083	3020012	7535264	7771760	2839011	2030	7160989	44
17	6982071	2082	3017929	7537959	7769079	2841041	2032	7158959	43
18	6984153	2081	3015847	7540654	7766398	2843073	2032	7156927	42
19	6986234	2081	3013766	7543348	7763717	2845105	2032	7154895	41
20	6988315	2081	3011685	7546042	7761036	2847137	2033	7152863	40
21	6990396	2080	3009604	7548735	7758355	2849170	2034	7150830	39
22	6992476	2079	3007524	7551428	7755674	2851204	2034	7148796	38
23	6994555	2078	3005445	7554122	7752993	2853238	2035	7146762	37
24	6996633	2078	3003367	7556816	7750312	2855273	2036	7144727	36
25	6998711	2078	3001289	7559509	7747630	2857309	2036	7142691	35
26	7000789	2077	2999211	7562202	7744948	2859345	2037	7140655	34
27	7002866	2076	2997134	7564895	7742266	2861382	2037	7138618	33
28	7004942	2076	2995058	7567588	7739584	2863419	2038	7136581	32
29	7007018	2075	2992982	7570280	7736902	2865457	2039	7134543	31
30	7009093	2074	2990907	7572972	7734220	2867496	2039	7132504	30
31	7011167	2074	2988833	7575664	7731537	2869535	2039	7130465	29
32	7013241	2073	2986759	7578356	7728854	2871574	2041	7128426	28
33	7015314	2073	2984686	7581048	7726171	2873615	2041	7126385	27
34	7017387	2072	2982613	7583740	7723488	2875656	2041	7124344	26
35	7019459	2072	2980541	7586432	7720804	2877697	2043	7122303	25
36	7021531	2070	2978469	7589124	7718120	2879740	2042	7120260	24
37	7023601	2071	2976399	7591815	7715437	2881782	2044	7118218	23
38	7025672	2069	2974328	7594506	7712754	2883826	2044	7116174	22
39	7027741	2070	2972259	7597197	7710070	2885870	2044	7114130	21
40	7029811	2068	2970189	7599888	7707386	2887914	2045	7112086	20
41	7031879	2068	2968121	7602578	7704701	2889959	2046	7110041	19
42	7033947	2067	2966053	7605268	7702016	2892005	2047	7107995	18
43	7036014	2067	2963986	7607958	7699332	2894052	2047	7105948	17
44	7038081	2066	2961919	7610648	7696648	2896099	2047	7103901	16
45	7040147	2066	2959853	7613338	7693963	2898146	2048	7101854	15
46	7042213	2065	2957787	7616028	7691279	2900194	2049	7099806	14
47	7044278	2064	2955722	7618718	7688592	2902243	2050	7097757	13
48	7046342	2064	2953658	7621408	7685906	2904293	2050	7095707	12
49	7048406	2063	2951594	7624097	7683221	2906343	2050	7093657	11
50	7050469	2063	2949531	7626786	7680536	2908393	2051	7091607	10
51	7052532	2062	2947468	7629475	7677850	2910444	2052	7089556	9
52	7054594	2061	2945406	7632164	7675164	2912496	2053	7087504	8
53	7056655	2061	2943345	7634852	7672477	2914549	2053	7085451	7
54	7058716	2060	2941284	7637540	7669790	2916602	2053	7083398	6
55	7060776	2059	2939224	7640229	7667104	2918655	2054	7081345	5
56	7062835	2059	2937165	7642918	7664418	2920709	2055	7079291	4
57	7064894	2059	2935106	7645606	7661731	2922764	2056	7077236	3
58	7066953	2058	2933047	7648294	7659044	2924820	2056	7075180	2
59	7069011	2057	2930989	7650981	7656356	2926876	2056	7073124	1
60	7071068		2928932	7653668	7653668	2928932		7071068	0

′	Cosine	Diff.	Vers.	Co-chord	Chord	Covers.	Diff.	Sine	′

′	0°	1°	2°	3°	4°	5°	6°	′
0	0·0000000	0·0174551	0·0349208	0·0524078	0·0699268	0·0874887	0·1051042	60
1	·0002909	·0177460	·0352120	·0526995	·0702191	·0877818	·1053983	59
2	·0005818	·0180370	·0355033	·0529912	·0705115	·0880749	·1056925	58
3	·0008727	·0183280	·0357945	·0532829	·0708038	·0883681	·1059866	57
4	·0011636	·0186190	·0360858	·0535746	·0710961	·0886612	·1062808	56
5	·0014544	·0189100	·0363771	·0538663	·0713885	·0889544	·1065750	55
6	·0017453	·0192010	·0366683	·0541581	·0716809	·0892476	·1068692	54
7	·0020362	·0194920	·0369596	·0544498	·0719733	·0895408	·1071634	53
8	·0023271	·0197830	·0372509	·0547416	·0722657	·0898341	·1074576	52
9	·0026180	·0200740	·0375422	·0550333	·0725581	·0901273	·1077519	51
10	0·0029089	0·0203650	0·0378335	0·0553251	0·0728505	0·0904206	0·1080462	50
11	·0031998	·0206560	·0381248	·0556169	·0731430	·0907138	·1083405	49
12	·0034907	·0209470	·0384161	·0559087	·0734354	·0910071	·1086348	48
13	·0037816	·0212380	·0387074	·0562005	·0737279	·0913004	·1089291	47
14	·0040725	·0215291	·0389988	·0564923	·0740203	·0915938	·1092234	46
15	·0043634	·0218201	·0392901	·0567841	·0743128	·0918871	·1095178	45
16	·0046542	·0221111	·0395814	·0570759	·0746053	·0921804	·1098122	44
17	·0049451	·0224021	·0398728	·0573678	·0748979	·0924738	·1101066	43
18	·0052360	·0226932	·0401641	·0576596	·0751904	·0927672	·1104010	42
19	·0055269	·0229842	·0404555	·0579515	·0754829	·0930606	·1106955	41
20	0·0058178	0·0232753	0·0407469	0·0582434	0·0757755	0·0933540	. 0·1109899	40
21	·0061087	·0235663	·0410383	·0585352	·0760680	·0936474	·1112844	39
22	·0063996	·0238574	·0413296	·0588271	·0763606	·0939409	·1115789	38
23	·0066905	·0241484	·0416210	·0591190	·0766532	·0942344	·1118734	37
24	·0069814	·0244395	·0419124	·0594109	·0769458	·0945278	·1121680	36
25	·0072723	·0247305	·0422038	·0597029	·0772384	·0948213	·1124625	35
26	·0075632	·0250216	·0424952	·0599948	·0775311	·0951148	·1127571	34
27	·0078541	·0253127	·0427866	·0602867	·0778237	·0954084	·1130517	33
28	·0081450	·0256038	·0430781	·0605787	·0781164	·0957019	·1133463	32
29	·0084360	·0258948	·0433695	·0608706	·0784090	·0959955	·1136410	31
30	0·0087269	0·0261859	0·0436609	0·0611626	0·0787017	0·0962890	0·1139356	30
31	·0090178	·0264770	·0439524	·0614546	·0789944	·0965826	·1142303	29
32	·0093087	·0267681	·0442438	·0617466	·0792871	·0968763	·1145250	28
33	·0095996	·0270592	·0445353	·0620386	·0795798	·0971699	·1148197	27
34	·0098905	·0273503	·0448268	·0623306	·0798726	·0974635	·1151144	26
35	·0101814	·0276414	·0451183	·0626226	·0801653	·0977572	·1154092	25
36	·0104724	·0279325	·0454097	·0629147	·0804581	·0980509	·1157039	24
37	·0107633	·0282236	·0457012	·0632067	·0807509	·0983446	·1159987	23
38	·0110542	·0285148	·0459927	·0634988	·0810437	·0986383	·1162936	22
39	·0113451	·0288059	·0462842	·0637908	·0813365	·0989320	·1165884	21
40	0·0116361	0·0290970	0·0465757	0·0640829	0·0816293	0·0992257	0·1168832	20
41	·0119270	·0293882	·0468673	·0643750	·0819221	·0995194	·1171781	19
42	·0122179	·0296793	·0471588	·0646671	·0822150	·0998133	·1174730	18
43	·0125088	·0299705	·0474503	·0649592	·0825078	·1001071	·1177679	17
44	·0127998	·0302616	·0477419	·0652513	·0828007	·1004009	·1180628	16
45	·0130907	·0305528	·0480334	·0655435	·0830936	·1006947	·1183578	15
46	·0133817	·0308439	·0483250	·0658356	·0833865	·1009886	·1186528	14
47	·0136726	·0311351	·0486166	·0661278	·0836794	·1012824	·1189478	13
48	·0139635	·0314263	·0489082	·0664199	·0839723	·1015763	·1192428	12
49	·0142545	·0317174	·0491997	·0667121	·0842653	·1018702	·1195378	11
50	0·0145454	0·0320086	·0494913	·0670043	·0845583	0·1021641	·1198329	10
51	·0148364	·0322998	·0497829	·0672965	·0848512	·1024580	·1201279	9
52	·0151273	·0325910	·0500746	·0675887	·0851442	·1027520	·1204230	8
53	·0154183	·0328822	·0503662	·0678809	·0854372	·1030460	·1207182	7
54	·0157093	·0331734	·0506578	·0681732	·0857302	·1033399	·1210133	6
55	·0160002	·0334646	·0509495	·0684654	·0860233	·1036340	·1213085	5
56	·0162912	·0337558	·0512411	·0687577	·0863163	·1039280	·1216036	4
57	·0165821	·0340471	·0515328	·0690499	·0866094	·1042220	·1218988	3
58	·0168731	·0343383	·0518244	·0693422	·0869025	·1045161	·1221941	2
59	·0171641	·0346295	·0521161	·0696345	·0871956	·1048101	·1224893	1
60	0·0174551	0·0349208	0·0524078	0·0699268	0·0874887	0·1051042	0·1227846	0
′	89°	88°	87°	86°	85°	84°	83°	′

NATURAL COTANGENTS.

′	7°	8°	9°	10°	11°	12°	13°	′
0	0·1227846	0·1405408	0·1583844	0·1763270	0·1943803	0·2125566	0·2308682	60
1	·1230798	·1408375	·1586826	·1766269	·1946822	·2128606	·2311746	59
2	·1233752	·1411342	·1589809	·1769269	·1949841	·2131647	·2314811	58
3	·1236705	·1414308	·1592791	·1772269	·1952861	·2134688	·2317876	57
4	·1239658	·1417276	·1595774	·1775270	·1955881	·2137730	·2320941	56
5	·1242612	·1420243	·1598757	·1778270	·1958901	·2140772	·2324007	55
6	·1245566	·1423211	·1601740	·1781271	·1961922	·2143814	·2327073	54
7	·1248520	·1426179	·1604724	·1784273	·1964943	·2146857	·2330140	53
8	·1251474	·1429147	·1607708	·1787274	·1967964	·2149900	·2333207	52
9	·1254429	·1432115	·1610692	·1790276	·1970986	·2152944	·2336274	51
10	0·1257384	0·1435084	0·1613677	·1793279	0·1974008	0·2155988	·2339342	50
11	·1260339	·1438053	·1616662	·1796281	·1977031	·2159032	·2342410	49
12	·1263294	·1441022	·1619647	·1799284	·1980053	·2162077	·2345479	48
13	·1266249	·1443991	·1622632	·1802287	·1983076	·2165122	·2348548	47
14	·1269205	·1446961	·1625618	·1805291	·1986100	·2168167	·2351617	46
15	·1272161	·1449931	·1628603	·1808295	·1989124	·2171213	·2354687	45
16	·1275117	·1452901	·1631590	·1811299	·1992148	·2174259	·2357758	44
17	·1278073	·1455872	·1634576	·1814303	·1995172	·2177306	·2360829	43
18	·1281030	·1458842	·1637563	·1817308	·1998197	·2180353	·2363900	42
19	·1283986	·1461813	·1640550	·1820313	·2001222	·2183400	·2366971	41
20	0·1286943	0·1464784	0·1643537	0·1823319	0·2004248	0·2186448	0·2370044	40
21	·1289900	·1467756	·1646525	·1826324	·2007274	·2189496	·2373116	39
22	·1292858	·1470727	·1649513	·1829330	·2010300	·2192544	·2376189	38
23	·1295815	·1473699	·1652501	·1832337	·2013327	·2195593	·2379262	37
24	·1298773	·1476672	·1655489	·1835343	·2016354	·2198643	·2382336	36
25	·1301731	·1479644	·1658478	·1838350	·2019381	·2201692	·2385410	35
26	·1304690	·1482617	·1661467	·1841358	·2022409	·2204742	·2388485	34
27	·1307648	·1485590	·1664456	·1844365	·2025437	·2207793	·2391560	33
28	·1310607	·1488563	·1667446	·1847373	·2028465	·2210844	·2394635	32
29	·1313566	·1491536	·1670436	·1850382	·2031494	·2213895	·2397711	31
30	0·1316525	0·1494510	0·1673426	0·1853390	0·2034523	0·2216947	0·2400788	30
31	·1319484	·1497484	·1676417	·1856399	·2037552	·2219999	·2403864	29
32	·1322444	·1500458	·1679407	·1859409	·2040582	·2223051	·2406942	28
33	·1325404	·1503433	·1682398	·1862418	·2043612	·2226104	·2410019	27
34	·1328364	·1506408	·1685390	·1865428	·2046643	·2229157	·2413097	26
35	·1331324	·1509383	·1688381	·1868439	·2049674	·2232211	·2416176	25
36	·1334285	·1512358	·1691373	·1871449	·2052705	·2235265	·2419255	24
37	·1337246	·1515333	·1694366	·1874460	·2055737	·2238319	·2422334	23
38	·1340207	·1518309	·1697358	·1877471	·2058769	·2241374	·2425414	22
39	·1343168	·1521285	·1700351	·1880483	·2061801	·2244429	·2428494	21
40	0·1346129	0·1524262	0·1703344	0·1883495	0·2064834	0·2247485	0·2431575	20
41	·1349091	·1527238	·1706338	·1886507	·2067867	·2250541	·2434656	19
42	·1352053	·1530215	·1709331	·1889520	·2070900	·2253597	·2437737	18
43	·1355015	·1533192	·1712325	·1892533	·2073934	·2256654	·2440819	17
44	·1357978	·1536170	·1715320	·1895546	·2076968	·2259711	·2443902	16
45	·1360940	·1539147	·1718314	·1898559	·2080003	·2262769	·2446984	15
46	·1363903	·1542125	·1721309	·1901573	·2083038	·2265827	·2450068	14
47	·1366866	·1545103	·1724304	·1904587	·2086073	·2268885	·2453151	13
48	·1369830	·1548082	·1727300	·1907602	·2089109	·2271944	·2456236	12
49	·1372793	·1551061	·1730296	·1910617	·2092145	·2275003	·2459320	11
50	0·1375757	0·1554040	0·1733292	0·1913632	0·2095181	0·2278063	0·2462405	10
51	·1378721	·1557019	·1736288	·1916648	·2098218	·2281123	·2465491	9
52	·1381685	·1559998	·1739285	·1919664	·2101255	·2284184	·2468577	8
53	·1384650	·1562978	·1742282	·1922680	·2104293	·2287244	·2471663	7
54	·1387615	·1565958	·1745279	·1925696	·2107331	·2290306	·2474750	6
55	·1390580	·1568939	·1748277	·1928713	·2110369	·2293367	·2477837	5
56	·1393545	·1571919	·1751275	·1931731	·2113407	·2296429	·2480925	4
57	·1396510	·1574900	·1754273	·1934748	·2116446	·2299492	·2484013	3
58	·1399476	·1577881	·1757272	·1937766	·2119486	·2302555	·2487102	2
59	·1402442	·1580863	·1760271	·1940784	·2122525	·2305618	·2490191	1
60	0·1405408	0·1583844	0·1763270	0·1943803	0·2125566	0·2308682	0·2493280	0
′	82°	81°	80°	79°	78°	77°	76°	′

′	14°	15°	16°	17°	18°	19°	20°	′
0	0·2493280	0·2679492	0·2867454	0·3057307	0·3249197	0·3443276	0·3639702	60
1	·2496370	·2682610	·2870602	·3060488	·3252413	·3446530	·3642997	59
2	·2499460	·2685728	·2873751	·3063670	·3255630	·3449785	·3646292	58
3	·2502551	·2688847	·2876900	·3066852	·3258848	·3453040	·3649588	57
4	·2505642	·2691967	·2880050	·3070034	·3262066	·3456296	·3652885	56
5	·2508734	·2695087	·2883201	·3073218	·3265284	·3459553	·3656182	55
6	·2511826	·2698207	·2886352	·3076402	·3268504	·3462810	·3659480	54
7	·2514919	·2701328	·2889503	·3079586	·3271724	·3466068	·3662779	53
8	·2518012	·2704449	·2892655	·3082771	·3274944	·3469327	·3666079	52
9	·2521106	·2707571	·2895808	·3085957	·3278165	·3472586	·3669379	51
10	0·2524200	0·2710694	·2898961	·3089143	·3281387	0·3475846	·3672680	50
11	·2527294	·2713817	·2902114	·3092330	·3284610	·3479107	·3675981	49
12	·2530389	·2716940	·2905269	·3095517	·3287833	·3482368	·3679284	48
13	·2533484	·2720064	·2908423	·3098705	·3291056	·3485630	·3682587	47
14	·2536580	·2723188	·2911578	·3101893	·3294281	·3488893	·3685890	46
15	·2539676	·2726313	·2914734	·3105083	·3297505	·3492156	·3689195	45
16	·2542773	·2729438	·2917890	·3108272	·3300731	·3495420	·3692500	44
17	·2545870	·2732564	·2921047	·3111462	·3303957	·3498685	·3695806	43
18	·2548968	·2735690	·2924205	·3114653	·3307184	·3501950	·3699112	42
19	·2552066	·2738817	·2927363	·3117845	·3310411	·3505216	·3702420	41
20	0·2555165	0·2741945	0·2930521	0·3121036	0·3313639	0·3508483	0·3705728	40
21	·2558264	·2745072	·2933680	·3124229	·3316868	·3511750	·3709036	39
22	·2561363	·2748201	·2936839	·3127422	·3320097	·3515018	·3712346	38
23	·2564463	·2751330	·2939999	·3130616	·3323327	·3518287	·3715656	37
24	·2567564	·2754459	·2943160	·3133810	·3326557	·3521556	·3718967	36
25	·2570664	·2757589	·2946321	·3137005	·3329788	·3524826	·3722278	35
26	·2573766	·2760719	·2949483	·3140200	·3333020	·3528096	·3725590	34
27	·2576868	·2763850	·2952645	·3143396	·3336252	·3531368	·3728903	33
28	·2579970	·2766981	·2955808	·3146593	·3339485	·3534640	·3732217	32
29	·2583073	·2770113	·2958971	·3149790	·3342719	·3537912	·3735532	31
30	0·2586176	0·2773245	0·2962135	0·3152988	0·3345953	0·3541186	0·3738847	30
31	·2589280	·2776378	·2965299	·3156186	·3349188	·3544460	·3742163	29
32	·2592384	·2779512	·2968464	·3159385	·3352424	·3547734	·3745479	28
33	·2595488	·2782646	·2971630	·3162585	·3355660	·3551010	·3748797	27
34	·2598593	·2785780	·2974796	·3165785	·3358896	·3554286	·3752115	26
35	·2601699	·2788915	·2977962	·3168986	·3362134	·3557562	·3755433	25
36	·2604805	·2792050	·2981129	·3172187	·3365372	·3560840	·3758753	24
37	·2607911	·2795186	·2984297	·3175389	·3368610	·3564118	·3762073	23
38	·2611018	·2798322	·2987465	·3178591	·3371850	·3567397	·3765394	22
39	·2614126	·2801459	·2990634	·3181794	·3375090	·3570676	·3768716	21
40	0·2617234	0·2804597	0·2993803	0·3184998	0·3378330	0·3573956	0·3772038	20
41	·2620342	·2807735	·2996973	·3188202	·3381571	·3577237	·3775361	19
42	·2623451	·2810873	·3000144	·3191407	·3384813	·3580518	·3778685	18
43	·2626560	·2814012	·3003315	·3194613	·3388056	·3583801	·3782010	17
44	·2629670	·2817152	·3006486	·3197819	·3391299	·3587083	·3785335	16
45	·2632780	·2820292	·3009658	·3201025	·3394543	·3590367	·3788661	15
46	·2635891	·2823432	·3012831	·3204232	·3397787	·3593651	·3791988	14
47	·2639002	·2826573	·3016004	·3207440	·3401032	·3596936	·3795315	13
48	·2642114	·2829715	·3019178	·3210649	·3404278	·3600222	·3798644	12
49	·2645226	·2832857	·3022352	·3213858	·3407524	·3603508	·3801973	11
50	0·2648339	0·2835999	0·3025527	0·3217067	0·3410771	0·3606795	0·3805302	10
51	·2651452	·2839143	·3028703	·3220278	·3414019	·3610082	·3808633	9
52	·2654566	·2842286	·3031879	·3223489	·3417267	·3613371	·3811964	8
53	·2657680	·2845430	·3035055	·3226700	·3420516	·3616660	·3815296	7
54	·2660794	·2848575	·3038232	·3229912	·3423765	·3619949	·3818629	6
55	·2663909	·2851720	·3041410	·3233125	·3427015	·3623240	·3821962	5
56	·2667025	·2854866	·3044588	·3236338	·3430266	·3626531	·3825296	4
57	·2670141	·2858012	·3047767	·3239552	·3433518	·3629823	·3828631	3
58	·2673257	·2861159	·3050946	·3242766	·3436770	·3633115	·3831967	2
59	·2676374	·2864306	·3054126	·3245981	·3440023	·3636408	·3835303	1
60	0·2679492	0·2867454	0·3057307	0·3249197	0·3443276	0·3639702	0·3838640	0
′	75°	74°	73°	72°	71°	70°	69°	′

NATURAL COTANGENTS.

′	21°	22°	23°	24°	25°	26°	27°	′
0	0·3838640	0·4040262	0·4244748	0·4452287	0·4663077	0·4877326	0·5095254	60
1	·3841978	·4043646	·4248182	·4455773	·4666618	·4880927	·5008919	59
2	·3845317	·4047031	·4251616	·4459260	·4670161	·4884530	·5102585	58
3	·3848656	·4050417	·4255051	·4462747	·4673705	·4888133	·5106252	57
4	·3851996	·4053804	·4258487	·4466236	·4677250	·4891737	·5109919	56
5	·3855337	·4057191	·4261924	·4469726	·4680796	·4895343	·5113588	55
6	·3858679	·4060579	·4265361	·4473216	·4684342	·4898949	·5117259	54
7	·3862021	·4063968	·4268800	·4476708	·4687890	·4902557	·5120930	53
8	·3865364	·4067358	·4272239	·4480200	·4691439	·4906166	·5124602	52
9	·3868708	·4070748	·4275680	·4483693	·4694988	·4909775	·5128275	51
10	0·3872053	0·4074139	0·4279121	0·4487187	0·4698539	0·4913386	0·5131950	50
11	·3875398	·4077531	·4282563	·4490682	·4702090	·4916997	·5135625	49
12	·3878744	·4080924	·4286005	·4494178	·4705643	·4920610	·5139302	48
13	·3882091	·4084318	·4289449	·4497675	·4709196	·4924224	·5142980	47
14	·3885439	·4087713	·4292894	·4501173	·4712751	·4927838	·5146658	46
15	·3888787	·4091108	·4296339	·4504672	·4716306	·4931454	·5150338	45
16	·3892136	·4094504	·4299785	·4508171	·4719863	·4935071	·5154019	44
17	·3895486	·4097901	·4303232	·4511672	·4723420	·4938689	·5157702	43
18	·3898837	·4101299	·4306680	·4515173	·4726978	·4942308	·5161385	42
19	·3902189	·4104697	·4310129	·4518676	·4730538	·4945928	·5165069	41
20	0·3905541	0·4108097	0·4313579	0·4522179	0·4734098	0·4949549	0·5168755	40
21	·3908894	·4111497	·4317030	·4525683	·4737659	·4953171	·5172441	39
22	·3912247	·4114898	·4320481	·4529188	·4741222	·4956794	·5176129	38
23	·3915602	·4118300	·4323933	·4532694	·4744785	·4960418	·5179818	37
24	·3918957	·4121703	·4327386	·4536201	·4748349	·4964043	·5183508	36
25	·3922313	·4125106	·4330840	·4539709	·4751914	·4967669	·5187199	35
26	·3925670	·4128510	·4334295	·4543218	·4755481	·4971297	·5190891	34
27	·3929027	·4131915	·4337751	·4546728	·4759048	·4974925	·5194584	33
28	·3932386	·4135321	·4341208	·4550238	·4762616	·4978554	·5198278	32
29	·3935745	·4138728	·4344665	·4553750	·4766185	·4982185	·5201974	31
30	0·3939105	0·4142136	0·4348124	0·4557263	0·4769755	0·4985816	0·5205671	30
31	·3942465	·4145544	·4351583	·4560776	·4773326	·4989449	·5209368	29
32	·3945827	·4148953	·4355043	·4564290	·4776899	·4993082	·5213067	28
33	·3949189	·4152363	·4358504	·4567806	·4780472	·4996717	·5216767	27
34	·3952552	·4155774	·4361966	·4571322	·4784046	·5000352	·5220468	26
35	·3955916	·4159186	·4365429	·4574839	·4787621	·5003989	·5224170	25
36	·3959280	·4162598	·4368893	·4578357	·4791197	·5007627	·5227874	24
37	·3962645	·4166012	·4372357	·4581877	·4794774	·5011266	·5231578	23
38	·3966011	·4169426	·4375823	·4585397	·4798352	·5014906	·5235284	22
39	·3969378	·4172841	·4379289	·4588918	·4801932	·5018547	·5238990	21
40	0·3972746	0·4176257	0·4382756	0·4592439	0·4805512	0·5022189	0·5242698	20
41	·3976114	·4179673	·4386224	·4595962	·4809093	·5025832	·5246407	19
42	·3979483	·4183091	·4389693	·4599486	·4812675	·5029476	·5250117	18
43	·3982853	·4186509	·4393163	·4603011	·4816258	·5033121	·5253829	17
44	·3986224	·4189928	·4396634	·4606537	·4819842	·5036768	·5257541	16
45	·3989595	·4193348	·4400105	·4610063	·4823427	·5040415	·5261255	15
46	·3992968	·4196769	·4403578	·4613591	·4827014	·5044063	·5264969	14
47	·3996341	·4200190	·4407051	·4617119	·4830601	·5047713	·5268685	13
48	·3999715	·4203613	·4410526	·4620649	·4834189	·5051363	·5272402	12
49	·4003089	·4207036	·4414001	·4624179	·4837778	·5055015	·5276120	11
50	·4006465	·4210460	·4417477	·4627710	·4841368	·5058668	·5279839	10
51	·4009841	·4213885	·4420954	·4631243	·4844959	·5062322	·5283560	9
52	·4013218	·4217311	·4424432	·4634776	·4848552	·5065977	·5287281	8
53	·4016596	·4220738	·4427910	·4638310	·4852145	·5069633	·5291004	7
54	·4019974	·4224165	·4431390	·4641845	·4855739	·5073290	·5294727	6
55	·4023354	·4227594	·4434871	·4645382	·4859334	·5076948	·5298452	5
56	·4026734	·4231023	·4438352	·4648919	·4862931	·5080607	·5302178	4
57	·4030115	·4234453	·4441834	·4652457	·4866528	·5084267	·5305906	3
58	·4033496	·4237884	·4445318	·4655996	·4870126	·5087929	·5309634	2
59	·4036879	·4241316	·4448802	·4659536	·4873726	·5091591	·5313364	1
60	0·4040262	0·4244748	0·4452287	0·4663077	0·4877326	0·5095254	0·5317094	0
′	68°	67°	66°	65°	64°	63°	62°	′

288   NATURAL COTANGENTS.

′	28°	29°	30°	31°	32°	33°	34°	′
0	0·5317094	0·5543091	0·5773503	0·6008606	0·6248694	0·6494076	0·6745085	60
1	·5320826	·5546894	·5777382	·6012566	·6252739	·6498212	·6749318	59
2	·5324559	·5550698	·5781262	·6016527	·6256786	·6502350	·6753553	58
3	·5328293	·5554504	·5785144	·6020490	·6260834	·6506490	·6757790	57
4	·5332029	·5558311	·5789027	·6024454	·6264884	·6510631	·6762028	56
5	·5335765	·5562119	·5792912	·6028419	·6268935	·6514774	·6766268	55
6	·5339503	·5565929	·5796797	·6032386	·6272988	·6518918	·6770509	54
7	·5343242	·5569739	·5800684	·6036354	·6277042	·6523064	·6774752	53
8	·5346981	·5573551	·5804573	·6040323	·6281098	·6527211	·6778997	52
9	·5350723	·5577364	·5808462	·6044294	·6285155	·6531360	·6783243	51
10	0·5354465	0·5581179	0·5812353	·6048266	·6289214	0·6535511	0·6787492	50
11	·5358208	·5584994	·5816245	·6052240	·6293274	·6539663	·6791741	49
12	·5361953	·5588811	·5820139	·6056215	·6297336	·6543817	·6795993	48
13	·5365699	·5592629	·5824034	·6060192	·6301399	·6547972	·6800246	47
14	·5369446	·5596449	·5827930	·6064170	·6305464	·6552129	·6804501	46
15	·5373194	·5600269	·5831828	·6068149	·6309530	·6556287	·6808758	45
16	·5376943	·5604091	·5835726	·6072130	·6313598	·6560447	·6813016	44
17	·5380694	·5607914	·5839627	·6076112	·6317667	·6564609	·6817276	43
18	·5384445	·5611738	·5843528	·6080095	·6321738	·6568772	·6821537	42
19	·5388198	·5615564	·5847431	·6084080	·6325810	·6572937	·6825801	41
20	0·5391952	0·5619391	0·5851335	·6088067	0·6329883	0·6577103	0·6830066	40
21	·5395707	·5623219	·5855241	·6092054	·6333959	·6581271	·6834333	39
22	·5399464	·5627048	·5859148	·6096043	·6338035	·6585441	·6838601	38
23	·5403221	·5630879	·5863056	·6100034	·6342113	·6589612	·6842871	37
24	·5406980	·5634710	·5866965	·6104026	·6346193	·6593785	·6847143	36
25	·5410740	·5638543	·5870876	·6108019	·6350274	·6597960	·6851416	35
26	·5414501	·5642378	·5874788	·6112014	·6354357	·6602136	·6855692	34
27	·5418263	·5646213	·5878702	·6116011	·6358441	·6606313	·6859969	33
28	·5422027	·5650050	·5882616	·6120008	·6362527	·6610492	·6864247	32
29	·5425791	·5653888	·5886533	·6124007	·6366614	·6614673	·6868528	31
30	0·5429557	0·5657728	0·5890450	·6128008	0·6370703	0·6618856	0·6872810	30
31	·5433324	·5661568	·5894369	·6132010	·6374793	·6623040	·6877093	29
32	·5437092	·5665410	·5898289	·6136013	·6378885	·6627225	·6881379	28
33	·5440862	·5669254	·5902211	·6140018	·6382978	·6631413	·6885666	27
34	·5444632	·5673098	·5906134	·6144024	·6387073	·6635601	·6889955	26
35	·5448404	·5676944	·5910058	·6148032	·6391169	·6639792	6894246	25
36	·5452177	·5680791	·5913984	·6152041	·6395267	·6643984	·6898538	24
37	·5455951	·5684639	·5917910	·6156052	·6399366	·6648178	·6902832	23
38	·5459727	·5688488	·5921839	·6160064	·6403467	·6652373	·6907128	22
39	·5463503	·5692339	·5925768	·6164077	·6407569	·6656570	·6911425	21
40	0·5467281	0·5696191	0·5929699	·6168092	0·6411673	0·6660769	0·6915725	20
41	·5471060	·5700045	·5933632	·6172108	·6415779	·6664969	·6920026	19
42	·5474840	·5703899	·5937565	·6176126	·6419886	·6669171	·6924328	18
43	·5478621	·5707755	·5941501	·6180145	·6423994	·6673374	·6928633	17
44	·5482404	·5711612	·5945437	·6184166	·6428105	·6677580	·6932939	16
45	·5486188	·5715471	·5949375	·6188188	·6432216	·6681786	·6937247	15
46	·5489973	·5719331	·5953314	·6192211	·6436329	·6685995	·6941557	14
47	·5493759	·5723192	·5957255	·6196236	·6440444	·6690205	·6945868	13
48	·5497547	·5727054	·5961196	·6200263	·6444560	·6694417	·6950181	12
49	·5501335	·5730918	·5965140	·6204291	·6448678	·6698630	·6954496	11
50	0·5505125	0·5734783	0·5969084	·6208320	0·6452797	0·6702845	0·6958813	10
51	·5508916	·5738649	·5973030	·6212351	·6456918	·6707061	·6963131	9
52	·5512708	·5742516	·5976978	·6216383	·6461041	·6711280	·6967451	8
53	·5516502	·5746385	·5980926	·6220417	·6465165	·6715500	·6971773	7
54	·5520297	·5750255	·5984877	·6224452	·6469290	·6719721	·6976097	6
55	·5524093	·5754126	·5988828	·6228488	·6473417	·6723944	·6980422	5
56	·5527890	·5757999	·5992781	·6232527	·6477546	·6728169	·6984749	4
57	·5531688	·5761873	·5996735	·6236566	·6481676	·6732396	·6989078	3
58	·5535488	·5765748	·6000691	·6240607	·6485808	·6736624	·6993409	2
59	·5539288	·5769625	·6004648	·6244650	·6489941	·6740854	·6997741	1
60	0·5543091	0·5773503	0·6008606	·6248694	0·6494076	0·6745085	0·7002075	0
′	61°	60°	59°	58°	57°	56°	55°	′

′	35°	36°	37°	38°	39°	40°	41°	′
0	0·7002075	0·7265425	0·7535541	0·7812856	0·8097840	0·8390996	0·8692867	60
1	·7006411	·7269871	·7540102	·7817542	·8102658	·8395955	·8697976	59
2	·7010749	·7274318	·7544666	·7822229	·8107478	·8400915	·8703087	58
3	·7015089	·7278767	·7549232	·7826919	·8112300	·8405878	·8708200	57
4	·7019430	·7283218	·7553799	·7831611	·8117124	·8410844	·8713316	56
5	·7023773	·7287671	·7558369	·7836305	·8121951	·8415812	·8718435	55
6	·7028118	·7292125	·7562941	·7841002	·8126780	·8420782	·8723556	54
7	·7032464	·7296582	·7567514	·7845700	·8131611	·8425755	·8728680	53
8	·7036813	·7301041	·7572090	·7850400	·8136444	·8430730	·8733806	52
9	·7041163	·7305501	·7576668	·7855103	·8141280	·8435708	·8738935	51
10	0·7045515	0·7309963	0·7581248	0·7859808	0·8146118	0·8440688	0·8744067	50
11	·7049869	·7314428	·7585829	·7864515	·8150958	·8445670	·8749201	49
12	·7054224	·7318894	·7590413	·7869224	·8155801	·8450655	·8754338	48
13	·7058581	·7323362	·7594999	·7873935	·8160646	·8455643	·8759478	47
14	·7062940	·7327832	·7599587	·7878649	·8165493	·8460633	·8764620	46
15	·7067301	·7332303	·7604177	·7883364	·8170343	·8465625	·8769765	45
16	·7071664	·7336777	·7608769	·7888082	·8175195	·8470620	·8774912	44
17	·7076028	·7341253	·7613363	·7892802	·8180049	·8475617	·8780062	43
18	·7080395	·7345730	·7617959	·7897524	·8184905	·8480617	·8785215	42
19	·7084763	·7350210	·7622557	·7902248	·8189764	·8485619	·8790370	41
20	0·7089133	0·7354691	0·7627157	0·7906975	0·8194625	0·8490624	0·8795528	40
21	·7093504	·7359174	·7631759	·7911703	·8199488	·8495631	·8800688	39
22	·7097878	·7363660	·7636363	·7916434	·8204354	·8500640	·8805852	38
23	·7102253	·7368147	·7640969	·7921167	·8209222	·8505653	·8811017	37
24	·7106630	·7372636	·7645577	·7925902	·8214093	·8510667	·8816186	36
25	·7111009	·7377127	·7650188	·7930640	·8218965	·8515684	·8821357	35
26	·7115390	·7381620	·7654800	·7935379	·8223840	·8520704	·8826531	34
27	·7119772	·7386115	·7659414	·7940121	·8228718	·8525726	·8831707	33
28	·7124157	·7390611	·7664031	·7944865	·8233597	·8530750	·8836886	32
29	·7128543	·7395110	·7668649	·7949611	·8238479	·8535777	·8842068	31
30	0·7132931	0·7399611	0·7673270	0·7954359	0·8243364	0·8540807	0·8847253	30
31	·7137320	·7404113	·7677893	·7959110	·8248251	·8545839	·8852440	29
32	·7141712	·7408618	·7682517	·7963862	·8253140	·8550873	·8857630	28
33	·7146106	·7413124	·7687144	·7968617	·8258031	·8555910	·8862822	27
34	·7150501	·7417633	·7691773	·7973374	·8262925	·8560950	·8868017	26
35	·7154898	·7422143	·7696404	·7978134	·8267821	·8565992	·8873215	25
36	·7159297	·7426655	·7701037	·7982895	·8272719	·8571037	·8878415	24
37	·7163698	·7431170	·7705672	·7987659	·8277620	·8576084	·8883619	23
38	·7168100	·7435686	·7710309	·7992425	·8282523	·8581133	·8888825	22
39	·7172505	·7440204	·7714948	·7997193	·8287429	·8586185	·8894033	21
40	0·7176911	0·7444724	0·7719589	0·8001963	0·8292337	0·8591240	0·8899244	20
41	·7181319	·7449246	·7724233	·8006736	·8297247	·8596297	·8904458	19
42	·7185729	·7453770	·7728878	·8011511	·8302160	·8601357	·8909675	18
43	·7190141	·7458296	·7733526	·8016288	·8307075	·8606419	·8914894	17
44	·7194554	·7462824	·7738176	·8021067	·8311992	·8611484	·8920116	16
45	·7198970	·7467354	·7742827	·8025849	·8316912	·8616551	·8925341	15
46	·7203387	·7471886	·7747481	·8030632	·8321834	·8621621	·8930569	14
47	·7207806	·7476420	·7752137	·8035418	·8326759	·8626694	·8935799	13
48	·7212227	·7480956	·7756795	·8040206	·8331686	·8631768	·8941032	12
49	·7216650	·7485494	·7761455	·8044997	·8336615	·8636846	·8946268	11
50	0·7221075	0·7490033	0·7766118	0·8049790	0·8341547	0·8641926	0·8951506	10
51	·7225502	·7494575	·7770782	·8054584	·8346481	·8647009	·8956747	9
52	·7229930	·7499119	·7775448	·8059382	·8351418	·8652094	·8961991	8
53	·7234361	·7503665	·7780117	·8064181	·8356357	·8657181	·8967238	7
54	·7238793	·7508212	·7784788	·8068983	·8361298	·8662272	·8972487	6
55	·7243227	·7512762	·7789460	·8073787	·8366242	·8667365	·8977739	5
56	·7247663	·7517314	·7794135	·8078593	·8371188	·8672460	·8982994	4
57	·7252101	·7521867	·7798812	·8083401	·8376136	·8677558	·8988251	3
58	·7256540	·7526423	·7803492	·8088212	·8381087	·8682659	·8993512	2
59	·7260982	·7530981	·7808173	·8093025	·8386041	·8687762	·8998775	1
60	0·7265425	0·7535541	0·7812856	0·8097840	0·8390996	0·8692867	0·9004040	0
′	54°	53°	52°	51°	50°	49°	48°	′

′	42°	43°	44°	45°	46°	47°	48°	′
0	0·9004040	0·9325151	0·9656888	1·0000000	1·0355303	1·0723687	1·1106125	60
1	·9009309	·9330591	·9662511	1·0005819	1·0361333	1·0729943	1·1112624	59
2	·9014580	·9336034	·9668137	1·0011642	1·0367367	1·0736203	1·1119127	58
3	·9019854	·9341479	·9673767	1·0017469	1·0373404	1·0742467	1·1125635	57
4	·9025131	·9346928	·9679399	1·0023298	1·0379445	1·0748734	1·1132146	56
5	·9030411	·9352380	·9685035	1·0029131	1·0385489	1·0755006	1·1138662	55
6	·9035693	·9357834	·9690674	1·0034968	1·0391538	1·0761282	1·1145182	54
7	·9040979	·9363292	·9696316	1·0040807	1·0397589	1·0767561	1·1151706	53
8	·9046267	·9368753	·9701962	1·0046651	1·0403645	1·0773845	1·1158235	52
9	·9051557	·9374216	·9707610	1·0052497	1·0409704	1·0780132	1·1164768	51
10	0·9056851	0·9379683	0·9713262	1·0058348	1·0415767	1·0786423	1·1171305	50
11	·9062147	·9385153	·9718917	1·0064201	1·0421833	1·0792718	1·1177846	49
12	·9087446	·9390625	·9724575	1·0070058	1·0427904	1·0799018	1·1184391	48
13	·9072748	·9396101	·9730236	1·0075918	1·0433977	1·0805321	1·1190941	47
14	·9078053	·9401579	·9735901	1·0081782	1·0440055	1·0811628	1·1197495	46
15	·9083360	·9407061	·9741569	1·0087649	1·0446136	1·0817939	1·1204053	45
16	·9088671	·9412545	·9747240	1·0093520	1·0452221	1·0824254	1·1210616	44
17	·9093984	·9418033	·9752914	1·0099394	1·0458310	1·0830573	1·1217183	43
18	·9099300	·9423523	·9758591	1·0105272	1·0464402	1·0836896	1·1223754	42
19	·9104619	·9429017	·9764272	1·0111153	1·0470498	1·0843223	1·1230329	41
20	0·9109940	0·9434513	0·9769956	1·0117038	1·0476598	1·0849554	1·1236909	40
21	·9115265	·9440013	·9775643	1·0122925	1·0482702	1·0855889	1·1243493	39
22	·9120592	·9445516	·9781333	1·0128817	1·0488809	1·0862228	1·1250081	38
23	·9125922	·9451021	·9787027	1·0134712	1·0494920	1·0868571	1·1256674	37
24	·9131255	·9456530	·9792724	1·0140610	1·0501034	1·0874918	1·1263271	36
25	·9136591	·9462042	·9798424	1·0146512	1·0507153	1·0881269	1·1269872	35
26	·9141929	·9467556	·9804127	1·0152418	1·0513275	1·0887624	1·1276478	34
27	·9147270	·9473074	·9809833	1·0158326	1·0519401	1·0893984	1·1283088	33
28	·9152615	·9478595	·9815543	1·0164239	1·0525531	1·0900347	1·1289702	32
29	·9157962	·9484119	·9821256	1·0170155	1·0531664	1·0906714	1·1296321	31
30	0·9163312	0·9489646	0·9826973	1·0176074	1·0537801	1·0913085	1·1302944	30
31	·9168665	·9495176	·9832692	1·0181997	1·0543942	1·0919460	1·1309571	29
32	·9174020	·9500709	·9838415	1·0187923	1·0550087	1·0925840	1·1316203	28
33	·9179379	·9506245	·9844141	1·0193853	1·0556235	1·0932223	1·1322839	27
34	·9184740	·9511784	·9849871	1·0199786	1·0562388	1·0938610	1·1329479	26
35	·9190104	·9517326	·9855603	1·0205723	1·0568544	1·0945002	1·1336124	25
36	·9195471	·9522871	·9861339	1·0211664	1·0574704	1·0951397	1·1342773	24
37	·9200841	·9528420	·9867079	1·0217608	1·0580867	1·0957797	1·1349427	23
38	·9206214	·9533971	·9872821	1·0223555	1·0587035	1·0964201	1·1356085	22
39	·9211590	·9539526	·9878567	1·0229506	1·0593206	1·0970609	1·1362747	21
40	0·9216969	0·9545083	0·9884316	1·0235461	1·0599381	1·0977020	1·1369414	20
41	·9222350	·9550644	·9890069	1·0241419	1·0605560	1·0983436	1·1376086	19
42	·9227734	·9556208	·9895825	1·0247381	1·0611742	1·0989857	1·1382761	18
43	·9233122	·9561774	·9901584	1·0253346	1·0617929	1·0996281	1·1389441	17
44	·9238512	·9567344	·9907346	1·0259315	1·0624119	1·1002709	1·1396126	16
45	·9243905	·9572917	·9913112	1·0265287	1·0630313	1·1009141	1·1402815	15
46	·9249301	·9578494	·9918881	1·0271263	1·0636511	1·1015578	1·1409508	14
47	·9254700	·9584073	·9924654	1·0277243	1·0642713	1·1022019	1·1416206	13
48	·9260102	·9589655	·9930429	1·0283226	1·0648918	1·1028463	1·1422908	12
49	·9265506	·9595241	·9936208	1·0289212	1·0655128	1·1034912	1·1429615	11
50	0·9270914	0·9600829	0·9941991	1·0295203	1·0661341	1·1041365	1·1436326	10
51	·9276324	·9606421	·9947777	1·0301196	1·0667558	1·1047823	1·1443041	9
52	·9281738	·9612016	·9953566	1·0307194	1·0673779	1·1054284	1·1449762	8
53	·9287154	·9617614	·9959358	1·0313195	1·0680004	1·1060750	1·1456486	7
54	·9292573	·9623215	·9965154	1·0319199	1·0686233	1·1067219	1·1463215	6
55	·9297996	·9628819	·9970953	1·0325208	1·0692466	1·1073693	1·1469949	5
56	·9303421	·9634427	·9976756	1·0331220	1·0698702	1·1080171	1·1476687	4
57	·9308849	·9640037	·9982562	1·0337235	1·0704943	1·1086653	1·1483429	3
58	·9314280	·9645651	·9988371	1·0343254	1·0711187	1·1093140	1·1490176	2
59	·9319714	·9651268	·9994184	1·0349277	1·0717435	1·1099630	1·1496928	1
60	0·9325151	0·9656888	1·0000000	1·0355303	1·0723687	1·1106125	1·1503684	0
′	47°	46°	45°	44°	43°	42°	41°	′

′	49°	50°	51°	52°	53°	54°	55°	′
0	1·1503684	1·1917536	1·2348972	1·2799416	1·3270448	1·3763819	1·4281480	60
1	1·1510445	1·1924579	1·2356319	1·2807094	1·3278483	1·3772242	1·4290326	59
2	1·1517210	1·1931626	1·2363672	1·2814776	1·3286524	1·3780672	1·4299178	58
3	1·1523979	1·1938679	1·2371030	1·2822465	1·3294571	1·3789108	1·4308039	57
4	1·1530754	1·1945736	1·2378393	1·2830160	1·3302624	1·3797551	1·4316906	56
5	1·1537532	1·1952799	1·2385762	1·2837860	1·3310684	1·3806001	1·4325781	55
6	1·1544316	1·1959866	1·2393136	1·2845566	1·3318750	1·3814458	1·4334664	54
7	1·1551104	1·1966938	1·2400515	1·2853277	1·3326822	1·3822922	1·4343554	53
8	1·1557896	1·1974015	1·2407900	1·2860995	1·3334900	1·3831392	1·4352451	52
9	1·1564693	1·1981097	1·2415290	1·2868718	1·3342984	1·3839869	1·4361356	51
10	1·1571495	1·1988184	1·2422685	1·2876447	1·3351075	1·3848353	1·4370268	50
11	1·1578301	1·1995276	1·2430086	1·2884182	1·3359172	1·3856844	1·4379187	49
12	1·1585112	1·2002373	1·2437492	1·2891922	1·3367276	1·3865342	1·4388114	48
13	1·1591927	1·2009475	1·2444903	1·2899669	1·3375386	1·3873847	1·4397049	47
14	1·1598747	1·2016581	1·2452320	1·2907421	1·3383502	1·3882358	1·4405991	46
15	1·1605571	1·2023693	1·2459742	1·2915179	1·3391624	1·3890876	1·4414940	45
16	1·1612400	1·2030810	1·2467169	1·2922943	1·3399753	1·3899401	1·4423897	44
17	1·1619234	1·2037932	1·2474602	1·2930713	1·3407888	1·3907934	1·4432862	43
18	1·1626073	1·2045058	1·2482040	1·2938488	1·3416029	1·3916473	1·4441834	42
19	1·1632916	1·2052190	1·2489484	1·2946270	1·3424177	1·3925019	1·4450814	41
20	1·1639763	1·2059327	1·2496933	1·2954057	1·3432331	1·3933571	1·4459801	40
21	1·1646615	1·2066468	1·2504388	1·2961850	1·3440492	1·3942131	1·4468796	39
22	1·1653472	1·2073615	1·2511848	1·2969649	1·3448658	1·3950698	1·4477798	38
23	1·1660334	1·2080767	1·2519313	1·2977454	1·3456832	1·3959272	1·4486808	37
24	1·1667200	1·2087924	1·2526784	1·2985265	1·3465011	1·3967852	1·4495825	36
25	1·1674071	1·2095085	1·2534260	1·2993081	1·3473198	1·3976440	1·4504850	35
26	1·1680947	1·2102252	1·2541742	1·3000904	1·3481390	1·3985034	1·4513883	34
27	1·1687827	1·2109424	1·2549229	1·3008733	1·3489589	1·3993636	1·4522923	33
28	1·1694712	1·2116601	1·2556721	1·3016567	1·3497794	1·4002245	1·4531971	32
29	1·1701601	1·2123783	1·2564219	1·3024407	1·3506006	1·4010860	1·4541027	31
30	1·1708496	1·2130970	1·2571723	1·3032254	1·3514224	1·4019483	1·4550090	30
31	1·1715395	1·2138162	1·2579232	1·3040106	1·3522449	1·4028113	1·4559161	29
32	1·1722298	1·2145359	1·2586747	1·3047964	1·3530680	1·4036749	1·4568240	28
33	1·1729207	1·2152562	1·2594267	1·3055828	1·3538918	1·4045393	1·4577326	27
34	1·1736120	1·2159769	1·2601792	1·3063699	1·3547162	1·4054044	1·4586420	26
35	1·1743038	1·2166982	1·2609323	1·3071575	1·3555413	1·4062702	1·4595522	25
36	1·1749960	1·2174199	1·2616860	1·3079457	1·3563670	1·4071367	1·4604632	24
37	1·1756888	1·2181422	1·2624402	1·3087345	1·3571934	1·4080039	1·4613749	23
38	1·1763820	1·2188650	1·2631950	1·3095239	1·3580204	1·4088718	1·4622874	22
39	1·1770756	1·2195883	1·2639503	1·3103140	1·3588481	1·4097405	1·4632007	21
40	1·1777698	1·2203121	1·2647062	1·3111046	1·3596764	1·4106098	1·4641147	20
41	1·1784644	1·2210364	1·2654626	1·3118958	1·3605054	1·4114799	1·4650296	19
42	1·1791595	1·2217613	1·2662196	1·3126876	1·3613350	1·4123506	1·4659452	18
43	1·1798551	1·2224866	1·2669772	1·3134801	1·3621653	1·4132221	1·4668616	17
44	1·1805512	1·2232125	1·2677353	1·3142731	1·3629963	1·4140943	1·4677788	16
45	1·1812477	1·2239389	1·2684940	1·3150668	1·3638279	1·4149673	1·4686967	15
46	1·1819447	1·2246658	1·2692532	1·3158610	1·3646602	1·4158409	1·4696155	14
47	1·1826422	1·2253932	1·2700130	1·3166559	1·3654931	1·4167153	1·4705350	13
48	1·1833402	1·2261211	1·2707733	1·3174513	1·3663267	1·4175904	1·4714553	12
49	1·1840387	1·2268496	1·2715342	1·3182474	1·3671610	1·4184662	1·4723764	11
50	1·1847376	1·2275786	1·2722957	1·3190441	1·3679959	1·4193427	1·4732983	10
51	1·1854370	1·2283081	1·2730578	1·3198414	1·3688315	1·4202200	1·4742210	9
52	1·1861369	1·2290381	1·2738204	1·3206393	1·3696678	1·4210979	1·4751445	8
53	1·1868373	1·2297687	1·2745835	1·3214379	1·3705047	1·4219766	1·4760688	7
54	1·1875382	1·2304997	1·2753473	1·3222370	1·3713423	1·4228561	1·4769938	6
55	1·1882395	1·2312313	1·2761116	1·3230368	1·3721806	1·4237362	1·4779197	5
56	1·1889414	1·2319634	1·2768765	1·3238371	1·3730195	1·4246171	1·4788463	4
57	1·1896437	1·2326961	1·2776419	1·3246381	1·3738591	1·4254988	1·4797738	3
58	1·1903465	1·2334292	1·2784079	1·3254397	1·3746994	1·4263811	1·4807021	2
59	1·1910498	1·2341629	1·2791745	1·3262420	1·3755403	1·4272642	1·4816311	1
60	1·1917536	1·2348972	1·2799416	1·3270448	1·3763819	1·4281480	1·4825610	0
′	40°	39°	38°	37°	36°	35°	34°	′

′	56°	57°	58°	59°	60°	61°	62°	′
0	1·4825610	1·5398650	1·6003345	1·6642795	1·7320508	1·8040478	1·8807265	60
1	1·4834916	1·5408460	1·6013709	1·6653766	1·7332149	1·8052860	1·8820470	59
2	1·4844231	1·5418280	1·6024082	1·6664748	1·7343803	1·8065256	1·8833690	58
3	1·4853554	1·5428108	1·6034465	1·6675741	1·7355468	1·8077664	1·8846924	57
4	1·4862884	1·5437946	1·6044858	1·6686744	1·7367144	1·8090086	1·8860172	56
5	1·4872223	1·5447792	1·6055260	1·6697758	1·7378833	1·8102521	1·8873436	55
6	1·4881570	1·5457647	1·6065672	1·6708782	1·7390533	1·8114969	1·8886713	54
7	1·4890925	1·5467510	1·6076094	1·6719818	1·7402245	1·8127430	1·8900006	53
8	1·4900288	1·5477383	1·6086525	1·6730864	1·7413969	1·8139904	1·8913313	52
9	1·4909659	1·5487264	1·6096966	1·6741921	1·7425705	1·8152391	1·8926635	51
10	1·4919039	1·5497155	1·6107417	1·6752988	1·7437453	1·8164892	1·8939971	50
11	1·4928426	1·5507054	1·6117878	1·6764067	1·7449213	1·8177405	1·8953322	49
12	1·4937822	1·5516963	1·6128349	1·6775156	1·7460984	1·8189932	1·8966688	48
13	1·4947225	1·5526880	1·6138829	1·6786256	1·7472768	1·8202473	1·8980068	47
14	1·4956637	1·5536806	1·6149320	1·6797367	1·7484564	1·8215026	1·8993464	46
15	1·4966058	1·5546741	1·6159820	1·6808489	1·7496371	1·8227593	1·9006874	45
16	1·4975486	1·5556685	1·6170330	1·6819621	1·7508191	1·8240173	1·9020299	44
17	1·4984923	1·5566639	1·6180850	1·6830765	1·7520023	1·8252767	1·9033738	43
18	1·4994367	1·5576601	1·6191380	1·6841919	1·7531866	1·8265374	1·9047193	42
19	1·5003821	1·5586572	1·6201920	1·6853085	1·7543722	1·8277994	1·9060663	41
20	1·5013282	1·5596552	1·6212469	1·6864261	1·7555590	1·8290628	1·9074147	40
21	1·5022751	1·5606542	1·6223029	1·6875449	1·7567470	1·8303275	1·9087647	39
22	1·5032229	1·5616540	1·6233599	1·6886647	1·7579362	1·8315936	1·9101162	38
23	1·5041716	1·5626548	1·6244178	1·6897856	1·7591267	1·8328610	1·9114691	37
24	1·5051210	1·5636564	1·6254768	1·6909077	1·7603183	1·8341297	1·9128236	36
25	1·5060713	1·5646590	1·6265368	1·6920308	1·7615112	1·8353999	1·9141795	35
26	1·5070224	1·5656625	1·6275977	1·6931550	1·7627053	1·8366713	1·9155370	34
27	1·5079743	1·5666669	1·6286597	1·6942804	1·7639007	1·8379442	1·9168960	33
28	1·5089271	1·5676722	1·6297227	1·6954069	1·7650972	1·8392184	1·9182565	32
29	1·5098807	1·5686784	1·6307867	1·6965344	1·7662950	1·8404940	1·9196186	31
30	1·5108352	1·5696856	1·6318517	1·6976631	1·7674940	1·8417709	1·9209821	30
31	1·5117905	1·5706936	1·6329177	1·6987929	1·7686943	1·8430492	1·9223472	29
32	1·5127466	1·5717026	1·6339847	1·6999238	1·7698958	1·8443289	1·9237138	28
33	1·5137036	1·5727126	1·6350528	1·7010559	1·7710985	1·8456099	1·9250819	27
34	1·5146614	1·5737234	1·6361218	1·7021890	1·7723024	1·8468923	1·9264516	26
35	1·5156201	1·5747352	1·6371919	1·7033233	1·7735076	1·8481761	1·9278228	25
36	1·5165796	1·5757479	1·6382630	1·7044587	1·7747141	1·8494613	1·9291956	24
37	1·5175400	1·5767615	1·6393351	1·7055953	1·7759218	1·8507479	1·9305699	23
38	1·5185012	1·5777760	1·6404082	1·7067329	1·7771307	1·8520358	1·9319457	22
39	1·5194632	1·5787915	1·6414824	1·7078717	1·7783409	1·8533252	1·9333231	21
40	1·5204261	1·5798079	1·6425576	1·7090116	1·7795524	1·8546159	1·9347020	20
41	1·5213899	1·5808253	1·6436338	1·7101527	1·7807651	1·8559080	1·9360825	19
42	1·5223545	1·5818436	1·6447111	1·7112949	1·7819790	1·8572015	1·9374645	18
43	1·5233200	1·5828628	1·6457893	1·7124382	1·7831943	1·8584965	1·9388481	17
44	1·5242863	1·5838830	1·6468687	1·7135827	1·7844107	1·8597928	1·9402333	16
45	1·5252535	1·5849041	1·6479490	1·7147283	1·7856285	1·8610905	1·9416200	15
46	1·5262215	1·5859261	1·6490304	1·7158751	1·7868475	1·8623896	1·9430083	14
47	1·5271904	1·5869491	1·6501128	1·7170230	1·7880678	1·8636902	1·9443981	13
48	1·5281602	1·5879731	1·6511963	1·7181720	1·7892893	1·8649921	1·9457896	12
49	1·5291308	1·5889979	1·6522808	1·7193222	1·7905121	1·8662955	1·9471826	11
50	1·5301023	1·5900238	1·6533663	1·7204736	1·7917362	1·8676003	1·9485772	10
51	1·5310746	1·5910505	1·6544529	1·7216261	1·7929616	1·8689065	1·9499733	9
52	1·5320479	1·5920783	1·6555405	1·7227797	1·7941883	1·8702141	1·9513711	8
53	1·5330219	1·5931070	1·6566292	1·7239346	1·7954162	1·8715231	1·9527704	7
54	1·5339969	1·5941366	1·6577189	1·7250905	1·7966454	1·8728336	1·9541713	6
55	1·5349727	1·5951672	1·6588097	1·7262477	1·7978759	1·8741455	1·9555739	5
56	1·5359494	1·5961987	1·6599016	1·7274060	1·7991077	1·8754588	1·9569780	4
57	1·5369270	1·5972312	1·6609945	1·7285654	1·8003408	1·8767736	1·9583837	3
58	1·5379054	1·5982647	1·6620884	1·7297260	1·8015751	1·8780898	1·9597910	2
59	1·5388848	1·5992991	1·6631834	1·7308878	1·8028108	1·8794074	1·9612000	1
60	1·5398650	1·6003345	1·6642795	1·7320508	1·8040478	1·8807265	1·9626105	0
′	33°	32°	31°	30°	29°	28°	27°	′

′	63°	64°	65°	66°	67°	68°	69°	′
0	1·9626105	2·0503038	2·1445069	2·2460368	2·3558524	2·4750869	2·6050891	60
1	1·9640227	2·0518185	2·1461366	2·2477962	2·3577590	2·4771612	2·6073558	59
2	1·9654364	2·0533349	2·1477683	2·2495580	2·3596683	2·4792386	2·6096259	58
3	1·9668518	2·0548531	2·1494021	2·2513221	2·3615801	2·4813190	2·6118995	57
4	1·9682688	2·0563732	2·1510378	2·2530885	2·3634946	2·4834023	2·6141766	56
5	1·9696874	2·0578950	2·1526757	2·2548572	2·3654118	2·4854887	2·6164571	55
6	1·9711077	2·0594187	2·1543156	2·2566283	2·3673316	2·4875781	2·6187411	54
7	1·9725296	2·0609442	2·1559575	2·2584016	2·3692540	2·4896706	2·6210286	53
8	1·9739531	2·0624716	2·1576015	2·2601773	2·3711791	2·4917660	2·6233196	52
9	1·9753782	2·0640008	2·1592476	2·2619554	2·3731068	2·4938645	2·6256141	51
10	1·9768050	2·0655318	2·1608958	2·2637357	2·3750372	2·4959661	2·6279121	50
11	1·9782334	2·0670646	2·1625460	2·2655184	2·3769703	2·4980707	2·6302136	49
12	1·9796635	2·0685994	2·1641983	2·2673035	2·3789060	2·5001784	2·6325186	48
13	1·9810952	2·0701359	2·1658527	2·2690909	2·3808444	2·5022891	2·6348271	47
14	1·9825286	2·0716743	2·1675091	2·2708807	2·3827855	2·5044029	2·6371392	46
15	1·9839636	2·0732146	2·1691677	2·2726729	2·3847293	2·5065198	2·6394549	45
16	1·9854003	2·0747567	2·1708283	2·2744674	2·3866758	2·5086398	2·6417741	44
17	1·9868387	2·0763007	2·1724911	2·2762643	2·3886250	2·5107629	2·6440969	43
18	1·9882787	2·0778465	2·1741559	2·2780636	2·3905769	2·5128890	2·6464232	42
19	1·9897204	2·0793942	2·1758229	2·2798653	2·3925316	2·5150183	2·6487531	41
20	1·9911637	2·0809438	2·1774920	2·2816693	2·3944889	2·5171507	2·6510867	40
21	1·9926087	2·0824953	2·1791631	2·2834758	2·3964490	2·5192863	2·6534238	39
22	1·9940554	2·0840487	2·1808364	2·2852846	2·3984118	2·5214249	2·6557645	38
23	1·9955038	2·0856039	2·1825119	2·2870959	2·4003774	2·5235667	2·6581089	37
24	1·9969539	2·0871610	2·1841894	2·2889096	2·4023457	2·5257117	2·6604569	36
25	1·9984056	2·0887200	2·1858691	2·2907257	2·4043168	2·5278598	2·6628085	35
26	1·9998590	2·0902809	2·1875510	2·2925442	2·4062906	2·5300111	2·6651638	34
27	2·0013142	2·0918437	2·1892349	2·2943651	2·4082672	2·5321655	2·6675227	33
28	2·0027710	2·0934085	2·1909210	2·2961885	2·4102465	2·5343231	2·6698853	32
29	2·0042295	2·0949751	2·1926093	2·2980143	2·4122286	2·5364839	2·6722516	31
30	2·0056897	2·0965436	2·1942997	2·2998425	2·4142136	2·5386479	2·6746215	30
31	2·0071516	2·0981140	2·1959923	2·3016732	2·4162013	2·5408151	2·6769951	29
32	2·0086153	2·0996864	2·1976871	2·3035064	2·4181918	2·5429855	2·6793725	28
33	2·0100806	2·1012607	2·1993840	2·3053420	2·4201851	2·5451591	2·6817535	27
34	2·0115477	2·1028369	2·2010831	2·3071801	2·4221812	2·5473359	2·6841383	26
35	2·0130164	2·1044150	2·2027843	2·3090206	2·4241801	2·5495160	2·6865267	25
36	2·0144869	2·1059951	2·2044878	2·3108637	2·4261819	2·5516992	2·6889190	24
37	2·0159592	2·1075771	2·2061934	2·3127092	2·4281864	2·5538858	2·6913149	23
38	2·0174331	2·1091611	2·2079012	2·3145571	2·4301938	2·5560756	2·6937147	22
39	2·0189088	2·1107470	2·2096112	2·3164076	2·4322041	2·5582686	2·6961181	21
40	2·0203862	2·1123348	2·2113234	2·3182606	2·4342172	2·5604649	2·6985254	20
41	2·0218654	2·1139246	2·2130379	2·3201160	2·4362331	2·5626645	2·7009364	19
42	2·0233462	2·1155164	2·2147545	2·3219740	2·4382519	2·5648674	2·7033513	18
43	2·0248289	2·1171101	2·2164733	2·3238345	2·4402736	2·5670735	2·7057699	17
44	2·0263133	2·1187057	2·2181944	2·3256975	2·4422982	2·5692830	2·7081923	16
45	2·0277994	2·1203034	2·2199177	2·3275630	2·4443256	2·5714957	2·7106186	15
46	2·0292873	2·1219030	2·2216432	2·3294311	2·4463559	2·5737118	2·7130487	14
47	2·0307769	2·1235046	2·2233709	2·3313017	2·4483891	2·5759312	2·7154826	13
48	2·0322683	2·1251082	2·2251009	2·3331748	2·4504252	2·5781539	2·7179204	12
49	2·0337615	2·1267137	2·2268331	2·3350505	2·4524642	2·5803800	2·7203620	11
50	2·0352565	2·1283213	2·2285676	2·3369287	2·4545061	2·5826094	2·7228076	10
51	2·0367532	2·1299308	2·2303043	2·3388095	2·4565510	2·5848421	2·7252569	9
52	2·0382517	2·1315423	2·2320433	2·3406928	2·4585987	2·5870782	2·7277102	8
53	2·0397519	2·1331559	2·2337845	2·3425787	2·4606494	2·5893177	2·7301674	7
54	2·0412540	2·1347714	2·2355280	2·3444672	2·4627030	2·5915606	2·7326284	6
55	2·0427578	2·1363890	2·2372738	2·3463582	2·4647596	2·5938068	2·7350934	5
56	2·0442634	2·1380085	2·2390218	2·3482519	2·4668191	2·5960564	2·7375623	4
57	2·0457708	2·1396301	2·2407721	2·3501481	2·4688816	2·5983095	2·7400352	3
58	2·0472800	2·1412537	2·2425247	2·3520469	2·4709470	2·6005659	2·7425120	2
59	2·0487910	2·1428793	2·2442796	2·3539483	2·4730155	2·6028258	2·7449927	1
60	2·0503038	2·1445069	2·2460368	2·3558524	2·4750869	2·6050891	2·7474774	0
′	26°	25°	24°	23°	22°	21°	20°	′

′	70°	71°	72°	73°	74°	75°	76°	′
0	2·7474774	2·9042109	3·0776835	3·2708526	3·4874144	3·7320508	4·0107809	60
1	2·7499661	2·9069576	3·0807325	3·2742588	3·4912470	3·7363980	4·0157570	59
2	2·7524588	2·9097089	3·0837869	3·2776715	3·4950874	3·7407546	4·0207446	58
3	2·7549554	2·9124649	3·0868468	3·2810907	3·4989356	3·7451207	4·0257440	57
4	2·7574561	2·9152256	3·0899122	3·2845164	3·5027916	3·7494963	4·0307550	56
5	2·7599608	2·9179909	3·0929831	3·2879487	3·5066555	3·7538815	4·0357779	55
6	2·7624695	2·9207610	3·0960596	3·2913876	3·5105273	3·7582763	4·0408125	54
7	2·7649822	2·9235358	3·0991416	3·2948330	3·5144070	3·7626807	4·0458590	53
8	2·7674990	2·9263152	3·1022291	3·2982851	3·5182946	3·7670947	4·0509174	52
9	2·7700199	2·9290995	3·1053223	3·3017438	3·5221902	3·7715185	4·0559877	51
10	2·7725448	2·9318885	3·1084210	3·3052091	3·5260938	3·7759519	4·0610700	50
11	2·7750738	2·9346822	3·1115254	3·3086811	3·5300054	3·7803951	4·0661643	49
12	2·7776069	2·9374807	3·1146353	3·3121598	3·5339251	3·7848481	4·0712707	48
13	2·7801440	2·9402840	3·1177509	3·3156452	3·5378528	3·7893109	4·0763892	47
14	2·7826853	2·9430921	3·1208722	3·3191373	3·5417886	3·7937835	4·0815199	46
15	2·7852307	2·9459050	3·1239991	3·3226362	3·5457325	3·7982661	4·0866627	45
16	2·7877802	2·9487227	3·1271317	3·3261419	3·5496846	3·8027585	4·0918178	44
17	2·7903339	2·9515453	3·1302701	3·3296543	3·5536449	3·8072609	4·0969852	43
18	2·7928917	2·9543727	3·1334141	3·3331736	3·5576133	3·8117733	4·1021649	42
19	2·7954537	2·9572050	3·1365639	3·3366997	3·5615900	3·8162957	4·1073569	41
20	2·7980198	2·9600422	3·1397194	3·3402326	3·5655749	3·8208281	4·1125614	40
21	2·8005901	2·9628842	3·1428807	3·3437724	3·5695681	3·8253707	4·1177784	39
22	2·8031646	2·9657312	3·1460478	3·3473191	3·5735696	3·8299233	4·1230079	38
23	2·8057433	2·9685831	3·1492207	3·3508728	3·5775794	3·8344861	4·1282499	37
24	2·8083263	2·9714399	3·1523994	3·3544333	3·5815975	3·8390591	4·1335046	36
25	2·8109134	2·9743016	3·1555840	3·3580008	3·5856241	3·8436424	4·1387719	35
26	2·8135048	2·9771683	3·1587744	3·3615753	3·5896590	3·8482358	4·1440519	34
27	2·8161004	2·9800400	3·1619706	3·3651568	3·5937024	3·8528396	4·1493446	33
28	2·8187003	2·9829167	3·1651728	3·3687453	3·5977543	3·8574537	4·1546501	32
29	2·8213045	2·9857983	3·1683808	3·3723408	3·6018146	3·8620782	4·1599685	31
30	2·8239129	2·9886850	3·1715948	3·3759434	3·6058835	3·8667131	4·1652998	30
31	2·8265256	2·9915766	3·1748147	3·3795531	3·6099609	3·8713584	4·1706440	29
32	2·8291426	2·9944734	3·1780406	3·3831699	3·6140469	3·8760142	4·1760011	28
33	2·8317639	2·9973751	3·1812724	3·3867938	3·6181415	3·8806805	4·1813713	27
34	2·8343896	3·0002820	3·1845102	3·3904249	3·6222447	3·8853574	4·1867546	26
35	2·8370196	3·0031939	3·1877540	3·3940631	3·6263566	3·8900448	4·1921510	25
36	2·8396539	3·0061109	3·1910039	3·3977085	3·6304771	3·8947429	4·1975606	24
37	2·8422926	3·0090330	3·1942598	3·4013612	3·6346064	3·8994516	4·2029835	23
38	2·8449356	3·0119603	3·1975217	3·4050210	3·6387444	3·9041710	4·2084196	22
39	2·8475831	3·0148926	3·2007897	3·4086882	3·6428911	3·9089011	4·2138690	21
40	2·8502349	3·0178301	3·2040638	3·4123626	3·6470467	3·9136420	4·2193318	20
41	2·8528911	3·0207728	3·2073440	3·4160443	3·6512111	3·9183937	4·2248080	19
42	2·8555517	3·0237207	3·2106304	3·4197333	3·6553844	3·9231563	4·2302977	18
43	2·8582168	3·0266737	3·2139228	3·4234297	3·6595665	3·9279297	4·2358009	17
44	2·8608863	3·0296320	3·2172215	3·4271334	3·6637575	3·9327141	4·2413177	16
45	2·8635602	3·0325954	3·2205263	3·4308446	3·6679575	3·9375094	4·2468482	15
46	2·8662386	3·0355641	3·2238373	3·4345631	3·6721665	3·9423157	4·2523923	14
47	2·8689215	3·0385381	3·2271546	3·4382891	3·6763845	3·9471331	4·2579501	13
48	2·8716088	3·0415173	3·2304780	3·4420226	3·6806115	3·9519615	4·2635218	12
49	2·8743007	3·0445018	3·2338078	3·4457635	3·6848475	3·9568011	4·2691072	11
50	2·8769970	3·0474915	3·2371438	3·4495120	3·6890927	3·9616518	4·2747066	10
51	2·8796979	3·0504866	3·2404860	3·4532679	3·6933469	3·9665137	4·2803199	9
52	2·8824033	3·0534870	3·2438346	3·4570315	3·6976104	3·9713868	4·2859472	8
53	2·8851132	3·0564928	3·2471895	3·4608026	3·7018830	3·9762712	4·2915885	7
54	2·8878277	3·0595038	3·2505508	3·4645813	3·7061648	3·9811669	4·2972440	6
55	2·8905467	3·0625203	3·2539184	3·4683676	3·7104558	3·9860739	4·3029136	5
56	2·8932704	3·0655421	3·2572924	3·4721616	3·7147561	3·9909924	4·3085974	4
57	2·8959986	3·0685694	3·2606728	3·4759632	3·7190658	3·9959223	4·3142955	3
58	2·8987314	3·0716020	3·2640596	3·4797726	3·7233847	4·0008636	4·3200079	2
59	2·9014688	3·0746400	3·2674529	3·4835896	3·7277131	4·0058165	4·3257347	1
60	2·9042109	3·0776835	3·2708526	3·4874144	3·7320508	4·0107809	4·3314759	0
′	19°	18°	17°	16°	15°	14°	13°	′

′	77°	78°	79°	80°	81°	82°	83°	′
0	4·3314759	4·7046301	5·1445540	5·6712818	6·3137515	7·1153697	8·1443464	60
1	4·3372316	4·7113686	5·1525557	5·6809446	6·3256601	7·1304190	8·1639786	59
2	4·3430018	4·7181256	5·1605813	5·6906394	6·3376126	7·1455308	8·1837041	58
3	4·3487866	4·7249012	5·1686311	5·7003663	6·3496092	7·1607056	8·2035239	57
4	4·3545861	4·7316954	5·1767051	5·7101256	6·3616502	7·1759437	8·2234384	56
5	4·3604003	4·7385083	5·1848035	5·7199173	6·3737359	7·1912456	8·2434485	55
6	4·3662293	4·7453401	5·1929264	5·7297416	6·3858665	7·2066116	8·2635547	54
7	4·3720731	4·7521907	5·2010738	5·7395988	6·3980422	7·2220422	8·2837579	53
8	4·3779317	4·7590603	5·2092459	5·7494889	6·4102633	7·2375378	8·3040586	52
9	4·3838054	4·7659490	5·2174428	5·7594122	6·4225301	7·2530987	8·3244577	51
10	4·3896940	4·7728568	5·2256647	5·7693688	6·4348428	7·2687255	8·3449558	50
11	4·3955977	4·7797837	5·2339116	5·7793588	6·4472017	7·2844184	8·3655536	49
12	4·4015164	4·7867300	5·2421836	5·7893825	6·4596070	7·3001780	8·3862519	48
13	4·4074504	4·7936957	5·2504809	5·7994400	6·4720591	7·3160047	8·4070515	47
14	4·4133996	4·8006808	5·2588035	5·8095315	6·4845581	7·3318989	8·4279531	46
15	4·4193641	4·8076854	5·2671517	5·8196572	6·4971043	7·3478610	8·4489573	45
16	4·4253439	4·8147096	5·2755255	5·8298172	6·5096981	7·3638916	8·4700651	44
17	4·4313392	4·8217536	5·2839251	5·8400117	6·5223396	7·3799909	8·4912772	43
18	4·4373500	4·8288174	5·2923505	5·8502410	6·5350293	7·3961595	8·5125943	42
19	4·4433762	4·8359010	5·3008018	5·8605051	6·5477672	7·4123978	8·5340172	41
20	4·4494181	4·8430045	5·3092793	5·8708042	6·5605538	7·4287064	8·5555468	40
21	4·4554756	4·8501282	5·3177830	5·8811386	6·5733892	7·4450855	8·5771838	39
22	4·4615489	4·8572719	5·3263131	5·8915084	6·5862739	7·4615357	8·5989290	38
23	4·4676379	4·8644359	5·3348696	5·9019138	6·5992080	7·4780576	8·6207833	37
24	4·4737428	4·8716201	5·3434527	5·9123550	6·6121919	7·4946514	8·6427475	36
25	4·4798636	4·8788248	5·3520626	5·9228322	6·6252258	7·5113178	8·6648223	35
26	4·4860004	4·8860499	5·3606993	5·9333455	6·6383100	7·5280571	8·6870088	34
27	4·4921532	4·8932956	5·3693630	5·9438952	6·6514449	7·5448699	8·7093077	33
28	4·4983221	4·9005620	5·3780538	5·9544815	6·6646307	7·5617567	8·7317198	32
29	4·5045072	4·9078491	5·3867718	5·9651045	6·6778677	7·5787179	8·7542461	31
30	4·5107085	4·9151570	5·3955172	5·9757644	6·6911562	7·5957541	8·7768874	30
31	4·5169261	4·9224859	5·4042901	5·9864614	6·7044966	7·6128657	8·7996446	29
32	4·5231601	4·9298358	5·4130906	5·9971957	6·7178891	7·6300533	8·8225186	28
33	4·5294105	4·9372068	5·4219188	6·0079676	6·7313341	7·6473174	8·8455103	27
34	4·5356773	4·9445990	5·4307750	6·0187772	6·7448318	7·6646584	8·8686206	26
35	4·5419608	4·9520125	5·4396592	6·0296247	6·7583826	7·6820769	8·8918505	25
36	4·5482608	4·9594474	5·4485715	6·0405103	6·7719867	7·6995735	8·9152009	24
37	4·5545776	4·9669037	5·4575121	6·0514343	6·7856446	7·7171486	8·9386726	23
38	4·5609111	4·9743817	5·4664812	6·0623967	6·7993565	7·7348028	8·9622668	22
39	4·5672615	4·9818813	5·4754788	6·0733979	6·8131227	7·7525366	8·9859843	21
40	4·5736287	4·9894027	5·4845052	6·0844381	6·8269437	7·7703506	9·0098261	20
41	4·5800129	4·9969459	5·4935604	6·0955174	6·8408196	7·7882453	9·0337933	19
42	4·5864141	5·0045111	5·5026446	6·1066360	6·8547508	7·8062212	9·0578867	18
43	4·5928325	5·0120984	5·5117579	6·1177943	6·8687378	7·8242790	9·0821074	17
44	4·5992680	5·0197078	5·5209005	6·1289923	6·8827807	7·8424191	9·1064564	16
45	4·6057207	5·0273395	5·5300724	6·1402303	6·8968799	7·8606423	9·1309348	15
46	4·6121908	5·0349935	5·5392740	6·1515085	6·9110359	7·8789489	9·1555436	14
47	4·6186783	5·0426700	5·5485052	6·1628272	6·9252489	7·8973396	9·1802838	13
48	4·6251832	5·0503690	5·5577663	6·1741865	6·9395192	7·9158151	9·2051564	12
49	4·6317056	5·0580907	5·5670574	6·1855867	6·9538473	7·9343758	9·2301627	11
50	4·6382457	5·0658352	5·5763786	6·1970279	6·9682335	7·9530224	9·2553035	10
51	4·6448034	5·0736025	5·5857302	6·2085106	6·9826781	7·9717555	9·2805802	9
52	4·6513788	5·0813928	5·5951121	6·2200347	6·9971806	7·9905756	9·3059936	8
53	4·6579721	5·0892061	5·6045247	6·2316007	7·0117441	8·0094835	9·3315450	7
54	4·6645832	5·0970426	5·6139680	6·2432086	7·0263662	8·0284796	9·3572355	6
55	4·6712124	5·1049024	5·6234421	6·2548588	7·0410482	8·0475647	9·3830663	5
56	4·6778595	5·1127855	5·6329474	6·2665515	7·0557905	8·0667394	9·4090384	4
57	4·6845248	5·1206921	5·6424838	6·2782868	7·0705934	8·0860042	9·4351531	3
58	4·6912083	5·1286224	5·6520516	6·2900651	7·0854573	8·1053599	9·4614116	2
59	4·6979100	5·1365763	5·6616509	6·3018866	7·1003826	8·1248071	9·4878149	1
60	4·7046301	5·1445540	5·6712818	6·3137515	7·1153697	8·1443464	9·5143645	0
′	12°	11°	10°	9°	8°	7°	6°	′

NATURAL COTANGENTS.

′	84°	85°	86°	87°	88°	89°	′
0	9·5143645	11·430052	14·300666	19·081137	28·636253	57·289962	60
1	9·5410613	11·468474	14·360696	19·187930	28·877089	58·261174	59
2	9·5679068	11·507154	14·421230	19·295922	29·122005	59·265872	58
3	9·5949022	11·546093	14·482273	19·405133	29·371106	60·305820	57
4	9·6220486	11·585294	14·543833	19·515584	29·624499	61·382905	56
5	9·6493475	11·624761	14·605916	19·627296	29·882299	62·499154	55
6	9·6768000	11·664495	14·668529	19·740291	30·144619	63·656741	54
7	9·7044075	11·704500	14·731679	19·854591	30·411580	64·858008	53
8	9·7321713	11·744779	14·795372	19·970219	30·683307	66·105473	52
9	9·7600927	11·785333	14·859616	20·087199	30·959928	67·401854	51
10	9·7881732	11·826167	14·924417	20·205553	31·241577	68·750087	50
11	9·8164140	11·867282	14·989784	20·325308	31·528392	70·153346	49
12	9·8448166	11·908682	15·055723	20·446486	31·820516	71·615070	48
13	9·8733823	11·950370	15·122242	20·569115	32·118099	73·138991	47
14	9·9021125	11·992349	15·189349	20·693220	32·421295	74·729165	46
15	9·9310088	12·034622	15·257052	20·818828	32·730264	76·390009	45
16	9·9600724	12·077192	15·325358	20·945966	33·045173	78·126342	44
17	9·9893050	12·120062	15·394276	21·074664	33·366194	79·943430	43
18	10·018708	12·163236	15·463814	21·204949	33·693509	81·847041	42
19	10·048283	12·206716	15·533981	21·336851	34·027303	83·843507	41
20	10·078031	12·250505	15·604784	21·470401	34·367771	85·939791	40
21	10·107954	12·294609	15·676233	21·605630	34·715115	88·143572	39
22	10·138054	12·339028	15·748337	21·742569	35·069546	90·463336	38
23	10·168332	12·383768	15·821105	21·881251	35·431282	92·908487	37
24	10·198789	12·428831	15·894545	22·021710	35·800553	95·489475	36
25	10·229428	12·474221	15·968667	22·163980	36·177596	98·217943	35
26	10·260249	12·519942	16·043482	22·308097	36·562659	101·10690	34
27	10·291255	12·565997	16·118998	22·454096	36·956001	104·17094	33
28	10·322447	12·612390	16·195225	22·602015	37·357892	107·42648	32
29	10·353827	12·659125	16·272174	22·751892	37·768613	110·89205	31
30	10·385397	12·706205	16·349855	22·903766	38·188459	114·58865	30
31	10·417158	12·753634	16·428279	23·057677	38·617738	118·54018	29
32	10·449112	12·801417	16·507456	23·213666	39·056771	122·77396	28
33	10·481261	12·849557	16·587396	23·371777	39·505895	127·32134	27
34	10·513607	12·898058	16·668112	23·532052	39·965460	132·21851	26
35	10·546151	12·946924	16·749614	23·694537	40·435837	137·50745	25
36	10·578895	12·996160	16·831915	23·859277	40·917412	143·23712	24
37	10·611841	13·045769	16·915025	24·026320	41·410588	149·46502	23
38	10·644992	13·095757	16·998957	24·195714	41·915790	156·25908	22
39	10·678348	13·146127	17·083724	24·367509	42·433464	163·70019	21
40	10·711913	13·196883	17·169337	24·541758	42·964077	171·88540	20
41	10·745687	13·248031	17·255809	24·718512	43·508122	180·93209	19
42	10·779673	13·299574	17·343155	24·897826	44·066113	190·98419	18
43	10·813872	13·351518	17·431385	25·079757	44·638596	202·21875	17
44	10·848288	13·403867	17·520516	25·264361	45·226141	214·85762	16
45	10·882921	13·456625	17·610559	25·451700	45·829351	229·18166	15
46	10·917775	13·509799	17·701529	25·641832	46·448862	245·55198	14
47	10·952850	13·563391	17·793442	25·834823	47·085343	264·44080	13
48	10·988150	13·617409	17·886310	26·030736	47·739501	286·47773	12
49	11·023676	13·671856	17·980150	26·229638	48·412084	312·52137	11
50	11·059431	13·726738	18·074977	26·431600	49·103881	343·77371	10
51	11·095416	13·782060	18·170807	26·636690	49·815726	381·97099	9
52	11·131635	13·837827	18·267654	26·844984	50·548506	429·71757	8
53	11·168089	13·894045	18·365537	27·056557	51·303157	491·10600	7
54	11·204780	13·950719	18·464471	27·271486	52·080673	572·95721	6
55	11·241712	14·007856	18·564473	27·489853	52·882109	687·54887	5
56	11·278885	14·065459	18·665562	27·711740	53·708587	859·43630	4
57	11·316304	14·123536	18·767754	27·937233	54·561300	1145·9153	3
58	11·353970	14·182092	18·871068	28·166422	55·441517	1718·8732	2
59	11·391885	14·241134	18·975523	28·399397	56·350590	3437·7467	1
60	11·430052	14·300666	19·081137	28·636253	57·289962	Infinite.	0
′	5°	4°	3°	2°	1°	0°	′

NATURAL COTANGENTS.

′	0°	1°	2°	3°	4°	5°	6°	′
0	1·0000000	1·0001523	1·0006095	1·0013723	1·0024419	1·0038198	1·0055083	60
1	1·0000000	1·0001574	1·0006198	1·0013877	1·0024623	1·0038454	1·0055391	59
2	1·0000002	1·0001627	1·0006300	1·0014030	1·0024829	1·0038711	1·0055699	58
3	1·0000004	1·0001679	1·0006404	1·0014185	1·0025035	1·0038969	1·0056009	57
4	1·0000007	1·0001733	1·0006509	1·0014341	1·0025241	1·0039227	1·0056319	56
5	1·0000011	1·0001788	1·0006614	1·0014497	1·0025449	1·0039486	1·0056631	55
6	1·0000015	1·0001843	1·0006721	1·0014655	1·0025658	1·0039747	1·0056943	54
7	1·0000021	1·0001900	1·0006828	1·0014813	1·0025867	1·0040008	1·0057256	53
8	1·0000027	1·0001957	1·0006936	1·0014972	1·0026078	1·0040270	1·0057570	52
9	1·0000034	1·0002015	1·0007045	1·0015132	1·0026289	1·0040533	1·0057885	51
10	1·0000042	1·0002073	1·0007154	1·0015293	1·0026501	1·0040796	1·0058200	50
11	1·0000051	1·0002133	1·0007265	1·0015454	1·0026714	1·0041061	1·0058517	49
12	1·0000061	1·0002194	1·0007376	1·0015617	1·0026928	1·0041326	1·0058834	48
13	1·0000072	1·0002255	1·0007489	1·0015780	1·0027142	1·0041592	1·0059153	47
14	1·0000083	1·0002317	1·0007602	1·0015944	1·0027358	1·0041859	1·0059472	46
15	1·0000095	1·0002380	1·0007716	1·0016109	1·0027574	1·0042127	1·0059792	45
16	1·0000108	1·0002444	1·0007830	1·0016275	1·0027791	1·0042396	1·0060113	44
17	1·0000122	1·0002509	1·0007946	1·0016442	1·0028009	1·0042666	1·0060435	43
18	1·0000137	1·0002575	1·0008063	1·0016609	1·0028228	1·0042937	1·0060757	42
19	1·0000153	1·0002641	1·0008180	1·0016778	1·0028448	1·0043208	1·0061081	41
20	1·0000169	1·0002708	1·0008298	1·0016947	1·0028669	1·0043480	1·0061405	40
21	1·0000187	1·0002776	1·0008417	1·0017117	1·0028890	1·0043753	1·0061731	39
22	1·0000205	1·0002845	1·0008537	1·0017288	1·0029112	1·0044028	1·0062057	38
23	1·0000224	1·0002915	1·0008658	1·0017460	1·0029336	1·0044302	1·0062384	37
24	1·0000244	1·0002986	1·0008779	1·0017633	1·0029560	1·0044578	1·0062712	36
25	1·0000264	1·0003058	1·0008902	1·0017806	1·0029785	1·0044855	1·0063040	35
26	1·0000286	1·0003130	1·0009025	1·0017981	1·0030010	1·0045132	1·0063370	34
27	1·0000308	1·0003203	1·0009149	1·0018156	1·0030237	1·0045411	1·0063701	33
28	1·0000332	1·0003277	1·0009274	1·0018332	1·0030464	1·0045690	1·0064032	32
29	1·0000356	1·0003352	1·0009400	1·0018509	1·0030693	1·0045970	1·0064364	31
30	1·0000381	1·0003428	1·0009527	1·0018687	1·0030922	1·0046251	1·0064697	30
31	1·0000407	1·0003505	1·0009654	1·0018866	1·0031152	1·0046533	1·0065031	29
32	1·0000433	1·0003582	1·0009783	1·0019045	1·0031383	1·0046815	1·0065366	28
33	1·0000461	1·0003660	1·0009912	1·0019225	1·0031615	1·0047099	1·0065702	27
34	1·0000489	1·0003739	1·0010042	1·0019407	1·0031847	1·0047383	1·0066039	26
35	1·0000518	1·0003820	1·0010173	1·0019589	1·0032081	1·0047669	1·0066376	25
36	1·0000548	1·0003900	1·0010305	1·0019772	1·0032315	1·0047955	1·0066714	24
37	1·0000579	1·0003982	1·0010438	1·0019956	1·0032551	1·0048242	1·0067054	23
38	1·0000611	1·0004065	1·0010571	1·0020140	1·0032787	1·0048530	1·0067394	22
39	1·0000644	1·0004148	1·0010705	1·0020326	1·0033024	1·0048819	1·0067735	21
40	1·0000677	1·0004232	1·0010841	1·0020512	1·0033261	1·0049108	1·0068077	20
41	1·0000711	1·0004317	1·0010977	1·0020699	1·0033500	1·0049399	1·0068419	19
42	1·0000746	1·0004403	1·0011114	1·0020887	1·0033740	1·0049690	1·0068763	18
43	1·0000782	1·0004490	1·0011251	1·0021076	1·0033980	1·0049982	1·0069108	17
44	1·0000819	1·0004578	1·0011390	1·0021266	1·0034221	1·0050275	1·0069453	16
45	1·0000857	1·0004666	1·0011529	1·0021457	1·0034463	1·0050569	1·0069799	15
46	1·0000895	1·0004756	1·0011670	1·0021648	1·0034706	1·0050864	1·0070146	14
47	1·0000935	1·0004846	1·0011811	1·0021841	1·0034950	1·0051160	1·0070494	13
48	1·0000975	1·0004937	1·0011953	1·0022034	1·0035195	1·0051456	1·0070843	12
49	1·0001016	1·0005029	1·0012096	1·0022228	1·0035440	1·0051754	1·0071193	11
50	1·0001058	1·0005121	1·0012239	1·0022423	1·0035687	1·0052052	1·0071544	10
51	1·0001101	1·0005215	1·0012384	1·0022619	1·0035934	1·0052351	1·0071895	9
52	1·0001144	1·0005309	1·0012529	1·0022815	1·0036182	1·0052651	1·0072248	8
53	1·0001189	1·0005405	1·0012676	1·0023013	1·0036431	1·0052952	1·0072601	7
54	1·0001234	1·0005501	1·0012823	1·0023211	1·0036€81	1·0053254	1·0072955	6
55	1·0001280	1·0005598	1·0012971	1·0023410	1·0036932	1·0053557	1·0073310	5
56	1·0001327	1·0005696	1·0013120	1·0023610	1·0037183	1·0053860	1·0073666	4
57	1·0001375	1·0005794	1·0013269	1·0023811	1·0037436	1·0054164	1·0074023	3
58	1·0001423	1·0005894	1·0013420	1·0024013	1·0037689	1·0054470	1·0074380	2
59	1·0001473	1·0005994	1·0013571	1·0024216	1·0037943	1·0054776	1·0074739	1
60	1·0001523	1·0006095	1·0013723	1·0024419	1·0038198	1·0055083	1·0075098	0
′	89°	88°	87°	86°	85°	84°	83°	′

NATURAL COSECANTS.

′	7°	8°	9°	10°	11°	12°	13°	′
0	1·0075098	1·0098276	1·0124651	1·0154266	1·0187167	1·0223406	1·0262041	60
1	1·0075459	1·0098689	1·0125118	1·0154787	1·0187743	1·0224039	1·0262731	59
2	1·0075820	1·0099103	1·0125586	1·0155310	1·0188321	1·0224672	1·0263421	58
3	1·0076182	1·0099518	1·0126055	1·0155833	1·0188899	1·0225307	1·0265113	57
4	1·0076545	1·0099934	1·0126524	1·0156357	1·0189478	1·0225942	1·0265806	56
5	1·0076908	1·0100351	1·0126995	1·0156882	1·0190059	1·0226578	1·0266499	55
6	1·0077273	1·0100769	1·0127466	1·0157408	1·0190640	1·0227216	1·0267194	54
7	1·0077639	1·0101187	1·0127939	1·0157934	1·0191222	1·0227854	1·0267889	53
8	1·0078005	1·0101607	1·0128412	1·0158462	1·0191805	1·0228493	1·0268586	52
9	1·0078372	1·0102027	1·0128886	1·0158991	1·0192389	1·0229133	1·0269283	51
10	1·0078741	1·0102449	1·0129361	1·0159520	1·0192973	1·0229774	1·0269982	50
11	1·0079110	1·0102871	1·0129837	1·0160050	1·0193559	1·0230416	1·0270681	49
12	1·0079480	1·0103294	1·0130314	1·0160582	1·0194146	1·0231059	1·0271381	48
13	1·0079851	1·0103718	1·0130791	1·0161114	1·0194734	1·0231703	1·0272082	47
14	1·0080222	1·0104143	1·0131270	1·0161647	1·0195322	1·0232348	1·0272785	46
15	1·0080595	1·0104568	1·0131750	1·0162181	1·0195912	1·0232994	1·0273488	45
16	1·0080968	1·0104995	1·0132230	1·0162716	1·0196502	1·0233641	1·0274192	44
17	1·0081343	1·0105422	1·0132711	1·0163252	1·0197093	1·0234288	1·0274897	43
18	1·0081718	1·0105851	1·0133194	1·0163789	1·0197686	1·0234937	1·0275603	42
19	1·0082094	1·0106280	1·0133677	1·0164327	1·0198279	1·0235587	1·0276310	41
20	1·0082471	1·0106710	1·0134161	1·0164865	1·0198873	1·0236237	1·0277018	40
21	1·0082849	1·0107141	1·0134646	1·0165405	1·0199468	1·0236889	1·0277727	39
22	1·0083228	1·0107573	1·0135132	1·0165946	1·0200064	1·0237541	1·0278437	38
23	1·0083607	1·0108006	1·0135618	1·0166487	1·0200661	1·0238195	1·0279148	37
24	1·0083988	1·0108440	1·0136106	1·0167029	1·0201259	1·0238849	1·0279860	36
25	1·0084369	1·0108875	1·0136595	1·0167573	1·0201858	1·0239504	1·0280573	35
26	1·0084752	1·0109310	1·0137084	1·0168117	1·0202457	1·0240161	1·0281287	34
27	1·0085135	1·0109747	1·0137574	1·0168662	1·0203058	1·0240818	1·0282002	33
28	1·0085519	1·0110184	1·0138066	1·0169208	1·0203660	1·0241476	1·0282717	32
29	1·0085904	1·0110622	1·0138558	1·0169755	1·0204262	1·0242135	1·0283434	31
30	1·0086290	1·0111061	1·0139051	1·0170303	1·0204866	1·0242795	1·0284152	30
31	1·0086676	1·0111501	1·0139545	1·0170851	1·0205470	1·0243456	1·0284871	29
32	1·0087064	1·0111942	1·0140040	1·0171401	1·0206075	1·0244118	1·0285590	28
33	1·0087452	1·0112384	1·0140536	1·0171952	1·0206682	1·0244781	1·0286311	27
34	1·0087842	1·0112827	1·0141032	1·0172503	1·0207289	1·0245445	1·0287033	26
35	1·0088232	1·0113270	1·0141530	1·0173056	1·0207897	1·0246110	1·0287755	25
36	1·0088623	1·0113715	1·0142029	1·0173609	1·0208506	1·0246776	1·0288479	24
37	1·0089015	1·0114160	1·0142528	1·0174163	1·0209116	1·0247442	1·0289203	23
38	1·0089408	1·0114606	1·0143028	1·0174719	1·0209727	1·0248110	1·0289929	22
39	1·0089802	1·0115054	1·0143530	1·0175275	1·0210339	1·0248779	1·0290655	21
40	1·0090196	1·0115502	1·0144032	1·0175832	1·0210952	1·0249448	1·0291383	20
41	1·0090592	1·0115951	1·0144535	1·0176390	1·0211566	1·0250119	1·0292111	19
42	1·0090988	1·0116400	1·0145039	1·0176949	1·0212180	1·0250790	1·0292840	18
43	1·0091386	1·0116851	1·0145544	1·0177509	1·0212796	1·0251463	1·0293571	17
44	1·0091784	1·0117303	1·0146050	1·0178069	1·0213413	1·0252136	1·0294302	16
45	1·0092183	1·0117755	1·0146556	1·0178631	1·0214030	1·0252811	1·0295034	15
46	1·0092583	1·0118209	1·0147064	1·0179194	1·0214649	1·0253486	1·0295768	14
47	1·0092984	1·0118663	1·0147572	1·0179757	1·0215268	1·0254162	1·0296502	13
48	1·0093386	1·0119118	1·0148082	1·0180321	1·0215888	1·0254839	1·0297237	12
49	1·0093788	1·0119575	1·0148592	1·0180887	1·0216510	1·0255518	1·0297973	11
50	1·0094192	1·0120032	1·0149103	1·0181453	1·0217132	1·0256197	1·0298711	10
51	1·0094596	1·0120489	1·0149616	1·0182020	1·0217755	1·0256877	1·0299449	9
52	1·0095001	1·0120948	1·0150129	1·0182588	1·0218379	1·0257558	1·0300188	8
53	1·0095408	1·0121408	1·0150643	1·0183158	1·0219004	1·0258240	1·0300928	7
54	1·0095815	1·0121869	1·0151158	1·0183728	1·0219630	1·0258923	1·0301669	6
55	1·0096223	1·0122330	1·0151673	1·0184298	1·0220257	1 0259607	1·0302411	5
56	1·0096631	1·0122793	1·0152190	1·0184870	1·0220885	1·0260292	1·0303154	4
57	1·0097041	1·0123256	1·0152708	1·0185443	1·0221514	1·0260978	1·0303898	3
58	1·0097452	1·0123720	1·0153226	1·0186017	1·0222144	1·0261665	1·0304643	2
59	1·0097863	1·0124185	1·0153746	1·0186591	1·0222774	1·0262352	1·0305389	1
60	1·0098276	1·0124651	1·0154266	1·0187167	1·0223406	1·0263041	1·0306136	0
′	82°	81°	80°	79°	78°	77°	76°	′

′	14°	15°	16°	17°	18°	19°	20°	′
0	1·0306136	1·0352762	1·0402994	1·0456918	1·0514622	1·0576207	1·0641778	60
1	1·0306884	1·0353569	1·0403863	1·0457848	1·0515617	1·0577267	1·0642905	59
2	1·0307633	1·0354378	1·0404732	1·0458780	1·0516612	1·0578328	1·0644033	58
3	1·0308383	1·0355187	1·0405602	1·0459712	1·0517608	1·0579390	1·0645163	57
4	1·0309134	1·0355998	1·0406473	1·0460646	1·0518606	1·0580453	1·0646294	56
5	1·0309886	1·0356809	1·0407346	1·0461581	1·0519605	1·0581517	1·0647425	55
6	1·0310639	1·0357621	1·0408219	1·0462516	1·0520604	1·0582583	1·0648558	54
7	1·0311393	1·0358435	1·0409094	1·0463453	1·0521605	1·0583649	1·0649693	53
8	1·0312147	1·0359249	1·0409969	1·0464391	1·0522607	1·0584717	1·0650828	52
9	1·0312903	1·0360065	1·0410845	1·0465330	1·0523610	1·0585786	1·0651964	51
10	1·0313660	1·0360881	1·0411723	1·0466270	1·0524614	1·0586855	1·0653102	50
11	1·0314418	1·0361699	1·0412601	1·0467211	1·0525619	1·0587926	1·0654240	49
12	1·0315177	1·0362517	1·0413481	1·0468153	1·0526625	1·0588999	1·0655380	48
13	1·0315936	1·0363337	1·0414362	1·0469096	1·0527633	1·0590072	1·0656521	47
14	1·0316697	1·0364157	1·0415243	1·0470040	1·0528641	1·0591146	1·0657663	46
15	1·0317459	1·0364979	1·0416126	1·0470986	1·0529651	1·0592221	1·0658807	45
16	1·0318222	1·0365801	1·0417009	1·0471932	1·0530661	1·0593298	1·0659951	44
17	1·0318985	1·0366625	1·0417894	1·0472879	1·0531673	1·0594376	1·0661097	43
18	1·0319750	1·0367449	1·0418780	1·0473828	1·0532686	1·0595454	1·0662243	42
19	1·0320516	1·0368275	1·0419667	1·0474777	1·0533699	1·0596534	1·0663391	41
20	1·0321282	1·0369101	1·0420554	1·0475728	1·0534714	1·0597615	1·0664540	40
21	1·0322050	1·0369929	1·0421443	1·0476679	1·0535730	1·0598697	1·0665690	39
22	1·0322818	1·0370757	1·0422333	1·0477632	1·0536747	1·0599781	1·0666842	38
23	1·0323588	1·0371587	1·0423224	1·0478586	1·0537765	1·0600865	1·0667994	37
24	1·0324359	1·0372417	1·0424116	1·0479540	1·0538785	1·0601951	1·0669148	36
25	1·0325130	1·0373249	1·0425009	1·0480496	1·0539805	1·0603037	1·0670302	35
26	1·0325903	1·0374082	1·0425903	1·0481453	1·0540826	1·0604125	1·0671458	34
27	1·0326676	1·0374915	1·0426798	1·0482411	1·0541849	1·0605214	1·0672615	33
28	1·0327451	1·0375750	1·0427694	1·0483370	1·0542873	1·0606304	1·0673774	32
29	1·0328227	1·0376585	1·0428591	1·0484330	1·0543897	1·0607395	1·0674933	31
30	1·0329003	1·0377422	1·0429489	1·0485291	1·0544923	1·0608487	1·0676094	30
31	1·0329781	1·0378260	1·0430388	1·0486253	1·0545950	1·0609580	1·0677255	29
32	1·0330559	1·0379098	1·0431289	1·0487217	1·0546978	1·0610675	1·0678418	28
33	1·0331339	1·0379938	1·0432190	1·0488181	1·0548007	1·0611770	1·0679582	27
34	1·0332119	1·0380779	1·0433092	1·0489146	1·0549037	1·0612867	1·0680747	26
35	1·0332901	1·0381621	1·0433995	1·0490113	1·0550068	1·0613965	1·0681914	25
36	1·0333683	1·0382463	1·0434900	1·0491080	1·0551101	1·0615064	1·0683081	24
37	1·0334467	1·0383307	1·0435805	1·0492049	1·0552134	1·0616164	1·0684250	23
38	1·0335251	1·0384152	1·0436712	1·0493019	1·0553169	1·0617265	1·0685420	22
39	1·0336037	1·0384998	1·0437619	1·0493989	1·0554204	1·0618367	1·0686591	21
40	1·0336823	1·0385844	1·0438528	1·0494961	1·0555241	1·0619471	1·0687763	20
41	1·0337611	1·0386692	1·0439437	1·0495934	1·0556279	1·0620575	1·0688936	19
42	1·0338399	1·0387541	1·0440348	1·0496908	1·0557318	1·0621681	1·0690110	18
43	1·0339188	1·0388391	1·0441259	1·0497883	1·0558358	1·0622788	1·0691286	17
44	1·0339979	1·0389242	1·0442172	1·0498859	1·0559399	1·0623896	1·0692463	16
45	1·0340770	1·0390094	1·0443086	1·0499836	1·0560441	1·0625005	1·0693641	15
46	1·0341563	1·0390947	1·0444001	1·0500815	1·0561485	1·0626115	1·0694820	14
47	1·0342356	1·0391800	1·0444917	1·0501794	1·0562529	1·0627227	1·0696000	13
48	1·0343151	1·0392655	1·0445833	1·0502774	1·0563575	1·0628339	1·0697182	12
49	1·0343946	1·0393511	1·0446751	1·0503756	1·0564621	1·0629453	1·0698364	11
50	1·0344743	1·0394368	1·0447670	1·0504738	1·0565669	1·0630568	1·0699548	10
51	1·0345540	1·0395226	1·0448590	1·0505722	1·0566718	1·0631684	1·0700733	9
52	1·0346338	1·0396085	1·0449511	1·0506706	1·0567768	1·0632801	1·0701919	8
53	1·0347138	1·0396945	1·0450433	1·0507692	1·0568819	1·0633919	1·0703106	7
54	1·0347938	1·0397806	1·0451357	1·0508679	1·0569871	1·0635038	1·0704295	6
55	1·0348740	1·0398669	1·0452281	1·0509667	1·0570924	1·0636158	1·0705484	5
56	1·0349542	1·0399532	1·0453206	1·0510656	1·0571978	1·0637280	1·0706675	4
57	1·0350346	1·0400396	1·0454132	1·0511646	1·0573034	1·0638403	1·0707867	3
58	1·0351150	1·0401261	1·0455060	1·0512637	1·0574090	1·0639527	1·0709060	2
59	1·0351955	1·0402127	1·0455988	1·0513629	1·0575148	1·0640652	1·0710254	1
60	1·0352762	1·0402994	1·0456918	1·0514622	1·0576207	1·0641778	1·0711450	0
′	75°	74°	73°	72°	71°	70°	69°	′

′	21°	22°	23°	24°	25°	26°	27°	′
0	1·0711450	1·0785347	1·0863604	1·0946363	1·1033779	1·1126019	1·1223262	60
1	1·0712647	1·0786616	1·0864946	1·0947781	1·1035277	1·1127599	1·1224927	59
2	1·0713844	1·0787885	1·0866289	1·0949201	1·1036775	1·1129179	1·1226592	58
3	1·0715043	1·0789156	1·0867634	1·0950622	1·1038275	1·1130761	1·1228259	57
4	1·0716244	1·0790427	1·0868979	1·0952044	1·1039777	1·1132345	1·1229928	56
5	1·0717445	1·0791700	1·0870326	1·0953467	1·1041279	1·1133929	1·1231598	55
6	1·0718647	1·0792975	1·0871675	1·0954892	1·1042783	1·1135516	1·1233269	54
7	1·0719851	1·0794250	1·0873024	1·0956318	1·1044289	1·1137103	1·1234942	53
8	1·0721056	1·0795527	1·0874375	1·0957746	1·1045795	1·1138692	1·1236616	52
9	1·0722262	1·0796805	1·0875727	1·0959174	1·1047303	1·1140282	1·1238292	51
10	1·0723469	1·0798084	1·0877080	1·0960604	1·1048813	1·1141874	1·1239969	50
11	1·0724678	1·0799364	1·0878435	1·0962036	1·1050324	1·1143467	1·1241648	49
12	1·0725887	1·0800646	1·0879791	1·0963468	1·1051836	1·1145062	1·1243328	48
13	1·0727098	1·0801928	1·0881148	1·0964902	1·1053349	1·1146658	1·1245010	47
14	1·0728310	1·0803212	1·0882506	1·0966337	1·1054864	1·1148255	1·1246693	46
15	1·0729523	1·0804497	1·0883866	1·0967774	1·1056380	1·1149854	1·1248377	45
16	1·0730737	1·0805784	1·0885226	1·0969212	1·1057898	1·1151454	1·1250063	44
17	1·0731953	1·0807071	1·0886589	1·0970651	1·1059417	1·1153056	1·1251750	43
18	1·0733170	1·0808360	1·0887952	1·0972091	1·1060937	1·1154659	1·1253439	42
19	1·0734388	1·0809650	1·0889317	1·0973533	1·1062458	1·1156263	1·1255130	41
20	1·0735607	1·0810942	1·0890682	1·0974976	1·1063981	1·1157869	1·1256821	40
21	1·0736827	1·0812234	1·0892050	1·0976420	1·1065506	1·1159476	1·1258514	39
22	1·0738048	1·0813528	1·0893418	1·0977866	1·1067031	1·1161084	1·1260209	38
23	1·0739271	1·0814823	1·0894788	1·0979313	1·1068558	1·1162694	1·1261905	37
24	1·0740495	1·0816119	1·0896159	1·0980761	1·1070087	1·1164306	1·1263603	36
25	1·0741720	1·0817417	1·0897531	1·0982211	1·1071616	1·1165919	1·1265302	35
26	1·0742946	1·0818715	1·0898904	1·0983662	1·1073147	1·1167533	1·1267003	34
27	1·0744173	1·0820015	1·0900279	1·0985114	1·1074680	1·1169148	1·1268705	33
28	1·0745402	1·0821316	1·0901655	1·0986568	1·1076214	1·1170766	1·1270408	32
29	1·0746631	1·0822618	1·0903032	1·0988023	1·1077749	1·1172384	1·1272113	31
30	1·0747862	1·0823922	1·0904411	1·0989479	1·1079285	1·1174004	1·1273819	30
31	1·0749095	1·0825227	1·0905791	1·0990936	1·1080823	1·1175625	1·1275527	29
32	1·0750328	1·0826533	1·0907172	1·0992395	1·1082363	1·1177248	1·1277237	28
33	1·0751562	1·0827840	1·0908554	1·0993855	1·1083903	1·1178872	1·1278948	27
34	1·0752798	1·0829149	1·0909938	1·0995317	1·1085445	1·1180498	1·1280660	26
35	1·0754035	1·0830458	1·0911323	1·0996779	1·1086989	1·1182124	1·1282374	25
36	1·0755273	1·0831769	1·0912709	1·0998243	1·1088533	1·1183753	1·1284089	24
37	1·0756512	1·0833081	1·0914097	1·0999709	1·1090079	1·1185383	1·1285806	23
38	1·0757753	1·0834395	1·0915485	1·1001175	1·1091627	1·1187014	1·1287524	22
39	1·0758995	1·0835709	1·0916876	1·1002644	1·1093176	1·1188647	1·1289244	21
40	1·0760237	1·0837025	1·0918267	1·1004113	1·1094726	1·1190281	1·1290965	20
41	1·0761481	1·0838342	1·0919659	1·1005584	1·1096277	1·1191916	1·1292687	19
42	1·0762727	1·0839661	1·0921053	1·1007056	1·1097830	1·1193553	1·1294412	18
43	1·0763973	1·0840980	1·0922448	1·1008529	1·1099385	1·1195191	1·1296137	17
44	1·0765221	1·0842301	1·0923845	1·1010004	1·1100940	1·1196831	1·1297864	16
45	1·0766470	1·0843623	1·0925243	1·1011480	1·1102498	1·1198472	1·1299593	15
46	1·0767720	1·0844947	1·0926642	1·1012957	1·1104056	1·1200115	1·1301323	14
47	1·0768971	1·0846271	1·0928042	1·1014436	1·1105616	1·1201759	1·1303055	13
48	1·0770224	1·0847597	1·0929444	1·1015916	1·1107177	1·1203405	1·1304788	12
49	1·0771477	1·0848924	1·0930846	1·1017397	1·1108740	1·1205051	1·1306522	11
50	1·0772732	1·0850252	1·0932251	1·1018879	1·1110304	1·1206700	1·1308258	10
51	1·0773988	1·0851582	1·0933656	1·1020363	1·1111869	1·1208350	1·1309996	9
52	1·0775246	1·0852913	1·0935063	1·1021849	1·1113436	1·1210001	1·1311735	8
53	1·0776504	1·0854245	1·0936471	1·1023335	1·1115004	1·1211653	1·1313475	7
54	1·0777764	1·0855578	1·0937880	1·1024823	1·1116573	1·1213308	1·1315217	6
55	1·0779025	1·0856912	1·0939291	1·1026313	1·1118144	1·1214963	1·1316961	5
56	1·0780287	1·0858248	1·0940702	1·1027803	1·1119716	1·1216620	1·1318706	4
57	1·0781550	1·0859585	1·0942116	1·1029295	1·1121290	1·1218278	1·1320452	3
58	1·0782815	1·0860924	1·0943530	1·1030789	1·1122865	1·1219938	1·1322200	2
59	1·0784080	1·0862263	1·0944946	1·1032283	1·1124442	1·1221600	1·1323950	1
60	1·0785347	1·0863604	1·0946363	1·1033779	1·1126019	1·1223262	1·1325701	0
′	68°	67°	66°	65°	64°	63°	62°	′

′	28°	29°	30°	31°	32°	33°	34°	′
0	1·1325701	1·1433541	1·1547005	1·1666334	1·1791784	1·1923633	1·2062179	60
1	1·1327453	1·1435385	1·1548945	1·1668374	1·1793928	1·1925886	1·2064547	59
2	1·1329207	1·1437231	1·1550887	1·1670416	1·1796074	1·1928142	1·2066917	58
3	1·1330962	1·1439078	1·1552830	1·1672459	1·1798222	1·1930399	1·2069288	57
4	1·1332719	1·1440927	1·1554775	1·1674504	1·1800372	1·1932658	1·2071662	56
5	1·1334478	1·1442778	1·1556722	1·1676551	1·1802523	1·1934918	1·2074037	55
6	1·1336238	1·1444630	1·1558670	1·1678599	1·1804676	1·1937181	1·2076415	54
7	1·1337999	1·1446484	1·1560620	1·1680649	1·1806831	1·1939446	1·2078794	53
8	1·1339762	1·1448339	1·1562572	1·1682701	1·1808988	1·1941712	1·2081175	52
9	1·1341527	1·1450196	1·1564525	1·1684755	1·1811146	1·1943980	1·2083559	51
10	1·1343293	1·1452055	1·1566480	1·1686810	1·1813307	1·1946251	1·2085944	50
11	1·1345060	1·1453915	1·1568436	1·1688867	1·1815469	1·1948523	1·2088331	49
12	1·1346829	1·1455776	1·1570394	1·1690926	1·1817633	1·1950796	1·2090720	48
13	1·1348600	1·1457639	1·1572354	1·1692986	1·1819798	1·1953072	1·2093112	47
14	1·1350372	1·1459504	1·1574315	1·1695048	1·1821966	1·1955350	1·2095505	46
15	1·1352146	1·1461371	1·1576278	1·1697112	1·1824135	1·1957629	1·2097900	45
16	1·1353921	1·1463238	1·1578243	1·1699178	1·1826306	1·1959911	1·2100297	44
17	1·1355697	1·1465108	1·1580209	1·1701245	1·1828479	1·1962194	1·2102696	43
18	1·1357476	1·1466979	1·1582177	1·1703314	1·1830654	1·1964479	1·2105097	42
19	1·1359255	1·1468852	1·1584146	1·1705385	1·1832830	1·1966767	1·2107500	41
20	1·1361036	1·1470726	1·1586118	1·1707457	1·1835008	1·1969056	1·2109905	40
21	1·1362819	1·1472602	1·1588091	1·1709531	1·1837188	1·1971346	1·2112312	39
22	1·1364603	1·1474479	1·1590065	1·1711607	1·1839370	1·1973639	1·2114721	38
23	1·1366389	1·1476358	1·1592041	1·1713685	1·1841554	1·1975934	1·2117132	37
24	1·1368176	1·1478239	1·1594019	1·1715764	1·1843739	1·1978230	1·2119545	36
25	1·1369965	1·1480121	1·1595999	1·1717845	1·1845927	1·1980529	1·2121960	35
26	1·1371755	1·1482005	1·1597980	1·1719928	1·1848116	1·1982829	1·2124377	34
27	1·1373547	1·1483890	1·1599963	1·1722013	1·1850307	1·1985131	1·2126795	33
28	1·1375341	1·1485777	1·1601947	1·1724099	1·1852500	1·1987435	1·2129216	32
29	1·1377135	1·1487665	1·1603933	1·1726187	1·1854694	1·1989741	1·2131639	31
30	1·1378932	1·1489555	1·1605921	1·1728277	1·1856890	1·1992049	1·2134064	30
31	1·1380730	1·1491447	1·1607911	1·1730368	1·1859089	1·1994359	1·2136491	29
32	1·1382529	1·1493340	1·1609902	1·1732462	1·1861289	1·1996671	1·2138920	28
33	1·1384330	1·1495235	1·1611894	1·1734557	1·1863490	1·1998985	1·2141351	27
34	1·1386133	1·1497132	1·1613889	1·1736653	1·1865694	1·2001300	1·2143784	26
35	1·1387937	1·1499030	1·1615885	1·1738752	1·1867900	1·2003618	1·2146218	25
36	1·1389742	1·1500930	1·1617883	1·1740852	1·1870107	1·2005937	1·2148655	24
37	1·1391550	1·1502831	1·1619882	1·1742954	1·1872316	1·2008258	1·2151094	23
38	1·1393358	1·1504734	1·1621883	1·1745058	1·1874527	1·2010582	1·2153535	22
39	1·1395169	1·1506638	1·1623886	1·1747163	1·1876740	1·2012907	1·2155978	21
40	1·1396980	1·1508544	1·1625891	1·1749270	1·1878954	1·2015234	1·2158423	20
41	1·1398794	1·1510452	1·1627897	1·1751379	1·1881171	1·2017563	1·2160870	19
42	1·1400608	1·1512361	1·1629905	1·1753490	1·1883389	1·2019804	1·2163319	18
43	1·1402425	1·1514272	1·1631914	1·1755603	1·1885609	1·2022226	1·2165770	17
44	1·1404243	1·1516185	1·1633925	1·1757717	1·1887831	1·2024561	1·2168223	16
45	1·1406062	1·1518099	1·1635938	1·1759833	1·1890055	1·2026898	1·2170678	15
46	1·1407883	1·1520015	1·1637953	1·1761951	1·1892280	1·2029236	1·2173135	14
47	1·1409706	1·1521932	1·1639969	1·1764070	1·1894508	1·2031577	1·2175594	13
48	1·1411530	1·1523851	1·1641987	1·1766191	1·1896737	1·2033919	1·2178055	12
49	1·1413356	1·1525772	1·1644007	1·1768314	1·1898968	1·2036264	1·2180518	11
50	1·1415183	1·1527694	1·1646028	1·1770439	1·1901201	1·2038610	1·2182983	10
51	1·1417012	1·1529618	1·1648051	1·1772566	1·1903436	1·2040958	1·2185450	9
52	1·1418842	1·1531543	1·1650076	1·1774694	1·1905673	1·2043308	1·2187919	8
53	1·1420674	1·1533470	1·1652102	1·1776824	1·1907911	1·2045660	1·2190390	7
54	1·1422507	1·1535399	1·1654130	1·1778956	1·1910152	1·2048014	1·2192864	6
55	1·1424342	1·1537329	1·1656160	1·1781089	1·1912394	1·2050370	1·2195339	5
56	1·1426179	1·1539261	1·1658191	1·1783225	1·1914638	1·2052725	1·2197816	4
57	1·1428017	1·1541195	1·1660224	1·1785362	1·1916884	1·2055088	1·2200296	3
58	1·1429857	1·1543130	1·1662259	1·1787501	1·1919132	1·2057450	1·2202777	2
59	1·1431698	1·1545067	1·1664296	1·1789642	1·1921381	1·2059814	1·2205260	1
60	1·1433541	1·1547005	1·1666334	1·1791784	1·1923633	1·2062179	1·2207746	0
′	61°	60°	59°	58°	57°	56°	55°	′

NATURAL COSECANTS.

′	35°	36°	37°	38°	39°	40°	41°	′
0	1·2207746	1·2360680	1·2521357	1·2690182	1·2867596	1·3054073	1·3250130	60
1	1·2210233	1·2363293	1·2524102	1·2693067	1·2870628	1·3057261	1·3253482	59
2	1·2212723	1·2365909	1·2526850	1·2695955	1·2873663	1·3060451	1·3256837	58
3	1·2215215	1·2368526	1·2529601	1·2698845	1·2876700	1·3063644	1·3260194	57
4	1·2217708	1·2371146	1·2532353	1·2701737	1·2879740	1·3066839	1·3263554	56
5	1·2220204	1·2373768	1·2535108	1·2704632	1·2882782	1·3070038	1·3266918	55
6	1·2222702	1·2376393	1·2537865	1·2707529	1·2885827	1·3073239	1·3270284	54
7	1·2225202	1·2379009	1·2540625	1·2710429	1·2888875	1·3076442	1·3273663	53
8	1·2227703	1·2381647	1·2543387	1·2713331	1·2891925	1·3079649	1·3277024	52
9	1·2230207	1·2384278	1·2546151	1·2716235	1·2894977	1·3082858	1·3280399	51
10	1·2232713	1·2386911	1·2548917	1·2719142	1·2898032	1·3086069	1·3283776	50
11	1·2235222	1·2389546	1·2551685	1·2722052	1·2901090	1·3089284	1·3287156	49
12	1·2237732	1·2392183	1·2554456	1·2724963	1·2904150	1·3092501	1·3290559	48
13	1·2240244	1·2394823	1·2557229	1·2727877	1·2907213	1·3095720	1·3293925	47
14	1·2242758	1·2397464	1·2560005	1·2730794	1·2910278	1·3098943	1·3297314	46
15	1·2245274	1·2400108	1·2562782	1·2733712	1·2913346	1·3102168	1·3300706	45
16	1·2247793	1·2402754	1·2565562	1·2736634	1·2916416	1·3105396	1·3304100	44
17	1·2250313	1·2405402	1·2568345	1·2739557	1·2919489	1·3108626	1·3307497	43
18	1·2252836	1·2408052	1·2571129	1·2742484	1·2922564	1·3111860	1·3310897	42
19	1·2255361	1·2410704	1·2573916	1·2745412	1·2925642	1·3115095	1·3314301	41
20	1·2257887	1·2413359	1·2576705	1·2748343	1·2928723	1·3118334	1·3317707	40
21	1·2260416	1·2416016	1·2579497	1·2751276	1·2931806	1·3121575	1·3321115	39
22	1·2262947	1·2418675	1·2582291	1·2754212	1·2934892	1·3124820	1·3324527	38
23	1·2265480	1·2421336	1·2585087	1·2757151	1·2937980	1·3128066	1·3327942	37
24	1·2268015	1·2423999	1·2587885	1·2760091	1·2941071	1·3131316	1·3331359	36
25	1·2270552	1·2426665	1·2590686	1·2763034	1·2944164	1·3134568	1·3334779	35
26	1·2273091	1·2429333	1·2593489	1·2765980	1·2947260	1·3137823	1·3338203	34
27	1·2275633	1·2432003	1·2596294	1·2768928	1·2950359	1·3141081	1·3341629	33
28	1·2278176	1·2434675	1·2599102	1·2771878	1·2953460	1·3144341	1·3345058	32
29	1·2280722	1·2437349	1·2601912	1·2774831	1·2956564	1·3147604	1·3348489	31
30	1·2283269	1·2440026	1·2604724	1·2777787	1·2959670	1·3150870	1·3351924	30
31	1·2285819	1·2442704	1·2607539	1·2780744	1·2962779	1·3154139	1·3355362	29
32	1·2288371	1·2445385	1·2610356	1·2783705	1·2965890	1·3157410	1·3358802	28
33	1·2290924	1·2448069	1·2613175	1·2786667	1·2969004	1·3160684	1·3362246	27
34	1·2293480	1·2450754	1·2615997	1·2789632	1·2972121	1·3163961	1·3365692	26
35	1·2296039	1·2453442	1·2618820	1·2792600	1·2975240	1·3167240	1·3369141	25
36	1·2298599	1·2456131	1·2621647	1·2795570	1·2978362	1·3170523	1·3372594	24
37	1·2301161	1·2458823	1·2624475	1·2798543	1·2981487	1·3173808	1·3376049	23
38	1·2303725	1·2461518	1·2627306	1·2801518	1·2984614	1·3177096	1·3379507	22
39	1·2306292	1·2464214	1·2630140	1·2804495	1·2987743	1·3180386	1·3382968	21
40	1·2308861	1·2466913	1·2632975	1·2807475	1·2990876	1·3183680	1·3386432	20
41	1·2311432	1·2469614	1·2635813	1·2810457	1·2994011	1·3186976	1·3389898	19
42	1·2314004	1·2472317	1·2638653	1·2813442	1·2997148	1·3190274	1·3393368	18
43	1·2316579	1·2475022	1·2641496	1·2816430	1·3000288	1·3193576	1·3396841	17
44	1·2319156	1·2477730	1·2644341	1·2819419	1·3003431	1·3196881	1·3400316	16
45	1·2321736	1·2480440	1·2647188	1·2822412	1·3006576	1·3200188	1·3403795	15
46	1·2324317	1·2483152	1·2650038	1·2825407	1·3009724	1·3203498	1·3407276	14
47	1·2326900	1·2485866	1·2652890	1·2828404	1·3012875	1·3206810	1·3410761	13
48	1·2329486	1·2488583	1·2655745	1·2831404	1·3016028	1·3210126	1·3414248	12
49	1·2332074	1·2491302	1·2658601	1·2834406	1·3019184	1·3213444	1·3417738	11
50	1·2334664	1·2494023	1·2661460	1·2837411	1·3022343	1·3216765	1·3421232	10
51	1·2337256	1·2496746	1·2664322	1·2840418	1·3025504	1·3220089	1·3424728	9
52	1·2339850	1·2499471	1·2667186	1·2843428	1·3028667	1·3223416	1·3428227	8
53	1·2342446	1·2502199	1·2670052	1·2846440	1·3031834	1·3226745	1·3431729	7
54	1·2345044	1·2504929	1·2672921	1·2849455	1·3035003	1·3230078	1·3435234	6
55	1·2347645	1·2507661	1·2675792	1·2852472	1·3038175	1·3233413	1·3438742	5
56	1·2350248	1·2510396	1·2678665	1·2855492	1·3041349	1·3236750	1·3442253	4
57	1·2352852	1·2513133	1·2681541	1·2858514	1·3044526	1·3240091	1·3445767	3
58	1·2355459	1·2515872	1·2684419	1·2861539	1·3047706	1·3243435	1·3449284	2
59	1·2358069	1·2518613	1·2687299	1·2864566	1·3050888	1·3246781	1·3452804	1
60	1·2360680	1·2521357	1·2690182	1·2867596	1·3054073	1·3250130	1·3456327	0
′	54°	53°	52°	51°	50°	49°	48°	′

NATURAL COSECANTS.

′	42°	43°	44°	45°	46°	47°	48°	′
0	1·3456327	1·3673275	1·3901636	1·4142136	1·4395565	1·4662792	1·4944765	60
1	1·3459853	1·3676985	1·3905543	1·4146251	1·4399904	1·4667368	1·4949596	59
2	1·3463382	1·3680699	1·3909453	1·4150370	1·4404246	1·4671948	1·4954431	58
3	1·3466914	1·3684416	1·3913366	1·4154493	1·4408592	1·4676532	1·4959270	57
4	1·3470449	1·3688136	1·3917283	1·4158619	1·4412941	1·4681120	1·4964113	56
5	1·3473987	1·3691859	1·3921203	1·4162749	1·4417295	1·4685713	1·4968961	55
6	1·3477528	1·3695586	1·3925127	1·4166883	1·4421652	1·4690309	1·4973813	54
7	1·3481072	1·3699315	1·3929054	1·4171020	1·4426013	1·4694910	1·4978670	53
8	1·3484619	1·3703048	1·3932985	1·4175161	1·4430379	1·4699514	1·4983531	52
9	1·3488168	1·3706784	1·3936918	1·4179306	1·4434748	1·4704123	1·4988397	51
10	1·3491721	1·3710523	1·3940856	1·4183454	1·4439120	1·4708736	1·4993267	50
11	1·3495277	1·3714266	1·3944796	1·4187605	1·4443497	1·4713354	1·4998141	49
12	1·3498836	1·3718011	1·3948740	1·4191761	1·4447878	1·4717975	1·5003020	48
13	1·3502398	1·3721760	1·3952688	1·4195920	1·4452262	1·4722600	1·5007903	47
14	1·3505963	1·3725512	1·3956639	1·4200082	1·4456651	1·4727230	1·5012791	46
15	1·3509531	1·3729268	1·3960593	1·4204248	1·4461043	1·4731864	1·5017683	45
16	1·3513102	1·3733026	1·3964551	1·4208418	1·4465439	1·4736502	1·5022580	44
17	1·3516677	1·3736788	1·3968512	1·4212592	1·4469839	1·4741144	1·5027481	43
18	1·3520254	1·3740553	1·3972477	1·4216769	1·4474243	1·4745790	1·5032387	42
19	1·3523834	1·3744321	1·3976445	1·4220950	1·4478651	1·4750440	1·5037297	41
20	1·3527417	1·3748092	1·3980416	1·4225134	1·4483063	1·4755095	1·5042211	40
21	1·3531003	1·3751867	1·3984391	1·4229323	1·4487478	1·4759754	1·5047131	39
22	1·3534593	1·3755645	1·3988369	1·4233514	1·4491898	1·4764417	1·5052054	38
23	1·3538185	1·3759426	1·3992351	1·4237710	1·4496322	1·4769084	1·5056982	37
24	1·3541780	1·3763210	1·3996336	1·4241909	1·4500749	1·4773755	1·5061915	36
25	1·3545379	1·3766998	1·4000325	1·4246112	1·4505181	1·4778431	1·5066852	35
26	1·3548980	1·3770789	1·4004317	1·4250319	1·4509616	1·4783111	1·5071793	34
27	1·3552585	1·3774583	1·4008313	1·4254529	1·4514055	1·4787795	1·5076739	33
28	1·3556193	1·3778380	1·4012312	1·4258743	1·4518498	1·4792483	1·5081690	32
29	1·3559803	1·3782181	1·4016315	1·4262961	1·4522946	1·4797176	1·5086645	31
30	1·3563417	1·3785985	1·4020321	1·4267182	1·4527397	1·4801872	1·5091605	30
31	1·3567034	1·3789792	1·4024330	1·4271407	1·4531852	1·4806573	1·5096569	29
32	1·3570654	1·3793602	1·4028343	1·4275636	1·4536311	1·4811278	1·5101538	28
33	1·3574277	1·3797416	1·4032360	1·4279868	1·4540774	1·4815988	1·5106511	27
34	1·3577903	1·3801233	1·4036380	1·4284105	1·4545241	1·4820702	1·5111489	26
35	1·3581532	1·3805053	1·4040403	1·4288345	1·4549712	1·4825420	1·5116472	25
36	1·3585164	1·3808877	1·4044430	1·4292588	1·4554187	1·4830142	1·5121459	24
37	1·3588800	1·3812704	1·4048461	1·4296836	1·4558666	1·4834868	1·5126450	23
38	1·3592438	1·3816534	1·4052494	1·4301087	1·4563149	1·4839599	1·5131446	22
39	1·3596080	1·3820367	1·4056532	1·4305342	1·4567636	1·4844334	1·5136447	21
40	1·3599725	1·3824204	1·4060573	1·4309600	1·4572127	1·4849073	1·5141452	20
41	1·3603372	1·3828044	1·4064617	1·4313863	1·4576621	1·4853817	1·5146462	19
42	1·3607023	1·3831887	1·4068665	1·4318129	1·4581120	1·4858565	1·5151477	18
43	1·3610677	1·3835734	1·4072717	1·4322399	1·4585623	1·4863317	1·5156496	17
44	1·3614334	1·3839584	1·4076772	1·4326672	1·4590130	1·4868073	1·5161520	16
45	1·3617995	1·3843437	1·4080831	1·4330950	1·4594641	1·4872834	1·5166548	15
46	1·3621658	1·3847294	1·4084893	1·4335231	1·4599156	1·4877599	1·5171581	14
47	1·3625324	1·3851153	1·4088958	1·4339516	1·4603675	1·4882369	1·5176619	13
48	1·3628994	1·3855017	1·4093028	1·4343805	1·4608198	1·4887142	1·5181661	12
49	1·3632667	1·3858883	1·4097100	1·4348097	1·4612726	1·4891920	1·5186708	11
50	1·3636343	1·3862753	1·4101177	1·4352393	1·4617257	1·4896703	1·5191759	10
51	1·3640022	1·3866626	1·4105257	1·4356693	1·4621792	1·4901489	1·5196815	9
52	1·3643704	1·3870503	1·4109340	1·4360997	1·4626331	1·4906280	1·5201876	8
53	1·3647389	1·3874383	1·4113427	1·4365305	1·4630875	1·4911076	1·5206942	7
54	1·3651078	1·3878266	1·4117517	1·4369616	1·4635422	1·4915876	1·5212012	6
55	1·3654770	1·3882153	1·4121612	1·4373932	1·4639973	1·4920680	1·5217087	5
56	1·3658464	1·3886043	1·4125709	1·4378251	1·4644529	1·4925488	1·5222166	4
57	1·3662162	1·3889936	1·4129810	1·4382574	1·4649089	1·4930301	1·5227250	3
58	1·3665863	1·3893832	1·4133915	1·4386900	1·4653652	1·4935118	1·5232339	2
59	1·3669567	1·3897733	1·4138024	1·4391231	1·4658220	1·4939940	1·5237433	1
60	1·3673275	1·3901636	1·4142136	1·4395565	1·4662792	1·4944765	1·5242531	0
′	47°	46°	45°	44°	43°	42°	41°	′

NATURAL COSECANTS.

′	49°	50°	51°	52°	53°	54°	55°	′
0	1·5242531	1·5557238	1·5890157	1·6242692	1·6616401	1·7013016	1·7434468	60
1	1·5247634	1·5562634	1·5895868	1·6248743	1·6622819	1·7019831	1·7441715	59
2	1·5252741	1·5568035	1·5901584	1·6254799	1·6629243	1·7026653	1·7448969	58
3	1·5257854	1·5573441	1·5907306	1·6260861	1·6635673	1·7033482	1·7456230	57
4	1·5262971	1·5578852	1·5913033	1·6266929	1·6642110	1·7040318	1·7463499	56
5	1·5268093	1·5584268	1·5918766	1·6273003	1·6648553	1·7047160	1·7470776	55
6	1·5273219	1·5589689	1·5924504	1·6279083	1·6655002	1·7054010	1·7478060	54
7	1·5278351	1·5595115	1·5930247	1·6285169	1·6661458	1·7060867	1·7485352	53
8	1·5283487	1·5600546	1·5935996	1·6291261	1·6667920	1·7067730	1·7492651	52
9	1·5288627	1·5605982	1·5941751	1·6297359	1·6674389	1·7074601	1·7499958	51
10	1·5293773	1·5611424	1·5947511	1·6303462	1·6680864	1·7081478	1·7507273	50
11	1·5298923	1·5616871	1·5953276	1·6309572	1·6687345	1·7088362	1·7514595	49
12	1·5304078	1·5622322	1·5959048	1·6315688	1·6693833	1·7095254	1·7521924	48
13	1·5309238	1·5627779	1·5964824	1·6321809	1·6700328	1·7102152	1·7529262	47
14	1·5314403	1·5633241	1·5970606	1·6327937	1·6706828	1·7109058	1·7536607	46
15	1·5319572	1·5638708	1·5976394	1·6334070	1·6713336	1·7115970	1·7543959	45
16	1·5324746	1·5644181	1·5982187	1·6340210	1·6719850	1·7122890	1·7551320	44
17	1·5329925	1·5649658	1·5987986	1·6346355	1·6726370	1·7129817	1·7558687	43
18	1·5335109	1·5655141	1·5993790	1·6352507	1·6732897	1·7136750	1·7566063	42
19	1·5340297	1·5660628	1·5999600	1·6358664	1·6739430	1·7143691	1·7573446	41
20	1·5345491	1·5666121	1·6005416	1·6364828	1·6745970	1·7150639	1·7580837	40
21	1·5350689	1·5671619	1·6011237	1·6370997	1·6752517	1·7157594	1·7588236	39
22	1·5355892	1·5677123	1·6017064	1·6377173	1·6759070	1·7164556	1·7595642	38
23	1·5361100	1·5682631	1·6022896	1·6383355	1·6765629	1·7171525	1·7603057	37
24	1·5366313	1·5688145	1·6028734	1·6389542	1·6772195	1·7178501	1·7610478	36
25	1·5371530	1·5693664	1·6034577	1·6395736	1·6778768	1·7185484	1·7617908	35
26	1·5376752	1·5699188	1·6040426	1·6401936	1·6785347	1·7192475	1·7625345	34
27	1·5381980	1·5704717	1·6046281	1·6408142	1·6791933	1·7199472	1·7632791	33
28	1·5387212	1·5710252	1·6052142	1·6414354	1·6798525	1·7206477	1·7640244	32
29	1·5392449	1·5715792	1·6058008	1·6420572	1·6805124	1·7213489	1·7647704	31
30	1·5397690	1·5721337	1·6063879	1·6426796	1·6811730	1·7220508	1·7655173	30
31	1·5402937	1·5726887	1·6069757	1·6433027	1·6818342	1·7227534	1·7662649	29
32	1·5408189	1·5732443	1·6075640	1·6439263	1·6824961	1·7234568	1·7670133	28
33	1·5413445	1·5738004	1·6081528	1·6445506	1·6831586	1·7241609	1·7677625	27
34	1·5418706	1·5743570	1·6087423	1·6451754	1·6838219	1·7248657	1·7685125	26
35	1·5423973	1·5749141	1·6093323	1·6458009	1·6844857	1·7255712	1·7692633	25
36	1·5429244	1·5754718	1·6099228	1·6464270	1·6851503	1·7262774	1·7700149	24
37	1·5434520	1·5760300	1·6105140	1·6470537	1·6858155	1·7269844	1·7707672	23
38	1·5439801	1·5765887	1·6111057	1·6476811	1·6864814	1·7276921	1·7715204	22
39	1·5445087	1·5771479	1·6116980	1·6483090	1·6871479	1·7284005	1·7722743	21
40	1·5450378	1·5777077	1·6122908	1·6489376	1·6878151	1·7291096	1·7730290	20
41	1·5455673	1·5782680	1·6128843	1·6495668	1·6884830	1·7298195	1·7737845	19
42	1·5460974	1·5788289	1·6134783	1·6501966	1·6891516	1·7305301	1·7745409	18
43	1·5466280	1·5793902	1·6140728	1·6508270	1·6898208	1·7312414	1·7752980	17
44	1·5471590	1·5799521	1·6146680	1·6514581	1·6904907	1·7319535	1·7760559	16
45	1·5476906	1·5805146	1·6152637	1·6520898	1·6911613	1·7326663	1·7768146	15
46	1·5482226	1·5810776	1·6158600	1·6527221	1·6918326	1·7333798	1·7775741	14
47	1·5487552	1·5816411	1·6164569	1·6533550	1·6925045	1·7340941	1·7783344	13
48	1·5492882	1·5822051	1·6170544	1·6539885	1·6931771	1·7348091	1·7790955	12
49	1·5498218	1·5827697	1·6176524	1·6546227	1·6938504	1·7355248	1·7798574	11
50	1·5503558	1·5833348	1·6182510	1·6552575	1·6945244	1·7362413	1·7806201	10
51	1·5508904	1·5839005	1·6188502	1·6558929	1·6951990	1·7369585	1·7813836	9
52	1·5514254	1·5844667	1·6194500	1·6565290	1·6958744	1·7376764	1·7821479	8
53	1·5519610	1·5850334	1·6200504	1·6571657	1·6965504	1·7383951	1·7829131	7
54	1·5524970	1·5856007	1·6206513	1·6578030	1·6972271	1·7391145	1·7836790	6
55	1·5530335	1·5861685	1·6212528	1·6584409	1·6979044	1·7398347	1·7844457	5
56	1·5535706	1·5867369	1·6218549	1·6590795	1·6985825	1·7405556	1·7852133	4
57	1·5541081	1·5873058	1·6224576	1·6597187	1·6992612	1·7412773	1·7859817	3
58	1·5546462	1·5878752	1·6230609	1·6603586	1·6999407	1·7419997	1·7867508	2
59	1·5551848	1·5884452	1·6236648	1·6609990	1·7006208	1·7427229	1·7875208	1
60	1·5557238	1·5890157	1·6242692	1·6616401	1·7013016	1·7434468	1·7882916	0
′	40°	39°	38°	37°	36°	35°	34°	′

NATURAL COSECANTS.

′	56°	57°	58°	59°	60°	61°	62°	′
0	1·7882916	1·8360785	1·8870799	1·9416040	2·0000000	2·0626653	2·1300545	60
1	1·7890633	1·8369013	1·8879589	1·9425445	2·0010083	2·0637484	2·1312205	59
2	1·7898357	1·8377251	1·8888388	1·9434861	2·0020177	2·0648328	2·1323880	58
3	1·7906090	1·8385498	1·8897197	1·9444288	2·0030283	2·0659186	2·1335570	57
4	1·7913831	1·8393753	1·8906016	1·9453725	2·0040402	2·0670056	2·1347274	56
5	1·7921580	1·8402018	1·8914845	1·9463173	2·0050532	2·0680940	2·1358993	55
6	1·7929337	1·8410292	7.8923684	1·9472632	2·0060674	2·0691836	2·1370726	54
7	1·7937102	1·8418574	1·8932532	1·9482102	2·0070828	2·0702746	2·1382475	53
8	1·7944876	1·8426866	1·8941391	1·9491583	2·0080994	2·0713670	2·1394238	52
9	1·7952658	1·8435166	1·8950259	1·9501075	2·0091172	2·0724606	2·1406015	51
10	1·7960449	1·8443476	1·8959138	1·9510577	2·0101362	2·0735556	2·1417808	50
11	1·7968247	1·8451795	1·8968026	1·9520091	2·0111564	2·0746519	2·1429615	49
12	1·7976054	1·8460123	1·8976924	1·9529615	2·0121779	2·0757496	2·1441438	48
13	1·7983869	1·8468460	1·8985832	1·9539150	2·0132005	2·0768486	2·1453275	47
14	1·7991693	1·8476806	1·8994750	1·9548697	2·0142243	2·0779489	2·1465127	46
15	1·7999524	1·8485161	1·9003678	1·9558254	2·0152494	2·0790506	2·1476993	45
16	1·8007365	1·8493525	1·9012616	1·9567822	2·0162756	2·0801536	2·1488875	44
17	1·8015213	1·8501898	1·9021564	1·9577402	2·0173031	2·0812580	2·1500772	43
18	1·8023070	1·8510281	1·9030522	1·9586992	2·0183318	2·0823637	2·1512684	42
19	1·8030935	1·8518672	1·9039491	1·9596593	2·0193618	2·0834708	2·1524611	41
20	1·8038809	1·8527073	1·9048469	1·9606206	2·0203929	2·0845792	2·1536553	40
21	1·8046601	1·8535483	1·9057457	1·9615829	2·0214253	2·0856890	2·1548510	39
22	1·8054582	1·8543903	1·9066456	1·9625464	2·0224589	2·0868002	2·1560482	38
23	1·8062481	1·8552331	1·9075464	1·9635110	2·0234937	2·0879127	2·1572469	37
24	1·8070388	1·8560769	1·9084483	1·9644767	2·0245297	2·0890265	2·1584471	36
25	1·8078304	1·8569216	1·9093512	1·9654435	2·0255670	2·0901418	2·1596489	35
26	1·8086228	1·8577672	1·9102551	1·9664114	2·0266056	2·0912584	2·1608522	34
27	1·8094161	1·8586138	1·9111600	1·9673805	2·0276453	2·0923764	2·1620570	33
28	1·8102102	1·8594612	1·9120659	1·9683507	2·0286863	2·0934957	2·1632633	32
29	1·8110052	1·8603097	1·9129729	1·9693220	2·0297286	2·0946164	2·1644712	31
30	1·8118010	1·8611590	1·9138809	1·9702944	2·0307720	2·0957385	2·1656806	30
31	1·8125977	1·8620093	1·9147899	1·9712680	2·0318168	2·0968620	2·1668915	29
32	1·8133953	1·8628605	1·9156999	1·9722427	2·0328628	2·0979869	2·1681040	28
33	1·8141937	1·8637126	1·9166110	1·9732185	2·0339100	2·0991131	2·1693180	27
34	1·8149929	1·8645657	1·9175230	1·9741954	2·0349585	2·1002408	2·1705335	26
35	1·8157930	1·8654197	1·9184362	1·9751735	2·0360082	2·1013698	2·1717506	25
36	1·8165940	1·8662747	1·9193503	1·9761527	2·0370592	2·1025002	2·1729693	24
37	1·8173958	1·8671306	1·9202655	1·9771331	2·0381114	2·1036320	2·1741895	23
38	1·8181985	1·8679875	1·9211817	1·9781146	2·0391649	2·1047652	2·1754113	22
39	1·8190021	1·8688453	1·9220990	1·9790972	2·0402197	2·1058998	2·1766346	21
40	1·8198065	1·8697040	1·9230173	1·9800810	2·0412757	2·1070359	2·1778595	20
41	1·8206118	1·8705637	1·9239366	1·9810659	2·0423330	2·1081733	2·1790859	19
42	1·8214179	1·8714244	1·9248570	1·9820520	2·0433916	2·1093121	2·1803139	18
43	1·8222249	1·8722859	1·9257784	1·9830393	2·0444515	2·1104523	2·1815435	17
44	1·8230328	1·8731485	1·9267009	1·9840276	2·0455126	2·1115940	2·1827746	16
45	1·8238416	1·8740120	1·9276244	1·9850172	2·0465750	2·1127371	2·1840074	15
46	1·8246512	1·8748764	1·9285490	1·9860080	2·0476386	2·1138815	2·1852417	14
47	1·8254617	1·8757419	1·9294746	1·9869997	2·0487036	2·1150274	2·1864775	13
48	1·8262731	1·8766082	1·9304013	1·9879927	2·0497698	2·1161748	2·1877150	12
49	1·8270854	1·8774755	1·9313290	1·9889869	2·0508373	2·1173235	2·1889541	11
50	1·8278985	1·8783438	1·9322578	1·9899822	2·0519061	2·1184737	2·1901947	10
51	1·8287125	1·8792131	1·9331876	1·9909787	2·0529762	2·1196253	2·1914370	9
52	1·8295274	1·8800833	1·9341185	1·9919764	2·0540476	2·1207783	2·1926808	8
53	1·8303432	1·8809545	1·9350505	1·9929752	2·0551203	2·1219328	2·1939262	7
54	1·8311599	1·8818266	1·9359835	1·9939753	2·0561942	2·1230887	2·1951733	6
55	1·8319774	1·8826998	1·9369176	1·9949764	2·0572695	2·1242460	2·1964219	5
56	1·8327959	1·8835738	1·9378527	1·9959788	2·0583460	2·1254048	2·1976721	4
57	1·8336152	1·8844489	1·9387889	1·9969823	2·0594239	2·1265651	2·1989240	3
58	1·8344354	1·8853249	1·9397262	1·9979870	2·0605031	2·1277267	2·2001775	2
59	1·8352565	1·8862019	1·9406646	1·9989929	2·0615836	2·1288899	2·2014326	1
60	1·8360785	1·8870799	1·9416040	2·0000000	2·0626653	2·1300545	2·2026893	0
′	33°	32°	31°	30°	29°	28°	27°	′

′	63°	64°	65°	66°	67°	68°	69°	′
0	2·2026893	2·2811720	2·3662016	2·4585933	2·5593047	2·6694672	2·7904281	60
1	2·2039476	2·2825335	2·3676787	2·4602008	2·5610599	2·6713906	2·7925444	59
2	2·2052075	2·2838967	2·3691578	2·4618106	2·5628176	2·6733171	2·7946641	58
3	2·2064891	2·2852618	2·3706390	2·4634227	2·5645781	2·6752465	2·7967873	57
4	2·2077323	2·2866286	2·3721222	2·4650371	2·5663412	2·6771790	2·7989140	56
5	2·2089972	2·2879974	2·3736075	2·4666538	2·5681069	2·6791145	2·8010441	55
6	2·2102637	2·2893679	2·3750949	2·4682729	2·5698752	2·6810530	2·8031777	54
7	2·2115318	2·2907403	2·3765843	2·4698943	2·5716462	2·6829945	2·8053148	53
8	2·2128016	2·2921145	2·3780758	2·4715181	2·5734199	2·6849391	2·8074554	52
9	2·2140730	2·2934906	2·3795694	2·4731442	2·5751963	2·6868867	2·8095995	51
10	2·2153460	2·2948685	2·3810650	2·4747726	2·5769753	2·6888374	2·8117471	50
11	2·2166208	2·2962483	2·3825627	2·4764034	2·5787570	2·6907912	2·8138982	49
12	2·2178971	2·2976299	2·3840625	2·4780366	2·5805414	2·6927480	2·8160529	48
13	2·2191752	2·2990134	2·3855645	2·4796721	2·5823284	2·6947079	2·8182111	47
14	2·2204548	2·3003988	2·3870685	2·4813100	2·5841182	2·6966709	2·8203729	46
15	2·2217362	2·3017860	2·3885746	2·4829503	2·5859107	2·6986370	2·8225382	45
16	2·2230192	2·3031751	2·3900828	2·4845929	2·5877058	2·7006061	2·8247071	44
17	2·2243039	2·3045660	2·3915931	2·4862380	2·5895037	2·7025784	2·8268796	43
18	2·2255903	2·3059588	2·3931055	2·4878854	2·5913043	2·7045538	2·8290556	42
19	2·2268783	2·3073536	2·3946201	2·4895352	2·5931077	2·7065323	2·8312353	41
20	2·2281681	2·3087501	2·3961367	2·4911874	2·5949137	2·7085139	2·8334185	40
21	2·2294595	2·3101486	2·3976555	2·4928421	2·5967225	2·7104987	2·8356054	39
22	2·2307526	2·3115490	2·3991764	2·4944991	2·5985341	2·7124866	2·8377958	38
23	2·2320474	2·3129513	2·4006995	2·4961586	2·6003484	2·7144777	2·8399899	37
24	2·2333438	2·3143554	2·4022247	2·4978204	2·6021654	2·7164719	2·8421877	36
25	2·2346420	2·3157615	2·4037520	2·4994848	2·6039852	2·7184693	2·8443891	35
26	2·2359419	2·3171695	2·4052815	2·5011515	2·6058078	2·7204698	2·8465941	34
27	2·2372435	2·3185794	2·4068132	2·5028207	2·6076332	2·7224735	2·8488028	33
28	2·2385468	2·3199912	2·4083469	2·5044923	2·6094613	2·7244804	2·8510152	32
29	2·2398517	2·3214049	2·4098829	2·5061663	2·6112922	2·7264905	2·8532312	31
30	2·2411585	2·3228205	2·4114210	2·5078428	2·6131259	2·7285038	2·8554510	30
31	2·2424669	2·3242381	2·4129613	2·5095218	2·6149624	2·7305203	2·8576744	29
32	2·2437770	2·3256575	2·4145038	2·5112032	2·6168018	2·7325400	2·8599015	28
33	2·2450889	2·3270790	2·4160484	2·5128871	2·6186439	2·7345630	2·8621324	27
34	2·2464025	2·3285023	2·4175952	2·5145735	2·6204888	2·7365892	2·8643670	26
35	2·2477178	2·3299276	2·4191442	2·5162624	2·6223366	2·7386186	2·8666053	25
36	2·2490348	2·3313548	2·4206954	2·5179537	2·6241872	2·7406512	2·8688474	24
37	2·2503536	2·3327840	2·4222488	2·5196475	2·6260406	2·7426871	2·8710932	23
38	2·2516741	2·3342152	2·4238044	2·5213438	2·6278969	2·7447263	2·8733428	22
39	2·2529964	2·3356482	2·4253622	2·5230426	2·6297560	2·7467687	2·8755961	21
40	2·2543204	2·3370833	2·4269222	2·5247440	2·6316180	2·7488144	2·8778532	20
41	2·2556461	2·3385203	2·4284844	2·5264478	2·6334828	2·7508634	2·8801142	19
42	2·2569736	2·3399593	2·4300489	2·5281541	2·6353506	2·7529157	2·8823789	18
43	2·2583029	2·3414002	2·4316155	2·5298630	2·6372211	2·7549712	2·8846474	17
44	2·2596339	2·3428432	2·4331844	2·5315744	2·6390946	2·7570301	2·8869198	16
45	2·2609667	2·3442881	2·4347555	2·5332883	2·6409710	2·7590923	2·8891960	15
46	2·2623012	2·3457349	2·4363289	2·5350048	2·6428502	2·7611578	2·8914760	14
47	2·2636376	2·3471838	2·4379045	2·5367238	2·6447323	2·7632267	2·8937598	13
48	2·2649756	2·3486347	2·4394823	2·5384453	2·6466174	2·7652988	2·8960475	12
49	2·2663155	2·3500875	2·4410624	2·5401694	2·6485054	2·7673744	2·8983391	11
50	2·2676571	2·3515424	2·4426448	2·5418961	2·6503962	2·7694532	2·9006346	10
51	2·2690005	2·3529992	2·4442294	2·5436253	2·6522901	2·7715355	2·9029339	9
52	2·2703457	2·3544581	2·4458163	2·5453571	2·6541868	2·7736211	2·9052372	8
53	2·2716927	2·3559189	2·4474054	2·5470915	2·6560865	2·7757100	2·9075443	7
54	2·2730415	2·3573818	2·4489968	2·5488284	2·6579891	2·7778024	2·9098553	6
55	2·2743921	2·3588467	2·4505905	2·5505680	2·6598947	2·7798982	2·9121703	5
56	2·2757445	2·3603136	2·4521865	2·5523101	2·6618033	2·7819973	2·9144892	4
57	2·2770987	2·3617826	2·4537848	2·5540548	2·6637148	2·7840999	2·9168121	3
58	2·2784546	2·3632535	2·4553853	2·5558022	2·6656292	2·7862059	2·9191389	2
59	2·2798124	2·3647265	2·4569882	2·5575521	2·6675467	2·7883153	2·9214697	1
60	2·2811720	2·3662016	2·4585933	2·5593047	2·6694672	2·7904281	2·9238044	0
′	26°	25°	24°	23°	22°	21°	20°	′

′	70°	71°	72°	73°	74°	75°	76°	′
0	2·9238044	3·0715535	3·2360680	3·4203036	3·6279553	3·8637033	4·1335655	60
1	2·9261431	3·0741507	3·2389678	3·4235611	3·6316395	3·8679025	4·1383939	59
2	2·9284858	3·0767525	3·2418732	3·4268251	3·6353316	3·8721112	4·1432339	58
3	2·9308326	3·0793590	3·2447840	3·4300956	3·6390315	3·8763293	4·1480856	57
4	2·9331833	3·0819702	3·2477003	3·4333727	3·6427392	3·8805570	4·1529491	56
5	2·9355380	3·0845860	3·2506222	3·4366563	3·6464548	3·8847943	4·1578243	55
6	2·9378968	3·0872066	3·2535496	3·4399465	3·6501783	3·8890411	4·1627114	54
7	2·9402597	3·0898319	3·2564825	3·4432433	3·6539097	3·8932976	4·1676102	53
8	2·9426265	3·0924620	3·2594211	3·4465467	3·6576491	3·8975637	4·1725210	52
9	2·9449975	3·0950967	3·2623652	3·4498568	3·6613964	3·9018395	4·1774438	51
10	2·9473725	3·0977363	3·2653149	3·4531735	3·6651518	3·9061250	4·1823785	50
11	2·9497516	3·1003805	3·2682702	3·4564969	3·6689151	3·9104203	4·1873252	49
12	2·9521348	3·1030296	3·2712311	3·4598269	3·6726865	3·9147254	4·1922840	48
13	2·9545221	3·1056835	3·2741977	3·4631637	3·6764660	3·9190403	4·1972549	47
14	2·9569135	3·1083422	3·2771700	3·4665073	3·6802536	3·9233651	4·2022380	46
15	2·9593090	3·1110057	3·2801479	3·4698576	3·6840493	3·9276997	4·2072333	45
16	2·9617087	3·1136740	3·2831316	3·4732146	3·6878532	3·9320443	4·2122408	44
17	2·9641125	3·1163472	3·2861209	3·4765785	3·6916652	3·9363988	4·2172606	43
18	2·9665205	3·1190252	3·2891160	3·4799492	3·6954854	3·9407633	4·2222928	42
19	2·9689327	3·1217081	3·2921168	3·4833267	3·6993139	3·9451379	4·2273373	41
20	2·9713490	3·1243959	3·2951234	3·4867110	3·7031506	3·9495224	4·2323943	40
21	2·9737695	3·1270886	3·2981357	3·4901023	3·7069956	3·9539171	4·2374637	39
22	2·9761942	3·1297862	3·3011539	3·4935004	3·7108489	3·9583219	4·2425457	38
23	2·9786231	3·1324887	3·3041778	3·4969055	3·7147105	3·9627369	4·2476402	37
24	2·9810563	3·1351962	3·3072076	3·5003175	3·7185805	3·9671621	4·2527474	36
25	2·9834936	3·1379086	3·3102432	3·5037365	3·7224589	3·9715975	4·2578671	35
26	2·9859352	3·1406259	3·3132847	3·5071625	3·7263457	3·9760431	4·2629996	34
27	2·9883811	3·1433483	3·3163320	3·5105954	3·7302409	3·9804991	4·2681449	33
28	2·9908312	3·1460756	3·3193853	3·5140354	3·7341446	3·9849654	4·2733029	32
29	2·9932856	3·1488079	3·3224444	3·5174824	3·7380568	3·9894421	4·2784738	31
30	2·9957443	3·1515453	3·3255095	3·5209365	3·7419775	3·9939292	4·2836576	30
31	2·9982073	3·1542877	3·3285805	3·5243977	3·7459068	3·9984267	4·2888543	29
32	3·0006746	3·1570351	3·3316575	3·5278660	3·7498447	4·0029347	4·2940640	28
33	3·0031462	3·1597876	3·3347405	3·5313414	3·7537911	4·0074532	4·2992867	27
34	3·0056221	3·1625452	3·3378294	3·5348240	3·7577462	4·0119823	4·3045225	26
35	3·0081024	3·1653078	3·3409244	3·5383138	3·7617100	4·0165219	4·3097715	25
36	3·0105870	3·1680756	3·3440254	3·5418107	3·7656824	4·0210722	4·3150336	24
37	3·0130760	3·1708484	3·3471324	3·5453149	3·7696636	4·0256332	4·3203090	23
38	3·0155694	3·1736264	3·3502455	3·5488263	3·7736535	4·0302048	4·3255977	22
39	3·0180672	3·1764095	3·3533647	3·5523450	3·7776522	4·0347872	4·3308996	21
40	3·0205693	3·1791978	3·3564900	3·5558710	3·7816596	4·0393804	4·3362150	20
41	3·0230759	3·1819913	3·3596214	3·5594042	3·7856760	4·0439844	4·3415438	19
42	3·0255868	3·1847899	3·3627589	3·5629448	3·7897011	4·0485992	4·3468861	18
43	3·0281023	3·1875937	3·3659026	3·5664928	3·7937352	4·0532249	4·3522419	17
44	3·0306221	3·1904028	3·3690524	3·5700481	3·7977782	4·0578615	4·3576113	16
45	3·0331464	3·1932170	3·3722084	3·5736108	3·8018301	4·0625091	4·3629943	15
46	3·0356752	3·1960365	3·3753707	3·5771810	3·8058911	4·0671677	4·3683910	14
47	3·0382084	3·1988613	3·3785391	3·5807586	3·8099610	4·0718374	4·3738015	13
48	3·0407462	3·2016913	3·3817138	3·5843437	3·8140399	4·0765181	4·3792257	12
49	3·0432884	3·2045266	3·3848948	3·5879362	3·8181280	4·0812100	4·3846638	11
50	3·0458352	3·2073673	3·3880820	3·5915363	3·8222251	4·0859130	4·3901158	10
51	3·0483864	3·2102132	3·3912755	3·5951439	3·8263313	4·0906272	4·3955817	9
52	3·0509423	3·2130644	3·3944754	3·5987590	3·8304467	4·0953526	4·4010616	8
53	3·0535026	3·2159210	3·3976816	3·6023818	3·8345713	4·1000893	4·4065556	7
54	3·0560675	3·2187830	3·4008941	3·6060121	3·8387052	4·1048374	4·4120637	6
55	3·0586370	3·2216503	3·4041130	3·6096501	3·8428482	4·1095967	4·4175859	5
56	3·0612111	3·2245230	3·4073382	3·6132957	3·8470006	4·1143675	4·4231224	4
57	3·0637898	3·2274011	3·4105699	3·6169490	3·8511622	4·1191498	4·4286731	3
58	3·0663731	3·2302846	3·4138080	3·6206101	3·8553332	4·1239435	4·4342382	2
59	3·0689610	3·2331736	3·4170526	3·6242788	3·8595135	4·1287487	4·4398176	1
60	3·0715535	3·2360680	3·4203036	3·6279553	3·8637033	4·1335655	4·4454115	0
′	19°	18°	17°	16°	15°	14°	13°	′

′	77°	78°	79°	80°	81°	82°	83°	′
0	4·4454115	4·8097343	5·2408431	5·7587705	6·3924532	7·1852965	8·2055090	60
1	4·4510198	4·8163258	5·2486979	5·7682867	6·4042154	7·2001996	8·2249952	59
2	4·4566428	4·8229357	5·2565768	5·7778350	6·4160216	7·2151653	8·2445748	58
3	4·4622803	4·8295643	5·2644798	5·7874153	6·4278719	7·2301940	8·2642485	57
4	4·4679324	4·8362114	5·2724070	5·7970280	6·4397666	7·2452859	8·2840171	56
5	4·4735993	4·8428774	5·2803587	5·8066732	6·4517059	7·2604417	8·3038812	55
6	4·4792810	4·8495621	5·2883347	5·8163510	6·4636901	7·2756616	8·3238415	54
7	4·4849775	4·8562657	5·2963354	5·8260617	6·4757195	7·2909460	8·3438986	53
8	4·4906889	4·8629883	5·3043608	5·8358053	6·4877944	7·3062954	8·3640534	52
9	4·4964152	4·8697299	5·3124109	5·8455820	6·4999148	7·3217102	8·3843065	51
10	4·5021565	4·8764907	5·3204860	5·8553921	6·5120812	7·3371909	8·4046556	50
11	4·5079129	4·8832707	5·3285861	5·8652356	6·5242938	7·3527377	8·4251105	49
12	4·5136844	4·8900700	5·3367114	5·8751128	6·5365528	7·3683512	8·4456629	48
13	4·5194711	4·8968886	5·3448620	5·8850238	6·5488586	7·3840318	8·4663165	47
14	4·5252730	4·9037267	5·3530379	5·8949688	6·5612113	7·3997798	8·4870721	46
15	4·5310903	4·9105844	5·3612393	5·9049479	6·5736112	7·4155959	8·5079304	45
16	4·5369229	4·9174616	5·3694664	5·9149614	6·5860587	7·4314803	8·5288923	44
17	4·5427709	4·9243586	5·3777192	5·9250095	6·5985540	7·4474335	8·5499584	43
18	4·5486344	4·9312754	5·3859979	5·9350922	6·6110973	7·4634560	8·5711295	42
19	4·5545134	4·9382120	5·3943026	5·9452098	6·6236890	7·4795482	·8·5924065	41
20	4·5604080	4·9451687	5·4026333	5·9553625	6·6363293	7·4957106	8·6137901	40
21	4·5663183	4·9521453	5·4109903	5·9655504	6·6490184	7·5119437	8·6352812	39
22	4·5722444	4·9591421	5·4193737	5·9757737	6·6617568	7·5282478	8·6568805	38
23	4·5781862	4·9661591	5·4277835	5·9860326	6·6745446	7·5446236	8·6785889	37
24	4·5841439	4·9731964	5·4362199	5·9963274	6·6873822	7·5610713	8·7004071	36
25	4·5901174	4·9802541	5·4446831	6·0066581	6·7002699	7·5775916	8·7223361	35
26	4·5961070	4·9873323	5·4531731	6·0170250	6·7132079	7·5941849	8·7443766	34
27	4·6021126	4·9944311	5·4616901	6·0274282	6·7261965	7·6108516	8·7665295	33
28	4·6081343	5·0015505	5·4702342	6·0378680	6·7392360	7·6275923	8·7887957	32
29	4·6141722	5·0086907	5·4788056	6·0483445	6·7523268	7·6444075	8·8111761	31
30	4·6202263	5·0158517	5·4874043	6·0588580	6·7654691	7·6612976	8·8336715	30
31	4·6262967	5·0230337	5·4960305	6·0694085	6·7786632	7·6782631	8·8562828	29
32	4·6323835	5·0302367	5·5046843	6·0799964	6·7919095	7·6953047	8·8790109	28
33	4·6384867	5·0374607	5·5133659	6·0906219	6·8052082	7·7124227	8·9018567	27
34	4·6446064	5·0447060	5·5220754	6·1012850	6·8185597	7·7296176	8·9248211	26
35	4·6507427	5·0519726	5·5308129	6·1119861	6·8319642	7·7468901	8·9479051	25
36	4·6568956	5·0592606	5·5395786	6·1227253	6·8454222	7·7642406	8·9711095	24
37	4·6630652	5·0665701	5·5483726	6·1335028	6·8589338	7·7816697	8·9944354	23
38	4·6692516	5·0739012	5·5571951	6·1443189	6·8724995	7·7991778	9·0178837	22
39	4·6754548	5·0812539	5·5660460	6·1551738	6·8861195	7·8167656	9·0414553	21
40	4·6816748	5·0886284	5·5749258	6·1660674	6·8997942	7·8344335	9·0651512	20
41	4·6879119	5·0960248	5·5838343	6·1770003	6·9135239	7·8521821	9·0889725	19
42	4·6941660	5·1034443	5·5927719	6·1879725	6·9273089	7·8700120	9·1129200	18
43	4·7004372	5·1108835	5·6017386	6·1989843	6·9411496	7·8879238	9·1369949	17
44	4·7067256	5·1183461	5·6107345	6·2100359	6·9550464	7·9059179	9·1611980	16
45	4·7130313	5·1258309	5·6197599	6·2211275	6·9689994	7·9239950	9·1855305	15
46	4·7193542	5·1333381	5·6288148	6·2322594	6·9830092	7·9421556	9·2099934	14
47	4·7256945	5·1408677	5·6378995	6·2434316	6·9970760	7·9604003	9·2345877	13
48	4·7320524	5·1484199	5·6470140	6·2546446	7·0112001	7·9787298	9·2593145	12
49	4·7384277	5·1559948	5·6561584	6·2658984	7·0253820	7·9971445	9·2841749	11
50	4·7448206	5·1635924	5·6653331	6·2771933	7·0396220	8·0156450	9·3091699	10
51	4·7512312	5·1712128	5·6745380	6·2885295	7·0539205	8·0342321	9·3343006	9
52	4·7576596	5·1788563	5·6837734	6·2999073	7·0682777	8·0529062	9·3595682	8
53	4·7641058	5·1865228	5·6930393	6·3113269	7·0826941	8·0716681	9·3849738	7
54	4·7705699	5·1942125	5·7023360	6·3227884	7·0971700	8·0905182	9·4105184	6
55	4·7770519	5·2019254	5·7116636	6·3342923	7·1117059	8·1094573	9·4362033	5
56	4·7835520	5·2096618	5·7210223	6·3458386	7·1263019	8·1284860	9·4620296	4
57	4·7900702	5·2174216	5·7304121	6·3574276	7·1409587	8·1476048	9·4879984	3
58	4·7966066	5·2252050	5·7398333	6·3690595	7·1556764	8·1668145	9·5141110	2
59	4·8031613	5·2330121	5·7492861	6·3807347	7·1704556	8·1861157	9·5403686	1
60	4·8097343	5·2408431	5·7587705	6·3924532	7·1852965	8·2055090	9·5667722	0
′	12°	11°	10°	9°	8°	7°	6°	′

NATURAL COSECANTS.

′	84°	85°	86°	87°	88°	89°	′
0	9·5667722	11·473713	14·335587	19·107323	28·653708	57·298688	60
1	9·5933233	11·511990	14·395471	19·213970	28·894398	58·269755	59
2	9·6200229	11·550523	14·455859	19·321816	29·139169	59·274308	58
3	9·6468724	11·589316	14·516757	19·430882	29·388124	60·314110	57
4	9·6738730	11·628372	14·578172	19·541187	29·641373	61·391050	56
5	9·7010260	11·667693	14·640109	19·652754	29·899026	62·507153	55
6	9·7283327	11·707282	14·702576	19·765604	30·161201	63·664595	54
7	9·7557944	11·747141	14·765580	19·879758	30·428017	64·865716	53
8	9·7834124	11·787274	14·829128	19·995241	30·699598	66·113036	52
9	9·8111880	11·827683	14·893226	20·112075	30·976074	67·409272	51
10	9·8391227	11·868370	14·957882	20·230284	31·257577	68·757360	50
11	9·8672176	11·909340	15·023103	20·349893	31·544246	70·160174	49
12	9·8954744	11·950595	15·088896	20·470926	31·836225	71·622052	48
13	9·9238943	11·992137	15·155270	20·593409	32·133663	73·145827	47
14	9·9524787	12·033970	15·222231	20·717368	32·436713	74·735856	46
15	9·9812291	12·076098	15·289788	20·842830	32·745537	76·396554	45
16	10·010147	12·118522	15·357949	20·969824	33·060300	78·132742	44
17	10·039234	12·161246	15·426721	21·098376	33·381176	79·949684	43
18	10·068491	12·204274	15·496114	21·228515	33·708345	81·853150	42
19	10·097920	12·247608	15·566135	21·360272	34·041994	83·849470	41
20	10·127522	12·291252	15·636793	21·493676	34·382316	85·945609	40
21	10·157300	12·335210	15·708096	21·628759	34·729515	88·149244	39
22	10·187254	12·379484	15·780054	21·765553	35·083800	90·468863	38
23	10·217386	12·424078	15·852676	21·904090	35·445391	92·913869	37
24	10·247697	12·468995	15·925971	22·044403	35·814517	95·494711	36
25	10·278190	12·514240	15·999948	22·186528	36·191414	98·223033	35
26	10·308866	12·559815	16·074617	22·330499	36·576332	101·11185	34
27	10·339726	12·605724	16·149987	22·476353	36·969528	104·17574	33
28	10·370772	12·651971	16·226069	22·624126	37·371273	107·43114	32
29	10·402007	12·698560	16·302873	22·773857	37·781849	110·89656	31
30	10·433431	12·745495	16·380408	22·925586	38·201550	114·59301	30
31	10·465046	12·792779	16·458686	23·079351	38·630683	118·54440	29
32	10·496854	12·840416	16·537717	23·235196	39·069571	122·77803	28
33	10·528857	12·888410	16·617512	23·393161	39·518549	127·32526	27
34	10·561057	12·936765	16·698082	23·553291	39·977969	132·22229	26
35	10·593455	12·985486	16·779439	23·715630	40·448201	137·51108	25
36	10·626054	13·034576	16·861594	23·880224	40·929630	143·24061	24
37	10·658854	13·084040	16·944559	24·047121	41·422660	149·46837	23
38	10·691859	13·133882	17·028346	24·216370	41·927717	156·26228	22
39	10·725070	13·184106	17·112966	24·388020	42·445245	163·70325	21
40	10·758488	13·234717	17·198434	24·562123	42·975713	171·88831	20
41	10·792117	13·285719	17·284761	24·738731	43·519612	180·93496	19
42	10·825957	13·337116	17·371960	24·917900	44·077458	190·98680	18
43	10·860011	13·388914	17·460046	25·099685	44·649795	202·22122	17
44	10·894281	13·441118	17·549030	25·284144	45·237195	214·85995	16
45	10·928768	13·493731	17·638923	25·471337	45·840260	229·18385	15
46	10·963476	13·546758	17·729753	25·661324	46·459625	245·55402	14
47	10·998406	13·600205	17·821520	25·854169	47·095961	264·44269	13
48	11·033560	13·654077	17·914243	26·049937	47·749974	286·47948	12
49	11·068940	13·708379	18·007937	26·248694	48·422411	312·52297	11
50	11·104549	13·763115	18·102619	26·450510	49·114062	343·77516	10
51	11·140389	13·818291	18·198303	26·655455	49·825762	381·97230	9
52	11·176462	13·873913	18·295005	26·863603	50·558396	429·71873	8
53	11·212770	13·929985	18·392742	27·075030	51·312902	491·10702	7
54	11·249316	13·986514	18·491530	27·289814	52·090272	572·95809	6
55	11·286101	14·043504	18·591387	27·508035	52·891564	687·54960	5
56	11·323129	14·100963	18·692330	27·729777	53·717896	859·43689	4
57	11·360402	14·158894	18·794377	27·955125	54·570464	1145·9157	3
58	11·397922	14·217304	18·897545	28·184168	55·455034	1718·8735	2
59	11·435692	14·276200	19·001854	28·416997	56·359462	3437·7468	1
60	11·473713	14·335587	19·107323	28·653708	57·298688	Infinite.	0
′	5°	4°	3°	2°	1°	0°	′